THE GREAT INDIAN POVERTY DEBATE

Editors

Angus Deaton and Valerie Kozel

MACMILLAN

First published, 2005

MACMILLAN INDIA LTD.
Delhi Chennai Jaipur Mumbai Patna Bangalore
Bhopal Chandigarh Coimbatore Cuttack Guwahati
Hubli Hyderabad Lucknow Madurai Nagpur Pune
Raipur Thiruvananthapuram Visakhapatnam

Companies and representatives throughout the world

ISBN 1403 92644 1

Published by Rajiv Beri for Macmillan India Ltd.
2/10 Ansari Road, Daryaganj, New Delhi 110 002

Printed at Sanat Printers, Kundli.

Foreword

Montek Singh Ahluwalia
Deputy Chairman
Planning Commission, Government of India

Measurement of the extent of poverty, trends over time and the role of economic policy and development strategy in reducing poverty have been at the centre of the policy debate in India for many years. This is only to be expected in a low-income country that is also a vibrant and highly participatory democracy. The poor are numerous and they vote – often decisively – and it is only natural that the impact of policy on the welfare of a large segment of the population should attract interest.

Debate on issues related to poverty has been greatly facilitated by a feature that distinguishes India from most developing countries – the existence of regular household surveys of consumption conducted almost annually by the National Sample Survey Organization. But if India is blessed with rich time series data on poverty, it is even more plentifully endowed with economists skilled at pointing out the limitations of the available data and also teasing out different conclusions from the same data! Both features have been especially evident in the 1990s. This was a period which saw a major reorientation of economic policy, away from the earlier control-oriented economic system with a dominant role for the public sector to a more liberal system with a much greater role for markets and the private sector, and a gradual opening of the economy to world trade and foreign investment. The shift in policy was bound to provide controversy and it did. The effectiveness of the reforms in achieving their declared objective was a subject of intense public scrutiny, and the key litmus test was their impact on poverty. There was, therefore, an intensification of scrutiny of this important issue.

This book provides a thorough documentation of the state of the debate as it stood in 2004. It brings together papers which reflect the differing viewpoints expressed by the principal protagonists in the debate at that time, leavened by a few seminal papers from earlier years which give the reader a sense of the pedigree of the literature in India. The introduction by Angus Deaton and Valerie Kozel is a masterful summary of the issues because they have dealt extensively with the many technical considerations which have to be kept in mind when evaluating the work of different contributors. I am tempted to use this Foreword primarily to set the context in which the debate unfolded from the perspective of the policy-making community.

The reforms of 1991 were initiated in the backdrop of a severe balance of payments crisis which began in late 1990 and reached crisis proportions by mid-1991. Initially, the focus of scrutiny was first on whether the reforms would be successful in managing the crisis, and second whether they would have an adverse impact on economic growth as had often been observed in stabilization programmes. The reforms passed both tests very well. Not only was the payments crisis indisputably overcome within two years, but there was also no relapse in any of the years since then, no mean achievement considering that in 1997 the East Asian crisis created an environment in which most Asian economies seemed vulnerable. On growth as well, the performance was commendable. India experienced no sign of the economic slowdown often associated with stabilization programmes. Instead, there was an acceleration in economic growth in the five years following the crisis compared to the five years preceding it, and the average GDP growth in the three years 1993-94 to 1996-97 actually exceeded 7 per cent per annum, suggesting that India had moved to a distinctly higher growth path.

The area where the reforms appeared most vulnerable was on the impact on poverty. When introducing the economic reforms, the government had consistently argued that these reforms would lead to a reduction in poverty, partly because of the impact of accelerated growth with a sectoral composition which paid special attention to agriculture, and partly because there were a number of programmes aimed specifically at the poor. This judgement was based on the fact that the growth in the 1980s, compared with the 1970s, had led to a steady decline in poverty and it was reasonable to expect that the trend of reduction in poverty would continue and hopefully even accelerate. This is not the pattern that emerged from the NSS data in the 1990s. On the contrary, the various sample surveys after 1991 appeared to show that despite the high rate of growth of GDP recorded in the national accounts, the percentage of population below the poverty line seemed to be unchanged, a distinct break from the pattern in the 1980s.

Critics argued that the economic reforms had promoted a type of growth that was distributionally malign, with benefits accruing only to the better-off sections of the population, while the poorer groups experienced little, if any, progress. The issue was obviously important substantively from an economic point of view, but it was also politically important because no reform programme could possibly receive general endorsement – essential in a democratic policy – if it was not perceived as generating an adequate flow of benefits to the poor.

Initially the debate was confined to academic circles since there were no official estimates of poverty after 1993-94. Official estimates of poverty were traditionally made by the Planning Commission on the basis of "full sample" National Sample Surveys (NSS) which appear every five years, ignoring the annual "thin sample" surveys. The 1993-94 NSS was a full sample survey and the next one was expected only in 1999-2000. The results of the 1999-2000 NSS became available only in 2001 and as it happened they opened up a new area for debate. The NSSO had been concerned about a long-standing problem of a growing discrepancy between estimates of per capita consumption emerging from the surveys and that from the national accounts. To test for the possible effects of different recall periods for measuring different items of consumption, the NSSO had been experimenting with alternative recall periods. In the 1999-2000 NSS two different recall periods were used and households were questioned about consumption using both recall periods. The NSSO presented the results for 1999-2000 using both reference periods. The new reference period showed distinctly higher levels of per capita consumption.

On the basis of the 1999-2000 survey results the government pronounced that on a comparable basis (i.e. using the same reference period as in 1993-94) the percentage of poverty had declined significantly between the estimate yielded by the full sample in 1993-94 (37.1 per cent in rural areas, 32.9 per cent in urban areas) and the new estimates of 26.8 per cent rural and 24.1 per cent urban yielded by the full sample survey of 1999-2000. The decline was less than had been projected in the Ninth Plan, but then growth was also significantly lower. Most importantly, the basic proposition that economic growth of the type experienced in India was continuing to contribute to reducing poverty appeared to be vindicated.

This conclusion was promptly challenged by critics who argued that the decision to administer questions based on both recall periods to the same household made the surveys non comparable even for estimates based on the same recall period since the response to the traditional questionnaire would be biased upwards. This sparked the new contributions by Deaton, and Sundaram and Tendulkar which are included in this volume. Both papers attempt to tease out poverty estimates that would not be subject to this bias. Both authors concluded that there was a decline in poverty in the 1990s though it was less than that claimed by the government. Sundaram and Tendulkar went further to argue that the growth process in the 1990s showed an acceleration in the pace of poverty reduction as compared to the 1980s. The paper in this volume by Sen and Himanshu however challenges the methodology used by Deaton and implies a less upbeat outcome on poverty.

Others who have contributed to the debate have come to much more optimistic conclusions. Surjit Bhalla is one of the principal contributors to the debate on trends in poverty both on a global scale and on poverty in India. On global poverty, Bhalla[1] has argued passionately that the World Bank is the most influential exponent of the consensus view of development outcomes but it understates the extent of reduction in poverty that has taken place in the world. This is because it relies on measurement methods which do not give adequate recognition to the growth that has taken place in some large developing countries, especially India. He has somewhat mischievously speculated that this may be because the Bank has anchored its *raison d'être* on poverty reduction and is unwilling to accept that its relevance may be shrinking! Bhalla's estimates show a dramatic reduction in poverty to as low as 15 per cent in 1999-2000 using the same consumption-based poverty line that is used in the other Indian studies. The principal reason for this dramatically different conclusion is that Bhalla adjusts the mean consumption level from the surveys for the discrepancy between the national accounts estimates of per capita consumption and the estimate from the surveys. His adjustment is not a crude expansion of consumption levels for all households to close the discrepancy; that would be questioned immediately on the grounds that the bulk of the discrepancy may arise from under-reporting by the rich. Bhalla recognizes this problem and devises a special adjustment whereby the consumption of different households is adjusted to different degrees, depending on their consumption of individual products and the adjustment for each product depends on the discrepancy between the survey estimates of total consumption of these products and estimates from the national accounts.

Is Bhalla's adjustment a valid procedure? This is clearly a critical issue. The adjustment makes a big difference in trends because the NSS estimates of consumption, which at one time were around 80 per cent of the national accounts based estimates, have fallen to as low as 55 per cent (in 1999-2000). As pointed out in this volume, any mechanical assumption that national income estimates are to be preferred is unsustainable, but equally the increasing discrepancy between the two estimates also undermines confidence in the survey.

A late entrant into the debate on poverty was a set of studies based on an entirely different data source – the periodic Market Information Surveys of Households (MISH) conducted by the National Council of Applied Economic Research. The conclusions derived from these surveys are presented in the paper by Bery and Shukla. The NCAER data differ from those generated by the NSSO in that respondents are asked to report their income, what the survey refers to as "perceived monetary income". They conclude that there was a sharp reduction in income poverty between 1987-88 and 1998-99 from 39.1 per cent to 16.2 per cent of the rural population and 38.3 per cent to 10.9 per cent of the urban population, almost as sharp as claimed by Bhalla. These income poverty lines have been calibrated against the Planning

---

[1] Surjit S. Bhalla, (2003) *Imagine There's No Country: Poverty, Inequality and Growth in the Era of Globalization,* Penguin Books, New Delhi.

Commission's expenditure headcount ratios in 1987-88, adjusted thereafter by the price deflators used by the Planning Commission to update its own expenditure poverty line. As rightly pointed out by the editors, the NCAER data suffer from the disadvantage that income is an internally difficult concept to define, let alone measure, and the NCAER survey estimate is based on a household response to a single question. This must certainly introduce errors, but it is not easy to discard the data set completely especially when it appears to correspond more closely to estimates of trends which take account of national accounts estimates. The fact that Bhalla, using NSS-adjusted estimates, and Bery and Shukla, using the NCAER data, come up with much more optimistic estimates of underlying trends, illustrates the difficulty in ensuring that the debate on politically sensitive issues is sufficiently anchored in "good practice" before it becomes a guide to policy. Life is probably much simpler for policy-makers when there are fewer data sources, but it is probably also less interesting.

An obvious solution to the problem is that we need better survey data and improvements in the data must be continuously attempted, though, as the Indian experience amply demonstrates, efforts to improve the system could create problems of comparability. Parallel with improvements in survey data there must be an attempt to broaden the indicators by which poverty is measured. There are several indicators that are relevant in this context including literacy, primary and secondary school enrolment, infant mortality rates, life expectancy, maternal mortality rates, access to potable drinking water and sanitation services. Broad based progress on all these fronts combined with progress on the traditional income or consumption poverty measures would provide convincing assurance that the welfare of the common people is indeed improving.

That said, it is also necessary to point out that while the focus on reducing absolute poverty is an overriding priority of the international development community, the distributional objective that policy-makers have to keep in mind is never unidimensional. Other distributional objectives are also relevant and often become the focus of attention. It is easy to imagine a situation where a particular pattern with respect to poverty reduction is accompanied by very different outcomes in other critical areas. Regional imbalance is a case in point since it is perfectly possible for a development strategy to achieve a steady reduction in poverty while showing a continuous increase in regional imbalance because the better-off states or regions do much better than those that are less well off, even if the latter show significant reductions in poverty. Similarly, the same pattern in poverty reduction may be accompanied by an increase or decrease in the equality of opportunity across income classes, or an increase or decrease in income security across income classes.

All these are clearly important for practical policy-making but we are as yet far from being able to measure changes in those dimensions.

MONTEK SINGH AHLUWALIA

Preface

Hundreds of millions of Indians are poor by national and international standards. Indian policy-making and politics are dominated by discussions of poverty, and measures of poverty rightly attract a great deal of attention and debate. In the second-half of the 1990s, India's GDP grew rapidly by historical standards, and many commentators have associated this acceleration with the process of economic reform that began in the 1990s. Yet the reforms themselves, and the limited opening of the Indian economy that they involved, remain controversial, as does their effect on poverty.

This debate is far from unique to India. The worldwide controversy about globalization and its effects on poverty and inequality has followed much the same lines as the internal debate in India. And indeed, India accounts for about 20 per cent of the global count of those living on less than $1 a person per day, so that what happens in India is not only a reflection of worldwide trends, but one of their major determinants.

This book brings together the key papers in the Indian poverty debate, together with a new introductory chapter that provides an overview and synthesis.

Many of the chapters in this volume are based on work that was first presented at a workshop on *Poverty Measurement, Monitoring, and Evaluation in India*, jointly organized by the Indian Planning Commission and World Bank in New Delhi on 11-12 January 2002 (www.worldbank.org/ Indiapovertyworkshop). The collection also contains some seminal papers that link the current debates to the earlier literature, as well as discussions of the issues in other countries.

Acknowledgements

The initial impetus for this book was provided by a workshop on *Poverty Measurement, Monitoring, and Evaluation in India*, jointly sponsored by the Indian Planning Commission and World Bank in January 2002. The editors are grateful for additional support provided by the World Bank for preparation of the book. However, the findings, interpretations, and conclusions expressed in this volume are entirely those of the co-editors and contributors, and should not be attributed to the World Bank or any of its affiliated organizations.

The National Sample Survey Organization (NSSO) must be acknowledged for making various rounds of India's National Sample Survey readily available to national and international researchers, including the much-debated NSS 55th Round, and for their openness and willingness to engage in experimentation and discussions of survey design and data. We would also like to thank the *Economic and Political Weekly* for publishing many of the workshop papers in a special volume of the journal, and for graciously allowing us to publish these and other papers in this volume. All royalties from sales of this book will accrue to the EPW Trust.

In closing, we would like to extend heartfelt thanks to the contributors as well as to the many other people who participated in the Delhi workshop and helped over the past three years in producing earlier publications as well as this final volume.

Contents

PART III
BROADER PERSPECTIVES ON POVERTY

Contributors

KATHARINE G. ABRAHAM
University of Maryland, USA

ABHIJIT BANERJEE
Massachusetts Institute of Technology, USA

SUMAN BERY
National Council for Applied Economic Research, India

SURJIT S. BHALLA
Oxus Research

NIKHILESH BHATTACHARYA (Retired)
Indian Statistical Institute, Kolkata

LATE G.S. CHATTERJEE
Indian Statistical Institute, Kolkata

GAURAV DATT
World Bank

ANGUS DEATON
Princeton University, USA

JEAN DREZE
GB Pant Social Science Institute, Allahabad

HIMANSHU
JNU, Delhi

ALOKE KAR
Central Statistical Organisation, Government of India

VALERIE KOZEL
World Bank

A.C. KULSHRESHTHA
Central Statistical Organisation, Government of India

GUY LAROQUE
INSEE-CREST, France

J.V. MEENASKHI
HarvestPlus, International Food Policy Research Institute

B.S. MINHAS
Independent

LATE M. MUKHERJEE
Indian Statistical Institute, Kolkata

RINKU MURGAI
World Bank

BARBARA PARKER
Independent

THOMAS PIKETTY
ENS-CEPREMAP, Paris

P.N. RADHAKRISHNAN
Perspective Planning Division, Planning Commission of India

MARTIN RAVALLION
World Bank

LATE ASHOK RUDRA
Indian Statistical Institute, Kolkata

N. S. SASTRY
Retired Director General, National Sample Survey Organization, Government of India

ABHIJIT SEN
Planning Commission, Government of India

R.K. SHUKLA
National Council for Applied Economic Research, India

T.N. SRINIVASAN
Yale University, USA

K. SUNDARAM
Delhi School of Economics, India

M.H. SURYANARAYANA
International Poverty Center, Brasilia, Brazil

ALESSANDRO TAROZZI
Duke University, USA

SURESH TENDULKAR
Delhi School of Economics, India

A. VAIDYANATHAN (Retired)
   Perspective Planning Division, Planning Commission of India, and Madras Institute of Development Studies

BRINDA VISWANATHAN
   WIDER and Madras School of Economics, India

SALMAN ZAIDI
   World Bank

Introduction

Angus Deaton and Valerie Kozel

Hundreds of millions of Indians are poor by national and international standards. Indian policy making and politics are dominated by discussions of poverty, and measures of poverty rightly attract a great deal of attention and debate. In the second half of the 1990s, India's GDP grew rapidly by (Indian) historical standards, and many commentators have associated this acceleration with the process of economic reform that began in the 1990s. Yet the reforms themselves, and the limited opening of the Indian economy that they involved, remain controversial, as does their effect on poverty. This debate is far from unique to India. The worldwide controversy about globalisation and its effects on poverty and inequality has followed much the same lines as the internal debate in India. And indeed, India accounts for about 20 per cent of the global count of those living on less than $ 1 a person per day, so that what happens in India is not only a reflection of worldwide trends, but one of their major determinants.

Historically, the Indian statistical system led the world in the measurement of poverty. The sample surveys that were pioneered by Mahalanobis at the Indian Statistical Institute in Kolkata in the 1940s and 1950s were moved into the government statistical system as the National Sample Survey Organisation (NSSO), whose household surveys are the basis for the regular publications on poverty by the Planning Commission. Where Mahalanobis and India led, the rest of the world has followed, so that today, most countries have a recent household income or expenditure survey from which it is possible to make a direct assessment of the living standards of the population. Mahalanobis and his colleagues in Kolkata also conducted experiments on the design of household surveys, investigating how they can most accurately measure the levels of consumption that are the raw material for the estimation. Such experiments are too infrequently carried out today, although, as we shall see, the NSSO has recently used them to investigate a number of important questions of survey design.

National statistical systems collect more than survey data, and much non-survey information is relevant for the monitoring of living standards. Most important are the National Accounts Statistics (NAS), which provide widely used measures of aggregate performance, particularly GDP and its components, particularly consumption. Although these consumption estimates rely on surveys for several of their components, much also comes from other sources. And although there are important differences in definition between the survey and national accounts concepts of consumption, a well-functioning statistical system will use multiple estimates to cross-check and validate one another. And indeed, there is a long and distinguished tradition of empirical work in India on such cross-checking and validation of the consumption estimates. Of course, poverty depends not only on average consumption, but also on its distribution, particularly at the bottom of the distribution, so that the National Accounts cannot by themselves provide a direct estimate of poverty. Even so, the existence of serious discrepancies between mean consumption from the surveys and from the National Accounts casts doubt on at least one of the two estimates, and if the discrepancy affects a number as important as the growth rate of average living standards, conflicts in measurement stop being the arcane purview of statisticians, and move into the public and political debate.

This is what happened in India in the late 1990s. The growth of average consumption measured from the National Accounts Statistics exceeded its measured rate of growth in the National Sample Surveys, with the result that measures of poverty, which are based entirely on the survey data, declined less rapidly than seemed to be warranted by the rate of growth of consumption (and GDP) in the national accounts. Given the political divisions that surrounded the reforms, the discrepancy quickly ceased to be a purely statistical issue. Those with a stake in the success of the reforms emphasised the national accounts statistics, as well as the lack of evidence that the distribution of consumption had widened among the poor. According to this view, surveys are inherently unreliable and error prone, and some commentators (although without producing any evidence) went so far as to paint pictures of enumerators filling out the questionnaires in tea-shops, avoiding the time-consuming and repetitive task of actually interviewing respondents. On the other side, reform skeptics argued that the survey data showed exactly what *they* had expected, that the reforms, while benefiting the better-off groups in society, had failed to reach the poor, particularly the rural poor, and that the distribution of consumption had indeed widened. They also pointed to the differences in definition between the national accounts and survey measures of consumption, arguing that the latter were more relevant for assessing poverty. They also identified many areas where the National Accounts estimates of consumption are weak and prone to error.

Once again, the Indian debate is mirrored in the global debate about trade, development and poverty. In many other countries, including many rich countries who spend a great deal more on their statistical systems, estimates of growth rates from National Accounts are larger than and inconsistent with those from household surveys. Mean consumption from the United States Consumer Expenditure Survey grows more slowly than does mean consumption in the national accounts, and the difference in the two growth rates is remarkably similar to the difference in India. And global poverty, measured from household income and consumption surveys from around the world, is not falling as rapidly as appears to be warranted from global growth rates and the limited change in global inequality. In consequence, the issues that roiled the Indian debate in the 1990s are actual or potential issues in a number of countries, and are an immediate threat to the estimation of global poverty, of which Indian poverty is an important component.

Statistical agencies do not exist outside the societies that they serve, so that debates over important numbers tend, quite properly, to provoke reviews of practice, and experimentation with new practices. To its credit, the National Sample Survey Organisation of India organised a series of experiments with its consumption surveys in the late 1990s. These were primarily designed to investigate the effects of different reporting periods on the amount of consumption reported, for example whether people reported a higher or lower rate of consumption of rice when the question was posed with reference to consumption over the last 30 days, or over the last 7 days. The experimental questionnaires, which collected data on food, paan, and tobacco at 7 days, clothing, durables, and educational and institutional medical expenses at 365 days, and other goods at 30 days, generated a modest increase in reported consumption over the traditional questionnaires, which collected all goods with a 30-day recall. For per capita total household expenditure, the average increase was between 15 to 18 per cent, but this turned out to be enough to halve the measured number of poor in India, because a large fraction of households have consumption near the poverty line. While this apparently stunning result reveals more about the inadequacy of poverty counts and headcount ratios than it does about poverty in India, it had an important effect on the debate. Not only did it provide ammunition to those who argued that surveys were inherently unreliable for measuring poverty, but it turned an apparently arcane statistical issue – the choice of reporting periods – into one that was politicised and intensely debated. These debates were 'resolved' by adopting a compromise design for the important consumption survey that was carried out in 1999/2000, the 55th Round of the NSS. This survey, which was the first large-scale survey since 1993/94, and the first that would provide relevant information on the effects of the reforms, was eagerly awaited. But in the event, the compromise design made it difficult to compare its results with earlier surveys. In consequence, the official poverty measures from that survey, which were published in February 2001 and which showed a very large decline in poverty rates, only fuelled the debate, instead of settling it.

As the debates on poverty counts continued, there was an increasing focus on other, broader lines of poverty research. In part this reflected a well-justified impatience with an exclusive focus on one set of numbers, which even if perfectly measured, have serious theoretical inadequacies, and in part, it reflected the worldwide trend in looking beyond consumption poverty to other important measures of living standards, in particular to indicators of human development, such as mortality, morbidity, and education. Much of this work has been pioneered in India, and it continues to be a necessary and vital part of poverty assessment in India and in the world.

Most of the research published in this book was carried out in response to the events described above. A good deal of it was first presented at a workshop in Delhi, in January 2002, co-sponsored by the Planning Commission and the World Bank, although there has been time since then for revisions and for some rethinking. Also included are papers that were written by workshop participants after the event, and which played no part in it, but which are important in continuing the debate. The papers are selected to represent all points of view, as well as to acknowledge, in a way that has not always been done, that these questions have been debated in India for at least thirty years, and that much can still be learned from the earlier contributions of Indian economists and statisticians. To that end, four earlier papers are included, three written during previous debates on poverty in India around 1970, and one published in 1988, whose discussion of the discrepancies between National Accounts Statistics and the National Sample Surveys is arguably the best available, even today, and whose implications for the measurement of poverty extend beyond India to many other countries in the world.

PART I: THE STATISTICAL BASIS FOR POVERTY MEASUREMENT

I.1 The Statistical System

The book begins with two chapters that step back from the details of the Indian debate to consider the broad purposes of national statistical systems, and how they can best be designed to function in an environment where measurement is imperfect and data are often politically charged. These general issues have great salience in India now, where it can reasonably be argued that at least some of the current difficulties with the system of poverty measurement could have been avoided had decisions about data collection been made in a more transparent and accountable fashion. For example, the contamination of the important 55th Round data by an ill-judged change in the questionnaire points to a systemic failure in the way such decisions are taken. (Similar problems have occurred in a number of other countries, particularly in Africa.) On the positive side of the ledger, the National Sample Survey

Organisation is to be congratulated on its open data access policy which, in recent years, has permitted academics and commentators to have access to the unit record data which opens up NSS activities to public scrutiny as well as allowing some of India's best researchers, not only to participate in an informed and lively debate, but also to feed back their experience into the design of future surveys.

These opening chapters are by two scholars with great experience of producing and disseminating statistics, Katharine Abraham, former Commissioner of the United States Bureau of Labor Statistics, and Guy Laroque, *Inspecteur Général* of the French National Statistical Institute (L'Institut National de la Statistique et des Études Économiques, or INSEE). Both chapters highlight the fact that in most of the developed countries there is extensive use of household survey data to inform policy making. In contrast, developing countries tend to rely more on administrative data, which can be of uneven quality. In the United States, a great deal of data is collected specifically for public policy purposes and serves three functions, namely, monitoring current conditions, assessing long-term trends, and analysing causal factors associated with observed outcomes. There are numerous examples of good collaboration between the administration and research institutes and universities. In France, most of the statistical information is produced by INSEE which tends to work in a highly centralised way. However, INSEE also works closely with economists and statisticians in the production of data and execution of economic analyses. Both chapters stressed the central importance of the independence of statistical agencies from policy makers. While statistical agencies must collect the information that serves the needs of policy makers, and must ultimately be accountable to elected officials, the public credibility of their data can only be protected if they are seen to be independent in their day-to-day professional activities. Both in the United States Bureau of Labour Statistics, and at INSEE in Paris, top staff are professionally distinguished; for example at INSEE from 1974 through 2002, successive directors were all fellows of the Econometric Society. Further discussion on the issues raised by Abraham and Laroque, particularly the guiding principles of policy relevance, credibility among users, and trust among data providers, can be found in the volume *Principles and Practices for a Federal Statistical Agency*, prepared by the National Research Council of the United States (Martin, Straf, and Citro, 2002).

The Indian statistical system has recently come under intense scrutiny by a National Statistical Commission chaired by Dr C. Rangarajan, Government of India (Rangarajan, 2001). The Commission noted that despite commendable achievements, there is a growing concern about the reliability, timeliness and adequacy of available data. In particular, the Indian statistical system relies heavily on administrative records that are not fully accurate, and there is poor coordination between central and state ministries with regard to data sharing. Chapter 3, by T.N. Srinivasan, discusses the NSC's report. Srinivasan emphasises the fact that there has been no recent, systematic appraisal of the information needs of the Indian economy, and argues that the extensive list of recommendations in the NSC would benefit from better prioritisation and more explicit cost-benefit analysis; indeed such cost-benefit analysis should serve as an overarching framework for decisions about which data ought to be collected. He argues for greater efficiency and better utilisation of the information that is being produced, as well as bolder measures to reform and modernise India's statistical system. Srinivasan draws particular attention to the sections of the NSC report on the inadequacies of the National Accounts Statistics, and argues that the material should be compulsory reading for those who otherwise mechanically use the national accounts measures of consumption to 'correct' the information collected in the household surveys.

I.2 Conflicts between the National Accounts and Sample Surveys

Estimates of mean consumption are generated both by the National Accounts Statistics (NAS) and by the National Sample Survey Organisation (NSSO) from their regular surveys of consumers' expenditures. The two sets of estimates can be used to cross-check one another, both at the level of total consumers' expenditure, and at the level of individual commodities, or groups of commodities, such as foodgrains, clothing or services. There is a long tradition of this work in India, and we include reprints of two short papers published in 1974, by M. Mukherjee and G.S. Chatterjee, Chapter 4, and by T.N. Srinivasan, P.N. Radhakrishnan, and A. Vaidyanathan, Chapter 5. These two chapters examine the match between the two estimates of consumption and its distribution, using NSS and NAS information from the 1950s and 1960s. For the decade up to 1963/64, Mukherjee and Chatterjee are able to write that 'the agreement between the revised series (for NAS consumption) and the NSS estimates remains surprisingly close,' although they note that the NSS estimates are systematically and (on average) increasingly below the NAS estimates in the period up to the end of the 1960s. They also note discrepancies in the distribution of consumption over commodities, with the surveys recording a higher share of food in the budget than does national accounts consumption. Srinivasan, Radhakrishnan and Vaidyanathan's analysis is broadly consistent with that of Mukherjee and Chatterjee, though they find that the survey estimates are lower than the NAS estimates from an earlier date. They also note that the distribution of consumption over categories is broadly similar in the two sources.

If the early comparisons of national accounts' and survey, estimates of consumption were relatively reassuring, more recent ones are anything but the gap between the two estimates of mean consumption has continued to widen, and has currently reached levels that would have been viewed with horror by the early writers. Depending on which set of adjustments we make, the NSS estimate is currently around two-thirds of the NAS estimate of consumption, and has been falling steadily since the late 1960s, by 5 to 10 percentage points per decade. It is worth noting that this differential rate of growth in consumption estimates is far from unique to India. As best we can tell, there is a similar discrepancy between survey and national accounts estimates of the growth rate of consumption for the world as a whole (see Deaton, 2004), and to take a specific example at a very different level of development, the differential rate of growth in the United States is very similar to that in India (see Triplett, 1997 and Garner et al., 2003). While there are certainly errors in both sets of estimates, the view of what is happening to poverty in India (and in the world) depends a good deal on how much of the discrepancy is attributed to each.

For many economists, who are well-versed in the concepts of national income accounting, but much less so in survey practice, the automatic reaction is to trust the national accounts over the surveys. That there is little basis for such a judgement is splendidly argued by B.S. Minhas, in a paper published in *Sankhya* in 1988, and reprinted here as Chapter 6. Minhas' paper should be compulsory reading for anyone concerned with the issue of national accounts versus surveys, particularly anyone who does not understand the complexities and approximations involved in the construction of the former. Minhas' chapter lays out the issues that have dominated the contemporary debate, the differential definition and coverage of NAS and NSS consumption, differences in timing, and the heavy reliance in national accounting practice on various 'rates and ratios' that link observable but irrelevant quantities to the relevant but unobservable ones. These ratios are in principle derived from surveys, for example surveys that link the earnings of those employed in services to the value added in the service sector, but are frequently many years, often decades, out of date. The use of outdated 'rates and ratios' in an economy undergoing growth and structural development will typically lead to systematic *trend* errors in the accounts. A prime example is the netting out of intermediate production from the value-added, which is frequently done using some fixed ratio. But the degree of intermediation tends to grow as the economy becomes more complex and more monetised, so that the rate of growth of GDP and of consumption will be systematically overstated.

Minhas notes that 'Many discussions of sampling errors seem to imply as if only the NSS estimates suffer from those errors. This is a gross misconception.' It ends by warning against adjustments which assume that only the survey estimates are at fault. In particular, he writes:

> It is indeed hazardous to carry out prorata adjustment in the observed size distribution of consumer expenditure in a particular NSS round by multiplying it with a scalar derived from ratio between the NAS estimates of aggregate private consumption for the nearest financial year and the total NSS consumer expenditure available from that particular round of household budget survey. This kind of mindless tinkering with the NSS size distribution of consumer expenditure, as practiced by the Planning Commission in the Seventh Five Year Plan documents, does not seem permissible either in theory or in light of known facts.

Given that NAS consumption is growing at more than 1 per cent per annum faster than NSS consumption, the application of the prorata adjustment, either 'correction' or 'mindless tinkering', depending on one's point of view, makes an enormous difference to the trend in measured Indian poverty. It is unfortunate that so much of the current debate over this issue should have been little informed by what Minhas wrote 15 years ago.

Contemporary discussions of the discrepancy are represented by two chapters in the current volume by A.C. Kulshreshtha and Aloke Kar and by K. Sundaram and Suresh Tendulkar. Kulshreshtha and Kar are the statisticians at the Central Statistical Organisation who are primarily responsible for the production of the national accounts, and whose views on the accuracy of the consumption estimates should, therefore, be accorded great weight. They document the growing discrepancy between the two sources, from 5 per cent in 1957/58 to more than 38 per cent in 1993/94, and note that the discrepancy for non-food is both larger and more rapidly growing than the discrepancy for food. They then go on to explore the food items in detail, because it is in this area where the most is known, and because often there is enough additional information to make an informed judgement about the likely balance of accuracy. Although there are some exceptions, the general finding is the same as Minhas (who comes at the issue from the survey side, as opposed to Kulshreshtha and Kar, who are national income statisticians), that when there is a discrepancy, it is the National Accounts estimates that are typically less plausible and more likely to be in error. They note that the food and tobacco discrepancy can be attributed to a few specific commodities (fruit, milk products, chicken, eggs, fish, minor cereals and their products, vanaspati, oilseeds and tobacco), and that for major subgroups that are important in poverty studies (major cereals, more commonly used pulses, edible oils, liquid milk, and vegetables), the two estimates are relatively close. They conclude that there is nothing in their findings that would 'render the NSSO data on household consumption expenditure unfit for measurement of poverty incidence'.

Sundaram and Tendulkar's chapter is complementary to that by Kulshreshtha and Kar. It reports on the findings of a joint CSO-NSSO exercise concerned with the cross-validation of the two sets of estimates. They draw particular attention to the 'fluidity' of the NAS estimates, that revisions for some categories are often so large as to cast serious doubt on the estimates in general. This is closely related to the outdated 'rates and ratios' point emphasised by Minhas; when eventually a long-used ratio is abandoned by the CSO, and new survey or other information collected, information based on actual data paints a very different picture to that based on the long-used approximation. Such revisions, while always welcome, do little for the large number of items still hostage to the accuracy of old, and aging, ratios. Sundaram and Tendulkar also argue that survey data is to be preferred because they measure living standards *directly*, as opposed to NAS statistics, which derive consumption as a residual at the end of a long chain of calculations.

Sundaram and Tendulkar also emphasise the importance of items included in the NAS estimates but not in the surveys, such as the imputed rents of owner occupiers and expenditures by non-profit institutions serving households. Like Kulshreshtha and Kar, they demonstrate the increasing importance of a relatively new item, introduced in accord with the recommendations of the 1993 version of the United Nations *System of National Accounts* (SNA), 'financial intermediation services indirectly measured' or FISIM, for short. FISIM is measured as the difference between interest paid to banks and other financial intermediaries and interest paid by them. The idea is that interest charged to borrowers contains, in addition to the market rate of interest, a charge for intermediation services to lenders, while interest paid to lenders is lower than the market, with the difference attributed to financial intermediation services to depositors. The difference between interest paid and interest received is, therefore, a measure of the value of financial intermediation to borrowers and lenders, and since the 1993 revision of the SNA, has been added to national accounts estimates of household consumption, with some backdating into the 1980s. A similar item is included for risk-bearing services, measured as the profits of insurance companies. In India, the value of FISIM increased from close to zero in 1983/84 to 2.5 per cent of consumption in 1993/94, so that this item alone accounts for a quarter of a percentage point per year of the difference in annual growth rates between NAS and survey consumption in India. Also note that, to the extent we are interested in measuring the living standards of the poor, it can reasonably be doubted whether any of the value of financial intermediation is relevant.

I.3 Revisions and Extensions to the NSS Methodology

The design of the Indian surveys has evolved over time, and is constantly under discussion. The NSS runs large consumption surveys every fifth year (in theory, though in recent years the gap has been more typically six years), with smaller consumption surveys in the 'off' years, when the main topic of the enquiry is something else, such as health, or small enterprises. Official poverty estimates are calculated only for the large surveys, on the grounds that sample sizes from the other rounds are too small for accurate estimation of state-level poverty. Yet it has never been made clear how much precision is needed, nor why the smaller rounds could not be used in a limited way, for example, to estimate poverty rates for All India, or for some of the larger states. Similarly, there has been little discussion of the suitability of NSS data for calculating more disaggregated poverty estimates, for example, for regions or districts, although there is widespread interest in these more local estimates. How big should the sample size be for these surveys?

A number of other design issues have also been the subject of recent discussions. We have already noted the issue of the recall period, the length of time over which respondents are asked to report their expenditures. Another perennial issue is the degree of detail in the consumption questionnaire, something that gets adjusted from survey to survey in response to special requests (for example, on the operations of the Public Distribution System), but which has always involved a long list of several hundred separate items. Are such detailed lists really necessary, or could interview time be saved by working with a list of, say, 30 or 40 items? In the past, up to the 50th Round in 1993/94, the consumption survey was canvassed simultaneously with the employment-unemployment survey, with the same households receiving both. This practice was abandoned in the 55th Round, in which the two questionnaires were given to different households, making it impossible to link material from the two modules at the unit record level.

Two of these issues are taken up in the next chapters. Chapter 9 by N.S. Sastry takes up an issue that has long been of interest to researchers on Indian poverty, which is whether it is possible to use NSS data to calculate district-level estimates of poverty. Sastry is a former Director General of the NSSO, so his analysis of the issue carries a great deal of authority. It is often said that the NSS surveys are 'representative' only down to the 'region' level, groupings of districts that are used by the NSSO as part of its stratification design for the surveys. It has never been entirely clear what exactly this warning means, or whether it should prevent a careful analysis of district-level data. And indeed, Sastry shows that with a few exceptions, the NSS data is sufficient to estimate poverty rates district by district within reasonable confidence intervals. This ability will be much enhanced by the increasing availability of state-level sample data. These 'state samples' of the NSS, which are equal in size to the 'central' samples, are tabulated and used in only a few states, and it is much to be desired that the data will be of greater use in future as the technology for processing, tabulating, and analysing it becomes cheaper and easier to use.

The final chapter in this section is a report by Nikhlesh Bhattacharya on behalf of an NSSO Working Group on Non-sampling Errors. Between 1994 and 1998, the NSSO ran experimental surveys on consumers' expenditures that experimented with different reference periods, both for 'high-frequency' purchases, such as food, paan and tobacco, and for 'low frequency' items such as clothing, durable goods, and institutional medical care. The NSSO tradition, based on experiments in the 1950s by Mahalanobis, is to use a 30-day recall period for all goods. The new experiments used two alternative questionnaires, one with the traditional 30-day recall for all goods, and one with three recall periods, 7 days for food, paan, and tobacco, 365 days for low frequency items such as clothing, footwear, durables, education, and institutional medical expenditures, and 30 days for other goods. Because households (or at least first-stage sampling units) were randomised to one questionnaire or the other, it is straightforward to see the effect of the change from one questionnaire to the other. Although there are differences from one commodity group to another, the experimental questionnaire increases measured total expenditure by about 15 to 18 per cent, compared with the traditional one. The increase for some of the high frequency items was a good deal more, for example, 30 to 35 per cent for food. These differences turn into much larger differences in measured rates of poverty, by about a half, at least if the standard poverty lines are used. (It is likely that the poverty lines would have been *lower*, and measured poverty even *lower*, if the experimental questionnaire had been in use at the time that the lines were set. The experimental questionnaires cause more food to be reported relative to other goods, so that calorie norms are attained at a lower level of total household expenditure, see Deaton, 2001, Figure 1.) These experimental results brought the choice of reporting period into the forefront of the debate on poverty.

The Working Group on Non-sampling Errors was charged with discovering which reporting period gives more accurate results, and did so by repeating and updating the experiments that had been carried out by Mahalanobis and Sen (1954). Alternative questionnaires are randomised over the experimental households, using three different reporting periods, 7 days, 30 days, and a 'gold standard' of daily visits accompanied by direct measurement. A pilot study was undertaken in five Indian states from January through June 2000. In the rural households in the experiment, the 7-day estimates were on average 23 per cent higher than the 30-day estimates, somewhat lower than the discrepancy in the large-scale

NSSO 'thin' round surveys. But comparison with the daily estimates shows that, for many important commodities, including cereals and cereal products, the 30-day estimates are *more* accurate than the 7-day estimates. Over all the goods examined, there is no clear superiority of one recall period over another, and there is little evidence that the traditional 30-day reporting period is seriously inadequate. This important study does not support the apparently sensible hypothesis that high-frequency items in India are better measured with a 7-day than a 30-day recall (for example, because people forget), nor does it support the idea that the discrepancy between the NAS and NSS measures of consumption is largely due to underestimation in the latter associated with an overly long-reporting period.

How the choice of reporting period affects estimates of consumption and poverty is a general one that affects many countries other than India. Nor is it the only issue. In literate populations, respondents can be asked to keep diaries as an alternative or supplement to interviews. It is also possible for surveyors to visit the households on multiple occasions, for example to take account of seasonality in expenditures, or because it is thought that respondents cannot remember accurately for anything other than short periods, so that longer reference periods must be gathered a day or two at a time. There has been a good deal of international experience on these issues, reviewed for example in Deaton and Grosh (2000), although there can be no presumption that a good design for one country will be a good design for another. Indeed, the results of the Indian experiments came as something of a surprise, in that prevailing opinion would certainly have judged the 30-day recall period as much too long for most foods.

PART II: INTERPRETING THE EVIDENCE

II.1 What Happened to Poverty in India in the 1990s?

At the end of the 1990s, there had not been a large-scale consumers' expenditure survey since 1993/94, hence there were no official estimates of national or state poverty rates for any later date. The NSSO runs smaller consumers' expenditure surveys between the quinquennial rounds, but poverty estimates based on them are not endorsed by the Planning Commission, even though the sample sizes are large enough to support accurate poverty estimates at the national level. These 'thin' surveys, the last of which was a half year survey in 1998, appeared to show that there had been little or no progress in reducing poverty, see for example the widely noted paper by Gaurav Datt (1999). It is widely believed that there was some problem with the sampling in the rounds from 1994 through 1998, but no official statement has ever confirmed such a problem, nor is it clear that whatever problems there were, seriously affected the results so that, until the results from the 1999/2000 survey were due in March 2001, these surveys provided the only survey data on trends in consumption poverty at the end of the decade. So the results of the 55th Round, the large survey canvassed in 1999/2000, assumed more than the usual importance.

However, there was an immediate problem. As we have seen, the 51st through 54th Rounds had tried out a new questionnaire, the results of which showed more consumption, and less poverty. The NSSO therefore had to face the question of what design to use in the all important 55th Round. Of course, the results of the working group discussed above were not available when the decision had to be made, so there was little solid scientific guidance. By contrast, the consequences for poverty estimation of adopting the new questionnaire were well understood. In the event, and after a good deal of controversy, a 'compromise' solution was adopted whereby, for food, *paan*, and tobacco, each household was asked to report all items over both a 7-day and 30-day recall period. At the same time, the traditional 30-day recall period for durables, footwear, clothing, education, and institutional medical expenses was replaced by a 365-day recall only. While this new, compound, design might well be defended on its own terms, it is clearly not comparable to any previous survey, so that the consumption and poverty estimates based upon it cannot reliably be used to assess trends. Because the experimental questionnaire generates higher responses than the traditional questionnaire, we would expect the presence of both to prompt respondents to reconcile the two reports. We would therefore expect, for example, the reported consumption of milk over 30 days often to be quite similar to (30/7) times the reported consumption of milk over the last 7 days, something that might not happen if the same respondent were asked one, or the other, but not both. And indeed, the means of total estimated consumption using the new and old questionnaires are much more similar in the 55th Round than was the case in the experimental thin rounds, where each household was randomly assigned to one or the other questionnaire. It remained unclear whether this meant that consumption reported with 30-day recall was pulled up to meet the 7-day reports, or whether the latter was pulled down by the presence of the traditional questions, or some combination of both.

The presence of both questionnaires on the survey increased the interviewing time, and forced a number of other changes to the survey. The employment and unemployment survey, usually given to the same households who answer the consumers' expenditure schedules, was given to separate households in the 55th Round. But even within the consumer expenditure schedule, there were important changes, nearly all in the interests of compression and time saving. Questions about the source of consumption, from purchases, home production, in kind, or gifts, were asked in an abbreviated form, and several items of consumption that had previously been asked separately, were now asked together. For example, there is a single question about wheat and atta, rather than questions about each.

In spite of all these difficulties, the 30-day responses were adopted as the new official poverty totals, although the Planning Commission, in its Press Release, also provided (lower) estimates of poverty using the 7-day recall. The estimates based on 30-day recall, which were the only ones even nominally comparable with the previous poverty estimates from 1993/94, showed a remarkable reduction in poverty rates from 1993/94 to 1999/2000. Among rural households estimated poverty fell from 37 to 27 per cent, and among urban households from 33 to 24 per cent, so that all-India poverty fell a full ten points over the 6-year period, from 36 to 26 per cent. Although these estimates were accepted by the Government of India, and vigorously defended by at least one government minister, there was widespread skepticism about their validity, with a fairly general belief that estimated poverty was too low because reported consumption over the 30-day reporting period had been upwardly biased by the simultaneous presence of the 7-day questions. But no one knew by how much the official estimates were out. Note once again that such problems are far from unique to India. There is always a conflict between updating and improving a survey instrument on the one hand, and consistency of estimation on the other. Yet there have been few cases as dramatic as the Indian one, or where the consequences of the change were so little anticipated in advance.

Chapter 11, by Abhijit Sen, first appeared in *Economic and Political Weekly* in 2000, before the final results of the 55th Round were published. It provides the first clear delineation of the combination of problems that were to dominate the interpretation of the full results of the 55th Round, which Sen refers to as a 'failed experiment'. He believes that the traditional 30-day recall period is more reliable, based on a review of relative standard errors, though that argument would not convince a skeptic who believed that the longer recall period led to more bias. (Although Sen's priors were at least partially supported by the later experiments reported in Chapter 10.) Like Minhas earlier, he cautions against using the NAS means to scale up the survey measures of consumption, noting that, to the extent that the NSS understates consumption, it is most likely by undercounting the rich and their expenditures, so that most of the shortfall of NSS from NAS will be accounted for by expenditures by those at the top of the distribution. He argues that, in these circumstances, the NSS will underestimate the degree of inequality, so that scaling up the NSS data to match the NAS mean will understate poverty, and if inequality is widening, overstate the rate of decline of poverty. Such a procedure, by spreading the discrepancy proportionally over all households, effectively attributes to the poor some of the unmeasured consumption of the rich.

Interestingly, recent work by Mistiaen and Ravallion (2003) has shown that this apparently obvious argument does not necessarily hold, and that higher refusal rates by better-off households will have an ambiguous effect on measured inequality. Sen's chapter is also notable for its argument that the rate of divergence between NAS and NSS consumption in nominal terms has been overstated, at least in the 1990s, and at least using earlier, unrevised national accounts estimates. This is a result that contradicts a good deal of earlier research, and appears not to hold using the most recent data. Indeed, Sen's own results using the most recent data shows the ratio of NSS consumption to NAS consumption declining at around one percentage point a year from 1990 through 1997, and that rate of decline has been maintained into 2000 and 2001.

Chapter 12, by Deaton, is one of several attempts to use the 55th Round data in a way that makes it comparable with the 50th Round data, and thus allows a comparison of poverty rates between them. His work, like the similar approach used by Tarozzi (2003), is based on the fact that an important part of the questionnaire was unchanged between the 50th and 55th Rounds, and can, therefore, be compared between them. These are the items that are neither 'high-frequency' nor 'low-frequency' and for which a 30-day reporting period was used in all surveys. This group of '30-day' goods comprises six broad categories, fuel and light, miscellaneous goods, miscellaneous services, non-institutional medical expenses, rent, and consumer cesses and taxes. These items have always been asked using the 30-day reporting period. The first four are important items, and the first three are purchased by almost all households in all surveys. Total expenditure on the six categories accounts for more than 20 per cent of all rural household expenditures, and more in urban areas. Importantly, expenditure on these items is also very well correlated with total household expenditure; in the 50th Round, the correlation between (the logarithm of) per capita total household expenditure and (the logarithm of) per capita household expenditure on these '30-day' goods is 0.79 in the rural sector and 0.86 in the urban sector. As a result, we have a part of the expenditure that is consistently measured across the surveys, and that is highly correlated with total expenditure whose direct measurement cannot be trusted in the 55th Round. Deaton uses the 50th Round data to calculate the probability of being poor as a function of household per capita expenditure on the 30-day goods. This estimated probability can then be taken to the 55th Round, and used together with the (inflation-adjusted) expenditures on the 30-day goods in that round, to estimate for each household a probability that it is poor according to the procedures and definitions of the 50th Round. Adding up these probabilities over all households gives an estimate of the fraction in poverty as it would have been measured had the 55th Round questionnaire been identical to that in the 50th Round.

The validity of Deaton's (and Tarozzi's) procedure depends on two key assumptions: first, that changes elsewhere in the survey do not affect the way that the 30-day goods are reported, and second, that the probability of being poor (i.e. of the poverty line being more than per capita expenditure, measured according to 50th Round protocols) is the same function of 30-day expenditures in 1999/ 2000 as it was in 1993/94. The first assumption is unlikely to be problematic, and if it is, the whole of the 55th Round is almost certainly worthless. The second assumption could potentially fail. For example, if it were the case that, at any given level of per capita total expenditure, households are buying more of these 30-day goods now than they used to, then the procedure would understate poverty, and overstate its rate of decline over time. Tarozzi (2003) shows that there is no evidence of any such trend in the rounds between 1993/94 and 1999/2000, but the possibility of failure remains and indeed, Himanshu and Sen, in Chapter 14, provide some indirect evidence that there is indeed a problem.

According to Deaton's calculations, most of the 'official' decline in poverty is real. For rural households, where the official calculations show the headcount ratio falling from 37.3 per cent in 1993/94 to 27.0 per cent in 1999/2000, Deaton finds that the fall is from 37.3 to 30.2 per cent, so that seven out of the ten points are confirmed. In the urban sector, he estimates a headcount ratio of 24.7 per cent, as opposed to the official 23.6 per cent, so that the fall in the poverty rate is reduced from 8.8 points to 7.5 points. The basic 'fact' behind these results is that there was a substantial increase in consumers' expenditures on the six expenditure categories that were consistently surveyed using 30-day recall, and that it is hard to reconcile that increase without there having been a substantial increase in total expenditure, and thus in the fraction of the population that is poor.

Chapter 13 presents a different set of internal corrections to the 55th Round data by K. Sundaram and Suresh Tendulkar. Because the questionnaire for the 55th Round asked households to report their high-frequency purchases (food, paan, and tobacco) at *both* thirty and seven days, the length of the interview was much longer than had been the case in the 50th Round. In consequence, the NSSO abandoned the traditional practice of asking the same households who answered the consumer expenditure schedule also to answer the questions on the employment and unemployment schedule, instead using different sample of households for each schedule. Such a procedure has the disadvantage that there is no measure of household expenditure for the households in the employment-unemployment sample, so the NSSO introduced a new, abbreviated (one-page) questionnaire on consumers' expenditure that was used for the households in this sample. The reporting period for this supplementary survey is 30 days for all of the 'high' and 'intermediate' frequency goods, so that, in principle, the data can be used instead of the data on food, paan and tobacco in the CE survey, avoiding any contamination of the 30-day reports by the inclusion of the 7-day recall in the questionnaire. But when Sundaram and Tendulkar compare the 30-day reports from the employment and unemployment survey with the comparable 30-day expenditures from the consumption expenditure survey, they find that, at least at the mean, there is a reasonably good match. They use this evidence to argue that the 30-day reports in the main CE survey are more or less accurate, at least on average, in spite of the presence of the potentially contaminating 7-day recall questions. If this much is accepted, the only remaining source of inconsistency between the 50th and 55th Round questionnaires is the treatment of the low frequency items, clothing, durables, educational expenses, and institutional medical expenditures, which were surveyed at 30 days in the 50th Round, but at 365 days in the 55th. But Sundaram and Tendulkar note that the 50th Round actually solicited expenditures on these goods at *both* 30 days and 365 days, so that, if total expenditure for the 50th Round is reconstructed using the latter, it is possible to construct a notionally consistent measure of per capita expenditure in both 50th and 55th Rounds, and hence an estimate of poverty.

Any correction procedure requires a number of untestable assumptions, and, as with Deaton's method, there are a number of potentially weak links in Sundaram and Tendulkar's procedure. The concordance of the reports from the employment-unemployment and consumer-expenditure surveys is evidence only that those two measures are equal, and not necessarily that they are both equal to the hypothetical measure that would have been obtained had the 55th Round been carried out in the same way as was the 50th Round. This is more than a hypothetical point, because the survey literature, as reviewed for example in Deaton and Grosh (2001), shows that abbreviation of questionnaires by aggregating groups of goods tends to reduce the total amount reported. It is, therefore, surprising that the highly aggregated employment-unemployment questionnaire should give the same results as the highly disaggregated consumer-expenditure questionnaire. And indeed the match is far from exact. The abbreviated questions generate less reported consumption for all food items, and much less for tobacco and paan. Second, the 50th Round's reports of expenditure on low frequency items (durables, footwear, education, etc.) over the last 365 days were collected side by side with reports of such expenditures over the last 30 days, while in the 55th Round, the 30-day question was not asked for these items. Much of the concern about the food items in the 55th Round has come from the possibility that dual reporting periods generate different results than a single reporting period, and it is not clear why we can ignore this problem for the low frequency items in the 50th Round.

Sundaram and Tendulkar estimate that there has been substantial poverty decline in India in the 1990s, though less than not only the official figures, but also than those calculated by Deaton's method. Based on the mixed reference periods for the 50th Round, (365 days for low frequency, 30 days for everything else,) they estimate that rural poverty in 1993/94 was 34 per cent and that this had fallen to 29 per cent in 1999/2000 so that the Sundaram and Tendulkar decline is about half of the official one, as opposed to Deaton's, which is about 70 per cent of the official one. For urban households, they estimate poverty in 1993/94 to be 26 per cent and find that it has fallen to 23 per cent in 1999/2000 so that they confirm only about a third of the official decline, whereas Deaton confirms 85 per cent of it. Note that Sundaram and Tendulkar's estimates are not comparable with the official ones, in part because of their use of the mixed reference periods in the 50th Round, also because they use different poverty lines from those used by the Planning Commission. Rather than work with the Planning Commission's state- and sector-specific poverty lines, which have been called into doubt by a number of authors (and see Part III.2 and the associated chapters below), they use the All India lines for 1973/74, updated only for the general rate of price inflation. Sundaram and Tendulkar have also extended their results to the major states, and have used the same corrections to investigate what has happened to the poverty rates for different social and economic groups. In line with other work (in particular see Deaton and Dreze in Chapter 18) it is clear that some groups have done much better than others. In particular, Sundaram and Tendulkar find that while some of the most vulnerable groups (scheduled castes, agricultural labourers, and urban casual labourers) have had poverty reductions in line with those of the general population, others, such as the scheduled tribes, have been left behind.

In Chapter 14, the most recently written in the book, Himanshu and Abhijit Sen have rejoined the argument, challenging both Deaton's and Sundaram and Tendulkar's conclusions. On Deaton's results, they show that the Deaton (and Tarozzi) corrections to the 55th Round data have some unexpected consequences. Starting from the 50th Round estimates of total expenditure from the 'mixed' reference period (365 days for the low-frequency items and 30 days for everything else), they follow Deaton (who used total expenditure from the 'uniform' reference period of 30 days), and calculate the probability of being poor conditional on expenditures on the consistently measured 30-day goods. Turning to the (contaminated) 55th Round, they repeat the calculation, to give the probability of being poor conditional on the consistently measured 30-day goods, with poverty calculated from total expenditure from 30-day responses for all but low frequency items, and 365-day responses for the latter. This second calculation is not to be trusted because of the contamination of the 30-day food responses by the presence of the 7-day questions though, if the 30-day responses are biased upwards by the presence of the 7-day questions, as generally expected, this 'probability of being poor' function would be too low. For any given expenditure on the consistently measured 30-day goods, food estimates are upwardly biased so that total expenditures are too high and poverty too low. In consequence, if Deaton's assumption of stability of the relationship is correct, the contaminated probability-of-poverty function from the 55th Round should lie *below* the similar function from the 50th Round, provided that the 365-day responses in the 50th Round are truly comparable to the 365-day responses in the 55th Round. In fact, as Himanshu and Sen show, the contaminated 'probability of being poor' function for the 55th Round is actually *above* the function from the 50th Round. In consequence, if food expenditures were indeed biased upwards in the 55th Round, Deaton's stability assumption must be false, for example, because the food Engel curve has shifted, with people at the same total expenditure-level spending *less* on food relative to other things, such as the consistently-measured 30-day goods. If so, assessing poverty decline by looking at the increase in those expenditures will overstate the decline in poverty.

These findings are puzzling, not because it is impossible or even implausible that consumers have switched their expenditures from food to non-food, but because there is no evidence of them doing so prior to the 55th Round. Indeed, Tarozzi (2003) looked for such shifts in the rounds between the 50th and 55th, and found none. More investigation of Engel curves is certainly called for, particularly in the recently available 56th and 57th Round data. In the meantime, while Himanshu and Sen's work has certainly shown that Deaton's method, and the poverty estimates based on it, use assumptions that have implications that are hard to explain, it is far from clear that these problems do indeed come from a genuine shift in the food Engel curve that would cause the method to understate poverty. For example, there were many other changes in the 55th Round questionnaire (particularly compressions in the food schedule and in the treatment of home-produced items) that might have affected the amount of food reported.

Himanshu and Sen also criticize Sundaram and Tendulkar's justification for their use of the uncorrected 30-day expenditures for food, paan, and tobacco (on grounds similar to those outlined above), and produce new and lower estimates using their own set of corrections. They use the following procedure. For each category of consumers' expenditure, they calculate three possible estimates: (a) the mean from the consumer's expenditure section of the questionnaire, (b) the mean from the corresponding category from the employment-unemployment section of the questionnaire, and (c) a 'counterfactual' based on extrapolation to the 55th Round of results from the 53rd and 56th Rounds. Given that the estimates from the employment-unemployment part of the survey are likely to be biased down (because the categories are broadly aggregated), they first take the larger of (b) and (c), and then finally choose the smaller of this and the original estimate (a). Their estimate of the mean is thus the minimum of (a) and whichever is the larger of (b) and (c). Like the assumptions underlying all the other estimates, these procedures are unlikely to command universal assent. If the 53rd Round estimates are too low (and indeed there has always been at least some suspicion of these rounds) and if the downward bias in the employment and unemployment schedule estimates is large (as it may well be), then taking the minimum will yield estimates of poverty that are too high.

Himanshu and Sen's final estimates are in line with Sen's original view, that there has been very little decline in headcount poverty in India in the 1990s. Using comparable mixed reference periods for both rounds, they estimate that between the 50th and 55th Rounds the rural headcount ratio fell by only 2.7 percentage points, from 31.9 per cent to 29.1 per cent, and the urban headcount ratio by 3.1 percentage points, from 29.2 per cent to 26.1 per cent. These estimates define the 'pessimistic' pole in the Indian poverty debate. While we shall probably never know for sure what the results of the 55th Round would have been had the questionnaire been the same as previous rounds, there are few who would accept that there has been so little reduction in poverty in the 1990s. Indeed, there is a great deal of evidence from sources other than the consumption surveys, for example, on wage rates, on the ownership rates of durable goods, and on incomes in other surveys, none of which are perfect indicators on their own, but which taken together are extremely difficult to reconcile with an India in which poverty is not declining. Some of this other evidence is discussed in Chapters 15 through 23 which are introduced in the next two subsections.

II.2 The Selection of Poverty Lines

The calculation of poverty measures requires two components, a distribution of household expenditure, and a poverty line or cut-off that separates poor from non-poor households. As is true in many countries, the history of Indian poverty lines is a case study in the interaction of science and politics, with essentially political decisions often claiming a scientific basis, sometimes with justification, and sometimes not. Although poverty lines are often linked to the amount of money that households need, to be able to buy a minimally satisfactory diet, the use and long-term survival of poverty lines depends on policy makers and others accepting them as useful. Chapter 15, by Ashok Rudra, originally published in the Bardhan and Srinivasan (1974), discusses the history of Indian poverty lines up to that time. He writes about the 'magic number' of Rs 20 per head in 1960/61 prices, and shows that a food-based analysis would lead to a considerably higher number. Yet the 'magic number' persisted, as similar magic numbers have persisted in other countries, not because it was correct in any scientific or nutritional sense, but, because, once established as useful in economic and political discussions, poverty numbers are resistant to change, unless they are wildly at variance with people's intuitive notions of the amount of money needed to stay out of poverty.

From late 1970s into the mid-1990s, the Planning Commission used only two poverty lines for per capita household expenditure in India, Rs 49 for rural households, and Rs 57 for urban households, so that prices were taken to be about 16 per cent higher for urban households, close to the 15 per cent urban price differential estimated by Chatterjee and Bhattacharya in 1974. The poverty lines were held constant in real terms, and were converted to current rupees using the implicit price deflator of consumption in the National Accounts. This process had the disadvantage of ignoring interstate differences in price levels, as well as variations from state to state in urban to rural price differential. Furthermore, it might be doubted whether the national accounts consumption deflator was an ideal measure of inflation for households near the poverty line. These problems (and several others) were dealt with by an Expert Group in 1993, whose recommendations for new poverty lines were adopted (in a somewhat modified form) by the Planning Commission, and these 'Expert Group' poverty lines have been used in the official calculations of poverty in India from 1983 (back-casting the methodology) to the present day. According to these procedures, poverty lines are defined at the state level, separately for urban and rural households. Each line is updated by a state-specific price index, the state consumer price index for agricultural labourers (CPIAL) for rural lines, and the state consumer price index for industrial workers (CPIIW) for urban lines. (Separate procedures are followed for the small states and territories, sometimes assuming the poverty *line* of a nearby state, and sometimes its poverty *rate*.) There is no countrywide poverty line as such; instead, once the all-India rural and urban headcount ratios have been calculated, the all-India lines are defined implicitly as the lines which, when applied to all households, give the all-India poverty rates.

The Expert Group poverty lines have a serious problem in that the urban to rural price differentials that are implied by them are too large to be credible. It is unclear how this happened, whether there was an error in the calculations, or whether the price indexes that went into the calculations produced the result through some unfortunate cumulative effect. Certainly, the state by state urban and rural poverty lines were calculated independently, without consideration of the implicit urban to rural price differentials. In any case, the average ratio of urban to rural poverty lines is around 1.4, and varies widely across states; in the 50th Round (1993/94), it is more than 1.7 in Andhra Pradesh, and nearly as much in Maharashtra, Madhya Pradesh, and Karnataka, but actually less than unity in Assam. As a result, the official headcount ratio measures of poverty are actually *higher* in urban than rural areas in some states, and the all-India headcount ratios differ little between the two sectors. Perhaps less serious, although the issue has attracted more comment, is the question of the accuracy of the state-level price indexes. These are reweighted only infrequently, so that, for example, the CPIAL used weights based on a 1960/61 survey until 1995. And although the CPIAL and CPIIW indexes are almost certainly better than the price deflator of national accounts consumption, it is unclear whether the prices or the weights that go into these indexes are the right ones for a national poverty measure.

Alternative price indexes can be calculated directly from the NSSO's consumption surveys. For almost all of the foods in the survey, as well as for tobacco, alcohol, and fuels, respondents report both expenditures and quantities. It is, therefore, possible to calculate a price, or more accurately a unit value, for each good for each household, and these can be used to form price indexes, for urban, for rural, for states, and for different rounds of the survey. The details of this work were originally laid out in Chapter 16 by Deaton and Alessandro Tarozzi, which is published here for the first time. Deaton and Tarozzi's results are brought up to date in the short Chapter 17, by Deaton, who presents a set of poverty lines based on the indexes. These price indexes are quite different from the price indexes implicit in the official poverty lines, and much closer to the uniform 16 per cent urban/rural price differential that was originally calculated, using similar procedures, by Chatterjee and Bhattacharya (1974). As a result, headcount ratios calculated using Deaton and Tarozzi's lines show much higher rates of rural relative to urban poverty than do the traditional lines. Their price indexes also rise somewhat less rapidly than do the official indexes, with the result that the associated poverty rates for the country as a whole decline somewhat more rapidly than do the official rates, at least until we reach the 55th Round in 1999/2000, where the contamination becomes an issue.

Deaton's poverty lines, together with his procedures for correcting the 55th Round data, form the basis for the analysis of poverty and inequality in the paper by Deaton and Jean Dreze, included here as Chapter 18. According to these estimates, there has been a fairly steady poverty decline in India in the 1970s, 1980s, and 1990s, with neither acceleration nor deceleration over the last decade. Deaton and Dreze argue that their estimates are broadly consistent with a range of other evidence, including state-level growth rates from state GDP accounts and the growth of agricultural wages. They also note that there has been a marked increase in consumption inequality in the late 1990s, between states, with the already better-off states in the south and west growing more rapidly than the poorer states in the north and east, between rural and urban households, with growth a good deal more rapid for the latter, and within the urban sectors of many states, where consumption has been growing more rapidly among the best off.

It is important to note that the trends in inequality are obscured by the questionnaire changes in the 55th Round. The substitution of a 365-day for a 30-day reference period for the low frequency items pulls up the bottom tail of the distribution of expenditures for those items, while simultaneously depressing its mean, so that expenditures on low frequency items are less unequally distributed using a 365-day as opposed to 30-day recall. This effect carries through to the distribution of per capita total household expenditure, whose distribution is artificially compressed in the 55th Round compared with the 50th. This questionnaire-driven reduction in measured inequality offsets and obscures the underlying increase in inequality if the old and new questionnaires are compared without explicit correction.

Deaton and Dreze also note that progress on consumption poverty is only one dimension of progress on poverty, and that broader perspectives reveal a picture that is a good deal more mixed. Although there has been rapid and most welcome progress in enrolment rates in elementary education, there has been a slowing down in progress in reducing the infant mortality rate. And even the economic progress has been far from even, with some groups losing out as others made historically impressive gains. We return to these broader issues in the final chapters of this book.

II.3 Other Data, Other Assessments

While some researchers have tried to work within the 55th Round data, trying to salvage and interpret, others have taken different approaches using alternative sources of data. Chapter 19, by Gaurav Datt, Valerie Kozel, and Martin Ravallion, takes a forecasting approach based on an econometric model that links poverty rates to their plausible determinants, including agricultural yields, non-farm growth, development spending and inflation. They use the estimated model to project poverty in 1999/2000, ignoring the flawed data from the 55th Round. According to their calculations, the changes in the explanatory variables would have warranted a decrease in the headcount ratio from 39 per cent of India's population in 1993/94 to 34 per cent in 1999/2000, suggesting that the pace of poverty reduction in the 1990s was slightly lower than in the 1980s, and lower than might be expected given India's high rate of economic growth in the latter half of the 1990s. The differences between official and predicted rates of progress are in large part due to slower progress in some of India's largest and poorest states, particularly Bihar, Uttar Pradesh, and Maharashtra. Bihar and Uttar Pradesh alone account for over half the difference between official estimates and predicted poverty levels. Datt, Kozel and Ravallion's projections are similar to the adjusted calculations by Sundaram and Tendulkar, but show a good deal less poverty reduction than does Deaton's method. Unlike the calculations based on the adjustment of the 55th Round data, the econometric results are predictions, not measurements, and will fail if the process of poverty reduction involves a change in the estimated relationship that would, in principle, be captured by direct measurement. Econometric predictions also have standard errors that depend on the fit of the model. Of course, because of the contamination of the survey, direct, comparable measurement is impossible, and all adjustment procedures rest on assumptions that can be challenged.

Chapter 20, by Suman Bery and R.K. Shukla, presents another method for estimating poverty trends, based on information collected from the Market Information Surveys of Households (MISH) that are run by the National Council on Applied Economic Research (NCAER.) MISH is a series of large-scale annual surveys of household expenditures on consumer durables and other items of consumption. Because the design, sample size and the survey methodology have been consistent over time, Bery and Shukla argue that the MISH is useful for identifying trends in consumption patterns. The MISH also asks several questions on household incomes, and these are used to provide alternative estimates of poverty. The analysis of the MISH data suggests that poverty has fallen sharply in India, whether estimated from the income data, or from the increase in the ownership of durable goods. One major concern about the MISH surveys is the adequacy of a single income question 'What is your annual household income from all sources?' Household income is always a difficult concept to explain and to measure, especially for rural households, many of whom are self-employed in agriculture. Incomes for such households require a great deal of imputation, as well as a careful separation of business from personal expenses. In consequence, most creators and users of household surveys would not work with such a question. Unfortunately, it is difficult to explore these issues in detail, because the MISH data are proprietary and have never been made available to independent researchers, even many years after their proprietary value has expired.

In Chapter 21, Surjit Bhalla argues that there has been a very sharp decline in poverty in India in the 1990s, and that the official estimate of 24 per cent in 1999/2000 is an underestimate. He writes that 'it is almost incontrovertible that poverty in India was less than 15 per cent in 1999/2000.' He also argues that inequality has *improved* in the late 1990s. Bhalla's conclusions are based on the argument that the national accounts estimates of consumption are more reliable than the survey estimates, and on a procedure that scales each household's consumption of each item so that the totals from the survey agree with the totals from the national accounts on an item by item basis, at least up to a scale factor. Not surprisingly, these imputations induce a rapid decrease in poverty. Bhalla does not address the detailed arguments by Minhas against this sort of adjustment, nor Kulshreshtha and Kar's demonstration of the inferiority of the numbers that Bhalla treats as correct compared with those that he rejects. Indeed, Bhalla does not reference their papers. His inequality measures also appear to be taken directly from the unadjusted 1999/2000 survey, and are compared with similar measures from earlier surveys. But as we have seen, and as is documented in detail in Deaton and Dreze's chapter, the unadjusted data from the 55th Round understate measured inequality. Yet, even if most researchers remain unpersuaded by Bhalla's arguments, his work is important because it represents one of the poles in the current debate on the Indian poverty numbers.

Chapter 22, by Abhijit Banerjee and Thomas Piketty, also takes up the issue of changing inequality previously raised in the chapters by Deaton and Dreze and by Bhalla. Their data come from the individual income-tax returns which, under some fairly heroic assumptions, can be used to document the very top end of the Indian income distribution. As many observers have conjectured, Indians with the highest incomes have done extremely well during the boom of the 1990s. Banerjee and Piketty calculate that the average incomes of the top 1 per cent have increased by 70 per cent in real terms, while at the very top, among the top 1 per cent of 1 per cent, average incomes tripled. Banerjee and Piketty provide the first good evidence on the extent to which there has been increasing inequality among the very best-off Indians. It is also relevant for the debate between the national accounts and the surveys; if inequality is increasing, and if people are less likely to cooperate with the survey – the higher their income, then the ratio of measured consumption in the surveys to true consumption will fall. And indeed, Banerjee and Piketty show that around a quarter of the increase in the NAS/NSS gap can plausibly be attributed to the increase in inequality among high income Indians that is documented in their chapter.

PART III: BROADER PERSPECTIVES ON POVERTY

The recent debate on Indian poverty has focused primarily on the headcount index, or proportion of people whose per capita consumption falls below the poverty line. But estimates of poverty that rely exclusively on income and consumption measures fail to capture important aspects of deprivation experienced by the poor. Human development is one of these: the Human Development Index (HDI) is based on a multidimensional concept of human development that has been developed under the overall leadership of the United Nations Development Program (UNDP). In India, there are several initiatives being pursued at the national and the state level to build database on human development indicators.

Insecurity, including food insecurity, violence, social exclusion, and lack of basic human rights are other important aspects of deprivation in India. The final chapters of the book explore some of these broader perspectives in the context of the debate on the 55th Round and poverty levels and trends in the 1990s.

Valerie Kozel and Barbara Parker in Chapter 23, describe multiple dimensions of poverty in Uttar Pradesh (UP), the largest state in India and one of the poorest. Poverty in UP is linked not only to material deprivation but also deprivation of human resources, social contacts, voice and power. Material deprivation is measured through the conventional headcount index; despite slow growth in mean per-capita consumption levels (on the order of 1.4 per cent per annum), poverty was estimated to fall by some 5–8 percentage points between 1993/94 and 1999/2000. However, the reduction is in part explained by the fact that many households are clustered around the poverty line so that a little growth can result in a sharp reduction in the number of people in poverty. Many of the erstwhile poor still have very low consumption levels and therefore remain vulnerable to income and other shocks that can pull them back into poverty.

Kozel and Parker, see poverty in UP, in terms of lack of assets combined with low and uncertain returns to the limited stock of assets owned by the poor. Thus poor men and women suffer from poverty of private resources, poverty of access to public goods and services, and poverty of social relationships. The poor are a heterogeneous group, characterised by many different forms of deprivation. To be effective, programmes and policies designed to redress poverty must be cognizant of its various dimensions and underlying causes.

Chapter 24, by J.V. Meenakshi and Brinda Viswanathan, examines calorie deprivation as a dimension of poverty; it explores nutrient intake patterns in rural India and shows that calorie intakes in India as a whole have declined since the early 1980s. Estimates of poverty based on calorie intakes are much higher than poverty estimates based on reported aggregate consumer expenditure measures, Meenakshi and Viswanathan argue that this finding highlights the need for a revision of the official poverty lines to better capture calorie norms. The research reveals that inequality in calorie intake has declined with the wealthy consuming less and the poor consuming more. Whether it makes sense to measure poverty through calorie consumption, as 'nutritional' poverty, remains a controversial issue. To the extent that the lower calorie consumption is a choice, in some cases reflecting higher incomes or different patterns of work, it is not a matter of great concern. On the other hand, it is clear that, for some groups at least, declining calorie consumption is a marker of increased poverty.

Finally, in Chapter 25, Rinku Murgai, M.H. Suryanarayana and Salman Zaidi discuss regional poverty estimates for the state of Karnataka, which are derived from a merged NSS 55th Round central, and matching state sample. (The method was discussed by Sastry in Chapter 9 of this volume.) They find substantial regional heterogeneity in poverty levels: districts in northern parts of the state are much poorer than those in other regions. They compare regional patterns of poverty with regional patterns of living standards based on other sources of information – agricultural wages, district domestic product, and employment shares in agriculture and non-farm activities; these are found to be largely consistent with regional poverty levels. However, urban-rural poverty differentials are not consistent with urban-rural differentials in other indicators: official estimates suggest that urban poverty was 6 percentage points higher than rural poverty in 1999/2000 (18.2 per cent of the rural population live below the poverty line, as compared to 24.5 per cent of the urban population), despite superior educational attainments, access to services, etc., in urban areas. The authors re-estimate poverty levels using Deaton's revised poverty lines (see the earlier discussion on poverty lines, also Chapters 17 and 18) and find a sharp drop in the headcount rate in urban Karnataka, and a significantly stronger statewide correlation between poverty levels and other measures of living conditions. The findings of the study highlight the need to update the Expert's Group poverty lines, also to assess poverty in the context of a wider set of indicators of well-being.

PART IV: SUMMARY AND NEXT STEPS

First, despite an extensive body of empirical work by eminent researchers, the debate on what happened to Indian poverty in the 1990s continues. And there is a good deal more fuelling this debate than concerns about data or poverty measurement: its persistence (and passion) reflect the complexity of the issues at hand as well as the great diversity of India. There is little doubt that things have changed in India and in many cases changed for the better. But there are still important concerns, e.g. about differences in opportunities and growing regional disparities, characterised by lagging progress in some states in the face of impressive and uncontestable progress in others. And there are concerns about perceived discrimination and continuing disparities across social, ethnic, and religious groups, all of which contribute to the mixed regional picture. Even with perfect data, there would be no single answer to the question 'what has happened to poverty in India in the 1990s?'

The difficulties in interpreting the data from the 55th Round have permitted a wide range of views about the rate of poverty reduction. These are unlikely to be resolved quickly. At the time of writing, two smaller NSSO surveys have been conducted following the 55th Round, the 56th and 57th. Unfortunately, these do not provide any clear resolution to the debate. The 56th Round, conducted in 2000/2001, shows a further reduction in poverty, very much along the trend line calculated by Deaton and Dreze in Chapter 19. The 57th Round data shows that there was a sharp *increase* in poverty compared with the previous year. (Both 56th and 57th Rounds use the 30/30/365 Schedule, which is the same as the 55th Round, but without the dual reporting periods for the high frequency goods, and so are nominally comparable with it.) It is unclear why poverty should have risen, and there is no obvious economic event that would have been expected to generate it. Yet the results from this latest round are more in line with the poverty estimates from the 51st through 53rd Rounds, in line with the arguments by Sen and Himanshu in Chapter 14 that there has been little or no reduction in poverty. Yet the other evidence on living standards appears to contradict such a view.

The workshop helped to build a consensus, although perhaps a short-lived one, on the situation of the poor in India and on recent progress. There was also wide agreement on the need to put the NSS back on a sound footing, as well as to improve the procedures for changes in survey design and for the calculation of poverty rates. Work needs to be done both on survey design, and on the official poverty lines. On the former, it would be extremely desirable if the next large round of the NSS provides a good link with the past, as well as setting the standard for the future. This could be done by randomly splitting the sample, giving one set of households a questionnaire that is identical or close to identical to that from the 50th Round in 1993/94, while the other half receive a new, best-practice, questionnaire that will be redesigned based on what has been learned from the experiments of the past decade. By randomising within first-stage sample units (villages or city blocks), such a design can permit each arm of the survey to have large sample sizes with minimal increase in cost. With luck, and no new missteps, we can hope that the 61st Round, unlike the 55th Round, will provide a much closer consensus on what has been happening to living standards in India.

We can only speculate on what might be recommended by a new Expert Group on poverty measurement, although it should certainly deal with the deficiencies of the current set of lines. But it should have a wide mandate, and it should consider other, far-reaching changes in methodology. At the same time the government of India needs to look at ways to strengthen the overall statistical system, in line with recommendations of the National Statistical Commission report (Rangarajan, 2001). As a result of these various initiatives, India should soon be in much better a place to take stock of the impact of her development strategy and programmes on poverty.

It is hard not to add a final word on the relationship between poverty measurement in India, and the surprising results of the election in May 2004, which has been interpreted by many as a confirmation that the 1990s, however good to the urban middle classes, left the rural poor behind. The election campaign of the ruling BJP had featured 'India Shining' a vision that is consistent with the views of the poverty optimists, that the 1990s saw the virtual elimination of poverty in India, and that extrapolated the successes of the urban middle classes to all of India. The testing of a link between the poverty estimates and the election would be a major undertaking, and it is wise to remember that the complexities of coalition politics in India make any single explanation more than usually hazardous. Nonetheless, these results have given new impetus to the debate on growth, inequality and poverty reduction in India, and the many challenges still facing politicians and policy makers.

REFERENCES

Bardhan, P.K. and J.N. Srinivasan, eds. (1974), *Poverty and Income Distribution in India*, Indian Statistical Institute, Calcutta.

Chatterjee, G.S., and N. Bhattacharya (1974), 'Between State Variations in Consumer Prices and Per Capita Household Consumption in Rural India' in *Poverty and Income Distribution in India*, T.N. Srinivasan and Pranab Bardhan, eds., Calcutta: Statistical Publishing Society.

Datt, Gaurav (1999), 'Has Poverty Declined since Economic Reforms? Statistical Data Analysis', *Economic and Political Weekly*, 11–17 December, pp. 11–17.

Deaton, Angus (2001), 'Counting the World's Poor, Problems and Possible Solutions', *World Bank Research Observer*, 16(2), Fall, pp. 125–47.

Deaton, Angus (2005), 'Measuring Poverty in a Growing World: Or Measuring Growth in a Poor World', *Review of Economics and Statistics*, Vol. 87, No. 1, pp. 1–19.

Deaton, Angus and Margaret Grosh (2000), 'Consumption' in *Designing Household Questionnaires for Developing Countries: Lessons from Fifteen Years of the Living Standard Measurement Study*, Margaret Grosh and Paul Glewwe, eds., Washington, DC: World Bank, pp. 91–133.

Garner, Thesia I., George Janini, William Passero, Laura Paszkiewicz and Mark Vendemia (2003), 'The Consumer Expenditure Survey in Comparison: Focus on Personal Consumption Expenditures', Washington, DC: Bureau of Labor Statistics, processed.

Government of India (2000), *Final Report of the National Statistical Commission*, New Delhi.

——— (1993), *Report of the Expert Group on Estimation of Proportion and Number of Poor*, New Delhi: Planning Commission.

Mahalanobis, P.C. and S.B. Sen (1954), 'On Some Aspects of the Indian National Sample Survey', *Bulletin of the International Statistical Institute*, 34.

Martin, Margaret E., Miron E. Straf and Constance F. Citro (2002), *Principles and Practices for a Federal Statistical Agency*, 2nd edn., Washington, DC: National Research Council.

Mistiaen, Johan A. and Martin Ravallion (2003), *Survey Compliance and the Distribution of Income*, Washington, DC, The World Bank, processed.

Rangarajan, C. (2001), 'The National Statistical Commission: An Overview of Recommendations', *Economic and Political Weekly,* October.

Tarozzi, Alessandro (2003), 'Calculating Comparable Statistics from Incomparable Surveys, with an Application to Poverty in India', Duke University, Department of Economics, processed, March.

Triplett, Jack E. (1997), 'Measuring Consumption: The Post-1973 Slowdown and the Research Issues', *Federal Reserve Bank of St Louis Review*, May-June, pp. 9–42.

Part I

The Statistical Basis for Poverty Measurement

I.1 THE STATISTICAL SYSTEM

1. Meeting Policy Makers' Information Needs: Lessons from the US Experience

2. Statistics vs Economics and Politics: Insights from the French Experience

3. India's Statistical System: Critiquing the Report of the National Statistical Commission

1

Meeting Policy-Makers' Information Needs
Lessons from the US Experience

Katharine G. Abraham

My subject in this note, is the contributions that household survey data can make to informing the public policy process. By training, I am an economist. Following a number of years in teaching and research positions at MIT, the Brookings Institution and the University of Maryland, I spent eight years, from October 1993 through October 2001, as Commissioner of the US Bureau of Labor Statistics (BLS). Together with the Census Bureau, the BLS is one of the two largest statistical agencies in the US federal government structure, and is responsible for producing a wide range of data, including information on employment, unemployment, prices, consumption patterns, occupational safety and health, and productivity, among other subjects. In my position at the BLS, I had a front-row seat for observing the contributions that the right data available in the right form can make to the development of effective policy.

My comments are focused on the policy uses of household survey data, as opposed to business survey data, with particular reference to the monthly Current Population Survey (CPS), the National Longitudinal Survey (NLS) programme, and the Panel Study of Income Dynamics (PSID). The CPS is the US government's flagship monthly household survey, the source of our monthly data on unemployment, among much other information. The NLS programme consists of a set of longitudinal surveys that have followed selected age cohorts over periods of many years. The PSID is another large-scale longitudinal survey that has been in existence for more than three decades. In contrast to the NLS surveys, which focus on specific age groups, the PSID was designed to be representative of the entire US population.

In thinking about policy makers' needs for information, it may be useful to consider the different sorts of questions that are likely to need answers. Although the boundaries between the following categories may be fuzzy, one can distinguish among information needs related to: (a) monitoring current conditions, (b) assessing longer-term trends, and (c) analysis and evaluation. Examples of specific topics that fit into each of the three categories are listed in Box 1.1; some of these are touched on, briefly below. Cross-sectional household surveys, such as the CPS, can contribute greatly to meeting monitoring and trend assessment needs, but longitudinal surveys, such as the various NLS surveys and the PSID, are often better suited to meeting analysis and evaluation needs.

Box 1.1 Selected Examples of Policy-relevant Topics Addressed Using CPS, NLS and PSID Data

Monitoring Current Conditions
- Movements in the unemployment rate
- Distribution of unemployment across demographic groups
- Number and characteristics of minimum wage workers

Trend Assessments
- Changes in earnings inequality associated with differing levels of educational attainment
- Changes in the incidence and demographic distribution of poverty over time
- Changes in women's labour market attachment compared to men's, together with changes in women's relative earnings
- Changes in the incidence of union membership

Analysis and Evaluation
- Persistence of adverse states (poverty, welfare receipt, low earnings)
- Effect of time spent by young children in day care, on their cognitive and emotional development
- Effect of unemployment benefits on youth unemployment
- Effect of training on subsequent earnings
- Effect of military service on the subsequent earnings of disadvantaged youth
- Effect of teen childbearing on mothers' later success in the labour market.

The CPS is a monthly household survey of approximately 50,000 to 60,000 households (the exact size of the survey has varied somewhat over time). Information on the characteristics and labour force status of all household members aged 16 and above is collected as part of the core CPS questionnaire. This information includes, among other things, the gender, race, ethnicity, age, and education of each eligible household member; for those who are employed, what kind of work they do, how many hours they work and how much they earn; and for those who are unemployed, whether they had worked previously and how long they have been searching for work.[1]

In addition, the CPS has served as a vehicle for supplemental questionnaires, added to the basic questions in selected months. These questionnaires would have been prohibitively expensive to administer as stand-alone surveys. By way of illustration, the topics covered by these supplements over a recent six-year period are shown in Box 1.2. Some of the supplements, most notably the annual income and work experience supplement that has been administered for many years each March, have become a regular part of the CPS programme.

Some of the CPS supplements are funded by policy departments to address specific information needs. Since the mid-1980s, for example, the Employment and Training Administration in the Department of Labor has funded a biennial supplement to provide information about workers displaced from their jobs. To take another example, the Department of Agriculture, which has responsibility for administering a food stamp programme that reduces food costs for low-income families, has on several occasions, sponsored a supplement related to families' concerns about adequate access to food. Giving policy departments the option of sponsoring such a supplement is one vehicle for ensuring that their information needs are met.

With respect to monitoring current conditions, the CPS is the source of perhaps the single-most watched statistic about the US economy, the monthly unemployment rate. The unemployment rate data are so important, partly because they are so timely. Each month's figures are released just three weeks

---

[1] A more detailed description of the CPS may be found in the US Bureau of Labor Statistics (1997), available in an updated form at http://www.bls.gov/opub/hom/homch1_itc.htm

Box 1.2 Current Population Survey Supplement Topics, 1996/2001

Topic	Dates	Sponsor(s)
Alimony and child support	April 1996, April 1998, April 2000	Office of Child Support Enforcement
Annual income and work experience	March of every year	Census Bureau, Bureau of Labour Statistics, Department of Health and Human Services
Computer use	August 2000	Department of Commerce
Computer and Internet use	September 2001	Bureau of Labor Statistics, National Technical Information Administration, Department of Commerce and others
Contingent and alternative work arrangements	February 1997, February 1999, February 2001	Bureau of Labor Statistics
Displaced workers	February 1996, February 1998, February 2000	Employment and Training Administration
Fertility and birth expectations	June 1996, June 1998, June 2000	Census Bureau
Food security	September 1996, April 1997, August 1998, April 1999, September 2000, April 2001	Department of Agriculture
Home-based work	May 1997, May 2001	Bureau of Labor Statistics
Job tenure	February 1996, February 1998, February 2000	Bureau of Labor Statistics
Lead paint awareness	June 1997	Department of Housing and Urban Development
Race and ethnicity	July 2000	Bureau of Labor Statistics
School enrolment	October of every year	Census Bureau
Tobacco use	January 1996, May 1996, September 1998, January 1999, May 1999, January 2000, May 2000, June 2001, November 2001	National Cancer Institute
Veterans' labour market experience	September 1997, September 1999, August 2001	Bureau of Labor Statistics, Veterans Employment and Training Administration
Voting and registration	November 1996, November 1998, November 2000	Census Bureau
Work schedules	May 1997, May 2001	Bureau of Labor Statistics

Source: US Bureau of Labor Statistics and US Census Bureau.

after the mid-month reference period, generally the first Friday of the following month, which makes them especially useful for policy makers and others concerned about the current state of the economy. Some indication of the attention paid to these figures, can be found in the sensitivity of interest rates, especially at the shorter end of the term structure, to surprises in the reported unemployment rate (Krueger and Fortson, 2003).

Because it has such a long history – the CPS has existed since the 1940s and a continuous time series on a great many items of interest can be constructed from 1967 forward – the CPS also makes valuable contributions to assessments of long-term trends in the US economy. One major concern of US policy makers in recent years, has been the dramatic growth in the inequality of earnings, especially the growing gap in earnings between more- and less-educated workers. Most of the research, documenting the growth in earnings inequality during the 1980s and early 1990s that has drawn policy makers' attention to this issue, has been based on CPS data.[2] A related topic is how the incidence and distribution of poverty in society in the US has changed over time. Thanks to the availability of CPS data, the dramatic decline in poverty among the elderly and the growth in child poverty that has occurred since the early 1960s are well-documented (see Census 2003 of the US Bureau). Another significant focus of attention for US policy makers, has been the changing position of women in the labour market. Although women remain less likely than men to be employed for pay and continue to earn less than men when they are employed, gender outcomes in the labour market have become much more equal than in the past (see Blau and Kahn, 1997). Again, most of what policy makers know about this subject, is based on research using the CPS data.

One important issue for the statistical agency staff who manage the CPS is how to reconcile the desire to improve the survey, as opportunities to do so present themselves with the need for comparability in the survey data over time. Because comparability is so important, changes to the CPS questionnaire have not been made lightly. The core questionnaire was essentially static, for example, between 1967 and 1994. By the late 1980s, however, the survey had become outdated in certain respects, and a major redesign of the CPS was introduced in January 1994. As a part of this redesign, the questions used to measure official labour force concepts were refined, some of the labour force concepts were modified and new questions were added to the survey. At the same time, collection of the survey was converted from a pencil-and-paper to a computer-assisted format. A major concern about these changes was that survey estimates for the post-1994 period would not be comparable to those for earlier years. To address this concern, a large-scale parallel survey employing the new methods was carried out from July 1992 through December 1993, and respondents to the parallel survey were administered the old version of the survey during the early months of 1994. The availability of these parallel survey data permitted the development of 'adjustment factors' that analysts could use in comparing pre- and post-redesign data (Polivka and Miller, 1998).

Although the CPS has proven to be an enormously flexible instrument for collecting information on current conditions and long-term trends, there are issues it cannot address that *can* be addressed using longitudinal or panel surveys such as the various NLS surveys and the PSID. The groups surveyed as part of the NLS programme include men aged 14–24 (young men) and 45–59 (older men) when first interviewed in 1966; women aged 14–24 (young women) and 30–44 (mature women) when first interviewed in 1968; youth aged 14–22 when first interviewed in 1979; the children of the women in the 1979 youth cohort; and youth aged 12–17 when first interviewed in 1997. Surviving members of all, except the original men's cohorts continued to be interviewed on a regular, ongoing schedule.[3] The first PSID interviews were conducted in 1968 and provide a similarly long set of observations for continuing respondents. The PSID is structured to provide information about households. As children in the original households leave to form their own households, these new households are added to the survey so that the sample continues to represent the population as a whole.[4] The NLS and PSID surveys are a key component of the statistical infrastructure relevant for policy makers in the United States.

One simple but important feature of longitudinal data is that they allow the analyst to study the persistence of adverse states over time. A cross-sectional survey can provide information on, for example,

---

[2] Two landmark studies are Katz and Murphy (1992) and Juhn, Murphy and Pierce (1993).

[3] More detailed descriptions of the various surveys conducted as part of the NLS programme may be found at http://www.bls.gov/nls/home.htm

[4] For additional information about the PSID, see http://psidonline.isr.umich.edu/

the number of people with incomes below the poverty line. A longitudinal survey will reveal whether those below the poverty line, tend to move upwards in the income distribution over time and, if some people move upwards, what their characteristics tend to be, or whether the poor tend to remain poor. Seminal research by Bane and Ellwood (1986) using PSID data demonstrated that, while many spells of poverty are short, most of those who are poor at any point in time are in the midst of rather long spells of poverty. In an interesting recent extension of Bane and Ellwood's work, also using PSID data, Stevens (1999) shows that many of those who exit poverty, subsequently slip back below the poverty line. This sort of information about the dynamics of poverty is clearly apt to be helpful for thinking about poverty policy.

Longitudinal data also offers considerable potential for identifying the causal factors influencing outcomes of interest. One of the great concerns in American life, for example, has been the effects of women's labour market participation on their children's well-being. Both NLS and PSID data have been used extensively to address this question. To take just one example, Waldfogel, Han and Brooks-Gunn (2002) conclude from their analysis of NLS data that, at least among non-Hispanic white children, maternal employment during the first year of life has adverse effects on the child's subsequent cognitive development, but that maternal employment during the second and third years of life has positive effects on subsequent cognitive development. Research on this important topic continues. At the other end of the life cycle, data for the older NLS cohorts have been used by researchers interested in studying retirement behaviour, a subject of great relevance to policy makers concerned with social security and pension policy (see, for example, Gustman and Steinmeier, 2000, who use NLS data to study retirement decisions in dual career families, documenting the strong tendency for these couples to coordinate their retirement dates despite the younger ages of wives as compared to their husbands).[5]

It is interesting that in the United States, even more so than in most other Western countries, there has been much heavier reliance on household survey data than on administrative data to inform policy making. This reflects not only the relatively unregulated nature of the US economy, which means that administrative data are perhaps less available than elsewhere, but also the relative advantages offered by available household survey data, such as that from the CPS, NLS and PSID, in terms of comparability over time and the quality controls built into the survey process.

This brings me to the lessons that might be drawn from the US experience about how data should be collected – as opposed to what data should be collected – to meet policy makers' information needs. Box 1.3 summarises a set of principles and practices for statistical agencies, developed by the Committee on National Statistics of the National Research Council, to which I believe most US observers would wholeheartedly subscribe. Although these principles were developed with official federal statistical agencies in mind, similar principles are applicable to other survey organisations that receive public support for their survey work, such as the Survey Research Center at the University of Michigan. I restrict myself here to a few brief observations regarding some selected aspects of how the official US statistical agencies operate, that seem to me to be particularly important.

It goes almost without saying, that the information produced by any statistical agency can be of value only to the extent that data users find it credible. The perceived independence of a statistical agency is a

---

[5] Questions about retirement planning and behaviour are of sufficient interest to US policy makers that two separate longitudinal studies of older Americans, specifically focused on retirement decisions, have been carried out – the Retirement History Survey, for which respondents were interviewed bienially from 1969 to 1979, and the Health and Retirement Study, begun in 1992. Both have been federally funded, with the former carried out by the Census Bureau and the latter by the University of Michigan's Survey Research Center.

Box 1.3 Statistical Agency Principles and Practices

Principles
- Relevance to policy issues
- Credibility among data users
- Trust among data providers and data subjects

Practices
- Define mission clearly
- Maintain a strong position of independence
- Treat data providers fairly
- Cooperate with data users
- Be open about strengths and weaknesses of data products
- Commit to data quality
- Strive to make data more useful
- Disseminate data widely
- Maintain an active research programme
- Advance professional staff on merit
- Coordinate with other statistical agencies

Source: Committee on National Statistics (1992, 2001).

---

very important ingredient in ensuring the credibility of its data. In the context with which I am most familiar, the independence of the BLS is guarded in a variety of ways. First, the agency head, the Commissioner of Labor Statistics, is appointed to serve a term appointment, rather than serving at the pleasure of the President, as do other Assistant-Secretary-level appointees in the Department of Labor. Second, all of the other staff of the agency serve in career civil service positions and continue in their jobs across changes of administration. Third, the data produced by the agency are first seen by policy officials only a very short time before they become public, and even then only after the accompanying press release has been finalised and sent to the printer. All of this helps to prevent the possibility – as well as the perception of there being a possibility – that the statistical agency's calculations or its interpretation of the numbers have been subject to political influence.

The professionalism of an agency's staff and their work, also are important ingredients in the credibility of the agency's data. For starters, the statistical agencies need to be able to offer salaries and working conditions that enable them to hire and retain well-qualified staff. Another dimension of agency professionalism that is important to the credibility of the agencies' data is the careful documentation of how those data are collected and processed. Ideally, such documentation should be readily accessible to interested data users and should include sufficient information to allow these data users to make judgements about potential sampling, non-response, coverage, measurement and processing errors.[6] This is something on which I believe the US statistical agencies have made progress, but on which there is still room for improvement.

As important as independence and professionalism are, it is equally important that agency staff be actively engaged with users of their data in deciding what information will be produced. The organisation of the US statistical system is somewhat unusual, in that there is no single, central statistical office, but rather a number of statistical agencies located around the government in different policy departments. This structure has drawbacks and complications, to be sure, but one advantage it offers is that agency officials have the opportunity to observe at close quarters, the ways in which their data are used and the

---

[6] For a thorough discussion of these issues, see Federal Committee on Statistical Methodology (2001).

information gaps it might be beneficial to fill. Without this sort of decentralised structure, there clearly need to be other mechanisms for close consultation between the top officials of the statistical agency and key policy officials.

Perhaps in part because of my background, I also would emphasise the importance of having statistical agency staff engaged in substantive research and the importance of close collaboration between the staff of the statistical agencies and the academic research community. Having researchers on the staffs of the statistical agencies is important because those who do not use data themselves, are unlikely to understand fully their value, their limitations or how they might be improved. Statistical agency research staff can contribute, in addition, by serving as liaisons to the academic research community. Innovative ideas about public policy in the United States frequently have their origins in academia or policy 'think tanks'. Making data widely available to researchers attached to these institutions can have a considerable payoff. For publicly-funded US surveys, it has become common practice to provide researchers with public use microdata files and, where information cannot be released in that form, because of confidentiality concerns, to grant bona fide researchers access to research data centres where the individual survey records can be analysed under controlled conditions. Having researchers on the staffs of the statistical agencies who are familiar with the data problems that policy researchers encounter as they work with the agencies' data can be of significant help in making subsequent improvements to the information that is produced.

In short, I would argue for a statistical system that is both profoundly independent and professionally excellent, but at the same time is actively engaged with policy users of its data in an effort to ensure that its data are as relevant and useful as possible. All of this requires, of course, a budget for the statistical agencies that is adequate for attracting well-qualified staff and for supporting the other activities I have described. There is, however, a large potential payoff to making this investment.

REFERENCES

Bane, Mary Joe and David T. Ellwood (1986), 'Slipping Into and Out of Poverty: The Dynamics of Spells', *Journal of Human Resources,* Winter, pp. 1–23.

Blau, Francine, and Lawrence Kahn (1997), 'Swimming Upstream: Trends in the Gender Wage Differential in the 1980s', *Journal of Labor Economics*, January, pp. 1–42.

Committee on National Statistics (1992), Commission on Behavioral and Social Sciences and Education, National Research Council, *Principles and Practices for a Federal Statistical Agency*, Margaret Martin and Miron Straf, eds., Washington, DC: National Academy Press, 2nd ed., 2001.

Federal Committee on Statistical Methodology (2001), *Measuring and Reporting Sources of Error in Surveys*, Statistical Policy Working Paper 31, June.

Gustman, Alan L. and Thomas L. Steinmeier (2000), 'Retirement in Dual-Career Families: A Structural Model', *Journal of Labor Economics*, July, pp. 503–45.

Juhn, Chinhui, Kevin M. Murphy and Brooks Pierce (1993), 'Wage Inequality and the Rise in Returns to Skill', *Journal of Political Economy*, Vol. 101(3), pp. 410–42.

Katz, Lawrence F. and Kevin M. Murphy (1992), 'Changes in Relative Wages, 1963/1987: Supply and Demand Factors', *Quarterly Journal of Economics*, February, pp. 35–78.

Krueger, Alan and Kenneth N. Fortson (2003), 'Do Markets Respond More to More Reliable Labor Market Date? A Test of Market Rationality', working paper, Princeton University, January.

Polivka, Anne and Stephen M. Miller (1998), 'The CPS After the Redesign: Refocusing the Economic Lens', in John Haltiwanger, Marilyn E., Manser and Robert Topel, eds., *Labor Statistics Measurement Issues*, Chicago: University of Chicago Press, pp. 249–89.

Stevens, Ann Huff (1999), 'Climbing Out of Poverty, Falling Back In: Measuring the Persistence of Poverty Over Multiple Spells', *Journal of Human Resources*, Summer, pp. 557–88.

US Bureau of Labor Statistics (1997), *Handbook of Methods*, Washington, DC: Government Printing Office, April.

US Bureau of the Census (2003), *Poverty in the United States: 2002*, Washington, DC: Government Printing Office, September.

Waldfogel, Jane, Wen-Jui Han and Jeanne Brooks-Gunn (2002), 'The Effects of Early Maternal Employment on Child Cognitive Development', *Demography*, May, pp. 369–92.

2

Statistics vs. Economics and Politics
Insights from the French Experience

Guy Laroque

INTRODUCTION

The production and dissemination of statistics are organised very differently in the countries around the world.

The gathering of the data can be decentralised, private or public, for instance in the case of traditional surveys, although there is a need for a reliable nationwide basis to draw the samples. Along with technological progress in computers, the statistical activity relies more and more on the use of large registers and data banks, often a side product of the administrative activities of the state. Pending arrangements compatible with privacy, this often reinforces the role of the public statistical agency, while the professional users of statistics show a growing interest in a direct access to individual data.

Statistical information in itself has a lot of the characteristics of a pure public good. Most importantly, it is the basis of the decisions of citizens in a democracy. It must be credible, free of manipulation, which requires some independence of the statistical agency from the political party in power.

Gathering data at minimal cost to the tax payer, issuing reliable and credible information, these are the two main goals of a modern statistical system. The French statistical system stands apart in its organisation towards these two goals: more than elsewhere, the training of statisticians and the production of economic, demographic or sociological studies are integrated with the processing of statistics. Such an integration helps adjusting to technological progress and to the availability of individual data and also may improve the credibility of the statistical agency. The argument is based on a stylised description of the French statistical institutions, and can be considered as an exercise in applied industrial organisation, in the spirit of Wilson (1989).

SOME BASIC FEATURES OF THE FRENCH STATISTICAL SYSTEM

The French central statistical office, INSEE, *Institut National de la Statistique et des Études Économiques,* has been created in 1946, in the wave of reorganisations following the Second World War. It is part of the Ministry of Finance, but has responsibility for all French statistics, including those collected in other ministries (labour, etc.) or public institutions (e.g. the central bank).

A privileged channel to relay to INSEE and to coordinate the social demands for statistical information is the National Board for Statistical Information (CNIS in French), an advisory body of about 100 members. The members represent both the main users of public statistics (firms and labour unions, universities, both parliamentary houses) and the producers of public statistics (INSEE, Ministerial Statistical Offices, EUROSTAT). CNIS is chaired by the Minister of Finance, and its permanent secretariat is harboured by INSEE.

Rather specific to France, the CNIS is quite useful (but costly to manage), to get a feeling on the demands for information and to get general public approval of the statistical projects. To quote one example, after the 1990 population census, a number of organisations started a press campaign on the grounds that the homeless were not properly accounted for. A working group was created inside CNIS and attended by most of these lobbies. It was explained and agreed, in an atmosphere more congenial to scientific discussion than a public debate, that the general census technique and questionnaire were ill adapted to the homeless, and even could raise ethical issues. The group recommended that a specific survey be carried out after the 1999 census, which was implemented successfully with the help of these organisations.

INSEE is an administrative division of the *Ministère de l'Économie des Finances et de l'Industrie,* or MINEFI for short. INSEE has five main missions:

- Production of statistics.
- Economic analysis.
- Coordination of public statistical works.[1]
- Training of statisticians/economists.
- Information dissemination.

INSEE has a unique (to the best of my knowledge) feature among statistical offices around the world: It has its own schools, recruiting two years after the end of high school, and a large research centre;[2] as explicitly stated in its name (national institute of statistics and economic studies), it undertakes economic studies and produces forecasts, close to the place where the data are collected and processed.

Compared to the more usual, restrictive, mandate of other countries' statistical agencies, this wide set of missions goes with some added costs of monitoring and managing a large organisation. The heads of the statistical units in far away ministries are chosen by the director of INSEE, who must follow their performance. The organisation, on the positive side, brings a number of benefits which I shall describe in some details now.

STATISTICS AND ECONOMICS

Training at INSEE

The statistical system has a specific body of civil servants at the executive level, the 'administrateurs de l'INSEE'. Apart from internal promotion, they are recruited through competitive exams and from the

---

[1] All public collection of statistics has to be coordinated through INSEE.
[2] The Norwegian statistical office also has a research centre.

top 'grandes écoles', such as the École Polytechnique. Then they receive, along with other non-civil servants students, a two-to-three years in-house education at the INSEE school. The curriculum bears equally on statistics and economics, with a strong third major in computer science. In an environment where the universities were not quantitatively oriented, the INSEE school took a pre-eminent position in economics in France under the direction of Edmond Malinvaud.

A sizeable part of the influence of INSEE comes from the reputation of its civil servants and from the fact that the director of INSEE manages the statistician civil servants and allocates them to the various statistical departments of central and local governments. Moreover, a number of statisticians in the private sector have graduated from the same INSEE school, and a significant fraction of the civil servants slip into the private sector after some 5 to 10 years in the public service. All of these are, therefore, familiar with INSEE.

Research and Diffusion of Technical Innovations

A research centre, CREST, is associated with the school. It hosts the equivalent of eighty full-time researchers, on a variety of topics, from mathematical statistics to sociology, including microeconometrics, macroeconomics, finance, industrial organisation and survey methodology. A substantial fraction of the members of CREST are on a leave position from the academic world, paid by INSEE. The main aim of the research centre is to train graduate students that will join the university or the private sector.

Aside from its academic activities, an important task of CREST is to facilitate the diffusion of research advances into the day-to-day practice of INSEE. This takes place in a number of ways. There are regular seminars on the new outputs of the production departments of INSEE; the heads of these departments have a scientific advisor from CREST whom they can ask for specific studies; days of training on specific topics (panel data, treatment of missing data, etc.) are organised three or four times a year.

What has turned out to be the most fruitful channel of innovation dissemination is a practice initiated by Edmond Malinvaud, thirty years ago. Every civil servant of INSEE who has a scientific project can ask for a sabbatical of two to three years to carry out his/her study inside CREST (with possibly a year of study abroad). The number of people taking this opportunity is small (one or two persons every year, i.e. about 10 per cent of the average annual inflow of 'administrateurs de l'INSEE'), but the leverage on this investment in human capital is large: typically these persons work on the data they have been responsible for, thereby improving the collection procedure and, in a few (non-publicised) cases, correcting errors; furthermore, after their sabbatical, they often go back to production, carrying with them new ideas, computer programs, etc., which they have experimented at CREST.

Statistics and Economic Studies

Apart from research, there is a sizeable group of around thirty young professionals belonging to a department that produces applied economic studies. They are geographically located close to CREST. But contrary to researchers at CREST, they work on topics that are selected by the hierarchy of INSEE. The aim is to be competitive with the university and the other institutes that produce similar studies. The subjects range from macroeconomics (the evolution of productivity is followed closely and there is a quarterly macroeconometric model), to social issues (pensions and retirement, family composition, etc.) and firms' behaviour (labour demand, investment, localisation of production activities, etc.).

As for research, as mentioned above, there is a strong positive externality between statistics and economics in the course of these studies. The economists benefit from an intimate knowledge of the data and from access to information covered by privacy laws. This last point is of particular importance for all studies on firms' behaviour. The statisticians improve the questionnaires and get a better understanding of the strengths and weaknesses of the data.

On the other hand, there are also some drawbacks. Data collection is by and large a natural monopoly, while the production of economic studies takes place in a competitive environment. It is not always easy to have them live side by side. An economic study is more easily criticised and not as 'objective' than the publication of regular statistics. Some people believe that the reputation of INSEE could be jeopardised by ill-conceived studies and therefore that it would be better to separate the two activities, at least in terms of supports of publication. There is truth in this statement and the economic studies should be tightly monitored. But, in my opinion, these concerns are overstated: the reputation of INSEE largely comes from the quality of its past studies and of the analysis of the data it produces, which is due to the association of economists and statisticians. Breaking the association would hit the reputation for sure!

The real danger is with independence. INSEE has to avoid studies that could either vindicate or criticise government policies.

STATISTICS AND POLITICS

About Independence

Like all statistical offices, INSEE is part of the executive branch of government. The main orientations of INSEE activities are decided by the political authorities and reflected in INSEE's budget. Independence therefore has to be understood as *professional* independence. Once the statistical program is defined and funded, the civil servants have full responsibility for carrying it out and making public its results. This professional independence is a condition for the credibility of the public statistics. Most politicians understand the issue and agree *ex ante* with this sharing of roles.

The head of INSEE is nominated by the council of ministers, on the proposal of the Minister of Finance. Typically this is considered a job of high technicality assigned to a politically neutral insider: from 1974 until 2002, Edmond Malinvaud, Jean-Claude Milleron, Paul Champsaur, the three successive directors, were fellows of the Econometric Society. INSEE has a valuable reputation with the media which is reinforced by the training and scientific culture of its civil servants.

Publication

An important instrument of professional independence is a direct access to the media and full responsibility for publication of data or studies without interference from the political authorities. In practice, to avoid a breach of commitment in the wake, say, of disputed elections, this has to be organised with care and procedures have to be spelled out in details.

On sensitive short run statistics, the IMF Data Dissemination Standard has turned out to be very helpful. At the end of every month, INSEE announces a predetermined timetable for the coming four months on short run statistics to be issued by the whole statistical system. The political authorities are informed prior to the public, typically in the evening before an early morning release the following day.

More generally, INSEE has its own journals and web site. A press office has direct access to the director and press briefings are regularly organised to directly comment the important news to the journalists.

Short Run Forecasts

To my knowledge, INSEE is the only statistical agency to publish a forecast with a six-month horizon on a regular basis, four times a year. This is a good example of the trade offs associated with doing economic analysis in a statistical agency.

First, the benefits. The same persons who compile the short run statistics, collect the opinion surveys, or build the national accounts, are involved in forecasting. It follows that the data is studied in detail and depth, and any deviation from the usual behaviour of a series is scrutinised. Since the horizon is short (six months), forecasting is very much extrapolating current data, INSEE appears to be more reliable than its competitors in the field, due to its proximity with the data: for instance, the individual answers of large firms to different surveys can be compared in case of discrepancies between sources.

Now, the risks. There is always an element of judgement in forecasting. The forecast may turn out to be difficult to reconcile with the official (two years ahead) government forecast, which serves to plan the budget voted in parliament. Then the independence of INSEE is in danger. At the end of the 1970s, the government, worried that INSEE's forecasts were biased against its policy, created five (private with public support) forecasting institutes, attached to the university, to the employers' confederation and to the unions. This move, which initially was thought by some observers, as a blow to INSEE, turned out to be beneficial for its credibility and independence. It is now publicly acknowledged, from comparison with the competition, that INSEE's forecasts are unbiased.

CONCLUSION

A broad mandate for the central statistical agency comes with costs and benefits. The costs are, as standard from the theory of the firm, the management of a set of very diverse activities in the firm. The benefits are an easier incorporation of methodological advances, a high reputation of independence of the institution, allowed by a strong group of highly skilled personnel. It would be hard to put a number on the balance of costs and benefits.

Can the French experience be useful to another country, such as India? A major element is the intellectual resources available to the statistical agency. Has the public service access to highly skilled personnel? Can the existing higher education and research institutions be easily convinced of the statistical needs of the country? How strong and helpful can the academic world be on statistical matters? History and culture play an important role, and the French experience may not be easily transferable elsewhere.

REFERENCE

Wilson, J.Q. (1989), *Bureaucracy: What Government Agencies Do and Why They Do It,* Basic Books, New York.

3

India's Statistical System
Critiquing the Report of the National Statistical Commission

T.N. Srinivasan

In response to 'The National Statistical Commission: An Overview of Recommendations' (Rangarajan, 2001): The National Statistical Commission should be commended for its broad, 'fivefold' remedial approach to the problems besetting India's statistical system. But its failure to offer any methods for judging the adequacy, timeliness and accuracy of statistical data and to undertake cost-benefit analyses of its concomitant recommendations undermines the utility of its work. Without such information, how can the government decide how to apportion its scarce resources among competing priorities?

The National Statistical Commission was appointed with very broad terms of reference. These included critically examining the deficiencies of the present statistical system, in terms of its timeliness, reliability and adequacy, as well as evaluating its administrative and organisational structures and legislative underpinnings. These terms of reference have indeed been met. The Commission's recommendations fill 81 pages. The largest number, 139, pertain to socio-economic statistics, closely followed by 122 recommendations concerning organisational aspects of the statistical system. The lowest number of recommendations, 11, relate to financial statistics.

It would be near-impossible for me to meaningfully evaluate individual recommendations, which range widely in their import, from that of paragraph 14.3.23, for instance, which discusses the need to fill vacancies in the Indian Statistical Service, to paragraph 14.5.2, which recommends the creation of a permanent and statutory National Commission on Statistics. In my comments, I will rather focus primarily on the organising principle or framework embodied in the Commission's approach, or rather, whether such a framework is indeed evidenced. I will then also comment on select issues that I deem to be particularly important and urgent.

The Commission adopted a 'fivefold' remedial approach to overcoming the problems identified in the present system of data collection and dissemination, based on an examination of its credibility, timeliness and accuracy. These remedies are as follows:

1. Reform in the administrative structure of the Indian Statistical System.
2. Improvement in the collection of existing data.
3. Exploration of alternative techniques for collecting existing data.

4. Identification of new data to keep pace with an expanding economy.
5. Development of appropriate methodologies for the collection of new data.

Prima facie, the Commission's approach may seem adequate. A deeper evaluation reveals that it is not. Crucially, I did not find any discussion in its report about how to judge the adequacy, timeliness and accuracy of the data produced by the statistical system. Moreover, the report does not incorporate any form of social cost-benefit analysis, which should be contained in an overarching framework for the examination of a statistical system. After all, the collection and dissemination of data by the government absorbs resources that could have other worthwhile uses.

A framework that is practicable, would accordingly require answers to several questions. For instance, are the benefits from collecting new data, or improving existing data collection, worth the cost? And is it indeed worthwhile to sustain all existing collection efforts? I was very disappointed that the Commission did not attempt to put any of its recommendation to such cost-benefit tests. The net result is that while the report provides many recommendations – 619 according to my count – they are of varied significance. It would take a lot of effort on the part of the government to sort out which of these are really worth implementing.

Let me turn to the Commission's three desiderata for the Statistical System, namely credibility, timeliness and adequacy. In Chapter 14 on the Indian Statistical System, six systemic deficiencies are said to have attracted the media's attention: gaps in availability of necessary data; delays in the publication of data; large and frequent revisions of published data; discrepancies between sources of official data; disagreement between summary and underpinning basic data; and lack of transparency.

The commission asserts, without any supporting analysis or cited evidence, that 'these deficiencies have led to a serious loss of credibility of official statistics'. Unless I missed something however, credibility is discussed in detail only in the context of the National Accounts Statistics (NAS). Their credibility is in turn, questioned on two counts. First, that there are frequent and large revisions in its estimates and second, that there is a large underestimation of GDP. The latter is indeed a common assertion.

However, the fact that large revisions are made is not in and of itself grounds for questioning the credibility of a statistical system. Revisions of official statistics are common even in industrialised countries – even large revisions. Preliminary estimates may be based on incomplete data that cannot be deemed representative. As long as this is known and understood, along with the extent and characteristics of this incompleteness, there should be no credibility issue on this score.

An underestimation of GDP need not undermine credibility either, as long as the underestimation – if any – is not politically or otherwise motivated, but arises only because of biases inherent in estimation procedures. Unless there are reasons to believe that this proportionate bias has changed over time, its mere existence need not affect the analysis of trends. Furthermore, the specific claim that the underestimation bias has increased since the emergence of the software industry need also not be valid. New areas of activity arise all the time, and it is typically sometime before data pertaining to them are collected. However, it is not obvious whether such activities – including software – are quantitatively and qualitatively different from existing activities.

As regards other issues to which the media is said to have drawn attention, a few points should also be made. Disagreements among sources of official data need not undermine credibility if, once again, the respective methods of data collection are known, allowing the possible sources of discrepancy to be identified. The same can be said of discrepancies between summary data and raw data. For their part, publication delays, unless politically or otherwise motivated, do not raise questions of credibility. I have discussed these issues in some detail only to illustrate the credulity of the Commission in accepting at face value, uninformed media criticism.

There is another point that needs some emphasising. Biases, whether large or small, whether increasing or decreasing over time, need not affect all analyses. By example, whether or not, the non-poor understate or overstate their consumption in NSS surveys, is totally irrelevant for the analysis of trends in poverty ratios or poverty gaps as they are conventionally measured in India, as long as the poor respond truthfully. Of course, NAS estimates of private consumption would clearly differ from NSS estimates if NAS are based on estimates of consumption that do not involve household responses, and these estimates are unbiased. Again however, this difference would not be relevant for poverty analyses.

So what does one do? The Commission has come up with a lofty mission statement for the Indian Statistical System in paragraph 14.5.7 of its report, exhorting that the system 'should provide timely and credible social and economic statistics to assist decision making within and outside the government, to stimulate research and promote informed debate relating to condition of people's life.' Though laudable, this statement is too vague as an operational guide.

I have already pointed out the superficiality of the Commission's analysis of credibility. Adequacy and timeliness are also ill-defined concepts. First, it should be noted that what is inadequate or late is contingent. It depends on the extent to which data being more plentiful and more rapidly available, makes a difference to the quality of the decision it informs.[1] Unless policy making and economic debates utilise data in a meaningful, analytical way, not much of an improvement in data gathering can be expected.

My second point is indeed, that the timeliness and adequacy of data depend on its analytic or policy uses, as well as on volatility in the data itself. For example, whereas the Commission bemoans long lags in the publication of data from the population censuses of 1991 and 2000, it does not specify what policies would have been better formulated, had unpublished census data become available earlier. I do not mean to suggest that long lags in the publication of census data are irrelevant. But I would ask the question: should more public resources be devoted to speeding up publication of Census data rather than to collecting some other data, or indeed, to allocation of these resources to some other public purpose? In any case, why not let the private sector undertake the tabulation and publication of the Census by making public, say 1 per cent of its sample? Incidentally, the Commission generally does not adequately explore the involvement of the private sector in data collection, analysis and dissemination.

Timeliness is also related to the frequency of data. Largely in response to pressure from the IMF, quarterly GDP data are now being published by the government. As far as I know however, no serious analysis has been done to ascertain whether the signal-to-noise ratio in the quarterly series is sufficiently high to warrant its publication. Has the availability of this quarterly series improved macroeconomic policy making in India, or the policy advice given by the IMF to India? Maybe it has, but it is hard to tell. Generally speaking, it is a waste of scarce resources to mechanically comply with a commitment to provide a number for 'India', to be slotted into some table or another in a publication by the IMF, the

---

[1] I was a member of the Data Improvement Committee, appointed in the early seventies by the Ministry of Finance and chaired by the inimitable, and one and only, Dr B.S. Minhas. We went around various ministries and talked to the chief bureaucrats. We first heard their litany of complaints about the data. We then asked them: suppose by waving a magic wand, we could make available to you all the data you want, as soon as you want them, what difference would it have made to the decisions you made? The response to this question was almost always a long silence. I am willing to bet that the situation has not changed over the three decades since we reported. The quality of Indian economic journalism is also not much influenced by the availability of data and I would be pleasantly surprised if the quality of the debate in the economic media is improved by better and timely data.

World Bank or the UN, or for that matter, to adopt the UN system of national accounts lock, stock and barrel, without examining whether doing so is meaningful in the Indian context. Unfortunately expert groups, such as those from National Accounts, often view data collection as costless and therefore recommend the collection of more detailed, disaggregated and frequent data.[2] I am afraid the Commission seems to have fallen into a similar trap, loading a lot more into the system, without taking much out.

I would now like to turn to a more specific commentary, by turning to a few of the more important data series produced by the Indian Statistical System. The Commission has rightly drawn attention to serious problems with agricultural production data. These owe to the breakdown of the *Girdawari* process for collecting crop-area statistics and also failures of the system of crop-cutting experiments. The Commission accordingly recommends that the *Patwari* and their supervisors should be made to accord the highest priority to the *Girdawari* and the *Patwari* shall be spared other duties during this time. It is all very well for the Commission to then recommend that the supervisory staff be held accountable, and that schemes for a Timely Reporting System (TRS) and Establishment of an Agency for Reporting Agricultural Statistics (EARAS) be regarded as programmes of national importance and so forth. However, I am not convinced that much can be accomplished by such exhortations.

The Commission should have explored the possibility of side-stepping the *Patwari* and supervisors altogether, and reverting to sample surveys for crop-area estimation across the entire country. This procedure that was abandoned decades ago because of large discrepancies between the Patwari estimates and sample estimates. These discrepancies were examined several times, once by M.S. Avadhani and myself, on behalf of the NSSO's governing council. If my memory does not fail, there was then no convincing reason for abandoning sample survey estimates in favour of the Patwari estimates. To boot, the solution adopted to address the discrepancy between Patwari and sample survey estimates, namely to discontinue the survey, has apparently not improved the credibility of the former!

Moreover, the Commission did not examine whether the so-called agricultural census, which is mostly a re-tabulation of poorly maintained land records, was serving any useful purpose, other than supplying dubious data to the FAO. It recommends the continuation of the census on a sample basis in 20 per cent of the sample villages. I am not persuaded that even with these changes, the quinquennial census would add anything of value to the data collected by the decennial NSS landholdings survey. Notably, resources saved by the abolition of the Census could be used for improving other agricultural statistics.

The Commission's discussion of crop-cutting experiments also does not address the issues of any biases, nor the reliability of yield estimates broken down by irrigation status and the variety of crop grown. There is also the question of whether the design of the General Crop Estimation Survey (GCES) is adequate, given the changing relative importance of Kharif, Rabi and summer seasons for different crops and crop varieties.

On the matter of industrial statistics, the Commission is right in focusing attention on the need for a proper sample frame for industrial units and also on the problems attending to the list of factories maintained by the Chief Inspector of Factories. Its recommendation that the CSO and NSSO should prepare directories of establishments using the data generated by the fourth economic census and its

---

[2] I was once a member of the NSSO's governing council. The council was often asked either to add more questions to already long questionnaires, or to collect new data. However, those making such demands did not think of the cost of adding questions, either in terms of the quality of the response. Nor, for that matter, did they say what question they would take out in order to maintain the length of the questionnaire.

follow up surveys, is well taken. However, it is unclear how a one-time census of industrial units could be undertaken. While they are eligible for registration, some may not be registered and there is no easy way of identifying the latter.

The chapter on National Accounts Data, especially in regard to GDP, Savings and Investment, in Volume II of the Commission's report, is well worth reading, particularly by secondary retailers of national data such as the World Bank and the IMF. It points out that Indian national accounts data are based on a mish-mash of income, production and expenditure methods, as well as combinations of data referring both to the relevant year and extrapolations from past years. The Commission notes that even when so-called 'direct' estimates are based on annually available statistics, 'their translation with national accounts often requires the use of certain norms, rates, and ratios and other assumptions'. Some of these norms are based on data from a remote past, the origins of which can most likely no longer be traced! Incidentally, there is no CSO publication that lists *all* the ratios and norms currently being used, as well as their sources.

However, these norms and ratios play a very major role in the estimation of Gross Capital Formation (GCF) through the commodity-flow approach. In turn, GCF is the starting point for determining household savings and investment – the latter in the form of physical assets, in their capacity as a residual. Quick estimates for 2000/01 show that this residual accounted for as much as 42 per cent of gross domestic savings. As the Commission notes, the Raj Committee in 1972 and the Chelliah Committee in 1986, were both 'uncomfortable with household saving in the form of physical assets being arrived at as a residual, but did not suggest any alternative method'. In fact, financial savings of the household sector is also estimated as a residual, by subtracting the savings of public and corporate sectors from total financial savings in the economy. However, no serious and credible macroeconomic analysis can be done if a large component of savings and investment in the economy is estimated as a residual. This is the case for the household sector – which is itself a residual, being the sector *other than* the public and corporate sectors.

The Commission notes that in National Accounts Statistics (NAS), three estimates of aggregate capital formation are available. The first is the financial aggregate of domestic savings and net capital inflow from abroad; the second is provided by adding assets, i.e. construction, machinery and changes in stocks, and the third; by aggregating industries of use. The second estimate is the same as the GCF, but is derived by the commodity flow approach. For 2000/01, total gross capital formation was Rs 5,013 billion from the financing side, Rs 4,782 billion by the type of assets, and Rs 4,098 billion by industry of use. The NAS treat the first figure as the control total because it deems it to be 'more reliable and firmer' and treats the difference between the first and second, namely Rs 231 billion, as Errors and Omissions (E and O). Thus E and O were 4.6 per cent of the control total in 2000/01, and even higher in some past years. The difference between the control total and the estimate by industry of use, is Rs 923 billion, which is as much as 18.4 per cent of the control total!

In fact, the above discussion somewhat understates the seriousness of the problem of E and O. The reason is that the residual, 'household savings in the form of physical assets', which is derived from GCF or the second of the two aforementioned estimates, is also a part either of the first estimate or the control total. In other words, the only two 'firm' numbers on the financing side are the *aggregate financial savings* in the economy, as provided by financial institutions, and *the net capital inflow* from abroad. The two together add up to finances available for investment, which came to Rs 2,943 billion in 2000/01. Since by definition, direct investment by households in physical assets does not involve financial intermediation, this entire sum is available for investment by the public and corporate sectors. The two together invested Rs 2,712 billion. The difference between the estimates of available financing on the one hand, and of investment on the other, is Rs 231 billion. This number is the same as the previous E and O. Thus, E and O as a proportion of the 'firm' number, i.e. financial savings available for intermediation, is a whopping 7.8 per cent. One can reduce the relative magnitude of E and O only by adding the residual category of household savings in physical assets, equalling Rs 2,071 billion, to both the financing and investment sides of the calculation. This raises their values to Rs 5,014 and Rs 4,783 billion, respectively.

There is another related and serious problem. The estimates of E and O have been consistently positive since the 1993/94 rebasing of the NAS. This means that finance available for investment exceeds estimated investment derived through the commodity flow approach. Since the former is deemed firmer and hence treated as the control total, it follows that there was in fact more investment in the economy than imputed by commodity flow estimate. However, there is no satisfactory way of distributing this excess investment among public, corporate and household sectors. The reason is that the estimated investment figures for the public and corporate sectors are derived from their accounts and treated as firm. Adding the excess investment to the household sector investment in physical assets would not solve the problem; then total household savings would go up by the same amount, which in turn means that finances available for investment also increases by the same amount!

Of course, one could attribute all the excess investment to the corporate sector. The reason would be that there are errors associated with the procedure for inflating estimated investment of companies in the RBI sample, in order to obtain a figure for investment by the corporate sector as a whole. However, this is not a valid ground, since there is no reason to believe that such errors have to be consistently positive, in order to be considered a consistently positive E and O. On the other hand, dividing the excess investment between public and corporate sectors would be arbitrary.

I have described the situation in some detail for a reason. Trends in aggregate savings and investments that exclude household savings in physical assets are not likely to differ from trends that include them. Only the latter are relevant, if the focus of analysis is financial intermediation, involved in translating savings into investment. But then one has to deal with the excess investment in some fashion and how one does so, has implications for macroeconomic analysis.

The NAS provides data on capital formation, for industry of use in the aggregate and for the public sector. However, corresponding data pertaining to household and corporate sectors are not published. This precludes a comparison between household investment in physical assets and that investment accounted for, by the industry of use method. In this light, the information provided in Table 13.12 of the Commission's report on sources of data and methods of estimation, are sobering to say the least. Household investment in construction is obtained by using the current year's output of agriculture and livestock and the base year 1991/92, in conjunction with the data on investment in construction in the All-India Debt and Investment Survey (AIDIS) of 1991/92. The index used to update AIDIS data for household investment in machinery and equipment, is derived from the output of machinery, as per the Annual Survey of Industries. However, my favourite estimate is 'household investment in the forestry sector'. This figure is obtained by merely inflating by 5.4 per cent, the estimates of investment in forestry by the public sector. Clearly, these procedures reflect implicit assumptions that, as far as I know, have not been tested.

The estimates of savings and investment are obtained by using accounts of the sample of companies in the annual survey of the Reserve Bank of India, and adjusting them 'for full coverage on the basis of data on paid up capital for all companies'. Since the problems with this procedure are well-known, I will refrain from listing them. The Commission's recommendation for addressing the problems of residual estimation of household investment in physical assets is twofold. First, it proposes to examine the feasibility of reintroducing the receipts and disbursement block, using its last 365 days as the reference period, in NSS household surveys. This was the case in the integrated household schedule of the current annual surveys of household consumer expenditure of NSS, as implemented in the period 1964/65 (19th Round) to1970/71 (25th Round). Second, it recommends experimenting with the survey methodology used to improve the estimation of capital formation using enterprise surveys.

However, I wish the Commission had explained the reasons for why the integrated household survey schedule was abandoned after 1970/71. If my memory serves me right, this was because the data collected proved unreliable, primarily because in the Indian context, it is virtually impossible to collect reliable data on incomes and receipts from household surveys – NCAER surveys notwithstanding. I do not think the situation is any different now, than it was 30 years ago, though, I could of course be wrong. Again, it is unfortunate that the Commission did not delve into the reason for making its recommendation.

Meanwhile, the Commission rightly draws attention to the various 'rates and ratios' used not only in the estimates of capital formation, but also in every other component of the NAS. Table 13.7 in the report provides information on sources of data and methods of estimation for National Income Estimates with base year 1993/94. Unfortunately, this table does not adequately explain the role played by various rates and ratios. Another item, Table 13.2 on direct and indirect estimates of GDP, shows that the proportion of direct estimates for the year 1996/97 fell to 60 per cent from 89.6 per cent in the base year 1993/94. Presumably, the reason for this decline is that as the base year recedes in time, the role of rates and ratios becomes more significant.

In summation, as regards such crucial series as GDP, Savings and Capital Formation, the data situation continues to be alarming.[3] By further example, value-added by the service sector, which accounts for nearly half of the estimated GDP, is based on indirect estimation. This involves multiplying value-added per worker in a base-year survey, by the growth rate of employment. With such a constant base-year price, value-added estimates are then inflated by a consumer price index to obtain current price estimates.

It is also noteworthy that the Commission in various places throughout its report, recommends the publication of sampling errors. However, it does not recommend undertaking for a recent year, an overall error estimate – both as regards sampling and non-sampling – of GDP and its components. The Final Report of the National Income Committee (GOI, 1954, pp. 147-48) chaired by Professor Mahalanobis provided an error estimate of 10 per cent in 1948/49 for net domestic product. Errors in the value-added in each sector, ranged between less than 10 per cent, to nearly a third. Unfortunately, this exercise has not been repeated since. If it was done for a recent year, I suspect that error margins would be found to be much larger than the Mahalanobis Committee's estimate.

In addition, the Commission several times in its report, urges closer integration and collaboration among statistical agencies of the central and state governments. It is indeed a scandal and a huge waste of resources that the state samples of NSS surveys are not analysed, and published results are based

[3] It is possible that this alarming situation endures because of a lack of interest in India, in serious macroeconomic analysis employing state-of-the-art theory and econometric tools. Most analyses forthcoming from economists inside or outside the government, are descriptive stories. This is not the case in other developing countries, for example, in Latin America. Macroeconometric modelling in India, including modelling by the Reserve Bank, appears very old-fashioned. In Europe and the US, large multi-equation models are no longer at the frontiers of macroeconometric analysis, but survive only among forecasters.

only on the Central sample. Although I cannot prove it, I strongly suspect that the resources currently expended on data collection by the Central and state governments, might also be adequate to collect, analyse and disseminate the needed data, if these resources were only more efficiently utilised.

Lastly, among the Commission's most weighty recommendations, is the creation of a permanent and statutory National Commission on Statistics (NCS) through an Act of Parliament, tasking an official agency, the National Statistical Organisation, to implement its policy decisions. The recommendation is based on the view that the main reason for the loss of credibility of official statistics is the absence of a 'policy making and coordination body with legal authority, independent of the producers of statistics and free from covert or overt political and bureaucratic pressures that can serve as a link between producers and users of statistics'. Having neither been a member of the Commission, nor a participant in its deliberations, I am not in a position to evaluate either its diagnosis of the problem or its prescriptions. I have no doubt that bureaucrats and politicians have occasionally attempted to put pressures on statistical authorities. However, have there been many such instances? There are no examples cited in the report as far as I could ascertain. More importantly, if, as I believe, such attempts at pressure are not unique to the statistical system but are commonly observed within the entire administrative system, then reorganising the statistical system cannot solve the problem. To put it differently, deploying the clichéd terminology of the World Bank and other international organisations: if the problem is one of general governance, it is extremely unlikely that the statistical system could be insulated from it, whether or not a NCS is created.

In conclusion, it would seem that the Commission missed a valuable opportunity to probe deeply the undoubtedly serious problems besetting macroeconomic statistics in India – which are essential for policy making – and to recommend corrective actions adequate to the task. Rather, it dissipated its powers of scrutiny by examining, often superficially, problems besetting all statistical series, regardless of their relative importance for monitoring of the economy, society and polity. This is indeed a pity. After all, between 1972 and 1992, the Indian Econometric Society has held five seminars and published five volumes on the Data Base of the Indian Economy. These volumes had made several recommendations. Other institutions have also probed into data issues. The Commission could simply have taken note of these studies and updated them if necessary, rather than delve *de novo* into the very same problems which they had already identified. This would have allowed it to concentrate on some of the important problems that have yet to be tackled.

ACKNOWLEDGEMENT

An earlier version of this chapter was published in *Economic and Political Weekly*, Vol. 37, 25–31 January 2003.

REFERENCES

GOI (1954), *Final Report of the National Income Committee*, Department of Economic Affairs, Ministry of Finance, Government of India.

Rangarajan, C. (2001), 'The National Statistical Comission: An Overview of Recommendations', *Economic and Political Weekly*, October.

I.2 CONFLICTS BETWEEN NATIONAL ACCOUNTS AND SURVEYS

4

On the Validity of NSS Estimates of Consumption Expenditure

M. Mukherjee and G.S. Chatterjee

We propose to examine here the National Sample Survey (NSS) estimate of consumption expenditure as a measure of the aggregate private consumption expenditure. Private consumption expenditure, today, is of the order of 80 per cent of the Net National Product (NNP) at market prices. The estimate of NNP in India does not depend on survey consumption data, and is based largely on information on output. A substantial part of the aggregate NNP in a particular year is based on projections and surmises and does not depend on direct information pertaining to the year. Consequently, corroboration of a sizeable part of it by a completely independent survey estimate will be welcome provided we are satisfied about its validity and accuracy.

We propose to examine here only the aggregates obtained by the NSS and not the composition of the aggregates. An examination of the composition is one method of assessing validity of an aggregate. We, however, do not propose to take this up in this paper. It is well-known that the pattern exhibited by the NSS estimates of consumption expenditure is, by and large, consistent in the sense that it does not change widely from one round to another, though certain shares change systematically. On the other hand, the NSS pattern is different from the one based on product flow estimates of consumption expenditure, showing a higher share for foodgrains and a lower share for services. Since the empirical basis of the product flow estimate is even weaker than that of the survey estimates for the components of consumption expenditure, in view of the application of relatively arbitrary allocation ratios and distributive margins on the values of output as produced, this discordance does not unequivocally establish that the survey estimates are at fault, in view of their stable pattern and systematic change. Also, when the detailed pattern is considered, the survey, being limited in size, is naturally less accurate for the components of expenditure depending on a fraction of the sample, than for the aggregate. Thus one could even conceive of a case in which all the components, other than those consumed by all or most households in the sample remain inaccurate, and yet the aggregate is accurate enough to be used.

The NSS estimates are based on a sample survey in which the households are asked about their consumption during a past period, and what we record in the schedule is what the respondents tell. In the process, apart from recall lapses, there could be biases. Respondents may have a tendency to overestimate some items of consumption and underestimate some other items. There is no way to get over this response bias completely, and we do not know definitely whether there is any systematic overestimation or underestimation in the aggregate. One may hope, however, that the bias is uniform over time, and the trend shown by the NSS series either overestimates or underestimates the aggregate household consumption expenditure systematically. Attempts at actual measurement in some case studies have shown that the response biases are not large, but these investigations were sporadic, without enabling us to draw a firm conclusion about the nature of the biases. Finally, it is not improbable that the biases change in unusual situations. For example, when prices increase very sharply, the expenditure as reported may be more than what is warranted by price rise, due to biases. Or, when the design of the schedule (or the order of asking questions) is changed, this may lead to overestimation or underestimation. Also, theoretically, one could not rule out the possibility of biases rising or falling systematically in time, though the chance here appears to be remote. But despite all these, the NSS estimates represent what a large sample of households tell about their consumption expenditure, and there is reason to be satisfied when the reported consumption expenditure is rising, because this at least is the consensus of the respondents. This remark, however, does not apply to real consumption expenditure which is a derived magnitude.

The NSS estimate represents household consumption expenditure while the comparable estimate obtained from the national income statistics represents the private consumption expenditure which includes the final consumption expenditure of private non-profit institutions apart from that of individuals and households. The magnitude of consumption expenditure of private non-profit institutions is not known. It follows, however, that the NSS estimate measures something which is smaller than what is measured by the corresponding official estimate.

The procedure of obtaining an estimate of private consumption expenditure from the official national income statistics is well-known and need not be repeated here. A few points, however, need some discussion. First, for the period under consideration, two official national income series exist, and one is free to choose either, though it is more or less agreed that the revised series is relatively better than the conventional series. Second, to get the estimate of national income at market prices from that at factor cost, it is necessary to add net indirect taxes to the latter. It is not obvious that what is classified as indirect taxes in the Central Statistical Organisation's (CSO) annual White Papers is the only aggregate suitable for this purpose. One could use a lower aggregate, depending on one's notion of cost of raising taxes, thus getting a smaller estimate of private consumption expenditure from the official sources. Finally, there are alternative series of net capital formation at market prices, which could be used as items of deduction in the process of obtaining the estimate of private consumption expenditure from the NNP at market prices. The reason for harping on these points is that there is no unique series of private consumption expenditure based on the official national income statistics, and a fair amount of variation is possible here depending on the choice one makes of the constituent series. It is necessary to keep this in view while comparing the NSS and national income-based estimates of consumption expenditure.

Since the revised national income series is available from 1954/55 onwards, we have confined our comparison to the period 1954/55 to 1968/69 only. The revised estimates at constant prices have been converted to current prices by using the deflator implicit in the conventional national income series. We have used the estimates of government consumption expenditure as given in the White Papers on national income up to the year for which the estimates are available, and projected these on the basis of aggregate revenue expenditure of the central and state governments for the remaining years. The capital formation estimates up to 1965/66 have been taken from R.N. Lal's paper; it may be observed that these are identical with the official estimates for the period 1960/61 to 1965/66. For the subsequent period, we have projected the estimates in relation to the aggregate provision for consumption of fixed capital implicit in the official national income statistics, because of the relatively stable relation between net and gross capital formation during the period 1960/61 to 1965/66. We are aware that the non-official estimates of capital formation proportion, (for example, by V.V. Bhatt, in a paper in *Commerce* and also by the Commerce Research) more recently show a large decline. Our procedure, on the other hand, leads to relatively stable proportions. The non-official estimates we may note, are only remotely linked with the official national income statistics. In view of the rising trend in the estimates of consumption of fixed capital in the official statistics, we suspect that the official capital formation estimates, when available, cannot possibly be as discouraging as the two non-official estimates considered. Obviously, there is no logical necessity for this because the level of depreciation provision should be linked with the stock rather then the flow of capital. This choice pulls down the estimates of private consumption expenditure based on official national income statistics.

The procedure for obtaining the NSS based estimates has been discussed in a book by one of us, and this does not require any detailed consideration. In sum, we have accepted the NSS estimates of per capita consumption expenditure for the period covered by the rounds, and assumed that the intensity of per capita consumption expenditure during a period between two rounds is the arithmetic average of the per capita consumption expenditures of the two rounds. The population used to obtain the aggregates is identical with that used in national income statistics. Finally, we have scaled up the NSS estimates for the imputed payment of rentals which is included in the official estimates but not in the NSS estimates. We have made use of data relating to all the rounds from the 8th to the 22nd, and in two cases tabulations based on a few subrounds have been used. The number of months missed is small and does not appreciably affect the overall trend shown.

The comparison attempted is entirely based on estimates at current prices. Deflation using a consistent system of price index numbers, however, should not give a discordant result. The available deflators which strictly apply to our data are presented in Table 4.1. If we extend the revised series national income deflator by the conventional series deflator, we find that the overall price rise in both national income and capital formation during the period 1954/55 to 1965/66 was identical, being about 63 per cent. This shows that the implicit price increase in a deflator for aggregate consumption expenditure has to be 63 per cent. Since little is known about the price level of government consumption, and in any case because it forms a small part of total consumption expenditure, one could take 63 per cent as an estimate of price rise in private consumption as well. For the period 1960/61 to 1965/66, however, the consumer price level must have risen more than the national income deflator if we accept the revised series deflator, and less than the national income deflator if we accept the conventional series. But the difference in either case is not large. It should be stressed here that one is not permitted to use consumer price index numbers relating to small sections of the population for deflating either the NSS or the official estimates of private consumption expenditure.

If, however, we obtain the national income deflators by working out estimates of national income at current market prices and base period market prices, thus assuming that base period net indirect taxes persist throughout the period for the real series, then the national income deflators rise a little more sharply. For example, the figure of 137.3 for 1965/66 in the revised series changes to 142.2 while 126.7 in the conventional series changes to 131.8. Thus, a somewhat larger rise in the consumer price index is warranted if we use the revised series, but prices of consumption and capital formation move similarly, if the conventional series is used.

Table 4.1 National Income and Capital Formation Deflators
with 1960/61 as Base, 1954/55 to 1965/66

Year	Conventional National Income	Revised National Income	Capital Formation
(1)	(2)	(3)	(4)
1954/55	84.1	–	80.5
1955/56	85.7	–	80.3
1956/57	92.5	–	82.1
1957/58	94.1	–	81.5
1958/59	97.3	–	89.4
1959/60	98.2	–	105.6
1960/61	100.0	100.0	100.0
1961/62	101.8	102.9	104.6
1962/63	104.0	105.9	110.9
1963/64	110.9	115.2	114.2
1964/65	112.5	133.6	123.0
1965/66	126.7	137.3	131.3

The basic estimates of our study are presented in Table 4.2.

The estimates in cols. (2)–(6) have been plotted in the Figure 4.1. It shows that, by and large, the three series depicted by figures in cols. (4)–(6) show similar trend. It can be observed, however, that up to 1962/63, the NSS estimates lay between the two estimates based on the official statistics, but since then, while the two official estimates tended to be closer, the NSS estimates were systematically slightly

Table 4.2 Private Consumption Expenditure at Current Market Prices
according to Different Sources: Rs ABJA

Year	NSS			Official		Per Cent Difference	
	ss 1	ss2	Comb.	Rev.	Conv.	Rev./Comb.	Conv./Comb.
(1)	(2)	(3)	(4)	(5)	(6)	(7)	(8)
1954/55	79.3	83.2	81.3	81.1	88.2	– 0.25	+ 8.49
1955/56	85.0	86.2	85.6	82.1	88.3	– 4.09	+ 3.15
1956/57	94.0	92.0	93.0	95.2	101.7	+ 2.37	+ 9.35
1957/58	100.7	97.5	99.0	98.4	105.4	– 0.61	+ 6.46
1958/59	109.1	110.2	109.6	109.5	116.3	– 0.09	+ 6.11
1959/60	113.1	114.4	113.8	110.2	117.2	– 3.16	+ 2.99
1960/61	121.6	121.5	121.6	118.8	127.4	– 2.30	+ 4.77
1961/62	127.9	128.1	128.0	125.4	132.7	– 2.03	+ 3.67
1962/63	133.6	134.7	134.1	131.1	136.1	– 2.24	+ 1.49
1963/64	141.3	142.6	142.0	147.8	148.9	+ 4.08	+ 4.86
1964/65	164.0	162.3	163.2	176.1	179.5	+ 7.90	+ 9.99
1965/66	173.9	177.0	175.5	178.4	179.1	+ 1.65	+ 2.05
1966/67	192.3	195.3	193.8	206.3	206.3	+ 6.45	+ 6.60
1967/68	218.1	220.8	219.3	248.7	241.4	+ 13.41	+ 10.08
1968/69	228.0	230.8	229.2	242.4	235.9	+ 5.76	+ 2.92

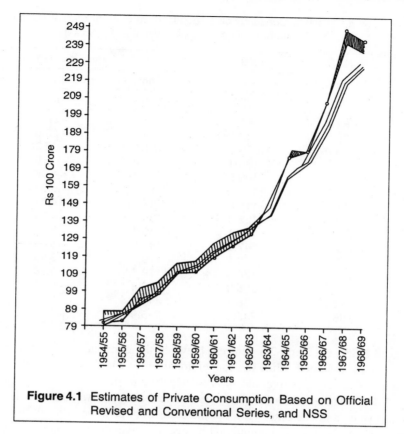

Figure 4.1 Estimates of Private Consumption Based on Official Revised and Conventional Series, and NSS

below the official estimates. But the divergence between the official and NSS estimates reduced very appreciably in 1965/66 and somewhat in 1968/69, and on the whole, the agreement between the revised series and the NSS estimates remains surprisingly close. The divergence in 1967/68 and the pronounced tendency of the official estimates since 1963/64 to lie above the NSS estimates, however, appear to be significant features of the difference between the series.

One could take a stand that an estimate of consumption expenditure based on a product flow approach must have a time reference prior to one based on data on final expenditures. To meet this argument, we have made an arbitrary assumption that the actual final expenditure takes place, on an average, six months after the date of production. If we make this assumption, Table 4.3 emerges.

The procedure brings the NSS series closer to the revised series in the recent past, but the close correspondence between the revised and NSS series for the earlier period is disrupted. If there is some reason to believe that the earlier revised estimates are underestimated, then only can this procedure be taken to show a generally closer relation between the NSS and the revised series. The procedure, however, definitely improves the correspondence between the conventional and NSS series.

In whichever way we try to compare the NSS and the other two series, we obtain, in general, differences, which are well within the range of uncertainty of this type of aggregates. The arithmetic averages of the absolute values of the fifteen percentage differences are 3.8 per cent between the revised and NSS series, 5.5 per cent between the conventional and NSS series, 4.2 per cent between the

Table 4.3 Private Consumption Expenditure at Current Market Prices: NSS Data Moved Forward by 6 Months (Rs ABJA)

| Year | NSS | Official | Per Cent Difference | | |
	Comb.	Rev.	Conv.	Rev./Comb.	Conv./Comb.
(1)	(2)	(3)	(4)	(5)	(6)
1954/55	83.4	81.1	88.2	− 2.76	+ 5.76
1955/56	89.3	82.1	88.3	− 8.06	− 1.12
1956/57	96.0	95.2	101.7	− 0.83	+ 5.94
1957/58	104.3	98.4	105.4	− 5.66	+ 1.05
1958/59	111.7	109.5	116.3	− 1.97	+ 4.12
1959/60	117.7	110.2	117.2	− 6.37	− 0.42
1960/61	124.8	118.8	127.4	− 4.81	+ 2.08
1961/62	131.0	125.4	132.7	− 4.28	+ 1.30
1962/63	138.0	131.1	136.1	− 5.00	− 1.38
1963/64	152.6	147.8	148.9	− 3.15	− 2.42
1964/65	169.4	176.1	179.5	+ 3.96	+ 5.96
1965/66	184.6	178.4	179.1	− 3.36	− 2.98
1966/67	206.6	206.3	206.3	− 0.15	0.00
1967/68	224.2	248.7	241.4	+ 10.93	+ 7.67
1968/69	236.6	242.4	235.9	+ 2.45	− 0.30

revised and lagged NSS series and 2.8 per cent between the conventional and lagged NSS series. In addition, when no lag is assumed, while the conventional series wholly lies above the NSS series, seven out of fifteen differences are positive and the rest negative in the comparison between the NSS and revised series. When a lag is assumed, the revised series almost always lies below the NSS series, except for last two years and one other year, but there are eight positive differences out of fifteen in the comparison between the NSS and conventional series. The average of annual percentage differences between the revised and conventional estimates works out at about 4.6 per cent, and this is of the same dimensional order as the average of differences between the official and NSS series. Consequently, except for the particular features of the difference we have already pointed out, one would have been surprised if the NSS and the two official series exhibited closer agreement.[1] It has to be stressed that when the two official series, based on more or less similar data and prepared by the same institution, exhibit large difference mainly due to methodological reasons, the NSS estimates depending almost entirely on an independent set of data of a different type, cannot be expected to show closer agreement with either of the official series, in view of the conceptual and methodological differences and the inherent variability of the statistical information used. In fact, the nature of correspondence is such that it partially validates the national income trends depicted by the two official series, and definitely suggests that a continuing NSS series on consumption expenditure could be a useful corroborative information for coming to a judgement about the trend of development of the national economy.

ACKNOWLEDGEMENT

Reprinted from *Artha Vijnana*, Vol. 14, June 1972.

[1] The subsample agreement in the case of NSS estimates is closer, having an average value of 1.6 per cent only, the subsample difference being expressed as a percentage of the combined estimate.

5

Data on Distribution of Consumption Expenditure in India
An Evaluation

T.N. Srinivasan, P.N. Radhakrishnan and A. Vaidyanathan

Much of the current discussion on consumption inequalities draws heavily on National Sample Survey (NSS) data. This is understandable because the NSS is the only source which provides a more or less comparable time series information on the levels and patterns of consumption and the distribution of population by per capita consumption levels. The information is gathered by a nationwide field organisation on the basis of a scientific sampling procedure and using a rather elaborate questionnaire. Nevertheless, doubts have been expressed about the reliability of NSS data and of analysis based on them. The object of this note is to clarify the nature of these doubts and to examine their validity. It should be emphasised that we are unable to offer any categorical answers. Our purpose would be adequately met if the subsequent discussion helps to clarify the issues involved and to focus more sharply on the directions in which further inquiries might be fruitful.

In relation to analysis of consumption inequalities, the following questions pertaining to NSS data are relevant:

1. How accurate is the NSS estimate of aggregate and per capita consumption in any given year?
2. How accurate is the NSS estimate of changes in aggregate and per capita consumption over time?
3. Are there any biases in the consumption reported by different classes and do these biases vary systematically over time?

LEVEL OF CONSUMPTION

The sample households selected for NSS investigation are usually divided into a number of independent interpenetrating subsamples. Information on all important aspects is available by subsamples. The variation between subsample estimates provides a measure of the error (both sampling and non-sampling) in NSS data: the closer the subsample estimates, the smaller the margin of error. However, the mere fact of close agreement between subsample estimates is no proof that the sample survey gives an accurate measure of the 'true value'. Systematic biases on the part of respondents can lead to a situation where the sample estimates diverge from true value and yet subsample variations are small. For instance if every household understates its consumption by 10 per cent say, the subsample estimates can be close and yet the expected value of each of the subsample estimates is below the 'true value' by 10 per cent. Since we are interested in the 'true value', it becomes necessary to check the sample data, with other independent sources of information.

In respect of the level and pattern of consumption, such an independent source of information exists in the official series of production trends in national income and the related magnitudes. It is possible to estimate aggregate personal consumption expenditures at current prices from the national income series by adjusting for indirect taxes and subsidies, trade deficit, capital formation and public consumption. Such estimates have been made by Mukherjee (1969), Mukherjee and Chatterjee (1972), Kansal (1965) and Kansal and Saluja (1961). An alternate method used by Kansal proceeds from a detailed analysis of the goods and services entering final consumption. Their quantities are weighted by relevant prices and aggregated to obtain the magnitude of aggregate consumption.

In a pioneering work Mukherjee (1969) reconstructed two series of private consumption expenditure for the period 1950/51 to 1962/63, one based on NSS with appropriate adjustments for coverage, reference period and methods of estimation to ensure comparability over time with the concepts of the official series; and the second derived from the CSO's national income series. He found the two series to be remarkably close both in terms of absolute level and of changes over time. More recently Mukherjee and Chatterjee (1972) have attempted a similar comparison for the period 1954/55 to 1968/69. They find that (a) up to 1963/64, the official (revised) series is consistently below the NSS but the differences are quite small and (b) thereafter, the official series is consistently higher than the NSS series and the differences are quite large.

We made an independent attempt to derive estimates of per capita private consumption from the official National Income Series (Estimate I) and from the NSS (Estimate II), following roughly the same procedures as used by Mukherjee. Our estimates (see Table 5.1) are quite close up to 1962/63 and begin to show substantial differences thereafter. However, unlike the Mukherjee estimate, ours suggest that the NSS series is consistently below the official series throughout the period (with a lone exception in 1959/60).

Estimates of per capita real consumption (valued at 1960/61 prices) corresponding to the official and the NSS series are presented in Table 5.2. These have been derived by dividing the per capita consumption expenditure at current prices with the implicit national income deflator in the case of official series (Estimate I) and with a weighted index of wholesale prices (using the relative proportions of different commodity groups in total consumption) in the case of NSS series (Estimate II). For purposes of comparison a third estimate of real per capita consumption for 1954/55 to 1963/64 made by Kansal (1965) using the commodity flow approach is also given in the Table 5.2.

While the estimates of consumption at current prices derived from National Income and the NSS data are in close agreement for the period 1954/55 to 1963/64, the estimates of real consumption differ substantially. This is essentially a reflection of the differences in the deflators used to adjust current price consumption for price changes. The National Income deflator implies a much slower increase in prices up to 1960/61 than the index applied to the NSS series. The latter is in principle superior because it approximates more closely to an index of consumer prices. Because of this difference in deflators, the increase in per capita real consumption according to Estimate I is considerably more than obtained by

Table 5.1 Estimates of Per Capita Private Consumption Expenditure
at Current Prices (Rs)

Year	Estimate I	Estimate II	Estimate II Expressed as a Per Cent of I
1954/55	208.9	207.0	99.1
1955/56	213.0	211.3	99.2
1956/57	242.3	225.4	93.0
1957/58	238.0	235.8	99.1
1958/59	259.3	254.8	98.3
1959/60	257.4	260.9	101.4
1960/61	277.6	274.2	98.8
1961/62	253.6	282.3	99.5
1962/63	289.3	289.0	99.9
1963/64	318.6	295.9	92.9
1964/65	369.0	339.4	92.0
1965/66	369.2	353.3	95.7
1966/67	423.2	N.A.	
1967/68	498.1	432.9	86.9
1968/69	487.7	433.1	88.8

Table 5.2 Estimate of Per Capita Private Consumption Expenditure
at 1960/61 Prices (Rs)

Year	Estimate I	Estimate II	Kansal Estimate	Deflators Used for		Index of Wholesale Prices 1960/61 = 100
				Estimate I	Estimate II	
1954/55	248.1	262.3	266.6	84.2	78.9	78.1
1955/56	248.3	278.3	270.9	85.8	75.9	74.1
1956/57	262.7	262.0	277.1	92.6	86.0	84.3
1957/58	252.7	265.7	266.4	94.2	88.7	86.8
1958/59	266.2	272.1	280.7	97.4	93.6	90.4
1959/60	262.9	269.0	276.6	98.3	97.0	93.8
1960/61	277.6	274.2	285.8	100.0	100.0	100. 0
1961/62	277.8	279.8	287.3	102.1	100.9	100.2
1962/63	273.4	279.6	278.3	105.8	103.3	102 .4
1963/64	277.0	276.9	281.6	115.0	106.9	108.3
1964/65	293.3	266.7		125.8	127.3	122.3
1965/66	269.5	262.5		137.0	134.6	132.1
1966/67	270.9	N.A.		156.2	N.A.	153.2
1967/68	291.8	240.4		170.7	180.1	170.2
1968/69	287.2	243.2		169.8	178.1	168.3

Estimate II. The extent of increase in real consumption is debatable, but all the estimates point to a modest, rising trend up to 1962/63. But thereafter, the two series show divergent trends in both real and nominal consumption.

In making these comparisons, it is important to bear in mind that each series is made up of point estimates in each year and hence are subject to a margin of error. The magnitude of error attaching to

NSS series can be calculated from the subsample comparisons. Rough estimates (see Table 5.3) suggest that on the whole the margin of errors in the NSS data are quite low, especially for rural areas.

Table 5.3 Approximate Precision Levels of Estimate with 95 Per Cent Probability

NSS Rounds	Rural (%)	Urban (%)
7	± 66.44	± 1.0
8	± 2.22	± 24.78
9	± 1.84	± 2.20
12	± 1.52	± 6.12
13	± .20	± 5.98
15	± 7.82	± 1.42
16	± 1.12	± 4.26
17	± 8.08	± 11.38
18	± 1.60	± .03
22	± 1.60	± 5.94
23	± 2.38	± .12

The official series, based as they are on incomplete production data and 'relatively arbitrary allocation ratios and distributive margins on the values of output as produced', also cannot be free of estimational errors, though their precise magnitude is not known. Once this fact is recognised, it is clear that a simple comparison of the two series may exaggerate the true significance of the difference. It is possible that even after allowing for this, some difference in the relative behaviours of the two series before and after 1962/68 may remain and needs to be explained.

Mukherjee and Chatterjee have argued that since there is a lag between production and consumer spending, it would be more appropriate to make allowance for this lag in comparing the two series. While there is justification in their basic point, the assumption of a six month lag is debatable. Also, in converting the NSS series to a fiscal year basis various assumptions have been made, which may introduce aberrations. It may not therefore be inappropriate to compare the NSS series (which relate to July–June) with the official series (which relate to the fiscal year) directly.

PATTERNS OF CONSUMPTION

Kansal (1965) compared the composition of aggregate consumption in 1957/58 estimated on the basis of the commodity flow approach using official data and the composition revealed by the NSS. There are significant differences of coverage and methods of valuation between the two sets of figures. Thus the commodity-flow estimates include government purchase of goods and services on current account while NSS relates strictly to household consumption. Unlike NSS, the commodity-flow method includes imputed rent on owner-occupied housing. There is also difference in methods of valuation: for instance the NSS (since the 9th Round), values of foodgrains consumed from home-grown stock are at harvest prices and cash purchases at retail prices. It is not clear whether estimates by the commodity-flow method follow the same procedure. Problems may also arise because of difference in classification. In the NSS, 'edible oils' and 'sugar' would cover direct household consumption. Indirect consumption through purchase of prepared foods would come under other food. In the commodity-flow approach the calculated availability would include both categories.

Subject to these limitations, the comparison reveals the following:

(a) When one considers broad commodity groups, as food and non-food, the patterns of expenditure distribution obtained by the two methods are quite close.

(b) However, there are large differences when the comparison is made by specific commodities. For instance, NSS estimates of foodgrains consumption in 1957/58 is 16 per cent higher than implied in official data (Table 5.4). But in most other food items, NSS shows a much lower level consumption than official estimates. The difference ranges from 10 per cent in meat, fish and eggs to 52 per cent in milk products. Among the non-food items, the NSS estimate is higher than the commodity-flow estimate in the case of fuel and light but lower in services and in conveyance.

Similar differences are noticed in 1960/61 as well. In general, compared to the product-flow estimates, the NSS pattern shows a larger share of expenditure on foodgrains, and a lower share for other food and services. To what extent these reflect the differences in concept, coverage and valuation mentioned earlier is a question deserving further study.

Table 5.4 Pattern of Consumption Expenditure at Current Prices,
India, 1957/58 and 1960/61

(Rs Million)

	1957/58		1960/61	
	Estimated*	*NSS*	*Estimated*	*NSS*
(1)	*(2)*	*(3)*	*(4)*	*(5)*
1. Foodgrains and cereal substitutes	34,360	39,740	39,424	44,109
2. Milk and milk products	11,230	5,430	12,470	9,781
3. Meat, fish and eggs	3,110	2,800	3,850	3,304
4. Sugar	3,780	2,220	5,236	3,247
5. Salt	180	240	276	268
6. Oils	3,220	2,740	4,062	3,643
7. Fruits and vegetables	5,920	3,590		
8. Spices	2,470	2,130		
9. Tobacco	2,370	2,020		
10. Other food products	2,629	4,750	20,022	16,523
11. Total of food products	69,200	66,260	85,940	81,175
12. Fuel and light	2,600	5,970	2,840	7,209
13. Clothing and footwear	9,970	9,410	10,640	9,706
14. Rent	6,120	1,190	6,620	1,237
15. Ornaments	570	680		
16. Domestic utensils	400	380		
17. Conveyance	2,360	1,600		
18. Medicine	1,170	1,470		
19. Amusement	520	520		
20. Services	7,440	5,680		
21. Other non-food items	3,460	5,513	22,920	23,143
22. Total of non-food products and services	34,610	32,410	43,020	41,295
23. Total (11 + 22)	1,03,310	98,670	1,28,960	1,22,470

Note: * Kansal and Saluja (l961).

The per capita consumption level of selected major commodities in 1961/62 obtained from the official statistics and the NSS are shown in Table 5.5. The NSS estimate for cereal consumption is nearly 38 per cent higher than the figure derived from official production and trade data. In fact, throughout the period under review, the NSS figures are consistently higher though the difference has narrowed down markedly since around 1964/65. The per capita consumption of pulses, vanaspati, edible oils, cotton clothing, tea in 1961/62, as revealed by the NSS, is uniformly below the official estimates of availability. Coffee is the only exception. The NSS figure is about 10 per cent or less below the official estimates in the case of edible oils, cotton clothing and tea, but the differences is about 25 per cent in the case of pulses and 50 per cent in vanaspati. In evaluating these comparisons it needs to be remembered that there are lags between production and consumption, that the official estimates do not make full allowance for stock changes and that the official estimates relate to total availability for internal consumption while the NSS figures in most cases relate to direct household consumption. The last mentioned factor implies that the direct household consumption should be less than the total availability for domestic consumption. This is corroborated by the comparison.

Table 5.5 Comparison of NSS Estimates of Per Capita Consumption with Official Estimates for Selected Commodities in 1961/62

Commodities	Unit	NSS Estimates	Official Estimates
Cereals	kg	203.6	147.2
Pulses	kg	18.4	24.1
Vanaspathi	kg	0.4	0.8
Edible oils	kg	3.3	3.4
Cotton clothing	m	13.2	14.7
Tea	g	293.0	316.0
Coffee	g	85.0	59.0

TRENDS IN CONSUMPTION

In an attempt to carry this analysis a bit further we have compared the time pattern of changes in consumption revealed by the NSS and official data in respect of the following four groups of commodities namely, foodgrains, edible oils, sugar and gur, and clothing (see Figures 5.1–5.4). The per capita consumption expenditure on each of these groups at current market prices is directly available from the NSS. For the official series the index of per capita availability is computed from the Annual Economic Surveys and other published sources. This index is multiplied by the index of wholesale prices for each of these commodity groups to arrive at index of per capita consumption at current prices. (However, the official series relates to total consumption, while NSS relates to household consumption only.) The trends of consumption of edible oils and sugar revealed by the two series are in surprisingly close agreement. In the case of foodgrains while the pattern of movement in the two series is broadly similar, the NSS indicates distinctly slower increase in per capita expenditure at current prices than implied in the official series. In the case of clothing there is little correspondence between the time pattern growth of consumption obtained by the two methods. While the official data point to a sharp and sustained increase in per capita expenditures in clothing, the NSS shows a little, if any, positive trend.

One of the main conclusions to emerge from the discussion of the previous section is that the relatively close agreement between the NSS and official series for some years does not necessarily

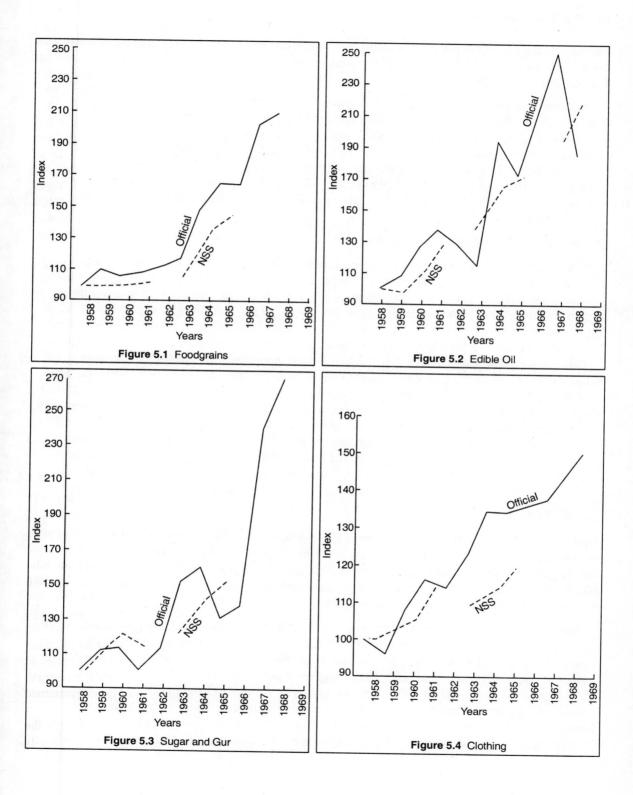

Figure 5.1 Foodgrains

Figure 5.2 Edible Oil

Figure 5.3 Sugar and Gur

Figure 5.4 Clothing

indicate the absence of systematic bias in either series; equally the divergence between the two series for other years does not necessarily indicate the presence of such bias. Thus we find it hard to agree with Dandekar and Rath (1971) who assert:

'It seems that the NSS estimate of per capita private consumer expenditure for 1967/68 is an underestimate. This becomes clear if we compare it with the NSS estimate for 1960/61. It will be seen that, compared at constant 1960/61 prices, the NSS estimate for 1967/68 (Rs 256.2) is below the NSS estimate for 1960/61 (Rs 278.8) by as much as 8.1 per cent. Hence, if we rely on the NSS estimates, it would appear that the per capita consumption declined by as much as 8.1 per cent during the seven years from 1960/61 to 1967-68. This appears unlikely. Hence we must conclude that the NSS estimate of per capita consumer expenditure in 1967/68 is in fact an underestimate.'

The reasons they offer for their conclusions are:

'If we examine . . . the estimates of per capita consumer expenditure in 1967/68 as percentages of per capita consumption in 1960/61, it will be seen that the middle and upper middle classes have done comparatively better than the lower middle and the poorer classes. For instance, the per capita consumption of the poorest 5 per cent is only 93.9 per cent of its level in 1960/61. This percentage gradually rises until, for the class of population lying between 60–70 per cent counted from the poorest, the per capita consumption in 1967/68 is 99.1 per cent of its level in 1960/61. This appears plausible namely that the middle and upper middle classes should have done comparatively better than the lower middle and the poorer classes. However, judging by the NSS estimates, it seems that the richer classes have done worse than the upper middle classes and indeed very much worse than even the poorest classes. Thus, it seems that in 1967/68, the per capita consumption of the population lying between 80–90 per cent was only 95.0 per cent of its level in 1960/61; of the population lying between 90–95 per cent, the per capita consumption in 1967/68 was only 91.1 per cent of its level and finally, of the richest 5 per cent population, the per capita consumption in 1967/68 was just 72.9 per cent of its level in 1960/61. This is incredible.'

EVALUATION

Bardhan has pointed out, that if a more appropriate deflator than the national income deflator is used to convert consumption expenditure at 1967/68 prices to the prices of 1960/61, Dandekar and Rath may find the pattern of change in levels of living of different fractile groups between 1960/61 and 1967/68 considerably less incredible. However, what are incredible are some of the *prima facie* reasons offered by them in support of their conclusions. We quote:

'The NSS secures its estimates of consumer expenditures by interviewing a random sample of rural and urban households and inquiring from them about their consumer expenditure during the previous month. The limitations of this procedure are well known. For instance, a number of items of consumer expenditure, such as clothing and other consumer durables, which a household would purchase less frequently than once every month, are likely to be missed by this procedure and hence the expenditure on them is likely to be underestimated. These are the items which are more important in the consumer expenditure of the rich than the poor and they become more important as the rich become richer. It is also known that the upper middle and the richer households, both in rural and urban areas, have become increasingly inaccessible to the NSS investigators who are after all class III government servants.'

First, the relative infrequency of purchase of certain consumer items does not lead to an underestimation in the NSS. The reasons for this are two: (i) The NSS is canvassed in a number of sub-rounds spread throughout the year and hence any seasonality in the purchase of an item leads to no bias. For instance, if cloth is purchased mainly during Diwali and Puja seasons, such a purchase will get reflected in the sub-rounds covering these periods. (ii) In any given sub-round the random sampling procedure of the survey will ensure that purchasers of cloth are not systematically excluded. Second, Dandekar and Rath have not established that underestimation of such purchases, if present at all, has increased between 1960/61 and 1967/68. Thirdly, there is *absolutely* no independent evidence other than the words of the distinguished authors to suggest that the upper income households have become increasingly inaccessible to the poor NSS investigator! One could device a crude test of their assertion by comparing the non-response rates in 1960/61 and 1967/68 classified according to some variable closely related to income. But this is possible only if data on such a variable had been collected at the time of preparing the household lists in each chosen village or urban block.

Suppose for the sake of argument, we assume that the NSS has been increasingly underestimating consumption expenditure. What does this imply for: (a) the estimates of the proportion of the population having consumption expenditure below some normative level; and (b) the extent of redistribution involved if the people below the poverty line were to be raised to the line?

It is clear that if: (i) the consumption as stated to the NSS investigator is an increasing function (not necessarily the same from round to round) of the true consumption expenditure and (ii) the consumers at the poverty line neither overstate nor understate their true consumption in any round, then the estimates of the proportion of the population below the poverty line based on the observed NSS distribution will not be biased. If the consumers at the poverty line understate (overstate) their true consumption such an estimate will be an overestimate (underestimate) of the true proportion. This is illustrated in Table 5.2. In deriving these figures we have assumed that, Rs 15 at 1960/61 prices is equivalent to Rs 28.3 at 1968/69 prices. We have chosen the percentages of bias in such a way as to read out without interpolation the proportion of population below the specified level of per capita expenditure!

Table 5.6 Proportion of Rural Population Having a Per Cent Monthly Consumption Expenditure below Rs 15 at 1960/61 Prices

1960/61		1968/69	
Bias (%)	Proportion of Poor	Bias (%)	Proportion of Poor
−13.3	0.28	−12.5	0.43
0.0	0.38	0.0	0.54
+20.0	0.52	+15.3	0.64

Thus if the consumers having a true consumption expenditure of Rs 15 per month had understated this by 13.3 per cent, i.e. they had reported a per capita expenditure of Rs 13 per month, then the true proportion of people below the line will be 28 per cent, while the estimate based on ignoring this bias will be 38 per cent. Similarly if there is no bias in 1960/61 while there is an understatement by 12.5 per cent in 1968/69, the true proportion of poor people will go up from 38 per cent to 43 per cent while a comparison ignoring the bias will suggest an increase from 38 per cent to 54 per cent. If the proportion of poor people is to be the same at 38 per cent, then one has to assume an understatement larger than 12.5 per cent.

Thus, for the limited question of estimating the incidence of poverty all one needs to be concerned with is the degree of bias (and its variation over time) at the chosen normative poverty line provided the reasonable assumption that stated consumption is an increasing function of true consumption is satisfied. But, if one is interested in quantifying the magnitude of income transfers from the 'rich' to the 'poor' required to reduce the incidence of poverty, it is essential to know the extent of bias at all levels of consumption.

Our main conclusions can now be summarised:

1. In comparing the series of consumption expenditure derived from the official estimates of national income and the National Sample Survey, allowance must be made for the inevitable margins of error for both estimates. If this were done, the divergence between the 2 series after 1962/63 may not be as great as suggested by the comparison of the point estimates.
2. Even allowing for the margins of error, it is possible that the pattern of divergence after 1962/63 is still different compared to the pattern in the previous years. A closer study of the data including any changes in the methods estimation, differences in concept, coverage and evaluation is necessary.
3. The mere fact of close agreement between the 2 series is no guarantee of the absence of bias, nor is the divergence between the 2 series proof of bias in either series.
4. For purposes of assessing the incidence of poverty it is enough to know whether or not persons near the normative poverty line have under/over reported the true income and by how much. Even if the precise degree of bias is not known it is possible to assess the sensitivity of conclusions under alternative assumptions about bias.
5. However, in order to estimate the magnitude of resource transfers required to reduce the incidence of poverty it is essential to know the direction and magnitude of the bias over the entire range of consumption.

ACKNOWLEDGEMENT

Reprinted from *Poverty and Income Distribution in India*, P.K. Bardhan and T.N. Srinivasan (eds.), Indian Statistical Institute, Calcutta, 1974.

REFERENCES

Dandekar, V.M. and N. Rath (1971), 'Poverty in India', *Economic & Political Weekly*, 2 and 9 January.

Kansal, S.M. (1965), Preliminary Estimates of Total Consumption Expenditure in India, 1950/51 to 1963/64, I.S.I., Planning Unit Discussion Paper No. 5, September (mimeo).

Kansal, S.M. and M.R. Saluja (1961), Preliminary Estimates of Total Consumption Expenditure in India; 1957/58 to 1960/61; Paper contributed to the Third Indian Conference on Research in National Income.

Mukherjee, M. (1969), *National Income of India: Trends and Structure*, Statistical Publishing Society, Calcutta.

Mukherjee, M. and G.S. Chatterjee (1972), On the Validity of NSS Estimates of Consumption Expenditure, *Arthavignana*, July.

6

Validation of Large-Scale Sample Survey Data
Case of NSS Estimates of Household Consumption Expenditure

B.S. Minhas

INTRODUCTION

Validation of the National Sample Survey (NSS) estimates of household consumption expenditure, or for that matter any other primary data set generated by a large-scale sample survey, involves many complicated issues. For expositional convenience, most of these issues can be discussed under two broad categories. One class of issues are more germane to the common, textbook variety, assessments of the internal validity of NSS estimates themselves. The other category of issues go much beyond the more easily tractable area of the internal validity of the survey estimates, and relate more to the examination of whether or not the sample survey estimates are in agreement with 'comparable' external data sets.

As strictly comparable external data sets are indeed rare to find, the comparisons with external data have to contend with inherent differences between concepts, definitions, coverage, time periods, methods of data collection, estimation procedures, etc. In view of all this, the question of external validation of sample survey data has to be approached with fairness and scientific detachment. The results of such comparisons are difficult to foresee: scientific scrutiny may, or may not, lead to mutual validation of both data sets under examination. It may, nevertheless, provide important clues for improving the reliability of either one or both data sets.

Out of the wide variety of primary data sets generated by the NSS over the past thirty-five years, the data on household consumption expenditure have been the most extensive, and have been made available to the public quite regularly. These data sets on consumption expenditure have also been most widely used, both by research workers and policy makers. A number of instances (see the concluding section) of abuse of this data have also come to light. These abuses and misuses have arisen partly from certain misunderstandings arising out of lack of adequate familiarity with the NSS estimates, but more importantly on account of the fact that external validations have been attempted on the basis of superficial comparisons.

Although we do not intend to ignore altogether the question of inherent variability and internal validity of the NSS estimates of household consumption expenditure, the main focus of this paper is on the issues relating to external validation. The external data sets for purposes of this comparison are the Central Statistical Organisation's (CSO) estimates of total private consumption, which are indirectly derived by adjusting production and income flows of consumer goods and services in the framework of the National Accounting System (NAS). Our emphasis shall mainly be on the methodology of external validation, and less on detailed numerical comparisons of the two sets of estimates, which are available elsewhere (Minhas et al., 1986). The questions relating to scrutiny and editing of raw data are not the concern of this paper. Further this investigation is confined to the analysis of only the central sample data.

INHERENT LIMITS TO THE COMPARABILITY OF THE SO-CALLED 'COMPARABLE' ESTIMATES

The basic rationale of comparisons between the estimates of household consumption expenditure obtained from the NSS, and the estimates of total private consumption from the NAS would seem to run along the following lines: the estimates of the NSS are subject to both sampling and non-sampling errors, each of which in turn is composed of a systematic component (bias) and a random component (variance). As the estimation procedures adopted in the NSS are unbiased for large sample sizes, the sampling bias can be neglected and the sampling errors and non-sampling variance would be rather small. One could, therefore, hope that but for the non-sampling bias of the survey results, the NSS estimates of household consumption expenditure for a particular year should be broadly comparable with the accounting estimates of total private consumption of NAS for the same year. In other words such comparisons, among other things, are expected to throw some light on the non-sampling bias of the NSS estimates. However, this reasonable expectation of comparability could hold only if the external (NAS) estimates of private consumption were either based fully on 'directly observed' data in the national accounting system, or the indirectly derived components of the NAS data – derived from old benchmark estimates and ad hoc sample studies – did not suffer from sampling and non-sampling errors which were not negligible. This basic rationale of comparisons of NSS estimates with external data has to be kept firmly in mind.

Differences in Coverage

The coverage of the NSS and the NAS estimates is not identical. The NSS covers only private households and tends to exclude the houseless population and the population residing in institutional households such as prisons, orphanages, barracks and hospitals. The NAS estimates include the latter along with the private households. In addition, the NAS also includes the consumption expenditure of non-profit and charitable institutions which are engaged in social welfare and religious activities and provide free or subsidised educational, medical, religious and other welfare services to the households. In view of this larger coverage, the NAS estimates would be expected to be higher than the NSS estimates.

In order to compare them with the estimates of private consumption of the NAS, the item-wise NSS per capita expenditure data can be used in conjunction with the total population of the country. This procedure is expected to give us detailed NSS-based estimates of total private consumption expenditure, reasonably comparable (in terms of coverage) with the NAS estimates, after certain minor adjustments to the latter. One such adjustment relates to government expenditure on several consumer items such as foodgrains, fruits and vegetables, and clothing, which are provided by the government to individuals (e.g. defence personnel), either free or at subsidised rates, and are included under government expenditure. These should be added to the NAS estimates of private consumption expenditure before comparing them with the NSS.

In consequence of the foregoing adjustments, the NSS total consumption could be slightly overestimated (underestimated) if the actual per capita consumption of the defence and security personnel in barracks and the houseless and institutional population is lower (higher) than the average per capita consumption of the NSS. On balance, the two estimates might nevertheless be regarded as reasonably comparable (from the point of view of coverage alone), especially for the food group items.

Differences in Time Periods

The NSS was never expected or specifically asked to produce estimates of household consumption expenditure on a regular, annual, or financial year basis. Its own anticipation of the periodicity of user demands for any particular set of data, or need for synchronisation with similar periodic activities of outside agencies, has determined the frequency of the reappearance of certain subject matters in the cycle of NSS work. Selection of time periods for different rounds by the NSS (both in regard to choice of dates and length of period for fieldwork) has generally been guided by certain technical as well as logistic considerations for the deployment of field staff all over the country.

The NAS estimates of total private consumption are presented every year and relate to the financial year, April to March. As far as the national accounts are concerned, the agricultural production year, July to June, is accounted for in the twelve-month period ending with 31 March – 3 months prior to end of June when the agricultural year ends. NSS, on the other hand uses variable time periods, varying in length as well as timing for different rounds. The detailed NSS estimates of household consumption expenditure are now presented only once in a quinquennium. The latest three such estimates pertain to 1972/73 (27th Round, from October 1972 to September 1973), 1977/78 (32nd Round, from July 1977 to June 1978) and 1983 (38th Round, from January to December 1983). It should be evident that it is not easy to establish any straightforward time correspondence between the NSS estimates and the external data sets of the NAS for different financial years.

Whatever is reported to the NSS as current consumption by the households is unlikely to have been concurrently produced by the production units. Although the NSS estimates of consumption expenditure are generally free from seasonality effects when the survey period spans a year, the available external data (annual product flow estimates of CSO) may contain a substantial portion of goods and services produced during intervals of time outside the survey period of the NSS. As the production of goods does not, by and large, have the characteristics of a steady-state flow in time, the product flow data of any particular year is likely to be impacted by the cyclical and seasonal elements in a manner different from the effects captured in the NSS estimates based on direct observations in the nearest survey period. This task of adjusting for time period differences between the NSS and NAS estimates of consumption is difficult, particularly, for the products originating in agriculture – the sector most vulnerable to the vagaries of weather.

The importance of differences in time periods outlined above can be best illustrated by comparing the NSS 38th Round (1983) estimates of household consumption with the NAS estimates for the financial year 1983/84. The latter estimate was 22 per cent higher than the estimate derived from the NSS round (1983) of the NSS. It can nevertheless be shown that this large magnitude of the discrepancy is largely illusory. While the NAS estimates of private consumption in 1983/84 are based on the production of the agricultural year July 1983–June 1984, the consumption of agricultural products reported to the NSS in the 38th Round January to December 1983, mostly pertain to agricultural production realised during the period July 1982 to June 1983. First crop of 1983/84 (kharif) would have been harvested from October 1983 onwards. Therefore, during the first ten months of the 38th Round survey (i.e. from January to October 1983), the reported consumption of foodgrains by the households would entirely be from the kharif and rabi crops of 1982/83. Only in the last two months of the survey period (November and December), the reported foodgrain consumption could have been from the kharif crop of 1983/84. For wheat, gram and barley, household consumption during the whole survey year (1983) would be from the rabi crops of 1982/83. In fact, in the first sub-round of the survey (January to March 1983), reported consumption of rabi grains would have been from the rabi crops of 1981/82. For all practical purposes, therefore, one can assume that the NSS estimates of expenditure on foodgrains in 1983 were out of the harvests realised in 1982/83 (July 1982 to June 1983).

Since there was a big jump in foodgrain production in 1983/84 over 1982/83 (of about 22 million tonnes), and all this would have been included in the NAS consumption estimates of 1983/84, the latter is naturally higher than the NSS (1983) estimates by about Rs 5,000 crore (accounting for 5 percentage points out of the apparent difference of 22 per cent in total consumption) due to foodgrains alone. The same considerations would also apply in comparing the consumption estimates of oilseeds and their products from the two data sources, as the production of oilseeds recorded a big increase of 27 per cent from 10 million tonnes in 1982/83 to 12.7 million tonnes in 1983/84. As most of the consumption of agricultural commodities and related products reported by the households to the NSS in 1983 was from 1982/83 crops, a rough adjustment of the time period effects for the agricultural sector alone would make the apparent discrepancy between the NAS and NSS estimates of total private consumption come down to about 12 per cent in comparison with the unadjusted difference of 22 per cent in 1983/84. The remaining difference of 12 per cent should narrow down further when the effects of the big harvests of 1983/84 on the other sectors of the economy are also suitably adjusted.

Similar adjustments for differences in time periods have also been made in case of a large number of agricultural products, to bring the NAS estimates of private consumption for 1972/73 and 1977/78 (financial years) in line for comparability with the NSS estimates of the 27th (October 1972–September 1973) and 32nd (July 1977–June 1978) Rounds of the survey. Detailed results are presented elsewhere (Minhas et al., 1986). It is sufficient to note here that these adjustments for time period differences between the NAS and the NSS do not always affect the NAS estimates of private consumption equally or in the same direction. The extent of adjustment is indicated by the time discordance between the survey period of a particular NSS round and the corresponding agricultural year; and the direction of adjustment (positive or negative) depends on whether the previous agricultural year/season was a year/season of significantly different (larger or smaller) production compared to the agricultural year corresponding to a specific NSS round.

Differences in Methods of Data Collection and Estimation Procedures

In addition to differences in coverage and time periods, the other major cause of lack of comparability between the NSS and NAS estimates of total private consumption may reside in the shortcomings in their respective methods of data collection and estimation procedures. An understanding of these methods is a necessary prerequisite for negotiating comparability between the two data sets.

NSS Procedures

The NSS collects detailed item-wise consumption data in value and quantity (wherever possible) terms for the last 30 days[1] preceding the date of inquiry from the sample households by interviewing the head of the household (and other members). The survey period of a round, normally of one-year duration, is generally subdivided into four sub-rounds. The sample villages and urban blocks are distributed over the four sub-rounds in equal numbers for either of the subsamples in which the total sample is divided. The sample households are canvassed in a staggered fashion all through the survey period and the estimates based on all the four sub-rounds taken together are free from seasonal variations.

The sampling scheme of the NSS consumer expenditure surveys is generally based on a stratified two stage sampling design. The rural and urban sectors of the country are separately divided into hundreds of strata. Villages and urban blocks are the first stage units (FSUs) in rural and urban sectors, respectively, and households comprise the second stage units (SSUs). The FSUs are usually selected from within the strata in the form of two independent subsamples. The FSUs, when selected with varying probabilities, are chosen either with replacement (PPS with replacement), or by systematic selection (PPS systematic). The SSUs (Households) are selected, either linear or circular, systematically. It must also be mentioned that various methods of sub-stratification and/or arrangements of households are also used by the NSS for selection of the SSUs from each selected FSU.

In the latest three full rounds of the NSS dealing with consumer expenditure namely: the 27th (1972/73), 32nd (1977/78) and 38th (1983), the sample size has been very large, comprising about 13,000 to 14,000 FSUs and 121,000 to 158,000 SSUs. The sampling errors of the NSS estimates of private consumption, based as they are on very large samples, are indeed very small at the all-India level.

Even at the state level, the relative standard errors of total expenditure in the bigger states vary between 2 and 3 per cent; whereas for expenditure on food the relative standard errors are less than 2 per cent. Further, although the precision of NSS estimates (Sarma, Rao, 1980)[2] of expenditure on individual items of most common consumption is satisfactory, nevertheless, for some items, such as quality foods, clothing, footwear, durable goods, medicines and consumer services, the standard errors of the estimates of sub-group-wise and item-wise expenditure at the state-level tend to be high. At the all-India level, the sampling errors of these item-wise estimates of expenditure would be far less than at the state level; nevertheless, for certain individual items they might turn out to be quite large.

Although an in-depth discussion of sampling errors will have to be deferred to a later occasion, a somewhat detailed treatment of the non-sampling errors, which have been considered likely to affect the NSS estimates of consumption, belongs here, and is given below:

(a) *Failure to recall precise information on the consumption of individual items within a broad group.* It may not be possible for the household members to recall correctly the quantity and value, say, of individual fruits and vegetables, or each of the grains in the foodgrains group, or each spice and condiment in the spices group, or each individual oil and fat, consumed during the last thirty days. In view of this, the detailed item-wise household consumption expenditure within the group is not likely to be correctly apportioned by the reporting households. In other words, there is likelihood of some misclassification within the group, although the total expenditure on the item-group might be more correctly reported. NSS appear to be conscious of this difficulty.

---

[1] In recent rounds, consumption data have also been collected for the last 365 days for durable and semi-durable goods.

[2] See, V.R.R. Sarma and G.D. Rao (1980), and the Supplementary Note in Appendix B of this chapter.

Nevertheless, very detailed listing of individual items comprising a group is adhered to in the schedules of inquiry to facilitate recall and minimise the chances of total omission of minor items by the respondents.

(b) *Wilful suppression or under-reporting of certain consumption expenditures.* The consumption of liquor and tobacco is frowned upon, or is considered unacceptable, by certain sections of society. Also, quite often the head of the household or the informant may not be aware even if some members of the household are casual or regular consumers of liquor and tobacco. There are also certain sensitive items, such as gold and jewellery, whose purchases may not be fully reported by the households to the investigators. The NSS consumption estimates of these sensitive or socially unacceptable items are therefore likely to be gross underestimates.

(c) *Underestimation of rents on dwellings.* The NSS collects data only on the actual rent paid by households. All imputed rentals from owner-occupied dwellings are excluded from the NSS rental estimates, whereas the NAS covers both rented as well as owner-occupied dwellings for the estimation of rent.

(d) *NSS design and estimates of certain items of expenditure associated with affluent sections of society.* Some scholars have argued that the current sampling design of the NSS might be leading to systematic underestimation of certain aggregates, like consumption of consumer durables, which are specifically associated with the rich. Murthy (1977), for instance, observed that 'since the NSS estimates are based on general purpose design with emphasis on point parameters, the estimates of tails, in which the users are specifically interested, are subject to larger sampling errors and hence not amenable to deeper analysis' (Murthy, 1977). Nevertheless these estimates are approximately unbiased. It is also known that the larger sampling errors in the upper tail does not vitiate the usual estimates of incidence of poverty, nevertheless the precision of the estimates of aggregate expenditure on modern consumer durables, important consumer services and certain other luxury goods might be affected. In order to ensure adequate representation of the consumption patterns of the more affluent sections of society, the sample selection procedures, both for FSUs (particularly in large cities) and SSUs, have been more carefully designed for the 43rd Round (1987/88), for which fieldwork is currently in progress. It is hoped that this would ensure better estimation of certain aggregates of expenditure which are specifically associated with the households in the upper tail of the distribution.

(e) *Possibility of duplication of expenditure on certain items, particularly foodgrains.* The NSS estimates of aggregate consumer expenditure on foodgrains, especially cereals, obtained by multiplying the total population of India with the NSS per capita consumption estimates, have been found to be consistently higher than the corresponding estimates of the NAS. As the NAS estimates are derived from independent estimates of production of cereals and other foodgrains released by the Ministry of Food and Agriculture (MFA), a number of possibilities of duplication and non-sampling biases in the NSS budget estimates of foodgrain consumption have been surmised by different scholars over the past 30 years. Since foodgrains constitute a very substantial proportion of the average household budget in India, it is very essential that in this paper, where the primary concern is validation of consumer survey data, we seek a satisfactory resolution of the doubts and suspicions raised about the possibilities of duplication in the NSS budget estimates. We find that most of these doubts and suspicions are based on *a priori* reasoning, or on facts whose relevance to the issues under examination is extremely far-fetched. Notwithstanding the lack of firm supportive evidence, the suspicions might nevertheless linger on. The situation demands new methodological studies to settle this question. The National Sample Survey Organisation (NSSO) has shown some renewed vigour in recent years in undertaking methodological work. One methodological study, bearing on the question of long vs short consumer expenditure schedule, has just been completed, and another study on the suitability of different reference periods, etc., is under progress, in collaboration with the Indian Statistical Institute (ISI). One hopes that the NSS would also undertake methodological work on the question of duplication, in household budgets, of expenditure on cereals. Meanwhile, considerable light on this question can also be thrown by computing standard errors (SES) of the estimates of expenditure on cereals, based on subsamples X states (the old one degree of freedom estimates), and comparing them with those derived directly from the household data. As both these estimates of SES are known to be unbiased (although quite different in regard to their efficiency), the direction of change in the ratios of SE estimates from the two procedures over the states could tell us a lot about the presence/absence of non-sampling bias in the NSS estimates. No such comparisons, however, seem to have been reported in the literature thus far, but we intend to take up this exercise on a later occasion.

CSO's Procedures for NAS Estimates of Private Consumption

The NAS estimates of private consumption are based on production data of all consumer goods and services obtained from various agencies outside the control of the CSO. These data are processed and adjusted by the CSO by deducting exports, intermediate uses, and net increases in stocks, and adding in imports to arrive at the availability of various goods and services for domestic consumption and capital formation. This volume and value of all goods and services available for domestic consumption is apportioned by the CSO among government, business and private consumption. It is this last use-category, i.e. private consumption, which is supposed to be comparable with the NSS estimates of household consumer expenditure.

The quantities of various consumer items (especially the food products) are subdivided into home-produced consumption, and purchases from markets, and these are separately evaluated at producer prices and retail prices, respectively. Private consumption expenditure estimates are derived by deducting government consumption expenditure from the total final consumption expenditure (CSO, 1980).

For many consumer services, such as recreation, personal services, etc., CSO follows the income approach to estimate the value of output and then makes allocation between intermediate, private and government uses. Under this approach the census data on the number of persons engaged in different services and the average earnings per person (taken from ad hoc survey reports) are utilised. Since the average earnings per person are not available on current basis, the base-year figures are updated with the help of consumer price indices of urban, non-manual employees for urban areas, and wages of rural skilled workers for rural areas. The above procedure provides the value-added figures which are inflated to obtain output figures by using output to value-added ratios taken from the old survey reports.

Although the CSO makes sincere efforts to use all available information on production, intermediate uses, etc., still the NAS estimates suffer from a number of shortcomings which basically are due to non-availability of reliable and currently observed information to make various adjustments. Some of these shortcomings, which affect the NAS estimates of private consumption, are:

(a) Data on changes in stocks are not only partial, but also of poor quality. Very little information is available about the stocks held by traders, producers and households (especially the producer households). With the availability of 1978/79 ASI data on changes in stocks, and similar data available in ASI summary reports from 1979/80 onward, the reliability of the NAS estimates for some sectors might improve a little. Nevertheless, the prospects are not encouraging for improvement in data relating to food stock with traders and farmers. However, the currently available NAS estimates, against which validation of NSS estimates is being attempted suffer from this weakness.

(b) Data on marketable surplus (i.e. allocation between home-grown consumption and market purchases) of various consumer products are based on the old reports of Directorate of Marketing and Inspection (DMI) issued in the fifties and early sixties. Adjustment made on the basis of stale information (collected three decades ago) do not inspire much confidence in the end product. However, efforts are now being made through the Ministry of Agriculture to collect current data on marketable surplus ratios and the CSO proposes to use them as and when such data become available.

(c) Data on intermediate uses are very weak and partial. For most foodgrains, base-year ratios of intermediate uses (like animal feed, wastages, etc.), which are 20 or more years old, are used in the absence of current information. There are problems also in adjusting the production of major foodgrains for amounts used as seed.

(d) In a few cases the data and the estimation procedure of the NAS are revised in the light of current data. All these revisions are not always carried backward; however, for major revisions the CSO adjusts the series backward for earlier years. Examples of revisions carried backward only for a limited number of years include the consumption estimates of other sugars, gram, salt and medical services, which have undergone substantial revisions at different points of time. Although the estimates for individual items are affected, the effects are insignificant at the overall level. In other words, the NAS estimates of private consumption for different years may not be strictly comparable among themselves. Their comparability with the NSS estimates for different (specific) years is likely to be affected in differential ways for different items, depending on whether the consequences of the revisions in NAS procedures are equally reflected in years selected for comparison.

(e) Data based on production of consumer goods in the unorganised sector is terribly weak. This is likely to affect seriously the NAS consumption estimates of several consumer products like transistor radios, matches, non-alcoholic beverages, biscuits, confectionary, etc. However, efforts are now being made to incorporate such data from the Directory and Non-directory Establishment Survey results for 1979/80. Nevertheless, the current NAS estimates are without the benefit of this data.

(f) The data on trade and transport margins, wherever used, appear to be rather inadequate. CSO has initiated studies in this regard and has approached a number of dealers for the purpose. The pay off from these efforts would take time in arriving. In the meanwhile, the attempted adjustments for trade and transport margins in the NAS estimates would continue to inspire only limited confidence in their reliability.

(g) For some items, such as match boxes and alcoholic beverages, the expenditure appears to be underestimated as the excise duty collections alone on such items are only marginally different from the corresponding NAS estimate of private expenditure (inclusive of excise) on these items.

(h) For certain categories of expenditure, such as education, medicines and medical services, the CSO use, a combination of survey (NSS) and administrative data. This practice has given rise to some duplication and overstatement of expenditure in NAS data, particularly for the education sector.

(i) CSO's estimates of expenditure on communications and railway services are based on firm accounting data on gross receipts. Nevertheless the difficulty arises in determining the share of the households in these receipts. Currently these shares seem to be based on subjective judgements. It is, therefore, necessary for the NAS to undertake/sponsor studies to work out the share of expenditure attributable to households in these sectors. In the meanwhile, sectoral aggregates of expenditure estimated by the NSS have to be judged against external evidence which is no better than informed/ill-informed guesswork.

(j) The allocation of total production of consumer durables between households and industry (for the NAS estimates of private consumption of durables) is another murky area. The CSO assumes certain fixed proportions (identical for many years) of production of durables in the economy as consumption by the households. This assumption is based on subjective judgements. This is indeed an unhappy situation, with implications also for the estimates of capital formation. Comparison with NSS data for this sector therefore have to be taken with caution.

Incomparability Caused by Unrecorded Data in Official Records *vs* Directly Reported Consumption

The NAS consumption estimates for various consumer goods are based on official data on production, exports and imports. Circumstances are known to exist which lead to deliberate under-recording of production of certain items. For example, the manufacturers might under-report production of many items to evade excise duty. Such unrecorded production would also be missing from the corresponding private consumption estimates of the CSO. On the other hand, consumers are likely to report the purchases of all such items irrespective of whether or not their production was entered into the records of the enterprises.

Some exports and imports also take place without being recorded in the official data. Besides organised smuggling, petty trade across the long open borders is not an uncommon phenomenon. Examples of such unrecorded imports relate to items such as watches, electronic consumer goods, gold and many kinds of textiles. Similarly there are many items, such as sugar, gur, liquor, tobacco and certain varieties of textiles, which are carried across the borders to the neighbouring countries without entry into official records.

All such transactions, missing from official records cannot be taken into account by the CSO in their estimates of private consumption. On the other hand, the NSS data can reflect all such transactions, as it does not depend on any official data records for its estimates of consumer expenditure. It is, therefore, natural to expect that the comparability of CSO and NSS consumption estimates for certain items would be severely affected.

Sampling and Non-sampling Errors: NSS *vs* the National Accounts

Many discussions of sampling errors seem to imply as if only the NSS estimates suffer from these errors. This is a gross misconception. The national accounts data get their copious share of sampling errors, not from one but many sample surveys from which the production database of the national accounts gets built up. Some of these surveys are conducted regularly every year, and others are of ad hoc nature. The data on per hectare yields (and therefore total output) of principal crops and a large part of industrial production, for instance, are based on regular sample surveys. Where the data on production are not being collected regularly, the value of output is often estimated by the CSO from the results of old surveys conducted at different points of time. All these diverse production surveys, which form the building blocks of the National Accounts, carry their sampling errors into the edifice of the NAS in the most confounded manner. This confounding of sampling errors in the NAS is so intractable that many scholars even fail to recognise them. No estimates of sampling errors of the NAS estimates are known to exist and no demand for such estimates of errors seems to have been made by the users of the NAS data. On the other hand, the sampling errors of the consumption estimates from NSS, even when these errors are known to be small, are expected to be routinely estimated without due appreciation of the costs involved in these computations.

In the discussion of differences in the methods of data collection and estimation procedures, we have provided fairly full details of the incidence of non-sampling errors in both data sets. Nevertheless, it is worth noting once again that the process of indirect derivation of numbers (not directly observed), by making all manner of adjustments on the basis of auxiliary data (which are stale, partial in coverage and often of very poor quality) and informed guesswork, leads to fast breeding of non-sampling errors which get cumulated (or get cancelled?) in unknown ways in the NAS estimates of private consumption. On the other hand, the non-sampling biases (if any) in the NSS data are likely to be small and uniform or subject to very slow change over time; and similarly over space and socio-economic groups. To put it differently, the control of non-sampling errors should be a matter for much deeper concern in the NAS data than in the case of consumption estimates obtained from any single consumer expenditure survey. In the context of the latter, it is much easier to improve concepts, tighten up methods of data collection and field supervision, to control suspected non-sampling errors.

It is quite obvious that the database of NAS estimates of private consumption would need to be improved in a number of directions. Many of these improvements are planned for the future. At this stage it would, however, be fair to conclude that the currently available NAS estimates of private consumption (with which NSS estimates are being compared) fall far short of the touchstone standard expected of an external validator data set. Matters relating to the degree of precision and biases in the NAS estimates of many items and item-groups are yet much too dependent on guesswork and subjective judgements to permit assessment of the limits within which scientifically valid comparisons can be undertaken with the corresponding survey (NSS) estimates.

Differences due to Different Price Sets

An examination of consumer prices, derived from the value and quantity estimates of different cereals and pulses, revealed that NSS (implicit) prices were consistently higher for almost all the foodgrains than the CSO prices in 1972/73 and 1977/78. The relevant data are presented in Appendix A-II. When the NSS quantities of different cereals and pulses are evaluated at CSO (NAS) prices, the apparent difference between the two sets of expenditure estimates for the foodgrains group gets reduced by about one-third in 1972/73 and by two-thirds in 1977/78.

In terms of its conceptual relevance, and comprehensiveness of fully representative coverage in space and time, the implicit prices set of the NSS is the ideal a welfare economist could wish for. They should be much better than the NAS prices for measuring cost of living and consumer welfare. Nevertheless, it is not obvious why NSS prices of foodgrains might be more or less consistently higher than the NAS prices. A firm answer to this question can be provided only on the basis of an empirical study, which is outside the scope of this paper.

Differences due to Unmatched Classification Schemes

There are many differences in the classification schemes of the two data sets. This should have little significance for the comparison of total consumption expenditure estimates, nevertheless, the item-wise/group-wise comparisons often get vitiated. In the national system of accounts, for instance, the expenditure in hotels and restaurants is classified under non-food in consumer services. In the NSS, on the other hand, the expenditure incurred by households in hotels and restaurants is included in the food group.

APPROXIMATE ADJUSTMENTS FOR NEGOTIATING COMPARABILITY

To adjust for all the seven major causes of apparent differences between the two sets of estimates is an almost impossible task. Nevertheless, some approximate adjustments can be made and their effects can be quantified. Some of the differences (for want of relevant information, or because of conceptual difficulties) on the other hand cannot be quantified, although their significance is capable of being assessed in qualitative terms.

The first crucial step in this process is to work out the item-wise details of consumer expenditure independently reported (without adjustments) by the two agencies for some recent years. One such exercise (Minhas et al., 1986) was undertaken to disaggregate and reclassify total private consumption expenditure into about fifty comparable commodity/service groups. For the purposes of this paper, however, these details of expenditure have been aggregated into nine broad groups. The NSS as well as NAS estimates (unadjusted) for these groups are given in Appendix AI. Prior to giving some answers to the question of external validation, it is this raw material which has to be processed and adjusted to negotiate comparability.

As can be seen from Table 6.1, the unadjusted CSO (NAS) estimates of total private consumption were higher by about 6 per cent in 1972/73 and about 12 per cent in 1977/78 than the corresponding NSS estimates. However, the differences were much larger in total non-food expenditure – NAS estimates were higher by 37 and 28 per cent respectively in 1972/73 and 1977/78. As regards the total expenditure

Table 6.1 Aggregate Private Consumption Expenditure Effect of Adjustment for Differences in Classification

(Rs Crore)

	1972/73			1977/78		
	CSO	*NSS*	*CSO/NSS %*	*CSO*	*NSS*	*CSO/NSS%*
(A) Food	21,770 + 444 (22,214)	23,420	93 (95)	37,400 +757 (38,157)	36,500	102 (105)
(B) Non-food	13,390 – 444 (12,946)	9,790	137 (132) (132)	25,680 –757 (24,923)	20,030	128 (124)
(C) Total consumption	35,160	33,210	106	63,080	56,530	112

on food, the differences were much smaller, and also they did not go in the same direction in the two years under study. The NAS estimate was about 7 per cent lower in 1972/73, whereas in 1977/78 it was about 2 per cent higher than the NSS estimate.

At this level of aggregation, the only adjustment that can be easily made is the one relating to differences in classification. As indicated earlier, the expenditure in hotels and restaurants is booked under consumer services in the NAS and is classified in the non-food group. Upon inclusion of this item in the food group in the NAS data, the difference between the two estimates narrows down from 7 to 5 per cent in 1972/73, but increases from 2 to 5 per cent in 1977/78. In other words, in consequence of this adjustment, the NAS estimate of total expenditure on food is lower by five per cent (−5 per cent) in 1972/73 and higher by five per cent (+5 per cent) than the NSS estimate for 1977/78. For the non-food group, the apparent excess of the NAS over the NSS estimate is reduced from 37 to 32 per cent in 1972/73 and from 28 to 24 per cent in 1977/78.

At this stage, one might be tempted to draw some facile conclusions:

First, as the NSS estimate of expenditure on food in India is (5 per cent) higher in 1972/73 and (5 per cent) lower in 1977/78 than the NAS estimates (partially adjusted for differences in classification only), one might conclude that there is no evidence of systematic non-sampling bias in the household consumer expenditure survey estimates (NSS) for the food group.

Second, Although the NSS has not computed standard errors of their estimates of food expenditure for the 27th (1972/73) or the 32nd (1977/78) Round, nevertheless, on the basis of results relating to the 28th Round (1973/74) data, one can safely assume that relative standard errors of the NSS estimates of food expenditure are no larger than 1 per cent at the all-India level (Appendix B). However, the apparent differences of the order of 5 per cent between the NAS and NSS estimates, although not insignificant, might not be considered as a cause for serious alarm.

Third, as the differences in the estimates of expenditure on the non-food group between the NAS and NSS are indeed large and as the NAS estimates are higher in both the years, the NSS estimates might be regarded as biased in the downward direction.

These conclusions are not warranted at this stage. The story of validation has just begun and can brook no haste in jumping to premature conclusions. We need to decompose the total expenditure on food and non-food into smaller subgroups of items to enable us to sort out at least those genuine differences (on account of factors enumerated earlier in this chapter) which are amenable to approximate adjustments.

Foodgrains. Foodgrains (cereals + pulses) account for a major part of the total expenditure on food in India. They constitute about 47.5 and 47.0 per cent of total food expenditure in CSO estimates and about 57 and 53 per cent in NSS estimates, respectively, for 1972/73 and 1977/78. The actual expenditure also shows (Table 6.2) that the NAS estimates were substantially lower than the NSS estimates in both the years – lower by about 23 per cent in 1972/73 and 9 per cent in 1977/78. These apparent differences can be investigated in quantitative terms with regard to the inherent discrepancies in implicit prices and reference periods of the two sets of data.

Adjustment for Consumer Prices. By evaluating the NSS quantities of different cereals and pulses at the NAS prices and then comparing them with the reported NAS estimates of expenditure, we find that the apparent differences were reduced from 23 to 16 per cent in 1972/73 and from 9 to about 3 per cent in 1977/78. Details are provided in Table 6.2.

As noted earlier, the CSO prices for all cereals and (especially) pulses where higher than the NSS

Table 6.2 Consumption Expenditure on Cereals and Pulses

(Rs Crore)

Items	1972/73					1977/78				
	NSS		CSO	CSO/NSS%		NSS		CSO	CSO/NSS%	
	I	II		I	II	I	II		I	II
(0)	(1)	(2)	(3)	(4)	(5)	(6)	(7)	(8)	(9)	(10)
Cereals	11,911	11,175	9,331	78.3	83.5	16,919	15,964	15,271	90.2	95.6
Gram	259	243	226	87.2	93.0	418	533	876	209.6	164.6
Pulses	1,249	894	806	64.5	90.2	1,964	533	876	209.6	164.6
Foodgrains	13,419	12,312	10,363	77.2	84.2	19,301	18,172	17,561	91.0	96.6

Notes: I. Gives the consumption expenditure as reported by the NSS.

II. Gives the consumption expenditure by evaluating the NSS quantities of different items at CSO prices.

prices in both the years. The only exception is the case of gram in 1977/78, where the NAS implicit price was 27 per cent higher than the corresponding NSS price. The reason for this appears to be that the CSO booked more than 90 per cent of total gram consumption under gram dal (dehusked split gram) and evaluated it at gram dal prices which are substantially higher than the whole gram prices. In the NSS, on the other hand the directly observed proportion of gram consumed as gram dal comes to only about 50 per cent. Another reason for the big jump in gram consumption in 1977/78 in the NAS estimates is a purely procedural quirk. In 1972/73, 35 per cent of reported gram output was deducted as animal feed in the NAS, whereas in 1977/78 only about 8 per cent was assumed as animal feed. The big jump in consumption expenditure on gram in 1977/78, therefore, is a consequence of the change in assumptions in regard to the proportion of gram deducted as animal feed from the official estimates of gram production. This revision in assumptions, although made on the basis of a (then recent) survey report on the estimates of concentrates fed to cattle in household dairy establishments, was inappropriately extended to the entire cattle population of India. The case of gram is an illustration of how assumption-driven estimates of NAS private consumption can go awry.

It is worth repeating that deduction for feed and wastages for all cereals and pulses are still based on the old marketing reports of the fifties and these deductions are made as fixed proportions of the reported production figures. These proportions need to be revised on the basis of fresh observations. The deductions, as made at present, do not inspire confidence about their reliability.

We might also note that the aggregate seed requirements for various crops do not seem to fall in line with the increases in cereal productivity during the 1970s. The area under high-yielding varieties of rice and wheat increased but the yields per hectare for these two crops increased far more rapidly. Nevertheless the deductions for seed requirements (in the NAS framework) as a proportion of total output of rice and wheat hardly show any fall.

Time Period Adjustments. The reference period differences can be roughly adjusted, particularly, in the case of important crops. This exercise (Minhas et al., 1986) was undertaken in details by us. I do not wish to repeat it here, except for recalling our results for the estimates of consumer expenditure on foodgrains. Adjusting for difference in the reference periods between the NAS and NSS estimates, the apparent discrepancy in 1972/73 gets reduced by 4 percentage points, whereas in 1977/78 the discrepancy gets further elevated by about 3 percentage points.

The estimates of expenditure on foodgrains alone, comprising about half of the total expenditure on the food group, works out to be substantially higher (23 per cent in 1972/73 and 9 per cent in 1977/78) in the NSS as compared with the unadjusted estimates of the NAS. However, adjusting for differences in prices and time periods the picture comes out to be as given in Table 6.3.

Table 6.3 Discrepancy in Foodgrain Consumption (Value) Estimates

	(CSO less than NSS by %)	
	1972/73	*1977/78*
Observed (Unadjusted)	22.8%	9.0
Due to implicit prices	7.0	5.6
Due to time period	3.8	−3.4
Due to other factors	12.0	6.8

In conclusion, adjustments for differences in prices and time periods do close the gaps between the two sets of estimates for both the years. Nevertheless, substantial differences still remain – 12 per cent in 1973/74 and 6.8 per cent in 1977/78.

We have been unable to fathom any sound basis to suspect the presence of systematic bias in the NSS estimates of expenditure on foodgrains. Also the magnitudes of the relative standard errors of the estimates of expenditure on foodgrains are far too small to bridge the gap of 12 per cent in 1972/73 and 7 per cent in 1977/78 between the NSS and CSO estimates of foodgrains consumption (say, at ± 2.0 s.e. level). On the other hand, it is strongly suspected that adjustments for seeds, feeds, wastages (and other assumptions about certain ratios in the NAS framework) may have led to systematic underestimation of private (human) consumption of foodgrains in the CSO data set in 1972/73 and 1977/78. The official estimates of area reported for different foodgrain crops might also deserve to be looked into with some care.

Other Food

The unadjusted NAS estimates of expenditure on other food (total food minus foodgrains) were much higher than the NSS – by 14 per cent in 1972/73 and 15 per cent in 1977/78. On reclassifying and including the NAS expenditure in hotels and restaurants in the other food groups, this discrepancy increased further to 18 per cent and 20 per cent respectively in 1972/73 and 1977/78. The causes of this large one-sided difference in each of the two years needs to be investigated. This investigation is all the more necessary as the respective differences between the two data sets at the subgroup level (Appendix A-III) do not go in the same direction for all the subgroups, or in both years, for the same subgroup.

The NAS estimates in both the years were higher for milk and milk products, edible oils and vanaspati, fruits and vegetables, and sugar and gur; whereas the estimates for salt and spices, and miscellaneous foods were higher in the NSS data. For meat, fish and eggs group, the NAS and NSS estimates were only marginally different.

Since milk and milk products, edible oils, sugar and gur are also used as inputs in commercial establishments, and these intermediate uses are not separately netted out in the NAS procedure for dealing with hotels, restaurants and sweets shops, the NAS and NSS estimates for these commodities are not therefore comparable. Also appropriate deductions for unrecorded exports of sugar and gur just cannot be made. In case of estimates of consumption of edible oils, the NAS includes expenditure on oilseeds under edible oils, whereas the NSS does not book any expenditure on oilseeds under this head. The reliability of NAS estimates for milk products and edible oils is also affected by the use of old ad hoc ratios in earmarking a certain proportion of milk output for conversion into curds, cheese, butter and ghee and the proportion of different oilseeds taken as available for oil extraction. The time period differences also vitiate comparability between the two data sets for sugars as well as edible oils. For instance, the production of oilseeds in the agricultural year 1977/78 was about 8 per cent higher than in the previous year. Bulk of the edible oils consumption observed by the NSS in 1977/78, however, would have come from the oils extracted from oilseeds produced in the previous year. The product flow estimates of edible oils consumption in 1977/78, based on the current year output, should therefore be higher than the NSS estimates of household expenditure for the survey year 1977/78.

Milk and Milk Products. The unadjusted NAS estimate of expenditure on this group was higher by 6 per cent in 1972/73 and 10 per cent in 1977/78. Nevertheless, estimated expenditure on liquid milk in the NAS data was lower than the NSS in both years (−11 per cent in 1972/73, and −4 per cent in 1977/78). Since some liquid milk is also used in hotels and restaurants and it is not separately accounted for in the NAS estimates of private consumption of milk and milk products, there is an element of incomparability in the two data sets. One should nevertheless expect the NAS estimates to be somewhat higher than the NSS. We can nevertheless adjust for difference in implicit prices which were higher in the NSS data for both the years. After carrying out this adjustment, the NAS estimates remain higher by only about 5 per cent in both the years. Disregarding the difference on account of the known element of incomparability, the NSS estimates of household expenditure on milk and milk products, which are quite precise, should be taken as validated.

Edible Oils and Vanaspati. The NAS estimates for this group were considerably higher (+14 per cent in 1972/73, and +37 per cent in 1977/78) than NSS. However for vanaspati which, though a smaller fraction of this subgroup, is the most popular cooking medium in sweets shops, hotels and restaurants, the differences in the two sets of data were even higher. After removing the expenditure on oilseeds from the CSO estimates, the expenditure on edible oils (other than vanaspati) in 1972/73 was almost exactly equal in the two data sets. Upon making similar deduction for expenditure on oilseeds, the CSO estimates of edible oils for 1977/78 still remain higher (+24 per cent) than the NSS. We must nevertheless remember that this large difference should come down appreciably when account is taken of the large increase (8 per cent) in oilseeds output in 1977/78 as compared with the previous agricultural year, and due regard is taken of the edible oils contained in sweets, etc., bought by the households from outside. If proper account of edible oils and vanaspati entering purchased food items could be taken in the NSS estimates, the two sets of estimates may not differ in the same direction in the two years.

Sugar, Gur and Other Sugars. The NAS estimates of expenditure on crystal sugar were higher by 12 and 16 per cent respectively in the two years. As indicated earlier the NAS estimates are expected to be higher than the NSS estimates. Also one need not be unduly disturbed on account of this difference in crystal sugar. However, one does need to worry about the staggering differences in gur and other sugars which are shown in Table 6.4.

We may be inclined to regard the NSS estimates of household expenditure on gur to be on the low side. However the CSO estimates of gur (and other sugars) consumption do not seem credible. The production estimates of gur, on the basis of cane utilisation data, were placed around 8.7 and 9.0 million tonnes respectively in 1972/73 and 1977/78. Whereas the CSO estimates of consumption (which are supposed to be smaller than production) come to 13.7 and 9.4 million tonnes for the same two years.

Table 6.4 Consumption Expenditure on Sugar, Gur and Other Sugars

(Rs Crore)

	1972/73			1977/78		
	CSO	NSS	CSO/NSS%	CSO	NSS	CSO/NSS%
Sugar	743	661	112	1,017	877	116
Gur	1,316	529	249	1,411	593	238
Other sugars	200	44	454	49	58	84
Total	2,259	1,234	183	2,477	1,528	162

While there might have been some unrecorded exports, there were no imports of gur in these two years. The story for other sugars is also difficult to trust: The NAS estimates of expenditure on other sugar was Rs 200 crore in 1972/73, which fell down to Rs 49 crore five years later in 1977/78; whereas the NSS estimate was Rs 44 crore in 1972/73 and Rs 58 crore in 1977/78. The NAS estimates of gur and other sugars seem to be too unreliable (both in 1972/73 and 1977/78) to serve as the validator data set for NSS expenditure on this subgroup.

Fruits and Vegetables. For the group as a whole, the CSO estimates were higher than the NSS by about 70 per cent in each of the two years. Part of this big difference is due to classification problems; some fruit products and processed fruits are included in this group by the CSO, whereas they appear under spices and miscellaneous food in the NSS. Nevertheless, more serious problem in assessing the reliability of the NAS estimates of consumption of fruits and vegetables arises from the fact that we have little solid data available to us on a regular basis relating to the production of a vast multitude of items composing this subgroup. Informed guesswork and judgemental projections are difficult to accept as validators of data obtained through other methods. The NSS estimates of household expenditure on many items in this subgroup seriously lack in precision. Nevertheless for the total of fruits (fruits and nuts) the estimates are reasonably precise.

In the vegetables group, potato is the only item for which regular estimates of production are available annually. The NAS estimates of potato consumption were lower by 33 per cent in 1972/73 but were higher by 19 per cent in 1977/78 as compared to NSS. A major part of this difference was due to differences in implicit prices in the two sources. In 1972/73 the CSO's implicit prices were 14 per cent lower than the NSS prices, but in 1977/78 the CSO prices were 12 per cent higher. Also the 1977/78 potato crop was 14 per cent larger than the 1976/77 crop. Adjusting for the price and time period difference the NAS and NSS estimates of household expenditure on potato come close to each other, but the remaining discrepancies do not go in the same direction in the two years. Also, the NSS estimate of potato consumption is characterised by low relative standard errors.

Salt and Spices. Since 1975/76 the ESO has been using NSS estimates of salt consumption and the estimates for 1977/78 are identical. Nevertheless, CSO estimates of consumption of spices were considerably lower than NSS – by about 53 per cent in 1972/73 and 45 per cent in 1977/78. The underestimation by the CSO seems to be resulting from its non-inclusion of many processed spices (which are far more expensive than the original ingredients). Also some of the spices, such as green chillies, are classified in the vegetables group by the CSO; in NSS they are included in the spices group. In the NSS, dried mango powder (amchur) is classified with spices; whereas the CSO seems to account for it in mangoes under fruits. There are also considerable differences in prices between the two data sets. The

CSO estimates of expenditure on salt and spices seem to be underestimates. On the other hand, the NSS estimates are not only precise but are likely to be bias-free.

Miscellaneous Food Group. This group includes tea (leaf), coffee (powder), other non-alcoholic beverages, biscuits and confectionery, tea and coffee cups (taken outside home), hotels and restaurants, sweets, refreshments and other miscellaneous foods. There are all manner of classification problems in this sundry-group – including exclusions and inclusions in one or the other data set. Nevertheless, in an earlier study (Minhas et al., 1986) we did try to carry out all the adjustments that seemed reasonable as well as practical. The NSS estimates of consumer expenditure on this miscellaneous group were Rs 1,273 crore and Rs 2,082 crore, respectively, in 1972/73 and 1977/78. The CSO estimates, on a comparable basis, were lower than NSS in both the years (being Rs 884 crore in 1972/73 and Rs 1,630 crore in 1977/78). It is difficult to decide which set of estimates is better. Some of the excess of the NAS estimates for milk, edible oils and sugars, for instance, might be offset against the relative excess of the NSS estimates over the NAS in this miscellaneous group.

Non-food Expenditure

Estimates of aggregate non-food expenditure, broken down into 8 subgroups, are shown in Appendix A.I. For detailed comparisons between the NAS and NSS estimates for these 8 subgroups and their components, the reader may refer to our earlier paper (Minhas et al., 1986). We shall address brief comments to the question of validation here. The first step in this regard is to adjust the two data sets for the obvious differences in classification and coverage.

As indicated earlier, the expenditure in hotels and restaurants is booked under consumer services in the NAS whereas the NSS estimates include this item under other food. Also the NSS estimates of expenditure on house rent do not include imputed rents of owner-occupied houses, whereas the NAS estimates are inclusive of imputed rents. Further, the NSS estimates of expenditure on education relate only to the household expenditure on education, whereas the NAS estimates also include expenditures undertaken by the non-profit educational institutions (as the latter are in the nature of transfers to the household sector). Taking account of the above-said differences in classification and coverage, the comparative picture of aggregate non-food expenditure is presented in Table 6.5.

In other words, in consequence of these adjustments, the gap between the NAS and NSS estimates of aggregate expenditure on non-food items narrows down from 37 to 14 per cent in 1972/73 and from 28 to 13 per cent in 1977/78.

Table 6.5 Aggregate Non-food Expenditure Adjusted for Coverage and Classification

(Rs Crore)

	1972/73			1977/78		
	NAS	*NSS*	*Ratio*	*NAS*	*NSS*	*Ratio*
Total non-food (unadjusted)	13,390	9,790	137	25,680	20,030	128
(i) Hotel and restaurants	−444			−757		
(ii) Imputed rents		+807			+1,040	
(iii) Education		+745			+1,023	
	12,946	11,342	114	24,923	22,093	113

Paan, Tobacco and Liquor. As argued earlier, the NSS is likely to underestimate by a big margin the household expenditure on tobacco and intoxicants: it is difficult to get correct consumption data on these two items through the interview method in our social setting where the consumption of these items is frowned upon. However, the CSO estimates of consumption of these two items, although substantially higher than the NSS estimates, also appear to be downward biased, particularly in case of liquor. The CSO's estimates of expenditure on liquor are only marginally higher than the actual collection of excise duty on this item in both the years.

In other words, the sample survey estimates of household expenditure on tobacco and liquor are better ignored because of the inherent social inhibitions of the respondents in reporting the consumption of these two items. While in theory, it would be possible to derive reliable estimates for tobacco and intoxicants from the production data by making proper adjustments for exports, imports, trade and transport margins, particularly for excise and custom duties, nevertheless, the available NAS estimates (following this method) seem to have serious flaws. Under the circumstances, it might not be inappropriate to drop these two items from both the data sets and compare only the expenditure on all non-food (ANF) minus the expenditure on tobacco and intoxicants. Dropping tobacco and intoxicants from both data sets, the comparative picture of aggregate expenditure on all non-food (ANF-tobacco and intoxicants) can be seen in Table 6.6.

Table 6.6 Aggregate Non-food Expenditure (ANF) Minus Tobacco and Intoxicants

(Rs Crore)

	1972/73			1977/78		
	NAS	*NSS*	*Ratio*	*NAS*	*NSS*	*Ratio*
ANF	12,946	11,342	114	24,923	22,093	113
(i) Tobacco	1,117	612		1,533	1,000	
(ii) Intoxicants	364	195		528	288	
ANF (i + ii)	11,465	10,535	109	22,862	20,805	110

As there is no tabboo against paan, supari, etc., the NSS estimates are quite precise and may be bias-free. The NSS estimates were 30 per cent higher than NAS in 1972/73 but were lower by 8 per cent in 1977/78. The wide variation between the two year is explained by the sudden rise in supari prices towards the end of 1977, which was fully reflected in the NAS (one shot) computations, but only slowly in the last two sub-rounds of the 32nd Round survey.

After negotiating comparability in classification, coverage differences in the treatment of imputed rents and expenditure of non-profit educational institutions, and excluding from both data sets the expenditure on tobacco and intoxicants, the aggregate estimates of expenditure on all non-food in the NAS data set were higher by 9 and 10 per cent, respectively, in 1972/73 and 1977/78. This remaining discrepancy between the two data sets pertains to other subgroups in the non-food sector and these subgroups are discussed below:

Clothing and Footwear. The NAS estimates for this subgroup are higher than the NSS by 11 per cent in 1972/73 and 14 per cent in 1977/78. Unlike certain other items of daily consumption, clothing and footwear are not bought by households in a regular fashion. The NSS estimates of expenditure on this subgroup are characterised by large sampling errors. Taking into account the standard errors of the point estimates of the NSS for this subgroup, one might conclude that the aggregate household expenditure on clothing and footwear in the two sets of data is not too different from each other. The differences in time periods between the NSS and NAS may not be important here. Nevertheless the NAS estimates of expenditure on this subgroup, taken by themselves, might not be free from underestimation.

Gross Rent, Fuel and Light. We have dealt with imputed rents already and adjusted the NSS data for incomplete coverage. The NSS estimates of expenditure on fuel and light are appreciably higher than the NAS. The NAS estimates, particularly for non-commercial fuels, seem to be gross underestimates. The CSO might be advised to use the NSS estimates of expenditure on fuel and light in its estimation of private consumption and other national income aggregates. The basis for this observation was fully elaborated in our earlier paper.

Medical Care and Health Services. The CSO estimates of private expenditure on this subgroup are based on the combined use of NSS estimates (for medicines) and administrative data on medical services. The two estimates were almost equal in 1972/73. However, the NAS estimate was 24 per cent lower than the NSS in 1977/78. It is instructive to note that the NAS estimate for 1977/78 was not at all comparable with its own estimate for 1972/73. The NAS procedure for estimation of expenditure on medical services was very different in 1977/78 as compared with 1972/73. Also the NAS estimate of expenditure on medicines was grossly underestimated in 1977/78. This happened because the NSS estimates for 1977/78 were not available to the CSO when the national income estimates for 1977/78 were released. The CSO took the NSS per capita expenditure on medicines in 1972/73 and carried it forward to 1977/78 by inflating it with the wholesale price index for drugs. This procedure took the price increases into account but totally ignored the quantitative increase in consumption of medicines during the intervening five-year period. The CSOs projected per capita consumption of medicines in 1977/78 was Rs 1.48 as compared with the NSS observed figures of Rs 2.26. In consequence, the NAS estimate of consumption of medicines was about 25 per cent lower than the NSS estimate of household expenditure in 1977/78. To conclude, the NSS estimates for this subgroup were comparable for both the years, whereas the CSO estimates not only lacked comparability in time but were also lower than the NSS estimates in both the years. The CSO could adopt both medicines as well as medical services estimates of NSS, as its experience with independently worked out estimates of medical services has been unsatisfactory.

Recreation, Entertainment, Cultural Services and Education. Assuming that the excess of expenditure on education in the NAS is the correct estimate of institutional expenditure on education (not covered by the NSS as it covers only the direct expenditure by households), and adding this difference in each of the two years to the NSS estimates for this subgroup, the comparative figures, adjusted for differences in coverage, show that NAS estimates for 1972/73 were higher than the NSS estimates by 4 per cent (Rs 1,402 crore in the NAS vs 1,384 crore in the NSS). For 1977/78 the NAS estimates (Rs 2,084 crore) were lower than the NSS estimates (Rs 2,323 crore) by 10 per cent.

Expenditure on entertainment, sports goods, etc., is higher by 4 per cent in 1972/73 in the NAS but lower than NSS by about 10 per cent in 1977/78. In fact, the CSO estimate of entertainment expenditure for 1977/78 is a gross underestimate: the receipts from entertainment tax levies by states were by themselves more than double the total entertainment expenditure reported in the NAS. Despite the apparently close correspondence between the two sets of estimates in consequence of due adjustments, there is room to believe that both sets of estimates might be on the low side.

Miscellaneous Goods and Services. This subgroup consists of a large number of goods and services and the figures of expenditure shown against the group (Appendix A.I) are not easy to sort out for negotiating comparability between the two sets. However, the expenditure in hotels and restaurants (Rs 444 crore in 1972/73 and Rs 757 crore in 1977/78), which is classified with miscellaneous services by the CSO, does not belong here. After this deduction, as these amounts have been taken account of in the other food group, the comparable figures are shown in parentheses (Appendix A.I). The aggregate expenditure on this group works out to be less in CSO estimates as compared with the NSS – by about 14 and 6 per cent respectively, in 1972/73 and 1977/78.

Overview for Non-food. Adjusting for differences in coverage and classification, and dropping out tobacco and intoxicants from both data sets the NAS estimate of private consumption expenditure on the non-food group was higher than the NSS estimates by 9 per cent (Rs 935 crore) in 1972/73, and by 10 per cent (Rs 2,057 crore) in 1977/78. The NSS point estimate of expenditure on clothing and footwear, allowing for sampling errors which are rather large for this subgroup, are not significantly different from the corresponding NAS estimates. The NAS estimates for fuel and light, medical care and health services, entertainment and sports goods, and miscellaneous goods and services subgroup, on the other hand, seem to be underestimates and are lower than the point estimates of household expenditure provided by the NSS for the same subgroups. However, for the remaining two subgroups, namely, consumer durables and transport and communications, the CSO estimates of expenditure are substantially higher than the NSS in both the years. The main reasons for the overall discrepancy in the aggregate estimates of expenditure on all non-food between the NAS and NSS would have to be located in the respective estimates of expenditure for these two subgroups. We must deal with them in some detail.

Furniture, Furnishing, Household Appliances (Operations and Repairs). The NAS estimate of expenditure on this subgroup was higher than the NSS by 54 per cent (+Rs 351 crore) in 1972/73 and by 34 per cent in 1977/78 (+Rs 504 crore). One major drawback in estimating the expenditure on consumer durables (furniture, radio, TV, musical instruments, bicycles, scooters, motor cycles, passenger cars, household appliances, ornaments, etc.) from product flow method is the absence of reliable information of their distribution by use – categories. Most of these goods are used by households as consumer durables, and also by establishments as capital goods. The current NAS practice of taking certain proportion of their total supplies as private consumption is essentially based on subjective judgements. Another difficulty that stares in the face of product flow methods is that a good many of the consumer durables are produced in the unorganised sector and reliable estimates of their production are not directly available. Thus derived data suffer from all manner of subjective correctives applied to incomplete and partial (often false and deliberately falsified) facts.

One can accept the proposition that the production-based estimates of consumption of consumer durables could be quite realistic provided their total supplies were estimated from current production data with adequate coverage and the total availability thus estimated was distributed between capital goods and consumer durables on some sound basis. However, this does not seem to be the case at present. The NSS estimates of household expenditure on consumer durables, on the other hand, are based on current data. Nevertheless, they are characterised by very large standard errors. In other words, there are deficiencies in both the data sets as far as the estimates of expenditure for this subgroup are concerned. The validator data set is far short of the touchstone quality and the survey estimates are not precise. Both need improvements and one can suspend final judgement on the relative merits of the two till the planned improvements are executed both by the CSO and NSS.

Transport and Communications. The estimates of expenditure on the modern consumer services – post, telephones, railway, taxi, bus, other conveyance, etc., are widely at variance between the NSS and

CSO. The NAS estimates are nearly three times the NSS in 1972/73 and well over three times in 1977/78. In money terms the difference amounts to Rs 1,134 crore in 1972/73 and Rs 2,921 crore in 1977/78. These are staggeringly large differences. Are these differences true? What is the degree of underestimation in the NSS estimates? Have the NAS judgements gone astray and produced gross overestimates of private expenditure on consumer services? These are the questions that need answers, but precise quantitative answers do not seem possible at this stage.

Reliable accounting data are available on gross receipts of post and communications department as well as the railways. However, the problems arise in distributing these receipts among households, businesses and government. The NAS assume 40 per cent of total receipts from postal and communication services as private expenditure, while NSS (observed) household share comes only to 10 per cent. Similarly, NAS assumes 80 per cent of total passenger receipts as private expenditure, whereas the NSS estimate of household expenditure on rail services is much less. The NAS estimates of expenditure on other modes of conveyance (including owner-driven vehicles) are also nearly twice (or more) as large as the NSS estimates.

Once again one may be tempted to regard the NSS estimates of household expenditure on communications and transport services as underestimates, nevertheless, the NAS ratios of use of these services among households, business enterprises and government also need to be revised on the basis of fresh studies. The relevant blocks in the consumer expenditure schedule of the NSS for the 43rd Round have been redesigned to capture adequately the household expenditure on these services. The CSO are also taking steps to improve the data that forms the basis of their judgements regarding the various ratios.

VALIDATION OF NSS ESTIMATES: AN OVERVIEW

We are now in a position to sum up our findings on the question of validation of the NSS estimates of household consumption expenditure against external evidence:

(a) Disregarding those differences which might be genuine but cannot be adequately adjusted, there does not seem to be any straightforward evidence of non-sampling bias in the NSS estimate of total expenditure on food consumption in the two years. NSS estimates are higher (+5 per cent) in 1972/73 and lower (–5 per cent) in 1977/78 in comparison with the NAS estimates.

(b) Considering the expenditure on foodgrains alone, the NSS estimates are higher than NAS in both years (being +12 per cent and +6.8 per cent respectively in 1972/73 and 1977/78), even after making the adjustments for differences in implicit prices and time periods. Although our search has failed to turn up any convincing evidence to suspect the presence of systematic bias in the NSS procedures for collecting data on foodgrain (cereal) consumption, some suspicions would linger on, unless the issue is resolved through appropriate methodological studies. On the other hand, our search has led us to the strong suspicion that the total consumption of foodgrains is underestimated in the NAS. Many suggestions have been offered for improving the database of the NAS estimates particularly in regard to various deductions (for seed, feed, wastages and other important ratios) which are so crucial in calculating the unduplicated net output of foodgrains available for human consumption.

(c) The NAS estimates of private expenditure on milk and milk products, edible oils and vanaspati, and sugar and gur are expected to be higher as the CSO is unable to take separate account of intermediate uses of these commodities. The discrepancy between the NAS and NSS estimates for these commodities was also caused by differences in implicit prices, time periods, and wrong derivations of production and/or availability for private consumption.

(d) Adjusting for differences in implicit prices and keeping in mind the upward bias in the NAS estimates, the NSS estimates of household expenditure on milk and milk products in both the years stand fully validated.

(e) After making adjustments in the NAS estimates of expenditure on edible oils (for seeds and appropriate time periods), the NSS estimates seem to pass the external validation test. However, the NAS estimates of vanaspati seem to be gross overestimates, as they are not appropriately netted for its use in commercial establishments.

(f) The NAS estimates of private consumption of gur and other sugars are so severely flawed that they are not worthy of being considered as an external validator set. The NAS estimate of other sugars for 1972/73 is about five times the NSS estimate, whereas the NAS estimate for 1977/78 is less than one fourth of its own estimate for 1972/73 and also slightly lower than the corresponding estimate of the NSS for 1977/78. The NAS estimates of private consumption of gur in both the years are even higher than gur production derived from cane utilisation data.

(g) The NSS estimates of household expenditure on salt and spices and miscellaneous foods are appreciably higher than the corresponding NAS estimates. A part of this difference is attributable to unadjustable differences in classification between the two data sets and partly due to underestimation of expenditure on spices in the NAS. On the whole the NSS estimates for this subgroup are quite precise and appear to be reliable.

(h) NSS estimates of household expenditure on meat, fish and eggs stand completely validated; ignoring, of course, the possibility that both might be bad.

(i) The NAS estimates of private consumption of vegetables and fruits are about 1.7 times the corresponding estimates of the NSS for 1972/73 as well as 1977/78 – larger than the NSS by Rs 1,262 crore in 1972/73 and by Rs 2,289 crore in 1977/78. These are very large differences for this one subgroup and account for about two-thirds of the total difference in aggregate expenditure between the NAS and NSS (on all the seven subgroups of other food taken together) in 1972/73 as well as in 1977/78. Although there are no regular official estimates of production of fruits and vegetables (except for bananas, papaya and potato), which could serve as a reliable database for deriving the NAS private consumption estimate of fruits and vegetables in the national accounting framework, one may nevertheless be inclined to consider that the point estimates of the household expenditure on many individual fruits and vegetables provided by the NSS (except for potato) might not be fully reliable – besides their large sampling errors, one could also suspect them to be underestimates. This would, of course, be a subjective judgement, difficult to maintain, lest the NAS estimates of private consumption got anchored to regular production estimates of fruits and vegetables over time.

(j) The unadjusted estimates of aggregate expenditure on other foods, dropping gur and other sugars from both data sets (as the latter were not worthy of being used in a validation exercise), are given in Table 6.7.

Notice that on eliminating the expenditure on gur and other sugars from both data sets, the point estimates of NSS aggregate household expenditure on all six subgroups of other food (other than foodgrains) differ from the corresponding NAS estimates only by Rs 907 crore (10 per cent) in 1972/73 and Rs 2,591 crore (16 per cent) in 1977/78. This, of course, is the situation without making any allowance whatever for the known (and shown) upward bias of the NAS estimates

Table 6.7 Unadjusted Estimates of Aggregate Expenditure on Other Foods

(Rs Crore)

	1972/73			1977/78		
	CSO	*NSS*	*CSO/NSS%*	*CSO*	*NSS*	*CSO/NSS (%)*
(i) Other foods	11,852	10,002	–	20,594	17,198	–
(ii) Gur and other sugars	1,516	573	–	1,460	652	–
(i) – (ii)	10,336	9,429	110	19,137	16,546	116

of private consumption of milk and milk products, vanaspati and edible oils, and crystal sugar in 1972/73 as well as 1977/78.

(k) Comparing these differences in aggregate expenditure (NAS > NSS by Rs 907 crore (+10 per cent) in 1972/73 and Rs 2,591 crore (+16 per cent) in 1977/78) on the six subgroups of 'other food' with the apparent differences in just one of the six subgroups, viz., 'fruits and vegetables' (NAS > NSS by Rs 1262 crore in 1972/73 and Rs 2,289 crore in 1977/78), one gets a clear perspective on the validity of the NSS estimates vis-á-vis the external data set. Leaving aside gur and other sugars, if one took the point estimates of the NSS as the only correct estimates of expenditure on each of the subgroups which have passed the validation test, the overall excess of the NAS estimates of aggregate private consumption of other food in 1972/73 (Rs 907 crore) will be less than Rs 1,262 crore, the amount by which the fruits and vegetables estimate alone exceeds the NSS estimate for this subgroup in 1972/73. Similarly the overall excess of the NAS estimate of aggregate consumption on all other food (Rs 2,591 crore) will be only slightly larger than the excess of Rs 2,289 crore by which the NAS estimate of private consumption of fruits and vegetables (alone) exceeds the NSS point estimate of household consumption for this subgroup in 1977/78.

(l) Adjusting for classification and coverage differences in the non-food group and dropping tobacco and intoxicants from both the data sets (Table 6.6), the NAS estimate of aggregate private consumption (value) of all non-food items was larger by 9 per cent (Rs 930 crore) in 1972/73 and by 10 per cent (Rs 2,057 crore) in 1977/78. We have shown that these apparent differences between the two aggregates are traceable mainly to just two subgroups, consumer durables and modern services.

(m) Taking account of the relative standard errors of the NSS point estimates of household expenditure on clothing and footwear, the NSS estimates for this group may pass the validation test although the fact of NSS point estimates of clothing (not footwear) being lower than NAS in both the years is less than reassuring.

(n) The NSS point estimates of household expenditure on fuel and light are quite robust and appreciably higher than the assumption-driven NAS estimates of private consumption for this group. The CSO might use the NSS estimates for this subgroup in the construction of national accounts.

(o) The NSS estimates of household expenditure on medical care and health services are better both in terms of consistency in procedure in the two year as well as in terms of reliability. The NAS estimates, on the other hand, seem to suffer both from inconsistency and underestimation.

(p) The aggregate household expenditure on miscellaneous goods and services subgroups, based on NSS point estimates, works out to be higher than the NAS in both the years. The NSS estimates for this sundry group of items, based as they are on current observations are more reliable than the corresponding miscellany of items and indirect procedures of the NAS.

(q) The NAS estimates of private consumption of consumer services (i.e. post, telephone and conveyance), although based on unverified assumptions regarding the distribution of gross receipts among household business and government, were much higher than the NSS in both the years – by Rs 1,485 crore (351 + 1,134) in 1972/73 and by Rs 3,425 crore (504 + 2,921) in 1977/78. In other words, the discrepancy between the expenditure estimates of the NAS and NSS for consumer durables and services is more than the overall discrepancy (of Rs 930 crore in 1972/73 and Rs 2,057 crore in 1977/78) for all non-food subgroups put together, including consumer durables and consumer services. The whole question of the validation of the total non-food sector estimates therefore, revolves around the views/judgements one takes in regard to underestimation/overestimation of expenditure on consumer durables and services – just these two subgroups only. However, it is better if such judgements are suspended till more and better data are collected and properly analysed.

(r) It is true that the NSS point estimates of household expenditure on consumer durables and consumer services are subject to very large sampling errors. Nevertheless one would have little confidence in stretching the error band to bridge the big, one-sided gaps between the NAS estimates of private consumption and the household expenditure of the NSS for these two sub-

Table 6.8 Cross Validation of Consumer Expenditure: NSS *vs* NAS

(Rs Crore)

	1972/73				1977/78			
	NSS	*CSO*	*CSO-NSO*	*CSO/NSS%*	*NSS*	*CSO*	*CSO-NSO*	*CSO/NSS%*
Foodgrains								
1. Unadjusted	13,419	10,363		77	19,301	17,561		91
2. NSS at CSO prices	12,312	–		–	18,172	–		–
3. Adjusted for time period	–	10,835		–	–	16,940		–
Foodgrains (adjusted)	12,312	10,835		88	18,172	16,940		93
Other Food								
1. Other food adjusted for classification difference	10,002	11,852		118	17,198	20,594		120
2. Gur and other sugars	573	1,516		–	652	1,460		–
1 minus 2	9,429	10,336	**907**	110	16,546	19,137	**2,591**	116
3. Fruits and vegetables	1,835	3,097	**1,262**	169	3,228	5,517	**2,289**	171
All Non-food (ANF)								
1. ANF unadjusted	9,790	13,390		137	20,030	25,680		128
(i) Hotels and restaurants	–	–444		–	+1,040	–757		–
(ii) Imputed rents	+807	–		–	+1,040	–		–
(iii) Education	+745	–		–	+1,023	–		–
2. ANF adjusted for coverage	11,342	12,946		114	22,093	14,923		113
3. Tobacco and intoxicants	807	1,481		–	1,288	2,061		–
2 minus 3	10,535	11,465	**930**	109	20,805	22,862	**2,057**	110
4. Consumer durables and services	1,284	2,769	**1,485**	216	2,650	6,075	**3,425**	229

groups. As imprecise point estimates with large sampling errors are a poor guide for the discovery of true values, one might, for the time being (until the results of the 43rd Round of NSS become available in 1989) adopt the NAS estimates (assumption-driven, hence not objective) of private consumption expenditure on consumer durables and services. This should also oblige us to accept the finding that a 9 to 10 per cent difference between the NAS and NSS estimates of aggregate expenditure on all non-food (minus tobacco and liquor) items is more than fully accounted for by the differences between the estimates of the two agencies for just two subgroups, i.e. consumer durables and transport and communication services, in 1972/73 as well as 1977/78.

The substance and pith of this validation exercise is presented in a capsule form in Table 6.8. Every step and number appearing in this table has already been explained earlier in this chapter. The independent data set (NAS), it would seem fair to conclude, is far short of the touchstone quality expected of an external validator data set. A number of its components are based on such weak evidence and unverified assumptions which seriously diminish its value in a cross-validation exercise. On the other hand, the NSS estimates of expenditure on minor vices, such as tobacco and intoxicants, and consumer durables, and modern consumer services are of doubtful reliability. Nevertheless, despite these difficulties, which need to be overcome in both data sets, an overwhelming proportion of household consumer expenditure data of the NSS and the independent private consumption estimates of the NAS do get cross validation.

SOME GENERAL LESSONS AND SUGGESTIONS FOR RESEARCH

This validation exercise suggests some obvious lessons for data users in the academic community and the policy making bodies. We also have some suggestions for further research work.

(a) The results presented in this paper should make it clear that it is hazardous to carry out pro rata adjustment in the observed size distribution of consumer expenditure in a particular NSS round by multiplying it with a scalar derived from the ratio between the NAS estimate of aggregate private consumption (for some financial year) and the total household expenditure available from the NSS round. This kind of mindless tinkering with the NSS distribution, as practised by the Planning Commission in the Seventh Plan documents, does not seem permissible either in theory or in the light of known facts.

(b) It would also seem equally wrong to attempt studies of comparative trends in respective (NSS vs NAS) aggregates, or components of these broad aggregates, by using raw data which have not been adjusted for differences in coverage, time periods, classification schemes, implicit prices, etc.[3] Quite aside from this question of genuine adjustments for negotiating comparability, the data thrown up by different cross-sectional cuts taken at varying intervals of time by the NSS and those obtained from continuous time series by the CSO are rooted in quite different objectives and operational strategies. The intention of this remark is not to suggest that the area of common intersection between the two data sets is small. On the contrary the area of this common intersection is indeed very large. Nevertheless often it is not realised that the likelihood of these two domains being coterminous (and the two methods throwing up identical estimates of total private

---

[3] Among some others, Vaidyanathan (1986) has also indulged in faulty comparisons of this kind, particularly in his Table 1, p. 135.

consumption, or its main components) at many points in calendar time is indeed small. We do not live in a steady-state world: the cross-sectional results are likely to have more rough edges for the comfort of those who unwittingly get used to reading smooth trends in time series data of national accounts.[4] The latter data set, one must remember, is conditioned by ad hoc judgements, check totals, benchmarks, ratios and informal adjustments provided by many diverse official agencies outside the control of the CSO.

(c) The NSS estimates of the distribution of consumer expenditure over the households are controlled only by the scientific considerations explicitly incorporated into the design of the sample survey in a particular round and not by any other extraneous consideration. It is perfectly legitimate to compare the NSS estimates of per capita consumption over different rounds of the survey. The non-sampling bias in the NSS estimates, if any, has been rather small and may have remained more or less constant over time.

(d) The few major differences between the two data sets, which still remain, do not seem amenable to explanation in terms of sampling errors. There are inherent difficulties in the collection of certain types of data in the NSS; whereas there are enormous gaps in production data and also many other difficulties in the derivation of private consumption estimates in the NAS framework. Frequent resort to unverified judgements and assumption driven estimation in national income accounting may seem unavoidable at present, nevertheless, it is unwise to assert, as some experts seem to have done,[5] that judgements can do just as well or better than directly observed data.

(e) It must be stressed that the conclusions of our validation exercise are based on two specific rounds of the NSS. There is need to further validate these results by examining some other rounds of the NSS. The 38th Round (1983) is the obvious candidate as the detailed data for the earlier rounds in the sixties are not easily retrievable.

ACKNOWLEDGEMENT

Reprinted from *Sankhya*, Series B, Vol. 50, Part 3, Supplement, 1988.

REFERENCES

Central Statistical Organisation (CSO) (1980), *National Accounts: Sources and Methods*, Government of India, New Delhi.

Chatterjee, G.S. and N. Bhattacharya (1975), *Some Observations on NSS Household Budget Data,* in V.M. Dandekar and P. Venkataramaiah (eds) *Data Base of Indian Economy*, Vol. II, Statistical Publishing Society, Calcutta, pp. 97–109.

Directorate of Economics and Statistics (1974), *Bulletin on Food Statistics,* Ministry of Agriculture, Government of India, New Delhi.

Jain, L.R. and S.D. Tendulkar (1987), 'On a Relationship between the Real and the Nominal Relative Disparities in the Consumption of Cereals in Rural India', *Technical Report No. 8715*, Indian Statistical Institute, Delhi Centre (mimeo).

Kansal, S.M. (1965), 'Preliminary Estimates of Total Consumption Expenditure in India', Indian Statistical Institute, Planning Unit, Discussion Paper No. 5, New Delhi (mimeo).

[4] See, for instance, Mukherjee, M. (1986).
[5] See, for instance, Mukherjee, M. (1986).

Mahalanobis, P.C. (1962), 'A Preliminary Note on the Consumption of Cereals in India', *Bulletin of the International Statistical Institute*, XXXIX, No. 4, pp. 53–76.

Minhas, B.S., S.M. Kansal, J. Kumar and P.D. Joshi (1986), 'On the Reliability of the Available Estimates of Private Consumption Expenditure in India', Read at the *IARNIW Seminar on Tangible Wealth and Consumption*, Bhopal.

Mukherjee, M. (1969), *National Income of India: Trends and Structure*, Statistical Publishing Society, Calcutta.

—— (1986), 'Statistical Information and Final Consumption in India and the National Sample Survey', *Economic and Political Weekly*, XXI, No. 5, pp. 206–09.

Mukherjee, M. and G.S. Chatterjee (1972), 'On the Validity of NSS Estimates of Consumption Expenditure', *Arthavijnana*, XIV, pp. 113–21.

Murthy, M.N. (1977), 'Use of Empirical Studies in Evaluating Sample Design for Estimating Frequency Distribution', *Bulletin of the International Statistical Institute*, XLVII, No. 3, pp. 191–211.

Sarma, V.R.R. and G.D. Rao (1980), 'Standard Errors of Estimates from the NSS 28th Round Consumer Expenditure Survey', *Sarvekshana*, III, No. 4, pp. 87–106.

Suryanarayana, M.H. and N.S. Iyengar (1986), 'On the Reliability of NSS Data', *Economic and Political Weekly*, XXI, No. 6, pp. 261–64.

Vaidyanathan, A. (1986), 'On the Validity of NSS Consumption Data', *Economic and Political Weekly*, XXI, No. 3, pp. 129–37.

Appendices

APPENDIX A

AI Unadjusted Consumption Expenditure in India at Current Prices
1972/73 and 1977/78

(Rs Crore)

Item	1972/73			1977/78		
	CSO	NSS	CSO/ NSS %	CSO	NSS	CSO/ NSS %
A. Food*	21,770	23,420	93	37,400	36,500	102
1.1 Foodgrains	10,362	13,418	77	17,560	19,302	91
1.2 Other food	11,408	10,002	114	19,840	17,198	115
B. Non-food	13,390	9,790	137	25,680	20,030	128
2. Paan, tobacco and liquor	1,613	994	162	2,397	1,595	150
3. Clothing and footwear	2,755	2,482	111	6,241	5,475	114
3.1 Clothing	2,563	2,319	111	5,888	5,068	116
3.2 Footwear	192	163	118	353	407	87
4. Gross rent, fuel and power	2,487	2,271	109	4,149	4,462	94
4.1 Gross rent and water	1,272	465	273	2,079	1,039	199
4.2 Commercial fuel	500	436	114	877	1,052	83
4.3 Non-commercial fuel	715	1,370	52	1,238	2,371	52
5. Furniture, furnishings – household appliances (operations and repairs)	1,003	652	154	1,984	1,480	134
6. Medical care and health services	799	854	94	1,458	1,915	76
7. Transport and communication	1,766	632	279	4,091	1,170	350
8. Recreation, entertainment education and cultural services	1,402	603	232	2,084	1,300	160
8.1 Education*	1,092	347	315	1,515	492	308
9. Miscellaneous goods* and services	1,565 (1,121)	1,302 (1,302)	120 (86)	3,231 (2,474)	2,633 (2,633)	123 (94)
Total private consumption expenditure (A + B)	35,160	33,210	106	63,080	56,530	112

Note: * Not comparable: The expenditure in restaurants and hotels in the case of NSS is included in item 1 (Food) and under miscellaneous goods and services in NAS; the NAS estimates for education include institutional expenditure on education, which is not covered by the NSS.

AII Unadjusted Consumption Expenditure on Foodgrains by Subgroup

(Rs Crore)

Item	1972/73			1977/78		
	CSO	NSS	CSO/NSS %	CSO	NSS	CSO/NSS %
1. Rice	1.38	1.42	97.2	1.74	1.82	95.6
2. Wheat	0.94	1.05	90.0	1.25	1.37	91.2
3. Jowar	0.97	1.09	89.4	1.08	1.14	94.7
4. Bajra	0.99	1.05	94.3	1.27	1.24	102.4
5. Maize	0.82	0.93	88.2	1.13	1.18	95.8
6. Barley	0.99	0.98	101.0	0.98	1.04	94.2
7. Ragi	0.83	0.94	88.3	1.04	1.15	90.4
8. Small millets	0.71	0.86	82.6	0.81	1.08	75.0
9. Gram (whole)	1.42	1.27 ⎫ 1.52	94.3	2.93	2.03 ⎫ 2.30	127.4
10. Gram (dal)		1.77 ⎭			2.57 ⎭	
11. Arhar (dal)	1.50	2.26	66.4	3.43	4.04	84.9
12. Moong (dal)	2.15	2.68	80.2	2.87	3.39	84.7
13. Urd (dal)	2.08	2.63	79.1	3.01	3.41	88.3
14. Masur (dal)	1.37	2.02	67.8	2.92	3.66	79.8
15. Other pulses	1.21	1.65	73.3	2.41	2.71	88.9

AIII Unadjusted* Consumption Expenditure on Other Food by Subgroup

(Rs Crore)

Item	1972/73			1977/78		
	CSO	NSS	CSO/NSS %	CSO	NSS	CSO/NSS %
1. Milk and milk products	2,765	2,606	106	5,227	4,749	110
1.1 Milk (liquid)	1,564	1,760	89	3,038	3,173	96
2. Edible oils	1,465	1,286	114	3,077	2,243	137
2.1 Vanaspati	307	188	162	561	322	174
3. Sugar, gur, etc.	2,259	1,234	183	2,477	1,528	162
4. Vegetables and fruits	3,097	1,835	169	5,517	3,228	171
4.1 Potato	231	347	67	778	655	119
4.2 Other tubers/cereal substitutes	191	143	133	225	155	144
5. Meat, fish and eggs	915	891	103	1,690	1,677	101
6. Salt and spices	467	877	53	979	1,690	58
7. Miscellaneous food	884	1,273	69	1,630	2,082	78
Total of other food	11,852	10,002	118	20,597	17,198	120

Note: * Except for the miscellaneous food subgroup, where a partial adjustment in the NAS data for expenditure on this item in hotels and restaurants has already been affected.

APPENDIX B

Standard Errors of NSS Estimates of Consumer Expenditure (A Supplementary Note)

Prior to computerisation of the tabulation of NSS data, the estimates of standard errors (SEs) were be worked out from estimates relating to different subsamples. Because of the interpenetrating network of samples provided in the sampling design, it was possible to obtain unbiased estimates of standard errors in this manner. Nevertheless these estimates were not efficient as they were based on very few degrees of freedom (DF). Quite often, these estimates used to be based on a single pair of half-samples with just 1 DF. Nevertheless, using stratum X subsample-wise estimates or State X subsample-wise estimates, DFs for such estimates of SEs could be increased to a reasonable number.

With the use of electronic computers to process NSS data, it has become possible to estimate standard errors directly from household data. However, the NSS have eschewed regular reporting of standard errors in recent years. The samples are now very large and the standard errors of estimates of consumer expenditure are expected to be very small. Also the amount of computational labour and expense involved in producing the estimates of standard errors (in multi-subject surveys, with the number of sample households being around 150,000 or more) is a real deterrent.

Although the number of sample FSUs in the 27th (1972/73), 32nd (1977/78) as well as 28th (1973/74) Rounds of the NSS was around 13,000, the number of households selected from each FSU (village/block) for the 28th Round survey was restricted to two on an average. In other words, in comparison with the 32nd Round, the total number of sample households in the 28th Round was only around one-seventh – about 23,000 as against 158,000 households.[1] Sarma and Rao (1980) used the data of this smallest round to estimate the SEs of estimates of expenditure on food, non-food, a large number of subgroups and individual items for 17 major states of the Union. This is the only recent consumer survey round for which SEs of estimates of consumer expenditure are available. Probably the purpose of Sarma and Rao exercise was to evaluate the precision of state-level estimates corresponding to certain allocations of FSUs at the state level. They did not, therefore, bother with the computation of RSEs at the all-India level. However, we are comparing the NSS estimates of household expenditure against the national accounting estimates of private consumption in India. We need the RSEs of all-India estimates of value of some aggregates, such as food, non-food and total expenditure.

Had Sarma and Rao given the estimated aggregates ($\hat{Y}_s$) of food, non-food and total expenditure along with the RSEs (as they did in their appendix tables for many item-groups and individual items), we could have easily obtained the statewise variances $V(\hat{Y}_s)$ by calculating (RSE) × (estimate)^2, then summed over states (S) both the estimates and their variances to yield the all-India estimate of expenditure ($\hat{Y}$) and its variance $V(\hat{Y})$, respectively:

$$(\hat{Y}) = \sum_s (\hat{Y}_s) \text{ and } V(\hat{Y}) = \Sigma\, V(\hat{Y}_s).$$

In the absence of the estimated aggregates, we have to calculate $\hat{Y}_s$ and $V(\hat{Y}_s)$ from the value of RSEs (Table 6.2 of Sarma and Rao) and of A and B (Table 6.3 of Sarma and Rao), the first and second

[1] For comparative details of sample size and methods of sample selection in the 28th and 32nd Rounds, see Table B-3.

stage components of variance, respectively. To obtain approximate value of SEs, we proceed as under:

$$V(Y_s) = \frac{A_s}{n_s} + \frac{B_s}{n_s m} = \frac{A_s}{n_s} + \frac{B_s}{2n_s}$$

where n_s is the average value of number of FSUs per stratum, which was obtained by dividing total number of FSUs in a state (sectorwise) by the number of strata formed in the 28th Round; and m (the number of SSUs per FSU) was equal to 2 in the 28th Round.

Now $\qquad (RSE)_s^2 = \dfrac{V(\hat{Y}_s)}{\hat{Y}_s^2}$

Therefore, $\qquad \hat{Y}_s = \sqrt{V(Y_s)} \div (RSE)_s$

For each state the sum of food and non-food expenditure should agree with the independently derived total expenditure. However, in our computations this did not happen in a few states. Nonetheless for most of the states there is good agreement. The values of RSEs for all the 17 states pooled together are as follows:

RSEs (28th Round)

(in %)

Sector	Food	Non-food	Total Expenditure
Rural	0.68	1. 42	0.74
Urban	1.29	1. 98	1.29

Naturally these all-India values of RSEs are lower than the lowest values obtained for the largest state, Uttar Pradesh (UP). All-India sample is manifold in size in comparison with UP.

Our interest in this note is not to compute RSEs of estimates of consumer expenditure directly from the household data of the 27th or 32nd Round. Rather we intend to demonstrate how one can use the already available 28th Round estimates to get approximate estimates of RSEs for the 32nd Round, as the set of strata and the sampling scheme were very similar for these two rounds. Writing the variance of all-India estimates of expenditure ($\hat{Y}$) as:

$$V = \sum_{s=1}^{17} \frac{A_s}{n_s} + \frac{1}{m} \sum_{s=1}^{17} \frac{B_1}{n_s} \qquad (1)$$

where n_s is the average number of sample FSUs per stratum in the sth state, $\dfrac{A_s}{n_s}$ and $\dfrac{B_s}{m.n_s}$ are the first stage and second stage components of variance of the aggregate estimate of the sth state and m is the average number of sample SSUs per FSU. We can rewrite (1) as:

$$V = \left(\sum \frac{B_s}{n_s} \right) \left[\frac{\sum (A_s/n_s)}{\sum (B_s/n_s)} + \frac{1}{m} \right].$$

In the case of 28th Round, variance of Y_{28} is given by

$$V_{28} = \left(\sum \frac{B_s}{n_s} \right) \left[\frac{\sum (A_s/n_s)}{\sum (B_s/n_s)} + \frac{1}{2} \right]. \tag{2}$$

Expressing this as relative variance,

$$\frac{V_{28}}{\hat{Y}_{28}^2} = \frac{\sum (B_s/n_s)}{\hat{Y}_{28}^2} \left[\frac{\sum (A_s/n_s)}{\sum (B_s/n_s)} + \frac{1}{2} \right] \tag{3}$$

Similarly the relative variance of the aggregate estimate of 32nd Round, $\hat{Y}_{32}$ is given by

$$\frac{V_{32}}{\hat{Y}_{32}^2} = \frac{\sum (B_s'/n_s)}{\hat{Y}_{32}^2} \left[\frac{\sum (A_s'/n_s)}{\sum (B_s'/n_s)} + \frac{1}{12} \right] \tag{4}$$

where the symbols with prime are for the 32nd Round,

$$\frac{(\text{Rel. var.})_{32}}{(\text{Rel. var.})_{28}} = \frac{\dfrac{\sum (B_s'/n_s)}{\hat{Y}_{32}^2} \left[\dfrac{\sum (A_s'/n_s)}{\sum (B_s'/n_s)} + \dfrac{1}{12} \right]}{\dfrac{\sum (B_s/n_s)}{\hat{Y}_{28}^2} \left[\dfrac{\sum (A_s/n_s)}{\sum (B_s/n_s)} + \dfrac{1}{2} \right]}$$

Now, as the sampling design, up to the selection of first stage units, in the 28th and 32nd Round, was exactly the same and the periods covered were close by, it can safely be assumed that approximately

$$\frac{\sum (B_s/n_s)}{\hat{Y}_{28}^2} = \frac{\sum (B_s^l/n_s)}{\hat{Y}_{32}^2}$$

and $$\frac{\sum (A_s/n_s)}{\sum (B_s/n_s)} = \frac{\sum (A_s'/n_s)}{\sum (B_s'/n_s)}$$

Therefore $\dfrac{(\text{Rel. var.})_{32}}{(\text{Rel. var.})_{28}}$ is approximately equal to K; where

$$K = \frac{\dfrac{\sum (A_s/n_s)}{\sum (B_s/n_s)} + \dfrac{1}{12}}{\dfrac{\sum (A_s/n_s)}{\sum (B_s/n_s)} + \dfrac{1}{2}}$$

Hence $(\text{RSE})_{32} = \sqrt{K} \ (\text{RSE})_{28}$.

The projected values of RSEs for 32nd Round are given in Table B-1.

The projected values of RSEs for 32nd Round are given in Table B-1.

Table B-1　RSEs (Projected) of the 32nd Round All-India Estimates of
Aggregate Values of Consumer Expenditure

Item	$(RSE)_{28}$	K	$\sqrt{K}$	$(RSE)_{32}$
(1)	(2)	(3)	(4)	(5)
		Rural		
Food	0.0068 (0.68%)	0.3486	0.5904	0.0040 (0.40%)
Non-food	0.0142 (1.42%)	0.4057	0.6369	0.0090 (0.90%)
Total	0.0074 (0.74%)	0.3998	0.6323	0.0047 (0.47%)
		Urban		
Food	0.0129 (1.29%)	0.3305	0.5749	0.0074 (0.74%)
Non-food	0.0198 (1.98%)	0.4293	0.6552	0.0130 (1.30%)
Total	0.0129 (1.29%)	0.4588	0.6773	0.0087 (0.87%)

Note: As the sample size in the 32nd Round was many times larger than that of 28th Round (about 158,000 households as against 23,000) the RSEs of the aggregate expenditures on food, non-food and total (food + non-food) in the 32nd Round come out to be lower than those of 28th Round.

In Table B-2 we have reproduced the highest and the lowest values of RSEs at the state level for many subgroups and items from Sarma and Rao (1980) from the 28th Round data, separately from the rural and urban sectors. The name of the state is given in parentheses along with RSE value. With a few easily understandable exceptions, the lowest RSEs, as expected, are found in relatively large states (UP in most cases) where the sample size is large; in comparison, the smaller states turn up relatively larger RSEs. I do not have the time or interest in computing all India RSEs for the aggregates of expenditure at the subgroup level. Nevertheless, one can make the following observations to enhance the appreciation (and confidence) of certain non-statistical economists and economic statisticians in regard to the precision of all India level NSS estimates of expenditure on the subgroups-items listed in Table B-2.

(a) The RSE of estimate of expenditure at the all-India level for any subgroup/item can at most be as large (in general it will be much smaller) as the highest estimate for the same subgroup/item computed for any state.[2]

---

[2] Thanks are due to Dr J.K. Ghosh (Editor) for the following proof:

$$V = \frac{\Sigma R_s^2 Y_s^2}{(\Sigma Y_s)^2} \text{ , where } R_s = \text{RSE for } s\text{-th state}$$

$$= \frac{\Sigma R_s^2 Y_s^2}{\Sigma Y_s^2} \cdot \frac{\Sigma Y_s^2}{(\Sigma Y_s^2)^2}$$

The first factor, being a weighted average, is less than or equal to the maximum R_s^2 and the second factor is ≤ 1, since all $Y_s \geq 0$. Therefore

$$V \leq \max_s R_s^2.$$

(b) The RSE at all-India level can be smaller than the smallest estimate obtained at the state level for the same subgroup. Nevertheless for certain commodities/services the RSE at all-India level might come out to be higher than the smallest estimate at the state level.

NSS might compute RSEs for a recent round. Nevertheless, the 28th Round results can safely be assumed for the time being to provide the outer limits to the magnitudes of relative standard errors of the estimates of consumer expenditure for all aggregates and almost all subgroups of items in the 32nd Round, or any other recent round where the set of strata and the sampling scheme might be similar to the 28th Round.

Table B-2 Percentage Standard Error of Estimate of Consumer Expenditure (Value) on All Commodities, Selected/Subgroups and Items
[highest and lowest values of RSE (%) among selected states based on 28th Round data]

Total/Subgroup/Item	Rural		Urban	
	Lowest	Highest	Lowest	Highest
(0)	(1)	(2)	(3)	(4)
Total expenditure	2.04 (UP)	4.81 (HP)	3.33 (UP)	9.72 (HP)
All food	1.87 (UP)	3.54 (HP)	2.92 (UP)	10.31 (HP)
All non-food	3.82 (UP)	9.00 (HP)	5.24 (UP)	14.20 (OR)
Food				
Milk and milk products	3.63 (Pb)	15. 28 (WB)	4.86 (UP)	17.21 (KL)
Edible oils	2.37 (UP)	5.04 (KL)	3.67 (UP)	9.76 (KL)
(Vanaspati)	5.10 (Pb)	11.11 (HP)	6.92 (Pb)	17.21 (HP)
Meat, fish and eggs	4.13 (AP)	10.43 (Pb)	5.31 (TN)	17.95 (Pb)
Vegetables	2.11 (UP)	5.85 (KL)	3.48 (UP)	9.83 (KL)
(Potato)	2.89 (UP)	6.37 (HP)	4.31 (Mah)	6.45 (J&K)
Fruits and nuts	5.32 (KL)	13.09 (WB)	6.06 (Mah)	11.42 (MP)
Sugar	2.75 (Mah)	4.81 (TN)	3.58 (Mah)	8.32 (KL)
Gur	3.69 (UP)	10.31 (HP)	–	–
Spices	2.13 (UP)	3.20 (KL)	3.27 (UP)	6.56 (Pb)
Beverages and refreshments	4.18 (Pb)	10.65 (WB)	5.00 (Mah)	10.95 (Pb)
Non-food				
Clothing	5.59 (MP)	10.58 (Pb)	8.39 (Mah)	17.55 (KL)
Footwear	9.38 (MP)	30.51 (TN)	16.61 (Pb)	36.22 (KL)
Fuel and light	1.62 (UP)	2.81 (KL)	3.05 (UP)	7.43 (KL)
(Electricity)	9.84 (Pb)	23.31 (UP)	8.60 (Pb)	18.95 (HP)
(Firewood)	2.44 (TN)	3.96 (KN)	–	–
Medicines	8.34 (Pb)	19.82 (UP)	12.11 (UP)	33.90 (Pb)
Durable goods	20.79 (UP)	49.50 (AP)	31.58 (WB)	64.49 (TN)
Misc. goods and services	4.65 (Pb)	6.92 (UP)	5.43 (Mah)	10.61 (KL)

Source: Various tables in Sarma and Rao (1980). State names have been abbreviated as follows Andhra Pradesh (AP), Himachal Pradesh (HP), Jammu & Kashmir (J&K), Karnataka (KN), Kerala (KL), Madhya Pradesh (MP), Maharashtra (Mah), Orissa (OR), Punjab (Pb), Tamil Nadu (TN), Uttar Pradesh (UP) and West Bengal (WB).

Table B-3 Number and Method of Selection of FSUs and SSUs for Schedule 1–0 in Recent NSS Consumer Expenditure Surveys

(0)	Rural (1)	Urban (2)	Total (Rural + Urban) (3)
28th Round (1973/74)			
1. No. of FSUs	8680	4,859	13,539
2. Method of Selection	Randomly with probability proportional to population and with replacement	Randomly with probability proportional to size and with replacement.	
3. No. of SSUs	15,467	7,881	23,348
4. Method of Selection	Linear systematically from the arranged frame prepared as follows: All the households were arranged into six classes on the basis of their means of livelihood (landless labour –1, cultivatora –2 and others –3) and whether visited health centre or not.	Linear systematically from the arranged frame prepared as follows: All the households in a sample arranged into six classes of occupation division	
32nd Round (1977/78)			
1. No. of FSUs	8,216	4,871	13,087
2. Method of selection	Randomly with probability proportional to population and with replacement	Randomly with probability proportional to size* and with replacement.	
3. No. of SSUs	99,766	58,162	157,982
4. Method of selection	Circular systematically from the arranged frame obtained by arranging the households in the sample village by the means of livelihood classes self-employed – non-agricultural –1, rural labour –2, and others –3.	Circular systematically from the arranged frame obtained by arranging the households into four classes on the basis of their nature of employment (self-employed, not self-employed) and their per capita expenditure level.	

Note: *Size is defined here in terms of block population in thousands rounded up to the next higher integer.

7

Estimates of Food Consumption Expenditure from Household Surveys and National Accounts

A.C. Kulshreshtha and Aloke Kar

Debates on the changing incidence of poverty inevitably converge to issues concerning the nature and acceptability of statistical evidence. In recent times, the Indian database for measurement of poverty have been questioned in both academic as well as policy circles. Questions relating to validity of the survey results on which the poverty measurements are based were raised when they did not show any decline in rural poverty during the 1990s, despite higher rate of growth in the aggregate GDP. Again, when the survey results showed a sharp decline in the incidence of poverty in 1999/2000 as compared to that in 1993/94, from 37.3 per cent to 27.1 per cent in rural poverty incidence and from 32.4 per cent to 23.6 per cent in urban poverty incidence, a great deal of controversy was generated regarding comparability of the results, particularly because of a major deviation that was made in the survey methodology.

POVERTY MEASUREMENT IN INDIA

The measure for incidence of poverty used in India requires setting up of a 'poverty line' based on established norms of food requirement. The Task Force on Projections of Minimum Needs and Effective Consumption Demand (1979) defined the poverty line as the per capita expenditure level at which the calorie norms established – 2,400 calories per capita per day for rural areas and 2,100 calories per capita per day for urban areas – were met on the basis of an all-India consumption basket of 1973/74. The 'poverty line' thus defined for 1973/74 was, till recently, updated for changes in price levels over time, using the price deflator implicit in the constant and current price estimates of *private final consumption expenditure* (PFCE) of the National Accounts Statistics (NAS). At present, however, following the recommendations of the Expert Group on Proportion and Number of Poor (1993) separate deflators are used for rural and urban areas of different states. The state-specific Consumer Price Index (CPI) of selected commodity-groups for agricultural labourers were used as price deflators for rural areas, and state-specific retail price movement of Consumer Price Index for industrial workers were used for urban areas.

Having set the 'poverty line', the estimates of poverty-incidence were worked out from the distribution of population by per capita consumption expenditure, estimated from the results of household surveys, as the proportion of the population having per capita consumption expenditure below the poverty line. The partly normative and partly behavioural measure of poverty used in India is based on the statistical data collected in the household surveys on consumption expenditure conducted by the National Sample Survey Organisation (NSSO). The NSSO's household survey on consumption expenditure of 1973/74 has provided the basis for establishing the 'poverty line', while the data to measure the incidence of poverty for the subsequent period are available from the following surveys on household consumption expenditure. Till recently, the Planning Commission, the official agency responsible for estimating poverty-incidence, had been scaling up the NSSO-based distribution of population by the level of consumption expenditure, by a factor equal to the ratio of the PFCE from the NAS and the estimate of aggregate consumption expenditure based on NSSO survey results. The Expert Group on Proportion and Number of Poor (1993), however, found this procedure unacceptable and recommended exclusive use of NSSO-based distribution of population by the level of consumption expenditure for estimation of 'head-count ratio'. The Planning Commission has adopted the procedure recommended by the Expert Group. Thus, the deflator-related issues apart, the acceptability of the measure of incidence of poverty in India now depends exclusively on the quality of the basic data collected by the NSSO from a large sample of households by canvassing a fairly detailed schedule of enquiry.

The Expert Group recommended against the use of PFCE aggregate to scale up the distribution of the population by level of consumption expenditure obtained from the (household) consumption expenditure surveys (HCES) of the NSSO, because of the following reasons:

(i) Not only did the estimates of domestic consumption expenditure of the household sector derived from the NSSO fail to agree reasonably with the PFCE estimates of the NAS, but the gap between the two sets of estimates is also found to widen over time.

(ii) The PFCE estimate of the NAS is estimated indirectly, depending upon the availability of data on production of a sizeable segment of the economy, and uses subjective judgements for deriving the estimates of private consumption.

(iii) The scaling up of the NSSO-based distribution was based on the assumption that the difference between the two estimates of aggregate consumption expenditure at the national level was uniformly distributed across the states, as well as all sections of the population.

ESTIMATES OF PFCE OF NAS AND HOUSEHOLD CONSUMPTION EXPENDITURE OF NSSO

The CSO's estimate of *private final consumption expenditure* is derived following what is called the 'commodity flow' approach. This approach consists of obtaining the quantum and value of different commodities flowing finally into the consumption process of the households and the private non-profit institutions serving households (NPISHs), from the quantum and value of the commodities produced and available during the accounting year. The national accounts statistics of India generally pertain to a financial year, extending from the beginning of April of one calendar year, till the end of March of the next. The sum of all the commodity-wise estimates of value gives the aggregate estimate of

PFCE, which in fact represents the value of goods and services consumed by the households and NPISHs.

The NSSO, on the other hand, employs the technique of survey sampling, in which the consumption expenditure of a random sample of households is ascertained directly by canvassing a well-designed schedule of enquiry, whose coverage is broad enough to include every item of household consumption expenditure. But the surveys conducted for this purpose, called (Household) Consumption Expenditure Surveys, are required to cover only the households and not the NPISHs. Moreover, these surveys are usually carried out over a period of one year that generally corresponds to an agricultural year, i.e. the beginning of July of one calendar year till the end of June of the next.

WIDENING GAP BETWEEN NAS AND NSS ESTIMATES

Evidently, the two data sets are not strictly comparable, hence disagreement between the estimates is, but expected. But, what appears to be a matter of serious concern is that the gap between the two sets of estimates has been widening progressively since the 1980s. A number of studies comparing the two sets of estimates conducted in the past, reveal that the estimates for the individual years of the 1950s, 1960s and 1970s were in fairly close agreement. Most of these studies pertain to estimates for the individual years of the 1950s and 1960s and contain comparisons at broad levels of aggregation. Only two of the latter studies (Minhas et al., 1986, and Minhas, 1988) deal with the estimates for two years of the 1970s and contain a comprehensive, disaggregated level comparison of the two sets of estimates.

The NAS estimates of PFCE and the NSS estimates of household consumption expenditure for different years are compared in Table 7.1, to reveal how the divergence between the two estimates has grown progressively over the years. Until the 1970s as Table 7.1 shows, the difference between the two estimates of total consumption expenditure was of the order of 13 per cent or less, that the divergence between the estimates, which was about 10 per cent in 1977/78, had soared to a level of about 25 per cent by 1982/83, remained at almost the same level in 1987/88, and then mounted to as high as 38 per cent in 1993/94. So far as the expenditure on food consumption is concerned, the estimates from the two sources varied by only about 5 per cent, that too either way, till the 1970s. But during the following period the increment in the NAS estimate has been at a much faster rate than that in the NSS estimate. So much so, that the difference between the NSS and NAS estimates rose to a level of 19 per cent by the 1980s and by 1993/94 the difference was about 29 per cent. Much in the same way, the divergence between the estimates of non-food consumption, which was of the order of 5 per cent till 1960/61, has grown manifold to a shade below 50 per cent in 1993/94. A divergence as wide as this is indeed unacceptable. It is necessary to mention here that the NSS estimates of all the years of the 1970s, 1980s and 1990s given in the table are based on quinquennial surveys, which were conducted on a larger, second-stage sample than the other years for which the estimates are available.

This paper presents the main findings of a recent study carried out jointly by the National Accounts Division of the CSO and Survey Design and Research Division of NSSO for a Study Group on Non-Sampling Errors. The study includes an analytical investigation for the underlying causes of the widening gap between the two sets of estimates, using the disaggregated item-level estimates from the HCES of NSSO (50th Round) 1993/94, and the disaggregated item-level data used for compiling PFCE for the National Accounts Statistics (NAS).

Table 7.1 Divergence between the NSS and NAS Estimates of
Consumption Expenditure for Selected Years

(Rs Crore)

Year	Source	Food	Non-food	Total
1957/58	NSS	6,626	3,241	9,867
	NAS	6,920	3,461	10,381
	% difference	−4.25	−6.36	−4.95
1960/61	NSS	8,118	4,130	12,247
	NAS	8,594	4,302	12,896
	% difference	−5.54	−4.00	−5.03
1967/68	NSS	16,373	5,537	22,695
	NAS	17,238	9,017	26,255
	% difference	−5.02	−16.55	−13.56
1972/73	NSS	23,420	9,790	33,210
	NAS	22,214	12,946	35,160
	% difference	5.43	−24.38	−5.55
1977/78	NSS	36,500	20,030	56,530
	NAS	38,157	24,923	63,080
	% difference	−4.34	−19.63	−10.38
1983/84	NSS	69,735	39,996	1,09,731
	NAS	85,613	60,471	1,46,084
	% difference	−18.55	−33.86	−24.88
1987/88	NSS	1,06,205	67,560	1,73,765
	NAS	1,22,805	1,01,256	2,24,061
	% difference	−13.52	−33.28	−22.45
1993/94	NSS	2,24,066	1,31,704	3,55,770
	NAS	3,15,243	2,59,529	5,74,772
	% difference	−28.92	−49.25	−38.10

Notes: 1. Percentage difference stands for (NSS − NAS)/NAS expressed in percentage.
2. The estimates for 1957/58 and 1960/61 are quoted from Srinivasan et al. (1974), who in turn have used the estimates for 1957/58 compiled by Kansal and Saluja (1961) for the NAS estimates.
3. The estimates for 1972/73 and 1977/78 are quoted from Minhas et al. (1986).
4. Sources for NAS estimates for 1983/84, 1987/88 and 1993/94 are the National Accounts Statistics of 1990, 1992 and 2000 respectively.

COMPARABILITY OF THE ESTIMATES

Many of the known causes of divergence between the two sets of estimates are inherent in the different approaches adopted by the two agencies. Apart from the differences in the coverage and reference time frames that are apparent, comparability of the two sets of estimates is constrained by the differences in the concepts and methods of estimation inherent in the very approaches employed by the two agencies. The differences that are inherent in the methods of estimation used by the two agencies relate to the: (i) coverage, (ii) reference time frames, (iii) unmatched classification schemes, (iv) treatment of cooked meals, and (v) the notional components in the NAS estimate of PFCE. A number of studies taken up in the past have dealt with these causes. Particularly, Minhas (1988) provides a comprehensive account of the limitations of comparing the two sets of estimates. Nevertheless, the divergence between the two sets of estimates is too wide to be justified by the methodological differences.

Among the differences cited above, the notional components in the NAS estimate, however, account for a substantial part of the divergence between the two estimates. Only the rent actually paid on dwellings is included in the NSS estimate, while the NAS estimate includes all imputed rentals of owner-occupied dwellings. Another such notional component in the NAS estimate is the financial intermediation services indirectly measured (FISIM). This is being included in PFCE since the 1980/81 series of national accounts. Thus, the NSS and NAS estimates of consumption do not suffer from non-comparability in this respect for the earlier years. Inclusion of these notional components in the NAS estimate of private consumption is, however, in strict adherence to the standards set by the internationally accepted system of national accounts. Table 7.2 illustrates how these notional components of the NAS estimates affect the comparability. In the table, the figures given in column 2 are the unadjusted NSS estimates, while those given in column 7, called 'adjusted NSS estimates', are the NSS estimates including the notional components of rent and FISIM.

Table 7.2 Comparison between the NSS Estimates and NAS Estimates Adjusted for Rent on Dwellings and FISIM

(Rs Crore)

Year	Unadjusted NSS	NAS	% Difference Cols. (2) & (3)	Imputed Rentals	FISIM	Adjusted NSS	% Difference Cols. (7) & (3)
(1)	(2)	(3)	(4)	(5)	(6)	(7)	(8)
1983/84	1,09,731	1,46,084	−24.88	10,478	758	1,20,967	−17.19
1987/88	1,73,765	2,24,061	−22.45	15,416	1,513	1,90,694	−14.89
1993/94	3,55,771	5,74,772	−38.10	37,297	11,801	4,04,869	−29.59

Notes: 1. Percentage difference stands for (NSS − NAS)/NAS expressed in percentage.
2. Sources same as those for Table 7.1.

COMPARISON OF ESTIMATES OF FOOD CONSUMPTION FOR 1993/94

As the classification schemes followed by the two agencies differ, the individual items have been regrouped suitably to make their estimates from the two sources comparable. For this purpose, the subgroups like those of gram products, pulses products, cereal products, cereal substitutes, vegetables, vegetable products, and confectionery items have been regrouped suitably taking individual item-level estimates which are available from both the sources. The regrouping involves both the sets of estimates. For the present study, expenditure on paan, tobacco and beverages is included in the estimates of food consumption.

Table 7.3 gives the NAS and NSS estimates for the different food subgroups made comparable by suitably regrouping the food items. The NAS and NSS estimates of quantity consumed are compared for the items for which quantity estimates are available from both the sources. For a valid comparison between the estimates of consumption expenditure (henceforth called value estimates) for the item-groups, the NAS value estimates have been adjusted for prices to eliminate the effect of differential implicit prices in the divergence between the two sets of estimates. For the items for which quantity and value estimates are available from both the sources, the adjusted NAS value estimates are arrived at by evaluating the NAS quantity estimates at NSS implicit prices. For the other items, the adjusted NAS estimates are taken same as the unadjusted value.

Table 7.3 Comparison of NSS Estimates with the Unadjusted and Price-adjusted NAS Estimates for Different Item-groups of Food Consumption for 1993/94

(Rs Crore)

Item-group	Unadjusted NAS				Adjusted NAS	
	NSS Estimate	*NAS Estimate*	*NSS– NAS*	*% Difference*	*NAS*	*% Difference*
1. Cereals and cereal products	72,188	77,655	–5,467	–7.04	77,338	–6.66
2. Bread	560	554	6	1.08	554	1.08
3. Gram (Whole)	530	265	265	100.00	308	72.08
4. Pulses and pulses products	12,665	11,993	672	5.60	13,430	–5.70
5. Cereal substitute (tapioca, etc.)	309	1,024	–715	–69.82	1,024	–69.82
6. Sugar and Gur	9,956	19,881	–9,925	–49.92	19,748	–49.58
7. Milk and milk products	33,737	46,594	–12,857	–27.59	44,714	–24.55
8. Edible oils and oilseeds	15,674	23,204	–7,530	–32.45	20,001	–21.63
9. Meat, egg and fish	11,923	21,737	–9,814	–45.15	21,153	–43.63
10. Fruits, vegetables and their products	28,851	68,036	–39,185	–57.59	66,839	–56.84
11. Salt	595	595	0	0.00	595	0.00
12. Spices	8,015	8,015	0	0.00	8,015	0.00
13. Non-alcoholic beverages	9,156	6,422	2,734	42.57	6,422	42.57
14. Processed/Other foods	5,910	5,436	474	8.72	5,436	8.72
15. Paan	1,830	2,988	–1,158	–38.76	2,988	–38.76
16. Tobacco	5,877	12,309	–6,432	–52.25	12,309	–52.25
17. Alcoholic beverages and other intoxicants	2,525	2,393	132	5.52	2,393	5.52
18. Hotel and restaurant/Cooked meals	3,765	6,142	–2,377	–38.70	5,589	–32.64
Food: Total	*2,24,066*	*3,15,243*	*–91,177*	*–28.92*	*3,08,856*	*–27.45*

Table 7.3 shows that the estimates for that total food consumption differ by over Rs 91,000 crore, the NSS estimate being smaller than the NAS estimate by about 29 per cent of the latter. The main contributor, it is seen, is the 'fruits, vegetables and their products' item-group, which alone accounts for Rs 39,000 crore out of the Rs 91,000 crore difference between the estimates of food consumption. This is followed by the 'milk and milk products' and 'sugar and gur' item-groups, accounting for Rs 13,000 and Rs 10,000 crore respectively. The NSS estimates are higher than the NAS estimates for only a few item-groups like 'pulses and pulses products', 'non-alcoholic beverages' and 'gram (whole)'. The differences between the estimates for such groups are much smaller in comparison. The estimates for the item-groups 'salt' and 'spices', it is seen, do not vary at all. This is because the NAS estimate for both the item-groups is directly taken from the HCES.

In the following paragraphs, the divergence between the two sets of estimates of the major item-groups is discussed at a more disaggregated level, which reveals more specific reasons for the divergence. The attempt is to identify the items within the item-groups that are mainly responsible for the divergence between the two estimates for the item-groups.

FOODGRAINS

Since the subgroups 'cereals and cereal products' and 'pulses and pulses products' have major shares in total consumption expenditure on food, it is necessary to undertake a disaggregated-level comparison of NAS and NSS estimates of cereals and pulses consumption. The following paragraphs contain a detailed comparison of the quantity and value estimates of consumption of individual constituents of foodgrains in 1993/94. Besides the cereals and pulses, foodgrains comprise cereals and pulses products and whole gram. Bread produced in bakeries, being principally a wheat product, is also included in this group of food items.

Cereals and Cereal Products

Table 7.4 gives a comparison of the NSS and NAS estimates of consumption of cereals and their products for 1993/94. It also provides comparable estimates for the items 'gram (whole grain)' and 'bread'. Both the NAS and NSS value estimates for the items in the rice and wheat groups represent the expenditure actually incurred on the items. The quantity available from the Public Distribution System (PDS) is evaluated at the administered price in the NAS, while the cost actually paid by the households for the quantity obtained from the PDS is recorded in the HCES. Thus, the implicit prices that can be worked out from the NAS and NSS estimates of value and quantity given in the table, represent the (weighted) average of the open market and administered prices. The adjusted NAS value estimates too, are given in the table alongside the unadjusted NAS estimates of value.

The estimates of quantity of wheat products are not worked out separately in the NAS. To segregate the NAS estimate of the quantity of wheat products, the estimates of suji and maida have been taken directly from the ASI. The estimate of the quantity of atta has been obtained by deducting the ASI quantity estimates of suji and maida from the NAS estimate of total quantity of wheat products.

Table 7.4 Itemwise Comparison between NAS and NSS Estimates of Quantity (*000 Tonnes*) and Value (*Rs Crore*) of Consumption of Cereals, Pulses and their Products for 1993/94

Item	NSS		NAS		Difference (NSS – NAS)	NAS Adjusted by NSS Price	Adjusted Difference
	Quantity	Value	Quantity	Value			
Rice and rice products	71,104	45,584	71,088*	45,243	341	47,209	−1,625
Wheat and its products	48,108	20,867	46,522@	20,885	−18	20,417	450
Other cereals and their products	17,536	5,737	29,808	11,527	−5,790	9,713	−3,976
Total cereals	1,36,748	72,188	1,47,418	77,655#	−5,467	77,338	−5,150
Pulses and products: Total	−	12,665	−	11,993$	672	13,430	−764

Notes: * The NAS quantity figures quoted for rice products are in terms of quantity of rice used for production of the rice product.

@ The NAS quantity estimates of output for wheat products like suji and maida are taken directly from the ASI, for the study. The quantity and value of atta, given above, is derived from the estimates of NAS and the ASI results for suji and maida.

\# Includes change in stocks.

$ Includes change in stocks.

The following observations emerge from the estimates presented in Table 7.4:

(i) The unadjusted NAS estimate of total cereals consumption is higher than the NSS estimate by Rs 5,467 crore, which reduces by over three hundred crores once the NAS quantity estimates are evaluated at NSS implicit prices. The unadjusted NSS and NAS estimates for the major cereal items like rice and rice products, and wheat and its products compare closely both in terms of quantity and value. With the adjustments made for prices, however, the difference increases and the order relations are reversed. The adjusted difference still remains within acceptable limits.

(ii) The NSS and NAS estimates also differ appreciably for the minor cereals and their products. A substantial part of the difference between the two sets of value estimates for these items may be attributed to the differential implicit prices. Adjustment for prices brings about a considerable reduction in the discrepancy between the estimates of value.

(iii) The estimates for pulses and their products do not differ much, though the implicit prices differ substantially. Adjustment for prices of the NAS estimates of value changes the direction of the gap between the estimates. In fact, the adjusted NAS estimate for pulses and pulses products exceeds the NSS estimate.

Milk and Milk Products

This item-group is only next to the 'fruits and vegetable' group in its contribution towards the discrepancy between the estimates of food consumption. Table 7.5 gives the comparable item-wise estimates for 1993/94, as available from the two sources. The NAS and NSS estimates of consumption of liquid milk, both in terms of quantity and value, compare closely with each other. However, while the NSS estimate of quantity is higher by about 2 per cent, that for value is less by about 5 per cent than the respective NAS estimates. After adjustment for prices, the NSS estimate turns out to be higher than NAS estimate. It may be noted here that, unlike the years for which the earlier comparative studies were conducted, the NSS and NAS estimates of consumption of milk, both in liquid form and otherwise, are in principle comparable for 1993/94, so far as the method of data collection in the HCES and that of compilation of NAS are concerned.

Estimation of value of consumption of milk products poses a more serious problem. In fact, this subgroup alone contributes Rs 12,000 crore in an overall discrepancy of Rs 91,000 crore between the estimates for the 'food' group as a whole. The NSS estimate for 'milk products' (Rs 3,000 crore) is found to be only a fifth of that of the NAS estimate (Rs 15,000 crore).

The NAS estimate for milk products is arrived at as the sum of the ASI value estimate of output of dairy products,[1] marked up by 20 per cent for 'Trade and Transport Margin' (TTM), and the estimated value of production of butter and lassi in the unorganised sector. For the production in the organised segment, CSO takes the ASI estimate for only the enterprises falling in the National Income Code (NIC) (1987) activity group 201, i.e. manufacturing of dairy products, which includes the production of pasteurised and other forms of liquid milk, apart from all kinds of milk products. Thus, the output of the enterprises falling in NIC 201 includes not just milk products but also liquid milk. It is seen from the detailed results of ASI 1994/95 (CSO, 1998), that only a part (about 40 per cent) of the ASI estimate of output of NIC activity group 201 is actually milk product and the rest, liquid milk. On the other hand, the

---

[1] This represents the production of dairy products in the organised segment of the economy.

present procedure altogether ignores intermediate consumption in the unorganised-sector enterprises like halwais, tea shops, hotels and restaurants.

Table 7.5 Itemwise Comparison between NAS and NSS Estimates of Quantity and Value (*Rs Crore*) of Consumption of 'Milk and Milk Products' for 1993/94

Item	NSS		NAS		Difference (NSS − NAS)	NAS Adjusted by NSS Price	Adjusted Differ-ence
	Quantity	Value	Quantity	Value			
Liquid Milk (000 Ltrs)	45,439	31,059	44,661	32,407	−1,348	30,528	532
Milk products (from ASI)	−		−	7,950	−7,950	7,950	−7,950
Butter and Lassi	−		−	7,178	−7,178	7,178	−7,178
Milk products: Total	−	2,678	−	15,128	−12,450	15,128	−12,450
Milk and milk products	−	33,737	−	46,594	−12,857	44,714	−10,977

Note: The NAS estimate of value for 'milk and milk products' are net of government final consumption and changes in stock, which are included in the estimates of the individual components.

Edible Oil and Oilseeds

For the study, the estimates of edible oils for 1993/94 available from the two sources have been re-grouped to make them comparable. For this purpose, the oils used less commonly have been clubbed together in the 'others' category for the NSS estimates. The comparable estimates thus arrived at from the two sources are presented in Table 7.6. The estimates of oilseeds consumption are also given in the table.

It is seen that the NSS estimate of consumption expenditure of 'edible oils and oilseeds' for 1993/94 is lower than the NAS estimate by 32 per cent. However, for the two most commonly used edible oils, mustard oil and groundnut oil, the estimates from the two sources are fairly close to each other. The major part of the big difference between the estimates for the group as a whole is caused by vanaspati and oilseeds. In the earlier study (Minhas et al., 1986) too it was found that the estimates for edible oils other than vanaspati differed little in the year 1972/73, though for the year 1977/78 the difference was substantial.

For the NAS estimates, the CSO uses the estimates of oilseeds production available from the Directorate of Economics and Statistics, Ministry of Agriculture (DESAg), and those of edible oils production from the Ministry of Food and Civil Supplies. These estimates of edible oils are in fact, derived on the basis of certain assumptions on the utilisation of oilseeds for different purposes like seed, feed, waste, etc., and oil extraction rates.

For deriving the NAS estimates, varying ratios of intermediate consumption are used for edible oils, but for vanaspati no adjustment is made for its use in other industries. This appears to be an important reason for the difference between the estimates of vanaspati consumption, since it is used extensively in commercial establishments like halwais, hotels and restaurants. As for the edible oils other than vanaspati, though the estimates for the entire subgroup compare closely, the estimates for individual oils are found to differ substantially in some cases. The difference is most pronounced for coconut oil. The estimates of both quantity and value differ widely. In particular, the NSS estimate of value is only a fourth of the

Table 7.6 Item-wise Comparison between NAS and NSS Estimates of Quantity (*000 Tonnes*) and Value (*Rs Crore*) of Consumption of 'Edible Oils and Oilseeds' for 1993/94

Item	NSS		NAS		Difference (NSS – NAS)	NAS Adjusted by NSS Price	Adjusted Differ- ence
	Quantity	Value	Quantity	Value			
Vanaspati	411	1,533	919	3,526	–1,994	3,322	–1,790
Mustard oil	1,785	5,558	1,584	5,249	308	4,882	676
Groundnut oil	1,645	6,125	1,445	5,420	705	5,303	822
Coconut oil	108	462	347	1,948	–1,486	1,275	–812
Gingelly (Til) oil	108	363	101	482	–119	326	36
Linseed oil: Total	80	173	22	98	75	45	127
Edible oil (Others)	411	1,429	497	2,091	–662	1,339	90
Edible oils: Total	–	15,642		18,814	–3,173	16,493	–851
Oilseeds	–	33	–	3,508	–3,475	3,508	–3,475
Edible oil and oilseeds	–	15,674	–	23,204	–7,530	20,001	–4,327

Notes: 1. The NSS estimate for the group 'other edible oils' includes those for Margarine, 'Refined oil', Palm oil and Rapeseed Oil.
2. NAS estimate for the entire group 'Edible oils and oilseeds' include imports and change in stock which are not shown separately in the table.

NAS estimate. This is mainly due to the varying prices implicit in the two sets of estimates. The gap between the two estimates of 'edible oils: total' reduces substantially by adjusting the NAS estimates for prices.

The difference in the estimates of consumption is most pronounced for oilseeds. The NSS estimate is found to be less than 1 per cent of that of the NAS. It may be noted that groundnuts used as such, are not included here. Notwithstanding the possibility of under-reporting in the NSS, the NAS estimate for oilseeds is based on the assumption that the entire amount of oilseeds retained by producers is consumed as oilseeds.

Meat, Fish and Egg

This is another item-group of food items for which the estimates for 1993/94 from the two sources vary widely. The value estimates for this item-group differ by about Rs 10,000 crore, the NSS estimate being lower than the NAS estimate by as much as 45 per cent. Table 7.7 gives the comparable NSS and NAS estimates of consumption of individual items of the item-group for 1993/94. For the meat subgroup, the table shows, the estimates from the two sources are fairly close to each other. The NAS estimate exceeds the NSS estimates by only about 400 crore, even as the NSS estimate is higher than the NAS estimate for 'goat meat and mutton'. It is seen that the NSS estimates, both in terms of value and quantity, are higher than the NAS estimates, though the combined implicit price is higher in the NAS. Thus, the gap between the two value estimates widens when the NAS value estimate is adjusted for prices.

The problem evidently is in the rest of the items of this item-group. The NSS estimate for 'chicken' is only about a fourth of that of the NAS estimate, that for eggs and egg products is only about half and

Table 7.7 Item-wise Comparison between NAS and NSS Estimates of Quantity (*000 Tonnes*) and Value (*Rs crore*) of Consumption of 'Meat, Egg and Fish' Item-group for 1993/94

Item	NSS		NAS		Difference (NSS – NAS)	NAS Adjusted by NSS Price	Adjusted Differ- ence
	Quantity	Value	Quantity	Value			
Goat meat *plus* mutton	794	4,201	703	3,803	398	3,781	420
Beef	246	503	286	633	−130	585	−82
Pork	80	208	150	546	−338	389	−182
Buffalo meat	246	302	331	643	−341	407	−104
Other meat	−	51	−		51		51
Meat: Total	−	5,265	−	5,625	−360	5,162	103
Other meat (by-product)	−		−	1,422	−1,422	1,422	−1,422
Chicken	−	994	−	4,133	−3,139	4,133	−3,139
Other birds (No.)	−	48	−	499	−450	499	−450
Eggs and egg products	−	1,146		2,487	−1,341	2,487	−1,341
Fish	−	4,437	−	7,450	−3,013	7,450	−3,013
Meat, egg and fish: Total	−	11,923		21,737	−9,814	21,153	−9,229

for fish, about 60 per cent. The subgroup 'other meat products' comprises glands, other poultry killed and other meat product in the NAS. In the NSS survey, no data is collected separately for these items. The expenditure on these items is embedded in the expenditure on meat. In the NAS, this subgroup contributes about Rs 1,422 crore and is a major factor for the discrepancy between the two sets of estimates.

Fruits and Vegetables

In terms of magnitude, the divergence between the NAS and NSS estimates of consumption expenditure is the widest for 'fruits and vegetables and their products' among all the item-groups of food consumption. Of the inter-agency difference of about Rs 91,000 crore in the estimates of consumption of all food items in 1993/94, about Rs 39,000 crore owes to the difference between the estimates for this item-group. Consistent with the observations made in the earlier studies (Minhas et al., 1988; Srinivasan et al., 1974) on the estimates for 1957/58, 1972/73 and 1977/78, the NSS estimate for this subgroup is found to be considerably lower than the corresponding NAS estimate for 1993/94.

The different classification schemes used by the two agencies render the NAS and NSS estimates of expenditure on fruits and vegetables directly non-comparable. In order to make them comparable, the item-wise estimates for 1993/94, available from both the sources, have been suitably regrouped. The items of fruits and vegetables for which separate estimates are available from the two agencies have been re-classified into comparable groups. The redefined group consists of fruits and vegetables (including their products) group, and the items potato, sweet potato and sugarcane for chewing, appearing in the classification scheme of the NAS. The NAS estimate for this group includes fruit products like pickles, sauces, jams and jellies. The estimates for these items are usually put in the 'miscellaneous food products' by the NSSO. The NSS estimates for these items have been added to its estimates of fruits (fresh), fruits (dry) and vegetables, to arrive at a comparable estimate. Further, the estimated consumption of green coconut, which is classified under 'non-alcoholic beverages' by the NSSO, has also been included in the NSS estimate, as it is included in the NAS estimate of fruit consumption. It may also be noted that, to make the NSS estimate comparable with the NAS estimate for the 'vegetable' group, which includes consumption of floriculture produce, the NSS estimate for consumption of flowers has been included in this group. The NAS estimate also includes consumption of the produce of the kitchen gardens, since kitchen gardens are used mostly for growing vegetables. Table 7.8 presents an item-by-item comparison between the estimates of quantities and values of consumption, to the extent the classification schemes adopted by the two agencies permit.

The item-specific estimates from the two sources reveal that the big difference between the estimates for this group is chiefly owed to the diverging estimates of fruit consumption. For the 'fruit' subgroup, as a whole, the NSS estimate falls far short of the NAS estimate. In sharp contrast, for the 'vegetable' group, not only is the difference between the NSS and NAS estimates smaller but also, the former is higher than the latter.

Table 7.8 Itemwise Comparison between NAS and NSS Estimates of Quantity (*000 Tonnes*) and Value (*Rs Crore*) of Consumption of 'Fruits and Vegetables and Their Products' for 1993/94

Items	NSS		NAS		Difference (NSS – NAS)	NAS Adjusted by NSS Price	Adjusted Difference
	Quantity	Value	Quantity	Value			
Potato	12,983	4,290	11,840	4,698	−408	3,907	383
Onion	5,274	2,588	3,555	2,132	456	1,746	843
Sweet potato	188	48	–	487	−439	487	−439
Other vegetables	–	13,823	–	8,044	5,779	8,044	5,779
Flowers	–	286	–	1,093	−807	1,093	−807
Kitchen garden	–		–	1,396	−1,396	1,396	−1,396
Total vegetables	–	21,035	–	17,850	3,185	16,673	4,362
Banana	–	1,720	–	4,067	−2,347	4,067	−2,347
Coconut	3,871	1,523	8,118	3,299	−1,776	3,190	−1,667
Mango	823	692	3,638	3,115	−2,423	3,060	−2,368
Grapes	195	327	482	689	−362	809	−482
Copra	108	296	–	660	−364	660	−364
Groundnut	354	609	1,892	3,232	−2,623	3,256	−2,647
Cashewnut	–	101	57	1,343	−1,242	1,343	−1,242
Other fruits	–	2,191	–	31,673	−29,482	31,673	−29,482
Total fruits (dry and fresh)	–	7,459	–	48,078	−40,619	48,057	−40,598
Total fruits and vegetables	–	28,494	–	65,928	−37,434	64,731	−36,237
Fruits and vegetable products	–	357	–	2,108	−1,751	2,108	−1,751
Fruits and vegetables and their products	–	28,851	–	68,037	−39,186	66,839	−37,988

Note: The category 'other fruits and vegetables', other than horticulture, classified in the NAS has been distributed to 'other vegetables' and 'other fruits' of the table in proportion to the value of their gross value of output. The NAS estimate for the item-group 'other fruits' includes that for the 'horticulture crops not elsewhere covered'.

Item-wise comparison within the vegetable group shows that the NSS estimate of the quantity of potato consumed, though higher, compares closely with that of the NAS, even as the implicit prices in the NAS estimates are higher than those in NSS estimates by about 20 per cent. In case of onion consumption, the NSS estimates of both quantity and value are substantially higher than those of the NAS.

For the NAS, the National Horticulture Board (NHB) is the main source for the production and price data for fruits not covered in area and production statistics of the DESAg. The NHB compiles data on area, production and productivity through the State Horticulture Boards (SHB). It has, however, been noticed that there is a sizeable divergence between the figures the SHBs supply to the DES and those to the NHB. The primary data on prices of these fruits is collected by the NHB through 33 Market Information Centres spread over the wholesale markets of the country. But the price data the NBH thus collects relate to wholesale prices rather than the prices representing the first point of sale.

There is a possibility that the reporting of fruits suffers severely from recall lapse in the HCES. Fruits consumed outside home, whether purchased or collected free, are most likely not captured in the HCES. As an evidence, one can take the example of banana, for which the production estimate used for deriving the NAS estimate is based on the data available from the regular crop reporting scheme and is thus expected to be fairly reliable. But even for this fruit crop, the NSS consumption estimate is less than half of the NAS estimate. Apprehending the possibility of non-reporting of fruit consumption, a set of probing questions, 'whether some specific fruits were consumed by any member of the household' was introduced in the schedule of enquiry of the HCES, in its 43rd Round. This was included in the HCES of the 50th Round as well. There was, however, hardly any improvement in the NSS estimate of fruit consumption, owing to the introduction of these questions. Thus, on the one hand the NAS estimate of fruit consumption appears to be on the higher side, on the other, the NSS estimate seems to suffer from underestimation.

Cooked Meals and Hotels and Restaurants

The NAS estimate for hotels and restaurants includes accommodation charges in addition to the value of food served by the hotels and restaurants. This estimate has been adjusted by netting out the estimated accommodation charges for comparison. The results of the Enterprise Survey on hotel and restaurants, 1993/94, published by the CSO (1999b) reveal that only about 9 per cent of the total receipts of hotels and restaurants were for accommodation charges and the rest largely for food served. The adjusted NAS figure in Table 7.3 represents the value of food served in hotels and restaurants. Moreover, the NAS estimate for hotels and restaurants includes not only meals served to the consumers but also a variety of other food items like tea, snacks and beverages. The NSSO, on the other hand, does not provide any estimate of consumption for this item-group as such. Instead it provides separate estimates of value of 'cooked meals', snacks, beverages, and 'other processed food' purchased by households. But, the entire value of the snacks, beverages and 'other processed food' consumed by households cannot be attributed to the restaurants. Thus the comparison between the NAS estimate for 'hotels and restaurants' and the NSS estimate of purchased 'cooked meals', is severely constrained by the difference in coverage. However, if the estimates for 'hotels and restaurants', 'non-alcoholic beverages' and 'processed/other food' are all considered together, the estimates from the two sources are found to agree fairly well.

Other Food Items

The item-groups 'salt', 'spices' and 'paan', for which the NAS estimates are based on the NSS estimates, 'tobacco', for which the estimates differ little, and those like 'beverages and intoxicants' and 'tobacco', for which the respondents are known to be reluctant in reporting consumption, are excluded from the discussion. We also refrain from discussing the divergence between the estimates for the items like 'sugar and gur', though it is rather wide, as the detailed analysis at further disaggregated level do not reveal any specific reason for the divergence.

COMPARISON OF ESTIMATES OF NON-FOOD CONSUMPTION FOR 1993/94

Private final consumption expenditure other than that on 'food, paan, tobacco and intoxicants' is referred to as 'non-food consumption' throughout the study. Services and manufactured goods, in national accounting, are further classified according to their nature and use. In the HCES, household non-food consumer goods and services, other than fuel and 'clothing and footwear' are, by convention, classified into 'durable goods' and 'miscellaneous goods and services'. Using the detailed and disaggregated item-level NAS and NSS estimates for 1993/94, the individual items have been appropriately regrouped into comparable item-groups.

Apparently, the NSS estimate for non-food consumption is only about a half of the NAS estimate (Table 7.1). But, the NAS estimate includes two important components of consumption that cannot be obtained directly from the reported consumption of the households, and are thus called 'notional' in the study. The NAS estimate of 'gross rent' includes the notional element of imputed rent of owner-occupied dwellings, and FISIM embodied in the banking services. Evidently, a valid comparison between the two sets of estimates requires adjustment of the NSS estimate for the notional elements that are not included in the NSS-based estimate of aggregate consumption.

Having adjusted the NSS estimates for the items house rent and banking services by replacing them by the NAS estimates (Table 7.9), and reclassifying accommodation charges of hotels in 'Misc. goods

Table 7.9 Comparison of NAS and NSS Estimates of Different Items of Non-food Consumption for 1993/94 Adjusted for the Notional Elements

(Rs Crore)

Item-group	Adjusted NSS	NAS	NSS – NAS	% Difference
1. Clothing and footwear	21,382	34,999	−13,617	−38.91
2. Gross (house) rent and water charges	45,476	46,854	−1,378	−2.94
3. Fuel and power	24,527	21,385	3,142	14.69
4. Furniture, furnishings, appliances and services	6,055	17,610	−11,555	−65.62
5. Medical care and health services	18,221	19,543	−1,322	−6.76
6. Transport equipment and operational cost	7,178	24,592	−17,414	−70.81
7. Transport services	8,450	36,143	−27,693	−76.62
8. Communication	1,048	4,258	−3,210	−75.39
9. Recreation, Education and Cultural services	11,811	17,626	−5,815	−32.99
10. Misc. goods and services	36,655	37,072	−417	−1.12
Total non-food	*1,80,803*	*2,60,082*	*−79,279*	*−30.48*
Total consumption expenditure	*4,04,869*	*5,74,772*	*−1,69,903*	*−29.56*

and services' of the NAS estimate, it is seen that the NSS estimate for non-food adjusted for the notional elements is less than the NAS estimate by only Rs 79,000 crore, which is 30.48 per cent of the latter. The difference between the estimates for total consumption expenditure reduces from Rs 2,19,000 crore to Rs 1,70,000 crore, i.e. from 38.10 per cent to 29.56 per cent, as a result of the adjustment.

Comparison of individual item-groups reveals that for all item-groups, except 'fuel and light', the NAS estimate is much higher than the NSS estimate. The two item-groups that account for the major part of the divergence between the NAS and the adjusted NSS estimates are 'transport services' and 'transport equipment and operational cost'. Together they account for Rs 45,000 crore out of a total difference of Rs 79,000 crore for non-food consumption, i.e. about 57 per cent of the excess of NAS estimate over the NSS estimate. The two item-groups 'clothing and footwear' and 'furniture, furnishings, appliances and services' also contribute substantial amounts of about Rs 14,000 crore and Rs 12,000 crore respectively towards the divergence between the two estimates. Apart from the item-groups for which estimates have been adjusted, or the NAS estimate is based on the NSS estimate, for most of the item-groups the estimates from the two sources differ by about 70 per cent. Only for 'clothing and footwear' and 'recreation, education and cultural services' the difference between the estimates, though still large, is not as wide – the NSS estimate is less than the NAS estimate by 39 and 33 per cent respectively.

CONCLUSION

Comparison between the item-wise estimates from the two sources help identify a multiplicity of underlying factors responsible for the wide divergence between the two sets of estimates. It also leaves differences between estimates for some of the item-groups unreconciled, thereby demarcating the relatively weak areas of the statistical system. That some items are being under-reported in the HCES, appears to be quite a conceivable possibility, though it requires to be substantiated by adequate evidences. Some errors are also possibly inherent in the NAS estimates as they depend on an assortment of direct and indirect estimates of output along with various rates and ratios, some of which are based on the results of studies carried out in the distant past.

The study reveals that the estimates of consumption expenditure on food differ by about 29 per cent, the NSS estimate being smaller than the NAS estimate. However, this divergence between the aggregate estimates of expenditure on food consumption owes principally to the divergence between the estimates for a few specific subgroups of food items. The major contributors towards the divergence between the estimates of expenditure on food are 'fruits', 'milk products', 'chicken', 'eggs' and 'fish', minor cereals and their products, 'vanaspati', oilseeds and the subgroup 'tobacco'. The other significant difference between the NAS and NSS estimates is in the subgroup 'sugar and gur'. These items together account for 27 percentage points.

What is more significant in the context of poverty studies is that the NAS and NSS estimates for the important subgroups of food items like major cereals, more commonly used pulses and edible oils, liquid milk and vegetables do not differ much. The gaps between the NSS and NAS estimates for these subgroups are so narrow that they could as well be attributed to the differences in coverage, sampling errors and those relating to differences in reference time frames.

As for the estimates of expenditure on non-food consumption, four item-groups, viz., 'transport services', 'transport equipment and operational cost', 'clothing and footwear' and 'furniture, furnishings, appliances and services', account for Rs 70,000 crore out of a total difference of Rs 79,000 crore for the non-food consumption.

Except for 'minor cereals and their products', the NAS estimates for all the food item-groups that account for a large part of the divergence, appear to suffer from some limitations. Apart from the possibility that errors are inherent in these estimates of the NAS, any shortfall in the NSS estimates for these items is not expected to affect poverty measurement seriously, since these are the items that account for only a minor part of the consumption expenditure of the vulnerable sections of the population. The same is also most likely true for the non-food item groups 'transport services' and 'transport equipment and operational cost'. The high order of divergence between the estimates from the two sources for these groups of food and non-food items, therefore, is not enough to render the NSSO data on household consumption expenditure unfit for measurement of poverty incidence.

REFERENCES

CSO (1980), *National Accounts Statistics – Sources and Methods*, April 1980.

——— (1978), *National Accounts Statistics – 1970/71 to 1975/76,* January 1978.

——— (1989), *National Accounts Statistics – Sources and Methods*, October 1989.

——— (1998), *Annual Survey of Industries, 1994/95 (Factory Sector),* Vols. II & III, February 1998.

——— (1999a), New Series on National Accounts Statistics (Base Year 1993/94), May 1999.

——— (1999b), *Report on Hotels and Other Lodging Places and Restaurants, Cafes and Other Eating and Drinking Places.* Enterprise Survey 1993/94, June 1999.

——— (1990), *National Accounts Statistics*, 1990.

——— (1992), *National Accounts Statistics*, 1992.

——— (2000), *National Accounts Statistics*, 2000.

Kansal, S.M. and M.R. Saluja (1961), 'Preliminary Estimates of Total Consumption Expenditure in India', Paper presented in the Third Indian Conference on Research in National Income, 1961.

Minhas, B.S. (1988), 'Validation of Large Scale Sample Survey Data – Case of NSS Estimates of Household Consumption Expenditure', *Sankhya*, Series B, Vol. 50, Part 3, Supplement (Chapter 6 of this book).

Minhas, B.S., S.M. Kansal, Jagdish Kumar and P.D. Joshi (1986), 'On Reliability of the Available Estimates of Private Consumption Expenditure in India', *The Journal of Income and Wealth,* Vol. 9, No. 2.

Minhas, B.S. and S.M. Kansal (1990), 'Firmness, Fluidity and Margins of Uncertainty in the National Accounts Estimates of Private Consumption Expenditure in the 1980s', *The Journal of Income and Wealth,* Vol. 12, No. 1.

Mukherjee, M. and G.S. Chatterjee (1974), 'On Validity of NSS estimates of Consumption Expenditure', in P.K. Bardhan and T.N. Srinivasan, eds., *Poverty and Income Distribution in India* (Chapter 4 of this book).

NSSO (1985), *Report on the Third Quinquennial Survey on Consumer Expenditure*, Report No. 319, June.

——— (1990), *Fourth Quinquennial Survey on Consumer Expenditure: Pattern of Consumption of Cereals, Pulses, Tobacco and Some Other Selected Items*, Report No. 374, September 1990.

——— (1993), *Design, Concepts, Definitions and Procedures: Instruction to Field Staff*, Vol. I., Fiftieth Round (July 1993 – June 1994), *Mimeo.* June 1993.

——— (1997a), *Consumption of Some Important Commodities in India*, Report No. 404, March 1997.

———— (1997b), *Use of Durable Goods by Indian Households: 1993/94*, Report No. 426, September 1997.

———— (1999), *Design, Concepts, Definitions and Procedures: Instruction to Field Staff*, Vol. I, 55th Round (July 1999 – June 2000), *Mimeo*. May 1999.

Planning Commission (1993): *Report of the Expert Group on Estimation of Proportion and Number of Poor*. July 1993.

Srinivasan, T.N., P.N. Radhakrishnan and A. Vaidyanathan (1974): 'Data on Distribution of Consumption Expenditure in India: An Evaluation', in Bardhan, P.K. and Srinivasan, T.N., eds. *Poverty and Income Distribution in India*.

Sundaram, K. and S.D. Tendulkar (2001), 'NAS-NSS Estimates of Private Consumption for Poverty Estimation – A Disaggregated Comparison for 1993/94', *Economic and Political Weekly*, Vol. XXXVI, No. 2.

8

NAS-NSS Estimates of Private Consumption for Poverty Estimation
A Further Comparative Examination

K. Sundaram and Suresh D. Tendulkar

INTRODUCTION

Concerns have recently been voiced about the use of National Sample Surveys (NSS) on Household Consumer Expenditure (HCE) as the sole data source for calculating the prevalence measure of poverty, i.e. the estimated percentage of population living below a pre-specified poverty line, or headcount ratio. These have centred on a comparison of NSS-based HCEs with estimates of Private Final Consumption Expenditure (PFCE) based on National Accounts Statistics (NAS). NSS estimates of HCE have been found to be significantly *lower* than PFCE. Also, it is alleged that the NAS-NSS gap itself has widened over the 1990s, which would affect the level of the headcount ratio as well as its trends over time. Pursuant to this, it has been suggested to resurrect an old practice for adjusting the NSS-based size distribution by a uniform scalar correction obtained by shifting the NSS distribution uniformly to the right by the ratio of per capita PFCE to per capita HCE. Though once used by the Planning Commission, this practice has been discarded on the recommendation of the Lakdawala Expert Group (GOI, 1993). Nevertheless, critics of NSS estimates of HCE now advocate its revival. Hence this further critical examination of the issue.

In an earlier paper (Sundaram and Tendulkar, 2001) we had undertaken a comparison of NAS and NSS estimates for the year 1993/94 to ascertain the appropriateness of uniform scalar correction. The exercise was based on published data disaggregated by commodity/item groups from NAS and by different fractile groups from NSS. We used two estimates for 1993/94 at current prices drawn from the NAS: one taken from the old series with a 1980/81 price base, and the other from the new series with 1993/94 price-base. These were compared with two estimates from the NSS: one with uniform reference period and another, a synthetic estimate, with mixed reference period. Two conclusions were reached.

First, those item groups that accounted for a very large proportion of the aggregate discrepancy between NAS and NSS estimates had a relatively small budget share in the consumption basket of the bottom 30 per cent of the rural and the urban populations. Contrary to this, in those item groups that together accounted for over 75 per cent of this consumption basket, the divergence between the two estimates was much smaller than the average for all of the above item groups, and, in some cases, *negative* in value. In other words, a uniform scalar correction would result in a significant *overstatement* of the consumer expenditure of the bottom 30 per cent and would, therefore, show a spuriously low level of poverty. If the discrepancy between NAS and NSS estimates has been rising, as alleged by the critics, such a correction would also show a decline in head count ratio where none existed. If there were a decline, a correction would exaggerate its magnitude.

The second and more important conclusion that we reached was that it was far from clear if NAS estimates of PFCE would be more correct and reliable than NSS-based HCE estimates.

In this chapter, we draw on a more recent, systematic, detailed and painstaking NAS-NSS comparison exercise carried out by the National Accounts Division (NAD) of the Central Statistical Organisation (CSO) and the Survey Design and Research Division (SDRD) of the National Sample Survey Organisation (GOI-NAD-SDRD 2001). Their work in turn updated an earlier joint CSO-NSSO effort carried out in the same context (see Minhas et al., 1986). We use the updated study to assess relative accuracy and reliability of the NAS and NSS. (Also see Chapter 7 in the present volume.)

The next section provides a discussion of the basic differences in coverage, estimation procedures and data bases of NAS and NSS in order to provide a general perspective on the problem being discussed. This is followed by a section on empirical comparison across various NAS-based estimates of PFCE for the year 1993/94, which emphasises the continued lack of firmness in the NAS estimates of PFCE – what Minhas and Kansal (1990) described as 'fluidity'. The chapter further draws on a detailed comparison in the NAD-SDRD study to assess weaknesses in both the data sources. The final section re-examines the advisability of adjusting the NSS estimates of HCE on the basis of NAS estimates of PFCE.

NAS-NSS DIFFERENCES IN COVERAGE, ESTIMATION METHODS AND DATABASES

It is useful for our purposes to start by outlining the major differences in coverage, estimation procedures and databases underlying consumption expenditure from National Accounts Statistics (NAS) and National Sample Surveys (NSS).

With respect to coverage, consistency with national accounting conventions requires that Private Final Consumption Expenditure (PFCE) in NAS be subject to a *wider* coverage than Household Consumer Expenditure (HCE) drawn from NSS. HCE relates to a directly observed estimate during the survey period of NSS, which is usually a year. PFCE is wider in scope than HCE in three respects. First, it includes, in addition to HCE, private final consumption expenditure of non-governmental Non-Profit Institutions Serving Households (NPISH). These include institutions that deliver religious, educational and health services. In addition, PFCE also includes two *notional* elements which are not captured by NSS through directly observed, *actual* HCE. The first element is *imputed* rents on owner-occupied dwellings. The second is described in the Indian NAS as 'Financial Intermediation Services Indirectly Measured' (FISIM). These are the price-cost margins on banking and insurance services which are deemed to be part of PFCE. Thirdly, HCE being based on a household frame, excludes by definition, houseless and institutional sections of the population, like inhabitants of orphanages, prisons and hospitals.

While estimates of notional elements are available from NAS and can be netted out, no independent estimates of consumption expenditure relating to (a) NPISH or (b) houseless and institutional populations, are available. These elements can therefore not be netted out in order to obtain an estimate comparable in coverage to HCE. It is the case that (b) is expected to be negligibly small in relation to total HCE or PFCE. Further, the GOI-NAD-SDRD (2001) also offers the judgement that as regards (a) 'there are reasons to believe that it is rather small'. Our judgement is that the share of NPISH in PFCE has actually been rising over time with the increasing role that various non-governmental organisations have come to play in the areas of education and health. However, HCE is in any case expected to be *lower* than PFCE because of the above-mentioned differences in coverage.

Turning to the estimation procedures, the basic point to note is that HCE from NSS is a *directly* observed stand-alone estimate relating to a given survey period (usually a year, as noted above) while PFCE from NAS is an *indirect*, *residual* macro-level estimate of aggregate PFCE derived from GDP estimates. Also, as noted above, it must be consistent with national accounts conventions and derived from *ex-post* national accounting identities. The residual nature of PFCE arises from its use of the commodity-flow method at the disaggregated level of a commodity or service. This method employs an *ex-post* aggregate commodity-flow balance in which economy-wide domestic production is equated to its various uses. These include, in addition to PFCE: governmental final consumption expenditure, investment, changes in stocks, intermediate uses in inter-industrial consumption and *net* exports to the rest of the world. PFCE is indirectly derived by netting out from domestic production all other elements in the *ex-post* commodity flow balance.

These differences in estimation procedures naturally lead to a discussion of differences in databases between NAS and NSS. Being *derived* from GDP the basic data underpinning PFCE in NAS are provided by estimates of the aggregate production within national geographical boundaries of all the goods and services produced in an accounting year (April-March). These are drawn from year to year, according to their availability as annual figures, from a large variety of administrative statistics with uneven quality across different sectors of production. Our subsequent discussion further elucidates this latter point. For a recent stocktaking in this respect, reference may also be made to the report of the National Statistical Commission (GOI-NSC 2001b, 346–427).

In addition, NAS has to resort to what can be described as the indirect method of estimation to account for contribution to GDP by sectors/units for which annual estimates of production are not regularly available. These relate to outputs of goods and services originating in the unorganised segments of the economy. These segments consist of a large number of small workshops and own-account household enterprises whose income-streams are irregular, uncertain and fluctuating from year to year; which are too small to keep accounts; are marked by frequent entry and exit even within an accounting year; and for which annual production estimates cannot be collected because there exists no regular machinery. In order to capture their contribution to GDP, periodical benchmark sample surveys are conducted, usually spanning a five or more years. The estimates from the benchmark survey year are extrapolated backward and forward to other years on the basis of some indicators of physical activity in the sector, which are often indirectly estimated.

In addition to weaknesses in the production data noted above, there are weak links in the commodity-flow balance estimation of elements other than PFCE, which are, however, transmitted to PFCE. In particular, data on changes in private stocks are conspicuously absent or scanty. Also, estimates of inter-industrial consumption and investment are frequently based on arbitrary or often outdated rates, ratios and norms.

Having discussed the NAS, we turn now to the NSS. In the HCE, as opposed to the PFCE, the basic unit of observation is a household defined by a common-kitchen criterion. Trained investigators elicit from each sample household information about the goods and services consumed or purchased by household members during a pre-specified recall period(s), preceding the date of interview. This recall, or reference period has been set at 30 days for most of the items purchased with low or intermediate frequency in HCE. The exception is a group of certain infrequently purchased items – clothing, footwear, durables, education and (institutional) health expenditure – for which the recall period currently stands at 365 days. As obtained from the NSS, HCE is an estimate of sample-design-consistent aggregation of sample household responses. Since the household is the primary unit of observation, NSS provides estimated size-distributions of per capita total household consumer expenditure for the rural and the urban population separately, both at the all-India level, and at the level of individual states. This makes possible the calculation of poverty measures at a considerable level of disaggregation, which is not possible on the basis of the nation-level aggregates yielded by NAS.

Notably however, previous experimentation with sample survey methods and practices have shown that HCE's from NSS are sensitive to the choice of recall period, the design and length of the questionnaire, (GOI-NSSO, 2000), the training, motivation and commitment of the field staff, the quality of supervision, and, finally, the degree of cooperation from respondent households included in the sample.

Finally, we may note that NSS estimates of HCE, although available with a fair degree of regularity, are stand-alone estimates whose periodicity and dates of release have not been fixed. In contrast, estimates of NAS have to be released every year at pre-specified dates, as they are required for the monitoring of changes in the economy and economic policy formulation of the government. However, the administrative statistics that are required for the compilation of NAS, are generally not available with the kind of regularity demanded by the pre-specified release dates of the NAS. As a result, NAS estimates undergo periodical revision with the availability of more information or more complete coverage. Consequently, in NAS there is an inescapable element of what Minhas and Kansal (1990) describe as 'fluidity' or lack of firmness. This 'fluidity' is periodically accentuated when a comprehensive exercise is undertaken to update the price-base underlying NAS – usually every ten years. This exercise seeks to improve the quality of NAS by introducing new methods of estimation, update rates and ratios used in the estimation of NAS, and sometimes incorporate information from newer data, or data sources. The manner in which this incorporates an element of 'fluidity' in NAS is illustrated here. Conversely, the estimates of HCE from NSS incorporate an element of 'finality', in the sense of not undergoing revisions after the survey is conducted and findings are released. Furthermore, there is no scope for correcting sampling and non-sampling errors, except in the following survey round.

THE CONTINUED FLUIDITY OF NAS ESTIMATES

In an earlier paper (Sundaram and Tendulkar, 2001), we had pointed out very considerable revisions in the 1993/94 NAS estimates of private final consumption expenditure (PFCE) at current prices, as reported in NAS 1998 and NAS 1999 (GOI-CSO, 1998, 1999). We find that NAS 2000 (GOI-CSO, 2000) has made *further revisions* to their estimates of PFCE for 1993/94, at 1993/94 prices. To get an idea of the extent of differences in the NAS estimates of PFCE for one year (1993/94) at current prices in three successive issues (1998, 1999 and 2000) of National Accounts Statistics, we present these estimates according to the level of detail provided in the published documents. In addition, following Minhas and Kansal (1990), we present, for each broad item-group as well as for the total PFCE, the sum of the absolute differences (i.e. ignoring signs) between the estimates for two pairs of years (NAS 1999 relative to NAS 1998 and NAS 2000 relative to NAS 1999). These are presented in columns (4) and (5) of Table 8.1.

Table 8.1 Alternative NAS Estimates of Private Final Consumption Expenditure, by Broad Items for 1993/94 at Current Prices

PFCE – Estimates

(Rs Crore)

Item of Expenditure	NAS 1998	NAS 1999	NAS 2000	NAS 1999 Minus NAS 1998	NAS 2000 Minus NAS 1999
1. **Food, beverage and tobacco**	**271,474**	**318,065**	**315,243**	**56,731***	**13,994***
Food	246,521	298,182	290,841	51,661	8,871
– Cereals and bread	74,482	82,264	80,267	7,782	(–)1,997
– Pulses	11,160	11,615	11,994	455	379
– Sugar and gur	21,389	21,815	20,162	426	(–)1,653
– Oils and oil seeds	22,342	24,144	23,204	1,802	(–)940
– Fruits and vegetables	30,993	62,338	62,570	31,345	232
– Potato and other tubers	6,088	6,145	6,205	57	60
– Milk and milk products	45,788	47,502	46,594	1,714	(–)908
– Meat, egg and fish	22,107	22,946	21,737	839	(–)1,209
– Coffee, tea and tobacco	4,596	5,787	5,852	1,191	65
– Spices	6,186	7,988	8,015	1,802	27
– Other foods	1,390	5,638	4,237	4,248	(–)1,401
Beverages, paan and intoxicants	8,144	5,929	5,951	(–)2,215	122*
– Beverages	3,692	2,875	2,947	(–)817	72
– Pan and other Intoxicants	4,452	3,054	3,004	(–)1,398	(–)50
Tobacco and its products	10,968	8,534	12,309	(–)2,434	4,475
Hotels and restaurants	5,841	5,420	6,142	(–)421	722
2. **Clothing and footwear**	**52,510**	**30,573**	**34,999**	**22,321***	**4,988***
Clothing	48,359	26,230	30,937	(–)22,129	4,707
Footwear	4,151	4,343	4,062	192	(–)281
3. **Gross rent, fuel and power**	**48,421**	**68,880**	**70,869**	**20,845***	**2,013***
Gross rent and water charges	27,601	47,483	49,484	19,882	2,001
Fuel and power	20,820	21,397	21,385	963*	(–)12
– Electricity	3,926	3,926	3,926	NIL	NIL
– LPG	1,714	1,521	1,521	(–)193	NIL
– Kerosene oil	2,906	2,906	2,906	NIL	NIL
– Other fuel	12,274	13,044	13,032	770	(–)12
4. **Furniture, furnishing appliances and services**	**14,849**	**16,940**	**17,610**	**3,411***	**1058***
Furniture, furnishing and repair	909	1,458	1,312	549	(–)146
Refrigerator, cooking, washing appliances	1,689	1,530	1,559	(–)159	29
Glassware, tableware and utensils	7,825	7,324	7,679	(–)501	355
Other goods	2,687	3,209	3,689	522	480
Services	1,739	3,419	3,371	1,680	(–)48

(Contd...)

(Contd...) (Rs Crore)

Item of Expenditure	NAS 1998	NAS 1999	NAS 2000	NAS 1999 Minus NAS 1998	NAS 2000 Minus NAS 1999
5. **Medical care and health services**	**10,984**	**19,543**	**19,543**	**8,559**	**NIL**
6. **Transport and communication**	**60,940**	**64,376**	**64,993**	**3,678***	**617**
Personal trspt. eqpt	2,391	2,284	2,294	(–)107	10
Operation of trspt. eqpt	18,794	22,290	22,298	3,496	8
Purchase of trspt. service	35,861	35,847	36,143	(–)14	296
Communication	3,894	3,955	4,258	61	303
7. **Recreation, education and cult. services**	**16,690**	**17,554**	**17,626**	**1,916***	**110***
Eqpt, paper and stationery	5,208	6,349	6,330	1,141	(–)19
Recreation and cult. services	1,639	1,113	1,204	(–)526	91
Education	9,843	10,092	10,092	249	NIL
8. **Misc. goods and services**	**23,059**	**31,308**	**36,519**	**8,249**	**5,537***
Personal care and effect	4,926	5,758	10,897	832	5,139
Personal goods n.c.c.	10,862	11,860	11,697	998	(–)163
Other misc. services	7,271	13,690	13,925	6,419	235
Total PFCE	**498,927**	**567,239**	**577,402**	**125,710***	**28,317***

Note: The values marked with * relate to the sum of absolute differences in the appropriate subgroups.

In the aggregate, the PFCE estimate for 1993/94 in NAS 1999 was higher than that published in NAS 1998 by close to 14 per cent. However, this aggregate difference is a net effect of increases for some items and decreases for others. If we aggregate the absolute differences (ignoring signs) between the two estimates, the overall difference between the two estimates is closer to 25 per cent. And of the 37 items/item groups distinguished in the published documents, the absolute difference as a percentage of the NAS 1998 estimates, was 5 per cent or more in 26 cases, and 20 per cent or more in 14 out of these 26 cases. In the case of 'other foods', the difference was more than 300 per cent (see also Sundaram and Tendulkar, 2001).

These large changes were not justified by the mere fact that NAS 1999 was reporting the NAS estimates under the New Series, using 1993/94 as the base year, while NAS 1998 was reporting the old series with a 1980/81 base. *This is because both the estimates pertain to the same year, 1993/94 and are set at 1993/94 prices – which are of course the 'current prices' for 1993/94. If price changes are ruled out, the reported changes must therefore reflect changes in the estimates of underlying quantities.*

To understand these changes, note that NAS estimates of PFCE are predominantly based on the commodity flow method. This method requires firm data on: (i) domestic production, (ii) net exports, and (iii) changes in stocks. When the last two elements are netted out, along with intermediate uses, we obtain what is available for domestic absorption. To derive, *residually*, from the portion available for domestic absorption the net quantity available for private consumption, one has to net out capital formation, and consumption by government and business. Further, in order to use appropriate valuation, the portion consumed by households from home-grown stocks needs to be distinguished from market purchases. Therefore, *the data on marketed surplus* is also needed. In the case of agriculture crops, we also require information on seeds, feed and wastage. At virtually every step of this procedure, there are significant gaps and weaknesses of database, which are papered over by the use of a number of *rates, ratios and norms of varying vintages.*

As more current data becomes available, *NAS estimates are also modified* through subsequent revisions. At the time when a new price-based NAS is introduced, a big-bang effort is made to bring as much fresh evidence as possible to bear on these estimates. Accordingly, at the time of a changeover in a series, large changes, as that between NAS 1998 and NAS 1999, are understandable. However, even with the introduction of the new series, in this case one using a 1993/94 base, the reliance on rates and ratios remains substantial (see GOI-NSC, 2001).

Less understandable is the need for a *further set of revision between NAS 1999 and NAS 2000.* The changes in many sectors are less than 5 per cent of the corresponding estimates in NAS 1999 – this is the case for 25 of the 37 item-groups. Despite this however, in the remaining 12 items/item-groups, the differences are large enough to take the NAS 1999 ratio of absolute difference-to-aggregate PFCE perilously close to the 5 per cent limit (4.99 per cent to be exact). These 12 item/item-groups are listed below, alongside the respective difference between their estimates in NAS 2000 and NAS 1999, as a percentage of NAS 1999.

Sugar and gur (7.58); meat, egg and fish (5.26); other foods (24.85); tobacco and its products (50.09); hotels and restaurants (13.32) in the food, beverages and tobacco group; clothing (17.95); footwear (6.47); furniture, furnishing and repair (10.01); other goods in furniture, furnishing appliances and services category (14.96); communications (7.66); recreations and cultural services (8.10); and personal care and *effects* (89.25). It is particularly worth noting the revisions of fifty per cent or more in tobacco and products, as well as personal care and effects. To observe changes of this magnitude in one year, is truly astonishing.

The case of *revisions in the NAS estimates of clothing is also worth highlighting.* The basic explanation given for the sharp drop in the NAS 1999 estimate relative to that given in NAS 1998, was to bring these estimates in line with the underlying GDP estimates, rather than having to use the 'independent' estimates from the Office of the Textile Commissioner (GOI-CSO, 1999b, 34). So far so good. However, *why then raise the new estimates by 18 per cent?* Tangentially, there is an interesting sidelight to this issues: Dr Bhalla, an otherwise ardent advocate of aligning the NAS and NSS estimates of private consumption expenditure, prefers to use the NAS 1998 estimates for clothing rather than the ones aligned with the GDP estimates!

The point of drawing attention to the continued fluidity of the NAS estimates is of course neither to argue that the concomitant revisions are necessarily unwarranted, nor to detract from the massive effort that goes into the preparation of a system of National Accounts. It is merely to highlight that it is problematic to use *NAS estimates as an unqualified 'touchstone' to test the validity of the NSS estimates: even with the new NAS series, the 'currentness' of the database for the NAS falls considerably short of what is required for these purposes.*

It is important to stress that by 'currentness of the database' we mean that the data in question would reflect the actual flow of goods and services during the accounting year for which the estimates are presented. Accordingly, the mere use of the 'latest' survey reports for updating benchmark values and/or for revising some of the rates and ratios used in the NAS estimates, does not render data 'current'. That a number of sample survey-based results, albeit the latest available, are nevertheless widely used in the NAS estimates – reinforces the following important point made by Professor Minhas over a decade ago: *'The national accounts data get their copious share of sampling errors, not from one but many sample surveys from which the production data base of the national accounts gets built up'* (Minhas, 1988, 14). This continues to be the case even today.

NAS-NSS COMPARISON: RESULTS FROM A RECENT CROSS-VALIDATION EXERCISE

As mentioned in the introduction, the National Accounts Division (NAD) of the CSO and the Survey Design and Research Division (SDRD) of the NSSO carried out a detailed joint study (GOI-NAD-SDRD, 2001) aimed at cross-validating private consumption expenditure available from household survey and national accounts – hereafter referred to as the NAD-SDRD study. The study presents a comparison of estimates of PFCE for 1993/94 based on NAS 2000, with estimates of household consumer expenditure based on the NSS 50th Round Consumer Expenditure Survey, carried out for the same year. This is a major and painstaking effort at rendering comparable the said estimates: close to 200 items are distinguished in the exercise. Whenever feasible, it also presents the implicit unit values from the two sources and undertakes comparisons *with and without adjustment for prices.* In general, the adjustment for prices narrows the gap. Wherever possible, the study also corrects for differences at the level of data collection and compilation in the detailed classification schemes used in NAS and NSS.

In discussing these results, we first get the notional elements in the NAS estimates out of the way that unnecessarily inflate the divergence between the two estimates. These are imputed rent and Financial Intermediation Services Indirectly Measured (FISIM), which are included in miscellaneous goods and services in the non-food group of PFCE. As per NAS 2001, these items contributed Rs 49,098 crore[1] to the Rs 2,19,001 crore difference between the two estimates, i.e. over 22 per cent of the aggregate difference. Excluding these items, the difference between the two estimates becomes Rs 1,69,903 crore. In total, the exclusion of notional estimates reduces the divergence between NSS and NAS from 38 per cent to 30 per cent of the NAS estimate. In the following subsections we discuss in detail each of the items/item-groups that are of concern to us in our comparison of NAS and NSS.

Food, Beverages and Tobacco Group

We first focus on the food, beverages and tobacco group. In the net, NAS estimates exceed NSS estimates for this group by Rs 91,177 crore, notwithstanding that there are some items, notably non-alcoholic beverages, where the NSS estimates exceed the NAS. This number is equivalent to about 54 per cent of the aggregate difference between NAS and NSS, excluding notional elements. This is also the group which accounted for 76 and 72 per cent of the expenditure of the bottom 30 per cent of the population in rural and urban India, respectively (Sundaram and Tendulkar, 2001).

Effect of Adjustments for Differences in Unit Values

In the food, beverages and tobacco group, revaluing the NAS estimates of PFCE at NSS-based unit values reduces the NAS estimate by Rs 5,835 crore. For the NSS, these values are mostly lower, with pulses and products being the major exception. Correspondingly, without any other adjustment, the excess of NAS PFCE estimate over the corresponding NSS-based estimate is also reduced by the same amount. It may be noted that this is a little over 3 per cent of the aggregate difference between the two

[1] Note that 100 crore equal 1 billion.

estimates, excluding the notional elements.[2] As a percentage of the difference in the food category, this would be equivalent to 6.4 per cent.

Assumptions about Intermediate Consumption and Private Stocks

The NAS estimates of PFCE for a number of commodities in the food, beverages and tobacco group are based on the assumption of *zero use for intermediate consumption.* The products/items affected by this assumption, as is indeed explicitly stated, are the following: *pulses and products, milk and milk products, vanaspati, chicken and eggs.* Though not stated to be the case, the same is also likely to be true for *maida* and *fish.* Also, it may be asked why vanaspati would fall in this category, but not other edible oils? It should be obvious from the commodity flow balance that understatement of intermediate consumption would, *ceteris paribus,* lead to overstatement of PFCE.

After adjusting for NSS-based unit values wherever quantities are reported, the excess of NAS PFCE estimates over the corresponding NSS-based estimates in respect of items so affected adds up to Rs 18,466 crore. This is a little over 20 per cent of the difference between the two sources for food, beverages and tobacco, taken as a group. The breakdown by items is as follows: pulses and products – Rs 764 crore; milk and milk products – Rs 10,977 crore; vanaspati – 1,790 crore; chicken and other birds – Rs 3,589 crore, and; eggs and products – Rs 1,341 crore. To this may be added the excess of NAS estimates over NSS-based estimates with respect to *maida* – Rs 1,705 crore, and fish – Rs 3,013 crore.

A further example is provided by the case of *sugar and gur,* where the price-adjusted NAS estimate exceeds the NSS-based estimate by close to Rs 10,000 crore, the NAS-assumption is that 5 per cent of the production is used for intermediate consumption. Yet, as the NAD-SDRD study puts it: '. . . it appears that *taking 5 per cent of gur and sugar production as intermediate consumption is unrealistic.*' As Professor Minhas noted in 1988, there is also in the case of sugar and gur, the additional problem of not inconsiderable *unrecorded exports* of the said items across the long and porous land border.

Of course, it cannot be anybody's argument that all of the observed differences between the NAS and the NSS-based estimates with respect to the items listed above are due simply to the assumption of zero or low use for intermediate consumption that underlies the NAS estimates. The idea is to bring out weaknesses in the underlying database. But by overstating PFCE, such assumptions are likely to have contributed substantially to the observed divergence.

Absence of Data on Privately Held Stocks

In the food group, we have the NAS estimate of PFCE on *oilseeds,* amounting to Rs 3,508 crore, compared to the NSS-based estimate of Rs 33 crore (the consumption of *groundnuts* is shown elsewhere as part of the estimates of consumption of *fruits and nuts.*) In part, the difference could flow from the underlying assumption about what part of the output is marketed. But, primarily, this flows from the assumption underlying the NAS estimates that '*the entire amount of oilseeds retained by the producers is consumed as oilseeds!*' Besides being implausible, this assumption primarily reflects the absence of information about privately held stocks.

---

[2] It is possible that the effect of the adjustment for the differences in unit values is somewhat greater than what is indicated in this text. The detailed tables in the NAD-SDRD study place the value of consumption of tapioca and its products at Rs 1,024 crore, as against the NSS-based estimate of Rs 290 crore – a difference of Rs 734 crore. It is possible that, as in the case of coarse cereals, the NAS unit values are higher (by about 16 per cent). If so, the difference would come down by a further Rs 163 crore.

Recall Period Sensitivity of NSS

There is another important issue pertaining to comparison of NSS and NAS that is relevant with respect to NSS-based estimates of household consumer expenditure on food, beverages, paan, tobacco and intoxicants. This is the fact that all the comparisons are being conducted by reference to NSS estimates on a uniform recall period of 30 days, for all items of expenditure. However, experiments with an alternative seven-day recall period in the annual, 'thin sample' rounds for 1994/95, 1995/96 and 1996/97, covering food, paan, tobacco and intoxicants, revealed that estimates of per capita expenditure on these items when reported on the basis of a shorter recall, were substantially higher than those obtained on the 30-day recall. Deaton (2001) has rightly cautioned about the possibility of 'telescoping' error being present in estimates on the 7-day recall. Accordingly, 'higher' is not necessarily better. Nevertheless, one must accept that a long recall period of 30 days with respect to these frequently purchased items which are not salient in respondents' memory could have resulted in depressing the reported per capita consumption such that it was lower than some 'true' value. Accordingly, a part of the difference that is observed between NAS and NSS-based estimates based on the 30-day reference period could be, and *is* perhaps real.

Fruits: A Weak Database in NAS

The aforementioned recall-period sensitivity would also affect the difference between NAS and NSS estimates for the consumption of vegetables and fruits. However, the detailed NAD-SDRD study shows that with respect to *vegetables,* the NSS-based estimates are *higher* by Rs 4,362 crore when adjusted for differences in unit values. In fact, this is the case even without such an adjustment. Accordingly, the overall excess of NAS-estimates over the NSS-based estimates for the group of vegetables and fruits, which is 38,000 crore, is primarily due to *divergent estimates for consumption of fruits.* These differences are sizeable in the case of *banana, coconut and mango, among fruits where the database for estimates of production are relatively firmer, and in the case of groundnuts.*[3]

But, by far the largest contributor to the NAS-NSS difference is a catch-all category of *'other fruits'.* In this respect, NAS estimates exceed NSS estimates by Rs 29,482 crore. In other words, *this single item accounts for a little over 32 per cent of the difference between the NAS and the NSS-based estimates for Food, Beverages and Tobacco as a group.*

As the NAD-SDRD study itself notes, 'while the cereal and pulses consumption is estimated to be Rs 78,000 and Rs 12,000 crore respectively in the NAS, that for 'fruits' alone is Rs 48,000 crore. Moreover, the estimated consumption of fruits alone is found to exceed the consumption of vegetables and that of 'meat, fish and eggs, taken together.' It appears that the heart of the problem lies in the underlying database for *output and prices of fruit.* For the NAS, as the NAD-SDRD study notes, 'the National Horticulture Board (NHB) is the main source for the production and price data for the fruits not covered *in area and production statistics* of the Directorate of Economics and Statistics (DES) of the Ministry of Agriculture. The NHB compiles data on area, production and productivity through the State Horticulture Board (SHB). It has however been noticed that there is a *sizeable divergence between the figures the SHBs supply to DES and those to NHB.'* In light of this, further comment on the sizeable divergence between the two estimates of consumption of fruits is superfluous.

---

[3] With respect to banana as also cashew nut, the NAS estimates *assume* 'that *none* of the two fruits are used in other industries as intermediate consumption.' And in the case of mango, only 30 per cent of the market supplies are assumed to be used for intermediate consumption.

Tobacco and Intoxicants: NAS and NSS Estimates both Equally Bad

As regards the estimates of consumption of *tobacco and products*, Professor Minhas commented over a decade ago that household surveys are poor instruments for collecting data on the consumption of products which are associated with *social stigma* or *taboo*. Consequently, it may be readily accepted that 'true' levels of consumption of these products are significantly higher than what is reported in the NSS surveys. However, without a clear understanding of how and why the relevant NAS estimate of consumption for 1993/94 jumps by nearly 50 per cent from Rs 8,534 crore in NAS 1999 to 12,309 crore in NAS 2000, the *extent* of the Rs 6,432 crore divergence between the two estimates remains a puzzle, and is less readily acceptable. Curiously, the agreement between the NAS and NSS estimates is, in fact, rather close in the case of alcoholic beverages and intoxicants – the difference being just 5.5 per cent. This is just one clear example of an instance in which both estimates are perhaps equally bad.

Cooked Meals (NSS) and Hotels and Restaurants (NAS)

Finally, a brief comment on the difference between the NSS-based estimate for purchased *cooked meals* and NAS estimate for Hotels and Restaurants. This difference is of the order of Rs 2,377 crore, equivalent to a little over 2 per cent of the aggregate difference for food, beverages and tobacco. In part at least, this is attributable to the fact that the *NAS estimate includes accommodation charge* (about 9 per cent of the receipts as per the Enterprise Survey) *as well as receipts from the sale of food and beverages other than cooked meals.*

Food, Beverages and Tobacco Group: Major Findings

It is useful to summarise the major findings about NAS-NSS differences in the estimation of expenditures on the food, beverages and tobacco group, before we turn to the differences in the case of non-food items. As noted above, the former is an important group which accounted for 54 per cent of the aggregate excess of NAS estimates over the NSS-based estimates excluding notional elements. To recap then, the major findings are as follows:

- Over 6 per cent of the NAS-NSS difference with respect to this group can be eliminated by adjusting for differences in unit values.
- 29 per cent of the difference is due to unrealistic assumptions about there being zero or low, 5 per cent use for intermediate consumption in regard to a number of items, including *maida, fish, banana and cashewnut.* The value of this difference aggregates to Rs 26,473 crore.
- 7 per cent of the divergence for the group, or about Rs 6,122 crore, is due to groundnuts and other oilseeds. This is the result of an assumption underlying the NAS estimates, namely that the entire amount retained by producer households is taken to be consumed by them as groundnuts and oil seeds. Essentially, the problem is therefore a reflection of a lack of information on privately held stocks.
- NSS estimates are higher in respect of consumption of vegetables.
- 32 per cent of the difference for all foods – over Rs 29,000 crore – is due to the category fruits, (consumption of which is larger in absolute size than the total NAS estimate for consumption of 'meat, eggs and fish'. This seems to arise largely from the weak data base underlying the production figures and prices used as inputs for NAS estimates particularly of 'other fruits'.
- NAS estimate of consumption of tobacco and products are higher than NSS estimates. The *direction* of this difference can be readily accepted, but there are questions about the total difference

of Rs 6,432 crore, because of the unexplained Rs 4,275 crore jump in the NAS estimates for the same year as between NAS 1999 and NAS 2000.

- Part of the explanation for the NAS estimate for food, paan, tobacco and intoxicants being higher, may also be traced to a possible understatement of consumer expenditure in the NSS Consumer Expenditure Surveys due to recall lapse manifesting over the 30-day reference period.

- Overall, *as much as 75 per cent of the divergence between NAS and NSS estimates with respect to all food, beverages and tobacco items may be traced to divergence of unit values, poor or infirm databases, or patently untenable assumptions about zero or very low use for intermediate consumption of some items in NAS.* The full extent, to which this is the case, is contingent on the allowance to be made for 'recall lapse' – related understatement in the NSS Surveys.

Consumption Expenditure on Non-food Items

With respect to expenditure on 'non-food' items as a group, adjustment for 'notional' element in the NAS estimates – imputed rent, banking services and insurance services – reduces the excess of NAS estimates over the NSS-based estimates, from Rs 79,000 crore to Rs 128,000 crore. Four item groups *account for over 89 per cent of the excess of NAS estimates* for the non-food items group, relative to the corresponding NSS-based estimates. These are *clothing and footwear, furniture, furnishing, appliances and services, transport equipment and operational cost, and transport services.*

Two other items, Medical Care and Health Services and Education, account for a further 9 per cent of the overall difference between NAS and NSS estimates of private consumption expenditure on all non-food items. In absolute numbers, the respective differences are Rs 1,322 crore and Rs 5,508 crore. In the case of Medical Care and Health Services, for which NAS estimates are directly carried over from the NSS, the excess of Rs 1,322 crore is seen to be due to an error arising from double-counting of employees' contributions to CGHS. With respect to education, almost all of the difference reflects the activities of the non-profit institutions that serve households.

As for expenses on fuel and power, NSS estimates exceed the NAS estimates for the group as a whole. This is also true of individual components, except charcoal and gobar gas.

The following subsections further detail the divergence between NAS and NSS estimates for these and other aforementioned items in the non-food group.

The Commodity Flow Method and Non-food Expenditure

However, before we consider the 'big ticket' items mentioned above, it is useful to recall the general method for deriving NAS estimates of private consumption of manufactured goods. As the NAD-SDRD study notes, 'the commodity-wise value of consumption of manufactured goods is derived from the estimate of value of production, by applying various ratios and norms respectively: (i) percentage share of consumables, (ii) gross distributive margin, (iii) percentage shares used for fixed capital formation and inter-industry consumption and Government Consumption.' In fact, the only firm and current database used is that pertaining to government consumption.

For registered manufacturing, the Annual Survey of Industries (ASI) provides a firm database, but since detailed results from the ASI are made available only with a fair time lag, the use of ratios from an earlier ASI are inevitably resorted to. This is the case for commodity shares of consumable items in the total output – both of product and by-products. However, this does not affect the comparison for 1993/94, as the ASI-based NAS estimates use detailed results from 1993/94 Annual Survey of Industries.

As regards the *unregistered manufacturing, product and by-product ratios to value-added have been worked out from the Enterprise Survey in Unorganised Manufacturing, 1994/95.*[4] The concomitant percentage shares of capital formation are based on norms worked out on the basis of the results of the All-India Debt and Investment Survey, 1981/82. What this means, in other words, is that there are a number of rates and ratios at work in the estimation of non-food expenditure, including one set of such numbers dating back to 1981/82!

Clothing and Footwear: Difference due to Different Recall Periods

With respect to clothing and footwear, the NSS estimates based on the 365 day reference period canvassed and reported in the 50th Round Survey, are significantly higher than estimates based on the 30-day recall period, which are the ones used in this cross validation exercise. The difference is close to Rs 8,000 crore with respect to clothing and about Rs 650 crore for footwear. Coincidentally, the difference between NSS (30-day) estimates of Rs 18,203 crore and the NAS 1999 estimate of PFCE on clothing, amounting to Rs 26,230 crore, is also about Rs 8,000 crore. The extra difference of about Rs 4,700 crore comes about precisely because of the unexplained jump in the NAS estimates between NAS 1999 and NAS 2000, with the latter serving as the comparator estimate.

Furniture Group: No Plausible Explanation for Divergence

The broad item group, Furniture, Furnishing, Appliance and Services, accounts for close to 15 per cent of the difference between NAS and NSS estimates for 'all non-food', after netting out 'notional' elements. Of this, more than half is accounted for by the subgroup 'glassware, tableware and utensils'. More than half the difference with respect to this category is in turn attributable to the item 'other metal/household utensils'. Unfortunately, there is really no satisfactory explanation for this large difference between NAS and NSS estimates with respect to these goods.

Durables: Divergence, but Not as much as Claimed by Critics

The really significant part of the story of NAS-NSS differences with respect to durables, is what does *not* contribute to this difference. With respect to the subgroup, 'Freeze, cooking, washing appliances', NSS estimates are about 20 per cent lower than the NAS estimates. Even with respect to 'Refrigerators and Air Conditioners' the difference, though higher, is well below 40 per cent. With respect to the purchase of 'Mobike, Scooter and Cycle', also found under the 'Transport Equipment and operational costs' category, the NSS estimate is lower than the NAS estimate by just about 8 per cent. With respect to wooden and steel furniture, the difference between the two estimates is also a shade below 11 per cent. In light of this, *claims of vast underestimation of private consumption of durables in the NSS Consumer Expenditure Survey, putatively by a factor of four or five, appear to be vastly exaggerated.* It needs to be noted that many of these durables are, in NAS parlance, partly capital goods. So that simple comparisons of NAS figures for their production and sale with NSS estimates of household consumption would appear to miss their dual-use nature.

NPISH and Operational Cost of Transport Equipment

The divergence between NAS and NSS estimates for *Transport Equipment and Operational Cost* accounts

---

[4] Note that the annual estimates of Gross Value Added (GVA) in unorganised manufacturing are themselves obtained by moving forward benchmark estimates for a base year by reference to some physical indicators (often based on ASI) and current-price estimates obtained by adjusting for price inflation.

for 22 per cent of the difference for 'all non-food' items. The *single largest source of divergence is found in figures for the Consumption of Petrol and Diesel, amounting to over Rs 12,000 crore.* Related Repairs and Repair Services add a further Rs 4,500 crore. Part of this is due to a measure of duplication in the calculation of repair costs in the NAS estimates. The sizeable difference between the two estimates, however, would appear to turn on the method of allocation of vehicles on the road, as belonging to the households and non-profit institutions serving the households, and on the use of the per vehicle operating cost derived from 'the allowance prescribed for computing rebate on income tax with respect to repairs and maintenance of different vehicles'. Both these issues would bear further scrutiny.

Transport Services: Dubious Ratios at Work

The final item-group for consideration is Transport Services, for which ratios play a large role in NAS estimates. In the respective NSS survey, underestimation of household expenditure with respect to Air fare and Rail fare may be conceded. As for the other modes of mechanised road transport covered in the NAS, gross passenger earnings are estimated as the product of an estimated average 'earnings per vehicle' and estimates of total number of vehicles, which are available from the Ministry of Surface Transport (MoST). As the study itself recognises, the key issues as regards this estimation are: (i) whether the MoST estimates represent the actual number of vehicles in operation, (ii) the validity of estimates of per vehicle earnings used at present, and (iii) the validity of the assumed ratios of private consumption of these services used for deriving NAS estimates of PFCE for these items. The latter ratio is given as 50 per cent for taxis and 90 per cent for autorikshaws and buses.

In the cases of railways and air transport, gross passengers earnings estimates are annually available but arbitrarily fixed ratios of 80 per cent for railways and 5 per cent for air travel for these earnings are assumed in calculating PFCE for ever year.

Non-food Expenditure: Overall Conclusion

In the overall non-food category, a fair measure of underestimation in the NSS-estimates *must be conceded, pertaining to consumption of clothing, footwear, durables and some items of personal goods – jewellery for example.* However, the validity of some of the key rates and ratios underlying the NAS estimates remain open to question – including in the case of Transport Services, the proportion of vehicles in actual operation, average earnings per vehicle, and the assumed ratios of private consumption, as discussed above. There are also other sources of divergence, including duplication in repair services and medical services; the allocation of expenses incurred by non-profit institutions serving households in the case of education; and operational costs of transport equipment; and possible overvaluation with respect to domestic services.

So how do we conclude? The key point to note in considering collectively the estimates of consumption of non-food items, is that *items affected by as yet unresolved doubts about NAS estimates contribute the lion's share of the total difference between NAS and NSS estimates.* Notably, this mirrors also our conclusion, in the earlier section regarding the causes of differences between NAS and NSS estimates for the consumption of food items.

CONCLUSION

This paper has re-examined the underlying issues that should be considered in the comparison of NAS estimates of private final consumption expenditure (PFCE) and NSS estimates of household consumer expenditure (HCE), in the light of suggestions to revive the officially discarded practice of adjusting NSS estimates by NAS estimates using uniform scalar correction.

After outlining differences in coverage, estimation procedures and databases of PFCE and HCE we illustrated the inherent and hence continued 'fluidity' of NAS-based estimates. We then discussed the results of the important cross-validation of NAS and NSS estimates undertaken jointly by the National Accounts Division (NAD) of the Central Statistical Organisation (CSO) and the Survey Design and Research Division (SDRD) of the National Sample Survey Organisation (NSSO). We presented its results in considerable detail in order to bring out the weaknesses of both NAS and NSS. Accordingly, we did not deny the presence of underestimation of HCE in NSS.

However, the basic question at hand is whether a residually estimated PFCE from NAS provides an independent and more reliable yardstick for correcting directly observed NSS-based HCE estimates for the purposes of poverty estimation. Our unambiguous conclusion is that this is not the case. We base this assessment on an empirical examination, highlighting the inherent and inescapable 'fluidity' of NAS estimates, weaknesses in their underlying database, and the fragility of the host of rates, ratios and norms used in the commodity-flow balance that underpins the residually estimated PFCE. Accordingly, the suggested pro rata adjustment of NSS on the basis of NAS was found to be based on patently implausible assumptions, and to be empirically unacceptable – as we have shown earlier (Sundaram and Tendulkar 2001, p. 124). In addition, our discussion in the present chapter found little basis for using the NAS-NSS differences at the level of distinct commodity groups to adjust the NSS estimates.

Accordingly, the basic argument for relying on NSS as the best available source for calculating poverty measures, as provided by the Expert Group (GOI, 1993, pp. 12-13) still holds true. It rests on two important considerations. First, NSS provides a valid estimate based on direct observations relating to the survey period. Second, unlike NAS, NSS avoids recourse to adjustments based on arbitrary assumptions. This is not to deny that there is scope for continuously refining and improving NSS survey design and procedures. However, as long as reasonable comparability of NSS estimates is ensured over time, NSS will enable the monitoring of *changes* in poverty over time, even though level comparability in a continuous fashion over time may be subject to difficulties (Sundaram and Tendulkar, 2002). In addition to our findings, both Ravallion (2000), as well as Deaton and Dreze (2002) independently confirm the appropriateness of continuing to use NSS as the sole source for poverty measurement.

As mentioned in the introduction, critics have also questioned the NSS on account of its comparability over time. They maintain that the extent of underestimation of HCE based on NSS has been *increasing in the 1990s*. We have not examined this issue in the present chapter because a critical assessment is already available (Sen, 2000, Section III). Using a detailed examination of NSS and NAS estimates of aggregate private consumption at current prices, covering the thirteen NSS rounds from 1972/73 to 1997, he shows that loud claims of increasing divergence between NAS and NSS are based on incorrect comparisons.

He shows that, contrary to what is claimed by critics of the NSS, the NAS-NSS discrepancy – if based on correct comparisons – was in fact wider in the 1970s and the 1980s than in the 1990s; (a) that the NAS to NSS ratios in the 1990s varied within a narrow band of 0.68 to 0.72; and (b) that the critics failed to take note of a break in the NAS series occurring due to the transition from the earlier 1980/81 price-base to a new 1993/94 price-base, and accordingly based their conclusions on incorrect comparisons. Consequently, there is no substance whatever to the hypothesis of a *growing* underestimation of HCE based on NSS.

Nearly a decade and a half ago, Minhas (1988) warned against 'mindless tinkering' with the NSS size distribution of consumer expenditure, which he saw manifested in the pro rata adjustment that the Planning Commission used to make in deriving official headcount ratios. His detailed validation exercise did not find the pro rata adjustment 'permissible either in theory or in the light of known facts'. Our earlier work, as well as this paper, also fails to find valid grounds for making NAS-based adjustments at a more detailed commodity group-level. Nevertheless, 'mindless tinkering' is reportedly being taken to a new and bizarre level, by a practice of adjusting, at the level of individual surveyed households, reported consumption of individual items, by a number of item-specific scalars that are derived from NAS that remain invariant across households. If true, this represents a conscious attempt to alter the observed-size distribution of NSS without any objective basis whatsoever. The patent absurdity of this is too obvious to warrant any serious comment.

ACKNOWLEDGEMENT

This chapter draws on a paper presented by S.D. Tendulkar at the workshop organised jointly by the Indian Planning Commission and the World Bank in New Delhi, as well as on a special lecture by K. Sundaram at the Indian Econometric Society Meeting in Chennai, January 2002.

The authors would like to thank Anjali for her efficient typing. They have benefited from comments by participants in the aforementioned New Delhi workshop and Chennai meeting, as well as seminars at Princeton University and the World Bank. In Particular, they thank Angus Deaton, Valerie Kozel, Martin Ravallion and A. Vaidyanathan.

REFERENCES

Bhalla, Surjit S. (2001), 'How to Over-Estimate Poverty: Detailed Examination of the NSS 1993 Data', Paper Presented at the International Seminar on 'Understanding Socio-Economic Changes Through National Surveys' organised by the National Sample Survey Organisation, 12-13 May, New Delhi.

Deaton, A. and J. Dreze (2002), 'Poverty and Inequality in India: A Re-examination', *Economic and Political Weekly*, 7 September, (Chapter 18 of this book).

Deaton, A. (2001), 'Survey Design and Poverty Monitoring in India', processed.

Government of India, Perspective Planning Division of the Planning Commission (1993), *Report of the Expert Group on the Estimation of Proportion and Number of Poor*, New Delhi.

Government of India, Central Statistical Organisation (1998), *National Accounts Statistics*, New Delhi.

———— (1999a), *National Accounts Statistics,* New Delhi.

———— (1999b), *New Series on National Accounts Statistics* (base year 1993-94), New Delhi, July.

———— (2000), *National Accounts Statistics*, New Delhi.

Government of India, National Accounts Division (CSO) and Survey Design and Research Division (NSSO) (2001), 'Cross-Validation Study of Estimates of Private Consumption Expenditure Available from Household Survey and National Accounts', Report of the Study Group on Non-Sampling Errors, June.

Government of India (GOI), National Sample Survey Organisation (NSSO) (2000), *Choice of Reference Period for Consumption Data*, Report Number 447, March.

GOI-NSC (2001a), Government of India, (2001) *Report of the National Statistical Commission*, New Delhi, August.

GOI-NSC (2001b), Government of India, (2001) *Report of the National Statistical Commission*, Vol. II, chapter 13, New Delhi, August.

Minhas, B.S., S.M. Kansal, Jagdish Kumar and P.D. Joshi (1986), 'On Reliability of the Available Estimates of Private Consumption Expenditure in India', (Indian) *Journal of Income and Wealth*, Vol. 9, No. 2.

Minhas, B.S. (1988), 'Validation of Large Scale Sample Survey Data: Case of NSS Estimates of Household Consumption Expenditure', *Sankhya*, Series B, Vol. 50, Part 3, Supplement (Chapter 6 of this book).

Minhas, B.S. and S.M. Kansal (1990), 'Firmness, Fluidity and Margins of Uncertainty in the national Accounts Estimates of PCE in the 1980s', *The Journal of Income and Wealth*, Volume 12, No.1.

Ravallion, M. (2000), 'Should Poverty Measures be Anchored on National Accounts?' *Economic and Political Weekly*, Vol. XXXV, Nos. 35 and 36, 26 August–2 September, pp. 3245–52.

Sen, Abhijit (2000), 'Estimates of Consumer Expenditure and its distribution: Statistical Priorities after NSS 55th Round', *Economic and Political Weekly*, Vol. XXXV, No. 51, 16–22 December, pp. 4499–4518 (Chapter 11 of this book).

Sundaram, K. and Suresh D. Tendulkar (2001), 'NAS-NSS Estimates of Private Consumption for Poverty Estimation: A Disaggregated Comparison for 1993/94', *Economic and Political Weekly*, Vol. XXXVI, No. 2, 13 January, pp. 119–29.

Sundaram, K. and Suresh D. Tendulkar (2002), 'Poverty in India Has Declined in the 1990s: A Resolution of Comparability Problems of NSS on Consumer Expenditure', Delhi School of Economics, July.

I.3 REVISIONS AND EXTENSIONS OF NSS METHODOLOGY

9

On the Feasibility of Using NSS Household Consumer Expenditure Survey Data for District-Level Poverty Estimates

N.S. Sastry

The distribution of people by Monthly Per Capita Expenditure (MPCE) classes obtained from National Sample Survey (NSS) quinquennial consumer expenditure surveys is widely used to estimate the percentage of people living below the local poverty line at the state level in India. The following paper examines the feasibility of using NSS consumer expenditure survey data to estimate corresponding district-level poverty ratios. Inter alia, this entails defining district poverty lines and then estimating the percentage of people falling below these lines, using NSS data. However, the chapter does not discuss issues raised in the definition of district-level poverty lines, *per se*.

On the basis of quinquennial NSS consumer expenditure surveys, the NSSO estimates the distribution of persons by MPCE classes both for distinct states and union territories, as well as for rural and urban sectors. This data is included in its published reports. The areas in question include the union territories of Chandigarh, Daman and Diu, and Dadra and Nagar Haveli, as well as Lakshadweep, which all comprise only one district. In this sense, district-specific distributions are therefore already available through the NSS reports.

Sometime ago, the Survey Design and Research Division (SDRD) of the NSSO undertook to determine the reliability of district-level distributions of persons by MPCE classes, derived from the NSS 55th Round conducted between July 1999 and June 2000. As usual, a stratified two-stage sampling design was adopted for this survey exercise. The sample First-Stage Units (FSUs) for rural areas were villages, or panchayat wards in the case of Kerala; the FSUs for urban areas were Urban Frame Survey (UFS) blocks; and the Ultimate Stage Units (USUs) were households. The households were selected from the corresponding frame in the FSU by the method of circular systematic sampling. Large FSUs were subdivided into hamlet groups in rural areas and sub-blocks in urban areas. These were grouped into two segments, and USUs were selected independently from each of these segments. Further details of sample design are given in the Appendix. Six thousand forty-six villages and panchayat wards in rural areas were surveyed as FSUs, along with 4,116 UFS blocks in urban areas. Twelve households from each FSU were surveyed as USUs.

SDRD estimated the relative standard errors (RSE) of average monthly per capita expenditure of households in each district, and in each MPCE class, by using subsample estimates. The degrees of freedom of these estimates depend on the number of subsample estimates available in respect to each district. A summary of these results is provided in Table 9.1. Of note, it may be seen that as many as 451 districts in the rural areas and 252 districts in the urban areas have RSEs of less than 5 per cent. The study also shows that only 10 districts in rural areas and 49 districts in urban areas have RSEs of 10 per cent or more. In rural and urban areas, an average of 13 FSUs had been surveyed in districts having RSEs of less than 5 per cent.

The average number of households surveyed per district in the MPCE class has been computed using data on the distribution of sample households by MPCE class for rural and urban areas in the different districts, or NSS regions of the country. (Data on district, or NSS region-wide sample households by MPCE class can be obtained from the author.) The results are shown in Table 9.2. In rural areas, an average of 98 households were surveyed in the maximum of 190 districts, followed by 195 households in 138 districts. In the case of urban areas, an average of 23 households were surveyed in 171 districts, followed by 63 households in 127 districts. For rural areas, treating districts as strata resulted in an increase in the number of households surveyed in the respective districts; this as compared to urban areas, where the stratum is constituted by groups of towns, based on the population within the respective NSS region.

The district-level estimates based on all the households surveyed in both rural and urban areas were obtained by adopting the following method:

Let y be the value of monthly consumer expenditure for a household and x be the corresponding household size. We may define two new variables as given below:

$$y' = I \times y$$
$$x' = I \times x$$

where $I = \begin{cases} 1 \text{ if a household belongs to the district} \\ 0, \text{ otherwise} \end{cases}$

By applying the estimation procedure of the 55th Round of the NSS to the above variables, district-level estimates were obtained.

In a few districts where central sample data is not adequate for deriving the distribution of persons by MPCE class, or for estimating the average MPCEs, relevant state and central sample data can be pooled. To pool the estimates of MPCE or distributions at district level, one has to use the information that is available about all the households surveyed by state and central agencies. Since the sample designs for both state and central samples are exactly the same, the sampling and non-sampling errors attributable to the corresponding estimates will be alike, except for the 'agency bias'. However, before pooling state and central samples, it should be ensured that divergence between state and central estimates is not significant at the district level. In case of wide variations, pooling of the estimates may not be advisable and may worsen the estimates. As a rule of thumb, pooling may be undertaken if difference between the central and state estimates at district level is within 30 per cent of pooled estimates. The other necessary conditions for obtaining pooled estimates are the following:

Table 9.1 Average RSE of MPCE (by Levels of RSE for Different MPCE Classes at District Level)

Rural

	Avg. No.	Average RSE (%) in MPCE (Rs) Class												All	No. of
RSE Class (%)	of FSUs Surveyed	000–225	225–255	255–300	300–340	340–380	380–420	420–470	470–525	525–615	615–775	775–950	≥950	Classes	Districts
(1)	(2)	(3)	(4)	(5)	(6)	(7)	(8)	(9)	(10)	(11)	(12)	(13)	(14)	(15)	(16)
0–5	12.65	1.21	0.46	0.49	0.42	0.45	0.46	0.58	0.82	1.05	1.44	1.16	2.79	1.65	451
5–10	7.62	1.90	0.60	0.67	0.70	0.58	0.75	1.02	1.30	1.27	1.80	0.47	1.56	6.75	29
10–20	6.00	1.92	0.94	0.65	0.81	0.32	0.52	0.17	1.61	1.38	0.96	0.00	1.65	14.73	8
20 and above	9.00	1.60	0.17	1.87	0.94	0.01	0.04	0.21	0.51	0.14	3.15	0.00	13.44	22.85	2

Urban

	Avg. No.	Average RSE (%) in MPCE (Rs) Class												All	No. of
RSE Class (%)	of FSUs Surveyed	000–300	300–350	350–425	425–500	500–575	575–665	665–775	775–915	915–1120	1120–1500	1500–1925	≥1925	Classes	Districts
0–5	13.03	1.55	0.51	0.72	0.55	0.52	0.5	0.54	0.49	0.72	1.00	0.85	2.93	1.912	252
5–10	6.26	1.45	0.75	0.79	0.73	0.61	0.76	0.65	0.72	0.83	1.06	0.96	3.15	7.06	80
10–20	3.76	1.08	0.71	0.61	0.86	0.7	0.87	0.97	0.79	1.452	1.69	1.43	4.93	13.62	42
20 and above	12.43	0.87	0.84	0.88	0.81	0.71	0.59	0.31	0.1	1.1	0.76	0.62	49.14	27.51	7

Table 9.2 Average Number of Households Surveyed per District by MPCE Class

Rural

No. of Sample Households	Average Number of Households Surveyed per District in MPCE (Rs) Class												All Classes	No. of Districts
	000–225	225–255	255–300	300–340	340–380	380–420	420–470	470–525	525–615	615–775	775–950	≥950		
(1)	(2)	(3)	(4)	(5)	(6)	(7)	(8)	(9)	(10)	(11)	(12)	(13)	(14)	(15)
0–36	1	1	1	2	2	2	2	2	3	4	3	4	26	35
37–95	3	2	4	4	5	5	5	6	9	10	7	11	72	59
96–108	4	4	8	8	8	8	9	10	11	12	7	9	98	190
109–189	4	4	9	9	10	10	13	13	17	22	13	24	147	41
190–216	7	7	15	17	17	17	19	18	22	25	14	18	195	138
217–276	3	3	7	8	14	15	19	23	34	48	32	47	252	10
277–300	11	10	23	24	25	26	28	28	35	36	19	27	292	13
301–468	12	13	29	30	33	36	41	37	46	42	23	35	376	20
468 and above	14	16	39	49	86	83	105	101	103	117	46	57	816	1

Urban

No. of Sample Households	Average Number of Households Surveyed per District												All Classes	No. of Districts
	000–300	300–350	350–425	425–500	500–575	575–665	665–775	775–915	915–1120	1120–1500	1500–1925	≥1925		
(1)	(2)	(3)	(4)	(5)	(6)	(7)	(8)	(9)	(10)	(11)	(12)	(13)	(14)	(15)
0–36	1	1	2	2	2	2	2	2	2	2	1	1	23	171
37–95	3	3	6	6	6	6	6	6	6	6	4	4	63	127
96–108	5	5	9	10	8	10	10	11	10	12	6	6	101	33
109–189	6	6	11	13	13	13	14	14	15	16	10	9	141	61
190–216	7	6	11	13	13	19	19	24	24	30	17	19	202	14
217–276	8	9	19	22	23	24	25	25	26	33	20	18	252	21
277–300	6	8	14	19	22	26	37	37	40	48	22	17	294	4
301–468	5	5	16	24	27	34	41	42	51	63	37	36	383	15
468 and above	7	8	27	37	47	61	74	91	117	153	94	120	836	12

- Data entry layout for both state and central samples should be identical, or at least compatible.
- Estimates should be generated at the district level. If any district is composed of more than one stratum, estimates are to be generated first at the stratum level and then at the district level by combining the stratum estimates.

Notably, the results of the SDRD study need to be confirmed by undertaking a similar exercise using 50th Round data for the year 1993/94. If the RSEs of the district-level average MPCEs are below 5 per cent (as is the case of a large number of districts in the 50th Round) and these districts are part of the same set of districts evincing a lower than 5 per cent RSE in 55th Round, it may be feasible to derive valid distributions for these districts spanning the years 1993/94 and 1999/2000. However, it may be useful to undertake separate studies for expenditure on food and non-food items, using data from both 50th and 55th Rounds. Also, wherever central sample data is not adequate for deriving district-level estimates, it is necessary to examine the desirability of pooling state sample data.

Encouragingly, since household-level data sets are now being made available by the NSSO under the aegis of the government's data dissemination policy, any institution – including international agencies, central and state government organisations, and research centres – could now embark on such feasibility studies and use the aforementioned data sets for deriving district-level poverty estimates. Such exercises have the potential of providing useful insights into the changes in poverty that have taken place at district level between 1993/94 and 1999/2000.

ACKNOWLEDGEMENT

Reprinted from *Economic and Political Weekly*, Vol. 37, 25–31 January 2003.

Appendix

SAMPLE DESIGN ADOPTED IN NSS 55TH ROUND SURVEY ON CONSUMER EXPENDITURE

General

A stratified sampling design has been adopted for selection of the sample first-stage units (FSUs). The FSUs are villages (panchayat wards for Kerala) for rural areas, and Urban Frame Survey (UFS) blocks for urban areas. The ultimate stage units (USUs) are households, which are selected by the method of circular systematic sampling from the corresponding frame in the FSU. Large FSUs are subdivided into hamlet-groups (rural)/sub-blocks (urban), that are grouped into two segments, and USUs are selected independently from each of these segments.

Sampling Frame for First Stage Units

A list of villages (panchayat wards for Kerala) as per the 1991 Census and the latest lists of UFS blocks are respectively used for selection of rural and urban sample FSUs. For selection of sample villages from Jammu and Kashmir, the list of villages as per the 1981 Census has been used as the sampling frame. It may be mentioned that all the uninhabited villages of the country as per the 1991 Census, interior villages of Nagaland situated beyond 5 km of a bus route, and inaccessible villages of Andaman and Nicobar Islands, are left out of the survey coverage of the NSS 55th Round.

Stratification

Rural

Two special strata are formed at the *state/UT-level*, viz.

    Stratum 1: all FSUs with population between 1 and 100, and
    Stratum 2: FSUs with population more than 15,000.

    The above two strata are spread across a given state and are not confined to any particular administrative division within the state.

    Above strata of either type are formed if at least 50 such FSUs are there in the respective frames. Otherwise, they are merged with the general strata.

    While forming general strata (consisting of FSUs other than those covered under strata 1 and 2), efforts have been made to treat each district as a separate stratum. If limitation of sample size does not allow forming so many strata, smaller districts within a particular NSS region are merged to form a stratum. As usual, each district with rural population of 2 million or more as per the 1991 Census (1.8 millions or more as per the 1981 Census in case of Jammu & Kashmir) is split into a number of strata.

Urban

Strata are formed within NSS regions as follows:

Stratum Number	Composition of Strata by Considering Population of Various Towns as per the 1991 Census
1, 3, 5 *	'Hospital area' (HA)/'industrial area' (IA)/'bazaar area' (BA) blocks taken together of each single city with a population of 10 lakh or more (there could be a maximum of three such cities within an NSS Region)
2, 4, 6 *	Other blocks of each single city with a population of 10 lakh or more
7	HA, IA, or BA blocks of all towns with population between 50,000 and less than 10 lakh
8	Other blocks of all towns with population between 50,000 and less than 10 lakh
9	HA, IA, or BA blocks of all towns with population less than 50,000
10	Other blocks of all towns with population less than 50,000

* Stratum numbers 3, 4, 5, and 6 remain void if there is only one city in an NSS region with a population of 10 lakh or more.

If limitation of sample size does not allow forming so many strata, all blocks of stratum 7 are merged with those of stratum 8 and all blocks of stratum 9 are merged with those of stratum 10.

Sample Size

A total of 10,384 FSUs were selected for survey in the *central sample* at the all-India level (rural and urban combined) in the 55th Round. For *state samples*, there is a matching sample size as per the usual matching pattern being followed over the last few rounds. The sample size for the whole round for each state/UT and sector (i.e. rural/urban) is allocated equally among the four sub-rounds. Sample FSUs for each sub-round are selected afresh in the form of two independent subsamples.

Allocation of FSUs

The State/UT-level rural sample size is allocated among the rural strata in proportion to population. The State/UT-level urban sample size is first allocated among the three classes of towns (i.e. 10 lakh +, 50000 to less than 10 lakh and less than 50,000) in proportion to population. Then sample allocation for each of the three classes of towns, within an NSS region, is further allocated between two strata types consisting of: (i) HA/IA/BA blocks, and (ii) the rest, in proportion to total number of FSUs in the respective frames with double weightage given to the first category of blocks. Stratum-level allocations for both rural and urban areas of a sub-round are made in even numbers in order to facilitate selection of FSUs in the form of two independent subsamples. Subsample numbers are 1 and 2 for sub-round 1; 3 and 4 for sub-round 2; 5 and 6 for sub-round 3, and 7 and 8 for sub-round 4.

Selection of FSUs

For each sub-round, sample FSUs from each stratum are selected in the form of two independent sub-samples by following circular systematic sampling with: (a) probability proportional to population for all rural strata other than stratum 1, and (b) equal probability for rural stratum 1 as well as all urban strata.

Formation of Hamlet-groups in Large Villages and Number of Hamlet-groups Selected for Survey

Depending upon the values of approximate present population (P) and approximate total number of non-agricultural enterprises (E), decision is taken to divide the FSU into a fixed number of hamlet-groups (hgs – the term applicable for rural samples)/sub-blocks (sbs – the term applicable for urban samples) as per the rules given below:

Value of P	No. of hgs/sbs Formed in the FSU as per Population Criterion	Value of E	No. of hgs/sbs Formed in the FSU as per Enterprise Criterion
(1)	(2)	(3)	(4)
Less than 1200	1 @	Less than 100	1 @
1200 – 1999	5	100 – 249	5
2000 – 2399	6	250 – 299	6
2400 – 2799	7	300 – 349	7
2800 – 3199	8	350 – 399	8
(and so on)		(and so on)	

@ No. of hbs/sbs = '1' means the whole FSU is considered for listing.

(For rural areas of Himachal Pradesh, Sikkim, and the Poonch, Rajouri, Udhampur and Doda districts of Jammu & Kashmir, number of hgs formed in the village as per population criterion is: 1 for P < 600, 5 for P = 600 to 999, 6 for P = 1000 to 1199, 7 for P = 1200 to 1399, 8 for P = 1400 to 1599, and so on.)

The number (D) of hgs/sbs formed in the FSU is such that the higher of the two values, as per population and enterprise criteria, is chosen. If value of P is less than 1200 (600 for certain hilly areas specified above) as well as value of E is less than 100 for an FSU, hg/sb formation is not resorted to and the whole FSU is considered for listing. In case hgs/sbs are formed in the sample FSU, the same is done by equalising the population in each hg/sb.

Formation of Segments within FSU

The hg/sb having maximum concentration of non-agricultural enterprises is selected with probability equal to one for listing of households/enterprises. This hg/sb is referred to as segment 1. From the remaining (D-1) hgs/sbs of the FSU, two more are selected using circular systematic sampling and these two selected hgs/sbs together are referred to as segment 2 for doing a combined listing of households/enterprises. Thus listing of households/enterprises is done only in segments 1 and 2 of the FSU. If it is not necessary to break the FSU into segments, then the whole FSU is treated as segment 1.

Stratification of Households

All the households listed in a segment (both rural and urban) are stratified into two *second stage strata*, viz., 'affluent households' (forming second stage stratum 1) and *the rest* (forming second stage stratum 2). In rural sector, a household is classified as 'affluent' if the household owns certain items like four-wheeler, colour TV, telephone, etc., or owns land/livestock in excess of certain limits. In the urban sector, the households having MPCE (monthly per capita consumer expenditure) greater than a certain limit for a given town/city are treated as 'affluent' households, and are included in the frame of second-stage stratum 1. The rest of the urban households are included in the frame of second-stage stratum 2.

Number of Households/Enterprises Selected for Survey

The number of households/enterprises selected for survey from each FSU in general, is given below:

Segment	Number of Households Allotted for Consumer Expenditure Schedule		
	Second Stage Stratum		
	1	2	Total
(1)	(2)	(3)	(4)
FSU with hg/sb formation:			
1	1	3	4
2	1	7	8
FSU with no hg/sb formation:			
1	2	10	12

10

Results of a Pilot Survey on Suitability of Different Reference Periods for Measuring Household Consumption

NSSO Expert Group on Non-sampling Errors[1]

INTRODUCTION AND BACKGROUND

The following chapter is a report on the results of an NSSO (National Sample Survey Organisation) pilot survey set up primarily to ascertain the most suitable reference period for collecting data on certain key items of household consumption. The periods evaluated were 'last month', 'last week', and 'yesterday'. The survey was conducted in January–June 2000 in five Indian states, as well the country's four big cities, under the guidance of an expert group set up by the government's Department of Statistics and Programme Implementation. It is the latest in a series of exercises conducted over the late 1980s and 1990s to evaluate appropriate reference periods for collecting various household consumption expenditure data. This survey was motivated in part by results from these experiments, showing considerable divergence between reported expenditure based on different reference periods. Meanwhile, concern about the reliability of NSS consumer expenditure data has been fuelled by reports of a growing divergence between NSS household consumer expenditure estimates, and those based on Indian National Account Statistics.

Sample surveys on household consumption expenditure have been carried out in many rounds of the NSS since its inception in 1950. During this time, much attention has been paid to the choice of appropriate reference periods for collecting household consumption expenditure data through the interview method. In the quinquennial surveys conducted during 1972/73 (27th Round), 1977/78 (32nd Round), 1983 (38th Round), 1987/88 (43rd Round), and 1993/94 (50th Round), the reference period used was 'last month', or 'last 30 days' for all items of the budget. From round 32 onwards, a reference period of 'last 365 days' was also used for some item-groups, in order to eliminate the effects of seasonal and other transitory factors. In rounds 32, 38, and 43, these item-groups were clothing, footwear, and durable goods. Education and medical expenses were added to this list in round 50.[2] However, only data relating

[1] Under the direction of Nikhilesh Bhattacharya.
[2] The interviews of sample households were evenly staggered over the survey period of one year.

to the reference period 'last 30 days' was used for obtaining the main estimates, and for measuring the incidence of absolute poverty in India (Report of the Expert Group of the Planning Commission, 1993). The choice of the 'last month' reference period was based on experience from the early NSS rounds, especially the 4th and 5th Rounds (1952/53), as well as some field tests carried out by Mahalanobis and Sen (1954) in rural areas of West Bengal.[3]

However, doubts were being expressed from time to time about the suitability of the 'last month' reference period. Accordingly, in 1986/87, a pilot survey was conducted by the NSSO in the rural and urban areas of five states, in order to examine, among other things, the quality of data collected by alternate interview methods – one using 'last month' as a reference period, and the other using 'last week'. This data was compared with data collected through daily visits to sample households spanning three or four consecutive days and incorporating, if possible, the weighing of household stocks of cereals and pulses in order to create a record of consumption. Unfortunately, because of processing problems, no results from this pilot study have yet been made available.

In the meantime, at the instigation of Professor Pravin Visaria, the late chairman of the NSSO's governing council, comparative studies of canvassing using 'last week' and 'last month' reference periods were carried out through the annual, thin sample enquiries of consumer expenditure conducted through NSS rounds 51 through 54, from July 1994 to June 1998. In each of these rounds, two types of schedules were canvassed in two half-samples drawn from the total sample of households. In schedule type 1, the reference period was 'last 30 days' for all items of the budget, but in schedule type 2, the reference period was 'last 7 days' for food, paan, tobacco, and intoxicants; 'last 30 days' for fuel and light, miscellaneous goods and services, and medical (non-institutional); and 'last 365 days' for clothing, footwear, durable goods, education, and medical (institutional). The major finding of this exercise was that week-based estimates were on average about 30 per cent higher than month-based estimates for the items of food, paan, tobacco, and intoxicants (Government of India, NSSO, 2000).

Subsequently, in the NSS quinquennial 55th Round conducted in 1998/99, two different reference periods of 'last 7 days' and 'last 30 days' were employed in the collection of data on consumption of food, paan, tobacco, and intoxicants, for every sample household. For the other items of the budget, the reference periods were the same as in schedule type 2 of rounds 51 through 54. However, the use of two reference periods for collecting information from the same sample households considerably narrowed the earlier observed differences between the week-based and month-based estimates for food, paan, tobacco, and intoxicants, thus, raising serious questions about the inter-temporal comparability between the two sets of estimates.

Meanwhile, more sources for potential concern over the reliability of NSS estimates have arisen. Historically, studies by Mukherjee and others (1974, 1981) and by Minhas and others (1986,1988, 1989), had shown reasonable agreement between NSS-based estimates of aggregate household consumption expenditure, and NAS estimates of private consumption expenditure up to the year 1977/78 (NSS 32nd Round). However, in later years, the NSS-based figures appeared to have fallen way below the corresponding NAS-based figures. All the above developments carry important implications for measurement of inter-temporal changes in poverty and the level of living in the country.

It is against this background that Professor Visaria and the governing council of NSSO initiated the pilot survey that is the subject of this paper. As noted earlier it was conducted during January-June 2000 in five Indian states, including the metropolitan areas of Delhi, Mumbai, Chennai, and Kolkata. The field-

[3] See, Appendix A for details of these early studies.

work was done by the Field Operations Division of the NSSO and the data processing mainly by the Data Processing Centre of the NSSO's Data Processing Division in Bangalore. The NSSO's Survey Design and Research Division in Kolkata undertook the planning and designing of schedules and tabulations, as well as reporting of results. This paper discusses this work as follows: The section that follow outlines the survey's design, and give a brief report on the fieldwork, stressing a discussion of the extent of cooperation received from sample households. The main findings of the survey, including the key tables, are presented subsequently. The report concludes with some discussion on related issues. Appendix A contains a note on some early studies on reference periods and Appendix B displays some detailed tables based on the pilot survey data.

DESIGN OF THE PILOT SURVEY

The main objective of the pilot survey was to collect data on household consumption with three different reference periods – 'last month', 'last week', and 'day (or yesterday)' – for items of food, paan, tobacco, and intoxicants, with a view to ascertaining the most suitable reference period in each instance.

The survey was carried out between 2 January and 9 July 2000 in the states of Haryana, Orissa, Maharashtra, Tamil Nadu, and Uttar Pradesh. In each of these states, both rural and urban areas were covered. However, owing to resource constraints, the survey was conducted in only one or two NSS regions in each state, selected on the basis of region-wise poverty estimates furnished by Dubey and Gangopadhyay (1998).[4] The study's coverage of the urban sector was also extended to include Kolkata and Delhi, in addition to the cities of Mumbai and Chennai, which were included in the survey by virtue of being located in to the states of Maharashtra and Tamil Nadu, respectively. This was done with the intention of comparing results for India's four big cities, with those for other urban areas, designated respectively as 'metro urban' and 'non-metro urban'.

The state-regions selected for this pilot survey are listed below, along with their codes, as used in Tables A8 and A9 of Appendix B.[5]

Code	State: Region	Number of Sample Households		
		Schedule 1.0(M)	Schedule 1.0(W)	Schedule 1.0(D)
082	Haryana: Western	96	96	192
311	Delhi (only metropolis)	48	48	96
253	Uttar Pradesh: Central	144	144	288
254	Uttar Pradesh: Eastern	144	144	288
145	Maharashtra: Inland Eastern	96	96	192
141	Mumbai (only metropolis)	48	48	96
192	Orissa: Southern	96	96	192
263	Kolkata (only metropolis)	48	48	96
234	Tamil Nadu: Inland	96	96	192
231	Chennai (only metropolis)	48	48	96

[4] The region-wise head-count ratios of poverty during 1993/94 based on the official poverty line (OPL) varied from 22 to 74 per cent across the rural regions, and from 2 to 41 per cent for the urban regions chosen for the pilot survey.

[5] Note that these codes have recently been changed.

A two-stage stratified sampling design was adopted in the survey, taking 1991 census villages as FSUs in the rural sector, and UFS blocks in the urban sector. Households were the second stage units in both sectors.

In the rural sector, the entire rural area of each NSS region was treated as a separate stratum. In the urban sector, each of the four big cities constituted a stratum by itself, while the remaining urban areas of each region formed a stratum.

The sample FSUs from each stratum were selected in the form of two independent subsamples of equal size, by CSS: (a) with Probability Proportional to Size (PPS) (size being measured by population) in the rural sector, and (b) with equal probability in the urban sector. FSUs in the frame of any rural stratum were arranged as in the 1991 census. Following usual procedures, a large village (or block) was subdivided into a suitable number of hamlet-groups (or sub-blocks) having equal population content, with one of them being selected at random for the survey. The total number of FSUs in the sample was as follows: rural areas consisted of 96 villages; metropolitan urban areas, i.e. the four big cities, consisted of 48 blocks; and other urban areas consisted of 72 blocks.

All households in a sample village/hamlet-group in the rural sector were listed and then arranged by their means of livelihood code and the amount of land they possessed, as ascertained at the time of listing. In the urban sector, all households in a sample block/sub-block were listed and then arranged by monthly per capita expenditure (MPCE), as ascertained at the time of listing. In each sample village/block, 16 households comprising four groups, each consisting of four consecutive households in the arrangement, were selected for the survey. Each group of four consecutive households was selected for canvassing using four different schedules, which are explained below – one each for Schedule 1.0(M), Schedule 1.0(W), Schedule 1.0(D3), and Schedule 1.0(D4). In both sectors, the first household of each group was selected by a slight modification of linear systematic sampling, following which Schedule 1.0(M) was canvassed for that household. The three following households of the group were canvassed for Schedule 1.0(W), Schedule 1.0(D3), and Schedule 1.0(D4), respectively. The following indicates the scope and content of each of these schedules.

Schedule 1.0(M). This was similar to the NSS 55th Round schedule for collecting consumer expenditure data through an interview method using the reference period 'last 30 days' for food, paan, tobacco, and intoxicants, fuel and light, miscellaneous goods and services – including medical (non-institutional). However, the reference period was 'last 365 days' for the five remaining items groups, namely, clothing, footwear, durables, education, and medical (institutional).

Schedule 1.0(W). This was similar to the NSS 55th Round schedule for collecting consumer expenditure data through an interview method employing 'last 7 days' as the reference period for food, paan, tobacco, and intoxicants. For the rest of the items, the reference periods were the same as in Schedule 1.0(M).

Schedule 1.0(D3)/Schedule 1.0(D4). These were consumer expenditure schedules using 'yesterday' as reference period for collecting data on food, paan, tobacco, and intoxicants only. This was done by visiting the respective household on three consecutive days in the case of Schedule 1.0(D3), or on four consecutive days for Schedule 1.0(D4). It was hoped that data collected in this fashion should to a large extent be free from memory errors. For households canvassed for Schedule 1.0(D3 or D4), the interview method was followed, but special efforts were made to collect accurate data through daily interviews and by measurement of key items, as far as possible. First, each household was supplied with a notebook and dot pen and requested to keep a record of consumption of each spending member of the household. More important, each household was supplied with two transparent graduated containers with volume markers, one measuring 500 ml and the other 100 ml, and were urged to measure cereals and cereal products, pulses and pulse products, and liquid milk consumed each day using these containers, instead of their own containers.[6] With a view to obtaining accurate figures on the amount of salt consumed, each household was requested to consume from one or more 0.5 kg packets supplied to them. The quantity of salt left unused at the end of the three-four days was then weighed, in order to estimate the quantity of salt consumed over the said period. A 'day' was taken to mean a period bounded by consecutive midnights.

Schedules 1.0(D3/D4) were designed to record consumption only of food, paan, tobacco, and intoxicants and to obtain such data as accurately as possible, because as noted earlier, the focus of the pilot survey was to establish what were the appropriate reference periods for these specific items. Schedules 1.0(M)/1.0(W), however, used the conventional schedules and included all items of the budget. This was done to confirm that the conditions obtaining during which simultaneous NSS enquiries through Schedules 1.0(D3/D4), were normal.

In the daily schedules, Schedules 1.0(D3/D4), there were columns for recording the volume of consumption (in ml), for each item of cereals and pulses and their products and for liquid milk, using one or the other of the containers supplied by NSSO staff. The measurements were to be taken after shaking the container, levelling the contents and slightly pressing the contents, if necessary. Conversion factors were then used to convert these volumes into quantity figures in standard unit (kg). These conversion factors were estimated by NSSO field staff for each separate item and for each NSSO FOD region under study. In those cases where the quantity of consumption could be reported in standard units by the respondent, this quantity was entered in the schedule under a column earmarked for this purpose.

Notably, for several items in Schedules 1.0(D3/D4), such as spices, the quantity/volume of consumption tended to be small for any particular day, and fieldworkers were asked to enter on the last day the total quantity/volume of consumption for the entire three or four-day period.

The number of sample households per FSU (village/block) was four for each of Schedules 1.0(M), 1.0(W), 1.0(D3), and 1.0(D4). Thus, the total number of sample households allotted for the pilot survey was 864 for each of the four schedules. The corresponding total number of daily schedules would be 2,592 for Schedule 1.0(D3) and 3,456 for Schedule 1.0(D4).

During each month of the six-month period, interviews and measurements for schedules with different reference periods were evenly distributed across the days of the week and the weeks of the month, in order to ensure that results based on Schedule 1.0(W) or on Schedule 1.0(D3/D4) were meaningful and comparable with results based on Schedule 1.0(M). A detailed programme for allocation among the four schedules were laid down in the instructions and was generally followed by the field staff. This procedure was replicated as far as possible for each state, sector, and stratum.[7]

Tables A3 to A7 in Appendix B depict the quality of the match among the three samples of households canvassed for the three reference periods. Due to space constraints, the results are presented for all

---

[6] The conversion factors from ml to kg were determined by the field workers for different items and separately for each NSS region.

[7] Tables A1 and A2 in Appendix B show the distribution of sample households canvassed for each type of schedule over the different months, and over different weeks of the month.

states and regions combined, though separately for the three sectors. It may be seen that the three samples of households agreed fairly well in respect of average household size and also in respect of their distributions over categories, by household type, i.e. broad household occupation, by religion, by social group and, in the rural sector, by size of land holding.

A BRIEF REPORT ON FIELDWORK

At the outset, investigators explained the objectives of the pilot survey to all their respondents, especially those chosen for Schedules 1.0(D3/D4), and appealed for their cooperation. There were few casualties for the four schedules. The number of households actually canvassed is shown below, listed by sectors and type of schedule:

Sector	Number of Households Canvassed by Type of Schedule*		
	Schedule 1.0(M)	Schedule 1.0(W)	Schedule 1.0(D3/D4)
Rural	384 (384)	383 (384)	768 (768)
Non-metro	288 (288)	288 (288)	574 (576)
Metro	188 (192)	187 (192)	384 (384)
Total	860 (864)	858 (864)	1,726 (1,728)

Note: * Number of households allotted for the survey are shown within brackets.

The fieldwork experience was satisfactory overall, though some problems were noted. Generally, relatively affluent households were less cooperative than poorer households and found the use of containers too time-consuming. Furthermore, the less educated informants could not record the details in the diary very well. Also, in regards to salt, some households did not accept salt as they were not accustomed to the use of the powdered variety supplied by the NSSO. Accordingly, no information on salt consumption could be collected for a small percentage of households canvassed for Schedule 1.0(D3/D4). However, some of them were able to provide reliable data because the opening stock of salt used by them, and the balance left on the last day could be measured. Some households also did not like daily visits for three or four consecutive days and it was noted in the context of both Schedules 1.0(M) and 1.0(W) that many informants looked tired and reluctant towards the end of the interview. According to entries made by the investigators in their schedules, the average times, in minutes, required for canvassing the different types of schedules were as follows:

Sector	Schedule 1.0(M)	Schedule 1.0(W)	Schedule 1.0(D3/D4)
Rural sector	182	175	125 (per day)
Non-metro urban	179	173	117 (per day)
Metro urban	177	170	90 (per day)

Clearly, the 'day' schedules were canvassed with maximum care. Nevertheless, there was some variation across NSS regions in the average time taken to canvass the schedules. This could be attributed to factors like the literacy level of the informants, the income/consumption level of the households, the extent of cooperation of respondents and the number of visits needed to canvass the schedule in different regions.

For some items, like pulses, the quantities consumed per day were small, which means that measurement with a container could involve large errors, in relative terms. For liquid milk, the poorer households consumed very small quantities and did not use the container.

Tables 10.1 to 10.3 present some information on the extent of cooperation received from households responding to Schedules 1.0(D3/D4). As stated earlier, all the 1,728 sample households, excepting only two, were canvassed.

Table 10.1 shows that out of 1,728 sample households selected for collection of data through the daily Schedule 1.0 (D3/D4), as many as 1,544 – i.e. about 89 per cent – accepted the packet(s) of salt supplied to them by NSSO field workers in the interest of collecting accurate data on consumption of this commodity. At about 95 per cent, this acceptance rate was higher for rural households, but appreciably lower for the four big cities, where it was only around 76 per cent. For other urban areas, the corresponding percentage was roughly the same as the overall figure of about 90.

Table 10.2 presents the frequencies with which the two containers supplied by NSSO staff were actually used by those sample households selected under Schedule 1.0(D3/D4) for measuring consumption of different items. Only the major items are shown in the table. (Similar figures for the detailed items are presented in Table A8 of Appendix B.) Note that the specified counts refer to the number of daily schedules, and not to the number of households.

It appears that for most of the important items, the households cooperated to a great extent, and 80–90 per cent of them reported that they had used the containers wholly for their measurements. However, there are exceptions to this general pattern, of which liquid milk is the most notable. About 45–50 per cent of households in rural and non-metro sectors, and only about 13 per cent of metro households, had used the containers wholly in the measurement of liquid milk. These low percentages can be explained by the fact that many households had obtained their milk supply from external sources and depended on the volume measurements made at that stage.

A closer examination also shows inter-sectoral differences in the extent to which households used containers for measurement. On the whole, rural households reported that the containers had been wholly used in a much higher proportion of cases than did their counterparts in the metro urban sector. Households in non-metro urban population occupied an intermediate position in this respect.

In addition, there were variations in the extent to which households selected for Schedules 1.0(D3/D4) had complied with the request by NSSO staff to record daily consumption in a diary supplied to them. Table 10.3 illustrates this. It appears that roughly half of the sample households in rural and non-metro sectors had used the diary quite often, whereas in this matter, households in the metro

Table 10.1 No. of Sample Households Accepting Salt Supplied by NSSO Field Staff

| Sector | Households for Schedule 1.0(D3) | | Households for Schedule 1.0(D4) | | Percentage of Households Accepting Salt | |
	Total No. in Sample	No. Accepting Salt	Total No. in Sample	No. Accepting Salt	Schedule 1.0(D3)	Schedule 1.0(D4)
(1)	(2)	(3)	(4)	(5)	(6)	(7)
Rural	384	362	384	365	94	95
Non-metro	288	266	288	261	92	90
Metro	192	145	192	145	76	76
All	864	773	864	771	89	89

Table 10.2 Percentage of Daily Schedules in Schedule 1.0(D3/D4) where Containers were used for Measuring Consumption of Selected Items

Item		Sector	% of Daily Schedules Reporting Use of Container			No. of Daily Schedules
Code	Description		Wholly	Partly	Not Used	Reporting the Item
(1)	(2)	(3)	(4)	(5)	(6)	(7)
101	Rice – PDS	Rural	94.1	0.0	5.9	153
		Non-metro	95.1	0.0	4.9	82
		Metro	71.8	0.0	28.2	71
		All	89.2	0.0	10.8	306
102	Rice – other sources	Rural	90.5	2.8	6.6	1,955
		Non-metro	88.4	0.1	11.5	1,591
		Metro	80.5	0.1	19.4	1,032
		All	87.5	1.2	11.2	4,578
107	Wheat – other sources	Rural	96.4	0.0	3.6	252
		Non-metro	91.4	0.0	8.6	243
		Metro	86.0	0.0	14.0	43
		All	93.3	0.0	6.7	538
110	Wheat atta – other sources	Rural	91.7	0.1	8.3	1,510
		Non-metro	84.2	0.3	15.5	1,165
		Metro	71.8	0.1	28.1	755
		All	84.8	0.2	15.1	3,430
112	Suji, rawa	Rural	26.5	0.0	73.5	49
		Non-metro	49.6	2.9	47.5	139
		Metro	61.5	0.0	38.5	65
		All	48.2	1.6	50.2	253
140	Arhar (tur)	Rural	92.0	0.1	7.9	1,213
		Non-metro	83.3	0.0	16.7	1,094
		Metro	71.3	0.0	28.7	387
		All	85.5	0.0	14.5	2,694
141	Gram (split)	Rural	72.5	0.0	27.5	109
		Non-metro	40.8	0.0	59.2	103
		Metro	58.0	0.0	42.0	69
		All	57.3	0.0	42.7	281
143	Moong	Rural	57.1	0.7	42.2	147
		Non-metro	59.7	0.0	40.3	268
		Metro	62.4	0.0	37.6	173
		All	59.9	0.2	40.0	588
144	Masur	Rural	51.3	18.6	30.2	199
		Non-metro	65.7	0.0	34.3	70
		Metro	51.8	0.0	48.2	255
		All	53.4	7.1	39.5	524

(Contd. . .)

(Contd. . .)

Item		Sector	% of Daily Schedules Reporting Use of Container			No. of Daily Schedules
Code	Description		Wholly	Partly	Not Used	Reporting the Item
(1)	(2)	(3)	(4)	(5)	(6)	(7)
145	Urad	Rural	86.2	1.1	12.7	189
		Non-metro	69.6	0.7	29.7	148
		Metro	65.1	0.0	34.9	86
		All	76.1	0.7	23.2	423
146	Peas	Rural	85.1	0.0	14.9	194
		Non-metro	59.5	0.0	40.5	37
		Metro	80.0	0.0	20.0	15
		All	80.9	0.0	19.1	246
150	Other pulses	Rural	39.7	3.2	57.1	63
		Non-metro	30.0	0.0	70.0	80
		Metro	40.1	0.0	59.9	157
		All	37.3	0.7	62.0	300
152	Besan	Rural	43.8	1.5	54.7	137
		Non-metro	39.5	0.0	60.5	119
		Metro	52.3	0.0	47.7	44
		All	43.3	0.7	56.0	300
160	Milk: liquid	Rural	48.6	0.8	50.5	1,686
		Non-metro	46.8	0.5	52.7	1,696
		Metro	13.2	0.0	86.8	1,016
		All	39.7	0.5	59.8	4,398

sector had cooperated to a lesser extent. Lastly, data on the number of meals consumed by individuals other than usual members of the households was examined. It was found that such meals were relatively small in number, and that they therefore did not materially influence the results (see Table A11 in Appendix B).

Table 10.3 Percentage of Daily Schedules Reporting Use of Diary for Recording Daily Consumption in Schedule 1.0(D3/D4)

Sector	% of Daily Schedules Reporting Use of Diary				No. of Daily Schedules
	Quite Often	A Little	Not at All	Not Recorded	
(1)	(2)	(3)	(4)	(5)	(6)
Rural	52.9	24.6	18.9	3.6	2,688
Non-metro	50.2	26.8	15.3	7.7	2,016
Metro	36.0	33.5	25.4	5.1	1,344
All	48.3	27.3	19.1	5.3	6,048

MAIN FINDINGS OF THE PILOT SURVEY

Tables 10.4 and 10.5 present the main results of the pilot survey, and, as discussed further below, indicate that for many items or item groups, reporting based on monthly reference periods is indeed inferior to weekly or daily periods.

Table 10.4 shows estimates of per capita monthly consumption in quantity and value terms for some important items and item-groups. With the exception of potato, these were items or item-groups for which attempts had been made to collect relatively accurate data through the use of containers – packets in the case of salt – supplied by NSSO staff. Because differentials across the three reference periods can conceivably vary across populations, three sectors are distinguished, namely: rural areas, the four big cities (metro) and other urban areas (non-metro). For the sake of interest, the table also shows the number of sample households reporting each item or item-group. Overall results for the urban sector were obtained as weighted averages of estimates for non-metro urban and metro urban, using weights 255 and 31, respectively, based on the 2001 census populations of the two sectors, for the country as a whole. Results for all-India rural-plus-urban were similarly computed using weights 742 and 285 for rural and urban, respectively. Table 10.5 is similar to Table 10.4, but covers other item groups under food, paan, tobacco, and intoxicants, and does not show any estimates of quantity.[8]

Both Tables 10.4 and 10.5 present the estimates separately by sub-samples and also for the combined sample. The divergence between subsample estimates indicates the margin of uncertainty associated with the combined estimate. The subsample estimates show a good deal of divergence. However,

Table 10.4 Item-wise Estimates of Quantity and Value of Consumption per Person per 30 Days by Schedule Type for Some Major Food Items

			Consumption per Person per 30 Days						No. of Sample Households Reporting Consumption		
			Quantity (in Kg)*			Value (in Rs)					
Item	Sector	Sub-sample	1.0(M)	1.0(W)	1.0(D)	1.0(M)	1.0(W)	1.0(D)	1.0(M)	1.0(W)	1.0(D)
(1)	(2)	(3)	(4)	(5)	(6)	(7)	(8)	(9)	(10)	(11)	(12)
Rice	Rural	1	4.96	6.36	5.45	45.24	58.84	52.44	178	164	338
		2	5.90	6.43	6.52	50.74	56.43	61.90	184	169	337
		Comb.	5.41	6.39	5.95	47.90	57.66	56.83	362	333	675
	Non-metro	1	3.25	3.85	3.04	38.39	44.85	35.99	137	137	262
		2	3.51	3.84	3.29	41.48	44.44	40.35	141	133	266
		Comb.	3.35	3.85	3.13	39.56	44.68	37.64	278	270	528
	Metro	1	4.57	5.10	4.31	61.97	69.17	60.10	88	86	174
		2	4.59	4.80	4.84	56.49	60.09	64.30	83	79	163
		Comb.	4.58	4.95	4.56	59.36	64.77	62.14	171	165	337
	Urban	1	3.39	3.98	3.18	40.91	47.45	38.57	225	223	436
		2	3.63	3.94	3.46	43.09	46.11	42.91	224	212	429
		Comb.	3.48	3.97	3.28	41.68	46.83	40.26	449	435	865
	Rural + urban	1	4.52	5.70	4.82	44.04	55.68	48.59	403	387	774
		2	5.27	5.74	5.67	48.61	53.56	56.62	408	381	766
		Comb.	4.87	5.72	5.21	46.17	54.65	52.23	811	768	1,540

(Contd. . .)

[8] Region-wise estimates parallel to those presented in Tables 10.4 and 10.5 are shown in Tables A9 and A10 in Appendix B.

(Contd. . .)

Item	Sector	Sub-sample	Consumption per Person per 30 Days						No. of Sample House-holds Reporting Consumption		
			Quantity (in Kg)*			Value (in Rs)					
			1.0(M)	1.0(W)	1.0(D)	1.0(M)	1.0(W)	1.0(D)	1.0(M)	1.0(W)	1.0(D)
(1)	(2)	(3)	(4)	(5)	(6)	(7)	(8)	(9)	(10)	(11)	(12)
Rice and products	Rural	1	4.99	6.50	5.51	45.69	60.73	53.40	179	166	340
		2	5.98	6.58	6.59	52.07	58.73	62.80	184	169	339
		Comb.	5.47	6.54	6.01	48.78	59.75	57.76	363	335	679
	Non-metro	1	3.33	3.88	3.10	39.46	45.31	37.05	138	137	262
		2	3.57	3.89	3.33	42.45	45.22	40.92	141	133	267
		Comb.	3.42	3.89	3.19	40.59	45.27	38.51	279	270	529
	Metro	1	4.64	5.16	4.38	63.13	70.24	61.39	90	87	177
		2	4.73	4.98	4.93	58.53	62.98	65.87	84	80	165
		Comb.	4.68	5.07	4.64	60.94	66.73	63.57	174	167	342
	Urban	1	3.47	4.02	3.24	41.99	47.98	39.65	228	224	439
		2	3.69	4.01	3.50	44.17	47.12	43.59	225	213	432
		Comb.	3.55	4.02	3.35	42.77	47.57	41.19	453	437	871
	Rural + urban	1	4.57	5.81	4.88	44.66	57.19	49.58	407	390	779
		2	5.34	5.86	5.73	49.88	55.50	57.46	409	382	771
		Comb.	4.94	5.84	5.27	47.11	56.36	53.16	816	772	1,550
Wheat, flour and maida	Rural	1	5.07	6.12	5.08	34.07	42.02	33.84	160	149	281
		2	4.60	5.81	6.02	30.48	39.23	40.03	152	143	279
		Comb.	4.84	5.97	5.52	32.33	40.65	36.72	312	292	560
	Non-metro	1	6.47	6.71	6.10	47.02	49.83	45.95	133	127	245
		2	6.18	6.99	6.42	46.93	54.45	51.38	126	118	238
		Comb.	6.36	6.82	6.22	46.98	51.71	48.00	259	245	483
	Metro	1	3.36	2.99	2.60	33.62	31.75	28.72	82	78	139
		2	3.91	3.88	3.37	38.74	39.66	34.12	73	62	134
		Comb.	3.62	3.42	2.97	36.05	35.58	31.34	155	140	273
	Urban	1	6.14	6.31	5.73	45.59	47.90	44.11	215	205	384
		2	5.94	6.66	6.09	46.05	52.87	49.53	199	180	372
		Comb.	6.07	6.46	5.87	45.81	49.98	46.22	414	385	756
	Rural + urban	1	5.37	6.17	5.26	37.27	43.65	36.69	375	354	665
		2	4.97	6.05	6.04	34.81	43.02	42.67	351	323	651
		Comb.	5.18	6.11	5.62	36.08	43.24	39.36	726	677	1,316
Wheat and products	Rural	1	5.16	6.29	5.15	35.42	44.57	34.84	162	152	288
		2	4.67	5.95	6.13	31.71	40.79	41.60	156	149	287
		Comb.	4.92	6.12	5.60	33.62	42.72	37.98	318	301	575
	Non-metro	1	6.66	6.97	6.26	50.35	54.42	48.67	139	134	254
		2	6.40	7.40	6.76	50.97	62.61	57.49	135	127	249
		Comb.	6.56	7.15	6.45	50.59	57.76	52.00	274	261	503
	Metro	1	3.94	3.62	3.04	44.03	42.97	35.64	88	87	158
		2	4.25	4.30	3.72	45.88	47.62	40.89	80	72	148
		Comb.	4.09	3.95	3.37	44.91	45.22	38.19	168	159	306
	Urban	1	6.37	6.61	5.92	49.67	53.20	47.28	227	221	412
		2	6.17	7.07	6.43	50.43	61.01	55.71	215	199	397
		Comb.	6.30	6.81	6.12	49.98	56.42	50.52	442	420	809
	Rural + urban	1	5.50	6.38	5.36	39.38	46.97	38.30	389	373	700
		2	5.09	6.26	6.21	36.91	46.41	45.52	371	348	684
		Comb.	5.30	6.31	5.74	38.17	46.53	41.46	760	721	1,384

Cereals	Rural	1	12.13	15.03	12.57	92.01	117.23	98.71	188	186	377
		2	13.29	15.03	14.34	98.06	113.29	113.35	191	192	384
		Comb.	12.69	15.03	13.39	94.94	115.30	105.51	379	378	761
	Non-metro	1	10.03	10.96	9.44	90.12	100.36	86.27	143	143	286
		2	10.08	11.35	10.13	94.39	108.20	98.75	144	142	288
		Comb.	10.05	11.12	9.70	91.74	103.56	90.98	287	285	574
	Metro	1	8.61	8.84	7.59	107.56	114.16	99.05	90	89	182
		2	9.13	9.31	8.78	106.19	110.94	108.30	84	81	175
		Comb.	8.86	9.07	8.17	106.91	112.60	103.54	174	170	357
	Urban	1	9.88	10.73	9.24	91.99	101.84	87.64	233	232	468
		2	9.98	11.13	9.99	95.65	108.49	99.77	228	223	463
		Comb.	9.92	10.90	9.54	93.36	104.53	92.32	461	455	931
	Rural + urban	1	11.50	13.84	11.65	92.00	112.95	95.63	421	418	845
		2	12.37	13.95	13.13	97.39	111.96	109.58	419	415	847
		Comb.	11.92	13.88	12.32	94.50	112.31	101.85	840	833	1,692
Pulses and products	Rural	1	0.90	1.32	1.18	21.06	30.75	28.37	187	182	359
		2	0.95	1.17	1.17	21.57	27.33	28.78	191	190	371
		Comb.	0.92	1.25	1.17	21.31	29.07	28.56	378	372	730
	Non-metro	1	0.80	1.18	0.97	20.09	30.99	25.55	143	139	272
		2	0.77	0.97	0.97	19.13	24.30	25.14	144	142	279
		Comb.	0.79	1.09	0.97	19.72	28.26	25.40	287	281	551
	Metro	1	1.15	0.86	1.14	33.81	26.24	35.45	88	86	171
		2	0.84	0.86	0.96	24.85	25.85	29.49	83	80	167
		Comb.	1.00	0.86	1.05	29.55	26.05	32.55	171	166	338
	Urban	1	0.84	1.15	0.99	21.56	30.48	26.61	231	225	443
		2	0.78	0.96	0.97	19.74	24.47	25.61	227	222	446
		Comb.	0.81	1.07	0.98	20.77	28.02	26.16	458	447	889
	Rural + urban	1	0.88	1.27	1.13	21.20	30.68	27.88	418	407	802
		2	0.90	1.11	1.11	21.06	26.53	27.90	418	412	817
		Comb.	0.89	1.20	1.12	21.16	28.78	27.89	836	819	1,619
Milk: Liquid	Rural	1	5.09	4.51	4.34	56.27	49.67	48.22	133	129	264
		2	4.00	4.33	4.40	39.87	43.10	45.26	137	118	252
		Comb.	4.56	4.42	4.37	48.32	46.45	46.85	270	247	516
	Non-metro	1	6.01	7.15	6.08	73.28	88.07	79.71	126	123	260
		2	4.90	5.27	4.85	61.60	66.35	59.75	125	126	245
		Comb.	5.59	6.38	5.62	68.85	79.20	72.18	251	249	505
	Metro	1	5.61	5.05	5.03	78.96	69.45	67.72	78	79	154
		2	5.13	4.90	5.02	69.24	65.60	69.74	76	73	157
		Comb.	5.38	4.98	5.02	74.34	67.59	68.70	154	152	311
	Urban	1	5.97	6.93	5.97	73.89	86.08	78.43	204	202	414
		2	4.92	5.23	4.87	62.42	66.27	60.82	201	199	402
		Comb.	5.57	6.23	5.56	69.44	77.96	71.81	405	401	816
	Rural + urban	1	5.33	5.18	4.79	61.17	59.79	56.61	337	331	678
		2	4.26	4.58	4.53	46.13	49.54	49.58	338	317	654
		Comb.	4.84	4.92	4.70	54.19	55.20	53.78	675	648	1,332
Sugar	Rural	1	0.80	1.05	0.96	11.92	16.28	15.42	172	156	288
		2	0.85	1.00	1.09	12.93	15.43	17.43	170	163	308
		Comb.	0.82	1.03	1.02	12.41	15.86	16.35	342	319	596
	Non-metro	1	1.36	1.48	1.28	20.68	22.96	19.95	142	140	274
		2	1.06	1.23	1.16	15.78	18.52	18.02	140	135	265
		Comb.	1.25	1.38	1.23	18.82	21.15	19.22	282	275	539

(Contd. . .)

			Consumption per Person per 30 Days						No. of Sample House- holds Reporting Consumption		
			Quantity (in Kg)*			Value (in Rs)					
Item	Sector	Sub-sample	1.0(M)	1.0(W)	1.0(D)	1.0(M)	1.0(W)	1.0(D)	1.0(M)	1.0(W)	1.0(D)
(1)	(2)	(3)	(4)	(5)	(6)	(7)	(8)	(9)	(10)	(11)	(12)
	Metro	1	0.81	0.81	0.82	12.09	12.20	12.79	88	85	169
		2	0.75	0.73	0.81	11.63	11.15	13.65	79	76	157
		Comb.	0.78	0.77	0.81	11.87	11.69	13.21	167	161	326
	Urban	1	1.30	1.41	1.23	19.76	21.81	19.18	230	225	443
		2	1.03	1.18	1.12	15.34	17.73	17.55	219	211	422
		Comb.	1.20	1.31	1.19	18.08	20.14	18.58	449	436	865
	Rural + urban	1	0.94	1.15	1.04	14.10	17.82	16.47	402	381	731
		2	0.90	1.05	1.10	13.60	16.07	17.46	389	374	730
		Comb.	0.93	1.11	1.07	13.98	17.05	16.97	791	755	1,461
Gur	Rural	1	0.16	0.25	0.15	1.77	2.87	1.85	82	60	118
		2	0.29	0.27	0.23	2.98	2.86	2.57	87	67	121
		Comb.	0.22	0.26	0.19	2.36	2.87	2.18	169	127	239
	Non-metro	1	0.06	0.03	0.02	0.72	0.32	0.33	24	9	19
		2	0.02	0.06	0.03	0.24	0.78	0.42	22	16	24
		Comb.	0.04	0.04	0.03	0.54	0.51	0.36	46	25	43
	Metro	1	0.04	0.02	0.01	0.68	0.24	0.23	10	4	6
		2	0.02	0.03	0.02	0.44	0.46	0.33	12	10	15
		Comb.	0.03	0.02	0.02	0.56	0.35	0.28	22	14	21
	Urban	1	0.06	0.03	0.02	0.72	0.31	0.32	34	13	25
		2	0.02	0.06	0.03	0.26	0.75	0.41	34	26	39
		Comb.	0.04	0.04	0.03	0.54	0.49	0.35	68	39	64
	Rural + urban	1	0.13	0.19	0.11	1.48	2.16	1.42	116	73	143
		2	0.21	0.21	0.17	2.22	2.27	1.97	121	93	160
		Comb.	0.17	0.20	0.15	1.85	2.21	1.67	237	166	303
Sugar group	Rural	1	0.96	1.31	1.12	13.73	19.20	17.29	177	168	319
		2	1.14	1.27	1.32	15.91	18.30	20.17	177	174	330
		Comb.	1.05	1.29	1.21	14.79	18.76	18.63	354	342	649
	Non-metro	1	1.42	1.51	1.31	21.40	23.28	20.37	142	140	276
		2	1.08	1.30	1.19	16.02	19.30	18.44	141	137	269
		Comb.	1.29	1.42	1.26	19.36	21.66	19.64	283	277	545
	Metro	1	0.85	0.83	0.83	12.83	12.45	13.02	88	85	170
		2	0.77	0.75	0.83	12.10	11.62	13.97	79	76	158
		Comb.	0.81	0.79	0.83	12.48	12.04	13.49	167	161	328
	Urban	1	1.36	1.44	1.26	20.48	22.12	19.58	230	225	446
		2	1.05	1.24	1.15	15.60	18.48	17.96	220	213	427
		Comb.	1.24	1.35	1.21	18.62	20.63	18.98	450	438	873
	Rural + urban	1	1.07	1.35	1.16	15.61	20.01	17.93	407	393	765
		2	1.11	1.26	1.27	15.82	18.35	19.56	397	387	757
		Comb.	1.10	1.31	1.21	15.86	19.28	18.73	804	780	1,522
Salt	Rural	1	0.34	0.41	0.36	1.07	1.35	1.42	187	184	376
		2	0.30	0.36	0.35	0.95	1.16	1.39	185	186	383
		Comb.	0.32	0.38	0.35	1.01	1.26	1.40	372	370	759
	Non-metro	1	0.26	0.31	0.28	1.29	1.56	1.42	143	142	283
		2	0.26	0.31	0.28	1.24	1.45	1.42	143	140	285
		Comb.	0.26	0.31	0.28	1.27	1.51	1.42	286	282	568

Item	Sector	Sub-sample									
	Metro	1	0.30	0.30	0.28	1.70	1.64	1.58	88	84	172
		2	0.27	0.26	0.26	1.51	1.44	1.43	83	78	165
		Comb.	0.28	0.28	0.27	1.61	1.54	1.51	171	162	337
	Urban	1	0.26	0.31	0.28	1.33	1.57	1.44	231	226	455
		2	0.26	0.30	0.28	1.27	1.45	1.42	226	218	450
		Comb.	0.26	0.31	0.28	1.31	1.51	1.43	457	444	905
	Rural + urban	1	0.32	0.38	0.34	1.14	1.41	1.42	418	410	831
		2	0.29	0.34	0.33	1.04	1.24	1.40	411	404	833
		Comb.	0.30	0.36	0.33	1.09	1.33	1.41	829	814	1,664
Edible oil	Rural	1	0.39	0.46	0.49	14.32	17.16	18.57	181	179	355
		2	0.43	0.50	0.48	15.84	17.74	18.04	183	181	358
		Comb.	0.41	0.48	0.48	15.06	17.44	18.32	364	360	713
	Non-metro	1	0.53	0.62	0.65	20.48	24.15	25.32	139	139	283
		2	0.67	0.65	0.70	25.35	25.18	27.31	144	141	288
		Comb.	0.58	0.64	0.67	22.33	24.57	26.07	283	280	571
	Metro	1	0.76	0.81	0.77	31.91	34.72	30.87	88	86	177
		2	0.72	0.61	0.71	28.99	25.83	29.39	83	80	172
		Comb.	0.74	0.71	0.74	30.52	30.42	30.15	171	166	349
	Urban	1	0.55	0.64	0.66	21.70	25.28	25.91	227	225	460
		2	0.68	0.65	0.70	25.74	25.25	27.53	227	221	460
		Comb.	0.60	0.65	0.68	23.21	25.20	26.51	454	446	920
	Rural + urban	1	0.44	0.51	0.54	16.37	19.42	20.61	408	404	815
		2	0.50	0.54	0.54	18.59	19.83	20.68	410	402	818
		Comb.	0.46	0.53	0.53	17.32	19.59	20.59	818	806	1633
Potato	Rural	1	1.58	1.91	1.88	5.02	6.82	7.17	186	175	324
		2	1.29	1.81	1.94	4.31	5.99	6.66	186	179	325
		Comb.	1.44	1.86	1.91	4.68	6.42	6.93	372	354	649
	Non-metro	1	1.70	2.25	2.22	5.17	6.74	7.31	139	128	249
		2	1.30	1.87	1.84	4.63	6.90	6.79	143	136	252
		Comb.	1.55	2.09	2.08	4.97	6.80	7.11	282	264	501
	Metro	1	0.98	1.39	1.42	4.97	7.19	7.54	82	78	151
		2	1.36	1.85	1.80	5.93	8.34	7.99	80	76	144
		Comb.	1.16	1.61	1.60	˙5.42	7.75	7.76	162	154	295
	Urban	1	1.62	2.16	2.13	5.15	6.79	7.33	221	206	400
		2	1.31	1.87	1.84	4.77	7.05	6.92	223	212	396
		Comb.	1.51	2.04	2.03	5.02	6.90	7.18	444	418	796
	Rural + urban	1	1.59	1.98	1.95	5.06	6.81	7.22	407	381	724
		2	1.29	1.83	1.91	4.44	6.29	6.73	409	391	721
		Comb.	1.46	1.91	1.94	4.77	6.55	7.00	816	772	1,445

Note: * Unit of quantity is litre for liquid milk.

because sampling errors are large, some of the differentials observed from Tables 10.4 and 10.5 across the three reference periods may not emerge as significant in strict statistical testing. This is confirmed by results listed in Tables A9 and A10, which show separate region-wise estimates for the three sectors. In principle, one might examine region x subsample-wise estimates, but such examination hardly appears to be necessary. The subsample-wise and region-wise estimates give a fairly good idea of the variability of the material and, hence, of the statistical significance of the differentials across the reference periods of 'last month', 'last week', and 'day (yesterday)'.

Table 10.4 suggests that 'last month' estimates may be closer to the 'yesterday' estimates compared to the 'last week' estimates for several items or item groups covered in Table 10.4. However, this is the

Table 10.5 Item-wise Estimates of Value of Consumption per Person per 30 Days by Schedule Type for Some Major Food and Non-food Items

Item	Sector	Sub-sample	Value of Consumption per Person per 30 Days (in Rs)			No. of Sample Households Reporting Consumption		
			1.0(M)	1.0(W)	1.0(D)	1.0(M)	1.0(W)	1.0(D)
(1)	(2)	(3)	(4)	(5)	(6)	(7)	(8)	(9)
Milk products (excluding liquid milk)	Rural	1	10.84	12.87	18.8	48	35	84
		2	6.1	3.33	8.89	46	21	63
		Comb.	8.54	8.19	14.2	94	56	147
	Non-metro	1	30.34	23.81	32.74	62	50	112
		2	11.26	8.39	15.48	56	45	104
		Comb.	23.1	17.52	26.23	118	95	216
	Metro	1	11.69	9.75	13.91	50	43	90
		2	8.81	11.18	15.7	37	37	76
		Comb.	10.32	10.45	14.78	87	80	166
	Urban	1	28.34	22.31	30.73	112	93	202
		2	11.00	8.69	15.50	93	82	180
		Comb.	21.73	16.76	25.01	205	175	382
	Rural + urban	1	15.70	15.49	22.11	160	128	286
		2	7.46	4.82	10.73	139	103	243
		Comb.	12.21	10.57	17.20	299	231	529
Egg, fish and meat	Rural	1	15.02	17.02	24.55	87	61	90
		2	11.24	14.51	19.77	92	66	91
		Comb.	13.19	15.79	22.33	179	127	181
	Non-metro	1	9.76	17.25	20.3	76	66	123
		2	20.79	21.86	21.14	85	67	114
		Comb.	13.95	19.13	20.61	161	133	237
	Metro	1	48.26	49.32	59.94	71	64	119
		2	37.37	36.7	50.95	59	50	104
		Comb.	43.08	43.21	55.57	130	114	223
	Urban	1	13.88	20.68	24.54	147	130	242
		2	22.56	23.45	24.33	144	117	218
		Comb.	17.07	21.71	24.35	291	247	460
	Rural + urban	1	14.70	18.04	24.55	234	191	332
		2	14.39	16.99	21.04	236	183	309
		Comb.	14.27	17.43	22.89	470	374	641
Vegetables	Rural	1	24.88	33.19	36.19	188	186	376
		2	23.77	31.53	38.28	191	192	383
		Comb.	24.34	32.37	37.16	379	378	759
	Non-metro	1	39.37	46.16	52.23	142	143	286
		2	32.56	44.18	47.97	144	142	288
		Comb.	36.79	45.35	50.62	286	285	574
	Metro	1	61.09	63.36	71.62	88	87	177
		2	45.63	56.59	62.48	83	80	172
		Comb.	53.73	60.09	67.18	171	167	349
	Urban	1	41.69	48.00	54.30	230	230	463
		2	33.96	45.51	49.52	227	222	460
		Comb.	38.60	46.93	52.39	457	452	923

	Rural +	1	29.55	37.30	41.22	418	416	839
	urban	2	26.60	35.41	41.40	418	414	843
		Comb.	28.30	36.41	41.39	836	830	1,682
Fruit (fresh)	Rural	1	6.48	9.53	13.08	146	111	215
		2	5.57	8.23	11.44	124	91	145
		Comb.	6.04	8.89	12.32	270	202	360
	Non-metro	1	16.01	18.5	28.69	128	96	201
		2	10.73	17.73	17.58	111	102	162
		Comb.	14	18.18	24.5	239	198	363
	Metro	1	31.29	39.67	45.65	92	77	137
		2	27.07	36.5	42.67	86	82	151
		Comb.	29.28	38.13	44.2	178	159	288
	Urban	1	17.64	20.76	30.50	220	173	338
		2	12.48	19.74	20.26	197	184	313
		Comb.	15.63	20.31	26.61	417	357	651
	Rural +	1	9.58	12.65	17.92	366	284	553
	urban	2	7.49	11.43	13.89	321	275	458
		Comb.	˙8.71	12.06	16.29	687	559	1,011
Fruit (dry)	Rural	1	1.32	2.37	1.85	61	40	67
		2	1.91	1.28	1.48	46	26	37
		Comb.	1.61	1.84	1.68	107	66	104
	Non-metro	1	4.06	3.34	4.46	69	35	77
		2	3.75	1.58	2.82	50	26	37
		Comb.	3.94	2.62	3.84	119	61	114
	Metro	1	3.39	2.49	3.85	29	13	33
		2	4.66	1.88	2.91	32	22	37
		Comb.	3.99	2.2	3.39	61	35	70
	Urban	1	3.99	3.25	4.39	98	48	110
		2	3.85	1.61	2.83	82	48	74
		Comb.	3.95	2.58	3.79	180	96	184
	Rural +	1	2.06	2.61	2.56	159	88	177
	urban	2	2.45	1.37	1.85	128	74	111
		Comb.	2.26	2.04	2.27	287	162	288
Spices	Rural	1	13.5	19.46	25.32	188	186	374
		2	12.85	18.84	21.77	191	192	381
		Comb.	13.18	19.15	23.67	379	378	755
	Non-metro	1	12.47	19.05	23.5	143	143	283
		2	13.9	20.29	23.08	144	142	287
		Comb.	13.01	19.55	23.34	287	285	570
	Metro	1	15.17	19.08	23.74	86	85	172
		2	15.44	18.68	21.79	83	78	164
		Comb.	15.3	18.89	22.79	169	163	336
	Urban	1	12.76	19.05	23.53	229	228	455
		2	14.06	20.12	22.94	227	220	451
		Comb.	0.39	0.58	0.69	456	448	906
	Rural +	1	13.29	19.35	24.82	417	414	829
	urban	2	13.19	19.20	22.10	418	412	832
		Comb.	5.06	7.38	9.09	835	826	1,661

(Contd. . .)

(Contd. . .)

Item	Sector	Sub-sample	Value of Consumption per Person per 30 Days (in Rs)			No. of Sample Households Reporting Consumption		
			1.0(M)	1.0(W)	1.0(D)	1.0(M)	1.0(W)	1.0(D)
(1)	(2)	(3)	(4)	(5)	(6)	(7)	(8)	(9)
Tea and coffee	Rural	1	12.95	18.81	18.47	166	153	309
		2	12.51	14.76	19.34	174	157	304
		Comb.	12.73	16.82	18.88	340	310	613
	Non-metro	1	19.77	21.66	27.16	143	142	278
		2	21.92	25.81	31.89	143	144	276
		Comb.	20.59	23.35	28.95	286	286	554
	Metro	1	31.64	32.69	43.53	94	92	190
		2	26.41	35.61	42.61	92	90	186
		Comb.	29.16	34.1	43.09	186	182	376
	Urban	1	21.04	22.84	28.91	237	234	468
		2	22.40	26.86	33.04	235	234	462
		Comb.	0.61	0.69	0.86	472	468	930
	Rural + urban	1	15.20	19.93	21.37	403	387	777
		2	15.26	18.12	23.15	409	391	766
		Comb.	5.22	6.74	7.68	812	778	1,543
Beverages, etc.	Rural	1	33.04	48.58	44.53	182	172	363
		2	22.05	36.64	57.74	182	170	345
		Comb.	27.72	42.73	50.67	364	342	708
	Non-metro	1	42.63	46.07	71.77	143	144	284
		2	37.56	44.2	70.63	144	144	280
		Comb.	40.71	45.31	71.34	287	288	564
	Metro	1	171.51	99.93	129.32	96	93	191
		2	104.8	143.77	167.55	92	93	191
		Comb.	139.79	121.15	147.89	188	186	382
	Urban	1	56.42	51.83	77.93	239	237	475
		2	44.75	54.85	81.00	236	237	471
		Comb.	1.21	1.35	2.12	475	474	946
	Rural + urban	1	39.54	49.48	53.81	421	409	838
		2	28.36	41.70	64.20	418	407	816
		Comb.	11.20	16.55	20.35	839	816	1,654
Food total	Rural	1	302.48	377.02	375.47	192	191	384
		2	274.74	334.1	384.98	192	192	384
		Comb.	289.04	355.99	379.89	384	383	768
	Non-metro	1	380.03	441.03	470.92	144	144	286
		2	347.03	401.55	428.08	144	144	288
		Comb.	367.51	424.91	454.75	288	288	574
	Metro	1	607.46	540.62	594.15	96	94	192
		2	485.15	545.13	614.95	92	93	192
		Comb.	549.29	542.8	604.25	188	187	384
	Urban	1	404.36	451.68	484.10	240	238	478
		2	361.81	416.91	448.07	236	237	480
		Comb.	10.92	12.63	13.52	476	475	958

	Rural +	1	330.79	397.77	405.65	432	429	862
	urban	2	298.93	357.11	402.51	428	429	864
		Comb.	114.44	139.80	149.24	860	858	1,726
Paan	Rural	1	3.14	4.51	5.83	79	68	145
		2	4.17	4.93	7.92	75	53	131
		Comb.	3.64	4.72	6.8	154	121	276
	Non-metro	1	2.34	7.37	6.35	48	53	107
		2	2.73	4.03	6.48	49	52	105
		Comb.	2.49	6.01	6.4	97	105	212
	Metro	1	4.61	3.78	2.99	22	17	27
		2	2.72	1.7	3.92	19	17	31
		Comb.	3.71	2.78	3.44	41	34	58
	Urban	1	2.58	6.99	5.99	70	70	134
		2	2.73	3.78	6.21	68	69	136
		Comb.	0.07	0.18	0.19	138	139	270
	Rural +	1	2.99	5.20	5.87	149	138	279
	urban	2	3.77	4.61	7.44	143	122	267
		Comb.	1.35	1.87	2.60	292	260	546
Tobacco	Rural	1	7.83	10.12	11.64	150	138	294
		2	8.39	9.94	11.67	150	139	289
		Comb.	8.1	10.03	11.65	300	277	583
	Non-metro	1	8.31	7.28	9.36	70	59	130
		2	12.03	8.87	14.57	75	74	163
		Comb.	9.72	7.93	11.32	145	133	293
	Metro	1	9.43	6.68	13.29	29	26	79
		2	4.49	10.21	13.58	26	37	76
		Comb.	7.08	8.39	13.43	55	63	155
	Urban	1	8.43	7.22	9.78	99	85	209
		2	0.36	0.26	0.43	101	111	239
		Comb.	2.26	2.57	4.07	200	196	448
	Rural +	1	8.00	9.31	11.12	249	223	503
	urban	2	3.38	3.78	4.61	251	250	528
		Comb.	5.91	7.00	9.64	500	473	1,031
Intoxicants	Rural	1	8.53	4.26	11.14	38	25	59
		2	5.34	11.14	10.88	43	33	68
		Comb.	6.99	7.63	11.02	81	58	127
	Non-metro	1	5.48	5.65	9.71	14	11	31
		2	7.97	8.02	9.58	15	17	23
		Comb.	6.43	6.62	9.66	29	28	54
	Metro	1	5.9	11.47	8.69	12	11	11
		2	3.45	6.43	4.57	8	6	8
		Comb.	4.74	9.03	6.69	20	17	19
	Urban	1	5.52	6.27	9.60	26	22	42
		2	0.24	0.24	0.28	23	23	31
		Comb.	1.51	2.71	2.15	49	45	73
	Rural +	1	7.70	4.82	10.71	64	47	101
	urban	2	2.16	4.16	4.13	66	56	99
		Comb.	4.49	6.37	6.76	130	103	200

case only for one or two of the three sectors, while 'last week' is found to be closer for the remaining sector – or sectors. Only in the case of cereals and products does 'last month' seem to be appropriate for all three sectors. The following is a tentative summary of conclusions which might be drawn from the quantity estimates in Table 10.4:

Item/Item-group	Appropriate Reference Period by Sector				
	Rural	Non-metro Urban	Metro Urban	Urban	Rural plus Urban
Rice and products	Month/week	Month	Month	Month	Month
Wheat and products	Week	Month	Week	Month	Month
Cereals and products	Month	Month	Month	Month	Month
Pulses and products	Week	Week	Month	Week	Week
Milk (liquid)	Week	Month	Week	Month	Month/week
Sugar group	Week	Month	Month/week	Month	Month/week
Salt	Month/week	Month/week	Month/week	Month/week	Month/week
Edible oil	Week	Week	Month	Week	Week
Potato*	Week	Week	Week	Week	Week

Note: * The conclusion as to the appropriate reference period for reporting on consumption of potato, is in keeping with that for vegetables group as a whole.

While figures in Table 10.4 suggest that 'last month' is a relatively inappropriate reference period, those in Table 10.5 do so in no uncertain terms. The week-based estimates of consumption expenditure are by and large appreciably higher than the corresponding month-based estimates, and are generally much closer to the day-based estimates. This shows that 'last week' would be more appropriate than 'last month' in many cases.

Table 10.6 brings out the fairly systematic differentials between week-based and month-based estimates of consumption expenditure for different groups of items included under food, paan, tobacco and intoxicants. In summation, the following observations may be made on the basis of Tables 10.5 and 10.6:

(i) For food group as a whole, week-based estimates appear to be higher than month-based estimates by 23 per cent for rural areas, and by 16 per cent for non-metro urban sectors. However, for the metro sector, the difference seems to be negligible. The corresponding differences for the urban sector and for the rural and urban sectors combined, are about 14 per cent and 21 per cent, respectively.

(ii) For most of the items across all sectors, week-based estimates are appreciably higher than corresponding month estimates. There are, however, exceptions.
With respect to milk and products, the week-month differences are not clear for any of the sectors. This is also the case for pulses and products, edible oil, egg, fish and meat, sugar, salt, beverages, etc., and tobacco, with respect to the metro sector. Notably, the differential with respect to tobacco is also not clear in the non-metro urban sector. Uncertainty also remains in the case of intoxicants, as reported for in the rural and non-metro urban sectors. Finally, it is also notable that for dry fruits, month-estimates appear to be higher than week-estimates, for the non-metro and metro urban sectors.

(iii) Beverages, etc., is one of the item-groups contributing to the large week-month differential for the rural sector. The same differential is much smaller, or negligible, for the other two sectors. This is likely explained by the fact that this group is highly heterogeneous, comprising items like tea and coffee, cold beverages, fruit juice, biscuits, cake and pastry, salted refreshments, prepared sweets, and cooked meals. However, even in the case of the rural sector, the week-month differential for the food group does not change by much if beverages, etc., are excluded.

In Table 10.4, the differentials across the three reference periods appear to be slightly larger for consumption expenditure than for consumption in quantity terms. Accordingly, conclusions about appropriate reference periods might be marginally different, depending on what estimates are used. Table 10.8 was drawn up to examine this matter. It presents the average prices implicit in the estimates of consumption presented in Table 10.4, both in terms of quantity and value. However, only the combined sample estimates are presented. According to the table, it appears that for many items and item-groups of the food group, the average implicit price was the highest for 'day (or yesterday)' reference period, and the lowest for the 'last month' reference period, with 'last week' prices occupying an intermediate position. Whether or not this pattern is illusory, created by differential reporting errors, is hard to say.

There is another issue that potentially clouds the results obtained so far. As many of the sizeable differences in Tables 10.4 and 10.5 are not clearly significant, one might conclude that the sample size, e.g. the scale of the pilot survey, was not sufficiently large that it would allow even fairly sizeable differences to be interpreted as statistically significant. Nevertheless, it seems reasonable to conclude that for many groups of items, as reported for in both rural and urban sectors, the 'last week' reference period would on the whole be more appropriate than the 'last month' reference period. These items include vegetables, fruits (fresh), and spices. This is because the week-based estimates of consumption expenditure appear to be *closer* to the corresponding day-based estimates, *which are taken as standard*. Similar conclusions may also be drawn in regards to the 'all food' group as a whole, and for paan, tobacco, and intoxicants. However, for some item-groups that are particularly important for nutrition-oriented studies, including cereals and products, 'last month' estimates may still be more reasonable.

The finding that week-based estimates from this pilot survey for many food items – including those for paan, tobacco, and intoxicants – are much higher than the corresponding month-based estimates, is broadly similar to earlier evaluations based on NSS rounds 51 to 54 (see NSS Report No. 447, Government of India, NSSO, 2000). Notwithstanding that the week-month differentials seem to be narrower for this study. The difference for salt is particularly striking.

However, the findings of this paper *do* differ from those of an earlier paper presenting some preliminary results of this survey, entitled 'Impact of Reference Periods . . .' which was prepared by the NSSO Expert Group on Non-Sampling Errors. This paper had focused on quantities of consumption of cereals and products, pulses and products, liquid milk, and items of the sugar group and salt, in an attempt to check the conclusions of Mahalanobis and Sen (1954). As noted above, for most of these item-groups, especially for cereals and products, the revised estimates presented in this report *do indeed* indicate that the 'last month' reference period is fairly appropriate.

However, there is a specific reason for this. In the case of items of the cereals group, for example, most households consume only a few items, and consume them at a more or less fixed daily rate over a period such as 30 days. Accordingly, consumption estimates for 'last month' are likely to be both relatively easy to estimate, and fairly close to estimates for 'day (or yesterday)'. If estimates for last week are on the higher side, this may be due to telescoping effects, or other errors.

Table 10.6 Week-estimates of Value of Consumption Expressed as Percentages of Corresponding Month Estimates, by Subsamples

Item-group	Rural			Non-metro			Metro			Urban			Rural + Urban		
	ss1	ss2	Comb.	ss1	ss2	Comb.	ss1	ss2	Comb.	ss1	ss2	Comb.	ss1	ss2	Comb.
(1)	(2)	(3)	(4)	(5)	(6)	(7)	(8)	(9)	(10)	(11)	(12)	(13)	(14)	(15)	(16)
Cereals	127.4	115.5	121.5	111.4	114.6	112.9	106.1	104.5	105.3	110.8	113.5	112.1	122.8	114.9	118.9
Pulses and products	146.0	126.7	136.4	154.3	127.0	143.3	77.6	104.0	88.2	146.1	124.5	137.4	146.0	126.1	136.7
Milk and products	93.2	101.0	96.1	108.0	102.6	105.2	100.5	97.3	98.8	107.2	102.0	104.5	97.1	101.3	98.4
Edible oil	119.8	112.0	115.8	117.9	99.3	110.0	108.8	89.1	99.7	116.9	98.2	108.9	119.0	108.2	113.9
Egg, fish and meat	113.3	129.1	119.7	176.7	105.2	137.1	102.2	98.2	100.3	168.7	104.5	133.2	128.7	122.3	123.4
Vegetables	133.4	132.7	133.0	117.3	135.7	123.3	103.7	124.0	111.8	115.8	134.4	122.1	128.5	133.2	130.0
Fruits (fresh)	147.1	147.8	147.2	115.6	165.2	129.9	126.8	134.8	130.2	116.8	161.9	129.9	138.7	151.7	142.4
Fruits (dry)	179.6	67.0	114.3	82.3	42.1	66.5	73.5	40.3	55.1	81.4	41.9	65.3	152.3	60.0	100.7
Sugar	136.6	119.3	127.8	111.0	117.4	112.4	100.9	95.9	98.5	109.9	115.1	110.9	129.2	118.1	123.1
Salt	126.2	122.1	124.8	120.9	116.9	118.9	96.5	95.4	95.7	118.3	114.6	116.4	124.0	120.0	122.5
Spices	144.2	146.6	145.3	152.8	146.0	150.3	125.8	121.0	123.5	149.9	143.3	147.4	145.8	145.7	145.9
Beverages, etc.	147.0	166.2	154.2	108.1	117.7	111.3	58.3	137.2	86.7	102.8	119.8	108.7	134.7	153.3	141.5
Food exclude beverages, etc.	121.9	117.7	119.9	117.1	115.5	116.2	101.1	105.5	103.0	115.4	114.4	114.8	120.1	116.8	118.5
Food total	124.6	121.6	123.2	116.1	115.7	115.6	89.0	112.4	98.8	113.2	115.3	113.8	121.4	119.9	120.6
Paan	143.6	118.2	129.7	315.0	147.6	241.4	82.0	62.5	74.9	290.1	138.5	223.6	184.3	123.8	155.8
Tobacco	129.3	118.5	123.8	87.6	73.7	81.6	70.8	227.4	118.5	85.8	90.1	85.5	117.2	110.6	113.2
Intoxicants	49.9	208.6	109.2	103.1	100.6	103.0	194.4	186.4	190.5	112.9	109.8	112.4	67.4	181.1	110.1
Food, paan, tobacco and intoxicants	125.2	126.1	125.5	115.6	114.6	115.0	82.9	117.8	97.1	112.1	114.9	113.1	121.6	123.0	122.1

Table 10.7 Month and Week-estimates of Value of Consumption Expressed as Percentages of Day Estimates, by Subsamples

Item-group	Sector	Month-estimates as Percentages			Week-estimates as Percentages		
		ss 1	ss 2	Comb.	ss 1	ss 2	Comb.
(1)	(2)	(3)	(4)	(5)	(6)	(7)	(8)
Cereals	Rural	93.2	86.5	90.0	118.8	99.9	109.3
	Non-metro	104.5	95.6	100.8	116.3	109.6	113.8
	Metro	108.6	98.1	103.3	115.3	102.4	108.8
	Urban	105.0	95.9	101.1	116.2	108.7	113.2
	Rural + urban	105.4	96.1	101.4	116.1	108.1	112.7
Pulses and products	Rural	74.2	74.9	74.6	108.4	95.0	101.8
	Non-metro	78.6	76.1	77.6	121.3	96.7	111.3
	Metro	95.4	84.3	90.8	74.0	87.7	80.0
	Urban	81.0	77.1	79.4	114.6	95.5	107.1
	Rural + urban	82.8	77.9	80.7	109.5	94.7	103.9
Milk and milk products	Rural	100.1	84.9	93.1	93.3	85.7	89.5
	Non-metro	92.1	96.8	93.4	99.5	99.3	98.3
	Metro	111.0	91.4	101.4	97.0	89.9	93.5
	Urban	93.7	96.2	94.2	99.3	98.2	97.8
	Rural + urban	94.9	95.7	94.8	99.1	97.3	97.5
Edible oil	Rural	77.1	87.8	82.2	92.4	98.3	95.2
	Non-metro	80.9	92.8	85.7	95.4	92.2	94.2
	Metro	103.4	98.6	101.2	112.5	87.9	100.9
	Urban	83.8	93.5	87.5	97.6	91.7	95.1
	Rural + urban	86.0	94.0	89.0	99.2	91.3	95.7
Egg, fish and meat	Rural	61.2	56.9	59.1	69.3	73.4	70.7
	Non-metro	48.1	98.3	67.7	85.0	103.4	92.8
	Metro	80.5	73.3	77.5	82.3	72.0	77.8
	Urban	56.6	92.7	70.1	84.3	96.4	89.1
	Rural + urban	61.5	89.2	71.5	83.9	91.9	86.9
Vegetables	Rural	68.7	62.1	65.5	91.7	82.4	87.1
	Non-metro	75.4	67.9	72.7	88.4	92.1	89.6
	Metro	85.3	73.0	80.0	88.5	90.6	89.4
	Urban	76.8	68.6	73.7	88.4	91.9	89.6
	Rural + urban	77.8	69.1	74.4	88.4	91.7	89.6
Fruit (fresh)	Rural	49.5	48.7	49.0	72.9	71.9	72.2
	Non-metro	55.8	61.0	57.1	64.5	100.9	74.2
	Metro	68.5	63.4	66.2	86.9	85.5	86.3
	Urban	57.8	61.6	58.8	68.1	97.4	76.3
	Rural + urban	59.3	61.9	59.9	70.7	95.2	77.8
Fruit (dry)	Rural	71.4	129.1	95.8	128.1	86.5	109.5
	Non-metro	91.0	133.0	102.6	74.9	56.0	68.2
	Metro	88.1	160.1	117.7	64.7	64.6	64.9
	Urban	90.8	136.0	104.0	73.9	57.0	67.9
	Rural + urban	90.5	138.4	105.2	73.1	57.7	67.6

(Contd. . .)

(Contd. . .)

Item-group	Sector	Month-estimates as Percentages			Week-estimates as Percentages		
		ss 1	ss 2	Comb.	ss 1	ss 2	Comb.
(1)	(2)	(3)	(4)	(5)	(6)	(7)	(8)
Sugar group	Rural	79.4	78.9	79.4	111.0	90.7	100.7
	Non-metro	105.1	86.9	98.6	114.3	104.7	110.3
	Metro	98.5	86.6	92.5	95.6	83.2	89.3
	Urban	104.6	86.9	98.1	113.0	102.9	108.7
	Rural + urban	104.2	86.8	97.7	111.8	101.4	107.3
Salt	Rural	75.4	68.3	72.1	95.1	83.5	90.0
	Non-metro	90.8	87.3	89.4	109.9	102.1	106.3
	Metro	107.6	105.6	106.6	103.8	100.7	102.0
	Urban	92.8	89.3	91.4	109.1	102.0	105.8
	Rural + urban	94.4	90.9	92.9	108.6	101.8	105.5
Spices	Rural	53.3	59.0	55.7	76.9	86.5	80.9
	Non-metro	53.1	60.2	55.7	81.1	87.9	83.8
	Metro	63.9	70.9	67.1	80.4	85.7	82.9
	Urban	54.2	61.3	56.9	81.0	87.7	83.7
	Rural + urban	55.2	62.2	57.9	80.9	87.5	83.6
Beverages, etc.	Rural	74.2	38.2	54.7	109.1	63.5	84.3
	Non-metro	59.4	53.2	57.1	64.2	62.6	63.5
	Metro	132.6	62.5	94.5	77.3	85.8	81.9
	Urban	72.4	55.3	64.5	66.5	67.7	67.2
	Rural + urban	81.5	56.6	69.5	68.1	71.0	69.6
Food excluding beverages, etc.	Rural	81.4	77.2	79.4	99.2	90.9	95.2
	Non-metro	84.5	86.6	85.2	99.0	100.0	99.0
	Metro	93.8	85.0	89.7	94.8	89.7	92.4
	Urban	85.7	86.4	85.8	98.4	98.6	98.2
	Rural + urban	86.5	86.2	86.2	98.0	97.6	97.5
Food total	Rural	80.6	71.4	76.1	100.4	86.8	93.7
	Non-metro	80.7	81.1	80.8	93.7	93.8	93.4
	Metro	102.2	78.9	90.9	91.0	88.6	89.8
	Urban	83.5	80.7	82.2	93.3	93.0	92.9
	Rural + urban	85.7	80.5	83.3	93.0	92.5	92.6
Paan	Rural	53.9	52.7	53.5	77.4	62.2	69.4
	Non-metro	36.9	42.1	38.9	116.1	62.2	93.9
	Metro	154.2	69.4	107.8	126.4	43.4	80.8
	Urban	43.1	44.0	43.1	116.6	60.9	93.1
	Rural + urban	48.7	45.6	46.8	117.1	59.8	92.4
Tobacco	Rural	67.3	71.9	69.5	86.9	85.2	86.1
	Non-metro	88.8	82.6	85.9	77.8	60.9	70.1
	Metro	71.0	33.1	52.7	50.3	75.2	62.5
	Urban	86.2	77.6	81.7	73.8	62.3	69.1
	Rural + urban	84.3	73.5	78.5	70.8	63.5	68.4
Intoxicants	Rural	76.6	49.1	63.4	38.2	102.4	69.2
	Non-metro	56.4	83.2	66.6	58.2	83.7	68.5
	Metro	67.9	75.5	70.9	132.0	140.7	135.0

	Urban	57.5	82.8	66.9	65.3	86.8	73.6
	Rural + urban	58.5	82.4	67.2	71.2	89.6	78.0
Food, paan, tobacco	Rural	79.7	70.4	75.2	98.0	86.7	92.4
and intoxicants	Non-metro	79.8	80.6	80.1	92.9	92.1	92.4
	Metro	101.3	77.8	90.0	90.9	88.5	89.7
	Urban	82.6	80.2	81.4	92.7	91.6	92.0
	Rural + urban	84.8	79.9	82.4	92.5	91.2	91.7

The problem of recall is more serious for items of groups like vegetables, fruits (fresh), spices, or beverages, etc. For such items, the level of consumption often fluctuates from day to day; much more so, for instance, than for items like rice or wheat. Thus, the informant may not clearly recall on how many days of the last month his/her household consumed items like brinjal, onion, banana, or biscuits, and what the quantities consumed were. Also, he/she may not make any serious effort to recall such facts, consulting other members of the household during the hurried process of interview, particularly if the respondent burden is proving to be too great. Recalling such consumption-related events during the 'last week' is obviously easier. Under-reporting of past consumption through recall lapse is thus likely to be smaller for item groups like vegetables when 'last week' reference period is used.

DISCUSSION AND CONCLUDING OBSERVATIONS

In this closing discussion, we would like to explain and further test the results noted in the previous section, besides outlining the implications of these results for the implementation of future surveys. To this end we note some practical obstacles to overhauling present survey practices. For the sake of completeness, we also discuss more generally the choice of appropriate reference periods for item-groups of the household budget other than food, paan, tobacco, and intoxicants.

Designs using bounded recall and fairly short reference periods have become increasingly popular. The UN NHSCP (National Household Survey Capability Programme) manual on non-sampling errors (1982, see, in particular pp. 134, 135) sums up the experience on recall lapse in surveys of income and expenditure, as well as other retrospective surveys. According to this approach, each household is interviewed for several consecutive time periods. The NHSCP manual notes that after the first time, the interviews become dependent, because the interviewer reminds the respondent of what they reported the last time, as a basis for inquiring about subsequent expenditure. In other words, the first report is not included in the tabulation, but is only used for establishing the basis for subsequent interviews. This practice was hardly meant for situations where households are interviewed for several consecutive *days*. In this pilot survey, each sample household selected for the 'day' reference period was visited on a day preceding day 1, in order to prepare it for the subsequent visits. Hence, data for day 1 was unlikely to be seriously affected by recall errors.

Nevertheless, for this pilot survey an attempt was made to tabulate separately the information collected across three or four days through Schedules 1.0(D3/D4), in order to find out whether the results would change if data for day 1 were excluded in the process of estimation. Some results from this exercise are presented in Table A12 in Appendix B. Reassuringly, it appears that the variation in estimates across the three or four days was small and inconsequential.[9]

[9] For some items/item-groups like spices and beverages, etc., the figures for the last day of the three- or four-day reference period appear to be much higher than those for the earlier days. For these items/-item-groups, the total consumption for the three- or four-day period was entered on the last day.

Table 10.8 Item-wise Estimates of Average Implicit Prices by Schedule Type for Some Major Food Items

| Item | Sector | Average Price (in Rs) per Kg* | | |
| | | Schedule 1.0(M) | Schedule 1.0(W) | Schedule 1.0(D) |
(1)	(2)	(3)	(4)	(5)
Rice	Rural	8.85	9.02	9.55
	Non-metro	11.81	11.61	12.03
	Metro	12.96	13.08	13.63
Rice and products	Rural	8.92	9.14	9.61
	Non-metro	11.87	11.64	12.07
	Metro	13.02	13.16	13.70
Wheat, flour and maida	Rural	6.68	6.81	6.65
	Non-metro	7.39	7.58	7.72
	Metro	9.96	10.40	10.55
Wheat and products	Rural	6.83	6.98	6.78
	Non-metro	7.71	8.08	8.06
	Metro	10.98	11.45	11.33
Cereals and products	Rural	7.48	7.67	7.88
	Non-metro	9.13	9.31	9.38
	Metro	12.07	12.41	12.67
Pulses and products	Rural	23.16	23.26	24.41
	Non-metro	24.96	25.93	26.19
	Metro	29.55	30.29	31.00
Milk: liquid (litre)*	Rural	10.60	10.51	10.72
	Non-metro	12.32	12.41	12.84
	Metro	13.82	13.57	13.69
Sugar	Rural	15.13	15.40	16.03
	Non-metro	15.06	15.33	15.63
	Metro	15.22	15.18	16.31
Gur	Rural	10.73	11.04	11.47
	Non-metro	13.50	12.75	12.00
	Metro	18.67	17.50	14.00
Sugar group	Rural	14.09	14.54	15.40
	Non-metro	15.01	15.25	15.59
	Metro	15.41	15.24	16.25
Salt	Rural	3.16	3.32	4.00
	Non-metro	4.88	4.87	5.07
	Metro	5.75	5.50	5.59
Edible oil	Rural	36.73	36.33	38.17
	Non-metro	38.50	38.39	38.91
	Metro	41.24	42.85	40.74
Potato	Rural	3.25	3.45	3.63
	Non-metro	3.21	3.25	3.42
	Metro	4.67	4.81	4.85

Note: * Unit of quantity is litre for liquid milk.

From the point of view of *sampling in time*, the reference period of 'last 30 days' nets a larger sample of consumption expenditure events than the reference period of 'last 7 days'. This is why the relative standard errors (RSEs) of estimates are generally smaller for month-based estimates than for week-based estimates. Indeed, owing to its small sample sizes, the present pilot survey did not yield dependable estimates of RSEs for the three reference periods. We therefore reproduce in Table 10.9 the relevant portion of Table T2 from NSS Report No. 447 (Government of India, NSSO, 2000) which compares RSEs of month-based and week-based estimates of per capita consumption for all-India, rural and urban, obtained from NSS rounds 52 and 53.

It is important to note that many practical and more prosaic factors also often impinge significantly on the reliability of surveys. For instance, as noted in a 2001 Report of the National Statistical Commission (see p. 57 of Vol. 1 and pp. 278–81 of Vol. 2), shortening the consumer expenditure schedule is as important an imperative for survey designers, as is choosing appropriate reference periods. It has long been recognised that Indian informants, especially those in the cities, have become increasingly busy. This has been accompanied by an increasingly cynical and somewhat resistant attitude to the long interview required for canvassing the detailed NSS schedule for consumer expenditure. To complicate matters further, consumption patterns have also become more diversified, even as events from other spheres of life increasingly impinge on the consciousness of informants. Thus, the salience of consumption-related events was no longer as easily remembered as in the 50s and 60s. In this context, an interview method asking responders to recall all salient consumption events during the last 30 days preceding the date of interview, imposes too great a *respondent burden*. Time is often a part of it. Thanks to improvements in roads and transport facilities, the typical field investigator was no longer setting up camps in sample villages, but was commuting daily from some nearby town and conducting the interviews at times not necessarily convenient to the informants. Many of the interviews were therefore being conducted in a hurried manner, especially in the larger towns and cities. The use of the 'last month' reference period again aggravates the problem.

There are further practical considerations. For instance, it is important to note that if one adopts last week as the reference period, one has to *stagger the interviews evenly over the 52 weeks of the survey year* and not merely over the 12 months of the survey year. This would, of course, impose severe restrictions on the work programme of the field staff. With this in mind, we have reproduced Table 10.10 from NSS Report No. 447 (Table T8, 29), which presents some figures pertaining to NSS rounds 51 to 53, across the all-India rural and urban populations. These show that when no special instructions were given to the investigators about whether or how they should spread the reference week over the calendar month designated by schedule type 2, the investigators tended to interview relatively few households during dates 1–7 of the calendar month.[10] In this instance, the last week reference period was used for items of food, paan, tobacco and intoxicants; the last 30 days for item groups like fuel and light; and last 365 days for item-groups like education. Table 10.10 also presents figures extracted from the above table, which show that average monthly per capita expenditure (MPCE) of sample households would be higher when the interviewing is done during the first week of the calendar month, rather than the remaining weeks of the same month. As a corollary, it may be noted that the use of a last-week reference period may also introduce biases if weeks that include festival days are not covered in the right proportion.

---

[10] This was mainly because the investigators drew their salaries in the first week of the month.

Table 10.9 Percentage Increase in RSE of All-India Estimate of Per Capita Consumption Obtained by Adopting Schedule Type 2 Instead of Schedule Type 1', for Rural and Urban India, NSS Rounds 52 and 53

Item-group	52 Rural			53 Rural			52 Urban			53 Urban			All
	RSE of Est. by Schedule Type		% Incr.	RSE of Est. by Schedule Type		% Incr.	RSE of Est. by Schedule Type		% Incr.	RSE of Est. by Schedule Type		% Incr.	% Incr.
	1	2		1	2		1	2		1	2		
(1)	(2)	(3)	(4)	(5)	(6)	(7)	(8)	(9)	(10)	(11)	(12)	(13)	(14)
Cereals	0.73	0.89	22	1.30	1.99	53	0.63	0.83	32	1.00	1.64	64	43
Gram	7.29	6.87	−6	8.00	12.01	50	4.16	4.87	17	4.39	5.48	25	22
Cereal subst.	6.74	7.74	15	8.89	8.28	−7	7.37	7.19	−2	7.20	7.60	6	3
Pulse and products	1.45	1.48	2	1.83	2.70	48	1.07	1.75	64	1.39	1.95	40	38
Milk and products	2.32	2.56	10	2.82	4.55	61	1.49	3.57	140	2.37	2.82	19	57
Edible oil	1.23	2.05	67	1.87	1.95	4	0.82	2.40	193	1.18	1.60	36	75
Meat, egg and fish	2.28	2.73	20	3.18	5.00	57	2.59	3.09	19	2.81	2.88	2	25
Vegetables	1.17	1.2	3	2.05	2.08	1	1.39	2.79	101	1.89	2.33	23	32
Fruits (fresh)	3.15	2.85	−10	4.23	4.33	2	3.16	4.61	46	3.03	3.54	17	14
Fruits (dry)	5.56	6.29	13	8.45	9.30	10	6.06	4.76	−21	4.87	7.03	44	11
Sugar	1.7	1.96	15	2.48	3.45	39	1.18	1.86	58	1.22	1.65	35	37
Salt	1.03	1.61	56	1.66	2.26	36	1.21	2.09	73	1.60	1.95	22	47
Spices	1.22	1.32	8	2.81	2.28	−19	0.93	2.00	115	1.55	1.65	6	28
Beverages, etc.	3.15	2.75	−13	3.00	4.25	42	3.03	2.68	−12	3.86	4.71	22	10
Food total	*0.85*	*0.93*	*9*	*1.29*	*1.85*	*43*	*0.95*	*1.96*	*106*	*1.35*	*1.55*	*15*	*43*
Paan	4.07	3.89	−4	4.86	5.03	3	5.08	5.08	0	4.15	4.59	11	3
Tobacco	1.98	2.61	32	2.55	3.70	45	2.87	5.16	80	4.00	4.52	13	42
Intoxicants	5.57	6.91	24	6.59	11.22	70	5.35	7.16	34	7.05	8.03	14	35

Note: * For item-groups shown here, the reference period was 'last 7 days' for schedule type 2 but 'last 30 days' for schedule type 1.

The finding that day-based estimates are even appreciably higher than the week-based estimates cannot be ignored. However, the adoption of 'day or yesterday' as reference period for nationwide surveys conducted by NSSO seems to be infeasible. Cost would rise manifold. Furthermore, cooperation from informants, of the kind received in this pilot survey, cannot be guaranteed in the case of repetitive surveys. Indeed, it would not be feasible to implement large-scale, year-on-year repeated interviews for the same household, spanning three or four consecutive days, along with collection of data on the volume of consumption through use of containers. One alternative suggestion is that the NSSO consider conducting small-scale enquiries at suitable intervals, in order to monitor the divergence between day-based and week-based estimates. However, such exercises should make note of the fact that it is possible that the day-based estimates obtained in this pilot survey were on the high side, due to various types of bias.

For the sake of completeness, we conclude this discussion by making a few observations on appropriate reference periods for item-groups of the household budget other than food, paan, tobacco, and intoxicants.

Table 10.10 Some Aspects of the Canvassing of Schedule Type 2 during
NSS Rounds 51 to 53: All-India, Rural plus Urban

Date of Canvassing	No. of Schedules of Type 2 Canvassed			Average MPCE of Sample Households (Rs)		
	Round 51	Round 52	Round 53	Round 51	Round 52	Round 53
1–7	1,798	1,758	2,026	464	556	620
8–14	6,026	6,087	4,882	442	514	605
15–21	7,256	6,791	5,258	440	506	616
22–31	10,862	9,431	8,383	442	505	603
All	26,437	24,141	20,601	442	511	612

While further field tests, as well as analytical studies, are necessary for making these choices, existing evidence does provide indications. In the aforementioned experiments in the annual NSS rounds 51 to 54, using two types of schedules, a reference period of 'last 30 days' was adopted in both schedule types for fuel and light, miscellaneous goods and services, and medical care (non-institutional). This seems to be appropriate, as these groups do not appear to pose any special problems. For clothing and footwear, the advantages of adopting 'last 365 days' as a reference period instead of 'last 30 days', seem to be clear, and in the annual round experiments with two types of schedules, the estimates were not very different for the two reference periods. The longer reference period with a lower RSE is therefore more appropriate, considering also its stabilising effect on seasonal and other short-run fluctuations.

In this regard, it may also be noted that the use of 'last 365 days' instead of 'last 30 days' as the reference period for item-groups like clothing, footwear, etc., provides a more stable measure of monthly per capita consumer expenditure (MPCE) and shifts the Lorenz curve of MPCE inward (Government of India, NSSO, 1992). A more subtle effect is observed if the Engel curves are estimated by regressing per capita item consumption on MPCE. In this instance, Engel elasticities for items like clothing change appreciably if the MPCE is computed utilising annual expenditures on item-groups like clothing and footwear, instead of last-month expenditures on these item-groups (Ghose and Bhattacharya, 1994).

Contrarily, in regards to limitations on the use of longer reference periods, there are apparent problems with the item-groups of education, medical care (institutional), and durables. The estimates from rounds 51 to 54 showed that for these three groups, 'last month' gave appreciably higher figures than 'last year'. The difference was 26 per cent for education, 41 per cent for medical care (institutional) and 44 per cent for durable goods. The drop in RSE when 'last year' is used cannot compensate for such downward bias in the estimates. It should be noted however that there are doubts about the quality of data collected in rounds 51–54, suggesting that further checks against NAS figures would be useful and important.

ACKNOWLEDGEMENT

A few early results of this pilot survey were reported in a paper entitled, 'Impact of Reference Periods on Measuring Household Consumption: Preliminary Results of a Pilot Survey', presented to the international seminar on 'Understanding Socio-Economic Changes through National Surveys', organised by the NSSO, 12-13 May 2001 in New Delhi, as part of the Golden Jubilee celebrations of the NSSO. More detailed results were later presented to the Workshop on Poverty Measurement, Monitoring and

Evaluation, organised by the Planning Commission, India, and the World Bank, in New Delhi on 11-12 January 2002. The full report will be available in *Sarvekshana*.

This chapter is reprinted from *Economic and Political Weekly*, Vol. 37, 25–31 January 2003.

REFERENCES

Dubey, Amaresh and Shubhashis Gangopadhyay (1998), Counting the Poor: Where are the Poor in India, *Sarvekshana* Analytical Report, No. 1, Department of Statistics & P.I., Government of India.

Ghose, Suchismita and Nikhilesh Bhattacharya (1994), 'Effect of Reference Period on Engel Elasticities of Clothings and Other Items', *Sarvekshana*, Vol. XVII, No. 3, January–March, pp. 35–39.

Government of India (2001), Report of the National Statistical Commission.

———, The Cabinet Secretariat (1959), Report on Pattern of Consumer Expenditure – Second to Seventh Rounds: April 1951–March 1954, NSS Report No. 20.

Government of India, National Sample Survey Organisation (2000), Choice of Reference Period for Consumption Data, NSS Report No. 447.

———, (1992), Report on the Fourth Quinquennial Survey on Consumer Expenditure: Consumption of Clothing, Footwear and Durable Goods (with month and year as reference period), NSS Report No. 384.

———, Perspective Planning Division, Planning Commission (1993), Report of the Expert Group on Estimation of Proportion and Number of Poor, New Delhi.

Mahalanobis, P.C. and S.B. Sen (1954), 'On Some Aspects of the Indian National Sample Survey', *Bulletin of the International Statistical Institute*, Vol. 34, p. 2.

Minhas, B.S. (1988), Validation of Large-Scale Sample Survey Data: Case of NSS Household Consumption Expenditure, *Sankhya*, Series B, Vol. 50 (Supplement), pp. 1–63 (Chapter 6 of this book).

Minhas, B.S. and S.M. Kansal (1989), Comparison of NSS and CSO Estimates of Private Consumption: Some Observations based on 1983 Data, *Journal of Income and Wealth*, Vol. 11, pp.7–24.

Minhas, B.S., S.M. Kansal, Jagdish Kumar and P.D. Joshi (1986), On the Reliability of Available Estimates of Private Consumption Expenditure in India, *The Journal of Income and Wealth*, Vol. 9, No. 2, pp. 71–93.

Mukherjee, M. and G.S. Chatterjee (1974), 'On the Validity of NSS Estimates of Consumption Expenditure' in P.K. Bardhan and T.N. Srinivasan (eds), *Poverty and Income Distribution in India*, Calcutta: Statistical Publishing Society, pp. 139–47 (Chapter 4 of this book).

Mukherjee, M. and S. Saha (1981), Reliability of National Income and Allied Estimates, *Journal of Income and Wealth*, Vol. 5, No. 2, pp. 131–36.

UN National Household Survey Capability Programme (1982), Non-Sampling Errors in Household Surveys: Sources, Assessment and Control, New York.

Appendices

A NOTE ON SOME EARLY STUDIES ON REFERENCE PERIODS

In the 4th and 5th Rounds of NSS, conducted during 1952/53, it was decided to compare the 'last week' and 'last month' reference periods for ascertaining the correct volume of consumption of food, as well as a few other items. Two schedules were used for these items, with two reference periods: 'last month', and 'last week'. Otherwise, however, the schedules were identical. The sample households allotted to each investigator were divided into two subsamples. The weekly schedules were completed for one of them, and the monthly schedules for the other. In view of the importance of the questions being posed, two investigators were sent to each village to investigate a different sample of households, in order to obtain replicated data. Hence, for any sample village, readings for a weekly period and a monthly period were obtained from each of the two investigators. It was then seen that the figures obtained for the 'last week' reference period were higher than the figures obtained with 'last month' as reference period. However, the degree of difference between the two sets of estimates did not manifest consistency over the two rounds, except in the case of foodgrains (cereals-plus-cereals substitutes). For this group, the week estimates were about 7 per cent higher in rural areas and about 11-12 per cent higher in urban areas in both the rounds, compared to month-based estimates. For all food, the corresponding differences were found to be as follows:

			(Per Cent)
Rural		Urban	
4th Round	5th Round	4th Round	5th Round
10.4	22.3	13.7	14.4

As described below, a special study by Mahalanobis and Sen (1954) was carried out to settle the question as to which of the two reference periods was providing the more correct figures.

The special study was conducted in March-April 1952 in 76 villages in West Bengal. A total of 1,254 sample households were selected from these villages and these were divided into four subsamples. Items under study were clean rice, pulses, sugar, and salt. Information was collected from the first and the second subsamples of households by interview method, using last week and last month reference periods, respectively. For the two remaining subsamples, particulars of consumption were obtained by the actual weighing of these food items by the investigators. The investigators requested the households to place the supplies for about 10 days in some suitable receptacles and to draw from these stocks for consumption during the next seven days. The investigators weighed the opening stock and also the balance left a week later. In the third group of households, the weighing was done at an interval of seven days, while for the fourth group, the weighing was done twice in seven days. These operations were repeated for three weeks. The starting days of the seven-day periods for the different households were scattered over the different days of the week. The study showed that the figures obtained through interviews with last month as reference period agreed fairly well with those based on weighing, while the figures based on last week were appreciably higher. This could have been due to border effects or telescoping in reporting food consumption during the last week (see also UN National Household Survey Capability Programme, 1982, pp. 127–29).

APPENDIX B

Table A1 Number of Sample Households Canvassed on Different Days of the Month by Type of Schedule

	No. of Sample Households Canvassed			
Date of Canvassing	Schedule 1.0(M)	Schedule 1.0(W)	Schedule 1.0(D3)	Schedule 1.0(D4)
(1)	(2)	(3)	(4)	(5)
Sector: Rural				
1–7	63	96	97	91
8–14	127	104	96	103
15–21	74	95	95	96
22–28	117	47	96	89
29+	3	41	0	5
All	384	383	384	384
Sector: Non-metro				
1–7	53	71	73	71
8–14	91	72	72	75
15–21	56	73	68	70
22–28	88	37	72	72
29+	0	35	1	0
All	288	288	286	288
Sector: Metro				
1–7	35	46	48	48
8–14	57	49	48	48
15–21	34	45	48	48
22–28	62	23	48	48
29+	0	24	0	0
All	188	187	192	192

Table A2 Number of Sample Households Canvassed in Different Months by Type of Schedule

Month when Canvassing	No. of Sample Households Canvassed			
	Schedule 1.0(M)	Schedule 1.0(W)	Schedule 1.0(D3)	Schedule 1.0(D4)
(1)	(2)	(3)	(4)	(5)
Sector: Rural				
January	26	25	27	26
February	60	61	59	62
March	82	76	82	80

April	82	85	81	82
May	60	62	61	60
June	61	61	60	60
July (1–8)	13	13	14	14
All	384	383	384	384

Sector: Non-metro

January	58	58	58	58
February	52	52	53	53
March	30	30	30	30
April	32	33	32	33
May	50	49	50	50
June	52	52	49	51
July (1–8)	14	14	14	13
All	288	288	286	288

Sector: Metro

January	24	23	24	24
February	30	30	32	32
March	32	31	32	32
April	32	31	32	32
May	31	32	33	32
June	31	32	31	32
July (1–8)	8	8	8	8
All	188	187	192	192

Table A3 Average Household Size of Sample Households by Type of Schedule and by Sector

	Average Household Size		
Sector	Schedule 1.0(M)	Schedule 1.0(W)	Schedule 1.0(D3/D4)
(1)	(2)	(3)	(4)
rural	4.68	4.63	4.73
non-metro	4.99	4.85	5.06
metro	4.12	4.23	4.37

Table A4R Per 1,000 Distribution of Sample Households by Household Type and by Type of Schedule

(Sector: Rural)

Type of Schedule	No. of Sample Households per 1,000 Households by Household Type					
	Self-employed in Non-agriculture	Agriculture Labour	Other Labour	Self-employed in Agriculture	Others	Total
(1)	(2)	(3)	(4)	(5)	(6)	(7)
Schedule 1.0 (M)	80	459	92	273	96	1000
Schedule 1.0 (W)	93	439	94	257	118	1000
Schedule 1.0 (D3/D4)	95	460	74	261	109	1000

Table A4U Distribution per 1,000 of Sample Households by Household Type and by Type of Schedule

Sector	Type of Schedule	No. of Sample Households per 1,000 Households by Household Type				
		Self-employed	Regular Wage/ Salary Earner	Casual Labour	Others	Total
(1)	(2)	(3)	(4)	(5)	(6)	(7)
Non-metro	Schedule 1.0(M)	480	339	69	111	1,000
	Schedule 1.0(W)	430	417	82	71	1,000
	Schedule 1.0(D3/D4)	410	414	90	80	1,000
Metro	Schedule 1.0(M)	304	550	81	65	1,000
	Schedule 1.0(W)	322	568	50	57	1,000
	Schedule 1.0(D3/D4)	328	529	77	67	1,000

Table A5 Distribution per 1,000 of Sample Households over Social Groups Separately by Type of Schedule and by Sector

Sector	Type of Schedule	No. of Sample Households per 1,000 Households by Social Group				
		ST	SC	OBC	Others	Total
(1)	(2)	(3)	(4)	(5)	(6)	(7)
Rural	Schedule 1.0(M)	91	244	544	120	1,000
	Schedule 1.0(W)	81	258	548	112	1,000
	Schedule 1.0(D3/D4)	86	246	549	117	1,000
Non-metro	Schedule 1.0(M)	35	162	316	487	1,000
	Schedule 1.0(W)	42	166	356	436	1,000
	Schedule 1.0(D3/D4)	11	182	367	434	1,000
Metro	Schedule 1.0(M)	11	112	223	654	1,000
	Schedule 1.0(W)	10	143	244	604	1,000
	Schedule 1.0(D3/D4)	13	134	223	627	1,000

Table A6R Distribution per 1,000 of Rural Households by Size Class of Land Possessed and by Type of Schedule

Type of Schedule	No. of Sample Households per 1,000 Households by Size Class of Land Possessed (Hectares)						
	< 0.01	0.01 – 0.40	0.41 – 1.00	1.01 – 2.00	2.01 – 4.00	> 4.00	Total
(1)	(2)	(3)	(4)	(5)	(6)	(7)	(8)
Schedule 1.0(M)	59	483	209	148	68	33	1,000
Schedule 1.0(W)	56	512	176	152	73	30	1,000
Schedule 1.0(D3/D4)	57	480	210	132	89	32	1,000

Table A7 Distribution per 1,000 of Sample Households by Religion, Separately by Type of Schedule and by Sector

		No. of Households per 1,000 Households by Religion				
Sector	Type of Schedule	Hinduism	Islam	Christianity	Others	Total
(1)	(2)	(3)	(4)	(5)	(6)	(7)
Rural	Schedule 1.0(M)	917	33	13	36	1,000
	Schedule 1.0(W)	890	38	8	64	1,000
	Schedule 1.0(D3/D4)	902	31	13	52	1,000
Non-metro	Schedule 1.0(M)	846	113	9	31	1,000
	Schedule 1.0(W)	842	115	14	29	1,000
	Schedule 1.0(D3/D4)	858	108	2	33	1,000
Metro	Schedule 1.0(M)	831	75	44	50	1,000
	Schedule 1.0(W)	833	68	58	41	1,000
	Schedule 1.0(D3/D4)	855	67	36	42	1,000

Table A8 Pattern of Use of Container for Measuring Consumption of Items Reported in Schedule 1.0(D3D4)

Item			No. of Daily Schedules Reporting Use of Container			
Code	Description	Sector	Wholly	Partly	Not Used	All
(1a)	(1b)	(2)	(3)	(4)	(5)	(6)
101	Rice – PDS	Rural	144	0	9	153
		Non-metro	78	0	4	82
		Metro	51	0	20	71
102	Rice – other sources	Rural	1,770	55	130	1,955
		Non-metro	1,407	1	183	1,591
		Metro	831	1	200	1,032
103	Chira	Rural	7	0	24	31
		Non-metro	8	1	55	64
		Metro	6	0	4	10
104	Khoi, lawa	Rural	0	0	6	6
		Non-metro	–	–	–	–
		Metro	5	0	1	6
105	Muri	Rural	34	0	34	68
		Non-metro	11	1	25	37
		Metro	0	0	131	131
106	Other rice products	Rural	11	0	1	12
		Non-metro	7	0	16	23
		Metro	0	0	2	2
107	Wheat/atta – PDS	Rural	243	0	9	252
		Non-metro	222	0	21	243
		Metro	37	0	6	43

(Contd. . .)

Item			No. of Daily Schedules Reporting Use of Container			
Code	Description	Sector	Wholly	Partly	Not Used	All
(1a)	(1b)	(2)	(3)	(4)	(5)	(6)
108	Wheat/atta – other sources	Rural	59	0	0	59
		Non-metro	72	0	12	84
		Metro	18	0	5	23
110	Maida	Rural	1,384	1	125	1,510
		Non-metro	981	4	180	1,165
		Metro	542	1	212	755
111	Suji, rawa	Rural	5	0	5	10
		Non-metro	30	0	29	59
		Metro	11	0	11	22
112	Sewai, noodles	Rural	13	0	36	49
		Non-metro	69	4	66	139
		Metro	40	0	25	65
113	Bread (bakery)	Rural	0	0	5	5
		Non-metro	0	0	35	35
		Metro	0	0	31	31
114	Other wheat products	Rural	0	0	37	37
		Non-metro	0	0	168	168
		Metro	0	0	166	166
115	Jowar and products	Rural	7	0	0	7
		Non-metro	2	0	3	5
		Metro	2	0	1	3
116	Bajra and products	Rural	157	0	7	164
		Non-metro	10	0	3	13
		Metro	25	0	0	25
117	Maize and products	Rural	–	–	–	–
		Non-metro	1	0	1	2
		Metro	3	0	0	3
118	Barley and products	Rural	17	0	4	21
		Non-metro	14	0	0	14
		Metro	8	0	1	9
121	Ragi and products	Rural	4	6	6	16
		Non-metro	2	0	0	2
		Metro	2	0	0	2
139	Cereal substitutes (tapioca, jackfruit seed, etc.)	Rural	3	0	8	11
		Non-metro	4	0	34	38
		Metro	2	0	8	10
140	Arhar (tur)	Rural	1,116	1	96	1,213
		Non-metro	911	0	183	1,094
		Metro	276	0	111	387
141	Gram (split)	Rural	79	0	30	109
		Non-metro	42	0	61	103
		Metro	40	0	29	69
142	Gram (whole)	Rural	25	0	11	36
		Non-metro	33	0	25	58
		Metro	17	0	11	28

143	Moong	Rural	84	1	62	147
		Non-metro	160	0	108	268
		Metro	108	0	65	173
144	Masur	Rural	102	37	60	199
		Non-metro	46	0	24	70
		Metro	132	0	123	255
145	Urad	Rural	163	2	24	189
		Non-metro	103	1	44	148
		Metro	56	0	30	86
146	Peas	Rural	165	0	29	194
		Non-metro	22	0	15	37
		Metro	12	0	3	15
147	Soyabean	Rural	2	0	0	2
		Non-metro	1	0	1	2
		Metro	1	0	3	4
148	Khesari	Rural	38	0	3	41
		Non-metro	2	0	0	2
		Metro	–	–	–	–
150	Other pulses	Rural	25	2	36	63
		Non-metro	24	0	56	80
		Metro	63	0	94	157
151	Gram products	Rural	7	0	10	17
		Non-metro	9	0	23	32
		Metro	5	0	21	26
152	Besan	Rural	60	2	75	137
		Non-metro	47	0	72	119
		Metro	23	0	21	44
153	Other pulse products	Rural	0	0	24	24
		Non-metro	0	0	35	35
		Metro	0	0	34	34
160	Milk: liquid	Rural	820	14	852	1,686
		Non-metro	793	9	894	1,696
		Metro	134	0	882	1,016

Table A9 Item-wise Estimates of Quantity and Value of Consumption per Person per 30 Days by Schedule Type and by NSS Region for Some Major Food Items

			Consumption per Person per 30 Days						No. of Sample Household Reporting Consumption		
		State Region Code	Quantity (in kg)*			Value (in Rs)					
Item	Sector		1.0(M)	1.0(W)	1.0(D)	1.0(M)	1.0(W)	1.0(D)	1.0(M)	1.0(W)	1.0(D)
(1)	(2)	(3)	(4)	(5)	(6)	(7)	(8)	(9)	(10)	(11)	(12)
Rice	Rural	082	0.30	0.26	0.31	3.67	3.41	3.53	36	18	37
		253	4.79	5.13	5.13	39.17	43.71	43.09	95	92	186
		254	6.27	6.90	6.05	52.17	56.89	51.05	96	96	190
		145	1.75	2.06	2.23	17.89	22.35	25.18	43	35	76
		192	12.59	16.80	15.07	99.61	133.64	125.30	45	45	90
		234	8.92	10.76	10.49	85.60	108.54	115.52	47	47	96
		All	5.41	6.39	5.95	47.90	57.66	56.83	362	333	675

(Contd. . .)

(Contd. . .)

Item	Sector	State Region Code	Consumption per Person per 30 Days						No. of Sample Household Reporting Consumption		
			Quantity (in kg)*			Value (in Rs)					
			1.0(M)	1.0(W)	1.0(D)	1.0(M)	1.0(W)	1.0(D)	1.0(M)	1.0(W)	1.0(D)
(1)	(2)	(3)	(4)	(5)	(6)	(7)	(8)	(9)	(10)	(11)	(12)
	Non-metro	082	0.78	1.19	0.70	9.24	13.97	9.12	39	33	53
		253	3.66	3.84	2.97	36.96	39.03	31.80	48	48	94
		254	4.41	4.15	3.61	45.92	46.47	40.59	47	48	95
		145	3.11	3.48	3.48	35.50	41.89	44.27	48	46	95
		192	10.65	10.44	11.14	112.28	100.92	115.35	48	47	96
		234	8.32	9.39	7.00	118.33	123.77	94.85	48	48	95
		All	3.35	3.85	3.13	39.56	44.68	37.64	278	270	528
	Metro	311	3.06	3.05	2.39	38.38	38.33	31.77	43	40	76
		141	3.50	3.93	3.95	49.10	55.25	59.02	42	40	88
		263	6.19	6.37	5.71	82.37	84.89	74.30	44	42	86
		231	6.24	7.08	6.72	74.37	86.91	86.48	42	43	87
		All	4.58	4.95	4.56	59.36	64.77	62.14	171	165	337
Rice and products	Rural	082	0.30	0.26	0.32	3.67	3.41	3.60	36	18	38
		253	4.79	5.13	5.14	39.33	43.76	43.20	95	92	186
		254	6.30	7.13	6.09	52.52	58.50	51.39	96	96	190
		145	1.84	2.20	2.35	19.36	24.84	27.01	44	37	79
		192	12.82	17.34	15.28	103.13	142.74	128.35	45	45	90
		234	8.92	10.76	10.50	85.60	108.54	115.60	47	47	96
		All	5.47	6.54	6.01	48.78	59.75	57.76	363	335	679
	Non-metro	082	0.81	1.19	0.70	9.63	13.97	9.15	40	33	53
		253	3.70	3.84	2.98	37.40	39.03	32.00	48	48	95
		254	4.52	4.24	3.65	47.32	47.69	41.67	47	48	95
		145	3.31	3.58	3.78	38.72	43.57	48.86	48	46	95
		192	10.72	10.47	11.18	113.32	101.44	115.87	48	47	96
		234	8.38	9.48	7.01	119.37	124.82	94.92	48	48	95
		All	3.42	3.89	3.19	40.59	45.27	38.51	279	270	529
	Metro	311	3.06	3.05	2.39	38.38	38.33	31.77	43	40	76
		141	3.63	4.04	4.00	50.86	56.87	59.83	42	40	88
		263	6.44	6.77	6.02	87.07	91.75	80.00	47	44	91
		231	6.24	7.08	6.72	74.37	86.91	86.52	42	43	87
		All	4.68	5.07	4.64	60.94	66.73	63.57	174	167	342
Wheat and atta	Rural	082	12.29	12.86	12.86	76.14	79.20	77.46	48	46	94
		253	10.66	11.33	8.55	69.68	73.03	58.46	96	95	192
		254	7.74	8.67	7.01	54.36	61.36	48.60	96	95	186
		145	2.89	5.03	5.04	20.03	37.84	36.67	43	39	72
		192	0.12	0.09	0.01	1.21	1.00	0.14	5	1	2
		234	0.31	0.57	0.15	3.30	5.59	1.87	24	16	14
		All	4.84	5.97	5.52	32.33	40.65	36.72	312	292	560
	Non-metro	082	8.18	8.89	8.44	53.84	59.52	57.20	48	48	95
		253	7.07	8.86	6.29	54.76	69.33	52.89	48	48	96
		254	6.62	7.18	5.92	55.09	60.66	51.54	47	48	96
		145	6.34	5.49	6.63	53.61	46.04	55.94	48	45	96
		192	1.20	1.95	1.37	11.29	22.67	15.33	27	28	59
		234	0.74	0.70	0.70	8.22	9.19	9.18	41	28	41
		All	6.36	6.82	6.22	46.98	51.71	48.00	259	245	483

	Metro	311	6.18	6.66	5.44	57.63	63.67	50.92	43	42	88
		141	4.15	3.39	3.42	43.36	37.85	39.21	42	36	83
		263	3.08	2.87	2.27	31.05	30.05	23.84	38	36	68
		231	0.68	0.78	0.41	7.20	9.59	5.38	32	26	34
		All	3.62	3.42	2.97	36.05	35.58	31.34	155	140	273
Wheat and product	Rural	082	12.32	13.05	12.92	76.54	80.59	78.18	48	47	94
		253	10.72	11.35	8.60	71.01	73.69	59.16	96	95	192
		254	7.77	8.71	7.06	54.90	62.15	49.43	96	95	186
		145	3.01	5.17	5.12	22.28	40.31	37.64	45	39	73
		192	0.14	0.11	0.04	1.46	1.23	0.48	6	3	6
		234	0.44	0.92	0.35	5.20	10.64	5.25	27	22	24
		All	4.92	6.12	5.60	33.62	42.72	37.98	318	301	575
	Non-metro	082	8.38	9.14	8.62	57.20	63.66	60.34	48	48	95
		253	7.30	9.18	6.64	59.82	76.15	60.10	48	48	96
		254	6.71	7.51	6.06	56.50	67.28	54.51	47	48	96
		145	6.57	5.97	6.73	58.10	56.09	58.00	48	46	96
		192	1.54	2.46	1.85	15.66	29.31	21.52	39	35	68
		234	0.95	1.00	1.05	11.47	14.22	13.94	44	36	52
		All	6.56	7.15	6.45	50.59	57.76	52.00	274	261	503
	Metro	311	6.51	7.04	5.90	63.70	70.41	57.71	43	42	90
		141	4.77	4.14	3.58	55.44	52.22	42.14	42	40	84
		263	3.41	3.24	2.82	36.74	35.62	32.72	44	41	76
		231	1.18	1.27	1.00	16.88	18.69	17.12	39	36	56
		All	4.09	3.95	3.37	44.91	45.22	38.19	168	159	306
Cereals	Rural	082	14.10	14.88	13.60	88.98	93.47	83.87	48	47	95
		253	15.52	16.49	13.74	110.36	117.45	102.36	96	95	192
		254	14.09	15.90	13.17	107.57	121.04	100.94	96	96	192
		145	11.34	13.45	12.66	76.48	96.71	92.54	47	48	96
		192	14.07	18.71	16.75	110.27	150.94	136.68	45	45	90
		234	10.47	13.49	12.00	97.28	129.81	128.02	47	47	96
		All	12.69	15.03	13.39	94.94	115.30	105.51	379	378	761
	Non-metro	082	9.23	10.33	9.34	67.07	77.70	69.64	48	48	95
		253	11.00	13.02	9.63	97.22	115.18	92.14	48	48	96
		254	11.24	11.74	9.80	103.92	114.97	96.85	47	48	96
		145	10.21	10.09	10.80	99.68	103.06	108.89	48	46	96
		192	12.26	12.93	13.03	128.98	130.75	137.41	48	47	96
		234	9.33	10.51	8.06	131.18	139.25	109.02	48	48	95
		All	10.05	11.12	9.70	91.74	103.56	90.98	287	285	574
	Metro	311	9.57	10.09	8.31	102.08	108.74	89.64	43	42	90
		141	8.66	8.32	7.96	109.40	111.01	106.49	42	40	88
		263	9.85	10.01	8.85	123.81	127.37	112.76	47	45	92
		231	7.41	8.34	7.77	91.25	105.59	103.96	42	43	87
		All	8.86	9.07	8.17	106.91	112.60	103.54	174	170	357
Cereal substitutes	Rural	253	0.07	0.24	0.00	0.41	1.66	0.00	1	1	0
		145	0.06	0.11	0.02	1.31	2.28	0.48	21	22	7
		234	0.01	0.00	0.01	0.05	0.00	0.26	1	0	3
		All	0.02	0.05	0.01	0.39	0.72	0.17	23	23	10
	Non-metro	082	0.10	0.00	0.00	0.35	0.00	0.00	1	0	0
		253	0.00	0.17	0.00	0.00	1.20	0.00	0	1	0
		254	0.00	0.00	0.00	0.00	0.09	0.00	0	1	0
		145	0.09	0.08	0.10	1.88	1.71	2.31	31	19	27
		234	0.01	0.00	0.10	0.07	0.00	0.93	1	0	3
		All	0.06	0.04	0.03	0.42	0.46	0.43	33	21	30

(Contd. . .)

(Contd. . .)

Item	Sector	State Region Code	Consumption per Person per 30 Days						No. of Sample Household Reporting Consumption		
			Quantity (in kg)*			Value (in Rs)					
			1.0(M)	1.0(W)	1.0(D)	1.0(M)	1.0(W)	1.0(D)	1.0(M)	1.0(W)	1.0(D)
(1)	(2)	(3)	(4)	(5)	(6)	(7)	(8)	(9)	(10)	(11)	(12)
	Metro	311	0.00	0.00	0.00	0.00	0.00	0.00	1	0	0
		141	0.11	0.05	0.03	2.66	1.30	0.76	16	6	8
		263	0.00	0.00	0.01	0.00	0.00	0.16	0	0	1
		All	0.04	0.02	0.01	0.91	0.44	0.31	17	6	9
Pulses and products	Rural	082	0.64	0.80	0.56	14.39	18.26	13.22	48	45	84
		253	1.22	1.57	1.32	28.47	37.32	32.30	95	93	187
		254	1.05	1.42	1.36	21.17	28.45	32.02	96	96	189
		145	1.21	1.67	1.44	27.33	37.57	34.73	47	48	91
		192	0.36	0.51	0.71	8.64	11.61	16.32	45	43	83
		234	0.88	1.29	1.44	23.38	35.75	37.57	47	47	96
		All	0.92	1.25	1.17	21.31	29.07	28.56	378	372	730
	Non-metro	082	0.56	0.72	0.66	13.90	18.41	16.78	48	45	83
		253	0.95	1.55	1.07	22.87	38.24	27.88	48	47	92
		254	0.94	1.20	1.23	22.30	31.50	32.86	47	48	96
		145	1.01	1.13	1.13	23.70	27.21	28.29	48	46	92
		192	0.67	0.74	1.10	18.04	19.83	30.80	48	47	94
		234	0.96	1.49	1.24	27.13	43.09	33.47	48	48	94
		All	0.79	1.09	0.97	19.72	28.26	25.40	287	281	551
	Metro	311	1.05	0.91	1.38	28.47	26.25	39.77	43	42	87
		141	1.29	0.92	0.97	36.94	26.97	29.91	42	40	86
		263	0.53	0.63	0.73	16.90	19.71	22.58	44	42	83
		231	0.94	0.91	1.17	30.81	30.16	38.92	42	42	82
		All	1.00	0.86	1.05	29.55	26.05	32.55	171	166	338
Milk: liquid*	Rural	082	17.78	16.13	14.74	185.10	165.77	159.03	48	46	96
		253	4.26	4.15	3.86	42.00	40.98	38.18	74	71	161
		254	3.33	2.87	2.74	35.30	29.27	29.07	72	61	117
		145	1.23	1.46	1.69	13.03	15.85	18.00	40	41	84
		192	0.35	0.11	0.14	2.64	0.88	1.19	4	2	6
		234	2.88	2.57	2.72	34.25	31.58	30.47	32	26	52
		All	4.56	4.42	4.37	48.32	46.45	46.85	270	247	516
	Non-metro	082	8.22	10.01	7.96	102.40	127.97	105.60	48	48	94
		253	4.01	4.71	4.53	47.29	57.48	54.58	44	44	89
		254	3.98	4.23	4.18	50.66	48.90	53.32	40	41	83
		145	3.04	4.26	3.55	38.49	53.66	46.76	45	40	91
		192	4.10	2.63	2.94	41.76	24.87	29.18	30	31	59
		234	4.41	4.64	4.90	52.82	54.49	60.08	44	45	89
		All	5.59	6.38	5.62	68.85	79.20	72.18	251	249	505
	Metro	311	7.33	7.35	7.78	102.99	99.99	109.33	44	42	89
		141	5.19	4.59	4.49	84.93	76.21	70.53	40	42	89
		263	4.10	3.69	3.83	48.65	40.17	41.14	35	32	63
		231	4.81	4.37	4.28	51.99	47.44	50.30	35	36	70
		All	5.38	4.98	5.02	74.34	67.59	68.70	154	152	311
Sugar	Rural	082	1.64	2.09	2.12	24.98	33.19	34.25	48	47	96
		253	0.84	0.91	1.00	13.48	14.41	16.84	91	83	168
		254	0.44	0.56	0.47	6.86	8.85	7.57	87	80	150

		145	1.13	1.38	1.35	16.98	21.29	21.52	47	46	92
		192	0.31	0.39	0.29	4.54	5.91	5.03	34	30	37
		234	0.49	0.51	0.55	6.69	6.88	7.97	35	33	53
		All	0.82	1.03	1.02	12.41	15.86	16.35	342	319	596
	Non-metro	082	1.74	1.73	1.64	27.02	27.48	25.97	48	48	94
		253	0.99	1.31	0.96	14.25	19.61	15.26	46	48	89
		254	0.77	1.19	0.84	11.01	17.13	12.46	46	45	87
		145	1.16	1.40	1.32	17.54	22.00	20.72	48	46	95
		192	0.69	0.55	0.88	9.46	8.29	13.05	47	46	84
		234	0.79	0.96	0.86	10.92	13.52	12.52	47	42	90
		All	1.25	1.38	1.23	18.82	21.15	19.22	282	275	539
	Metro	311	0.91	0.78	1.07	13.63	11.99	17.58	44	43	89
		141	0.91	0.95	0.85	13.99	14.52	13.88	41	40	85
		263	0.57	0.51	0.64	9.61	8.67	11.06	44	41	84
		231	0.64	0.71	0.67	8.84	9.91	9.68	38	37	68
		All	0.78	0.77	0.81	11.87	11.69	13.21	167	161	326
Gur	Rural	082	0.39	0.48	0.25	4.62	5.87	3.06	28	20	38
		253	0.41	0.39	0.21	3.90	3.79	2.09	51	35	57
		254	0.34	0.55	0.47	3.79	5.83	5.08	76	61	119
		145	0.26	0.20	0.15	2.67	2.13	1.93	12	10	23
		192	0.00	0.00	0.00	0.05	0.00	0.00	2	0	0
		234	0.00	0.01	0.03	0.00	0.15	0.47	0	1	2
		All	0.22	0.26	0.19	2.36	2.87	2.18	169	127	239
	Non-metro	082	0.07	0.01	0.02	0.81	0.08	0.29	8	1	8
		253	0.03	0.06	0.03	0.30	0.64	0.43	5	6	9
		254	0.08	0.11	0.05	0.87	1.34	0.63	15	10	12
		145	0.03	0.07	0.02	0.39	1.08	0.34	11	7	7
		192	0.01	0.00	0.03	0.11	0.02	0.40	7	1	6
		234	0.00	0.00	0.01	0.00	0.00	0.14	0	0	1
		All	0.04	0.04	0.03	0.54	0.51	0.36	46	25	43
	Metro	311	0.01	0.03	0.02	0.14	0.42	0.29	5	2	4
		141	0.08	0.03	0.02	1.42	0.56	0.35	12	10	12
		263	0.01	0.01	0.02	0.16	0.32	0.23	2	2	2
		231	0.00	0.00	0.01	0.06	0.00	0.20	3	0	3
		All	0.03	0.02	0.02	0.56	0.35	0.28	22	14	21
Sugar group	Rural	082	2.04	2.58	2.38	29.74	39.19	37.82	48	47	96
		253	1.26	1.30	1.21	17.38	18.20	18.93	94	91	180
		254	0.78	1.11	0.94	10.65	14.68	12.65	96	93	186
		145	1.39	1.58	1.51	19.65	23.42	23.45	47	48	96
		192	0.32	0.39	0.29	4.58	5.91	5.03	34	30	37
		234	0.49	0.53	0.58	6.69	7.03	8.44	35	33	54
		All	1.05	1.29	1.21	14.79	18.76	18.63	354	342	649
	Non-metro	082	1.80	1.74	1.66	27.83	27.56	26.33	48	48	94
		253	1.02	1.37	0.99	14.54	20.25	15.69	46	48	92
		254	0.84	1.30	0.89	11.88	18.47	13.09	47	46	89
		145	1.19	1.47	1.35	17.92	23.08	21.28	48	47	95
		192	0.70	0.55	0.91	9.57	8.31	13.45	47	46	85
		234	0.79	0.96	0.87	10.92	13.52	12.67	47	42	90
		All	1.29	1.42	1.26	19.36	21.66	19.64	283	277	545
	Metro	311	0.92	0.81	1.09	13.77	12.41	17.87	44	43	89
		141	0.99	0.99	0.87	15.44	15.08	14.22	41	40	85
		263	0.58	0.53	0.65	9.79	8.99	11.29	44	41	84
		231	0.64	0.71	0.68	9.05	9.91	9.88	38	37	70
		All	0.81	0.79	0.83	12.48	12.04	13.49	167	161	328

(Contd. . .)

(Contd. . .)

Item	Sector	State Region Code	Consumption per Person per 30 Days						No. of Sample Household Reporting Consumption		
			Quantity (in Kg)*			Value (in Rs)					
			1.0(M)	1.0(W)	1.0(D)	1.0(M)	1.0(W)	1.0(D)	1.0(M)	1.0(W)	1.0(D)
(1)	(2)	(3)	(4)	(5)	(6)	(7)	(8)	(9)	(10)	(11)	(12)
Salt	Rural	082	0.28	0.30	0.31	1.15	1.22	1.27	48	47	95
		253	0.26	0.28	0.28	0.63	0.67	0.82	92	91	192
		254	0.24	0.29	0.30	0.68	0.86	1.69	94	93	191
		145	0.30	0.35	0.32	0.98	1.20	1.12	47	47	95
		192	0.32	0.50	0.34	1.02	1.49	1.36	44	45	90
		234	0.46	0.55	0.52	1.34	1.81	1.91	47	47	96
		All	0.32	0.38	0.35	1.01	1.26	1.40	372	370	759
	Non-metro	082	0.27	0.27	0.25	1.54	1.47	1.42	48	48	94
		253	0.20	0.24	0.26	0.92	1.30	1.35	47	48	94
		254	0.24	0.23	0.26	0.94	1.02	1.40	47	47	95
		145	0.27	0.33	0.28	1.07	1.57	1.11	48	46	96
		192	0.26	0.40	0.29	1.47	2.28	1.82	48	46	95
		234	0.36	0.58	0.42	1.43	2.27	1.73	48	47	94
		All	0.26	0.31	0.28	1.27	1.51	1.42	286	282	568
	Metro	311	0.23	0.22	0.23	1.53	1.44	1.31	43	41	79
		141	0.29	0.24	0.21	1.89	1.60	1.49	42	39	86
		263	0.31	0.29	0.28	1.67	1.62	1.63	44	42	85
		231	0.31	0.37	0.41	1.20	1.48	1.63	42	40	87
		All	0.28	0.28	0.27	1.61	1.54	1.51	171	162	337
Edible oil	Rural	082	0.23	0.27	0.26	8.38	10.06	9.48	33	29	52
		253	0.62	0.56	0.53	20.02	17.99	17.98	96	95	190
		254	0.44	0.44	0.44	16.10	16.51	16.63	96	96	191
		145	0.56	0.72	0.68	20.61	25.62	25.63	47	48	95
		192	0.16	0.17	0.21	6.63	6.87	8.33	45	45	89
		234	0.39	0.54	0.63	15.02	20.43	24.88	47	47	96
		All	0.41	0.48	0.48	15.06	17.44	18.32	364	360	713
	Non-metro	082	0.51	0.60	0.63	19.68	23.08	24.61	45	44	92
		253	0.68	0.77	0.69	24.58	27.72	25.07	48	48	96
		254	0.48	0.46	0.60	18.32	17.58	23.97	47	48	96
		145	0.80	0.86	0.88	31.40	33.26	34.72	48	46	96
		192	0.41	0.49	0.49	18.11	21.99	20.08	47	47	96
		234	0.55	0.58	0.65	22.29	24.84	26.51	48	47	95
		All	0.58	0.64	0.67	22.33	24.57	26.07	283	280	571
	Metro	311	0.65	0.58	0.79	28.56	24.85	35.56	43	42	89
		141	0.91	0.85	0.71	37.97	36.80	30.51	42	40	89
		263	0.74	0.72	0.76	31.77	31.34	28.82	44	42	85
		231	0.58	0.64	0.72	19.77	25.61	25.39	42	42	86
		All	0.74	0.71	0.74	30.52	30.42	30.15	171	166	349
Potato	Rural	082	1.24	1.75	1.39	4.97	7.11	5.63	48	46	73
		253	4.39	4.41	4.02	9.24	9.43	8.81	96	95	186
		254	3.67	4.63	4.84	9.33	11.71	13.02	96	96	192
		145	0.53	0.63	0.61	2.88	3.51	3.87	45	43	65
		192	0.73	1.39	1.82	3.82	7.27	9.86	44	44	87
		234	0.23	0.44	0.55	1.77	3.25	3.86	43	30	46
		All	1.44	1.86	1.91	4.68	6.42	6.93	372	354	649

Non-metro	082	1.22	1.35	1.32	4.32	4.74	4.97	46	44	82
	253	2.66	4.12	4.05	5.69	9.40	10.14	48	48	93
	254	3.58	3.96	3.93	10.88	11.91	11.82	47	47	96
	145	0.65	1.00	0.83	3.46	5.38	4.79	48	44	84
	192	0.81	1.51	2.45	4.29	7.69	12.20	47	47	96
	234	0.23	0.43	0.50	2.05	3.82	4.00	46	34	50
	All	1.55	2.09	2.08	4.97	6.80	7.11	282	264	501
Metro	311	1.30	2.06	2.04	5.84	9.40	9.32	38	40	85
	141	0.85	1.20	1.16	4.73	6.72	6.83	41	35	76
	263	2.39	3.00	3.27	8.80	10.90	11.95	44	42	85
	231	0.33	0.55	0.42	2.87	4.85	4.01	39	37	49
	All	1.16	1.61	1.60	5.42	7.75	7.76	162	154	295

Table A10 Item-wise Estimates of Value of Consumption per Person per 30 Days by Schedule Type and by NSS Region for Some Major Items of Food, Paan, Tobacco, and Intoxicants

Item	Sector	NSS Region	Value of Consumption per Person per 30 Days (in Rs)			No. of Sample Household Reporting Consumption		
			1.0(M)	1.0(W)	1.0(D)	1.0(M)	1.0(W)	1.0(D)
(1)	(2)	(3)	(4)	(5)	(6)	(7)	(8)	(9)
Milk products (exclude liquid milk)	Rural	082	43.04	42.32	60.74	20	18	40
		253	6.46	3.47	10.31	32	16	56
		234	3.50	0.00	3.60	9	0	22
		192	0.05	0.78	1.49	2	2	18
		254	1.59	1.47	3.81	12	9	4
		145	2.10	1.75	4.26	19	11	147
		All	8.54	8.19	14.20	94	56	25
	Non-metro	082	50.66	40.94	54.13	32	32	64
		253	3.28	3.86	10.39	16	10	7
		234	2.17	1.18	7.17	4	5	22
		254	3.93	1.29	8.17	15	6	48
		192	5.02	1.31	11.32	21	14	38
		145	10.17	12.04	10.70	30	28	19
		All	23.10	17.52	26.23	118	95	216
	Metro	311	17.76	16.75	32.88	32	29	66
		141	13.17	8.39	12.04	19	15	42
		263	4.36	7.32	8.68	18	14	38
		231	3.81	10.09	7.05	18	22	20
		All	10.32	10.45	14.78	87	80	166
Egg, fish and meat	Rural	082	3.56	0.18	4.07	4	1	4
		253	8.14	10.39	11.15	30	22	26
		254	9.21	10.63	11.33	39	23	34
		145	10.08	9.82	20.95	27	16	34
		192	10.63	17.40	25.73	40	35	45
		234	29.88	43.11	53.90	39	30	38
		All	13.19	15.79	22.33	179	127	181
	Non-metro	082	7.12	5.01	0.87	12	5	6
		253	19.22	20.34	19.63	28	23	35

(Contd. . .)

(Contd. . .)

Item	Sector	NSS Region	Value of Consumption per Person per 30 Days (in Rs)			No. of Sample Household Reporting Consumption		
			1.0(M)	1.0(W)	1.0(D)	1.0(M)	1.0(W)	1.0(D)
(1)	(2)	(3)	(4)	(5)	(6)	(7)	(8)	(9)
		254	12.60	24.02	33.24	21	23	45
		145	12.85	15.21	27.81	25	16	41
		192	25.77	33.42	52.32	40	37	71
		234	27.63	51.80	47.48	35	29	39
		All	13.95	19.13	20.61	161	133	237
	Metro	311	8.62	6.56	13.10	18	13	28
		141	49.63	25.03	48.89	31	22	50
		263	70.47	77.06	103.33	42	40	76
		231	42.54	75.95	65.83	39	39	69
		All	43.08	43.21	55.57	130	114	223
Vegetables	Rural	082	37.45	43.61	38.73	48	47	95
		253	25.31	32.69	26.50	96	95	192
		254	26.02	36.86	40.24	96	96	192
		145	20.34	23.31	23.51	47	48	94
		192	19.71	35.13	47.48	45	45	90
		234	20.99	28.92	48.90	47	47	96
		All	24.34	32.37	37.16	379	378	759
	Non-metro	082	47.27	52.09	51.57	47	48	95
		253	25.39	38.80	38.30	48	48	96
		254	36.21	44.92	58.76	47	48	96
		145	30.96	40.32	47.56	48	46	96
		192	39.74	57.10	72.87	48	47	96
		234	26.01	36.96	48.98	48	48	95
		All	36.79	45.35	50.62	286	285	574
	Metro	311	46.40	58.50	75.17	43	42	89
		141	77.84	69.84	75.01	42	40	88
		263	37.18	49.60	63.68	44	42	85
		231	39.48	56.52	49.15	42	43	87
		All	53.73	60.09	67.18	171	167	349
Fruit (fresh)	Rural	082	9.03	18.05	17.80	42	37	54
		253	4.74	6.60	11.70	59	40	81
		254	3.45	5.19	10.44	65	50	89
		145	5.70	5.67	8.05	33	21	29
		192	1.76	1.19	3.66	23	8	20
		234	9.25	14.58	20.43	48	46	87
		All	6.04	8.89	12.32	270	202	360
	Non-metro	082	21.99	24.74	36.92	45	39	66
		253	5.30	9.30	9.17	33	23	44
		254	4.75	8.24	10.91	33	24	42
		145	10.67	22.31	20.29	43	31	59
		192	8.62	13.80	25.21	37	33	62
		234	15.33	21.24	29.04	48	48	90
		All	14.00	18.18	24.50	239	198	363

	Metro	311	22.36	33.35	54.70	45	38	66
		141	46.67	46.92	53.17	45	42	88
		263	16.57	33.80	30.37	42	33	55
		231	21.49	33.68	31.07	46	46	79
		All	29.28	38.13	44.20	178	159	288
Fruit (dry)	Rural	082	2.19	2.46	1.91	14	6	10
		253	1.60	1.11	1.60	22	12	25
		254	0.98	1.52	1.68	25	17	24
		145	3.54	4.06	3.45	37	30	43
		192	0.15	0.00	0.00	4	0	0
		234	0.19	0.08	0.21	5	1	2
		All	1.61	1.84	1.68	107	66	104
	Non-metro	082	3.78	3.41	4.17	19	10	20
		253	4.06	2.99	2.69	24	11	20
		254	5.02	0.22	2.34	19	5	12
		145	7.41	5.55	10.33	44	30	55
		192	0.82	0.44	0.35	9	3	4
		234	0.10	0.38	0.16	4	2	3
		All	3.94	2.62	3.84	119	61	114
	Metro	311	1.22	0.88	1.74	10	4	7
		141	8.90	4.12	6.00	33	22	40
		263	0.73	1.09	1.88	4	2	8
		231	2.38	1.62	1.97	14	7	15
		All	3.99	2.20	3.39	61	35	70
Spices	Rural	082	12.95	15.64	17.54	48	47	94
		253	9.87	13.44	15.16	96	95	191
		254	10.29	15.70	17.75	96	96	190
		145	14.27	20.70	24.18	47	48	94
		192	7.17	9.37	12.87	45	45	90
		234	18.80	31.98	44.73	47	47	96
		All	13.18	19.15	23.67	379	378	755
	Non-metro	082	12.39	17.02	20.07	48	48	93
		253	11.01	18.70	22.28	48	48	96
		254	11.32	19.05	24.69	47	48	95
		145	14.19	19.65	21.29	48	46	96
		192	14.30	17.35	21.27	48	47	96
		234	17.79	29.44	36.05	48	48	94
		All	13.01	19.55	23.34	287	285	570
	Metro	311	12.02	16.22	21.82	41	39	79
		141	15.53	16.69	19.98	42	40	87
		263	11.31	13.69	13.50	44	42	84
		231	21.80	29.38	36.91	42	42	86
		All	15.30	18.89	22.79	169	163	336
Tea and coffee	Rural	082	16.26	21.02	21.90	48	47	94
		253	5.85	7.89	9.52	81	66	144
		254	7.82	8.10	11.34	84	77	144
		145	11.40	15.80	15.03	48	48	94
		192	3.13	4.66	6.85	35	34	56
		234	23.49	33.96	39.91	44	38	81
		All	12.73	16.82	18.88	340	310	613

(Contd. . .)

(Contd. . .)

Item	Sector	NSS Region	Value of Consumption per Person per 30 Days (in Rs)			No. of Sample Household Reporting Consumption		
			1.0(M)	1.0(W)	1.0(D)	1.0(M)	1.0(W)	1.0(D)
(1)	(2)	(3)	(4)	(5)	(6)	(7)	(8)	(9)
	Non-metro	082	19.86	21.11	28.42	48	48	94
		253	17.84	21.89	25.83	47	48	90
		254	12.52	15.80	29.65	47	47	95
		145	26.05	26.78	32.68	48	48	95
		192	10.34	9.70	9.95	48	47	89
		234	31.26	42.69	36.30	48	48	91
		All	20.59	23.35	28.95	286	286	554
	Metro	311	22.43	24.91	39.27	46	45	93
		141	41.48	47.44	51.06	46	45	94
		263	14.54	19.83	28.92	47	48	95
		231	30.56	36.06	46.08	47	44	94
		All	29.16	34.10	43.09	186	182	376
Beverages, etc.	Rural	082	25.02	47.59	47.51	48	47	96
		253	12.23	17.40	25.00	90	78	174
		254	14.67	17.91	30.03	90	84	177
		145	21.21	24.54	32.83	48	48	95
		192	16.43	25.39	36.40	41	41	74
		234	59.38	106.80	116.62	47	44	92
		All	27.72	42.73	50.67	364	342	708
	Non-metro	082	42.61	43.15	79.29	48	48	95
		253	24.68	35.06	42.30	47	48	93
		254	50.64	32.51	70.48	48	48	95
		145	43.71	46.62	74.72	48	48	96
		192	29.40	65.36	53.71	48	48	91
		234	46.98	74.34	90.26	48	48	94
		All	40.71	45.31	71.34	287	288	564
	Metro	311	76.39	85.86	112.97	46	45	95
		141	254.89	180.73	191.14	46	46	96
		263	47.95	67.77	100.39	48	48	96
		231	113.80	115.05	151.72	48	47	95
		All	139.79	121.15	147.89	188	186	382
Food total	Rural	082	459.83	496.61	491.74	48	47	96
		253	286.60	317.04	311.17	96	96	192
		254	256.99	299.22	306.61	96	96	192
		145	234.34	289.02	311.58	48	48	96
		192	188.68	265.48	295.18	48	48	96
		234	318.62	450.08	517.77	48	48	96
		All	289.04	355.99	379.89	384	383	768
	Non-metro	082	416.70	461.08	489.97	48	48	95
		253	299.45	387.92	360.13	48	48	96
		254	331.55	361.67	428.67	48	48	96
		145	341.15	401.98	452.63	48	48	96
		192	340.12	394.54	467.97	48	48	96
		234	380.34	490.54	500.88	48	48	95
		All	367.51	424.91	454.75	288	288	574

	Metro	311	460.64	490.35	604.54	46	45	96
		141	751.32	617.79	657.90	46	46	96
		263	419.49	477.90	538.42	48	48	96
		231	448.15	541.00	572.15	48	48	96
		All	549.29	542.80	604.25	188	187	384
Paan	Rural	082						
		253	4.50	2.46	3.00	28	16	36
		254	5.51	6.09	9.89	53	43	104
		145	5.46	8.96	11.76	40	39	83
		192	1.61	0.32	2.99	13	3	14
		234	3.29	5.70	7.75	20	20	39
		All	3.64	4.72	6.80	154	121	276
	Non-metro	082	0.00	0.00	0.01	0	0	1
		253	0.89	8.06	3.46	7	11	15
		254	5.96	16.36	20.19	22	24	70
		145	8.43	10.98	14.92	41	42	80
		192	4.98	1.78	7.40	17	16	34
		234	1.68	2.79	2.64	10	12	12
		All	2.49	6.01	6.40	97	105	212
	Metro	311	0.00	0.83	0.00	0	2	0
		141	7.24	2.19	5.25	24	11	29
		263	3.00	1.84	3.81	8	7	13
		231	2.80	6.39	3.44	9	14	16
		All	3.71	2.78	3.44	41	34	58
Tobacco	Rural	082	17.71	16.26	21.16	40	35	84
		253	10.01	12.17	13.32	76	76	159
		254	5.28	6.44	7.38	78	71	145
		145	4.42	7.42	7.43	38	34	64
		192	5.34	6.82	9.19	42	40	84
		234	9.00	12.58	13.21	26	21	47
		All	8.10	10.03	11.65	300	277	583
	Non-metro	082	11.74	9.01	13.29	29	25	52
		253	8.57	9.18	15.21	29	27	54
		254	2.80	4.43	5.96	19	17	54
		145	6.63	6.21	12.49	28	27	67
		192	2.33	2.72	6.32	21	20	43
		234	17.31	11.40	6.70	19	17	23
		All	9.72	7.93	11.32	145	133	293
	Metro	311	3.93	2.25	5.44	9	8	26
		141	4.68	6.85	11.19	20	16	39
		263	14.69	10.82	20.36	18	22	56
		231	6.82	14.54	18.90	8	17	34
		All	7.08	8.39	13.43	55	63	155
Intoxicants	Rural	082	17.16	25.06	18.86	14	9	16
		253	2.36	6.06	8.59	13	10	20
		254	2.10	4.78	8.13	14	12	31
		145	5.78	4.19	3.49	13	10	12
		192	2.02	2.84	4.94	13	13	23
		234	9.69	3.48	21.36	14	4	25
		All	6.99	7.63	11.02	81	58	127

(Contd. . .)

Item	Sector	NSS Region	Value of Consumption per Person per 30 Days (in Rs)			No. of Sample Household Reporting Consumption		
			1.0(M)	1.0(W)	1.0(D)	1.0(M)	1.0(W)	1.0(D)
(1)	(2)	(3)	(4)	(5)	(6)	(7)	(8)	(9)
	Non-metro	082	11.68	12.92	13.35	11	8	9
		253	4.24	0.99	7.30	2	2	9
		254	1.28	5.92	3.79	2	4	8
		145	3.33	3.88	18.67	5	6	18
		192	1.24	0.89	2.05	6	5	8
		234	2.86	1.95	1.22	3	3	2
		All	6.43	6.62	9.66	29	28	54
	Metro	311	5.15	7.85	2.81	4	3	4
		141	5.22	11.57	8.31	7	6	7
		263	3.31	1.43	1.60	3	1	2
		231	4.84	13.20	12.36	6	7	6
		All	4.74	9.03	6.69	20	17	19

Table A11 Average Number of Meals Consumed per Household by Household Members and Others During a Period of 30 Days by NSS Region and by Quintile Group for All Regions Combined

NSS Region/ Quintile Group (%)	Type of Schedule	Number of Meals per Household Taken by Household Members				Number of Meals per Household Served to Others		
		Free of Cost	On Payment	At Home	Total	Guests at Cere-monials	Casual Members	Agricultural Labour and Employees
(1)	(2)	(3)	(4)	(5)	(6)	(7)	(8)	(9)
								Rural
082	1.0 (M)	10.4	2.4	400.3	413.1	0.9	13.6	0.9
	1.0 (W)	10.9	2.5	485.7	499.1	0.6	25.8	7.7
	1.0 (D)	–	–	–	456.5	1.0	34.7	0.1
253	1.0 (M)	7.2	0.1	369.5	376.8	1.4	7.8	0.0
	1.0 (W)	5.1	0.4	422.5	428.0	0.0	9.5	0.0
	1.0 (D)	–	–	–	404.2	6.0	18.2	0.0
254	1.0 (M)	8.7	0.2	455.0	463.9	2.9	6.5	0.0
	1.0 (W)	9.8	0.0	452.9	462.7	3.1	6.9	1.0
	1.0 (D)	–	–	–	457.6	5.7	21.7	0.6
145	1.0 (M)	12.3	1.0	286.3	299.6	0.6	11.9	0.0
	1.0 (W)	17.1	0.0	292.8	309.9	0.0	4.9	0.0
	1.0 (D)	–	–	–	258.5	2.9	23.3	0.0
192	1.0 (M)	1.4	0.0	287.4	288.8	1.9	0.3	0.0
	1.0 (W)	0.4	0.0	505.9	506.3	3	0.6	0.0
	1.0 (D)	–	–·	–	292.3	3.2	0.7	0.0
234	1.0 (M)	20.3	10.8	327.2	358.3	0.0	14.4	0.0
	1.0 (W)	16.1	5.9	289.1	311.1	4.5	12.7	1.0
	1.0 (D)	–	–	–	312.0	0.2	19.2	1.1

NSS region: All

0 – 20	1.0 (M)	16.8	0.2	394.1	411.1	1.4	2.1	0.0
	1.0 (W)	22.0	0.0	466.3	488.3	1.4	6.9	0.0
	1.0 (D)	–	–	–	336.2	0.1	8.8	0.1
20 – 40	1.0 (M)	14.6	0.1	379.3	394.0	0.7	4.5	0.0
	1.0 (W)	11.5	0.0	461.5	473.0	2.4	4.3	0.0
	1.0 (D)	–	–	–	389.5	0.5	8.0	0.0
40 – 60	1.0 (M)	11.5	1.7	312.3	325.5	0.2	11.5	0.0
	1.0 (W)	14.4	0.1	367.0	381.5	0.0	6.6	1.9
	1.0 (D)	–	–	–	380.6	1.8	20.5	0.1
60 – 80	1.0 (M)	11.9	2.4	323.0	337.3	0.4	17.6	0.0
	1.0 (W)	5.8	1.7	332.5	340.0	0.9	9.6	0.9
	1.0 (D)	–	–	–	337.1	1.8	13.2	1.4
80 – 100	1.0 (M)	5.4	10.7	307.1	323.2	2.3	12.1	0.6
	1.0 (W)	8.0	6.0	309.5	323.5	4.9	17.6	3.4
	1.0 (D)	–	–	–	279.7	6.7	39.9	0.2
All	1.0 (M)	11.6	3.4	339.2	354.2	1.0	10.1	0.1
	1.0 (W)	11.8	1.9	378.3	392.0	2.1	9.6	1.4
	1.0 (D)	–	–	–	338.8	2.6	19.9	0.4

Non-metro

082	1.0 (M)	8.6	0.1	399.4	408.1	0.4	14.9	0.1
	1.0 (W)	12.3	0.0	401.7	414.0	1.4	17.6	1.5
	1.0 (D)	–	–	–	373.3	0.8	24.0	0.8
253	1.0 (M)	3.8	0.0	353.0	356.8	0.0	1.2	0.0
	1.0 (W)	7.1	1.0	323.5	331.6	0.7	6.6	0.0
	1.0 (D)	–	–	–	324.3	3.0	8.1	0.0
254	1.0 (M)	5.6	3.3	326.3	335.2	4.4	3.0	0.0
	1.0 (W)	6.9	0.1	431.6	438.6	0.0	7.1	0.0
	1.0 (D)	–	–	–	393.9	6.2	11.4	0.0
145	1.0 (M)	14.6	0.9	321.6	337.1	0.2	6.9	0.0
	1.0 (W)	26.4	1.2	322.7	350.3	0.0	11.6	0.0
	1.0 (D)	–	–	–	306.7	0.3	30.1	0.0
192	1.0 (M)	1.0	0.0	234.0	235.0	2.6	2.2	0.7
	1.0 (W)	20.2	3.3	270.7	294.2	4.7	1.3	0.7
	1.0 (D)	–	–	–	302.2	6.3	3.9	0.4
234	1.0 (M)	11.8	1.7	363.4	376.9	1.0	11.3	0.0
	1.0 (W)	15.4	2.1	345.3	362.8	0.5	8.4	0.0
	1.0 (D)	–	–	–	358.4	3.3	11.9	0.0

NSS region: All

0 – 20	1.0 (M)	12.5	0.4	429.8	442.7	0.7	2.2	0.0
	1.0 (W)	35.1	0.0	396.7	431.8	0.0	7.1	0.0
	1.0 (D)	–	–	–	413.3	0.0	5.0	0.0
20 – 40	1.0 (M)	3.9	0.2	382.5	386.6	0.8	4.9	0.0
	1.0 (W)	15.6	0.1	422.5	438.2	3.3	2.3	0.0
	1.0 (D)	–	–	–	398.4	2.8	14.8	0.0
40 – 60	1.0 (M)	6.0	0.0	358.4	364.4	0.4	8.5	0.2
	1.0 (W)	10.5	0.0	405.2	415.7	0.9	10.2	0.0
	1.0 (D)	–	–	–	357.1	1.1	16.3	0.0

(Contd. . .)

NSS Region/ Quintile Group (%)	Type of Schedule	Number of Meals per Household Taken by Household Members				Number of Meals per Household Served to Others		
		Free of Cost	On Payment	At Home	Total	Guests at Cere-monials	Casual Members	Agricultural Labour and Employees
(1)	(2)	(3)	(4)	(5)	(6)	(7)	(8)	(9)
60 – 80	1.0 (M)	6.5	0.2	334.5	341.2	2.9	5.1	0.0
	1.0 (W)	10.4	0.7	318.3	329.4	0.0	18.6	2.7
	1.0 (D)	–	–	–	346.7	2.5	20.4	0.0
80 – 100	1.0 (M)	13	3.0	320.3	336.3	0.1	20.9	0.1
	1.0 (W)	4.5	2.4	333.1	340.0	0.8	15.2	0.1
	1.0 (D)	–	–	–	290.8	4.4	27.7	1.3
All	1.0 (M)	8.4	0.9	359.4	368.7	1.0	9.1	0.1
	1.0 (W)	13.5	0.8	368.2	382.5	0.9	11.6	0.6
	1.0 (D)	–	–	–	353.7	2.4	18.1	0.3
								Metro
311	1.0 (M)	0.0	5.1	364.3	369.4	0.0	0.0	7.9
	1.0 (W)	0.0	7.1	377.1	384.2	0.0	0.0	5.9
	1.0 (D)	–	–	–	317	1.9	4.4	5.3
141	1.0 (M)	7.5	6.1	223.4	237	10.4	4.9	0.1
	1.0 (W)	15.2	10.1	213.2	238.5	0.0	2.1	0.0
	1.0 (D)	–	–	–	263.4	0.0	14.1	0.1
263	1.0 (M)	3.1	2.1	242.9	248.1	0.8	4.7	0.8
	1.0 (W)	2.5	3.4	246	251.9	2.8	9.2	0.0
	1.0 (D)	–	–	–	239.9	2.3	7.8	0.9
231	1.0 (M)	40.6	19.6	290.1	350.3	0.0	11.9	0.7
	1.0 (W)	26.8	13	346.9	386.7	3.8	7.7	2.5
	1.0 (D)	–	–	–	347.8	2.4	24.3	1.3
NSS region: All								
0 – 20	1.0 (M)	14.9	3.6	370.6	389.1	0.0	3.9	0.0
	1.0 (W)	20.3	1.3.0	360	381.6	0.0	4.6	0.0
	1.0 (D)	–	–	–	348.4	0.0	2.9	0.0
20 – 40	1.0 (M)	15.6	7.8	309.8	333.2	0.3	0.4	0.0
	1.0 (W)	13.5	4.3	318.9	336.7	0.0	0.8	0.0
	1.0 (D)	–	–	–	332.6	4	12.5	0.0
40 – 60	1.0 (M)	7.5	3.4	316.6	327.5	0.2	2.5	0.0
	1.0 (W)	11.1	1.4	372.1	384.6	2.9	6.4	0.0
	1.0 (D)	–	–	–	327.5	0.0	6.5	0.7
60 – 80	1.0 (M)	14.6	1.8	282	298.4	0.4	11.6	0.8
	1.0 (W)	13.2	9.4	300.2	322.8	2.7	8.4	1.3
	1.0 (D)	–	–	–	301.6	0.8	15	0.5
80 – 100	1.0 (M)	11.1	18.0	163.3	192.4	12.7	7.1	6.5
	1.0 (W)	6.2	19.1	167	192.3	1.3	2.3	5.4
	1.0 (D)	–	–	–	202.5	2.1	21.2	4.8
All	1.0 (M)	12.5	8.2	273.1	293.8	3.8	5.4	2
	1.0 (W)	12.0	8.7	285.9	306.6	1.4	4.4	1.9
	1.0 (D)	–	–	–	289.5	1.4	13.1	1.7

Table A12 Estimates of Value of Consumption per Person per 30 Days based on Schedules 1.0(D3/D4) Separately for each Day of Canvassing, for Selected Items/Item-groups*

Item/Item-group	Based on Schedule 1.0(D3)			Based on Schedule 1.0(D4)			
	Day 1	Day 2	Day 3	Day 1	Day 2	Day 3	Day 4
(1)	(2)	(3)	(4)	(5)	(6)	(7)	(8)
							Sector: Rural
Rice and products	56.0	54.7	56.4	60.2	62.3	63.6	59.4
Wheat and products	40.6	37.9	35.8	33.7	37.9	40.3	34.4
Cereals	107.0	103.0	103.2	102.7	108.5	112.4	104.1
Pulses and products	31.1	27.4	30.2	30.7	27.2	27.1	25.6
Milk and products	15.3	13.4	14.6	11.4	16.1	17.2	11.3
Edible oil	17.5	18.0	18.9	17.6	17.8	22.5	16.5
Vegetables	36.0	36.6	40.2	36.0	36.1	38.7	36.5
Fruits (fresh)	10.5	11.5	15.4	10.7	12.3	13.4	12.5
Fruits (dry)	2.0	1.1	0.9	2.1	1.0	4.0	0.9
Gur	2.4	2.2	2.3	2.5	1.5	2.3	2.0
Sugar group	20.0	18.0	18.8	18.2	17.8	20.9	16.7
Salt	–	0.0	4.6	–	–	–	5.1
Spices	–	0.1	76.2	–	–	–	87.9
Beverages, etc.	33.4	47.9	75.8	41.6	37.0	34.7	83.4
All food	339.9	348.2	467.8	328.2	345.9	366.8	461.7
Paan	1.6	1.6	19.5	2.1	1.9	1.9	18.3
Tobacco	8.9	8.7	21.9	6.9	6.8	6.4	20.8
Intoxicants	15.9	11.4	9.6	13.2	10.0	8.1	7.7
Potato	6.7	7.2	7.3	7.2	6.8	6.9	6.5
							Sector: Non-metro
Rice and products	40.5	41.7	40.8	37.8	37.0	36.0	34.8
Wheat and products	48.7	50.0	50.5	53.8	56.3	53.3	49.6
Cereals	90.2	92.3	91.7	92.2	94.2	90.0	85.0
Pulses and products	27.1	24.9	27.6	26.0	24.7	22.7	23.7
Milk and products	25.8	29.5	32.0	20.9	26.2	23.8	22.6
Edible oil	25.5	25.4	27.9	24.1	26.5	27.1	25.6
Vegetables	50.2	48.8	51.6	46.8	50.8	54.0	52.0
Fruits (fresh)	22.2	24.6	29.0	17.0	26.0	27.5	24.3
Fruits (dry)	4.8	3.8	6.4	2.5	3.4	2.0	2.9
Gur	0.4	0.4	0.4	0.5	0.3	0.2	0.2
Sugar group	19.5	19.3	20.5	19.0	20.7	19.2	19.0
Salt	–	0.0	4.2	–	0.1	–	5.7
Spices	–	0.4	72.0	–	–	0.0	89.7
Beverages, etc.	62.8	56.5	104.5	52.9	51.6	52.5	115.0
All food	421.2	423.9	546.3	393.9	418.0	416.0	551.2
Paan	3.0	2.8	12.9	2.3	2.4	2.3	19.1
Tobacco	8.7	8.3	21.1	8.3	8.0	7.8	15.7
Intoxicants	17.6	6.3	7.8	9.3	9.6	11.6	4.7
Potato	6.8	6.8	7.0	7.1	7.2	7.6	7.6

(Contd. . .)

(Contd. . .)

Item/Item-group	Based on Schedule 1.0(D3)			Based on Schedule 1.0(D4)			
	Day 1	Day 2	Day 3	Day 1	Day 2	Day 3	Day 4
(1)	(2)	(3)	(4)	(5)	(6)	(7)	(8)
							Sector: Metro
Rice and products	63.9	62.3	63.9	65.6	65.7	63.6	68.5
Wheat and products	40.5	37.1	35.5	40.3	41.3	38.9	36.2
Cereals	104.9	100.9	100.9	108.5	109.4	107.3	106.8
Pulses and products	32.8	34.0	28.8	31.0	32.3	35.0	38.7
Milk and products	11.3	15.8	14.4	13.2	13.4	15.8	22.8
Edible oil	28.8	30.3	30.4	29.0	31.9	31.3	33.4
Vegetables	67.0	65.8	67.3	64.8	68.1	72.8	73.6
Fruits (fresh)	46.5	45.2	50.6	39.6	38.2	42.9	48.8
Fruits (dry)	4.1	1.8	5.3	2.4	2.6	3.6	4.1
Gur	0.3	0.4	0.4	0.1	0.2	0.4	0.3
Sugar group	12.9	14.4	13.9	12.9	13.6	13.9	14.3
Salt	–	–	5.1	–	–	–	5.8
Spices	–	–	75.2	–	–	–	90.5
Beverages, etc.	124.0	138.6	185.1	137.9	136.5	132.9	201.0
All food	541.8	560.0	704.2	571.2	580.7	589.8	770.1
Paan	1.8	2.0	7.9	1.7	1.5	1.8	7.8
Tobacco	9.2	8.9	13.6	14.6	14.4	14.1	24.7
Intoxicants	5.3	10.3	10.2	4.4	7.6	5.0	2.6
Potato	8.5	7.2	7.9	8.3	7.1	8.1	8.2

Note: * See Footnote 6 in the text.

Part II

Interpreting the Evidence

II.1 WHAT HAPPENED TO POVERTY IN INDIA IN THE 1990s?

11. Estimates of Consumer Expenditure and Its Distribution: Statistical Priorities after NSS 55th Round

12. Adjusted Indian Poverty Estimates for 1999/2000

13. Poverty Outcomes in India in the 1990

14. Poverty and Inequality in India: Getting Closer to the Truth

11

Estimates of Consumer Expenditure and Its Distribution
Statistical Priorities after the NSS 55th Round

Abhijit Sen

ISSUES

For sometime now, data available periodically from the National Sample Survey (NSS) have figured significantly in policy-related discussions on the effects of the economic strategies of the 1990s on the incidence of poverty, especially rural poverty. Throughout the 1990s, the NSS results on household consumption expenditure generated much interest in both academic and policy circles.[1] These results, which many independent researchers have analysed, had led to a general consensus that rural poverty at the all-India level did *not* show any declining trend over the 1990s (see Table 11.1).[2] That this had happened despite the somewhat higher rates of aggregate GDP growth during the period became an important issue in the ongoing policy debate on the effects of the liberalising economic policies instituted by successive governments over the 1990s.

[1] With nine NSS surveys on Consumer Expenditure conducted during the nineties, there is more information on the matter than during the previous two decades. Results are currently available for July–June 1990/91 (46th Round), July–December 1991 (47th Round), January–December 1992 (48th Round), January–June 1993 (49th Round), July–June 1993/94 (50th Round), July–June 1994/95 (51st Round), July–June 1995/96 (52nd Round), January–December 1997 (53rd Round) and January–June 1998 (54th Round). However, of these, only the 50th Round is a quinquennial large sample survey, while the rest are based on 'thin samples' involving a much smaller sample size. Moreover, Rounds 47, 49 and 54 are half-year surveys which are not necessarily comparable to the rest because of possible seasonal biases and, for this reason, have not been considered in the discussion to follow. During July 1999-June 2000, the NSS has completed another quinquennial large sample survey, the 55th Round, results of which are expected later this year.

[2] Three internally consistent series on poverty incidence are available for the nineties, all of which are based on the NSS distribution of nominal consumption expenditure and on the official poverty line but use somewhat different deflators: Datt (1999), Gupta (1999), and Sundaram and Tendulkar (2000). Each of these show that the headcount poverty ratio in Rural India declined almost steadily between 1972/73 and 1989/90, and that after July 1991 this has fluctuated at levels which in every subsequent year has been higher than during 1989/90. Urban poverty is, however, seen to be declining during the nineties by all the three series.

Table 11.1 Estimates of Poverty in India (Headcount Ratios)

NSS Round	Year	Rural			Urban		
		Datt	Gupta	Tendulkar-Sundaram	Datt	Gupta	Tendulkar-Sundaram
27	October 72–September 73	55.4	NA	57.2	45.7	NA	47.0
28	October 73–June 74	55.7	NA	56.2	48.0	NA	49.2
32	July 77–June 78	50.6	NA	54.5	40.5	NA	42.9
38	January–December 83	45.3	45.6	49.0	35.7	40.8	38.3
42	July 86–June 87	38.8	NA	45.2	34.3	NA	35.4
43	July 87–June 88	39.2	39.1	44.9	36.2	38.2	36.5
44	July 88–June 89	39.1	NA	42.2	36.6	NA	35.1
45	July 89–June 90	34.3	33.7	36.7	33.4	36.0	34.8
46	July 90–June 91	36.4	35.0	37.5	32.8	35.3	35.0
47	July 91–December 91	37.4	NA	40.1	33.2	NA	34.8
48	January–December 92	43.5	41.7	46.1	33.7	37.8	36.4
49	January 93–June 93	NA	NA	44.2	NA	NA	38.9
50	July 93–June 94	36.7	37.3	39.7	30.5	32.4	30.9
51	July 94–June 95	41.0	38.0	43.6	33.5	34.2	34.1
52	July 95–June 96	37.2	38.3	40.1	28.0	30.0	28.7
53	January–December 97	35.8	38.5	38.3	30.0	33.9	31.0
54	January 98–June 98	NA	45.3	44.9	NA	34.6	31.6

Sources: (a) Ozler, Datt and Ravallion (1996), as updated by Datt (1999); (b) Gupta (1999); (c) Sundaram and Tendulkar (2000).

Those questioning the economic reform package have argued that these policies have involved neglect of rural investment and of the food security system, resulting in slow agricultural growth, reduced employment opportunities in rural areas, and high food prices. All of these are likely to be associated with persistent or even increasing rural poverty. Also, that NSS surveys show stagnation or even decline in rural non-agricultural employment, which is in conformity with their argument that the reform package increased the urban-rural divide by reducing the spill-overs that public sector effort can contribute by way of mitigating inter-sectoral and inter-regional inequalities.

By contrast, proponents of the economic policies of the 1990s have by and large held that the NSS results so far available did not allow such conclusions, and that nothing could be said conclusively about rural consumption or poverty until the next large sample results were available. The serious economists amongst these have not contested the NSS data which show that rural poverty has failed to decline, but have argued that the reforms process should not be implicated for this. They have questioned the critics' association of economic liberalisation and public expenditure cuts with the lower growth of rural real consumption implied by the NSS, and argued essentially that extraneous factors may be involved.[3]

A view often expressed in this context was that the matter of causation cannot be settled since the last large sample NSS round in 1993/94 was too close to the beginning of the reform period, and that the more recent results are from 'thin samples'. Because of their smaller sample size, and the associated higher variance of sample estimates, these are not reliable for analysis below the national level. Since it is generally agreed that the somewhat higher GDP growth during the 1990s has been associated with

[3] See, Tendulkar and Jain (1995), Datt and Ravallion (1997), Ravallion (2000a, b, c), and Sundaram and Tendulkar (2000 op. cit.).

larger interstate differences in growth rates, correlation of these with poverty trends at the state level are of particular importance to test the relationship between economic growth and poverty reduction.

However, in the course of this debate, some defenders of the economic reform strategy went much further and questioned the NSS database itself. These observers found it impossible to accept that income poverty at the national level can increase during a period of rapid GDP growth and claimed that the NSS consumption expenditure estimates from the thin samples must be flawed even at the national level simply because these were out of line with estimates of GDP growth.[4] Interestingly, this fundamentalist position, that economic growth is not only necessary for poverty reduction but also sufficient, was at this very time being questioned by the World Bank's draft 'World Development Report'. In the subsequent effort to stall this rethinking, a leading role was played by some influential Indian economists abroad who, among other things, questioned the Indian data in this context.

Thus, there emerged a view that the association of higher GDP growth rates with the persistence of rural poverty was not a real fact which needed to be understood and addressed, but a failure of the statistical system to capture the actual increase in consumption in rural areas. Unfortunately, this direction of attack sought to undermine the credibility of a consistent and comparable time series of estimates, which not only has an almost incomparable statistical pedigree among survey sources of economic data anywhere in the world, but has also so far been accepted as reliable by economists, whatever their differences on the interpretation of the results thus thrown up.

With this background, considerable importance attached to results of the 55th Round (1999/2000) of the NSS, which is the first 'large sample' since 1993/94. These results were being awaited to be examined closely, not only for an assessment of the actual material condition, consumption and employment patterns of people in the country, but also for policy implications regarding actual implementation of the economic reforms process and its effects on the welfare of the poor. But it now appears that this round, instead of providing the necessary statistical material for serious analysis of actual trends, may only add to confusion regarding the data.

There have already been a spate of newspaper reports about the results of the first two of the four sub-rounds of the 55th Round which have been tabulated. First reports had suggested that these show a dramatically lower estimate of poverty than those obtained from the earlier rounds of the 1990s. Predictably, the media took the opportunity to both hail this as evidence that the reforms have reduced poverty, and, noticing the incongruity of the NSS reporting such a dramatic reduction within such a short time, to also rubbish the country's statistical system (*Indian Express*, 23 September 2000). Since then, newspaper reports on the matter have been even more intriguing. Not only have there been claims that the data might be flawed, but also that differences exist within government (*Business Standard*, 28 and 31 October 2000).

Obviously, nothing definite can be said either about the 55th Round results, or about the official position on this, until the data from all the four sub-rounds are released. But it is already evident that this NSS Round will be less relevant for analysis or policy assessment, and more interesting for another reason. This is because in the 55th Round, the National Sample Survey Organisation (NSSO) has made a major deviation from the technique it has been using so far to establish household consumption levels.

The basic change is in terms of the reference periods used in questions asked on consumption. In all NSS Rounds after the early 1950s, the reference period has essentially been uniform, with respondents asked about their consumption during the 'past 30 days'. But, after experimenting briefly with an

---

[4] See, Aiyer (2000), Bhalla (2000a), Lal, Natarajan and Mohan (2000), and Srinivasan (2000).

alternative questionnaire using a 'past week' reference period for food and 'past 365 days' for certain other items, and having obtained higher consumption, especially for lower income households, the NSSO has changed its questionnaire. During the 55th Round, questions on consumption of clothing, footwear, education, health (institutional) and durable goods were asked only for the 'past 365 days', and, for food, tobacco and intoxicants, all sample households were put both the '30-day' and 'one-week' questions.

This appears to have been a concession by the NSSO to its critics who had alleged an increase in the underestimation of household consumption during the nineties. At least one of these critics has already hailed this change, though 'belatedly only 40 years later', because, in his opinion, the 30-day recall 'leads to unreasonably low estimates of actual consumption'. Moreover, he has claimed that the 55th Round shows 'poverty has *declined*, concomitant with economic growth' (Bhalla, 2000b, emphasis added), although he is aware that changes in methodology, even if these improve point estimates, make time series comparisons difficult.

He, and many others, see in this data 'a reason for some celebration' because of the 'joy that there are less joyless in India', and find any argument for further scrutiny to be mere carping. But, since statistics should reflect the truth, killjoys will abound among serious analysts on both sides of the policy debate if in the process of methodology change the 55th Round has become non-comparable with all past rounds, and thus lost utility for the analysis that had made it so eagerly awaited. In view of this, and the criticism to which the NSS has been subjected recently, there is a need to examine the consistency of the available NSS data, including the data so far released from the 55th Round, without this getting embroiled in the policy debate.

This is the objective of this chapter. Further, the chapter discusses the issue of the reference period used by the NSS: why the NSS has so far used the '30-day' reference period, why recently a need was felt for further methodological experiments on the matter, and what results were actually obtained from the experiments conducted by the NSSO during the 51st to 54th Rounds. The preliminary results from the 55th Round are considered in this context, and, in the light of this, it is apprehended that *the 55th Round may be an experiment which has failed.*

It is, however, extremely important to appreciate that this is an inherent risk in all scientific endeavour, which should not reflect negatively on the NSSO. Indeed the main objective of this article is to stress the basic integrity of India's statistical system and to emphasise that prejudices, however plausible, should not be allowed to override statistical method. Since differences do exist between the NSS and alternative data, there was a strong scientific need for the experiments carried out by the NSSO during Rounds 51 to 54. The results of these experiments are important, and need to be analysed in full.

These experiments, with alternative reference periods, had shown significantly higher food consumption by the one-week recall but also larger sampling errors of these estimates. For clothing, durable goods and certain services, the 365-day recall had suggested both lower consumption and smaller sampling errors than by the 30-day recall, but also a much more equal distribution. Compared to the usual 30-day schedule, the alternative schedule had thus shown higher mean consumption and lower inequality, but with much higher sampling error of the distribution itself, especially at its lower tail.

There was thus strong evidence that the reference period used does systematically effect reported consumption and its distribution across commodities and expenditure groups, for example, that choosing a 'one-week' reference period increases estimates of food consumption. This had certainly warranted further experimentation. But, these experiments had not established greater reliability of estimates from the alternative schedule. It was, therefore, necessary to proceed cautiously to preserve continuity of data and draw proper inferences. Unfortunately, pressure to reflect quickly in the 55th Round, the higher food consumption obtained earlier in the experimental schedules, appears to have led to these being administered in a manner that has contaminated the data.

A disturbing consequence of this is that the 55th Round is unlikely to provide any conclusive indication of the trend in poverty. Initial analysis of the partial data released by the NSSO from the 55th Round suggests that newspaper reports were correct in reporting that the 55th Round shows a large decline in the incidence of poverty during 1999/2000 as compared to 1993/94. However, this comparison is vitiated by differences in reference periods used. *The reference periods used in the 55th Round make its results conceptually non-comparable to all previous officially released estimates from the NSS.*

The *only* conceptually valid comparison possible is of the 55th Round results from the one-week recall with those obtained from the alternative experimental schedule canvassed during Rounds 51 to 54. On this basis, *the presently available results from the 55th Round show higher poverty than during each of the previous four thin sample NSS rounds.* Since rural poverty in at least three out of these four rounds was earlier found to have been higher than during 1993/94 by using the mutually comparable 30 day recall, there is greater validity to the opposite claim: that poverty during 1999/2000 was higher than in 1993/94. However, *the real problem at this stage is the threat posed by such highly contradictory conclusions to the credibility of the country's statistical system.*

The root of this problem of credibility lies in differences between NSS estimates of household consumption and those available from the National Accounts Statistics (NAS). And, particularly, in a perception that these differences had increased so markedly during the nineties that an immediate review of the NSS methodology was necessary. This issue is taken up later and it is shown that there *are* certain persistent differences between the NSS and NAS estimates, which did diverge increasingly during the seventies and the eighties. But, contrary to the perception, *there had actually not been any further significant increase in the divergence between the NSS and NAS estimates of nominal consumption during the nineties.*

Since the NSS measures nominal consumption only, this implies that underestimation by the NSS did not increase during the nineties and that the perception of increased divergence is largely extraneous to the NSS. This has arisen because of the use of different deflators and on account of recent revisions by the Central Statistical Organisation (CSO) to the NAS data. Moreover, it is well known that the NSS has always under-enumerated the rich, leading to lower estimates of non-food consumption than by the NAS. Any disproportionate increase in the consumption of the rich would, therefore, bias downward both the mean consumption and the inequality as measured by the NSS. This would also introduce errors in any attempt to validate alternative NSS reference periods through comparisons with the NAS. On making the necessary adjustments, it is found that estimates of food consumption by the one-week recall may actually be overestimates.

Detailed analysis of the available data thus suggests that there is as yet no statistical warrant to prefer the reference periods used in the 55th Round over the 30-day recall. First, the experimental rounds did not provide any in-sample evidence of the inferiority of the 30-day recall. Second, there is no basic inconsistency between consumption trends from earlier NSS rounds and the NAS. And, third, even point comparisons between the two sources do not necessarily imply that the 30-day recall underestimates consumption.

Nonetheless, with poverty having failed to decline by NSS data during the nineties despite the somewhat higher GDP growth, scepticism will continue, unless it is established that there was an increase in inequality. Validation of NSS data is, therefore, not complete without an identification of the sources of such increased inequality. This is done in the Section entitled 'Consistency of Estimates, Inequality and Poverty', where it is shown that *inequality increased both through the impact of higher relative food prices and through changes in the distribution of nominal consumption between the rural and urban areas and within each of these areas.*

An important aspect of these distributional changes relates to the rural-urban differential. Even those who insist that there has not been any increase in the inequality of incomes within each of these sectors, and argue the primacy of income growth for poverty reduction, would agree that rural poverty is unlikely to have declined if rural per capita incomes have stagnated. A calculation of rural incomes based on the National Accounts Statistics is, therefore, presented. Again recent revisions in the NAS cause some complication, but the results of this analysis are quite conclusive in indicating that *there was a very significant deceleration of the growth of per capita incomes in rural areas during the nineties, because the rapid growth of the non-agricultural incomes did not spill over to rural areas.*

However, it is important to keep separate the trends evident in the data currently available from the issue of data collection and the credibility of the NSS. While there is enough consistency between the existing NSS and NAS estimates to reject the charge that somehow the former has become less relevant recently, it is certainly the case that the NSS has always missed out on some part of the consumption that is actually being carried out by the residents of the country. It is, therefore, quite possible that all currently available estimates of poverty are overestimates, although it remains extremely unlikely that the trends so far available for the nineties are in any way erroneous.

As in any survey-based method, there are two possible sources of error in the NSS data. There could be non-sampling biases in recall and response, which might be reduced by choosing a different reference period or by some other change in the survey methodology. And, there is almost definitely a sampling bias with respect to the underreporting of consumption by richer households. These certainly require further investigation, and there is clearly a need for systematic work through experimental sampling techniques to try and minimise such biases. But for such experimentation to be valid, these must be conducted in a manner that allows for comparability of the data over time and is completely transparent, with separate data from different survey methods made available separately. Further, in order to preserve the integrity of the statistical system, such experiments must be analysed statistically by statisticians and comparable estimates generated, without interference from economists, policy makers and others who have their own priors, and perhaps even biases, to defend.

This is particularly important because the utility of NSS consumer expenditure surveys is wider than its use in the measurement of poverty. Although this is an important and politically sensitive use, the NSS is also the main data-source for estimates of consumer demand, which are required for various policy purposes. Since the reference periods used for these surveys do appear to affect estimates of consumption and its distribution across expenditure classes, it is necessary to ensure that choice in this matter does not distort the input required for policy. This is an especially relevant priority today, when the economy is facing a situation of large excess stocks of several food items despite relatively low increase in their output. An assessment of why current demand is low, and what can be expected in the future, is possible only if the data available allows for comparability over time and is not distorted because of changes in survey methodology.

THE CHOICE OF REFERENCE PERIOD

Since the 1950s, NSS consumption surveys have been using a uniform reference period of one month, and spreading interviews evenly over months to iron out the problem of seasonal variations. However, in recent years the NSSO has revived the issue of whether a one-week reference period is more suitable for determining food consumption than the one-month reference period currently used.

This is not a new issue. Indeed, this question has been of concern to the NSS since the very inception of the surveys in the early 1950s. In fact, in the formative years of the NSS, considerable attention was paid to the length of reference period suitable for ascertaining the correct level of consumption of different items of goods and services. A special report on the suitability of reference period was brought out covering the period April 1951 to March 1954.

Most interestingly, a special investigation into this very issue was carried out during March-April 1952 under the guidance of P.C. Mahalanobis, based on 1254 households of 76 villages of West Bengal. The households were divided into two groups. For one group, consumption details were procured by actual weighing of food items (clean rice, pulses, sugar and salt) by field staff. For the other group, data collection was by questioning, and here again the group was divided equally between those for whom the questions pertained to a reference period of one-week and those for whom the reference period was one month.

The results were revealing. It was found that the two sets of data obtained by questioning differed quite sharply, with the consumption estimates obtained on the basis of the one-week reference period being higher than those obtained on the basis of one-month recall. It was also found that the one-month recall generated information that corresponded much more closely to the data on the basis of actual weighing of food items (Mahalanobis and Sen, 1954). This led to the conclusion that the one-month reference period was better suited for the purpose of estimating food consumption through the survey methodology in India, although even then a one-week reference period was standard in budget surveys in the West.

Since then, the National Sample Survey has consistently used the one-month reference period for food items, although both the one-month and one-year reference period have been used for some non-food items. In the five quinquennial surveys of household consumption expenditure between 1972/73 and 1993/94, information for clothing, footwear and durable goods was collected from each sample household for two reference periods – 'last 30 days' and 'last 365 days'. In the 50th Round, 'educational' and 'institutional medical' expenses were also added to the list of items for which data were collected by these two reference periods. Nonetheless, in order to maintain comparability, the final results for all these past quinquennial rounds, as published in the relevant NSS reports and used by researchers, was only by the '30-day' recall.

However, during the 1990s, the question of the most suitable reference period for food consumption has resurfaced. This is for many reasons, but essentially because past NSS rounds have been throwing up certain puzzles regarding food consumption, which have yet to be resolved. First, the NSS estimates of cereals consumption have shown lower growth than the official estimates of cereals production, and, consequently, from having exceeded the official cereals availability figures till the late 1980s have since fallen below. Second, although the relatively slow growth of cereal consumption in the NSS has been attributed to a shift in food consumption patterns towards other food, the NSS itself has consistently estimated lower consumption of most non-cereals food than the NAS. Third, although the food consumption data from the NSS imply a very high incidence of nutritional inadequacy when converted to nutrient terms, this contrasts markedly with the very high percentage of respondents who report that they have had two square meals in subjective questions to this effect asked by the NSS itself since 1983.

In an effort to test whether some of these differences are due to recall, the NSS had in its recent thin samples experimented with alternative schedules administered to independent subsamples during the course of the same survey. This was done for the 51st Round (1994/95), the 52nd Round (1995/96), the 53rd Round (1997) and the 54th Round (January–June 1998). In all of these rounds, one half of the sample (Type 1) had a reference period of 30 days for all items. For the other half (Type 2) the reference periods were as follows: one week for all food, paan, tobacco and intoxicants; one month for fuel and light and miscellaneous goods and services; and one year for clothing, footwear and durable goods as well as education and institutional medical expenses. But, since the Type 2 schedule was not comparable to earlier NSS surveys, the results by this schedule were not tabulated in the NSS Reports on Consumer Expenditure for the relevant rounds. All available analyses of consumer expenditure and of poverty during the nineties are based on the Type 1 schedule.

However, in a separate report, the NSSO has recently released the comparative results on consumer expenditure, and its distribution, as obtained from the Type 1 and Type 2 schedules canvassed during the 51st, 52nd, 53rd and 54th Rounds (NSSO, 2000a). It is, therefore, possible to examine the effect of choosing one reference period over another. These results, based on the alternative schedules, are extremely interesting. It emerges that the 'one-week' recall gives much higher estimates of overall food consumption, *exactly as Mahalanobis had found in the early NSS surveys and confirmed through pilot investigation in West Bengal villages in 1952.*[5]

Total expenditure on food was about 30 per cent higher according to the Type 2 schedule than from the Type 1 schedule, with the difference ranging from about 14 per cent in the case of cereals and milk to almost 75 per cent in the case of spices. These differences between the one-month and one-week responses were found to be fairly stable across each of the experimental rounds, but, interestingly, the differences were found to be systematically larger for richer households (Table 11.2). *The one-week response thus implies greater inequality in food expenditure and also higher income elasticity of food than by the one-month recall.*

Equally interesting are the results for the goods and services canvassed by the 365-day recall in the Type 2 schedule. In the case of these, with the exception of clothing, the results by the Type 2 schedule generally indicate much lower mean consumption than by the 30-day recall used in the Type 1 schedule. However, even for these goods and services, including clothing, the consumption reported by the bottom half of the population turns out to be much higher by the Type 2 schedule than by the Type 1 schedule and, simultaneously, the consumption reported by the richest households is much lower. While the top quartile reports 40 to 50 per cent less consumption of these goods by the 365-day recall than by the one-month recall, the poor report a consumption which is more than double by the Type 2 schedule than by the Type 1. As a result, *the 365-day recall indicates a much lower income elasticity of demand for clothing, durables and expenditure on education and health than hitherto estimated with the 30-day recall, and also a much more equal distribution of the consumption of these items across household groups.*

[5] The issue of why there should be such a discrepancy, and why the seven-day recall should provide a higher estimate, has not been resolved adequately. Intuitively it would appear that a seven-day recall should be more accurate, particularly for items consumed infrequently, since informants are less likely to forget their consumption by a shorter recall. But one possibility is that there is a certain 'overhead' characteristic to food consumption which may result in overestimation by recall relating to a shorter period. Thus, suppose that a certain item of food is consumed during a particular week without there being any purchase or household production of that item during that week. There would be double counting if the seven-day response leads to respondents reporting accurately their expenditure during the reference week, but are then prompted by the questionnaire to report consumption of items which were not purchased or otherwise acquired during that week but were consumed nonetheless. A related problem is the difficulty faced by informants in calculating consumption for a week in cases where this is less than the quantity normally purchased at a time. Since the quantity best known to the informant is the latter, this might be reported without making tedious calculations.

Table 11.2 Percentage Difference between Consumption Estimates from Type 2 and Type 1 Schedules in Experimental Rounds (All-India Rural)

Round	Quartile 1	Quartile 2	Quartile 3	Quartile 4	All
Items canvassed by 7-day recall in schedule Type 2					
51	23	28	31	37	31
52	22	26	29	44	33
53	23	25	26	34	28
Items canvassed by 365-day recall in schedule Type 2					
51	176	77	31	−54	−26
52	214	101	22	−47	−16
53	145	71	16	−46	−22
Items canvassed by 30-day recall in schedule Type 2					
51	−2	−2	−1	−11	−6
52	−4	−3	−2	2	−1
53	−2	−2	−5	−5	−4
All items					
51	24	25	25	3	15
52	24	25	22	11	18
53	23	23	19	3	13

Source: Computed from NSSO Report No. 447.

The net consequence of these differences, which are substantial and systematic in the four experimental rounds, is that total consumer expenditure is reported higher according to the Type 2 schedule, and the distribution of this expenditure across households is also reported more equal. For the bottom half of the population, total consumer expenditure by the Type 2 schedule is about 25 per cent higher than by the Type 1 schedule, with about 75 per cent of the difference due to food and 25 per cent due to the items canvassed by the 365-day recall. As a result, the proportion of population below any expenditure level is always higher by the Type 1 schedule than by Type 2, with this difference very large at the lower expenditure ranges. Poverty estimates obtained from the Type 2 schedules are, therefore, much lower than by the one-month recall used so far.

Visaria (2000a) has compared the poverty estimates as obtained from these two consumer expenditure schedules canvassed during Rounds 51 to 54. He finds, for example, that although about 38 per cent of the rural population was found to have consumption below the poverty line in 1995/96 (52nd Round) by the Type 1 schedule, this percentage was only around 19 per cent by the Type 2 schedule. The corresponding percentages for urban areas were 30 and 15. Similar large differences are obtained for the 51st, 53rd and 54th Rounds which all show almost half the poverty incidence by the Type 2 schedule as compared to the Type 1 schedule (Table 11.3).

In the large sample 55th Round of 1999/2000, this experiment has been carried one step further. In this round, estimates for clothing, footwear, durable goods and expenditure incurred on education and on health (institutional) were obtained *only* with a 365-day recall. For, food and intoxicants, every sample household was canvassed by both the one week and the one month reference periods. The idea obviously was to prepare for a transition to the Type 2 schedule. This would not only make the NSS methodology similar to that followed in budget surveys carried out in developed countries, it would also

Table 11.3 Poverty Estimates from Type 1 and Type 2 Schedules of Rounds 51 to 54, and by the 30-day and 7-day recalls in sub-rounds 1&2 of the 55th Round

Round	Year	Rural		Urban	
		Type 1	Type 2	Type 1	Type 2
51	July 94–June 95	41.2	22.8	35.5	18.3
52	July 95–June 96	37.6	19.1	29.9	15.2
53	January–December 97	35.9	20.7	32.3	17.8
54	January–June 98	42.6	23.6	32.9	20.0
55*	July–December 99	27.6	24.8	25.2	23.4

Source: Visaria (2000b). For the 55th Round, the result from the 30-day recall for food is shown under Type 1, although this schedule in Rounds 51 to 54 did not use the 365-day recall, and is not strictly comparable. That from the 7-day recall is under Type 2.

increase the NSS estimate of food and total consumption. These would then be closer to the alternative estimates obtained from the NAS, reducing the discrepancy that currently exists between nutritional adequacy as calculated from the NSS consumption data and the results that the NSS has obtained from subjective questions regarding the incidence of hunger.

Visaria, who is Chairman of the NSSO Governing Council, has expressed preference for the one-week recall for food in precisely these terms. He recognises that poverty estimates by this recall are not comparable with earlier estimates, and in fact argues that there is a case to revise upwards the poverty line to make these rather low estimates 'more realistic and relevant'. He, however, stresses the prior that 'the incidence of stark hunger in the country may be much less than generally believed'. And writes that: 'The overstatement of the level of poverty has thus quite likely been a consequence of a long reference period adopted for the collection of the data on food consumption by our people. To confirm this hypothesis, the quinquennial survey for 1999/2000, due to be completed by 30 June, has collected data from each household according to the two reference periods of a week and the 30 days preceding the date of survey. Its findings will perhaps help to clinch the issue' (Visaria, op. cit.).

However, in the process, not enough thought appears to have been given to the comparability of the 55th Round results with those from earlier rounds. First, to the extent that the 55th Round has canvassed certain items by only the 365-day recall, this makes estimates for these items non-comparable with estimates from all previous rounds, and, as discussed above, also has serious implications for the distribution so obtained. Second, since the two schedules canvassed in Rounds 51 to 54 had given varying results for food consumption, incorporating them so that all the households respond by both the one week and one month reference periods was obviously problematic since it could bias the results of either or both.

The problem is that, since all households were questioned on food consumption by both types of recall, there would have been a pressure for consistency between answers to the one-week and the 30-day reference periods on the part of both respondents and investigators. It is very likely that when a household is questioned using both the one-week and one-month recall, the answers will be tested by simple multiplication of the one-week reply for the monthly response as well. Hence, although the 55th Round gives results on food consumption by both the reference periods, these can no longer be seen as independent. Both are likely to differ from earlier rounds, depending upon the exact conflation of the reference periods.

Now that some results are available from the first half of the 55th Round (Table 11.4), and preliminary estimates of poverty can be made on this basis, it is worth considering these to get an idea of the problems involved (NSSO, 2000b).[6] Using the distribution obtained from answers to food consumption *by the 30-day recall* in the 55th Round, the incidence of poverty during July–December 1999 are 27.4 and 25.2 per cent respectively for Rural and Urban India.[7] *By the one-week recall*, the same poverty lines give esti-mates of 24.4 and 23.4 per cent respectively. Visaria (2000b) reports very similar results (Table 11.3).

It is these figures which have been compared to the much higher figures reported in Table 11.1 for the poverty incidence found from the 50th Round in 1993/94 to conclude that actual poverty has declined. However, since all available results from the 50th Round are based on answers by the 30-day

Table 11.4 Distribution of Consumer Expenditure in the 55th Round
(*Subsamples 1 and 2*) All-India, July–December 1999

	Rural					Urban			
	30-Day Recall for Food, etc.		7-Day Recall for Food, etc.			30-Day Recall for Food, etc.		7-Day Recall for Food, etc.	
Expendi-ture Class	Per cent Persons	Average MPCE	Per cent Persons	Average MPCE	Expendi-ture Class	Per cent Persons	Average MPCE	Per cent Persons	Average MPCE
0–220	4.8	186	4.3	185	0–290	4.5	242	4.1	242
220–250	4.5	237	3.7	237	290–330	4.2	310	3.3	311
250–290	9.0	271	7.9	272	330–405	9.4	369	9.1	368
290–330	9.6	311	8.9	311	405–480	10.0	443	9.7	443
330–370	10.2	351	9.8	351	480–550	9.9	516	9.1	514
370–410	10.2	390	9.7	390	550–630	9.1	591	9.6	589
410–460	10.4	435	10.5	434	630–735	9.9	682	10.6	681
460–515	9.9	487	10.6	487	735–855	9.7	792	9.7	792
515–605	10.9	556	11.8	557	855–1040	10.2	943	10.3	940
605–765	10.3	676	11.4	677	1040–1315	9.4	1167	10.1	1167
765–945	5.3	843	5.8	842	1315–1535	4.5	1422	4.6	1418
945 +	5.0	1331	5.7	1324	1535 +	9.1	2371	9.9	2352
All	100.0	484	100.0	502	All	100.0	839	100.0	860

Source: NSSO (2000b), Report No. 453.

[6] NSSO (2000b) contains a set of key results giving expenditure class-wise distribution of persons and average monthly consumption expenditure by all-India and states from sub-rounds 1 and 2 of the 55th Round, covering the period July–December 1999. This is available by both the one-week and one month recall for food consumption. However, the only details of consumption by commodities are in a single table. This gives a breakdown of the all-India consumption by items at the aggregate rural and urban levels without any expenditure class-wise distribution.

[7] Since the NSSO does not make any poverty calculations on its own, this must be derived from the distribution of consumer expenditure using some poverty line. We assume poverty lines of Rs 328 and Rs 458 per capita per month for rural and urban areas for July–December 1999. These are obtained by updating the Planning Commission's official poverty lines with available consumer price indices as recommended by the Expert Group (Planning Commission, 1993). It should be noted, however, that we have updated the national poverty line using national-level price indices and have applied this to the national distribution, and have not followed the Expert Group's recommendation of constructing state-wise poverty lines to derive poverty estimates separately by states. As a result, our estimates will differ from those obtained by proper application of the Expert Group method, but are conceptually similar to all the estimates in Table 11.1, which also apply a national poverty line to the national distribution.

recall only, two assumptions are necessary for such a conclusion to be valid. First, that dropping the 30-day question for clothing, etc., and relying only on the 365-day recall, has made no difference. Secondly, that the presence of the one-week questions for food in the 55th Round questionnaire has not altered responses to the 30-day questions. In other words, the comparability of the 55th Round to earlier rounds requires assuming that its results using the 30-day recall for food are equivalent to those by the Type 1 schedule used in Rounds 51 to 54.

However, under this assumption, a comparison of results obtained from the 'one week' and '30-day' recalls in the 55th Round also constitutes a test of the crucial issue of whether the presence of questions by both reference periods in this round has contaminated responses. This is so, since with the one-week recall for food the 55th Round reference periods are exactly the same as those in the Type 2 schedule of Rounds 51 to 54. If there was no contamination, the poverty incidence calculated from the one-week recall would have been much lower than by the '30-day' recall, exactly as found on comparing the Type 1 and Type 2 schedules canvassed experimentally during Rounds 51 to 54. On the basis of the results of those experiments, a 27.4 per cent rural poverty incidence by the Type 1 schedule should imply an incidence of only 12 to 14 per cent by the Type 2 schedule independently canvassed; while for urban areas a poverty incidence of 25.2 per cent by the Type 1 schedule should similarly correspond to only 10 to 13 per cent by the Type 2 schedule.[8]

Had the poverty incidence by the 'one-week' recall in the 55th Round been at these low benchmark levels derived from the earlier experiments, this round could have been deemed a success in terms of what it had set out to do. The differences in consumption estimates by the two recalls observed in the 'thin sample' Rounds 51 to 54 would then have been maintained into the 55th Round large sample, and seen to be invariant to whether these were canvassed independently or together. This would have clinched the issue that there is a systematic bias on account of recall. Provided, further, that there was some independent basis to argue that estimates of food consumption by the one-week reference period were closer to the truth, a strong case could be made to adopt this reference period for future surveys, while adjusting downwards the poverty estimates of all past years. Such adjustment to past data would have been far from easy. And, much of the very large body of research carried out in the past using NSS data in a number of areas, for example, in demand analysis, would be rendered useless without any possibility of further time-series work on these topics for several years. Nonetheless, the decision to opt for the one-week reference period would then have had some vindication.

But, given the very small difference between poverty estimates actually found by the two recalls, the 55th Round must be judged to be a failed experiment, on precisely these grounds. Although the 55th Round does show a significant *increase* in real mean consumption compared to Rounds 51 to 53 by the 30-day recall in both rural and urban areas, this is found to *decline* when comparisons are made using data by the 7-day recall. In the earlier experimental rounds, the one-week recall had consistently shown about 30 per cent higher consumption of food, beverages, paan, tobacco and intoxicants than by the 30-day recall. But the 55th Round shows a difference of only about 5 to 6 per cent (Table 11.5). Thus, either the presence of the one-week question has biased upward the one-month estimates, or the presence of the one-month question has biased down the one-week replies, or, as is most likely, answers to both sets of questions have been influenced by the presence of the other. There is, therefore, strong evidence

---

[8] Using the distributions for the 51st, 52nd, 53rd and 54th Rounds, rural poverty estimates by the Type 2 schedule corresponding to a 27.4 per cent rural poverty by the Type 1 schedule work out to 12.2, 12.2, 14.2 and 12.1 respectively, giving an average of 12.7 per cent. Similarly, for urban poverty, an incidence of 25.2 per cent by the Type 1 schedule corresponds to an incidence by the Type 2 schedule of 9.9, 11.2, 12.5 and 13.4 in Rounds 51 to 54.

Table 11.5 Some Comparisons with Results of the 55th Round, Subsamples 1 and 2

		Round	50th	51st	52nd	53rd	55th
Real per capita mean consumption at 1993/94 prices	Urban	Type 1	458	464	502	480	524
		Type 2		549	568	548	537
	Rural	Type 1	281	277	280	294	303
		Type 2		316	329	331	314
Ratio of the one week to one month estimate of consumption of food, etc.	Urban			1.35	1.32	1.33	1.05
	Rural			1.31	1.33	1.28	1.06
Share of Bottom 40 per cent of population in total consumption	Urban	Type 1	19.9	18.8	18.8	19.2	19.8
		Type 2		21.0	21.3	21.4	19.9
	Rural	Type 1	23.1	22.7	23.4	22.3	24.2
		Type 2		24.7	25.0	24.2	24.1
Share of Top 20 per cent of population in total consumption	Urban	Type 1	42.8	45.4	45.8	44.5	42.2
		Type 2		40.2	40.1	40.2	42.1
	Rural	Type 1	38.4	39.9	38.1	39.7	36.6
		Type 2		35.3	35.0	35.5	36.3

Source: Computed from NSSO (2000b): Report No. 453.

that there was contamination across responses by different reference periods and that, as a consequence, the 55th Round results, even by the one-month recall, are not comparable with the 50th and earlier rounds.

Similarly, while the distribution by the Type 1 schedule had consistently exhibited greater inequality than by the Type 2 schedule in the earlier experimental rounds, this is not observed on comparing the 55th Round distributions using the one-week and 30-day recalls. In this case, there is some basis for assessing the direction of bias. In both areas, the 55th Round results by the two recalls are very close to each other, and intermediate between the results by the different schedules in Rounds 51 to 54. In urban areas the 55th Round distribution appears closer to the Type 1 schedule of the experimental rounds and similar to that in the 50th Round. For rural India, on the other hand, the evidence seems to suggest quite strongly that the 55th Round distribution is closer to that by the Type 2 schedules of Rounds 51 to 54, whereas the 50th Round distribution was closer to that by the Type 1 schedule. Consequently, the consumption share of the bottom 40 per cent of the rural population by the one-month recall of the 55th Round would be overestimated by at least 5 per cent.

Most importantly, on the basis of the only comparable results from the 55th Round, there is case for the claim that *poverty was higher during July–December 1999 than during 1993/94.* This is by the results from the one-week recall for food, etc., using which the 55th Round reference periods are exactly the same as in the Type 2 schedules used in Rounds 51 to 54. By these identical reference periods, the poverty estimates from the 55th Round are higher than all the estimates obtained from NSS Rounds 51 to 54. Moreover, poverty during, at least, three out of four of these thin sample rounds was higher than during the 50th Round by the mutually exactly comparable 30-day recall.[9]

[9] It should be noted that a 24.4 per cent rural poverty incidence by the Type 2 schedule corresponds to poverty incidences of 43.1, 44.4, 40.1 and 43.3 per cent by the Type 1 schedule using the distributions in Rounds 51, 52, 53 and 54 respectively. For urban areas, Type 1 estimates corresponding similarly to a Type 2 estimate of 23.4 per cent are 41.0, 38.9, 39.3 and 36.4 per cent respectively. On the basis of these correspondences, the poverty incidence found using the 7-day recall during July–December 1999 would be higher than not only in 1993/94 but also 1987/88.

However, although more valid conceptually than the claim of reduced poverty, any claim of increased poverty during the 55th Round must also be inconclusive since there is the possibility of the one-week recall being contaminated by the presence of the 30-day question. The essential problem is that of the comparability of the 55th Round with past rounds. The real matter of concern is that these contradictory indications by the two recall periods, and the strong evidence of contamination of both by the presence of the other, may push future discussion of trends in poverty into a statistical minefield which can only erode the credibility of the NSS. Moreover, since the question of what has happened to poverty is important not only to social scientists but to politicians as well, an unseemly debate could be set off with different camps arguing not just about how exactly the data should be interpreted but also about the motives behind the sudden change in methodology.

On interpretation, there are bound to be differences regarding by how much the 7-day questions have distorted the one-month response, and vice versa. But these will be impossible to settle with the 55th Round data. And much ink may be spilt on issues, which may not really be germane, such as the way in which the questionnaire was designed or the order in which the questions were asked. Indeed, Bhalla and Visaria have already raised the issue of the order in which questions by the one week and one month recall were asked. Apparently, the NSSO had decided to ask the one-month question first, but this order got reversed in some cases because of late issue of instructions.

This might not, however, be of much importance since the pressure for consistency across questions in a survey can arise irrespective of the order in which questions are asked and can lead respondents to revise their earlier answers. In any case, *the 'one-week' and 'one-month' questions were solicited in the 55th Round questionnaire for each commodity in two separate columns on the same page, with the 7-day response to be entered in the left column.* Given that English and most Indian languages are read from left to right, it is possible and even likely that the one-week question was asked first even if investigators were instructed otherwise. Unless it is asserted that the NSSO has so much authority that instructions from Delhi always override instincts of individuals in the field, there is no real basis to evaluate whether contamination was less from the one-week to the one-month recall, or the other way around.

Notwithstanding this, it is very important not to question past decisions taken by the NSSO Governing Council on operational matters concerning the actual conduct of surveys. It should be assumed that these were taken after full consideration of the statistical issues involved and implemented accordingly, subject, of course, to the usual administrative constraints and pressures. Reopening these will not improve the data but might embroil the NSSO in unnecessary controversy on matters which are best left internal.[10]

Things would, of course, be much worse if this becomes a political issue. There are then likely to be accusations that reference periods were changed in order to fudge results. And, in turn, there may be pressure to explain the contamination now confirmed by arguing either that *no inferences are possible from the thin samples*, or that the 55th Round results show that *the choice of reference period does not matter.* This would be untrue, and totally unscientific, negating not only the value of previous experiments but also the rationale for the change in reference period. Whatever the immediate outcome of such uninformed political intervention, this would in the longer run risk destroying an institution which is not only of extreme national importance but also one among the few government organisations in India which currently enjoys almost unparalleled world repute as regards both its competence and its integrity.

---

[10] This is especially so because, according to Visaria (2000b), the decision on the 55th Round schedule was 'a last minute compromise'.

The only way out of this difficult and potentially dangerous situation for the credibility of the country's statistical system is to be honest and transparent. It should be obvious to all serious analysts that changes in the reference periods used in the 55th Round were taken in good faith as part of a larger experiment, but that this has turned out to be a failure. For this reason, the credibility of the NSSO can be salvaged if the experimental nature of the 55th Round is stressed, and all data available from it is released for independent research. However, another Consumer Expenditure Survey using a large sample will need to be conducted as soon as possible to give results which are comparable with previous rounds, while incorporating whatever valid lessons might have been learnt in this and the experimental surveys.

In this context, of the design of future NSS rounds, certain other results from the experiments conducted during Rounds 51 to 54 should be noted. First, estimates of consumer expenditure obtained from the Type 2 schedule were found to be sensitive to the positioning of the survey date within a month, with higher consumption reported in the first week of the month. There is thus an additional source of sampling error in the one-week consumption estimates. To avoid this, samples would need to be drawn uniformly over weeks, and not just uniformly over months. To achieve this, without sacrificing statistical reliability at the state and lower levels, *a substantial increase in sample size would be required, involving a corresponding large increase in survey cost*. Moreover, this also raises the question of how to interpret the resulting distribution of consumption across households, since selecting samples uniformly over weeks might reduce the bias in the consumption estimates but at the same time introduce an additional bias in the distribution so obtained.

Second, and more important, interpenetrating subsamples were drawn independently by each type of schedule during Rounds 52 and 53. These subsample differences enabled computation, separately from the Type 1 and Type 2 schedules, of the Relative Standard Errors (RSE) for most estimates obtained, thus allowing some conclusions regarding the relative sampling variability of estimates across schedules. These show: (a) that the RSE of the mean consumer expenditure estimates was higher in the case of almost every commodity in almost every state by the one-week recall than by the 30-day recall, indicating that consumption estimates from the one-week recall were statistically less reliable *in general* than corresponding estimates by the 30-day recall, although in the case of many food items, notably cereals, the RSE of mean consumption was low by both reference periods; (b) that the RSE of mean consumption of almost every commodity for which a 365-day recall was used, was lower by this longer reference period than by the 30-day recall; and (c) that the RSE of estimates of the proportion of households and persons falling in every expenditure class below the poverty line was found to be much higher by the Type 2 schedule than by the Type 1 schedule, indicating much lower statistical stability of the distribution obtained from the Type 2 schedule, at least, at the lower tail (Table 11.6). This third point is perhaps the most important from the point of view of the reliability of poverty estimates.

These in-survey diagnostics of the statistical reliability of samples obtained by different recalls had, therefore, indicated much greater stability of the distribution obtained from the Type 1 schedule used so far, and had also indicated lower errors with a longer reference period. Indeed, the NSSO (2000a) acknowledges the second point transparently, and cites this as a reason to chose the 365-day recall for clothing, etc. But in the case of food and intoxicants, a different criterion was followed. After noting, correctly, that 'the substantial and systematic differences between the week and month-based estimates indicate that one or both methods are not depicting the real-life situation,' it went on to make the judgement that 'because the RSEs arising from schedule Type 1 and schedule Type 2 do not differ very substantially for these item groups (food, paan, tobacco and intoxicants), the RSE criterion

Table 11.6 Relative Standard Errors of Estimated Distribution of Persons by MPCE Class

| | Rural | | | | | Urban | | | |
| | 52nd Round | | 53rd Round | | Expendi- | 52nd Round | | 53rd Round | |
Expendi-ture Class	Type 1	Type 2	Type 1	Type 2	ture Class	Type 1	Type 2	Type 1	Type 2
0–120	12.9	30.6	28.5	39.4	0–160	14.3	23.6	15.2	20.7
120–140	12.4	21.3	18.8	28.7	160–190	9.5	20.5	11.1	21.3
140–165	7.3	16.7	17.2	18.5	190–230	7.2	15.7	7.4	16.1
165–190	5.5	9.6	9.1	14.7	230–265	6.5	10.5	6.7	11.9
190–210	6.0	8.5	9.7	14.1	265–310	4.4	7.2	5.2	9.8
210–235	4.8	6.8	8.2	11.2	310–355	4.5	6.4	5.1	11.5
235–265	4.1	5.0	6.9	9.8	355–410	4.4	5.5	4.8	6.3
265–300	3.6	4.7	6.5	6.1	410–490	3.7	4.4	4.7	5.9
300–355	3.4	3.8	5.4	5.9	490–605	3.3	3.2	3.8	4.1
355–455	3.7	3.0	4.1	3.9	605–825	3.6	3.0	4.3	3.5
455–560	5.2	4.1	5.3	6.1	825–1055	4.4	4.5	6.1	5.3
560+	4.9	4.2	5.0	5.4	1055+	4.4	4.9	6.4	5.5

Source: NSSO (2000a).

does not really clinch the issue in favour of schedule Type 1, and the question of bias becomes all-important.'

However, precisely because the matter of bias cannot be settled without an independent procedure to arrive at the 'true' estimate, Mahalanobis and his associates had considered it necessary, almost fifty years ago, to include through the methodology of independent and interpenetrating samples a test by physical measurement to provide the benchmark for judging bias in survey estimates simultaneously obtained by different reference periods. Although the NSSO does not report any such independent benchmark in the surveys recently carried out, it does note that the earlier survey by Mahalanobis had also obtained higher consumption by the 'one-week' recall, and that '*the present survey(s) can be taken as confirming the findings of the earlier survey because the data appear to follow the same pattern.*' A similar benchmark survey is an obvious priority for the NSSO.

Nonetheless, since no in-survey benchmark was available, the NSSO compared the consumption estimates from the two schedule types for food, beverages and tobacco taken together with the corresponding estimate of consumption from the NAS. At this aggregate level, the consumption of food, beverages and tobacco taken together was found to be 20 to 25 per cent lower than the NAS estimate by the one-month recall, whereas the estimates by one-week recall ranged from 6 per cent higher in 1995-96 to 2 per cent lower in 1997 as compared to NAS estimates for those years. It is on this basis that the NSSO concluded that 'further methodological survey on this important subject would be advisable', leading to the choice of reference periods used in the 55th Round.

It should, therefore, be evident that, quite apart from the very important issue of comparability with past NSS rounds raised thereby, *the inclusion of the 'one-week' questions in the 55th Round, and the effective changeover to the Type 2 schedule with its less reliable distribution, had no in-survey statistical warrant from the experiments conducted during Rounds 51 to 54.* The only justification for the one-week recall was that this gave an estimate for aggregate expenditure on food, beverages and tobacco which was closer to that obtained from the CSO's National Account Statistics than the corresponding estimate by the one-month recall. However, even here, there is some inconsistency. The decision to adopt the 365-day recall for a number of items was taken despite earlier rounds indicating that this was likely to increase the even larger gap that exists between the NAS and NSS estimates for these items, and lead to a reduction in the measured inequality in NSS consumption data. These systematic differences between different recalls are important and deserved further analysis but, instead, the issue of the choice of reference period appears to have been linked inextricably to another old issue: that of comparisons of the NSS with the NAS data.

COMPARING NSS AND NAS ESTIMATES OF CONSUMER EXPENDITURE

With the change in reference periods made essentially because previous experimental rounds had indicated that a one-week reference period might give estimates of food consumption closer to those estimated in the National Accounts, the 55th Round has reopened an old question in an entirely new way. Differences between NSS and NAS consumption estimates have been the subject of much academic and official assessment ever since the 1950s. The system of official statistics has in the past incorporated results of such research by sometimes revising NAS estimates to correspond to the NSS. For a time poverty estimates were also anchored to the NAS by using a hybrid of NAS mean consumption and the NSS distribution. But never before has the NSS survey methodology been changed as a result.

The most recent official assessment of differences between the NSS and NAS estimates of consumption expenditure was in 1993, by the Expert Group on Estimation of Proportion and Number of Poor which had been constituted to review the official methodology for poverty estimation. At that time, official poverty measures were anchored to the NAS consumption estimates, by applying the NSS distribution to the NAS mean consumption. This practice was stopped because of the Expert Group's recommendation that poverty ratios be calculated exclusively from the NSS consumption data without any adjustment for the discrepancy between these and the NAS.

In this context, the Expert Group had noted that 'The NAS estimate of private consumption is derived as a residual by deducting from estimated production of the various goods and services (adjusted for foreign trade), the estimated use for capital formation and public consumption. Apart from the lack of reliable direct data on production for a sizeable segment of the economy, the adjustments for uses other than private consumption are based on scanty data, often of the distant past, and subjective judgements.' It went on to state that 'NSS data are of course not free from errors, biases, comparability over time and other problems. The nature of these have been widely debated and there is a sustained effort to refine and improve the survey design and procedure. Even as these efforts continue – as of course they must – the NSS remains the best available source of assessing poverty incidence and the characteristics of the poor across space and time.' In this, the Expert Group had put special emphasis on the fact that the NSS surveys 'are carefully organised and use uniform concepts' (Planning Commission, 1993).

In view of this rather categorical assessment, the NSSO's recent decision to change the reference periods in the 55th Round, and to thus disturb the uniformity of NSS concepts, appears somewhat strange. This would, at least, have been understandable had the in-survey diagnostics from the experiments in Rounds 51 to 54 indicated much greater statistical reliability of the distribution obtained by the Type 2 schedule. But not only was there no such statistical warrant, the decision to include the one-week recall appears to have been taken purely on the consideration that this would bring the NSS estimates of food consumption closer to those from the NAS. Since the official view so far has been that there is no strong basis to prefer the NAS estimates over those from the NSS, this is perhaps an indication of the extent to which the NSSO felt pressured from arguments that the NSS was increasingly underestimating consumption during the nineties, and thus overestimating poverty.

Ravallion (2000c) has drawn attention to a recent upsurge in criticism of the NSS consumption data by those who 'have clearly been worried that the NSS-based poverty numbers will help fuel a backlash against economic reform in India'. He has reviewed their argument to re-anchor poverty measures to the NAS consumption estimates, and notes: (a) that the alternative estimates from the NAS are not free from error and, unlike the NSS, includes 'non-household' consumption which might be increasing; (b) that some of the claims of increasing underestimation by the NSS, e.g. in case of cereals, are weak; (c) that the NSS misses out some of the rich, and hence the difference between the two consumption estimates could enlarge without this biasing poverty measures if an increasing proportion of measured NAS consumption is consumed by the rich; and (d) that the NSS surveys do indicate much faster increase in the consumption of the top quintile so that this is a distinct possibility. His basic conclusions are that there is no *a priori* reason to prefer the NAS mean consumption, and no basis to adjust poverty measures downwards on the assumption that errors (if any) in the NSS data are distribution-neutral. In response to the recent criticism, this is essentially an endorsement of the position taken in 1993 by the official Expert Group, but, curiously, Ravallion does not examine whether the gap between the NAS and NSS estimates of consumption has actually increased in recent years, accepting somewhat uncritically that it has.

However, the question of whether this gap between the NAS and the NSS has increased during the nineties is of rather crucial importance. This is because recent criticism of the NSS has at its starting point the observation that although GDP growth has increased somewhat during the nineties, and is reflected in the growth of real per capita private consumption expenditure from the NAS, measures of real per capita mean consumption obtained from the NSS show much lower growth during the nineties than during the seventies and eighties, particularly in rural India. This observation, which recent critics of the NSS have raised *ad nauseam* as evidence that something terrible must have gone wrong with the NSS during the nineties, appears to have convinced many who had earlier been in agreement with the Expert Group to swing around to the view that there was a need to reconsider the matter. This added weight to the opinion which appears to have led the NSSO to consider anchoring its estimates of food consumption to the NAS, paying less attention to the purely statistical in-sample results of its own experiments.

But did the gap between the NSS and NAS consumption estimates actually increase by so much after the Expert Group's widely accepted observations to warrant this outcome? An important matter which seems to have been overlooked in this context is that the NSS measures only nominal consumption on the date of the survey and that estimates of real consumption are derived later by users of this data by deflating it with price indices which they chose to be most suitable for their purpose. Since the most important use of NSS data is to calculate poverty estimates, the deflators most commonly applied to NSS data are base weighted price indices constructed for population groups close to the poverty line, and these cannot be the same as the current weighted price indices for total consumption implicit in the NAS estimates. For this reason, a correct assessment of whether there was increasing divergence between the NAS and the NSS requires comparison, not of the derived measures of real consumption, but of the direct estimates of nominal consumption from the two sources.

On making this proper comparison, the striking result is that *there is no evidence of any large widening of the gap between the NAS and NSS estimates of nominal consumption during the 1990s*. The ratio of the NSS consumption expenditure to the corresponding estimate from the NAS (with 1980/81 as base) did fall from 0.82 to 0.69 between 1977/78 and 1990/91. But, during the subsequent years for which this NAS series is available, this ratio has remained more or less constant, varying in the range 0.68 to 0.72 (Table 11.7). Matters have been confused somewhat because the CSO has after 1998 shifted to a new series of national income with base year 1993/94, and estimates from 1997/98 onwards are available only on this basis. This has involved a revision of the NAS nominal consumption for 1993/94 by almost 16 per cent over the corresponding estimate according to the NAS series with 1980/81 as base, reducing the NSS to NAS ratio from 0.69 to 0.60 for that year. Some analysts failed to notice this break in the NAS series, and, by mistakenly attributing the resulting fall in the ratio to increased NSS underestimation, added fuel to the fire from the critics of the NSS.[11]

Table 11.7 Comparison of NSS and NAS Nominal Consumption

NSS Round	Year	NSS Per Capita Monthly Consumption (Rs/Month)			Annual Per Capita Consumption (Current Prices)			Ratio of NSS Nominal Consumption to	
		Rural	Urban	Total	NSS	NAS 1980/81	NAS 1993/94	NAS 1980/81	NAS 1993/94
27	Oct. 72/Sep. 73	44.17	63.33	48.11	585	744	907	0.79	0.65
32	Jul. 77/Jun. 78	68.89	96.15	74.89	911	1109	1352	0.82	0.67
38	Jan. 83/Dec. 83	112.45	164.03	124.72	1517	1967	2330	0.77	0.65
42	Jul. 86/Jun. 87	140.93	222.65	161.24	1962	2657	3092	0.74	0.63
43	Jul. 87/Jun. 88	158.10	249.93	181.19	2204	2938	3406	0.75	0.65
44	Jul. 88/Jun. 89	175.10	266.85	198.45	2414	3296	3818	0.73	0.63
45	Jul. 89/Jun. 90	189.46	298.00	217.37	2645	3639	4244	0.73	0.62
46	Jul. 90/Jun. 91	202.12	326.75	234.49	2853	4108	4764	0.69	0.60
48	Jan. 92/Dec. 92	247.21	398.95	287.24	3495	4871	5612	0.72	0.62
50	Jul. 93/Jun. 94	281.40	458.04	328.68	3999	5801	6680	0.69	0.60
51	Jul. 94/Jun. 95	309.41	508.07	363.08	4417	6505	7506	0.68	0.59
52	Jul. 95/Jun. 96	344.29	599.26	413.74	5034	7202	8523	0.70	0.59
53	Jan. 97/Dec. 97	395.01	645.44	465.00	5658	8178	10031	0.69	0.56

Sources: NSSO (various) and National Accounts Statistics (1998, 2000). The NAS data by financial years has been interpolated linearly to correspond to the period of NSS rounds.

The new revised NAS series (with 1993/94 as base) does show higher consumption growth than the older series, and the ratio of the NSS to NAS mean consumption does fall somewhat in 1997. But, nonetheless, even by this, the increase in the discrepancy between the two consumption estimates during the nineties is modest compared to the increase which occurred between 1977/78 and 1990/91, especially by the old series to which the Expert Group had access when it decided on the matter. What

---

[11] Thus, Datt (1999) writes 'in nominal terms, NSS consumption grew by 198 per cent between 1990/91 and 1997, while NAS consumption grew by 233 per cent in the same period'. In fact, NSS nominal per capita consumption increased 98 per cent between 1990/91 and 1997. The corresponding growth in NAS, interpolating linearly to NSS survey mid-points is 99 per cent when the old 1980/81 series is extended from 1996/97 to 1997/98 using the new 1993/94 series and 111 per cent with the new series as reported in NAS 2000. The NAS consumption growth would be 145 per cent if the 1997 figure from the series with 1993/94 as base is compared incorrectly to the 1990/91 figure from the series with 1980/81 as base. Thus Datt appears to have reported the level of indices as their growth and, using an earlier estimate for 1997 from the NAS with 1993/94 as base, compared this with the 1990/91 figure from the NAS with 1980/81 as base.

is, however, most surprising about the new series are the revisions to the pre 1993/94 data which have only just been released.[12] These show much higher consumption during the seventies and eighties than earlier estimated, and as a consequence the discrepancy between the NAS and NSS is much higher in the earlier years by the new series than by the old, and show a correspondingly lower subsequent increase. The oddity of this is that the NSS estimates for 1972/73 and 1977/78, which Minhas had earlier validated, are now seen to be gross underestimates by the new NAS series.[13] Unfortunately, no commodity details of this series have yet been released for the years before 1993/94 to judge what new insight the CSO now has about consumption in those years.

The nature of these revisions to the NAS, and also the issue of alternative deflators, will be discussed later. Here, the important point to note is that when the claim was made that the divergence between the NSS and the NAS had increased sharply during the nineties, there was absolutely no substance for this in the NAS series then available. The only significant increase in divergence between the NSS and the NAS during the nineties is by the new series for the single year 1997. And, even by this, the increased divergence is much smaller than what the Expert Group had noticed with the old NAS series when it had decided not to anchor poverty estimates to the NAS data.

To take the comparisons further, Table 11.8 presents the ratios of the NSS to NAS estimates of consumption by broad items over successive full-year NSS rounds beginning 1977/78. Since only the NAS estimates with base 1980/81 cover this entire period with full commodity breakdown, these ratios have been calculated with these NAS estimates rather than the new estimates with 1993/94 as base. As may be seen there are certain persistent differences between these two data sets at the level of individual

Table 11.8 Ratio of NSS Nominal Consumption by Items to Corresponding Estimates from the NAS (*1980/81 Base*)

	1977/ 78	1983	1987/ 88	1988/ 89	1989/ 90	1990/ 91	1992	1993/ 94	1994/ 95	1995/ 96	1997
Cereals	1.09	1.08	1.02	1.02	1.02	0.96	1.03	0.95	0.99	0.95	0.98
Pulses	1.09	1.12	1.29	1.17	1.24	1.23	1.30	1.17	1.27	1.41	1.50
Sugar	0.60	0.49	0.50	0.60	0.52	0.51	0.46	0.45	0.45	0.49	0.48
Edible oils	0.73	0.65	0.67	0.64	0.73	0.81	0.72	0.68	0.71	0.71	0.66
Fruits and vegetables	0.58	0.70	0.75	0.74	0.71	0.75	0.68	0.71	0.62	0.69	0.65
Milk and products	0.86	0.74	0.73	0.74	0.75	0.72	0.73	0.72	0.68	0.73	0.79
Meat, fish and eggs	0.96	0.77	0.68	0.71	0.67	0.64	0.60	0.51	0.48	0.49	0.48
Other food and beverages	1.22	1.34	1.59	1.56	1.54	1.49	1.57	1.46	1.28	1.16	1.03
Paan, tobacco, etc.	0.51	0.52	0.62	0.63	0.60	0.58	0.52	0.51	0.45	0.38	0.35
Fuel and light	1.20	1.08	1.07	1.06	1.10	1.13	1.16	1.17	1.17	1.30	1.42
Clothing	0.61	0.63	0.46	0.50	0.44	0.34	0.43	0.36	0.43	0.49	0.47
Footwear	1.03	1.00	0.83	0.73	0.76	0.52	0.74	0.75	0.86	1.14	1.24
Other goods and services	0.62	0.52	0.53	0.49	0.49	0.47	0.50	0.53	0.52	0.56	0.56
Total	0.81	0.76	0.73	0.72	0.72	0.69	0.71	0.68	0.67	0.69	0.69

[12] The *National Accounts Statistics 2000* gives macroeconomic aggregates by the revised (1993/94 base) series from 1950/51 onwards in a special statement, but no commodity-wise break-ups are available as yet.

[13] See Minhas (1988). The present NAS estimates of total consumer expenditure for 1972/73 and 1977/78 are about 34 per cent higher than those used in this article.

items. Thus, for cereals, the ratio has always been close to unity but with some tendency to decline over time. For sugar, edible oils, fruits and vegetables, milk and products, and other goods and services, the NSS has consistently measured lower consumption but with no obvious time trend in these ratios. In the case of meat, fish and eggs, paan, tobacco and intoxicants, and clothing, NSS has lower consumption and the ratio has fallen over time. But for pulses, other food, and fuel and light, the NSS has consistently measured higher consumption than the NAS.

These persistent differences between NSS and NAS data have in the past been analysed by independent researchers, notably by B.S. Minhas and his associates.[14] Their detailed item by item comparison of consumption by the two sources, which is impossible for us to replicate, had led to validation of the NSS data despite the large apparent differences with the NAS. It was noted in this past research that it is normal all over the world for items like intoxicants to be under-reported by respondents, and something similar is probably true also for non-vegetarian items in a country such as India. Moreover, these researchers noted reasons to doubt the reliability of the NAS data for meat, egg and fish and for fruits and vegetables, estimates of which undergo persistently large revisions and there also appears to be some double counting. For sugar, edible oils and milk and products, a considerable proportion is purchased by hotels, restaurants and food manufacturers as intermediate goods to produce final goods purchased by households. A large part of such processed and prepared food appear differently in the NSS and NAS data, with the former including these under 'other foods' while the latter includes them directly under the item concerned. This explains why the NSS measures higher expenditure under 'other food'. The relative overestimation by the NSS of fuel and light has likewise been explained by failure of the NAS to adequately capture fuel wood collected directly by households.

Thus, for most of the above items, the differences are not particularly surprising or unexpected, especially given that the NSS leaves out 'non-household' consumption such as in hostels, prisons and ceremonials and, unlike the NAS, does not impute any rental on owned residential dwellings. However, for certain items such as clothing and 'miscellaneous non-food goods and services' the differences are large and have been attributed in past analysis both to a failure of the NAS to measure household consumption correctly and to a failure of the NSS to adequately capture the consumption of the relatively richer household who consume relatively more of these. In this context it should be noted that if indeed much of the underestimation of non-food items is due to the inability of the NSS to sample the rich, this would also have led to considerable underestimation of food consumption by the NSS.

With this background, it is possible to return to the issue of the NSS reference period to see to what extent the change in recall improves the correspondence between the NSS and NAS. Table 11.9 gives the absolute values of consumption estimates for 1995/96 from both the Type 1 and Type 2 NSS schedules and from both the NAS estimates with base 1980/81 and base 1993/94. For the new NAS series, the estimates for 1995/96 as shown by both NAS 1999 and NAS 2000 are also presented to give an idea of the revisions which continue even after considerable lag.[15]

Comparing the estimates by the two NSS schedules with NAS (1980/81), it may be noticed that for all items of food, beverages and intoxicants taken together, the Type 1 NSS estimates are 20 per cent lower than the NAS, while the Type 2 NSS estimates are about 7 per cent higher. However, although at

[14] See, for example, Minhas, Kansal and Joshi (1986), Minhas (1988), and Minhas and Kansal (1989).

[15] The reason for considering 1995/96 is that this is the latest year for which full details are available both by the two schedules in the NSS and by the two alternative series of the NAS. The only other year for which such details are available is 1994/96, and this shows similar differences.

this aggregate level of comparison the Type 2 NSS schedule (with one-week recall) is closer to the NAS, this greater apparent concordance is something of a statistical artefact. This is so since the one week recall gives higher estimates for all these items including for those, such as pulses and spices, where NSS estimates with the 30-day recall are much higher than the NAS estimate. As a consequence, if correspondence between the NSS and NAS for food, beverage and intoxicants is judged on the statistically correct basis of *absolute* or squared differences, this is in fact slightly better by the one-month recall than by the one-week recall.[16] Also the large gap between the NAS and NSS for non-food items by the usual 30-day schedule is even wider by the Type 2 schedule. Thus, even treating the NAS as benchmark, the 30-day NSS schedule cannot be judged unambiguously inferior to the alternative schedule on the basis of NAS estimates available at the time that the experimental results from Rounds 51 to 54 were obtained.

However, as discussed above, the CSO has revised its estimates of private consumption expenditure as part of constructing its new series of National Accounts with 1993/94 as base. For 1995/96, these new estimates are higher than the older NAS estimates with 1980/81 as base by about 16 per cent for total consumption and about 20 per cent for consumption of food, beverages and intoxicants. This has involved upward revisions for most items, with particularly large increases for fruits and vegetables, gross rent, medical services and miscellaneous goods and services. But for two items, 'paan, tobacco and intoxicants' and 'clothing', the NAS has substantially revised downwards its consumption estimates. Although the net result is to increase the discrepancy between the NAS and NSS estimates of total consumption further, these revisions between the 1980/81 and 1993/94 series, particularly for fruits and vegetables and clothing, have the effect of increasing the divergence much more with the NSS Type 1 schedule than with the Type 2 schedule. In this sense, the revisions to NAS appear to have reflected to some extent the information obtained in these experimental NSS rounds. Nonetheless, as is evident from the changes made to the 1995/96 revised data between 1999 and 2000, these revisions are far from stable.

Thus, in the case of fruits and vegetables, sugar, edible oils, tobacco and clothing, the revisions earlier made while shifting base have been reversed within a period of one year by varying extents. For example, the estimate of fruit and vegetable consumption was increased by as much as 117 per cent in the new series when it was first released, but this has been revised downward by about 9 per cent this year. Nonetheless, even now the NAS estimate for fruits and vegetables is three times the NSS 30-day estimate and almost double even the higher NSS one-week estimate, making it highly suspect. Similarly, the original downward revision in the estimate for clothing was by as much as 43 per cent, although this has since been increased by 12 per cent, while the estimate for tobacco was first reduced by 33 per cent and then upped by 54 per cent. It, therefore, still remains true, as Minhas and Kansal (1989) had pointed out over a decade ago, that 'the margin of uncertainty (error) in NAS estimates – uncertainty caused by subjective adjustments, methodological innovations and changes in production data – is uncomfortably too large to sustain a healthy degree of confidence in them.'

With recent revisions not inspiring greater confidence in the NAS than what had been concluded from earlier research to validate the NSS, there are obvious problems in treating the NAS as benchmark. But, from the point of view of the choice of reference period in the NSS, there is a further problem in the

---

[16] The sum of absolute differences between the NSS and NAS 1980/81 estimates for food items are Rs 69,514 crore and Rs 77,028 crore by schedules 1 and 2 respectively. This is as against the corresponding algebraic differences of Rs 54,303 crore and Rs (–) 31,213 crore.

validity of such comparisons. Since a large gap exists between the NSS and NAS estimates of non-food consumption, and since this is wider with the Type 2 schedule than with the Type 1 schedule and widens further if NAS 1993/94 rather than NSS 1980/81 is considered, there is a strong presumption that the NSS does under-enumerate the rich systematically. If so, tests of consistency between the NAS and NSS, and judgements about the best reference period for the NSS, must take into account explicitly the implications of such under-enumeration and also the fact that 'non-household' private consumption is not covered by the NSS. Any underestimation of consumption resulting from these would not only have biased the NSS estimates of non-food consumption but also of food consumption.

The last two columns of Table 11.9 give details of a synthetic construction from the NSS data for 1995/96, separately for the Type 1 and Type 2 schedules, to give an idea of what the NSS estimates are likely to be if these are adjusted for such underestimation. For this, it is assumed that the difference between the NSS and NAS estimates of total consumption of non-food items (other than paan, tobacco and intoxicants and gross rent) arises entirely because of under-enumeration or non-coverage. And, using this as a controlling total, the item-wise NSS estimates from both schedules have been adjusted

Table 11.9 Nominal Consumer Expenditure Estimates 1995/96

(Rs in Crore)

| | National Accounts Statistics | | | National Sample Survey | | | |
| | 1980/81 Base | 1993/94 Base | | Unadjusted | | Adjusted for Under-enumeration | |
	NAS 1998	NAS 1999	NAS 2000	Type 1	Type 2	Type 1	Type 2
Cereals	90,616	103,671	102,330	90,714	103,227	102,592	125,696
Pulses	11,569	13,602	13,589	16,844	25,774	20,448	34,979
Sugars	21,375	23,216	21,537	11,009	14,332	13,170	18,877
Edible oils	27,848	29,113	26,892	20,651	25,872	25,479	36,848
Fruits and vegetables	46,297	100,674	91,733	33,547	53,232	44,340	83,350
Milk and products	59,046	63,326	62,283	44,116	51,315	58,597	81,912
Meat, fish and eggs	29,783	30,857	30,957	14,917	23,551	19,425	35,035
Spices and salt	8,158	9,677	9,759	10,344	17,906	12,279	23,950
Other food and beverages	23,499	26,758	25,231	21,653	34,044	34,342	68,471
Paan and intoxicants	5,275	3,708	3,644	4,957	7,652	6,283	10,952
Tobacco	17,347	11,706	18,046	6,268	8,008	7,608	11,059
Total food, beverages, etc.	340,813	416,308	406,001	275,113	365,064	344,654	531,281
Clothing	69,453	39,879	44,503	35,119	34,168	55,450	50,419
Footwear	4,592	4,646	4,693	5,500	5,119	9,132	8,595
Rent	33,775	54,004	58,953	32,070	30,360	40,240	43,683
Fuels	24,270	25,745	25,647	32,070	22,042	26,939	37,652
Medical	14,222	30,207	30,207	18,435	22,042	32,416	27,703
Education	12,998	13,466	13,466	16,771	12,792	32,416	27,703
Durable goods	18,529	18,896	18,698	24,615	12,450	49,558	27,426
Other goods and services	130,442	154,233	156,489	51,938	49,874	79,968	98,226
Total non-food excluding rent	274,506	287,072	293,703	184,448	166,806	293,703	293,703
Total consumption	649,094	757,384	758,657	468,785	542,956	657,422	856,716

Sources: National Accounts Statistics (1998, 1999, 2000) and NSSO (2000a).

upwards, making the further assumption that the commodity composition of the underestimated consumption is the same as that of the top 15 per cent of the urban population from the relevant NSS schedule.[17] Thus, each of these adjusted estimates have a total consumption for non-food (other than paan, tobacco and intoxicants and gross rent) which is the same as in NAS 1993/94, but the estimates of food consumption, as also the item-wise distribution of non-food consumption, are derived entirely from the NSS. The purpose is to arrive at NSS-based estimates of food consumption which are consistent with the assumption that the unexplained non-food consumption is due to under-enumeration of the rich and non-coverage of 'non-household' private consumption.

Comparing these to the NAS shows that, as far as total food consumption is concerned, the adjusted estimates from the Type 1 schedule are fairly close to the NAS, while the adjusted estimates from the Type 2 schedule are considerably higher. The total consumption of food, beverages and intoxicants by the adjusted one-month recall is 1 per cent higher than in NAS 1980/81 and 15 per cent lower than in NAS 1993/94; while by the adjusted one-week recall this is 56 and 31 per cent higher than the two NAS estimates. There are, of course, even larger differences at the individual commodity level, but these are within plausible levels with the one-month recall, especially if allowance is made for differences in the way the NSS and NAS treat items such as sugar which are used to produce other food and if it is agreed that the estimate for fruits and vegetables in the NAS 1993/94 might be an overestimate. On the other hand, the adjusted estimates by the Type 2 schedule are much higher compared to both the NAS 1980/81 and the NAS 1993/94 for every item except sugar and fruits and vegetables. This suggests that Mahalanobis may, in fact, have been correct to suspect gross overestimation by the one-week recall prevalent elsewhere, and to prefer the one-month response.

Thus, allowing for under-enumeration and non-coverage, there is a much stronger case for continuing with the one-month recall for food than to adopt the one-week recall, especially if it is accepted that the large revision to 'fruits and vegetables' in NAS 1993/94 is suspect. The revised estimate for fruits and vegetables is 133 per cent higher than the adjusted Type 1 estimate and 10 per cent higher than the adjusted Type 2 NSS estimate. Similarly, the revision to clothing in NAS 1993/94 deserves a re-look, and there also appears to be considerable difference between the NAS and the NSS in the definition of which goods are 'durable'.

None of this can, of course, be taken as settling either the issue of the most appropriate recall period for the NSS, or of the precise reasons for differences between the NAS and the NSS. There is evidence that the NSS does underestimate consumption, but it is unclear to what extent this is due to poor recall as against an under-enumeration of the rich. Both of these would lead to the NSS overestimating poverty, although this would be much more if errors of recall dominate over those due to under-enumeration. Also, these two sources of error have very different implications for demand estimation. If under-enumeration were the main problem, the NSS would be expected to underestimate the income elasticity of relative luxuries. On the other hand, accepting the reference periods used in the 55th Round would require upward revision to the income elasticity for food derived from the 30-day recall and a downward revision to the elasticity for non-food items. Since the NSS is the most important source of data for

---

[17] In, other words, the adjustment consists of first estimating the NAS-NSS difference in total non-food consumption. From this, the total underestimated consumption is derived by dividing by the share of non-food in the consumption bundle of the rich. The commodity composition of the consumption bundle of the rich is also used to distribute item-wise the derived estimate of total underestimated consumption. This exercise was also done using the NAS 1980/81 as the controlling total for non-food consumption, and with the assumption that the missing consumption had a commodity composition similar to the consumption of the top decile of the rural population. The qualitative results are similar to those reported.

demand assessment, ignoring these to concentrate only on the implications for poverty may lead to inappropriate policy input. Clearly, there is considerable need for further research.

Nonetheless, some conclusions are possible. First, that if the validity of the NSS reference period is tested by comparing with the NAS, then the one-month recall for food in the NSS is not necessarily inferior to the one-week recall. On making allowance for the fact that the NSS does under-enumerate the rich, it is in fact superior. Second, that the validation of the NSS by the NAS is itself a suspect procedure because of frequent and large revisions to the NAS, and that, in this context, there is a strong case to re-examine the revised NAS 1993/94, especially for 'fruits and vegetables' and clothing. Moreover, there is the important observation that although there is a fairly large difference between the NSS and NAS estimates of total consumer expenditure, this divergence did not increase significantly during the nineties. On the basis of these, it can be concluded that *not only was there no in-survey warrant from the earlier experimental rounds for the revised schedule used in the 55th Round, comparisons with the NAS also did not warrant the change in reference period leading to non-comparability with past data.*

CONSISTENCY OF ESTIMATES OF GROWTH, INEQUALITY AND POVERTY

Notwithstanding all the above, some reservations can be expected from those who find it inconsistent that rural poverty has failed to decline during a period of fairly rapid economic growth. A priori, of course, there can be a lack of correspondence between trends in income growth and poverty incidence if inequality has increased, but this can also be a result of measurement problems. The argument so far would suggest increased inequality, but the presumption among many is that it is otherwise. This presumption is informed to a considerable extent by the findings of Ravallion and Datt (Datt and Ravallion, 1992; Ravallion and Datt, 1996), based on the widely used World Bank database on Poverty and Growth in India constructed by them with NSS data. They had found that almost the entire reduction in poverty in India during the 1970s and 1980s was due to growth rather than to redistribution. This was reinforced by Datt (1999) who concluded that poverty as measured from the NSS had failed to decline during the 1990s, not so much because of any increase in inequality as measured by the NSS but because measured rural consumption from the NSS failed to reflect the income growth in the NAS. This was widely interpreted to imply that there must have been measurement problems in the NSS which caused poverty to be overestimated during the nineties.

However, although Datt did not rule this out as a possibility, he had himself been rather more careful about the matter. He had noted that it was well known that the NSS under-enumerates the rich, and that, therefore, the income growth estimated by the NAS during the nineties might not have been captured fully by the NSS if this had accrued disproportionately to the under-enumerated rich. If so, the NSS would not only underestimate true income growth but also fail to measure the increase in true inequality. This possibility, that sampling biases at the upper tail of the distribution may cause the NSS to underestimate both the mean consumption and the inequality of distribution, was essentially why the Expert Group on Poverty Estimates had recommended against constructing hybrid poverty estimates using the NAS consumption mean and the NSS distribution. As discussed earlier, Ravallion (2000c) has also come out strongly against anchoring poverty estimates to the NAS, noting that errors, if any, in the NSS are unlikely to be distribution-neutral, buttressing this by providing evidence from within the NSS of a significant increase in inequality during the nineties.

Thus, Ravallion-Datt have themselves diluted considerably the support claimed from their earlier research by those who argue that the existing NSS estimates overestimate poverty. But, nonetheless, their recent writings continue to suggest: (a) that the gap between the NAS and NSS estimates of consumption expenditure has widened during the nineties, and (b) that although there is strong evidence of an increase in inequality at the national level during the nineties, this is entirely a result of a widening of the urban-rural gap and not of inequalities within either sector. Since such ambiguities can lead to persisting doubts on the credibility of the NSS data, which show no decline in poverty despite measured income growth from the NAS, it is important to emphasise that both these suggestions are somewhat misleading.

On the first of these, i.e. the issue of divergence between the NAS and the NSS, it has already been shown that there is very little evidence of any widening of the gap between the NAS and NSS estimates of *nominal* consumption during the nineties. However, it is important to note that, despite this, the *real* per capita consumption calculated from these two sources do show differential movement during the nineties (Table 11.10). Real per capita consumption obtained directly from the two national accounts series have increased much more than the real consumption estimates derived by Datt (1999) from the NSS. The latter shows an increase of less than 8 per cent between 1990/91 and 1997 against increases of 18 and 20 per cent according to the old and new NAS series.

With this fairly large difference in movements of real consumption between the NAS and NSS occurring without any corresponding difference in movements of nominal consumption, the conclusion must be that that the price deflators used to move from nominal to real consumption are of central importance in the so-called poverty puzzle. And, as is evident from Table 11.10, the Ravallion-Datt deflator did increase more during the 1990s than those implicit in the NAS estimates. Thus the ratio of the Ravallion-Datt deflator to the NAS 1980/81 deflator increased 9 per cent between 1990/91 and 1997,

Table 11.10 Indices of Real Per Capita Consumption and Relative Deflators

| NSS Round | Year | Indices of Real Per Capita Consumption | | | | | Ratio of Datt Deflator to NAS Deflator | |
| | | National Sample Survey (Datt) | | | National Accounts | | | |
		Rural	Urban	Total	1980/81 Base	1993/94 Base	1980/81 Base	1993/94 Base
27	Oct. 72/Sep. 73	81.8	84.7	74.8	70.3	72.5	98.3	102.1
32	Jul. 77/Jun. 78	87.3	90.4	86.6	76.3	77.7	101.5	100.9
38	Jan. 83/Dec. 83	92.1	96.0	92.1	84.9	85.9	103.3	101.5
42	Jul. 86/Jun. 87	100.4	103.0	100.6	91.6	90.6	98.9	95.4
43	Jul. 87/Jun. 88	99.8	97.8	98.9	93.5	92.3	102.2	100.9
44	Jul. 88/Jun. 89	99.8	99.4	99.5	96.8	95.7	102.6	101.6
45	Jul. 89/Jun. 90	103.4	102.4	103.0	98.8	98.2	100.4	99.3
46	Jul. 90/Jun. 91	100.0	100.0	100.0	100.0	100.0	100.0	100.0
48	Jan. 92/Dec. 92	95.6	102.2	97.8	101.4	100.6	107.0	107.0
50	Jul. 93/Jun. 94	101.1	105.3	102.7	105.7	104.2	102.2	101.5
51	Jul. 94/Jun. 95	99.5	105.9	102.0	109.3	107.8	104.8	104.0
52	Jul. 95/Jun. 96	101.0	113.6	105.6	113.0	113.3	107.6	105.9
53	Jan. 97/Dec. 97	106.0	109.3	107.6	118.3	120.1	109.2	105.1

Sources: Computed from Datt (1999) and National Accounts Statistics (1998, 2000).

explaining almost totally the difference in the measured increase in real per capita consumption between the two series.[18]

It is important to recognise that this difference between the two deflators is not due to any measurement error. The implicit deflators from the NAS relate to the consumption basket of the nation as a whole and is properly measured as such by the CSO. On the other hand, the Ravallion-Datt deflators are for poverty calculations, and are again properly constructed to reflect more closely the consumption basket near the poverty line. There may well be errors in the construction of National Accounts, and differences can exist on how to construct the best deflator for the poverty line, but conceptually the latter cannot be the same as the NAS deflator and errors in these, if any, have nothing to do with the NSS data.[19]

In practice, the deflators used to convert NSS rural and urban nominal expenditures into real trends are based on the official consumer price indices for agricultural labourers (CPIAL) and industrial workers (CPIIW). Both these consumer price indices have increased faster than the implicit NAS consumption deflators during the 1990s, essentially because food items have a larger weight in the indices of consumer prices and because prices of various food items, particularly cereals, have increased much more during the nineties than the prices of other items which are consumed more by the rich (Table 11.11). This has reversed a past trend. Thus, the main reason why there is a stagnation in per capita real consumption according to the Ravallion-Datt series (as indeed in all similar series derived from the NSS to calculate poverty), despite the NAS showing fairly substantial growth in this, is because of the reality that food prices have increased faster during the nineties than the prices of other goods. At least in this purely statistical sense *the increase in the relative price of food, particularly of cereals, is a major factor explaining why the incidence of poverty did not decline during the 1990s despite an increase in the mean real per capita consumption as measured by the NAS.*

On the second issue of inequality, it is important to note that in the presence of these significant shifts in relative prices during the nineties, Gini coefficients calculated from the distribution of nominal consumption are only partial indicators of true inequality. Even with unchanged distribution of nominal consumption, the higher relative price of foodgrains would have increased real inequality (as measured by any welfare measure) in both rural and urban areas, while simultaneously *reducing* the gap between rural and urban incomes. This needs to be emphasised since advocates of anchoring poverty estimates to the NAS have claimed that inequality has not increased, and because Ravallion's disclaimer to this, pointing out that there *was* an increase in inequality at the national level, is a qualified one. This stresses the increase in rural-urban disparity during the nineties but not the trends in inequality in either the rural or urban areas.

In fact, the Gini coefficients calculated by Ravallion and Datt from the NSS distribution of nominal consumption show a clear, and statistically significant, reversal during the nineties of an earlier trend of declining rural inequality between 1977/78 and 1990/91.[20] Since then, this has fluctuated wildly around

---

[18] The ratio of the Ravallion-Datt deflator to the consumption deflator in NAS 1993/94 increases less, by 5 per cent between 1990/91 and 1997, leaving some unexplained gap between the two real consumption estimates. But this corresponds exactly to the difference found earlier between the NSS nominal consumption and that according to NAS 1993/94.

[19] Differences in deflators explain most of the differences in the different poverty estimates in Table 11.1, but this does not alter the basic conclusion. All these deflators are constructed from data external to the NSS. See, however, Deaton and Tarozzi (1999), who have constructed Tornquist indices from prices implicit in the NSS.

[20] There is evidence of a significant trend-break in rural inequality after 1990/91, although, unlike for urban areas or the national, the trend fitted to rural Gini coefficients during the nineties is not statistically significant. Fitting a kinked exponential model to all full year rounds between 1972/73 and 1997 shows the rural Gini declining at 0.5 per cent per annum

Table 11.11 Ratio of Various Price Indices to the Wholesale Price Index
(*All Commodities*)

Year	WPI Cereal	CPIAL Food	CPIAL General	NAS (1993/94) Consumption Deflator	CPIAL Non-food
1977/78	119.3	109.3	109.2	101.3	108.6
1978/79	116.6	105.8	106.8	104.0	111.9
1979/80	109.5	99.4	99.6	97.6	100.2
1980/81	104.0	96.8	96.0	91.4	91.7
1981/82	106.5	102.6	101.0	93.9	92.5
1982/83	113.2	102.4	101.3	95.3	95.2
1983/84	114.1	106.4	106.5	97.1	106.9
1984/85	101.9	99.1	98.7	97.5	96.6
1985/86	103.9	99.1	99.0	98.1	98.9
1986/87	104.0	97.9	98.1	99.8	98.9
1987/88	103.4	99.7	99.7	99.6	99.5
1988/89	107.3	105.3	104.2	100.2	98.5
1989/90	102.2	102.9	102.6	100.8	100.8
1990/91	100.0	100.0	100.0	100.0	100.0
1991/92	108.4	106.0	104.9	99.2	98.7
1992/93	111.8	108.8	107.2	98.7	98.6
1993/94	108.9	103.0	102.3	100.1	98.4
1994/95	109.4	104.2	103.3	98.4	98.5
1995/96	107.7	107.0	106.1	98.4	101.0
1996/97	114.7	110.8	109.0	100.6	99.3
1997/98	113.2	107.4	107.3	101.7	106.7
1998/99	114.8	118.4	116.0	103.8	103.0
1999/2000	126.0	117.6	114.9	NA	100.3

a *rising* trend, exhibiting movements very similar to that of the national inequality (Table 11.12). Urban inequality, which had no trend earlier, also shows a statistically significant increase during the nineties. Thus, even ignoring the strong possibility of the NSS missing out on increasing consumption by the rich which it does under-enumerate, there is clear evidence that inequality increased during the nineties in three different ways. First, the differential impact on the poor of the increase in the relative price of food; second, the increased inequality of nominal consumption in urban areas and the reversal during the nineties of an earlier trend of declining inequality in rural areas; and, third, as Ravallion has correctly emphasised, the increased disparity between urban and rural areas.

This last point is particularly important because a noteworthy feature of the trend revealed by the NSS during the 1990s is that the absence of any reduction in poverty is confined only to the rural areas. The NSS ratio of urban to rural mean per capita consumption has increased during the 1990s in both nominal and real terms. Although this increase in nominal terms continues a trend observed during the previous two decades, the increase in real disparity reverses an earlier decreasing trend. Thus, according to Ravallion-Datt estimates from the NSS, the real per capita consumption in rural areas, which had

between 1972/73 and 1990/91 and increasing at 0.6 per cent per annum thereafter, with both the earlier negative trend and the break after 1990/91 statistically significant. The statistically significant negative trend in rural Gini between 1972/73 and 1990/91 was not picked up by the earlier Ravallion-Datt analysis because of inclusion of the 28th Round which is not a full year round.

Table 11.12 Some Indicators of Inequality

NSS Round	Year	Gini Coefficients (Datt-Ravallion)		Ratio of Urban to Rural Mean Consumption		
		Rural	Urban	National	Nominal	1973/74 Prices
27	Oct. 72/Sep. 73	30.67	34.70		1.43	1.41
32	Jul. 77/Jun. 78	30.92	34.71		1.40	1.41
38	Jan. 83/Dec. 83	30.10	34.08	32.06	1.46	1.42
42	Jul. 86/Jun. 87	30.22	36.75	33.68	1.58	1.40
43	Jul. 87/Jun. 88	29.39	34.64	33.08	1.58	1.34
44	Jul. 88/Jun. 89	29.51	34.80	32.93	1.52	1.36
45	Jul. 89/Jun. 90	28.23	35.59	31.84	1.57	1.35
46	Jul. 90/Jun. 91	27.72	33.98	31.21	1.62	1.37
48	Jan. 92/Dec. 92	29.88	35.11	34.31	1.61	1.46
50	Jul. 93/Jun. 94	28.58	34.34	31.52	1.63	1.42
51	Jul. 94/Jun. 95	30.17	37.18	36.32	1.64	1.45
52	Jul. 95/Jun. 96	28.43	35.53	32.86	1.74	1.54
53	Jan. 97/Dec. 97	30.56	36.54	37.83	1.63	1.41

Source: Datt (1999) and Ravallion (2000c).

increased 14 per cent between 1977/78 and 1987/88, averaged only 2 per cent higher during 1993/94 to 1997, than the average for 1987/88 to 1990/91. The corresponding figures for urban areas are 8 and 9 per cent respectively. Even in 1997, when the rural-urban gap had closed considerably and rural real consumption reached its highest ever level, this was less than 6 per cent higher than during 1990/91. Moreover, according to the NSS, the share of the bottom 40 per cent of the rural population declined 5 per cent to 22.3 per cent in 1997 from 23.4 per cent in 1990/91. As a result, the real consumption of the bottom 40 per cent of the rural population in 1997 was virtually unchanged from that in 1990/91.

Thus, the picture from the NSS is quite clear. Rural poverty did not decline during the nineties both because there was somewhat higher inequality within the rural sector and because the rural real mean consumption lagged behind its urban counterpart, causing negligible or even negative growth in the real consumption of the bottom 40 per cent of the rural population. The growth of overall mean consumption as measured by the NSS has already been validated against that revealed by the NAS. But, in order to clinch the matter, it is necessary to examine whether the NAS is consistent with the Ravallion-Datt result from the NSS that per capita *rural* consumption grew by only around 6 per cent between 1990/91 and 1997, as against a growth of around 20 per cent in real national per capita consumption according to the NAS. For this, it is useful to consider measures of rural output and incomes, remembering that there does exist a strong likelihood of the NSS underestimating increases in the incomes of the rich, and that if anything, consumption is likely to have lagged behind income. Even those who may doubt whether inequality has increased would agree that rural poverty is unlikely to have declined if average rural per capita incomes have stagnated.

The easiest comparison in this context is with measures of agricultural income and output per head of rural population. Table 11.13 gives indices of agricultural output per capita of rural population computed from the official Index Numbers of Agricultural Production (IAP) and from the CSO's constant price estimates of the Gross Domestic Product in Agriculture, Forestry and Fishing, by both the series with base 1980/81 and 1993/94. The IAP shows that per capita agricultural output during the nineties peaked in 1996/97 (when there was no NSS survey) at a level less than 8 per cent higher than in 1990/91, with

Table 11.13 Indices of Rural Per Capita Output and Incomes

| | | Indices of Agricultural Output Per Capita of Rural Population | | Indices of Rural Indices of Per Capita | | |
| | Agricultural Production | GDP from Agriculture, etc. | | NAS 1980/81 Deflated by | | NAS 1993/94 |
		1980/81 Base	1993/94 Base	Output Price	CPIAL	CPIAL Deflated
1977/78	86.3	89.0	–	73.0	61.0	–
1978/79	87.7	89.4	–	74.7	64.6	–
1979/80	72.6	76.5	–	67.2	62.0	–
1980/81	82.1	84.8	85.8	72.2	65.1	–
1981/82	86.5	88.5	88.9	75.4	65.8	–
1982/83	81.4	85.7	86.7	74.9	67.1	–
1983/84	90.5	93.3	93.2	80.4	70.1	–
1984/85	88.4	91.6	92.8	80.9	75.5	–
1985/86	88.0	90.2	91.7	81.7	78.2	–
1986/87	83.3	87.1	89.5	82.1	80.6	–
1987/88	81.9	85.8	86.6	83.2	81.4	–
1988/89	97.6	98.1	98.1	93.2	87.1	–
1989/90	98.0	98.0	97.8	97.5	94.1	–
1990/91	100.0	100.0	100.0	100.0	100.0	100.0
1991/92	96.5	96.1	96.8	94.2	91.7	91.7
1992/93	99.0	100.4	100.7	98.2	91.5	91.5
1993/94	100.8	102.2	102.7	101.2	100.4	100.4
1994/95	105.0	105.8	106.2	105.7	103.0	102.3
1995/96	100.6	100.8	103.5	106.5	101.9	102.1
1996/97	107.9	107.3	111.9	111.6	103.1	107.0
1997/98	101.0	103.5	108.3	110.6	103.7	108.8
1998/99	107.6	–	114.5	–	–	115.5
1999/00	104.6	–	114.5	–	–	–

Source: Chandrasekhar and Ghosh (2000) for rural income estimates.

the average for 1993/98 only 3 per cent higher than in 1990/91. A more or less similar picture is obtained from the GDP series with 1980/81 as base, according to which agricultural income per capita of rural population averaged only 4 per cent higher during 1993–98 than in 1990/91, with a peak in 1996/97 which was 7 per cent higher. However, the series with 1993/94 as base shows better performance, with per capita agricultural income 12 per cent higher in 1996/97 than in 1990/91 and the average for 1993/98 higher by 6 per cent.

On re-tabulating the data to correspond to the NSS rounds (Table 11.14), both the IAP and NAS 1980/81 show somewhat lower growth between 1990/91 and 1997 than the NSS. Also, although the NAS 1993/94 does show higher growth, this is not so seriously out of line as to be outside the range of error likely to be caused by under-enumeration of the rich. Thus, *the NSS-based estimates of the growth of rural consumption are not out of line with agricultural growth.* Nonetheless, it is important to note the difference between the two NAS series. While agricultural growth is similar by the old GDP series and the IAP, the new series diverges considerably, especially after 1996/97. On the basis of provisional estimates for 1999/2000, per capita agricultural output by this series is 14.5 per cent higher than in 1990/91 compared to an increase of only 4.6 per cent by the IAP. Further, it can be argued that agricultural growth is an insufficient measure of the growth of rural incomes. Non-agricultural incomes have

Table 11.14 Indices of Rural Per capita Output and Incomes

Year	Index of NSS Real Rural Consumption	Indices of Agricultural Output Per Capita of Rural Population			Indices of Rural Income Per Capita		
		IAP	GDP from Agriculture		NAS 1980/81 Output Price	Deflated	NAS 1993/94
			1980/81 Base	1993/94 Base		CPIAL	CPIAL Deflated
Jul. 77/Jun. 78	87.3	87.5	90.0		74.5	63.2	–
Jan. 83/Dec. 83	92.1	89.0	92.3	92.3	80.2	70.8	–
Jul. 86/Jun. 87	100.4	83.7	87.6	89.5	83.6	82.5	–
Jul. 87/Jun. 88	99.8	86.6	89.8	90.2	87.0	84.6	–
Jul. 88/Jun. 89	99.8	98.6	99.0	98.8	95.7	90.7	–
Jul. 89/Jun. 90	103.4	99.4	99.5	99.2	99.6	97.6	–
Jul. 90/Jun. 91	100.0	100.0	100.0	100.0	100.0	100.0	100.0
Jan. 92/Dec. 92	95.6	99.2	100.3	100.5	98.6	93.5	93.5
Jul. 93/Jun. 94	101.1	102.8	104.1	104.4	103.9	103.2	103.0
Jul. 94/Jun. 95	99.5	104.9	105.6	106.3	107.5	104.9	104.4
Jul. 95/Jun. 96	101.0	103.3	103.5	106.4	109.3	104.3	105.5
Jan. 97/Dec. 97	106.0	103.6	105.5	110.0	112.5	105.8	110.6

percolated to rural areas in the past, particularly during 1983 to 1987 when per capita agricultural output and income was stagnant but poverty declined significantly.

The first of these, i.e. the revision of CSO's national accounts, is interesting since almost the entire increase in both the level and the rate of growth of agricultural output and incomes is because the coverage of fruits, vegetables and floriculture has been enlarged in the new NAS series with 1993/94 as base. The data source for output of these crops has been shifted partly from the Directorate of Economics and Statistics, Ministry of Agriculture (DESAg) to the National Horticulture Board (NHB), and the prices used to calculate value of horticultural output have also been revised. For 1993/94, these revisions have led to an increase in the value of horticultural output by over 60 per cent, leading to an upward revision of total agricultural GDP by about 7 per cent. Also, the rate of growth of horticultural output has been put at more than double the rate of growth of remaining crops, so that about 35 per cent of the total increase in the value of crop output between 1993/94 and 1998/99 is attributed to fruits and vegetables alone. Fruits and vegetables are thus currently estimated to account for over 25 per cent of the value of total crop output (almost the same as that of rice and wheat put together), although grown on only 4.5 per cent of crop area.

These revisions were made because it was felt that the DESAg was missing out on a considerable part of horticultural production. But, although there is certainly evidence that changing patterns of demand *have* caused significant diversification of agriculture during the nineties, the magnitude of these revisions to fruits and vegetables output appear inexplicably large. Unlike the DESAg estimates of forecast crops for which a system of area statistics exists and scientific crop-cutting estimates are done to determine yields, the system of estimation for horticultural crops is weak. Reliance on NHB data has meant including some estimates of output which are based purely on seed distribution, while some of the prices used are inclusive of high trade and transport margins. In the earlier discussion, it has already been observed that the resulting revisions have led to estimates of consumption of fruits and vegetable which are totally out of line with the NSS data. Accepting these revisions would thus require reassessment of all recent research into factor productivity in Indian agriculture and of all earlier estimates of future demand. Such reassessment should, of course, be carried out if there is compelling evidence, but before this there is a need for the CSO to review its changed methodology for horticultural crops which leads to estimates of production and consumption that are totally out of line with other data. Pending such review, it is safer to rely on the data by 1980/81 as base.

As for the second point, that proper assessment of trends in rural incomes requires considering non-agricultural incomes as well, the problem is that, excepting for the two base years 1980/81 and 1993/94, the CSO does not give a break-up of sectoral and total incomes by rural and urban areas. However, the rural-urban break-up of the sectoral employment estimates from the NSS, which the CSO now uses for the NAS, is available. On the basis of these, and the assumption that the growth of labour productivity is the same in rural and urban areas, Chandrasekhar and Ghosh (2000) have made some estimates of rural incomes, indices of which are also presented in Tables 11.13 and 11.14.[21] It should, however, be noted that there is no independent evidence for the assumption of equal productivity growth, which would, if anything, exaggerate the growth of rural incomes.

These estimates suggest a sharp slowdown in the growth of per capita rural output and real incomes during the nineties. Such incomes can be measured in two ways: either using the implicit NAS deflators for or by deflating nominal income with the CPIAL as in the poverty calculations. The first method based on the NAS 1980/81 shows a decline in growth rate from 3.1 per cent per annum during the Triennium Ending (TE) 1980/81 to TE 1990/91 to 1.8 per cent per annum during TE 1990/91 to TE 1997/98. The second method, also based on NAS 1980/81, shows an even larger decline, from 3.9 to 1.4 per cent per annum. As discussed earlier, the new NAS with base 1993/94 shows higher incomes and higher growth, but if this is spliced backward to the old series, the result is still a decline in per capita rural income (CPIAL deflated) from 3.9 to 1.8 per cent. As against these, the residual estimates of per capita urban incomes show sharp acceleration in growth (increasing from less than 2.5 per cent per annum during TE 1980/81 to TE 1990/91 to almost 5 per cent during TE 1990/91 to TE 1997/98), confirming a very significant increase in rural-urban disparity.

One reason for this increased disparity is the fall in agriculture's share in GDP, but an even more significant reason is the trend in rural non-agricultural employment. According to NSS data, rural non-agricultural employment had increased from 36 million in 1977/78 to 66 million in 1989/90, but this fell sharply in 1991/92 and has since fluctuated at between 58 and 63 million. As a result, the rural share in non-agricultural employment, which had increased from 47 to 52 per cent between 1977/78 and 1989/90, has declined almost continually during the nineties to reach only 43 per cent in 1997. Because of the methodology adopted, this fall in employment share is reflected in the estimates of rural incomes above. These show fairly rapid growth during 1977/78 to 1987/88, explaining why NSS consumption increased significantly despite stagnation in per capita agricultural output. But, with productivity gains neutralised by declining non-agricultural employment thereafter, the rates of growth of real rural per capita incomes during the nineties are very similar to those of agricultural output.

[21] The method adopted for this is as follows. Since both sectoral employment and income figures for rural and urban areas are available for 1980/81 and 1993/94, it is possible to compute sectoral productivities for the primary, secondary and tertiary sectors in the rural areas and urban areas. This allows computation of the ratio of urban to rural productivities for each sector for those years. It is assumed that these ratios remain constant in all subsequent or previous years. Based on this assumption, and using the overall GDP figures and the figures on rural and urban sectoral employment from the NSS, the level of rural and urban sectoral incomes is estimated for the remaining years.

Since NSS estimates of real consumption growth during the nineties have already been validated against the latter, the validation extends also to rural incomes including non-agriculture, especially using the CPIAL deflator as for the NSS. This implies basically that *the rapid growth of non-agriculture measured by the NAS at the national level during the nineties did not spill over into rural areas.* In conjunction with the small increase in intra-rural inequality measured by the NSS, this large increase in rural-urban disparity makes the *trends* in NSS estimates of consumption compatible with the NAS estimates of national income.

In fact, even the *level* of NSS rural consumption is not unreasonably low compared to the NAS estimate of rural income. As base for its new series, the NAS has estimated rural NDP per capita in 1993/94 at Rs 5,783, of which Rs 3,052 originates in agriculture. These are likely to be overestimates for reasons already discussed, and are about 9 per cent higher than by the old series. But even compared to these, the corresponding NSS estimate of annual per capita rural consumption, at Rs 3,424, is not implausible. In addition to savings by rural households, the NSS excludes imputed rental on rural dwellings (put at Rs 240 per capita in the NAS) and factor incomes originating in rural areas but appropriated elsewhere. The latter is not insignificant. On the basis of NAS sector-wise factor shares and the sector break-up of rural NDP, operating surpluses accruing to the organised sector account for almost 10 per cent of rural NDP. Deducting these, NSS rural consumption in 1993/94 would be about 70 per cent of rural disposable incomes by the new NAS series and around 75 per cent by the old series. This still implies that the NSS underestimates rural consumption, but clearly any such underestimation is disproportionately more in urban areas since total NSS consumption is only around 50 per cent of total personal disposable incomes.[22]

Thus, NSS estimates of rural consumption during the nineties are not seriously out of line with NAS-based estimates of rural incomes. In particular, there is no essential discrepancy between the growth of real rural consumption from the NSS and of real rural incomes from the NAS, provided NSS employment trends are accepted and the same deflator is used in both cases. Hence, GDP growth during the nineties can be reconciled with the NSS-based trend in rural poverty without assuming much more inequality than what the NSS already shows. Nonetheless, since the issue of rural-urban differentials is important, and the CSO does have the required data, a priority is that the NAS provide regular annual estimates of rural and urban NDP. Also, there is a need to re-examine some of the revisions made in NAS 1993/94, particularly to the value of output from fruits and vegetables.

CONCLUSION

In anticipation of the full results of the 55th Round, this article has attempted to validate the existing NSS series and consider the issue of the most appropriate reference period for the NSS. Comparison of the existing NSS series by the 30-day recall with the NAS shows that although the NSS does estimate a

---

[22] The simple ratios of NSS consumption to NDP (new series) are 0.59 and 0.41 for rural and urban India respectively in 1993/94. Adjusting the respective numerators upward for the NAS-NSS difference in estimates of rent on dwellings, these become 0.63 and 0.46. And further, on deducting from the respective denominators, the operating surpluses accruing to the organised sector, these are 0.70 and 0.57. To arrive at the correct ratio of consumption to disposable income, further adjustments to the denominators are required, i.e. deduction of personal taxes and interest payments by unorganised enterprises and addition of receipts on account of transfer payments and distribution of profit and interest by the organised sectors. The data available does not allow these further adjustments, which in the net are likely to add much more substantially to urban incomes.

lower level of consumption as compared to the NAS, the trend during the nineties are very similar. Also, any underestimation is likely to be disproportionately in urban areas. Especially on trends in rural consumption, the two sources agree if proper deflators are used and the available evidence on the rural-urban distribution of the workforce is considered. From the point of view of valid poverty calculations using the NSS, nothing of substance has changed since the exhaustive analysis of the matter in 1993 by the Expert Group on Estimation of Proportion and Number of Poor. If anything, the correspondence between the trends revealed by the NSS and those by alternative data is much closer during the nineties than these were during the seventies and eighties.

It remains true, however, as the Expert Group had observed, that there is need for 'a sustained effort to refine and improve the survey design and procedure' in order that NSS estimates are considered reliable not only in regard to trends, but also the level of consumption. To this end, experiments involving alternative reference periods are not only desirable but are also a scientific necessity. However, since errors in the NSS are unlikely to be on account of recall alone, an equal emphasis requires to be put on improving the sampling procedure to better capture the consumption of the rich, or, at least, to provide some reliable estimate of errors involved.

In such experimentation particular attention needs to be paid to two issues. First, since comparison with external benchmarks cannot discriminate between errors due to under-enumeration in the samples and the non-sampling errors of recall, it is impossible to judge the relative accuracy of alternative schedules unless there is in-survey validation. Validation of NSS schedules by comparison with the NAS are thus prone to error even if the NAS were error-free, which it is not. Second, it is vital in all experimentation to continue in parallel with the existing 30-day schedule canvassed independently. This is required not only because of the need for comparable time-series data for policy purposes, but also because this is a benchmark necessary to draw valid conclusions from alternative schedules.

Analysis of the experiments in rounds 51 to 54 shows certain systematic differences in results across schedules, which are very important and require further investigation. However, these did not provide any in-survey statistical warrant for the change in schedule used in the 55th Round. Nor is there any statistical warrant for this from valid comparisons with the NAS. Thus, although the one-week recall leads to higher survey estimates of food consumption, apparently closer to the NAS, this does not necessarily imply greater accuracy of this recall if the NSS under-enumerates the rich. Indeed, there is some evidence that on correction for such under-enumeration the schedule used in the 55th Round may be overestimating food consumption. For this reason, it is necessary that the NSSO include some in-survey test of bias in its design of experiments by different recalls and also that an analysis be conducted of the pattern of non-response in its samples. Further, since the 365-day recall alters substantially the distribution obtained for the consumption of certain goods and services, it is necessary that there be an analysis of the comparative results obtained in past rounds in which both the 30-day and 365-day questions were asked.

Moreover, the limited results now available from the 55th Round show clearly that answers to both the one-week and 30-day questions have been contaminated by the presence of the other. Quite possibly, exclusive reliance on the 365-day question in the case of clothing, etc., has also altered responses. As a result, consumption estimates from this round are not comparable to those from previous NSS rounds, and will probably be virtually useless for any assessment of changes in consumer demand. This also leads to a major contradiction whereby the 55th Round shows both large reductions in poverty by the 30-day recall and also significant increases in poverty by the 7-day recall.

For this reason, it is important for the credibility of the NSSO to stress the experimental nature of the 55th Round and its non-comparability with past rounds. While experiments with different schedules canvassed separately should continue, it is absolutely necessary to conduct another large sample Consumer Expenditure Survey using the 30-day reference period as soon as possible. Failure to do this, for whatever reason, could not only give misleading indicators to policy makers using this data, it would also compromise the reputation of India's statistical system. To admit the non-comparability of the 55th Round may mar some celebrations, but in order to maintain the integrity of the statistical system it is vital that truth continues to be given priority over joy.

In this context, it is also necessary to re-examine some of the revisions that have been made in the National Accounts series with 1993/94 as base. This series has involved some very welcome changes in methodology – most notably in the use of workforce data from the NSS rather than the Census. But it is also known that certain extraneous considerations had led the CSO to make large upward revisions in some sectors where the database was weak. In particular, the estimates of the value of 'fruits and vegetables' in the new series appear to be totally out of line with other data and lead to conclusions about agricultural growth and productivity which are at variance with those derived from the more reliable data for forecast crops. This is an important matter that ultimately requires that the system of agricultural statistics be modernised to cope with requirements of an agricultural sector undergoing diversification towards horticulture and livestock. However, till then, NAS estimates for non-forecast crops should at least bear consistency with area statistics and with independent estimates of consumption. Also, since most of the recent scepticism about data has concerned rural poverty, it is desirable that the CSO make available on a regular annual basis the estimates of the rural-urban break-up that are already implicit in the NAS data.

ACKNOWLEDGEMENT

Reprinted from *Economic and Political Weekly,* Vol. 35, 16 December 2000.

REFERENCES

Aiyer, S. (2000), 'Has economic reforms bypassed the poor?', *The Times of India*, 23 April.

Bhalia, Surjit (2000a), 'Growth and Poverty in India – Myth and Reality', mimeo.

——— (2000b), 'Poverty Falls: What, Me Worry?', *Business Standard*, 30 September 2000.

Chandrasekhar, C.P. and Jayati Ghosh (2000), 'Poverty Puzzle', Macroscan, *Businessline*, February.

Datt, G. (1999), 'Has Poverty Declined since Economic Reforms? Statistical Data Analysis', *Economic and Political Weekly*, 11 December.

Datt, G. and M. Ravallion (1992), 'Growth and Redistribution Components of Changes in Poverty Measures: A Decomposition with Application to Brazil and India in the 1980s', *Journal of Development Economics*, Vol. 38.

Datt and Ravallion (1997), 'Macroeconomic Crises and Poverty Monitoring', *Review of Development Economics*, 1(2).

Deaton, A, and A. Tarozzi (1999), *Prices and Poverty in India*, mimeo, Woodrow Wilson School, Princeton.

Gupta, S.P. (1999), 'Trickle Down Theory Re-visited: The Role of Employment and Poverty', V.B. Singh Memorial Lecture, Indian Society of Labour Economics, 18–20 November.

Lal, Deepak, I. Natarajan and Rakesh Mohan (2000), 'Economic Reforms and Poverty Alleviation: A Tale of Two Surveys', mimeo, UCLA and NCAER.

Mahalanobis and Sen (1954), *Bulletin of the International Statistical Institute*, Vol. 34, Part II, 1954.

Minhas, B.S. (1988), 'Validation of Large Scale Sample Survey Data – Case of NSS Estimates of Household Consumption Expenditure', *Sankhya*, Series B, Vol. 50, Part 3, May.

Minhas, B.S., S.M. Kansal, Jagdish Kumar and P.D. Joshi (1986), 'On the Reliability of the Available Estimates of Consumer Expenditure in India', *Journal of Income and Wealth*, Vol. 9, No. 2, July.

Minhas, B.S. and S.M. Kansal (1989), 'Comparisons of the NSS and CSO Estimates of Private Consumption', *Journal of Income and Wealth*, Vol. 11, No. 1, January.

NSSO (2000a), Report No. 447: Choice of Reference Period for Consumption Data, NSSO, March 2000.

——— (2000b), 'Report No. 453: Household Consumer Expenditure in India, Key Results, July–December 1999.

Ravallion, M. (2000a), 'Food Prices, Real Wages and Rural Poverty', *Food Policy*, August.

——— (2000b), 'What is needed for a more pro-poor growth prospect in India?', *Economic and Political Weekly*, Special Number.

——— (2000c), 'Should Poverty Measures be Anchored to the National Accounts?', *Economic and Political Weekly*, 26 August.

Ravallion, M. and G. Datt (1996): 'India's Checkered History in Fight Against Poverty – Are There Lessons for the Future?', *Economic and Political Weekly*, Special Number.

Sundaram, K. and S. Tendulkar (2000), 'Poverty in India: An Assessment and Analysis', mimeo, Delhi School of Economics.

Tendulkar, S. and L.R. Jain (1995), 'Economic Reforms and Poverty', *Economic and Political Weekly*, 10 June.

Visaria, Pravin (2000a), 'Alternative Estimates of Poverty in India', *Economic Times*, 29 June.

——— (2000b), 'Polemics on Poverty', *Business Standard*, 30 October 2000.

Srinivasan, T.N. (2000), 'Growth, Poverty Reduction and Inequality', mimeo, Yale University.

12

Adjusted Indian Poverty Estimates for 1999/2000

Angus Deaton

INTRODUCTION: POVERTY AND POVERTY DEBATES IN THE 1990s

What has happened to Indian poverty in the 1990s has been hotly debated. After the economic reforms in the early 1990s, there was a historically rapid rate of growth in GDP per head but, until the publication of estimates from the 55th Round of the National Sample Survey (NSS) for 1999/2000, little apparent reduction in the fraction of the population in poverty. Official poverty estimates in India are based on large household surveys of consumption carried out by the NSS approximately every fifth year. The 50th Round survey, carried out in 1993/94, produced poverty rates that were only slightly lower than the previous quinquennial survey, the 43rd, carried out in 1987/88. After 1994, there were four 'thin' survey rounds, which have smaller samples and which are not primarily designed to collect household consumption data, and these also showed little if any evidence of a reduction in poverty up to the middle of 1998. But there have always been some doubts about the reliability of these surveys; not only are they smaller, and therefore less precise, but their sample design differs from that of the quinquennial rounds, so there remain questions about their reliability as guides to the evolution of consumers' expenditure and poverty.

In consequence, the results of the 55th Round quinquennial survey of 1999/2000 were eagerly awaited. The estimates, published in February 2001, showed a marked reduction in the fractions of people in poverty. Among rural households, the fraction estimated to be in poverty fell to 27.1 per cent in 1999/2000, compared with 37.3 per cent in 1993/94, while among urban households, the fractions were 23.6 per cent in 1999/2000, compared with 32.4 per cent in 1993/94. However, because the design of the 55th Round questionnaire was different from that in earlier rounds, the comparability of these new estimates has been challenged (see for example Sen, 2000).

In this paper, I explain a method that can be used to adjust the 55th Round poverty estimates so as to make them comparable with earlier official estimates. This method is only as good as its assumptions which are plausible, but not necessarily correct. Given that the 55th Round is not comparable with earlier rounds, some assumptions are needed to make progress at all. As I shall show, my estimates suggest that much, if not all, of the official fall in poverty is real. Indeed, there are some basic facts of the 55th Round which were not compromised by the survey design, and which make it clear that there has been a substantial improvement in levels of living since the 50th Round in 1993/94.

The chapter explains the source of the non-comparability of the 55th Round estimates and the basis for adjustments. Inevitably, there are some formulae, but I have tried to keep them to a minimum, and I explain what each of them means. Further, it discusses the results, and includes adjusted headcount ratios for all India and each of the large states, for both urban and rural sectors. These estimates are a first cut at the issue, and should not be treated as the best estimates that are currently available. My preferred estimates of poverty and inequality in India in 1999/2000, together with comparable estimates for earlier years, are given in Deaton and Dreze (2002). Lastly, some broader issues about poverty monitoring in India, including those raised by the incomparability that is my main topic, but looking further to issues of future survey design, and to the choice of poverty lines, are discussed.

SURVEY DESIGN AND NON-COMPARABILITY

The comparability problems came about as follows. In the 51st through 54th (thin) Rounds, the NSS experimented with the recall periods over which respondents were asked to report their consumption. NSS consumption surveys have traditionally used a 30-day recall period for all goods, a decision that was based on some experiments in the early 1950s (Mahalanobis and Sen, 1954). Most statistical offices around the world use a shorter recall period for high-frequency items, such as food, and longer recall period for low-frequency items, such as large durable goods. The NSS experiments in the 51st through 54th Rounds compared a traditional 30-day recall questionnaire (Schedule 1) with an experimental questionnaire with three reporting periods, 7, 30, and 365 days, applied to different classes of goods (Schedule 2). Households were randomly assigned to one or other schedule, and it was found that, on average, the experimental 7/30/365 Schedule generated more reported total expenditures. This effect was large enough to cut estimated poverty rates by approximately a half when the experimental schedule was used in place of the traditional schedule (Visaria, 2000). Shorter reporting periods typically generated higher rates of consumption flow, so that the seven-day recall in Schedule 2 produced higher average consumption than the 30-day recall in Schedule 1, while the 365-day recall in Schedule 2 produced lower average consumption. However, the 365-day recall also has the consequence of pulling up the bottom tail of the distribution of expenditures on these infrequently purchased items, such as durables, clothing, or hospital expenditures, and many fewer Schedule 2 than Schedule 1 households report no purchases of these items over the reporting period.

The 55th Round differed both from earlier rounds and from either of the Schedules in the experimental rounds. For the high-frequency items, households were asked to report their expenditures for both recall periods. The questionnaires were printed with the list of goods down the leftmost column, with the next four columns requesting quantities and expenditures over the last seven days and over the last 30 days respectively. Such multiple reporting periods are often used in household expenditure surveys, and may well produce excellent estimates in their own right. But the results are unlikely to be comparable with those from a questionnaire in which only the 30-day questions are used. For example, when they are asked both questions, respondents are effectively being prompted to reconcile the rates of consumption across the two periods. Indeed, there is some evidence that is consistent with this sort of reconciliation. In the 51st through 54th Rounds, where different households were assigned one or other of the two Schedules, the ratio of mean per capita expenditure in Schedule 2 to mean per capita expenditure in

Schedule1 lay between 1.13 and 1.18 for both urban and rural sectors in all four rounds. Yet in the 55th Round, the ratio of the two measures of per capita expenditure fell to 1.04 among rural and 1.03 among urban households. This was in spite of the fact that the low-frequency items were asked only at the 365-day reporting period, which should have reduced the Schedule 1 estimates and further inflated the ratio of the Schedule 2 to Schedule 1 totals.

Although we have no way of knowing exactly what happened, one reasonable hypothesis is that the immediate juxtaposition of the two Schedules prompted households to reconcile their two reports, pulling up the rate of consumption at 30-day recall above what it would have been if asked in isolation, and pulling down the rate of consumption at 7-day recall above what it would have been if asked in isolation. If so, the 30-day estimates of consumption from the 55th Round are too high compared with the 30-day estimates of consumption from earlier large rounds, particularly the 50th, and the reduction in poverty is overstated. Given the very large drop in the headcount ratios, this is a plausible story. The 7-day estimates cannot be used to repair the poverty estimates because there are no 7-day estimates from earlier large rounds. The best that can be done is to compare the 55th with the immediately preceding thin rounds, a procedure that shows an increase in poverty in 1999/2000 compared with the period from mid-1994 through mid-1998.

ADJUSTING THE POVERTY ESTIMATES

This section outlines a procedure for adjusting the poverty estimates from the 55th Round to make them comparable with earlier large rounds, particularly the 50th. Because the new survey does not contain all the information that is needed to make it fully comparable, the method, like any effective procedure, rests on a number of assumptions. I shall provide some evidence to suggest that these assumptions are plausible, but they cannot be fully tested without the information that, if it existed, would obviate the need for them.

The key idea is that there are a group of goods for which the questionnaire is the same across all rounds. There are six broad categories, fuel and light, miscellaneous goods, miscellaneous services, non-institutional medical services, rent, and consumer cesses and taxes. These items have always been asked using the 30-day reporting period. The first four are important items, and expenditures on the first three are reported by virtually all households. Non-institutional medical expenditures are also important on average, with a mean that is comparable in size to expenditures on miscellaneous goods or expenditures on miscellaneous services, but they are incurred by less than half of households over a 30-day period. Taken together, expenditures on the six broad categories account for more than 20 per cent of all expenditures, and more in urban areas. Total expenditure on these '30-day' goods is also highly correlated with total household expenditure; in the 50th Round, the correlation between the logarithm of total household per capita expenditure and the logarithm of per capita expenditure on these 30-day goods is 0.79 and 0.86 in the rural and urban sectors respectively. I can, therefore, use expenditures on these comparably surveyed goods to get an idea of trends in total expenditures, and therefore, of trends in poverty.

Rather than estimating per capita expenditure as a first stage and then going on to estimate poverty, I use a more direct procedure. Denote the logarithm of household total expenditure per head by x, and the logarithm of total expenditure per head on 30-day goods by m. The logarithm of the poverty line is written z, and everything is measured in constant price rupees. If the headcount ratio is denoted by P, I can write

$$P = F(z),\tag{1}$$

where $F(\ )$ is the cumulative distribution function of the logarithm of per capita expenditure (PCE). $F(z)$ is simply the fraction of people who live in households with a logarithm of pce less than the logarithm of the poverty line, or just the fraction of people who live in households with pce less than the poverty line.

We are interested in using the amount of m to predict the level of poverty. Consider then the probability of being poor conditional on spending m on 30-day goods, $F(z|m)$. I can rewrite equation (1) as

$$P = \int_0^\infty F(z|m)g(m)dm = E_m[F(z|m)],\tag{2}$$

where $g(m)$ is the density function of the logarithm of expenditure on 30-day goods m. Equation (2) invites us to consider what is the probability of being poor overall, given expenditure on 30-day goods. The headcount ratio for the population as a whole is the average of this probability over everyone.

Equation (2) cannot be evaluated using data from the 55th Round any more than can equation (1). However, if there are grounds to suppose that the probability of being poor conditional on m, $F(z|m)$, is constant over time, and if the density of m, $g(m)$, is the same in the 55th Round as it would have been with a traditional schedule, then we can use the actual marginal distribution of m from the 55th Round together with the conditional headcount function $F(z|m)$ from an earlier round to compute corrected headcount estimates. In particular, I use the 50th Round to compute the headcount conditional on m and estimate the 55th Round poverty rate according to

$$\hat{P}_{55} = \int_0^\infty \hat{F}_{50}(z|m)\hat{g}_{55}(m)dm = \hat{E}_{m55}[\hat{F}_{50}(z|m)],\tag{3}$$

where the 'hats' denote estimates, and the subscripts denote the relevant NSS rounds. According to equation (3), we use the probabilities of being poor given expenditure on 30-day goods, estimated from the 50th Round, and combine them with the distribution of expenditures on 30-day goods from the 55th Round, expenditures that were collected in a comparable way in the 50th and 55th Rounds. Put differently, we can observe directly expenditures on 30-day goods in the 55th Round. These tell us something about poverty in that round. Exactly what can be calculated by using each household's 30-day expenditures to calculate its probability of being poor, given the relationship between being poor and 30-day expenditures from the 50th Round, and then averaging over all households to get the estimated poverty count.

The procedure here is very different from another method that is sometimes used. This alternative uses expenditure on 30-day goods and on all goods in the 50th Round to calculate the value of 30-day expenditures that correspond to the overall poverty line, effectively a 30-day expenditure poverty line. It then uses this 30-day poverty line in the 55th Round to calculate the fraction of people whose 30-day expenditure is below this cut off, and uses that as an estimate of poverty. The problem with this method is that there are some people whose 30-day expenditure is low, but who will not be poor overall, and some who are poor overall, but not poor in 30-day expenditures. These households are recognised in equations (1), (2) and (3), but missed in the alternative. Indeed, it is easy to use equations (2) and (3) to show that the alternative method will be correct only when 30-day poverty is a *perfect* predictor of overall poverty.

Note too that the procedure deals simultaneously with the changes from 30 days to 7 days, and the change from 30 days to 365 days. We make no use of the 7-day or 365-day expenditures from the 55th Round, relying only on the 30-day expenditures, which are comparable across both.

What assumptions are required for equation (3) to work, and why might they be valid? The most plausible assumption is that the density of m is the same in the 55th Round as it was actually conducted as it would have been had the 55th Round been run in the traditional way. Remember that the questionnaire for the 30-day goods is identical to earlier questionnaires, so that the issue is whether changes elsewhere in the questionnaire altered the responses to the parts that remained the same. This is certainly possible, although there is no reason to think so. There is also relevant evidence from the thin rounds, which can be used to compare the distributions of 30-day goods in Schedule 1 and in Schedule 2, where the questions on all the other goods were different. Tarozzi (2001) runs these tests and is unable to reject the hypothesis that the distributions of reported expenditure on 30-day goods are the same in the two Schedules.

The second assumption is about the stability from the 50th to the 55th Rounds of the function $F(z|m)$ and its validity depends, among other things, on the stability of the Engel curve relating the logarithm of expenditures per capita on 30-day goods to the logarithm of total household expenditure per capita. If this Engel curve is stable over time, and the distribution of households around the Engel curve does not change, then the fraction of people who are poor at any given level of m will be constant. Note that it is not required that expenditure on 30-day goods be a fixed ratio of total expenditure, only that the relationship between them remain stable. To see how this works, and to see potential problems, suppose that the Engel curve can be written as

$$m = \varphi(x) + u \tag{4}$$

where $\varphi(x)$ is monotone increasing in x and the CDF of u, which is independent of x, can be written $H(u)$. Then we have

$$
\begin{aligned}
F(z|m) &= \Pr\,(x \le z|m) \\
&= \Pr\,[u \ge m - \varphi(z)|m] \\
&= 1 - H[m - \varphi(z)].
\end{aligned}
\tag{5}
$$

By equation (5), the regression of poverty on m, $F(z|m)$, will be constant over time if the Engel curve remains fixed, and if the distribution of u remains constant. The equation also highlights a potential source of difficulty. If the Engel curve depends on other variables, perhaps most obviously on relative prices, and if these variables shift, the poverty regression will also shift, and the estimates will likely be biased. If such variables are identifiable, and if the data are available, they can be used to condition the distribution of x along with m in equations (2) and (3). Note finally that, while it is useful to consider the Engel curve when justifying the procedure, the estimation does not work with the Engel curve nor its inverse, the projection of total expenditure on 30-day expenditure, but directly with the regression of poverty on 30-day expenditures through equation (3).

Once again, without the missing data from the 55th Round, there is no way of checking the validity of the assumption. But once again robustness can be checked by calculating the regression functions $F(z|m)$ from the thin rounds – albeit less precisely than for the 50th Round – and the results inserted into equation (3) in place of the estimates from the 50th Round. I have done some experiments along these lines for the all-India estimates shown here, and while there are some changes, they are well within the range of uncertainty given the standard errors.

EMPIRICAL METHODS, RESULTS AND DISCUSSION

I calculate the adjusted poverty estimates by direct application of equation (3). Using data from the 50th Round first, I calculate a dummy variable for each household indicating whether its members are poor or not, according to whether its household per capita expenditure is below the official poverty line for the 50th Round. When the calculations are for All-India, I use the All-India poverty line; when they are for a specific state, I use that state's specific poverty line. All calculations are done separately for urban and rural sectors. I then use a locally weighted regression procedure, to locally regress the poverty dummy on the logarithm of 30-day expenditures. I do this at each point on a 50-point grid. These regressions are weighted by the NSS-supplied household inflation factors multiplied by household size so that everything is effectively done at the individual, not household, level.

Turning to the 55th Round, I first deflate 30-day expenditures by the consumer price index implicit in the appropriate official poverty line. For example, the official poverty line for rural Bihar was Rs 212.16 in the 50th Round and Rs 333.07 in the 55th Round, so that the deflator for rural Bihar is 333.07 divided by 212.16. While it might be preferable to work with a price index for the 30-day goods, the real issue is the stability of the Engel curve with respect to changes in relative prices, which my preliminary calculations suggested was not too much of a problem. After deflation, I compute a kernel density estimate for the logarithm of deflated 30-day expenditures, using the same grid points as in the 50th Round regression. The corrected poverty estimate is then a weighted average of the 50th Round regression predictions using the estimated density as weights.

Before looking at the estimates, it is useful to consider the Figure 12.1. The Figure 12.1 shows, for All-India rural, the two estimated densities for the logarithm of real per capita expenditure on 30-day goods in the 50th and 55th Rounds. These estimates, weighted and averaged over the population, give

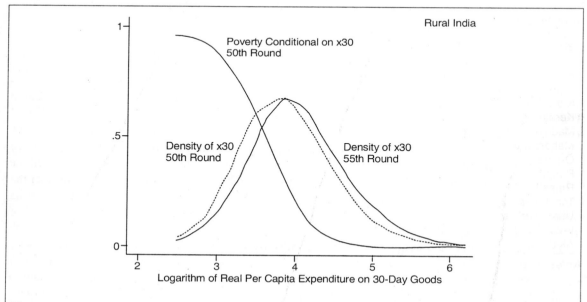

Figure 12.1 Distribution of Expenditures on 30-Day Goods in the 50th and 55th Rounds, and Probability of being Poor Conditional on 30-Day Expenditures, Estimated from 50th Round

us our estimates of the poverty headcount ratio. The important point to note is the extent to which the density of 30-day goods has moved to the right from the 50th to the 55th Rounds. At all levels of the distribution, among the poor, the middle, and the best-off, there are more 30-day expenditures in 1999/2000 than there were in 1993/94. It is this fact that drives the reduction in estimated poverty, and that makes it so unlikely that there has been no improvement in living standards. Expenditures on 30-day goods are translated into poverty estimates using the probability of being poor given expenditures on 30-day goods. This is shown as the solid line in the figure, falling from left to right. Among those with very low expenditures on 30-day goods, the probability of being poor is nearly one, but falls steadily the more 30-day expenditures there are. Again, these are probabilities; I am not assuming that there is any deterministic relationship between being poor and the amount of 30-day expenditures. The poverty headcount ratios reported below are calculated by weighting the density of 30-day purchases, in Figure 12.1 the dotted line, by the probability of being poor conditional on 30-day expenditure, the solid declining line.

Table 12.1 shows the results for rural India, and Table 12.2 for urban India. I have shown my own recalculation of the official headcount ratios along with the official estimates themselves. The two sets of estimates are slightly different, presumably because the official numbers are not calculated from the unit record data, but from interpolation using published tabulations of the size distribution of per capita expenditure. I present both sets of numbers because the adjusted estimates are calculated from the unit

Table 12.1 Headcount Poverty Ratios *(Rural India, Per Cent)*

	50th Round		55th Round		55th Round	
	Official	*Estimate*	*Official*	*Estimate*	*Adjusted*	*St Error*
Andhra Pradesh	15.9	15.9	11.1	10.5	14.9	0.64
Assam	45.0	45.2	40.0	40.3	44.1	2.05
Bihar	58.2	58.0	44.3	44.0	49.2	1.18
Gujarat	22.2	22.2	13.2	12.4	15.4	1.17
Haryana	28.0	28.3	8.3	7.4	12.7	1.06
Himachal Pradesh	30.3	30.4	7.9	7.5	18.9	1.32
Karnataka	29.9	30.1	17.4	19.8	25.7	1.59
Kerala	25.8	25.4	9.4	9.4	12.6	0.67
Madhya Pradesh	40.8	40.7	37.1	37.3	36.4	1.47
Maharashtra	37.9	37.9	23.7	23.2	29.2	1.43
Orissa	49.7	49.8	48.0	47.8	47.3	1.75
Punjab	12.0	11.7	6.4	6.0	5.9	0.43
Rajasthan	26.5	26.4	13.7	13.5	19.6	1.59
Tamil Nadu	32.5	33.0	20.6	20.0	19.9	1.02
Uttar Pradesh	42.3	42.3	31.2	31.1	33.7	0.86
West Bengal	40.8	41.2	31.9	31.7	37.1	1.50
All-India	37.3	37.2	27.1	27.0	30.2	0.43

Notes: The 'official' estimates for the 50th and 55th Rounds are those published in the Planning Commission's press releases. The 'estimate' in Columns 2 and 4 are my calculations from the unit record data. These differ from the official numbers because the latter are extrapolated from published tables rather than directly calculated from the data. The last two columns show the adjusted poverty estimates using the procedures detailed in the text, together with standard errors calculated from 100 replications of a bootstrap that takes into account the cluster structure of the data, but ignores stratification.

Table 12.2 Headcount Poverty Ratios *(Urban India, Per Cent)*

	50th Round		55th Round		55th Round	
	Official	*Estimate*	*Official*	*Estimate*	*Adjusted*	*St Error*
Andhra Pradesh	38.3	38.8	26.6	27.2	27.7	1.45
Assam	7.7	7.9	7.5	7.5	8.3	1.23
Bihar	34.5	34.8	32.9	33.5	33.8	1.77
Gujarat	27.9	28.3	15.6	14.8	16.0	1.69
Haryana	16.4	16.5	10.0	10.0	9.5	1.45
Himachal Pradesh	9.2	9.3	4.6	4.6	4.5	0.68
Karnataka	40.1	39.9	25.3	24.6	25.5	1.96
Kerala	24.6	24.3	20.3	19.8	18.7	1.03
Madhya Pradesh	48.4	48.1	38.4	38.5	37.9	1.63
Maharashtra	35.2	35.0	26.8	26.7	28.1	1.49
Orissa	41.6	40.6	42.8	43.5	41.4	3.80
Punjab	11.4	10.9	5.8	5.5	6.3	0.42
Rajasthan	30.5	31.0	19.9	19.4	22.8	2.23
Tamil Nadu	39.8	39.9	22.1	22.5	24.4	1.21
Uttar Pradesh	35.4	35.1	30.9	30.8	30.4	1.64
West Bengal	22.4	22.9	14.9	14.7	19.5	1.24
Delhi	16.0	16.1	9.4	9.2	6.5	0.68
All-India	32.4	32.6	23.6	23.5	24.7	0.41

Notes: The 'official' estimates for the 50th and 55th Rounds are those published in the Planning Commission's press releases. The 'estimate' in Columns 2 and 4 are my calculations from the unit record data. These differ from the official numbers because the latter are extrapolated from published tables rather than directly calculated from the data. The last two columns show the adjusted poverty estimates using the procedures detailed in the text, together with standard errors calculated from 100 replications of a bootstrap that takes into account the cluster structure of the data, but ignores stratification.

record data, and to demonstrate that the difference between the adjusted and official estimates does not come from my inability to reproduce the official counts. The penultimate column of the tables shows the adjusted headcount ratios, and the last column shows bootstrapped standard errors. These should be thought of as standard errors around the true poverty rates, not around the estimates that would have been produced by the 55th Round had it been run along traditional lines. Because I have allowed for the cluster structure of the data, but not the stratification, they are likely somewhat too large. Once again, note that these estimates have been updated for other factors and fully recalculated in Deaton and Dreze (2002).

The adjusted rural poverty estimates are somewhat higher than the official 30-day estimates. For all-India, the official estimate of 27.1 per cent is replaced by 30.2 per cent. Instead of there being a drop in rural poverty since 1993/94 of 10.2 percentage points, the adjusted figures show a reduction of only 7.0 percentage points, so that a little more than two-thirds of the official reduction appears to be real. Most of the states show a similar pattern, though in the cases of Madhya Pradesh, Orissa, Punjab, and Tamil Nadu, the adjusted estimates are lower than the official numbers. In the urban sector, Table 12.2 shows adjusted urban estimates that are typically very close to the official estimates. For all-India urban, the official estimate of 23.6 per cent is raised only to 24.7 per cent, so that I estimate that 7.9 percentage points of the official reduction of 9.1 percentage points is real. Across the states, some of the adjusted figures are lower and some higher than the official figures. Notable changes are in Rajasthan and West Bengal where the adjusted poverty counts are considerably higher than the official ones.

In summary, the calculations suggest that the official poverty counts based on the 30-day questionnaire are not seriously misleading, though in the rural sector, it appears that only around two-thirds of the officially measured decline in poverty is real. The other third is an artefact, presumably induced by changes in the survey instrument between the 50th and 55th Rounds.

The corrected figures raise a number of questions of their own. First, if the changed survey design has its effects through the way that respondents react to the questionnaire, it is unclear why the effects should be different from one state to another, and in particular, between rural and urban households. Perhaps the difference has something to do with other changes, for example in the way that respondents were asked about home-produced foods, or in the uniform adoption of a 365-day questionnaire for the low-frequency items. Both of these changes surely altered reported expenditures on durables and on homegrown food, and would have done so differently depending on whether or not the respondent was engaged in agriculture and on his or her level of living. Agriculture is more important in the countryside, and durables are more important in towns. Second, the results are very different from the prior expectations of many researchers, including my own. That reported 30-day expenditure would be pulled up by the presence of questions about 7-day expenditures seems entirely plausible, yet the results in the tables suggest that most of the distortion was to the seven day reports, not to the 30-day reports. There is one other shred of evidence relevant to this. The NSS has recently repeated the 7-day versus 30-day experiments that were done by Mahalanobis in the 1950s. The preliminary results appear to suggest that the 30-day estimates are more reliable than the 7-day estimates, which appear to be overstated. If so, it is possible that the 30-day responses are generally reliable, and that 7-day recall is less accurate, and more prone to being changed by changes in questionnaire design.

POVERTY MONITORING IN INDIA

It is worth stepping back from the results, and considering the broader implications for poverty monitoring in India. That it is necessary to adjust the official estimates at all is unfortunate, although the NSS is surely to be congratulated for its willingness to conduct experiments in the interests of long-run improvements in data collection and poverty estimation. That said, it is most desirable that survey practice and design be stabilised soon so that, when the next large round is done, we will be able to have poverty counts that are compatible with at least some earlier estimates, and that do not need to be adjusted by statistical techniques. Exactly what the questionnaire should look like is still not clear. Many people have assumed that, because Schedule 2 produced more expenditures, it is therefore better, but that is not necessarily true. Recent NSS experiments, suggest that, at least for some goods, the 30-day reporting periods may be more accurate, as Mahalanobis and Sen originally found. So it may be better to go back to something like the traditional Schedule, with its uniform 30-day reporting period. The choice between 30 days and 365 days for low-frequency items is a particularly difficult one. The reduction in mean that accompanies the move to 365 days is likely to come from people's inability to remember purchases made 10 or 12 months ago. On the other hand, the longer recall period allows more people to report something, and raises reported expenditures the bottom tail of the per capita expenditure distribution. Compared with the earlier practice, this change tends to reduce measured poverty below what it would have been with the original, 30-day, questionnaire. Indeed, as argued by Sundaram and Tendulkar (2002), the change from 30-days to 365-days for the low-frequency items may by itself be responsible for much of the understatement of poverty (relative to earlier methods) in the official estimates for the 55th Round.

It should also be noted that the choice of recall period, important though it has been in the current discussions, is far from the only, or even most important, issue in poverty counts. Issues of comparability between NSS and NAS estimates are now being seriously addressed, and it appears that earlier claims that NSS estimates were wild underestimates were themselves greatly exaggerated. Nevertheless, given the importance of the poverty estimates in India, not to mention the worldwide interest in the relationship between growth and poverty reductions, it would be useful to maintain a close dialogue between the producers of the two kinds of data.

Finally, poverty counts depend only in part on the survey data. They also depend on the poverty lines that are used as cut offs. I have argued elsewhere that the current set of poverty lines used by the Planning Commission are not defensible and ought to be changed (see, Chapters 16 and 17 of this volume) and my companion paper in this issue. The distribution over states and sectors of the current poverty lines makes very little sense, and there are better alternatives available.

ACKNOWLEDGEMENTS

An earlier version of this chapter was published in *Economic and Political Weekly*, Vol. 37, 25–31 January 2003.

I am grateful to Jean Dreze, Bo Honoré, Nick Stern, and Elie Tamer for helpful discussions during the preparation of this paper. I should particularly like to acknowledge discussions with and help from Alessandro Tarozzi whose paper, Tarozzi (2001), develops an alternative methodology and covers many important issues not dealt with here.

REFERENCES

Deaton, Angus and Alessandro Tarozzi (2000), 'Prices and Poverty in India', Princeton, Research Programme in Development Studies, processed. Available at http://www.wws.princeton.edu/~rpds (Chapter 16 of this book).

Deaton, Angus and Jean Dreze (2002), 'Poverty and Inequality in India: a Reexamination', *Economic and Political Weekly*, 7 September (Chapter 18 of this book).

Mahalanobis, P.C. and S.B. Sen (1954), 'On Some Aspects of the Indian National Sample Survey', *Bulletin of the International Statistical Institute*, 34.

Sen, Abhijit (2000), 'Estimates of Consumer Expenditure and Its Distribution: Statistical Priorities after the NSS 55th Round', *Economic and Political Weekly*, December 16, pp. 4499–518.

Sundaram, K. and Suresh Tendulkar (2002), 'Recent Debates on Data Base for Measurement of Poverty in India', Delhi School of Economics, processed. Presented at Joint GOI/World Bank Poverty Workshop, Delhi, January 2002. Available at http://www.worldbank.org/indiapovertyworkshop.

Tarozzi, Alessandro (2001), 'Estimating Comparable Poverty Counts from Incomparable Surveys: Measuring Poverty in India', Princeton University, Department of Economics, processed.

Visaria, Pravin (2000), Poverty in India during 1994–98: Alternative Estimates, *Institute for Economic Growth*, New Delhi, processed (June 9).

13

Poverty Outcomes in India in the 1990s

K. Sundaram and Suresh D. Tendulkar

This is a consolidated version of three papers (Sundaram and Tendulkar: 2003a, 2003b, and 2003d) after incorporating the correction for an inadvertent error in the first two papers (Sundaram and Tendulkar, 2003c) that was pointed out by Abhijit Sen (Sen and Himanshu, 2004 also Chapter 14). It deals with poverty outcomes in terms of four well-known poverty measures: headcount ratio (HCR); poverty-gap index (PGI) denoting the depth of poverty; squared poverty gap (FGT* in subsequent discussion) reflecting the severity dimension; and the estimated size of the poor population. The comparable outcomes are presented mostly for the two (July–June) years 1993/94 and 1999/2000 of the 1990s. We have also presented outcomes for the third time-point of (January–December) 1983 at the all-India level and 15 major states enabling a comparison of change between the six years of the 1990s and the previous 10 years constituting the 1980s in the subsequent discussion. The poverty outcomes are presented separately for the rural and the urban population: (a) at the all-India level in aggregate;[1] (b) for social and economic groups of households separately at the all-India level; and (c) for 15 major states in India.

Doubts have been raised about the comparability of the size distributions and of the poverty measures based on them from the 50th (1993/94) and the 55th (1999/2000) Rounds of Consumer Expenditure Surveys (CES) carried out by the National Sample Survey Organisation. We resolve the comparability problems by using the unit-level records of the 50th Round of CES and those relating to consumer expenditure from the employment-unemployment survey (EUS) of the 55th Round. We show (a) that the estimated monthly per capita consumer expenditure (MPCE) from the 55th Round of CES based on the 30-day recall has not been biased upwards (as maintained by the critics) by an alleged extrapolation by the respondents of the prior responses to questions on the 7-day recall (if the latter were canvassed first) and that therefore, it is comparable to the (recalculated) 50th Round estimates.

Using comparable estimates of four measures of poverty and the Sen index at the all-India level, it is shown that poverty in India has declined in the 1990s in terms of all the five measures of poverty in rural India and in the country as a whole, and in urban India on all the measures of poverty except the number

---

[1] In this analysis, we also include the Sen index of severity of poverty in addition to the four poverty measures mentioned above.

of urban poor. Also, normalised for the length of the time interval and the base year levels of poverty measures, the average annual rate of reduction in poverty was higher in the last six years of the 1990s than that recorded during the ten-and-a-half year period preceding 1993/94. This is particularly true for the number of poor in the country.

Later, the chapter examines, again at the all-India level, the issue of whether and how far households belonging to different social groups (the scheduled castes, scheduled tribes, and others) and economic groups (based on a major source of means of livelihood) shared the overall decline in poverty in the 1990s. It may be noted that social and economic groups are defining characteristics of *households* while subsequent poverty measures are defined in terms of *persons and not households*. Thus, headcount ratio for Scheduled Caste (SC) households indicate the proportion of the estimated total SC persons who are located in the SC households located below the poverty line. In terms of changes in poverty in the 1990s, it is found that while the SC and agricultural labour (rural), and casual labour (urban) households experienced decline in poverty on par with the total population, the Scheduled Tribe (ST) households fared badly in both the segments. A further disaggregated analysis brings out the consequences for poverty of combined social and economic vulnerabilities.

The chapter further undertakes an assessment of poverty outcomes in the 1990s for 15 major states in terms of four poverty indicators, namely, headcount ratio, absolute size of the poor population, the depth of poverty, and severity measures of poverty. These are examined for the three (rural, urban, and total – rural plus urban) segments of population separately. Over the 1990s, taking both the rural and urban populations together, except for Assam and Orissa which show a rise in poverty on all the four indicators, and, Madhya Pradesh which shows a rise in headcount ratio, depth measure and the number of poor (but not in the severity measure), all the remaining 12 major states show an unambiguous decline in poverty in terms of all the four indicators. In terms of the pace of decline too, although a mixed picture emerges across individual poverty indicators and across individual states, the overwhelming impression is one of generally better performance in poverty reduction in the 1990s than in the previous ten-and-a-half year period.

Finally, the chapter discusses some implications of the empirical results for the design of a strategy for poverty reduction.

CES COMPARABILITY PROBLEMS, SOLUTIONS, AND IMPLICATIONS

The Problems and Their Resolution: An Outline

The primary and most widely debated problem is that information in the 55th Round CES concerning household spending on a group of frequently purchased food items – comprising 'food, paan, tobacco, and intoxicants' and, henceforth, referred to as the 'the food group',[2] was canvassed on two alternative reference or recall periods of 30 days and 7 days, among the *same set of* households, and recorded on the schedule of enquiry in blocks located side-by-side. While only the 30-day reporting was published in the 55th Round CES, critics maintained that this reporting might have been biased upwards if households were first canvassed on the 7-day reference period and they subsequently extrapolated their response on the 7-day reporting to the 30-day entry by rough multiplicative adjustments (which was found to be higher than comparable 30-day reporting from the responses based on independent samples in the earlier

---

[2] We will use 'food group' to denote food, beverages, paan, tobacco, and intoxicants, whereas 'total food' is used to denote the total for food and beverages only and excludes paan, tobacco, and intoxicants.

51st through 54th 'thin' Rounds). If this were indeed true, then there would be strong grounds to believe that the 55th Round overstated consumer expenditures on these items in comparison with all the earlier quinquennial rounds.

The second and less widely recognised problem is that, in the 55th Round, consumer expenditure on certain infrequently purchased items, namely 'clothing', 'footwear', 'durables', 'education' and 'health care' (institutional), was collected only on a 365-day reference period. The published results for all remaining items were based on a 30-day reference period. Accordingly, in the published results, the size-distribution of monthly per capita total expenditure (PCTE) as per the NSS 55th Round consumer expenditure survey for 1999/2000 is based on a mixed reference period (MRP). In contrast, the published size-distribution of PCTE from the NSS 50th and all the earlier rounds is based on data collected with a uniform reference period (URP) of 30 days for all items of expenditure. In particular, this was also true for the published results of all the quinquennial surveys carried out earlier in 1972/73, 1977/78, 1983, and 1987/88.

These comparability problems are not intractable, however. We resolve the first one, showing that the size-distribution of consumer expenditure on the food group collected in the 55th Round of CES indeed reflects 30-day recall. To establish this we compare the CES results with consumer expenditure data from the 55th Round's Employment-Unemployment Survey (EUS) which was canvassed on an *independent sample of households* distinct from those in CES but from the same universe of population and *used only 30-day recall period* for items in the food group and a 365-day recall period for the above-listed infrequently purchased items. So that, *on this score*, a size-distribution based on the EUS would be comparable to the published 55th Round CES results with a 30-day reference period for the food group. It is then ascertained whether the observed difference between the CES and EUS could be attributed to the possible biases introduced in the CES estimates by the canvassing of the household expenditures on these items on two alternative recall periods. This is done by comparing the CES-EUS differential with the corresponding average differential in the estimates of consumer expenditure of these items emerging from independent schedules with 7- and 30-day recall periods canvassed on independent samples during the experimental annual CES surveys conducted from the 51st to the 54th Rounds of NSS and by reference to size of the CES-EUS differential.

However, in making this comparison between the estimates of the consumer expenditure from the 55th Round CES and EUS, note needs to be taken of the fact that the latter are based on a highly abridged recording schedule (a worksheet) used by the EUS, which imparts a downward bias to its estimates of Monthly Per Capita Expenditutre[3] (MPCE).

An independent estimate for the possible magnitude of difference that would be expected between a 7-day recall and a 30-day recall is provided by the 4 annual 'thin' rounds (51st to 54th) of CES conducted in 1994/95, 1995/96, 1996/97 and January–June 1998. For the specified items, these canvassed both a 30-day and a 7-day reference period for the food group on *independent sets of sample households* in each round. A key finding of this exercise was that *estimates based on 7-day recall were considerably higher than corresponding estimates based on 30-day recall* over the four rounds. The difference, averaged over the four rounds, accordingly provides a benchmark for evaluating the observed differences between the CES and EUS.

[3] As discussed further on in the paper, monthly per capita consumer expenditure was merely a classificatory variable for tabulation of employment characteristics in the EUS, and not the main subject of enquiry. Therefore, consumer-expenditure details were canvassed with a considerably abridged schedule. The implications of abridgement are set out in the section 'EUS as a Reference Point for CES'.

Given the underestimation inherent in the EUS because of the use of an abridged schedule, *the presumption that the CES estimates on the 30-day recall had indeed been biased upwards by interference from the 7-day reference canvassing, would be strong if the CES estimates exceed the corresponding EUS estimates by a margin greater than the average 7-day versus 30-day difference indicated by the annual rounds.*[4]

As set out in Section entitled 'Comparing EUS and CES by Commodity Groups', this is not the case. Rather, it is shown that for as many as eight item groups out of nine distinguished in the EUS under the food group, the excess of CES estimates over the corresponding EUS estimates, as a percentage of EUS estimates, is well below the benchmark average 7-day/30-day difference derived from the four annual rounds. Equally important is the fact that, in a number of categories (together accounting for 60 per cent or more of food expenditure reported by CES) the differentials are quite small – well below 5 per cent. So that the observed CES-EUS differences can be taken as being consistent with the expected effects of the use in the EUS of a highly abridged schedule. This result is shown to hold not only at the aggregate level of entire population, but also at the disaggregated level comprising fractile groups for the rural and urban populations, each taken separately. We accordingly draw the conclusion that the 55th Round CES estimates on the 30-day recall had not been biased upwards by the canvassing from the same households of consumer expenditures on these items also on the 7-day recall.

This, in turn, leads us to infer that the published MRP-based results of the 55th Round consumer expenditure survey are comparable to the size-distribution of the 50th Round – once the latter has been recalculated on an MRP basis in order to resolve the second comparability problem noted above.

This recalculation of the 50th Round size-distribution is discussed in Section entitled 'Correcting for Mixed Reference Periods in 50th Round'.

In the 50th Round, information about expenditures on 'clothing', 'footwear', durables', and 'institutional health care' were elicited from surveyed households both on the basis of the 30-day reference period and on the basis of 365-day reference period. However, the latter data was recorded in a separate block. The published size-distribution of PCTE for this round is based on a uniform reference period of 30-days for all items, including those listed above. It is, however, possible to reconstruct from the unit record data an alternative size-distribution comparable in recall periods to that in the 55th Round. This is based on consumer expenditure from the 365-day reference period pertaining to the above listed items, and on the 30-day reference period pertaining to all other items. In both instances, the information is as reported by the surveyed households. We, thus, generate a size-distribution for the 50th Round on a mixed reference period comparable to the 55th Round consumer expenditure survey. Our presentation of these results in the Section on 'Correcting Mixed Reference Periods' is preceded by a brief discussion about the possibility of the reported expenditure on the 365-day recall being influenced by household responses on the 30-day recall in the 50th Round.

Possibilities for Bias in 55th CES Round

As mentioned earlier, concerns about the comparability of the 55th Round CES with the 50th Round have arisen primarily because in the former, two recall periods of 7 days and 30 days were canvassed on

---

[4] Even this does not constitute a strict proof that the stated interference from the 7-day canvassing had indeed occurred. Since, in principle, the effect of abridgement on the EUS estimates could be so large as to produce a difference between the CES and EUS estimates larger than the average 7-day *versus* 30-day difference indicated by the annual rounds even in the absence of such an interference.

the same set of households, in blocks positioned side-by-side for the same set of items – the food group. Accordingly, there is a possibility that reporting for one of two canvassed reference periods influenced and, hence, biased – the reporting for the other. Critics of the NSS 55th Round maintain that reported 30-day estimates from CES have been biased upward by the responses on the 7-day recall and consequently overstate consumer expenditures in the food group.

Indeed, in the 55th Round, respective MPCE on the food group from the 7- and 30-day reference periods converge to an unexpectedly high degree in comparison to the results from the set of four experimental annual, 'thin' rounds of CES conducted prior to the 55th Round. In these rounds, the 7- and 30-day recall periods had been canvassed on two independent sets of sample households, and in the case of the shorter reference period, the estimates of MPCE were considerably higher than those based on corresponding and comparable 30-day recall-based estimates (NSSO, 2000a).

To illustrate, in the 55th Round, the difference between the two estimates (on the 7-day relative to the 30-day recalls) of overall mean per capita expenditure on 'total food' was 6.5 per cent and 5.7 per cent for the all-India rural and urban population respectively (NSSO, 2000b). Over the four rounds of annual surveys, however, the corresponding differences averaged 30 per cent and 33 per cent.

Since the food group dominates the consumption basket of poor households, in the annual surveys, headcount ratios based on the size-distribution of PCTE from the 7-day recall-based reporting were also about half the magnitude of those based on the 30-day recall (Visaria, 2000). In the 55th Round, the comparable differential considerably narrowed to 10–12 per cent.

The divergence between the 7- and 30-day results in the annual surveys was an expected consequence of two types of possible errors – recall error and telescoping error – which operate on the frequent and less salient expenditures in the food group, respectively. Whereas the former increases with a longer recall period, the latter increases with a shorter recall period. For this reason both phenomena skew results for the 7- and 30-day recalls in opposite directions (Deaton and Grosh, 2000).

The narrowing differential in the 55th Round may have arisen as follows: when confronted with having to report consumption for the same list of items, involving frequently consumed items which are non-salient events in respondent's memory on two alternative recall periods, the respondents would try to economise on their effort by adjusting their reporting for the second reference period on the basis of a rough extrapolation from the first one.

Accordingly, there are *two possibilities that could result in the narrow difference* between the 7- and 30-day recalls observed in the 55th Round of CES. Possibility 1 (P1) is that the 7-day recall was the first to be canvassed, and that respondents subsequently reported the 30-day equivalent by making a rough multiplicative adjustment. P1 would clearly impart a downward bias in the estimated headcount ratio for 1999/2000 in comparison with the earlier rounds. Hence it would overstate the comparable extent of decline in poverty, as asserted by critics of officially released poverty estimates. If P1 is true for a sizeable proportion of household, the results of the 55th Round with respect to the specified items would therefore be non-comparable with respect to all previous NSS rounds.

The other possibility, (P2), is that respondents may have been asked first to recall consumption for the past 30 days, and subsequently reported their consumption during the previous 7 days by use of crude division. It can easily be seen that either P1 or P2 would produce the narrowed 7- versus 30-day differential observed in the 55th Round CES. P1 would bias upwards the reporting for the 30-day recall, whereas P2 would bias downward the results for the higher 7-day recall.[5] However, if P2 were true, the

---

[5] The initial instructions to NSS field staff did not explicitly mention the sequence in which information from respondents was to be elicited for the two recall periods. However, nearly one-and-a-half months after the field work was launched for

results of the 55th Round would indeed turn out to be comparable to the 50th Round – provided one adjusts the latter for the mixed reference period used in the 55th Round – as discussed further. The test procedure whether P1 or P2 holds true is further examined in the following sections.

EUS as a Reference Point for CES

As noted in the outline given in the introduction, a reference point for assessing bias in the CES is provided by the EUS also conducted in the 55th NSS Round. This is because the EUS was canvassed on *an independent sample drawn from the same universe of population* as the CES, and also used reporting based only on a 30-day reference period for the food group (NSSO, 2001a). On this score, a comparison of per capita consumer expenditures from the 55th Round of CES and EUS could provide an indication of bias in the published CES estimates.

However, this comparison needs to take account of the fact that the EUS is likely to understate consumer expenditures compared with the CES. In the EUS, per capita consumer expenditure was merely a classificatory variable for tabulation of employment characteristics and not the main subject of enquiry. Therefore, consumer-expenditure details were canvassed with a considerably abridged schedule. International experience and *a priori* reasoning suggest that for a given recall period, a detailed listing of items helps reduce recall error. Conversely, an abridged listing leads to a greater recall lapse and hence to an understatement of consumer expenditure in comparison to reporting based on a more detailed listing (Deaton and Grosh, 2000).

Whereas the CES enquiry canvassed a detailed schedule of 330-odd items spread over some 15 pages, the EUS enquiry canvassed a one-page schedule comprising only 33 items. According to the explanation provided on the relevant enquiry block, this part of the survey was deemed to serve as a 'worksheet' for recording household consumer expenditure. However, all the items would not have been affected by abridgement to the same degree. For a given recall period, understatement from recall lapse is expected to be the greater the more heterogeneous the basket contained in the abridged description. The recall lapse is affected by the diversity in consumer purchases and fluctuations in their consumption during the recall period, as well as the concomitant frequency and salience of the respective consumption events in the respondent's memory.

So, given the impact of the abridgement effect, we can expect the 30-day CES estimates based on a detailed schedule to be higher than the corresponding EUS estimates using an abridged schedule. If, in addition, P1 had indeed eventuated as has been maintained by the critics, then the reported 30-day recall-based estimates from CES would also have been pulled up by the 7-day reporting, compared with what they would have been had the 30-day recall been canvassed independently. This would accentuate the EUS-CES difference beyond that arising from the use in the EUS of an abridged schedule. In order to test the possibility P1, relative differences in Tables 13.1R and 13.1U provide the excess of CES estimates over those from the EUS, as a percentage of the latter. *Accordingly, the CES-EUS relative differences indicate the excess of allegedly overstated CES estimates in relation to expectedly understated EUS-based estimates.*

---

the 55th Round, a letter was sent by the sampling design and research division of NSSO, dated 19 August 1999, *asking the investigators to elicit information first for the 30-day recall for all items of the food group and then seek the same (again from the beginning) for the last 7 days.* Which sequence was in fact followed, however, remains an open question. We bypass this aspect of the issue by directly examining the outcome through a comparison of the CES estimates of MPCE on the specified items with the EUS-based estimates of MPCE canvassed with a single 30-day reference period – albeit with an abridged schedule.

Now, the central question is *how large should this excess be in order to validate P1?* As noted earlier, the annual 51st to 54th 'thin sample' Rounds of the NSS provide unbiased estimates of the order of magnitude of this excess. Accordingly, given the expected understatement in the EUS, if P1 holds, we expect the excess of CES over EUS to be unequivocally greater than the excess of the 7-day estimates over the corresponding estimates, averaged over the 4 'thin' Rounds (or average 7-day–30-day difference for short). If this does not hold, P1 is not proven. This leaves us with possibility P2 as having eventuated. If this is so, then, the 55th Round would indeed have captured the 30-day recall rendering it comparable to all the earlier rounds of NSS as far as food group is concerned.

It needs to be stressed that the empirical support for P2 does not rest solely on the absence of validation of P1. Specifically, as we shall see presently, in the case of many significant item groups, the size of the CES-EUS differential is quite small and thus consistent with P2 being true, after allowing for abridgement effect and sample variability.

Comparing EUS and CES by Commodity Groups

The All-India Picture

In the light of the foregoing *a priori* considerations, we now undertake an empirical implementation of the suggested test procedure to resolve the 7-day–30-day recall controversy. It is organised in two parts. The first compares the CES-EUS at the aggregate level of the total rural/urban population but separately across all the comparable commodity groups identified in the abridged EUS schedule. This information is collected in Tables 13.1R and 13.1U, for the rural and urban populations, respectively. The second part performs a similar comparison, but only for the contested commodity groups, and at a disaggregated level, dividing the population into 20 fractile groups of 5 per cent each. A CES-EUS comparison is given for each fractile group. The commodity group details in this part are confined only to those item groups that are affected by the 7-day–30-day controversy. The information is presented for rural and urban population in Appendix Tables A.1R and A.1U.

Let us turn to an examination of Tables 13.1R and 13.1U. For as many as eight out of the nine items in the food group in both tables, the differences between CES and EUS estimates are well short of the benchmark average 7-day–30-day difference emerging from the 51st to 54th annual Rounds. In fact, the estimates are amazingly close to each other, given the impact of the use of an abridged schedule in the EUS.[6]

The only exception to the above result is the omnibus category of 'other food', comprising sugar, salt, spices, beverages and processed foods including cooked meals. This shows the highest percentage excess within the food group. An excess of 54 per cent almost touches the 7-day–30-day norm for the rural population, whereas for the urban population the CES-EUS difference for this item group at 67 per cent overshoots the 53 per cent norm emerging from the 'thin' rounds. This item group by itself accounts for nearly two thirds (61 per cent in rural India and 64 per cent in urban India) of the total difference (disregarding sign) between the CES and EUS in the total food category.

---

[6] The only item group where the percentage difference between the CES and EUS estimates, though less than the difference between the 7- and 30-day estimates, is somewhat close to the latter, is milk and milk products. This too is a somewhat heterogeneous item group that accounted for less than 5 per cent of total consumption for the lowest 30 per cent of the rural population in 1993/94. For urban India, the corresponding proportion was a little over 7 per cent (Sundaram and Tendulkar, 2002).

Table 13.1R A Comparison of Estimates of MPCE from CES and EUS
NSS 55th Round July 1999 to June 2000 for all-India rural population: By item group   *(Rs 0.00)*

S. No.	Item	CES	EUS	Diff	Diff (%)	Avg. Diff 7 Days vs 30 Days (%)
1.	All goods and services	486.16	443.11	43.05	9.71 .	–
2.	Cereals and substitutes	108.11	106.24	1.87	1.76	12.92
3.	Pulses and products	19.14	18.19	0.95	5.22	48.18
4.	Milk and milk products	42.56	37.47	5.09	13.58	19.62
5.	Edible oil	18.16	18.05	0.11	0.61	22.83
6.	Vegetables	29.98	29.75	0.23	0.77	55.25
7.	Fruits (fresh + dry fruits)	8.36	6.65	1.72	25.71	60.27
8.	Egg, fish, and meat	16.14	15.72	0.42	2.67	54.16
9.	Other food (sugar, salt, spices and beverages)	46.36	30.04	16.32	54.32	54.57
10.	Total food	288.81	262.11	26.7	10.19	30.01
11.	Paan, tobacco and intoxicants	13.96	12.11	1.85	15.28	43.13
12.	Fuel and light	36.56	32.03	4.53	14.14	–
13.	Entertainment	2.02	1.02	1.00	98.03	–
14.	Non-institutional medical services	22.94	22.43	0.51	2.27	–
15.	Toilet articles	11.62	14.66	–3.04	–20.74	–
16.	Travel/conveyance	14.28	10.70	3.58	33.46	–
17.	Rent	1.89	1.95	-0.06	–3.08	–
18.	Other miscellaneous goods and services	26.65	12.69	13.96	110.01	–
19.	Education (tuition + newspapers + books, stationery, etc.)	9.38	13.91	–4.53	–32.57	–
20.	Institutional medical services	6.66	6.32	0.34	5.38	–
21.	Cloth and clothing	33.28	32.68	0.60	1.84	–
22.	Footwear	5.37	5.39	–0.02	–0.37	–
23.	Durable goods	12.76	15.62	–2.86	–18.31	–

Notes: 1. CES and EUS – Mean MPCE from CES & EUS respectively.
2. Diff – Difference between CES & EUS.
3. Diff – Diff as per cent of mean MPCE for respective item from EUS.
4. Avg. Diff 7 day–30 day – Excess of estimated MPCE as per Schd. Type 2 (with 7-day reference period for food, paan, tobacco and intoxicants) over that based on Schd. Type 1 (with uniform reference period of 30 days) as a percentage of the estimates on the 30-day reference period, averaged over the four 'Annual' Rounds (1994/95, 1995/96, 1996/97 and January–June 1998).

Source: All EUS estimates represent the average of subsample estimates generated from Unit Record Data. CES estimates are drawn from: GOI, NSS Report No. 457 (55/100/3), Level and Pattern of Consumer Expenditure in India, 1999/2000, May 2001.

Before proceeding to discuss further the CES-EUS difference in respect of the items in the food group it is useful to review the relative difference between CES and EUS estimates for items outside the food group. Identical reference periods are used for these items in both the 55th Round CES and EUS.[7]

[7] This is strictly not true with respect to two items forming a part of the category education. Unlike in the CES, two components, namely, tuition fees, and newspapers, magazines, etc., have a 30-day reference period in the EUS, whereas

Table 13.1U A Comparison of Estimates of MPCE from CES and EUS
NSS 55th Round July 1999 to June 2000 for all-India rural population: By item group   (*Rs 0.00*)

S. No.	Item	CES	EUS	Diff	Diff (%)	Avg. Diff 7 Days vs 30 Days (%)
1.	*All goods and services*	*854.92*	*762.93*	*91.99*	*12.06*	–
2.	Cereals and substitutes	106.02	102.34	3.68	3.60	15.94
3.	Pulses and products	25.20	24.22	0.98	4.05	42.08
4.	Milk and milk products	74.17	66.91	7.26	10.85	12.24
5.	Edible oil	26.81	27.02	−0.24	−0.78	22.30
6.	Vegetables	43.90	47.86	−3.96	−8.27	52.48
7.	Fruits (fresh + dry fruits)	20.68	17.26	3.42	19.81	69.28
8.	Egg, fish, and meat	26.78	25.90	0.91	3.40	50.44
9.	Other food (sugar, salt, spices and beverages)	87.39	52.26	35.13	67.22	53.42
10.	*Total food*	*410.95*	*363.77*	*47.18*	*12.96*	*32.91*
11.	Paan, tobacco and intoxicants	16.22	13.79	2.43	17.62	41.50
12.	Fuel and light	66.26	58.79	7.47	12.71	–
13.	Entertainment	9.88	4.87	5.01	102.87	–
14.	Non-institutional medical services	30.95	29.57	1.38	4.67	–
15.	Toilet articles	26.34	25.41	0.93	3.66	–
16.	Travel/conveyance	47.19	30.14	17.05	56.57	–
17.	Rent	38.16	38.58	−0.42	−1.09	–
18.	Other miscellaneous goods and services	67.02	33.06	33.96	102.72	–
19.	Education (tuition + newspapers + books, stationery, etc.)	37.06	55.83	−18.77	−33.62	–
20.	Institutional medical services	12.33	11.60	0.68	6.29	–
21.	Cloth and clothing	51.76	50.33	1.43	2.84	–
22.	Footwear	10.05	10.22	−0.17	−1.66	–
23.	Durable goods	30.85	36.98	−6.13	−16.58	–

Notes: 1. CES and EUS – Mean MPCE from CES and EUS respectively.
2. Diff – Difference between CES and EUS.
3. Diff – Diff as per cent of mean MPCE for respective item from EUS.
4. Avg. Diff 7 day–30 day – Excess of estimated MPCE as per Schd. Type 2 (with 7-day reference period for food, paan, tobacco and intoxicants) over that based on Schd. Type 1 (with uniform reference period of 30 days) as a percentage of the estimates on the 30-day reference period, averaged over the four 'Annual' Rounds (1994/95, 1995/96, 1996/97 and January–June 1998).

Source: All EUS estimates represent the average of sub-sample estimates generated from Unit Record Data. CES estimates are drawn from: GOI, NSS Report No. 457 (55/100/3), Level and Pattern of Consumer Expenditure in India, 1999/2000, May 2001.

Therefore, if CES estimates are higher, it is due entirely to the abridgement effect in the EUS. So that, this would provide some benchmarks for the pure abridgement effect.

---

they – along with school books and other educational articles – are all canvassed with a 365-day reference period in the CES. This could be a factor in explaining why the EUS estimates exceed the CES estimates.

Only for three item groups – 'entertainment, travel/conveyance' and the catch-all category of 'other miscellaneous goods and services' – do CES estimates exceed EUS estimates by more than 30 per cent. This does not account for items for which the EUS estimates actually exceed the CES estimates namely 'education', 'footwear' and 'durable goods'. In both rural and urban India, the difference is more than 100 per cent in the cases of both 'entertainment' and 'other miscellaneous goods and services'. Each of these constitutes a heterogeneous basket where the abridgement effect is expected to be significant, as has been observed in similar cases all over the world.

Notably, the catch-all category of 'other miscellaneous goods and services' accounts for a major part of the compounded difference between CES and EUS estimates outside the food group: 40 per cent of the sum of absolute differences in rural India, and 36 per cent in urban India. To reiterate, any observed excess of CES estimates over the EUS estimates in respect of *all the items outside the food group* are due to the impact of abridgement in the EUS and of sampling variability and *not* the result of any interference due to recall on any alternative recall period.

With this assessment of abridgement effect outside the food group that is free from recall-period effect, let us now revert to a consideration of the CES-EUS differences for items in the food group where both the effects are present.

In eight out of the nine item groups, as noted previously, the excess of CES estimates over the corresponding EUS estimates (as a percentage of the latter) are well below the average 7-day–30-day difference observed in the 4 'thin' rounds preceding the 55th Round Survey, with only the heterogeneous group of 'other food' as the exception. The exception is on expected lines as it is consistent with *a priori* reasoning and attributable to the abridgement effect based on the evidence from international surveys.

Further, in rural India, for four item groups (cereals and substitutes, edible oils, vegetables, and egg, fish and meat), the CES-EUS difference is less than 3 per cent, with this difference slightly exceeding 5 per cent for pulses and products. In urban India, the CES-EUS difference is below 5 per cent for the same five item groups (including two cases, edible oils and vegetables, where the EUS estimates exceed the CES estimates). In both segments, these five item groups accounted for close to two-thirds of the average expenditure on all food in CES.

In respect of all these item groups, a CES-EUS difference of the order of 5 per cent or less (and way below the 7-day–30-day difference in the 'thin' rounds), is quite consistent with the absence of an effect on the 30-day response of a *prior response* on the 7-day reference – if the latter was canvassed first – allowing for the presence of abridgement effects and sampling variability.

This leaves us with three item groups; milk and milk products (CES-EUS difference of above 5 per cent, but close to the 7-day–30-day difference); paan, tobacco and intoxicants (CES-EUS difference above 10 per cent but well below the 7-day–30-day difference); and the heterogeneous group of 'other food' with CES-EUS difference being large and close to or above the 7-day–30-day difference.

In respect of milk and milk products (where the CES-EUS difference is 14 per cent in rural India and 11 per cent in urban India), a plausible benchmark for the 'order of magnitude' of CES-EUS difference that is unaffected by the 7-day–30-day controversy and that reflects only the effects of abridgement and sampling variability is provided by the case of another compositionally diverse group of fuel and light which also has a sizeable share in overall PCTE. In the case of fuel and light, the CES-EUS difference is 14 per cent in rural India and 13 per cent in urban India. Further, given that there are five major item-categories where the size of the CES-EUS difference is small enough (5 per cent or less) to be consistent with the hypothesis of no upward bias in CES on account of the presence of 7-day questions, it does not appear plausible to argue that the responses of the households on the 7-day recall influenced their reporting on the 30-day recall for *milk and milk products* but not for, say, *vegetables* when these item categories are not very dissimilar in terms of salience and frequency of purchase.

In respect of 'other food' and, paan, tobacco, and intoxicants, a rough indication of the size of the CES-EUS differential that can be expected for a very heterogeneous group – *even in the complete absence of any influence of an alternative reference period on the 30-day recall, and reflecting only the effects of abridgement and sampling variability* – is provided by the differential for the group 'miscellaneous goods and services' in the non-food category: 100 per cent for rural India and 103 per cent for urban India. As can be readily seen, in respect of both 'other food' and paan, tobacco, and intoxicants, the observed CES-EUS differences are well below these benchmark levels. If this is accepted, even in respect of the two heterogeneous item groups in the food category which show a large CES-EUS difference, the 55th Round CES estimates can be taken to reflect the responses on the 30-day recall.

In all these cases, therefore, the size of the CES-EUS differential, allowing for the abridgement effect and sampling variability, is consistent with the hypothesis P2 rather than P1, that is to say, *the 55th Round CES estimates on items in the food group indeed reflect responses on the 30-day recall and hence are comparable to those in the earlier NSS rounds.*

Critics of the 55th Round might argue that the test for resolving the 7-day–30-day controversy, when implemented at the aggregate level for the entire population may conceal uneven incidence of the recall problem at the disaggregated level, affecting certain population groups. Indeed, if the 7-day recall had biased upward the 30-day estimate in CES at the lower end of the size distribution, this would overstate consumer expenditure for poorer groups, and hence lead to an understatement in corresponding poverty indicators.

In order to evaluate this possibility, the percentage excess of CES estimates over EUS estimates are mapped across 20 fractile groups of 5 per cent size each in Appendix Tables A.1R and A.1U, respectively for the rural and urban populations. As mentioned earlier, we apply this analysis only to those items which have been involved in the 7-day–30-day controversy, namely, food, beverages, paan, tobacco, and intoxicants. The first line in both tables provides the respective norms for the 7-day–30-day difference derived from the average over the 'thin' 51st to the 54th Rounds, as used also in Tables 13.1R and 13.1U for all-India rural and urban populations. These broad yardsticks continue to be used as the common standard of comparison because differentials derived from comparable 'thin samples' at the fractile-group level are expected to carry higher relative standard errors.

Remarkably, in both Appendix Tables A.1R and A.1U, CES-EUS differences for all but one of the item groups lie well below the yardsticks provided by the 51st through 54th Rounds. The exception is provided by the same group that stood out in Tables 13.1 and 13.2 – namely 'other food'. The reason is also the same: this is an aggregate of heterogeneous items for which abridgement effect is expected to be very pronounced. However, it is remarkable that for the bottom 40 per cent of the rural population, even this diverse group of items registers relative CES-EUS differences that are well below their respective yardsticks.

Further, in almost all fractile groups in the bottom 40 per cent, the CES-EUS difference is 5 per cent or less for at least four item categories.

What we have, therefore, shown is that the observed differences between the 30-day-based CES estimates and EUS estimates overwhelmingly reflect the combined impact of the abridged schedule in the EUS and sampling variability. *These differences in turn are too small to support the hypothesis that the CES estimates on the 30-day reference period have been artificially inflated because households extrapolated their 30-day reporting from a 7-day recall.* Therefore, the narrowed differential between the 7- and 30-day recall-based estimates in the 55th Round CES that we noted earlier has to be due to possibility P2 which, as outlined, requires that the households predominantly recorded expenditures on the 30-day recall and may subsequently have adjusted their 7-day estimates accordingly.

The EUS-CES Comparisons: The State-level Picture

The state-level EUS-CES comparisons at the level of 15 major states, and separately for the rural and the urban populations in these states are presented in Appendix Tables A.2R and A.2U. They present the percentage excess of CES-estimates over EUS-estimates for each of the 15 major states but restricted to items in food group.

As regards the standard of comparison, we continue to use the difference or rather the excess of 7-day estimates over the 30-day estimates at the all-India level (but separately for the rural and the urban areas) averaged over the four 'thin sample' rounds preceding the 55th Round Surveys.

The use of all-India level estimates as a common standard of comparison has been preferred to state-specific standards on a view that, given the small sample size at the level of individual states in the 'thin sample' rounds, state-specific estimates may be expected to carry higher relative standard errors than the all-India estimates.

Before proceeding to examine these results in detail, it is useful to recall that the use of the 'excess of 7-day estimates over the 30-day estimates averaged over the four 'thin' sample rounds preceding the 55th Round Surveys' as a standard of comparison for the CES-EUS differences reported in Tables A.2R and A.2U is designed to test the evidence in favour of the hypothesis that the CES-30-day estimates have been artificially pulled up by the extrapolation of their prior responses to the 7-day question. If, *after allowing for the abridgement effect and sampling variability (expected to be higher at the level of individual states than at the all-India level),* the CES-EUS differences are *equal to* or *greater than those* revealed by the standard of comparison, then that would be a strong presumptive evidence in favour of the stated hypothesis. As we shall see presently, the results do not offer such a presumptive evidence favouring the hypothesis that the 30-day estimates in CES have been artificially pulled up by the prior responses on the 7-day reference period.

The results for rural Rajasthan and rural Uttar Pradesh – the two states where the NSS investigators are reported to have canvassed the 7-day questions first – are particularly striking. *In rural Rajasthan, the EUS-estimates exceed, albeit marginally in most of the cases, the CES-estimates of MPCE on cereals and substitutes; edible oil; vegetables; fruits and nuts; and egg, fish, and meat.* Of the remaining four item groups distinguished in the EUS (where the CES-estimates exceed the EUS-estimates), in three of them, namely, pulses and products; other food; and, paan, tobacco, and intoxicants, the difference between the two estimates – expressed as a percentage of the EUS-estimates – are seen to be way below the average difference between the 7-day and the 30-day estimates in the four 'thin sample' rounds. Particularly noteworthy in this regard is the fact that, even in respect of the omnibus 'other food', the difference between the two estimates for rural Rajasthan is just half of the difference between the 7-day and the 30-day estimates, while in respect of the other two items, the CES-EUS difference was less than 15 per cent of that between the 7-day and the 30-day estimates. In only one case, namely, milk and milk products, the CES-EUS difference (in percentage terms) is fractionally greater than the 7-day–30-day difference. Given the negligible differences in respect of other items in the food group noted above, this can be plausibly attributed to the abridgement effect and sampling variability.

In rural Uttar Pradesh too, the EUS estimates of MPCE on cereals and substitutes; vegetables; and egg, fish, and meat are higher than the corresponding CES-estimates. In all other cases, though the CES-estimates are higher, the relative differences are lower (in all but one case, much less) than that between the 7-day and the 30-day estimates. In respect of the omnibus category 'other food', the difference between the CES and the EUS estimates, though substantial (47.5 per cent), is less than the average difference of 55 per cent between the 7-day estimate and the 30-day estimate of MPCE on these items.

Broadly, the same picture also holds true for the urban areas of Rajasthan and Uttar Pradesh.

More generally, except in respect of 'milk and milk products' in both segments of Gujarat, Madhya Pradesh, and Rajasthan, and, in respect of the heterogeneous group of 'other food' – especially in the southern states – the percentage excess of CES-estimates over the corresponding EUS-estimates is much lower than the 7-day–30-day difference from the 'thin sample' rounds.

Considering the 15 states and nine item groups together, of the possible 135 (9 × 15) cases, only in 13 cases in rural India and 14 cases in urban India the CES-EUS difference exceeded the 7-day–30-day difference. And, of these 13 cases in rural India (14 in urban India) a majority of cases seven (nine in urban India) pertain to the heterogeneous group 'other food' comprising sugar (including gur, khandsari, and honey), salt, spices, beverages, and processed food including cooked meals. The rural/urban breakdown of the remaining cases is: milk and milk products (three each), paan, tobacco, and intoxicants (one case rural and two cases urban) and fruits and nuts (two cases, only rural). These groups are marked by within group heterogeneity. The cases where the CES-EUS differences are more substantial (say, exceeding 15 per cent) but less than the average 7-day–15-day difference emerging from the 'thin' rounds are all found in the four heterogeneous groups mentioned here.

At the other end, this difference is either negative or less than 5 per cent in 58 (out of 135) cases in rural India and in 71 cases in urban India. More specifically, the CES-EUS difference is negative or less than 5 per cent for four or more of the nine item groups in as many as nine of the 15 states in rural India. And, the same was true in 11 of the 15 states in urban India. Further, except for Karnataka in rural India and Uttar Pradesh in Urban India (with two cases each) in all the other 14 states, the CES-EUS difference is negative or less than 5 per cent for a minimum of three item groups.

It needs to be noted that in all the three (four in urban India) cases, this sizeable excess of CES over EUS estimates for milk and milk products (and, additionally eggs, fish, and meat in urban India) co-exist alongside CES-EUS differences that are either negative or small for other item groups such as edible oils, and/or vegetables and/or (in rural India) also eggs, fish, and meat, that are broadly comparable with milk and milk products in terms of salience and frequency of purchase.

As noted in our summary of all-India results on this issue, the CES-EUS differences in respect of the item group 'miscellaneous goods and services' falling outside the 7-day–30-day controversy and reflecting only the effects of abridgement and sampling variability, are higher than the observed CES-EUS differences in respect of 'other food' and paan, tobacco, and intoxicants. And this is true for each and all of the 15 states and in both population segments.

Thus, *our state-level results too indicate that the observed differences between the 30-day recall-based CES-estimates and the corresponding EUS-estimates (based on an independent sample of households and with only a 30-day reference period in respect of the food group of items) is consistent with the presence of abridgement effects rather than offering support for the hypothesis that the 30-day recall-based responses in the Consumer Expenditure Survey have been artificially pulled up by the prior responses on the basis of a 7-day recall.*

To conclude, the close correspondence between the 30-day-based CES estimates and the corresponding EUS-estimates, after making due allowance for the sampling variability and the abridgement of the schedule of enquiry, leads us to believe that irrespective of the sequence in which the 7-day and the 30-day recall periods were canvassed in the CES, the reported 30-day-based estimates in CES have not been affected much by the 7-day questions. Consequently, the 55th Round CES size distribution (using the 30-day recall for the food group) are comparable to the results from our alternative, MRP-based size-distributions based on the unit record data for the 50th Round once we correct for the problem of mixed reference periods pertaining to 50th Round.

Correcting for Mixed Reference Periods in 50th Round

As mentioned in Section on 'The Problems and Their Resolution' in the CES for 1993/94 (50th Round), information on clothing, footwear, durables, education, and health (institutional) was collected from each sample household for two alternative reference periods of 30 days and 365 days. Notably, for all the remaining items in the 50th Round, a uniform 30-day recall was used. It is thus possible to compute two alternative size-distributions for the 50th Round – one based on a uniform reference period (URP) of 30 days, and another based on a mixed reference period (MRP) of 365 days for above-mentioned items, and 30 days for the remaining items. This is important for establishing recall-period comparability between the 50th Round and the 55th Round, in view of the shift to MRP in the latter.

Before we report the results of our exercise, it is useful to raise the question of whether canvassing two alternative recall periods in the case of the 50th Round raises possible problems of the first recall influencing the reporting for the second, of the kind discussed in connection with the food group in the previous sections. In the 50th Round CES, the items of concern are: (a) clothing, (b) footwear, (c) durables, (d) education, and (e) institutional health expenditures. As noted above, information on these items was collected in the 50th Round on two alternative recall periods of 30 days and 365 days, from the same set of sample households. In the schedules of enquiry, the blocks relating to (a) to (c) were placed one after the other, with the 30-day recall coming first, whereas for (d) and (e), they were side by side. *Prima facie*, it cannot be completely ruled out that this might pose problems.

In our judgement, however, their incidence is likely to be minimal, for the following reasons. First, expenditures on (a) to (e) relate to events that are relatively less frequent and more salient in the respondent's memory than those in the food group. Accordingly, expenditures over the last 30 days can be more easily distinguished from those in the last 365 days. This is not the case with the items in the food group. Purchases of these food items are likely to have been more frequent and less memorable, providing greater incentive to minimise the additional effort required to accurately recall expenditures. Second, it is deemed significant that there was some previous experience in the use of the two recall periods in the case of clothing, etc. Information on items (a) to (c) had been collected from the same set of households, eliciting information on the basis of the same two alternative recall periods, for the three quinquennial rounds preceding the 50th Round. In addition, field officials had been explicitly instructed to check the recorded entries against the two recall periods, presumably to keep some check on the investigators.

What light does the evidence from the 'thin' rounds throw on this issue of the 50th Round estimates of consumer expenditure on the 365-day reference period being influenced by the prior responses on the 30-day recall in respect of items of low-frequency purchase? We have tabulated, for all-India, but separately for the rural and the urban populations, the estimates of consumer expenditure on the two recall periods for the 50th Round and three full-year, 'thin' rounds (51st, 52nd and 53rd) for clothing and durables. This has been done for broad fractile groups – the bottom 40 per cent and the middle 40 per cent, with the top 20 per cent being split into three groups: the 80th–90th percentile; the 90th–95th percentile, and the top 5 per cent. For the 50th Round these are exact percentiles, but, for the 'thin' rounds, they would be approximate – obtained by aggregating the estimates for (fixed) expenditure – classes.[8] The outcome is presented in Tables 13.2R and 13.2U.

For the population as a whole, in the 'thin' rounds, the expenditure reported on the two reference periods are fairly close to one another for clothing in the rural population while the urban population reported higher expenditure on 365-day recall than that for 30 days. However, in respect of durables the 365-day estimates are substantially lower than the estimates on the 30-day recall, for both the segments.

In the 50th Round, the overall MPCE on clothing on the 365-day recall was about 40 per cent higher than that on the 30-day recall. In the case of durables, however, the estimated expenditure on the 365-day recall was *lower* by about 14 per cent (rural) and 20 per cent (urban).

Tables 13.2R and 13.2U show that there are differences in consumer behaviour in respect of these relatively infrequently purchased items across fractile groups.

Now, *focusing on the bottom 40 per cent*, we find that the estimates of expenditure on clothing on the 365-day recall are substantially higher than those on the 30-day recall in both the 50th Round and in the 'thin' rounds – but the differential is greater in the 50th Round. Broadly, the same is also true in respect of the durables: an excess of estimates on the 365-day recall over those on the 30-day recall of between 4 and 54 per cent in the 'thin' rounds and of 160 per cent in the 50th Round (see Tables 13.2R and 13.2U). In other words, for the poor population these items are much more infrequent in their purchases of the last 30 days as compared to those during the last 365 days.

For purposes of poverty estimates we may focus on the above-stated results for the bottom 40 per cent: that the excess of the estimates of expenditures on clothing and durable on the 365-day recall over those on the 30-day recall are greater in the 50th Round relative to the differentials yielded by the 'thin' rounds. If the argument is that canvassing the two alternative recall periods on the same set of households has biased the estimates on the 365-day recall because of their *prior* responses on the 30-day recall by minimising their recall efforts, then such an interference should have brought the comparable *monthly* estimates on the two recall periods *closer* relative the differences emerging from the 'thin' rounds. This has *not* happened. The estimates on the two recall periods appear to be indeed based on independent recall efforts on the part of the respondents.

Appendix Tables A.3R and A.3U present the size-distributions of total household consumer expenditure according to 5 per cent fractile groups for the rural and urban populations, respectively. The households are ranked according to the size of monthly per capita total consumer expenditure (PCTE).

It may be noted that a shift from 30-day recall to 365-day recall in respect of clothing, footwear, durables, education, and institutional health expenditure leads to a higher mean PCTE for fractile groups in the bottom 85 per cent and 95 per cent of the rural and urban populations, respectively. In other words, for these sections of the population, mean per capita monthly expenditure on the above-mentioned items was higher on the basis of 365-day recall than it was for the preceding 30-day recall. In contrast, for the top 10 per cent and 5 per cent of the respective rural and urban population, the mean monthly per capita household expenditure on these items was lower with a 365-day reference period in this instance.

---

[8] Ideally, one would have preferred to have set up a similar comparison in respect of fractile groups formed after excluding the expenditures on the items on the 365-day recall. Unfortunately, the unit record data for the NSS Rounds 51 through 54 provide information only on the 30-day reference period. Efforts are on in this regard.

Table 13.2R 30-day/365-day Estimates of MPCE for Clothing and Durables by Broad Fractile Group in the 50th, 51st, 52nd and 53rd Rounds of the NSS Consumer Expenditure Surveys: All-India Rural

Clothing (Rs 0.00)

	50th Round		51st Round		52nd Round		53rd Round	
	30 Days	365 Days	30 Days	365 Days	30 Days	365 Days	30 Days	365 Days
Bottom 40%	2.63	14.09	3.43	10.64	2.84	12.38	2.59	10.79
Middle 40%	10.14	21.29	12.54	16.44	10.44	18.91	8.44	18.07
80–90	27.03	29.23	31.68	23.88	28.44	26.79	21.73	27.28
90–95	47.48	33.21	49.94	28.48	56.39	32.86	36.84	28.60
95–100	98.74	46.92	136.85	44.88	130.48	45.88	105.45	48.80
All	15.12	21.18	21.78	21.21	26.63	26.43	27.60	28.11

Durables (Rs 0.00)

	50th Round		51st Round		52nd Round		53rd Round	
	30 Days	365 Days	30 Days	365 Days	30 Days	365 Days	30 Days	365 Days
Bottom 40%	1.00	2.60	1.18	1.23	1.12	1.33	0.70	1.08
Middle 40%	3.04	5.22	3.40	2.46	3.76	2.85	3.45	2.67
80–90	7.28	10.33	8.84	5.71	8.68	5.81	7.25	6.10
90–95	11.09	14.70	17.49	8.54	16.40	8.79	14.58	8.59
95–100	95.54	33.44	196.91	30.41	113.80	29.96	85.82	26.54
All	7.67	6.57	16.12	6.29	15.36	8.25	17.34	9.28

Table 13.2U 30-day/365-day Differences in MPCE for Clothing and Durables by Broad Fractile Group in the 50th, 51st, 52nd and 53rd Rounds of the NSS Consumer Expenditure Surveys: All-India Urban

Clothing (Rs 0.00)

	50th Round		51st Round		52nd Round		53rd Round	
	30 Days	365 Days	30 Days	365 Days	30 Days	365 Days	30 Days	365 Days
Bottom 40%	3.58	18.51	3.75	14.11	3.31	15.71	2.44	14.73
Middle 40%	15.94	32.90	17.68	26.62	16.84	27.97	14.02	25.81
80–90	40.46	48.47	41.97	39.82	49.43	42.56	36.55	41.77
90–95	62.07	62.07	66.62	49.57	73.72	54.57	67.00	54.07
95–100	129.62	84.12	154.25	72.67	213.29	79.00	150.86	95.06
All	21.43	32.72	28.11	34.26	42.65	40.10	37.62	43.61

Durables (Rs 0.00)

	50th Round		51st Round		52nd Round		53rd Round	
	30 Days	365 Days	30 Days	365 Days	30 Days	365 Days	30 Days	365 Days
Bottom 40%	1.20	3.02	1.72	1.71	1.48	1.60	1.30	1.59
Middle 40%	5.14	8.82	5.04	3.89	5.08	4.79	4.43	4.53
80–90	13.77	18.62	14.72	11.81	16.72	13.82	14.37	16.27
90–95	26.53	32.95	21.44	19.75	26.26	15.13	23.22	22.46
95–100	198.64	78.44	226.09	59.00	308.81	74.58	198.94	92.94
All	15.16	12.17	22.89	12.47	38.75	18.31	32.33	23.44

The overall mean PCTE turns out to be marginally higher (by 1.6 per cent in rural India and by 1.2 per cent in urban India) with the mixed reference period.

The corresponding Lorenz curves (LCs) presented in Figure 13.1 for the rural population and in Figure 13.2 for the urban population, show that the LC based on a mixed reference period (MRP) lies

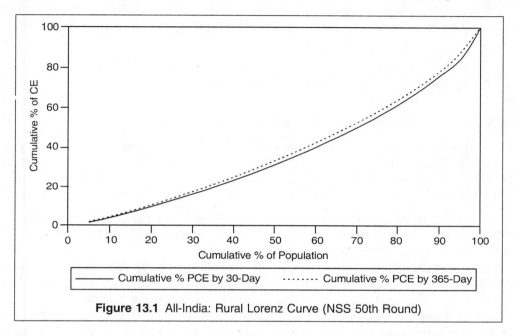

Figure 13.1 All-India: Rural Lorenz Curve (NSS 50th Round)

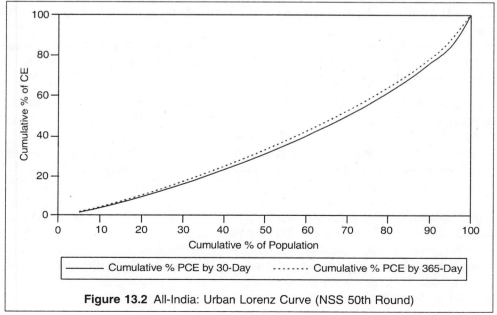

Figure 13.2 All-India: Urban Lorenz Curve (NSS 50th Round)

uniformly inside the LC based on 30-day uniform reference period (URP). Consequently, the summary measure of relative inequality based on the LC, namely the Gini coefficient, is distinctly lower when it is based on an MRP than on a URP. The respective Gini coefficients for rural and urban population are 0.2581 and 0.3184 for the MRP, and 0.2859 and 0.3438 for the URP.

Since the reported PCTE for the bottom fractile groups is higher under MRP than that under URP, the headcount ratio based on MRP, as presented in the following section, is expected to be lower than that based on URP.

POVERTY OUTCOMES IN THE 1980s AND THE 1990s: THE ALL-INDIA PICTURE

Comparable Headcount Ratios and Related Measures of Poverty

In the previous section we discussed the problems of comparability pertaining to consumer expenditure surveys from the 50th and 55th Rounds of the NSS, which have been highlighted during recent debates about poverty trends in the 1990s in India. Our empirical analysis, based partly on the published results, and partly on unit-level records of the 50th and the 55th Rounds of NSS, have established the following:

- First, the published size-distribution of the first five quinquennial rounds, including the 50th Round in 1993/94, are based on a uniform, 30-day reference period (URP) and headcount ratios calculated from them are comparable.
- Second, the published size-distributions of the 50th Round for 1993/94, and the 55th Round for 1999/2000 are not directly comparable because of the differences in the recall period, namely, URP in the 50th Round and a mixed reference period (MRP) in the 55th Round.
- Third, as regards the 7-day–30-day controversy besetting the CES in the 55th Round, evidence presented earlier suggests that the size-distribution of the CES in the 55th Round based on 30-day recall for the food group is comparable to the MRP-based size-distribution of the 50th Round.
- Fourth, the size-distribution of the 50th Round can be recast for MRP, and we have recalculated it with MRP in Section entitled 'Correcting for Mixed Reference Periods in 50th Round', to make it directly comparable to the 55th Round.

These points enable us to calculate comparable poverty indicators in order to assess India's much-debated aggregate poverty outcomes over the 1980s and 1990s. To this end we use five summary indicators that capture different dimensions of absolute deprivation.

The first and generally the most widely-used indicator is HCR, which specifies the proportion of the population that is estimated to be at or below an exogenously defined poverty line. However, it ignores size of the poverty gap, that is, how far below poverty line different poor households are in terms of their PCTE. It also does not reflect relative inequality among the poor.

The second indicator is PGI, which sums up the poverty gaps of poor households and normalises the resulting aggregate (weighted) poverty gap. This is done by reference to the maximum possible poverty gap for the entire poor and non-poor population, derived from the product of the poverty line and the total population. Accordingly, given two populations with the same level of HCR, the one with higher PGI will have a larger concentration of the poor population living farther away from the poverty line. Hence it is taken to describe the depth of poverty.

The third and fourth indicators are the squared poverty gap (SPG, denoted as FGT* in subsequent discussion) and the Sen Index (SI) (Sen, 1976). In addition to the headcount ratio and the poverty gap, these indicators take into account the relative inequality among the poor. However, SPG and SI differ from each other in terms of the underlying summary measure of relative inequality. SPG incorporates squared coefficient of variation, whereas the SI uses the Gini coefficient among the poor population. Because of their sensitivity to relative inequality, SPG and SI are taken to measure the severity of poverty. Indeed, because they incorporate as component measures both the HCR and the poverty gap, as well as the measure of relative inequality among the poor, these indicators are by far the most comprehensive measures of absolute deprivation. Accordingly, given the same HCR and PGI for two populations, the one with higher SPG and SI reflects a greater severity of poverty. A reference may be made to Sundaram and Tendulkar (1993) for a discussion of these measures.

We may add that HCR, PGI, and SPG, or FGT* belong to the class of decomposable poverty indicators suggested by Foster et al. (1984).

The fifth and final indicator of poverty used in this paper is the size of the poor population – variously described also as the 'absolute headcount', 'the numerical magnitude', or simply 'the number of poor people'. It is given by a multiplication of the sample survey-based *estimated* HCR and the *estimated* total population at the midpoint of the survey period. The *qualifying* adjective 'estimated' is to be underlined because both components of the product are estimated independently of each other and are not based on direct observations: HCR is based on the estimated size-distribution of PCTE among the universe of all households, which is in turn based on an appropriately selected sample of households. Similarly, 'total population at the midpoint of the survey period' is an interpolated, or projected figure. Consequently, the size of the poor population is to be regarded as a probabilistic point estimate of the aggregate macro-level order of magnitude of the poor population.

Three comments are warranted on the interpretation of the last indicator. First, it does not permit physical identification of poor persons or households at the micro level. This would require a complete census. Second, a change in the size of the poor population during the time interval between the two surveys merely indicates the net change in the estimated number of poor people between the midpoints of the two survey periods from all sources. Third, this change in size has two components: (a) change due to changes in the HCR between two time-points, which is then applied to the base year population; (b) change in the total population between two time-points, which is applied to the HCR in the terminal year. Notice that (b) is always positive while (a) will be negative in cases where the headcount ratio declines. Either component may dominate the other.

The five summary indicators of poverty are presented in Table 13.3. They are shown for the rural, urban, and total population at the all-India level, mapped across three time-points: 1983, 1993/94, and 1999/2000. The choice of years is governed by a specific set of considerations. The idea is to monitor descriptively the progress in poverty reduction over the last two decades and in the process also bring out differences in the level comparability of HCR, arising from uniform and mixed reference periods. To represent the decade of the 1980s, we could have chosen to compare the 43rd Round for 1987/88 with the 38th Round for 1983. However, poverty – in particular, rural poverty – is known to be affected by abnormal harvests and 1987/88 was a meteorological drought year. Hence it was excluded.

Table 13.3 provides two estimates for 1993/94, one based on URP and the other based on MRP. The estimates based on URP are comparable to the 1983 estimates while the MRP-based estimates for 1993/94 are comparable to the estimates for 1999/2000.

Table 13.3 Alternative Measures of Poverty in India: All-India Rural, Urban all Areas: 1983–1999/2000

Segment/Measure	Measures on URP		Measures on MRP	
	1983	*1993/94*	*1993/94*	*1999/2000*
(1)	(2)	(3)	(4)	(5)
All-India Rural				
1. Headcount ratio (%)	49.02	39.66	**34.19**	28.93
2. Poverty-gap index	0.1386	0.0928	**0.0728**	0.0579
3. FGT*	0.0545	0.0315	**0.0232**	0.0173
4. Sen index	0.1882	0.1278	**0.1014**	0.0806
5. *Number of poor ('000)*	268,062	261,369	225,321	210,498
All-India Urban				
1. Headcount ratio (%)	38.33	30.89	**26.41**	23.09
2. Poverty-gap index	0.0995	0.0749	**0.0600**	0.0504
3. FGT*	0.0366	0.0265	**0.0202**	0.0160
4. Sen index	0.1362	0.1034	**0.0833**	0.0695
5. *Number of poor ('000)*	65,720	72,586	62,061	63,827
All-India All Areas				
1. Headcount ratio (%)	46.47	37.35	**32.15**	27.32
2. Poverty-gap index	0.1293	0.0881	**0.0694**	0.0558
3. FGT*	0.0502	0.0302	**0.0224**	0.0170
4. Sen index	0.1758	0.1214	**0.0966**	0.0775
5. *Number of poor ('000)*	333,782	333,955	287,382	274,325
Memorandum item				
Total (all areas) population ('000)	718,300	894,006	**894,006**	1004,086
Share of urban population (%)	23.87	26.28	**26.28**	27.53

Notes: 1. Official all-India poverty lines in terms of monthly per capita total expenditure (MPCTE) of Rs 49.09 (rural) and Rs 56.64 (urban) at 1973/74 prices have been used in the calculations in this table. They have been adjusted for changes in prices using the price indices specifically compiled for the poor population. The numerical values of the price adjusted poverty lines in terms of MPCTE at current prices are given below for the years used in this study

	1983	1993/94	1999/2000
Rural	093.16	211.30	335.05
Urban	111.25	274.88	451.19

2. All numbers in Column 4 are the revised estimates.

Sources: Estimates HCR, PGI, FGT*, and SI for 1983 are drawn from, Tendulkar, Sundaram, and Jain (1993), Parallel estimates for 1993/94 with uniform and mixed reference periods and with mixed reference period for 1999/2000 have been estimated from unit record data for the 50th Rounds of consumer expenditure survey.

Poverty Outcomes in India in the 1980s

To contextualise this exercise, and to provide a point of reference for the changes in poverty over the 1990s, let us first consider briefly the changes in poverty over the ten-and-a-half years between 1 July 1983 and 1 January 1994. In both rural and urban India, and hence, also at the all-India level, there is a clear reduction in the headcount ratio, poverty-gap index, FGT*, and Sen Index. In rural India, the annual average decline in the headcount ratio over the ten-and-a-half year period was a little under 0.9 percentage points. In urban India, the corresponding decline was 0.7 percentage points per year. For rural and urban areas taken together, the average decline in HCR was close to, but below 0.9 percentage points per annum.

In terms of the estimated number of people living below the poverty line, or, the poor population, there is a clear rural-urban contrast. While in rural India, the size of the poor population declined by a little under 6.7 million over the ten-and-a-half year period – translating into an annual average decline of 0.64 million – in urban India, the number of poor people increased by 6.9 million between 1 July 1983 and 1 January 1994, despite the reduction in the corresponding headcount ratio. Consequently, for both rural and urban areas taken together, the number of poor people in India increased marginally by 0.17 million.

However, the rise in population of the poor in urban India, which more than offset the decline in the size of the poor population in rural India, has to be seen in the context of a rapid growth in urban population, from 171.5 million to 235.0 million. This corresponds to a growth rate of over 3 per cent per annum.

We may caution also that the entire increase in urban population cannot be attributed to rural-urban migration. A rise in the urban population also takes place (a) because of natural population growth in areas which remain classified as urban across survey years; (b) because of an addition of population in the areas that in the base year were rural but re-classified as urban in the terminal year; and (c) because of inter-censal growth of this population.

Poverty in India in 1990s

What has been the record on poverty in India over the 1990s?

To start with, notice that a shift from URP to MRP for 1993/94 results in a HCR for 1993/94 that is nearly five-and-a-half percentage points lower than that on the URP for rural India. For urban India, the difference is much lower (4.5 percentage points). For the country as a whole (that is taking the rural and the urban population together), the HCR for 1993/94 on the mixed reference period is lower by 5.2 percentage points. Accordingly, an uncorrected and hence inappropriate comparison based on the published results (URP for 1993/94 and MRP for 1999/2000) would overstate the decline over the six years by the same magnitude.

Using comparable MRP-based measures for both 1993/94 and 1999/2000, we find that, except in respect of the number of poor in urban India, all measures of poverty showed a clear decline in both rural and urban areas and, therefore, also for the country as a whole.

Consider first the rural population. At the all-India level over the six-year period from 1 January 1994 to 1 January 2000, the HCR declined by over 5 percentage points translating to an average decline of a slightly under 0.9 percentage points per annum – roughly the same as that realised between 1983 and 1993/94. It is necessary further to normalise by reference to the initial level value of the indicator for more appropriate comparability.[9] By taking the annual average decline by reference to the base year level values (of 49 per cent on URP for 1983 and of 34 per cent on MRP for 1993/94), the rate of annual average decline between 1993/94 and 1999/2000 at 2.6 per cent is higher than that achieved between 1983–1993/94 (1.8 per cent). In terms of the number of rural poor, the 1990s witnessed a decline of close to 15 million over the six-year period: an annual average decline of close to 2.5 million. This may be contrasted with the annual average decline of a little over 0.6 million between 1983 and 1993/94.

As noted above, PGI, FGT*, and Sen Index also record a decline for the rural population between 1993/94 and 1999/2000.

For urban India too, HCR, PGI, FGT*, and Sen Index record a decline between 1993/94 and 1999/2000. Taken as they are, the annual average decline in all these indices are slightly smaller in the 1990s than that between 1983 and 1994. However, when normalised by reference to the relevant base year values, the rates of annual average decline are slightly higher between 1993/94 and 1999/2000. In terms of the *number of poor in urban India we have an increase in both periods*. However, aided by slightly a growth slower in urban population, the annual average increase (0.3 million) between 1993/94 and 1999/2000 was less than half the annual average increase in the number of urban poor between 1983 and 1993/94 (0.66 million).

The picture for the country as a whole (i.e. taking the rural and urban population together) parallels that for the rural population with declines in all the poverty indicators between 1993/94 and 1999/2000, with the normalised (with reference to base year values) annual average fall being higher for the 1990s than for the 1980s. Particularly noteworthy is the decline in the absolute number of poor at over 2 million per annum compared to an increase (albeit marginal) between 1983 and 1993/94.

Finally, a word of caution in interpreting these results.

In the chapter, we have deliberately avoided bringing in a discussion of the possible factors explaining the decline in poverty. In this vein, we would also like to caution that the average annual percentage point decline is not expected to be spread evenly over the intervening years. In an earlier work, one of us had brought out the complexity of causal mechanisms impacting poverty on the basis of poverty calculations from 1970/71 to 1993/94 (Tendulkar, 1998). It was argued that a poverty outcome in a given year is a combined consequence of (a) the impact of economic reforms and reform-related factors; (b) the impact of other secular factors operating since pre-reform years; and (c) the impact of year-specific abnormal factors, such as a drought.

We may also emphasise that the expected favourable effects of economic reforms and reform-related factors on poverty operate through their impact on raising the long-term growth path of the economy. Higher growth rates, in turn, generate sustainable productive employment opportunities which provide the only enduring solution to poverty-eradication (Sundaram and Tendulkar, 2002).

POVERTY AMONG SOCIAL AND ECONOMIC GROUPS IN INDIA IN THE 1990s

In this section, we examine the levels and changes in poverty indicators in the 1990s for the rural and the urban population disaggregated by (a) social groups, and (b) household types distinguished according to major source of livelihood of a household during the 365 days preceding the date of interview. This is

---

[9] We hold the view that it is important to normalise the average annual decline by reference to the initial level value of the poverty indicator. Alternatively, one may opt for compound annual change which is also normalised in a similar fashion. Both procedures yield the same conclusion, namely, the pace of poverty decline was higher in the six-year period of 1990s than in the previous ten-and-a-half years.

carried out on the basis of comparable estimates on the MRP computed from the unit record data for the 50th (1993/94) and 55th (1999/2000) Rounds of CES carried out by NSSO. The key issue here is how far the different social and economic groups shared the overall average decline in poverty over the 1990s noted in the last section.

The Social and Economic Groups

Social Groups

The 50th Round of the NSS distinguished two socially disadvantaged groups of SC and ST which have been specifically mentioned in the Constitution of India for affirmative state action. SCs have been at the lowest end of the Hindu (social) caste hierarchy based on birth. Over long periods in the past, the social system ascribed occupations to this group which were not only low in social order but were also characterised by very low productivity. With ascription on the basis of birth, the system did not permit occupational mobility. Consequently, this group remained at the lowest end of the economic hierarchy as well. While the intensity of caste-based discriminatory social practices varied in different parts of the country and was partially moderated with the penetration of the impersonal market forces in varying degrees, this group remained on the fringe of the traditional village society and rural economy practising lowly occupations with little exposure to educational opportunities.

STs in contrast, had not been part of the Hindu social hierarchy. Their social and economic backwardness was derived from their long habitation in geographically isolated areas with difficult terrain and practice of shifting cultivation. Lack of exposure to education and isolation from the social mainstream made them vulnerable to exploitation by the non-tribals and uprooting from their traditional habitation and occupations so that they were relegated to the lowest end of the economic hierarchy.

The residual omnibus social group of 'others' consisted of castes other than SC in the Hindu social hierarchy and non-ST members of other religious communities. In the 55th Round this residual (non-SC/ST) group has been further subdivided into 'other backward castes' (OBC) in the Hindu social hierarchy announced by the state governments as being socially 'backward' for eligibility to state-initiated programmes of affirmative action and the remaining 'others'.[10] Comparable poverty indicators for both the 50th (1993/94) and the 55th (1999/2000) Rounds can be computed for three social groups: SC, ST, and others. We have aggregated (by computing population-weighted averages) OBC and others in the 55th Round to make it comparable with 'others' in the 50th Round.

Economic Groups or Household Types

In addition to social groups, NSS also makes possible disaggregation of the surveyed households according to economic groups, what the NSS reports describe as 'household types'. These are classified on the basis of the reported major source of income or livelihood during the last year for the household as a whole.

Five household types are distinguished for the rural households on the basis of ownership or lack of physical or human capital, namely,

---

[10] The foregoing social groups derive relevance for state action in the traditional rural social structure where social interaction is mostly face-to-face and where the age-old attitudes and belief systems stubbornly persist. The intensity of social discrimination associated with these social groupings goes down considerably in large and impersonal urban settlements although their self-reported social identities have been recorded in the urban areas as well.

   (i) Self-employed in agriculture;
  (ii) Self-employed in non-agriculture;
 (iii) Rural agricultural labour;
 (iv) Other (than agricultural) rural labour; and
  (v) (residual) Others.

In the first two categories, deployment of land [category (i)] and non-agricultural physical or human capital assets [category (ii)] in the production process provide the major source of livelihood. The next two categories of households possess virtually no physical or human capital assets but subsist on the basis of their endowments of abundant manual labour which they supply to agricultural activities [category (iii)] or non-agricultural manufacturing or service activities [category (iv)] on non-contractual casual basis. After accounting for self-employment [household types (i) and (ii)] and non-contractual casual employment [types (iii) and (iv)], the fifth residual category of 'others' covers two types of earnings, namely (a) those households whose major source of income arises mostly from contractual employment with regular wages and salaries, and (b) those who earn their living from non-labour assets without direct participation in gainful economic activity. The latter category of non-participatory earnings [as distinct from participatory earnings in (a) as well as in types (i) to (iv)] may include current returns from ownership of immovable assets (land or real estate) or from past financial investments, or receipts from public or private transfers (including pension and remittances).

For the urban households, four categories of household types are distinguished, namely,

  1. self-employed households;
  2. wage and salaried income households;
  3. casual labour households; and
  4. (residual) others.

In this classification, the second and the third categories are well-defined and distinguished on the basis of (contractual or non-contractual casual) nature of hired employment and the major source of income earned therefrom by supplying labour. The first category is a heterogeneous aggregate ranging from high income professionals earning their incomes from technical skills and education to the unskilled low productivity trading and personal services with meagre physical or human capital. In the urban context, after accounting for self-employment and contractual as well as non-contractual paid employment in the first three categories, the fourth residual category of 'others' is taken to include those households whose major source of income is derived from non-participatory earnings as described under (v)(b) for rural household type.

With these prefatory remarks to help interpretation, we start by providing an overview across social groups and across household types on the basis of all-India size distribution and a uniform all-India poverty line applicable to all the social and economic categories of households.

Composition of Total and Poor Population Across Social and Economic Groups

To provide an overview, Tables 13.4R and 13.4U provide the composition of rural and urban total as well as poor population located in households classified alternatively according to social groups and household types discussed above along with the widely-used HCR measure of poverty. Also indicated is the absolute size of the total population as well as poor population whose percentage composition is

Table 13.4R Composition of Total and Poor Population Located in Households Classified by Means of Livelihood Categories and Social-Group Affiliation: All-India Rural 1993/94–1999/2000

Category	1993/94			1999/2000		
	Percentage Share of the Household Type in		HCR	Percentage Share of the Household Type in		HCR
	Total Rural Population	Rural Poor Population		Total Rural Population	Rural Poor Population	
I. Social groups						
Scheduled castes	21.10	28.19	45.69	20.43	27.10	38.38
Scheduled tribes	10.83	15.46	48.81	10.49	17.41	48.02
Others	68.07	56.35	28.30	69.08	55.49	23.23
All households	100.01	100.00	34.20	100.00	100.00	28.93
Population (000)	(659,025)	(225,392)		(727,611)	(210,498)	
II. Means of livelihood						
Self-employed in agriculture	42.40	32.33	26.08	37.78	28.25	21.62
Self-employed in non-agriculture	13.08	11.16	29.18	13.84	11.53	24.09
Agricultural labour	27.51	42.62	52.97	31.10	48.01	44.64
Other labour	7.49	7.84	35.82	7.40	7.12	27.79
Others	9.52	6.04	21.69	9.87	5.09	14.93

Table 13.4U Composition of Total and Poor Population Located in Households Classified by Means of Livelihood Categories and Social-Group Affiliation: All-India Urban 1993/94–1999/2000

Category	1993/94			1999/2000		
	Percentage Share of the Household Type in		HCR	Percentage Share of the Household Type in		HCR
	Total Urban Population	Urban Poor Population		Total Urban Population	Urban Poor Population	
I. Social groups						
Scheduled castes	13.85	22.48	42.85	14.38	23.57	37.84
Scheduled tribes	3.21	4.09	33.63	3.40	5.18	35.15
Others	82.94	73.43	23.39	82.22	71.26	20.01
All households	100.00	100.00	26.41	100.00	100.00	23.09
Population (000)	(234,981)	(67,675)		(276,425)	(63,827)	
II. Means of livelihood						
Self-employed	38.77	41.86	28.50	39.23	44.48	26.11
Regular wage/ salaried workers	42.66	25.24	15.62	40.00	19.73	11.36
Casual labour	13.18	28.60	57.25	14.33	31.08	49.95
Others	5.39	4.30	21.05	6.44	4.71	16.85

presented. *In the subsequent discussion, whenever we refer to the share or poverty indicator of a given household type, it refers to the share or poverty indicator for the population located in that household type.* The purpose is to avoid tedious repetition of the phrase 'population located in'. For instance, the share of self-employed households in total or poor rural population indicates the share of total or poor population located in self-employed households. In addition, unless otherwise indicated, level comparisons of poverty indicators across social, economic, or socio-economic groups in the immediately following discussion are by reference to the estimates for 1999/2000.

The composition of the *total rural population* indicates that in 1999/2000, *SC and ST* population accounted for a little over *one fifth and one-tenth, respectively, of the total rural population*. The social disadvantage of these groups is reflected in their above average HCRs: 38 per cent (SC) and 48 per cent (ST) in comparison with 29 per cent average HCR for all rural households. Consequently, they are over-represented in the poor population with the two socially disadvantaged groups together accounting for nearly 45 per cent of the rural poor population.

As between SC and ST, the latter is worse-off with a higher HCR than the former. Also, the share of ST in rural poor population has increased by 2.0 percentage points over the six-year period. This is *despite* a slight reduction in the share of ST in the total rural population-reflecting a lower-than-average growth in ST population (Table 13.4R). In the large and impersonal urban settlements, SCs and STs have much lower share of urban total as well as poor population while sharing with their rural counterparts the characteristic of a higher than average HCR. However, *urban STs register lower HCR than urban SCs, thereby reversing the rural ordering between these two social groups.* These rural-urban comparisons and contrasts at the all-India level are also repeated in most of the 15 major states as well. The state-level results would be presented in a separate paper.

Turning to rural household types, *population located in self-employed (agricultural as well as non-agricultural) households accounted for nearly 52 per cent of the total rural population in 1999/2000 whereas the share of the population located in the rural (agricultural as well as non-agricultural) manual labour households was over 38 per cent.* Residual (non-manual, non-self-employed) households were less than a tenth of total rural population. Within each of the two major groups of the self-employed and rural labour households, agricultural ones predictably dominated over the non-agricultural. With a rate of growth of population well above the average for the total rural population, three household types, namely, agricultural labour households, households self-employed in non-agricultural activities, and, the residual Means of Livelihood (MoL) category of 'other' households (see Table 13.4R) record a rise in their share in the total rural population between 1993/94 and 1999/2000.

This rise in population share is particularly marked (close to 4 percentage points) in the case of population in agricultural labour households. In the rural context, this is mainly a reflection of the demographic pressure on land resulting in fragmentation of agricultural holdings and the consequent burgeoning of the virtually assetless agricultural labour population. These households record the highest headcount ratio (across MoL categories) of nearly 45 per cent which is nearly 30 percentage points higher than the lowest HCR (14.9 per cent) recorded by the residual MoL category 'others', and about 16 percentage points higher than the HCR for the total rural population. These households possess little, if any, physical or human capital assets and depend for their livelihood on the irregular, fluctuating, and uncertain casual labour employment tied mainly to seasonal agricultural activities and dependent on the vagaries of weather.[11] *The agricultural labour households constituting 31 per cent of the total rural*

---

[11] Population in all the remaining other household types, namely, other rural labour, self-employed (agricultural and non-agricultural), and (residual) other households are marked by below-average HCRs, the lowest one by the (residual)

population but accounting for an overwhelming 48 per cent of the rural poor, clearly, represent the most vulnerable segment of the rural economy.

In urban India, two dominant household types of wage-and-salaried households and self-employed households, each with a share of 40 per cent, accounted for around four-fifths of the total population. Population located in casual labour households formed 14 per cent of the total with the residual category of 'Others' accounting for the balance 6 per cent.

With the highest urban headcount ratio of nearly 50 per cent in 1999/2000 (which was more than twice the average of 23 per cent for the entire urban population) *the population in casual labour households accounted for 31 per cent of the urban poor population.* The self-employed urban population reported the second highest (and above-average) HCR of 26 per cent. But with a share of nearly 40 per cent in total population, *the self-employed constituted the numerically dominant (at 45 per cent) section of the urban poor population.* As noted earlier, the households engaged in low skilled, low-productivity commodity production, personal services, and petty trading services in the urban informal sector are most likely to account for the urban poor population among the self-employed households. *The lowest urban headcount ratio of a little over 11 per cent was recorded by the regular wage-and-salaried population.* So that, despite a 40 per cent share in the total urban population, *their share in the urban poor population was less than 20 per cent.*

To recapitulate the overview on social and economic groups in the society, population located in SC and ST households recorded above-average HCR among both the rural and the urban population. As between the two socially disadvantaged groups, SCs recorded a higher HCR than STs in the rural population but the ranking was reversed in the urban population. Rural agricultural labour and urban casual labour households constitute the most vulnerable economically disadvantaged segments with the highest HCRs across household types in the rural and the urban population, respectively. The former, i.e. the agricultural labour households, also account for the numerically dominant share of the rural poor population. In the urban poor population, the self-employed poor are numerically dominant. The lowest HCR is recorded by the (residual non-self-employed, non-casual labour) other households in rural India and, by the regular wage-and-salaried households in the urban population. In 1999/2000 (but not in 1993/94) the HCR for the urban self-employed was higher than that for the self-employed (both agricultural and non-agricultural) in rural India. Further, in both years the HCR for the urban casual labour households were higher than those for the agricultural and other rural labour households.

Poverty among Social Groups Classified by Means of Livelihood

In this section, we carry out a more disaggregated analysis of poverty among the social and economic groups at the all-India level by cross-classifying the population in each social group by reference to the principal means of livelihood of the households. So that, with three social groups (SC, ST, and others) and five economic groups (four in the case of the urban population), we will have 15 rural (12 urban) mutually exclusive and exhaustive categories into which the rural (urban) population can be classified and for which one can analyse the poverty situation and the changes therein over the 1990s. We may recall that while the classification of social and economic groups is on the basis of household characteristics, our analysis of shares, HCR, etc., are in terms of persons or the population located in households with the described characteristics.

---

other households in 1999/2000. In 1993/94, along with the agricultural labour households, the other rural labour households also had a headcount ratio above the average for the total rural population.

Composition of the Total and the Poor Population in Social Groups by Means of Livelihood

Tables 13.5R presents a cross-classification of the all-India total and poor population in rural India by social groups and means of livelihood (MoL for short) categories, for 1993/94 and 1999/2000. Parallel estimates for all-India urban population are presented in Table 13.5U. Given the cross-classification, one could examine the MoL composition of the population in each social group as well as the social group composition of the population in a given MoL category. However, our primary focus is on the former. The reasoning is that, while the *social disadvantage* of belonging to the SC/ST categories has to be taken as given, expanding employment opportunities in the process of rapid economic growth can, in

Table 13.5R Percentage Distribution of Rural Population and Rural Poor Population by Social Groups Cross-classified by Means of Livelihood: All-India 1993/94–1999/2000

Social Group/ Household Type	1993/94				1999/2000			
	Scheduled Castes	Scheduled Tribes	Others	All Social Groups	Scheduled Castes	Scheduled Tribes	Others	All Social Groups
Self-employed agriculture	4.77 (4.93)	4.52 (5.72)	33.12 (21.69)	42.40 (32.34)	3.91 (4.07)	4.13 (5.70)	29.75 (18.48)	37.79 (28.25)
Self-employed non-agriculture	2.35 (2.45)	0.68 (0.91)	10.04 (7.80)	13.08 (11.16)	2.62 (2.97)	0.58 (0.82)	10.62 (7.73)	13.82 (11.52)
Agricultural labour	9.96 (16.61)	3.82 (6.65)	13.74 (19.36)	27.52 (42.62)	10.47 (16.72)	4.34 (9.10)	16.30 (22.20)	31.11 (48.02)
Other labour	2.16 (2.42)	1.06 (1.43)	4.27 (3.99)	7.49 (7.84)	1.97 (2.23)	0.85 (1.30)	4.59 (3.59)	7.41 (7.12)
Others	1.86 (1.79)	0.75 (0.74)	6.90 (3.50)	9.52 (6.03)	1.50 (1.16)	0.60 (0.49)	7.77 (3.44)	9.87 (5.09)
All MoL categories	21.11 (28.19)	10.83 (15.45)	68.07 (56.35)	100.00 (100.00)	20.47 (27.15)	10.49 (17.41)	69.04 (55.44)	100.00 (100.00)

Table 13.5U Percentage Distribution of All-India Urban Population and Urban Poor Population by Social Groups Cross-classified by Means of Livelihood Categories 1993/94–1999/2000

Social Group/ MoL Categories	1993/94				1999/2000			
	Scheduled Castes	Scheduled Tribes	Others	All Social Groups	Scheduled Castes	Scheduled Tribes	Others	All Social Groups
Self-employed	3.66 (6.44)	0.86 (1.29)	34.26 (34.14)	38.78 (41.87)	4.02 (7.92)	0.86 (1.38)	34.36 (35.21)	39.24 (44.51)
Regular wage salaried workers	5.82 (5.98)	1.50 (1.25)	35.33 (17.99)	42.65 (25.22)	5.63 (4.43)	1.41 (1.23)	32.97 (14.07)	40.01 (19.73)
Casual labour	3.76 (9.18)	0.61 (1.31)	8.82 (18.12)	13.19 (28.61)	4.02 (10.22)	0.82 (2.29)	9.47 (18.54)	14.31 (31.05)
Others	0.62 (0.90)	0.25 (0.24)	4.52 (3.16)	5.39 (4.30)	0.71 (1.04)	0.28 (0.30)	5.45 (3.38)	6.44 (4.72)
All MoL categories	13.86 (22.50)	3.21 (4.09)	82.93 (73.41)	100.00 (100.00)	14.38 (23.60)	3.37 (5.20)	82.25 (71.20)	100.00 (100.00)

principle, facilitate a measure of upward mobility within and across means of livelihood categories. And, this process can be assisted by targeted policy intervention in education and skill development besides positive discrimination in public employment in favour of the socially disadvantaged. In practice, while there has been a measure of success in ensuring that the socially disadvantaged have their fair share in regular wage/salaried employment in urban India, demographic forces have proved stronger in pushing an increasing proportion of households – across all social groups – into the more vulnerable economic categories of agricultural and non-agricultural labour households in rural India and the casual labour households in urban India. Also, as we shall see presently, while there has been an improvement in living standards in these two MoL categories, upward mobility across MoL categories (in terms of a re-shuffle of population shares) over the six-year period 1993/94 to 1999/2000, while not totally absent, has been very limited.

Focusing on the MoL composition of the population in each social group, let us consider first the situation in rural India.

Overall, as was noted in earlier, the SCs accounted for a little over 21 per cent of the total population and 28 per cent of the rural poor population in 1993/94. These proportions fell marginally to 20.5 per cent and 27.2 per cent, respectively, in 1999/2000.

In both the years, the single largest economic group among the SCs was also the most disadvantaged group economically: namely, the agricultural labour households who accounted for 47 per cent of the rural SC population (and close to 10 per cent of the total rural population) in 1993/94. This share rose to 51 per cent of the SC (and 10.5 per cent of the total) rural population in 1999/2000. With a sharply higher headcount ratio than the average for the entire SC population (57.0 per cent against 45.7 per cent in 1993/94, see Table 13.6R HCR) and in fact the highest HCR across all household types (for the SC population) the agricultural labour households accounted for nearly 59 per cent of the poor population in SC households and about one-sixth of the total rural poor in 1993/94. The share of the agricultural labour population in the poor among the SCs went up to 62 per cent in 1999/2000.

Among the total rural SC population, with a 23 per cent share in 1993/94, those self-employed in agriculture were the next largest category. However, with a lower-than-average (for the SC population as a whole) HCR because of their access to cultivable land, they had a 17.5 per cent share in the poor among the SCs in 1993/94. Their share in the total and the poor population in SC households fell to 19

Table 13.6R HCR   Headcount Ratio for All-India Rural Population by Social Groups
Cross-classified by Means of Livelihood: 1993/94–1999/2000

(%)

Social Group/ Household Type	1993/94				1999/2000			
	Scheduled Castes	Scheduled Tribes	Others	All Social Groups	Scheduled Castes	Scheduled Tribes	Others	All Social Groups
Self-employed in agriculture	35.34	43.30	22.40	26.08	30.11	39.97	17.97	21.62
Self-employed non-agriculture	35.59	45.82	26.57	29.18	32.76	40.87	21.06	24.09
Agricultural labour	57.02	59.51	48.19	52.97	46.20	60.69	39.39	44.64
Other labour	38.34	46.25	31.99	35.82	32.82	44.22	22.59	27.79
Others	32.98	33.88	17.36	21.69	22.45	23.55	12.81	14.93
All MoL categories	45.69	48.81	28.30	34.19	38.38	48.02	23.23	28.93

Table 13.6R PGI Poverty Gap Index for All-India Rural Population by Social Groups Cross-classified by Means of Livelihood Categories: 1993/94–1999/2000

Social Group/ MoL Categories	1993/94				1999/2000			
	Scheduled Castes	Scheduled Tribes	Others	All Social Groups	Scheduled Castes	Scheduled Tribes	Others	All Social Groups
Self-employed agriculture	0.07223	0.10105	0.03911	0.04943	0.05347	0.08999	0.02889	0.03807
Self-employed non-agriculture	0.07184	0.10792	0.04959	0.05667	0.06338	0.09430	0.03826	0.04533
Agricultural labour	0.13735	0.15121	0.10902	0.12516	0.09958	0.15263	0.08021	0.09680
Other labour	0.07586	0.09597	0.06203	0.07079	0.07139	0.08951	0.04475	0.05696
Others	0.07670	0.08834	0.03746	0.04910	0.04226	0.06118	0.02424	0.02922
All MoL categories	0.10369	0.11780	0.05603	0.0728	0.07920	0.11451	0.04298	0.0579

Table 13.6R FGT* The FGT* Poverty Measure for All-India Rural Population by Social Groups Cross-classified by Means of Livelihood Categories: 1993/94–1999/2000

Social Group/ MoL Categories	1993/94				1999/2000			
	Scheduled Castes	Scheduled Tribes	Others	All Social Groups	Scheduled Castes	Scheduled Tribes	Others	All Social Groups
Self-employed agriculture	0.02220	0.03372	0.01072	0.01446	0.01441	0.02850	0.00725	0.01030
Self-employed non-agriculture	0.02207	0.03851	0.01460	0.01722	0.01838	0.03007	0.01037	0.01270
Agricultural labour	0.04700	0.05401	0.03561	0.04229	0.03100	0.05317	0.02407	0.03045
Other labour	0.02347	0.02958	0.01862	0.02156	0.02272	0.02613	0.01295	0.01705
Others	0.02583	0.03301	0.01184	0.01623	0.01274	0.02551	0.00747	0.00936
All MoL categories	0.03435	0.04072	0.01692	0.0232	0.02407	0.03842	0.01211	0.0173

Table 13.6U HCR Headcount Ratios for All-India Urban Population by Social Groups Cross-classified by Means of Livelihood Categories: 1993/94–1999/2000

(%)

Social Group/ MoL Categories	1993/94				1999/2000			
	Scheduled Castes	Scheduled Tribes	Others	All Social Groups	Scheduled Castes	Scheduled Tribes	Others	All Social Groups
Self-employed	46.44	39.71	26.30	28.50	45.28	36.95	23.59	26.11
Regular wage/ salaried workers	27.11	22.07	13.44	15.62	18.12	20.16	9.83	11.36
Casual labour	64.44	56.85	54.21	57.25	58.49	63.89	45.08	49.95
Others	38.14	25.74	18.45	21.05	33.89	24.91	14.26	16.85
All MoL categories	42.85	33.63	23.39	26.41	37.84	35.15	19.98	23.09

Table 13.6U PGI Poverty-gap Index for All-India Urban Population by Social Groups Cross-classified by Means of Livelihood Categories: 1993/94–1999/2000

Social Group/ MoL Categories	1993/94				1999/2000			
	Scheduled Castes	Scheduled Tribes	Others	All Social Groups	Scheduled Castes	Scheduled Tribes	Others	All Social Groups
Self-employed	0.11334	0.09626	0.05660	0.06285	0.09975	0.08711	0.04864	0.05472
Regular wage/ salaried workers	0.05513	0.04906	0.02466	0.02969	0.03432	0.04589	0.01762	0.02095
Casual labour	0.18176	0.16352	0.13852	0.1520	0.15094	0.17606	0.10951	0.12490
Others	0.12035	0.05242	0.04383	0.0530	0.08088	0.07719	0.03014	0.03769
All MoL categories	0.10778	0.08353	0.05110	0.0600	0.08766	0.08980	0.04209	0.0504

Table 13.6U FGT* The FGT* Poverty Measure for All-India Urban Population by Social Groups Cross-classified by Means of Livelihood Categories: 1993/94–1999/2000

Social Group/ MoL Categories	1993/94				1999/2000			
	Scheduled Castes	Scheduled Tribes	Others	All Social Groups	Scheduled Castes	Scheduled Tribes	Others	All Social Groups
Self-employed	0.03840	0.03366	0.01793	**0.02022**	0.03232	0.03058	0.01454	**0.01671**
Regular wage/ salaried workers	0.01686	0.01513	0.00727	**0.00886**	0.00909	0.01616	0.00471	**0.00573**
Casual labour	0.06928	0.06636	0.04920	**0.05572**	0.05277	0.06596	0.03746	**0.04336**
Others	0.06151	0.01507	0.01739	**0.02234**	0.03170	0.03896	0.01003	**0.01364**
All MoL categories	*0.03876*	*0.02975*	*0.01673*	*0.0202*	*0.02894*	*0.03350*	*0.01298*	*0.0160*

per cent and 15 per cent, respectively, in 1999/2000. Together, the agriculture-dependent households (both self-employed and casual labour) accounted for more than three-fourths (77 per cent) of the poor among rural scheduled caste population, and close to 21 per cent of the poor in the entire rural population in 1999/2000.

Among the STs in rural India, those self-employed in agriculture formed the numerically dominant economic group in 1993/94 and accounted for close to 42 per cent of the rural ST population, and with a lower-than-average HCR, a little over 37 per cent of the poor among them. In 1999/2000, with a reduced (39 per cent) share in total ST population in rural India, the self-employed among them accounted for a little under one-third of the poor in rural ST households.

In 1993/94, with 35 per cent share the agriculture labour households formed the second-largest economic group in the rural ST population. However, with the highest HCR (across all social groups and all households types, Table 13.6R HCR) of close to 60 per cent (against 49 per cent for the entire rural ST population), *ST households with agriculture labour as the principal means of livelihood accounted for 43 per cent of the poor population in rural ST households. This share of agriculture labour population rose sharply to a little under 52 per cent in 1999/2000.* In 1999/2000, the agriculture labour households also became the numerically single-largest economic group among the total rural ST population with a 41 per cent share – an increase of 6 points from the 35 per cent share in 1993/94. As we shall see presently, this combination of a sharp rise in the share of the agricultural labour households in the total ST population and a small (2 per cent) rise in HCR among such households is at the heart of the virtual absence of progress in poverty reduction over the 1990s among the rural ST population taken as a whole. The self-employed in agriculture and the agriculture labour households accounted for 85 per cent of the poor in ST households in rural India in 1999/2000.

Among the rural non-SC, non-ST population *(the social group categorised as 'others')*, the self-employed in agriculture dominated both the total and the poor population in 1993/94 with a share, respectively, of nearly 49 per cent (in total population in the non-SC, non-ST households) and 38.5 per cent (in the poor population in this social group). In 1999/2000, though their share in the (non-SC, non-ST) population declined to 43 per cent, they still remained the single-largest group. However, with a share of 33 per cent (relative to the 40 per cent share of the agricultural labour households) they yield first place to the agricultural labour population in terms of their share of the poor among the non-SC, non-ST population. The latter, i.e. the agricultural labour households, raise their share in the total rural non-SC, non-ST population from 20 per cent in 1993/94 to a little under 24 per cent in 1999/2000, while their share in the poor population in the non-SC, non-ST households went up from 34 to 40 per cent over the same period.

Let us shift the focus, briefly to the distribution across social groups of the total population in the different livelihood categories.

Given that the residual social group 'others', i.e. the non-SC, non-ST population had a dominant share in the total *rural population* (more than two-thirds), in both years, and, in almost all the MoL categories, this social group accounted for a clear majority of the population in the respective MoL categories. The sole exception to this result is provided by the agricultural labour households where the share of the social group 'others' at 49.9 per cent fell just short of the majority in 1993/94. And, except in respect of the two casual wage-labour-dependent categories of agricultural labour and other rural labour households, the non-SC, non-ST population group has more than two-thirds share in all the other three MoL categories in both the years.

The measure of over-representation of a social group in a given means of livelihood (MoL) category can be obtained by taking the *ratio* (call it k) of the share of the social group in a given MoL category to the share of that social group in the total rural/urban population. While a value of this ratio greater than 1 will imply over-representation, a value close to 1 will imply that the social group has its fair share in the MoL category under reference. On the stated criterion, *both the SCs and STs are seen to be over-represented in the economically disadvantaged categories of agricultural labour households and other rural labour households in rural India and in the category of casual labour households in urban India.* And this was so in both the years. In rural India, in both the MoL categories and in both the years *the extent of over-representation* was greater for the scheduled castes than for the scheduled tribes. And, over the six-year period, the extent of over-representation in the MoL category agricultural labour declined marginally for the SCs and increased marginally for the STs, while in respect of the MoL category 'other rural labour' both the social groups reported a decline in the extent of over-representation. Underlying these changes was a reduction in the share of SCs in both categories and a mix of a rise in share in the MoL category agricultural labour and a reduction in its share in 'other rural labour' for the SCs.

In the rural context, a major segment of the residual MoL category 'others' covers mostly those whose principal means of livelihood is regular wage/salaried employment. In this perspective, a k-ratio of less than 1 – and substantially so for both the disadvantaged social groups in 1999/2000 – would suggest that, at least in rural India, neither of the groups can be said to have had its fair share of regular wage/salaried employment. By the same measure, with a k-ratio close to or above 1 in both years in the MoL category 'regular wage/salaried work', both the SCs and the STs do appear to have succeeded in getting their fair share in such employment in urban India. So that, the policy of positive discrimination in public employment appears to have achieved a measure of success in urban India – though the same cannot be said in respect of rural India.

Judged by the same yardstick, while the STs (but not the SCs) are seen to be well-represented in the category 'self-employed in agriculture' in rural India, among the self-employed in non-agriculture it is the SCs who have a better representation relative to their share in the total rural population. In urban India, both the social groups are substantially under-represented in the MoL category, self-employed.

Not surprisingly, being better endowed with land, physical capital and human capital resources, the residual social group 'others' comprising the non-SC, non-ST population, have a better than even share in self-employment in both population segments and a fair share in the MoL categories of regular wage/ salaried work in urban India and in the MoL category 'others' in rural India. Equally unsurprising is the fact that in both the years and in both population segments, this residual social group of others is under-represented in the MoL categories reflecting dependence on uncertain and fluctuating employment as casual wage labourers.

We turn now to a discussion of the composition of the total and the poor population in social groups – each sub-classified on the means of livelihood criteria *in urban India* (Table 13.5U).

A key feature of the distribution of the total all-India urban population across the 12 sub-categories (three social groups and four household types on the means of livelihood criteria) is that, for each and all of the three social groups and in both years (with one exception) the numerically dominant economic group is the 'regular wage/salaried workers', with the self-employed coming a close second. The exception is provided by the omnibus social group 'others' where the self-employed had a one percentage point edge in 1999/2000. *In terms of the poor population*, however, the self-employed remain the numerically dominant group among the residual (non-SC, non-ST) social group of 'others'. For this residual social group of 'others', with a 26 per cent share, the casual labour households constituted the second-largest group of poor among them. In the case of the SCs and the STs, however, it is the casual labour households that dominate and this is so in both 1993/94 and 1999/2000.

A second common feature across the three social groups is the decline between 1993/94 and 1999/ 2000 in the share of the population in households with regular wage/salaried work as the principal means of livelihood (RWS households for short). Among the SCs, the share of RWS households went down from 42 per cent in 1993/94 to 39 per cent in 1999/2000. It declined from 47 per cent to 42 per cent among the STs and, more moderately, from 43 per cent to 40 per cent for the non-SC, non-ST population. Significantly, among the SCs, in 1993/94 (but not in 1999/2000), the HCR for the RWS households was higher than the average for the entire urban population, so that their share in the total urban poor was higher (6.0 per cent) than their share in total urban population (5.8 per cent).

As regards the casual labour households, their share in the respective urban population rose in all the three social groups. Further, with the highest HCR across all household types in each social group and significantly higher than the all-households average, they are over-represented among the urban poor. The extent of over representation has increased further between 1993/94 and 1999/2000 for the casual labour households among the urban ST population. This is attributable to a sharp rise in HCR (from 57 per cent to 64 per cent) in these households (Table 13.6U HCR) in a situation where all other household types among ST population (and all household types in all other social groups and, therefore, also the urban population as a whole), experienced a decline in their respective HCRs over the same period. This combination·of an increased share of casual labour households in the total ST population and a rise in HCR in such households has been a major factor underlying the rise in the HCR for the entire urban ST population in India from 33.6 per cent in 1993/94 to a little over 35 per cent.

Poverty Indicators for Social Groups and Means of Livelihood Categories

In this section, we present and analyse the estimates of HCR, PGI and the FGT* measures of poverty for the 15 rural and 12 urban mutually exclusive and exhaustive categories on the social group-cum-livelihood criteria for the rural (urban) population at the all-India level for 1993/94 and 1999/2000. These estimates are presented in Tables 13.6R HCR (13.6U HCR); 13.6R PGI (13.6U PGI); and 13.6R FGT* (13.6U FGT*).

In rural India, in respect of all the social groups, and, both in 1993/94 and in 1999/2000, the household types on the MoL criterion were ranked, in ascending order on the HCR measure, as follows: 'others' (with the lowest HCR); self-employed in agriculture; self-employed in non-agriculture; other rural labour; and the agricultural labour households with the highest HCR. This was also the rank-ordering on the PGI and FGT* measures in 1999/2000 for the SC households and on the PGI measure for the residual (non-SC, non-ST) social group of 'others' in both 1993/94 and in 1999/2000. For this residual social group of 'others', in both years, the rank-ordering on FGT* was broadly similar except that the MoL category self-employed in agriculture reported a lower level of deprivation than the 'others' on the MoL categorisation.

For the ST population in rural India, the rank-ordering on the PGI measure for both years and on the FGT* measure for 1999/2000 was such that the lowest level of deprivation was reported by the MoL category 'others', followed, in ascending order of deprivation, by: other (non-agricultural) labour; the self-employed in agriculture; the self-employed in non-agriculture; and the agricultural labour households. In 1993/94, however, among the rural ST population, the MoL category 'other labour' reports a lower level of FGT* than the 'others', which latter, in turn, was lower than the FGT* for the self-employed in agriculture.

In all the three social groups and in both the years, the agricultural labour households experienced the highest level of poverty (across MoL categories) on all the three poverty measures of HCR, PGI, and FGT.* Across social groups, the agricultural labour households in the rural ST population record the highest levels of poverty in terms of HCR, PGI, and FGT*, followed by the agricultural labour households among the SCs. The lowest HCR (and PGI and FGT*) among the agricultural labour households is recorded by such households belonging to the residual, non-ST, non-SC social group 'others'. Even though the levels of HCR (and PGI and FGT*) for the agricultural labour households belonging to the social group 'others' is the lowest across social groups, their levels of deprivation on all the three measures of poverty are greater than that recorded by any other MoL category in any social group. And this is true for both 1993/94 and 1999/2000.

In examining the changes between 1993/94 and 1999/2000 in respect of the prevalence, depth, and severity measures of poverty for the three social groups each further differentiated by household types on the MoL category (Table 13.7R), it would be useful to recollect that, while the SC households matched the performance of the total rural population in terms of poverty reduction on all the three measures, poverty-reduction was very sluggish for the ST population in terms of all the three measures.

Focusing first on the sluggish performance in poverty-reduction for the ST population, further disaggregation by MoL categories (see Table 13.7R) shows that, except in respect of the MoL category

Table 13.7R Percentage Change (1993/94 and 1999/2000) in Poverty Indicators by
Socio-Economic Categories of All-India Rural Population

Socio-economic Category	HCR	PGI	FGT*
Scheduled castes			
1. Self-employed agricultural	−14.80	−25.97	−35.09
2. Self-employed non-agricultural	−7.95	−11.78	−16.72
3. Agricultural labour	−18.98	−27.50	−34.04
4. Other labour	−14.40	−5.89	−3.20
5. Others	−31.93	−44.90	−50.68
All scheduled castes	*−16.00*	*−23.62*	*−29.93*
Scheduled tribes			
1. Self-employed agricultural	−7.69	−10.95	−15.48
2. Self-employed non-agricultural	−10.80	−12.62	−21.92
3. Agricultural labour	1.98	0.94	−1.56
4. Other labour	−4.39	−6.73	−11.66
5. Others	−30.49	−30.74	−22.72
All scheduled tribes	*−1.62*	*−2.79*	*−5.64*
Others			
1. Self-employed agricultural	−19.78	−26.13	−32.37
2. Self-employed non-agricultural	−20.74	−22.85	−28.97
3. Agricultural labour	−18.26	−26.43	−32.41
4. Other labour	−29.38	−27.86	−30.45
5. Others	−26.20	−35.29	−36.91
Social group others	*−17.92*	*−23.29*	*−28.42*
MoL category, all social groups			
MoL categories, all social groups	−17.10	−22.98	−28.77
Self-employed non-agricultural	−17.44	−20.01	−26.25
Agricultural labour	−15.73	−22.66	−28.00
Other labour	−22.42	−19.54	−20.92
Others	−31.17	−40.49	−42.33
All households	*−15.38*	*−20.47*	*−25.43*

'others' where the percentage reduction in HCR (but less so in respect of PGI and FGT*) matches that recorded by this MoL category in the entire rural population, in all the other MoL categories, *the performance of ST households has been worse than the average reduction in poverty in the comparative MoL category in the total rural population. Within the ST population, agriculture labour households have fared the worst on all three measures: a 2 per cent rise in HCR, a 1 per cent rise in PGI, and a small, 1.5 per cent decline in FGT*.* In contrast, in the total rural population, agricultural labour households recorded declines of 16, 23, and 28 per cent, respectively, in HCR, PGI, and FGT*. The performance of the other rural labour households in the rural ST population, though better than that of the agricultural labour households, is seen to be substantially below that for the total rural population as a whole as well as the poverty-reduction achieved by the other labour households in the total rural population. The poor performance of the labour households (especially the agricultural labour households) together with the rise in the share of such households in the total rural ST population has been a major factor underlying the relative poor performance in poverty reduction of the ST population in rural India.

Except for those of them located in the ST population, agricultural labour households – whether among the SC population or in the social group 'others' – have recorded reduction in poverty (on all the three measures) that are on par with or better than that recorded by the total rural population.

For the SCs, two MoL categories, namely, the self-employed in non-agriculture and the other (than agricultural) rural labour households have experienced smaller (percentage) reduction in poverty than the SC population as a whole. In respect of HCR (but not PGI and FGT*), the SC households self-employed in agriculture also experienced a smaller (percentage) decline than that for the rural SC population and that for the total rural population.

In respect of the omnibus group of 'others' on the social group affiliation, all household types on the MoL categorisation are seen to have experienced larger percentage declines (over the 1993/94 levels) in respect of HCR, PGI, and FGT* than that experienced by the entire rural population. In fact, in comparison with the percentage reduction experienced by a comparator MoL category in the total rural population, the comparable household type in the social groups 'others' have experienced (in all but one MoL category) greater percentage reduction in all three measures of poverty: HCR, PGI, and FGT*. The exception, surprisingly, is the residual MoL category 'others'.

We turn now to a consideration of the levels of and the changes in poverty indicators for each social group cross-classified by the principal means of livelihood in the *urban areas of all-India* (see Tables 13.6U HCR, 13.6U PGI, and 13.6U FGT* for the level and 13.7U for rates of change).

On all the three indicators, in both the years, and in all the three social groups, the lowest level of poverty is recorded by the regular wage/salaried worker households and the highest levels by the casual labour households. And, except in respect of PGI and FGT* for the urban SC households in 1993/94 and in respect of FGT* for the urban ST households in 1999/2000, poverty levels were lower for the MoL category 'others' than for the urban self-employed.

In terms of changes in poverty levels between 1993/94 and 1999/2000, we had noted earlier that, taken as a group, the urban SC households had experienced reductions in poverty (on all the three indicators) of an order broadly similar to or better than that for the total urban population. This was made possible by the fact that, in respect of each and all the three indicators, the regular wage/salaried earner households in the SC population experienced much higher percentage-reduction not only relative to the average for the social group in total urban population but also relative to that experienced by the regular wage/salary earner households in the total urban population (see Table 13.7U). Also, while the poverty-reduction experienced by the casual labour households in the SC population was smaller than that experienced by casual labour households in the total urban population, it was close to or above the percentage declines experienced by the total urban population in respect of PGI and FGT* (but not HCR). Significantly, among the scheduled caste population, the self-employed experienced the smallest percentage reduction in HCR, PGI, and FGT* across households types.

We had noted earlier that, while the total urban population experienced fairly sizeable declines in poverty (on all the three indicators) between 1993/94 and 1999/2000, the ST households, as a group, had experienced a rise in poverty on all the three indicators. A disaggregation by MoL categories reveals an interesting result: even among the urban ST population, two groups, namely the self-employed (on all three indicators) and the regular wage/salaried earner households (on HCR and PGI but not on FGT*)

Table 13.7U Percentage Change (1993/94–1999/2000) in Poverty Indicators by
Socio-economic Categories of All-India Urban Population

Socio-economic Category	HCR	PGI	FGT*
Scheduled castes			
Self-employed	−2.50	−11.99	−15.83
Wage/Salary earner	−33.16	−37.75	−46.09
Casual labour	−9.23	−16.96	−23.83
Others	−11.14	−32.80	−48.46
All scheduled castes	*−11.69*	*−13.67*	*−25.34*
Scheduled tribes			
Self-employed	−6.95	−9.51	−9.15
Wage/Salary earner	−8.65	−6.46	6.81
Casual labour	12.38	7.67	−0.60
Others	−3.22	47.25	158.53
All scheduled tribes	*4.52*	*7.51*	*12.61*
Others			
Self-employed	−10.30	−12.52	−18.91
Wage/Salary earner	−26.86	−28.55	−35.21
Casual labour	−16.84	−20.94	−23.86
Others	−22.71	−31.23	−42.50
Social group (others)	*−14.45*	*−17.63*	*−22.41*
MoL category, all social groups			
Self-employed	−8.39	−12.94	−17.36
Wage/Salary earner	−27.27	−29.43	−35.33
Casual labour	−12.75	−17.94	−22.18
Others	−19.95	−28.89	−38.94
All households	*−12.57*	*−16.00*	*−20.79*

do experience a reduction in poverty over the same period. Even the residual MoL category of 'others' experienced a small (3 per cent) reduction in HCR. However, for reasons not clear, the MoL category of 'others' in the ST population experienced a very large percentage rise in PGI and an even larger (percentage) rise in FGT*. Clearly, therefore, the overall increase in poverty in terms of HCR and PGI for the urban ST population (taken as a group) is driven by the sizeable rise in HCR and PGI for the casual labour households and the increase in the share of such households in the urban ST population. The 13 per cent rise in FGT* for the total ST population in the urban areas, on the other hand, is primarily driven by the (somewhat inexplicable) rise in FGT* for the regular wage/salaried worker households in the urban ST population.

As noted earlier for the rural population, in the residual (non-SC, non-ST) social group of 'others', all the MoL categories experience a greater reduction in poverty (in all the three indicators) than that experienced by the comparative household types in the total urban population. However, for the self-employed in this omnibus social group of 'others', the percentage reduction in HCR (as well as in PGI and in FGT*) has been less than that experienced by the total urban population. So that, relative to the total urban population, the poverty reduction of the urban self-employed in the social group, 'others' –

as also the self-employed in the SC and those in the ST population and, therefore, also the self-employed in the total urban population – has worsened relative to the total urban population.

POVERTY OUTCOMES IN THE 15 MAJOR STATES

State-level Changes in Poverty-indicators over the 1990s

In tracking the changes in poverty over the 1990s at the state-level, four indicators are used: the HCR; the size of the poor population; the PGI, which reflects the depth of poverty; and, the FGT* which is a measure of severity of poverty. Of the four measures, PGI and FGT* are sensitive to the distribution of the poor population below the poverty line. These distribution-sensitive measures are proportional to headcount ratio and, hence, usually (though not always) move in the same direction as HCR. We would be noting the exceptions in the subsequent analysis. Similarly, while a rise in HCR would necessarily lead

Table 13.8R HCR and the Size of Poor Population on Uniform and Mixed Reference Periods in 15 Major States: 1983–1999/2000

15 Major States Rural Population

States	HCR on URP (%)		HCR on MRP (%)		No. of Poor (000) on URP		No. of Poor (000) on MRP	
	1983	1993/94	1993/94	1999/2000	1983	1993/94	1993/94	1999/2000
(1)	(2)	(3)	(4)	(5)	(6)	(7)	(8)	(9)
Andhra Pradesh	34.91	28.60	23.86	22.01	14,923	14,418	12,028	11,975
Assam	49.21	57.85	51.08	53.41	8,391	12,046	10,636	12,202
Bihar	70.43	65.73	60.94	51.49	45,203	53,316	49,431	47,871
Gujarat	36.30	30.20	24.70	18.89	8,818	8,552	6,994	5,881
Haryana	24.00	30.05	24.43	7.83	2,544	3,938	3,202	1,148
Karnataka	40.24	38.27	29.88	24.09	11,040	12,288	9,295	8,279
Kerala	47.18	34.09	30.30	16.47	9,875	7,503	6,668	3,839
Madhya Pradesh	54.03	36.65	29.45	32.93	23,572	19,615	15,761	19,640
Maharashtra	54.02	51.06	44.83	37.65	22,950	27,589	24,223	20,650
Orissa	65.04	59.57	55.52	56.27	15,725	16,951	15,799	17,299
Punjab	18.44	11.68	12.00	8.73	2,326	1,727	1,774	1,383
Rajasthan	41.99	26.25	19.27	11.39	11,979	9,544	7,006	4,791
Tamil Nadu	56.82	37.87	32.89	27.69	18,989	13,807	11,992	9,750
Uttar Pradesh	49.76	39.14	34.03	25.50	47,481	46,352	40,300	34,293
West Bengal	65.86	53.37	48.33	44.18	27,744	27,546	24,945	25,048
15-States (Wt. Ave.) Total	51.27	43.01	37.47	31.86	271,560	275,192	240,054	224,049

Notes: 1. All numbers in Columns 4 and 8 (in italic) are the revised estimates.
2. Last line is population-weighted averages for the 15 states.
3. URP – Uniform reference period of 30 days for all items of consumer expenditure.
MRP – Mixed-reference period of 30 days for all items other than clothing, footwear, education, medical (institutional), and durables which have a reference period of 365 days.

Sources: 1. Tendulkar, Sundaram, and Jain (1993) for 1983.
2. Figures for 1993/94 and 1999/2000 are based on calculations of the authors from the unit-level records for the 50th and 55th Rounds.

to an increase in the size of poor population, the number of poor can increase despite a decline in HCR when the growth of estimated population exceeds the extent of decline in HCR.

Let us consider first the changes in *rural poverty*.

Table 13.8R presents the estimates of HCR and of the size of poor population for three time-points: 1983, 1993/94, and 1999/2000. (The underlying, state-specific and segment-specific poverty lines for 1983, 1993/94, and 1999/2000 are presented in Table A4).

For the year 1993/94, we present two sets of estimates: estimates on a URP of 30 days for all items of expenditure from the published results that are directly comparable with the estimates for 1983 (and all the previous quinquennial rounds); and, estimates on a MRP computed by us from unit record data that are comparable (as argued earlier) with the 55th Round Consumer Expenditure Survey (30-day for the food group) results. Parallel estimates of PGI and FGT* are presented in Table 13.9.

Table 13.9R PGI & FGT* on Uniform and Mixed Reference Periods: 1983–1999/2000

(15 Major States Rural Population)

States	PGI on URP		PGI on URP		FGT* on URP		FGT* on MRP	
	1983	1993/94	1993/94	1999/2000	1983	1993/94	1993/94	1999/2000
(1)	(2)	(3)	(4)	(5)	(6)	(7)	(8)	(9)
Andhra Pradesh	0.0807	0.0563	0.0445	0.0394	0.0282	0.0176	0.0134	0.0116
Assam	0.0997	0.1264	0.1008	0.1236	0.0294	0.0380	0.0288	0.0419
Bihar	0.2355	0.1820	0.1528	0.1099	0.1015	0.0671	0.0529	0.0335
Gujarat	0.0749	0.0612	0.0459	0.0347	0.0229	0.0185	0.0131	0.0100
Haryana	0.0464	0.0632	0.0458	0.0132	0.0141	0.0200	0.0136	0.0038
Karnataka	0.1117	0.0868	0.0617	0.0432	0.0429	0.0291	0.0194	0.0117
Kerala	0.1301	0.0830	0.0678	0.0280	0.0491	0.0291	0.0227	0.0076
Madhya Pradesh	0.1542	0.0821	0.0600	0.0646	0.0602	0.0277	0.0188	0.0190
Maharashtra	0.1527	0.1448	0.1132	0.0867	0.0582	0.0569	0.0408	0.0285
Orissa	0.2078	0.1529	0.1323	0.1478	0.0907	0.0551	0.0448	0.0534
Punjab	0.0358	0.0270	0.0185	0.0115	0.0105	0.0071	0.0044	0.0026
Rajasthan	0.1226	0.0517	0.0338	0.0170	0.0496	0.0155	0.0091	0.0041
Tamil Nadu	0.1842	0.0896	0.0744	0.0552	0.0801	0.0315	0.0252	0.0170
Uttar Pradesh	0.1337	0.0922	0.0707	0.0438	0.0525	0.0305	0.0214	0.0116
West Bengal	0.2238	0.1259	0.1062	0.0959	0.1015	0.0412	0.0330	0.0311
15-States (Wt. Ave.) Total	0.1491	0.1039	0.0831	0.0653	0.0603	0.0361	0.0269	0.0202

Notes: 1. All numbers in Columns (4) and (8) (in bold) are the revised estimates.
2. Last line is population-weighted averages for the 15 states.
3. URP: Uniform reference period of 30 days for all items of consumer expenditure.
   MRP: Mixed-reference period of 30 days for all items other than clothing, footwear, education, medical (institutional), and durables which have a reference period of 365 days.
4. PGI denotes poverty gap index and FGT* denotes squared poverty gap in the Foster-Grear-Thorebecke class of poverty indicators.

Sources: 1. Tendulkar, Sundaram, and Jain (1993) for 1983.
2. Figures for 1993/94 and 1999/2000 are based on calculations of the authors from the unit level records for the 50th and 55th Rounds.

Focusing on the changes over the 1990s, comparable MRP estimates for each of the 15 major states and a population-weighted measure for the 15 states taken together are presented in Columns 4 and 5 (for HCR in Table 13.8R and for PGI in Table 13.9R) and in Columns 8 and 9 (for the size of poor population in Table 13.8R and for FGT* in Table 13.9R).

Consider first the *direction and magnitude of changes in poverty ratio (HCR) and in the size of the poor population between 1993/94 and 1999/2000 in rural India.* In terms of the HCR, poverty has shown a distinct decline in all but three of the 15 states, with the population-weighted average for all the states taken together declining by a little over 5.5 percentage points or a little under 1 percentage point per annum. When further normalised by reference to the base year value of HCR, this will translate to a

Table 13.10U HCRs and the Size of Poor Population on Uniform and
Mixed Reference Periods: 1983–1999/2000

(15 Major States Urban Population)

States	HCR on URP (%)		HCR on MRP (%)		No. of Poor (000) on URP		No. of poor (000) on MRP	
	1983	1993/94	1993/94	1999/2000	1983	1993/94	1993/94	1999/2000
(1)	(2)	(3)	(4)	(5)	(6)	(7)	(8)	(9)
Andhra Pradesh	35.49	36.80	*32.13*	25.91	4,820	6,841	*5,973*	5,230
Assam	21.02	10.36	*6.71*	9.58	405	281	*182*	313
Bihar	51.29	46.30	*39.41*	44.11	4,754	5,711	*4,861*	6,280
Gujarat	37.34	29.44	*24.65*	16.81	4,241	4,544	*3,805*	3,073
Haryana	21.30	11.41	*7.70*	7.49	655	520	*350*	436
Karnataka	37.65	33.09	*28.87*	17.59	4,291	4,945	*4,314*	3,060
Kerala	47.78	27.90	*26.64*	23.49	2,547	2,188	*2,089*	1,926
Madhya Pradesh	51.95	46.62	*41.44*	38.89	5,988	7,742	*6,882*	7,633
Maharashtra	40.36	33.29	*29.22*	25.82	9,583	11,848	*10,399*	10,234
Orissa	52.54	38.49	*35.94*	41.92	1,755	1,755	*1,638*	2,235
Punjab	21.58	6.97	*5.16*	2.91	1,064	457	*338*	461
Rajasthan	37.22	32.30	*26.45*	15.72	2,901	3,512	*2,876*	2,011
Tamil Nadu	45.14	38.67	*34.69*	22.99	7,508	8,161	*7,321*	6,008
Uttar Pradesh	48.14	34.84	*30.40*	31.75	10.337	10,424	*9,096*	11,268
West Bengal	28.83	21.41	*16.08*	12.95	4,424	4,219	*3,169*	2,850
15-States (Wt. Ave.) Total	*40.61*	*33.05*	*28.60*	*24.58*	*65,273*	*73,148*	*63,293*	*63,018*

Notes: 1. All numbers in Columns 4 and 8 (in italics) are the revised estimates.
    2. Last line is population-weighted averages for the fifteen states.
    3. URP – Uniform reference period of 30 days for all items of consumer expenditure.
       MRP – Mixed-reference period of 30 days for all items other than clothing, footwear, education, medical (institutional), and durables which have a reference period of 365 days.
    4. PGI denotes poverty gap index and FGT* denotes squared poverty gap in the Foster-Grear-Thorebecke class of poverty indicators.

Sources: 1. Tendulkar, Sundaram, and Jain (1993) for 1983.
    2. Figures for 1993/94 and 1999/2000 are based on calculations of the authors from the unit-level records for the 50th and 55th Rounds.

rate of decline of a little over 4 per cent per annum. The three states that are an exception to this general and widespread decline in rural poverty are *Assam, Madhya Pradesh*, and *Orissa*.

In terms of the size of the poor population, in the 15 states taken together, there was a distinct decline in the number of poor by close to 16 million, from 240 million to 224 million. Despite a decline in HCR, *West Bengal* joins *Assam, Madhya Pradesh*, and *Orissa* in recording a rise in the number of poor: by 1.6 million in Assam, 3.9 million in Madhya Pradesh, and 1.5 million in Orissa and, a marginal 0.1 million in West Bengal.

The results in terms of the distribution-sensitive measures are in line with the changes in HCR noted above. The 15-state (population) weighted average PGI (on MRP) declines over the six years, from 0.0831 to 0.0653 (21 per cent), while FGT* declines from 0.0269 to 0.0202 (25 per cent).

Tables 13.10U and 13.11U present the estimates of poverty indicators for the *urban* population of the 15 major states.

Table 13.11U PGI & FGT* on Uniform and Mixed Reference Periods: 1983–1999/2000

(15 Major States Urban Population)

States	PGI on URP (%)		PGI on MRP		FGT on URP		FGT* on MRP	
	1983	1993/94	1993/94	1999/2000	1983	1993/94	1993/94	1999/2000
(1)	(2)	(3)	(4)	(5)	(6)	(7)	(8)	(9)
Andhra Pradesh	0.0868	0.0852	*0.0726*	0.0517	0.0309	0.0291	*0.0241*	0.0157
Assam	0.0392	0.0131	*0.0093*	0.0186	0.0110	0.0031	*0.0024*	0.0054
Bihar	0.1494	0.1157	*0.0944*	0.1061	0.0575	0.0415	*0.0327*	0.0357
Gujarat	0.0743	0.0663	*0.0519*	0.0283	0.0218	0.0213	*0.0158*	0.0077
Haryana	0.0409	0.0197	*0.0136*	0.0171	0.0122	0.0054	*0.0036*	0.0064
Karnataka	0.1038	0.0844	*0.0656*	0.0352	0.0400	0.0303	*0.0218*	0.0109
Kerala	0.1459	0.0669	*0.0608*	0.0493	0.0601	0.0235	*0.0209*	0.0151
Madhya Pradesh	0.1363	0.1270	*0.1018*	0.0968	0.0495	0.0470	*0.0355*	0.0338
Maharashtra	0.1166	0.0957	*0.0758*	0.0641	0.0466	0.0388	*0.0288*	0.0227
Orissa	0.1531	0.1022	*0.0901*	0.1040	0.0596	0.0373	*0.0314*	0.0362
Punjab	0.0463	0.0101	*0.0075*	0.0035	0.0141	0.0022	*0.0018*	0.0007
Rajasthan	0.0953	0.0732	*0.0544*	0.0287	0.0344	0.0238	*0.0161*	0.0073
Tamil Nadu	0.1289	0.0971	*0.0818*	0.0497	0.0515	0.0371	*0.0300*	0.0161
Uttar Pradesh	0.1327	0.0894	*0.0721*	0.0699	0.0498	0.0323	*0.0243*	0.0216
West Bengal	0.0662	0.0405	*0.0316*	0.0226	0.0231	0.0125	*0.0096*	0.0061
15-States (Wt. Ave.) Total	*0.1083*	*0.0837*	*0.0669*	*0.0544*	*0.0406*	*0.0301*	*0.0231*	*0.0176*

Notes: 1. All numbers in Columns 4 and 8 (in italics) are the revised estimates.
     2. Last line is population-weighted averages for the 15 states.
     3. URP – Uniform reference period of 30 days for all items of consumer expenditure.
       MRP – Mixed-reference period of 30 days for all items other than clothing, footwear, education, medical (institutional), and durables which have a reference period of 365 days.
     4. PGI denotes poverty gap index and FGT* denotes squared poverty gap in the Foster-Grear-Thorebecke class of poverty indicators.

Sources: 1. Tendulkar, Sundaram, and Jain (1993) for 1983.
     2. Figures for 1993/94 and 1999/2000 are based on calculations of the authors from the unit level records for the 50th and 55th Rounds.

Again focusing on the changes between 1993/94 and 1999/2000 (Columns 4 and 5, and 8 and 9 of the two tables) consider first the changes in HCR.

Four states – *Assam, Bihar, Orissa,* and *Uttar Pradesh* – show a rise in urban HCR ranging between 1.4 percentage points in Uttar Pradesh and 6 points in Orissa. *All the remaining 11 states record a decline in HCR* and this decline has been sizeable – 6 percentage points or more – in Andhra Pradesh, Gujarat, Karnataka, Rajasthan, and Tamil Nadu. The 15-state weighted average HCR also shows a decline of a little over 4 percentage points – from 28.6 per cent in 1993/94 to 24.6 per cent in 1999/2000.

In terms of the *size of the poor population,* in addition to the four states (*Assam, Bihar, Orissa,* and *Uttar Pradesh*) which experienced a rise in HCR, *Haryana, Madhya Pradesh* and *Punjab* also recorded a rise in the number of poor despite a decline in HCR. All other states show a decline in the *size* of poor population. For the 15 states taken together, the size of the urban poor population has declined only marginally from 63.3 million in 1994 to 63 million in 2000.

In terms of the distribution-sensitive measures, Haryana which recorded a marginal decline in HCR but a rise in the number of poor *showed an increase in PGI and FGT**. All other states recording a decline in HCR also showed a decline in PGI and FGT*. Among the four states which recorded a *rise* in headcount ratio, *Uttar Pradesh records a decline in both PGI and FGT**. In *Assam, Bihar* and *Orissa,* both the distribution-sensitive indicators show a rise in poverty in line with the rise in HCR in those states.

Table 13.12 HCRs and the Size of Poor Population on Uniform and Mixed Reference Periods: 1983–1999/2000

[15 Major States Total (Rural + Urban) Population]

States	HCR on URP (%)		HCR on MRP (%)		No. of Poor (000) on URP		No. of Poor (000) on MRP	
	1983	1993/94	1993/94	1999/2000	1983	1993/94	1993/94	1999/2000
(1)	(2)	(3)	(4)	(5)	(6)	(7)	(8)	(9)
Andhra Pradesh	35.05	30.81	26.09	23.07	19,743	21,259	18,001	17,205
Assam	46.35	52.37	45.96	47.94	8,796	12,327	10,818	12,515
Bihar	68.01	63.16	58.10	50.51	49,957	59,027	54,292	54,151
Gujarat	36.63	29.93	24.68	18.12	13,059	13,096	10,799	8,954
Haryana	23.40	25.24	20.11	7.73	3,199	4,458	3,552	1,584
Karnataka	39.48	36.63	29.55	21.91	15,331	17,233	13,609	11,339
Kerala	47.30	32.47	29.34	18.30	12,422	9,691	8,757	5,765
Madhya Pradesh	53.59	39.01	32.29	34.41	29,560	27,357	22,643	27,273
Maharashtra	49.12	44.00	38.67	32.69	32,533	39,437	34,622	30,884
Orissa	63.52	56.65	52.82	54.14	17,480	18,706	17,437	19,534
Punjab	19.32	13.69	9.89	7.75	3,390	2,923	2,112	1,844
Rajasthan	40.97	27.64	20.92	12.40	14,880	13,056	9,882	6,802
Tamil Nadu	52.94	38.16	33.55	25.69	26,497	21,968	19,313	15,758
Uttar Pradesh	49.46	38.27	33.30	26.80	57,518	56,776	49,396	45,561
West Bengal	55.97	44.54	39.42	35.45	32,168	31,765	28,114	27,898
15-States (Wt. Ave.) Total	48.79	40.46	35.19	29.92	336,833	349,079	303,347	287,067

Note: All numbers in Columns 4 and 8 (in italics) are the revised estimates.
Source: Population-weighted averages calculated from Tables 13.8R and 13.10U.

Taking both rural and the urban population together, i.e. for each state taken as a whole, *only three states recording a rise in HCR* (*Assam, Madhya Pradesh* and *Orissa*) also show an increase in poverty in terms of the size of poor population (Table 13.12).

In terms of PGI and FGT* (see Table 13.13) only two states, *Assam* and *Orissa* show an increase in poverty in both indicators. In Madhya Pradesh, while PGI shows a rise, FGT* in 1999/2000 is fractionally lower. *Thus, in an overwhelming majority of the 15 major states of India, all the measures of poverty show an unambiguous decline in poverty.* In all these states taken together, the size of poor population declined by a little over 16 million at an average rate of 2.7 million per annum. The 15-state weighted average HCR declined by 5.3 percentage points. In terms of the distribution-sensitive measure (PGI and FGT*) the 15-state weighted average ratios show fairly sizeable declines (by close to 19 per cent over the 1993/94 values for PGI and by a little over 25 per cent for FGT*).

Table 13.13 PGI and FGT* on URP and MRP: 1983–1999/2000

[15 Major States Total (Rural + Urban) Population]

States	PGI on URP		PGI on MRP		FGT on URP		FGT* on MRP	
	1983	1993/94	1993/94	1999/2000	1983	1993/94	1993/94	1999/2000
(1)	(2)	(3)	(4)	(5)	(6)	(7)	(8)	(9)
Andhra Pradesh	0.0822	0.0641	*0.0521*	0.0427	0.0289	0.0207	*0.0163*	0.0127
Assam	0.0936	0.1133	*0.0902*	0.1105	0.0275	0.0340	*0.0258*	0.0373
Bihar	0.2246	0.1732	*0.1451*	0.1094	0.0959	0.0637	*0.0502*	0.0338
Gujarat	0.0747	0.0630	*0.0480*	0.0323	0.0225	0.0195	*0.0141*	0.0091
Haryana	0.0452	0.0520	*0.0375*	0.0143	0.0137	0.0162	*0.0110*	0.0045
Karnataka	0.1094	0.0860	*0.0630*	0.0405	0.0420	0.0295	*0.0202*	0.0114
Kerala	0.1333	0.0788	*0.0660*	0.0335	0.0513	0.0280	*0.0222*	0.0096
Madhya Pradesh	0.1505	0.0927	*0.0699*	0.0726	0.0580	0.0323	*0.0228*	0.0227
Maharashtra	0.1398	0.1253	*0.0983*	0.0772	0.0540	0.0497	*0.0360*	0.0261
Orissa	0.2012	0.1459	*0.1265*	0.1413	0.0869	0.0526	*0.0430*	0.0509
Punjab	0.0388	0.0218	*0.0151*	0.0088	0.0115	0.0056	*0.0036*	0.0020
Rajasthan	0.1167	0.0566	*0.0385*	0.0197	0.0463	0.0174	*0.0107*	0.0048
Tamil Nadu	0.1658	0.0923	*0.0771*	0.0529	0.0706	0.0336	*0.0270*	0.0166
Uttar Pradesh	0.1335	0.0916	*0.0710*	0.0492	0.0520	0.0309	*0.0220*	0.0137
West Bengal	0.2126	0.1023	*0.0856*	0.0754	0.0806	0.0333	*0.0265*	0.0241
15-States (Wt. Ave.) Total	*0.1420*	*0.0988*	*0.0789*	*0.0642*	*0.0557*	*0.0346*	*0.0259*	*0.0194*

Note: All numbers in Columns 4 and 8 (in italics) are the revised estimates.
Source: Population-weighted averages calculated from Tables 13.9R and 13.11U.

Has Poverty Declined Faster in the 1990s?

In seeking to answer the question whether the performance of the economy in the area of poverty alleviation has been better (or worse) during the six years between 1993/94 and 1999/2000 than that during the preceding ten-and-a-half years between (1 July) 1983 and (1 January) 1994 we need to set up the comparisons carefully.

Note first that, the levels of poverty indicators for 1983, based as they are on size-distributions of per capita consumer expenditure with a URP of 30 days for all items of expenditure, are not directly comparable to the MRP-based estimates for 1999/2000. However, since, for 1993/94, we have both

URP- and MRP-based estimates, we can compare the changes in the comparable levels of poverty indicators between 1983 and 1993/94 on URP and between 1993/94 and 1999/2000 on MRP as we did in the previous section.

There are, however, two residual issues of comparability of the relative performance in poverty alleviation between the two periods.

The first of these problems is the more obvious one of unequal lengths of the time-intervals: ten-and-a-half years between 1983 and 1993/94 and 6 years between 1993/94 and 1999/2000. This is readily overcome by computing the average change per annum over the two periods.

The second issue in setting up valid comparisons of relative performance turns on the initial levels from which the changes are measured: a 10 percentage point decline in, say, HCR from an initial level of 35 per cent cannot be equated with a 10 percentage point decline from an initial level of 55 per cent.

Normalisation of the absolute average annual change for initial values is thus essential – both for comparisons over time and across states. This normalisation, of course, has to be over and above that for the differing lengths of the time-intervals between 1983 and 1993/94 on the one hand and that between 1993/94 and 1999/2000 on the other.

In view of the foregoing discussion, we present in Annexure Tables A.5R (for rural population), A.5U (for urban population) and A.5T (for the total rural-plus-urban population), the average annual change in poverty indicators between 1983 and 1993/94 and that between 1993/94 and 1999/2000 expressed as a percentage of the URP-based estimates for 1983 and the MRP-based estimates for 1993/94 respectively.

Rural Population

Let us consider first the poverty situation in the rural areas of the 15 major states.

To place the widespread decline in rural poverty during the 1990s in perspective it needs to be noted that the *ten-and-a-half years between 1983 and 1993/94 too had witnessed a significant and broad-based decline in poverty in terms of HCR, PGI, and FGT* – with only Assam and Haryana recording a rise in these indicators. In terms of the size of poor population,* however, *six of the 15 states* (Assam, Bihar, Haryana, Karnataka, Maharashtra, and Orissa) and, *the aggregate for 15 states taken as a group, recorded an increase in the size of the rural poor population between 1983 and 1993/94.*

Among the states that recorded a decline in rural poverty in terms of HCR during the 1980s, *Madhya Pradesh* (which also recorded a decline in poverty in terms of the number of poor, PGI, and FGT* during the 1980s) and *Orissa* (which recorded a decline in PGI and FGT* but not in the number of poor during the 1980s) are the two states which register a worsening of poverty situation in the 1990s in terms of a rise in HCR, in the number of rural poor and a rise in PGI and FGT*. *Among the other states that recorded a decline in HCR (as well as PGI and FGT*) during the 1980s, in three states – Andhra Pradesh, Tamil Nadu, and West Bengal – the annual average rate of reduction in the three indicators during the 1990s has been lower.* In Andhra Pradesh, the normalised average annual reduction in the number of rural poor is also lower in the 1990s than during the 1980s. In Tamil Nadu, aided by a very sharp drop in growth of rural population, the annual average decline in the number of rural poor is greater in the 1990s, despite a slower decline in HCR. In West Bengal, the number of rural poor recorded an increase in the 1990s after a decline in the 1980s.

As noted in the previous section, *Assam is the only state that recorded a rise in all the four indicators of rural poverty in the 1980s as well as in the 1990s. The normalised rate of rise in HCR and in the number of rural poor has been slower during the 1990s, but higher in the case of the distribution-sensitive PGI and FGT* poverty measures.*

For the 1980s, Haryana, in addition to Assam *recorded a rise in all the four poverty indicators. Haryana* parted company with Assam *during the 1990s and recorded a very sharp fall in all the four indicators* with the average annual decline as a percentage of the (MRP-based) levels for 1993/94 ranging between 11 and 12 per cent.

In the case of all other states and on all the four indicators the average annual rate of decline in rural poverty has been greater, with Bihar, Karnataka and Maharashtra recording a sizeable decline in the number of rural poor during the 1990s in contrast to the rise in the size of the population of rural poor in these states between 1983 and 1993/94. The worsening of rural poverty in the three large states between 1983 and 1993/94 and an improvement between 1993/94 and 1999/2000 get reflected in the aggregate performance of 15 major states: an increase in the size of rural poor population by 3.6 million during the ten-and-a-half years (1983/94) and a decline of 16 million in the following six years (Table 13.8R).

Urban Population

We turn now to a consideration of changes in urban poverty in the 15 major states in the two periods.

Prima facie, in a number of states, 1980s appear better for urban poverty outcomes than the 1990s on the basis of the normalised average rate of annual changes (Table A.5U). A remarkable feature of the 1980s was that in respect of both the distribution-sensitive indicators, namely, PGI and FGT*, each and all of the 15 major states experienced a decline in *urban poverty.* In respect of HCR, 14 of the 15 states, recorded a decline in urban poverty, with Andhra Pradesh as the sole exception. However, in terms of the size of urban poor population, as many as nine of the 15 states, and therefore, also the 15 states taken together, registered a rise in poverty between 1983 and 1993/94 or an increase of 7.9 million in the size of the urban poor population (Table 13.10U).

In contrast, a mixed picture appears to emerge during the 1990s. Three states, namely, *Assam, Bihar,* and *Orissa,* record a rise in urban poverty on all the four indicators while a fourth state, *Haryana,* records a rise in PGI, FGT*, and in the number of urban poor despite a decline in HCR. *Uttar Pradesh,* like Haryana, is another state where the size of the urban poor population shows an increase during the 1990s despite a fall in the HCR. Unlike Haryana, however, Uttar Pradesh also records a decline in urban poverty during the 1990s in terms of PGI and FGT*. However, in terms of the pace of decline (measured the average annual change as a percentage of respective base year values), the decline in HCR, PGI, and FGT* was slower, while the rise in the number of urban poor was faster in Uttar Pradesh during the 1990s than during the 1980s.

Kerala records a decline in urban poverty on all the indicators in both periods, but the normalised annual average rate of decline is smaller between 1993/94 and 1999/2000 than between 1983 and 1993/ 94 on all the four indicators.

In eight of the nine remaining states (with the exception of Punjab), the performance in urban poverty reduction on all the four indicators has been better between 1993/94 and 1999/2000 than during the preceding ten-and-a-half years. In Andhra Pradesh, a rise in HCR and in the number of urban poor during the 1980s is converted into a decline between 1993/94 and 1999/2000. In *Gujarat, Karnataka, Maharashtra, Rajasthan,* and *Tamil Nadu, and,* also when *the 15 states are considered together,* a rise in the number of urban poor between 1983 and 1993/94 is converted into a decline in the number of urban poor between 1993/94 and 1999/2000. In *Madhya Pradesh,* even though *the number of urban poor* does record a rise between 1993/94 and 1999/2000, *the average annual rise as a percentage of base year value is smaller during the 1990s* than that recorded for the 1980s. *In terms of all the other three indicators,* namely, the HCR, PGI, and FGT*, *the average annual rate of decline in urban Madhya*

Pradesh has been greater during the 1990s than between 1983 and 1993/94. *In Punjab, the poverty-reduction performance was better in the 1990s in terms of HCR, PGI, and FGT*.* But, in terms of the number of poor, we have a decline over the 1980s and a rise over the 1990s.

In the aggregate for the 15 major states as a group, when we use the urban population in the states as weights for aggregating the urban poverty outcomes, a mixed picture for the individual states in the 1990s turns into a decisively better one than the 1980s on all the four indicators. That is to say, a higher rate of reduction in urban poverty (and, in respect of the number of urban poor, a lower rate of increase) on the basis of the normalised average annual rate of change (Table A.5U, last line).

Total (Rural-plus-Urban) Population

Finally, we consider the performance of each state in the two periods when both the rural and the urban populations are considered together (Table A.5T).

In terms of HCR only one state, namely *Assam*, records a rise in poverty in both periods. However, the pace of rise was slower during the 1990s than in the 1980s. Except for *Madhya Pradesh, Orissa –* where a decline in HCR during the 1980s gets converted to a rise during the 1990s – and *West Bengal –* where the pace of decline in HCR is slower in the 1990s – *for the remaining 11 states the normalised pace of decline was faster in the 1990s. The same result also holds true for the two distribution-sensitive indicators, namely PGI and FGT*.* In three states (Madhya Pradesh, Orissa, and West Bengal), the poverty-reduction performance is worse in the 1990s also in terms of PGI and FGT*, with Madhya Pradesh and Orissa recording a rise in PGI and FGT* during the 1990s. In Assam, where the pace of rise in HCR was lower during the 1990s, there was a faster rise in PGI and FGT* during the nineties.

In terms of the *size of the poor population*, in one state, *Madhya Pradesh*, a decline during the 1980s is reversed and the number of poor shows a rise between 1993/94 and 1999/2000, while in *Orissa*, the normalised *rate* of *rise* in the number of poor *was faster during the 1990s* relative to the 1980s. In *Assam*, while the number of poor rose both during the 1980s and the 1990s, *the average annual increase* (as a percentage of the base year size of the poor population) at 2.8 per cent *was smaller in the 1990s* than the corresponding figure for the 1980s (3.8 per cent). In West Bengal, while there was a reduction in the number of poor in both periods, the normalised annual average decline was fractionally lower, during the 1990s. *In all the remaining 11 (out of 15) major states, where the number of poor declined during the 1990s, the performance in poverty reduction was significantly better during the 1990s.* While in six states (Andhra Pradesh, Bihar, Gujarat, Haryana, Karnataka, and Maharashtra), a rise in the number of poor during the 1980s gets converted to a clear decline during the 1990s, in the remaining five states (Kerala, Punjab, Rajasthan, Tamil Nadu, and Uttar Pradesh) the pace of decline in the number of poor was quicker during the 1990s.

Thus, taking both the rural and the urban populations together, in an overwhelming majority of the states (with only Assam, Madhya Pradesh, Orissa, and West Bengal as the exceptions), there was not only a reduction on the four poverty indicators but also a faster rate of normalised average annual decline during the 1990s than in the 1980s and not surprisingly, the same result holds good for the 15 states considered together.

SOME IMPLICATIONS

What implications do the foregoing results have for the design of a strategy for poverty reduction?

One notable feature of the above-stated results is that notwithstanding their social and economic disadvantages, the SC and the agricultural labour households as well as the double-disadvantaged group of agricultural labour households located among the SC population have experienced rates of reduction in all the three poverty indicators HCR, PGI and FGT* that have matched or bettered the poverty reduction experienced by the rural population on the average. The same is true for the urban SCs, the casual labour households as well as the casual labour households in the SC population in urban India. This fact holds the important message that the benefits of growth have indeed helped reduce deprivation of the socially and economically disadvantaged groups in India. Thus, one can, and should, pursue a growth-centred strategy for poverty reduction in India. This is not to deny, however, that, despite matching the average rate of reduction the current *levels* of poverty indicators in these groups continue to be unconscionably high. The failure of the ST population and, in particular, the casual-wage-labour dependent households among them to experience commensurate rates of reduction in poverty would appear to be, in part at least, a reflection of the poverty outcomes in specific states, namely, Assam, Madhya Pradesh, and Orissa (where poverty has increased between 1993/94 and 1999/2000) where the ST population is concentrated.

The second feature relevant to the design of anti-poverty policies and programmes is the sizeable share of the self-employed in the poor in India: 40 per cent in rural India and 44 per cent in urban India with this group being numerically dominant group among the urban poor. At this point it is important to emphasise one neglected feature of the employment situation of the usual status (principal-plus-subsidiary status) workforce in self-employed households that tends to get submerged in general discussions about underemployment in the country. Male workers in these households are at work, on the average, for 344 days in a year in rural India and for 349 days in the year in urban India. Even allowing for the fact that women workers work fewer days in the year (260 days in rural India and 282 days in urban India), usual status workers (males-plus-females) in self-employed households are at work for between 315 (in the case of self-employed in agricultural activities) and 321 days (for self-employed in non-agriculture) in a year in rural India, while in urban India they are at work for 337 days out of the 365 days in the year. Characterisation of this situation as one of underemployment is a serious misrepresentation of the problem: Do we or should we, expect them to be at work on all 365 days in the year?[12] *More important, such a characterisation shifts the focus away from quality of employment in general and productivity in particular towards quantity of employment in terms of number of days of employment.* The central problem of poverty in the self-employed households is *not* that they are at work for only a few days in the year but that the returns to their labour input are too low. So, policy should focus more on raising the returns from the asset-base of the self-employed – chiefly land in rural India – and raising their skill profile – especially in urban India.

In the rural context, this requires a strong push for growth in public investment in rural infrastructure including, but not limited to, irrigation, water conservation, and management. In particular, it must be extended to cover rural roads; telecommunication network; and facilities for storage, preservation, and

---

[12] Admittedly, the participation in economic activity on current daily status (on which are based the number of days at work in a year reported in the text) reflect the self-perceived employment situation on the time-criterion as reported by the respondents. In principle, therefore, the reported number of days at work could conceal a measure of work-sharing and work-spreading in the self-employed households. Inherently, this cannot be quantified. Note, however that, in the Survey, for each of the 7 days in the reference week, a further classification of the reported activity status by intensity (in terms of half intensity and full intensity) is possible, with work on half-intensity on any given day treated as half-a-day's work. And, the reported daily-status situation represents an aggregation (across calendar days) of such half-days and full-days of work. If this situation still reflects a measure of underemployment arising from work-sharing and work-spreading, it cannot be captured in measures based on the current daily status. More important, as argued in the text, the solution to the problem of poverty among the self-employed lies *not* in raising the number of days they are at work in a year – again measured by reference to the current daily status reporting – but by raising the returns to their labour input.

transportation of perishable commodities like vegetables, fruits, and flowers which have a considerable market both domestically and internationally. Given the parlous fiscal situation in virtually all states and the drain on the exchequer – both in the centre and the states – arising from 'remunerative' procurement prices and a host of non-transparent input subsidies, the desired push for public investment in rural infrastructure will not be possible without a conscious effort at fiscal stabilisation along with a switch in government spending from revenue to capital expenditure. From a longer-term perspective, expansion of social services in education, health, water, and sanitation would help improve the quality of rural human resources. This, in turn, would complement and contribute to raising productivity in, what would still remain, a largely agriculture-centred rural growth strategy.

In the urban context, a central component of a strategy to combat poverty among the self-employed would be a conscious effort to raise their skill-profile so that they move up the productivity chain. Skill-development programmes have the further advantage that they can be consciously targeted towards the socially disadvantaged groups of the SCs and STs. Equally important, if not more, we need to expand rapidly the market – both domestic and international – for the goods and services produced in the urban informal sector. And hurdles, such as exclusive reservation for the small-scale sector, would need to be removed. There is also the need to reduce the dichotomy between the formal and the informal sector by the alleviation of labour market inflexibility generated by labour laws that emphasise, perhaps overemphasise, job security, often at the expense of other facets of working conditions.

What about the (casual) wage-labour-dependent households who are numerically the dominant group among the rural poor and account for close to a third of the urban poor?

Admittedly, with work for 278 days (294 days in urban India) in the year, the (casual) wage-labour households are better candidates for policies and programmes aimed at raising their number of days in employment during the year. Further, safety nets, in the form of special employment programmes must continue. And, if, along with raising the number of days at work in a year the real wage rates can be held firm it would certainly reduce poverty among such households. However, as the experience of the labour households over the 1990s has shown, growth in real wages is a strong force for reducing poverty in such households. Greater demand for wage labour at rising real wage rates would require rapid growth with rising labour productivity. *For individual sectors, raising labour productivity requires a slower growth in the number of workers than the growth in value-added.* Greater demand for labour would then have to come about by a faster growth of more labour-intensive sectors (apart from faster overall growth) rather than seeking to enhance the labour-intensity of individual sectors (Sundaram and Tendulkar, 2002).

Overall, therefore, rapid growth must occupy centre stage in any strategy for poverty reduction in India. And, as exemplified by the performance of the SCs and the agricultural labour households over the 1990s, it works.

ACKNOWLEDGEMENT

This chapter provides a consolidation of four papers (Sundaram and Tendulkar, 2003a to 2003d) published earlier in the *Economic and Political Weekly* over the calendar year 2003.

Considerable intellectual debt has been accumulated in this process. Particular thanks are due to Angus Deaton and Valerie Kozel for a rewarding process of dialogue, and Abhijit Sen and Himanshu for pointing out a key error in our earlier results which has since been corrected. Useful discussions and comments from Martin Ravallion, A. Vaidyanathan, and S. Subramanian are gratefully acknowledged. It can be said without exaggeration that without the excellent research support of Shilpa Bogra and Sanjeev Sharma and the typing of Anjali all this would not have been possible and to them we offer our thanks.

REFERENCES

Deaton, A. (2001), Adjusted Indian Poverty Estimates for 1999/2000, *Economic and Political Weekly*, Vol. 37, 25–31 January (Chapter 12 of this book).

Deaton, A. and M. Grosh (2000), 'Consumption', in M. Grosh and P. Glewwe (eds), *Designing Household Survey Questionaires for Developing Countries, Lessons from 15 Years of the Living Standards Measurement Study*, the World Bank, Washington, DC, pp. 91–134.

Foster, J.J. Greer and E. Thorebecke (1984), A Class of Decomposable Poverty Measures, *Econometrica*, Vol. 52, No. 3, pp. 571–76.

NSSO (2001a), 'Level and Pattern of Consumer Expenditure in India, 1999/2000', NSS 55th Round (July 1999–June 2000), Report No. 457, May.

———— (2001b), 'Employment and Unemployment Situation in India, 1999/2000', Part I, NSS 55th Round (July 1997–June 2000), Report No. 458, May.

———— (2000a), 'Choice of Reference Period for Consumption Data based on NSS 51st to 54th Rounds', Report No. 447, March.

———— (2000b), 'Household Consumer Expenditure in India, 1999/2000, Key Results', NSS 55th Round, (July 1999–June 2000), December.

———— (1996), 'Level and Pattern of Consumer Expenditure', 5th Quinquennial Survey, NSS 50th Round, 1993/94, Report No. 402, May.

Sen, Abhijit and Himanshu (2004), 'Poverty and Inequality in India – I', *Economic and Political Weekly*, Vol. 39, 18 September (Chapter 14 of this book).

———— (2004), 'Poverty and Inequality in India – II: Widening Disparities in the 1990s', *Economic and Political Weekly*, Vol. 39, 25 September (Chapter 14 of this book).

Sen, A. (1976), Poverty: An Ordinal Approach to Measurement, *Econometrica*, Vol. 44, No. 2, pp. 219–31.

———— (1993), Poverty in Asia and the Pacific: Conceptual Issues and National Approaches to Measurement, *Economic Bulletin for Asia and the Pacific*, Vol. XLIV, No. 2, December.

Sundaram, K. and Suresh D. Tendulkar (2003a), Poverty Has Declined in the 1990s: A Resolution of Comparability Problems in NSS Consumer Expenditure, *Economic and Political Weekly*, Vol. XXXVIII, No. 4 (January 25–31), pp. 327–37.

———— (2003b), Poverty in India in the 1990s: An Analysis of Changes in 15 Major States, *Economic and Political Weekly*, Vol. XXXVIII, No. 14 (April 15), pp. 1385–93.

———— (2003c), Poverty in India in the 1990s: Revised Results for All-India and 15 Major States, *Economic and Political Weekly*, Vol. XXXVIII, No. 46 (November 15), pp. 4865–72.

———— (2003d): Poverty among Social and Economic Groups in India in the 1990s, *Economic and Political Weekly*, Vol. XXXVIII, No. 50 (April 15), pp. 5263–76.

———— (2002), The Working Poor in India: Employment-Poverty Linkages and Employment Policy Options, Discussion Paper 4, Issues in Employment and Poverty, Recovery and Reconstruction Department, International Labour Office, Geneva, September.

Tendulkar, Suresh D., K. Sundaram and L.R. Jain (1993), Poverty in India, 1970/71 to 1988/89, Working Paper, Asian Regional Team for Employment Promotion (ARTEP), World Employment Programme, International Labour Organisation, New Delhi, December.

Tendulkar, Suresh D. (1998), 'India's Economic Policy Reforms and Poverty' in I.J. Ahluwalia and I.M.D. Little (eds), *Indian Economic Reforms and Development, Essays for Manmohan Singh*, New Delhi: Oxford University Press, pp. 280–309.

Visaria, Pravin (2000), Alternative Estimates of Poverty in India, *The Economic Times*, June 29.

Appendices

Table A.1R Percentage Excess of CES estimates over EUS Estimates of MPCE in Food, Paan, Tobacco, and Intoxicants in 1999/2000: All India: Rural Population for 5 per cent Fractile Groups

(Per Cent)

Fractile Group	Cereals and Substi- tutes	Pulses and Products	Milk and Milk Products	Edible Oils	Vege- tables	Fruits and Nuts	Eggs, Fish, and Meat	Other Food	Total Food	Paan, Tobacco, and Intoxicants
(1)	*(2)*	*(3)*	*(4)*	*(5)*	*(6)*	*(7)*	*(8)*	*(9)*	*(10)*	*(11)*
A. All-India Avg. Diff. 7 days vs 30 days (%)	12.9	48.2	19.6	22.8	55.3	60.3	54.2	54.6	30.0	43.1
B. Excess of CES over EUS (%) All fractile groups	1.8	5.2	13.6	0.6	0.8	25.7	2.8	54.3	10.2	15.3
B.1. 0–5	5.6	−7.1	−14.1	−2.5	12.7	30.7	−11.8	34.8	6.2	14.3
B.2. 5–10	3.4	−2.3	−2.8	−2.3	13.6	17.2	−17.8	42.7	6.2	15.6
B.3. 10–15	3.8	1.2	−2.3	−0.7	10.6	−1.7	−8.2	45.3	7.0	9.1
B.4. 15–20	3.0	−0.5	7.1	−2.8	6.6	3.4	−4.5	41.0	6.3	13.4
B.5. 20–25	0.7	2.3	15.0	0.0	6.9	13.8	−4.0	46.2	6.9	6.8
B.6. 25–30	1.8	3.6	9.3	−2.9	2.0	19.2	−7.6	46.3	6.4	18.4
B.7. 30–35	0.5	5.3	11.1	1.4	7.0	6.7	−4.0	49.8	7.4	17.4
B.8. 35–40	0.9	2.7	15.9	0.1	8.2	16.5	6.0	49.9	8.8	12.4
B.9. 40–45	2.3	5.8	11.0	−2.3	5.5	12.7	−2.4	53.2	8.7	14.1
B.10. 45–50	0.3	3.9	12.1	1.6	4.0	17.2	3.7	54.4	8.5	17.3
B.11. 50–55	0.5	6.9	14.6	2.7	6.1	29.5	2.7	49.3	9.4	12.7
B.12. 55–60	−0.4	8.3	11.1	2.9	0.6	34.8	16.1	56.2	9.6	9.8
B.13. 60–65	−0.4	5.4	14.1	3.2	1.8	20.9	−2.7	59.3	9.3	6.6
B.14. 65–70	2.2	4.6	16.7	4.0	−0.5	21.5	5.2	55.6	11.1	14.4
B.15. 70–75	1.0	7.5	13.7	1.8	1.5	21.0	4.2	51.6	10.2	9.7
B.16. 75–80	2.4	5.3	12.0	1.4	−1.5	25.1	6.7	54.9	10.8	13.2
B.17. 80–85	1.8	6.9	21.0	−0.7	−3.2	26.9	−4.4	57.7	11.9	5.6
B.18. 85–90	0.1	6.7	16.7	2.1	−4.9	28.8	11.6	51.3	11.5	12.1
B.19. 90–95	5.0	12.4	13.7	1.6	−7.6	32.5	13.4	52.9	13.7	19.7
B.20. 95–100	4.3	8.5	15.5	0.9	−7.0	39.3	8.8	67.9	17.4	38.2

Notes: 1. Avg. Diff. 7 days vs 30 days (%) – Ratio of 7-day-recall-based estimate to corresponding 30-day-recall-based estimate expressed as a percentage and averaged over 51st to 54th Rounds of NSS.
2. CES – Consumer Expenditure Survey.
3. EUS – Employment-Unemployment Survey.
4. 0–5 denotes bottom 5 per cent, 5–10, the next 5 per cent of the population and so on.

Sources: 1. NSSO (2000a) for the first row.
2. Our calculations based on unit level record for the 55th Round of NSS.

Table A.1U Percentage Excess of CES Estimates over EUS Estimates of MPCE in Food, Paan, Tobacco, and Intoxicants in 1999/2000: All-India: Urban Population for Five Per cent Fractile Groups

(Per Cent)

Fractile Group	Cereals and Substitutes	Pulses and Products	Milk and Milk Products	Edible Oils	Vege-tables	Fruits and Nuts	Eggs, Fish, and Meat	Other Food	Total Food	Paan, Tobacco, and Intoxicants
(1)	*(2)*	*(3)*	*(4)*	*(5)*	*(6)*	*(7)*	*(8)*	*(9)*	*(10)*	*(11)*
A. All-India avg. diff. 7 days vs 30 days (%)	15.9	42.1	12.2	22.3	52.5	69.3	50.4	53.4	32.9	41.5
B. Excess of CES over EUS (%) All fractile groups	3.6	4.1	10.9	−0.8	−8.3	19.8	3.4	67.22	13.0	17.6
B.1. 0–5	9.9	3.2	5.3	−3.3	1.8	−6.9	−14.1	60.8	10.9	9.3
B.2. 5–10	5.7	1.7	7.9	−0.7	3.2	1.7	2.3	56.9	10.3	8.2
B.3. 10–15	6.9	1.7	3.1	0.1	1.2	20.8	4.3	56.4	10.9	0.7
B.4. 15–20	2.1	4.2	7.2	0.6	−1.6	20.9	−3.3	64.4	9.5	2.5
B.5. 20–25	4.3	2.2	5.8	−0.3	−3.9	15.5	0.6	57.9	9.3	9.1
B.6. 25–30	2.2	9.1	4.5	2.8	−0.7	12.7	1.8	58.7	9.8	13.5
B.7. 30–35	5.0	2.8	2.9	2.4	−3.4	8.8	−0.6	60.1	9.8	28.4
B.8. 35–40	4.6	4.3	3.4	−1.5	−5.7	10.5	1.0	62.7	9.6	24.4
B.9. 40–45	8.1	9.8	4.4	−1.1	−5.0	13.2	3.7	58.6	11.3	3.5
B.10. 45–50	7.0	3.2	7.6	0.1	−4.1	12.3	8.0	58.0	11.6	16.9
B.11. 50–55	4.2	7.0	16.1	0.2	−5.0	17.3	−2.4	67.7	13.0	9.2
B.12. 55–60	6.3	4.3	11.1	0.7	−7.6	24.2	9.0	65.0	13.2	9.8
B.13. 60–65	2.6	6.2	15.2	1.7	−7.1	22.0	3.0	61.6	12.2	4.6
B.14. 65–70	−0.3	4.4	17.3	2.1	−9.5	24.1	−5.8	65.9	11.7	4.4
B.15. 70–75	−0.5	4.6	11.9	1.4	−14.6	25.7	7.4	69.7	11.9	24.3
B.16. 75–80	4.0	5.4	15.5	−1.7	−12.6	18.1	−0.4	55.8	12.0	1.5
B.17. 80–85	3.0	5.9	11.3	0.3	−10.8	19.2	6.1	65.7	13.5	16.9
B.18. 85–90	4.9	0.6	9.7	−2.7	−12.0	16.4	9.7	67.1	13.9	28.6
B.19. 90–95	−0.3	5.2	15.6	Neg	−12.7	30.2	2.0	61.4	14.6	18.1
B.20. 95–100	−2.5	9.7	9.1	−10.1	−18.2	20.4	12.1	65.2	14.3	57.2

Notes: 1. Avg. Diff. 7 days vs 30 days (%) – Ratio of 7-day-recall-based estimate to corresponding 30-day-recall-based estimate expressed as a percentage and averaged over 51st to 54th Rounds of NSS.
2. CES – Consumer Expenditure Survey.
3. EUS – Employment-Unemployment Survey.
4. 0–5 denotes bottom 5 per cent, 5–10, the next 5 per cent of the population and so on.

Sources: 1. NSSO (2000a) for the first row.
2. Our calculations based on unit level record for the 55th Round of NSS.

Table A.2R Percentage Excess of CES Estimates over EUS Estimates of MPCE on Item-groups in Food, Paan, Tobacco and Intoxicants in 1999/2000: All-India and 15 Major States: Rural Population

States/ Item-Group	Excess of CES-Estimates over EUS-Estimates as a Percentage of EUS-Estimates									
	Cereals and Substitutes	Pulses and Products	Milk and Milk Products	Edible Oils	Vegetables	Fruits and Nuts	Eggs, Fish, and Meat	Other Food	Total Food	Paan, Tobacco, and Intoxicants
(1)	(2)	(3)	(4)	(5)	(6)	(7)	(8)	(9)	(10)	(11)
All-India										
Avg. Diff. 7 days vs 30 days (%)	12.9	48.2	19.6	22.8	55.3	60.3	54.2	54.6	30.0	43.1
Excess of CES over EUS (%): All India	1.8	5.2	13.6	0.7	0.9	25.9	2.9	54.4	10.2	15.3
15 major states										
Andhra Pradesh	−0.2	−2.9	5.1	−9.0	0.4	23.7	−2.7	58.2	6.5	16.6
Assam	−0.5	6.4	10.8	−5.3	−4.7	−13.7	6.4	40.2	3.5	44.5
Bihar	−0.1	7.4	13.7	3.3	8.6	6.7	−3.5	49.1	6.7	14.3
Gujarat	−1.3	4.8	25.1	6.7	−8.8	32.0	−12.5	68.0	13.9	−4.8
Haryana	8.3	12.6	9.4	−7.7	−5.4	−1.9	−14.8	28.8	9.3	11.5
Karnataka	6.8	7.4	15.0	−1.9	14.2	86.3	3.3	69.7	19.2	20.1
Kerala	5.8	−12.0	2.8	−5.3	−2.8	39.9	12.7	88.0	18.7	24.4
Madhya Pradesh	2.0	7.9	27.5	2.3	0.8	7.0	−22.2	40.8	9.2	13.7
Maharashtra	6.5	13.9	11.6	1.2	1.3	66.2	−4.2	42.9	13.6	14.5
Orissa	1.3	−6.1	11.4	−1.6	4.9	15.1	0.7	59.1	6.1	21.9
Punjab	9.1	11.0	2.8	1.0	−4.7	13.6	17.0	43.0	10.6	56.6
Rajasthan	−0.6	6.7	19.8	−0.1	−4.0	−9.7	1.8	27.3	9.4	4.2
Tamil Nadu	4.9	13.6	6.6	−7.4	2.3	50.8	−0.4	87.7	18.4	26.0
Uttar Pradesh	2.9	7.3	10.8	7.6	−3.2	7.0	−5.6	47.5	6.6	9.5
West Bengal	4.1	−6.3	15.0	2.8	8.5	19.0	17.7	61.9	10.6	4.5

Notes: 1. Avg. Diff. 7 days vs 30 days (%) – Ratio of 7-day-recall-based estimate to corresponding 30-day-recall-based estimate expressed as a percentage and averaged over 51st to 54th Rounds of NSS.

2. CES – Consumer Expenditure Survey.

3. EUS – Employment-Unemployment Survey.

Sources: 1. NSSO (2000a) for the first row.

2. Our calculations based on unit-level records for the 55th Round of NSS.

Table A.2U Percentage Excess of CES Estimates over EUS Estimates of MPCE on Item-groups in Food, Paan, Tobacco and Intoxicants in 1999/2000: All-India and 15 Major States: Urban Population

States/ Item-Group	Excess of CES-Estimates over EUS-Estimates as a Percentage of EUS-Estimates									
	Cereals and Substitutes	Pulses and Products	Milk and Milk Products	Edible Oil	Vegetables	Fruits and Nuts	Eggs, Fish, and Meat	Other Food	Total Food	Paan, Tobacco, and Intoxicants
(1)	(2)	(3)	(4)	(5)	(6)	(7)	(8)	(9)	(10)	(11)
All-India										
Avg. Diff. 7 days vs 30 days (%)	15.9	42.1	12.2	22.3	52.5	69.3	50.4	53.4	32.9	41.5
Excess of CES over EUS (%): All-India	3.5	4.1	10.9	−0.8	−8.9	19.8	3.4	67.22	13.0	17.6
15 major states										
Andhra Pradesh	4.9	−0.2	6.8	−5.0	−6.2	12.9	−4.9	66.0	10.7	18.4
Assam	2.3	−0.1	14.7	−1.0	−14.2	−23.2	1.4	80.6	7.9	43.6
Bihar	−4.0	4.5	11.0	7.4	−2.3	−3.3	3.7	67.1	7.3	0.1
Gujarat	0.3	6.5	15.2	3.7	−10.2	17.0	13.1	59.3	13.0	−11.8
Haryana	13.2	0.5	7.6	−7.2	−29.9	−17.1	−6.9	13.0	1.3	35.3
Karnataka	3.9	−8.3	7.8	−2.4	−9.7	46.3	−0.5	93.3	16.4	12.5
Kerala	5.6	−5.6	8.9	−1.8	0.6	43.4	16.2	63.2	19.3	21.9
Madhya Pradesh	4.6	11.8	15.9	−1.9	−12.0	−0.8	0.5	42.4	9.3	24.1
Maharashtra	5.9	3.9	8.5	1.0	−10.0	34.6	0.9	64.1	14.1	23.9
Orissa	2.9	2.6	6.9	1.5	−8.9	6.1	1.9	79.2	9.1	8.0
Punjab	9.2	4.6	6.6	−14.7	−19.8	−3.8	7.5	42.3	7.2	52.7
Rajasthan	2.5	4.0	21.6	2.0	−7.8	−1.1	12.7	30.5	11.2	12.1
Tamil Nadu	1.1	10.7	5.0	−9.3	−4.4	44.3	1.4	76.3	15.4	31.3
Uttar Pradesh	4.1	12.3	9.6	6.9	−7.1	17.7	3.0	59.1	12.7	9.8
West Bengal	3.0	−13.1	5.2	−1.2	−6.6	−6.9	6.0	50.0	6.9	−6.4

Notes: 1. Avg. Diff. 7 days vs 30 days (%) – Ratio of 7-day-recall-based estimate to corresponding 30-day-recall-based estimate expressed as a percentage and averaged over 51st to 54th Rounds of NSS.
  2. CES – Consumer Expenditure Survey.
  3. EUS – Employment-Unemployment Survey.

Sources: 1. NSSO (2000a) for the first row.
  2. Our calculations based on unit level records for the 55th Round of NSS.

Table A.3R NSS 50th Round: A Comparison of Size-distribution by 5 Per cent Fractile Groups between Uniform and Mixed Reference Periods: All-India Rural Population

Fractile Group (%)	Cumulative % of Population	Average PCTE URP	Cumulative % CE by 30-Day	Average PCTE MRP	Cumulative % CE by 365-Day
0–5	5	**101.3139**	1.80	110.2837	1.93
5–10	10	**131.1899**	4.13	141.7052	4.41
10–15	15	**147.2251**	6.75	158.7001	7.18
15–20	20	**160.8434**	9.61	172.626	10.20
20–25	25	**172.7032**	12.67	184.7478	13.43
25–30	30	**183.6508**	15.94	196.1252	16.86
30–35	35	**195.0225**	19.40	207.5231	20.49
35–40	40	**206.4848**	23.07	218.9433	24.32
40–45	45	**218.0165**	26.94	231.0298	28.36
45–50	50	**230.531**	31.04	243.5303	32.61
50–55	55	**243.749**	35.37	256.804	37.10
55–60	60	**257.9355**	39.95	270.8079	41.84
60–65	65	**273.5705**	44.82	286.229	46.84
65–70	70	**291.2079**	49.99	303.3376	52.15
70–75	75	**312.0809**	55.53	322.6343	57.79
75–80	80	**337.115**	61.52	345.9822	63.84
80–85	85	**371.5535**	68.13	376.3839	70.42
85–90	90	**419.6128**	75.58	419.0215	77.75
90–95	95	**499.0608**	84.45	490.8102	86.33
95–100	100	**875.375**	100.00	781.9013	100.00
0–100		*281.4032*		*285.9563*	

Notes: 1. All numbers in bold are the revised estimates.
2. URP – Uniform (30-day) reference period for all items of consumer expenditure.
3. MRP – Mixed reference period: 365 days for clothing, footwear, education and health (institutional) and 30 days for all the remaining items.
4. CE – Aggregate consumer expenditure.
5. PCTE – Per capita total consumer expenditure.

Sources: Estimates by authors from the unit-level records of the 50th Round.

Table A.3U NSS 50th Round: A Comparison of Size-distribution by 5 Per cent Fractile Groups between Uniform and Mixed Reference Periods: All-India Urban Population

Fractile Group (%)	Cumulative % of Population	Average PCTE URP	Cumulative % CE by 30-Day	Average PCTE MRP	Cumulative % CE by 365-Day
0–5	5	133.0799	1.45	*144.2726*	*1.56*
5–10	10	175.8905	3.37	*188.5886*	*3.59*
10–15	15	201.9348	5.58	*215.6687*	*5.92*
15–20	20	222.8357	8.01	*237.9062*	*8.49*
20–25	25	242.3559	10.65	*258.9554*	*11.28*

25–30	30	261.9733	13.51	*279.101*	*14.29*
30–35	35	281.1159	16.58	*298.7234*	*17.51*
35–40	40	302.5225	19.88	*319.4199*	*20.96*
40–45	45	323.6575	23.42	*341.5709*	*24.65*
45–50	50	346.5325	27.20	*365.0693*	*28.59*
50–55	55	370.3242	31.24	*389.3419*	*32.79*
55–60	60	397.9061	35.58	*416.542*	*37.28*
60–65	65	430.2546	40.28	*447.7376*	*42.11*
65–70	70	467.1801	45.38	*484.4874*	*47.34*
70–75	75	513.6512	50.99	*528.6223*	*53.04*
75–80	80	569.3199	57.20	*583.3929*	*59.33*
80–85	85	641.3186	64.20	*651.9997*	*66.36*
85–90	90	742.1016	72.30	*747.8689*	*74.43*
90–95	95	911.4375	82.25	*911.5722*	*84.26*
95–100	100	1626.268	100.00	*1457.917*	*100.00*
0–100		*458.083*		*463.4379*	

Notes: 1. All numbers in bold are revised estimates.
2. URP – Uniform (30-day) reference period for all items of consumer expenditure.
3. MRP – Mixed reference period: 365-days for clothing, footwear, education and health (institutional) and 30-days for all the remaining items.
4. CE – Aggregate consumer expenditure.
5. PCTE – Per capita total consumer expenditure.

Source: Estimates by authors from the unit-level records of 50th Round.

Table A4 All-India and State-Specific Rural-Urban Poverty Lines 1983, 1993/94 and 1999/2000

(Rs 0.00)

States	Rural			Urban		
	1983	1993/94	1999/2000	1983	1993/94	1999/2000
Andhra Pradesh	80.30	190.55	308.79	104.70	271.06	449.11
Assam	103.48	258.16	407.16	96.23	271.06	449.11
Bihar	105.31	229.34	353.29	116.81	269.07	431.30
Gujarat	92.62	222.56	351.66	120.48	302.74	490.09
Haryana	95.26	241.06	366.34	103.46	236.37	399.91
Karnataka	87.36	204.20	339.63	110.36	271.83	452.34
Kerala	110.20	273.94	426.50	125.71	297.20	506.29
Madhya Pradesh	87.84	185.11	297.93	121.26	310.45	484.35
Maharashtra	97.43	228.71	380.79	126.05	320.81	531.84
Orissa	103.51	210.49	350.07	129.94	286.16	463.61
Punjab	96.76	250.11	383.05	98.12	231.31	355.43
Rajasthan	90.48	215.54	332.65	112.92	284.56	447.85
Tamil Nadu	99.75	208.97	336.03	117.26	291.42	480.34
Uttar Pradesh	87.46	205.24	316.94	106.80	257.79	423.35
West Bengal	109.67	248.07	389.40	100.12	240.77	399.43
All-India	*93.16*	*211.30*	*335.46*	*111.25*	*274.88*	*451.19*

Table A.5R Average Annual Rate of Change in Poverty Indicators between 1983/94 (on URP) and between 1994/2000 (on MRP) as a Percentage of Base Year Values: 15 Major States – Rural Population

(Per Cent)

Poverty Indicators	HCR		Number of Poor		PGI		FGT*	
States	1983/ 94	1994/ 2000	1983/ 94	1994/ 2000	1983/ 94	1994/ 2000	1983/ 94	1994/ 2000
(1)	(2)	(3)	(4)	(5)	(6)	(7)	(8)	(9)
Andhra Pradesh	−1.72	−1.29	−0.32	−0.07	−2.87	−1.91	−3.58	−2.24
Assam	1.67	0.76	4.15	2.45	2.55	3.77	2.79	7.58
Bihar	−0.64	−2.58	1.71	−0.53	−2.16	−4.68	−3.23	−6.11
Gujarat	−1.24	−3.92	−0.28	−2.65	−1.74	−4.07	−3.19	−3.94
Haryana	2.42	−11.32	5.23	−10.69	3.45	−11.86	3.97	−12.01
Karnataka	0.47	−3.23	1.08	−1.82	−2.12	−5.00	−3.05	−6.62
Kerala	−2.65	−7.61	−2.29	−7.07	−3.45	−9.78	−3.87	−11.09
Madhya Pradesh	−3.07	1.97	−1.60	4.10	−4.46	1.28	−5.15	0.18
Maharashtra	−0.52	−2.67	1.93	−2.46	−0.49	−3.90	−0.21	−5.02
Orissa	−0.80	0.23	0.74	1.58	−2.52	1.95	−3.74	3.20
Punjab	−3.47	−4.54	−2.45	−3.67	−2.35	−6.31	−3.05	−6.82
Rajasthan	−3.57	−6.82	−1.94	−5.27	−5.51	−8.28	−6.55	−9.16
Tamil Nadu	−3.17	−2.64	−2.60	−3.12	−4.89	−4.30	−5.78	−5.42
Uttar Pradesh	−2.03	−4.18	−0.23	−2.48	−2.95	−6.34	−4.00	−7.63
West Bengal	−1.81	−1.43	−0.07	0.07	−4.16	−1.62	−5.66	−0.96
15 States (Wt. Ave.)	−1.54	−2.50	0.13	−1.11	−2.89	−3.57	−3.81	−4.15

Note: Numbers in Columns 3, 5, 7 and 9 (in italics) are the revised estimates.

Sources: Tables 13.3 and 13.4.

Table A.5U Average Annual Rate of Change in Poverty Indicators between 1983/94 (on URP) and between 1994/2000 (on MRP) as a Percentage of Base Year Values: 15 Major States – Urban Population

(Per Cent)

Poverty Indicators	HCR		Number of Poor		Poverty Gap Index		FGT*	
States	1983/ 94	1994/ 2000	1983/ 94	1994/ 2000	1983/ 94	1994/ 2000	1983/ 94	1994/ 2000
(1)	(2)	(3)	(4)	(5)	(6)	(7)	(8)	(9)
Andhra Pradesh	0.37	−3.23	3.99	−2.07	−0.17	−4.80	−0.55	−5.81
Assam	−4.85	7.13	−2.92	12.00	−1.91	16.67	−6.82	20.83
Bihar	−0.94	1.99	1.92	4.87	−2.15	2.07	−2.64	1.53
Gujarat	−2.01	−5.30	0.68	−3.21	−1.02	−7.58	−0.23	−8.54
Haryana	−4.41	−0.45	−1.96	4.10	−4.94	4.29	−5.32	12.96
Karnataka	−1.14	−6.51	1.45	−4.84	−1.78	−7.72	−2.30	−8.33
Kerala	−3.96	−1.97	−1.34	−1.30	−5.15	−3.15	−5.81	−4.63
Madhya Pradesh	−0.98	−1.03	2.79	1.82	−0.65	−0.82	−0.48	−0.80
Maharashtra	−1.66	−1.94	2.25	−0.26	−1.71	−2.57	−1.59	−3.53
Orissa	−2.55	2.77	NIL	6.07	−3.17	2.57	−3.56	2.55

Punjab	−6.44	−7.27	−5.43	6.07	−7.45	−8.89	−8.01	−10.19
Rajasthan	−1.26	−6.76	2.01	−5.01	−2.20	−7.87	−2.94	−9.11
Tamil Nadu	−1.37	−5.62	0.83	−2.99	−2.35	−6.54	−2.66	−7.72
Uttar Pradesh	−2.68	0.74	0.08	3.98	−3.10	−0.51	−3.35	−1.85
West Bengal	−2.46	−3.24	−0.44	−1.68	−3.68	−4.75	−4.81	−6.08
15 States (Wt. Ave.)	−1.77	−2.34	1.15	−0.07	−2.16	−3.11	−2.46	−3.97

Note: Numbers in Columns 3, 5, 7 and 9 (in italics) are the revised estimates.

Sources: Tables 13.5 and 13.6.

Table A.5T Average Annual Rate of Change in Poverty Indicators between 1983–94 (on URP) and between 1994–2000 (on URP) and between 1994–2000 (on MRP) as a Percentage of Base Year Values: 15 Major States, Total (Rural + Urban) Population

(Per Cent)

Poverty Indicators	HCR		Number of Poor		Poverty Gap Index		FGT*	
States	1983/ 94	1994– 2000	1983– 94	1994– 2000	1983– 94	1994– 2000	1983– 94	1994– 2000
(1)	(2)	(3)	(4)	(5)	(6)	(7)	(8)	(9)
Andhra Pradesh	−1.15	−1.93	0.73	−0.74	−2.09	−3.01	−2.70	−3.68
Assam	1.24	0.72	3.82	2.61	2.01	3.75	2.23	7.43
Bihar	−0.68	−2.18	1.73	−0.04	−2.18	−4.10	−3.20	−5.44
Gujarat	−1.74	−4.43	0.03	−2.85	−1.49	−5.45	−1.29	−5.91
Haryana	0.75	−10.26	3.75	−9.23	1.44	−10.31	1.75	−9.85
Karnataka	−0.69	−4.31	1.18	−2.78	−2.04	−5.95	−2.83	−7.26
Kerala	−2.99	−6.27	−2.09	−5.69	−3.89	−8.21	−4.33	−9.46
Madhya Pradesh	−2.59	1.09	−0.71	3.41	−3.65	0.64	−4.28	−0.07
Maharashtra	−0.99	−2.58	2.02	−1.80	−0.99	−3.58	−0.76	−4.58
Orissa	−1.03	0.42	0.68	2.00	−2.62	1.95	−3.76	3.06
Punjab	−2.77	−3.61	−1.31	−2.11	−4.18	−6.95	−4.87	−7.41
Rajasthan	−3.10	−6.79	−1.17	−5.19	−4.90	−8.14	−5.94	−9.19
Tamil Nadu	−2.66	−3.90	−1.63	−3.07	−4.22	−5.23	−4.99	−6.42
Uttar Pradesh	−2.16	−3.25	−0.12	−1.29	−2.99	−5.12	−3.87	−6.29
West Bengal	−1.95	−1.68	−0.21	−0.13	−4.90	−1.99	−5.58	−1.51
15 States (Wt. Ave.)	−1.63	−2.50	0.35	−0.89	−2.89	−3.11	−3.61	−4.18

Note: Numbers in Columns 3, 5, 7 and 9 (in italics) are the revised estimates.

Sources: Tables 13.7 and 13.8.

14

Poverty and Inequality in India

Abhijit Sen and Himanshu

ISSUES AND BACKGROUND

In an earlier paper [Sen 2000], published before release of final results from the National Sample Survey (NSS)'s 55th Round (1999/2000), one of the present authors had warned that estimates of consumption expenditure and of poverty from this round would be controversial:

(i) Reference periods were changed in the Consumer Expenditure Survey of the 55th Round after all nine NSS rounds during 1990–98 had reported higher rural poverty than in 1989-90.

(ii) This had followed influential criticism that NSS was diverging increasingly from National Accounts (NAS) during the 1990s. But, in fact, growth of NSS nominal consumption during 1990–97 was very similar to that from the then current NAS (base 1980/81) and NSS growth of rural consumption also agreed with implicit NAS growth of rural incomes.

(iii) The existing NAS series was replaced by a new series (base 1993/94) in 1999, which implied higher 1990s growth of both consumer expenditure and rural incomes. This lent ex post credibility to claims of increased NSS-NAS divergence, but involved arbitrary and implausible revisions to production and consumption estimates of fruits and vegetables.

(iv) Alternative reference periods were experimented with in NSS rounds 51 to 54 (i.e. 1994–98) and found to halve measured poverty. But their validity over the uniform 30-day recall used hitherto was not established, and conflicting criteria were used for selection. The 7-day recall chosen for food, etc., gave estimates closer to NAS but with larger variance, while the 365-day recall for clothing, etc., gave lower variance but were even further from NAS. In 'a last minute compromise' the final choice for the 55th Round retained 30-day food questions also.

In anticipation of full 55th Round results, the paper had validated 1990s NSS data, pleaded against allowing users' priors to interfere in statistical design of data generation, and argued for a new 'large sample' survey with uniform 30-day recall. It was shown that inclusion of both 7 and 30-day questions for food, etc., had led to 'contamination', i.e. had made either or both non-comparable with previous estimates using corresponding recalls, and that contradictory conclusions were possible about the direction of poverty change depending on the reference periods compared.

There has been no subsequent survey using the uniform 30-day reference period. The Planning Commission's official 55th Round poverty estimates were based on its 30-day food recall, ignoring the 7-day food recall and accepting its 365-day recall for clothing, etc. This implied apparently that All-India poverty incidence had declined by 10 percentage points and the number of poor reduced by about 60 million since 1993/94 (i.e. the previous 'large sample' 50th Round). However, while releasing these, the Commission drew attention to 'changes in methodology of data collection' and qualified that 'estimates may not be strictly comparable to earlier estimates of poverty'.

Since then, a sizeable literature has grown up on the 55th Round. This was discussed intensively at a seminar organised by the National Sample Survey Organisation (NSSO) in May 2001 and was the subject of a joint Planning Commission-World Bank workshop in January 2002. In these, there was unanimity that the 55th Round was non-comparable with previous rounds and that official figures had overestimated poverty decline. However, differences emerged on how much the 55th Round may have underestimated poverty, and indeed, on whether it was even possible to quantify what actually happened. Nonetheless, the then World Bank chief economist reflected accurately the dominant view at the 2002 workshop when he observed that poverty had probably declined, although he then stated that this could have been by 'about 10 percentage points', i.e. the same as if the 55th Round had been fully comparable with earlier rounds.

The incredible implication – that methodological changes in 55th Round did not matter – was of course a slip, but minor. It was more accurately slight exaggeration of results from two serious attempts to 'correct' for changes in methodology [Sundaram and Tendulkar 2003a and 2003b, Deaton 2003a and 2003b and Deaton and Dreze 2002]. Sundaram-Tendulkar compared 55th Round Consumer Expenditure (CES) and Employment-Unemployment Surveys (EUS) to claim that presence of 7-day questions on food, etc., had not inflated 30-day responses. And, while agreeing that 365-day questions for clothing, etc., did matter, offered 'comparable' estimates from 50th Round (which asked 365-day questions also) that implied 8 percentage points reduction in All-India poverty ratio. Deaton used a different method, exploiting the fact that only 30-day questions were asked for some items in both rounds and assuming a stable relationship between spending on these and probability of being poor. His 'adjusted' 55th Round All-India poverty was 7 percentage points less than in 50th Round, correcting apparently for 7-day questions also. From these, it was claimed that poverty reduced more during 1990s than earlier, reversing the pre-55th Round consensus.

The present paper reports a re-examination, beginning with a critical appraisal of methods adopted by Sundaram-Tendulkar and Deaton. This was done, first, because uncritical acceptance of these may privilege ex post data adjustments over the crucial statistical priority of maintaining comparability at the data generation stage, and, second, because these results were prima facie implausible. In particular:

(i) The earliest problem noted about 55th Round CES was that its 7 and 30-day food estimates gave conflicting results on direction of poverty change [Sen 2000]. To resolve this, Sundaram (2001) used consumption data from 55th Round EUS that asked only 30-day food questions. He noted that although the EUS schedule was abridged, it too showed poverty reduced by 2.7 percentage points all-India between rounds 50 and 55. Thus, Sundaram-Tendulkar used EUS originally, not to argue against contamination, but to circumvent this. Sen (2001) observed that poverty decline from EUS was not robust since round 51-54 experiments suggested that its 365-day recall for clothing, etc., reduced measured poverty by 4 to 6 percentage points compared to 30-day recall.

(ii) During this stage of the debate, when the primary focus was on 'contamination' from 7-day food questions to 30-day answers, the NSSO released 55th Round Report No 471 on Nutritional

Intake, showing increase in proportion of people reporting inadequate nutrition. Since this was from CES, in which food estimates were, if anything, inflated, this not only implied increase in nutrition poverty but also, given the large reported reduction in income poverty, significant shift from food to non-food expenditures among the poor. Quite apart from conflict on poverty criteria, this contradicted Deaton's assumed stable relationship between poverty and non-food spending.

(iii) At the 2002 workshop, Datt, Kozel and Ravallion (2003) had reported projections from an econometric model fitted to data till 1993/94 that implied only 40 per cent of poverty reduction obtained from unadjusted 50th and 55th Round data. Although parametric projection with out-of-survey variables is different from Deaton's non-parametric method to 'adjust' using in-survey data on a subset of comparable items, both involve implicit models and require relational stability. Both confirmed 55th Round underestimation of poverty, but the large conflict in orders of magnitude suggested that much of this might not have been adjusted for.

(iv) An important point, made by both Deaton-Dreze and Sundaram-Tendulkar, was that although unadjusted data show inequality reduced between rounds 50 and 55, this inequality increases on adjusting for the 365-day reference period. But, very oddly, their 'comparable' poverty estimates did not reflect this. Rural poverty declines 7 percentage points if 50th Round distribution is scaled up to 55th Round mean consumption. This is exactly the decline claimed by Deaton, while Sundaram-Tendulkar claimed more.

In addition, there is the issue of sampling biases both in 55th and other NSS, especially 'thin sample', rounds. This is not a primary concern here, but cannot be avoided without ducking the matter of viewing the 55th Round in the context of nearby rounds. Although inconvenient 'thin samples' were ignored in the defence of 55th Round poverty estimates, except partially by Deaton-Dreze, any re-examination must take into account recently released thin sample NSS rounds 56 and 57, which retained only the 365-day recall for clothing, etc.

At the outset it must be stated that the re-examination carried out in light of the above was on comparability and consistency of NSS data and not their validity. The principal motivation was to assess the consensus that seemingly emerged after the 55th Round against the pre-55th Round consensus. Moreover, since the matter is sensitive, earlier versions of this paper were circulated widely in order to arrive at some general agreement on its technical content. In particular, clarification was sought on two points that had emerged early in this research, and which taken together was strong evidence against the consensus from Sundaram-Tendulkar and Deaton-Dreze. First, that Sundaram-Tendulkar had erroneously underestimated (by over 50 per cent) 50th Round difference in poverty ratios obtained from uniform 30-day (URP) and mixed 30-365-day (MRP) recalls. Second, that Deaton's adjustment, which among other things aimed to correct the likely upward bias in 55th Round food consumption estimates due to its 7-day questions, had in fact increased these further.

Sundaram and Tendulkar (2003c) have acknowledged an inadvertent error in their estimates. In correction, they have reduced their estimate of poverty reduction between rounds 50 and 55 from 8.2 to 4.8 percentage points or by over 30 million people. Deaton has also communicated that his method does unexpectedly involve an implicit upward revision of 55th Round food expenditures. It is therefore now agreed that they did not gauge 55th Round non-comparability fully. Further, during course of research, Peter Lanjouw drew attention to their work at the World Bank. This, and some recent NSSO comparisons of short and full schedules suggest that even the estimates presented here may overestimate poverty reduction. Nonetheless, these have been retained unchanged to inform a wider audience on ongoing research on this important subject, the literature on which has involved some rather misleading use of hyperbole, creating confusion in both academia and policy circles.

This chapter is organised as follows. The section that follows presents 'comparable' estimates in two steps. First, following Sundaram-Tendulkar, 50th Round estimates are obtained using its 365-day rather than 30-day reports for clothing, etc., and comparability checked against the 55th Round that used only 365-day recall for these items. It is found that distributions are not comparable, but poverty estimates are. Avoiding Sundaram-Tendulkar's error, 50th Round poverty using MRP is placed at 30.6 per cent all-India, against 35.9 per cent using URP. Second, 55th Round estimates of food, etc., are checked for possible 'contamination' from 7-day questions. This too follows Sundaram-Tendulkar, i.e. use of 55th Round CES and EUS. Their results, and information from nearby NSS rounds, are used to arrive at some bounds. At its lower bound, the extent of such 'contamination' does turn out to be small. But even this implies 55th Round all-India poverty incidence using MRP to be 27.8 per cent as against 26.1 per cent officially. The decline between 1993/94 and 1999/99 is thus only 2.8 percentage points at most. Moreover, MRP estimates show less poverty decline during 1993/94 to 1999/2000 than during 1987/88 to 1993/94. Since annual poverty reduction by official estimates had already halved during 1987/88 to 1993/94 compared to the previous decade, there is no doubt that poverty reduction did suffer serious setback in the 1990s, at least so long as NSS data and official poverty lines are accepted.

In the next section, Deaton's adjustment is examined in this light and is shown to fail because of shift in consumption patterns from food to non-food. However, slight modification of his method also leads to estimates close to the estimates described above. The subsequent section presents results at the level of NSS regions and assesses what disaggregated conclusions are possible. In the last part of this chapter, these estimates are put in context of longer time series, including data from subsequent rounds 56 and 57, to examine growth and distribution aspects that underlie the poverty changes.

An important finding of this chapter is that on proper comparison 55th Round results agree reasonably with trends from other NSS rounds during the 1990s, testifying to integrity of NSS field operations in face of fairly severe methodological shocks. This restores and gives confidence to the earlier assessment that poverty had increased significantly in the early 1990s when growth had faltered during crisis and stabilisation, and that poverty reduction has been held back during the subsequent growth recovery because of increased inequalities. However, the main lesson is that poverty estimates are very sensitive to both survey design and post-survey analysis. For poverty monitoring to be credible, not only should survey design be stable and kept free from users' priors, but some non-survey issues need urgent reopening too, e.g. poverty lines currently in use.

COMPARABILITY OF 55TH ROUND

The following are the uncontested facts regarding comparability of the 55th NSS Round:

(a) Official estimates before 55th Round were based on data using uniform 30-day reference period for all items (URP). But no URP estimates are available from 55th Round since this used only a 365-day recall for five low frequency items (clothing, footwear, durable goods, education and institutional medicine). Official 55th Round estimates are based on the 30-day recall for food and intoxicants from CES, which asked both 7 and 30-day questions on these items. The resulting 30-365-days mixed reference period (MRP) is not comparable to URP of previous rounds. Subsequent NSS rounds have also used this MRP, but without 7-day food questions.

(b) Although official estimates before 55th Round used URP, and thin samples before 50th Round did not ask 365-day questions, questions on the five low frequency items were asked by both 30 and 365-day recalls in the 50th Round. Thus, distributions and poverty ratios using the MRP used officially from 55th Round can be obtained from 50th Round unit level data. Although not identical, MRP estimates can also be obtained from the previous thick sample, i.e. the 43rd Round, in which both 30 and 365-day questions were asked for three of these low frequency items (i.e. for clothing, footwear and durable goods).

(c) However, while part of the comparability problem can thus be resolved objectively, MRP estimates from 50th and 55th Rounds may still be non-comparable despite identical reference periods. This is because of possible 'contamination', i.e. influence of questions by one recall on answers by another. First, 365-days answers on low frequency items in the 50th Round may have been affected by presence of 30-day questions on these items that were not present in 55th Round. Second, 30-day answers on food and intoxicants in 55th Round CES may have been affected by pre-sence of 7-day questions that were not present in the 50th Round.

(d) No in-survey test has been carried out of how answers to 365-day questions are affected by presence or absence of 30-day questions in the same questionnaire. The only information on this is the relative results of two different sets of contemporaneous URP and MRP estimates: the thick sample rounds 43 and 50 where both 30 and 365-day questions were asked to the same sample, and the thin sample rounds 51 to 54 where these were put to two independent samples.

(e) Similarly, no in-survey assessment has been done of how simultaneous presence of 7-day questions influence 30-day answers. But while both 7 and 30-day questions were put to the same respondents in 55th Round CES, the 55th Round EUS did simultaneously collect data using only 30-day food questions. Although the EUS used an abridged schedule whose estimates may not be comparable with the CES, comparison of their results with each other and with results of other nearby NSS rounds is the only available method of assessing this directly.

The main thrust of Sundaram and Tendulkar (2003a and 2003b) was to argue against contamination, i.e. to claim that 50th Round MRP estimates from step (b) above are 'comparable' to 55th Round CES. They reported 50th Round MRP results but, as mentioned in the introduction, they erred. As a result of oversight, they overestimated 50th Round poverty.[1] Comparing these erroneous estimates to 55th Round

[1] The NSS Compact Disk on 50th Round Consumption Expenditure Survey (CES) contains 14 data files, aggregating to about two Gigabytes of information, in addition to details on multipliers and documentation. Of these, two relatively small files D376SUMR and D376SUMU aggregating 43 Megabytes, contain unit-level summary information that the NSSO had generated for tabulation purposes from the other detailed files. Since the data layout on itemwise consumption in these summary files correspond to a summary block in the original questionnaire, and appear to contain information by both 30 and 365-day recalls for items on which a 365-day question was asked, these seem to be the obvious source files from which to obtain the alternative 50th Round distributions. Sundaram-Tendulkar used these. However, on closer examination of the data, it turns out that these summary files return incorrect estimates of the alternative 50th Round distributions using the 365-day recall. This is because while these files contain the requisite information to replace the 30-day responses by 365-day responses in case of clothing, footwear and durable goods, this is not possible for education and institutional medicine. In fact, data on education and medical expenses are aggregated together in these files, and are put in the data fields for education leaving empty the fields for medical care, probably because the break-up was not required in the NSSO tabulation plan to which these summary files were input. As a result, although separate data fields exist for 30 and 365-day entries under education and medicines, since only 30-day questions were asked on non-institutional medicines, expenditure on this is included in the aggregated entry with 30-day recall but excluded from the aggregated entry with 365-day recall. It is, therefore, not possible in these files to isolate the expenditure on non-institutional medical care and this gets dropped

CES they concluded that rural and urban poverty ratios had declined 8.9 and 5.7 percentage points respectively. Since this implied that the number of poor had reduced by nearly 45 million, they claimed 'greater improvement in the poverty situation in the 1990s than in the previous ten-and- half-year period', thus largely vindicating official estimates.

However, on receiving results of this paper, Sundaram and Tendulkar (2003c) have revised their estimates of 'comparable' poverty. Although they continue with hyperbole of 'better performance in poverty reduction in the 1990s', their revised estimate of 4.8 percentage points decline in All-India poverty ratio during 1993/2000 is not only less than half the official decline but actually implies less annual reduction than during the 1980s.[2] Also, although they report absolute numbers of poor reduced, their revised estimate of 13 million is well below quarter of the number measured officially. Thus, what they now report is no longer vindication of official estimates but huge differences with these. Further, such large differences are obtained still assuming that there was no 'contamination' from the 7-day questions on food and intoxicants asked in the 55th Round.

Tables 14.1 and 14.2 present key results from rounds 43 and 50 by both URP and MRP. Unlike Sundaram-Tendulkar, who use their own poverty lines, estimates here use official poverty lines to maintain consistency with a larger literature. But since doubts have been expressed about validity of state/sector cost of living differentials implicit in official state-specific poverty lines, headcount ratios are also presented applying national poverty lines uniformly over states. The poverty line choice has important bearing on matters such as interstate allocation of anti-poverty resources, and is discussed later. The more pertinent and immediately relevant point from these tables is that the MRP returns lower poverty than the URP, irrespective of round, state, sector or poverty measure used.

The 50th Round URP-MRP differences for All-India headcount ratios using official poverty lines are 5.6 percentage points rural and 4.7 urban, almost the same as Sundaram-Tendulkar report after correction. These large URP-MRP differences explain why they now accept so much less poverty reduction than official comparisons of 55th Round with 50th Round URP. Moreover, although these differences vary somewhat across states, sectors and rounds, their underlying causes are systematic:

(i) In all cases, i.e. irrespective of state, sector or round, the MRP Gini is less than URP.

---

altogether if the 30-day aggregate entries on education and health are replaced by the corresponding 365-day entries. Sundaram and Tendulkar did not notice this. Consequently, their 50th Round MRP estimates excluded non-institutional medical expenses, which account for 4 per cent of total consumer expenditure, and correspondingly overstated 50th Round poverty 'comparable' to the 55th Round. Luckily, however, this oversight can be rectified. The data on both education and medical expenses were collected in Block 8.1 of the original 50th Round questionnaire, and the detailed unit-level information from this are contained in files D150L89R and D150L89U of the 50th Round CES CD. The summary files can be made complete by entering data from these more detailed files into the separate fields for education, institutional and non-institutional medical care, distinguishing further between the 30 and 365-day responses on the first two of these.

[2] Sundaram and Tendulkar (2003c) continue to make this claim while reporting corrected 50th Round MRP results, and base this on some comparisons of poverty reduction during 1993/94 to 1999/2000 and 1983 to 1993/94. But this is hyperbole since the opposite also follows from their estimates. Sundaram-Tendulkar had earlier reported URP (rural + urban) headcounts of 51.9, 46.5, 42.8, 36.2 and 37.4 using their poverty lines for rounds 32, 38, 43, 45 and 50. They now report MRP counts of 32.1 and 27.3 for rounds 50 and 55. If their 50th Round URP-MRP difference is taken to be valid for 55th Round also, the 1999/2000 URP count is 32.6. The implied poverty reduction rates are 1.3 percentage points per annum during 1977-1990, 0.9 during 1983-1994, 0.8 during 1993/2000 and only 0.4 during 1989–2000. These also imply that, even ignoring 55th Round contamination, the number of poor increased 27 million between 1989/90 and 1999/2000 or over the '1990s' as usually understood, after decrease of more than 30 million during the previous 12 years.

Table 14.1(a) Key Results from Uniform and Mixed Recalls – 43rd Round Rural

| | Monthly Per Capita Consumer Expenditure | | | | Gini Index | Poverty Measures | | | |
| | | | | | | National Poverty Line | State-Specific Poverty Line | | |
	Poorest 40 Per cent	Next 40 Per cent	Richest 20 Per cent	All		Head-count Ratio	Head-count Ratio	Poverty Gap	Squared Poverty Gap
Uniform 30-day Reference Period									
Andhra Pradesh	88	149	322	158.90	30.9	40.0	21.0	4.4	1.4
Assam	104	156	275	158.80	23.0	27.7	39.4	7.5	2.0
Bihar	84	131	246	134.90	25.6	48.7	53.9	12.9	4.5
Gujarat	101	161	304	165.64	26.1	28.4	28.3	5.4	1.6
Haryana	125	215	428	221.44	29.2	13.9	15.4	3.6	1.3
Karnataka	85	145	295	150.78	29.7	41.2	32.6	7.9	2.8
Kerala	112	194	434	209.18	32.1	19.7	29.3	6.3	2.0
Madhya Pradesh	79	133	270	138.45	29.2	49.6	42.0	10.6	3.8
Maharashtra	88	145	323	157.96	31.2	40.6	40.9	9.6	3.2
Orissa	77	127	239	129.23	26.9	53.0	58.7	16.3	6.2
Punjab	135	228	472	239.66	29.7	9.6	12.8	2.0	0.5
Rajasthan	93	167	351	174.33	31.5	31.8	33.3	8.6	3.4
Tamil Nadu	82	145	328	156.38	33.0	44.3	46.3	12.6	4.8
Uttar Pradesh	86	143	291	149.89	28.8	42.9	42.3	10.0	3.3
West Bengal	93	147	275	151.04	25.8	36.6	48.8	11.6	4.0
All-India	*88*	*150*	*312*	*157.69*	*29.9*	*39.0*	*39.0*	*9.3*	*3.2*
Mixed 30/365 days Reference Periods									
Andhra Pradesh	92	150	286	153.72	26.9	36.7	17.7	3.4	1.1
Assam	108	161	277	163.19	22.2	24.1	34.8	6.2	1.6
Bihar	88	134	229	134.71	22.7	44.1	49.4	11.1	3.7
Gujarat	109	172	317	175.83	25.4	22.1	21.9	4.0	1.2
Haryana	135	220	388	219.18	25.1	10.1	12.5	2.5	0.9
Karnataka	85	145	292	150.64	29.2	40.5	32.0	7.7	2.7
Kerala	114	195	421	207.79	31.0	19.6	28.2	6.0	1.9
Madhya Pradesh	85	138	251	138.98	25.7	43.8	37.4	8.4	2.8
Maharashtra	95	151	285	155.31	26.1	34.6	34.9	7.4	2.3
Orissa	81	130	228	129.92	24.4	49.9	55.7	14.3	5.1
Punjab	147	237	453	244.11	26.8	5.3	8.0	1.1	0.3
Rajasthan	100	169	324	172.28	28.0	27.3	29.1	6.7	2.5
Tamil Nadu	85	149	311	155.98	30.7	41.2	43.5	11.3	4.2
Uttar Pradesh	91	146	271	148.62	25.8	39.6	39.0	8.4	2.6
West Bengal	96	150	264	151.56	24.0	33.9	45.9	10.4	3.4
All-India	*93*	*153*	*294*	*157.33*	*27.3*	*35.2*	*35.2*	*7.8*	*2.6*

Note: The MRP estimates are from distributions obtained using the 365-day recall for clothing, footwear and durable goods and 30-day recall for all other items. The state-wise poverty lines used in columns 8 to 10 are those that were used by the Planning Commission based on the Expert Group methodology. The national poverty line implied by these is Rs 115.20 and is used in Column 7. The All-India estimates in the table are those obtained by applying the national poverty line to the All-India distribution and need not correspond to the population weighted average of the state level poverty estimates.

Source: Unit-level data from NSS 43rd Round.

Table 14.1(b) Key Results from Uniform and Mixed Recalls – 43rd Round Urban

| | Monthly Per Capita Consumer Expenditure | | | | Gini Index | Poverty Measures | | | |
| | | | | | | National Poverty Line | State-Specific Poverty Line | | |
	Poorest 40 Per cent	Next 40 Per cent	Richest 20 Per cent	All		Head-count Ratio	Head-count Ratio	Poverty Gap	Squared Poverty Gap
Uniform 30-day Reference Period									
Andhra Pradesh	112	204	509	228.07	36.1	45.7	41.1	10.6	3.9
Assam	143	237	522	256.15	31.0	28.7	11.3	1.5	0.3
Bihar	104	172	384	187.21	31.0	57.9	51.9	13.0	4.6
Gujarat	138	224	448	234.32	27.8	32.1	38.5	8.2	2.6
Haryana	143	249	483	253.46	28.7	36.9	18.4	3.6	1.1
Karnataka	113	208	477	223.50	34.0	45.1	49.2	14.1	5.7
Kerala	123	237	591	261.70	36.9	38.2	38.7	10.0	3.9
Madhya Pradesh	119	218	492	232.98	33.2	40.9	47.4	13.6	5.3
Maharashtra	131	262	580	273.18	34.8	30.6	40.5	12.4	5.2
Orissa	119	213	446	222.01	31.0	39.2	42.6	11.1	4.2
Punjab	157	267	531	275.67	28.8	21.0	13.7	2.3	0.6
Rajasthan	126	219	535	245.11	34.6	36.9	37.9	9.6	3.4
Tamil Nadu	118	224	542	245.19	35.8	38.9	40.2	11.5	4.6
Uttar Pradesh	108	200	454	214.00	34.0	48.6	45.0	12.2	4.5
West Bengal	123	229	536	247.98	34.6	39.7	33.7	7.4	2.4
All-India	*121*	*227*	*533*	*245.71*	*35.0*	*38.7*	*38.7*	*10.2*	*3.8*
Mixed 30/365 days Reference Periods									
Andhra Pradesh	118	210	458	222.78	32.0	42.8	36.3	9.0	3.2
Assam	150	248	474	253.72	27.2	24.6	10.2	1.1	0.2
Bihar	110	177	360	186.71	28.0	55.6	46.8	10.9	3.7
Gujarat	149	244	463	249.74	26.6	24.5	29.8	6.1	1.8
Haryana	155	267	486	265.89	26.9	21.2	13.7	2.6	0.7
Karnataka	120	214	441	222.04	30.6	38.8	43.4	12.0	4.7
Kerala	129	249	596	270.06	35.8	34.8	35.4	8.6	3.2
Madhya Pradesh	129	226	472	236.45	30.4	35.3	43.3	11.0	4.0
Maharashtra	140	273	561	277.43	32.4	27.3	36.3	10.5	4.2
Orissa	126	218	434	224.56	29.1	36.6	38.1	9.6	3.3
Punjab	167	274	528	282.16	27.3	16.3	10.4	1.6	0.4
Rajasthan	134	229	504	246.32	31.2	32.7	33.8	7.7	2.5
Tamil Nadu	123	226	512	242.03	33.6	35.7	37.7	10.4	4.1
Uttar Pradesh	114	207	437	215.71	31.6	45.7	41.6	10.4	3.6
West Bengal	128	235	519	249.11	32.9	36.8	30.4	6.4	2.0
All-India	*128*	*235*	*514*	*247.99*	*32.7*	*34.9*	*34.9*	*8.6*	*3.1*

Note: The MRP estimates are from distributions obtained using the 365-day recall for clothing, footwear and durable goods and 30-day recall for all other items. The state-wise poverty lines used in columns 8 to 10 are those that were used by the Planning Commission based on the Expert Group methodology. The national poverty line implied by these is Rs 162.16 and is used in Column 7. The All-India estimates in the table are those obtained by applying the national poverty line to the All-India distribution and need not correspond to the population weighted average of the state level poverty estimates.

Source: Unit-level data from NSS 43rd Round.

Table 14.2(a) Key Results from Uniform and Mixed Recalls – 50th Round Rural

| | Monthly Per Capita Consumer Expenditure | | | | Gini Index | Poverty Measures | | | |
| | | | | | | National Poverty Line | State-Specific Poverty Line | | |
	Poorest 40 Per cent	Next 40 Per cent	Richest 20 Per cent	All		Head-count Ratio	Head-count Ratio	Poverty Gap	Squared Poverty Gap
Uniform 30-day Reference Period									
Andhra Pradesh	167	272	565	288.70	29.0	35.4	15.9	2.9	0.9
Assam	185	264	393	258.11	18.0	29.3	45.1	8.3	2.2
Bihar	143	219	368	218.30	22.6	55.3	58.0	14.7	5.1
Gujarat	192	304	526	303.32	24.0	23.9	22.2	4.1	1.2
Haryana	207	365	779	385.01	31.4	18.1	28.3	5.6	1.7
Karnataka	160	264	499	269.38	27.1	39.2	30.1	6.3	2.0
Kerala	218	371	773	390.41	30.1	15.3	25.4	5.6	1.8
Madhya Pradesh	147	243	479	252.01	28.0	46.5	40.7	9.5	3.3
Maharashtra	150	259	546	272.66	30.7	42.2	37.9	9.3	3.4
Orissa	138	216	391	219.80	24.7	56.7	49.8	12.0	4.1
Punjab	255	409	837	433.00	28.2	6.2	11.7	1.9	0.5
Rajasthan	194	317	590	322.39	26.5	22.3	26.4	5.2	1.6
Tamil Nadu	162	272	600	293.62	31.2	36.6	32.9	7.3	2.5
Uttar Pradesh	158	266	521	273.83	28.2	39.5	42.3	10.4	3.5
West Bengal	175	267	509	278.78	25.4	33.3	41.2	8.3	2.5
All-India	*162*	*271*	*541*	*281.40*	*28.6*	*37.2*	*37.2*	*8.5*	*2.8*
Mixed 30/365 days Reference Periods									
Andhra Pradesh	177	280	504	283.49	24.9	30.6	12.5	2.2	0.6
Assam	196	281	411	272.86	17.6	22.6	36.0	6.3	1.6
Bihar	153	231	367	227.15	20.9	48.8	52.9	11.8	3.9
Gujarat	206	328	527	319.08	22.3	18.3	16.6	2.9	0.8
Haryana	225	374	700	379.55	26.9	12.8	22.3	4.0	1.2
Karnataka	176	280	488	279.88	24.3	30.5	22.0	4.3	1.3
Kerala	232	386	732	393.75	27.2	11.3	21.9	4.4	1.4
Madhya Pradesh	161	257	459	258.78	25.0	38.8	32.8	7.0	2.2
Maharashtra	165	275	508	277.50	26.7	36.1	31.0	6.6	2.2
Orissa	146	222	375	222.49	22.4	53.0	45.6	10.0	3.2
Punjab	277	434	758	436.35	23.8	4.2	8.5	1.2	0.3
Rajasthan	212	330	568	330.38	23.5	16.6	19.2	3.4	0.9
Tamil Nadu	172	283	563	294.72	28.2	31.5	28.1	6.0	2.0
Uttar Pradesh	170	275	494	277.10	25.2	34.1	37.3	8.1	2.5
West Bengal	184	279	502	285.98	23.8	27.9	35.5	6.7	1.9
All-India	*174*	*283*	*519*	*286.58*	*25.8*	*31.6*	*31.6*	*6.6*	*2.1*

Note: The MRP estimates are from distributions obtained using the 365-day recall for clothing, footwear, durable goods, education and institutional medical care and 30-day, recall for all other items. The statewise poverty lines used in Columns 8 to 10 are those that were used by the Planning Commission based on the Expert Group methodology. The National poverty line implied by these is Rs 205.88 and is used in Column 7. The All-India estimates in the table are those obtained by applying the national poverty line to the All-India distribution and need not correspond to the population weighted average of the state level poverty estimates.

Source: Unit-level data from NSS 50th Round.

Table 14.2(b) Key Results from Uniform and Mixed Recalls — 50th Round Urban

| | Monthly Per Capita Consumer Expenditure | | | | Gini Index | Poverty Measures | | | |
| | | | | | | National Poverty Line | State-Specific Poverty Line | | |
	Poorest 40 Per cent	Next 40 Per cent	Richest 20 Per cent	All		Head-count Ratio	Head-count Ratio	Poverty Gap	Squared Poverty Gap
Uniform 30-day Reference Period									
Andhra Pradesh	214	385	845	408.60	32.3	39.9	38.8	9.3	3.2
Assam	257	444	892	458.57	29.0	25.9	7.9	0.9	0.2
Bihar	192	333	714	353.03	30.9	50.1	34.8	7.9	2.6
Gujarat	258	437	879	454.18	29.1	24.4	28.3	6.2	2.0
Haryana	269	464	903	473.92	28.4	22.0	16.5	3.0	0.9
Karnataka	217	416	849	423.14	31.9	35.7	39.9	11.4	4.4
Kerala	253	448	1,066	493.83	34.3	24.6	24.3	5.5	1.9
Madhya Pradesh	214	376	859	408.06	33.1	39.5	48.1	13.4	5.1
Maharashtra	247	507	1,142	529.80	35.7	25.5	35.0	10.2	4.2
Orissa	213	396	793	402.54	30.7	36.5	40.9	11.4	4.3
Punjab	290	506	960	510.73	28.1	16.3	10.9	1.7	0.4
Rajasthan	236	416	820	424.73	29.3	31.1	31.0	7.0	2.2
Tamil Nadu	221	397	957	438.29	34.8	35.7	39.9	10.2	3.9
Uttar Pradesh	201	369	804	388.97	32.6	42.3	35.1	9.0	3.3
West Bengal	235	450	1,000	474.19	33.9	31.1	22.9	4.5	1.4
All-India	*228*	*427*	*980*	*458.04*	*34.4*	*32.6*	*32.6*	*8.0*	*2.9*
Mixed 30/365 days Reference Periods									
Andhra Pradesh	225	399	817	413.06	30.3	35.0	34.2	7.9	2.7
Assam	275	463	922	479.73	28.3	18.9	4.6	0.7	0.2
Bihar	206	356	729	370.69	29.7	43.6	28.8	6.2	2.0
Gujarat	278	474	870	474.77	26.9	20.2	23.7	4.8	1.4
Haryana	290	488	906	492.97	26.7	17.0	10.0	2.0	0.6
Karnataka	234	441	861	442.10	30.4	31.0	36.0	9.2	3.3
Kerala	260	447	1,007	484.07	32.3	21.8	21.5	5.0	1.7
Madhya Pradesh	232	392	811	412.02	29.7	32.5	43.4	10.8	3.8
Maharashtra	268	522	1,128	541.70	33.5	20.5	30.2	8.1	3.1
Orissa	223	404	787	408.35	29.4	35.1	38.5	10.1	3.6
Punjab	308	522	953	522.90	26.5	12.3	7.6	1.3	0.3
Rajasthan	256	431	799	434.28	26.8	25.0	25.0	5.1	1.5
Tamil Nadu	234	412	928	443.99	32.8	31.6	36.0	8.6	3.2
Uttar Pradesh	216	388	782	397.78	30.2	37.2	30.6	7.3	2.4
West Bengal	248	469	1,018	490.47	32.7	27.8	18.2	3.5	1.1
All-India	*243*	*446*	*948*	*464.83*	*31.9*	*27.9*	*27.9*	*6.5*	*2.2*

Note: The MRP estimates are from distributions obtained using the 365-day recall for clothing, footwear, durable goods, education and institutional medical care and 30 days recall for all other items. The statewise poverty lines used in Columns 8 to 10 are those that were used by the Planning Commission based on the Expert Group methodology. The national poverty line implied by these is Rs 281.36 and is used in Column 7. The all-India estimates in the table are those obtained by applying the national poverty line to the all-India distribution and need not correspond to the population weighted average of the state level poverty estimates.

Source: Unit-level data from NSS 50th Round.

   (ii) It is this greater equality of MRP distribution than URP that drives differences in poverty, not differences in means. Mean per capita consumption expenditure (MPCE) is higher with URP than MRP in about a third of the cases, but nonetheless poverty is higher with URP.

  (iii) The greater equality of MRP is because in every case the bottom 80 per cent by this distribution report higher MPCE than corresponding fractiles of URP distribution, and because MPCE of the top quintile from MRP distribution is less than from the URP distribution.

  (iv) The reason why MPCE of poorer groups is higher by MRP than URP is because there is a large percentage of zero responses to the 30-day recall for low frequency purchases, which is reduced considerably with the longer 365-day recall. The frequency of zero response with URP is particularly marked for the bottom 40 per cent. For this fractile, the MRP-URP difference in MPCE is in almost all cases within a relatively narrow range of 4 to 9 per cent.

  (v) The reason why the top quintile reports lower consumption by MRP is less clear, but use of the longer recall does appear to lead to memory loss. In most cases, the average household in the top quintile reports higher expenditure on low frequency items during 'last 30 days' than the 30-day equivalent of what the same household reports as its annual expenditure on these items.

These observations are relevant to assess the possible 'contamination' of 365-day replies on low frequency items as a result of the presence of 30-day questions on these items in Round 50 but not in Round 55. Sundaram and Tendulkar have asserted that the influence from one recall to another is unlikely in the case of these low frequency expenditures since these are 'salient in memory of respondents'. But this is not correct. In the 50th Round, reported average expenditure on these items was higher by the 365-day recall, whereas in rounds 51 to 54, where the two recalls were used on separate samples, the 30-day recall returned higher average expenditure on these items. That presence of 30-day questions magnifies 365-day reports means that the 365-day estimates from the 50th Round are not fully comparable with those from the 55th Round.

However, detailed analysis summarised in Table 14.3, of 43rd and 50th Round differences between 30 and 365-day recalls with corresponding differences in rounds 51 to 53 shows this to be confined largely to the upper tail of the distribution.[3] The richest quintile not only report less consumption of low frequency items by the 365-day than the 30-day recall, this difference increases significantly when 365-day questions are asked without 30-day questions. In round 50, the top quintile by MRP reported 75–80 per cent of the spending on 365-day items than the top quintile by URP, but this ratio fell to half in round 51 to 53. This explains almost entirely why reported total consumption of these items was higher by MRP in the 50th Round but higher by URP in rounds 51 to 53. On the other hand, presence or absence of 30-day questions does not appear to matter for the poorest 40 per cent population since, irrespective of this, 365-day questions elicit many more non-zero replies. In particular, MRP-URP differences in MPCE for this fractile in rounds 51 to 53 are well within the 4–9 per cent range found from rounds 43 and 50. Sundaram-Tendulkar are correct that salience of low frequency purchases makes influence

---

[3] However, this analysis, although very strongly suggestive, cannot be conclusive. The NSS has so far not included a direct control to test how presence of 30-day queries affects 365-day answers within the same round. Moreover, rounds 51-54 had two schedules: one which used an uniform 30-day reference period and another which used not only the 365-day recall for low frequency items but also the 7-day recall for food and intoxicants. It therefore needs to be assumed that presence of 7-day questions on food did not affect outcomes by the 365-day recall for low frequency items. The analysis above has ignored the 54th Round since this was only a half-year round and may be affected by seasonality. More generally also, only full year NSS rounds have been used in the rest of this paper.

Table 14.3 Percentage Change in Fractile Specific MPCE Due to Shift from 30-Day to 365-Day Reference Period by Item

NSS Round	Rural				Urban			
	Bottom 40 Per cent	Next 40 Per cent	Top 20 Per cent	All	Bottom 40 Per cent	Next 40 Per cent	Top 20 Per cent	All
Clothing								
43	5.3	2.6	−3.7	0.7	5.8	3.6	−1.7	1.7
50	6.6	4.2	−3.7	2.3	6.2	4.0	−1.5	2.6
51	5.3	2.1	−5.4	−0.1	6.3	3.2	−2.5	1.2
52	6.5	2.6	−6.8	−0.1	6.2	2.0	−5.2	−0.5
53	5.8	2.3	−5.1	0.1	5.7	2.5	−2.4	0.9
Footwear								
43	0.2	0.1	−0.6	−0.1	0.4	0.1	−0.4	0.0
50	0.5	0.4	−0.6	0.1	0.6	0.5	−0.2	0.3
51	0.5	0.2	−0.5	0.0	0.8	0.6	−0.2	0.3
52	0.6	0.2	−0.9	−0.1	0.8	0.5	−0.8	0.0
53	0.4	0.2	−0.9	−0.2	0.8	0.5	−0.3	0.2
Durable Goods								
43	0.6	0.3	−2.6	−0.8	0.4	0.8	−2.7	−0.8
50	0.7	0.5	−2.6	−0.4	0.5	0.5	−2.9	−0.6
51	0.3	0.1	−8.1	−3.1	0.3	0.4	−4.9	−2.0
52	0.4	0.0	−5.6	−2.0	0.4	0.5	−8.3	−3.4
53	0.2	0.2	−5.4	−2.0	0.4	1.0	−4.1	−1.4
Above 3 items								
43	6.1	3.0	−6.9	−0.2	6.6	4.5	−4.8	0.9
50	7.8	5.1	−6.9	2.0	7.3	5.0	−4.6	2.3
51	6.1	2.4	−14.0	−3.3	7.4	4.3	−7.6	−0.5
52	7.5	2.8	−13.3	−2.2	7.4	2.9	−14.3	−3.9
53	6.4	2.8	−11.4	−2.1	7.0	4.1	−6.9	−0.2
Education								
50	0.2	0.1	−0.4	0.1	0.3	0.1	−1.8	−0.3
51	0.1	−0.2	−0.7	−0.4	0.7	0.3	−1.3	−0.4
52	0.1	−0.3	−0.9	−0.4	0.5	−0.3	−3.4	−1.5
53	−0.6	−1.1	−1.1	−1.0	−0.2	−1.4	−3.1	−1.9
Institutional Medicine								
50	0.1	0.2	−1.2	−0.2	0.2	0.2	−1.7	−0.5
51	0.1	0.0	−1.3	−0.5	−0.1	0.1	−1.0	−0.5
52	0.4	0.2	−0.5	0.0	0.4	0.1	−0.9	−0.3
53	0.1	0.2	−1.9	−0.7	0.2	0.3	−2.9	−1.1
Above 5 items								
50	8.1	5.5	−8.5	1.9	7.7	5.2	−8.0	1.5
51	6.2	2.2	−16.0	−4.1	7.9	4.7	−10.0	−1.4
52	8.0	2.7	−14.7	−2.7	8.3	2.8	−18.6	−5.8
53	5.9	1.8	−14.4	−3.7	7.0	3.0	−12.8	−3.3

Note: Each cell gives the value of $100 * (c^{365}_{ij} - c^{30}_{ij})/y^{30}_j$ by round/sector/item. Here, y^{30}_j is MPCE using the uniform 30-day recall of the jth fractile group formed using MPCE by this recall; c^{30}_{ij} is the 30-day consumption report on the ith item by the jth fractile group when fractiles are formed using the MPCE by uniform 30-day recall; and c^{365}_{ij} is the 365-day consumption report on the ith item by jth fractile group when fractiles are formed using the MPCE by mixed 30-365-day recall.

from 30-day questions to 365-day answers unlikely for most respondents. But the rich who are frequent buyers of these items do suffer memory lapse with the long reference period. This becomes more pronounced if not prompted by a shorter recall.

Certain important conclusions follow regarding the influence that presence of 30-day questions on low frequency items has on replies to 365-day questions on these items:

(a) First, since presence of 30-day queries lead to higher 365-day reports of low frequency items by the top quintile who are major consumers of these items, measured MPCE with MRP is higher.

(b) Second, since presence of 30-day queries increases consumption reports of only the relatively rich, measured inequality is higher. Although inequality is reported less with MRP than URP in all rounds, Gini differences in rounds 43 and 50 were only about half those in rounds 51 to 53.[4]

(c) Third, and crucially, since presence or absence of 30-day questions does not appear to affect the 365-day consumer expenditure estimates for the poorest 40 per cent of population, poverty counts from the MRP of 50th Round are almost fully comparable with the MRP in later rounds.

This closes discussion on comparability regarding 30 and 365-day recalls for low frequency items. Since 30-day queries on these were dropped in 55th and subsequent rounds, the 365-day recall in these is similar to those in experimental schedules of rounds 51 to 53. Consequently, both MPCE and inequality are likely to have been underestimated in these later rounds as compared to MRP of rounds 43 and 50. Nonetheless, it must be accepted that Sundaram-Tendulkar were correct in treating poverty estimates from the 50th Round MRP as a valid objective method of dealing with the 365-day issue. However, poverty comparisons from 55th Round remain subject to problems created by the 7-day questions on food and intoxicants in its Consumer Expenditure Survey (CES).

The nature of the problem created by 7-day queries for food, etc., is illustrated in Table 14.4 which compares poverty headcounts from the 43rd and 50th Round MRPs with two sets of 55th Round 30/ 365-day counts The first are from its Employment-Unemployment Survey (EUS) which, although free from 7-day problems, may overestimate poverty because of an abridged schedule. The second are official 55th Round counts that, although from the full CES schedule, may underestimate poverty because of its 7-day questions. It is evident that despite comparability provided by 50th Round MRP, even the direction of poverty change is contestable. With the number of poor up by over 50 million between 1993/94 and 1999/2000 according to its EUS, but down by 12 million according to its CES, objective comparisons from the 55th Round are inconclusive.

A third objective comparison, of counts using 7-day food recall from 55th Round CES with those from schedule type 2 of rounds 51 to 53 which used exactly the same recalls, also shows increased poverty [Sen 2000, 2001]. This clearly proves 'contamination', i.e. convergence of 7 and 30-day food reports in 55th Round CES, either because 7-day questions influenced 30-day answers or the other way round or, as is most likely, some combination of both. Although estimates of food expenditure by these two recalls did differ in 55th Round CES, this was by only 6 per cent as against 30 per cent in experimental Rounds 51 to 54 where these recalls were used on different samples. 55th Round poverty counts using 7-day reports are overestimated if presence of 30-day questions pulled down 7-day reports. But, similarly,

---

[4] The Ginis being compared are from the MRP and URP of the 43rd and 50th Round distributions reported above and from schedule types 1 and 2 in rounds 51 to 53. Inequality was lower by 2.5 and 2.8 Gini points by the mixed recall in urban and rural areas in the 50th Round, and by 2.7 and 2.3 points in round 43, as against an average difference of 5.3 and 5.0 Gini points in urban and rural areas between schedules 1 and 2 of rounds 51 to 53. It should be noted, however, that the comparison is not exact since schedule type 2 in rounds 51 to 53 contained 7-day questions on food.

Table 14.4 Headcount Poverty Ratios by 30/365 Days Reference Periods

	Using Official State-Specific Poverty Lines					Using National Poverty Lines for All States				
	43rd MRP	50th MRP-A	50th MRP	55th EUS	55th CES	43rd MRP	50rd MRP-A	50th MRP	55th EUS	55th CES
Rural										
Andhra Pradesh	17.7	12.7	12.5	13.8	11.1	36.7	30.8	30.6	31.6	27.8
Assam	34.8	36.9	36.0	48.3	40.0	24.1	23.5	22.6	35.0	28.5
Bihar	49.4	53.1	52.9	51.9	44.3	44.1	49.0	48.8	49.7	42.2
Gujarat	21.9	17.1	16.6	18.5	13.2	22.1	18.8	18.3	20.5	14.7
Haryana	12.5	21.6	22.3	14.2	8.3	10.1	12.8	12.8	9.4	4.8
Karnataka	32.0	22.4	22.0	30.1	17.4	40.5	31.4	30.5	35.1	21.4
Kerala	28.2	22.4	21.9	17.6	9.4	19.6	12.3	11.3	10.3	4.9
Madhya Pradesh	37.4	33.4	32.8	43.9	37.1	43.8	39.6	38.8	49.6	41.8
Maharashtra	34.9	31.2	31.0	32.9	23.7	34.6	36.2	36.1	36.3	26.0
Orissa	55.7	45.3	45.6	54.3	48.0	49.9	52.3	53.0	55.7	49.3
Punjab	8.0	8.5	8.5	11.5	6.4	5.3	4.7	4.2	7.6	3.3
Rajasthan	29.1	20.0	19.2	17.5	13.7	27.3	16.5	16.6	14.0	11.0
Tamil Nadu	43.5	28.3	28.1	31.5	20.6	41.2	31.8	31.5	37.0	25.6
Uttar Pradesh	39.0	37.7	37.3	35.7	31.2	39.6	34.6	34.1	32.9	28.6
West Bengal	45.9	35.6	35.5	43.8	31.9	33.9	28.0	27.9	36.3	26.1
All-India	*35.2*	*31.9*	*31.6*	*34.0*	*27.1*	*35.2*	*31.9*	*31.6*	*34.0*	*27.1*
Urban										
Andhra Pradesh	36.3	34.6	34.2	33.6	26.6	42.8	35.4	35.0	32.8	25.9
Assam	10.2	4.7	4.6	10.5	7.5	24.6	18.4	18.9	22.7	22.8
Bihar	46.8	29.4	28.8	33.1	32.9	55.6	44.3	43.6	48.6	47.3
Gujarat	29.8	23.6	23.7	19.6	15.6	24.5	20.0	20.2	16.8	12.8
Haryana	13.7	10.0	10.0	15.7	10.0	21.2	16.1	17.0	19.6	12.6
Karnataka	43.4	36.0	36.0	31.8	25.3	38.8	31.6	31.0	24.5	18.3
Kerala	35.4	22.0	21.5	27.7	20.3	34.8	22.4	21.8	24.6	17.6
Madhya Pradesh	43.3	44.1	43.4	45.6	38.4	35.3	32.3	32.5	41.1	33.8
Maharashtra	36.3	30.5	30.2	33.0	26.8	27.3	20.7	20.5	22.4	17.6
Orissa	38.1	38.1	38.5	48.7	42.8	36.6	34.6	35.1	45.2	39.5
Punjab	10.4	7.9	7.6	9.6	5.8	16.3	12.5	12.3	16.6	12.7
Rajasthan	33.8	25.0	25.0	27.9	19.9	32.7	25.1	25.0	25.2	17.8
Tamil Nadu	37.7	36.0	36.0	22.2	22.1	35.7	31.3	31.6	19.0	19.4
Uttar Pradesh	41.6	30.8	30.6	36.4	30.9	45.7	37.1	37.2	43.6	37.3
West Bengal	30.4	18.4	18.2	17.9	14.9	36.8	27.8	27.8	24.5	21.6
All-India	*34.9*	*28.0*	*27.9*	*28.9*	*23.6*	*34.9*	*28.0*	*27.9*	*28.9*	*23.6*
MEMO: Number of Poor (million)										
All-India	278	276	274	327	262	278	276	274	327	262
15 Major States	274	269	267	319	257	272	271	268	319	259

Note: Columns 2 and 7 are from 43rd Round unit level data, i.e. Tables 1a and 1b; Columns 4 and 9 are from 50th Round unit level data, i.e. Tables 2a and 2b; columns 3 and 8 are also from 50th Round unit level data but MRP-A is the MRP corresponding to the 43rd Round, i.e. 365-day estimates are used only for clothing, footwear and durable goods; column 6 gives the official counts from the 55th Round and column 11 reworks this applying the national poverty line uniformly to the grouped data of every state; columns 5 and 10 are obtained by applying the same poverty lines as in columns 6 and 11 to grouped data from the consumption schedule of the 55th Round Employment-Unemployment Survey. The All-India number of poor is obtained applying the all-India poverty ratios to all-India population. For the 15 major states, the number of poor in each state is obtained by applying the state poverty ratio to state population.

its 30-day counts are underestimates if 7-day questions pulled up 30-day reports. The real issue, since official estimates use 30-day reports and field instructions in 55th Round CES were also to ask the 30-day question first, is by how much were 30-day answers affected, i.e. what would these have been without the 7-day questions?

On this, the only direct check is the 55th Round EUS but, unfortunately, no independent analysis of this is possible. The official NSSO Compact Disk containing 55th Round EUS unit level data does not include its consumption schedule and no details, apart from distributions by expenditure class, have been published. This is a serious drawback since EUS estimates can mislead unless account is taken of its commodity composition. For example, not having access to this, Sen (2001) had assumed that the 10 per cent shortfall of EUS total expenditure from CES could be attributed entirely to food and intoxicants. Since this implied 25 per cent difference between 7-day CES and 30-day EUS food estimates, i.e. the same ball park as 7/30-day differences in rounds 51 to 54 where the two recalls were sampled separately, he had concluded that CES 'contamination' was mainly from 7-day queries to 30-day answers. It now turns out that this conclusion was incorrect.

Sundaram and Tendulkar (2003a), who did have access to unit level EUS consumption data, have clarified matters. They report that not all the difference between EUS and CES was on account of food, and that EUS estimates are about 10 per cent lower for both food and non-food. They note correctly that, since identical reference periods were used in EUS and CES for non-food items, lower EUS estimates for these must be attributed to abridgement in EUS. This must be the starting point for valid assessments of comparable estimates from EUS and of 'contamination' in the CES.

Fortunately, it is possible to purge the EUS of underestimation in non-food items that could not have been affected by 'contamination'. This requires synthetic distributions in which per capita consumption of each fractile is the fractile-specific sum of food, etc., from EUS and of remaining items from CES. Since full CES details are available, and Sundaram-Tendulkar have provided fractile-wise ratios of EUS to CES expenditure on food, etc., these could be computed. These imply poverty counts of 31.7 and 27.9 per cent for rural and urban India respectively, in-between corresponding counts from EUS and CES and almost identical to 50th Round MRP. This reduces the upper bound on comparable 55th Round poverty, but continues to imply that there was no reduction in poverty ratios between rounds 50 and 55. Nonetheless, since these counts are similar, there is the positive implication that comparable poverty ratios must have reduced if any part of CES-EUS difference in estimates of food, etc., was due to abridgement in EUS rather than due to 'contamination' in CES.

On this remaining issue of CES-EUS differences in estimates of food and intoxicants expenditure only, Sundaram-Tendulkar take the view that this was due entirely to abridgement in EUS and not at all to 'contamination' in CES. But they employ a curious logic. In a vast majority of cases they find 30-day CES estimates to be higher than corresponding EUS estimates but by less than the difference that was found between 7 and 30 days estimates in experimental rounds 51 to 54. From this, i.e. absence of full 'contamination', they conclude no 'contamination'. For some items, e.g. 'other food', they do find CES-EUS differences consistent with full 'contamination'. But even for these they deny any 'contamination', arguing that EUS underestimation is likely to have been greater for such heterogeneous items. They assume basically that only two outcomes are possible, either full 'contamination' or none, and that this must be similar across all item groups. Since full 'contamination' is not found for most food items, they cite evidence that abridgement in EUS did measure lower non-food consumption to argue that this rules out not only full 'contamination' in the few food items where this was a possibility but also any 'contamination' for any food item.

However, contrary to Sundaram-Tendulkar's assertions, past NSS evidence is that *schedule abridgement does not reduce reported food consumption*. A methodological survey in the 38th Round had found no difference in reported food expenditures between a short schedule and the full, and this result was repeated in the 52nd Round.[5] The short schedules in the 52nd Round, although more aggregated on non-food items, used exactly the same aggregation of food items as the 55th Round EUS.[6] As compared to the full 30-day (type 1) schedule of 52nd Round, these returned about 25 per cent lower reported non-food expenditure but reported identical total food expenditure.[7] This evidence refutes quite conclusively Sundaram-Tendulkar's claim that EUS food reports are necessarily less than comparable, just because it returned lower non-food reports than CES.

Since this exhausts what can be inferred using 55th Round data alone, it is worth summarising:

(a) If 30-day estimates of food and intoxicants in 55th Round CES are completely uncontaminated by presence of 7-day questions, poverty ratios declined 4.1 and 4.5 percentage points in rural and urban India compared to 50th Round MRP. If so, the absolute number of poor declined by about 12 million between 1993/94 and 1999/2000.

(b) At the other extreme, if EUS estimates of food and intoxicants are assumed unaffected by schedule abridgement, comparable 55th Round poverty ratios are same as 50th Round MRP. If so, the absolute number of poor increased by 33 million between 1993/94 and 1999/2000.

(c) This difference is due entirely to the 10 per cent higher expenditure on food and intoxicants estimated from the 30 days recall in the CES than from the same recall in the EUS.

(d) That the CES and EUS differ so much on food estimates makes it certain that a joint hypothesis of no effect of abridgement in EUS and no 'contamination' in CES can be rejected.

(e) Full 'contamination' either way, with or without effect of abridgement, can also be rejected because 7 and 30 days food estimates do differ in the CES.

(f) Sundaram-Tendulkar claim that the entire CES-EUS difference in food expenditure was due to abridgement in EUS with no 'contamination' from 7 to 30-day recall in CES. But this is not supported by past NSS evidence and is not based on sound logic regarding 'contamination'.[8]

[5] See 'A Note on the Results of the Methodological Survey on Integrated Short-Schedule on Consumer Expenditure', *Sarvekshana*, Vol. XI, No. 3, January 1988; and NSSO Expert Group on Non-sampling Errors: *Preliminary Comparison of Consumption data collected through Detailed and Abridged Schedules: NSS 52nd Round*, (mimeo).

[6] These 52nd Round worksheets (schedules 25.0 and 25.2) asked only 8 questions (all using 365-day recall) on broadly aggregated non-food items, as against 24 (10 using 30-day recall and 14 using 365-day recall) in 55th Round EUS. However, both asked only 30-day questions on the same 8 broadly aggregated food items, although, unlike 55th Round EUS, the 52nd Round worksheets also recorded break-down of food items by 'home-grown' and 'others'.

[7] Ratios of worksheet to full schedule All-India consumption estimates were 1.004, 0.774 and 0.914 for food, non-food and total in rural and 1.002, 0.731 and 0.867 in urban. However, within the food group, worksheet estimates were higher for fruits, vegetables and meat, etc, and lower for other items. Interestingly, despite lower MPCE and because of their 365-day recall non-food distribution, poverty counts from these worksheets were almost identical to those from the type 1 schedules of Round 52. These All-India counts were about 3 percentage points larger than from 55th Round EUS, reflecting almost entirely the much larger non-food underestimation in 52nd Round worksheets.

[8] The really curious aspect of Sundaram-Tendulkar's argument is that although they report most CES-EUS differences as between full and no 'contamination', they rule out the obvious. They do not even examine partial 'contamination', i e, that 7-day queries in the 55th Round CES led to average outcomes somewhere in between no 'contamination' and the 7-30-day difference expected from Rounds 51 to 54. Their logic underlying this appears to be that each individual is likely to have given either the 30-day or the 7-day reply, and that the final estimate must therefore be either of these and nothing in between. But, even ignoring that this rules out arbitrarily that different individuals may have had different in-between

In view of the above, it is not possible to accept (a) as correct comparison. On the other hand, since (b) is consistent with past NSS evidence on schedule abridgement, any acceptable bound must admit the possibility that poverty ratios did not decline between 1993/94 and 1999/2000.

Nonetheless, since schedule abridgement is generally believed to reduce estimates, it is reasonable to also admit the possibility that despite past NSS evidence there was probably both some effect of abridgement on EUS and some 'contamination' in CES. The issue then is of their relative extents. But this requires data external to the 55th Round and, since the purpose here is to assess 55th Round comparability not validity, the only suitable external references are estimates from other NSS rounds. In this context, it may be noted that 55th Round real per capita food consumption from CES is above, and from EUS below, all other full-year NSS rounds during 1987–2002. A simple model using time trend and relative prices shows the CES excess to be statistically significant and to account for about 70 per cent of CES-EUS difference. This implies poverty reduction, but by only 1–1.5 percentage points. However, this also suggests EUS underestimation.

In the light of this, and since an upper bound on comparable 55th Round poverty has already been established, a more detailed procedure was adopted to obtain a lower bound. This was based on Sundaram-Tendulkar's (2003b) finding that CES-EUS differences were concentrated on a few items, and were small for remaining items. Since they provided itemwise, statewise EUS details, these could be assessed individually against corresponding counterfactuals from neighbouring rounds, particularly 53rd and 56th. In many cases, e.g. pulses, edible oil, meat, etc., and vegetables, EUS estimates exceeded counterfactuals, while in other cases, e.g. other foods and milk and products, EUS estimates were well below counterfactuals. Given this asymmetry, it was decided to conclude 'contamination' only if the CES estimate was higher than both EUS and counterfactual; and to limit its measured extent to excess of CES over the higher of these two. This procedure, i.e. only upward adjustments itemwise, statewise, to EUS for its abridged schedule, and no adjustment of CES to below EUS, captures Sundaram-Tendulkar's intuition and confirms their assessment of substantial EUS underestimation of items such as other food. The results, in Table 14.5, attribute bulk of CES-EUS difference to EUS underestimation and return strikingly small estimates of CES 'contamination'.

The results are surprising for two reasons. First, implied extents of EUS underestimation are found to be much larger than had been found comparing estimates from 52nd Round worksheets with corresponding full schedule estimates.[9] Second, implied extents of 'contamination' from 7-day food questions in the 55th Round CES are almost unbelievably low. The 7-day questions in the 55th Round CES questionnaire had preceded 30-day ones and instructions to ask these in reverse order were not issued till six weeks (i.e. 11.5 per cent) of the survey was over. Even with full compliance, expected 'contamination' of 30-day reports of 55th Round CES would be about this proportion of the 7-30-day differences found in experimental rounds 51–54. However, most estimates in Table 14.5 are less than

---

responses for different items, there is the fact that each pairing of respondent and investigator in a random survey is an independent event. Given this, their argument that the aggregate outcome must be either the 30 or 7-day estimate, and nothing in-between, is in terms of logic dangerously close to the assertion that since a tossed coin can only come down head or tail, in many tosses too there can only be either all heads or all tails.

[9] Thus, for 'other foods', the ratio of EUS to the implied uncontaminated CES from Table 14.5 is 0.72 and 0.67 in rural and urban all-India while 52nd Round ratios of short to full schedule estimates were 0.98 and 0.87.

Table 14.5 Estimated Overestimation due to 'Contamination' in 30-Day Estimates of the 55th Round Consumer Expenditure Survey (As per cent of reported consumption)

	Cereals, etc.	Pulses, etc.	Milk, etc.	Edible Oils	Vegeta-bles	Fruits and Nuts	Meat, etc.	Other Food	Paan, Tobacco, etc.	All
Rural										
Andhra Pradesh	0.00	0.00	0.00	0.00	0.40	0.00	0.00	6.30	0.00	1.03
Assam	0.00	2.17	0.00	0.00	0.00	0.00	0.00	10.22	0.00	1.18
Bihar	0.00	6.89	0.00	3.19	7.92	6.28	0.00	16.13	0.00	3.29
Gujarat	0.00	4.58	1.21	0.00	0.00	0.23	0.00	0.71	0.00	0.72
Haryana	0.26	11.19	7.15	0.00	0.00	0.00	0.00	15.29	3.20	6.07
Karnataka	0.00	6.89	9.64	0.00	12.43	11.95	0.00	5.23	0.72	4.13
Kerala	0.00	0.00	0.00	0.00	0.00	16.38	2.67	12.95	9.00	5.06
Madhya Pradesh	1.96	7.32	13.19	2.25	0.79	0.00	0.00	9.40	0.00	4.61
Maharashtra	4.24	11.77	0.00	0.00	1.28	0.00	0.00	3.44	0.00	3.08
Orissa	0.00	0.00	0.00	0.00	4.67	0.00	0.70	0.00	14.87	1.22
Punjab	2.22	9.91	0.00	0.99	0.00	10.31	0.00	16.85	13.21	5.43
Rajasthan	0.00	6.28	1.94	0.00	0.00	0.00	1.77	12.23	4.03	2.92
Tamil Nadu	0.00	11.97	0.00	0.00	2.25	12.76	0.00	17.42	0.00	5.64
Uttar Pradesh	2.82	6.80	0.96	7.06	0.00	0.00	0.00	13.80	8.68	4.52
West Bengal	0.00	0.00	2.06	2.72	7.83	0.00	7.38	0.00	4.31	2.26
All-India	*0.95*	*6.35*	*2.43*	*2.04*	*2.81*	*5.03*	*1.78*	*9.90*	*3.23*	*3.38*
Urban										
Andhra Pradesh	3.61	0.00	0.00	0.00	0.00	0.00	0.00	1.57	4.84	1.67
Assam	2.25	0.00	12.82	0.00	0.00	0.00	1.38	20.56	13.98	6.14
Bihar	0.00	4.31	1.49	6.89	0.00	0.00	3.57	7.27	0.10	2.21
Gujarat	0.00	6.10	2.94	3.57	0.00	14.53	0.00	11.53	0.00	4.46
Haryana	0.11	0.50	3.94	0.00	0.00	0.00	0.00	0.00	26.09	2.48
Karnataka	3.62	0.00	7.24	0.00	0.00	18.79	0.00	15.06	0.00	6.65
Kerala	2.81	0.00	0.00	0.00	0.42	11.06	0.00	0.00	0.00	1.65
Madhya Pradesh	4.40	10.55	2.73	0.00	0.00	0.00	0.50	3.69	4.00	3.32
Maharashtra	2.46	3.75	0.72	0.99	0.00	3.73	0.89	8.11	4.98	3.22
Orissa	2.82	2.53	0.00	0.00	0.00	0.00	0.00	0.00	0.00	1.22
Punjab	2.50	4.40	0.00	0.00	0.00	0.00	6.98	6.41	0.00	2.21
Rajasthan	2.44	3.85	10.15	1.96	0.00	0.00	9.95	11.51	8.80	6.47
Tamil Nadu	0.41	9.67	4.76	0.00	0.00	20.30	1.38	20.63	6.86	8.19
Uttar Pradesh	1.67	10.95	0.00	6.45	0.00	15.04	0.81	8.50	0.00	3.90
West Bengal	0.00	0.00	4.94	0.00	0.00	0.00	5.66	24.02	0.00	6.09
All-India	*1.92*	*5.16*	*2.96*	*1.65*	*0.01*	*9.20*	*2.13*	*11.02*	*3.79*	*4.38*

Note: The table above reports the percentage difference between the reported CES estimate and its 'uncontaminated' counterpart CES*. The latter is estimated as CES* = Min[CES, Max(EUS, Z)] where CES and EUS are the relevant actual survey estimates and Z is a counterfactual. Z varies slightly from case to case but corresponds closely in all cases with interpolation to the 55th Round from corresponding estimates of NSS rounds 53 and 56. EUS is derived from figures in Sundaram and Tendulkar (2003a and 2003b). All-India figures are weighted averages of state-specific figures and, since no negative adjustment is being allowed at the state-level, are slightly higher than if all-India estimates of CES, EUS and Z were used.

this.[10] This does raise questions regarding both estimates and benchmarks. But since the calculations follow Sundaram-Tendulkar's intuition and use their tabulations (that could not be checked against primary data), these small 'contaminations' can safely be taken to be the minimum necessary correction to their unacceptable claim of no 'contamination' from 7-day queries.[11]

Table 14.6 presents key results on 55th Round distribution and poverty, both before any adjustment and after adjusting pro rata its unit level data itemwise and statewise with the corrections for 'contamination' in Table 14.5. Although these small corrections increase 55th Round all-India poverty headcounts from 27.0 per cent to 28.8 rural, and from 23.4 to 25.1 per cent urban, the 'food adjusted' counts are lower than from 50th Round mixed recall and imply reduction in poverty incidence. However, in view of all the other evidence presented and the deliberate downward bias used in computation, these must be treated as lower bounds to the range of comparable 55th Round poverty estimates at whose upper bound all-India poverty ratios may have remained unchanged from the 50th Round. Nonetheless, accepting these lower bounds for what follows, maximum poverty reduction between 1993/94 and 1999/2000 is placed finally at 2.8 percentage points. This implies increase in the absolute number of poor by about five million and some deterioration in poverty reduction performance compared to 1987/88 to 1993/94.

DEATON ADJUSTMENT

This conclusion contradicts Deaton's (2003a) claim that the poverty ratio declined 7 percentage points between rounds 50 and 55. Unlike Sundaram-Tendulkar's direct comparison on the 30/365-day issue and subjective view on 7-day questions, Deaton had attempted to deal simultaneously, but indirectly, with both. He exploited that, despite non-comparable recall, both 50th and 55th Rounds used only 30-day questions for non-food items other than clothing, footwear, durable goods, education and institutional medical care. He pointed out that poverty counts comparable with the 50th Round can be obtained for the 55th Round using its data for only this comparable set of goods and services, provided two assumptions hold:

(i) that the personal distribution of expenditure on this set of goods and services is unaffected by changes in reference periods used for other goods and services; and

(ii) that conditional probabilities of being poor, given the reported expenditure on the set of comparable goods and services, are identical in both rounds.

If these assumptions do hold, it is quite straightforward to obtain comparable poverty estimates. First, rank unit-level data from the 50th Round by per capita expenditure on the set of comparable items (say, m) and group them into suitable intervals. Second, for each interval of m, calculate the proportion of individuals whose total expenditure is less than the poverty line. Since both 30 and 365-day recall were used for clothing, etc., in the 50th Round, there are two sets of interval-specific poverty counts,

[10] The highest implicit CES 'contamination' obtained in Table 14.5 is for 'other foods', 10 and 11 per cent in rural and urban all-India. These are about a fifth of the average 7-30-day difference (of 55 and 53 per cent) found in rounds 51–54. In the experimental rounds, vegetables, fruits, and meat, fish and eggs also had large 7-30-days differences. For all these items, the implicit CES 'contamination' is less than a tenth of the average 7-30 days difference in round 51–54.

[11] In particular, 'contamination' is almost certainly underestimated for vegetables, fruits and for meat, fish and eggs. For these, 52nd Round full schedule estimates were lower than from worksheets (e.g. the ratio of short to full schedule estimates for vegetables was 1.20 rural and 1.34 urban) but the calculations above do not adjust CES below EUS.

Table 14.6a Key Results from the 30/365-Day Recall of 55th Round Rural

| | Monthly Per Capita Consumer Expenditure | | | | Gini Index | Poverty Measures | | | |
| | | | | | | National Poverty Line | State-specific Poverty Line | | |
	Poorest 40 Per cent	Next 40 Per cent	Richest 20 Per cent	All		Head-count Ratio	Head-count Ratio	Poverty Gap	Squared Poverty Gap
Unadjusted									
Andhra Pradesh	292	445	794	453.47	23.8	27.5	10.5	1.8	0.5
Assam	288	438	677	425.90	20.3	27.6	40.1	8.4	2.7
Bihar	261	386	628	384.45	20.8	42.2	44.1	8.8	2.5
Gujarat	348	553	952	551.24	23.8	14.3	12.4	2.2	0.6
Haryana	436	719	1,256	714.16	25.0	4.9	7.4	1.3	0.4
Karnataka	314	492	885	499.60	24.5	21.5	16.8	2.7	0.7
Kerala	437	734	1,486	765.57	28.9	4.4	9.4	1.5	0.4
Madhya Pradesh	252	399	706	401.33	24.4	42.1	37.3	7.7	2.3
Maharashtra	299	490	904	496.62	26.2	25.3	23.2	4.4	1.3
Orissa	231	371	660	372.95	24.7	49.5	48.1	11.7	4.0
Punjab	456	733	1,333	742.29	25.3	2.9	6.0	0.8	0.2
Rajasthan	367	554	900	548.77	21.3	10.6	13.5	2.1	0.5
Tamil Nadu	298	495	984	513.75	28.4	25.3	20.0	3.8	1.1
Uttar Pradesh	291	457	836	466.44	24.9	28.5	31.1	5.8	1.6
West Bengal	296	454	769	454.24	22.6	25.9	31.7	6.5	1.9
All-India	*293*	*476*	*892*	*485.87*	*26.3*	*27.0*	*27.0*	*5.3*	*1.5*
Adjusted for 7-day questions on food, etc.									
Andhra Pradesh	290	442	789	450.43	23.8	28.3	11.1	1.9	0.6
Assam	286	434	671	422.27	20.3	28.4	41.3	8.7	2.8
Bihar	255	377	614	375.73	20.8	44.8	46.7	9.6	2.8
Gujarat	347	551	948	548.75	23.8	14.4	12.6	2.3	0.6
Haryana	421	693	1,218	688.97	25.0	5.6	9.2	1.5	0.4
Karnataka	306	479	864	486.64	24.5	23.3	19.1	3.1	0.8
Kerala	424	711	1,448	743.86	29.0	5.5	10.7	1.7	0.4
Madhya Pradesh	246	387	684	389.97	24.2	44.3	39.6	8.4	2.6
Maharashtra	292	481	893	487.82	26.4	27.2	24.9	4.8	1.4
Orissa	229	368	655	369.92	24.7	50.4	49.3	12.1	4.1
Punjab	441	712	1,295	720.24	25.3	3.7	7.4	1.0	0.2
Rajasthan	361	544	884	538.68	21.3	11.6	14.3	2.3	0.6
Tamil Nadu	287	477	950	495.70	28.4	28.6	23.2	4.5	1.3
Uttar Pradesh	283	444	815	453.78	25.0	31.2	34.1	6.6	1.9
West Bengal	293	447	757	447.24	22.6	27.0	33.0	6.9	2.1
All-India	*287*	*466*	*873*	*475.63*	*26.3*	*28.8*	*28.8*	*5.7*	*1.7*

Note: The statewise poverty lines used in Columns 8 to 10 are those that were used by the Planning Commission based on the Expert Group methodology. The national poverty line implied by these is Rs 327.56 and is used in Column 7. The all-India estimates in the table are those obtained by applying the national poverty line to the all-India distribution and need not correspond to the population weighted average of the state level poverty estimates. The adjustment for 7-day questions uses the statewise, itemwise correction factors from Table 14.5 and applies these pro rata to the reported CES itemwise consumption of every sample household.

Source: Unit-level data from NSS 55th Round and adjustment factors from Table 14.5.

Table 14.6b Key Results from the 30/365-Day Recall of 55th Round Urban

| | Monthly Per Capita Consumer Expenditure | | | | Gini Index | Poverty Measures | | | |
| | | | | | | National Poverty Line | State-specific Poverty Line | | |
	Poorest 40 Per cent	Next 40 Per cent	Richest 20 Per cent	All		Head-count Ratio	Head-count Ratio	Poverty Gap	Squared Poverty Gap
Unadjusted									
Andhra Pradesh	407	743	1,565	773.34	31.6	26.8	27.2	5.6	1.7
Assam	425	798	1,622	813.82	31.2	23.0	7.2	1.5	0.4
Bihar	318	559	1,253	601.58	32.3	47.8	33.5	6.7	2.1
Gujarat	501	867	1,723	891.59	29.1	11.5	14.8	2.4	0.6
Haryana	501	914	1,734	911.82	29.1	13.5	10.0	2.0	0.8
Karnataka	462	880	1,871	910.78	32.8	17.7	24.6	5.6	1.8
Kerala	473	900	1,913	932.48	32.6	17.3	19.8	3.9	1.1
Madhya Pradesh	367	657	1,419	693.36	31.9	33.7	38.5	9.5	3.3
Maharashtra	468	908	2,114	973.16	35.4	17.4	26.7	6.7	2.4
Orissa	343	599	1,205	618.22	29.6	39.6	43.5	11.1	3.9
Punjab	504	860	1,764	898.59	29.4	11.0	5.5	0.6	0.1
Rajasthan	458	767	1,531	795.70	28.5	17.2	19.4	3.4	0.9
Tamil Nadu	451	845	2,265	971.34	38.9	19.7	22.5	4.8	1.5
Uttar Pradesh	355	641	1,459	690.07	33.2	36.6	30.7	6.6	2.0
West Bengal	433	796	1,873	866.32	34.7	21.5	14.7	2.5	0.7
All-India	*420*	*798*	*1,836*	*854.69*	*34.7*	*23.4*	*23.4*	*5.2*	*1.6*
Adjusted for 7-day questions on food, etc.									
Andhra Pradesh	402	736	1,556	766.93	31.7	27.6	28.3	5.8	1.8
Assam	411	768	1,565	784.70	31.2	25.9	8.6	1.7	0.5
Bihar	314	552	1,237	593.72	32.3	49.0	34.4	7.1	2.2
Gujarat	489	847	1,685	871.28	29.1	13.3	16.1	2.7	0.7
Haryana	494	902	1,716	901.02	29.2	13.9	10.5	2.2	0.8
Karnataka	445	851	1,817	881.99	33.0	20.2	27.1	6.3	2.1
Kerala	468	893	1,902	924.65	32.7	18.0	20.3	4.1	1.2
Madhya Pradesh	359	645	1,401	681.81	32.2	35.0	40.0	10.2	3.6
Maharashtra	459	894	2,087	958.49	35.5	18.2	27.9	7.1	2.6
Orissa	339	594	1,201	613.76	29.8	40.7	43.9	11.4	4.1
Punjab	498	850	1,747	888.83	29.4	11.7	6.1	0.7	0.1
Rajasthan	440	739	1,483	768.55	28.7	20.2	22.3	4.1	1.1
Tamil Nadu	431	811	2,189	933.78	39.1	22.4	24.7	5.6	1.9
Uttar Pradesh	347	627	1,433	675.91	33.3	38.0	32.4	7.1	2.2
West Bengal	422	772	1,800	837.53	34.3	23.9	16.0	2.9	0.8
All-India	*410*	*780*	*1,799*	*836.00*	*34.8*	*25.1*	*25.1*	*5.6*	*1.8*

Note: The statewise poverty lines used in Columns 8 to 10 are those that were used by the Planning Commission based on the Expert Group methodology. The national poverty line implied by these is Rs 454.11 and is used in Column 7. The all-India estimates in the table are those obtained by applying the national poverty line to the all-India distribution and need not correspond to the population weighted average of the state level poverty estimates. The adjustment for 7-day questions uses the statewise, itemwise correction factors from Table 14.5 and applies these pro rata to the reported CES itemwise consumption of every sample household.

Source: Unit-level data from NSS 55th Round and adjustment factors from Table 14.5.

say $P_{3030}{}^{50}(m)$ and $P_{30365}{}^{50}(m)$. These are 50th Round probabilities of being poor by each recall, conditional on being within a particular interval of m. Third, group the unit-level data from the 55th Round into the same intervals of m after suitable deflation for price change, and obtain 55th Round proportion of total population falling in each interval, say $N^{55}(m)$. Now by assumption (i), distribution $N^{55}(m)$ is unaffected by changes in reference periods and, by assumption (ii), each $P_i{}^{50}(m)$ is also the 55th Round poverty count for that interval of m by that recall as in 50th Round. Hence, the sum of $N^{55}(m)P_i{}^{50}(m)$ over all intervals of m gives comparable headcount ratios for the 55th Round, without requiring details about expenditure on items not in m.

Deaton obtained 'adjusted' 55th Round poverty counts using a refinement of the above.[12] For this he used only the URP from 50th Round, i.e. only conditional probabilities $P_{3030}{}^{50}(m)$, and thus his 'adjusted' 55th Round estimates are also by URP. He reports these as 30.2 and 24.7 per cent for rural and urban India using official poverty lines, against official counts of 27.1 and 23.4 per cent respectively. The logic of the exercise is as follows. Let $P_{3030}{}^{55}(m)$ and $P_{30365}{}^{55}(m)$ be interval-specific counts which would have been reported had the 55th Round used exactly the same recalls as in the 50th. These are unobservable, and different interval-specific counts, say $Q_{30365}{}^{55}(m)$, are obtained from 30/365-day reports of the 55th Round. Deaton accepts the prior that $Q_{30365}{}^{55}(m)$s are less than corresponding $P_{3030}{}^{55}(m)$s and that official 55th Round poverty, i.e. $\Sigma_m N^{55}(m)Q_{30365}{}^{55}(m)$, is an underestimate. The $Q_{30365}{}^{55}(m)$s are then replaced with $P_{3030}{}^{50}(m)$s to derive 'adjusted' counts. These are higher than the official counts. But the claim that these are 'comparable' to 50th Round is entirely assumption (ii), i.e. $P_{3030}{}^{55}(m) = P_{3030}{}^{50}(m)$, which cannot be tested.

This is a method both elegant and relatively simple to implement, and addresses quite generally the problem of comparing the distribution of a variable across different survey designs provided that a stable relationship exists with some other variable not affected by difference in survey design. However, like any surrogate, this works only up to tolerance of its assumptions. Deaton was unable to test the assumptions and relied on some validation by Tarozzi (2002) with data from rounds 51 to 54. He assumed that validity extended to 55th Round but was careful to point out that this made the results tentative. However, a simple test is possible directly with 55th Round data, using no more than the logic of the adjustment. Unfortunately, the method fails the test.

To see the nature of the test, note that it is agreed that presence of 7-day questions on food and intoxicants in the 55th Round led if, anything, to higher reported consumption and lower poverty estimates by 30-day recall than would be obtained if these questions were not present.[13] In other words, the accepted prior is that actual 30-day poverty counts from 55th Round data are lower, or at least no higher, than if 7-day questions for food had been absent and 30/365-day questions for other items been similar in the 55th Round to those in the 50th Round, i.e. $Q_{30365}{}^{55}(m) \leq P_{30365}{}^{55}(m)$.[14] Note, also, that if assumption (ii) is correct, this applies not only to poverty counts by the uniform 30-day recall but also

---

[12] He smoothed intervals and used kernel densities. See also Tarozzi (2002).

[13] Thus, on 55th Round food questions, Deaton (2001) wrote: 'when respondents were asked to report expenditures over both the last 7 and 30 days, they were in effect prompted to reconcile the two estimates of the rate of expenditure flow, bringing the two estimates closer together than would have been the case without the prompt. If the 30-day responses are shaded up by the reconciliation, and if the 7-day responses are shaded down to the same end, the new estimates would be too low on the 7-day count and too high on the 30-day count. Of course, there are other possibilities…prompting may lead to more expenditures being remembered, in which case both estimates would be higher.'

[14] This is so since it has already been shown that presence (as in Round 50) or absence (as in Round 55) of the 30-day question for clothing, etc., is unlikely to have affected the 30/365-day poverty counts significantly.

for counts by the mixed 30/365-day recall, i.e. $P_{30365}^{55}(m) \leq P_{30365}^{50}(m)$. It then follows trivially that a necessary condition for both the prior and the assumption to be correct is $Q_{30365}^{55}(m) = P_{30365}^{50}(m)$, which is testable. Thus, a test of assumption (ii) is that adjusted 55th Round poverty counts from this method must be higher (or at least no less) than official counts not only on implementation with 50th Round poverty counts by the uniform recall which Deaton used, but also the mixed recall. Unless this is so, either the presence of 7-day questions in the 55th Round increased measured poverty, which is a priori unlikely, or assumption (ii) is invalid.

Table14. 7 Deaton Adjustment using Both Uniform 30-Day and Mixed 30/365 Days Reference Periods

Range of Real Per Capita Consumption on 30-Day Items (m) 1993/94 Rs	Distribution of Persons		Poverty Counts		
	50th Round $N^{50}(m)$	55th Round $N^{55}(m)$	50th Round		55th Round
			Uniform Recall $P_{3030}^{50}(m)$	Mixed Recall $P_{30365}^{50}(m)$	Mixed Recall $Q_{30365}^{50}(m)$
Rural					
0–20	6.28	4.49	93.14	92.20	91.47
20–25	6.73	4.57	84.32	80.26	81.50
25–30	8.51	5.92	73.83	66.77	72.50
30–35	9.25	6.88	63.34	54.27	59.89
35–40	8.34	7.71	52.19	41.65	44.64
40–45	7.69	7.13	41.13	28.75	35.57
45–50	6.99	7.15	31.28	22.98	26.19
50–55	6.22	6.32	21.47	14.17	18.37
55–65	9.67	10.59	15.71	9.95	10.66
65–75	7.20	8.13	8.18	4.52	4.64
75–100	10.46	12.66	3.51	1.85	1.52
100–150	7.82	10.51	0.69	0.21	0.15
>150	4.84	7.93	0.02	0.01	0.00
Avg N^{50} weighted			37.23	31.56	
Avg N^{55} weighted			30.17	24.98	26.98
Urban					
0–40	11.67	7.97	92.85	91.46	91.85
40–45	4.18	2.95	81.69	76.70	83.10
45–50	4.33	3.19	76.55	67.43	76.91
50–55	4.43	3.25	69.50	60.75	67.40
55–60	4.05	3.12	61.01	47.28	60.48
60–65	4.09	3.10	54.34	41.27	50.85
65–70	3.86	3.04	42.72	29.57	43.79
70–75	3.57	3.06	39.70	29.09	33.80
75–100	15.24	13.68	21.30	14.08	18.95
100–125	10.56	10.89	7.36	3.96	4.40
125–150	7.38	8.36	2.06	0.96	1.06
150–175	5.65	6.40	0.57	0.16	0.17
>175	20.98	30.98	0.02	0.01	0.00
Avg N^{50} weighted			32.61	27.92	
Avg N^{55} weighted			24.54	20.67	23.41

Source: Unit level data from NSS 50th and 55th Rounds.

Table 14.7 summarises the Deaton method. Poverty counts using official poverty lines from the 55th and from uniform and mixed recalls of the 50th Round are juxtaposed against each other for various levels of real per capita spending on comparable 30-day items. It may be observed that almost all 55th Round grid-specific counts are less than corresponding counts from the 50th Round uniform recall but more than from the mixed recall. When implemented using 50th Round mixed recall counts, the adjusted 55th Round poverty estimates are 25.0 and 20.7 per cent for rural and urban India. Being 4–6 percentage points less than 'adjusted' counts by the uniform recall, these confirm the difference found earlier in poverty estimates by these two recalls. But since these are less than unadjusted estimates by 30/365-day recall, the method itself is put in doubt.

Table 14.8, which gives estimates of real consumption corresponding to poverty counts, indicates where the method goes awry. With 55th Round distribution of clothing, etc., similar to that by the 365-days recall in 50th Round, and different from 30 days recall, the method adjusts quite well for this. But 55th Round grid-specific poverty counts turn out higher than 50th Round MRP because 55th Round grid-specific food expenditures were lower than 50th. Deaton's use of 50th Round surrogates thus involved upward 'adjustment' to reported 55th Round food spending, in total contradiction to the maintained prior that these were likely overestimates. It is this contra-prior implicit revision of food estimates, which Deaton has since acknowledged did occur, that led his adjusted 55th Round poverty estimates to be lower than directly adjusting for 365-day recall as in the previous section.

Thus, either it must be accepted that presence of 7-day queries pulled down 55th Round food estimates, or Deaton's adjustment must be rejected. Given the unambiguous results of experiments in rounds 51 to 54 and the follow-up survey conducted by the NSSO in January-June 2000 (NSSO, 2003), there is now no room for doubt that the 7-day recall does elicit much higher reported food spending. Since no one has claimed the perverse outcome, that presence of 7-day questions pulls down 30-day replies, the conclusion must be that the method has failed in the present case, and led to underestimates of 55th Round poverty because the required assumptions did not hold.

But what does assumption (ii) mean and why does it fail? Deaton has explained that this is implied if Engel curves are stable, i.e. if item shares in consumer spending are constant unless real incomes change. Now suppose this is not the case, and some people reduce food consumption to increase expenditure on fuel, rent, medicine and conveyance, keeping total expenditure constant. This could reflect changes in tastes or circumstance (i.e. relative prices, access to commons or public supply, or simply need), and the reason may matter for welfare assessment. But whatever the reason, this change should not properly affect the income poverty status of these persons if their total real expenditure remains unchanged. However, the Deaton procedure would record the increased expenditure on fuel, rent, medicines and conveyance but not the decline in food consumption. On the contrary, since it assumes unchanged shares implicitly, it would deem an increase also in food consumption and record that real expenditure increased by more than the fall in food share. Consequently some persons below the poverty line will be adjusted above spuriously. Since the issue is about NSS recall periods for food and of perverse outcomes on this from the Deaton adjustment, it is important to note that the method is very sensitive to stability of food shares.

In this context, a pertinent and well known fact is that food shares, which were relatively stable during the 1980s, declined sharply in the 1990s. NSS food shares fell 10 and 13 percentage points in rural and urban India between 1990/91 and 2000/01, and the NAS trend is similar. By the underlying trend, food shares in1999/2000 were nearly 7 percentage points lower than in 1993/94, although, as would be expected from contamination, 55th Round food shares were about 3 percentage points above

Table 14.8 Real Per Capita Consumption of Different Items by Ranges of Real Consumption on 30-Day Items (at 1993/94 Prices)

Range of Real Per Capita Consumption on 30-Day Items (m) 1993/94 Rs	50th Round				55th Round		
	Items with Only 30-Day Recall	Clothing, etc.		Food, etc.	Items with Only 30-Day Recall	Clothing, etc.	Food, etc.
		30-Day Recall	365-Day Recall	30-Day Recall		365-Day Recall	30-Day Recall
Rural							
0–20	15.44	7.81	14.55	115.60	15.66	14.16	118.96
20–25	22.64	9.77	18.59	130.51	22.71	18.43	130.24
25–30	27.57	12.14	22.40	142.37	27.63	20.88	136.94
30–35	32.55	13.31	24.61	150.94	32.53	23.46	148.30
35–40	37.55	16.65	26.77	159.80	37.52	26.35	155.25
40–45	42.53	17.86	29.80	170.02	42.48	28.76	161.28
45–50	47.45	20.76	31.98	175.80	47.47	30.82	168.19
50–55	52.42	23.57	34.88	186.43	52.47	32.81	174.24
55–65	59.78	27.05	37.73	195.23	59.86	36.70	185.44
65–75	69.84	35.17	41.71	210.16	69.72	44.54	198.46
75–100	86.08	47.07	50.02	227.51	86.18	49.34	216.54
100–150	119.85	72.11	64.37	258.64	120.34	65.54	248.15
>150	264.12	146.01	100.21	336.65	240.77	113.93	314.34
Avg N^{50} weighted	*62.80*	*31.87*	*37.05*	*186.74*			
Avg N^{55} weighted	*74.67*	*38.80*	*41.63*	*199.21*	*72.90*	*42.36*	*190.31*
Urban							
0–40	30.32	12.47	22.83	148.13	30.53	24.84	145.54
40–45	42.61	17.15	29.23	173.10	42.57	29.29	161.61
45–50	47.43	24.22	33.86	181.21	47.47	34.02	194.29
50–55	52.61	26.32	36.26	186.54	52.52	34.22	175.26
55–60	57.45	30.69	39.48	195.68	57.48	36.56	207.73
60–65	62.54	31.19	43.00	201.43	62.58	40.15	189.56
65–70	67.51	33.60	45.30	212.25	67.45	41.06	193.19
70–75	72.40	36.76	46.56	215.01	72.37	45.39	199.57
75–100	86.71	47.70	57.04	234.17	87.28	53.24	213.33
100–125	112.02	78.39	71.26	261.88	112.16	64.98	239.76
125–150	136.89	71.95	76.89	284.04	136.86	73.04	261.76
150–175	162.06	75.48	90.42	306.06	162.04	83.19	277.90
>175	320.12	148.23	151.56	413.68	375.27	168.32	377.86
Avg N^{50} weighted	*131.26*	*65.75*	*72.54*	*261.09*			
Avg N^{55} weighted	*159.96*	*79.04*	*85.05*	*286.21*	*177.15*	*88.01*	*264.65*

Source: Unit level data from NSS 50th and 55th Rounds.

trend. More important, and directly relevant to Deaton, is that most of this decline in NSS food shares was a result of shifts of the Engel curve rather than of movements along this. This is evident from Figures 14.1 and 14.2, and from the finding by Ravi (2000) that decline in food shares, particularly of cereals, is explained not by movements along stable consumption functions but by time trends within fixed expenditure classes. The failure of assumption (ii) is thus not just in procedure; there is strong corroborative evidence of Engel shifts from food to non-food. Since even the unadjusted 55th Round

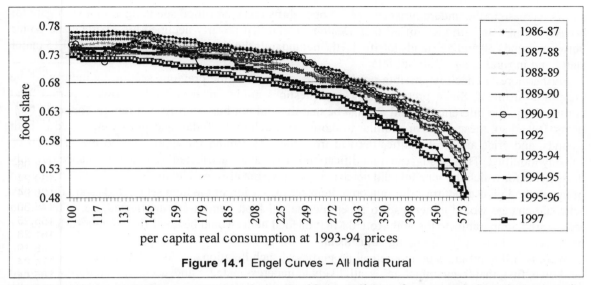

Figure 14.1 Engel Curves – All India Rural

Note: Food shares plotted at current prices (using the 30-day uniform reference period) against per capita consumption at constant 1993/94 prices for all full year NSS rounds from 1986/87 to 1997. This is from grouped data of different rounds, interpolated to a common grid of real per capita expenditure.

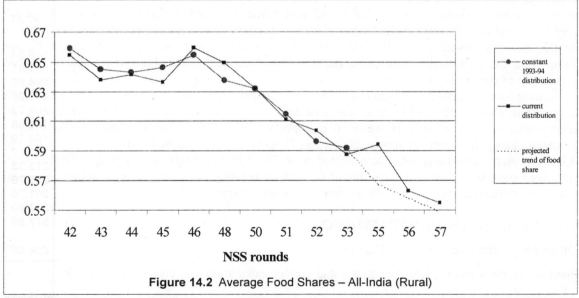

Figure 14.2 Average Food Shares – All-India (Rural)

Note: Average food share plotted from the above NSS rounds (see Figure 14.1), both as actually reported in a round and also applying the constant 1993/94 distribution of MPCE expenditure to the expenditure class specific food shares from the different rounds. The data till Round 53 pertains to the uniform 30-day recall. The constant distribution shares have not been plotted for rounds 54 to 57 because only the mixed 30/365 day recall is available, and the distribution by the two recalls are not comparable. The current distribution shares are by URP till Round 53 and by MRP for Rounds 55 to 57.

shows increase in the undernourished, these Engel shifts make non-food spending a poor surrogate for poverty estimation.[15] In view of all this, Deaton's claim that poverty declined by 7 percentage points between rounds 50 and 55 stands falsified. His method fails the test above in urban areas of all 15 major states and in rural areas of all but four.

Furthermore, a check is possible on the results obtained in the previous section by modifying the Deaton adjustment. Since presence of 7-day questions could not have pulled down reported food consumption, the inference should at most be that this did not bias 55th Round reports for some food items. But, if so, these items are similar to those for which only 30-day questions were asked in both Rounds, and grids and probabilities derived from the 50th Round for application to the 55th can be suitably modified. Thus, a suggested modification is to treat as unaffected by schedule change not only those items for which the schedule did not actually change but also food items for which implementation of the method gives a contra-prior outcome. Iterative expansion of the item set treated as unaffected by schedule change would either lead to accepting that all food items were unaffected, i.e. 55th Round results are 'comparable' to the 50th Round MRP, or food items would be identified as being affected per prior along with the corresponding adjustment.

Work is still in progress on theoretical properties of such iteration and its implementation. But it can be shown, first, that 'contamination' is still likely to underestimated;[16] and, second, that, if implemented with an expanded set of items considered unaffected by schedule change, the method agrees broadly with results of the previous section. It may be noted from Table 14.5 that two major food items with least evidence of 'contamination' are cereals and edible oils. The shares of these items declined, leading to large contra-prior imputation. When Deaton's adjustment is done with these two treated as belonging to the same set as 30-day items, with grids and probabilities obtained on this basis, this passes the test above in most cases. Accepting unadjusted 55th Round counts if the test fails, adjusted counts from this modification are presented in Table 14.9. Despite differences at State and sector levels, notably for Tamil Nadu, the all-India poverty count obtained is almost identical to that obtained from the direct food adjustment of the previous section.

Pending further work on modification of Deaton's method and verification of Sundaram-Tendulkar's calculations from 55th Round EUS, results from the earlier direct method are accepted tentatively and used further in what follows. However, it is important to note that, just as Sundaram-Tendulkar's estimates change drastically on proper calculation, Deaton's adjusted estimates are also likely to change if implemented consistently with the accepted prior. These two methods had seemingly converged on very large poverty reduction during 1993/2000. But on scrutiny and appropriate correction, absolute poverty as defined by the official poverty lines is seen to increase by both.

POVERTY MONITORING WITH 55TH ROUND

Other Estimates and Regional Patterns

Previous sections have established that while correct calculation and consistent estimation with the

---

[15] Besides growing divergence between nutrition and income poverty, this implies that surveys such as NCAER's Market Information Survey of Households (MISH), which ignore food consumption altogether, are likely to overestimate decline in income poverty This data was used to argue that NSS was increasingly underestimating consumption and overestimated poverty in the 1990s [Lal et al (2001) and Bery and Shukla (2003)]. But the NSS growth of per capita non-food consumption was itself double that of total consumption during 1987/88 to 1999/2000.

[16] In particular, it is possible that iterations conclude all food items are unaffected although there is 'contamination'.

Table 14.9 Comparing the Modified Deaton with Direct Estimates
(Headcount Percentages using Official State-specific Poverty Lines)

	50th Round		55th Round					
			Un-adjusted	Original Deaton Method		Modified Deaton Method		Direct Food Adjusted
	30/30	30/365	30/365	30/30	30/365	30/30	30/365	30/365
Rural								
Andhra Pradesh	15.9	12.5	10.5	14.9	11.3	16.8	13.4	11.1
Assam	45.1	36.0	40.1	44.1	35.8	48.2	40.2	41.3
Bihar	58.0	52.9	44.1	49.2	44.7	53.4	48.4	46.7
Gujarat	22.2	16.6	12.4	15.4	10.9	17.9	12.5	12.6
Haryana	28.3	22.3	7.4	12.7	9.0	13.4	10.1	9.2
Karnataka	30.1	22.0	16.8	25.7	18.3	27.3	19.5	19.1
Kerala	25.4	21.9	9.4	12.6	9.1	13.9	11.4	10.7
Madhya Pradesh	40.7	32.8	37.3	36.4	28.7	45.8	37.3	39.6
Maharashtra	37.9	31.0	23.2	29.2	23.1	29.7	23.2	24.9
Orissa	49.8	45.6	48.1	47.3	43.9	51.8	48.1	49.3
Punjab	11.7	8.5	6.0	5.9	3.9	7.9	6.0	7.4
Rajasthan	26.4	19.2	13.5	19.6	13.0	19.4	13.5	14.3
Tamil Nadu	32.9	28.1	20.0	19.9	14.7	34.4	29.6	23.2
Uttar Pradesh	42.3	37.3	31.1	33.7	28.1	36.1	31.1	34.1
West Bengal	41.2	35.5	31.7	37.1	31.4	42.4	37.2	33.0
Wt Av 15 States	37.5	31.9	27.3	30.9	25.5	34.6	29.3	29.2
Urban								
Andhra Pradesh	38.8	34.2	27.2	27.7	24.2	31.3	27.2	28.3
Assam	7.9	4.6	7.2	8.3	6.7	10.3	7.5	8.6
Bihar	34.8	28.8	33.5	33.8	27.3	39.0	33.5	34.4
Gujarat	28.3	23.7	14.8	16.0	12.5	20.0	16.2	16.1
Haryana	16.5	10.0	10.0	9.5	5.4	14.6	10.2	10.5
Karnataka	39.9	36.0	24.6	25.5	22.2	28.2	24.6	27.1
Kerala	24.3	21.5	19.8	18.7	16.0	21.9	19.8	20.3
Madhya Pradesh	48.1	43.4	38.5	37.9	33.9	42.6	38.5	40.0
Maharashtra	35.0	30.2	26.7	28.1	23.6	31.7	27.2	27.9
Orissa	40.9	38.5	43.5	41.4	39.6	46.0	43.5	43.9
Punjab	10.9	7.6	5.5	6.3	3.5	7.8	6.0	6.1
Rajasthan	31.0	25.0	19.4	22.8	16.3	24.6	19.4	22.3
Tamil Nadu	39.9	36.0	22.5	24.4	20.4	31.0	27.6	24.7
Uttar Pradesh	35.1	30.6	30.7	30.4	27.3	34.9	30.7	32.4
West Bengal	22.9	18.2	14.7	19.5	14.7	19.6	15.4	16.0
Wt Av 15 States	33.7	29.2	24.6	25.7	21.7	29.4	25.4	26.1
Memo: number of poor (millions)								
15 Major States	312.5	267.0	254.9	283.0	234.8	318.5	271.0	272.1

Note: In those cases where the implementation of the modified Deaton method gives an adjusted 30/365 day count less than unadjusted, the latter is accepted, and the modified 30/30-day count obtained by increasing the unadjusted 30/365 day count by the difference in adjusted 30/30 and 30/365 day counts.

Source: Computed from unit level data from Rounds 50 and 55.

methods of Sundaram-Tendulkar and Deaton do suggest decline in poverty ratios between 50th and 55th Rounds, the reduction was less than 3 percentage points. These revised estimates of poverty decline are not far from Datt, Kozel and Ravallion (2003)'s forecast from a model relating poverty to growth and inflation. Also, these agree with results reported recently by Kijima and Lanjouw (2003) from a completely independent exercise. The latter obtain adjusted counts from 55th Round distribution of household characteristics by applying a multivariate parametric model fitted to 50th Round data relating these characteristics to poverty. By this method, poverty ratios declined only 2.9 and 1.4 percentage points in rural and urban India, even less than obtained above. With measured decline thus clustering at much less than the 10 percentage points claimed officially, evidence is now overwhelming that comparable 55th Round poverty was underestimated very substantially.

However, given the extent of methodological change and the very different adjustments, it would be a miracle if full unanimity ever emerges regarding comparable results from 55th Round. Since comparable numbers at the level of states and NSS regions are required for poverty monitoring and policy, it is useful to highlight differences by different methods and ask to what extent can this round inform on regional patterns of poverty change? But a complication in this is the use of different poverty lines. Estimates in previous sections used official poverty lines. Deaton gives estimates both by these and his preferred lines based on NSS implicit prices. Kijima-Lanjouw use only the Deaton lines. Sundaram-Tendulkar and Datt et al use different sets of lines altogether.

State level estimates using official poverty lines have been presented already. Besides large EUS-CES differences, these are very sensitive to adjustment of CES. Thus the poverty ratio increased only in urban Orissa on official comparison and Deaton's adjustment adds only urban Assam. But, five more cases, rural Assam, Madhya Pradesh and Orissa and urban Bihar and Uttar Pradesh, are added comparing 50th Round MRP to unadjusted 55th Round CES. The food adjustment of the Section 'Comparability of 55th Round' adds urban Haryana, and the modified Deaton adjustment of the next Section expands this further to include rural Andhra Pradesh, Tamil Nadu and West Bengal. If the number of poor rather than proportion is considered, this increased also in rural Bihar and Uttar Pradesh and in urban Haryana, Maharashtra and Rajasthan by at least one of these adjustments.

Poverty estimates using Deaton's poverty lines are presented in Table 14.10. In no case is unadjusted 55th Round poverty ratio higher than 50th Round URP, and there are only two such cases, rural Assam and urban Orissa, with the Deaton adjustment. But the food adjusted MRP comparison with Deaton lines shows increase in rural Assam, Madhya Pradesh, Orissa and West Bengal and in urban Assam and Orissa. With these lines, Kijima-Lanjouw report adjusted counts higher in rural Assam, Punjab and West Bengal and in urban Assam, Bihar, Haryana, Orissa, Punjab and Tamil Nadu. Considering the number rather than proportion of poor using Deaton lines, at least one of these adjustments shows increase also in rural Andhra Pradesh, Rajasthan and Uttar Pradesh and in urban Madhya Pradesh, Rajasthan and Uttar Pradesh.

Similarly, there is not a single case where the unadjusted 55th Round returns higher poverty ratio than 50th Round URP with poverty lines used by World Bank and Datt et al. But food adjusted 55th Round poverty ratios are higher than 50th Round MRP in rural Assam, Madhya Pradesh and Orissa and in urban Assam and Bihar. Against this, Datt et al.'s projected headcount ratios increase in rural Assam and Bihar and imply additionally increase in the number of poor in rural Madhya Pradesh, Maharashtra and Uttar Pradesh and in urban Assam, Haryana, Punjab, Madhya Pradesh, Maharashtra, Orissa and Uttar Pradesh. But this projection also implies very large poverty reduction in rural West Bengal where most other adjustments show increase in the number of poor.

Table 14.10 Alternative Poverty Estimates with Deaton Lines
(Headcount Percentages using Deaton's State-specific Poverty Lines)

	50th Round		Un-adjusted	Deaton Adjusted	Kijima-Lanjouw Adjusted	Food Adjusted
	30-30	30-365	30-365	30-30	30-30	30-365
Rural						
Andhra Pradesh	29.2	24.5	22.3	26.2	23.6	22.9
Assam	35.4	27.7	31.6	35.5	36.8	32.6
Bihar	48.6	41.2	30.4	41.1	48.3	33.1
Gujarat	32.5	26.5	16.0	20.0	27.7	16.4
Haryana	17.0	12.0	3.4	5.7	14.2	4.6
Karnataka	37.9	29.3	20.5	30.7	31.0	22.4
Kerala	19.5	14.8	9.2	10.0	14.4	10.6
Madhya Pradesh	36.6	29.2	30.1	31.3	32.9	32.5
Maharashtra	42.9	36.8	23.5	31.9	35.5	25.2
Orissa	43.5	38.3	40.0	43.0	41.3	41.0
Punjab	6.2	4.3	2.7	2.4	6.4	2.9
Rajasthan	23.0	17.0	10.3	17.3	20.4	11.1
Tamil Nadu	38.5	33.3	27.7	24.3	31.8	30.5
Uttar Pradesh	28.6	22.7	15.7	21.5	26.2	17.6
West Bengal	25.1	20.3	21.4	21.9	26.4	22.3
Wt Av 15 States	33.4	27.4	21.8	26.7	30.4	23.4
Urban						
Andhra Pradesh	17.8	15.3	9.4	10.8	14.6	9.9
Assam	13.0	9.1	10.7	11.8	13.8	11.7
Bihar	26.7	20.1	18.0	24.7	31.1	18.9
Gujarat	14.7	10.7	4.0	6.4	11.9	4.5
Haryana	10.5	6.4	4.8	4.6	11.3	5.5
Karnataka	21.4	16.5	8.5	10.8	13.4	9.2
Kerala	13.9	12.6	8.7	9.6	10.5	9.2
Madhya Pradesh	18.5	13.6	10.7	13.9	17.8	11.9
Maharashtra	18.2	15.0	10.6	12.0	14.7	11.5
Orissa	15.2	13.2	13.3	15.6	17.9	13.4
Punjab	7.8	4.8	2.9	3.4	8.4	3.2
Rajasthan	18.3	12.9	6.1	10.8	15.7	8.0
Tamil Nadu	20.8	16.9	9.0	11.3	22.0	11.1
Uttar Pradesh	21.7	16.3	13.5	17.3	20.5	14.4
West Bengal	15.5	12.4	6.8	11.3	14.3	7.4
Wt Av 15 States	18.4	14.3	9.6	12.4	16.8	10.6
Memo: Number of poor (millions)						
15 Major States	252.8	205.6	177.6	218.9	256.2	191.4

Source: Unit level NSS data from rounds 50 and 55 for Columns 2, 3, 4 and 7; Deaton and Dreze (2002) for Column 5 and Kijima and Lanjouw (2003) for Column 6.

Thus, even ignoring the EUS, it is possible to be relatively sure of poverty decline only in rural Haryana, Gujarat, Karnataka and Kerala and in urban Andhra Pradesh, Gujarat, Karnataka, Kerala and West Bengal. But taken together these account for only a small proportion of the total number of poor in the country. The 50th Round URP measured 46, 38 and 49 million poor in this set of cases by official, Deaton and World Bank poverty lines and numbers were 37, 30 and 41 million using MRP. Corresponding 55th Round numbers are 30, 20 and 33 million unadjusted, 32, 21 and 35 million food adjusted and 40, 34 and 42 million by URP from modified Deaton, Kijima-Lanjouw and Datt et al.

On the other hand, it is almost certain that the number of poor did increase in both rural and urban areas of Assam, Madhya Pradesh and Orissa and in urban Uttar Pradesh. The 50th Round URP measured 66, 50 and 65 million poor in this set of cases by official, Deaton and World Bank poverty lines and the numbers were 56, 40 and 55 million using MRP. Corresponding 55th Round numbers are 67, 45 and 64 million unadjusted, 70, 48 and 66 million by food adjusted MRP and 78, 53 and 68 million by the URP from modified Deaton, Kijima-Lanjouw and Datt et al.

However, with the number of poor up by at least one adjustment/poverty line but not all, the direction of change is unclear elsewhere in the 15 major states analysed. These states/sectors account for the vast majority of India's poor. The 50th Round URP measured 201, 165 and 220 million poor in these by official, Deaton and World Bank poverty lines and the numbers were 173, 136 and 192 million using MRP. Corresponding unadjusted 55th Round numbers are 158, 113 and 171 million. These become 170, 123 and 183 million by food adjusted MRP and 201, 170 and 220 million by URP estimates from modified Deaton, Kijima-Lanjouw and Datt et al.

This large area of uncertainty does reduce somewhat if within-state inequality and demography are accounted for by implementing at the level of NSS regions.[17] For example, comparing food-adjusted (using official poverty lines) and Kijima-Lanjouw (using Deaton poverty lines) estimates, there is agreement on direction of change in two-thirds of the NSS regions/sectors that fall within states where there is disagreement – with these divided roughly equally between agreed increase and agreed decrease in the number of poor.[18] But huge disagreements still persist, making it impossible to be precise with the 55th Round on regional change in poverty incidence.[19]

Nonetheless, adjusted 55th Round counts at level of NSS regions overturn some conclusions that others have reached. First, contrary to a claim often made, there is no clear state-level pattern to divide

---

[17] In this section, and elsewhere in the paper, population figures at the state level are obtained by interpolating between Population Censuses. These are not necessarily the same as those implicit in NSS, and NSSO recommends application of survey ratios to Census population. However, the population figures used at the level of NSS regions were not obtained directly from the Census but calculated by applying the implicit NSS share of a region's population in the state to the state total obtained from the Census (separately, for urban and rural areas). This was necessary to ensure that poverty estimates at the level of NSS regions sum to estimates earlier reported at the state level.

[18] Overall, of the 58 NSS regions in the 15 major states, these two adjustments agree on increase in the number of poor in 17 rural and 25 urban NSS regions, accounting for 39 and 44 per cent of respective populations in the major states. The two also agree on reduction in number of poor in 26 rural and 16 urban NSS regions, accounting for 35 and 30 per cent of the respective populations. There is disagreement regarding direction of change in the remaining regions.

[19] For example, there is less agreement on change in poverty ratios than in number of poor. Poverty ratios increase in 18 rural and 19 urban NSS regions (accounting for 24 and 34 per cent of respective populations) by food adjusted MRP, and in 13 rural and 22 urban regions (accounting for 29 and 32 per cent of population) by the Kijima-Lanjouw adjustment. However the two agree on increase in only 7 rural and 11 urban regions (accounting for 11 and 18 per cent of population). Also, correlation between food adjusted and Kijima-Lanjouw adjusted percentage poverty change across NSS regions is only 0.29.

NSS regions by poverty reduction performance. By each adjustment, almost every major state had at least one rural or urban NSS region where the poverty ratio increased and also at least one region where this declined. Second, contrary to another usual claim, urban poverty reduction outcomes were, if anything, worse than rural in most NSS regions.[20] Third, contrary to the claim made by Deaton-Dreze with state level data, there is very little evidence of 'divergence' (i.e. of lower rates of poverty reduction in regions that had more poverty to start with) at the level of NSS regions.[21] Together, these amount to rejection of an assessment that is made quite frequently from 55th Round data: that despite increase in regional inequality, poverty reduction during 1993/2000 was significant and widespread, except possibly in a few backward, mainly rural, locations in East and Central India where growth failed to penetrate.

This does not of course mean that eastern and central regions did not have poor poverty reduction. They did, but so did a number of regions elsewhere. Nor does this imply that rural-urban disparities did not increase. Adjusted NSS data not only show growth of all-India urban real MPCE more than double rural but also that urban MPCE growth was higher than rural in an overwhelming majority of NSS regions.[22] That urban poverty reduction was nonetheless worse in most regions is because of increased within-region urban inequality. This increase was sizeable on average and occurred in 42 of the 58 NSS regions in the major states.[23] Similarly, absence of 'divergence' certainly does not mean that regional inequalities did not increase. Inequality of inter-regional distribution of MPCE increased quite sharply in both rural and urban areas by all measures and irrespective of deflation or adjustment. But changes in within-region inequality meant that this was not reflected fully in changes in inter-region inequality of adjusted poverty counts. In short, although poverty ratios did fall using adjusted NSS data, significant reduction was not widespread: increased inter-region and inter-sector inequality limited the spatial spread of MPCE growth and rise in within-region inequality caused insignificant poverty reduction (or even increase) in many regions where MPCE did grow significantly.

The above follows from both the food and Kijima-Lanjouw adjustments, although these approach 55th Round comparability very differently and differ at the level of specific regions. Kijima-Lanjouw's method is rather static on both growth and inequality,[24] and they do not discuss inequalities explicitly, but the message from the broad agreement is that 55th Round underestimated inequalities increase quite comprehensively. This is of course accepted. For example, despite unadjusted comparison of rounds 50 and 55 showing lower inequality in most states, Deaton-Dreze report inequality rising after adjustment in 8 rural and 12 urban areas of the 15 major states. They also report significant increase in MPCE

[20] In fact, the proportionate decline (increase) in poverty ratio was smaller (larger) in urban than in rural areas of 45 of 58 NSS regions by at least one of food or Kijima-LanjouwL adjustment and in 35 and 34 regions by these individually.

[21] Correlation between 50th Round poverty ratios and subsequent proportionate change is negligible across rural areas of NSS regions and of the wrong sign across urban areas of these regions These are −0.10 rural and −0.35 urban by the food adjustment and 0.04 rural and −0.23 urban by the Kijima-Lanjouw adjustment.

[22] Of the 58 NSS regions, urban MPCE growth exceeded rural in 38 and 41 by food and Kijima-Lanjouw adjustments respectively.

[23] The inequality measure used is the within-region standard deviation of the logarithms of household level MPCE using the 30/365 mixed recall. Kijima-Lanjouw do not report any measure of inequality but that urban inequality increased sharply by their adjustment also is implicit since they report real MPCE declining in only 12 of the 58 urban regions, the headcount ratio increasing in 22 and the poverty gap increasing in 32.

[24] Kijima-Lanjouw only measure changes in household characteristics, implicitly holding constant mean MPCE and variance associated with any vector of characteristics. Consequently, they underestimate changes in both MPCE and inequality compared to the food adjusted estimates that largely accept the 55th Round MPCE distribution, with the slight food correction made state/itemwise but irrespective of household characteristics.

inequality between urban and rural areas and across states. But although they too pointed to pockets of impoverishment below state level, they did not go below this level, and stressed 'divergence instead'. Since inter-region MPCE inequality did increase, poverty reduction would be expected to 'diverge' if growth were strongly poverty reducing and if insufficient growth in poor regions was the only reason for insufficient poverty reduction.

It is therefore necessary to emphasise that the poverty 'divergence' reported by Deaton-Dreze was largely a spurious outcome of change in recall and of their adjustment for this. First, the proportionate excesses of 50th Round URP poverty counts over MRP were systematically larger in states with lower poverty.[25] As a result, the spurious poverty reduction caused by 55th Round shift to MRP was systematically larger in richer states, and 'divergence' higher when unadjusted 55th Round is compared to 50th Round URP than when MRP from these rounds are compared.[26] Second, the measured interstate pattern of poverty reduction turns out to be very sensitive to the surrogates used to correct the 55th Round. The Deaton adjustment reinforces 'divergence', while this disappears completely with Kijima-Lanjouw's adjustment.[27] Not surprisingly, these correlations are also much weaker across NSS regions than across states.[28] The main conclusion from disagreement on 'divergence' is therefore that 55th Round underestimation of poverty was not proportionately uniform across regions and that different adjustments 'correct' differently. This is further reason to be sceptical regarding use of 55th Round data for conclusions on poverty change at state and lower levels, which is a pity. Food adjusted MRP comparisons suggest that important changes may have occurred in patterns of spillovers to actually blunt the ability of growth to reduce poverty.[29]

One aspect that does stand out however is that broad conclusions are clearer on considering the number rather than proportion of the poor.[30] This is of course in part a trivial consequence of population

[25] The state-level correlations between 50th Round URP counts using Deaton's poverty lines and proportionate difference of corresponding 50th Round MRP counts from these are 0.83, 0.36 and 0.78 for rural, urban and both.

[26] State-level correlations between 50th Round MRP counts using Deaton poverty lines and subsequent proportionate change to the corresponding unadjusted 55th Round counts are 0.43, −0.01 and 0.49 for rural, urban and rural + urban. State-level correlations between 50th Round URP counts using Deaton's poverty lines and subsequent proportionate change to unadjusted 55th Round counts are 0.53, 0.11 and 0.59.

[27] State-level correlations between 50th Round URP counts using Deaton poverty lines and subsequent proportionate change to Deaton's adjusted 55th Round counts are 0.69, 0.34 and 0.73. State-level correlations between 50th Round URP counts and subsequent proportionate change to Kijima-Lanjouw's adjusted 55th Round counts are −0.03, −0.12 and 0.01.

[28] Deaton (2003c) has subsequently provided region level adjusted poverty counts using his poverty lines. Adjusted with his original state-level non-parametric relation between poverty and consumption of 30-day items, correlations across NSS regions between 50th Round counts and subsequent percentage change to these 'adjusted' 55th Round counts are −0.24, −0.38 and −0.17 for rural, urban and both. These carry the wrong sign. He also presents alternative counts using regional level probits. Correlations using these are 0.22, −0.19 and 0.26. Although these do suggest some divergence in rural areas, this is much weaker than the same correlations at state-level. Interestingly, these Deaton counts correlate better with food adjusted estimates on poverty change across NSS regions than either of these do with Kijima-Lanjouw's counts. Further, almost every state has a region where the number of poor increases by these Deaton counts also.

[29] Regressions across NSS regions (not reported here but available from the authors) show no evidence of either divergence or convergence of rural poverty and in fact show conditional convergence of urban poverty. Growth and inequality change within each sector has the expected effect on poverty change within that sector. But importantly, rural growth is found to have no effect on urban poverty while urban growth does impact rural poverty – a result opposite to that found in studies using earlier Indian data. However, increase in urban inequality is found to be associated with lower rural poverty reduction and, significantly, a positive correlation is found between urban MPCE growth and inequality increase.

[30] Full details can be obtained from an extended version of this paper available on http://www.macroscan.org

growth, but it is important to note that the demographics had a pattern, important for poverty outcomes. Not surprisingly, urban population growth was higher than rural and, on classifying regions broadly by initial poverty, population growth turns out to have been highest in those urban regions that were the richer to start with. This was much higher than in the poorest urban regions. At the other end, population growth was slowest in the richest rural regions, much slower than in poorer rural regions. In addition to well known regional variations in natural growth, this pattern almost certainly reflects incentives regarding migrant destinations and constraints on ability to migrate. In fact, population growth averaged below natural growth in the richest rural areas and in the poorest urban areas. Average MPCE is similar in these two sets and lower than in other urban areas. But this is not only much higher than in other rural areas, connectivity is also much better.

The set of richest urban region,[31] the obvious magnet for migrants, did have the highest growth of total expenditure and did show significant decline in poverty ratios. But, since population growth was high, the change in adjusted number of poor was only marginal. On the other hand, despite lower MPCE growth, the number of the poor did decline quite significantly in the poorest urban areas[32] and in the richest rural areas,[33] which appear to have been major points of migrant origin. As compared to this, population growth was almost at the natural rate in poorer rural regions, much higher than in the richest rural regions despite lower initial MPCE and much lower subsequent MPCE growth. Not surprisingly, the largest absolute increase in the numbers of poor occurred in these already poor regions. But, interestingly, the proportionate increase in numbers of poor was highest in the set of middle urban regions, neither richest nor poorest. Population growth was only slightly less here than in the richest urban areas and, although MPCE growth was relatively high, these were the location of largest increase in within-region inequality and lowest decline in poverty ratios. On further break-up it is found that most of the increase in the number of rural poor also occurred in the rural hinterland of these middle urban regions.

The following may therefore be concluded about regional trends from the 55th Round. Consistent with the finding that all-India poverty reduction between 1993/94 and 1999/2000 was by at most 3 percentage points, there are only a few regions that can be identified definitely as having witnessed significant poverty decline. In fact, although some broad regional patterns do emerge that could otherwise have aided understanding of spatial linkages following economic 'reform', this round remains unreliable on poverty change across states and regions. Nonetheless, adjusted NSS 55th Round data does appear to indicate that the focus of poverty analysis should now be as much on ability of urban regions to offer escape and linkages and on determinants of mobility from poorer rural areas, as it must be on rural income growth.

---

[31] This comprises urban areas of Inland North Andhra Pradesh, Assam Eastern Plains, four of five Gujarat regions excluding East Gujarat, both regions of Haryana, South Karnataka, South Kerala, Coastal Maharashtra, both regions of Punjab, West and South Rajasthan, Inland Tamil Nadu, Himalayan Uttar Pradesh and West Bengal Central Plains.

[32] This comprises urban areas of Coastal and South-West Andhra Pradesh, North Bihar, North Karnataka, Central, South and South-West Madhya Pradesh, North, Central and Inland East Maharashtra, South Orissa, South-East Rajasthan, South Tamil Nadu and Central, East and South Uttar Pradesh.

[33] This comprises rural areas of Coastal, North and South Andhra Pradesh, Gujarat Northern Plains and Saurashtra, both regions of Haryana, Coastal and Eastern Karnataka, both regions of Kerala, North Madhya Pradesh, Coastal and Western Maharashtra, both regions of Punjab, West and North-East Rajasthan, Coastal and Inland Tamil Nadu, Himalayan and Western Uttar Pradesh and the Central Plains of West Bengal.

POVERTY AND INEQUALITY DURING THE 1990S

A crucial issue raised by the analysis therefore, is about the significance that ought to be attached to 55th Round results, since without adjustment these are completely at variance with those from the nine preceding rounds that the NSS had conducted during the 1990s. With the small adjustments of Deaton and Sundaram-Tendulkar, 55th Round results have been used to attempt a reversal of the consensus that had emerged from these previous rounds – that poverty reduction had suffered a serious setback during the 1990s. Being a quinquennial large-sample round, results from the 55th Round should normally have commanded greater credibility than the other, mostly 'thin' sample, results. However, given its acknowledged non-comparability and the limitations discussed earlier of both the Sundaram-Tendulkar and Deaton adjustment procedures, the normal credibility of a 'thick' sample is missing in this case. Against this are the earlier 1990s rounds, each of which may have had individual limitations but which together constituted a set of independent samples having comparable recall, with collective size far exceeding that of the 55th Round, and whose results were sufficiently consistent to have led to a consensus. In view of this, it is necessary to go beyond comparison of the 50th and 55th Rounds. This is particularly so because results have now become available from NSS 'thin' rounds 56 and 57 (2000/01 and 2001/02) which reverted to only 30-day recall for food while retaining only 365-day recall for clothing, etc. These and adjusted 55th Round results need to be compared with earlier NSS data.

Since 'thin rounds' do not command general credibility below the national level, it is useful to comment first on state-level results from the 43rd Round (1987/88), the last 'thick' 1980s round. The official URP comparison of the 43rd and 50th Rounds had shown only a 3 percentage point decline in the poverty ratio, a sharp deceleration from previous trends. The number of poor had increased 13 million nationally, and individually in rural Assam, Bihar, Haryana, Karnataka, Madhya Pradesh, Maharashtra and Uttar Pradesh, and in urban Andhra Pradesh, Haryana, Madhya Pradesh, Maharashtra, Orissa and Tamil Nadu. But MRP counts in Table 14.11, which summarises the analysis in this chapter thus far show larger poverty decline. This implies that MRP counts may be declining faster than URP as consumption patterns change. Also, in some cases, e.g. rural Haryana, the 50th Round appears to be an outlier. Overall, the conclusion from this table is that poverty change from round 43 to 50 MRP, though somewhat larger from that in round 50 to 55 MRP, was not too dissimilar.

Direct comparison of 43rd Round MRP counts with the 55th is slightly more complicated since in the former 365-day questions were asked only for clothing, footwear and durables and not for education and institutional health. However, this is surmountable since the 50th Round permits calculation of MRP counts with and without 365-day reports for education and institutional health, and the difference turns out to be small. Using official poverty lines and unadjusted 55th Round counts, there is a fall of 8 and 11 percentage points in rural and urban poverty ratios, and a reduction in the number of poor by about 13 million. With food-adjusted 55th Round counts, the decline in poverty ratios is 6.2 and 9.8 percentage points over the 12 years and the number of poor is seen to increase slightly. The pace of poverty reduction over this longer period (0.5 and 0.8 percentage points per annum in rural and urban areas) is similar to the 50th and 55th Rounds comparison, as is indication that this was not enough to reduce the absolute number of poor. Moreover, except that West Bengal is one of the better performing states on this longer comparison, the statewise pattern is also similar.[34] Comparing food-adjusted 55th Round counts with 43rd Round MRP, the number of poor increased in rural areas of Assam, Bihar, Madhya

[34] Correlations between state-level changes in headcount ratios between rounds 43 and 55 and the corresponding changes between rounds 43 and 50 or between rounds 50 and 55 are all in the range 0.55-0.85.

Table 14.11 Comparable MRP Poverty Changes over Rounds 43 to 55
(Based on state-specific official poverty lines)

	Headcount Ratio (Per Cent)			Poverty Gap (Per Cent)			Number of Poor (Million)		
	1987/88 to 1993/94	1993/94 to 1999/ 2000	1987/88 to 1999/ 2000	1987/88 to 1993/94	1993/94 to 1999/ 2000	1987/88 to 1999/ 2000	1987/88 to 1993/94	1993/94 to 1999/ 2000	1987/ 88 to 1999/ 2000
Rural									
Andhra Pradesh	−5.0	−1.4	−6.4	−1.2	−0.3	−1.5	−1.8	−0.3	−2.1
Assam	2.1	5.3	7.4	0.2	2.4	2.6	1.2	1.9	3.1
Bihar	3.7	−6.2	−2.5	0.8	−2.2	−1.4	7.9	0.8	8.7
Gujarat	−4.8	−4.0	−8.8	−1.0	−0.6	−1.6	−0.8	−0.8	−1.6
Haryana	9.1	−13.1	−4.0	1.4	−2.5	−1.1	1.4	−1.6	−0.2
Karnataka	−9.6	−2.9	−12.5	−3.4	−1.2	−4.6	−2.3	−0.5	−2.8
Kerala	−5.8	−11.2	−17.0	−1.5	−2.7	−4.2	−1.0	−2.3	−3.3
Madhya Pradesh	−4.0	6.8	2.8	−1.3	1.4	0.1	0.0	6.0	6.0
Maharashtra	−3.7	−6.1	−9.8	−0.7	−1.8	−2.5	−0.3	−2.0	−2.3
Orissa	−10.4	3.7	−6.7	−4.3	2.1	−2.2	−1.6	2.2	0.6
Punjab	0.5	−1.1	−0.6	0.1	−0.2	−0.1	0.2	−0.1	0.1
Rajasthan	−9.1	−4.9	−14.0	−3.2	−1.1	−4.3	−1.9	−1.0	−2.9
Tamil Nadu	−15.2	−4.9	−20.1	−5.3	−1.5	−6.8	−5.2	−2.1	−7.3
Uttar Pradesh	−1.3	−3.2	−4.5	−0.3	−1.5	−1.8	3.9	1.7	5.6
West Bengal	−10.3	−2.5	−12.8	−3.7	0.2	−3.5	−2.8	0.4	−2.4
15 Major States	−3.2	−2.8	−6.0	−1.4	−0.8	−2.2	−3.2	2.3	−0.9
All-India	−3.3	−2.8	−6.1	−1.2	−0.9	−2.1	1.2	1.5	2.7
Urban									
Andhra Pradesh	−1.7	−5.9	−7.6	−1.0	−2.1	−3.1	0.6	−0.7	−0.1
Assam	−5.5	4.0	−1.5	−0.4	1.0	0.6	−0.1	0.2	0.1
Bihar	−17.4	5.6	−11.8	−4.6	0.9	−3.7	−1.3	1.4	0.1
Gujarat	−6.2	−7.6	−13.8	−1.3	−2.1	−3.4	−0.2	−0.8	−1.0
Haryana	−3.7	0.5	−3.2	−0.7	0.2	−0.5	0.0	0.1	0.1
Karnataka	−7.4	−8.9	−16.3	−2.7	−2.9	−5.6	−0.2	−0.7	−0.9
Kerala	−13.4	−1.2	−14.6	−3.5	−0.9	−4.4	−0.6	0.0	−0.6
Madhya Pradesh	0.8	−3.4	−2.6	−0.2	−0.6	−0.8	1.4	0.7	2.1
Maharashtra	−5.8	−2.3	−8.1	−2.4	−1.0	−3.4	0.2	1.1	1.3
Orissa	0.0	5.4	5.4	0.5	1.3	1.8	0.3	0.5	0.8
Punjab	−2.5	−1.5	−4.0	−0.3	−0.6	−0.9	−0.1	0.0	−0.1
Rajasthan	−8.8	−2.7	−11.5	−2.5	−1.0	−3.5	−0.3	0.1	−0.2
Tamil Nadu	−1.7	−11.3	−13.0	−1.7	−3.0	−4.7	0.8	−1.1	−0.3
Uttar Pradesh	−10.8	1.8	−9.0	−3.2	−0.2	−3.4	−1.1	2.3	1.2
West Bengal	−12.0	−2.2	−14.2	−2.9	−0.6	−3.5	−1.6	−0.1	−1.7
15 Major States	−6.0	−3.2	−9.2	−2.1	−1.0	−3.2	−2.2	3.1	0.9
All-India	−6.9	−2.8	−9.7	−2.1	−0.9	−3.0	−2.9	3.7	0.8

Note: Changes from 1987/88 to 1993/94 are based on 365-day recall for clothing, footwear and durable goods for both rounds 43 and 50. Changes from 1993/94 to 1999/2000 are based on 365-day recall for clothing, footwear, durable goods, education and institutional health in both rounds 50 and 55. Estimates for 55th Round are food adjusted as in Tables 14.6a and 14.6b. Figures for '15 major states' are on basis of state-level poverty estimates and census population of states. Figures under all-India are based on estimates using the NSS all-India distribution and all-India poverty lines.

Pradesh, Orissa, Punjab and Uttar Pradesh and in urban areas of Assam, Bihar, Haryana, Madhya Pradesh, Maharashtra, Orissa and Uttar Pradesh. The best performers were Gujarat, Karnataka, Kerala, Rajasthan, Tamil Nadu and West Bengal, where the number of poor (urban + rural) declined by more than 15 per cent. At the level of NSS regions, although 55th Round poverty ratio is lower than the 43rd in most regions, the number of poor increased in 29 rural and 42 urban regions spread all over the 58 NSS regions in major states.[35] Further, as in the shorter comparison, this is associated with greater urban-rural disparity; and within-region urban inequality increased in 40 NSS regions.

This indication that 55th Round food-adjusted counts are not markedly differently from the MRP trend from the two previous 'thick' NSS rounds is important. It confirms that the shift to only a 365-day recall for low-frequency items was the main source of the misleading results obtained by comparing the unadjusted 55th Round with URP of previous rounds. It also suggests positively that simply juxtaposing may restore some inter-temporal comparability between existing URP and available MRP data with minimum further adjustment. For this, estimates by uniform 30-day recall from NSS rounds before the 55th can be plotted on separate axes against corresponding estimates using 365-day recall for clothing, etc., which was the only one used in rounds 55 to 57. Besides rounds 43 and 50, for which both URP and MRP estimates are available directly, 365-day questions for low-frequency items were canvassed in schedule type 2 of rounds 51 to 54 while schedule type 1 of these rounds used 30-day URP. Although direct 30/365-days MRP estimates are not available for these since type 2 schedules used a seven-day recall for food, etc., hybrid estimates are possible replacing deciles-wise the 30-day estimates for clothing, etc., in schedule 1 with the corresponding 365-day estimates from schedule 2. This is approximate, but unlikely to mislead.

To begin with, consider poverty counts. Headcount ratios from all full-year NSS rounds starting 1977/78 are plotted in Figures 14.3a, 14.3b and 14.3c. These are based on official poverty lines available for 'thick' samples, extended to 'thin' samples using appropriate price indices. The 55th Round estimates are food-adjusted. The separate axes differ only by an intercept shift equal to the average MRP-URP difference during Rounds 51–53. The important point to note is that wherever estimates by both recall types are available, their year-to-year movements are similar. This not only adds confidence to earlier comparisons with the 55th Round but also to comparison across other rounds without common recall. On this basis, adjusted 55th Round estimates are found consistent with the other 1990s NSS rounds. Thus, properly interpreted, the 55th Round is not so out of line with earlier 1990s NSS rounds as to require revising conclusions drawn earlier from them.

However, the 1990s 'thin' sample estimates do show large variation around the trend from 'thick' samples. If these are accepted, poverty reduced well below trend in Rounds 45 and 46 (1989/90 and 1990/91), rose very sharply in Round 48 (1992) and then fluctuated above trend till Round 55 (1999/2000) before falling below trend in Round 56 (2000/01). Moreover, although declining, the trend rural poverty ratio remained consistently above the low reached in 1989/90. The graphical picture thus bears out the pre-55th Round consensus: that rural poverty was higher in every 1990s NSS round than at the

[35] The 55th Round food-adjusted poverty ratios are higher than 43rd Round MRP in rural areas of south-west Andhra Pradesh, all three regions of Assam, south and central Bihar, west Haryana, Chhattisgarh, Vindhya, south and north Madhya Pradesh, eastern Maharashtra, south Orissa, Himalayan and central Uttar Pradesh and Himalayan West Bengal and in urban areas of Assam eastern plains, west Haryana, Chhattisgarh, north Madhya Pradesh, all three Orissa regions and south-east Rajasthan. As far as the number of poor is concerned, this declined in rural areas of all NSS regions in Kerala and Tamil Nadu and in urban areas of both Kerala regions. In all the remaining states, there was at least one NSS region where the number of poor was higher in 1999/2000 than in 1987/88.

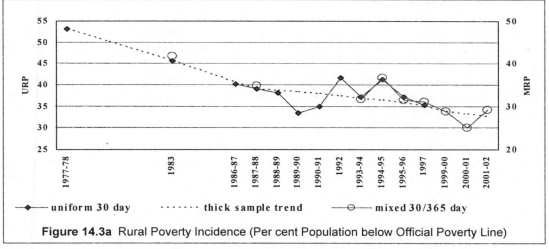

Figure 14.3a Rural Poverty Incidence (Per cent Population below Official Poverty Line)

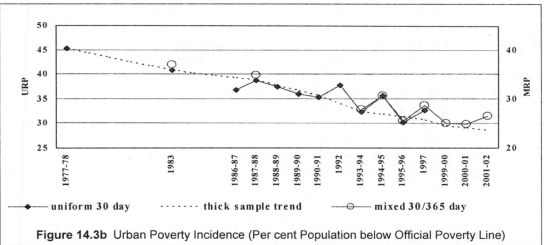

Figure 14.3b Urban Poverty Incidence (Per cent Population below Official Poverty Line)

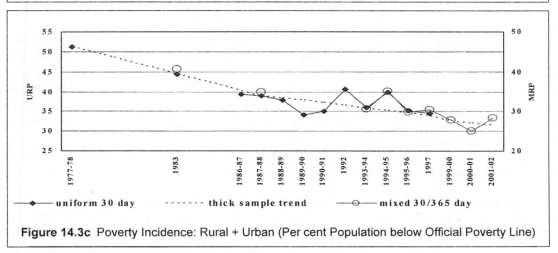

Figure 14.3c Poverty Incidence: Rural + Urban (Per cent Population below Official Poverty Line)

end of the 1980s. Furthermore, although the rural poverty ratio finally fell below 1989/90 in the 56th Round, it rose back again in the 57th Round. Figures 14.4a, 14.4b and 14.4c, which plot the numbers of poor, show that although India's 1980s poverty reduction performance was not spectacular, with increasing urban numbers eroding rural reduction, the number of poor did fall to a low in 1989/90. This has been exceeded in every subsequent year – by nearly 20 million in 2000/01 and much more in the other years. Should all this information be ignored?

This is important since, in addition to incorrect small adjustments to the 55th Round, the reversal of pre-55th Round consensus has involved ignoring the 'thin' rounds. These were potential input into time-series analysis not only of an eventful decade for the Indian economy but also of how aggregate world poverty and inequality were affected by economic 'reform' in the country with the largest number of poor. But since the unadjusted 55th Round is totally out of line with previous 'thin' rounds, it is not possible for both to be broadly comparable to previous thick rounds. Post-55th Round data uncertainty has virtually halted the time-series research on poverty change that till recently had grappled and debated the relative impact of various exogenous and policy variables.

This is not the place to detail results of past research that used time-series data. But, since the food-adjusted 55th Round does compare quite well with nearby rounds once the URP-MRP distinction is made, it is appropriate to note that econometric models available had explained much of the large year-to-year poverty variation found in the 'thin' rounds above. Although some of these rounds were outliers and different models did differ on the exact specification of explanatory variables, research had moved towards agreement that in addition to agricultural and non-agricultural growth, certain other variables such as prices, public expenditure and patterns of growth diffusion (for example, through rural non-agricultural opportunities) were important.[36] In particular, cereal prices and rural non-farm employment were found to affect rural poverty quickly; and large and opposite movements in these during the late 1980s and early 1990s were identified as a possible cause of the large swings observed in\ poverty ratios. The large poverty decline in the 56th Round can be explained in these terms. Cereals prices fell in 2000/01, reversing large real increase since 1990/91, and NSS also shows rural non-farm activity rising smartly from 1999/2000 after the large decline since 1989/90. The setback in the 57th Round is less easy to explain but this affected cultivators most and is probably the lagged effect of a poor 2000/01 harvest coinciding with general deflation of farm prices.

Recent Indian discussion has unfortunately neglected proper monitoring of short-run poverty change to focus solely on medium-term trends and on how 'reforms' may have affected this. This too has privileged 'thick' over 'thin' samples, although in fact the latter are of more than adequate size for reliable estimates at the all-India level. Nonetheless, since 'thin' rounds differ on principal subjects of enquiry, there could of course be bias if sampling frames or responses are affected. But for every 'thin' round after 1993/94, except 57, there is at least one previous round with the same purpose of enquiry and same sampling frame: rounds 56, 51 and 45 (unorganised manufacture), 53 and 46 (unorganised trade) and 52 and 42 (education). There is little reason for all-India trends from these mutually comparable rounds to be less valid than from the thick rounds.

Table 14.12 presents annualised changes in headcount ratios from all these comparable rounds. With the exception of comparisons involving the 51st round, which appears to be an outlier, the picture that

---

[36] Early research had established the significance of food prices and agricultural growth. Later research has established importance of public expenditure and the nature of diffusion of non-farm incomes, Sen (1996, 1997), Datt and Ravallion (1998 and 2002) Fan et al. (2000) and Lanjouw and Sharief (2000).

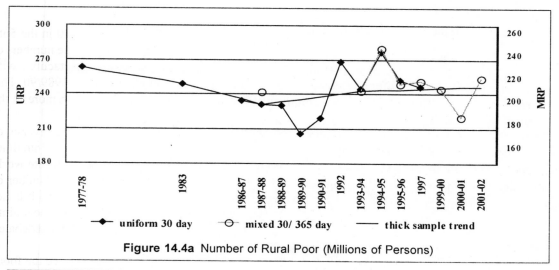

Figure 14.4a Number of Rural Poor (Millions of Persons)

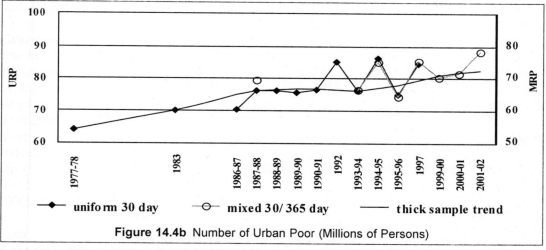

Figure 14.4b Number of Urban Poor (Millions of Persons)

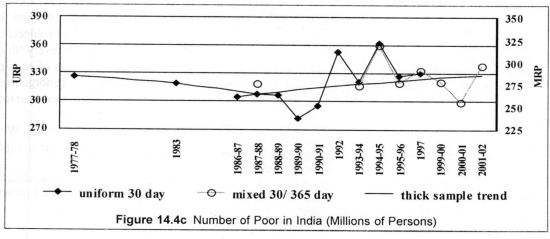

Figure 14.4c Number of Poor in India (Millions of Persons)

Table 14.12 Headcount Poverty Ratios and Comparable Change
(Based on official poverty lines)

| Year (NSS Round) | Headcount Ratios (Per cent HCR) | | | | Comparable Annual Change in HCR from | | | |
| | Rural | | Urban | | About 5 Years Ago | | About a Decade Ago | |
	Uni-from 30-Day	Mixed 30-365 Days	Uni-from 30-Day	Mixed 30-365 Days	Rural	Urban	Rural	Urban
1983 (38)	45.6	41.8	40.8	37.0	−1.4	−0.8	−1.1	−0.6
1986/87 (42)	40.2		36.7					
1987/88 (43)	39.0	(35.2)	38.7	(34.9)	−1.5 (−1.5)	−0.5 (−1.5)	−1.4	−0.7
1988/89 (44)	38.1		37.5					
1989/90 (45)	33.5		36.0					
1990/91 (46)	35.0		35.3					
1992 (48)	41.7		37.8					
1993/94 (50)	37.2	31.6 (31.9)	32.4	27.9 (28.0)	−0.3 (−0.6)	−1.1 (−1.2)	−0.8 (−1.0)	−0.8 (−0.9)
1994/95 (51)	41.3	36.6	35.7	30.7	1.6 (1.4*)	−0.1 (−0.3*)		
1995/96 (52)	37.1	31.5	30.2	25.5			−0.3 (−0.6*)	−0.7 (−0.8*)
1997 (53)	35.3	31.1	32.7	28.7	0.1 (0.3*)	−0.4 (−0.4*)		
1999/2000 (55)		28.8		25.1	−0.5* (−0.5)	−0.5* (−0.5)	−0.5* (−0.5)	−0.8* (−0.8)
2000/01 (56)		25.0		24.9	−1.9* (−1.9)	−1.0* (−1.0)	−0.3* (−0.4*)	−0.6* (−0.7*)
2001/02 (57)		29.1		26.6				

Note: All estimates use all-India distribution and all-India poverty lines. The MRP in 43rd Round had 365-day questions only for clothing, footwear and durable goods and the corresponding estimates for Round 50 are in brackets. All other MRP estimates used 365-day questions for clothing, footwear, durable goods, education and institutional medical care. MRP estimates for Rounds 51 to 53 are hybrid, replacing decileswise the 30-day estimates for low frequency items in schedule 1 with corresponding 365-day estimates from schedule 2, and 55th Round estimates are food adjusted. All other estimates use unadjusted original distributions. Comparable annualised change is either from one thick round to another (in bold), including from Rounds 27 and 32, or over the following comparable thin Rounds: 42 and 52; 45, 51 and 56; and 46 and 53. Each of these sets had the same principal purpose of enquiry and the same sampling frame. The change figures are on both URP basis (unbracketed) and MRP (bracketed). The change estimates with asterisk are those for which the same reference period was not available from the two rounds compared. These cases involve Rounds 42, 45 and 46 for which MRP is not available and it was assumed that the MRP-URP difference was the same as in Round 43; and Rounds 55 and 56 for which URP is not available and it was assumed that the MRP-URP difference was the same as the average for Rounds 51 to 53. Change figures without asterisk are direct, from comparable rounds using comparable reference periods.

emerges is consistent. Quinquennial comparisons suggest acceleration of urban poverty reduction in the late 1980s followed by a slowdown after the mid-1990s. However, decadal rates of decline obtained from the various 1990s rounds cluster at 0.6–0.8 percentage points per annum, the same as in the two previous decades. On the other hand, for rural areas, quinquennial comparisons show a sharp slowdown in poverty reduction during the early 1990s, followed by a revival in the late 1990s. Unlike the urban, however, the decadal pace of rural poverty reduction is found to reduce very significantly, from 1-1.5 percentage points per annum during 1970s and 1980s to at most 0.5 percentage points per annum in the 1990s. This or lower rates of poverty reduction are found for each of the full-year rounds 52, 53, 55 and 56 from comparable rounds about a decade earlier (that is, 42, 46, 43 and 45 respectively). All of these imply that the number of poor increased during the 1990s, by between 3 and 35 million.[37] In other words, mutually comparable nearby 'thin' rounds replicate almost fully the conclusion drawn earlier about 1990s poverty reduction from 'thick' round comparisons with the food-adjusted 55th Round.

This evidence, that 'thin' and 'thick' rounds match reasonably on decadal all-India comparison, vindicates both the food adjustment made to 55th Round data and the 'thin' round results usually ignored. Perhaps the most interesting aspect of this is the concordance found between decadal comparisons involving Rounds 52 and 53 on the one hand and Round 56 on the other. The former have been criticised for overestimating poverty compared even with other pre-55th Rounds and the latter shows less poverty than even the unadjusted 55th Round. Yet, valid comparisons from these and from adjusted 'thick' rounds agree that the earlier trend decline in the number of rural poor was reversed during the 1990s, and also on its broad statewise pattern.[38] Of course, some states do differently across comparisons, some rounds are outliers even on all-India estimates, and it appears certain that a part of the large variation seen over the thin rounds is due to sampling and other differences, which require care

[37] The lowest increase of 3 million is found comparing the 55th Round food-adjusted to the 43rd Round MRP. The highest increase of 35 million is comparing the URP from Rounds 53 and 46.

[38] State-level results for rural India have been computed for these comparisons. Between 1986/87 and 1995/96, rural poverty ratios increased in Assam, Bihar, Madhya Pradesh, Rajasthan and Uttar Pradesh; and decreased by more than 15 per cent in Gujarat, Haryana, Kerala, Tamil Nadu and West Bengal. Between 1990/91 and 1997, poverty ratios increased in Assam, Bihar, Haryana, Madhya Pradesh, Orissa, Punjab and Uttar Pradesh; and decreased by more than 15 per cent in Gujarat, Tamil Nadu and West Bengal. Using 43rd Round state-specific URP-MRP differences to make 45th Round counts comparable to MRP of 56th Round, rural poverty ratios increased between 1989/90 and 2000/01 in Gujarat, Madhya Pradesh, Punjab and Uttar Pradesh and the number of poor increased in Assam also; on this comparison, the number of poor declined more than 15 per cent in Karnataka, Kerala, Orissa and Tamil Nadu. These results, along with earlier comparison of 1987/88 and 1999/2000, all agree that rural poverty numbers increased in Assam, Madhya Pradesh and Uttar Pradesh and, except for one comparison each, in Bihar and Punjab as well. These states account for over 45 per cent of total rural population in the 15 major states. At the other end, Karnataka, Kerala, Tamil Nadu and West Bengal, accounting for 22 per cent of rural population in major states, show more than 15 per cent poverty reduction in most decadal comparisons without showing poverty increase in any. Andhra Pradesh and Maharashtra, accounting for 16 per cent of total rural population, show poverty decline in all these comparisons but do not figure among top performers in any. Thus, as far as ranking by poverty reduction is concerned, there is broad consistency across the different comparisons on the ranking of 11 of 15 major states, accounting for 83 per cent of rural population.

[39] In the above comparisons, Gujarat, Haryana, Orissa and Rajasthan figure among states showing increased rural poverty by some comparison and also among best performers by some other comparison. The reason could be either some year-specific event, e.g. weather, which is particularly variable in these states, or survey idiosyncrasy. That survey idiosyncrasy may be relevant is evident in case of the 51st round during which experimental schedules with alternative recall were initiated and which, although it had the same subject of enquiry and used the same sampling frame (the economic census) as rounds 45 and 56, returned higher poverty and lower estimates of rural non-farm activity compared not only to

in comparison.[39] However, quite apart from reference period change, there were sampling changes in the 55th Round also.[40] All this scarcely justifies ignoring the 'thin' samples to concentrate only on interpreting the 55th Round. Together, the information from each reinforces the other to confirm the pre-55th Round consensus, not its revision.

The main criticism of pre-55th Round 1990s NSS data was that it had increasingly underestimated growth. Figure 14.5a plots, for all full-year NSS rounds since 1977/78, the NSS average real MPCE for all-India (rural + urban) using official poverty lines as deflator. Once again, the 55th Round estimate is food-adjusted and estimates by uniform 30-day and mixed 30/365-day recall are against separate axes with intercept shift equal to average difference in Rounds 51 to 53, taking into account the fact that MRP means in Rounds 43 and 50 were higher than in other rounds because of 30-day questions for clothing, etc. The 1980s trend is also included.

This does show that NSS measured relative stagnation of real per capita consumption in the early 1990s, with MPCE in Rounds 42 (1986/87) to 45 (1989/90) above the 1980s trend and Rounds 48 (1992) to 51 (1994/95) below. However, MPCEs were back on trend in Rounds 52 (1995/96) and 53

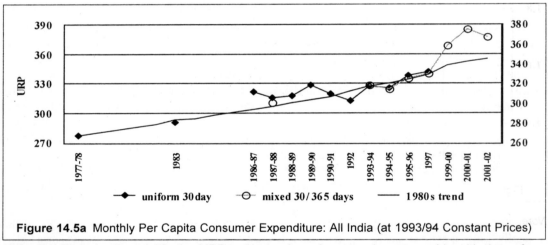

Figure 14.5a Monthly Per Capita Consumer Expenditure: All India (at 1993/94 Constant Prices)

Note: For Rounds 43 and 50, the MRP estimates have been made comparable with those from Round 51 to 57.

---

the trend from these rounds but also compared to neighbouring rounds. Other rounds that used this frame, i.e. 45, 46, 53, 56 and 57, returned systematically higher rural secondary sector activity and lower poverty than rounds that used population census as frame, and much more so in some states than in all-India. Also, census population weighted averages of state poverty counts in Rounds 56 and 57 are less than all-India counts using the implicit NSS population weights. Clearly, some of the variation observed over rounds is because of different sampling frames rather than any underlying change in population characteristics.

[40] For example, the 55th Round involved an enterprise survey for the non-organised sector as well and because of this non-agricultural sub-blocks were over-sampled purposively. This was unlike in any previous round but was repeated in the 56th Round. This may have contributed to why the 55th Round measured 18 per cent more rural non-agricultural employment than Round 53 and why this increased further by 12 per cent in Round 56. These are orders of magnitude much higher than any likely true increase in rural non-farm employment over a couple of years and, since poverty is related inversely with this, could potentially have introduced an additional downward bias to 55th Round measured poverty.

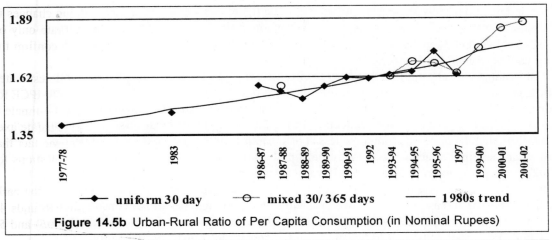

Figure 14.5b Urban-Rural Ratio of Per Capita Consumption (in Nominal Rupees)

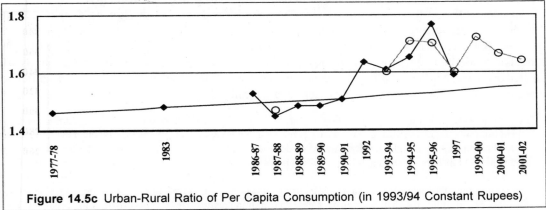

Figure 14.5c Urban-Rural Ratio of Per Capita Consumption (in 1993/94 Constant Rupees)

Note: In Figure 14.5a, the plotted MRP estimates for the 43rd and 50th Rounds (which had a 30-day question for low frequency items) have been reduced by 4.5 per cent to make them comparable with Rounds 51 to 57, which only had the 365-day question for low-frequency items. In Figures 14.5b and 14.5c, only a single axis is used since there is no significant difference in urban-rural MPCE ratios between MRP and URP. The deflation for Figures 14.5a and 14.5b is with official poverty lines for rural and urban India extended to thin samples using appropriate consumer price indices. The real MPCE in Figure 14.5a is the population weighted average of rural and urban.

(1997) and went well above this in Rounds 55 (1999/2000), 56 (2000/01) and 57 (2001/02). Since the concern of this paper is consistency and comparability of NSS estimates and not validation, NSS-NAS comparisons can be skirted to note simply that the NAS also shows a sharp deceleration in the early

---

[41] According to the current NAS series with 1993/94 as base, the rate of growth of real per capita private consumption expenditure was 2 per cent per annum during 1977/78 to 1990/91 and declined to only 0.9 per cent per annum during 1990/91 to 1993/94. Corresponding point-to-point growth rates from the NSS series used in Figure 14.5a are 1.1 and 0.8 per cent per annum. Clearly the major growth underestimation in NSS, if any, occurred before the 1990s. From 1997 to 2000/01, the NAS and NSS growth rates are 3.6 and 3.8 per cent per annum respectively.

1990s and that after 1997, NSS growth implicit in the figure is, if anything, higher than the NAS.[41] It is of course true that the NSS measures lower consumption than the NAS and it is also true that, since NSS-NAS differences enlarged in the 1980s, the difference in levels was larger in the 1990s. But this alone cannot explain the 1990s outcome.

The striking and relevant fact that emerges from these figures is that although comparable NSS real MPCE growth accelerated during the 1990s, the pace of comparable rural poverty reduction fell much short of that achieved earlier. This reinforces the point made by Sen (2000) with pre-55th Round NSS data that the slower pace of poverty reduction during the 1990s cannot be dismissed by simply repeating ad nauseam that the NSS was somehow less able to capture 1990s growth than it had been able to do in earlier decades. In the face of recent assertions by Deaton and Dreze (2002)[42] and Datt and Ravallion (2002),[43] this point needs to be restated. Poverty calculations use not only NSS data but also externally derived poverty lines, and the lower poverty reduction measured from NSS throughout the 1990s was despite higher, or at least not much lower, growth of NSS nominal per capita consumption deflated by these poverty lines than in the 1980s. This implies quite unambiguously that the cause of slower poverty reduction during the 1990s should be sought in the increase in sources of inequality.

One aspect of this is the urban-rural divide. Figure 14.5b shows that the growth of nominal urban MPCE outstripped the rural one throughout, and that the differential rose well above the 1980s trend from 1999/2000. A more significant trend break, shown in Figure 14.5c, occurred in the early 1990s and involved underlying deflators which caused the urban-rural gap to increase even more sharply when calculated using real MPCEs implicit in poverty calculations. As discussed in Sen (2000), these differential changes in deflators were largely a consequence of the much larger weight of cereals in the consumer

[42] They write 'aside from indicating no poverty decline in the late 1990s, the thin rounds also suggest that average per capita expenditure was stagnating during that period – something that is very hard to reconcile with other evidence'. In fact, this is misleading on both counts. First, there was some decline in the headcount ratio between 1993/94 or 1994/95 and 1997, i e, the thin rounds period that they refer to, although this was at a much slower pace than before the 1990s. Second, the NSS growth rate of real consumption during 1993–97 or 1994–97 was in fact marginally faster than the pre-1990s rate. Deaton-Dreze thus miss the real picture from the NSS during this period: that the rate of poverty reduction was much lower than in the pre-1990s despite growth of average per capita consumption being no less. They also miss an even bigger picture that emerges from available NSS rounds if official deflators are used: that the increase in poverty occurred not during 1994/95 to 1997 but during 1990/91 to 1994/95 when NSS real per capita consumption did fall below the pre-1990s trend, including in the thick 50th Round. This is missed since Deaton-Dreze do not consider rounds 45 and 46 at all, and in their comparison of the 43rd and 50th Rounds they use Deaton's alternative deflators which imply both more growth and greater poverty decline. A case does exist against the official deflators, but it is not proper to assess the thin rounds against a thick sample trend thrown up by use of alternative deflators without also deflating the thin rounds alternatively. Deaton and Dreze do not do this.

[43] They write: 'Comparing the nominal consumption aggregates from both sources over the period 1972–97, Sen (2001) finds that consumption by households in India implied by the NSS accounts for 60–70 per cent of the national private consumption implied by the national accounts. Moreover, the divergence between the NSS and the national accounts seems to be growing'. This misinterprets Sen, whose essential point was that, although the NSS measures less consumption than the NAS and although this divergence had increased during the 1980s, the divergence between NSS and NAS on nominal consumption did not grow during 1990/97 by the then current NAS with base 1980/81. In fact, during the crucial period of poverty increase, i.e. 1990/91 to 1993/94, this divergence did not grow even by the new NAS with 1993/94 as base. In the subsequent period, 1993/94 to 1997, there is increased divergence by the new series but not the old, and after 1997 there is again no growth divergence between the NSS and NAS 1993/94. It is surely too much to hang the NSS on such slender evidence from the NAS, especially since Sen had also made two other points. First, that the new NAS was suspect on some important revisions and, second, that the real difference was with deflators used for poverty calculation and those implicit in the NAS and that this has nothing at all to do with the NSS.

price index of agricultural labourers and of the fact that cereal prices, which had risen less than other prices during the 1980s, increased much more in the early 1990s. Since changes in cereal prices shift incomes between net buyers and net sellers, implicit in this is redistribution within rural areas, from the rich to the poor during the 1980s and from the poor to the rich for most of the 1990s. Another important aspect of this, that high relative cereal prices increase welfare inequality with unchanged income distribution, is missed by inequality measures applied not only to nominal consumption but even real, if obtained by uniform deflation.

But although there is no doubt either about movements in relative cereal prices or about the increase in nominal urban-rural disparity, Deaton has raised doubts about the extent of increase in real urban-rural disparity. Using NSS implicit prices, he has argued that official deflators overestimated rural, but not urban, inflation during 1987/88 to 1993/94 and thus underestimated rural poverty decline. This of course has nothing to do with the 55th Round, and analysis after 1993/94 shows less difference. But this is important since near complete agreement exists otherwise on increased real urban-rural disparities as a major source of 1990s inequality increase. By the usual measures, both rural poverty and this disparity (Figures 14.4a and 14.5c) jumped sharply in tandem during the early 1990s.

Deaton's alternative deflators do not reverse the conclusion of increased urban-rural disparity. But, while the NSS ratio of urban to rural real MPCEs increased 10 per cent between the 43rd and 50th Rounds by official deflators, as against 5 per cent increase in the nominal ratio, this rose by only 2 per cent by Deaton's implicit deflators. Purely as a result of this, Deaton estimated a 6 percentage point decline in rural poverty between 1987/88 and 1993/94, against only 2 percentage points officially. Carried over to the rest of the decade, this implies about 30 million less poor. This has nothing to do with the much-maligned NSS surveys, and in fact Deaton prefers implicit prices from the NSS to the independent price indices used officially. But excessive focus on the NSS-NAS difference has resulted in insufficient discussion of the very substantial issues raised thereby.

These cover a wide canvas, most significantly that official state and sector-specific price deflators mislead on true spatial variations in costs of living and that consequently the resulting region-specific poverty counts are inappropriate input for policy-making.[44] Matters are, however, less clear-cut on temporal change. Deaton's deflators cover items which form only part of the total consumption and, unlike direct price quotes, changes in implicit prices from the NSS also reflect changes in quality and source, for example, home produced, market purchase and purchase from the public distribution system. Moreover, the matter of appropriate weights for different items raises interesting conceptual issues quite apart from the usual index number problems. Given the much higher increase in cereal prices relative to other prices during this period and the fact that cereals' share in consumption has been falling, it is not surprising that base-weighted official deflators show higher inflation than current weighted or 'ideal' indices. There is of course warrant from consumer theory, rooted in the principle of consumer sovereignty, to take shifts in consumption patterns into account and prefer the latter as measures of cost of living. But it is not evident that this is preferable to a fixed base-year basket, or consistent, when carrying forward a poverty line from 1973/74 which was rooted on a nutrition norm and thus on a welfare

[44] State and sector-specific official poverty lines are in any case flawed since the 1993 expert group had applied interstate differentials for 1963/64 to price indices with different base without correcting for the intervening price change.

[45] The official deflation procedure has been criticised as being inconsistent with this norm, for example, by Mehta (2001) and Patnaik (2002), who note correctly that poverty reduction is much less using the direct calorie cut-off. Official deflators ensure at least that the original food bundle even if not actually consumed is affordable at the poverty line. Any shift from base to 'ideal' weights risks losing even this link between the original nutrition norm and later poverty lines.

criterion which put particular emphasis on affordability of adequate nutrition.[45]

Similarly, the implication from Deaton's deflators that real urban-rural disparity increased less than the nominal between 1987/88 and 1993/94 obtains some support from official measures of the domestic terms of trade of agriculture. The latter had improved quite substantially from the mid-1980s to the mid-1990s, before its subsequent decline. However, since improvement in agriculture's terms of trade during this period was almost entirely as a result of higher cereal prices, involving a relative loss not only for agricultural labourers but also for cultivators of other crops, this brings back the issue of inequality implications of relative cereal prices.

There are, therefore, strong reasons to be sceptical about official poverty lines, particularly at the state and sector levels and on their ability to capture shifting tastes even at the national level. But counter-arguments can also be offered to prefer these to Deaton's, that is, greater proximity to (and consistency with) consumption weights near the poverty norm and greater completeness both in item coverage and as time series. Nonetheless, the issues raised by Deaton are important enough to require a new expert group to re-examine existing poverty lines and the methods used to update these. Till then, there is really no alternative to the official deflators for deriving comparable poverty estimates over time although different levels of state and sector-specific poverty lines can be adopted as is already done by some independent researchers. On this basis at least, the data underlying Figures 14.5b and 14.5c do confirm a large increase in urban-rural disparity and also that, except for an absolute decline in cereals prices in 2000/01, nothing of substance has changed after the 55th Round to alter the detailed analysis offered on this in Sen (2000, 2002a and 2002b).

Turning to inequality within the urban and rural sectors, Figures 14.6a and 14.6b plot Gini indices of nominal consumption at the all-India level for all full-year NSS rounds since round 32 (1977/78). As before, estimates by uniform 30-day and mixed 30/365-day recall are against separate axes, with Ginis from schedule 2 of rounds 51 to 53 plotted against the 30/365-day axis. Again, the axes are aligned with an intercept shift equal to the average difference found in the URP and MRP from rounds 51 to 53. In interpreting these figures, it should be remembered that, as discussed in the Section 'Comparability of 55th Round', the presence of 30-day questions for clothing, etc., caused the 30/365-day distribution in the 43rd and 50th Rounds to be more unequal and thus non-comparable to the other rounds for which MRP estimates are available based on only the 365-day question. The figures also include fitted trends incorporating a kink after 1992, which are statistically significant.

These figures suggest that, despite claims to the contrary, such as by Bhalla (2003) and Singh et al (2003), inequality of nominal consumption increased during the 1990s, and was particularly sharp in urban areas. The contrary view is based on a simple comparison of the 55th with earlier rounds. For example, the rural Gini in the 55th Round was 26.4 as against 28.6 in the 50th Round. However, this comparison is incorrect because the Ginis in the 50th and earlier rounds are based on 30-day recall for clothing, etc., and, as discussed in the Section 'Comparability of 55th Round', the 55th Round's 365-day recall for clothing, etc., reduces measured inequality very considerably. Thus, in the 50th Round, which had both the 30 and 365-day questions, rural Ginis were 28.6 and 25.8 by these two recalls; and these averaged 29.7 and 24.8 in rounds 51 to 53 where the two recalls were put to separate samples. Adjusted for the fact that the 55th Round used only the 365-day recall, the correct change in rural inequality between the 50th and 55th Rounds is an almost 3-Gini point increase rather than a 2-Gini point decline.

Since the effect of shift to MRP on measured inequality is crucial to appreciate 1990s trends, Table 14.13 provides fractile-specific MPCE estimates, for the bottom 40 per cent, next 40 per cent and top

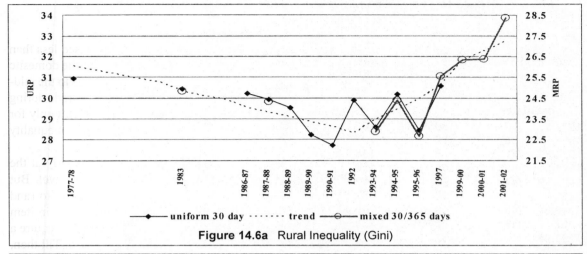

Figure 14.6a Rural Inequality (Gini)

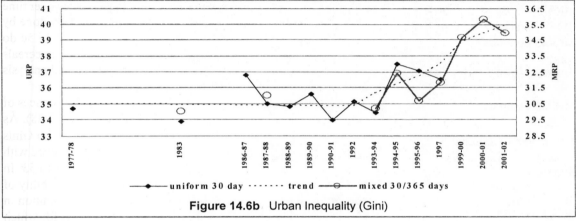

Figure 14.6b Urban Inequality (Gini)

Notes:

1. The trends plotted above are from the following fits obtained from the data in the figures:
   For rural areas:
   $$G = 394.7 + 5.05*D1 + 2.33*D2 - 0.19*T + 0.64*T1; \qquad R2 = 0.85$$
   $$ (7.14) \quad\;\; (2.45) \quad (3.02) \quad\; (4.21)$$
   For urban areas:
   $$G = 29.26 + 4.67*D1 + 1.58*D2 + 0.00*T + 0.57*T1; \qquad R2 = 0.79$$
   $$(6.50) \quad\;\; (1.67) \quad (0.01) \quad\; (3.71)$$
   where G is the Gini index, T is time, T1 is 0 till 1992 and thereafter the number of years elapsed since 1992, D1 is a dummy with value 1 if the estimate is by the uniform 30-day recall and 0 otherwise, and D2 is a dummy which is 1 only if the estimate is by the 30/365-day recall but the 30-day question for clothing, etc, is also present. Figures in parentheses are t-values. It may be noticed that both dummies are significant, implying that estimates by the 30-day recall return a higher Gini and that presence of the 30-day question also increases the Gini by the 30/365-day recall.

2. The trend lines are drawn with D1 = 1 and D2 = 0.

3. In order to make them comparable with rounds 51 to 57, the plotted values of the MRP Ginis of rounds 43 and 50 (where D2 was equal to 1) have been reduced by the coefficients of D2 in the fits above. All the other Ginis plotted are unadjusted. For rounds 51 to 53, URP Ginis are from schedule 1 and MRP from schedule 2.

Table 14.13 Fractile Specific Nominal MPCE by Different Recalls and Derived Linkage Factors

Year (NSS Round)	Rural			Urban		
	Bottom 40 Per cent	Next 40 Per cent	Top 20 Per cent	Bottom 40 Per cent	Next 40 Per cent	Top 20 Per cent
URP estimates						
1977/78 (32)	36	63	147	49	94	215
1983 (38)	62	107	222	82	153	348
1986/87 (42)	78	138	274	113	215	527
1987/88 (43)	88	150	312	121	227	533
1988/89 (44)	99	167	342	134	250	585
1989/90 (45)	110	187	353	147	271	655
1990/91 (46)	118	200	376	165	309	685
1992 (48)	140	238	481	193	368	869
1993/94 (50)	162	271	541	228	427	980
1994/95 (51)	176	290	612	239	454	1,154
1995/96 (52)	202	331	656	287	541	1,347
1997 (53)	221	375	785	309	585	1,436
MRP43 estimates						
1983 (38)	64	109	206	86	157	333
1987/88 (43)	93	153	294	128	235	514
1993/94 (50a)	174	283	523	243	446	965
MRP50 estimates						
1993/94 (50)	174	283	519	243	446	948
MRP51–57 estimates						
1994/95 (51)	187	296	514	258	475	1,039
1995/96 (52)	219	340	560	310	556	1,096
1997 (53)	234	382	671	331	603	1,252
1999/2000 (55)	287	466	873	410	780	1,799
2000/01 (56)	298	487	902	440	853	1,986
2001/02 (57)	286	488	942	465	884	1,977
Linkage factor A: Ratio of MRP43–50 to URP						
1983 (38)	1.049	1.019	0.928	1.049	1.026	0.957
1987/88 (43)	1.057	1.020	0.942	1.058	1.035	0.964
1993/94 (50a)	1.074	1.044	0.967	1.066	1.044	0.985
1993/94 (50)	1.074	1.044	0.959	1.066	1.044	0.967
Average	1.064	1.032	0.949	1.060	1.037	0.968
Linkage factor B: Ratio of MRP51–57 to URP						
1994/95 (51)	1.062	1.022	0.840	1.079	1.047	0.900
1995/96 (52)	1.080	1.027	0.853	1.083	1.028	0.814
1997 (53)	1.059	1.018	0.856	1.070	1.030	0.872
Average	1.067	1.022	0.850	1.077	1.035	0.862
Linkage factor C: Ratio of MRP43–50 to MRP51–57 (ratio of linkage factors A and B)						
Average	1.000	1.009	1.116	0.984	1.002	1.123

Note: MPCEs for 55th Round are food adjusted and for Rounds 51–53 these are hybrid, replacing decileswise the 30-day consumption estimates of low frequency items in schedule 1 with 365-day estimates from Schedule 2.

20 per cent rural and urban, for all full-year rounds from 32 onwards. The MRP-URP ratios from rounds with both recalls are linkage factors similar to those used to splice different series of index numbers. As discussed earlier, there are three different MRP specifications: MRP43 used in the 43rd Round where both 30 and 365-day questions were put to all respondents for clothing, footwear and durable goods, MRP50 used in the 50th Round where again both 30 and 365-day recalls were asked to the same sample but for education and institutional medicine as well, and MRP51-57 used in rounds 55 to 57 and also in schedule 2 of rounds 51 to 54 where only the 365-day recall was used for items where this recall was used in the 50th Round. Of these, MRP43 and MRP50 are very similar but MRP51-57 does differ, though only in case of the top quintiles for which it returns much lower MPCEs. Figure 14.7 presents indices of real MPCE on URP basis by fractile groups, applying linkage factor B from Table 14.12 to MRP estimates for rounds 55 to 57 and using the NAS consumption deflator.

These indices (with base 1993/94) in Figure 14.7 and their annualised decadal growth rates in Table 14.14 (over comparable rounds identified in Table 14.12) must remain somewhat tentative since, owing to the presence of seven-day food questions in schedule 2 of rounds 51 to 53, the estimates used to

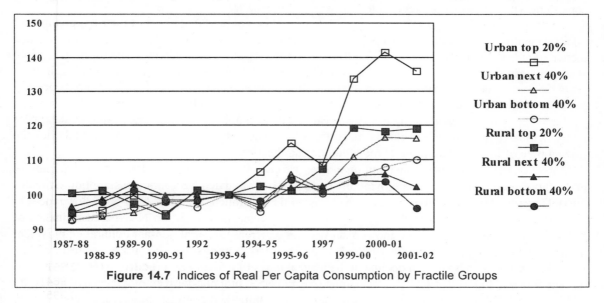

Figure 14.7 Indices of Real Per Capita Consumption by Fractile Groups

Table 14.14 Comparable Rates of Growth of Fractile Specific Real MPCE

	Rural			Urban		
	Bottom 40 Per cent	Next 40 Per cent	Top 20 Per cent	Bottom 40 Per cent	Next 40 Per cent	Top 20 Per cent
1977/78 to 1987/88	1.43	1.16	0.01	1.53	1.31	1.57
1983 to 1993/94	1.01	0.54	0.39	1.04	1.28	1.38
1986/87 to 1995/96	1.54	0.67	0.65	1.29	1.21	1.37
1987/88 to 1999/2000	0.78	0.73	1.41	1.02	1.48	2.88
1989/90 to 2000/01	0.21	0.24	1.76	1.03	1.87	3.22

Note: The deflator used is the NAS deflator for private consumption expenditure.

compute linkage factors B are hybrid. On the other hand, so long as the procedure is approximately correct, these indices and growth rates underestimate the true 1990s inequality increase because the same deflator (for overall aggregate consumption expenditure) is used for all fractile groups, ignoring that inflation was higher for items consumed by the poor during most of the 1990s. Moreover, even nominal inequality increase may be underestimated since there are strong reasons to believe that survey capture is poorer at the upper tail.

Nonetheless, if accepted, the procedure leads to the conclusion that the 1990s, particularly second half, saw very large increases in consumption by the relatively rich. The 40 per cent increase in real consumption of the top urban quintile during 1993/2001 is not only unprecedented since Indian surveys began, but also involves more than 50 million people – rare internationally. The nearly 20 per cent increases for the top rural quintile and the next urban 40 per cent (involving over 250 million people) are also higher than rates recorded previously for these fractiles. Further, although much lower than the others, the consumption increase of the bottom 40 per cent urban (about 100 million) was not significantly less than that recorded for this group during the 1970s and 1980s. Up to this point, the picture is consistent with claims of unprecedented growth and prosperity post-'reform'.

But the picture is no longer shining when it comes to the bottom 80 per cent of the rural population, numbering almost 600 million. Real NSS per capita consumption of this vast majority of Indians had increased at 1-1.5 per cent per annum (and more if differential cereal price movements are taken into account) during the 1970s and 1980s. But, from Figure 14.7, their 1990s consumption was less in most years than was reached in 1989/90, and the maximum attained since then (in 1999/2001) only about 3 per cent higher. It would of course be exaggeration for anyone to claim from this that the poor got poorer as the rich got richer during the 1990s. But the distortion involved in such a claim would appear minor compared with previous claims made from the same data. At least, this is what underlies the finding here of insignificant poverty reduction during the 1990s.

Moreover, these NSS rural consumption indices are consistent with independent data on agricultural production and rural non-farm employment. Sen (2000) had validated NSS rural consumption estimates till 1997 against NAS and other data, and had argued that the much discussed NSS-NAS differences in mean consumption are overwhelmingly urban and cast much less doubt on NSS-based estimates of rural poverty. Subsequent NSS rounds do show a large increase in rural non-agricultural employment from an earlier collapse during the 1990s. But, as Figure 14.8 brings out, this just about restored late 1980s levels and accompanied a decline in the official index of agricultural production (IAP) relative to rural population. Indexed at 1989/90, per capita IAP and NSS rural non-farm employment averaged only 100.9 and 100.0 during the triennium ending 2001/02 – in marked contrast to previous trends. Given this, claims of greater 1990s poverty reduction (or, indeed, of any significant 1990s rural poverty reduction) are difficult to sustain unless these indicators of rural growth are questioned or some counter-evidence produced to show that the distribution of rural incomes did improve substantially.

Perhaps because of this, Sundaram (2001), Deaton and Dreze (2002) and Bhalla (2003) have all relied on evidence of rising real agricultural wage rates for external support to their claims of large 1990s rural poverty reduction. The different time-series available agree that, although less than during the 1980s, 1990s growth of real agricultural wage rates averaged 2-3 per cent per annum at the national level and

---

[46] NSS real agricultural wage rates increased 4.2 per cent per annum from 1983 to 1987/88, 1.6 per cent per annum from 1987/88 to 1993/94 and 2.8 per cent per annum from 1993/94 to 1999/2000. Data from agricultural wages in India and comprehensive scheme for studying the cost of cultivation of principal crops in India also show real wage rate growth at about 2 per cent per annum during the 1990s, down from about 5 per cent during the 1980s, but unlike NSS do not show

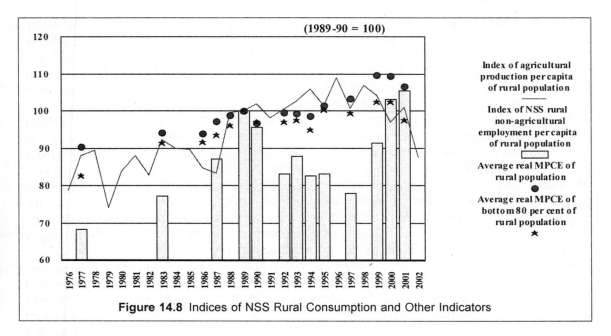

Figure 14.8 Indices of NSS Rural Consumption and Other Indicators

exceeded the growth per capita of either IAP or NSS rural consumption.[46] If wage rates were accurate measures of per capita incomes of agricultural labourers, this would indeed imply improved distribution of rural incomes, benefiting the poorest section of India's rural population. But since incomes depend not only on wage rates but also on days of employment, this needs to be taken into account to put matters in the correct perspective.

On this, the NSS reflects an underlying 1990s reality, corroborated by independent evidence:[47] that per capita incomes of agricultural labourers lagged behind wage rates because their numbers grew much more than available days of wage employment. The NSS estimates that the percentage of rural population in agricultural labour households increased from 27.6 to 31.1 between rounds 50 (1993/94)

---

acceleration in the mid-1990s. In this context, it should be noted that the NSS had specifically excluded overtime payments from wage rates before the 55th Round but included these in 1999/2000. This is yet another instance where 55th Round innovation may have biased results towards a rosier picture than would be obtained if earlier survey concepts had been retained.

[47] For example, data on 21 major crops in 14 major states from the comprehensive scheme for studying the cost of cultivation of principal crops in India (CS) show that total payments to hired labour increased at 3.1 per cent per annum in real terms (deflated by the CPIAL) during the 1990s, made up of over 2 per cent per annum growth in real daily wage rates but only 1 per cent growth in days of hired labour employed in the production of these crops. Simultaneously, real farm business incomes (value of crop output less paid-out costs including payments to hired labour) grew at only 1.5 per cent per annum. But although the share of labour in total crop income did increase quite significantly as a result, this does not imply that incomes of labourers increased more than that of cultivators. With the population census showing that the number of agricultural labourers increased at 3.7 per cent per annum over 1991 to 2001, and that of cultivators only 1.4 per cent per annum, this actually implies a decline in real hired labour payments per agricultural labourer and marginal increase in real farm business income per cultivator. However, this excludes horticulture and livestock and analyses costs and returns of only major crops. See Sen and Bhatia (2002) for details.

and 55 (1999/2000), implying 3.7 per cent annual growth of this population. Against this, it reports less than 1.5 per cent annual growth of wage-paid days of employment in agriculture. The consequent decline, through unemployment and lower work participation, of days of employment per member of agricultural labour households makes clear why although NSS reports real wage rate growth of 2.8 per cent per annum during 1993/2000, much higher than rural MPCE, it reports per capita consumption of these households increasing less than the rural average.[48]

This digression, which is cautionary against use of wage rates as proxy for income when other evidence suggests a growing employment deficit, plugs the main external support claimed by those who read large 1990s rural poverty reduction into recent NSS data.[49] However, it is also clear that the source of 1990s within-rural inequality increase was not factorial. With urbanisation slowing down during the 1990s despite faster growth in urban incomes and with farm incomes at best stagnant in most parts of the country after 1996/97, this was largely an outcome of demographic pressure and of very uneven rural linkages with the highly unequal urban growth.[50] The big picture, even ignoring other dimensions of true inequality, for example, the effect of relative price shifts on the poor and inability of NSS to capture consumption of the rich adequately, is that measured 1990s increase in nominal inequality caused consumption of the rural poor to rise by at most a fifth, and of the urban poor only half, of the average national per capita real growth measured by the NSS.

Nonetheless, although these results from adjusted NSS data may disturb some, it may be noted that of the distributional data presented so far, the 1990s urban Gini increase was similar to that in China, the percentage increase in nominal urban-rural ratio was two-thirds that of the Chinese, and the rural Gini increase in India was less than half. This still leaves space to argue that India's relative failure was in growth and not distribution, provided of course that the unequal growth observed in both countries is considered inevitable and put beyond policy discourse.

In this context, an aspect of inequality of particular importance in these continental countries is the regional dimension. In discussions of world inequality, where inclusion or exclusion of just these two giants can alter conclusions completely, it has been suggested that different results may follow if regions and sectors within these are treated like different countries. This is of course of greater relevance to

---

[48] To maintain consistency with data elsewhere, 55th Round consumer expenditure of agricultural labour households (ALH) are from CES, which shows both this and their population share (reported above) somewhat higher than EUS. The CES 55th Round MPCE of ALH is Rs 386 unadjusted and Rs 380 food-adjusted, against 50th Round MPCE of Rs 217 and Rs 224 by URP and MRP. Food-adjusted, this implies a CPIAL deflated real increase of 6.5 per cent over these six years. This is significantly less than for the rural population as a whole (8.9 per cent) when corrections outlined above are made to the 55th Round both for its overestimation of food expenditure and its underestimation of expenditure on 365-day items by the top quintile. It may also be noted that MPCE of ALH corresponds closely in both rounds to their implicit income as obtained by multiplying wage rates with days of employment. The 55th Round EUS reports average daily employment rate of 35.7 per cent (28.2 wage paid and 7.5 self-employed) per member of ALH against 38.1 per cent (29.9 wage paid and 8.2 self-employed) in the 50th Round. The reported average daily wage earnings of casual labourers in agricultural operations were Rs 18.98 and Rs 35.62 in rounds 50 and 55. Using these for returns to self-employment also, gives an average ALH monthly per capita income of Rs 217 (i.e. .381*18.98*30) in 50th Round and Rs 381 (.357*35.62*30) in the per cent. Compare these with the MPCE of ALH reported above.

[49] The most convoluted argument is Bhalla (2003). With NSS wage rates as proxy for rural income growth he projects from 1983 to arrive at a poverty ratio of only 12 per cent in 1999/2000. He ignores that the 1999/2000 wage rates, which he does accept, imply 44 per cent poverty ratio in agricultural labour households at current employment. This alone contributed to over 12 per cent rural poverty, even ignoring the poor in the remaining 70 per cent of rural population.

[50] Across rural household types, MPCE increase over 1993–2002 was least among the 'self-employed', especially farmers who are least mobile, and highest among 'non-agricultural labour' and 'others' who are most urban-linked.

China where between-region inequalities accounted for a much larger part of total inequality before 1978 and both between and within inequality have increased massively since then. But in India too, where almost every other aspect of the 1990s poverty and inequality is hotly contested, there is general agreement that regional inequality did increase significantly.

Since this is a matter where longer-term trends are of interest, Figures 14.9a, 14.9b and 14.9c cover the period 1959/60 to 2001/02 (using all full-year NSS rounds from 15 to 57) and plot population-weighted standard deviation of logarithms of nominal average MPCE across 15 major states. As before, these are calculated with both uniform 30 and mixed 30/365-day recalls, with the latter for rounds 51 to 53 derived from schedule 2, replacing seven-day estimates for food, etc, by corresponding 30-day estimates from schedule 1. For the 55th Round, estimates are from the Section on 'Comparability of 55th Round' as corrected for the presence of seven-day questions. The figures also include two different fitted trends to analyse changes over time. The first is a fourth degree polynomial, which picks up turning points endogenously, and the second a kinked trend fit with three imposed breaks: 'green revolution' after 1966, introduction of 'rural development' in 1976, and adoption of economic 'reforms' after 1991.

The 'green revolution' had reversed an earlier trend of decreasing interstate rural disparities. But, after increasing for about a decade from its onset in the mid-1960s, this was reversed again after the mid-1970s. If, anything, interstate rural inequality declined during the 1980s. Interstate urban inequality had declined continuously till the mid-1980s. Considering both rural and urban, interstate variance of per capita average consumption remained stable during the 1980s. For the 1990s, these figures reproduce with NSS data a result obtained by Ahluwalia (2002) using per capita state domestic product. There is clear and statistically significant evidence of a trend break from the 1980s, into large and sustained

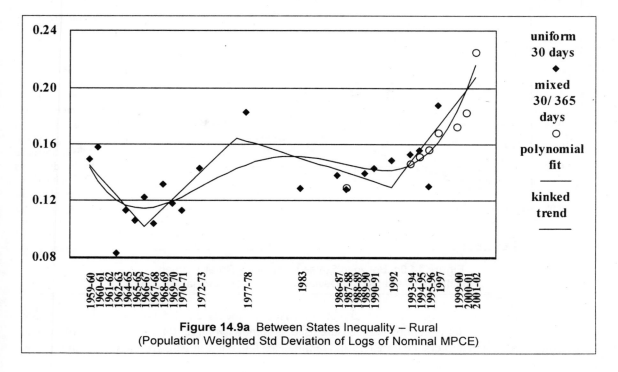

Figure 14.9a Between States Inequality – Rural
(Population Weighted Std Deviation of Logs of Nominal MPCE)

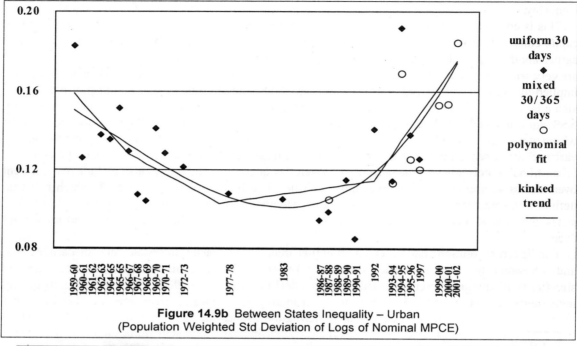

Figure 14.9b Between States Inequality – Urban
(Population Weighted Std Deviation of Logs of Nominal MPCE)

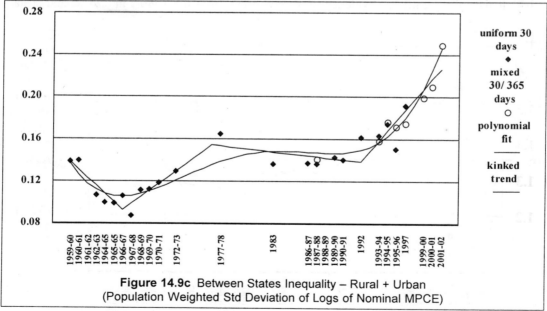

Figure 14.9c Between States Inequality – Rural + Urban
(Population Weighted Std Deviation of Logs of Nominal MPCE)

increase in interstate inequality, both rural and urban. Also, this increase in interstate inequality of NSS consumption, by about 50 per cent by the measure used, is somewhat larger than reported by Ahluwalia for income, implying that interstate transfers and remittances failed to mitigate growing regional income inequality.

This is consistent with Deaton-Dreze's claim of growth 'divergence' (that is, higher growth of per capita consumption in states where this was initially high) between rounds 50 and 55. But, as found earlier about their claim regarding poverty 'divergence', the evidence is weak.[51] Tests of 'divergence' are very sensitive and not robust to choice of deflator or adjustment. That 'divergence' is not necessarily implied by, nor implies, increase in population-weighted inequality measures applied across regions, is also a lesson from recent research on world inequality. Moreover, as the earlier discussion at level of NSS regions showed, evidence of 1990s increase in interstate inequality should not detract from inequality within states. In fact, even after the large increase in interstate inequality during the 1990s, interstate variance accounted for only 15 and 9 per cent of the total national variance of logarithms of rural and urban MPCEs obtained from unadjusted 55th Round unit-level data. Within-state inequality is still the overwhelming component of total inequality in India. Figure 14.10a plots within-state rural-urban disparity, defined as the population weighted average of state-level ratios of urban to rural MPCE for the 15 major states, for all full-year NSS rounds from 1959/60 to 2000/01. Although increasing throughout, this also accelerated in the 1990s. Figures 14.10b and 14.10c plot population-weighted averages of state-level Gini indices for rural and urban areas of the major states. As before, URP and MRP are on separate axis and polynomial and kinked trends are included. These show that a period of inequality decline (highly significant in rural India) starting mid-1970s was reversed in the early 1990s. Although the subsequent increase still leaves within-state rural inequality less than in the mid-1970s, within-state urban inequality

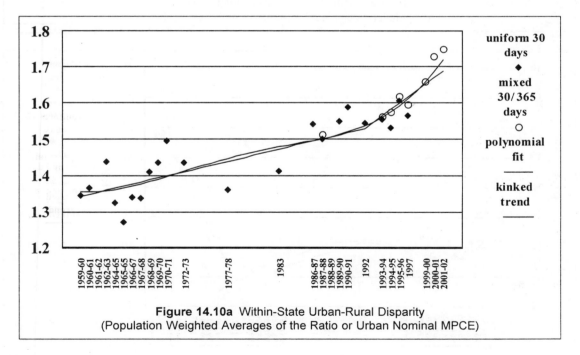

Figure 14.10a Within-State Urban-Rural Disparity
(Population Weighted Averages of the Ratio or Urban Nominal MPCE)

---

[51] The correlation between 50th Round nominal MPCE (urban + rural) using MRP and its growth between rounds 50 and 55 is only 0.32 across the 15 major states, much lower than what Deaton-Dreze report using their adjusted 55th Round data deflated by their state-specific cost of living indices.

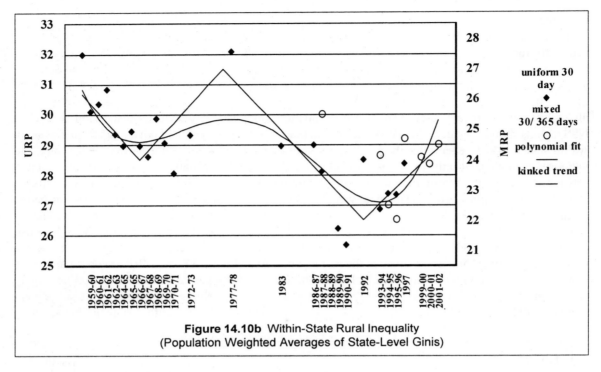

Figure 14.10b Within-State Rural Inequality
(Population Weighted Averages of State-Level Ginis)

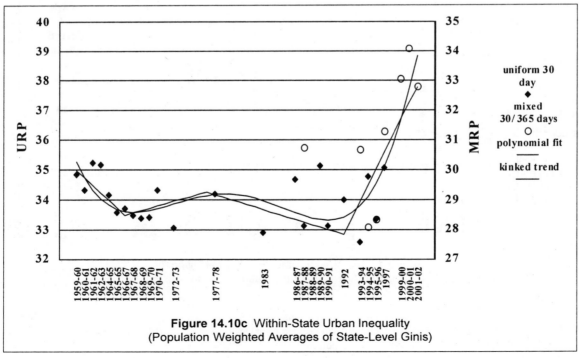

Figure 14.10c Within-State Urban Inequality
(Population Weighted Averages of State-Level Ginis)

has increased massively during the 1990s, probably more than in China. Along with between-state inequalities, these within-state inequalities increase explain why the 1990s were a relatively lost decade for poverty reduction.[52]

CONCLUSION

The 55th Round of the NSS was important and controversial. Conducted in 1999/2000, it was awaited eagerly for information on what had happened to poverty and inequality during this eventful decade. Unfortunately, methodological changes were made in this round, making it non-comparable to previous rounds, and its results different from the previous nine NSS rounds. In complete contrast to the picture of severe setback to poverty reduction that had emerged from earlier 1990s NSS surveys, including the previous 'thick' sample NSS 50th Round conducted in 1993/94, unadjusted comparison of the 55th with the 50th Round shows very large poverty reduction, by 10 percentage points of population, or about 60 million persons.

It is generally agreed that this magnitude of poverty reduction obtained from the 55th Round is an overestimate. A large literature has emerged on the comparability problems involved. In particular, it is known that the 365-day recall used in this round for low-frequency purchases, such as on durables goods and clothing, caused it to measure lower inequality compared with previous rounds, and that the presence of seven-day food queries probably measured higher consumption. Some alternative 'corrected' 55th Round poverty counts were presented at two seminars held in 2001 and 2002. All of these revised downward the extent of measured poverty reduction from the 55th Round and revised measured inequality upward, but the alternatives varied considerably on actual numbers.

This chapter has reviewed all available 55th Round estimates and reported comparable estimates of poverty and inequality. This exercise relied mainly on recalculation of unit-level NSS data from rounds 43, 50 and 55, making as few assumptions as possible. In particular, 43rd and 50th Round poverty counts and inequality measures were re-estimated with the mixed 30/365-day recall (MRP) used in the 55th Round, rather than the uniform 30-day recall (URP) used earlier. The only adjustment was to correct 55th Round estimates of food consumption for 'contamination' from the presence of seven-day questions. This food adjustment, based on the abridged consumption schedule of the 55th Round employment-unemployment survey and nearby trends, is *minimal* and within the margin expected simply on account of the fact that no instructions were issued to even ask 30-day food questions before the

---

[52] Full details of polynomial and kinked trends are available from the authors, but the following may be relevant:

(a) For rounds 43, 50 and 55 data are from this paper. Grouped data are used for rounds 56-57 and 51-53. For the latter, URP are from schedule 1, MRP Ginis from schedule 2 and MRP means hybrid. All other data are from Ozler et al. (1996).

(b) In addition to time variables, two dummies were included: D1 for cases where the 30-day recall was used for the low frequency items and D2 for cases where the 365-day recall was used but where the schedule had also included the 30-day question. In the case of all the fits in Figures 14.9a, b and c and Figure 14.10a, none of these dummies were found significant and were dropped. These charts are therefore plotted using only a single axis. For both types of trend in Figures 14.10b and c, both dummies were found significant. For rural areas, the coefficient on D1 was 4.54 and 4.67 for the polynomial and kinked trend equations and that on D2 was 1.73 and 1.99. The corresponding coefficients for urban areas were 4.86, 4.85, 1.95 and 1.98. In these cases, separate URP and MRP axis were used.

(c) In case of Figures 14.9a and c and Figures 14.10b and c, all four polynomial terms were found significant, but for Figures 14.9b and 14.10a only two of these terms were significant. Similarly, all three breaks in the kinked trend were found significant in case of Figures 14.9a and c and Figure 14.10b, but only two (1976 and 1992) were found significant for Figure 14.9b and only one (1992) was found significant in case of Figures 14.10a and c. In all cases, the break in the 1990s was found statistically significant.

seven-day ones till six weeks after the 55th Round survey had begun.

Comparison of these food-adjusted 55th Round counts with the 50th Round MRP shows that although poverty ratios may have declined, this was by *at most* 3 percentage points and the absolute number of poor did not decline. Since this magnitude of poverty reduction during 1993–2000 is less than that obtained for 1987–94 with previous NSS thick rounds and implies no reduction in the number of poor, it corresponds to the gut feeling expressed by many at the seminars referred to above and corroborates the pre-55th Round consensus that the 1990s were a relatively lost decade for poverty reduction. However, the result does contradict a different consensus that emerged from work by Deaton and Sundaram-Tendulkar: that although the 55th Round overestimated poverty decline, the number of poor did decline, by at least 30 million.

This is not just an intellectual matter. Poverty counts influence fiscal allocation, determine interstate distribution of anti-poverty funds, and fix the number of households entitled to below poverty line benefits (access to food subsidy, anti-poverty schemes, and increasingly to subsidised health care and education). All of these are under review and identification has begun of those entitled to targeted benefits. A mistaken consensus on Deaton-Sundaram-Tendulkar counts could cause withdrawal of entitlements from more existing poor beneficiaries than the entire population of Iraq. This may be the human cost of what had originated as sustained attacks on the earlier 1990s NSS rounds that had dissatisfied those who believe 'reforms' reduce poverty quickly, and which persist, despite Deaton and Dreze (2002) reporting that 'we have not been able to identify any "smoking gun" that would point to a specific problem with any of these rounds'.

It needs to be clarified in this context that the focus of the present paper has been comparability and consistency of NSS data, not their validity. The objective was to assess what can be concluded post-55th Round from NSS data about 1990s poverty change, not whether existing poverty estimates from previous NSS rounds were correct. Some conclusions on larger issues of poverty norms and measurement do emerge and are mentioned below. But the important point is that not only were all methodological changes in the 55th Round, made following earlier criticism of NSS, systematically in the direction of measuring reduced poverty, Sundaram-Tendulkar and Deaton-Dreze failed to gauge the true magnitude of this, in part because they chose to ignore the nearby 'thin' NSS rounds rather than use these to calibrate and critically assess their adjusted estimates.

As far as Sundaram and Tendulkar are concerned, the only conceptual difference between their method and that followed here is the correction for 55th Round 'contamination' from seven-day food questions. However, given the minimal food adjustment made here, this explains only a minor part of the difference in poverty results. The major difference was due to an inadvertent error in their calculation of 50th Round 30/365-day counts, which they have since acknowledged and corrected. Poverty reduction between 1993/94 and 1999/2000 is more than halved compared with official claims with this correction alone.

The conceptual difference with Deaton is more substantial. He used the 55th Round's retention of only 30-day questions for some non-food items, assuming a stable relationship between spending on these and the probability of being poor. Since this reported less poverty reduction than Sundaram-Tendulkar's original estimates, correcting not only for 365/30-day differences on low frequency purchases but also apparently for seven-day questions on food, this looked more credible. However, on Sundaram-Tendulkar revising their estimates, Deaton's original estimates become incongruous since these imply that the seven-day questions on food in the 55th Round *increased* measured poverty. It turns out that shifts in consumption patterns invalidated a basic assumption of his method and, as Deaton has now acknowledged, led to 'corrected' estimates of food consumption higher than uncorrected. Since his prior position was that presence of seven-day queries had inflated measured food consumption, these results must be deemed to be on the wrong side of credibility. Nonetheless, this method confirms that the switch to 365-day recall for clothing, etc, reduced measured inequality significantly. Moreover, slightly modified, treating some food items as unaffected by recall change, the method gives all-India counts very close to those used here, though with state-level differences.

In contrast to these two adjustments, flaws which have largely been reconciled with proper calculation and consistent estimation, two other adjustments conform more closely to the food-adjusted counts reported in this paper: Datt, Kozel and Ravallion, who used current macroeconomic data in an econometric model relating poverty to growth, inflation and public expenditure, and Kijima and Lanjouw, who put 55th Round household characteristics into a parametric model relating these to poverty. Like Deaton, these derive 55th Round counts assuming some stable relationship from the past. However, not only do these use much less of 55th Round information than the food-adjusted comparisons used here, and require much stronger assumptions, these do not allow direct analysis of inequality change. Moreover, although the all-India poverty change from these is close to the food-adjusted counts, there are significant differences at the state level.

This chapter has examined available data not only for states but also at the level of NSS regions. Some widely known facts, for example, higher growth in urban than rural areas and in southern and western states than elsewhere, are reflected in the adjusted NSS data. But more important are that the number of poor increased in urban areas of more NSS regions than rural despite much faster growth of urban MPCE, and that almost every state had both regions where poverty increased and others where it declined. Poverty numbers were found sensitive to patterns of inequality increase and demographic change, muting the link between growth and poverty reduction. Apart from low growth in many already poor rural regions and limited mobility from these, the other disturbing feature is that although urban growth was much higher than in the past, not only was this associated with increased within-urban inequality but also many urban areas failed to offer either linkage to their rural hinterlands or escape for the rural poor.

These broad patterns, and evidence that poverty reduction was held back by inequality increase, emerge not only from differently adjusted 55th Round data but also from nearby NSS rounds. However, it is difficult to analyse regional change fully because 55th Round methodological changes affected measured inequality and poverty differently across regions. A conclusion of this paper is that although adjusted 55th Round results are quite robust at the all-India level, this translates less clearly to the states. Although only for Assam is it possible to be certain that the poverty ratio increased between rounds 50 and 55, an increase in absolute number of the poor cannot be ruled out for any major state if all alternative estimates are considered, including from the consumption schedule of the 55th Round EUS. Consequently, this round remains inadequate for policy, for example, interstate allocation of poverty alleviation outlay.

But notwithstanding this, another conclusion is that, if adjusted properly, all-India data from round 55 onwards agree reasonably with previous 1990s NSS rounds. Given this, a big picture appears quite unambiguously: that the 1990s was the first post-independence decade when economic inequality increased sharply in all its dimensions. Long period time series presented here show that inequalities had increased in the initial decade of the 'green revolution' also. But, with urban gaps reducing, inequality increase in that period was largely confined to rural areas. Moreover, this was accompanied by a tendency for relative food prices to fall and was followed after the mid-1970s by a period of about one-and-a-half decades when rural inequalities declined. This, and better growth after the mid-1970s, caused poverty to fall almost throughout from then to 1990 when growth spluttered and food prices rose sharply during a payments crisis. It is not surprising that poverty increased then. But, importantly, poverty reduction appears to have faltered during the subsequent growth revival because every distributional indicator has since worsened.

As far as this big picture is concerned, the 55th Round is only one point in the figures presented here, and matters only on the nature of recovery from crisis and poverty increase in the early 1990s. Since this and later rounds do show that growth revived, the issue is distribution. Unanimity exists on inequality increase between states, across urban-rural and through food prices. And although shift to MRP from 55th Round onwards masks within-states inequality, most adjustments agree on inequality increase in urban areas and on the failure of earlier equalising rural trends to continue. Such inequality increase may not be unusual post-'reform' – China is an example – but high initial poverty and population growth seem to have ensured that India's growth revival after 1992 has largely by-passed the poor. The relatively rich did gain, and some states did perform better than others. But if NSS data and official poverty lines are accepted, there is little doubt that the 1990s saw an increase in the number of poor in many of India's more populated regions. This is consistent with evidence, such as on wage rates, which others have cited to underplay distribution and to argue that only growth matters. However, there is some uncertainty on the exact impact, especially regarding deflators.

Another important finding is of a large 1990s shift in spending from food to non-food (such as fuel, medicines and conveyance) even among the poor. This affected Deaton's adjustment, and means that disjuncture between income poverty and nutrition intake has widened, so that trends in income poverty understate a worsening nutrition situation.[53] There is thus no warrant at all to make the apparent fall in poverty numbers from unadjusted 55th Round an excuse to cut the number of those entitled to subsidised food. The expert group on identification of households below poverty line (BPL), 2002, recommended a new census but has stipulated that the number of BPL households identified in any state should not exceed by more than 10 per cent the Planning Commission estimates based on the 55th Round.[54] With this arbitrary 10 per cent revision, the national poverty count is almost exactly Deaton's adjusted estimate and, as stated earlier, could cut the number of beneficiaries by at least 30 million. To justify denial to so many based on what this paper has established is an incorrect estimate of reduction in the number of income poor (let alone of the nutrition deprived) would be travesty, not only of social justice but of truth as well. This also raises issues of how to match poverty estimates from the NSS with beneficiary

[53] According to the FAO's *State of Food Insecurity in the World – 2003*, the number of undernourished people in India went up by 19 million between 1995–97 and 1999–2001. These are, however, based on food balance sheets that return at least 10 per cent higher calorie intake than NSS, entirely on account of non-cereals, and could also mislead on changes over time since data on private stocks is poor. On an assessment that reviews both food balance sheet and NSS data and concludes that nutritional intake did worsen during the 1990s, see *Report of the High Level Committee on Long-term Grain Policy*, Ministry of Consumer Affairs, Food and Public Distribution, Government of India, 2002.

[54] The census recommended by this expert group was to collect data from all households on 13 indicators such as their education, health and migration status, indebtedness, possession of consumer durables, landholding, housing, food security, water supply and sanitation. Selection of below poverty line (BPL) households will be based on the average rank score of each household across these 13 indicators subject to ceiling on total number of BPL households obtained from the Planning Commission's poverty counts using NSS. Hirway (2003) has criticised this, pointing out that 'there is no logic in reducing the estimates of poverty of one kind to match the other kind of poverty!'

[55] This raises issues well beyond the scope of this paper, including the very large ones of whether NSS consumption expenditure surveys should at all be used to measure poverty and whether targeting if at all should aim at binary identification of poor and non-poor. But one relevant point does emerge from the previous discussion. If poverty counts from NSS are

selection.[55]

However, although no less painful for the excluded, those contemplating a cut in BPL numbers for fiscal or other reasons would be closer to at least some versions of truth if they justify this not by exaggerating poverty reduction but by the argument that poverty numbers from the 50th and earlier rounds may have been fixed too high. After all, claims that the NSS exaggerated poverty have been voiced using NAS-NSS comparisons ever since the expert group on estimation of proportion and number of poor (1993) ended the practice of applying the NSS distribution to NAS mean expenditure. Also, had they had been used, Deaton's alternative poverty lines would have cut the 1993/94 number of poor by 60 million. Similarly, poverty by the 30/365-day mixed recall was already almost 50 million less in the 50th Round than by the uniform 30-day recall.

But none of this is uncontested, and it is not just measurement but also norms that are at issue. For example, it is not proper if poverty is to be kept anchored to a nutrition norm to use the 30/365-day recall without revisiting Engel curves to fix new poverty lines.[56] But doing so now would require confronting the fact that nutrition poverty on existing norms has increased to well over twice income poverty.[57] Any new expert group will clearly have its hands full, especially since poverty numbers are sensitive to even small changes in poverty lines and measured inequality. Results presented here on how poverty counts change from 30 to 365-day recall for low-frequency items, and on sensitivity to the presence or absence of 30-day questions, should also be salutary against belief that possible underestimation in NSS can be set right merely by distribution-neutral adjustments. In any case, the evidence refutes strongly a basic assumption of those who argue for anchoring poverty estimates to the NAS: that distributional changes are small and slow.[58]

Finally, the much-maligned National Sample Survey Organisation (NSSO) emerges rather well, at least compared with its users. That the present analysis was at all possible is because changes were preceded by experiments whose results are almost entirely in the public domain. That, after all, some

---

to be used to set a ceiling and actual identification done on basis of household characteristics including health and education status and durables possession, it may be better to define poverty from NSS without including expenditure on durables, education or medical care and to set statewise ceilings specific to broad household characteristic. Much of the uncertainty stemming from URP-MRP difference would be reduced, and the effect of sampling errors in NSS poverty counts can also be minimised using the Population Census, which does provide information on the population distribution of many of these household characteristics.

[56] The evidence from all the rounds where both the 30 and 365-day reference period were used for low frequency items such as clothing, etc., is that shift to MRP increases total MPCE by 5 to 8 per cent (for the national distribution) in the neighbourhood of the current poverty line. Since this reference period choice does not affect food consumption, poverty lines for MRP consistent with existing nutrition norms must also be 5 to 8 per cent higher.

[57] See NSS Report No 471 and Meenakshi and Vishwanathan (2003). Given evidence of Engel shifts, two opposite arguments are possible on this separate matter of the nutrition norm. Either, that existing norms remain valid and poverty lines need to be revised upward since these do not correspond to norm nutrition with changed patterns of consumption. Or, that the consumption shifts reflect lower calorie requirement as result of better infrastructure or diet quality and that norms can be revised down to take this into account. Some support for this comes from Radhakrishna and Ravi (2003) who show using National Nutrition Monitoring Bureau and National Family Health Survey data that, despite lower calorie intake, there was some reduction in the anthropometric incidence of child malnutrition during the 1990s in all states except Rajasthan, Uttar Pradesh and possibly Madhya Pradesh, Orissa and Gujarat.

[58] Banerjee and Piketty (2003) provide independent evidence from income tax data that inequality at the top of the distribution, that is, income shares of the top percentile and above (that had decreased earlier), increased very sharply between 1983 and 1987 and again after 1992. They show that, if these very rich were not captured adequately by NSS, their increased share alone can explain 20 to 40 per cent of enlarging NAS-NSS differences. This is in addition to inequality increases discussed here, i.e. those captured by the NSS itself, and disregards possible NAS overestimation.

comparability is possible and the 55th Round turns out to correspond fairly well with nearby rounds is testimony to the integrity of NSS field operations in the face of fairly severe shocks. Further work is of course necessary, especially on sampling biases and on improving response of the relatively rich, for example, by reducing questionnaire size. Also, in the absence of direct control for these in any NSS round, some ambiguity remains on how the simultaneous presence of two recalls affect each other. But the NSSO comes out relatively unscathed even on this: 55th Round 'contamination' from seven-day queries to 30-day food estimates could well have been as small as assumed here and, if anything, 365-day estimates of low frequency items improve if 30-day queries are also present.

It is now by and large quite well known how different reference periods affect estimates; and, as this paper demonstrates, linkage factors can be obtained, with minimum arbitrary assumptions, from earlier thick rounds that used both URP and MRP and from the type 1 and type 2 schedules of rounds 51 to 54. Some in-survey calibration is necessary to eliminate differences that remain on how to adjust the 55th Round. But with the NSS having concluded a proper test of suitability of different recalls for different food items through a pilot survey, in-survey calibration of remaining ambiguities on exact linkage between earlier NSS rounds and rounds 55 to present are also probably best left to experimental pilot surveys. The overwhelming priority now is to restore the credibility of NSS time series and to close the entire issue of reference periods.

The strength of the NSS was the consistency of its survey design and uniformity of the concepts used. Given the sensitivity of poverty numbers to even small changes, experimentation confuses in surveys whose purpose is poverty monitoring. It is too early to tell whether past criticism of NSS and subsequent experiments will improve future estimates. Sadly for statistics, the 55th Round also became an opportunity, seized by a coalition of the willing, to degrade earlier 1990s NSS rounds just because these had revealed a poverty setback. This paper has reviewed the resulting literature. However, longer-run credibility of the statistical system requires consensus on a definite transition to an agreed set of reference periods in the next 'thick' round. This would be best accomplished by having two schedules canvassed separately, one which uses whatever is considered a preferred recall structure for consistent use in at least the medium-term future, and the other which uses the exact 50th Round reference periods and is implemented on an independent and inter-penetrating sample, large enough to provide linkage factors accurate at least to deciles level by states.

This need to agree on a stable survey design for the medium-term future and to simultaneously benchmark against past data, not only on consumption levels but also and more importantly on their distribution, is vital. The interpretation of 1990s NSS trends offered here differs significantly from what others have concluded from the same data. It is not just economic analysis that is affected critically by whether or not the Indian economy has been able to buck the trend in China and elsewhere by 'reforming' without large inequality increase. A huge gap exists today between what policy-makers often state in Washington, Delhi or even many state capitals and grass roots perception among social workers and activists or as becomes evident during elections. It may of course be that governance in this era of globalisation requires hype to 'feel good'. But unless the still excellent NSS consumer expenditure surveys regain sufficient agreement among analysts for them to be able to inform truthfully on serious issues of distribution and thus bridge gaps in perception, these will be of little or no practical value.

ACKNOWLEDGEMENT

This chapter is a consolidated version of a paper published in two parts in *Economic and Political Weekly*, Vol. 39, 18–25 September and 25 September–1 October 2004.

REFERENCES

Ahluwalia, Montek S (2000), 'Economic Performance of States in Post-Reforms Period', *Economic and Political Weekly*, 6–11 May.

Banerjee, Abhijit and T Piketty (2003), 'Top Indian Incomes, 1956–2000', BREAD Working Paper No. 46, available at http://www.ksg.harvard.edu/cid/bread/046.htm

Bhalla, Surjit S (2003), 'Recounting the Poor: Poverty in India, 1983–99', *Economic and Political Weekly*, 25–31 January, (Chapter 21 of this book).

Chadha, G K and Alakh N Sharma (1997), *Growth, Employment and Poverty: Change and Continuity in Rural India*, Vikas, Delhi.

Datt, Gaurav and Martin Ravallion (1998): 'Why Have Some Indian States Done Better than Others at Reducing Rural Poverty?' *Economica,* 65, pp. 17–38.

———— (2002), 'Is India's Economic Growth Leaving the Poor Behind?', *Journal of Economic Perspectives*, summer, Vol. 16, No. 3.

Datt, Gaurav, Valerie Kozel and Martin Ravallion (2003), 'A Model-based Assessment of India's Progress in Reducing Poverty in the 1990s', *Economic and Political Weekly*, 25–31 January, (Chapter 19 of this book).

Deaton, Angus (2001), 'Survey Design and Poverty Monitoring in India', research programme in development studies, Princeton University. Available at http://www.wws.princeton.edu/~rpds

———— (2003a), 'Adjusted Indian Poverty Estimates for 1999/2000', *Economic and Political Weekly*, 25–31 January, (Chapter 12 of this book).

———— (2003b), 'Prices and Poverty in India, 1987–2000', *Economic and Political Weekly*, 25–31 January, (Chapter 17 of this book).

———— (2003c), 'Regional Poverty Estimates for India, 1999–2000' research programme in development studies, Princeton University (mimeo).

Deaton, Angus and Jean Dreze (2002), 'Poverty and Inequality in India: A Re-examination', *Economic and Political Weekly*, 7 September, (Chapter 18 of this book).

Fan, Shenggen, Peter Hazell, and S K Thorat (2000), 'Impact of Public Expenditure on Poverty in Rural India', *Economic and Political Weekly*, 30 September.

FAO (2003), *State of Food Insecurity in the World – 2003*, Rome.

Government of India (2002), 'Report of the High Level Committee on Long-term Grain Policy', Ministry of Consumer Affairs, Food and Public Distribution.

Hirway, Indira (2003), 'Identification of BPL Households for Poverty Alleviation Programmes', *Economic and Political Weekly*, 8 November.

Kijima, Yoko and Peter Lanjouw (2003), 'Poverty in India during the 1990s: A Regional Perspective', World Bank Policy Research Working Paper 3141, World Bank, Washington, DC.

Lanjouw, Peter and Abusaleh Sharief (2000), 'Rural Non-Farm Employment in India: Access, Incomes and Poverty Impact', (processed), World Bank, Washington, DC.

Meenakshi, J V and Brinda Vishwanathan (2003), 'Calorie Deprivation in Rural India, 1983–1999/2000', *Economic and Political Weekly*, January, pp. 25–31, (Chapter 24 of this book).

Mehta, Jaya, (2001), 'Give Poverty A Face Please!' in *Alternative Economic Survey 2001/2002*, Rainbow Publishers, Delhi.

Ozler, B, Gaurav Datt, and Martin Ravallion (1996), 'A Data Base on Growth and Poverty in India', World Bank. available at http://www.worldbank.org

Patnaik, Utsa (2002), 'Deflation and Déjà vu' in V K Ramchandran and M Swaminathan (eds), *Agrarian Studies – Essays on Agrarian Relations in Less Developed Countries,* Tulika, Delhi.

Radhakrishna, R and C Ravi (1994), 'Food, Nutrition and Prices: Some Macro Issues', Working Paper No. 22, Centre for Economic and Social Studies, Hyderabad.

———— (2003), 'Malnutrition in India: Trends and Determinants', (processed), Centre for Economic and Social Studies, Hyderabad.

Ramchandran, V K and M Swaminathan (2002), *Agrarian Studies – Essays on Agrarian Relations in Less Developed Countries,* Tulika, Delhi.

Ravi, C (2000), 'Complete Demand Systems, Welfare and Nutrition: An Analysis of Indian Consumption Data', unpublished PhD thesis.

Sen, Abhijit (1996), 'Economic Reforms, Employment and Poverty: Trends and Options', *Economic and Political Weekly*, Special Number, September.

———— (1997), 'Structural Adjustment and Rural Poverty: Variables that Really Matter' in G K Chadha and Alakh N Sharma (eds), *Growth, Employment and Poverty: Change and Continuity in Rural India*, Vikas, Delhi.

———— (2000), 'Estimates of Consumer Expenditure and Its Distribution: Statistical Priorities after NSS 55th Round', *Economic and Political Weekly*, 16–22 December, (Chaptr 11 of this book).

———— (2001), 'Estimates of Consumer Expenditure and Implications for Comparable Poverty Estimates after the NSS 55th Round'. Paper presented at NSSO international seminar on 'Understanding Socio-Economic Changes through National Surveys', 12-13 May, New Delhi.

———— (2002), 'Agriculture, Employment and Poverty: Recent Trends in Rural India' in V K Ramachandran and Madhura Swaminathan (eds), *Agrarian Studies*, Tulika Books, New Delhi.

Sen, Abhijit and M S Bhatia (2002), 'Cost of Cultivation and Farm Income – A Study of the Comprehensive Scheme for Studying the Cost of Cultivation of Principal Crops in India and Results from It', *State of the Farmer in India: A Millennium Study*, Ministry of Agriculture, New Delhi.

Singh, Nirvikar, Laveesh Bhandari, Aoyu Chen and Aarti Khare (2003), 'Regional Inequality in India: A Fresh Look', *Economic and Political Weekly*, 15 March.

Sundaram, K (2001), 'Employment and Poverty in the 1990s: Further Results from NSS 55th Round Employment-Unemployment Survey 1999/2000', *Economic and Political Weekly*, 11–17 August.

Sundaram, K and Suresh D Tendulkar (2003a), 'Poverty *Has* Declined in the 1990s: A Resolution of Comparability Problems in NSS Consumer Expenditure Data', *Economic and Political Weekly*, 25–31 January.

———— (2003b), 'Poverty in India in the 1990s: An Analysis of Changes in 15 Major States', *Economic and Political Weekly*, 5–11 April.

———— (2003c): 'Poverty in India in the 1990s: Revised Results for All-India and 15 Major States for 1993/94', *Economic and Political Weekly*, 15–22 November.

Tarrozzi, Alessandro (2002): 'Estimating Comparable Poverty Counts from Incomparable Surveys: Measuring Poverty in India', Research Programme in Development Studies, Princeton University. Available at http://www.wws.princeton.edu/~rpds

II.2 THE SELECTION OF POVERTY LINES

15

Minimum Level of Living
A Statistical Examination

Ashok Rudra

A certain magic number has received currency in the growing literature on Poverty: Rs 20 per capita per month of consumption at 1960/61 prices. It is written in the Draft Fifth Five-Year Plan that 'In the Fourth Plan document, private consumption of Rs 20 per capita per month at 1960/61 prices was deemed a minimum desirable consumption standard.' The magic number however began its career much earlier. As a matter of fact, it is this figure that constitutes the keystone to the exercise in long-term planning that is presented in the Planning Commission document 'Notes on Perspective of Development, India: 1960/61 to 1975/76'. This document describes the first of its four basic objectives as, 'to ensure a minimum consumption of Rs 20 per capita per month to the entire population by the end of the Fifth Five-Year Plan . . . .'

The origin of the figure however is somewhat of a mystery. The way this figure gets cited, one would think that it is a generally accepted statistical magnitude. It is indeed generally accepted. But the basis of acceptance is obscure. The presumption seems to be that some competent statistical authority had arrived at the figure after careful calculations. But what is that competent authority and what kind of calculations did it carry out? Nobody seems to know the answer. Bardhan (1973) writes 'It is by now well known that in 1962 a distinguished study group set up by the Government of India is reported to have recommended per capita consumption of Rs 20 at 1960/61 prices per month (excluding expenditure on health and education, both of which are expected to be provided by the State according to the Constitution and in the light of its other commitments).' But what definition of minimum level of living did that distinguished group use? What statisticians did the statistical work, what statistical data did they use, what assumptions did they use to arrive at the figure of Rs 20? We have failed to get answers to any of the above questions from any published or unpublished sources, and have therefore set ourselves the task of making a critical examination of the figure of Rs 20 at the prices of 1960/61: how far real, and how far mythical a minimum level does it represent?

A minimum level of living is an elusive concept that is vaguely associated with the culture of a people and level of development of the economy to which they belong. For India, however, the minimum would have to mean an absolute minimum – a standard of living such that anything less is incompatible with the maintenance of physical well being. It has to be in terms of certain norms in regard to food, clothing, housing, medical and educational facilities, etc. Norms for medical and educational facilities have indeed been proposed, but in India these provisions for education and health for the masses are supposed to be accommodated in public consumption, so that they are not relevant to the Rs 20 type of calculation, the latter being concerned with private consumption alone. Of the items that belong to private consumption proper, it is only with regard to food that a normative approach can be taken – on considerations of nutrition. As to non-food items like clothing and housing, the concept of minimum requirements is far from being totally irrelevant. But no yardsticks have been worked out for them on any scientific basis. Quite a lot of work has, on the other hand, been done on low cost dietary patterns for meeting minimum nutritional needs. It is these dietary recommendations that constitute the core of any calculations regarding minimum consumption needs. We shall also begin with them.

MINIMUM DIET

Among the expert bodies that have worked on the problem of minimum dietary patterns, those associated with the Food and Agriculture Organisation (FAO) are the foremost. The FAO has worked out normative diets for groups of countries having comparable geographical and climatic conditions which would ensure similarity of physiological requirements as well as of food availability. The pattern that would be relevant for India is the one meant for South-East Asia (see FAO, 1973) and is presented in Table 15.1. Of course, South-East Asia is a highly heterogeneous region from all points of view, so that the diet recommended for the whole of South-East Asia would certainly require to be adjusted to make it suitable for India. For India, in particular, various recommendations have been made by the Nutrition Advisory Committee (NAC). But recommendations made purely from a nutritional point of view are of course not sufficient. Minimum cost considerations have also to be kept in mind and that calls for not only the expertise of dieticians but also those of economists and statisticians. The most careful and detailed work that has been done in this line is that by Sukhatme (1965). He took into account various recommendations

Table 15.1 Normative Minimum Daily Dietary Patterns

(Quantities in kg)

(1)	Sukhatme[a] (Minimum Target) (2)	FAO[a] (3)	Patwardhan[b] (4)	Price Multiplier per kg (5)
Cereals	0.403	0.395	0.425	0.400
Pulses	0.104[c]	0.075	0.113[c]	0.600
Starchy roots	0.046	0.160	–	0.375
Sugar	0.050	0.035	0.043	0.600
Milk	0.201	0.098	0.113	0.500
Meat	0.007	0.036	–	2.130
Fish and eggs	0.019	0.027	–	1.500
Fruits and vegetables	0.137	0.225	0.170	0.500
Oils and fats	0.018	0.016	0.035	2.250
Value of diet at 1960/61 prices (Rs)	0.5238	0.6087	0.4838	–

Notes: [a] per person, [b] per adult unit, [c] inclusive of nuts.

of the FAO and the NAC, various specific considerations for India in terms of availability as well as consumption habits, the different requirements of persons of different age-sex groups, and worked out two food baskets corresponding to a minimum concept and a medium concept. Sukhatme's minimum food basket is also presented in Table 15.1 (Column 2). Also presented in Column 4 is a third set of food consumption norms which is made use of in the Report of the Second Pay Commission as well as by Bardhan (1973). The figures are reportedly based on suggestions made by the NAC and modified in the light of advice given by a nutrition expert, Dr Patwardhan.[1]

VALUATION OF MINIMUM DIET

We now turn to the problem of expressing in value terms the minimum food basket. The problem consists in converting the quantities into values by the use of suitable price multipliers. By the very nature of the problem there cannot be any satisfactory solution to the problem of price weights. Given the temporal, spatial and quality-wise variation of prices for any one of the items of the basket any number standing for a 1960/61 price has to be the result of some kind of a crude averaging process which cannot be justified by any theory of averaging. Keeping in mind the essential arbitrariness of any price weights that we may use, we have chosen to use the average rural retail prices for 1960/61 as presented in the National Sample Survey (NSS) Report No. 123 for all items other than fruits, starchy vegetables, vegetables and fish.[2] For the latter we have mainly used prices as worked out and used by Kansal in his paper (see references). Results of the valuation exercise also are presented in Table 15.1 (Column 5). It may be seen that the food basket recommended by Sukhatme is worth Rs 15.71 per person per month; that recommended by the FAO is worth Rs 18.26 per person per month. The food basket taken by Bardhan from the report of the Second Pay Commission takes a much smaller value – Rs 14.51 per month *per adult unit,* which would correspond to an even smaller figure – Rs 11.61 – when converted to per month *per person* basis. Bardhan however arrives at a still lower figure – Rs 11.87 per month per adult unit and Rs 9.61 per month per person, even though he also uses NSS estimates of rural retail prices. It may be noted in this connection that Bardhan's figure is considerably lower than the figure set out in the Pay Commission Report itself which is Rs 17.33 per adult unit, higher than our figure. Bardhan's lower figures are partly explained by the following two elements in his calculation procedure:

(a) Bardhan ignores vegetables and nuts from the food basket taken by him from the Pay Commission Report (though this is taken care of in his 'blowing up' procedure).

(b) Before using the NSS based average retail prices, Bardhan marks them down to take account of the fact that the average rural consumer does not procure all his consumption needs from the market, a part of his supply being from his own home grown stock.

We have serious reservations about the procedure followed by Bardhan in effecting this latter adjustment, both from a conceptual and a methodological point of view, which we shall discuss in the Appendix. We may however state our view here that we do not see any particular reason to attach much importance to the food basket taken by Bardhan from the Pay Commission Report, as no information is available as to

---

[1] Food baskets based on nutritional norms have also been arrived at by Panikkar (1972) and Rajaraman (1974) for Kerala and Punjab respectively, by using the standard linear programming approach. We shall not consider these baskets as we are considering the concept of minimum level of living for the country as a whole.

[2] See note at the end of the article for further details.

the way the quantity figures referred to Patwardhan have been arrived at. By contrast, Sukhatme gives detailed explanations for all the considerations he has taken into account and all the comparisons he has made between different nutritional norms before working out the minimum food basket put forward by him. It is true that Sukhatme's norms include non-vegetable items and therefore would not be pertinent for vegetarian Indians. But the same difficulty would attach to any purely vegetarian basket in that it would not be relevant for meat and fish eating Indians. As a matter of fact if one were to think of dietary patterns acceptable to Indian consumers one would have to work out different normative patterns for different regions and different communities.

MINIMUM PER CAPITA CONSUMPTION EXPENDITURE

To arrive at a figure representing a level of per capita expenditure that would be such that a minimum normative diet could be accommodated in it, we have now to work out a figure that would represent the minimum expenditure that would have to go on all non-food items as well as such food items as are not covered by the basket considered above (e.g. salt, spices, etc.). As we have observed before, while conceptually one could think of minimum norms for clothings and housing, in fact such norms have not been worked out by any experts on any scientific considerations. The only reasonable course of action under the situation is to ask the question: 'What has to be the consumption budget of an average rural consumer facing average 1960/61 prices if he may be expected to spend a certain stipulated amount (say Rs 15.71) on a specified number of food items?' We shall answer this question by answering the following different question: 'What was the average per capita total consumption expenditure of those rural consumers in 1960/61 who spent that stipulated amount on those specified items of consumption?' The answer to the question is worked out by making use of the average expenditure pattern for 1960/61 as presented in NSS Report No. 138 for 1960/61 supplemented by NSS Report No. 189 for 1964/65.[3] The results are presented in Table 15.2. The figures for 'total food' are obtained by applying linear interpolation on expenditure data for 1964/65 of Table 1.1.2 of Report No. 189. The figure for 'all other non-food items' is similarly obtained from expenditure data for 1960/61 as presented in Table 1.7.0 of Report No. 138. It is seen that Sukhatme's minimum dietary pattern indicates a minimum per capita consumption of Rs 22.73 per month for rural consumers; the corresponding figure for the FAO norms

Table 15.2 Minimum Per Capita Monthly Consumption Expenditure for Rural Consumers

				(1960/61 Prices)
Sl. No.		Sukhatme (Minimum)	FAO	Patwardhan
1.	Value of minimum diet	15.71	18.26	11.61
2.	Total expenditure on food corresponding to minimum diet	16.59	19.59	12.24
3.	Total consumption expenditure corresponding to minimum diet	22.73	28.60	15.63

[3] This resort to 1964/65 is called for by the fact that the 1960/61 data do not give any figures separately for vegetables and fruits whereas the 1964/65 data do. The use we have made for 1964/65 data implies the assumption that the relative prices between all the items included in the diet taken as a group and the remaining food items do not change a great deal between 1960/61 and 1964/65.

is Rs 28.60 and for Patwardhan's norms, Rs 15.63, which is somewhat higher than what Bardhan calculates.

MINIMUM LEVEL OF LIVING OF URBAN CONSUMERS

In the plan documents, Rs 20 per capita per month at 1960/61 prices is presented as a national minimum and not for rural consumers alone. In our calculations, we have however till now kept in view only rural consumers: we have used rural retail prices and consumption expenditure proportions. It may however be interesting to repeat the calculations for urban consumers. Differences would arise on two accounts: urban prices being different from rural prices, and urban consumption expenditure proportions being also different from rural ones. Not having the same type of urban price data as the rural prices data we have used, we have, just to get an idea about the order of dimensions, made the rather conservative assumption that the expenditures on all food including the minimum diet, at urban prices, would be more than that at rural prices by 10 per cent.[4] To go from expenditure on food to the per capita consumptions levels, we have proceeded exactly as before with urban consumption expenditure proportions taken from Table 2.0.0 of Report No. 138. The results are presented in Table 15.3. It is seen that Sukhatme's dietary patterns would call for as much as about Rs 27 as minimum per capita monthly consumption expenditure, the FAO norms would call for Rs 33. Only Patwardhan's norms would call for an amount less than Rs 20.

Table 15.3 Minimum Per Capita Monthly Consumption Expenditure for Urban Consumers

(1960/61 Prices)

Sl. No.		Sukhatme (Minimum)	FAO	Patwardhan
1.	Total expenditure on food corresponding to minimum diet	18.25	21.35	13.46
2.	Total consumption expenditure corresponding to minimum diet	27.33	33.73	18.99

USES OF THE MINIMUM LEVEL CALCULATION

We have to conclude that the figure of Rs 20 per capita per month as minimum per capita CE does not represent any meaningful minimum. Rejecting both the high figures corresponding to the FAO norms and the low figures following from Patwardhan's norms, and tentatively accepting those of Sukhatme, it would appear that if a figure has to represent a national minimum it would lie between Rs 22 and Rs 27. But to what use can such a figure, standing for a kind of a national minimum level of living, be put? There have been two uses to which such calculations have been put in our country. The first use, in our opinion a valid one, is to set a target for the growth of aggregate consumption which has got some normative significance. If T be the end year of a plan, a macroeconomic target that would occur in practically any national economic planning would be C^T, measured in some base year prices. While quite often C^T is set by assuming an arbitrary rate of growth of aggregate consumption, a meaningful way of setting it that has been followed in certain plan model exercises using the Rs 20 norm is as follows:

[4] Bhattacharya and Chatterjee (1971) found that the average urban prices are 15 per cent higher then the average rural prices. We are assuming that the food prices' differential is lower than that for non-food prices.

(a) assume that a certain fractile group would have an average consumption level equal to the calculated minimum level, C;

(b) assume a certain degree of inequality of distribution of per capita consumption in the population measured by, say, Lorenz ratio θ;

(c) calculate the population average c_0 of per capita consumption that would be consistent with (a) and (b) above;

(d) calculate C^T by multiplying, c_0, by the population projection P^T for the end year.

The second use to which the results of such calculation have been put is to treat it as what has been called a poverty line, and estimate the proportion of consumers who fall below the line. This use is, in our view, invalid, for in counting the persons who cannot afford to buy a minimum diet, the diet itself has to be worked out separately for different areas and different communities, taking into account different availabilities and different food habits; then these different diets have to be valued differently for different areas by using different sets of local retail prices. No one dietary pattern valued at one set of national price average can be made use of for counting the persons who cannot afford this dietary pattern. For calculating what proportion of consumers cannot afford the minimum diet, it is not necessary to add to the value of minimum diet some figure representing expenditure on non-food items, as is customarily done. The National Sample Survey gives figures representing expenditure on different groups of consumer items for different expenditure groups and one can work out the proportion of people who spend less on food items less than the value of the minimum diet. What has however to be done is to recalculate the NSS expenditure figures for home grown food using the same set of retail prices as for purchased food. This matter is further elaborated in the Appendix.

ACKNOWLEDGEMENT

Reprinted from Poverty and Income Distribution in India, P.K. Bardhan and T.N. Srinivasan (eds), Indian Statistical Institute, Calcutta, 1974.

I am grateful to S.M. Kansal for helping me by drawing attention to certain references, to Pranab K. Bardhan for many stimulating discussions and to T.N. Srinivasan for encouraging me to work on the problem and for helping me in revising the first draft.

REFERENCES

Bardhan, P.K. (1973), 'On the Incidence of Poverty in Rural India of the Sixties', *Economic and Political Weekly*, Annual Number, February.

Bhattacharya, N. and G.S. Chatterjee (1971), 'On Rural-Urban Consumer Prices and Per Capita Household Consumption in India by Levels of Living', *Sankhyà*, Series B, 33, Parts 3 and 4.

FAO (1973), *Monthly Bulletin of Agricultural Economics and Statistics,* January.

Kansal, S.M., Preliminary Estimates of Total Consumption Expenditure in India 1950/51 to 1963/64, Discussion Paper No. 5, Planning Unit, Indian Statistical Institute, New Delhi.

Panikkar, P.G.K. (1972), 'Economies of Nutrition', *Economic and Political Weekly,* Annual Number.

Rajaraman, Indira (1974), 'Constructing the Poverty Line, Rural Punjab, 1960/61' (unpublished), Discussion Paper No. 43, Woodrow Wilson School, Princeton University, March.

Sukhatme, P.Y. (1965), *Feeding India's Growing Millions,* Asia Publishing House, Bombay.

Appendix

SOME ASPECTS OF BARDHAN'S CALCULATIONS

We have said before that the calculations behind the figure of Rs 20 are not available for scrutiny. But those of Bardhan are available, and as his estimate of minimum per capita consumption differs substantially from ours even when we use the same quantity figure as he does, namely those of Patwardhan, we may point out why certain statistical procedures Bardhan follows appear to us to be unacceptable. One of these procedures is the price adjustment carried out by him for home grown products. Presumably Bardhan is worried about the indubitable fact that the NSS rural retail price estimates do not represent the actual prices rural consumers would have paid in 1960/61 as they would confront a set of prices different from the average, depending on where they are located, during what part of the year they are making purchases and what part of the basket they would be able to procure from home production and what part they would have to purchase at the retail market. Bardhan wants to take care of this last factor alone, namely the difference arising from the fact that a part of the supply for consumption would come from home grown stock. But for that it is difficult to think of any justification for the procedure he adopts. Bardhan is ultimately interested in finding out the proportion of rural consumers for 1960/61 who had a consumption level that could hypothetically accommodate the food basket he has accepted as a normative minimum; and he is faced with the problem that 'in NSS expenditure data, while cash purchase part is evaluated at retail prices, the part of consumption that is out of home grown product is evaluated at ex-farm rates'. To take proper care of this problem what is called for is recalculation of the per capita expenditure of each expenditure group by revaluating the home grown part by local retail prices and also revaluation of the normative diet by local retail prices, the operation to be repeated for every area that has a set of prices different from those of other areas. Bardhan overlooks the fact that it is not only the home grown part that is evaluated in the NSS data in prices different from the average retail prices he uses to evaluate his food basket. The cash purchase part in NSS expenditure data is evaluated in actual prices paid by the consumers, and not by the average retail prices independently estimated and separately presented by the NSS. The price average implicit in the NSS expenditure data regarding cash purchases is a weighted average, whereas the rural retail prices are simple averages. It may, in this connection, be borne in mind that correcting the average rural retail prices themselves for evaluating the minimum food basket, as Bardhan does, would not yield the same result as would be obtained by correcting per capita expenditure levels for different expenditure groups by changing over to local retail prices and then comparing with the value of the minimum food basket evaluated at the local rural retail prices. Let us further note that the share of the home grown part and the purchased part of any item by a consumer would be related to absolute quantity consumed of that item by the consumer, as well as his overall per capita consumption level, however measured, and therefore this proportion would vary from one group of consumers to another. The proportions corresponding to no one particular group may be considered appropriate for correcting the average retail prices for evaluating the minimum food basket. Bardhan chooses the proportions for the lower 50 per cent of the consumers but does not give any arguments whatsoever for this totally arbitrary choice.

The other procedure followed by Bardhan that we find indefensible is the way he arrives at total consumption expenditure from expenditure on the food items taken by him from Patwardhan's dietary norms. The procedure, in his own words, is as follows. 'From NSS data we find that in 1960/61 total per capita expenditure for the bottom 50 per cent of the rural population, on an average, was 46 per cent above that of cereals, pulses, milk, sugar and gur and edible oils taken together . . . . In the absence of proper norms for non-food items (and of prices for food items like vegetables and ground nut) we use these percentages to get the blow-up estimates of per capita expenditure based on the cost of minimum diet.' The figure 46 per cent seems to be erroneous – the relevant percentage for the lower 50 per cent of consumers was around 35 per cent in 1960/61. But more seriously, why again the lower 50 per cent of consumers? Why is this group relevant?

Notes on Prices The prices used by us are mainly based on NSS Report No. 123 (16th Round) on rural retail prices. Considering the very crude nature of the simple averages which these estimates are, we have taken liberty to derive appropriate prices multipliers for our purpose on the basis of subjective judgement. (Unlike Bardhan who takes a lot of trouble in deriving weighted averages. Given his peculiar predeliction for the lower 50 per cent, he uses as weights the expenditures on different items by the bottom 5 deciles to arrive at price multipliers. Why the bottom five deciles are relevant and why expenditures constitute suitable weights for prices are not explained anywhere.) The price figures Rs 0.40 assumed by us for cereals corresponds to the price of bajra; it is less than the price of rice (coarse), wheat (coarse) and gram but is more than that of jower, maize and ragi. The price taken by us for pulses (Rs 0.60) correspond to that of masur – it is less than for moong and urad, but is more than that of gram (dal). The price for starchy roots (Rs 0.375) is made somewhat lower than that for potato (Rs 0.43) to take care of the lower prices of tapioca (Rs 0.344) and sweet potato (Rs 0.344) as worked out by Kansal (see references). For sugar (Rs 0.60) we have chosen a figure only slightly more than that of gur (0.57) and much less than that of sugar proper (Rs 1.23). For meat and milk we have taken the actual figures given in the NSS report. For fish we had once again taken resort to Kansal's estimates and for eggs, not having prices by weight, we have used the same price as for fish, which constitutes an underestimation. The most difficult problem was offered by vegetables and fruits. Given the huge variety of fruits and vegetables available to consumers and the very large seasonal fluctuations, obtaining a price average in weight terms is a very difficult task. We have used the figure of Rs 0.50 per kg which we think is not a serious overestimate. For oils and fats we have used the NSS price estimate for mustard oil which is lower than that for coconut oil and gingelly oil, but more than that for groundnut oil.

16

Prices and Poverty in India

Angus Deaton and Alessandro Tarozzi

INTRODUCTION

In India, as in other countries, indexes of consumer prices perform many important functions. Millions of workers have their wages indexed to some measure of the price level. Just as important is the issue that is our main focus here, the estimation of poverty. Indian poverty rates are defined as the fractions of people living in households whose real per capita total expenditure falls below the poverty line. Data on total expenditures is collected by the National Sample Survey (NSS) in money terms so that, for each new round of data, the real poverty line must be converted to current rupees by multiplying by an index of prices. Inaccuracy in the estimation of the index, for example overestimation of the price increase relative to the base, will result in corresponding inaccuracy of the poverty estimates, for example an underestimation in the rate of poverty reduction. At a time when the data shows historically high rates of GDP growth without much reduction in poverty, especially rural poverty, it is important to establish the accuracy of the price and poverty calculations.

The measurement of inflation is not the only role of price indexes in measuring poverty in India. Price indexes are required, not only to establish the rates of inflation in the urban and rural sectors of each state, but also to compare price *levels* between them. In a country where many states are larger than most nations in the world, price indexes are needed to make comparisons between states. Differences in poverty rates between Indian states affect the amounts of transfers from the Centre to the states, and influence discussions about poverty reduction strategies among international lenders such as the World Bank. In the broader context, India contributes more people to world poverty than does any other country and changes in the way the Indian poor are counted can have significant effect on the world total.

For purposes of tracking poverty over time, the two most important price indexes in India are the Consumer Price Index for Industrial Workers (CPIIW) and the Consumer Price Index for Agricultural Labourers (CPIAL). Reweighted versions of each are used to update the urban and rural poverty lines. Until it was revised in November 1995, the CPIAL itself was based on prices regularly collected from a sample of 422 villages, weighted using an expenditure pattern that dates back to 1960/61. By the time of the revision in 1995, which was later than any of the survey data used in this chapter, the weights for the

CPIAL were more than three decades out of date, an unusually long time period for any major price index anywhere in the world.

The CPIIW was revised in October 1988. Prior to that date, the base year was 1960, with weights derived from a survey of workers from 1958/59. Prices were collected from shops in a number of markets in 50 industrial centres throughout India. After October 1988, the weights were updated using a 1981/82 survey, with a new basis in 1982, some old centres were dropped and some new ones added, and the total rose to 70. For both indexes, and in order to maximise comparability over time, the specifications of items priced, the units, the shops, the markets, and the day and the time of the visits were held fixed throughout the life of the series. To the extent that there are problems with these price series, they are likely to come from the unusually long periods between revisions. Not only are the weights of these Laspeyres indexes long out of date by the time of transition, but there must also be concern about the continued representativeness of the villages, centres, and markets over such long periods. Whether or not the price indexes are seriously affected is ultimately an empirical question, though it is often supposed (for example, in the comparable debate over the CPI in the United States) that Laspeyres indexes will increasingly overstate inflation as the base period recedes into the past, a tendency that will be exacerbated by the failure to pick up new goods (whose prices are often falling rapidly) and discard old (whose prices may be stagnant or even rising).

For the purposes of updating the official poverty lines used by the Planning Commission, the CPIAL and CPIIW are reweighted using national level consumption patterns of people around the poverty line in 1973/74. The primitive price data are the same as for the CPIAL and CPIIW themselves, but the commodity level prices are weighted using the more recent (although still elderly by world standards) and more poverty-relevant weights. These indexes are clearly superior to the CPIAL and CPIIW themselves for the purposes of the poverty calculations, but they also inherit any deficiencies in the underlying prices.

The purpose of this paper is to provide an independent set of calculations of Indian price indexes using data for two year-long periods, 1987/88, and 1993/94, periods that are the same as those for the last two official poverty calculations. We provide estimates of the rate of inflation over the six-year period for all-India and for 17 of the largest states, by sector, plus Delhi. We also provide separate price indexes for the rural and urban sectors for each of the 17 states and for all-India in both periods, as well as estimates of price levels across states by sector in each of the two periods. The sources of data for both prices and expenditure patterns are the 43rd and 50th Rounds of the NSS, both of which collected extensive data on consumption of individual items. The use of expenditure surveys to calculate *weights* for consumer price indexes is standard practice throughout the world. The innovation here is the use of information from the surveys on the prices themselves. For most of the commodities in the NSS surveys, respondents are asked to provide information on how much they spent on the item and on the physical quantity purchased, for example Rs 8 on 2 kg of rice. The ratio of expenditure to volume provides a measure of price, or more precisely, a measure of unit value.

Compared with the use of the CPIAL and CPIIW, this approach has both advantages and disadvantages. One strength is the size of the samples involved and their representativeness across states and sectors. More than 3.5 million pairs of expenditures and quantities are sampled in each of the two rounds, and the NSS samples are designed to be representative at the state and sector levels (and indeed beyond). In consequence, it is possible to construct, not only price indexes that track inflation over time, but also price indexes that compare price levels across states and sectors. A second advantage of unit values is that they relate to actual transactions, not to prices listed or reported by shops. Third, because the transactions are linked to the people who made them, it is possible to stratify prices and price indexes by socioeconomic characteristics, such as level of living, or occupation, or demographic structure.

There are two main disadvantages to the use of unit values. Not all goods and services have readily defined quantities. In particular, while unit values are available for most foods, for alcohol and tobacco, and for fuels, they are not collected for such items as transportation or housing. In India, the covered goods comprise between two-thirds and three-quarters of the budget, which makes the exercise worth doing, but which would obviously not be the case in a country such as the United States. Even so, when using price indexes constructed from unit values, it is always important to keep in mind the likely effects of the excluded categories, and in particular the effects on comparisons between urban and rural sectors of omitting the prices of housing and of transportation.

The second disadvantage is that unit values are not prices. Even when goods are defined at the maximum feasible level of disaggregation, many goods are not perfectly homogeneous, so that any given unit value will reflect, not only price, but the mix of varieties within the category. As a result, unit values differ from one purchaser to another in a way that is not caused by differences in prices. In particular, richer households have higher unit values than poorer households, a fact that has been used to study the choice of *quality* since Prais and Houtkakker (1955) [see Deaton (1988, 1997, Chapter 5)] for modern treatments. The quality problem can be dealt with in part by disaggregating to the maximum extent permitted by the data. In the analysis below, we work with more than 200 items of expenditure. Even so, the literature shows that the total expenditure elasticity of unit values is small, even for fairly broad aggregates of goods – such as 'cereals' or 'pulses'. Beyond that, it is important to inspect the data on unit values and to document their price-like characteristics, for example that in a given round and state that a large number of people report the same unit value, and that the unit values have the appropriate patterns of variation over regions and seasons of the year.

The rest of this paper is organised as follows. To begin with, the chapter explains how the unit values and expenditure weights are calculated from the detailed survey data, and we provide summaries of the results and of the methods used to obtain them. Because there are so many observations, more than 7 million unit values, and because each must be examined before being incorporated into the price indexes, the data processing stage of this work has been both long and complex. Nevertheless, we have tried to provide enough detail to permit replication of our results, and our STATA code is available on request. The section on Alternative Price Indexes is methodological, and further presents the index number formulae used in the calculations, as well as the strengths and weaknesses of each. It also explains why some of the indexes are much more difficult to calculate than others, in particular, why the interstate comparisons of prices are likely to be much less reliable than comparisons over time, with comparisons between urban and rural prices somewhere in between. Subsequently, it presents the main results and compares the price index numbers calculated here with the two official price indexes. Later, in the chapter the implications for the calculations of poverty rates between 1987/88 and 1993/94, as well as for the 1993/94, rates and under alternative assumptions about interstate and intersector price variation are considered. Lastly, the chapter offers some tentative conclusions, as well as an outline of the work that remains to be done.

Using the NSS Data to Calculate Unit Values and Expenditure Patterns

The NSS samples from the 43rd and 50th Rounds are described in Table 16.1 which shows the distribution of sample households over states and sectors, as well as the total number of purchases recorded for the

Table 16.1 Numbers of Sample Households and Recorded Purchases

	43rd Round				50th Round			
	Rural		Urban		Rural		Urban	
	House-holds	Purchases	House-holds	Purchases	House-holds	Purchases	House-holds	Purchases
Andhra Pradesh	6,015	193,490	3,421	122,804	4,908	171,913	3,644	140,384
Assam	3,290	111,468	1,171	40,560	3,199	123,150	880	36,946
Bihar	7,740	194,271	2,083	61,473	6,979	195,356	2,155	71,788
Gujarat	2,795	95,164	2,260	85,016	2,219	85,015	2,372	100,054
Haryana	1,165	37,079	634	22,995	1,040	35,445	697	25,249
Himachal Pradesh	1,835	56,633	459	15,226	1,875	59,905	400	14,664
Jammu & Kashmir	3,197	87,786	1,488	45,082	820	27,606	528	21,050
Karnataka	3,254	120,783	2,307	90,819	2,617	108,986	2,469	106,555
Kerala	3,358	118,107	1,432	49,704	2,555	100,884	1,830	71,601
Madhya Pradesh	6,294	183,849	2,888	104,703	5,313	167,681	3,233	125,399
Maharashtra	5,726	212,872	5,497	222,693	4,440	175,356	5,528	238,136
Orissa	3,493	95,524	1,151	36,628	3,338	105,351	1,037	38,571
Punjab	2,665	84,939	1,901	65,264	2,046	71,961	1,947	72,250
Rajasthan	3,607	89,735	1,734	55,111	3,097	86,723	1,799	60,134
Tamil Nadu	4,567	155,196	4,109	156,221	3,901	155,420	4,042	170,104
Uttar Pradesh	10,395	292,021	4,497	145,020	9,010	297,803	4,451	170,499
West Bengal	4,983	164,005	3,433	124,574	4,480	170,649	3,338 *	135,564
Delhi	66	2,685	1,130	47,505	61	2,045	985	33,517
All-India	82,653	2,531,548	45,348	1,610,434	69,206	2,378,646	46,148 **	1,807,324

Note: Households are the numbers of sample households in each round; purchases are the numbers of recorded purchases of the list of commodities in Table A1.

   * This figure also includes 2,223 households with zero sampling weight.

   ** The total includes households in UP (2,223) that had a zero multiplier, and hence were not counted in any calculation.

food, alcohol, and tobacco, and fuel categories, the detailed components of which are listed in Table A1. Table 16.1 lists information for all-India, which is the complete sample, and for the 17 largest states plus Delhi; clearly it is only for urban Delhi that there are a significant number of sample households. There are 128,101 sample households in the 43rd Round and 115,354 in the 50th Round. By dividing the 'purchases' column by the 'households' column, we see that, on average, urban households, who have access to a wider range of goods and are typically better off than rural households, record expenditure on around 40 of the items used here, while rural households reported purchases of about 30 items. In total, over the two surveys, there are 8.3 million quantity/expenditure pairs available for analysis; as we shall see, this number will be reduced somewhat as we proceed.

For each item of expenditure, household respondents are asked to report both the quantity and value of purchases over the last 30 days. The NSS records expenditures in considerable detail which is shown (for the goods used here and for the 50th Round) in Table A1. The comparable list of goods for the 43rd Round is almost identical apart from the important difference that goods bought from the public distribution system (PDS in Table A1) are recorded separately from goods from other sources in the 50th Round but not in the 43rd. We have made no attempt to work with the data on clothing and footwear, where there is also some information on quantities purchased, e.g. dhotis and sarees in metres, or shoes in pairs.

For a few of the commodities listed in Table A1, it is effectively impossible to measure quantities, and the questionnaire does not attempt to do so. These commodities (or commodity groups) are therefore dropped from the analysis. They are as follows: egg products, other fresh fruits, other beverages (Horlicks, etc.), biscuits and confectionery, salted refreshments, prepared sweets, other processed food, other drugs and intoxicants, dung cakes, gobar gas, and other fuel and light. Several of these fall into the 'other' or residual category within a larger group; for example, other drugs and intoxicants is the residual category in a group that contains toddy, beer, liquor, ganja, and opium. As we shall see later, not only these but several other residual categories do not have well-defined units. There are also few cases where the units change between the two rounds. For example, lemons (guavas) were measured in kilogrammes (units) in the 43rd Round and in units (kilogrammes) in the 50th Round. We retain such items for comparisons between states or sectors within each round but, since we have no way of knowing how many lemons or guavas are in a kilo, we drop them when making comparisons between the two rounds.

For each consumption record, a unit value was calculated by dividing expenditure by quantity. The NSS collects data separately for commodities purchased in the market, for commodities produced or grown at home, and for commodities obtained as gifts or loans. Unit values were calculated by dividing the sum of the three kinds of expenditure by the sum of the three kinds of quantity. This procedure effectively weighs each of three possible unit values by the shares of expenditure devoted to each. Working commodity by commodity, the unit values were then checked for plausibility as indicators of price. There is no foolproof way of doing this. Nevertheless, there are a number of obvious problems to guard against, and procedures can be developed to detect them. One such is the difficulty of defining units for physical quantities. Expenditure is always measured in rupees, and the concept and its units are clear. For quantities, there is sometimes a choice of units; for example, items can be bought one by one, or by weight. There are also local variations in units, so that what works in one place may not work as well somewhere else. Some customary units are not well-defined in terms of weight; goods bought by the bunch, box, bag, or packet will be converted by the respondent or the enumerator, but the conversion may be less than accurate. To the extent that errors are made – eggs measured in units for some households, and in dozens for others – the unit values will have multi-modal distributions, with peaks corresponding to each distinct unit.

A second problem, which can also be detected by looking for multiple modes, is when two or more distinct goods are included within a single commodity. For example, if milk (liquid) and milk products (expensive sweets) are lumped together, the unit values will cluster around the milk price and the sweet price. While gross contamination is avoided by using the maximal detail, inspection of Table A1 shows that, even with so many items, there is still room for heterogeneity within many of the categories. If the compounded goods are sufficiently similar, the unit value may still give a useful indication of prices. The problem arises when there are spatial or temporal differences in the mixture, so that a compound of (cheap) A and (expensive) B is primarily A in state 1, but is primarily B in state 2.

Our procedures are part graphical, and part automatic. For each commodity, we draw histograms and one-way plots of the logarithms of the unit values, using each to detect the presence of gross outliers for further investigation. In some cases, outliers are isolated cases that result from errors of misreporting, miscoding, or misinterpretation of units, and are deleted. In other cases, a problem with units or with contamination can be identified and corrected. An automatic method for outlier detection was also used, and unit values eliminated whose logarithms lie more than 2.5 standard deviations from the mean of logarithms. Note that this does not remove the need for the graphical inspection, since gross bimodality would not necessarily be detected by the standard deviation rule. Log unit values were also inspected for plausibility after deletion of outliers. The resulting distributions of unit values were also examined to assess how many purchases clustered at the median – if the unit values are close to being prices, we would expect substantial such clustering – and tested using analysis of variance for cluster (PSU), district, and subround (seasonal effects) – which should be present if variation in unit values is dominated by price variation rather than quality effects or product heterogeneity within the commodity group.

The data examination led to the deletion of a number of goods where unit values appeared not to be reliable, or where there were other unsolved problems of interpretation. Tables A2 to A5 list the goods involved. Table A2 lists the goods omitted because the NSS instructions do not call for quantities to be collected; for reasons that we do not understand, quantity data exist for these commodities, but the associated unit values would have been deleted by our inspection procedures in any case. Tables A3 and A4 list the additional commodities that were excluded from the 43rd and 50th Rounds, respectively. Most of these cases are 'other' residual categories within larger subgroups, where the unit values showed dispersion to match the obvious heterogeneity in the definition of the group. Some are goods where there is clear evidence of bimodality. (For example, liquid petroleum gas in the 43rd Round, where there is apparently more than one unit of measurement, but where we were unable to make a suitable correction. There has apparently also been a black market in LPG in India, which may explain the price variation.) One or two of the goods lost (for example, cups of tea and coconuts) are important items in some states, there is no obvious reason for problems, and their loss is unfortunate. Table A5 lists the additional commodities that had to be eliminated in the comparisons between rounds, but not within them. In addition to the two goods whose units were changed according to the NSS documentation, there are five other commodities where the distributions of prices in the two rounds are so far apart that it seems likely that an undocumented change of units took place. (For example, coal gas is measured in 'standard units' which perhaps changed in the intervening six years.)

Summary unit values were calculated from the 'cleaned' data by commodity, by sector, by state, and by round. In addition to the 18 'large' states (as listed in Table 16.1), comparable calculations were made for all-India. In preference to means, we use medians for the summary unit values, largely because of their greater resistance to any remaining outliers. The calculations of medians are weighted using the household multipliers supplied by the NSS; since purchases are assumed to be made at the household level, it is appropriate to weigh using household weights.

For each household in the surveys, we calculated the share in the budget devoted to each commodity; more precisely, we used the total value of expenditures on the commodity (summing purchases, home production, gifts and loans, and other) divided by household total expenditure on all goods and services, constructed from the NSS – supplied per capita total household expenditure multiplied by household size. These budget shares were then averaged over all households in a given sector, state, and round, using as weights the NSS multipliers multiplied by household size. There are three points to notice about this construction. First, we use means rather than medians; because the budget shares are automatically bounded between 0 and 1, there is less concern about the effects of an isolated undetected outlier. Second, the weighing scheme, by multiplying by household size, puts the weights on an individual, rather than household, basis. Because individuals – not households – are the appropriate units for welfare analysis, the commodity weights for price indexes, which is what the budget shares will become, are better computed on an individual than a household basis.

Third, the use of averaged budget shares will generate 'democratic' price indexes (Prais, 1959, Pollak, 1987) rather than the 'plutocratic' price indexes that are routinely produced by national statistical offices. The weights for the latter are aggregate consumers' expenditure on each commodity divided by the aggregate of consumers' expenditure on all commodities; as is easily shown, this ratio of aggregates is the average of the individual household ratios weighted by total household expenditure. As a result, the ratio of aggregates weighs rich households more than poor households, hence the label of 'plutocratic'. Plutocratic indexes are not well suited for calculating the cost-of-living for poor people. Ideally, we might wish to use price indexes whose weights are tailored to the expenditure patterns of those below the poverty line, and it would be straightforward to do so using the NSS data. However, because Indian poverty lines are typically around the middle of the per capita expenditure distribution, democratic indexes will not differ much from poverty-line weighted indexes. Checking this conjecture is an important topic for further research.

There is also a (minor) data problem associated with the construction of the budget shares. In the 43rd Round, there are six pairs of commodity items (jowar and jowar products, bajra and bajra products, maize and maize products, barley and barley products, small millets and small millets products, and ragi and ragi products) where some expenditure is entered under one member of the pair, and some under another, so that it is only possible to work with the pair as a combined category, rather than with each separately. For each of these pairs, we work with the budget share of the two together, and with the unit value of the first. This appears to give sensible results.

Table 16.2 shows an illustrative selection of results, for 13 commodities for the rural sectors of Uttar Pradesh, and Kerala in the two rounds. These two states were chosen because their expenditure patterns are very different. Since it is clearly impossible to show all the commodities, we have selected for each case the 13 most important defined by the size of their average budget shares. Clearly, which commodities have the largest budget share is neither robust to the degree of disaggregation nor to the definition of commodities, and we claim no significance for our choice other than that the goods are ones purchased by large numbers of households. The table lists the commodity names, the units in which they are measured, the mean of their budget share over all households, the number of households recorded as making purchases of each, and the number of households deleted by the outlier elimination procedures. Finally, the last column in each panel shows the median unit values reported. A number of points should be noted.

The most important single item in all four tables is the main staple, flour in UP, and rice in Kerala, followed by milk, cooking oil, and firewood. In Kerala, the PDS is an important source of rice; in 1993/94, 44 per cent of rice expenditure was in PDS stores. Since rice from these stores was cheaper than rice purchased from other sources, more than half of rice by quantity came through the public system. Some flour in UP is also sold through the PDS, but the amounts are not important enough to show up in the table. [Note that PDS and other sources are not separated in the 43rd Round, so that the bottom panel shows combined budget shares. Hence, the 20.6 per cent budget share of rice in Kerala in the 43rd Round should be compared with 10.8 plus 8.6 (19.4) per cent in the 50th Round.]

The differences in the consumption patterns across the two states highlight the difficulty of making interstate price comparisons, as we shall see in more detail in section as Price Indexes: results. If we are to compare the price level in Kerala with the price level in UP, we will need to price flour in Kerala, which comprises more than 14 per cent of the budget in UP, but which is rarely bought in Kerala, and whose

Table 16.2 Select Budget Shares and Unit Values, Rural Areas of
Two States, 43rd and 50th Rounds

Rural Uttar Pradesh, 50th Round, 1993/94

Commodity	Units	Mean Share	No. of Obs.	Outliers	Median Unit Value
Flour	kg	14.3	5,575	39	3.533
Milk (liquid)	litre	10.8	6,618	88	6
Rice	kg	9.2	7,186	169	6
Mustard oil	kg	3.9	8,627	278	30
Firewood and chips	kg	3.4	4,871	107	0.7
Arhar (tur)	kg	2.6	6,568	210	16
Potatoes	kg	2.5	8,797	187	3
Bidis	no.	1.6	4,802	102	0.071
Sugar (crystal)	kg	1.5	5,529	145	12
Gur (cane)	kg	1.1	4,770	64	8
Urad	kg	0.9	4,589	69	12
Goat meat	kg	0.9	2,018	16	50
Leaf tea	gm	0.7	5,808	113	0.08

Rural Kerala, 50th Round, 1993/94

Commodity	Units	Mean Share	No. of Obs.	Outliers	Median Unit Value
Rice: other sources	kg	10.8	2,073	50	7.5
Rice: PDS	kg	8.6	1,916	27	5.52
Fresh fish	kg	5.8	2,158	30	17.6
Milk (liquid)	litre	4.6	1,776	37	8
Firewood and chips	kg	4.6	2,061	49	0.6
Coconuts	no.	4.5	2,334	25	4
Coconut oil	kg	2.8	2,229	50	38
Tea	cup	2.5	1,698	32	1
Sugar: other	kg	1.6	2,055	13	13.75
Sugar: PDS	kg	1.1	2,287	48	8.44
Bidis	no.	1.5	1,073	20	0.1
Leaf tea	gm	1.4	2,248	52	0.065
Cooked meals	no	1.3	403	11	7

Rural Uttar Pradesh, 43rd Round, 1987/88

Commodity	Units	Mean Share	No. of Obs.	Outliers	Median Unit Value
Flour	kg	16.5	4,862	26	2
Milk (liquid)	litre	9.1	7,069	217	4
Rice	kg	8.9	8,077	130	3.2
Mustard oil	kg	4.7	9,826	96	26
Firewood and chips	kg	3.5	6,845	127	0.5
Arhar (tur)	kg	3.1	7,305	278	10
Potatoes	kg	2.3	10,090	59	1.5
Bidis	no.	1.6	5,978	205	0.0333
Gur (cane)	kg	1.5	7,319	235	3.5
Sugar (crystal)	kg	1.3	6,650	37	6.5
Kerosene	litre	1.1	9,884	156	3
Urad	kg	0.9	4,693	169	8
Vanaspati	kg	0.8	2,574	16	26

Commodity	Units	Mean Share	No. of Obs.	Outliers	Median Unit Value
Rural Kerala, 43rd Round, 1987/88					
Rice	kg	20.6	3,271	27	3.6
Coconuts	no.	5.6	3,157	34	3
Firewood and chips	kg	5.4	2,984	43	0.43
Fresh fish	kg	5.3	2,777	36	10
Milk (liquid)	litre	3.9	2,286	27	4
Tea	cup	2.7	2,681	34	0.5
Cooked meals	no.	2.5	1,055	33	3.333
Sugar	kg	2.3	3,224	50	5.6
Coconut oil	kg	1.8	2,354	32	34
Bidis	no.	1.5	1,660	45	0.05
Dried chillies	gm	1.3	3,255	83	0.02
Leaf tea	gm	1.3	2,857	35	0.0333
Palm oil	kg	1.3	2,034	33	17

Notes: 1. In the 43rd Round, foods purchased from the Public Distribution System (PDS) are not distinguished from foods bought from other sources, see for example rice in Kerala in the 43rd Round versus rice in Kerala in the 50th Round.
2. In the 50th Round for Uttar Pradesh, the amounts shown for flour, rice, mustard oil, arhar, sugar, and urad are all purchases from sources other than PDS.
3. In Kerala for the 50th Round, PDS and other sources both appear in the table except for coconut oil, which is coconut oil from non-PDS sources.

price is irrelevant for most of its inhabitants. Similar issues arise for fresh fish, coconuts, and for coconut versus mustard oil. These differences of consumption patterns pose familiar problems for analysts of price indexes, although more usually for price comparisons between countries, not within them.

The table also shows that the number of outliers is small relative to the numbers of original purchases in the data. Note also that the median unit values are often whole numbers. Large numbers of purchases take place at or close to the numbers shown. For example, in UP in the 43rd Round (bottom left panel of the Table 16.2) 1,706 of the 4,862 recorded purchases of flour (or more than a third of total purchases when weighted) were at exactly Rs 2 per kg. More than half of purchases of liquid milk were at Rs 4 per litre, and although only 10 per cent of purchases of mustard oil were at exactly Rs 26, more than a half took place within 10 per cent of Rs 26.

Although it is difficult to use Table 16.2 to get an informal idea of price differences between Kerala and UP, it is straightforward to see the effects of inflation and to guess its extent. For many of the goods shown, prices in 1993/94 were between one-and-a-half and twice their levels in 1987/88. The relative ease of making intertemporal compared with spatial comparisons of prices will carry through to the more formal results in the subsequent section (Price Index: Results), where the estimates of price inflation will be more robust than the estimates of price differences across states or sectors.

Alternative Price Indexes: Theory

When price indexes are used to make comparisons over time, it is often the case that neither relative prices nor patterns of expenditure change very much between the two dates in the comparison. In such cases, different price indexes tend to look quite similar, and the choice of index is not of great importance. We shall see that this is the case here for comparisons of given sectors of given states between the two rounds. But relative prices and expenditure patterns are very different between states, and to a lesser extent between sectors within states, so that the precise choice of index is often important for these comparisons. In the calculations below, we work with four different indexes that are briefly presented and discussed here.

The Laspeyres index compares prices in period (state, sector) 1 with a base period (state, sector) 0 according to the formula

$$P_{10}^{L} = \sum_{k=1}^{n} q_{0k} p_{1k} \bigg/ \sum_{k=1}^{n} q_{0k} p_{0k} \tag{1}$$

where qs are quantities and ps are prices, where the first suffix on prices and quantities refers to the location (place) of the price, either base 0 or comparison 1, and the second suffix k refers to the commodity and runs over all n goods. The Paasche price index is written

$$P_{10}^{P} = \sum_{k=1}^{n} q_{1k} p_{1k} \bigg/ \sum_{k=1}^{n} q_{1k} p_{0k} . \tag{2}$$

For the purposes of the calculations of this paper, it is more convenient to write these indexes in terms of budget shares and price relatives. The budget share of good i in location 0 (say) is defined as

$$w_{0i} = p_{0i} q_{0i} \bigg/ \sum_{k=1}^{n} p_{0k} q_{0k} . \tag{3}$$

These budget shares will be taken to be the (weighted) average of the comparable budget shares over all households in the state, sector, and round under consideration. By rearranging equations (1) and (2), we can easily show that

$$P_{10}^{L} = \sum_{k=1}^{n} w_{0k} \left(\frac{p_{1k}}{p_{0k}} \right) \tag{4}$$

while the Paasche index takes the form

$$P_{10}^{P} = \left[\sum_{k=1}^{n} w_{1k} \left(\frac{p_{1k}}{p_{0k}} \right)^{-1} \right]^{-1} \tag{5}$$

In both cases, the price relatives of the individual goods convey the price information, and the budget shares provide the weights, the base period for the Laspeyres and the comparison period for the Paasche.

Neither the Laspeyres nor the Paasche is particularly suitable for making comparisons between Indian states. As we saw in the earlier section using the illustrative comparison between Kerala and UP, consumption patterns differed greatly across states even to the extent that a staple in one state may not be consumed at all in another. In consequence, prices for the staple in the 'wrong' state are either not observed at all, or at best will be poorly measured. For example, for the 43rd Round, Table 16.2 shows that 4,862 rural households in UP bought flour, but only 272 rural households in Kerala did so. Coconut oil, purchased by 2,354 households in rural Kerala, was purchased by only five households in UP. And even if the prices are available, and can be accurately measured, it is not clear that the price of coconut oil in UP, where people use mustard oil for cooking, is really relevant to calculations of the standard living. The usual way of thinking about this problem is to note that neither Laspeyres nor Paasche indexes do an adequate job of capturing consumer substitution, that when faced with differences in relative prices, consumers are likely to adjust their consumption patterns towards relatively cheap goods, and away from relatively more expensive ones. Of course, it also might be argued that the difference between UP and Kerala is not merely a difference in relative prices, but a difference in tastes or if not in tastes, in the environment, including not only the physical environment but such things as provision of public goods. If so, it is not clear that there exists any satisfactory basis for comparing price levels between them.

As noted long ago, the geometric mean of the Paasche and the Laspeyres, the Fisher Ideal Index, does a better job than either one in capturing substitution. The Fisher index is defined as

$$P_{10}^{F} = \sqrt{P_{10}^{L} P_{10}^{P}} \tag{6}$$

We shall also use the Törnqvist price index, which is defined by

$$\ln P_{10}^{T} = \sum_{k=1}^{n} \frac{w_{1k} + w_{0k}}{2} \ln\left(\frac{p_{1k}}{p_{0k}}\right). \tag{7}$$

Because both the Fisher and the Törnqvist indexes use both sets of budget shares, they mute the negative effects of using one or other (the budget share of flour in UP to measure prices in Kerala, or the budget share of coconut oil to measure prices in UP). More generally, both Törnqvist and Fisher Ideal indexes are *superlative* indexes, Diewert (1976), which means that they are exactly equal to a true cost-of-living index number for some utility-based demand system that is general enough to provide a second-order approximation to preferences, or a first-order approximation to the demand system. It should be noted that superlative indexes deal with substitution effects better than they deal with income effects. Superlative indexes are only exact in the case of homothetic preferences (preferences not only have to be the same in Kerala and UP, but expenditure patterns in both should not vary with the level of living), and when homotheticity is violated, offer an approximation only at some level of living intermediate between the two points being compared. It is not clear how this intermediate point should be interpreted, nor whether the superlative indexes answer the questions to which we most want answers. Even so, it is clear that, for comparisons between states and between sectors within states, it makes more sense to use Törnqvist or Fisher indexes than Paasche or Laspeyres.

Note that the Törnqvist and Fisher indexes have another advantage, which is that they satisfy the 'reversal' test. If prices are (say) 10 per cent higher in UP than Kerala, or more precisely, if the price index for UP relative to Kerala is 110, then prices are 10 per cent lower in Kerala than in UP (or the price index for Kerala relative to UP is 100/110 = 90.9). Because of the change in weights as we move from one base to another, neither Laspeyres nor Paasche index has this property. Since the 'reversal' property is so deeply ingrained in the way that we talk about prices, there is much to be said for index numbers that embody it.

Another, perhaps equally appealing, property is *not* satisfied by these index numbers. This is the 'circularity' or 'transitivity' property. Suppose that we have three situations, A, B, and C. We can calculate an index for B relative to A, and for C relative to B. If these are multiplied together, we get an 'indirect' price index for C relative to A, in contrast to the 'direct' estimate that comes from comparing

C with A in one step. Circularity is satisfied if these two indexes are the same. The failure of this property arises in the current context when we wish to combine urban to rural price indexes with state to all-India indexes. Suppose, for example, that in the rural sector, UP has an index of 110 relative to 100 for all-India, while in the urban sector, UP is 105 relative to 100 for all-India. If the all-India urban to rural price index is 115 (say), then the 'indirect' route gives us an urban to rural price index for UP of 120.75 (115 × 105) to 110 (110 × 100) or 109.8. But we can also use the 'direct' route to compare urban and rural prices in UP and there is no guarantee that we will get the same answer. As we shall see, this sort of 'circularity' failure has caused problems in the context of measuring poverty in India.

Price Indexes: Results

Table 16.3 shows the results of possibly the greatest interest, the comparison of price levels between the two rounds, by state, and by sector. Following a format that will be applied in all the tables in this section, we show first the total share of the budget covered by all of the goods that go into the price indexes, averaged over all households included. The closer these numbers to unity, the more complete the price index. Since the various price indexes involve two sets of budget shares, the 'base' and the 'comparison', there are generally two sets of budget shares in the tables. We then present the four price indexes – Laspeyres, Paasche, Fisher Ideal, and Törnqvist. In most cases, the last two indexes are very close to one another, and since both have the 'superlative' index property, they are our preferred estimates. In all cases, the code is written so as to exclude any good from the price indexes when in either base or comparison data set, there are less than 20 observations on its price. Although the choice of 20 is arbitrary, the results are not sensitive to reasonable variations, and some such rule is required to eliminate cases where there are only one or two observations on a given price.

Table 16.3 shows that, for all-India, goods comprising 74.6 per cent of the budget were included in the rural sector of the 43rd Round, falling to 70.7 per cent in the 50th Round. This decline is to be expected from Engel's Law if there is an increase in real incomes, and would be interpreted by some as evidence that real incomes have indeed been increasing. The shares covered are lower in the urban sector, 67.6 and 63.4 per cent, which is again to be expected if urban areas are somewhat better off, and because of the relatively greater importance for urban consumers of items such as housing and transportation. With a few exceptions, these patterns of shares between the rounds and between urban and rural sectors are replicated across the individual states shown in the Table 16.3. In the rural sector, the covered share rose in only three states, Haryana, Himachal Pradesh, and Punjab, and in the urban sector, increased only in Delhi (where the covered share is lower than anywhere else). Several states, particularly in urban sectors, show large decreases in the covered share. In the rural sector, Gujarat, Karnataka, Madhya Pradesh, and Maharashtra showed declines of more than 5 percentage points, while the same occurred in the urban sectors of Assam, Gujarat, Jammu and Kashmir, Karnataka, Kerala, Madhya Pradesh, and Maharashtra. While the share of the budget devoted to food is far from being an infallible guide to welfare, these results are consistent with an increase in well-being that is somewhat unevenly spread, and that is stronger in urban than rural sectors.

The all-India (Törnqvist) price index shows an increase between the rounds of 69.8 per cent for the rural sector, and of 73.8 per cent in the urban areas. The CPIAL, which is the relevant comparison for the rural sector, increased by 76.3 per cent, while the CPIIW, which is the relevant index for urban comparisons, increased by 75.1 per cent. The versions of the CPIAL and CPIIW used in the official poverty lines, and which are calculated by dividing the 50th Round lines by the 43rd Round lines, are

Table 16.3 Price Indexes for 1993/94 Relative to 1987/88

	Budget 43	Budget 50	Laspeyres	Paasche Index	Fisher Ideal	Törnqvist	CPI	PL Deflator
Rural							CPIAL	
Andhra Pradesh	69.9	68.5	177.5	174.1	175.8	175.9	177.3	177.3
Assam	81.9	81.6	174.8	172.5	173.6	173.7	181.6	182.1
Bihar	79.0	76.3	161.3	158.1	159.7	159.7	175.6	176.3
Gujarat	78.5	71.1	175.2	166.1	170.6	170.6	175.2	175.7
Haryana	68.5	69.3	175.7	173.0	174.3	174.2	–	190.2
Himachal Pradesh	68.4	69.2	171.6	162.9	167.1	167.1	–	190.2
Jammu & Kashmir	68.7	67.8	184.9	178.4	181.6	181.5	171.2	–
Karnataka	73.2	62.1	175.8	174.5	175.1	175.1	178.7	178.7
Kerala	69.7	68.5	174.7	169.4	172.1	172.3	186.4	186.7
Madhya Pradesh	75.9	70.9	174.7	169.1	171.9	171.9	179.8	180.5
Maharashtra	71.8	61.1	174.1	171.3	172.7	172.6	168.6	168.6
Orissa	79.9	79.1	167.4	162.1	164.7	164.6	159.9	159.8
Punjab	66.7	68.2	192.6	188.6	190.6	190.7	191.0	190.2
Rajasthan	72.7	68.1	169.4	164.2	166.8	166.9	186.1	183.7
Tamil Nadu	73.4	69.0	169.4	165.9	167.6	167.7	167.0	166.2
Uttar Pradesh	69.8	68.9	170.3	165.5	167.9	167.9	186.0	185.9
West Bengal	79.6	75.5	167.6	165.4	166.5	166.5	170.2	170.8
All-India	74.6	70.7	171.7	167.9	169.8	169.8	176.3	178.7
Urban							CPIIW	
Andhra Pradesh	64.8	62.4	179.7	174.6	177.1	177.2	175.9	183.1
Assam	72.4	66.4	179.4	175.9	177.6	177.7	179.7	167.8
Bihar	73.1	71.0	165.9	164.3	165.1	165.2	168.6	158.7
Gujarat	70.4	65.3	169.2	161.7	165.4	165.4	173.0	171.6
Haryana	68.5	60.5	178.6	176.7	177.6	177.6	180.6	180.3
Himachal Pradesh	62.1	58.7	179.7	170.8	175.2	175.2	–	176.0
Jammu & Kashmir	66.8	59.5	185.8	171.7	178.6	178.5	174.3	–
Karnataka	67.7	60.6	179.5	174.6	177.0	177.1	180.8	176.9
Kerala	69.0	63.4	175.5	171.2	173.3	173.5	174.9	171.8
Madhya Pradesh	72.2	63.9	173.5	168.2	170.8	170.9	174.1	177.8
Maharashtra	65.4	59.0	183.4	178.5	180.9	181.1	183.3	173.7
Orissa	70.7	66.6	169.1	166.5	167.8	167.8	178.7	180.3
Punjab	62.5	60.9	188.6	185.4	187.0	187.1	172.4	174.9
Rajasthan	67.1	64.5	173.7	169.9	171.8	171.8	173.1	169.8
Tamil Nadu	62.9	62.9	172.4	168.3	170.3	170.5	177.1	178.9
Uttar Pradesh	67.2	64.7	166.5	164.2	165.4	165.4	169.6	167.8
West Bengal	68.4	65.3	172.4	168.8	170.6	170.6	172.1	165.1
Delhi	55.8	56.9	180.1	170.5	175.2	175.7	177.1	174.9
All-India	67.6	63.4	175.1	172.3	173.7	173.8	175.1	173.5

Notes: 1. Budget 43 and Budget 50 are the total shares of the budget (in per cent) in the 43rd and 50th Rounds, respectively, of all the goods covered by the index.

2. Data for all-India are calculated from the complete survey, including those states and territories not listed separately. We do not have data for the CPIAL for Haryana nor for Jammu & Kashmir, nor the CPIIW for Jammu & Kashmir.

3. The final column is the implicit deflator of the official poverty lines; it is computed from the same prices collected for the CPIAL and CPIIW, but uses different weights in order to more closely reflect the experience of people near the poverty line.

shown in the final column. The rural poverty weighted index rose by a little more than the CPIAL, 78.7 per cent, and the urban poverty weighted index by a little less than the CPIIW, 73.5 per cent. The differences between our calculations and the 'official' numbers are not very large, but the direction of the difference, with the official prices overestimating inflation in the rural sector, appears in many of the entries in the Table 16.3. The Laspeyres index estimates more inflation than the two superlative indexes which allow for some substitution; in the urban sector, our all-India Laspeyres is identical to the CPIIW while in the rural sector, the Laspeyres takes us only about a third of the way from the superlative indexes to the CPIAL. Across (most but not all of) the states, as for all-India, our calculations show more overestimation of inflation in rural than in urban areas, so that recalculations of poverty rates in the next section will show more effect on calculated rural than urban poverty.

One possible reason why our calculations might systematically *understate* the rate of inflation would be if the rate of inflation of non-covered goods, including housing and transportation, has typically been higher than the rate of inflation of the covered goods. We do not currently have to hand the CPIAL and CPIIW disaggregated by commodity groupings. However, the Indian Labour Yearbooks show that, for all-India, the all-items or general versions of the two price indexes have been rising *less* rapidly than the food component alone. Hence, if we were to combine our indexes for the covered goods with the relevant components of the CPIAL and CPIIW for the non-covered items, the result would show less inflation than our current estimates.

At the state level, our calculations show less inflation over the period than do the corresponding CPIAL or CPIIW indexes in all the states shown except for rural Jammu & Kashmir, Maharashtra, Orissa, and Tamil Nadu, and for urban Andhra Pradesh, Jammu & Kashmir, and Punjab. (Note that we do not currently have data on the CPIAL for Haryana nor on either the CPIAL nor CPIIW for Himachal Pradesh.) The differences between the two sets of indexes are smaller in the urban areas, and the largest differences occur in the rural areas of a few states, notably Bihar, Kerala, Rajasthan, and Uttar Pradesh. It is worth noting that some of these states have relatively high poverty rates, where a reduction in the price level is likely to have the largest effects.

Indexes for urban prices relative to a rural base are presented in Table 16.4. The choice of which sector to use as base makes a difference to all but the two superlative indexes, although note that the Laspeyres index for rural relative to urban is the reciprocal of the Paasche index for urban relative to rural. For India as a whole, urban prices for covered goods were 11.4 per cent higher than rural prices in the 43rd Round. By the 50th Round, this difference had expanded to 15.6 per cent. Note that this difference is qualitatively consistent with the results in Table 16.3, where the urban rate of inflation was calculated to be somewhat higher than the rural rate. There is some variation across states in urban-rural price differentials, and these variations seem to be stable over time. Urban Kerala is only slightly more expensive than rural Kerala; the same appears to be the case for Himachal Pradesh and Jammu & Kashmir in 1987/88, though less so in 1993/94. At the other end of the scale, the urban price differential was highest in Uttar Pradesh, West Bengal, Maharashtra, Madhya Pradesh, Punjab, and Haryana.

For many years, until the Expert Group Report of 1993, Indian poverty lines were set (in 1973/74 prices) at Rs 49 of per capita household expenditure for rural areas and Rs 57 for urban areas, a difference of 15 per cent. Clearly, our estimates in Table 16.4, particularly for the latter round, are consistent with such a difference. Of course, our estimates exclude between a quarter and a third of the budget, including important items like housing and transportation so that a fuller account of the budget would presumably raise the relative cost of living in urban areas. There are no official price indexes for urban to rural differentials. Nevertheless, the Expert Group calculated a set of poverty lines for 1987/88

Table 16.4 Price Indexes for Urban Relative to Rural, 43rd and 50th Rounds

	Budget: Urban	Budget: Rural	Laspeyres Index	Paasche Index	Fisher Ideal Index	Törnqvist Index	PL Deflator	Uncovered Price
43rd Round								
Andhra Pradesh	68.8	74.7	111.8	109.5	110.6	110.7	165.2	456.6
Assam	75.0	83.5	109.1	107.0	108.1	108.0	99.3	72.1
Bihar	75.5	80.4	108.5	107.7	108.1	108.1	124.8	207.6
Gujarat	72.7	80.0	106.3	104.5	105.4	105.4	150.6	476.5
Haryana	71.5	69.4	114.1	110.3	112.2	112.1	116.5	127.8
Himachal Pradesh	66.5	67.8	111.6	96.1	103.6	104.8	117.2	147.5
Jammu & Kashmir	72.5	72.5	104.6	102.8	103.7	103.8	119.3	172.4
Karnataka	71.4	77.2	110.4	108.9	109.6	110.0	163.9	518.8
Kerala	73.0	74.4	103.7	103.4	103.5	103.5	125.0	212.3
Madhya Pradesh	74.2	76.6	116.9	109.4	113.1	113.0	166.7	548.7
Maharashtra	69.1	73.8	114.9	113.1	114.0	114.1	163.6	403.4
Orissa	73.5	81.2	112.9	107.6	110.2	110.2	136.2	281.0
Punjab	64.7	68.6	115.6	110.8	113.2	113.2	118.0	128.1
Rajasthan	70.2	74.3	108.2	105.3	106.7	106.7	140.7	289.3
Tamil Nadu	68.8	79.3	109.7	108.4	109.0	109.0	140.3	288.0
Uttar Pradesh	69.7	71.8	120.0	116.1	118.1	118.1	134.6	184.4
West Bengal	71.9	81.8	112.9	112.4	112.6	112.7	116.1	127.9
All-India	70.9	77.1	113.1	109.8	111.4	111.4	140.8	274.0
50th Round								
Andhra Pradesh	63.4	69.6	111.8	109.3	110.5	110.5	170.6	404.1
Assam	68.3	80.9	113.6	109.1	111.3	111.6	91.5	51.2
Bihar	71.7	77.0	112.6	112.3	112.5	112.5	112.4	112.2
Gujarat	67.6	74.6	106.9	103.4	105.1	105.2	147.1	335.3
Haryana	62.3	69.1	119.2	112.0	115.5	115.6	110.5	101.2
Himachal Pradesh	61.4	66.8	110.9	104.5	107.7	108.1	108.5	109.2
Jammu & Kashmir	58.2	67.1	109.2	104.9	107.0	107.0	n.a.	n.a.
Karnataka	64.3	69.1	111.3	109.9	110.6	110.6	162.3	349.9
Kerala	64.0	68.6	104.7	103.7	104.2	104.2	115.1	139.8
Madhya Pradesh	65.1	73.3	118.7	113.1	115.8	115.8	164.2	360.1
Maharashtra	61.7	67.4	121.2	115.4	118.3	118.2	168.5	321.6
Orissa	66.4	77.9	111.9	108.9	110.4	110.5	153.7	361.3
Punjab	62.8	68.5	116.3	112.0	114.1	114.2	108.5	98.3
Rajasthan	64.9	72.6	113.2	109.1	111.1	111.3	130.1	183.4
Tamil Nadu	63.3	70.1	111.0	108.5	109.8	109.7	150.9	286.0
Uttar Pradesh	66.2	69.2	118.3	114.5	116.4	116.5	121.4	132.4
West Bengal	65.3	75.4	119.6	115.0	117.3	117.5	112.1	100.4
All-India	65.8	73.7	117.5	113.7	115.6	115.6	136.7	201.1

that differed between urban and rural in each state, and so contained an implicit set of urban to rural price differences. The Planning Commission subsequently adopted a modified version of the Expert Group's proposals so that the official poverty lines also contain a set of implicit urban-to-rural price ratios and these can be obtained by dividing the urban by the rural lines. These are listed in the penultimate column of Table 16.4, labelled 'PL deflators'. (That these urban to rural indexes are *implicit* should be emphasised.) The Expert Group did not derive these price deflators from an explicit set of urban-to-rural price indexes. Instead, they started from the original urban poverty line, and adjusted it by a price index for the urban areas of the different states in Minhas, Jain, Kansal, and Saluja (1988). Similarly, they adjusted the original rural line by the statewise rural price differences from 1960/61 in Chatterjee and Bhattacharya (1974). The implicit price indexes for urban relative to rural are, therefore, generated in an indirect manner that did not make them conform to other evidence that placed limits on their plausibility (something that can be thought of as a failure of the circularity criterion).

As we might expect, given that the non-covered goods include housing and transportation, the urban-rural price differentials implicit in the poverty lines are always larger than those calculated in this paper. For all-India, the 'official' urban prices are higher than rural prices by 40.8 per cent, compared with 11.4 per cent for the Törnqvist index, and the official urban premium varies across states from a high of 65.2 per cent in Andhra Pradesh to low of only 15.3 per cent in West Bengal and is actually negative in Assam. Of course, such variability is not in itself implausible, given the variability in the cost of housing from one place to another. (Even so, it seems surprising that the second lowest differential should be in the state that contains India's largest city.) Another way of comparing our calculations with those of the official indexes is to work out the price index for non-covered goods that would be required to reconcile the two sets of results. We do this by calculating the price relative which, when inserted into a Törnqvist index with the covered goods, would yield a price index equal to the official estimate. These numbers are shown in the last column. For all-India, the price of uncovered goods in the urban areas would have to be 2.74 times its level in rural areas, and for individual states, the ratios range from 5.5 in Madhya Pradesh to 1.3 in West Bengal and 0.7 in Assam. It is hard to accept that the high figures are correct, and thence not to conclude that the official urban-to-rural price differentials are not too large. Indeed, they are sufficiently large as to cause measured poverty rates to be higher in urban than rural areas in several states where many observers have found the finding implausible, for example in comparison with other non-expenditure-based measures of poverty, such as levels of infant mortality or literacy.

Tables 16.5 and 16.6 present price indexes for differences in prices across states. For the reasons discussed in the theory section, these are the most difficult price indexes to compute, and are likely to be most sensitive to a few outliers, or to the fundamental problems of comparing groups of consumers whose tastes are very different. One symptom of these problems is the sensitivity of these calculations to the precise definition of the index. In these tables, the Paasche and Laspeyres tend to be further apart than in the urban rural or over time comparisons, and even the Törnqvist and Fisher indexes tend not to be the same. Rather than present the complete matrix of state-by-state comparisons, in which every state acts as a base for every other state, we have selected 'all-India' as the base, so that we have, as before, one index for each sector of each state. This procedure also has the advantage that the Laspeyres indexes, which price the same bundle in each of the states, are conceptually the same as the state price indexes calculated by the Expert Group. Table 16.5 shows the estimates from the 43rd Round and Table 16.6 those for the 50th Round.

According to these calculations, the differences in aggregate price levels across states are not large, at least not for the covered goods (for the cost of housing, matters may be different). In 1987/88, only

Table 16.5 Price Indexes for States Relative to All-India, 43rd Round, 1987/88

	Share of Budget	Laspeyres Index	Paasche Index	Fisher Ideal Index	Törnqvist Index	Poverty Lines Implicit
Rural						
Andhra Pradesh	75.5	98.3	90.9	94.6	94.0	79.8
Assam	84.3	108.1	104.2	106.1	106.7	110.6
Bihar	81.2	104.4	104.5	104.5	104.6	104.5
Gujarat	80.4	111.3	110.0	110.5	110.5	99.8
Haryana	70.4	104.0	94.7	99.3	98.9	106.7
Himachal Pradesh	70.8	103.9	100.0	101.9	101.6	106.7
Jammu & Kashmir	73.7	97.9	92.9	95.4	95.1	107.9
Karnataka	77.6	102.6	97.1	99.8	99.3	90.7
Kerala	74.7	111.5	99.2	105.2	104.9	113.4
Madhya Pradesh	77.8	96.6	92.9	94.8	94.2	92.9
Maharashtra	74.5	105.2	102.7	103.9	103.8	100.4
Orissa	82.4	99.1	94.3	96.7	96.6	105.4
Punjab	68.8	100.2	88.8	94.3	94.2	106.7
Rajasthan	75.3	112.2	97.7	104.7	103.9	102.0
Tamil Nadu	79.6	109.4	102.9	106.1	105.5	102.6
Uttar Pradesh	72.0	94.6	88.2	91.3	91.4	99.5
West Bengal	82.1	100.2	98.3	99.2	99.2	112.2
All-India	71.0*	100.0	100.0	100.0	100.0	100.0
Urban						
Andhra Pradesh	69.0	96.8	91.4	94.1	94.0	93.6
Assam	75.0	104.4	101.0	102.7	103.0	78.1
Bihar	75.7	102.6	98.7	100.6	100.5	92.7
Gujarat	73.3	112.0	107.9	110.0	109.5	106.8
Haryana	71.7	102.8	100.3	101.6	101.5	88.3
Himachal Pradesh	66.7	101.0	94.9	97.9	98.2	88.8
Jammu & Kashmir	72.6	94.9	90.3	92.6	92.2	91.5
Karnataka	71.6	99.6	96.8	98.2	98.2	105.6
Kerala	73.1	103.0	92.4	97.5	97.6	100.7
Madhya Pradesh	75.6	100.4	96.6	98.5	98.2	110.0
Maharashtra	69.4	109.1	106.6	107.9	107.8	116.7
Orissa	74.0	96.3	91.5	93.8	94.0	102.0
Punjab	64.9	99.3	94.7	97.0	96.6	89.4
Rajasthan	70.5	106.8	97.5	102.1	101.5	102.0
Tamil Nadu	68.9	102.0	99.8	100.9	100.8	102.2
Uttar Pradesh	69.8	102.0	96.3	99.1	98.8	95.1
West Bengal	72.2	102.8	98.4	100.6	100.1	92.5
Delhi	60.2	105.1	102.2	103.7	102.8	109.1
All-India	66.5*	100.0	100.0	100.0	100.0	100.0

Notes: * Indicates the average over all the states.

The implicit Expert Group price index is obtained from Table 4.1 of the Expert Group report by dividing the state poverty lines by the all-India poverty lines.

Table 16.6 Price Indexes for States Relative to All-India, 50th Round, 1994/94

	Share of Budget	Laspeyres Index	Paasche Index	Fisher Ideal Index	Törnqvist Index	Poverty Lines Implicit
Rural						
Andhra Pradesh	71.1	104.8	93.5	99.0	97.9	79.2
Assam	81.9	114.4	104.6	109.4	109.3	112.7
Bihar	77.4	98.9	96.9	97.9	98.1	103.1
Gujarat	75.4	118.7	114.5	116.6	116.5	98.2
Haryana	69.7	107.2	99.8	103.4	103.3	113.6
Himachal Pradesh	74.2	107.4	101.6	104.5	104.5	113.6
Jammu & Kashmir	71.1	105.9	102.2	104.0	104.1	–
Karnataka	72.8	105.7	101.7	103.7	103.5	90.7
Kerala	68.7	119.5	105.7	112.4	112.7	118.5
Madhya Pradesh	74.2	95.6	93.0	94.3	94.2	93.8
Maharashtra	69.5	110.0	100.7	105.2	105.7	94.7
Orissa	80.0	99.0	87.4	93.0	92.8	94.3
Punjab	68.9	109.9	101.1	105.4	105.0	113.6
Rajasthan	73.3	112.2	100.7	106.3	105.5	104.9
Tamil Nadu	70.8	114.1	102.0	107.9	107.0	95.5
Uttar Pradesh	70.0	94.8	89.4	92.1	91.8	103.5
West Bengal	75.6	99.7	94.2	96.9	96.6	107.2
All-India	66.9*	100.0	100.0	100.0	100.0	100.0
Urban						
Andhra Pradesh	63.6	98.0	90.9	94.4	94.0	98.9
Assam	68.6	109.1	102.4	105.7	105.9	75.5
Bihar	72.0	98.1	93.4	95.8	95.7	84.8
Gujarat	68.2	105.3	104.6	105.2	105.2	105.6
Haryana	63.0	101.6	100.1	100.9	100.9	91.8
Himachal Pradesh	61.7	101.4	97.3	99.4	99.3	90.1
Jammu & Kashmir	62.3	97.3	94.3	95.8	95.7	–
Karnataka	64.4	101.4	98.0	99.7	99.4	107.7
Kerala	64.1	106.8	94.9	100.7	100.5	99.7
Madhya Pradesh	65.6	95.6	94.0	94.8	94.8	112.7
Maharashtra	62.2	112.2	108.9	110.6	110.6	116.8
Orissa	67.7	93.8	87.1	90.4	90.6	106.0
Punjab	63.2	103.2	100.4	101.8	101.7	90.1
Rajasthan	65.6	104.9	95.8	100.2	99.7	99.8
Tamil Nadu	63.5	105.1	97.1	101.0	100.4	105.4
Uttar Pradesh	66.3	96.8	91.9	94.3	94.1	91.9
West Bengal	65.6	103.2	97.5	100.3	100.0	88.0
Delhi	58.6	109.3	103.4	106.3	106.3	110.0
All-India	60.5*	100.0	100.0	100.0	100.0	100.0

Note: * Indicates the average over all states.

rural Gujarat, rural Assam, and rural Tamil Nadu were more than 5 per cent more expensive than all-India, and rural Uttar Pradesh, Andhra Pradesh, Madhya Pradesh, and Punjab are more than 5 per cent less expensive. Among the urban areas, only Gujarat and Maharashtra are more than 5 per cent above the all-India estimate, and only Andhra Pradesh, Jammu & Kashmir, and Orissa are more than 5 per cent less. By 1993/94, there is somewhat more dispersion in the price indexes. Rural Gujarat and Kerala are more than 10 per cent more expensive than rural India as a whole, and Assam, Maharashtra, Punjab, Rajasthan, and Tamil Nadu are more than 5 per cent more expensive. Madhya Pradesh, Orissa, and Uttar Pradesh are more than 5 per cent below the average. In the urban sectors, in only Maharashtra is the price level more than 10 per cent above the all-India urban average, while Assam, Gujarat, and Delhi are 5 per cent or more above. Andhra Pradesh, Madhya Pradesh, Orissa, and Uttar Pradesh are the states with the lowest urban prices. Nevertheless, it would not be hard to make the case that, given the difficulties of these measurements, and given the lack of evidence for large price differentials, it would be better to ignore interstate price differences in setting poverty lines, even if only in the interests of transparency.

Once again, at least for the 43rd Round, it is possible to compare our results with the prices that are implicit in the Planning Commission's poverty lines which in turn derive from the Expert Group report. Dividing each state's official line by the official all-India line (within sectors) we can obtain a price index for comparison. The results are listed in the final columns of Tables 16.5 and 16.6. In both sectors, and for both years, these implicit prices are positively correlated with those calculated here, with correlation coefficients between 0.28 and 0.38, but none of these correlations is significantly different from zero. Our own state price relatives are strongly correlated with each other, both over time within sector (correlations greater than 0.7) and within states across sector (correlations again greater than 0.7). This similarity of rural and urban prices across different states is in sharp contrast to the correlations displayed by the official state indexes where the state rural and urban price differentials are *negatively* correlated across states within each round (correlation –0.40 in the 43rd Round and –0.60 in the 50th). This is in itself a strange result; spatial price differences are moderated by arbitrage, so that prices should be more similar between the urban and rural sectors of the same state than they are across states, precisely the opposite of the pattern in the official lines. The Expert Group statewise price differences, on which the Planning Commission lines are based, are taken from Chatterjee and Bhattacharya (1974) which were calculated for 1960/61, so that there must be some questions about their relevance after more than a quarter of a century, especially given the differential rate of inflation by state even over the relatively short period from 1987/88 to 1993/94 (Table 16.3) and the sizeable differences in our calculated statewise price indexes between Tables 16.5 and 16.6.

Consequences for Poverty Measurement

Even given a trial price index, there is no straightforward way to calculate its effect on estimated headcount ratios compared with the price index in current use. The problem lies in the need to choose a base year, and in the arbitrariness of any particular choice. In India, 1973/74 is frequently taken as base, and the poverty lines of Rs 49 (rural) and Rs 57 (urban) per head in 1973/74 prices have nearly always been taken as the base from which different updating schemes start. Following this tradition, the obvious way to assess the effects of different prices on poverty estimates would be to start from the assumption that the price indexes in 1973/74 are correct, and then to calculate new price indexes for subsequent years. If it were the case that a Laspeyres index with fixed base were to slowly come adrift from another (for example superlative) index, then the differences in poverty counts would also drift apart over the years. Armed with all the expenditure surveys since 1973/74, it would be possible in principle to repeat the calculations of this paper, and to carry out the repricing exercise. However, we have so far worked with only two full expenditure surveys, 1987/88 and 1993/94, so that our only estimate of the rate of inflation is between those two years. In consequence, the only feasible calculation of poverty rates is one that takes (at least some of) the 1987/88 rates as correct, and then compares the 'official' poverty rates in 1993/94 with those calculated using the different price indexes. From this, we can compare the 'official' and 'experimental' changes in the headcount ratio from 1987/88 to 1993/94. While this calculation is of considerable interest, and makes a first attempt to answer the question about whether price mismeasurement means that rural poverty is falling more rapidly than officially documented, it is certainly not the only possible answer. With another choice of base year (such as 1973/74), the nominal poverty lines in 1987/88 would be different, and because the effects of poverty lines on poverty counts are not the same at different points in the distribution, the effects on the change in the poverty rates between the two years would also be different, even though the inflation rate between them were the same. The change in poverty rates between any two dates is not a unique function of the change in nominal poverty lines between them, but also depends on the level of the lines.

A further complication is that the general agreement on poverty lines in 1973/74 has largely broken down since the publication of the Expert Group Report, with different analysts updating their lines in different ways, so that there is no obvious starting point for our first survey in 1987/88. We have chosen to start from the most 'official' of the lines, which are those used by the Planning Commission, which are modified versions of those put forward by the Expert Group. Given our previous criticism of these lines, this may seem like an odd choice. But any choice is more or less arbitrary, and in the absence of a more thoroughgoing analysis, we prefer to look at the effects of redefinition in the vicinity of lines that are currently in use for policy making within the Government of India. In any case, in our final recommended estimates presented below, we shall make only minimal use of the 1987/88 lines.

Table 16.7 lists the nominal official poverty lines for the two surveys, the associated headcount ratios, and the change in the headcount ratios over the six-year period. The poverty lines are taken from the updates of the Expert Group's recommendations in Government of India (1997). The headcount ratios were calculated using the individual record data from the 43rd and 50th Rounds; they are not quite identical to the headcount ratios in Government of India (1997) which are based on interpolations but are recognisably calculations of the same thing. Note that the all-India poverty estimates are calculated by adding up the estimated numbers of people in poverty in each state (including the small states and territories not listed here), and the all-India poverty lines are then derived implicitly as the lines that replicate the all-India counts from the state-level calculations. Because of the differences in the method of calculation between Table 16.7 and the Planning Commission, the implicit all-India lines, shown here as 'all-India (2)' are also slightly different from the official ones. The replication in Table 16.7 is important to check that there are no major differences of definition or procedures between the official figures and the experimental ones to be calculated below. In substance, the Table 16.7 shows the familiar picture of poverty rates falling in urban areas – by 6 percentage points for all-India, and much more in some states – but with a much more modest decrease in the rural areas – only 2 percentage points for the country as a whole, and five of the states actually show *increases* in the rural poverty rate over the period.

Table 16.8 repeats the four official price indexes, the CPIAL and the CPIIW themselves, together with their reweighted versions implicit in the official poverty lines in Table 16.7 and obtained by dividing the 1993/94 lines by the 1987/88 lines. The first two columns show that the reweighting of the CPIAL

Table 16.7 Official Poverty Lines and Headcount Ratios, 43rd and 50th Rounds

	Poverty Lines 1987/88	Headcount Ratio 1987/88	Poverty Lines 1993/94	Headcount Ratio 1993/94	Change in HCR
Rural					
Andhra Pradesh	91.94	21.04	163.02	15.89	−5.15
Assam	127.44	39.42	232.05	45.20	5.78
Bihar	120.36	53.92	212.16	57.95	4.03
Gujarat	115.00	28.56	202.11	22.16	−6.40
Haryana	122.90	15.34	233.79	28.26	12.92
Himachal Pradesh	122.90	16.68	233.79	30.36	13.68
Karnataka	104.46	32.63	186.63	30.11	−2.52
Kerala	130.61	29.46	243.84	25.38	−4.08
Madhya Pradesh	107.00	42.02	193.10	40.72	−1.30
Maharashtra	115.61	40.95	194.94	37.91	−3.04
Orissa	121.42	58.67	194.03	49.84	−8.83
Punjab	122.90	12.81	233.79	11.69	−1.12
Rajasthan	117.52	33.30	215.89	26.40	−6.90
Tamil Nadu	118.23	46.34	196.53	32.95	−13.39
Uttar Pradesh	114.57	41.92	213.01	42.32	0.40
West Bengal	129.21	48.80	220.74	41.18	−7.62
All-India (1)	115.20	39.01	205.84	37.21	−1.80
All-India (2)	115.70	39.40	205.67	37.13	−2.42
Urban					
Andhra Pradesh	151.88	41.09	278.14	38.82	−2.27
Assam	126.60	11.32	212.42	7.93	−3.39
Bihar	150.25	51.89	238.49	34.84	−17.05
Gujarat	173.18	38.53	297.22	28.26	−10.27
Haryana	143.22	18.38	258.23	16.47	−1.91
Himachal Pradesh	144.10	7.20	253.61	9.26	2.06
Karnataka	171.18	49.19	302.89	39.90	−9.29
Kerala	163.29	39.80	280.54	24.31	−15.49
Madhya Pradesh	178.35	47.25	317.16	48.08	0.83
Maharashtra	189.17	40.34	328.56	34.99	−5.35
Orissa	165.40	42.58	298.22	40.64	−1.94
Punjab	144.98	13.70	253.61	10.90	−2.80
Rajasthan	165.38	37.89	280.85	31.02	−6.87
Tamil Nadu	165.82	40.20	296.63	39.91	−0.29
Uttar Pradesh	154.15	44.93	258.65	35.09	−9.84
West Bengal	149.96	33.74	247.53	22.95	−10.79
Delhi	176.91	15.06	309.48	16.09	1.03
All-India (1)	162.16	38.64	281.35	32.63	−6.01
All-India (2)	163.30	39.10	283.44	33.15	−5.80

Notes: 1. The First and Third Columns, the two sets of poverty lines by state and sector, are those used by the Planning Commission in the official poverty counts.

2. The headcount ratios in the second and fourth Columns are computed from the unit record data from the 43rd and 50th Rounds, and estimate the proportions of people below the poverty line for the state and sector in which they live. These differ slightly from the official headcount ratios because the official calculations use grouped data; the numbers in the Table 16.7 are, therefore, somewhat more accurate than the official estimates.

3. The all-India (1) headcount ratios are computed from the official all-India rural and urban poverty lines as shown: Rs 115.20 (rural) and Rs 162.16 (urban) in the 43rd Round, and Rs 205.84 (rural) and Rs 281.35 (urban) in the 50th Round.
4. The all-India headcount ratios are the fractions of people in rural and urban India whose household per capita expenditure is below these lines. However, in the official methodology, these all-India lines are calculated implicitly from the state-level results; the headcount ratios for each state and territory are added up (weighted by population) to give an all-India headcount ratio, and an all-India poverty line calculated so as to yield that headcount ratio when directly applied to the all-India data. These calculations are replicated in the row labelled all-India (2).
5. We have followed the official methodology in assigning poverty lines or poverty rates to small states as follows: Goa and Dadra & Nagar Haveli are assigned the poverty lines of Maharashtra, and rural Delhi (not shown in the Table) the poverty line of rural Haryana. Other small states and territories are assigned the poverty *rates* of neighbours with rural matched to rural and urban to urban: Assam is used for Arunachal Pradesh, Manipur, Meghalaya, Mizoram, Nagaland, Sikkim, and Tripura; Tamil Nadu is used for the Andaman and Nicobar Islands and for Pondicherry; the *urban* poverty rate for Punjab is assigned to both rural and urban households in Chandigarh; Maharashtra is used for Daman and Diu; and Kerala for Lakshadweep.
6. In the 50th Round, the headcount ratio for Himachal Pradesh is used for Jammu & Kashmir. Assigning neighbouring poverty rates appears to be a less attractive strategy than assigning neighbouring poverty lines; the assumption that the price levels are the same is surely more appropriate than the assumption that the lower tails of the consumption distribution are similar. However, the small states and territories contain a small enough share of the population so that differences in methodology do not have much effect.
7. Using poverty lines rather than poverty rates, the all-India rural lines and headcount ratios are Rs 115.50 and 39.24 per cent in the 43rd Round and Rs 204.95 and 36.84 per cent in the 50th Round. The corresponding urban estimates are Rs 163.24 and 39.08 per cent in the 43rd Round and Rs 282.11 and 32.83 per cent in the 50th Round.

Table 16.8 Official Price Indexes and Implicit Price Deflators: 1993/94 versus 1987/88

	CPIAL	Implicit Rural Price Deflator	CPIIW	Implicit Urban Price Deflator
Andhra Pradesh	177.3	177.3	175.9	183.1
Assam	181.6	182.1	179.7	167.8
Bihar	175.6	176.3	168.6	158.7
Gujarat	175.2	175.7	173.0	171.6
Haryana	–	190.2	180.6	180.3
Karnataka	178.7	178.7	180.8	176.9
Kerala	186.4	186.7	174.9	171.8
Madhya Pradesh	179.8	180.5	174.1	177.8
Maharashtra	168.6	168.6	183.3	173.7
Orissa	159.9	159.8	178.7	180.3
Punjab	191.0	190.2	172.4	174.9
Rajasthan	186.1	183.7	173.1	169.8
Tamil Nadu	167.0	166.2	177.1	178.9
Uttar Pradesh	186.0	185.9	169.6	167.8
West Bengal	170.2	170.8	172.1	165.1
All-India	176.3	178.7	175.1	173.5

Notes: 1. The CPIAL and CPIIW are repeated from Table 16.3.

2. The implicit rural and urban price deflators come from the Planning Commission's poverty lines are obtained by dividing the 1993/94 poverty lines by the 1987/88 lines.

makes little difference, either state by state, or for the country as a whole; the updating index is very close to the CPIAL. This is what would be expected given the high poverty rates in India. For urban poverty lines, the reweighting appears to induce larger deviations from the CPIIW, particularly in a few states (Assam, Bihar, and Maharashtra). It is not transparent from the information to hand why these differences exist, and why they are larger than for the CPIAL.

Table 16.9 shows our own calculations of poverty rates using the inflation rates between 1987/88 and 1993/94 that were calculated in the earlier sections of this paper and that were reported in Table 16.3. In these first calculations, we are ignoring the other price indexes, those for interstate and intersectoral differentials; we take the 1987/88 official lines for each sector of each state as the base, and apply the Törnqvist inflation factors from Column 6 of Table 16.3. In this way, we isolate the effects of the different calculated rates of inflation, leaving the urban-rural and statewise differentials for later.

The Table 16.9 starts by examining the sensitivity to changes in the poverty lines of the headcount ratios in both rounds. Since the headcount ratio is the distribution function of per capita expenditure evaluated at the poverty line, the derivative of the ratio is the density evaluated at the same point. We have calculated these densities using a kernel smoother with a Gaussian kernel and with a bandwidth chosen according to Silverman's (1986) robust version of the optimal bandwidth. The density at the poverty line, multiplied by the poverty line, shows the derivative of the headcount ratio with respect to the logarithm of the poverty line, and the estimates for the two rounds are reported in the first two columns of the table. (Note that these two columns can also be interpreted as the derivatives of the poverty rates with respect to mean per capita expenditure holding its distribution constant.)

To interpret the derivatives in the first two columns, note for example that the figure of 0.70 for rural Andhra Pradesh in the 43rd Round shows that a 1 per cent decrease in the nominal poverty line (or equivalently a 1 per cent decrease in the price deflator) would cause the headcount ratio to fall by 0.70 percentage points, that is from the calculated headcount ratio of 21.04 per cent to 20.34 per cent. These estimates fall between 0.32 (urban Himachal Pradesh) and 1.11 (rural Assam and Bihar). They are larger, the larger is the density of the population at or nearer to the poverty line, so that given where poverty lines lie in the state distributions of per capita expenditure in India, they tend to be larger in the poorer states and smaller in the richer states. In the latter the poor are in the tail of the distribution, so that shifts in the mean have relatively little effect on their numbers, while in the poor states, where the poverty line is near the median, shifts in the line (or in economic growth) have much larger effects on the counts. These numbers should be seen as providing a rough rule of thumb for how much to expect differences in price indexes (or growth rates) to affect the poverty rates.

Column 3 in Table 16.9 $\Delta \ln P$ shows the difference (in percentage points) between the price indexes calculated in this paper and the change in the official price indexes from 1987/88 to 1993/94, where the official indexes are those implicit in the poverty lines. These figures are simply the difference between the logarithms of Column 6 and Column 8 in Table 16.3. Again we are looking only at inflation rates, making no correction for the interstate or intersectoral price differences. Column 4 repeats the headcount ratio for 1993/94, as reported in Table 16.7, while Column 5 reports what the headcount ratio would be if the nominal poverty lines in 1987/88 were updated, not as in the official lines, but by the Törnqvist price indexes in Column 6 of Table 16.3.

The last two columns show the changes in the headcount ratios between the two surveys, by the official counts in Column 6, and by our counts in Column 7. Although there are some differences on a state-by-state basis, our results for the urban sector are similar to the official results, and the official decline in the urban poverty rate of –6.01 percentage points is revised only to –5.87 percentage points.

Table 16.9 Sensitivity of Headcount Ratios and Alternative Estimates

	ΔHCR43	ΔHCR50	Δ ln P	HCR50	HCR50 New	Change 43–50	Change 43–50 New
Rural							
Andhra Pradesh	0.70	0.56	−0.8	15.89	15.49	−5.15	−5.55
Assam	1.11	1.17	−4.7	45.20	39.51	5.78	0.09
Bihar	1.11	0.87	−9.9	57.95	48.37	4.03	−5.55
Gujarat	0.93	0.76	−3.0	22.16	20.26	−6.40	−8.30
Haryana	0.70	0.73	−8.8	28.26	20.49	12.91	5.15
Himachal Pradesh	0.74	0.91	−13.0	30.36	17.14	13.68	0.46
Karnataka	0.84	1.00	−2.0	30.11	28.07	−2.52	−4.56
Kerala	0.92	0.66	−8.0	25.38	20.49	−4.08	−8.97
Madhya Pradesh	0.97	0.91	−4.9	40.72	36.16	−1.30	−5.86
Maharashtra	0.85	0.74	2.3	37.91	39.65	−3.04	−1.30
Orissa	0.93	1.03	3.0	49.84	52.68	−8.83	−5.99
Punjab	0.62	0.64	0.2	11.69	11.98	−1.12	−0.83
Rajasthan	0.80	0.92	−9.6	26.40	18.66	−6.90	−14.64
Tamil Nadu	0.78	0.86	0.9	32.95	33.41	−13.39	−12.93
Uttar Pradesh	0.88	0.86	−10.2	42.32	33.76	0.40	−8.16
West Bengal	0.89	0.96	−2.6	41.18	38.71	−7.62	−10.09
All-India	0.89	0.91	−5.1	37.21	32.78	−1.80	−6.23
Urban							
Andhra Pradesh	0.74	0.77	−3.3	38.82	35.83	−2.27	−5.26
Assam	0.46	0.66	5.7	7.93	10.82	−3.39	−0.50
Bihar	0.88	0.91	4.0	34.84	38.32	−17.05	−13.57
Gujarat	0.96	0.62	−3.7	28.28	26.10	−10.27	−12.43
Haryana	0.70	0.46	−1.5	16.47	15.79	−1.91	−2.59
Himachal Pradesh	0.32	0.32	−0.5	9.26	9.26	2.06	2.06
Karnataka	0.80	0.66	0.1	39.90	40.11	−9.29	−9.08
Kerala	0.78	0.69	1.0	24.31	25.16	−15.49	−14.64
Madhya Pradesh	0.77	0.69	−4.0	48.08	45.08	0.83	−2.17
Maharashtra	0.57	0.66	4.2	34.99	38.08	−5.35	−2.26
Orissa	0.98	0.80	−7.2	40.64	35.67	−1.94	−6.91
Punjab	0.57	0.66	6.7	10.90	14.43	−2.80	0.74
Rajasthan	0.75	0.77	1.2	31.02	31.93	−6.87	−5.96
Tamil Nadu	0.73	0.84	4.8	39.91	35.87	−0.29	−4.33
Uttar Pradesh	0.81	0.82	−1.4	35.09	33.76	−9.84	−11.17
West Bengal	0.91	0.56	3.3	22.95	24.57	−10.79	−9.17
Delhi	0.57	0.57	0.4	16.09	16.50	1.03	1.44
All-India	0.69	0.73	0.2	32.62	32.78	−6.01	−5.87

Notes: 1. ΔHCR is the estimated derivative of the headcount ratio with respect to the logarithm of the updating price index; it is also the derivative with respect to the logarithm of mean PCE with the distribution held constant.

2. Δ ln P is the logarithm of our Törnqvist price index less the logarithm of the official price index implicit in the poverty lines, and is the difference between the logarithms of Column 8 and Column 6 in Table 16.3.

3. HCR50 is replicated from Table 16.7. HCR50 new is the headcount ratio in 1993/94 when, instead of the official lines for the 50th Round, we use the official lines for the 43rd Round updated using the Törnqvist indexes in Table 16.3.

4. The change for 43–50 is replicated from Table 16.7, and the new change 43–50 is the difference between the HCR43 (Table 16.7) and HCR50 new.

The differences are much more important in the rural sector. For all-India, the reduction in the poverty rate from 1987/88 to 1993/94 moves from only 2 percentage points in the official counts to more than 6 per cent according to our price indexes. The differences are much larger for some states, particularly Assam, Bihar, Haryana, Himachal Pradesh (where the official very puzzling 14 percentage point rise in poverty is eliminated), Kerala, Madhya Pradesh, Rajasthan, and Uttar Pradesh, and in all these cases the adoption of the new price indexes would cause measured poverty to have fallen more rapidly than in the official counts. These calculations are consistent with the view that, between 1987/88 and 1993/94, there was no great difference in the rates of decline of urban and rural poverty in India.

Table 16.10 explores the effects of modifying the Expert Group lines for the urban-rural and interstate price differentials as measured in this paper. Again, we proceed in a series of steps. Column 1 shows the updated Expert Group headcount ratios for each state (other than Jammu & Kashmir). This column replicates the data from Column 4 of Table 16.9. Column 2 of Table 16.10 (labelled 'New 1') takes the updated Expert Group lines for the rural sector of each state as correct, but calculates the urban poverty lines by applying the urban-rural Törnqvist price indexes for 1993/94 shown in the bottom panel of Table 16.4. The associated headcount ratios are shown in this column; the top panel is unchanged by construction, but the urban headcount ratios in the bottom panel are often dramatically different from the official ratios. For example, according to these estimates, only 9.6 per cent of people in urban Andhra Pradesh are poor, as opposed to 38.8 per cent in the official estimates. There are similar dramatic declines in measured urban poverty in Gujarat, Karnataka, Madhya Pradesh, Maharashtra, Orissa, and Tamil Nadu, and the all-India rate of urban poverty falls from 33 per cent to 19 per cent. But this first step should not be taken too seriously. While it corrects for the almost certainly too large urban-rural price differences in the Expert Group lines, it takes their rural lines as correct, accepting their implicit interstate price differences. The low headcount ratio that we estimate for urban Andhra Pradesh (for example) owes as much to a low starting point in the rural line, as it does to a low price relative from urban to rural.

The next step is taken in Column 3, labelled 'New 2'. These estimates do a more comprehensive job of correcting the official calculations because they correct for state price differences as well as for sector differences. The calculations are done by starting with (our slightly recalculated version of) the official rural poverty line for all-India in 1993/94, Rs 205.67, see Table 16.7. This number is used to generate rural poverty lines for each state by multiplying by the rural Törnqvist price indexes for states relative to all-India for 1993/94 shown in the top panel of Table 16.6. The urban lines are then created, state-by-state, by multiplying by the urban to rural Törnqvist price differentials that are listed in the bottom panel of Table 16.4 (and that were already used in calculating Column 2). Note that the same price indexes could be used differently, converting the all-India rural poverty line to an urban poverty line using the all-India urban-to-rural price index, and then applying the state to all-India *urban* price indexes. Because circularity does not hold, the poverty lines derived in this way are different from those actually used, though here the differences are not important.

The 'New 2' poverty rates are now slightly higher in the urban areas, though still much less than the official counts. Again, there are large differences for individual states (21 per cent in urban Andhra Pradesh versus 39 per cent, 25 per cent in urban Karnataka versus 40 per cent), and our urban counts are typically lower than the corresponding rural counts. Our price indexes do not support the large interstate or intersectoral differences that are built into the official lines, so that our calculations, unlike the official ones, support the notion that poverty rates are higher in rural than in urban areas.

The fourth column ('New 3') in Table 16.10 is a further and final modification. Instead of starting

Table 16.10 Official and Alternative Headcount Ratios for 1993/94 and Change since 1987/88

	Official	New 1	New 2	New 3	New 43rd	Change
Rural						
Andhra Pradesh	15.89	15.89	33.47	29.17	35.00	−5.83
Assam	45.20	45.20	41.51	35.43	36.13	−0.70
Bihar	57.95	57.95	53.21	48.57	54.55	−5.98
Gujarat	22.16	22.16	37.22	32.45	39.43	−6.98
Haryana	28.26	28.26	19.67	17.01	13.58	3.43
Himachal Pradesh	30.36	30.36	21.15	17.14	13.26	3.88
Jammu & Kashmir	n.a.	n.a.	13.66	10.13	15.32	−5.19
Karnataka	30.11	30.11	42.46	37.90	40.81	−2.91
Kerala	25.38	25.38	22.36	19.48	23.77	−4.29
Madhya Pradesh	40.72	40.72	41.11	36.63	43.72	−7.09
Maharashtra	37.91	37.91	46.69	42.89	44.32	−1.43
Orissa	49.84	49.84	47.78	43.50	50.37	−6.87
Punjab	11.69	11.69	8.56	6.16	6.61	−0.45
Rajasthan	26.40	26.40	26.79	23.03	35.29	−12.26
Tamil Nadu	32.95	32.95	43.18	38.46	49.01	−10.55
Uttar Pradesh	42.32	42.32	32.35	28.65	34.92	−6.27
West Bengal	41.18	41.18	29.23	25.07	36.29	−11.22
All-India	37.13	37.13	37.10	32.94	38.96	−6.02
Urban						
Andhra Pradesh	38.82	9.61	20.75	17.78	23.44	−5.66
Assam	7.93	17.93	16.26	12.97	13.56	−0.59
Bihar	34.84	34.97	30.47	26.68	38.13	−11.45
Gujarat	28.28	8.08	17.62	14.72	16.42	−1.70
Haryana	16.46	18.99	14.85	10.55	11.79	−1.24
Himachal Pradesh	9.26	9.26	5.61	3.64	1.66	1.98
Jammu & Kashmir	n.a.	n.a.	3.89	3.10	3.82	−0.72
Karnataka	39.90	16.03	24.50	21.44	25.95	−4.51
Kerala	24.31	18.34	15.98	13.87	20.97	−7.10
Madhya Pradesh	48.08	20.83	21.22	18.50	20.70	−2.20
Maharashtra	34.99	15.67	20.57	18.24	21.16	−2.92
Orissa	40.64	18.97	17.89	15.18	20.82	−5.64
Punjab	10.90	14.19	9.11	7.75	6.56	1.19
Rajasthan	31.02	20.37	20.75	18.26	19.80	−1.54
Tamil Nadu	39.91	16.13	24.20	20.85	26.15	−5.30
Uttar Pradesh	35.09	32.13	24.15	21.71	29.29	−7.58
West Bengal	22.95	25.19	18.99	15.53	22.26	−6.73
All-India, weighted average	33.15	19.33	20.83	18.12	22.83	−4.71

Notes: 1. The first Column, 'Official', repeats the Planning Commission's poverty counts for 1993/94, and thus repeats Column 4 of Table 16.7. In the second column, labelled 'New 1', we take the Planning Commission's rural poverty lines as given, so that the rural figures are the same as in the first column. However, the urban poverty lines are calculated using the Planning Commission's rural poverty lines and multiplying by the urban to rural Törnqvist price indexes reported in the bottom panel of Table 16.4.

2. The third column, labelled 'New 2' uses only the all-India rural poverty line (Rs 205.67, see Table 16.7) from our reworking of the official counts. The rural lines for each state are created from the all-India line using the state Törnqvist price indexes from the top panel of Table 16.6, and the urban lines are created from the rural lines using the urban to rural price indexes as in Column 2. Note that the all-India rural poverty rate in column 3, 37.10 per cent, is not identical to the figure of 37.13 reported in Column 1 and in Table 16.7; this small discrepancy comes from the treatment of the all-India headcount ratio, which is derived here by imputing poverty lines or poverty rates to the small states (see the notes to Table 16.7 for details) and in addition using the official lines for urban and rural Delhi, and then weighting the state poverty rates by their shares in the population. Presumably the discrepancy could be eliminated by some iterative calculation.

3. Column 4, labelled 'New 3', uses the all-India official poverty line (as recalculated here) for 1987/88, 115.70, see Table 16.7. This is updated to 1993/94 using the all-India Törnqvist rural price index, 169.8 from Table 16.3.

4. The rural and urban state-level poverty lines are then created as in Column 3. Column 5, labelled 'New 43rd' uses the corresponding procedure for the 43rd Round, starting from 115.70, and creating rural poverty lines from the state indexes from the 43rd Round, and converting to urban lines using the urban to rural price indexes for the 43rd Round.

5. The final column, labelled 'Change' is Column 5 minus Column 4 and shows the estimated change in the headcount ratios using the preferred methodology.

6. In all cases, the all-India headcount ratios are derived from the state ratios following the 'official' methodology, imputing lines or rates to the small states, and adding over all states with the appropriate population weights, see notes to Table 16.7. In these calculations, the official lines for Delhi are used when needed; this avoids the need to calculate a rural price index from the small sample of households in rural Delhi.

from the official rural poverty line for 1993/94 of Rs 205.67, we start from the corresponding 1987/88 estimate of Rs 115.70, see again Table 16.7. This is updated to 1993/94 using the all-India rural Törnqvist index of 169.8 (Table 16.3) to give a 1993/94 line of Rs 196.46. This all-India rural poverty line then replaces Rs 205.67 as the base, and all poverty counts are thereby reduced compared with the previous column. These estimates, like those in the previous column, are the headcount ratios that come out of the price calculations in this paper, and we believe them to be both soundly based and sensible.

The fifth column ('New 43rd') reports the corresponding headcount ratios for the 43rd Round. Again, we start from the all-India rural poverty line of Rs 115.70, apply the 43rd Round rural state to all-India price indexes (top panel of Table 16.5) to get state-level rural poverty lines, which are converted to urban poverty lines using the 43rd Round urban to rural price indexes (top panel of Table 16.4). These headcount ratios are directly comparable to those from the 50th Round in the previous column ('New 3') and the changes in the last column are appropriate measures of the change in poverty between the two rounds. These estimates of change are not very different from those in the final column of Table 16.9, but are to be preferred because of their symmetrical treatment of the two rounds, and because of the fact that they make no use of the implicit urban-to-rural or statewise price indexes in the official lines. Of course, the levels from which these changes take place are quite different from the official levels, particularly in our much lower poverty rates in urban areas.

Further Work and Preliminary Conclusions

The calculations in this paper, although extensive in themselves, leave a great deal undone. In particular, it would be highly desirable to extend the calculations to both earlier periods and later periods. Among the large consumption surveys, the 38th Round (1983) is available and can be used in the same way as the 43rd and 50th Rounds. The 50th Round is the latest large consumption survey[1] that is currently available, but more recent surveys contain a good deal of consumption information, and could be used to give less precise, but probably still adequate estimates of inflation, if not of interstate or intersectoral price differences. It would also be desirable to extend the indices to cover all of consumption, which could be done by incorporating the appropriate components of the disaggregated CPIAL and CPIIW indexes. The calculations also need to be repeated to check what difference, if any, comes from reweighting our price indexes to more accurately reflect the consumption patterns of the poor. Finally, it would be extremely desirable if the NSS itself were to make similar calculations, as a cross-check, and because independent investigators cannot hope to match the resources, knowledge, and expertise of the government statisticians.

In spite of the preliminary nature of the work, we would like to emphasise some tentative conclusions. First, the unit value data from the NSS consumption surveys is a viable data base for cross-checking other price indexes. Second, the results presented here show good agreement between the rate of increase of the official CPIAL and CPIIW indexes and the prices reported by the large, national sample of respondents in the NSS surveys. Our calculations show little apparent bias in the CPIIW, but suggest that the CPIAL may have been growing too quickly, consistently with what might be expected from using a long outdated Laspeyres rather than a chain-linked or superlative index. If this conclusion is accepted, it is likely that the decline in rural poverty rates has been understated in the official poverty counts. Indeed, we are led to suggest as a working hypothesis that, between 1987/88 and 1993/94, there was no great difference in the rate of decline of urban and rural poverty, at least according to the headcount measure.

Our calculations suggest rather more serious problems with the Expert-Group based current procedures for calculating the official poverty lines. The data examined here suggests that their urban lines are too high relative to their rural lines; we find no support in the NSS purchase data for the argument that urban prices are so much higher than rural prices. Indeed the once standard procedure of assuming a uniform 15 per cent excess of urban over rural prices finds more support in the data than do the current differentials which are around 40 per cent. Nor does the purchase data generates interstate price indexes that are close to those incorporated in the Expert Group and official lines. Although interstate price differences are similar in 1993/94 and 1987/88, they are not identical, and so there is no reason to suppose that interstate price differentials from the early 1960s contain much useful information on price differentials today. There are difficult practical and conceptual problems with the computation of interstate price indexes in a country such as India, and there is a case based on transparency for not trying to do so. But if this case is not accepted, interstate price indexes should be calculated from the plentiful and recent NSS data. Doing so has dramatic effects on the distribution of poverty across the Indian states, and between the rural and urban sectors. Indeed, one of the main results of this paper is that current official practice causes much larger errors in calculating the distribution of poverty within the country than it does in calculating changes in overall poverty over time.

The Expert Group's recommendations are admirable in their attempt to use all the information available in order to improve the updating formulae for the poverty lines. But one unintended consequence of their recommendations has been to make the construction of the lines a great deal less transparent than used

---

[1] When this paper was being prepared the 50th Round was the latest large consumption survey that provided comparable estimates of consumer expenditures.

to be the case when there were only two lines – one urban and one rural – which were held fixed in real terms, and updated using a single all-India price index. Updating now involves two different price indexes, the CPIAL and the CPIIW which are reweighted in a way that makes the poverty lines increase at rates that are (somewhat) different from published price indexes. The base poverty lines that are updated are now also 'corrected' for urban-to-rural price differences, and for interstate differences. As we have seen, these corrections are difficult to make, and any specific numbers are subject to challenge, so that one result has been that there are now several different sets of poverty lines in use by different agencies. Simplicity and transparency are also virtues, and it is legitimate to ask whether the complexity and lack of transparency in the Expert Group's procedures have generated enough additional accuracy to make them worthwhile.

REFERENCES

Chaterjee, G.S. and N. Bhattacharya (1974), 'Between State Variations in Consumer Prices and Per Capita Household Consumption in Rural India' in T.N. Srinivasan and Pranab Bardhan (eds), *Poverty and Income Distribution in India*, Calcutta: Statistical Publishing Society.

Deaton, Angus S. (1988), 'Quantity, Quality and Spatial Variation in Price', *American Economic Review*, 78, pp. 418–30.

——— (1997), *The Analysis of Household Surveys: A Microeconometric Approach to Development Policy*, Baltimore, Md: Johns Hopkins University Press.

Diewert, W. Erwin (1976), 'Exact and Superlative Index Numbers', *Journal of Econometrics*, 4, pp. 114–45.

Government of India (1997), Estimate of Poverty, Press Information Bureau, 11 March.

——— (1993), Report of the Expert Group on the Estimation of Proportion and Number of Poor, Delhi: Planning Commission.

Minhas, B.S., L.R. Jain, S.M. Kansal and M.R. Saluja (1988), 'Measurement of General Cost of Living for Urban India – All-India and Different States', *Sarvekshana*, 12.

Pollak, Robert A. (1981), 'The Social Cost of Living Index', *Journal of Public Economics*, 15, pp. 311–36.

Prais, Sigbert (1959), 'Whose Cost of Living?', *Review of Economic Studies*, 26, pp. 126–34.

Prais, Sigbert and Hendrik S. Houtakker (1955), *The Analysis of Household Budgets*, Cambridge: Cambridge University Press.

Silverman, Bernard W. (1986), *Density Estimation for Statistics and Data Analysis*, London: Chapman and Hall.

Appendices

Table A1 List of Commodities in 50th Round

Paddy	Urad – PDS	Eggs	Mango	Cooked Meals
Rice – PDS	Urad – other sources	Egg Products	Kharbooza	Cake, Pastry
Rice – other sources	Khesari – PDS	Fish (fresh)	Pears (naspati)	Pickles
Chira	Khesari – other	Fish (dry)	Berries	Sauce
Khoi, Lawa	Peas	Fish (canned)	Leechi	Jam/Jelly
Muri	Soyabean	Other meat, etc.	Apple	Other Proc Food
Other Rice Products	Other Pulses	Potato	Grapes	Paan, leaf
Wheat – PDS	Besan	Onion	Other Fresh Fruits	Paan, finished
Wheat – other	Other Pulse Products	Radish	Coconut (copra)	Supari
Atta – PDS	Milk, liquid	Carrot	Groundnut	Lime
Atta – other sources	Baby Food	Turnip	Dates	Katha
Maida	Milk, cond./Powder	Beet	Cashew Nuts	Other Pan ingred.
Suji, Rawa	Curd	Sweet Potato	Walnuts	Bidi
Seewai, Noodles	Ghee	Arum	Other Nuts	Cigarettes
Bread, Bakery	Butter	Other Root Veg.	Raisins (kishmish	Leaf Tobacco
Other Wheat prods	Ice-cream	Pumpkin	Other Dry Fruits	Snuff
Jowar – PDS	Other Milk Products	Gourd	Sugar (crystal) PDS	Hookah Tobacco
Jowar – other	Vanaspati – PDS	Bitter Gourd	Sugar (crystal) other	Cheroot
Jowar Products	Vanaspati – other	Cucumber	Khandsari	Zarda, Kimam, Serti
Bajra – PDS	Margarine	Parwal/Patal	Gur (cane)	Other Tobacco prod
Bajra – other	Mustard Oil – PDS	Jhinga/Torai	Gur (others)	Ganja
Bajra Products	Mustard Oil – other	Snake Gourd	Sugar Candy (misri)	Toddy
Maize – PDS	Groundnut Oil, PDS	Other Gourd	Honey	Country Liquor
Maize – other	Groundnut Oil – other	Cauliflower	Sugar (others)	Opium, Bhangharas
Maize Products	Coconut Oil – PDS	Cabbage	Sea Salt	Beer
Barley	Coconut Oil – other	Brinjal	Other Salt	Foreign Ref. Liquor
Barley Products	Gingelly Oil – PDS	Lady's Finger	Turmeric	Other Drugs and
Small Millets	Gingelly Oil – other	Palak	Black Pepper	Intoxicants
Small Millets prods	Linseed Oil – PDS	Other Leafy Veg.	Dry Chillies	Coke
Ragi	Linseed Oil – other	French Beans	Garlic	Firewood and Chips
Ragi Products	Refined Oil – PDS	Tomato	Tamarind	Electricity
Gram (whole grain)	Refined Oil – other	Peas	Ginger	Dung Cake
Gram Products	Palm Oil – PDS	Chili (green)	Curry Powder	Kerosene – PDS
Tapioca/Sago	Palm Oil – other	Capsicum	Other Spices	Kerosene – other
Tapioca (green)	Rapeseed Oil PDS	Plantain (green)	Tea, cups	Matches
Mahua	Rapeseed Oil – other	Jackfruit (green)	Tea, leaf	Coal – PDS
Jackfruit seed	Oil seeds	Lemon	Coffee, cups	Coal – other sources
Other Cereal Subs	Edible Oils (others)	Other Vegetables	Coffee, powder	Coal Gas
Arhar (tur) – PDS	Goat Meat	Banana	Ice	LPG
Arhar – other	Mutton	Jackfruit	Cold Beverage	Charcoal
Gram (split) – PDS	Beef	Water Melon	Fruit Juice, Shake	Other Lighting Oils
Gram (split) – other	Pork	Pineapple	Coconut, green	Candles
Moong – PDS	Buffalo Meat	Coconut	Other Beverages	Methylated Spirits
Moong – other	Other Meat	Guava	Biscuits & Confect	Gobar Gas
Masur – PDS	Chicken	Singara	Salted Refreshment	Other Fuel and
Masur – other	Other Birds	Orange, Mausami	Prepared Sweets	Light

Table A2 List of Commodities Excluded because of Lack of Quantity Data

Egg products	Salted refreshments	Dung cakes
Other fresh fruit	Prepared sweets	Gobar gas
Other beverages	Other processed food	Other fuel and light
Biscuits and confectionery	Other drugs and intoxicants	

Table A3 List of Commodities Excluded from 43rd Round Calculations

(in Addition to Those Listed in Table A2)

Other wheat products	Other dried fruit	Other oil for lighting
Ice-cream	Ice	LPG
Other milk products	Fruit juice/shakes	Candles
Other nuts	Other pan ingredients	Methylated spirits

Table A4 List of Commodities Excluded from 50th Round Calculations

(in Addition to Those Listed in Table A2)

Other cereal substitutes	Coconuts	Other pan ingredients
Other spices	Tea (cups)	Hookah tobacco
Ice-cream	Coffee powder	Opium
Other milk products	Ice	Toddy
Other birds	Cold drinks	Other oil for lighting
Other meat, eggs, and fish	Cakes and pastries	
Other nuts	Paan leaf	

Table A5 List of Commodities Excluded from 43rd and 50th Round Comparisons

(in Addition to the Union of Commodities Listed in Tables A4 and A5)

Goods whose units changed:	Goods whose units appear to have changed:
Lemons	Coal gas
Guavas	Cheroots
	Zarda, kimam and serti
	Other tobacco
	Ganja

17

Prices and Poverty in India, 1987–2000

Angus Deaton

INTRODUCTION

This paper uses the consumption data from the 43rd, 50th, and 55th Rounds of the Indian National Sample Survey to compute consumer price indexes. For each of the large Indian states, by urban and rural sectors separately, I calculate a range of price indexes for 1999/2000 relative to 1993/94, and for 1993/94 relative to 1987/88. In all three years, I also calculate price indexes for each state relative to all-India, again separately for urban and rural households, as well as price indexes of urban relative to rural prices for each of the states. I use the price indexes to calculate a new set of poverty lines, by state and sector, and over time, and calculate headcount ratios based on them. Finally, I use the procedures of Deaton (2003) to adjust the 55th Round poverty estimates for the fact that changes in questionnaire design make results from the 55th Round incomparable with those from earlier rounds. The final tables contain estimates of headcount ratios based on a consistent set of price indexes from the 43rd to the 55th Rounds as well as on consistent, or adjusted to be consistent, consumption data.

Because my calculated inflation rates are somewhat lower than those used by the Planning Commission, my rural poverty lines, which take the official rural poverty line in 1987/88 as base, are lower than the official ones in both the later periods, especially in 1999/2000. However, my adjustment to the poverty rates in the 55th Round, to account for the incomparability in survey design, offsets a good deal of this effect, so that my final all-India rural headcount ratio is only slightly lower than the official one, 25.3 per cent as opposed to 27 per cent. Note however that my estimates of the reduction in the headcount ratio from 1993/94 to 1999/2000 are a good deal smaller than the official estimates because much of the decline in the new estimates took place between 1987/88 and 1993/94, not in the 1990s. Note also that my urban poverty lines are on average only 15 per cent higher than my rural poverty lines as opposed to nearly 40 per cent in the official lines, so that because I start from the same *rural* estimates for 1987/88 as the Planning Commission, I estimate urban poverty in all years to be much lower. As argued in Deaton and Tarozzi (2000), the urban to rural price differentials that are implicit in the official lines are quite implausible, so that the estimates in this paper are to be preferred to the official counts. My price indexes for the states relative to the average are also different from the official ones, so that the distribution of poverty across states is different from the official distribution. Again, I would argue that my estimates are more rationally based. Nevertheless, all of my calculations, like the official ones, are based on the NSS household survey data and make no attempt to correct it for any of the deficiencies (other than change of reporting period) that have sometimes been levelled against it.

The main focus of this paper is to explain the methodology underlying the new price indexes, and to incorporate them into poverty lines. A fuller discussion of the results, not only of poverty headcount ratios, but of poverty gap measures and various inequality indexes, is given in Deaton and Dreze (2002).

PRICE INDEXES: METHODOLOGY

The procedures for calculating price indexes are described in full in Deaton and Tarozzi (2000). The NSS consumer expenditure surveys collect data on both expenditure and quantity purchased for a large number of food, beverage, tobacco (and other intoxicants) and fuel items. In the 55th Round, for example, there are 173 separate items for which both quantity and expenditure data were collected. This is somewhat less than in previous rounds; a few previously separate items were combined in order to shorten the consumption questionnaire. Unlike previous large consumption surveys in India, respondents were asked to report expenditures and quantities over both 30 and 7 days for all the items used here. Here, I use only the 30-day reports; preliminary work showed that the results based on the 7-day reports would not be much different. However, in order to protect against any possible systematic differences, I did not attempt to increase the sample by combining unit values obtained at both frequencies.

For each recorded purchase of each good, a unit value was calculated by dividing the reported expenditure by the reported quantity. These unit values were inspected for outliers and for multi-modality, the presence of which would suggest that the category contained several distinct goods with very different unit values. For example, 'other milk products' (as well as several other 'other' categories) was usually deleted because it contains cheap items (like panir or yoghurt) and expensive items (like milk based sweets). For each sector within each state, the median unit value was calculated for each good. As in the earlier work, a large fraction of these often assumed the same value. For example, in the 55th Round, of 1,879 recorded purchases of liquid milk in rural Kerala, 600 were at exactly Rs 12 per litre, and 669 were at exactly Rs 13 per litre.

For each household, the expenditure on each good was used to calculate a budget share by division by the household's total monthly expenditure. These household budget shares, including the zero budget shares, were then averaged by sector and state. Although these are not poverty weighted, the use of the average of the budget shares, rather than the budget shares of the averages, imparts a 'democratic' bias to the weights and locates them well down the income distribution. The average budget shares were then combined with the median unit values to calculate Laspeyres, Paasche, Fisher Ideal, and Törnqvist price indexes according to standard formulae. The Laspeyres index is calculated according to the formula

$$P_{10}^{\mathrm{L}} = \sum_{k=1}^{n} w_{0k} \left(\frac{P_{1k}}{P_{0k}} \right) \tag{1}$$

where w_{0k} is the average household budget share for good k in period 0, and P_{1k} and P_{0k} are its median unit value in periods 1 and 0. The Paasche index uses current, not base period weights, and can be written in the form

$$\left[P_{10}^{\mathrm{L}} \right]^{-1} = \sum_{k=1}^{n} w_{1k} \left(\frac{P_{1k}}{P_{0k}} \right)^{-1} \tag{2}$$

also involving price relatives and budget shares, this time period 1's budget shares. The Fisher Ideal index is the square root of the product of (the geometric mean) of the Paasche and the Laspeyres. The Törnqvist index, which is perhaps the least familiar, is a weighted geometric index of prices, using the average of the budget shares from the two periods as weights. Formally,

$$\ln P_{10}^{T} = \sum_{k=1}^{n} \frac{w_{1k} + w_{0k}}{2} \ln \left(\frac{P_{1k}}{P_{0k}} \right) \tag{3}$$

The Fisher Ideal and Törnqvist indexes are *superlative* indexes, and so are capable of approximating some of the substitution effects that separate a cost-of-living index from a 'basket' price index such as the Paasche or Laspeyres. Compared with the Laspeyres basis of most official price indexes, these indexes will tend to grow somewhat less rapidly. They are particularly useful for calculating price indexes for urban versus rural households, or for states versus all-India, when the budget shares in the two places in the comparison are often very different. Another issue relates to choice of base period. One possibility would have been to use the 43rd Round as base for all calculations. However, I chose instead to chain indexes, by using the 43rd Round as base for the 50th Round, and the 50th Round as base for the 55th Round, and then multiplying the indexes to calculate inflation rates from the 43rd to 55th. The price index literature suggests that chaining the indexes is likely to give a more accurate estimate of underlying price trends.

PRICE INDEXES: RESULTS

Table 17.1 shows price indexes for the 55th Round (1999/2000) with the 50th Round (1993/94) as base. The top panel shows the rural results by state, and for all-India, and the bottom panel the corresponding urban results. The first two columns show the percentage of the total budget accounted for by the totality of all the goods in the index in both rounds. These numbers are lower in the urban than in the rural sector, and lower in the 55th Round than in the 50th Round. Given that most of these goods are foods, such a result is to be expected from the operation of Engel's law given that the cities are better off than the countryside (and their inhabitants do less heavy manual labour) and given that real incomes have been growing between the two surveys. The effect also has the undesirable result that the price indexes calculated here are based on an ever smaller share of the total budget. The official price indexes have more comprehensive coverage, at least in principle, although in practice it is unclear how well the prices and budget shares of the other goods are captured. Table 17.2 shows the comparable results for the 50th Round with the 43rd Round (1987/88) as base.

In both Tables, for 1993/94 compared with 1987/88, and for 1999/2000 compared with 1993/94, the rural Laspeyres index calculated from the unit values shows somewhat less inflation than the price index implicit in the poverty lines. In the earlier period (Table 17.2) the rural Laspeyres calculated here is 171.7 compared with 178.7 in the official poverty lines. In the second period, the comparison is 156.4 to 159.1. The superlative indexes make the discrepancy somewhat larger, 169.8 versus 178.7 and 154.5 versus 159.1. For urban households by contrast, the Laspeyres index from the unit values is close to (or even a little larger than) the implicit price deflator for the poverty lines, though the superlative indexes, which make some allowance for substitution, are very close to the official indexes, somewhat less in the second period, and somewhat more in the first period.

As always, there is dispersion across the states. For example, it is not always true that the price indexes are always less than the indexes implicit in the poverty lines. Occasionally, the calculated index

Table 17.1 Price Indexes for 1999/2000 Relative to 1993/94

	Budget 50	Budget 55	Laspeyres	Paasche Index	Fisher Ideal	Törnqvist	PL Deflator
Rural							
Andhra Pradesh	64.1	60.7	159.6	155.3	157.4	157.3	161.3
Assam	69.6	64.8	161.4	156.5	158.9	159.4	157.5
Bihar	70.3	65.4	162.5	158.1	160.3	160.4	157.0
Gujarat	68.8	59.6	150.2	147.4	148.8	148.6	157.8
Haryana	63.4	57.1	151.8	147.9	149.9	149.8	155.2
Himachal Pradesh	64.4	54.4	164.3	159.7	161.9	161.9	157.2
Jammu & Kashmir	65.0	58.8	162.7	161.4	162.0	162.5	–
Karnataka	62.8	57.0	165.0	158.1	161.5	161.7	165.9
Kerala	57.8	49.0	165.5	162.3	163.9	163.7	153.7
Madhya Pradesh	64.3	58.6	159.5	156.1	157.8	157.8	161.2
Maharashtra	59.1	52.6	163.6	155.6	159.5	159.1	163.5
Orissa	68.4	63.1	175.2	166.1	170.6	171.4	166.9
Punjab	62.5	53.5	153.9	150.6	152.2	152.3	155.1
Rajasthan	65.4	59.8	165.6	162.9	164.2	164.3	159.4
Tamil Nadu	63.4	55.9	160.0	155.6	157.8	157.8	156.5
Uttar Pradesh	64.4	58.2	163.4	158.7	161.0	161.1	158.2
West Bengal	66.5	62.5	162.7	159.7	161.2	161.4	158.6
All-India	65.5	59.6	156.4	152.5	154.5	154.5	159.1
Urban							
Andhra Pradesh	56.6	48.9	163.4	161.2	162.3	161.9	164.4
Assam	57.1	52.5	161.3	157.1	159.2	158.3	161.9
Bihar	63.3	58.4	156.5	154.2	155.3	155.2	159.2
Gujarat	60.9	50.1	159.2	137.8	148.1	155.9	159.6
Haryana	56.6	46.8	152.9	151.0	151.9	151.8	162.7
Himachal Pradesh	56.6	44.8	158.8	147.8	153.2	154.3	165.7
Jammu & Kashmir	56.9	50.4	163.4	161.5	162.4	162.1	–
Karnataka	56.2	46.1	163.7	160.6	162.1	162.0	168.9
Kerala	52.4	45.5	165.6	162.9	164.3	164.4	170.1
Madhya Pradesh	57.1	50.0	153.4	151.2	152.3	151.9	151.9
Maharashtra	54.1	46.2	155.3	151.9	153.6	153.2	164.3
Orissa	56.4	54.1	158.1	156.7	157.4	157.4	158.6
Punjab	55.3	48.5	148.5	145.2	146.9	146.8	153.1
Rajasthan	59.0	51.6	159.0	153.8	156.4	158.0	165.9
Tamil Nadu	55.2	47.2	165.0	161.7	163.4	163.2	160.3
Uttar Pradesh	58.6	52.2	161.2	157.3	159.3	159.0	160.9
West Bengal	55.5	50.0	156.9	155.9	156.4	156.2	165.3
Delhi	53.6	41.9	165.8	158.1	161.9	161.9	163.3
All-India	57.8	50.3	162.0	155.7	158.8	157.7	161.4

Note: Budget 50 and Budget 55 are the total shares of the budget (in per cent) in the 50th and 55th Rounds respectively of all the goods covered by the index. Data for all-India are calculated from the complete survey, including those states and territories not listed separately. The final column is the implicit deflator of the official poverty lines.

Table 17.2 Price Indexes for 1993/94 Relative to 1987/88

	Budget 50	Budget 55	Laspeyres	Paasche Index	Fisher Ideal	Törnqvist	PL Deflator
Rural							
Andhra Pradesh	69.9	68.5	177.5	174.1	175.8	175.9	177.3
Assam	81.9	81.6	174.8	172.5	173.6	173.7	182.1
Bihar	79.0	76.3	161.3	158.1	159.7	159.7	176.3
Gujarat	78.5	71.1	175.2	166.1	170.6	170.6	175.7
Haryana	68.5	69.3	175.7	173.0	174.3	174.2	190.2
Himachal Pradesh	68.4	69.2	171.6	162.9	167.1	167.1	190.2
Jammu & Kashmir	68.7	67.8	184.9	178.4	181.6	181.5	–
Karnataka	73.2	62.1	175.8	174.5	175.1	175.1	178.7
Kerala	69.7	68.5	174.7	169.4	172.1	172.3	186.7
Madhya Pradesh	75.9	70.9	174.7	169.1	171.9	171.9	180.5
Maharashtra	71.8	61.1	174.1	171.3	172.7	172.6	168.6
Orissa	79.9	79.1	167.4	162.1	164.7	164.6	159.8
Punjab	66.7	68.2	192.6	188.6	190.6	190.7	190.2
Rajasthan	72.7	68.1	169.4	164.2	166.8	166.9	183.7
Tamil Nadu	73.4	69.0	169.4	165.9	167.6	167.7	166.2
Uttar Pradesh	69.8	68.9	170.3	165.5	167.9	167.9	185.9
West Bengal	79.6	75.5	167.6	165.4	166.5	166.5	170.8
All-India	74.6	70.7	171.7	167.9	169.8	169.8	178.7
Urban							
Andhra Pradesh	64.8	62.4	179.7	174.6	177.1	177.2	183.1
Assam	72.4	66.4	179.4	175.9	177.6	177.7	167.8
Bihar	73.1	71.0	165.9	164.3	165.1	165.2	158.7
Gujarat	70.4	65.3	169.2	161.7	165.4	165.4	171.6
Haryana	68.5	60.5	178.6	176.7	177.6	177.6	180.3
Himachal Pradesh	62.1	58.7	179.7	170.8	175.2	175.2	176.0
Jammu & Kashmir	66.8	59.5	185.8	171.7	178.6	178.5	–
Karnataka	67.7	60.6	179.5	174.6	177.0	177.1	176.9
Kerala	69.0	63.4	175.5	171.2	173.3	173.5	171.8
Madhya Pradesh	72.2	63.9	173.5	168.2	170.8	170.9	177.8
Maharashtra	65.4	59.0	183.4	178.5	180.9	181.1	173.7
Orissa	70.7	66.6	169.1	166.5	167.8	167.8	180.3
Punjab	62.5	60.9	188.6	185.4	187.0	187.1	174.9
Rajasthan	67.1	64.5	173.7	169.9	171.8	171.8	169.8
Tamil Nadu	62.9	62.9	172.4	168.3	170.3	170.5	178.9
Uttar Pradesh	67.2	64.7	166.5	164.2	165.4	165.4	167.8
West Bengal	68.4	65.3	172.4	168.8	170.6	170.6	165.1
Delhi	55.8	56.9	180.1	170.5	175.2	175.7	174.9
All-India	67.6	63.4	175.1	172.3	173.7	173.8	173.5

Note: Budget 43 and Budget 50 are the total shares of the budget (in per cent) in the 43rd and 50th Rounds respectively of all the goods covered by the index. Data for all-India are calculated from the complete survey, including those states and territories not listed separately. We do not have data for the CPIAL for Haryana nor for Jammu & Kashmir, nor the CPIIW for Jammu & Kashmir. The final column is the implicit deflator of the official poverty lines.

is considerably less than the official deflator; for example, for the later period the Törnqvist index for rural Gujarat is 148.6 compared with the official index of 157.8. In spite of these differences, the cross-state correlation between the official and calculated (Törnqvist) index in Table 17.1 is 0.43 for rural households and 0.62 for urban households.

Table 17.3 shows, for all three rounds, the urban relative to rural price indexes for each state and for all-India. Here there is a good deal of consistency over time. In particular, the all-India ratio is 115.1 in 1999/2000, compared with 115.6 in 1993/94, and 111.5 in 1987/88. It is worth noting that the 15 per cent price difference between urban and rural is exactly the amount that was for many years incorporated into the poverty lines, until the 1993 Expert Group Report recommended separate rates for each state. As in previous rounds, the urban to rural price differentials are quite different from those that are implicit in the official poverty lines. In 1999/2000, the interstate correlation coefficient between the two sets of prices is only 0.24. In some cases, such as Andhra Pradesh, Karnataka and Maharashtra, the deflators implicit in the official poverty lines defy belief. Note that these implicit differentials were not explicitly set by the Expert Group who calculated separate urban and rural poverty lines (based on studies of interstate price differentials) and did not explicitly consider the urban to rural differentials that were embodied in them. Whatever their intent, the effect of the adoption of the Expert Group lines was to raise measured poverty in urban relative to rural areas. In 1999/2000, the urban to rural differential implicit in the official lines is 38.6 per cent, compared with 15.1 per cent in the unit values, and 15 per cent in the official lines prior to the adoption of the Expert Group lines. As I shall discuss in Section entitled 'Price Indexes: Results', it is the treatment of the urban-rural price difference that makes the biggest difference between the official poverty estimates and those presented in this chapter.

Table 17.3 Price Indexes for Urban Relative to Rural 43rd, 50th and 55th Rounds

	Budget Urban	Budget Rural	Laspeyres Index	Paasche Index	Fisher Ideal Index	Törnqvist Index	PL Deflator
43rd Round							
Andhra Pradesh	68.8	74.7	111.8	109.5	110.6	110.7	165.2
Assam	75.0	83.5	109.1	107.0	108.1	108.0	99.3
Bihar	75.5	80.4	108.5	107.7	108.1	108.1	124.8
Gujarat	72.7	80.0	106.3	104.5	105.4	105.4	150.6
Haryana	71.5	69.4	114.1	110.3	112.2	112.1	116.5
Himachal Pradesh	66.5	67.8	111.6	96.1	103.6	104.8	117.2
Jammu & Kashmir	72.5	72.5	104.6	102.8	103.7	103.8	119.3
Karnataka	71.4	77.2	110.4	108.9	109.6	110.0	163.9
Kerala	73.0	74.4	103.7	103.4	103.5	103.5	125.0
Madhya Pradesh	74.2	76.6	116.9	109.4	113.1	113.0	166.7
Maharashtra	69.1	73.8	114.9	113.1	114.0	114.1	163.6
Orissa	73.5	81.2	112.9	107.6	110.2	110.2	136.2
Punjab	64.7	68.6	115.6	110.8	113.2	113.2	118.0
Rajasthan	70.2	74.3	108.2	105.3	106.7	106.7	140.7
Tamil Nadu	68.8	79.3	109.7	108.4	109.0	109.0	140.3
Uttar Pradesh	69.7	71.8	120.0	116.1	118.1	118.1	134.6
West Bengal	71.9	81.8	112.9	112.4	112.6	112.7	116.1
All-India	70.9	77.1	113.1	109.8	111.4	111.4	140.8

(Contd...)

(Contd...)

	Budget Urban	Budget Rural	Laspeyres Index	Paasche Index	Fisher Ideal Index	Törnqvist Index	PL Deflator
50th Round							
Andhra Pradesh	63.4	69.6	111.8	109.3	110.5	110.5	170.6
Assam	68.3	80.9	113.6	109.1	111.3	111.6	91.5
Bihar	71.7	77.0	112.6	112.3	112.5	112.5	112.4
Gujarat	67.6	74.6	106.9	103.4	105.1	105.2	147.1
Haryana	62.3	69.1	119.2	112.0	115.5	115.6	110.5
Himachal Pradesh	61.4	66.8	110.9	104.5	107.7	108.1	108.5
Jammu & Kashmir	58.2	67.1	109.2	104.9	107.0	107.0	na
Karnataka	64.3	69.1	111.3	109.9	110.6	110.6	115.1
Kerala	64.0	68.6	104.7	103.7	104.2	104.2	164.2
Madhya Pradesh	65.1	73.3	118.7	113.1	115.8	115.8	168.5
Maharashtra	61.7	67.4	121.2	115.4	118.3	118.2	153.7
Orissa	66.4	77.9	111.9	108.9	110.4	110.5	108.5
Punjab	62.8	68.5	116.3	112.0	114.1	114.2	130.1
Rajasthan	64.9	72.6	113.2	109.1	111.1	111.3	150.9
Tamil Nadu	63.3	70.1	111.0	108.5	109.8	109.7	121.4
Uttar Pradesh	66.2	69.2	118.3	114.5	116.4	116.5	112.1
West Bengal	65.3	75.4	119.6	115	117.3	117.5	112.1
All-India	65.8	73.7	117.5	113.7	115.6	115.6	136.7
55th Round							
Andhra Pradesh	52.6	62.8	111.9	110.7	111.3	111.3	174.0
Assam	60.2	69.6	112.4	110.7	111.5	111.5	94.1
Bihar	61.4	66.3	108.9	107.7	108.3	108.3	114.0
Gujarat	52.0	56.1	110.5	108.9	109.7	109.5	148.7
Haryana	47.7	57.4	117.8	112.5	115.2	115.3	115.8
Himachal Pradesh	48.1	54.5	109.2	91.7	100.1	104.5	114.4
Jammu & Kashmir	56.4	62.5	106.2	102.7	104.5	104.7	na
Karnataka	49.3	58.3	115.8	112.4	114.1	113.8	165.2
Kerala	53.5	56.7	103.5	103.1	103.3	103.3	127.3
Madhya Pradesh	53.0	59.5	112.6	109.6	111.1	111.2	154.7
Maharashtra	50.3	54.4	121.8	119.3	120.5	120.5	169.4
Orissa	59.4	65.4	104.2	103.8	104.0	104.0	146.1
Punjab	49.7	53.9	111.8	109.7	110.7	110.8	107.0
Rajasthan	53.8	55.9	110.2	107.6	108.9	109.0	135.4
Tamil Nadu	52.5	60.5	109.3	108.4	108.8	108.8	154.6
Uttar Pradesh	55.1	59.8	115.2	113.1	114.1	114.2	123.6
West Bengal	56.7	68.8	113.2	110.5	111.8	112.0	116.9
All-India	53.2	61.1	115.9	114.0	115.0	115.1	138.6

The urban to rural price differences vary from one state to another, although the interstate patterns show some persistence over time. Using the Törnqvist price index, the 55th Round differentials have an interstate correlation coefficient with the 50th Round differentials of 0.75, falling to 0.70 with the 43rd

Round differentials. This is what we might expect. The ratios do not change rapidly, but nor are they fixed in stone, so that the further apart are the comparisons, the lower the correlations.

Tables 17.4A–C present the price indexes comparing the prices in each state to those for the country as a whole. These are the most difficult of the price indexes to estimate because consumption patterns vary greatly across the subcontinent, and when different people consume very different goods, there is little basis for a price index that compares between them. In the calculations, this shows up in relatively large differences between the Paasche and Laspeyres indexes, and in rather smaller differences between the two superlative indexes. Although there is a great deal of spatial variation in prices across India, when all prices are combined into an index, the spatial differences are relatively modest. In the 55th Round, rural Maharashtra has the highest prices relative to the country as a whole, 123.2, and rural Uttar Pradesh, at 92.4, has the lowest. As might be expected, the interstate variations are somewhat lower in urban areas, ranging from highs of 114.7 in Delhi and 109.6 in Maharashtra to a low of 88.6 in Orissa. Once again, the interstate patterns are persistent over time; the correlations of the 55th Round with the 50th and 43rd Rounds are 0.82 and 0.65 for the rural sector, and 0.84 and 0.59 in the urban sector. Once again, it is reasonable for these patterns to remain constant over short periods of time, but not over long periods. Indeed, these results serve as a warning against the official lines which, on the Expert Group recommendation, embody fixed interstate price differentials based on long outdated studies. Even so, there is still some correlation across the states between the official deflators and those shown in the table, 0.45 for the rural sector and 0.33 for the urban sector.

POVERTY ESTIMATES: METHODS AND RESULTS

Tables 17.5 and 17.6 present my recalculations of headcount ratios using the price indexes of Tables 17.1 through 17.4. The results update those presented in Table 17.10 of Deaton and Tarozzi (2000), and were obtained using the same procedures, as follows. The starting point is the official rural all-India poverty line for the 43rd Round, 1987/88. This is Rs 115.70 per head for 30 days. Rural poverty lines for each state are obtained by multiplying this base poverty line by the rural price indexes for each state relative to all-India. Finally, the urban poverty lines, for each state as well as for all-India, are calculated from the rural poverty lines by scaling up by the respective urban relative to rural price indexes. In all cases, I use the relevant Törnqvist price indexes. The case of Delhi is handled differently. Because there are few sample households in rural Delhi, it is not advisable to use the price index for rural Delhi as part of the calculations. The poverty line for urban Delhi is calculated from the all-India urban poverty line by multiplying it by the price index for urban Delhi relative to urban all-India.

To move to the 50th Round, the all-India rural line of Rs 115.70 is scaled up by the Törnqvist index for all-India rural for the 50th Round relative to the 43rd Round, 1.698 (Table 17.2, Column 6), to give an all-India rural poverty line for the 50th Round. This number is then used to generate an all-India urban poverty line, and state urban and rural poverty lines, following exactly the same procedure as for the 43rd Round. Finally, poverty lines for the 55th Round are calculated in the same way from an all-India rural line, which is the 50th Round all-India rural line scaled up by the inflation rate between the two surveys, 1.545, see Table 17.1, Column 6.

Table 17.5 shows some of the results. Columns 1 through 4 show the official calculations; the 55th Round official poverty lines are followed by the official headcount ratios for the 43rd, 50th, and 55th Rounds. (These have been recalculated for this paper from the unit-record data and differ somewhat from the headcount ratios published by the Planning Commission, which come from extrapolation from

Table 17.4A Price Indexes for States Relative to All-India, 55th Round, 1999/2000

	Share of Budget	Laspeyres Index	Paasche Index	Fisher Ideal Index	Törnqvist Index	Poverty Lines Implicit
Rural						
Andhra Pradesh	64.1	106.8	98.5	102.6	102.0	80.3
Assam	71.1	116.3	107.7	111.9	112.0	111.6
Bihar	67.6	99.5	96.5	98.0	97.8	101.7
Gujarat	63.4	113.2	109.1	111.1	111.1	97.4
Haryana	58.5	107.7	98.2	102.8	102.4	110.8
Himachal Pradesh	59.9	121.4	116.0	118.7	119.0	112.2
Jammu & Kashmir	65.0	117.3	111.1	114.2	114.7	na
Karnataka	62.1	108.7	104.0	106.4	106.3	94.5
Kerala	57.2	130.6	113.0	121.5	123.2	114.4
Madhya Pradesh	62.1	96.5	94.0	95.2	95.2	95.0
Maharashtra	57.7	107.9	102.8	105.3	105.4	97.3
Orissa	66.9	101.5	97.0	99.2	99.0	98.9
Punjab	55.3	111.6	98.6	104.9	104.3	110.7
Rajasthan	62.6	116.9	99.7	108.0	106.7	105.0
Tamil Nadu	61.6	117.4	106.1	111.6	110.9	93.9
Uttar Pradesh	60.8	94.9	90.6	92.7	92.4	102.8
West Bengal	69.0	103.9	99.0	101.4	101.1	106.9
All-India	59.8*	100.0	100.0	100.0	100.0	100.0
Urban						
Andhra Pradesh	53.2	101.6	94.7	98.1	97.7	100.7
Assam	60.5	110.8	105.0	107.9	107.9	75.8
Bihar	62.1	93.1	89.6	91.3	91.4	83.6
Gujarat	53.9	109.7	104.8	107.2	107.4	104.5
Haryana	49.3	100.7	100.1	100.4	100.5	92.5
Himachal Pradesh	50.1	109.7	95.2	102.2	104.3	92.5
Jammu & Kashmir	58.2	106.8	105.8	106.3	107.0	na
Karnataka	50.7	105.6	101.4	103.5	103.5	112.6
Kerala	54.2	113.6	102.6	107.9	108.5	105.1
Madhya Pradesh	54.1	94.1	91.4	92.8	92.7	106.1
Maharashtra	51.4	111.1	108.2	109.7	109.6	118.9
Orissa	60.5	91.2	86.2	88.6	88.6	104.2
Punjab	51.0	98.5	96.1	97.3	97.3	85.5
Rajasthan	55.3	102.6	96.5	99.5	99.1	102.6
Tamil Nadu	52.7	110.3	100.5	105.3	104.6	104.7
Uttar Pradesh	55.9	97.2	91.9	94.5	94.3	91.7
West Bengal	57.5	101.1	95.9	98.5	98.4	90.1
Delhi	47.1	117.7	111.7	114.6	114.7	111.3
All-India	52.0*	100.0	100.0	100.0	100.0	100.0

Note: * Indicates the average over all the states.

Table 17.4B Price Indexes for States Relative to All-India, 50th Round, 1994/94

	Share of Budget	Laspeyres Index	Paasche Index	Fisher Ideal Index	Törnqvist Index	Poverty Lines Implicit
Rural						
Andhra Pradesh	71.1	104.8	93.5	99.0	97.9	79.2
Assam	81.9	114.4	104.6	109.4	109.3	112.7
Bihar	77.4	98.9	96.9	97.9	98.1	103.1
Gujarat	75.4	118.7	114.5	116.6	116.5	98.2
Haryana	69.7	107.2	99.8	103.4	103.3	113.6
Himachal Pradesh	74.2	107.4	101.6	104.5	104.5	113.6
Jammu & Kashmir	71.1	105.9	102.2	104.0	104.1	–
Karnataka	72.8	105.7	101.7	103.7	103.5	90.7
Kerala	68.7	119.5	105.7	112.4	112.7	118.5
Madhya Pradesh	74.2	95.6	93.0	94.3	94.2	93.8
Maharashtra	69.5	110.0	100.7	105.2	105.7	94.7
Orissa	80.0	99.0	87.4	93.0	92.8	94.3
Punjab	68.9	109.9	101.1	105.4	105.0	113.6
Rajasthan	73.3	112.2	100.7	106.3	105.5	104.9
Tamil Nadu	70.8	114.1	102.0	107.9	107.0	95.5
Uttar Pradesh	70.0	94.8	89.4	92.1	91.8	103.5
West Bengal	75.6	99.7	94.2	96.9	96.6	107.2
All-India	66.9*	100.0	100.0	100.0	100.0	100.0
Urban						
Andhra Pradesh	63.6	98.0	90.9	94.4	94.0	98.9
Assam	68.6	109.1	102.4	105.7	105.9	75.5
Bihar	72.0	98.1	93.4	95.8	95.7	84.8
Gujarat	68.2	105.8	104.6	105.2	105.2	105.6
Haryana	63.0	101.6	100.1	100.9	100.9	91.8
Himachal Pradesh	61.7	101.4	97.3	99.4	99.3	90.1
Jammu & Kashmir	62.3	97.3	94.3	95.8	95.7	–
Karnataka	64.4	101.4	98.0	99.7	99.4	107.7
Kerala	64.1	106.8	94.9	100.7	100.5	99.7
Madhya Pradesh	65.6	95.6	94.0	94.8	94.8	112.7
Maharashtra	62.2	112.2	108.9	110.6	110.6	116.8
Orissa	67.7	93.8	87.1	90.4	90.6	106.0
Punjab	63.2	103.2	100.4	101.8	101.7	90.1
Rajasthan	65.6	104.9	95.8	100.2	99.7	99.8
Tamil Nadu	63.5	105.1	97.1	101.0	100.4	105.4
Uttar Pradesh	66.3	96.8	91.9	94.3	94.1	91.9
West Bengal	65.6	103.2	97.5	100.3	100.0	88.0
Delhi	58.6	109.3	103.4	106.3	106.3	110.0
All-India	60.5*	100.0	100.0	100.0	100.0	100.0

Note: * Indicates the average over all the states.

Table 17.4C Price Indexes for States Relative to All-India, 43rd Round, 1987/88

	Share of Budget	Laspeyres Index	Paasche Index	Fisher Ideal Index	Törnqvist Index	Poverty Lines Implicit
Rural						
Andhra Pradesh	75.5	98.3	90.9	94.6	94.0	79.8
Assam	84.3	108.1	104.2	106.1	106.7	110.6
Bihar	81.2	104.4	104.5	104.5	104.6	104.5
Gujarat	80.4	111.3	110.0	110.5	110.5	99.8
Haryana	70.4	104.0	94.7	99.3	98.9	106.7
Himachal Pradesh	70.8	103.9	100.0	101.9	101.6	106.7
Jammu & Kashmir	73.7	97.9	92.9	95.4	95.1	107.9
Karnataka	77.6	102.6	97.1	99.8	99.3	90.7
Kerala	74.7	111.5	99.2	105.2	104.9	113.4
Madhya Pradesh	77.8	96.6	92.9	94.8	94.2	92.9
Maharashtra	74.5	105.2	102.7	103.9	103.8	100.4
Orissa	82.4	99.1	94.3	96.7	96.6	105.4
Punjab	68.8	100.2	88.8	94.3	94.2	106.7
Rajasthan	75.3	112.2	97.7	104.7	103.9	102.0
Tamil Nadu	79.6	109.4	102.9	106.1	105.5	102.6
Uttar Pradesh	72.0	94.6	88.2	91.3	91.4	99.5
West Bengal	82.1	100.2	98.3	99.2	99.2	112.2
All-India	71.0*	100.0	100.0	100.0	100.0	100.0
Urban						
Andhra Pradesh	69.0	96.8	91.4	94.1	94.0	93.6
Assam	75.0	104.4	101.0	102.7	103.0	78.1
Bihar	75.7	102.6	98.7	100.6	100.5	92.7
Gujarat	73.3	112.0	107.9	110.0	109.5	106.8
Haryana	71.7	102.8	100.3	101.6	101.5	88.3
Himachal Pradesh	66.7	101.0	94.9	97.9	98.2	88.8
Jammu & Kashmir	72.6	94.9	90.3	92.6	92.2	91.5
Karnataka	71.6	99.6	96.8	98.2	98.2	105.6
Kerala	73.1	103.0	92.4	97.5	97.6	100.7
Madhya Pradesh	75.6	100.4	96.6	98.5	98.2	110.0
Maharashtra	69.4	109.1	106.6	107.9	107.8	116.7
Orissa	74.0	96.3	91.5	93.8	94.0	102.0
Punjab	64.9	99.3	94.7	97.0	96.6	89.4
Rajasthan	70.5	106.8	97.5	102.1	101.5	102.0
Tamil Nadu	68.9	102.0	99.8	100.9	100.8	102.2
Uttar Pradesh	69.8	102.0	96.3	99.1	98.8	95.1
West Bengal	72.2	102.8	98.4	100.6	100.1	92.5
Delhi	60.2	105.1	102.2	103.7	102.8	109.1
All-India	66.5*	100.0	100.0	100.0	100.0	100.0

Note: * Indicates the average over all the states. The implicit Expert Group price index is obtained from Table 4.1 of the Expert Group report by dividing the state poverty lines by the all-India poverty lines.

Table 17.5 Poverty Lines for the 55th Round and Headcount Ratios, 43rd through 55th Rounds

	Official: Planning Commission				Recalculated using New Prices			
	PL_{55}	HCR_{43}	HCR_{50}	HCR_{55}	PL_{55}	HCR_{43}	HCR_{50}	HCR_{55}
Rural								
Andhra Pradesh	262.94	21.0	15.9	10.5	309.62	35.0	29.2	22.3
Assam	365.43	39.4	45.2	40.3	339.94	36.1	35.4	31.8
Bihar	333.07	53.9	58.0	44.0	296.87	54.6	48.6	30.4
Gujarat	318.94	28.6	22.2	12.4	337.32	39.4	32.5	16.0
Haryana	362.81	15.3	28.3	7.4	310.77	13.6	17.0	3.4
Himachal Pradesh	367.45	16.7	30.4	7.5	361.34	13.3	17.1	6.7
Karnataka	309.59	32.6	30.1	16.8	322.60	40.8	37.9	20.5
Kerala	374.79	29.5	25.4	9.4	373.94	23.8	19.5	9.2
Madhya Pradesh	311.34	42.0	40.7	37.3	288.89	43.7	36.7	30.1
Maharashtra	318.63	41.0	37.9	23.2	319.85	44.3	42.9	23.5
Orissa	323.92	58.7	49.8	47.8	300.34	50.4	43.5	40.0
Punjab	362.68	12.8	11.7	6.0	316.49	6.6	6.2	2.7
Rajasthan	344.03	33.3	26.4	13.5	323.92	35.3	23.0	10.3
Tamil Nadu	307.64	46.3	33.0	20.0	336.52	49.0	38.5	27.7
Uttar Pradesh	336.88	41.9	42.3	31.1	280.49	34.9	28.7	15.7
West Bengal	350.17	48.8	41.2	31.7	306.84	36.3	25.1	21.4
All-India	327.56	39.4	37.1	27.0	303.52	39.0	32.9	21.6
Urban								
Andhra Pradesh	457.40	41.1	38.8	27.2	344.76	23.4	17.8	9.4
Assam	343.99	11.3	7.9	7.5	378.99	13.6	13.0	10.7
Bihar	379.78	51.9	34.8	33.5	321.64	38.1	26.7	18.0
Gujarat	474.41	38.5	28.3	14.8	369.36	16.4	14.7	4.0
Haryana	420.20	18.4	16.5	10.0	358.38	11.8	10.6	4.8
Himachal Pradesh	420.20	7.2	9.3	4.6	377.65	1.7	3.6	2.2
Karnataka	511.44	49.2	39.9	24.6	367.22	26.0	21.4	8.5
Kerala	477.06	39.8	24.3	19.8	386.23	21.0	13.9	8.7
Madhya Pradesh	481.65	47.3	48.1	38.5	321.29	20.7	18.5	10.7
Maharashtra	539.71	40.3	35.0	26.7	385.36	21.2	18.2	10.6
Orissa	473.12	42.6	40.6	43.5	312.34	20.8	15.2	13.3
Punjab	388.15	13.7	10.9	5.5	350.53	6.6	7.8	2.9
Rajasthan	465.92	37.9	31.0	19.4	353.15	19.8	18.3	6.1
Tamil Nadu	475.60	40.2	39.9	22.5	366.08	26.2	20.9	9.0
Uttar Pradesh	416.29	44.9	35.1	30.8	320.42	29.3	21.7	13.5
West Bengal	409.22	33.7	23.0	14.7	343.51	22.3	15.5	6.8
Delhi	505.45	15.1	16.1	9.2	400.43	4.7	8.8	3.2
All-India	454.11	39.1	33.2	23.5	349.22	22.8	18.1	9.5

Table 17.6 Headcount Ratios with Adjustment for 55th Round Expenditure Overstatement

	HCR_{43}	HCR_{50}	HCR_{55}	Change 43–50	Change 50–55	Change 43–55
Rural						
Andhra Pradesh	35.0	29.2	27.9	−5.8	−1.3	−7.1
Assam	36.1	35.4	35.7	−0.7	0.3	−0.4
Bihar	54.6	48.6	39.3	−6.0	−9.3	−15.3
Gujarat	39.4	32.5	20.4	−7.0	−12.1	−19.1
Haryana	13.6	17.0	6.5	3.4	−10.5	−7.1
Himachal Pradesh	13.3	17.1	12.5	−3.9	−4.6	−0.7
Karnataka	40.8	37.9	30.3	−2.9	−7.6	−10.5
Kerala	23.8	19.5	11.6	−4.3	−7.9	−12.2
Madhya Pradesh	43.7	36.7	31.2	−7.1	−5.5	−12.6
Maharashtra	44.3	42.9	30.8	−1.4	−12.1	−13.5
Orissa	50.4	43.5	41.3	−6.9	−2.2	−9.1
Punjab	6.6	6.2	2.8	−0.5	−3.4	−3.9
Rajasthan	35.3	23.0	16.2	−12.3	−6.8	−19.1
Tamil Nadu	49.0	38.5	25.6	−10.6	−12.9	−23.5
Uttar Pradesh	34.9	28.7	20.8	−6.3	−7.9	14.2
West Bengal	36.3	25.1	22.7	−11.2	−2.4	−13.6
All-India	39.0	32.9	25.3	−6.0	−7.6	−13.6
Urban						
Andhra Pradesh	23.4	17.8	11.3	−5.7	−6.5	−12.2
Assam	13.6	13.0	12.1	−0.6	−0.9	−1.5
Bihar	38.1	26.7	23.5	−11.5	−3.2	−14.7
Gujarat	16.4	14.7	6.6	−1.7	−8.1	−9.8
Haryana	11.8	10.6	5.1	−1.2	−5.5	−6.7
Himachal Pradesh	1.7	3.6	1.7	2.0	−1.9	0.1
Karnataka	26.0	21.4	11.5	−4.5	−9.9	−14.4
Kerala	21.0	13.9	10.5	−7.1	−3.4	−10.5
Madhya Pradesh	20.7	18.5	14.1	−2.2	−4.4	−6.6
Maharashtra	21.2	18.2	13.0	−2.9	−5.2	−8.1
Orissa	20.8	15.2	15.6	−5.6	0.4	−5.2
Punjab	6.6	7.8	4.0	1.2	−3.8	−2.6
Rajasthan	19.8	18.3	10.6	−1.5	−7.7	−9.2
Tamil Nadu	26.2	20.9	11.1	−5.3	−9.8	−15.1
Uttar Pradesh	29.3	21.7	16.5	−7.6	−5.2	−12.8
West Bengal	22.3	15.5	11.4	−6.7	−4.2	−10.9
Delhi	4.7	8.8	2.7	4.1	−6.1	−2.0
All-India	22.8	18.1	12.5	−4.7	−5.6	−10.3

published tables.) Column 5 shows the 55th Round poverty lines calculated as detailed in the previous paragraph. Because my deflators show less inflation than the official ones, the rural lines are lower than the official ones, at least on average, if not for every state. The urban lines, of course, are much lower than the official ones, because they incorporate the much lower (and much more reasonable) urban to rural price differentials.

My rural headcount ratio for the 43rd Round is, by construction, essentially the same as the official rural headcount ratio; this is because my calculations are based on the official all-India rural poverty line for the 43rd Round. In subsequent rounds, my all-India rural poverty lines diverge from the official ones to the extent of the cumulative divergence of my price indexes relative to the official ones. In consequence, the associated headcount ratios show a more rapid decline in poverty rates, by 1 percentage point a year from 1987/88 to 1993/94, and by 1.9 percentage points a year from 1993/94 to 1999/2000. Because the all-India urban price indexes grow at much the same rate as the official implicit deflators of the all-India urban poverty lines, the two sets of urban nominal poverty lines grow in parallel. The difference in their levels, and thus in the two sets of all-India urban poverty rates in the last row of Table 17.5, is driven by the fact that the price indexes from the unit values show only a 15 per cent difference between urban and rural prices, compared with the much larger differential in the official lines. By 1999/2000, the all-India urban headcount ratio in Table 17.5 is only 9.5 per cent. The headcount ratio fell by 0.8 percentage points a year from 1987/88 to 1993/94, and by 1.4 percentage points a year from 1993/2000.

The headcount ratios in Table 17.5, like the official ones, take no account of the fact that the 55th Round survey was carried out in a way that was not comparable with the surveys for the 43rd and 50th Rounds. In particular, respondents in the 55th Round were asked to report their expenditures on food, beverages, and intoxicants over *both* the last 30 days and the last 7 days, while for low frequency items, including durables and clothing, the response period was changed from 30 days in the earlier surveys to 365 days in the 55th Round. Experimental surveys in the 51st through 54th Rounds showed that changes in the reporting period can have substantial effects on the amounts reported, and very large effects on the headcount ratios. In particular, the 7-day reporting period for the high frequency items generates larger reported expenditures than does the 30-day period, at least when households are randomly allocated to one or the other. Because respondents were given both questionnaires in the 55th Round, we have no direct prior experience to tell us how responses were affected. Even so, a reasonable supposition is that, by being asked to report for both reporting periods side by side, respondents were unlikely to report wildly inconsistent patterns. If so, the presence of the 7-day questions, which tend to lead to higher reports, might have caused respondents to shade upwards their 30-day reports, thus overstating their total expenditures compared with what they would have reported given the questionnaires used in the 43rd and 50th Rounds. The move to 365 days for the low frequency items, although lowering the average amount reported, caused a much larger number of households to report something. These additional reports caused the bottom tail of the expenditure distribution to be pulled up compared with earlier rounds (Sundaram and Tendulkar, 2003). It is therefore likely that both changes to the questionnaire had the effect of increasing reported expenditures among the poor, so that the official headcount ratios, which use the 30-day reporting period for all but the low frequency items, which are reported at 365 days, are too low compared with earlier rounds. The existence and extent of this bias have been the subject of a good deal of debate.

In Deaton (2003), I show how it is possible to adjust the 55th Round figures to make them comparable with the earlier rounds. The method relies on the fact that, in all rounds, there is an important group of goods, including fuel and light and a long list of miscellaneous goods and services, the questionnaire for which is the same in all rounds. Expenditure on these items is highly correlated with total expenditures, and so can be used to develop an estimate of the headcount ratio that is, in principle, comparable with those from the earlier rounds. Assumptions are required to make this possible, and while they are plausible, there is no guarantee that they hold; given that the questions were asked differently, there is no assumption-free method of recovering what would have happened had the survey been run in the traditional manner! The most important assumption is that the probability of being poor, conditional on reported expenditures on the items collected in the same way, remains the same in the 55th Round as it was in the 50th Round. Some evidence for the validity of this assumption is presented in my earlier paper.

Table 17.6 presents the results of making the adjustments using the formulae in Deaton (2001), but with the poverty lines and price indexes of this paper in place of the official ones. The first two columns repeat the headcount ratios from the 43rd and 50th Rounds from Table 17.5. These need no adjustment. Column 3 then shows my 'final' estimate of the headcount ratios from the 55th Round. These estimates include both sets of adjustments, for potential overestimation of total per capita expenditures in the survey, as well as for the recalculated price indexes. The last three columns are based on the first three and show the changes in the headcount ratios from 1987/88 to 1993/94, from 1993/94 to 1999/2000, and over the whole period. The effect of the adjustment for the questionnaire design is typically to raise the headcount ratios for the 55th Round compared with the unadjusted figures in the last column of Table 17.5. About three quarters (rural) and two-thirds (urban) of the reduction in poverty from the unadjusted figures survives the adjustment. In the final analysis, I estimate that rural poverty fell by 1.3 percentage points a year from 1993/94 to 1999/2000, while the corresponding figure for the urban sector is 0.9 per cent points a year. Even with the adjustment, there has been very substantial poverty reduction in India in the 1990s.

As always, there is a good deal of difference in rates of poverty across the different states. There are two patterns that are particularly notable. The first is the widely noted superior performance of the southern and western states relative to those in the north and east. In rural Tamil Nadu, for example, nearly half of the population lived below the poverty line in 1987/88; 12 years later, it was only a quarter. What is more surprising, although it appears to a lesser extent in the official figures, is the large estimates of poverty reduction in some of the poorest states. There was a 15.3 percentage point reduction in the headcount ratio in rural Bihar between 1987/88 and 1999/2000, of which 9.3 percentage points took place between 1993/94 and 1999/2000. The corresponding figures for rural Rajasthan are 19.1 and 6.8 percentage points, and for rural Uttar Pradesh 14.2 and 7.9 per cent. A good deal of this mild convergence in headcount rates is a largely automatic consequence of the fact that, in states with high headcount rates, there is a relatively large fraction of the population near the poverty line, so that even modest growth is capable of having a large effect on the fraction in poverty. As explained in some detail in Deaton and Dreze (2002), the overall picture between the 50th and 55th Rounds is one of divergence and increasing inequality, between the more successful states in the south and west, between rural and urban sectors of each state, and within the urban sectors of many states.

ACKNOWLEDGEMENT

We wish to acknowledge the assistance of India's National Sample Survey Organisation, especially the late Pravin Vasaria and S.S. Shukla for providing the data as well as documentation and help on their use. We thank Shawna Samuel for assistance with the calculations. We would also like to acknowledge comments and assistance by Montek Ahluwalia, Pronab Sen and particularly K.L. Datta whose detailed comments led to great improvements and closer consistency with the official calculations. We also thank Surjit Bhalla, Anne Case, Gaurav Datt, Jean Dreze, Valerie Kozel, Rakesh Mohan, Martin Ravallion and Salman Zaidi for their assistance and comments.

This chapter is a revised version of the paper 'Computing Prices and Poverty Rates in India, 1999/2000', and also incorporates some of the tables from my joint paper with Alessandro Tarozzi 'Prices and Poverty in India'.

REFERENCES

Deaton, Angus (2003): 'Adjusted Indian Poverty Estimates for 1999/2000', Economic and Political Weekly, 25 January, pp. 322–26, (Chapter 12 of this book).

Deaton, Angus and Jean Dreze (2002): 'Poverty and Inequality in India: A Re-examination', *Economic and Political Weekly*, 7 September, pp. 3730–48, (Chapter 18 of this book).

Deaton, Angus and Alessandro Tarozzi (2000): 'Prices and Poverty in India', Research Program in Development Studies, processed, 29 July, Princeton, NJ, (Chapter 16 of this book).

Sundaram, K and Suresh D Tendulkar (2003): 'Poverty Has Declined in the 1990s: A Resolution of Comparability Problems of NSS on Consumer Expenditure', *Economic and Political Weekly*, 20 January.

18

Poverty and Inequality in India
A Re-Examination

Angus Deaton and Jean Dreze

Poverty trends in India in the nineties have been a matter of intense controversy.[1] The debate has often generated more heat than light, and confusion still remains about the extent to which poverty has declined during the period. In the absence of conclusive evidence, widely divergent claims have flourished. Some have argued that the nineties have been a period of unprecedented improvement in living standards. Others have claimed that it has been a time of widespread impoverishment.[2] Against this background, this paper presents a reassessment of the evidence on poverty and inequality in the nineties.

So far, the debate on poverty in the nineties has focused overwhelmingly on changes in the 'headcount ratio' – the proportion of the population below the poverty line. Accordingly, we begin the chapter with a reassessment of the evidence on headcount ratios and related poverty indexes, based on National Sample Survey (NSS) data. In particular, we present a new series of internally consistent poverty indexes for the last three 'quinquennial rounds' (1987/88, 1993/94 and 1999/2000). The broad picture emerging from these revised estimates is one of sustained poverty decline in most states (and also in India as a whole) during the reference period. It is important to note, however, that the increase in per capita expenditure associated with this decline in poverty is quite modest, e.g. 10 per cent or so between 1993/94 and 1999/2000 at the all-India level.

In the section on Further Evidence, we consider related evidence from three additional sources: the Central Statistical Organisation's 'national accounts statistics', the 'employment-unemployment surveys' of the National Sample Survey, and data on agricultural wages. We find that these independent sources are broadly consistent with the revised poverty estimates presented in section on Poverty Indexes in the Nineties. In particular, real agricultural wages in different states (which are highly correlated with headcount ratios of rural poverty) have grown at much the same rate as the corresponding NSS-based

---

[1] See Datt (1999a), Gupta (1999), Bhalla (2000a, 2000b), Deaton and Tarozzi (2000), Dreze (2000), Lal, Mohan and Natarajan (2001), Nagaraj (2000), Ravallion (2000), Sen (2000), Sundaram and Tendulkar (2000, 2001, 2002), Visaria (2000), Sundaram (2001a, 2001b, 2001c), Chandrasekhar and Ghosh (2002), Datt and Ravallion (2002), among others.

[2] On the first position, see e.g. Bhalla (2000a), Bhagwati (2001), Das (2000). On the other side, see Mehta (2001), Sainath (2001a, 2001b), Shiva (2001a), among others.

estimates of per capita expenditure in rural areas. While each of these sources of information, including the National Sample Survey, has important limitations, they tend to corroborate each other as far as poverty decline is concerned, and the combined evidence on this from different sources is quite strong.

The evidence on inequality is discussed in the section on Economic Inequalities in the Nineties, where we focus mainly on the period between 1993/94 and 1999/2000. Based on further analysis of National Sample Survey data and related sources, we argue that there has been a marked increase in inequality in the nineties, in several forms. First, there has been strong 'divergence' of per capita expenditure across states, with the already better off states (particularly in the southern and western regions) growing more rapidly than the poorer states. Second, rural-urban disparities of per capita expenditure have risen. Third, inequality has increased within urban areas in most states. The combined effects of these different forms of rising inequality are quite large. In the rural areas of some of the poorest states, there has been virtually no increase in per capita expenditure between 1993/94 and 1999/2000. Meanwhile, the urban populations of most of the better-off states have enjoyed increases of per capita expenditure of 20 to 30 per cent, with even larger increases for high-income groups within these populations.

The section on Qualification and Concerns takes up some qualifications and concerns. We pay special attention to the apparent decline of cereal consumption in the nineties, which is not obviously consistent with the notion that poverty has steadily declined during that period. We also consider the possibility of impoverishment among specific regions or social groups, in spite of the general improvement in living conditions. Finally, we comment on the unresolved puzzle of the 'thin rounds'.

In the section on Beyond Poverty Indexes, we argue for supplementing expenditure-based data with other indicators of living standards, focusing for instance on literacy rates, health achievements, nutritional levels, crime rates, and the quality of the environment. This broader approach sheds a different light on poverty trends in the nineties. In particular, it prompts us to acknowledge that social progress has been uneven across the different fields. For instance, the nineties have been a period of fairly rapid increase in literacy and school participation. On the other hand, there has been a marked slowdown in the rate at which infant mortality has been declining, and a significant increase in economic inequality. An integrated assessment of changes in living conditions has to be alive to these diversities. We also discuss other implications of this broader approach to the evaluation of living standards, going beyond the standard poverty indexes.

The concluding section sums up the insights of this enquiry.

POVERTY INDEXES IN THE NINETIES

Official Estimates

We begin with an examination of household per capita consumption and the associated poverty estimates. Consumption is only one element of well-being, but it is an important element, and much interest is rightly attached to the Planning Commission's periodical estimates of poverty-based on National Sample Survey data. The most widely-used poverty indicator is the 'headcount ratio' (hereafter HCR), i.e. the proportion of the population below the poverty line.

The latest year for which relatively uncontroversial HCR estimates are available is 1993/94, corresponding to the 50th Round of the National Sample Survey, a 'quinquennial' round. This round was followed by a series of so-called 'thin rounds', involving smaller samples and somewhat different sampling designs; indeed, in the last of these, the 54th Round, the survey was only in the field for six months rather than the customary year and is therefore most unlikely to be comparable with any previous survey. These thin rounds suggested not only that poverty remained more or less unchanged between 1993/94 and the first six months of 1998 (the reference period for the 54th Round), but also that average per capita expenditure stagnated during this period of rapid economic growth. This is very difficult to square with independent evidence, e.g. from national accounts statistics. As things stand, we do not have a good understanding of why the thin rounds give what appear to be anomalous results, and until that puzzle is resolved, our confidence in our other results must remain qualified. We shall return to this issue in later in the section on The 'Thin' Rounds and ignore the thin rounds in the meantime.

In contrast to the thin rounds, the official counts from the latest quinquennial round (the 55th Round, pertaining to 1999/2000) suggest considerable poverty decline between 1993/94 and 1999/2000. According to official estimates, widely relayed, the all-India headcount ratio declined from 36 to 26 per cent over this short period. As is well known, however, the 55th Round is not directly comparable to the 50th Round, due to changes in questionnaire design.

Briefly, the problem is as follows. After the 50th Round, the National Sample Survey introduced an experimental questionnaire with different recall periods for different classes of goods, in addition to the traditional '30-day recall' questionnaire. The experimental questionnaire used a seven-day recall period for food, paan, and tobacco, as well as a 365-day recall period for less frequently purchased goods such as durables, clothing, footwear, educational and institutional medical expenditures. Prior to 1999/2000, the traditional '30-day recall' questionnaire and the experimental questionnaire were administered to *different* (and independent) samples of households. These alternative questionnaires produced two independent series of expenditure estimates, with a fairly stable 'ratio' of the lower estimates based on the traditional questionnaire to the higher estimates based on the experimental questionnaire. In 1999/ 2000, the 30-day recall and 7-day recall periods for food, paan and tobacco were used for the same households, in two adjacent columns on the same pages of a single questionnaire. This effectively 'new' questionnaire design led to a sudden 'reconciliation' of the results obtained from the two different recall periods, perhaps reflecting efforts to achieve 'consistency' on the part of investigators and/or respondents. This reconciliation is likely to boost the expenditure estimates based on 30-day data, and therefore to pull down the official poverty counts, which are based on these 30-day expenditures. In addition, only the 365-day questionnaire was used for the less frequently purchased items, and this abandonment of the traditional 30-day recall for durables and other items also brings down the poverty count. Indeed, most people report no such purchases over 30 days, but report something over 365 days. The bottom tail of the consumption distribution is thereby pulled up, reducing both poverty and inequality compared with the previous design. For this reason, as well as because of possible reconciliation between 7-day and 30-day reports, the latest headcount ratios are biased down compared with what would have been obtained on the basis of the traditional questionnaire.

There is another, quite different problem with the official estimates, which does not concern the 55th Round specifically. This relates to the state and sector-specific poverty lines that are used by the Planning Commission to compute the poverty estimates. In several cases the poverty lines are implausible, particularly the very much higher urban than rural lines in several states. The source of the problem lies in the use of defective price indexes in adjustments of the poverty line over time and between states. In the next section, we discuss ways of overcoming this problem and other limitations of the official poverty estimates.

Proposed Adjustments

In this chapter, we present a new series of consistent poverty estimates for the most recent quinquennial rounds (1987/88, 1993/94 and 1999/2000).[3] Essentially, these involve four major departures from the official estimates. First, an attempt is made to 'adjust' the 55th-Round estimates to achieve comparability with the earlier rounds. Second, we use improved price indexes to update the 'poverty line' over time, and to derive state-specific poverty lines from the all-India poverty line. Third, a similar procedure is used to derive an explicit estimate of the appropriate gap between rural and urban poverty lines (in contrast with the often implausible rural-urban gaps that are implicit in the official estimates). Fourth, in addition to corrected 'headcount ratios', we present estimates of a potentially more informative poverty indicator, the 'poverty-gap index'. Each of these departures calls for further discussion.

The possibility of 'adjusting' the 1999/2000 poverty estimates arises from the fact that the 55th Round questionnaire retained the '30-day recall' (and 30-day recall only) approach for a number of items such as fuel and light, non-institutional medical care, and large categories of miscellaneous goods and services. Further, it turns out that expenditure on this intermediate group of commodities is highly correlated with total expenditure.[4] Expenditures on these comparably surveyed goods can therefore be used to get an idea of trends in total expenditures, and hence, of trends in poverty.

This procedure is valid if two assumptions hold. The first is that reported expenditures on the intermediate goods, for which the recall period is unchanged, are unaffected by the changes elsewhere in the questionnaire. The second is that the relation between intermediate-goods expenditure and total expenditure is much the same in 1999/2000 as in 1993/94.[5] The second assumption would be undermined by a major change in relative prices of the intermediate goods relative to other goods in the late 1990s. It can be checked to some extent by applying the proposed method to the 'thin rounds' instead of the 55th Round, and comparing the predicted distribution of total expenditure with the actual distribution. These checks suggest that the correction procedure works reasonably well (Deaton, 2001a and Tarozzi, 2001). However, this should not be regarded as a definitive validation of the proposed method, given the ambiguities associated with the thin rounds. There are other possible approaches to adjustment that have not yet been explored, and further work may lead to different conclusions. Meanwhile, we regard our adjusted figures as the best currently available in terms of dealing with the change in questionnaire design, without pretending that they represent the final word on the topic.

Turning to the price adjustments, one limitation of the price indexes that have been traditionally used to update poverty lines over time (e.g. the Consumer Price Index for Agricultural Labourers) is that they are based on fixed and frequently outdated commodity 'weights'. It is possible to calculate alternative price indexes using the information in the consumer expenditure surveys themselves. For more than 170 commodities, households report both quantities and expenditures, and the ratio of the latter to the former provides an estimate of the price paid. These prices can then be combined into consumer price index numbers that allow comparisons across states, and if we use data from different rounds, for states and the whole country at different points in time. One limitation of these price indexes is that their

---

[3] These estimates build on earlier work by Deaton and Tarozzi (2000), Deaton (2001a and 2001b) and Tarozzi (2001).

[4] In the 50th Round, the correlation between the logarithm of total household per capita expenditure and the logarithm of per capita expenditure on this subset of commodities is 0.79 and 0.86 in the rural and urban sectors, respectively.

[5] More precisely, and somewhat less restrictively, we require that the probability of being poor, given the amount of a household's expenditure on these intermediate goods, remains the same in the 55th Round as it was in the 50th. We require this on a state by state basis, one sector at a time, which allows the conditional probability to vary by state and by sector.

coverage of commodities is only partial (a little more than half the budget in the 55th Round, though more in earlier rounds), so that they cannot capture price changes in important items such as transportation, housing, most non-food goods, and services. However, CPIAL data suggest that the inflation rate for the uncovered items is not very different from that applying to the covered items.[6] The price indexes from the surveys have the advantage of being based on several million actual purchases in each round. They also make it possible to use formulae for superlative indexes, such as the Fisher ideal index or the Törnqvist index, that allow for substitution behaviour as households adapt to relative price changes over time.

The calculated Törnqvist indexes for the 43rd and 50th Rounds are reported in Deaton and Tarozzi (2000), and were updated to the 55th Round by Deaton (2001b).[7] These price indexes differ from the official indexes in a number of ways. In particular, they rise somewhat more slowly over time than do the official price indexes, especially in the rural sector. For example, the all-India rural Törnqvist index rises by 69.8 per cent from 1987/88 to 1993/94 and by a further 54.5 per cent from 1993/94 to 1999/2000, compared with 78.7 per cent and 59.1 per cent for the deflators implicit in the official all-India rural poverty line. For the urban sector over the two periods, the Törnqvist price indexes rise by 73.8 and 57.7 per cent versus 73.5 and 61.4 per cent for the implicit deflator of the urban poverty line. The price indexes for each state show rather modest differences from one state to another. They also differ from those implicit in the official poverty lines, although the two sets of deflators are correlated. This pattern is consistent with the fact that relative prices across states vary somewhat over time, and that the interstate prices used in the official deflators are outdated.

The third departure concerns the gap between rural and urban poverty lines. From the mid-1970s until the early 1990s, there were only two poverty lines for India, one for rural and one for urban. The urban line was around 15 per cent higher than the rural line, and both were held fixed in real terms, with updating on the basis of approximate price indexes such as the Wholesale Price Index or the CSO's private consumption deflator. The initial rural-urban gap of 15 per cent is anchored in 1973/74 calorie consumption data, but it is essentially arbitrary since the urban and rural 'calorie norms' themselves (2,100 and 2,400 calories per person per day, respectively) have a fragile basis.[8] More recently, the Planning Commission has adopted a modified version of the poverty lines recommended by a 1993 Expert Group (Government of India, 1993). The Expert Group retained the original rural and urban lines, but adjusted them for statewise differences in price levels, separately for urban and rural sectors, using estimates of statewise price differences calculated from NSS data on expenditures and quantities using similar methods to those adopted in this paper. The Expert Group lines used the then best-available

---

[6] In Deaton and Tarozzi (2000), it is shown that, between the 43rd and 50th Rounds, the component of the CPIAL for the uncovered items grew somewhat less rapidly than the component for the covered items. In consequence, if we were to supplement our price indexes for uncovered items from the CPIAL, the estimated rate of increase of consumer prices would come down, and correspondingly, there would be a faster decline in the poverty indexes, at least for the period falling between these two rounds (i.e. 1987/88 to 1993/94).

[7] The Törnqvist price index is a weighted geometric index with weights that are the average of the expenditure shares in the base and comparison periods. It is a superlative index in the sense of Diewert (1976).

[8] For further details, see EPW Research Foundation (1993). On the conceptual and practical problems involved in defining 'calorie norms', see Dasgupta and Ray (1990) and Osmani (1990), and the literature cited there. Note also that, if the calorie norms were to be reapplied today, they would not generate the same poverty lines. Updating calorie-norm based poverty lines for inflation does not preserve their calorie-norm status.

information on price differences across states, both urban and rural, but the information was outdated, especially for the rural sector.

Because the statewise adjustments were done separately for urban and rural households, the price differences between the urban and rural sectors of each state were derived only implicitly, and some are rather implausible, particularly the very much higher urban than rural lines in several states. For example, the most recent urban poverty lines for Andhra Pradesh and Karnataka are around 70 per cent higher than the corresponding rural lines, with the uncomfortable result that urban poverty is much *higher* than rural poverty in these two states (see Table 18.3). In Assam, by contrast, the rural poverty line is actually *higher* than the urban line, and based on these odd poverty lines, Assam turns out to be one of India's highest-poverty states for rural areas but lowest-poverty states for urban areas. It is hard to accept these and other implications of the Expert Group poverty lines.

There are grounds, of course, for questioning whether it is even possible to derive comparable rural and urban poverty lines. Comparisons of living standards in rural and urban areas are inherently difficult, since there are large intersectoral differences not only in the patterns of consumption but also in lifestyles, public amenities, epidemiological environments, and so on. One way forward is to avoid such comparisons altogether, and to focus on sector-specific (rural or urban) poverty estimates. Yet there is a case for attempting to compare private consumption levels across sectors, bearing in mind that this is at best a partial picture of the relevant differences in living standards.[9] These comparisons can be made by anchoring poverty estimates in a single poverty line, adjusted where appropriate to take into account rural-urban price differences, using the same method as that described earlier for adjusting poverty lines over time and between states. Based on this procedure, the urban poverty line tends be about 15 per cent higher than the rural poverty line, though there are variations across states. As it turns out, this rural-urban difference in poverty lines is broadly consistent with the original methodology used before the adoption of the Expert Group recommendations.

To recapitulate, the revised poverty lines used in this paper, which are presented in full in Table 18.4 of Deaton (2001b), are derived as follows. Our starting point is the official rural all-India poverty line for the 43rd Round (1987/88): Rs 115.70 per person per month.[10] Rural poverty lines for each state for the 43rd Round are obtained by multiplying this base poverty line by the rural price indexes for each state relative to all-India. The urban poverty lines for the 43rd Round, for each state as well as for all-India, are calculated from the rural poverty lines by scaling up by the respective urban relative to rural price indexes. In all cases, we use the relevant Törnqvist price indexes.[11] To move to the 50th Round, the original all-India rural line, Rs 115.70, is scaled up by the Törnqvist index for all-India rural for the 50th Round relative to the 43rd Round, 1.698, to give an all-India rural poverty line for the 50th Round. This

---

[9] Similar issues arise, of course, in the context of interstate comparisons, especially between states (e.g. Kerala and Uttar Pradesh) with radically different consumption patterns and social environments. In both cases, comparisons of living standards call for supplementing expenditure data with other types of information, relating for instance to public amenities, health achievements, educational levels, etc.

[10] The official line is actually 115.20. We use 115.70 because this is the figure yielded by the official methodology when the calculations are based on the unit record data, as opposed to the interpolations used by the Planning Commission. See notes to Table 18.3.

[11] The case of Delhi is handled differently. Because there are few sample households in rural Delhi, it is not advisable to use the price index for rural Delhi as part of the calculations. The poverty line for urban Delhi is calculated from the all-India urban poverty line by multiplying it by the price index for urban Delhi relative to urban India.

number is then used to generate rural and then urban poverty lines for each state, following exactly the same procedure as for the 43rd Round. Finally, poverty lines for the 55th Round are calculated in the same way from an all-India rural line, which is the 50th Round all-India rural line scaled up by the value of the Törnqvist index between the two surveys.[12]

The motivation for the fourth departure (or rather extension) arises from the limitations of the headcount ratio as an indicator of poverty. The headcount ratio has a straightforward interpretation and is easy to understand. In that sense it has much 'communication value'. Yet, the HCR has serious limitations as a poverty index. For one thing, it ignores the *extent* to which different households fall short of the poverty line. This leads to some perverse properties. For instance, an income transfer from a very poor person to someone who is closer to the poverty line may lead to a *decline* in the headcount ratio, if it 'lifts' the recipient above the poverty line. Similarly, if some poor households get poorer, this has *no effect* on the headcount ratio.

A related issue is that changes in HCRs can be highly sensitive to the number of poor households near the poverty line (since changes in the HCR are entirely driven by 'crossings' of the poverty line). If poor households are heavily 'bunched' near the poverty line, a small increase in average per capita income could lead to a misleadingly large decline in the headcount ratio. This 'density effect' has to be kept firmly in view in the context of comparisons of poverty *change*, involving questions such as 'has there been more poverty decline in Bihar than in Punjab during the nineties', or 'has poverty declined faster in the nineties than in the eighties?' Often such questions are answered by looking at, say, the respective changes (absolute or proportionate) in headcount ratios. These changes, however, are difficult to interpret in the absence of further information about the initial density of poor households near the poverty line in each case.

One way forward is to use more sophisticated poverty indexes such as the Foster-Greer-Thorbecke (FGT) indexes or the Sen index. In this paper, we focus on the simplest member of the FGT class (other than the headcount ratio itself), the 'poverty-gap index'. Essentially, the poverty-gap index (hereafter PGI) is the aggregate shortfall of poor people's consumption from the poverty line, suitably normalised.[13] The PGI can also be interpreted as the headcount ratio multiplied by the mean percentage shortfall of consumption from the poverty line (among the poor). This index avoids the main shortcomings of the headcount ratio, is relatively simple to calculate, and has a straightforward interpretation.[14]

Adjusted Estimates

Table 18.1 presents official and adjusted estimates of the all-India headcount ratio. In each panel, the

[12] Note that this is not the only way of using the indexes; another (but only one other) possibility would be to update the poverty line for each sector of each state by its own inflation rate. Because we are dealing with price indexes, not prices, the different alternatives will give different answers.

[13] More precisely, the poverty-gap index (PGI) calculates the total shortfall of consumption below the poverty line, per capita of the total population, and expressed as a percentage of the poverty line: $PGI \equiv (1/z) [(\Sigma (z - y_i)/n]$ where z is the poverty line, n is the population size, and y_i is the consumption level of the ith poor person.

[14] The poverty-gap index, however, retains one limitation of the headcount ratio: it is not sensitive to the distribution of per capita expenditure below the poverty line. This limitation is overcome by higher-order members of the FGT class, such as the 'squared poverty-gap index' (SPGI), and also by the Sen index. While we have calculated the SPGI estimates, we confine ourselves here to the poverty-gap index, for two reasons. First, it is easier to interpret. Second, SPGIs are highly sensitive to measurement errors at the bottom of the per capita expenditure scale, and their reliability calls for further scrutiny.

first row gives the official estimates; the second row retains the official poverty lines but adjusts the 1999/2000 estimates for the change in questionnaire design in the way described earlier; the third row gives fully-adjusted poverty estimates, which combine the adjustments for questionnaire design and for price indexes. Table 18.2 gives the corresponding poverty-gap indexes.

As the first two rows of each panel indicate, the official estimates are quite misleading in their own terms: the 1999/2000 poverty estimates are biased downward by the changes in questionnaire design. For headcount ratios, the estimates adjusted for changes in questionnaire design 'confirm' about two-thirds of the official decline in rural poverty between 1993/94 and 1999/2000, and about 90 per cent of the decline in urban poverty. For poverty-gap indexes, the corresponding proportions (62 per cent and 77 per cent) are lower, especially for the urban sector.

The fully adjusted estimates in the last row of each panel show somewhat lower rural poverty estimates and much lower urban poverty estimates for 1999/2000 than even the official estimates. Note, however, that because we are recalculating the poverty lines back to the 43rd Round, a good deal of the decrease took place in the six years prior to 1993/94, not only in the six years subsequent to 1993/94.

Table 18.1 All-India Headcount Ratios

			(Per Cent)
	1987/88	*1993/94*	*1999/2000*
Rural			
Official estimates	39.4	37.1	26.8
Adjusted estimates			
Step 1: Adjusting for changes in questionnaire design	39.4	37.1	30.0
Step 2: Revising the poverty lines	39.4	33.0	26.3
Urban			
Official estimates	39.1	32.9	24.1
Adjusted estimates			
Step 1: Adjusting for changes in questionnaire design	39.1	32.9	24.7
Step 2: Revising the poverty lines	22.5	17.8	12.0

Source: Planning Commission, Press Releases (11 March 1997 and 22 February 2001), Deaton (2001a and 2001b), and Table 18.3.

Table 18.2 All-India Poverty-Gap Indexes

	1987/88	*1993/94*	*1999/2000*
Rural			
Estimates from unadjusted data and official poverty lines	9.4	8.4	5.2
Adjusted estimates			
Step 1: Adjusting for changes in questionnaire design	9.4	8.4	6.4
Step 2: Revising the poverty lines	9.4	7.0	5.2
Urban			
Estimates from unadjusted data and official poverty lines	10.4	8.3	5.2
Adjusted estimates			
Step 1: Adjusting for changes in questionnaire design	10.4	8.3	5.9
Step 2: Revising the poverty lines	4.8	3.7	2.3

Source: Authors' calculations from unit record data from the 43rd, 50th, and 55th Rounds of the NSS.

The fully adjusted estimates for the headcount ratios and poverty-gap indexes suggest that poverty decline has been fairly evenly spread between the two sub-periods (before and after 1993/94), in contrast with the pattern of 'acceleration' in the second sub-period associated with the official estimates.

The rural-urban gaps in the poverty estimates are also of interest. Looking first at the base year (1987/88), the rural-urban gap based on adjusted estimates is much larger than that based on official estimates. Indeed, the latter suggest no difference between rural and urban poverty in that year. This is hard to reconcile with independent evidence on living conditions in rural and urban areas, such as a life-expectancy gap of about seven years in favour of urban areas around that time.[15] Our low estimate of the urban headcount ratio relative to the official estimate (22.5 per cent versus 39.1 per cent), and similar differences in 1993/94 and 1999/2000, come from the fact that we take the rural poverty line in 1987/88 as our starting point, and peg the urban poverty lines about 15 per cent higher than the rural poverty lines, in contrast to the much larger differentials embodied in the official lines.

Figure 18.1 shows the new estimates of the headcount ratios together with the official estimates going back to 1973/74. The fully adjusted figures are lower throughout because we treat the rural poverty line in the 43rd Round as our baseline so that, with larger rural-urban gaps in the poverty estimates, we estimate lower poverty overall. If instead, we had taken the urban poverty line as base, the adjusted figures would have been higher than the official figures. From 1987/88 to 1993/94, the adjusted headcount ratio falls more rapidly than the official headcount; this is because our price deflators are rising less rapidly than the official ones. From 1993/94, the adjusted figures fall more slowly because the effects of the price adjustment are more than offset by the correction for questionnaire design. The estimates for the thin rounds – which look very different – are included to remind us of the residual uncertainty about our conclusions, and will be discussed later.

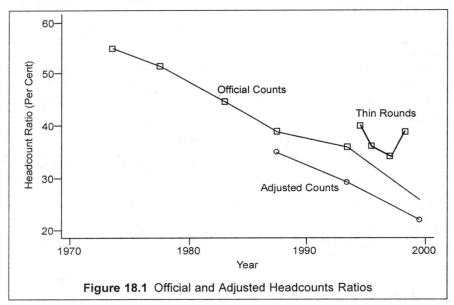

Figure 18.1 Official and Adjusted Headcounts Ratios

Source: Planning Commission, Press Releases (11 March 1997 and 22 February 2001), Deaton (2001a and 2001b), and Table 18.3 of this chapter.

[15] See Government of India (1993b), p. 16.

Regional Contrasts

State-specific headcount ratios are presented in Table 18.3.[16] The table has the same basic structure as Table 18.1, except that we jump straight from official to fully-adjusted estimates. The latter suggest that the basic pattern of sustained poverty decline between 1987/88 and 1999/2000, discussed earlier at the all-India level, also applies at the level of individual states in most cases. The main exception is Assam, where poverty has stagnated in both rural and urban areas. In Orissa, there has been very little poverty decline in the second sub-period, with the result that Orissa now has the highest level of rural poverty among all Indian states, according to the adjusted 1999/2000 estimates.[17] Reassuringly, the 'anomalies' noted earlier with respect to rural-urban gaps in specific states tend to disappear as one moves from official to adjusted estimates.

Table 18.4 shows the corresponding poverty-gap indexes. The general patterns are very much the same as with headcount ratios; indeed the PGI series are highly correlated with the corresponding HCR series, with correlation coefficients of 0.98 for rural and 0.95 for urban. Even the HCR and PGI *changes* between the 50th and 55th Rounds are highly correlated; the correlation coefficient between changes in HCR and changes in PGI is 0.95 for the rural sector, and 0.96 for the urban sector. Thus, in spite of its theoretical superiority over the headcount ratio, the poverty-gap index gives us very little additional insight in this case.

In interpreting and comparing poverty declines over time, it is useful to supplement the poverty indexes with information on the growth rate of average per capita consumption expenditure (hereafter APCE). State-specific estimates of APCE growth between 1993/94 and 1999/2000 are shown in Table 18.3, where states are ranked in ascending order of APCE growth for rural and urban areas combined.[18] Here, a striking regional pattern emerges: except for Jammu & Kashmir, the low-growth states form one contiguous region made up of the eastern states (Assam, Orissa and West Bengal), the so-called BIMARU states (Bihar, Madhya Pradesh, Rajasthan and Uttar Pradesh), and Andhra Pradesh. The high-growth states, for their part, consist of the southern states (except Andhra Pradesh), the western states (Gujarat and Maharashtra) and the northwestern region (Punjab, Haryana and Himachal Pradesh). Further, it is interesting to note that this pattern is reasonably consistent with independent data on growth rates of per capita 'state domestic product' (SDP); these are shown in the last column of Table 18.5. With a couple of exceptions on each side, all the states in the 'low APCE growth' set had comparatively low rates of per capita SDP between 1993/94 and 1999/2000 (say below 4 per cent per year), and conversely, all the states in the 'high APCE growth' set had comparatively high annual growth rates of per capita SDP (the correlation coefficient between the two series is 0.45).[19]

This broad regional pattern is a matter of concern, because the low-growth states also tend to be states that started off with comparatively low levels of APCE or per capita SDP. In other words, there

[16] In Table 18.3 and elsewhere in this paper, the terms 'Bihar', 'Madhya Pradesh' and 'Uttar Pradesh' refer to these states as they existed prior to the formation of Jharkhand, Chattisgarh and Uttaranchal in late 2000.

[17] In the first sub-period, the estimates suggest some increase in poverty in rural Haryana and Himachal Pradesh, and also in urban Himachal Pradesh, Punjab and Delhi. These patterns, however, should be interpreted with caution, given the relatively small sample sizes for these states and the possibility of transient fluctuations in poverty levels in specific years.

[18] Here and elsewhere, it is useful to remember that the period between 1993/94 and 1999/2000 was one of 'peak' economic growth for the Indian economy, with per capita GDP growing at a healthy 4.4 per cent per year.

[19] While the *relative* growth rates of APCE in different states are consistent with the corresponding relative growth rates of per capita SDP, the *levels* of per capita SDP growth tend to be higher than those of APCE growth. We shall return to this issue in the next section, with reference to the all-India figures.

Table 18.3 State-specific Headcount Ratios

(Per Cent)

	Official Methodology			Adjusted Estimates		
	1987/88	*1993/94*	*1999/2000*	*1987/88*	*1993/94*	*1999/2000*
Rural						
Andhra Pradesh	21.0	15.9	10.5	35.0	29.2	26.2
Assam	39.4	45.2	40.3	36.1	35.4	35.5
Bihar	53.9	58.0	44.0	54.6	48.6	41.1
Gujarat	28.6	22.2	12.4	39.4	32.5	20.0
Haryana	15.4	28.3	7.4	13.6	17.0	5.7
Himachal Pradesh	16.7	30.4	7.5	13.3	17.1	9.8
Jammu & Kashmir	25.9	30.4	4.7	15.3	10.1	6.1
Karnataka	32.6	30.1	16.8	40.8	37.9	30.7
Kerala	29.5	25.4	9.4	23.8	19.5	10.0
Madhya Pradesh	42.0	40.7	37.2	43.7	36.6	31.3
Maharashtra	41.0	37.9	23.2	44.3	42.9	31.9
Orissa	58.7	49.8	47.8	50.4	43.5	43.0
Punjab	12.8	11.7	6.0	6.6	6.2	2.4
Rajasthan	33.3	26.4	13.5	35.3	23.0	17.3
Tamil Nadu	46.3	35.9	20.0	49.0	38.5	24.3
Uttar Pradesh	41.9	42.3	31.1	34.9	28.6	21.5
West Bengal	48.8	41.2	31.7	36.3	25.1	21.9
All-India Rural	39.4	37.1	26.8	39.0	33.0	26.3
Urban						
Andhra Pradesh	41.1	38.8	27.2	23.4	17.8	10.8
Assam	11.3	7.9	7.5	13.6	13.0	11.8
Bihar	51.9	34.8	33.5	38.1	26.7	24.7
Gujarat	38.5	28.3	14.8	16.4	14.7	6.4
Haryana	18.4	16.5	10.0	11.8	10.5	4.6
Himachal Pradesh	7.2	9.3	4.6	1.7	3.6	1.2
Jammu & Kashmir	15.0	9.3	2.0	3.8	3.1	1.3
Karnataka	49.2	39.9	24.6	26.0	21.4	10.8
Kerala	39.8	24.3	19.8	21.0	13.9	9.6
Madhya Pradesh	47.3	48.1	38.5	20.7	18.5	13.9
Maharashtra	40.3	35.0	26.7	21.2	18.2	12.0
Orissa	42.6	40.6	43.5	20.8	15.2	15.6
Punjab	13.7	10.9	5.5	6.6	7.8	3.4
Rajasthan	37.9	31.0	19.4	19.8	18.3	10.8
Tamil Nadu	40.2	39.9	22.5	26.2	20.8	11.3
Uttar Pradesh	44.9	35.1	30.8	29.3	21.7	17.3
West Bengal	33.7	22.9	14.7	22.3	15.5	11.3
Delhi	15.1	16.1	9.2	4.7	8.8	2.4
All-India Urban	39.1	32.9	24.1	22.5	17.8	12.0

Notes: The headcount ratios labelled 'official methodology' are computed from the unit record data using the official poverty lines, as well as the official procedures for assigning poverty rates (or poverty lines) to small states. We have also followed the official treatment of Jammu & Kashmir. The all-India poverty rates are computed by adding up the number of poor in each state and dividing by the total population. Because the Planning Commission uses interpolation rather than computations from the unit record data, there are minor differences between these numbers and those published in the official releases. The adjusted estimates are computed as described in the text (and more fully in Deaton and Tarozzi, 2001 and Deaton, 2001b); they use price indexes computed from the unit record data, and correct for the changes in questionnaire design in the 55th Round. The final column is a somewhat refined version of the corresponding column in Deaton (2001b). The estimates for Jammu & Kashmir are calculated directly, and not by assuming the poverty line or poverty rate for any other state (as in the official methodology).

Source: Authors' calculations based on NSS unit record data from 43rd, 50th and 55th Rounds.

Table 18.4 State-specific Poverty-Gap Indexes

	Official Methodology			Adjusted Estimates		
	1987/88	1993/94	1999/2000	1987/88	1993/94	1999/2000
Rural						
Andhra Pradesh	4.4	2.9	1.8	8.0	5.8	4.8
Assam	7.4	8.3	8.5	6.5	5.7	6.1
Bihar	12.9	14.7	8.7	13.2	10.7	8.5
Gujarat	5.5	4.1	2.2	8.4	6.8	3.8
Haryana	3.6	5.6	1.3	2.8	3.0	0.7
Himachal Pradesh	2.6	5.6	1.0	2.1	3.0	1.5
Jammu & Kashmir	4.5	5.6	0.6	2.4	1.6	0.7
Karnataka	7.9	6.3	2.7	10.5	8.6	6.1
Kerala	6.4	5.6	1.5	4.8	3.9	1.7
Madhya Pradesh	10.6	9.5	7.7	11.2	8.2	6.6
Maharashtra	9.6	9.3	4.4	10.8	11.2	7.6
Orissa	16.3	12.0	11.7	13.0	9.7	10.5
Punjab	2.0	1.9	0.8	1.0	1.0	0.3
Rajasthan	8.6	5.2	2.1	9.2	4.4	3.0
Tamil Nadu	12.6	7.3	3.8	13.7	9.1	4.6
Uttar Pradesh	9.9	10.4	5.8	7.5	5.8	3.9
West Bengal	11.6	8.3	6.5	7.7	4.2	3.5
All-India Rural	9.4	8.4	5.2	9.2	7.0	5.2
Urban						
Andhra Pradesh	10.6	9.3	5.6	4.9	3.4	1.9
Assam	1.5	0.9	1.5	2.0	2.0	1.9
Bihar	13.0	7.9	6.7	8.2	5.6	5.0
Gujarat	8.2	6.2	2.4	2.8	2.6	1.0
Haryana	3.6	3.0	2.0	2.3	1.9	0.7
Himachal Pradesh	0.7	1.2	0.6	0.2	0.5	0.2
Jammu & Kashmir	2.4	1.2	0.2	0.5	0.5	0.2
Karnataka	14.1	11.4	5.6	5.7	4.5	2.1
Kerala	10.4	5.5	3.9	4.5	2.7	1.7
Madhya Pradesh	13.6	13.4	9.5	4.1	3.5	2.6
Maharashtra	12.3	10.1	6.7	5.3	4.6	2.8
Orissa	11.1	11.4	11.1	4.2	3.0	3.0
Punjab	2.3	1.7	0.6	1.0	1.1	0.4
Rajasthan	9.6	7.0	3.4	4.0	3.2	1.7
Tamil Nadu	11.5	10.2	4.8	6.2	4.5	2.0
Uttar Pradesh	12.2	9.0	6.6	6.3	4.6	3.3
West Bengal	7.4	4.5	2.5	4.2	2.9	1.9
Delhi	2.8	3.9	1.5	0.7	1.7	0.4
All-India Urban	10.4	8.3	5.2	4.8	3.7	2.3

Notes: The poverty-gap indexes labelled 'official methodology' are computed from the unit record data using the official poverty lines, and using rules for assigning poverty-gap indexes to small states (and to J&K) that mirror the rules used by the Planning Commission for computing the official headcount ratios. The adjusted indexes use the recomputed price indexes to update the poverty lines, and correct for the changes in questionnaire design in the 55th Round. All numbers are directly computed from poverty lines and unit record data for each state, and the all-India estimates are calculated as weighted averages of the state estimates.

Table 18.5 Growth Rates of APCE and per Capita SDP, 1993/94 to 1999/2000

	Six-year Growth of APCE ('Adjusted'), 1993/94 to 1999/2000			Annual Growth Rate of per Capita SDP, 1993/94 to 1999/2000
	Rural	Urban	Combined	
Assam	0.9	8.8	1.7	0.58
Orissa	1.4	−0.0	3.3	2.34
West Bengal	2.1	11.5	3.3	5.48
Jammu & Kashmir	5.4	8.0	5.3	2.49
Bihar	6.9	4.8	7.1	2.10
Madhya Pradesh	6.6	14.1	7.8	2.78
Andhra Pradesh	2.8	18.5	8.3	3.57
Rajasthan	7.0	15.4	8.6	4.60
Uttar Pradesh	8.3	10.1	9.0	2.99
India	8.7	16.6	10.9	4.36
Karnataka	9.5	26.5	14.0	5.82
Maharashtra	14.1	16.7	15.9	3.53
Gujarat	15.1	20.9	16.8	4.88
Himachal Pradesh	16.2	28.5	17.6	5.06
Tamil Nadu	15.7	25.1	18.9	5.39
Kerala	19.6	18.2	19.6	4.01
Punjab	20.2	17.9	19.9	2.74
Haryana	31.0	23.0	29.2	3.05
Delhi	−	30.7	30.7	5.69

Note: The states are arranged in ascending order of the growth rate of APCE for rural and urban area combined.

Sources: For APCE: Authors' calculations from unit record data for the 50th and 55th Rounds of the National Sample Survey. For SDP: Authors' calculations based on unpublished data kindly supplied by the Planning Commission. The figures in the last column should be taken as indicative, given the significant margin of error involved in SDP estimates.

has been a growing 'divergence' of per capita expenditure (and also of per capita SDP) across Indian states in the nineties.[20] The point is illustrated in Figure 18.2, which plots the average growth in APCE for each state between 1993/94 and 1999/2000 against the geometric mean of APCE in 1993/94.

It is worth asking to what extent these regional patterns, based on APCE data, are corroborated by regional patterns of poverty decline. One difficulty here is that there is no obvious way of 'comparing' the extent of poverty decline across states. For instance, looking at absolute changes in (say) HCRs would seem to give an unfair 'advantage' to states that start off with high levels of poverty, and where there tends be a large number of households close to the poverty line. To illustrate, the absolute decline of the rural HCR between 1993/94 and 1999/2000 was about twice as large in Bihar (7.4 percentage points) as in Punjab (3.8 points), yet over the same period APCE grew by only 6.9 per cent in Bihar compared with 20.2 per cent in Punjab, with virtually no change in distribution in either case.[21] The reason for this contrast is that Bihar starts off in 1993/94 with a very high proportion of households

[20] On the growing divergence of per capita SDP in the nineties, see also Ahluwalia (2000) and Dreze and Sen (2002).
[21] For inequality indexes, see Table 18.7 in section on Economic Inequality in the Nineties.

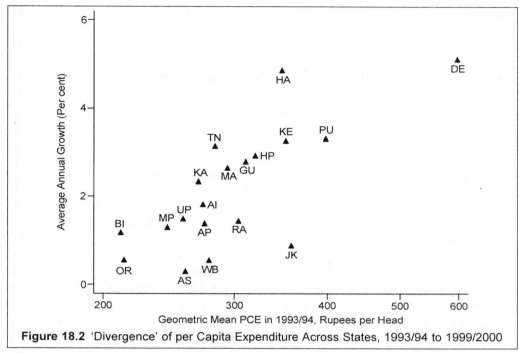

Figure 18.2 'Divergence' of per Capita Expenditure Across States, 1993/94 to 1999/2000

Note: AI = All India; AP = Andhra Pradesh; AS = Assam; BI = Bihar; DE = Delhi; GU = Gujarat; HA = Haryana; HP = Himachal Pradesh; JK = Jammu & Kashmir; KA = Karnataka; KE = Kerala; MA = Maharashtra; MP = Madhya Pradesh; OR = Orissa; PU = Punjab; RA = Rajasthan; TN = Tamil Nadu; UP = Uttar Pradesh; WB = West Bengal.

Source: Authors' calculations using unit record data from the 50th and 55th Rounds of the National Sample Survey.

close to the poverty line, so that small increases in APCE can produce relatively large absolute declines in the headcount ratio.

An alternative approach is to look at proportionate changes in HCRs or PGIs. These turn out to be highly correlated with the corresponding growth rates of APCE. The point is illustrated in Figure 18.3, where we plot the proportionate decline in the rural headcount ratio in each state against the growth rate of APCE in rural areas. The correlation coefficient between the two series is as high as 0.91. This reflects the fact that poverty reduction is overwhelmingly driven by the growth rate of APCE, rather than by changes in distribution – we shall return to this point later. From these observations, it follows that if we accept 'proportionate change in HCR' (or PGI) as an index of poverty reduction, then the broad regional patterns identified earlier for the growth rate of APCE also tend to apply to poverty reduction. In particular: (1) most of the western and southern states (with the important exception of Andhra Pradesh) have done comparatively well; (2) the eastern region has achieved very little poverty reduction between 1993/94 and 1999/2000; and (3) there is a strong overall pattern of 'divergence' (states that were poorer to start with had lower rates of poverty reduction). This reading of the evidence, however, remains somewhat tentative, since there is no compelling reason to accept the proportionate decline in HCR (or PGI) as a definitive measure of poverty decline.

We end this section with a caveat. From Table 18.2 and Figure 18.1, it may appear that the 'pace' of poverty decline in the nineties has been fairly rapid. It is important to note, however, that the associated increases in per capita expenditure have been rather modest in most cases. For instance, the decline of 6.6 percentage points in the all-India HCR (from 29.2 per cent to 22.7 per cent) between 1993/94 and 1999/2000 is driven by an increase of only 10.9 per cent in average per capita expenditure – not exactly a spectacular improvement in living standards. Similarly, Table 18.2(a) suggests that Bihar achieved a large step in poverty reduction in the nineties, with the rural HCR coming down from 49 per cent to 41 per cent. Yet, as Table 19.3 indicates, average APCE in rural Bihar increased by only 7 per cent between 1993/94 and 1999/2000.

Why are small increases in APCE associated with substantial declines in poverty indexes? It is tempting to answer that the *distribution* of consumer expenditure must have improved in the nineties. As discussed in section on Economic Inequality in the Nineties, however, this is not the case: indeed economic inequality has increased rather than decreased in the nineties. The correct answer relates to the 'density effect' mentioned earlier (see section on Proposed Adjustments): when many poor households are close to the poverty line, modest increases in APCE can produce substantial declines in standard poverty indexes. One reason for drawing attention to this is that the official poverty estimates have sometimes been used to claim that the nineties have been a period of spectacular achievements in poverty reduction. In fact, when the relevant adjustments are made, and the poverty indexes are read together with the information on APCE growth, poverty reduction in the nineties appears to be more or less in line with previous rates of progress.

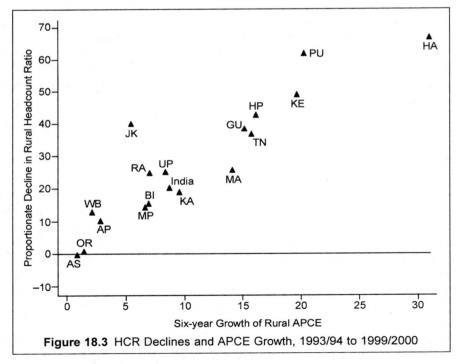

Figure 18.3 HCR Declines and APCE Growth, 1993/94 to 1999/2000

Source: Tables 18.3 and 18.5.

FURTHER EVIDENCE

National Accounts Statistics

There has been much discussion of the consistency between National Sample Survey data and the 'national accounts' published by the Central Statistical Organisation (CSO).[22] The latter include estimates of 'private final consumer expenditure', which is frequently compared with NSS estimates of 'household consumption expenditure'. Over time, the CSO estimates have tended to grow faster than the NSS estimates, leading some commentators to question the reliability of National Sample Survey data.

It is important to note that these two notions of 'consumer expenditure' are not exactly the same, and also that there are major methodological differences between the two sources. The NSS figures are direct estimates of household consumption expenditure. The CSO figures include several items of expenditure that are not collected in the NSS surveys; examples are expenditures by non-profit enterprises, as well as imputed rent by owner occupiers and 'financial intermediation services indirectly measured' (the last item is essentially the net interest earned by financial intermediaries, which is counted as expenditures on intermediation services by households). According to Sundaram and Tendulkar (2002), who quote a recent cross-validation study by the National Accounts Department, the last two items account for 22 per cent of the difference in levels between CSO and NSS estimates of consumer expenditure. Further, the CSO estimates are 'residual' figures, obtained after subtracting other items from the national product. Leaving aside these comparability issues, there is indeed a gap between the CSO-based and NSS-based growth rates of consumer expenditure. According to CSO data, per-capita consumer expenditure has grown at much the same rate as per capita GDP between 1993/94 and 1999/2000 – about 3.5 per cent per year in real terms.[23] The corresponding NSS-based estimate associated with our 'adjusted' APCE figures is around 2 per cent.[24]

This is quite different from the situation that prevailed prior to the 55th Round, when consumer expenditure was hardly growing at all according to the NSS 'thin rounds' but galloping forward according to the CSO data. Today, in the light of more recent estimates, the discrepancy looks much smaller. That discrepancy calls for further scrutiny and resolution, but meanwhile, it can hardly be regarded as an indictment of National Sample Survey data. For one thing, the reference categories are not the same. For another, there is no reason to believe that the CSO estimates are more accurate than the NSS estimates; indeed the cross-validation exercise raised serious questions about a number of the consumption categories in the CSO data.[25]

---

[22] See particularly Bhalla (2000a), Kulsheshtra and Kar (2002), Ravallion (2000), Sen (2000), Sundaram and Tendulkar (2001).

[23] Calculated from Central Statistical Organisation (2001), p. xxxii.

[24] In nominal terms, between 1993/94 and 1999/2000, consumer expenditure has been growing at about 11.5 per cent per year according to CSO data, and 10 per cent per year according to our NSS-based estimates. Both the CSO's implicit price deflator and our Törnqvist index have been growing at 8 per cent per year or so during this period. Thus, differences in price deflators do not seem to help to resolve the CSO-NSS discrepancy in this case, even though price-index differences may have played a role in enhancing that discrepancy in earlier periods (see Sen, 2000).

[25] The NSS surveys, for their part, almost certainly disproportionately miss wealthy households at the very top of the distribution, and as Banerjee and Piketty (2001) have shown, there has been a marked rise in incomes among the very highest earners. Even so, they show that the total amount of these earnings is not enough to explain the increasing disparity between the NSS and the CSO estimates of consumption expenditure.

Agricultural Wages

Agricultural wages provide an important source of further information on poverty. There are, in fact, two ways of thinking about the relevance of this information. First, real agricultural wages are highly correlated with standard poverty indexes such as headcount ratios: where poverty is higher, wages tend to be lower, and vice versa. Based on this statistical association, real wages can be used to provide some information about other poverty indexes. Second, it is also possible to think about the real wage as a rough poverty indicator in its own right. The idea is that, if the labour market is competitive (at least on the supply side), then the real wage measures the 'reservation wage', i.e. the lowest wage at which labourers are prepared to work. This has direct evidential value as an indication of the deprived circumstances in which people live (the more desperate people are, the lower the reservation wage), independently of the indirect evidential value arising from the statistical association between real wages and standard poverty indexes such as the headcount ratio.

Detailed information on agricultural wages is available from *Agricultural Wages in India* (AWI), an annual publication of the Directorate of Economics and Statistics, Ministry of Agriculture. The data initially come in the form of district-specific money wages.[26] These are typically aggregated using the numbers of agricultural labourers in different districts as weights, and deflated using the Consumer Price Index for Agricultural Labourers (CPIAL). The quality of this information is not entirely clear, but available evidence suggests that it is adequate for the purpose of broad comparisons.[27]

As Figure 18.4 illustrates, real agricultural wages in different states are highly correlated with expenditure-based poverty indexes (here and elsewhere in this section, the focus is on rural poverty). The main 'outlier' is Kerala, where real wages are far above the 'regression line'; it seems that the power of labour unions in Kerala has raised agricultural wages well above the level found in any other Indian states, but that this does not translate into a correspondingly low level of rural poverty, possibly because high wages are partly offset by high unemployment, or because other determinants of rural poverty are also at work. In 1999/2000, the correlation coefficient between real wages and headcount ratios in different states was 0.79 in absolute value, rising to 0.91 if Kerala is excluded. In 1993/94, the correlation coefficient was 0.87 in absolute value, with or without Kerala. Interestingly, if 'official' HCRs are used instead of our adjusted HCRs, the correlation coefficients come down quite sharply (e.g. from 0.91 to 0.73 in 1999/2000 and from 0.87 to 0.54 in 1993/94, without Kerala in both cases). This can be tentatively regarded as a further indication of the plausibility of the proposed adjustments.

Given the close association between real wages and rural poverty, the growth rates of real wages over time provide useful supplementary evidence on poverty trends. According to recent estimates based on AWI data, real agricultural wages were growing at about 5 per cent per year in the eighties and 2.5 per cent per year in the nineties.[28] Thus, real agricultural wages were growing considerably faster in the eighties than in the nineties. But even the reduced growth rate of agricultural wages in the nineties, at 2.5 per cent per year, points to significant growth of per capita expenditure among the poorer sections of the population and reinforces our earlier findings on poverty reduction. In fact, this reduced growth rate is a little *higher* than the growth rate of average per capita expenditure (1.5 per cent per year) that

[26] For details, see, e.g. Acharya (1989).

[27] See, e.g. Jose (1988) and Sarmah (2000). Note that the 'real wage' estimates used here ignore interstate differences in price levels.

[28] See Dreze and Sen (2002), p. 328; on the slowdown of the growth rate of real agricultural wages in the nineties (compared with the eighties), see also Sarmah (2000 and 2001).

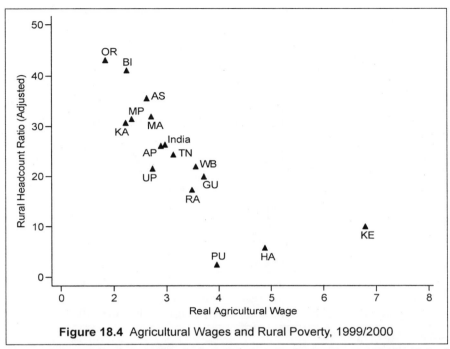

Figure 18.4 Agricultural Wages and Rural Poverty, 1999/2000

Source: Dreze and Sen (2002), Statistical Appendix, Table A3, and Table 18.3 of this paper. The 'real agricultural wage' is a three-year average ending in 1999/2000.

sustains our estimated declines of rural headcount ratios and headcount indexes between 1993/94 and 1999/2000.

The data on real wages also provide some independent corroboration of the state-specific patterns of poverty decline. This is illustrated in Figure 18.5, where we plot state-specific estimates of the growth rate of real agricultural wages in the nineties against the estimated proportionate decline in the headcount ratio (a very similar pattern applies to the poverty-gap index). Here the two main outliers are Punjab and Haryana, where the headcount ratio has declined sharply without a correspondingly sharp increase in real wages (indeed without any such increase, in the case of Punjab). Leaving out these two outliers, the association between the two series is remarkably close (with a correlation coefficient of 0.88).

An interesting sidelight emerging from Figure 18.5 is that a healthy growth of real agricultural wages appear to be a 'sufficient' condition for substantial poverty decline in rural areas: all the states where real wages have grown at more than, say, 2.5 per cent per year in the nineties have experienced a comparatively sharp reduction of the rural headcount ratio. Conversely, in states with low rates of reduction of the headcount ratio (say, 15 per cent or less over six years), real wages have invariably grown at less than 2 per cent per year. This applies in particular to the entire eastern region (Assam, Orissa, West Bengal and Bihar) and also to Andhra Pradesh and Madhya Pradesh.

Independent evidence on the growth rates of real wages has recently been presented by Sundaram (2001a and 2001b), based on the 'employment-unemployment surveys' (EUS) of the National Sample Survey for 1993/94 and 1999/2000. For the present purpose, these surveys are comparable. Sundaram estimates that the real earnings of agricultural labourers have grown at about 2.5 per cent per year

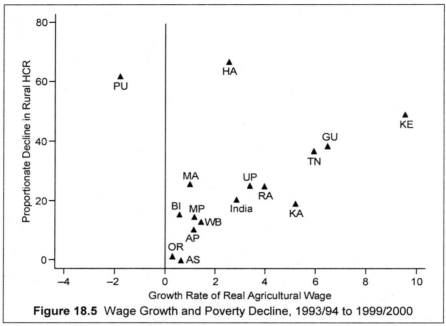

Figure 18.5 Wage Growth and Poverty Decline, 1993/94 to 1999/2000

Source: See Figure 18.4.

between 1993/94 and 1999/2000. These are tentative estimates, based as they are on data for two years only. Yet it is reassuring to find that they are consistent with the AWI-based estimates.

The 'Employment-Unemployment Surveys'

The National Sample Survey's 1993/94 and 1999/2000 employment-unemployment surveys (EUS) also include consumer expenditure data. These can be used for further scrutiny of poverty trends. This task has been undertaken in a recent paper by Sundaram and Tendulkar (2002). They note that the consumption survey in the 1999/2000 EUS uses the traditional 30-day reporting period, but differs from the standard questionnaire by only asking an abbreviated set of questions. However, the authors find that, in those cases where the questions have comparable coverage, the means from the EUS, using the traditional 30-day reporting period, are typically close to those from the 30-day questionnaire in the main consumption survey. Based on this correspondence, they argue that the 30-day questions in the main 1999/2000 survey were not much distorted by the seven-day questions that were asked alongside them. In this version of events, the major source of incomparability between the 55th and 50th Rounds is not the contamination of the 30-day questions, but rather the revised treatment of the low frequency items, for which the reporting period was 30 days in the 50th Round and 365 days in the 55th Round. As we have already noted, the 365-day reporting period for these items pulls up the lower tail of the consumption distribution, and thus biases down the headcount ratio compared with earlier methods. However, Sundaram and Tendulkar note that the 50th Round contained both 30-day and 365-day reporting periods for the low frequency items. Hence, by recalculating the 50th Round headcounts using the 365-day responses, they can put the 50th and 55th Rounds on a roughly comparable basis. When they do this, they find that, in both rural and urban sectors, they can confirm a little more than three-quarters of the official decline in the headcount ratios between the two rounds (Sundaram and Tendulkar, 2002: Table III.8). These calculations are not identical to our first-step adjustments (see Table 18.1), but they are close enough to inspire some confidence that both sets of results are in the right range.

To sum up, the all-India poverty indexes presented earlier in this paper are broadly consistent with independent evidence from the national accounts statistics and the employment-unemployment surveys, as well as with related information on agricultural wages. There is also some congruence between the interstate contrasts emerging from NSS data and independent information on state-specific growth rates of 'state domestic product' and real agricultural wages. The combined evidence from these different sources is fairly strong, even though each individual source has significant limitations.

ECONOMIC INEQUALITY IN THE NINETIES

Growth, Poverty and Inequality

It is possible to think about poverty decline, as captured by standard poverty indexes, in terms of two distinct components: a growth component and a distribution component. The growth component reflects the increase of average per capita expenditure. The distribution component captures any change that may take place in the distribution of per capita expenditure over households.

This decomposition exercise is pursued in Table 18.6, with reference to the headcount ratio (very similar results apply to the poverty-gap index). The first column repeats the headcount ratio for 1993/94 from Table 18.3. The second column (labelled 'derivative with respect to growth') shows our estimate of the percentage-point reduction in HCR associated with a distribution-neutral, 1 per cent increase in APCE in the relevant state. To illustrate, in rural Andhra Pradesh a 1 per cent increase in APCE in 1993/94, with no change in distribution, would have led to a decline of 0.9 percentage points in the rural headcount ratio.[29] This derivative depends positively on the fraction of people who are at or near the poverty line, which is typically larger in the poorer states. The figures in Column 2 vary from −1.27 in rural Assam to −0.15 in urban Jammu & Kashmir. Column 3 reproduces the total percentage growth between 1993/94 and 1999/2000 from Table 18.5.

If we multiply the second column (the derivative with respect to growth) by the third column (the amount of growth), we get an estimate of the amount of poverty reduction that we would expect from growth alone, in the absence of any change in the shape of the distribution. This is an approximation, because the derivative is likely to change as the headcount ratio falls. In Column 4, we report a more precise calculation: an estimate of what the headcount ratio would have been in 1999/2000 if the distributions of consumption in each state were identical to those in 1993/94, but had been shifted upwards by the amount of growth in real per capita expenditure that actually took place. This can be readily calculated by reducing the 1993/94 poverty lines by the amount of growth, and re-estimating the headcount ratios from these adjusted lines and the 1993/94 expenditure data. These hypothetical changes can then be compared with the *actual* reductions in the headcount ratios, shown in the final column. The difference between these last two columns is the change in the headcount ratio that is attributable to changes in the shape of the consumption distribution.

---

[29] Note that these derivatives are not elasticities in the usual sense, and are not the same as the elasticities sometimes quoted, which are the derivatives of the logarithm of the headcount ratio with respect to the logarithm of mean per capita expenditure.

Table 18.6 Growth and the Headcount Ratio, 1993/94 to 1999/2000

	HCR_{50}	Derivative with Respect to Growth	Six Years Growth	Change in HCR_{55} Inequality Fixed	Change in HCR_{55}, Actual
Rural					
Andhra Pradesh	29.2	−0.90	2.8	−2.5	−3.0
Assam	35.4	−1.27	0.9	−1.4	0.1
Bihar	48.6	−1.06	6.9	−8.2	−7.4
Gujarat	32.5	−0.91	15.1	−12.1	−12.4
Haryana	17.0	−0.63	31.0	−12.9	−11.3
Himachal Pradesh	17.1	−0.75	16.2	−8.3	−7.3
Jammu & Kashmir	10.1	−0.50	5.4	−2.6	−4.0
Karnataka	37.9	−0.91	9.5	−9.0	−7.2
Kerala	19.5	−0.62	19.6	−10.3	−9.5
Madhya Pradesh	36.6	−0.93	6.6	−6.5	−5.3
Maharashtra	42.9	−0.81	14.1	−10.9	−11.0
Orissa	43.5	−1.04	1.4	−1.2	−0.5
Punjab	6.2	−0.34	20.2	−4.0	−3.8
Rajasthan	23.0	−0.78	7.0	−5.5	−5.7
Tamil Nadu	38.5	−0.90	15.7	−13.3	−14.1
Uttar Pradesh	28.6	−0.79	8.3	−6.6	−7.2
West Bengal	25.1	−0.79	−2.1	−2.0	−3.2
All-India	33.0	−0.88	8.7	−6.8	−6.7
Urban					
Andhra Pradesh	17.8	−0.62	18.5	−9.0	−6.9
Assam	13.0	−0.64	8.8	−3.1	−1.2
Bihar	26.7	−0.79	4.8	−4.0	−2.0
Gujarat	14.7	−0.55	20.9	−8.7	−8.3
Haryana	10.5	−0.47	23.0	−6.3	−6.0
Himachal Pradesh	3.6	−0.26	28.5	−2.9	−2.4
Jammu & Kashmir	3.1	−0.15	8.0	−0.4	−1.8
Karnataka	21.4	−0.60	26.5	−12.9	−10.6
Kerala	13.9	−0.46	18.2	−7.1	−4.2
Madhya Pradesh	18.5	−0.63	14.1	−8.0	−4.6
Maharashtra	18.2	−0.45	16.7	−6.1	−6.2
Orissa	15.2	−0.54	0.0	0.1	0.4
Punjab	7.8	−0.38	17.9	−4.9	−4.4
Rajasthan	18.3	−0.59	15.4	−8.4	−7.5
Tamil Nadu	20.8	−0.66	25.1	−12.9	−9.6
Uttar Pradesh	21.7	−0.59	10.1	−6.0	−4.4
West Bengal	15.5	−0.56	11.5	−5.8	−4.3
Delhi	8.8	−0.26	30.7	−5.7	−6.4
All-India	17.8	−0.56	16.6	−7.4	−5.9

Source: Authors' calculations from the unit record data of the 43rd, 50th and 55th Rounds of the NSS. Note that the hypothetical all-India figures are calculated on the counterfactual assumption that each household received the state growth rate. They therefore do not show what would have happened had growth been more equally distributed across the states: see the text for this alternative calculation.

It is important to note that the last two columns are highly correlated. The correlation coefficients across the states are 0.97 (rural) and 0.93 (urban), so that growth alone can predict much of the cross-state pattern of reduction in HCRs. Nevertheless, the estimates are far from identical. In particular, the all-India calculations show that 'growth alone' would have reduced the poverty rate by *more* than actually happened, implying that there was an increase in inequality that offset some of the effects of growth, or put differently, that APCE growth among the poor was less than the average. These inequality effects vary somewhat from state to state and are much weaker in rural than in urban areas. In urban India, increasing inequality moderated the decline in the headcount ratio in all states except Delhi, Maharashtra, and Jammu & Kashmir. In some cases, such as urban Kerala and Madhya Pradesh, the 'moderating effect' is pronounced, with actual rates of reduction only a little over half those predicted by the growth in the mean.

For the urban sector as a whole (the last row of the table), the actual decline in the HCR is one and a half points lower (5.9 versus 7.4 per cent) than would have been the case had growth been equally distributed within each state. This estimate, which is the population-weighted average of the corresponding numbers for each state, calculates what would have happened if each household in each state had experienced the average growth for that state. An alternative, and equally interesting, counterfactual is what would have happened if, between 1993/94 and 1999/2000, each household in the country had experienced the countrywide growth rate of 10.9 per cent. Such a calculation yields an all-India HCR of 21.4 per cent (for rural and urban areas combined), compared with an actual all-India HCR of 22.7 per cent based on the 55th Round. In other words, the all-India HCR in 1999/2000 was 1.3 percentage points higher than it would have been (with the same growth rate of APCE) in the absence of any increase in inequality.

Aspects of Rising Inequality

Three aspects of rising economic inequality in the nineties have come up so far in our story. First, we found strong evidence of 'divergence' in per capita consumption across states. Second, our estimates of the growth rates of per capita expenditure between 1993/94 and 1999/2000 (Table 18.3) point to a significant increase in rural-urban inequalities at the all-India level, and also in most individual states. Third, the decomposition exercise in the preceding section shows that rising inequality within states, particularly in the urban sector, has moderated the effects of growth on poverty reduction.

Table 18.7 provides more systematic evidence on recent changes in consumption inequality within each sector of each state using two different measures of inequality. We show the logarithm of the difference of the arithmetic and geometric means (approximately the fraction by which the arithmetic mean exceeds the geometric mean), as well as the variance of the logarithm of per capita expenditure.

The table shows that the correction for questionnaire design is critical for understanding what has been happening. (Note that the correction for prices has no effect within sectors and states.) The direct use of the unit record data in the 55th Round, with no adjustment, shows a substantial *reduction* in inequality within the rural sectors of most states, with little or no increase in the urban sectors. With the correction, we see that within-state rural inequality has not fallen, and that there have been marked increases in within-state urban inequality. We suspect that the main reason why the unadjusted data are so misleading in this context is the change from 30 to 365 days in the reporting period for the low frequency items (durable goods, clothing and footwear, and institutional medical and educational expenditures). The longer reporting period actually reduces the mean expenditures on those items, but because a much larger fraction of people report *something* over the longer reporting period, the bottom tail of the consumption distribution is pulled up, and both inequality and poverty are reduced. Whether 365 days are a better or worse reporting period than 30 days could be argued either way, but the main point here is that the 55th and 50th Rounds are not comparable, and that the former artificially shows too little inequality compared with the latter. Once the corrections are made, we see that, in addition to increasing inequality between states, there has been a marked increase in consumption inequality within the urban sector of nearly all states.

Two further pieces of evidence are worth mentioning in this context. First, our findings on rising economic inequality within the urban sector are consistent with recent work by Banerjee and Piketty (2001), who use income tax records to document very large increases in income among the very highest income earners. They show that, in the 1990s, real incomes among the top one per cent of income earners increased by a half in real terms, while those of the top 1 per cent of 1 per cent increased by a factor of three in real terms.

Second, it is interesting to compare the growth rate of real wages for agricultural labourers with that of public sector salaries. As we saw earlier, real agricultural wages have grown at 2.5 per cent or so in the nineties. Public sector salaries, for their part, have grown at almost 5 per cent per year during the same period.[30] Given that public-sector employees tend to be much better off than agricultural labourers, this can be taken as an instance of rising economic disparities between different occupation groups. Since agricultural labourers and public-sector employees typically reside in rural and urban areas, respectively, this finding may just be another side of the coin of rising rural-urban disparities. Even then, it strengthens the evidence presented earlier on aspects of rising economic inequality in the nineties.

To sum up, except for the absence of clear evidence of rising intra-rural inequality within states, we find strong indications of a pervasive increase in economic inequality in the nineties. This is a new development in the Indian economy: until 1993/94, the all-India Gini coefficients of per capita consumer expenditure in rural and urban areas were fairly stable.[31] Further, it is worth noting that the rate of increase of economic inequality in the nineties is far from negligible. For instance, the compounding of interstate 'divergence' and rising rural-urban disparities produces very sharp contrasts in APCE growth between the rural sectors of the slow-growing states and the urban sectors of the fast-growing states (Table 18.3). This is further compounded by the accentuation of intra-urban inequality, which is itself quite substantial, bearing in mind that the change is measured over a short period of six years (Table 18.7).

It might be argued that a temporary increase in economic inequality is to be expected in a liberalising economy, and that this trend is likely to be short-lived. Proponents of the 'Kuznets curve' may even expect it to be reversed in due course. However, China's experience of sharp and sustained increase in economic inequality over a period of more than 20 years, after market-oriented economic reforms were initiated in the late 1970s, does not inspire much confidence in this prognosis.[32] It is, in fact, an important pointer to the possibility of further accentuation of economic disparities in India in the near future.

[30] Calculated from Government of India (2002), p. S-51. There have been further major increases in public-sector salaries after 1999/2000, with the gradual implementation of the recommendations of the Fifth Pay Commission by many state governments.

[31] See Dreze and Sen (2002), Statistical Appendix, Table A.6; also Datt (1999a and 1999b).

[32] On rising income inequality in China in the post-reform period, see Bramall and Jones (1993), Griffin and Zhao Renwei (1993), Yao Shujie (1999), Khan and Riskin (2001), among others.

Table 18.7 Inequality Measures

	Log AM – log GM[a]			Variance of Logs		
	50th Round	55th Round	55th Round Adjusted	50th Round	55th Round	55th Round Adjusted
Rural						
Andhra Pradesh	0.14	0.09	0.13	0.24	0.17	0.22
Assam	0.05	0.07	0.06	0.10	0.13	0.11
Bihar	0.08	0.07	0.08	0.16	0.13	0.16
Gujarat	0.10	0.09	0.11	0.17	0.18	0.18
Haryana	0.16	0.10	0.23	0.28	0.19	0.31
Himachal Pradesh	0.13	0.10	0.14	0.22	0.17	0.24
Jammu & Kashmir	0.10	0.06	0.07	0.16	0.12	0.14
Karnataka	0.12	0.10	0.12	0.21	0.18	0.22
Kerala	0.15	0.14	0.16	0.26	0.24	0.27
Madhya Pradesh	0.13	0.10	0.12	0.22	0.18	0.22
Maharashtra	0.16	0.11	0.16	0.27	0.20	0.28
Orissa	0.10	0.10	0.12	0.18	0.18	0.21
Punjab	0.13	0.10	0.14	0.22	0.19	0.24
Rajasthan	0.12	0.07	0.10	0.20	0.14	0.18
Tamil Nadu	0.16	0.14	0.15	0.27	0.23	0.24
Uttar Pradesh	0.13	0.10	0.12	0.23	0.18	0.21
West Bengal	0.11	0.09	0.08	0.17	0.15	0.15
All-India Rural	0.14	0.11	0.14	0.23	0.21	0.24
Urban						
Andhra Pradesh	0.17	0.16	0.17	0.30	0.29	0.33
Assam	0.13	0.16	0.14	0.25	0.30	0.27
Bihar	0.15	0.17	0.17	0.27	0.30	0.30
Gujarat	0.14	0.14	0.14	0.25	0.25	0.26
Haryana	0.13	0.14	0.15	0.24	0.27	0.28
Himachal Pradesh	0.38	0.16	0.42	0.37	0.29	0.40
Jammu & Kashmir	0.13	0.09	0.12	0.24	0.16	0.21
Karnataka	0.16	0.18	0.17	0.31	0.32	0.34
Kerala	0.20	0.17	0.22	0.31	0.32	0.37
Madhya Pradesh	0.18	0.17	0.18	0.29	0.29	0.33
Maharashtra	0.21	0.21	0.21	0.40	0.36	0.40
Orissa	0.15	0.14	0.16	0.29	0.26	0.29
Punjab	0.13	0.14	0.14	0.23	0.25	0.25
Rajasthan	0.14	0.13	0.14	0.25	0.23	0.26
Tamil Nadu	0.21	0.27	0.20	0.39	0.34	0.35
Uttar Pradesh	0.17	0.18	0.19	0.31	0.31	0.34
West Bengal	0.19	0.20	0.19	0.34	0.31	0.35
Delhi	0.29	0.21	0.30	0.43	0.39	0.46
All-India Urban	0.19	0.20	0.21	0.34	0.34	0.37
All-India	0.17	0.18	0.19	0.29	0.29	0.32

Note: An AM is the arithmetic mean and GM is the geometric mean: the difference in their logarithms is the mean relative deviation, a measure of inequality.

QUALIFICATIONS AND CONCERNS

Food Consumption

There have been major changes in India's food economy in the nineties. The eighties were a period of healthy growth in agricultural output, food production, and real agricultural wages. During the nineties, however, productivity increases slowed down in many states. The quantity index of agricultural production grew at a lame 2 per cent per year or so. The growth of real agricultural wages slowed down considerably. And cereal production barely kept pace with population growth.[33]

The virtual stagnation of per capita cereal production in the nineties has been accompanied by a gradual switch from net imports to net exports, and also by a massive accumulation of public stocks. Correspondingly, there has been no increase in estimated per capita 'net availability' of cereals (Table 18.6). If anything, net availability declined a little, from a peak of about 450 grammes per person per day in 1990 to 420 grammes or so at the end of the nineties. This is consistent with independent evidence, from National Sample Survey data, of a decline in per capita cereal consumption in the nineties. Between 1993/94 and 1999/2000, for instance, average cereal consumption per capita declined from 13.5 kg per month to 12.7 kg per month in rural areas, and from 10.6 to 10.4 kg per month in urban areas.[34] This comparison is based on the 'uncorrected' 55th Round data, and the 'true' decline may be larger still, given the changes in questionnaire design (see section on Official Estimates).

The reduction of cereal consumption in the nineties may seem inconsistent with the notion that poverty has declined during the same period. Indeed, this pattern has been widely invoked as evidence of 'impoverishment' in the nineties. If cereal consumption is declining, how can poverty be declining?

It is worth noting, however, that the decline of cereal consumption is not new. A similar decline took place (according to National Sample Survey data) during the seventies and eighties, when poverty was

Table 18.8 Cereal Availability in the Nineties (*Grams per person per day*)

	Net Production	Net Imports	Net Change in Public Stocks	'Net Availability' (1 + 2 – 3)
1985/89	422.7	2.0	–5.3	430.1
1990	456.9	0.3	5.0	452.1
1991	447.9	–1.4	0.4	446.1
1992	446.8	1.3	4.2	443.8
1993	446.4	2.5	16.6	432.3
1994	456.3	0.2	16.6	439.9
1995	448.6	–5.9	–2.3	445.1
1996	451.7	–6.9	–11.7	456.4
1997	445.5	–6.7	–4.2	443.0
1998	455.3	–4.7	11.0	439.6
1999	456.3	–5.4	25.3	425.6
2000	452.7	–5.2	30.7	416.8

Note: All figures (except first row) are three-year averages centred at the year specified in the first column.
Source: Calculated from Government of India (2002), p. S-21.

[33] On these and related trends, see Dreze and Sen (2002), chapter 9. On the growth of foodgrain production, see Government of India (2002), pp. S-21 and S-22.
[34] See Shariff and Mallick (1999), Table 18.7, and National Sample Survey Organisation (2001), pp. A-101 and A-134.

certainly declining. Hanchate and Dyson's (2000) recent comparison of rural food consumption patterns in 1973/74 and 1993/94 sheds some useful light on this matter. As the authors show, during this period per capita cereal consumption in rural areas declined quite sharply on average (from 15.8 to 13.6 kg per person per month), but rose among the poorest households. The decline in the average is driven by reduced consumption among the higher expenditure groups.[35]

The average decline is unlikely to be driven by changes in relative prices; indeed, there has been little change in food prices, relative to other prices, in the intervening period. Instead, this pattern appears to reflect a substitution away from cereals to other food items as incomes rise (at least beyond a certain threshold). The consumption of 'superior' food items such as vegetables, milk, fruit, fish and meat did rise quite sharply over the same period, across all expenditure groups. Seen in this light, the decline of average cereal consumption may not be a matter of concern per se. Indeed, average cereal consumption is inversely related to per capita income across countries (e.g. it is lower in China than in India, and even lower in the United States), and the same applies across states within India (e.g. cereal consumption is higher in Bihar or Orissa than in Punjab or Haryana).

Food intake data collected by the National Nutrition Monitoring Bureau (NNMB) shed further light on this issue. Aside from detailed information on food intake, the NNMB surveys include rough estimates of household incomes. These are used in Figure 18.6 to display the relation between per-capita income and food intake, for different types of food. The substitution from cereals towards other food items

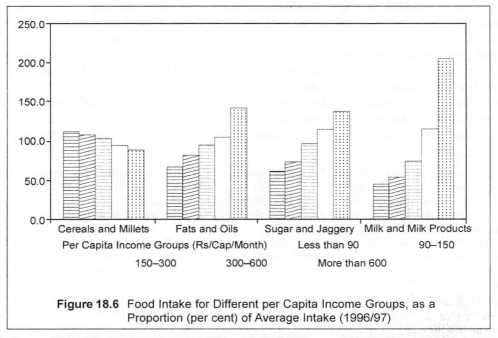

Figure 18.6 Food Intake for Different per Capita Income Groups, as a Proportion (per cent) of Average Intake (1996/97)

Source: Calculated from National Nutrition Monitoring Bureau (1999), Table 6.9. The data relate to rural areas of eight sample states.

---

[35] For similar observations based on a comparison of 1972/73 and 1993/94 NSS data, see Rao (2000).

with rising per-capita income emerges quite clearly.[36] This pattern, if confirmed, would fit quite well with the data on change over time.[37] It also implies that the decline of average cereal consumption in the nineties is not inconsistent with our earlier findings on poverty decline.[38]

Localised Impoverishment and Hidden Costs

The overall decline of poverty in the nineties does not rule out the possibility of impoverishment among specific regions or social groups. That possibility, of course, is not new, but it is worth asking whether its scope has expanded during the last decade. As the economy gives greater room to market forces, uncertainty and inequality often increase, possibly leading to enhanced economic insecurity among those who are not in a position to benefit from the new opportunities, or whose livelihoods are threatened by the changes in the economy. The increase of economic inequality in the nineties, noted earlier, suggests that tendencies of this kind may well be at work in India today. Adverse trends in living standards could take several distinct forms, including: (1) impoverishment among specific regions or social groups, (2) heightened uncertainty in general, and (3) growing 'hidden costs' of economic development.

In connection with the first point, we have already noted that some of the poorer states, notably Orissa and Assam, have not fared well at all in the nineties. It is quite possible that the poorer regions within these states have done even worse, to the point of absolute impoverishment for substantial sections of the population. In the case of Orissa, there is some independent evidence of localised impoverishment in the poorer districts, due inter alia to the destruction of the local environmental base and to the dismal failure of state-sponsored development programmes (Dreze, 2001).[39]

Similarly, the overall improvement of living standards may hide instances of impoverishment among specific occupation groups. The nineties have been a period of rapid structural change in the Indian economy, leading in some cases to considerable disruption of earlier livelihood patterns. Examples include a deep recession in the powerloom sector, a serious crisis in the edible oil industry after import tariffs were slashed, periodic waves of bankruptcy among cotton growers, the displacement of traditional fishing by commercial shrimp farms, and a number of sectoral crises associated with the abrupt lifting

[36] For further evidence, see also National Institute of Nutrition (1997). This pattern, sometimes known as the 'nutrition transition', is familiar to nutritionists (Drewnoski, 1999). It is worth noting that its implications for health are not uncontroversial; some nutrition experts have apparently 'pointed to the beneficial health effects of dire poverty, poor diets, and strenuous manual labour', presumably referring to the benefits of a low fat, low sugar, and high fibre diet, rather than low quantities (Drewnoski, 1999, p. 195).

[37] Unlike NNMB data, National Sample Survey data suggest that per capita cereal consumption rises monotonically with per capita expenditure. The contradiction between nutritional food intake and expenditure surveys is neither uncommon nor fully understood; for two different interpretations of the Indian case, see Subramanian and Deaton (1996) and Subramanian (2001).

[38] Also worth noting in this context is tentative evidence of recent improvement in nutritional indicators based on anthropometric measurements. According to NNMB data, the proportion of adults with a low 'body mass index' has declined in the nineties (see Vaidyanathan, 2002). The National Family Health Surveys also suggest that the proportion of undernourished children has declined between 1992/93 and 1998/99 (see International Institute for Population Sciences 1995: xxxiii, and International Institute for Population Sciences, 2000: 267 and 443).

[39] It should also be noted, however, that Orissa was hit by a devastating cyclone in October 1999, around the middle of the 55th Round survey period. The 1999/2000 poverty estimates for Orissa are therefore likely to be somewhat 'above trend'.

of quantitative restrictions on imports in mid-2001.[40] The destruction of local environmental resources is another common cause of disrupted livelihoods in many areas.

A related issue is the possibility of 'hidden hardships' associated with recent patterns of economic development. To illustrate, there is much evidence that, in many of the poorer regions of India, further impoverishment has been avoided mainly through seasonal labour migration.[41] The latter often entails significant social costs that are poorly captured, if at all, in standard poverty indexes or for that matter in the other social indicators examined in this paper. Examples of such costs include irregular school attendance, the spread of HIV/AIDS, the disruption of family life, and rising urban congestion.[42] Similarly, involuntary displacement of persons affected by large development projects such as dams and mines tends to have enormous human costs. These, again, are largely hidden from view in income-based analyses of poverty. In fact, the incomes of displaced persons often rise (with 'cash compensation') even as their lives are being shattered.[43] The 'informalisation' of labour markets is another example of economic change with substantial hidden costs (e.g. longer working hours, higher insecurity, lower status, and deteriorating work conditions).[44] These issues are not new, but it is important to acknowledge the possibility that the hidden costs of economic growth have intensified in the nineties.

This acknowledgement helps to reconcile the survey-based evidence reviewed earlier with widespread media reports, in recent years, of sectoral economic crises and localised impoverishment.[45] This issue calls for further scrutiny, based on more focused analysis of survey data as well as on micro-studies.

The 'Thin' Rounds: An Unresolved Puzzle?

We have so far said very little about the 'thin' rounds, and the poverty estimates that can be calculated from them. Yet Figure 18.1 shows that the recent thin rounds, from the 51st through the 54th Rounds, generate poverty estimates that are hard to reconcile with the quinquennial 'thick' rounds. If we were to connect up these points with the official HCR estimates, we would get a series in which poverty rose between 1993/94 and 1994/95, fell from 1994/95 to the end of 1997, rose very sharply in the first half of 1998, and then fell with extraordinary rapidity in 1999/2000. As we have seen, the official estimate for 1999/2000 is too low, and the last thin round, the 54th Round, ran for only the first six months of 1998, and may therefore not be fully comparable with other rounds. Even so, and with due allowance for corrections, it is very hard to integrate the poverty estimates based on the thin rounds with the picture that emerges from the thick rounds as well as from other sources surveyed in this paper.

The story is further complicated by the fact that these thin rounds were run in two versions, one of which resembled the standard questionnaire up to and including the 50th Round, and one of which – the

[40] For insightful case studies of localised economic crises in the nineties, see, e.g. Roy (1999), Breman (2001a), Krishna (2001), Jhabvala and Sinha (2002), Samal (2002), and Dabir-Alai (2002).

[41] See Rodgers and Rodgers (2000), Rogaly et al. (2001), Sharma (2001), Institute for Human Development (2002), among others.

[42] On the other hand, labour migration can also have positive roles, such as facilitating the diffusion of knowledge (Maharatna, 2001) and enabling the disadvantaged castes to 'escape from the clutches of the prevailing caste discrimination in the village', (Sharma, 2001: 18).

[43] For a telling case study of the human costs of involuntary displacement, see Bhatia (1997).

[44] On this, see particularly Breman (2001a and 2001b).

[45] See, e.g. Sainath (2001a, 2001b, 2001c and 2001d), Breman (2001b), Dreze (2001), Mehta (2001). We are not referring here to media reports of short-term hardship associated with the recent drought (in 2000 and 2001), but to stories of sustained impoverishment.

experimental questionnaire – had different reporting periods for different goods. Headcount ratios based on the experimental questionnaire (not shown in Figure 18.1) are lower than those from the standard questionnaire, because the experimental questionnaire generated higher reports of per capita expenditure. However, they also show rising HCRs from the 52nd through the 54th Rounds, and the increase continues into the 55th Round if we use comparable reporting periods from that round. Based on the experimental questionnaire, a case could be made that the all-India HCR has been rising since 1995-96 (Sen, 2000). As we have seen, there are good grounds for distrusting the experimental questionnaire in the 55th Round, because of the juxtaposition of the 7-day recall and 30-day recall data for food – paan and tobacco. Quite likely, the 'reconciliation effect' (see section on Official Estimates) pulled down the estimates of per capita expenditure from the experimental questionnaire, thus exaggerating poverty by this count. Even so, if poverty were genuinely falling, there is no obvious explanation why the experimental questionnaire should show a rise in poverty from 1995 through 1998.

The Planning Commission has never endorsed poverty counts from the thin rounds. In part, this has been because of the smaller sample sizes. The Planning Commission needs estimates of HCRs, not just for all-India, but for individual states, and the thin rounds are not large enough to support accurate estimates for some of the smaller (of the major) states. But inadequate sample size generates variance, not bias, and in any case, the thin round sample sizes are perfectly adequate to generate accurate estimates for the all-India HCRs. The discrepancies in Figure 18.1 cannot be explained by inadequate sample sizes.

There are other differences between thick and thin rounds. For example, the sampling frame for the 51st, 53rd, and 54th Rounds was not the census of population, but the 'economic' census. In the population census, each household is asked if it has a family business or enterprise, and only such households are included in the first-stage sampling from the economic census when 'first-stage units' are drawn with probability proportional to size. This means that a village with few or no such households has only a small or no chance of being selected as a first-stage unit. Even so, when the team reaches the village, *all* households are listed and have a chance of being in the sample, so it is unclear that this choice of frame makes much difference. Indeed, comparison of various socio-economic indicators (e.g. literacy rates, years of schooling, landholding, or family size) from the surveys suggests no obvious breaks between the 51st and 53rd Rounds on the one hand, and the 52nd Round (which used the population census) on the other. Conversations with NSS and Planning Commission staff sometimes suggest that there may be other (non-documented) differences in the sampling structure of the thin rounds. Certainly, a tabulation of the population sizes of the first-stage units shows that the 52nd Round contained relatively few large units compared with the 51st, 53rd, 54th, and 55th Rounds; this is a different issue from the use of the economic rather than population census (both the 52nd and 55th Rounds use the latter), and the finding suggests that the first-stage units in the 52nd Round were selected differently from other rounds in some way that is not documented. Moreover, the measurement of consumption is not the main purpose of any of these thin rounds, all of which have some other objective, so it is possible that consumption is not so fully or carefully collected as in the quinquennial rounds.

In short, there are grounds for scepticism about the validity of the thin rounds for poverty estimation purposes, and this is all the more so if we remember that aside from indicating no poverty decline in the late nineties, the thin rounds also suggest that *average* per capita expenditure was stagnating during that period – something that is very hard to reconcile with other evidence. Having said this, we have not been able to identify any 'smoking gun' that would point to a specific problem with any of these rounds and explain their apparently anomalous poverty estimates. Until that puzzle is resolved, we see the evidence from the thin rounds as casting a shadow of doubt over the interpretation of the poverty estimates presented earlier in this paper. Perhaps the thin rounds in the next five years will offer some useful clues.

BEYOND POVERTY INDEXES

The decline of poverty in the nineties, as captured in the indicators examined so far, can be seen as an example of *continued progress* during that period. Whether the rate of progress has been faster or slower than in the eighties is difficult to say, and the answer is likely to depend on how the rate of progress is measured. There is, at any rate, no obvious pattern of 'acceleration' or 'slowdown' in this respect.

It is important to supplement the evidence reviewed so far, which essentially relates to purchasing power, with other indicators of well-being relating, for instance to educational achievements, life expectancy, nutritional levels, crime rates, and various aspects of social inequality. This broader perspective reveals that social progress in the nineties has followed very diverse patterns, ranging from accelerated progress in some fields to slowdown and even regression in other respects. The point is illustrated in Figure 18.7, where simple measures of the progress of different social indicators in the nineties are compared with the corresponding achievements in the eighties.

Elementary education provides an interesting example of accelerated progress in the nineties.[46] This trend is evident not only from census data on literacy rates, but also from National Family Health Survey data on school participation. To illustrate, school participation among girls aged 6–14 jumped from 59 per cent to 74 per cent between 1992/93 and 1998/99.[47] The regional patterns are also instructive. It is particularly interesting to note evidence of rapid progress in Madhya Pradesh and Rajasthan, demarcating

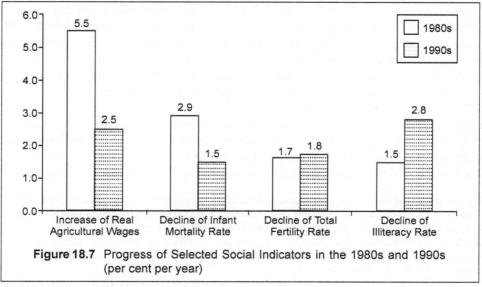

Figure 18.7 Progress of Selected Social Indicators in the 1980s and 1990s (per cent per year)

Source: Dreze and Sen (2002), Chapter 9.

[46] For further discussion, see Dreze and Sen (2002), Chapter 5.

[47] See Dreze and Sen (2002), p. 148; also International Institute for Population Sciences (1995 and 2000), for further details.

them clearly from Bihar and Uttar Pradesh, the other two members of the so-called BIMARU set.[48] There is an important pointer here to the relation between public action and social achievements. Indeed, Madhya Pradesh and Rajasthan are two states where there have been many interesting initiatives in the field of elementary education in the nineties (on the part of government as well as non-government institutions), in contrast with Bihar and Uttar Pradesh where schooling matters continue to be highly neglected. The fact the literacy rates and school participation have surged in the more 'active' states is an encouraging indication of the possibility of effective public intervention in this field.

Turning to instances of 'slowdown', we have already referred to the slackening of the growth rate of real agricultural wages in the nineties. Another important example is the slowdown of infant mortality decline. During the eighties, India achieved a reduction of 30 per cent in the infant mortality rate – from 114 deaths per 1,000 live births in 1980 to 80 per 1,000 in 1990. During the nineties, however, the infant mortality rate declined by only 12.5 per cent – from 80 to 70.[49] In fact, in the second half of the nineties, India's infant mortality rate has remained virtually unchanged. In some states, notably Rajasthan, the infant mortality rate has stagnated for as long as 10 years. These worrying trends have received astonishingly little attention in policy debates, and even in the debate on 'poverty in the nineties'.

Finally, there have also been some areas of 'regression' in the nineties. The increase of economic inequality, discussed earlier, can be seen in those terms. Given the adverse social consequences of economic inequality (ranging from elitist biases in public policy to the reinforcement of other types of inequality), this accentuation of economic disparities is not a trivial matter. Another example of adverse development in the nineties is the decline in the female-male ratio among children, from 945 girls per 1,000 boys (in the 0–6 age group) in 1991 to 927 girls per 1,000 boys in 2001.[50] This decline appears to be driven by the spread of prenatal sex-determination technology and sex-selective abortion, but this does not mean that it is a 'technological' phenomenon, unrelated to other recent economic and social trends. Economic growth, in particular, may facilitate the spread of sex-selective abortion, by making the use of sex-determination technology more affordable. In this connection, it is worth noting that the largest declines of the female-male ratio among children between 1991 and 2001 occurred in five states (Gujarat, Haryana, Himachal Pradesh, Punjab and Delhi) that are relatively well-off economically, and have also experienced comparatively high rates of growth of per capita expenditure in the nineties (Table 18.3).[51]

A detailed assessment of the progress of development indicators in the nineties is beyond the scope of this paper. However, a few general observations can be made on the basis of these illustrations. First, as noted already, poverty is not unidimensional. The poverty indexes used in the first part of this paper are useful indicators of inadequate purchasing power, but on their own do not do justice to the range of

---

[48] To illustrate, looking at the percentage reduction in illiteracy between 1991 and 2001, Madhya Pradesh and Rajasthan did better than any other major state except Himachal Pradesh; Uttar Pradesh is very close to the all-India average; and Bihar ranks second from the bottom (calculated from census data given in Government of India, 2001b). The comparison is particularly instructive because all four BIMARU states started off with similar (very low) levels of literacy in 1991. On the 'schooling revolution' in Himachal Pradesh (an even more remarkable example of successful promotion of elementary education), see PROBE Team (1999), Chapter 9.

[49] See Government of India (1999a), Table 18.1, and *Sample Registration Bulletin*, April 2001; also UNICEF (2001) and Mari Bhat (2002). The comparison with Bangladesh is also instructive: Bangladesh's infant mortality rate was much higher than India's in 1990 (91 and 80 per 1,000, respectively), but by 1999 it had come down to 61 as against India's 71. See *World Development Indicators 2001*, pp. 16-17.

[50] On this and related issues, see Dreze and Sen (2002), Chapter 7.

[51] The relevant female-male ratios are given in Government of India (2001b), pp. 92–94.

deprivations we ought to be concerned with. Following on this, it is important to acknowledge that recent progress in eliminating poverty and deprivation has been quite uneven in different fields. The debate on 'poverty in the nineties' has often overlooked this basic point.

Second, this recognition is also important in assessing the relation between poverty decline and economic growth. As noted earlier, the decline of poverty in the nineties, as captured by conventional indexes such as the headcount ratio or the poverty-gap index, has been overwhelmingly driven by the growth of average per capita expenditure. From this it may seem that the reduction of poverty is mainly a question of economic growth. However, there is an element of circularity in this argument: if poverty is defined as lack of income, it is not surprising that the growth of income plays a key role in reducing it. When the multi-dimensional nature of poverty is acknowledged, this relation appears in a different light. To illustrate, consider child mortality as an aspect of the deprivations associated with poverty. There is, of course, a significant (negative) relation between child mortality and purchasing power. But child mortality is also strongly influenced by other factors such as educational levels, fertility rates, public health provisions (including clean water and vaccinations), and various aspects of gender relations. Looking at interstate contrasts in India, the correlation between child mortality and average per capita expenditure (or even poverty indexes) is actually quite weak. Other factors, particularly female literacy, are often more important.[52] Similar comments apply in the context of elementary education: the nineties have demonstrated the possibility of rapid progress in this field through public intervention, with or without rapid economic growth. In short, the standard focus on headcount ratios and other expenditure-based poverty indexes tends to foster a simplistic view of the relation between economic growth and poverty decline.

Third, it is also interesting to re-examine the issue of trends in inequality, in the light of this broader perspective. As discussed in section on Economic Inequality in the Nineties, there is much evidence of rising economic inequality in the nineties, in the form of a widening rural-urban gap, enhanced interstate disparities, and also growing inequality within urban areas in most states. What about other types of social inequality, involving other dimensions of well-being (e.g. educational levels or life expectancy) and other bases of disadvantage (e.g. gender or caste)? The decline of the female-male ratio among children illustrates the fact that the phenomenon of rising inequality in the nineties is not confined to standard economic inequalities: 'natality inequality' between males and females is also rising.[53] But this is not to say that inequality has risen across the board. Even within the field of gender inequality, there are changes in the other direction, such as the emergence of a substantial gender gap in life expectancy in favour of *women*, overturning India's long history of female disadvantage in this respect. Similarly, it is interesting to note that while economic disparities between rural and urban areas have sharply risen in the nineties, there are trends in the opposite direction as well. The rural-urban gap in life expectancy, for instance, has declined from 10 years or so in the late 1970s to seven years or so today, and rural-urban differentials in school participation have also narrowed.[54] Here again, the picture is more diverse (and more interesting) than it appears on the basis of purchasing-power indicators alone.

[52] Across states, the correlation coefficient between child mortality and per capita expenditure is 0.4 (in absolute value), compared with 0.8 for the correlation coefficient between child mortality and female literacy. After controlling for female literacy, per capita expenditure bears no significant association with child mortality at the state level. For further discussion, see Dreze and Sen (2002), pp 87–89. On the determinants of mortality and fertility in India, see also Murthi, Guio and Dreze (1995) and Dreze and Murthi (2001), and further studies cited there.

[53] On 'natality inequality' and its significance, see Sen (2001).

[54] See, e.g. Government of India (1999), p. 16, and Dreze and Sen (2002), p. 148.

Fourth, the broad approach explored here calls for a correspondingly broad reading of the causal influences underlying the identified changes. In the debate on 'poverty in the nineties', there has been a tendency not only to view development trends in unidimensional terms, but also to attribute these trends in a somewhat mechanical manner to the economic reforms initiated around 1991. At one end of the spectrum, it has been claimed that the last decade has been a period of unprecedented improvement in living standards, thanks to liberalisation.[55] At the other end, the nineties have been described as a period of widespread 'impoverishment', attributed to liberalisation.[56] Clearly, these readings fail to do justice to the diversity of recent trends. But in addition, they ignore the diversity of causal influences that have a bearing on these trends. The accelerated progress of elementary education in the nineties, for instance, has little to do with liberalisation, and the same applies to the slowdown of infant mortality decline, not to speak of the decline of the female-male ratio among children. Much else than liberalisation has happened in the nineties, and while issues of economic reform are of course extremely important, so are other aspects of economic and social policy.

CONCLUSION

A number of useful lessons emerge from this re-examination of the evidence on poverty and inequality in the nineties. First, there is consistent evidence of continuing poverty decline in the nineties, in terms of the 'headcount ratio'. The extent of the decline, however, remains somewhat uncertain at this time. Given the methodological changes that took place between the 50th and 55th Rounds of the National Sample Survey, the official figures (implying a decline from 36 per cent to 26 per cent in the all-India headcount ratio between 1993/94 and 1999/2000) are, strictly speaking, invalid. We have discussed alternative estimates, based on comparable data from the two surveys. As it turns out, these adjusted estimates suggest that a large part of the poverty decline associated with official figures is 'real', rather than driven by methodological changes. While further corroboration and investigation of the adjustment procedure is required, the results have been supported by one independent study using an entirely different methodology (Sundaram and Tendulkar, 2002). Further, the adjusted figures fit reasonably well with related evidence from the national accounts statistics, the employment-unemployment surveys, and data on agricultural wages.

Second, we have discussed some important limitations of the headcount ratio as an index of poverty (even within the standard expenditure-based approach), and argued for wider adoption of alternative poverty indexes such as the poverty-gap index. The main argument for using headcount ratios is that they have good 'communication value', in so far as they are relatively easy to understand and interpret. However, this transparency is to some extent deceptive, and much caution is required in interpreting poverty trends on the basis of headcount ratios. For the purpose of the poverty comparisons examined

[55] To illustrate: 'Economic reforms initiated in 1991 have led to a radical transformation in the well-being of the bottom half of the population. From an approximate level of 38 per cent in 1987, poverty level in India in 1998 was close to 12 per cent' (Bhalla, 2000b, p. 7).

[56] To illustrate: 'Both under the World Bank structural adjustment, and from the finance ministry – it's feet might be in India, but it's head is in Washington – and then under the World Trade Organisation obligations, we're basically getting a fundamental destruction of notions of the rights of citizens . . . . Very vital resources we need both for survival – drinking water, all the resources people need for livelihoods – are just disappearing so rapidly that life is becoming impossible . . . we really have a very, very major crisis of survival at hand . . .' (Shiva, 2001b). For further contributions on both sides of the debate, see the literature cited in Footnote 2.

in this paper, the headcount ratio turns out to be no less informative than the poverty-gap index. Yet it was important to calculate the PGIs, if only to discover that this refinement does not, after all, make much difference in this particular context.

Third, growth patterns in the nineties are characterised by major regional imbalances. Broadly speaking, the western and southern states (Andhra Pradesh excluded) have tended to do comparatively well. The low growth states, for their part, form a large contiguous region in the north and east. This is a matter of concern, since the northern and eastern regions were poorer to start with. Indeed, National Sample Survey data suggest a strong pattern of inter-regional 'divergence' in average per capita expenditure (APCE): states that started off with higher APCE *levels* also had higher *growth rates* of APCE between 1993/94 and 1999/2000. In some of the poorer states, notably Assam and Orissa, there has been virtually zero growth of average per capita expenditure (and very little reduction, if any, in rural poverty) between 1993/94 and 1999/2000. These regional patterns are at least broadly consistent with independent estimates of the growth rates of state domestic product (SDP).

Fourth, the intensification of regional disparities is only one aspect of a broader pattern of increasing economic inequality in the nineties. Two other aspects are rising rural-urban disparities in per capita expenditure, and rising inequality of per capita expenditure within urban areas in most states. Further, the real wages of agricultural labourers have increased more slowly than per capita GDP, and conversely with public sector employees, suggesting some intensification of economic inequality between occupation groups.

Fifth, we have argued for assessing changes in living standards in a broader perspective, going beyond the standard focus on expenditure-based indicators. In that broader perspective, a more diverse picture emerges, with areas of accelerated progress in the nineties as well as slowdown in other fields. For instance, there is much evidence of rapid progress in the field of elementary education, but the rate of decline of infant mortality has slowed down. These and related trends deserve greater attention than they have received so far in the debate on 'poverty in the nineties'.

Sixth, the case for going beyond expenditure-based indicators applies also to the assessment of inequality. While expenditure-based data suggest rising disparities in the nineties, the same need not apply to other social indicators. For instance, while economic disparities between rural and urban areas have increased in the nineties, there has been some narrowing of the rural-urban gap in terms of life expectancy and school participation.

Finally, we have argued against reading these trends simply as evidence of the impact (positive or negative) of 'liberalisation'. For one thing, the impact of liberalisation is a 'counterfactual' question, and much depends on how the alternatives are specified. For another, much else has happened in the nineties, other than liberalisation. The evidence we have reviewed is of much interest in its own right, independently of the liberalisation debate. Much work remains to be done in terms of identifying the causal relations underlying the trends we have identified.

ACKNOWLEDGEMENT

Reprinted from *Economic and Political Weekly*, 7 September 2002.

REFERENCES

Acharya, Sarthi (1989): 'Agricultural Wages in India: A Disaggregated Analysis', *Indian Journal of Agricultural Economics*, 44.

Ahluwalia, Montek S (2000): 'Economic Performance of States in Post-reforms Period', *Economic and Political Weekly*, 6 May.

Banerjee, A. and Piketty, T. (2001): 'Are the Rich Growing Richer: Evidence from Indian Tax Data', MIT, Cambridge MA, and CEPREMAP, Paris, processed, (see Chapter 22 of this book).

Bhagwati, Jagdish (2001): 'Growth, Poverty and Reforms', *Economic and Political Weekly*, 10 March.

Bhalla, Surjit (2000a): 'Growth and Poverty in India: Myth and Reality', mimeo, Oxus Research and Investments, New Delhi.

———— (2000b): 'FAQs on Poverty in India', mimeo, Oxus Research and Investments, New Delhi.

Bhatia, Bela (1997): 'Forced Evictions in the Narmada Valley' in Dreze, J.P., Samson, M., and Singh, S. (eds) (1997), *The Dam and the Nation: Displacement and Resettlement in the Narmada Valley*, Oxford University Press, New Delhi.

Bramall, Chris, and Jones, Marion (1993): 'Rural Income Inequality in China since 1978', *Journal of Peasant Studies*, 21(1).

Breman, Jan (2001a): 'An Informalised Labour System: End of Labour Market Dualism', *Economic and Political Weekly*, 35(52).

———— (2001b): 'The State of Poverty in Urban India at the Beginning of the 21st Century', Sukhamoy Chakravarty Memorial Lecture, Delhi School of Economics, 16 November.

Central Statistical Organisation (2001): *National Accounts Statistics 2001,* CSO, New Delhi.

Chandrasekhar, C.P., and Ghosh, J. (2002): *The Market that Failed: A Decade of Neoliberal Economic Reforms in India,* Leftword Books, New Delhi.

Dabir-Alai, Parviz (2002): 'The Socio-Economics of Street Vending: A Case Study of Vulnerability for Delhi in the 1990s', mimeo, Richmond School of Business, London.

Das, Gurcharan (2000): *India Unbound,* Penguin, New Delhi.

Dasgupta, Partha, and Ray, Debraj (1990): 'Adapting to Undernourishment: The Biological Evidence and Its Implications' in Dreze and Sen (1990), vol i.

Datt, Gaurav (1999a): 'Has Poverty Declined since Economic Reforms?', *Economic and Political Weekly*, 11–17 December.

———— (1999b): 'Poverty in India: Trends and Decompositions', mimeo, World Bank, Washington, DC.

Datt, Gaurav, and Ravallion, Martin (2002): 'Is India's Economic Growth Leaving the Poor Behind?', mimeo, World Bank, Washington, DC.

Deaton, Angus (2001a): 'Adjusted Indian Poverty Estimates for 1999/2000', Princeton, Research Programme in Development Studies, processed. Available at http://www.wws.princeton.edu/~rpds.

———— (2001b): 'Computing Prices and Poverty Rates in India, 1999/2000', Princeton, Research Programme in Development Studies, processed, (see Chapter 17 of this book).

Deaton, Angus and Tarozzi, Alessandro (2000): 'Prices and Poverty in India', Princeton, Research Programme in Development Studies, processed, (see Chapter 16 of this book).

Diewert, W. Erwin (1976): 'Exact and Superlative Index Numbers', *Journal of Econometrics*, 4.

Drewnowski, Adam (1999): 'Fat and Sugar in the Global Diet: Dietary Diversity in the Nutrition Transition' in Grew, R. (ed), *Food in Global History*, Westview, Boulder.

Dreze, Jean (2000): 'Poverty: Beyond Headcount Ratios', *The Hindu*, 9 September.

———— (2001): 'No More Lifelines: Political Economy of Hunger in Orissa', *The Times of India*, 17 September.

Dreze, Jean, and Murthi, Mamta (2001): 'Fertility, Education, and Development: Evidence from India', *Population and Development Review*, 27.

Dreze, Jean and Sen, Amartya (eds) (1990): *The Political Economy of Hunger*, Clarendon, Oxford.

———— (2002): India: Development and Participation Oxford University Press, New Delhi.

EPW Research Foundation (1993): 'Poverty Levels in India: Norms, Estimates and Trends', *Economic and Political Weekly*, 21 August.

Government of India (1993a): *Report of the Expert Group on Estimation of Proportion and Number of Poor*, Planning Commission, New Delhi.

———— (1993b): *Sample Registration System: Fertility and Mortality Indicators 1990*, Office of the Registrar General, New Delhi.

———— (1999): *Compendium of India's Fertility and Mortality Indicators 1971/1997*, Office of the Registrar General, New Delhi.

———— (2001a): *Economic Survey 2000/2001*, Ministry of Finance, New Delhi.

———— (2001b): 'Provisional Population Totals', Census of India 2001, Series 1(India), Paper 1 of 2001, Office of the Registrar General, New Delhi.

———— (2002): *Economic Survey 2001/2002*, Ministry of Finance, New Delhi.

Griffin, K., and Zhao Renwei (eds) (1993): *The Distribution of Income in China*, Macmillan, London.

Gupta, S.P. (1999): 'Tricle Down Theory Revisited: The Role of Employment and Poverty', V B Singh Memorial Lecture, 41st Annual Conference of the Indian Society of Labour Economics, 18–20 November, Mumbai.

Hanchate, A. and Dyson, T. (2000): 'Trends in the Composition of Food Consumption and their Impact on Nutrition and Poverty in India', mimeo, London School of Economics.

Institute for Human Development (2002): 'Dynamics of Poverty, Employment and Human Development in Bihar', project report; to be published as a monograph.

International Institute for Population Sciences (1995): National Family Health Survey 1992/93: India, IIPS, Mumbai.

———— (2000): *National Family Health Survey 1998/99 (NFHS-2): India*, IIPS, Mumbai.

Jhabvala, R. and Sinha, S. (2002): 'Liberalisation and the Woman Worker', *Economic and Political Weekly*, 25 May.

Jose, A.V. (1988): 'Agricultural Wages in India', *Economic and Political Weekly*, 25 June.

Khan, A.R. and Riskin, C. (2001): *Inequality and Poverty in China in the Age of Globalisation*, Oxford University Press, New York.

Krishna, Sridhar (2001): 'Phasing Out of Import Licensing: Impact on Small-scale Industries', *Economic and Political Weekly*, 7 July.

Kulshreshtha, A.C. and Kar, A. (2002): 'Estimates of Food Consumption Expenditure from Household Surveys and National Accounts', paper presented at the joint Planning Commission/World Bank workshop on poverty measurement, Delhi, January (Chapter 7 of this book).

Lal, D., Mohan, R. and Natarajan, I (2001): 'Economic Reforms and Poverty Alleviation: A Tale of Two Surveys', *Economic and Political Weekly*, 24 March.

Maharatna, Arup (2001): 'On the 'Brighter Side' of Seasonal Migration: A Case Study of Fertility Transition in Tribal Population in Rural West Bengal, India', mimeo, Gokhale Institute of Politics and Economics, Pune.

Mari Bhat, P.N. (2002): 'Has the Decline in Infant Mortality Rate Slowed Down? A Review of SRS Evidence', paper presented at a national workshop on 'Infant Mortality: Levels, Trends and Interventions' held at New Delhi on 11-12 April.

Mehta, Jaya (2001): 'Give Poverty a Face Please!', in *Alternative Economic Survey 2000/2001,* Rainbow Publishers, Delhi.

Murthi, M., Guio, A.C. and Dreze, J.P. (1995): 'Mortality, Fertility and Gender Bias in India', *Population and Development Review,* 21.

Nagaraj, R. (2000): 'Indian Economy since 1980: Virtuous Growth or Polarisation?', *Economic and Political Weekly,* 5 August.

National Institute of Nutrition (1997): *25 Years of National Nutrition Monitoring Bureau,* NIN, Hyderabad.

National Nutrition Monitoring Bureau (1999): *Report of Second Repeat Survey – Rural (1996/97),* National Institute of Nutrition, Hyderabad.

National Sample Survey Organisation (2001a): 'Level and Pattern of Consumer Expenditure in India 1999/2000', Report 457, National Sample Survey Organisation, New Delhi.

———— (2001b): 'Consumption of Some Important Commodities', Report 461, National Sample Survey Organisation, New Delhi.

Osmani, Siddiq R. (1990): 'Nutrition and the Economics of Food: Implications of Some Recent Controversies' in Dreze and Sen (1990), Vol i.

PROBE Team (1999): *Public Report on Basic Education in India,* Oxford University Press, New Delhi.

Rao, C.H. Hanumantha (2000): 'Declining Demand for Foodgrains in Rural India: Causes and Implications', *Economic and Political Weekly,* 22 January.

Ravallion, Martin (2000): 'Should Poverty Measures be Anchored to the National Accounts?', *EPW,* 26 August– 2 September.

Rodgers, Gerry and Rodgers, Janine (2000): 'Semi-Feudalism Meets the Market: A Report from Purnia', Working Paper 6, Institute for Human Development, New Delhi.

Rogaly, B., Biswas, J., Coppard, D., Rafique, A., Rana, K. and Sengupta, A. (2001): 'Seasonal Migration, Social Change and Migrants' Rights: Lessons from West Bengal', *Economic and Political Weekly,* 8 December.

Roy, Tirthankar (1999): 'Growth and Recession in Small-Scale Industry: A Study of Tamil Nadu Powerlooms', *Economic and Political Weekly,* 30 October.

Sainath, P. (2001a): 'Will the Real National Calamity Please Stand Up?', *The Hindu,* 25 February.

———— (2001b): 'It's the Policy, Stupid, Not Implementation' (2 parts), *The Hindu,* September.

———— (2001c): 'Mass Media: Disconnected from Mass Reality', *The Hindu,* 2 September.

———— (2001d): 'Where Stomachaches are Terminal', *The Hindu,* 29 April.

Samal, K.C. (2002): 'Shrimp Culture in Chilika Lake: Case of Occupational Displacement of Fishermen', *Economic and Political Weekly,* 4 May.

Sarmah, Sasanka (2000): 'Agricultural Wages: Trends and Determinants', MPhil thesis, Delhi School of Economics.

———— (2001): 'Agricultural Wages in India: An Analysis of Regions and States', mimeo, Centre for Development Economics at the Delhi School of Economics; forthcoming in *Indian Journal of Labour Economics.*

Sen, Abhijit (2000): 'Estimates of Consumer Expenditure and its Distribution', *Economic and Political Weekly,* 16 December.

Sen, Amartya (2001): 'Many Faces of Gender Inequality', *Frontline,* 27 October.

Shariff, A. and Mallick, A.C. (1999): 'Dynamics of Food Intake and Nutrition by Expenditure Class in India', *Economic and Political Weekly*, 3 July.

Sharma, Alakh (2001): 'Agrarian Relations and Socio-Economic Change in Bihar', paper presented at a conference on 'Labour and Capitalist Transformation in Asia' held at the Centre for Development Studies, Thiruvananthapuram, 13–15 December.

Shiva, Vandana (2001a): 'India: Corporatisation of Agriculture Disastrous', *The Guardian*, 7 March.

——— (2001b): 'Is Globalisation Killing the Environment?', interview with Frederick Noronha; available at http://www.onweb.org/archive/features/shiva/shiva.html.

Subramanian, A. (2001): 'Are Income-Calorie Elasticities Really High in Developing Countries? Some Implications for Nutrition and Income', mimeo, National Council of Applied Economic Research, New Delhi.

Subramanian, Shankar and Angus Deaton (1996): 'The Demand for Food and Calories', *Journal of Political Economy*, 104, 133–62.

Sundaram, K. (2001a): 'Employment-Unemployment Situation in Nineties: Some Results from NSS 55th Round Survey', *Economic and Political Weekly,* 17 March.

——— (2001b): 'Employment and Poverty in 1990s: Further Results from NSS 55th Round Employment-Unemployment Survey, 1999/2000', *Economic and Political Weekly*, 11 August.

——— (2001c): 'Poverty in India: Some Issues in Measurement and Database', mimeo, Delhi School of Economics, Delhi.

Sundaram, K and Tendulkar, S (2000): 'Poverty in India: An Assessment and Analysis', draft report for the Asia Development Bank; mimeo, Delhi School of Economics, Delhi.

——— (2001): 'NAS-NSS Estimates of Private Consumption for Poverty Estimation: A Disaggregated Comparison for 1993/94', *Economic and Political Weekly*, 13 January.

——— (2002): 'Recent Debates on Data Base for Measurement of Poverty in India', Delhi School of Economics, processed. Presented at joint GOI/World Bank poverty workshop, Delhi, January 2002. Available at http://www.worldbank.org/indiapovertyworkshop.

Tarozzi, Alessandro (2001): 'Estimating Comparable Poverty Counts from Incomparable Surveys: Measuring Poverty in India', Research Programme in Development Studies, Princeton University, processed. Available at http://www.wws.princeton.edu/~rpds.

UNICEF (2001): 'GOI-UNICEF Country Programme of Cooperation 2003/2007', mimeo, UNICEF, New Delhi.

Vaidyanathan, A. (2002): 'Food Consumption and Nutrition Status: A Re-examination Based on Indian Evidence', mimeo, Madras Institute of Development Studies, Chennai.

Visaria, Pravin (2000): 'Alternative Estimates of Poverty in India', *The Economic Times*, 27 June.

Yao Shujie (1999): 'Economic Growth, Income Inequality and Poverty in China under Economic Reforms', *Journal of Development Studies*, 35.

II.3 OTHER DATA, OTHER ASSESSMENTS

19

A Model-Based Assessment of India's Progress in Reducing Poverty in the 1990s

Gaurav Datt, Valerie Kozel, and Martin Ravallion

INTRODUCTION

Poverty monitoring in India since the 1960s has been mainly based on the National Sample Survey (NSS). While there has often been a debate on the precise numbers, the NSS has been a well-respected survey instrument internationally, and a model for other countries. Recently, however, questions have been raised about the reliability of the NSS as an instrument for monitoring poverty in India.

One concern is the gap between aggregate private consumption as measured by the national accounts and mean consumption from the NSS. Depending on the precise measures used, the latter accounts for 60–70 per cent of the measure of private consumption implied by the national accounts.[1] Since there are differences in definitions and coverage between these two data sources one cannot expect that they will agree. More worrying is the fact that the divergence has been widening over time since the 1970s (Sen, 2001). Some observers have attributed the divergence entirely to underestimation of consumption in the NSS, and have assumed that this underestimation has been distribution-neutral – that the surveys get the mean wrong but inequality right. If one re-calculates India's poverty measures under that assumption then one finds an appreciably higher rate of poverty reduction than indicated by the NSS (Bhalla, 2000; Srinivasan, 2000). However, there is no basis for assuming that the divergence between the consumption numbers from the NSS and the national accounts is solely due to underestimation of consumption in the NSS; nor is it plausible that underestimation by the NSS is distribution neutral (Ravallion, 2000b and Sundaram and Tendulkar, 2001).

Another concern is that changes in the design of the latest survey, namely the 55th Round for 1999/2000, cast doubt on the comparability of the resulting poverty estimates with those from earlier rounds of the NSS. Since the NSS began in the 1950s, it has used 30-day recall for consumption. This changed with the 51st Round (Table 19.1). For the 51st through the 54th Rounds, the NSS administered two

---

[1] There was a revision to the NAS methods in the late 1990s, in line with the new international standards for national accounts. The extent of divergence depends on whether one uses the new series (base 1993/94) or the old one (base 1980/81). For further details see Sen (2001).

Table 19.1 Recall Periods in Different NSS Rounds

	Food	High-frequency Non-food	Low-frequency Non-food
Commodity group in NSS consumption module	Food, paan, tobacco, and intoxicants	Fuel and light miscellaneous goods and services, medical (non-institutional)	Educational, medical (institutional), clothing, footwear, and durable goods
Approximate budget share in recent surveys	60 per cent	20 per cent	20 per cent
Up to 50th Rounds (all households)	30-day	30-day	30-day
51st–54th Rounds			
Schedule 1 (independent subsample)	30-day	30-day	30-day
Schedule 2 (independent subsample)	7-day	30-day	365-day
55th Round (all households)	Both 7-day and 30-day	30-day	365-day

Source: Based on NSS reports.

different consumption schedules to two independent sub-samples of households. Schedule 1 used the traditional 30-day recall for all consumption items, while Schedule 2 applied multiple recall periods for different items: 7-day recall for food (food, paan, tobacco, and intoxicants), 30-day recall for high-frequency non-food (fuel and light, miscellaneous goods and services, non-institutional medical) and 365-day recall for low-frequency non-food (educational, institutional medical, clothing, footwear, and durable goods). This changed further in the 55th Round. In that round, food consumption (typically about 60 per cent of aggregate consumption) was obtained by both 7-day and 30-day recall for the same set of households, with the question on the last seven days' consumption of each commodity coming before that on the last 30 days. (The columns for 7- and 30-day recall appear side by side on the same page in the questionnaire.) Instructions were given to interviewers to ask the questions in reverse order, though apparently this was done after the survey had begun, and it is not known how well the instruction was followed. In contrast, spending on low-frequency non-food consumption items, typically with a budget share of about 20 per cent, was obtained only using a one-year recall – also a change from earlier rounds of the NSS. The 30-day recall period was only used for the high-frequency non-food items with a budget share of about 20.

The numbers for consumption from the two recall methods in the 55th Round are quite similar – far more so than in previous experimental Rounds 51 though 54, in which different households got different recall schedules (Visaria, 1999; Deaton, 2000 and GOI, 2000). Putting both 7-day and 30-day recall questions side-by-side on the same page of the questionnaire probably leads to convergence; interviewers and respondents naturally would tend to cross-check or validate the response based on one recall period with that based on the other.

The way one interprets the data from the 55th Round matters greatly to the conclusions one draws about what is happening to the incidence of poverty in India. Comparisons over time are problematic using the 55th Round given the changes in survey design. Notice first that two sets of estimates are possible from the 55th Round: one using 7/30/365-day recalls, the other using 30/30/365-day recalls (the first uses 7-day while the second uses 30-day recall for food). If one uses the 30/30/365-day recall estimates, ignoring the likely bias from the presence of the 7-day food recall questions in the same survey and the change in the recall period for high frequency non-food goods, then the consumption distributions in the 55th Round imply a sizable reduction in poverty. The Planning Commission's (2001) estimates along these lines indicate that the national poverty rate fell by about 10 percentage points between 1993/94 and 1999/2000, from 36 per cent in 1993/94 to only 26 per cent in 1999/2000. The rural poverty rate is likewise estimated to have fallen from 37 per cent to 27 per cent (Planning Commission, 2001).

If instead one compares the 7/30/365-day estimates from the 55th Round with the 7/30/365-day estimates from the past experimental rounds (51 through 54), then one gets an increase in poverty. While noting the comparability problems given the other changes to the 55th Round, Sen (2001) presents such a comparison of the poverty rates reporting estimates by Visaria (1999). The comparison suggests an increase of 2 percentage points in the rural poverty rate between 1994/95 and 1999/2000, and an increase of five points in the urban poverty rate.

Any attempt to adjust the data from the 55th Round to make it more comparable with previous rounds will of course require untestable assumptions. In one attempt to correct the data, Deaton (2001) has exploited the fact that there were some goods (viz. the high-frequency non-food consumption items) in the 55th Round that used the same (30-day) recall period as in previous surveys. These goods account for about one-fifth of mean consumption. Deaton estimates the distribution of total consumption as if there had been no change in survey design under two key assumptions.[2] First, he assumes that the marginal distribution of the goods with the common, 30-day, recall period is unaffected by the change in survey design. Second, he assumes that the distribution of total consumption conditional on consumption of the common-recall goods has not changed over time and so can be inferred from the 1993/94 Round (which was of course uncontaminated by the change in survey design). Applying this method, Deaton finds a fall in poverty in 1999/2000, though not as great as that implied by the 55th Round. His results suggest that 30 per cent of the fall in rural poverty incidence between the 50th and the 55th Rounds obtained by the Planning Commission (2001) is attributable to the change in survey design; for urban areas it is 15 per cent. Of course, these 'corrections' are only as good as the assumptions on which they are based. The estimates will be biased if, at a given level of total consumption, demand for the goods with the common recall period changed over time with changes in tastes, relative prices or survey design. The direction of bias could go either way.

This chapter takes a different approach to checking the results of the 55th Round. We use a model-based approach for projecting poverty in India after 1993/94. In constructing the model, we build on past research indicating that the key determinants of poverty in India at the state level are economic growth and its sectoral composition (depending on state initial conditions), development spending, and inflation (Datt and Ravallion, 1998a; Datt and Ravallion, 2001). From this starting point, we calibrate our model to the time series data by state up to 1993/94 and we then forecast forward, and compare the results to those of the 55th Round. The section on Data and Methods outlines the model which is followed by sections on Post-sample Projections of Poverty and Conclusion respectively.

[2] Similarly see Tarozzi (2001). The Deaton and Tarozzi method shares common features with the method proposed by Lanjouw and Lanjouw (2001) to deal with survey non-comparability. The Lanjouw- Lanjouw method assumes that the Engel curve for the commonly observed consumption components is inter-temporally stable. This will hold under somewhat weaker assumptions used by Deaton and Tarozzi.

DATA AND METHODS

We will only be concerned here with measures of absolute poverty, by which we mean that the standard of living of a household is measured by its consumption expenditure per capita and the poverty line is kept fixed in real terms over the entire (spatial and temporal) domain of poverty measurement.

Our projections of poverty measures after 1993/94 will be based on a model calibrated to the time series data of past measures based on the NSS, following Ravallion and Datt (2002). We ask in essence how much poverty reduction could have been expected after 1993/94 given the historical relationship between poverty and its identified covariates, and how those covariates evolved after 1994/94. This assumes of course that the historical relationship is maintained. If one thinks instead that the NSS has led to underestimation of the rate of poverty reduction (back to the 1960s) then one will also believe that our forecasts are underestimating the rate of poverty reduction at given growth rates. The position one takes on the reasons for the difference between the NSS and NAS consumption aggregates naturally spills over into the forecasting problem.

There is a large literature studying the evolution of India's poverty measures over time, following (and debating) the seminal contribution of Ahluwalia (1978) on rural poverty; Datt and Ravallion (1998b) survey this literature. The model we use here follows Datt and Ravallion (2001). The essential features are that (i) we model the state-wide poverty measures, and (ii) we relax the almost universal assumption in past work that poverty responses to growth are the same across all states. Thus we allow for state-specific growth elasticities of poverty. (Datt and Ravallion, 2001, attempt to explain the interstate differences in growth elasticities in terms of initial conditions at state level.) We condition out interstate differences in the levels of poverty, by including state fixed effects. We also allow for state-specific time trends as well as state effects in other time-varying factors that could well bias our results if they were omitted. The rest of this section describes the model in greater detail and our estimation results.

Model of Poverty

In modelling the impact of growth on poverty in India, the simplest starting point would be a regression of the poverty measure on mean income or consumption.[3] Here we want a richer model. One way in which such a model can be extended is to allow for interstate and inter-sectoral differences in the growth elasticities of poverty, and for differences in the sectoral composition of growth. Recent research has shown that India's states vary enormously in terms of initial conditions that are relevant to how much impact economic growth will have on poverty (Datt and Ravallion, 2001). Those differences also lead one to expect that the sectoral composition of growth will matter more in some states than others; in a state with high literacy, for example, there could be more scope for reducing poverty through non-agricultural growth.

We also allow for differences in state development spending, which is allowed to have a differing impact across states. And we allow for the effect of inflation. In Datt and Ravallion (1998b) we argued that the main channel through which inflation mattered to India's poor was through its short-term

---

[3] Another possibility is to use the analytic properties of poverty measures to derive the changes in measured poverty with growth in the mean. However, this has two problems for our purposes. First, it also requires an assumption about how the Lorenz curve is going to shift; distribution neutrality is a common assumption, but in practice distributions do change from one survey to another – even when there is little long-run trend. Second, it requires an assumption about how much the growth in aggregate output will be passed onto the survey mean consumption. Our approach effectively 'solves out' these problems, by looking directly at how the poverty measures move with growth in output.

adverse effect on the real wage rate for unskilled labour. While the rate of inflation varies little between states, it might also have a differing impact in different states, according to differences in labour market conditions.

Since we are interested here in modelling the evolution over time (rather than levels) of the poverty measures we also control for differences between states in the initial level of poverty, i.e. we include state dummy variables in all regressions.[4] As usual in fixed-effects regressions, this also means that our results will be robust to endogeneity due to the correlation of the explanatory variables with the time-invariant state-specific effects. To allow for any omitted (time-trended) variables we also include state-specific trends.

Combining these features, our projections of poverty use the following econometric model of poverty (described more fully in Datt and Ravallion, 2001):

$$\ln P_{it} = \beta_i^N \ln \text{NFP}_{it} + \beta_i^F \ln \text{YLD}_{it} + \beta_i^G \ln \text{GOV}_{it} + \gamma_i \text{INF}_{it} + \pi_i t + \eta_i + \epsilon_{it} \tag{1}$$
$$(i = 1, \ldots, n; t = 1, \ldots, T)$$

where P_{it} is the measure of absolute consumption poverty (on a per capita basis) in state i at date t, NFP_{it} is real non-farm product per head of the population in state i at date t, YLD is farm yield (output per hectare),[5] GOV is real state development expenditure per capita, and INF is the inflation rate. The state effect is η_i and ϵ_{it} is an innovation error term.[6] Consistently with Datt and Ravallion (1998a and 1998b), we found that the fit of this model was improved if we used the two-year moving averages of ln YLD and ln NFP, and the lagged value of ln GOV.

To be as flexible as possible, we initially allow all the β_is to vary by state. Since we have state fixed effects and state-specific time trends as well as differing effects of inflation, estimating equation (1) is then equivalent to running a separate regression for each state.

However, we found that a degree of pooling was consistent with the data. In particular, we could not reject the null hypothesis of constant coefficients across states at the 10 per cent level or better for all variables except non-farm output per person, and the state effects in the intercept. Thus, we impose a constant-coefficients restriction for YLD, GOV, and INF, leaving the coefficients on NFP free to vary between states while also retaining the state fixed effects. In addition, although we could not reject the hypothesis of common time trends across states, we nonetheless chose to retain state-specific trends to maintain a more general specification.

Data

The data is documented more fully in Özler, Datt, and Ravallion (1996) and Datt and Ravallion (2001, Appendix). Here we only summarise salient features.

---

[4] Alternatively one can interpret our regressions as models of the deviations from time mean or the rates of poverty reduction (difference in logs) as functions of the similarly transformed (state- and time-specific) explanatory variables.

[5] In past work on these data (Datt and Ravallion, 1998a and 1998b) it was found that farm output per hectare is a better predictor of poverty than output per person; on decomposing log output per person into output per hectare and hectares per person, the latter is insignificant. Output per hectare is probably the better measure of farm productivity (for further discussion see Datt and Ravallion, 1998b).

[6] We initially estimated the model allowing ϵ_{it} to be an AR1 error term, allowing for the uneven spacing of the surveys when estimating the autoregression coefficient (following the method in Datt and Ravallion, 1998a). However, the autoregression coefficient was not significantly different from 0 so we set it to 0 to simplify the estimation method.

We use measures of absolute poverty for India's 15 main states using distributions of per capita consumption from 20 rounds of the NSS spanning the period 1960/61 (Round 16) to 1993/94 (Round 50) at intervals of 0.9 to 5.5 years. All 20 rounds of the survey are covered for the 15 major states except Jammu & Kashmir, where surveys were not held for the 48th and 50th Rounds due to the prevailing political unrest.[7] Altogether, data from 298 consumption distributions were used to construct state-level poverty measures.[8]

The poverty lines we use are based on those initially proposed by the Planning Commission in 1979 (GOI, 1979). These lines were defined at the per capita monthly expenditure levels of Rs 49 for rural areas and Rs 57 for urban areas (rounded to the nearest rupee) at October 1973–June 1974 all-India prices. A substantial effort was invested into the construction of a consistent set of price indices across states and survey periods, using monthly data on consumer price indices from the Labour Bureau (disaggregated to the centre level for the urban index) over the whole 35-year period. Our primary deflators were the Consumer Price Index for Industrial Workers (CPIIW) for the urban sector and the *adjusted* all-India Consumer Price Index for Agricultural Labourers (CPIAL) for the rural sector. The adjustment carried out to the CPIAL was for the price of firewood that has been held constant in the official CPIAL series since 1960/61. The nominal state-level distributions were further normalised for interstate cost of living differentials estimated separately for urban and rural areas, anchored to the consumption pattern of households in the neighbourhood of the poverty line.[9] For further details on the construction of the price indices, see Özler, Datt, and Ravallion (1996), Datt (1999), and Datt and Ravallion (1998a).[10]

The poverty measures are estimated from published grouped distributions of per capita expenditure using parameterised Lorenz curves; for details on the methodology see Datt and Ravallion (1992).

We have collated the survey data with data on farm yields, non-farm output, government spending, and inflation from a number of official sources.[11] Datt and Ravallion (2002, Appendix) provides more details on the data and sources.

Regressions

Table 19.2 gives the estimated parameters of the restricted version of equation (1) for state headcount

---

[7] Punjab and Haryana had to be treated as a composite state because Haryana emerged as a separate state only in 1964. For NSS rounds since then, the poverty measures for the two states have been aggregated using population weights derived from the decennial censuses.

[8] There is considerable variation in the sample sizes. For all states, the samples range from 6,330 households for the 16th Round (July 1959–June 1960) to 157,928 households for the 32nd Round (July 1977–June 1978), with a median sample size of 25,761 households for the 43rd Round (July 1986–June 1987). The smallest sample size for any state and sector is 140 households for rural Gujarat for the 16th Round. Assuming a simple random sample for the rural sector within the state, this implies a maximum standard error, for a headcount index of 50 per cent, of 4.2 percentage points.

[9] However, since a single price index is used for a given state and sector, we do not allow for differences between expenditure groups (as would arise from non-homothetic preferences with changes in relative prices).

[10] The state-specific poverty lines implied by our price indices differ from the current poverty lines used by the Planning Commission for the 50th and the 55th Rounds, despite their common starting point in the original 1979 Planning Commission poverty lines of Rs 49 and 57 per capita per month at 1973/74 prices for rural and urban areas, respectively. This is because the Planning Commission uses a different set of spatial and temporal deflators to update the 1973/74 poverty lines. Note that the Planning Commission poverty lines are also utilised in Deaton (2001).

[11] The data on farm yields and non-farm output utilise Central Statistical Organisation's series on State Domestic Product (SDP). The SDP numbers since 1993/94 use the new base for India's national accounts. These were spliced with the data for the earlier series, with base 1980/81.

indices. Two sets of estimates are presented: for urban and rural sectors combined, and for rural headcount indices separately. The two sets of results are very similar, reflecting in part the large share of rural poverty in total state-level poverty. The model's explanatory power is clearly good, with over 90 per cent of the variance in poverty incidence (across states and over time) accounted for.

Higher farm yields and higher development spending reduce the incidence of poverty, and the coefficients are highly significant. Higher non-farm output per person lowers poverty in all states. Inflation is poverty increasing, confirming our earlier results (Datt and Ravallion, 1997, 1998a and 1998b). We also find a significant positive time trends for most (10 of the 15) states. These could arise from population pressure on agricultural land availability at given yield per acre or they could reflect an adverse distributional effect of population growth on poverty, as argued by van de Walle (1985). However, it might also reflect rising under-reporting of consumption in the NSS, as is thought to be the main source of the (arguably growing) divergence between the NSS-based consumption estimates and those from the National Accounts Statistics (NAS).[12] Datt and Ravallion (2001) test this further, and show

Table 19.2 Regressions for State Headcount Indices allowing for Interstate Differences in Elasticities to Non-farm Output and Time Trends

Independent Variable	Urban and Rural Dep. Var. ln (Headcount Index)		Rural Dep. Var. ln (Rural Headcount Index)	
	Parameter Estimate	t-ratio	Parameter Estimate	t-ratio
Real agricultural output per hectare of net sown area: current + lagged (*YLD*)	−0.097	−3.50	−0.097	−3.07
Real per capita state development expenditure: lagged (*GOV*)	−0.128	−2.16	−0.177	−2.63
Inflation rate (*INF*)	0.392	4.71	0.458	4.83
Real non-agricultural output per person: current + lagged (*NFP*)				
Andhra Pradesh	−0.141	−1.31	−0.126	−1.03
Assam	−0.361	−2.30	−0.339	−1.90
Bihar	−0.130	−2.02	−0.115	−1.58
Gujarat	−0.289	−2.36	−0.234	−1.68
Jammu & Kashmir	−0.369	−3.29	−0.392	−3.07
Karnataka	−0.332	−2.73	−0.347	−2.51
Kerala	−0.665	−4.02	−0.664	−3.53
Madhya Pradesh	−0.320	−3.83	−0.330	−3.46
Maharashtra	−0.251	−2.34	−0.310	−2.54
Orissa	−0.290	−4.63	−0.295	−4.13
Punjab and Haryana	−0.426	−2.09	−0.608	−2.62
Rajasthan	−0.270	−3.24	−0.256	−2.70
Tamil Nadu	−0.272	−2.03	−0.265	−1.74
Uttar Pradesh	−0.337	−4.14	−0.364	−3.93
West Bengal	−0.511	−5.56	−0.530	−5.07

(Contd...)

[12] The positive trends however are not just a 1990s phenomenon, as has sometimes been claimed for the NAS-NSS growth divergence in the context of the post-reforms debate. On the contrary, the conditional trends are the strongest for the 1970s and weaker for the 1980s and 1990s.

(Contd...)

Independent Variable	Urban and Rural Dep. Var. ln (Headcount Index)		Rural Dep. Var. ln (Rural Headcount Index)	
	Parameter Estimate	t-ratio	Parameter Estimate	t-ratio
Time trend $\times 10^{-2}$				
Andhra Pradesh	0.223	0.25	0.327	0.32
Assam	3.088	2.21	3.299	2.07
Bihar	1.530	3.72	1.857	3.96
Gujarat	1.575	1.75	1.435	1.40
Jammu & Kashmir	3.302	3.21	4.309	3.68
Karnataka	2.223	2.42	2.817	2.69
Kerala	2.500	2.16	2.703	2.05
Madhya Pradesh	2.611	4.48	3.101	4.68
Maharashtra	2.006	2.44	2.672	2.86
Orissa	1.266	2.38	1.428	2.35
Punjab and Haryana	2.339	1.24	4.635	2.15
Rajasthan	1.164	2.23	1.519	2.55
Tamil Nadu	1.545	1.46	1.813	1.51
Uttar Pradesh	2.172	3.80	2.652	4.08
West Bengal	0.979	1.94	1.038	1.81
Root mean square error	.0937		.1067	
R^2	0.923		0.905	
Test for common non-ag. growth elasticities across states: $F(14,238)$ with p-value in ( )	1.59 (0.08)		1.56 (0.09)	
Test for common time trends across states: $F(14,238)$ with p-value in ( )	1.12 (0.34)		1.48 (0.12)	

Note: All variables are measured in natural logarithms. A positive (negative) sign indicates that the variable contributes to an increase (decrease) in the headcount index. The estimated model also included state-specific intercept effects, not reported in the Table. The number of observations used in the estimation is 272.

Source: Datt and Ravallion (2001).

that the trends disappear if one allows for population growth effects. We also find that controlling for total population results in a switch in the sign of the trends from positive to negative in most states. However, these variables are so highly correlated that it is clearly hard to disentangle their effects, and standard errors on the trend coefficients rise considerably.

POST-SAMPLE PROJECTIONS OF POVERTY

Based on the actual growth performance by state and the values of the other explanatory variables discussed in the last section, Tables 19.3 and 19.4 give our projections of poverty incidence in 1999/2000, as implied by our model calibrated to the data up to 1993/94. We find an overall reduction in national poverty incidence, from 39 per cent in 1993/94 to 34 per cent in 1999/2000 (Table 19.3).

Table 19.3 Measures of Total (Urban plus Rural) Poverty Incidence
(% Living Below the Poverty Line)

State	1993/94 Survey Estimate: Headcount Index (%)	1999/2000 Forecast (One-step): Headcount Index (%)	1993/94– 1999/2000 (Forecast) Annual Percentage Point Reduction in Headcount Index (6 Years)	1999/2000 (55th Round) Survey Estimate: Headcount Index (%)	1993/94– 1999/2000 (55th Round) Annual Percentage Point Reduction in Headcount Index (6 Years)	Share of Aggregate Difference between Forecast and 55th Round Estimate (%)
Andhra Pradesh	29.5	24.1	0.89	21.9	1.25	2.6
Assam	44.5	46.9	-0.40	39.4	0.85	3.2
Bihar	60.3	61.8	-0.24	46.4	2.33	26.6
Gujarat	33.7	26.8	1.16	19.9	2.31	5.5
Karnataka	37.4	29.7	1.28	23.2	2.37	5.5
Kerala	28.8	14.4	2.39	14.4	2.40	0.0
Madhya Pradesh	44.0	41.5	0.43	37.7	1.06	4.9
Maharashtra	43.2	40.4	0.48	29.9	2.21	15.9
Orissa	40.3	34.3	1.00	37.9	0.40	-2.1
Punjab	21.4	17.0	0.73	8.8	2.09	5.8
Rajasthan	43.3	34.2	1.51	25.6	2.95	7.6
Tamil Nadu	34.9	28.2	1.11	21.5	2.23	6.7
Uttar Pradesh	40.1	35.4	0.78	28.1	2.00	20.2
West Bengal	25.9	16.1	1.64	18.1	1.31	-2.5
All-India	39.1	34.3	0.80	27.9	1.87	100.0

Note: Jammu & Kashmir omitted because of incomplete data.

How do these compare with the rates of poverty reduction suggested by direct estimates from the 55th Round? As discussed in the introduction, comparisons over time using the 55th Round are clouded by the changes in survey design. We shall compare the results using 30/30/365-day recall from that survey with the 30/30/30-day recall estimates from the previous quinquennial survey for the 50th Round for 1993/94.[13] In Tables 19.3 and 19.4 we present these estimates from the 50th and the 55th Rounds and the annualised rates of poverty reduction implied for major states and at the national level.

We cannot give similar calculations based on 7/30/365-day recalls since this requires experimental NSS rounds (Rounds 51 through 54) that are not available at state level.[14] The aggregate urban and rural poverty estimates using the 7/30/365-day recall, as indicated above, suggest an *increase* in urban poverty incidence of about one point per year during 1994/95 and the latter half of 1999, and an increase in rural incidence of about 0.4 points per year over the same period (Sen, 2001). While these rates of decline are a useful point of reference, their comparison with our model-based estimates below should however be tempered by the consideration that the two use different sets of poverty lines (see section on Data).

Our model predicts that the national poverty rate should have fallen from 39.1 per cent in 1993/94 to 34.3 per cent in 1999/2000, or at about 0.8 percentage points per year. The direct estimates for the 55th Round (using 30/30/365-day recall) indicate that 27.9 per cent of the population are poor 1999/2000,

[13] The switch to one-year recall for low frequency non-food items in the 55th Round would probably impart an upward bias in the poverty rate compared to previous 30-day recall periods for non-food goods. Without this effect, the 55th Round would have implied an even higher rate of poverty reduction.

[14] The state level consumption distributions from the experimental rounds are available only for Schedule 1 (30/30/30-day recalls), though the all-India distributions are available for both schedule 1 and Schedule 2 (using 7/30/365-day recalls).

Table 19.4 Measures of Rural Poverty Incidence (% Living Below the Poverty Line)

State	1993/94 Survey Estimate: Headcount Index (%)	1999/2000 Forecast (One-step): Headcount Index (%)	1993/94–1999/2000 (Forecast) Annual Percentage Point Reduction in Headcount Index (6 Years)	1999/2000 (55th Round) Survey Estimate: Headcount Index (%)	1993/94–1999/2000 (55th Round) Annual Percentage Point Reduction in Headcount Index (6 Years)	Share of Aggregate Difference between Forecast and 55th Round Estimate (%)
Andhra Pradesh	28.9	23.8	0.86	23.1	0.97	0.7
Assam	49.0	52.2	−0.53	43.7	0.89	4.1
Bihar	63.5	67.2	−0.61	48.5	2.51	36.4
Gujarat	35.4	28.4	1.17	22.7	2.12	3.7
Karnataka	41.0	32.9	1.34	27.4	2.26	4.0
Kerala	31.1	15.4	2.61	13.8	2.88	0.8
Madhya Pradesh	45.4	43.2	0.35	41.2	0.70	2.6
Maharashtra	47.8	44.7	0.52	33.7	2.35	12.7
Orissa	40.3	34.2	1.01	38.2	0.36	−2.5
Punjab	25.2	20.1	0.85	10.0	2.54	6.5
Rajasthan	47.5	38.2	1.55	29.1	3.07	8.1
Tamil Nadu	36.7	30.3	1.08	26.8	1.67	2.6
Uttar Pradesh	41.6	37.1	0.76	28.3	2.22	24.7
West Bengal	27.3	16.4	1.81	20.0	1.22	−4.2
All-India	41.9	37.5	0.72	30.7	1.85	100.0

Note: Jammu & Kashmir omitted because of incomplete data.

implying that the poverty rate is falling at 1.9 points per year.[15] On the other hand, estimates using the 7/30/365-day recalls, reported by Sen (2001), suggest a rate of increase in poverty incidence of about 0.6 point per year (over 1994/95–1999). So our projections suggest a little under half (43 per cent) of the rate of decline implied by the 30-day food recall estimates from the 55th Round, and the projected rate of decline is a little closer to the 30/30/365-day rate of decline than to the 7/30/365-day rate of decline implied by the 55th Round.

The discrepancy between our projections and the 30/30/365-day recall numbers from the 55th Round is similar for rural poverty (Table 19.4). For rural India as a whole, the 55th Round estimates imply a 1.85 percentage point annual rate of reduction in the poverty rate, from 41.9 per cent in 1993/94 to 30.7 per cent in 1999/2000. By contrast the model predicts a much slower rate of decline in rural poverty rate at about 0.7 percentage points per year, to 37.5 per cent in 1999/2000. Thus, the forecast rate of rural poverty reduction is about 39 per cent of the rate implied by the 55th Round (30/30/365-day recall estimates). And, this too is roughly half way between the rates of decline based on 30/30/365 and 7/30/365-day recalls (the latter was reported by Sen, 2001, to be a rate of increase of 0.4 percentage points per annum).

Our results can be compared with Deaton (2001). He also estimates a slower rate of rural poverty reduction than implied by the NSS 55th Round, though he finds a closer correspondence between his adjusted estimates and the 55th Round. By his estimates, the adjusted rate of poverty reduction between 1993/94 and 1999/2000 was about 69 per cent of the direct 30/30/365-day 55th Round estimate. The

[15] The Planning Commission's estimates for the 50th and 55th Rounds (using 30-day recall for food) imply that the poverty rate is falling at 1.7 points per year (over 1993/94–1999/2000).

comparison with our results is not strictly valid given the use of different poverty lines. Despite this, there is a measure of correspondence in the state-level results. For 11 of the 14 states, both Deaton's and our estimates predict a lower rate of rural poverty reduction than implied by the direct 55th Round estimates; in one state it is higher by both estimates. Only for two states is the direction of indicated bias different. Overall, the ratio of predicted rural poverty reduction to direct NSS-based reduction in our estimates has a mild positive correlation of 0.42 ($t = 1.6$) with Deaton's adjusted estimates based on the 55th Round.

One can also work out the rates of decline in urban poverty implicitly determined by our national and rural poverty estimates. The results suggest that the urban rates of decline were slightly higher than the rural rates. Based on the 55th Round survey (30/30/365-day recall estimates), urban poverty declined from 31.1 per cent in 1993/94 to 20.1 per cent in 1999/2000, or by about 1.8 per cent per year, while the model forecasts indicate a slower decline to 25.6 per cent in 1999/2000 or at about 0.9 percentage points per annum.

Of India's 15 largest states, Uttar Pradesh and Bihar, accounted for the largest share of national poverty in 1993/94 (18 per cent and 17 per cent, respectively; see Table 19.3). The model predicts that the rural poverty rate in Bihar has increased by 0.6 percentage point per year; here the model is reflecting the state's relatively weak agricultural and non-farm growth and low non-farm growth elasticity (Table 19.3). However, the 55th Round estimates (based on 30/30/365-day recalls) imply that the rural poverty rate in Bihar has been falling at 2.5 percentage points per year, from 64 per cent in 1993/94 to 49 per cent in 1999/2000 (Table 19.4). The discrepancies are less but still significant for UP: 55th Round estimates imply a 2.2 percentage points per year reduction in rural poverty, in contrast to a 0.8 percentage point reduction implied by the model. Maharashtra is another state that accounts for a significant share of poverty in India (10.8 per cent); the model forecasts a 0.5 percentage point per year decline in rural poverty incidence as compared to a rate of decline of 2.4 points per year implied by our 55th Round estimates. In contrast, the rates of rural poverty reduction agree quite closely for some states – Andhra Pradesh, Kerala, Madhya Pradesh, Tamil Nadu and West Bengal[16] – and reasonably closely for some others.

The last columns of Tables 19.3 and 19.4 give the shares of the aggregate difference due to each state.[17] The two contiguous northern states of Bihar and Uttar Pradesh account for a large share of the difference between our model predictions and 55th Round estimates at an all-India level; these two states account for 47 per cent of the difference in aggregate poverty, and for 61 per cent of the difference in rural poverty. Bihar alone accounts for 27 per cent of the aggregate (urban + rural) difference, and 36 per cent for rural areas.

Orissa presents an interesting case. In contrast to other states, the model predicts a higher rate of poverty reduction than evidenced in 55th Round estimates. The 55th Round estimates undoubtedly reflect the impact of a cyclone that devastated coastal regions of the state in the second half of 1999. It is of course difficult to say how much is due to the cyclone. One possible assumption is that the rate of poverty reduction in Orissa immediately prior to the cyclone would have continued without it. As in any reflexive comparison, that assumption can be questioned. For example, it might be the case that

---

[16] These are all states with an absolute difference in the rates of poverty reduction of under 0.6 percentage points per annum.

[17] This is the state's population share in 1999 times the ratio of the state-specific difference (forecast – 55th Round estimate) to the aggregate difference.

1999/2000 would have been an unusually good agricultural year if not for the cyclone, so that poverty would have been below trend under the counter-factual. We cannot say how the covariates of poverty would have evolved without the cyclone. But it is still of interest to see how far off Orissa's poverty rate for the cyclone year was from what one would expect based on the state's trend immediately prior to the cyclone.

We first re-estimate the rate of poverty reduction in Orissa predicted by the growth rates and other explanatory variables up to 1998/99 (the year before the cyclone). Based on this calculation, poverty is predicted to fall by 1.24 percentage points a year between 1993/94 and 1998/99. At this rate, poverty incidence in Orissa would have been 32.9 per cent by 1999/2000. Instead, despite the change in survey design, the 55th Round estimate indicates a poverty incidence of 37.9 per cent. Comparing the two estimates, we find that the poverty rate was five percentage points higher than we would have expected in 1999/2000. (Without the survey comparability problem the difference would be larger.) However, only a part of this is directly attributable to changes in the correlates of poverty included in the model; a comparison with the model forecast of 34.3 per cent suggests this part to be about 1.4 percentage points. Thus about 70 per cent of the difference between the poverty rate in Orissa based on the 55th Round and that implied by our forecast prior to the cyclone is due to idiosyncratic effects not captured by our model. However, it is not implausible that a shock such as a severe cyclone would entail a large idiosyncratic effect on consumption, not readily accountable to the covariates of poverty at normal times.

A large share of the cyclone-related impact in Orissa is likely to be short-lived, though we cannot of course say how much. But, the Orissa case illustrates a more general point: a household survey provides a snapshot of economic conditions at the time the survey is administered; a drought, crop failure, or severe economic shock can cause a sharp (and in some cases transitory) increase in poverty. It may give an erroneous picture of poverty trends; poverty levels may fall again, equally dramatically, once conditions change.[18]

Does our model suggest a slowing down in the rate of poverty reduction in the post-reform period of the 1990s? We compared the projected rates of poverty reduction from this paper with the rates of poverty reduction observed prior to 1993/94. Comparing 1993/94 with the earliest 'thick sample' round in Datt (1999), namely for 1977/78, one finds that national poverty incidence fell by about 1 per cent per year, slightly higher than the 0.8 per cent point rate predicted by our model for the period after 1993/94.[19] The pattern is similar for rural poverty. The rural rate of poverty reduction between 1977/78 and 1993/94 was 0.9 per cent points per year, while the model projects a slightly lower rate of 0.7 per cent points after 1993/94.

An annual rate of decline in the poverty rate of 0.8 is also lower than one would have expected given India's growth rate in the 1990s and the historical elasticities based on the 'pre-reform' data (1960–91), as given in Ravallion and Datt (1996). The growth rate in private consumption per capita from the national accounts was 4.1 per cent per annum between 1993/94 and 1999/2000, implying that the poverty rate would have fallen by 1.6 points per year over that period.[20]

---

[18] Also see the discussion in Datt and Ravallion (1997) related to the immediate post-reform round of the NSS.

[19] This is based on all-India poverty rates derived as population-weighted averages of poverty rates for the 15 states.

[20] This calculation uses the estimated elasticity of the headcount index w.r.t. private consumption per capita of –0.9; this is based on a regression of the changes in the log of the headcount index on changes in the log of private consumption per capita from the national accounts using 23 surveys spanning 1958–91 (Ravallion and Datt, 1996). The regression included a correction for bias due to differences between the deflators used for the poverty measures and the national accounts.

We suspect that the difference is due to the pattern of growth in the 1990s and other signs of rising inequality (Ravallion, 2000b). However, it should also be kept in mind that there is a degree of imprecision around these estimates. Our projected rate of poverty reduction after 1993/94 is within the 95 per cent confidence interval implied by the 'pre-reform' elasticities in Ravallion and Datt (1996).

The diverse experience of India's states in reducing poverty at a given rate of growth also holds some clues to what else needs to be done to assure more pro-poor growth in the future. Datt and Ravallion (2002) show that growth in the non-farm sector in the 1990s has generally not been any higher in the states where it would have had the most impact on poverty nationally; indeed, there is virtually zero correlation between growth rates and the (share-weighted) growth elasticities of poverty across states in the 1990s. This is not unique to the 1990s; trend growth rates in India's non-farm economy from 1960 to 1993/94 were also uncorrelated with the weighted growth elasticities of poverty (Ravallion and Datt, 2002). The differences across states in the non-farm growth elasticities of poverty are largely explicable in terms of differences in initial rural development, and initial human development (Ravallion and Datt, 2002). States that lagged in these areas faced limited longer-term prospects of pro-poor growth from their non-farm economies. Nor was the sectoral pattern of growth particularly pro-poor: the states with higher growth in agriculture yields were not the states with initial high levels of poverty. Agriculture as a whole lagged the non-farm sector in the 1990s; while India's aggregate GDP grew at 6.7 per cent per annum between 1993/94 and 1999/2000, the agriculture component (agriculture and allied services) grew at about 3.2 per cent per annum.

CONCLUSION

Different interpretations of the data from the latest round of India's NSS imply very different measured rates of poverty reduction in the 1990s. The consumption-poverty estimates based on 30-day recall for food in the 55th Round of the NSS imply a sizable drop in the poverty rate when compared to previous estimates based on 30-day recall. By contrast, the estimates based on 7-day recall from the same survey round indicate rising poverty incidence, when compared to (limited) prior surveys using this recall period. Given the design of the 55th Round it is hard to say which is right looking at the survey data alone.

Faced with this ambiguity in the results of the latest survey data, we have offered alternative estimates of progress against poverty. These have been based on an econometric model of the state-level poverty measures based on the NSS rounds spanning 1960/61 to 1993/94. The model allows for state fixed effects, state-specific time trends and state-specific elasticities of poverty to non-farm output growth, while also allowing poverty measures to depend on yield per hectare, per capita development spending and the inflation rate in the state. We then project forward using this model and the latest available data on its explanatory variables. These model-based projections are not intended as substitutes for better survey data. We only offer them as a form of triangulation, given the uncertainties about the most recent survey results.

Our state-level projections up to 1999/2000 suggest that the incidence of poverty has been falling in India. The overall rate of poverty reduction implied by our results is 0.8 percentage points per year for the period since 1993/94. This is a little more than halfway between the rates of poverty reduction implied by the 7-day recall and 30-day recall numbers from the 55th Round. And it is about 43 per cent of the rate of poverty reduction implied by the latter source. The projections for rural poverty reduction (of 0.7 percentage points per year) are about 39 per cent of the rate of decline implied by the 30-day estimates from the 55th Round, and they are also about halfway between the estimates for the 7- and 30-day recalls for the two 55th Round. Our estimates for the 1990s suggest that the rate of poverty reduction is slightly lower than India experienced in the 1980s and lower than one would have expected based on growth elasticities of poverty calibrated to the 'pre-reform' data. Our model-based rates of poverty reduction have quite a different geographic composition to those implied by the 55th Round. These differences largely reflect the geographic pattern of farm and non-farm growth in India in the 1990s.

ACKNOWLEDGEMENT

Reprinted from *Economic and Political Weekly*, Vol. 37, 25–31 January 2003.

REFERENCES

Ahluwalia, Montek S. (1978), 'Rural Poverty and Agricultural Performance in India', *Journal of Development Studies*, 14(3), pp. 298–323.

Bhalla, Surjit (2000), 'Growth and Poverty in India – Myth and Reality', available from *http://www.oxusresearch.com/economic.asp*

Datt, Gaurav (1999), 'Has Poverty in India Declined since the Economic Reforms?', *Economic and Political Weekly,* 34, 11–17 December.

Datt, Gaurav and Martin Ravallion (2002), 'Has India's Post-Reform Economic Growth Left India's Poor Behind?' mimeo, Development Research group, World Bank.

———— (1998b), 'Farm Productivity and Rural Poverty in India', *Journal of Development Studies,* 34, pp. 62–85.

———— (1998a), 'Why Have Some Indian States Done Better than Others at Reducing Rural Poverty?', *Economica*, 65, pp. 17–38.

———— (1997), 'Macroeconomic Crises and Poverty Monitoring: A Case Study for India', *Review of Development Economics*, 1(2), pp. 135–52.

———— (1992), 'Growth and Redistribution Components of Changes in Poverty Measures: A Decomposition with Applications to Brazil and India in the 1980s.' *Journal of Development Economics*, 38, pp. 275–95.

Deaton, Angus (2001), 'Adjusted Indian Poverty Estimates for 1999/2000', mimeo, Research Program in Development Studies, Princeton University.

———— (2000), 'Preliminary Notes on Reporting Periods in the Indian NSS 52nd through 54th Rounds', mimeo, Research Program in Development Studies, Princeton University.

Deaton, Angus and Alessandro Tarozzi (1999), 'Prices and Poverty in India', mimeo, Research Program in Development Studies, Princeton University.

Ghosh, Jayati (2000), 'Poverty Amidst Plenty?', *Frontline* 17(5), March 4-17 (available from *www.the-hindu,com/fline/fl1705*).

Government of India (2000), *Choice of Reference Period for Consumption Data,* National Sample Survey Organization, March.

———— (1979), *Report of the Task Force on Projections of Minimum Needs and Effective Consumption*, New Delhi: Planning Commission.

Jha, Raghbendra (2000), 'Reducing Poverty and Inequality in India: Has Liberalization Helped?, Indira Gandhi Institute of Development Research, Bombay, India.

Lanjouw, Jene and Peter Lanjouw (2001) 'How to Compare Apples and Oranges: Poverty Measurement Based on Different Definitions of Consumption', *Review of Income and Wealth*, 47(1), pp. 25–42.

Özler, Berk, Gaurav Datt and Martin Ravallion (1996). 'A Database on Poverty and Growth in India', mimeo, Policy Research Department, World Bank.

Planning Commission (2001), 'Poverty Estimates for 1999/2000', *http://planningcommission.nic.in/prfebt.htm*.

Ravallion, Martin (2000b), 'Should Poverty Measures be Anchored to the National Accounts?' *Economic and Political Weekly*, 34, 16 August, pp. 3245–52.

————— (2000a), 'What is Needed for a More Pro-poor Growth Process in India?', *Economic and Political Weekly*, 35, 25–31 March, pp. 1089–93.

————— (1996), 'How Well Can Methodology Substitute for Data? Five Experiments in Poverty Analysis', *World Bank Research Observer*, 11, pp. 199–222.

Ravallion, Martin and Gaurav Datt (2002), "Why Has Economic Growth Been More Pro-Poor in Some States of India than Others?', *Journal of Development Economics*, in press (earlier version available as Policy Research Working Paper WPS 2263, World Bank; *http://econ.worldbank.org/.*).

————— (1996), 'How Important to India's Poor is the Sectoral Composition of Economic Growth?' *World Bank Economic Review,* 10(1), pp. 1–25.

Sen, Abhijit (2001), 'Estimates of Consumer Expenditure and its Distribution: Statistical Priorities after the NSS 55th Round', *Economic and Political Weekly*.

Srinivasan, T.N. (2000), 'Growth and Poverty Alleviation: Lessons from Development Experience', mimeo, Yale University.

Sundaram, K., and Suresh D. Tendulkar (2001), 'NAS-NSS Estimates of Private Consumption for Poverty Estimation: A Disaggregated Comparison for 1993/94', *Economic and Political Weekly*, 13 January, pp. 119–29.

Tarozzi, Alessandro (2001), 'Estimating Comparable Poverty Counts from Incomparable Surveys: Measuring Poverty in India', mimeo, Princeton University.

van de Walle, Dominique (1985), 'Population Growth and Poverty: Another Look at the Indian Time Series Evidence', *Journal of Development Studies,* 34(4), pp. 62–85.

Visaria, Pravin (1999), 'Poverty in India During 1994–98: Alternative Estimates', mimeo, Institute of Economic Growth, Delhi, India, 1999.

20

NCAER's Market Information Survey of Households

Statistical Properties and Applications for Policy Analysis

Suman Bery and R.K. Shukla

INTRODUCTION

The Market Information Survey of Households (MISH) is a household survey conducted periodically by the National Council of Applied Economic Research (NCAER). It was initiated in 1985/86 to estimate market size and penetration for a variety of consumer goods, and has been undertaken more or less annually since then, with a few gaps. The MISH also provides a profile of consuming households in terms of income, occupation, and location. Because the first surveys were undertaken prior to the liberalisation of trade and investment in the Indian economy in 1991, the survey series provides a potential basis for chronicling the evolution of Indian spending habits in the course of liberalisation.

Following an initial period during which it was supported through sponsorship from the Indian government, MISH has been conducted by the NCAER using the organisation's own resources. Costs have been partially recovered through the sale of information on product penetration and other tabulations. In light of this, the design and analysis of the surveys has been directed toward their primary purpose, which is to understand consumer behaviour. However, as a corollary, the MISH surveys have also generated valuable demographic data, particularly on household incomes. It has been suggested that this data could throw light on broader social trends in the economy.

With this idea in mind, Lal et al. (2001) attempted to calculate poverty measures using MISH data stretching until 1997/98. The work was well-received by academics, researchers, and policy-makers, and enhanced interest in using MISH data for further analysis. Along these lines, this paper seeks to assess the relevance of MISH data to further demographic calculations, and to update and extend estimates of poverty obtained by Lal et al. using MISH data for the year 1998/99. To this end, it first discusses the methodological properties of the MISH, including elements of its sample design. Validation of the choices made is undertaken by comparing the results with the NCAER's earlier Micro Impacts of

Macroeconomic and Adjustment Policies (MIMAP) survey of income and consumption, and also with the National Accounts Statistics (NAS) of India. The paper discusses these results broadly and in its conclusion spells out the consequent outlook for MISH data usage in further demographic analysis.

SURVEY OUTLINE

The MISH is conducted in two rounds. Households in both urban and rural sample areas are first listed according to the sampling method described below. In addition to the basic demographic data, information on ownership of selected consumer durables is collected at this stage. From this list of households, a sub-sample is selected for more intensive canvassing of expenditure on consumables.

For all rounds of the MISH, a multi-stage, stratified sampling scheme has been adopted. Sample districts, villages, and households compose the first, second, and third stages, respectively, of selection for the rural sample. Cities/towns, urban blocks, and households compose the three stages of selection for the urban sample.

The sampling methodology – in particular the stages of selection, the number of sample locations and sample size – is approximately the same for all the rounds of MISH. However, actual locations, including sample villages and towns as well as households, are independently selected for each round. The survey covers all the states/union territories (UTs) of India, except those areas where it is particularly difficult for operational reasons to establish coverage.[1]

The rural sample has been selected from every district in the covered states – i.e. each of these districts was selected with probability 1. From each district, two villages were selected with probability proportional to the population of the village, as per the 1981 Census or 1991 Census, as appropriate.

The 1991 Census categorises cities/towns by their population, ranging from less than 5,000 to over 10 million. All cities with a population exceeding 500,000, as reported in the 1991 Census, were included in the sample. The remaining towns/cities were grouped into six strata on the basis of their population size, and from each stratum a sample of towns was selected independently. A progressively increasing sampling fraction with increasing town population class was used for determining the number of sample towns to be selected from each stratum, independently for each state (Table 20.1).

In building the sampling frame for the 1991 Census, the Office of the Registrar-General of India divided each city/town into a number of urban blocks. The blocks are a compact agglomeration of units

Table 20.1 Sampling Fraction for City/Town Groups (by State)

City/Town Size Group	Sampling Fraction	Number of Sample Cities/Towns
Over 500,000	1.00	53
200,000–500,000	0.80	65
100,000–200,000	0.60	98
50,000–100,000	0.30	102
20,000–50,000	0.10	97
10,000–20,000	0.05	62
Below 10,000	0.04	38
Total	0.14	515

[1] The states/UTs that are left out of MISH survey are Arunachal Pradesh, Manipur, Mizoram, Nagaland, Sikkim, Tripura, Jammu & Kashmir, Andaman and Nicobar Islands, Dadra and Nagar Haveli, and Lakshadweep. These account for about 3-4 per cent of the total population of the country.

with well-defined boundaries and with approximately equal population of around 600. A sample of blocks was randomly and independently selected from each selected town/city. The number of blocks selected ranged between 2 and 50, depending on the size of the town.

In the absence of a definitive list of households, those in the selected villages and urban blocks were listed through a specially designed pro forma, which sought information on identification particulars, household size, number of income earners, occupation of household head, annual income from all sources, and information related to consumer durable goods. In the case of large villages, a fraction of households were listed, due to time and cost constraints. These households were randomly chosen.

The size and breadth of the MISH sample has been determined by the need to capture the penetration of consumer durables with some precision at the zonal, or regional level, for example, north India, south India, etc. Accordingly, in 1998/99, nearly 92,000 households distributed over 840 villages in 420 districts were included in the rural listing. Similarly, the urban listing consisted of over 183,000 households distributed over 1,650 urban blocks in 515 towns/cities.

The levels of penetration of consumer expendable goods are generally high. In fact, for a few products they are close to 100 per cent, and for no product is the penetration level below 20 per cent. Therefore, it was felt that a small sample size around 25,000 would be adequate to provide reasonably reliable estimates of different levels of consumption at regional levels. The other considerations governing the sample size were time and cost constraints.

Consumption is highly correlated with level of income. However, households with higher incomes exhibit large variations both in variety and quantity of consumption, while constituting a small proportion of the total population. Accordingly, unless such households are adequately represented in the sample, estimates are likely to have large sampling errors. Therefore, to select representative households for consumer expendables, the listed households in each sample place (villages and urban blocks) were stratified into five income bands[2] on the basis of annual household income. These income bands are specific to NCAER and are adjusted in nominal terms each year to reflect constant levels of real household income in the initial year. Households were selected independently from each stratum/income band, with equal probability. Such a sampling procedure registered proportionately higher representation from high-income households in the sample. However, this is rectified using different household weights, inverse of probability of selection, for each of the five income bands. All households in a given income band in a particular location are assigned an equal weight.

The MISH survey, thus, results in two data sets. A large data set of around 300,000 households emerges directly from the listing operation. In addition to containing the demographic information for each household, this data set comprises information on the ownership of durable products. In addition, a second, small data set of around 25,000 households is drawn from a sub-sample of the above data set, containing information on consumer expendables, along with demographic particulars.

VALIDATION OF SAMPLING CHOICES

Sampling

The larger villages exhibit a high degree of variation in their ownership and purchases of consumer

---

[2] Income bands (Annual household income in rupees at 1998/99 prices): Low = Up to Rs 35,000; Lower Middle = Rs 35,001 to Rs 70,000; Middle = Rs 70,001 to Rs 105,000; Upper Middle = Rs 105,001 to Rs 140,000; and High = Above Rs 140,000.

goods. Therefore, varying probability selection was undertaken to ensure that larger villages were adequately represented in the sample. The distribution of sample villages in the 1998/99 MISH shows that over 15.8 per cent of the villages had a population above 5,000, while according to the 1991 census, only 2.3 per cent of all villages exceeded this size. Similarly, the smaller villages with population below 500, accounted for 42.2 per cent of all villages according to the 1991 census, but represent only 12.6 per cent of villages selected in the MISH sample. However, the estimated distributions of villages and population based on MISH are very close to distributions based on the 1991 Census (Figure 20.1).

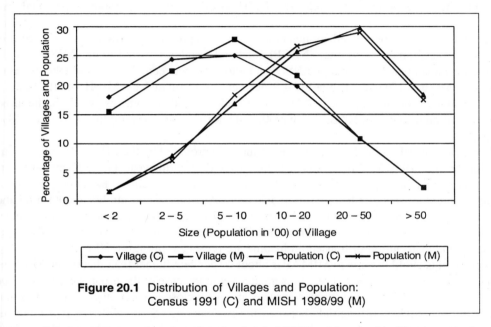

Figure 20.1 Distribution of Villages and Population:
Census 1991 (C) and MISH 1998/99 (M)

A further validation of appropriate sample selection in MISH can be obtained by a comparison of its population estimates with those available from the NAS at the national level (Table 20.2). At the all-India level, the MISH tracks official population estimates relatively closely – the MISH-based estimate of 948.5 million for the 16 states is within 1 per cent of the NAS-reported figure of 935.5 million.

Table 20.2 Comparison of MISH and National Accounts (NAS)
Estimates (1998/99)

Particulars	NAS	MISH	Ratio of MISH to NAS
Population (million)	935.5	948.5	1.01
NSDP (Rs '000 million) – 16 states	12,163	7,628	0.63
Per capita NSDP (Rs)	13,002	8,042	0.62

Income

The MISH is one of few consistent sources providing comparable household income data on a regular basis, notwithstanding the fact that in the strict sense, it is neither an income nor an expenditure survey. The main concept of income that has been used in the MISH is the concept of 'perceived monetary income', which includes all income received by the household as a whole, and by each of its members, during the reference year. The exact question that MISH asks of households is – 'What is your annual household income from all sources?' This income concept is different from the economic concept of income as defined by the NAS, which includes employers' contributions to provident fund (PF), interest on PF, interest on cumulative deposits, etc. MISH also does not include incomes in kind. Further, certain components of income are not perceived as income by the respondents and are, hence, excluded from incomes reported to MISH. Items like reimbursements for travel, medical, and such other expenses are not reported. Therefore income estimated from MISH is not directly comparable to 'personal disposable income'.

At the all-India level, perceived monetary income as captured by MISH is 63 per cent of NAS reported Net State Domestic Product (NSDP) for the 16 states covered under MISH (Table 20.2). However, the annual growth in per capita NSDP at factor cost between 1987/88 and 1998/99 as reported by NAS, was about 4.1 per cent, against 4.8 per cent as estimated by MISH for the same period. Therefore, in spite of the fact that the MISH surveys underestimate income as per NAS, the direction of change is very similar to that of NAS, which renders the former data meaningful for policy analysis (Lal et al., 2001).

Another means of validating MISH income estimates is provided by the MIMAP study conducted by NCAER for the year 1994/95. MISH was also conducted during this year. In the former study, primary data was collected from 5,000 households to obtain details of income, expenditure, savings and employment, and other social indicators, from different categories of households in both rural and urban India. Accordingly, coverage of income is better in the MIMAP, as it includes more components, such as imputed and accrued, but not realised incomes. The corresponding MIMAP and MISH estimates of both the level and distribution of household income are presented in Figure 20.2.

The average household income in MIMAP is about 20 per cent higher than that of the MISH estimate based on the small sample data set. The gap is greater yet in the case of the urban sample, at 32 per cent. However, the rural distributions of the two surveys are fairly close to each other. For its part, the urban distribution reflects higher differentials between the two surveys. Since MIMAP is a more intensive study on income and the distribution obtained, it is expected to be more reliable. Yet the difference between the two distributions appears to be only at their tails; while MISH has more households at the lower tail, MIMAP has more at the upper tail. Meanwhile, the distribution of income by quantile groups of population from the two surveys, obtained by converting the household income data to individual income data, is very similar for both rural and urban areas (Table 20.3).

The validity checks made above do reflect a fair degree of match between MISH and other surveys, in regard to the distributional properties. It is the case that the MISH survey does not adopt an economic concept of income because of its specific objectives. However, its consistency with regard to methodology and coverage provides us with a fair degree of confidence in using its data for demographic analyses oriented towards policy research. The following section further discusses the observations and trends outlined by this data.

RESULTS AND DISCUSSION

Estimated Population Profile

As per MISH data, the Indian population grew at 2.11 per cent per annum between 1987/88 and

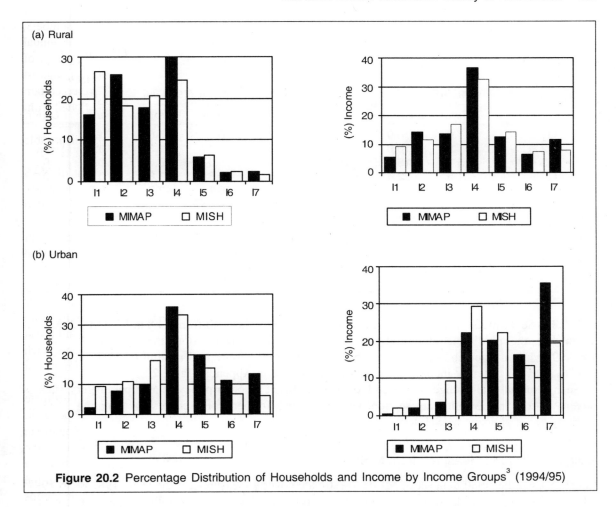

Figure 20.2 Percentage Distribution of Households and Income by Income Groups[3] (1994/95)

1998/99. Over the same period, the estimated per capita income grew at a rate of 4.84 per cent per annum, while the estimated number of households in the country increased by 37.6 million. Not surprisingly, the household income distribution has accordingly undergone a significant change since 1987/88. While the share of low-income households as defined by NCAER (see footnote 5) in the total population decreased sharply, from about 61 per cent in 1987/88 to 40 per cent in 1998/99, the other income classes increased in their respective sizes. In absolute terms, the number of lower-income households declined from 81.9 million in 1987/88, to 68.2 million – a drop of 21.3 per cent. The estimated population profile based on MISH data for two years is presented in Appendix Table 1.

Both rural and urban areas follow a similar trend with respect to the income distribution of households. The number of low-income households in rural areas dropped in absolute numbers from 67.2 million in

[3] Income Groups (Annual household income in Rs at 1994/95 prices)

I1 = Up to Rs 12,000; I2 = Rs 12,001 – Rs 18,000; I3 = Rs 18,001 – Rs 24,000; I4 = Rs 24,001 – Rs 48,000; I5 = Rs 48,001– Rs 72,000; I6 = Rs 72,001 – Rs 96,000; and I7 = Above Rs 96,000.

Table 20.3 Income Distribution by Quantile Groups (Percentage in Income)

Quantile Group	MIMAP (1994/95)		MISH (1994/95)		MISH (1998/99)		Difference between MIMAP and MISH (1994/95) (% Points)	
	Rural	Urban	Rural	Urban	Rural	Urban	Rural	Urban
Q1	7.0	6.0	6.0	5.3	6.0	5.6	1.0	0.7
Q2	11.2	10.6	10.8	9.9	10.4	11.3	0.6	0.9
Q3	15.7	15.5	15.4	15.1	15.0	16.6	0.2	0.3
Q4	21.5	22.4	22.3	22.6	22.5	23.8	−0.9	−0.3
Q5	44.6	45.5	45.5	47.1	46.1	42.7	−0.9	−1.6
Gini	0.38	0.39	0.43	0.38	0.39	0.36		
Average annual household income (Rs)	27,411	57,675	22,843	43,693	44,997	71,508		
Annual per capita income (Rs)	4,860	11,309	4,015	8,061	7,922	13,341		

1987/88 to 58.9 million in 1998/99, while in the urban areas it declined from 14.8 million to 9.3 million. Meanwhile, the middle-income group grew faster in rural areas, nearly doubling between 1987/88 and 1998/99, while in the urban population, this group expanded from 20.8 million to 33.6 million. The growth rates for different income categories are presented in Appendix Table 2.

Such distributional changes are bound to have an impact on other policy-related parameters, such as poverty ratios. In the following section, we discuss this further in the context of updating previous work by Lal et al. using MISH data.

Estimated Poverty Measures from MISH

Lal et al. used the small data set of MISH to estimate poverty measures for the years 1987/88 to 1997/98 on account of unavailability of a large data set prior to 1994/95. In the following exercise, we too have used the small data set for the years 1987/88, 1994/95, and 1998/99. Although the large data set is available for 1998/99, it has not been used for the current exercise due to constraints of time and resources. However, there is currently an effort underway to investigate how, and to what extent the large data set available for the later rounds of MISH could be used for policy research.

Meanwhile, poverty measures using a per capita income distribution from the small data set have been estimated, using two alternative approaches. The first follows Lal et al.,[4] while the second uses the Planning Commission's expenditure poverty line. The resulting estimates of various poverty measures are presented in the Appendix Tables 3 and 4.

---

[4] Lal et al. used the Planning Commission's poverty ratios – rural (39.1 per cent) and urban (38.2 per cent) – for 1987/88 as base, in order to calculate the income poverty line (IPL) from MISH data available for the same year. These ratios, when applied to MISH data, resulted in rural IPL of Rs 1,149 and urban IPL of Rs 1,701 per capita per annum for the year 1987/88. The Consumer Price Index (CPI) for agricultural laboures and CPI for industrial workers are used to update IPL for rural and urban areas, respectively, for the year 1998/99.

Using the first approach, estimates of income poverty measures show a drastic decline from 1987/88 to 1998/99. For instance, the urban headcount ratio has declined from 38.2 per cent in 1987/88 to 10.9 per cent in 1998/99. Similarly, in the case of the rural population, the estimate for the headcount ratio has declined from 39.1 per cent to 16.2 per cent. In absolute terms, there were 139 million poor people in 1998/99, of which 20 million (17 million in rural and 3 million in urban areas) lived in extreme poverty (the proportion of the population living below 50 per cent of IPL).

Two other important poverty measures, namely, the poverty gap and the squared poverty gap, also depict trends similar to that observed for the headcount ratio in both urban and rural areas. Although the respective headcount ratios were more or less same during the base year (1987/88), the rate of decline in the level of poverty is much faster in the case of the urban population during this period. Accordingly, by 1998/99, the rural poverty gap and squared poverty gap are approximately double those of urban areas.

Different, though roughly proportionate results were obtained using an expenditure poverty line for 1998/99 based on the Planning Commission's expenditure poverty line defined for 1999/2000 and applied to income data from MISH 1998/99. The estimated headcount ratio was about 25.9 and 15.1 for rural and urban areas, respectively, as against 16.2 and 10.9 obtained through Lal et al. approach.

CONCLUSION

In conclusion, the following can be said about the utility of MISH and the observations it yields. Foremost, the rounds of MISH have gone some way towards providing consistent and comparable household income data sets. Demographic parameters and poverty measures estimated on the basis of data sets available from this survey are presented in this paper. Importantly, the consistency test conducted on the results, comparing them with results from the NAS and MIMAP, suggests that we can use MISH data for policy research with a fair degree of confidence.

So what does this data tell us? Between 1987/88 and 1998/99, the income distribution of households has undergone a significant change. While the share of low income households in the total population decreased sharply, the other income classes increased in size. As expected, the results show that estimates of poverty ratios obtained from different sources of data vary, and that to some extent, they are also affected by the methodological approach adopted. However, of greater interest than the poverty ratio per se, is information about how fast, and in which direction it is moving. To this extent, it is encouraging to note that while the poverty lines estimated in this paper elicit a range of indications on the magnitude of poverty, the IPL estimated using Lal et al. approach shows consistency in the movement of poverty ratios.

For reasons mentioned earlier, poverty measures based on MISH have hitherto been derived from its small data set. However, it should be noted that the size of a sample in any case only ensures the relative quality of a particular estimate. In fact, no sample survey can provide the population parameter exactly. If a survey adopts consistency in its overall approach, the resulting estimate of a particular parameter is robust and a series of such surveys would be able to reflect consistency in a trend. This is exactly what is being reflected in the above poverty results.

Nevertheless, the possible utility of larger MISH data sets in the context of policy research is currently being assessed. Over the years, we expect such large sets to reproduce qualitatively improved and robust estimates of poverty, and to show more consistent trends that could also be more reliably interpreted.

ACKNOWLEDGEMENT

We would like to acknowledge the support of the NCAER MISH team, particularly S.P. Batra, S.D. Brahmankar, S.K. Dwivedi, and Asha Virmani, who we thanks for their guidance and support. Surjit Bhalla and Amaresh Dubey also provided criticism and comments well beyond the call of duty.

The survey was conducted in 1994/95 as part of an on going project – 'Micro Impact of Macroeconomic & Adjustment Policies' (MIMAP) – supported by International Development Research Centre (IDRC), Canada.

Reprinted from *Economic and Political Weekly*, Vol. 37, 25–31 January 2003.

REFERENCES

Lal, D., Rakesh Mohan and I. Natarajan (2001), 'Economic Reforms and Poverty Alleviation – A Tale of Two Surveys', *Economic and Political Weekly*, 24 March, pp. 1017–28.

Natarajan, I. (1998), *India Market Demographics Report,* NCAER, New Delhi.

NCAER (2000), *MIMAP India News*, Vol. 1, Issue 2.

Planning Commission (2002), *Poverty Estimates for 1999/2000, Press Note*, New Delhi.

Rao, S.L. and I. Natarajan (1996), 'Indian Market Demographics – The Consumer Classes', NCAER, New Delhi.

Reserve Bank of India (2001), *Handbook of Statistics on Indian Economy*, Mumbai.

Appendix

Appendix Table 1 Estimated Population Profile from MISH Data

Estimated Parameters	1987/88	1998/99
Rural		
Total households (million)	97.61	122.81
Distribution of households (%)		
Low income	68.8	47.9
Low-middle income	25.8	34.8
Middle income	4.3	10.4
Upper-middle income	0.7	3.8
High income	0.4	3.0
Total	100.0	100.0
Household size	5.73	5.68
Population (million)	550	693
Average household income (Rs per annum)	9,901	44,997
Per capita income (Rs per annum) at current price	1,728	7,922
Per capita income (Rs per annum) at constant price	3,051	5,241
Urban		
Total households (million)	36.69	49.11
Distribution of households (%)		
Low income	40.3	19.0
Low-middle income	35.5	33.8
Middle income	16.2	22.6
Upper-middle income	5.0	12.2
High income	3.1	12.5
Total	100.0	100.0
Household size	5.49	5.36
Population (million)	198	249
Average household income (Rs per annum)	17,101	71,508
Per capita income (Rs per annum) at current price	3,115	13,341
Per capita income (Rs per annum) at constant price	5,499	8,826
Total		
Total households (million)	134.30	171.92
Distribution of households (%)		
Low income	61.0	39.7
Low-middle income	28.4	34.5
Middle income	7.6	13.9
Upper-middle income	1.9	6.2
High income	1.1	5.7
Total	100.0	100.0
Household size	5.67	5.59
Population (million)	749	942
Average household income (Rs per annum)	11,868	52,570
Per capita income (Rs per annum) at current price	2,095	9,407
Per capita income (Rs per annum) at constant price	3,699	6,223

Appendix Table 2 Percentage Annual Growth in Estimated Population Parameters between 1987/88 and 1998/99

Estimated Parameters	Rural	Urban	Total
Low income households	−1.19	−4.11	−1.66
Low-middle income households	4.94	2.22	4.09
Middle income households	10.64	5.81	8.08
Upper-middle income households	18.66	11.42	13.97
High income households	23.72	16.76	18.82
Total households	2.11	2.69	2.27
Population	2.12	2.11	2.11
Per capita income at constant price	5.04	4.39	4.84

Appendix Table 3 Estimated Income Poverty Line (IPL) and Income-based Poverty Measures

Estimated Parameters	1987/88	1998/99	1998/99
Rural			
Poverty line (Rs per capita/annum)	1149*	3000*	3802**
Headcount ratio	39.1	16.2	25.9
Poverty gap	13.3	4.0	7.8
Squared poverty gap	6.5	1.7	3.3
Estimated population below income poverty line (million)	215	112	179
Urban			
Poverty line (Rs per capita/annum)	1701*	4455*	5271**
Headcount ratio	38.29	10.9	15.1
Poverty gap	13.7	2.2	3.9
Squared poverty gap	7.3	0.9	1.5
Estimated population below income poverty line (million)	76	27	38

* Income poverty line based on Lal et al. approach
** Expenditure poverty line based on Planning Commission

Appendix Table 4 Estimated Extreme IPL (50 per cent of IPL) and Income-based Poverty Measures

Estimated Parameters	1987/88	1998/99	1998/99
Rural			
Poverty line (Rs per capita/annum)	575*	1500*	1901**
Headcount ratio	10.6	2.48	4.62
Poverty gap	2.8	0.43	1.10
Squared poverty gap	1.1	0.16	0.37
Estimated population below income poverty line (million)	58	17	32
Urban			
Poverty line (Rs per capita/annum)	851*	2228*	2636**
Headcount ratio	11.9	1.18	1.93
Poverty gap	3.8	0.29	0.48
Squared poverty gap	1.8	0.11	0.18
Estimated population below income poverty line (million)	24	3	5

* Income poverty line based on Lal et al. approach
** Expenditure poverty line based on Planning Commission

21

Recounting the Poor
Poverty in India 1983–99

Surjit S. Bhalla

INTRODUCTION

The official source of information on poverty in India is the consumer expenditures survey undertaken by the National Sample Survey Organisation (NSSO). It has conducted such surveys for almost 50 years. Though annual surveys have been conducted in recent years, most analysis and debate has centred on the large survey, which the NSS undertakes every five years, incorporating more than 100,000 households. Since 1983, two such surveys have been conducted: the Consumer Expenditure Survey (CES) and the Employment and Unemployment (E&U) Survey. These have been conducted simultaneously, covering the same set of households for the survey years 1983, 1987/88, 1993/94,[1] but different households for the year 1999/2000. This paper is about the inferences one can make about the magnitude of and trends in poverty in India, on the basis of unit records made available by these eight household surveys since 1983.

What is the value-added of further research purporting to estimate poverty, when an official government agency has already undertaken this task? There are two major reasons why extra research into the basic topic of 'what is the magnitude of poverty in India' is worthwhile. First, for some years now, and certainly since the late seventies, the NSSO surveys on which official poverty estimates are now based, are capturing less and less of consumption as revealed by the National Accounts (NA). Second, for the latest survey year, 1999/2000, the survey authorities posed the *same* food expenditures questions to the *same* households, asking them to recall their estimates for both a 7- and a 30-day reference period. (In previous years, NSSO surveys had only used a 30-day recall period.) Thus, the possibility exists that the total 30-day recall-based food expenditures results could have been influenced by the expenditures reported for the 7-day reporting period; and that the 'bias' was likely to be upwards since typically a lower recall period for food results in higher reported mean expenditures. Since food is a large proportion of expenditures, there is therefore the theoretical possibility that estimates of the 'contaminated' 30-day recall period for 1999 cannot be used for inferring trends from the earlier years.

[1] For an analysis of this unusual property of the surveys, see Bhalla (2002e).

However, as argued in this paper, while some bias is admittedly present in the 1999/2000 survey due to its use of mixed reference period, the magnitude of this bias is likely to be small, especially in comparison to other mis-measurement caused by use of survey data. This is underlined by the growing divergence between NSSO- and NAS-based estimates of per capita consumption. Today, the NSSO surveys are capturing about 20 to 30 per cent less of aggregate consumption as revealed by the NAS, than they did just 15 years ago. If this mis-measurement also affects estimates of the consumption of the poor and, thus, the calculation of the headcount ratio (HCR), then it far outweighs a few percentage points error in mean consumption caused by the 7- or 30-day problem. It is therefore necessary to devise a method for 'correctly' estimating mean consumption in 1999/2000, and if need be, for other survey years. To this end, this paper offers an *NSS* non-expenditures survey-based method of arriving at a valid estimate of mean consumption that neither relies on the use of national accounts information[2] nor on the problematic CES of 1999/2000.

The need for such an alternative estimate is especially evident in light of the fact that poverty estimates, despite their simplicity, are the most contentious of all Indian statistics. Many public policies and perhaps even political fortunes hinge on these estimates. If the HCR of a state – or the country – goes down, it is considered to be doing well, and its policies are deemed deserving of praise and emulation. (On the other hand, if the HCR rises, the country/states may ask for more funds to fight poverty.) Accordingly, economists and statisticians who use this data, as well as the survey agencies that collect and process it, find themselves at the centre of contentious discussions about poverty trends, and the accuracy of associated economic policies.

The plan of this chapter is as follows. The section that follows summarises the controversy over the magnitude of Indian poverty. The next section discusses the trends in the survey capture ratio, i.e. the ratio of what household surveys indicate is the level of per capita consumption, to that corresponding estimate provided by an alternative source, such as the national accounts. The chapter further discusses the possible sources and magnitude of errors contained in both the households surveys and national accounts. Finally, the last section estimates poverty in India in 1999/2000 according to different methods, emphasising in particular a method which uses information about increases in real wages between 1983 and 1999, as measured by NSSO household surveys. As noted above, the former is the year of an 'uncontaminated' survey and the latter is that of a problematic expenditures survey – in neither year was the NSSO survey containing wage information 'contaminated'. This section also concludes, arguing in particular that in light of data from the national sample surveys, it is almost incontrovertible that poverty in India was less than 15 per cent in 1999/2000. Notably, this number is some conceptual distance away from the corresponding 35 to 40 per cent estimate poverty of the World Bank for the same year, and is nearly half of the official government of India estimates of 26 per cent. The term incontrovertible is not used lightly. If certain universal assumptions, made by all economists, political scientists, and sociologists are also made about the relationship between wages, income, and consumption, then it *has* to follow that poverty in India in the late nineties was in the teens. Other alternative estimates may of course be posited. As argued however, these are accordingly also plagued by severe, so-called 'smell test'[3] problems.

---

[2] A framework to analyse poverty using both survey and national accounts information is developed in Bhalla (2000a and 2002d).

[3] Smell tests and duck tests are offered in Bhalla (2002d) to differentiate between alternative claims about reality – for example, if it stinks, it cannot be a rose.

THE DEBATE OVER POVERTY IN INDIA

Over a 30-year period lasting until the early eighties, there was not much per capita income growth in India, and not surprisingly, not much reduction in poverty.[4] Indeed, there was almost no improvement in the HCR during this time; it was 45 per cent in 1951/52, 45.3 per cent in 1960/61, 52.9 per cent in 1970/71, and 43 per cent in 1983.[5] When Ahluwalia et al. (1979) constructed the first international poverty line, they based it on the 45th percentile of the Indian distribution.[6] This 45 per cent estimate of poverty is virtually identical to the official Indian poverty estimate for 1983, based on the NSS expenditures survey for that year.

However, India changed in the early 1980s. It was mysterious perhaps, but the fact remains that per capita income growth accelerated from about 1 per cent per annum to above 3 per cent per annum. This new trend has persisted for the two decades and all estimates and analysts agree that per capita consumption in India, as measured by national accounts, is at least 50 per cent higher in 1999/2000 than it was in 1983. This increase is based on a lower bound estimate of per capita consumption growth of 2.5 per cent per annum.

So how large a decline in poverty should result from a 50 per cent rise in consumption, assuming that the consumption distribution stayed the same?[7] Theoretical estimates of the elasticity of poverty reduction with respect to growth – referred to as the headcount elasticity – have been estimated by various authors.[8] This elasticity has been estimated to be about –1.3 for India (Ravallion and Datt, 1996) and about –2 for developing countries (see Collier-Dollar, 2000). Given an Indian poverty level of 45 per cent in 1983 and 50 per cent growth in per capita consumption, the elasticity estimate of –1.3 yields a predicted HCR of 23 per cent in 1999/2000.

Using unit-level data for India covering the years 1983, 1987, 1993, and 1999, and disaggregating each state and its distribution into rural and urban components, the mean survey-based growth between 1983 and 1999 is observed to be 26.2 per cent, and the elasticity of poverty reduction is –2.4. This elasticity is derived from a regression whose dependent variable is the log change in the poverty ratio, and whose independent variable is the log growth in surveyed real per capita expenditures. In total, there are 105 state-level urban/rural observations of changes in growth and poverty for 1987, 1993/94, and 1999/2000. On the basis of this growth rate and elasticity, the predicted poverty level in 1999 is 24 per cent. If the elasticity were –1.33, the predicted 1999 poverty level would be 31.8 per cent.

As discussed in World Bank (1991), Bhalla (2000a) and Bhalla (2002d), there are severe problems with the above method of deriving the elasticity, and in its use in forecasting or estimating levels of poverty. Changes in the HCR are critically dependent on the position of the poverty line and its interaction

[4] Poverty is correctly defined, and measured, in terms of per capita consumption. This is also the practice in this paper. However, while primarily discussing trends in consumption poverty it uses the terms income and consumption interchangeably, on the basis that there cannot be consumption growth without income growth. It should be noted however that poverty is of course not defined in terms of income alone; it also comprises consumption of social services such as education and health services. For discussion of international trends in living standards, see Bhalla (2002) and Asian Development Bank (2002).

[5] Estimates from World Bank (1997), p. 149.

[6] That this Indian poverty line is equivalent to the famous PPP one dollar-a-day poverty line is documented in Bhalla (2002d).

[7] In fact, as shown later in the chapter (Table 21.5), the distribution of consumption in India *improved* between 1983 and 1999.

[8] See Ravallion and Datt (1996) for a sampling.

with the distribution of consumption.[9] This can be illustrated by the following simple example. Assume the poverty line is Rs 100 and all the poor have income of Rs 99. A 1 per cent growth in incomes of the poor will lead to 0 poverty – an infinite elasticity of poverty reduction with respect to growth. Now assume all the poor are clustered at Rs 50, and the poverty line remains at Rs 100. Obviously, even a 60 per cent growth in the incomes of the poor will lead to a 0 reduction in the HCR – a zero elasticity.

Obviously, reality is not as extreme as this. However, by not adjusting *at all* for the interaction between the poverty line and the distribution, many researchers have led themselves to conclude erroneously that the growth-poverty elasticity has been low and, hence, that it is imperative to increase this elasticity, for example by achieving a better distribution of income. To evaluate such concerns, Bhalla (2002d) introduces the concept of the 'shape of distribution elasticity (SDE)'. This is defined as the amount by which the HCR will decline for a given amount of growth, assuming that there is no change in the distribution. This 'elasticity' has to be estimated in a non-linear manner, by shocking the Lorenz curve with small changes (+/– 2.5 per cent) at the poverty line. As developed in Bhalla (2002d), the SDE can help translate income and inequality changes into expected changes in poverty, via the following formula:

$$d\text{P} = (g + i)*\text{SDE} \tag{1}$$

where dP is the arithmetic change in the HCR of poverty, g is the (log) growth in *average* per capita consumption, and i is the (log) change in the share of consumption of the poor *at or near the poverty line*.[10] The above equation is *exact*, and has no room for a 'residual' term as argued by Ravallion and Datt (1999). For non-small changes, the relationship does not hold exactly, for the simple reason that the large changes in income most likely traverse a large portion of the Lorenz curve and the arc elasticity estimated by SDE is an average of several 'arcs'. However, as results for several Indian states show (Table 21.1), the approximation for large changes provided by equation (1) is reasonably close.

Table 21.1 presents SDE results for several states in India, outlining respective changes in their poverty rates over the 16-year period, 1983–99. Results are presented for rural and urban areas, and are also provided as pooled data for each state. A perusal of these results suggests the following:

1. The 'model' outlined by equation (1) is an excellent predictor of changes in poverty. Notably however, the model does *not* incorporate the 'initial inequality' effect on poverty reduction, as

---

[9] This point was first made in a World Bank study on Malaysia (World Bank, 1991), and subsequently in Bhalla (2000a, 2000b). The World Bank report was published in January 1991, but the work had been completed more than a year earlier. The report stated: 'Choice of a poverty line dictates the initial level of absolute poverty, which has an important bearing on subsequent achievements . . . Since poverty is defined in terms of a simple headcount measure (incomes above or below a fixed income) the decline is dependent on the defined poverty line . . . If there are many people slightly below the poverty line initially, then a relatively small amount of growth can have a large effect on reducing poverty'. The World Bank's *World Development Report* for 1990 articulates similar conclusions: 'For any given increase in the incomes of the poor, the reduction in poverty depends on where the poor are in relation to the poverty line. If they are concentrated just below the line, the increase in their incomes will have a bigger effect on poverty than if they are spread more evenly'. Prior to the publication of these 'findings', the poverty literature did not contend with this effect. Since then, it has been 'well known', but to wit, many pro-poor growth analysts have not to date incorporated it into their analyses.

[10] The reason Ravallion and Datt have a 'residual' term is because they *define* the arithmetic change in poverty to be equal to a growth component plus a redistribution component plus a residual equal to the 'difference between the growth (redistribution) components evaluated at the terminal and initial Lorenz curves (mean incomes) respectively'. As documented in Bhalla (2002d), the derivation of equation 1 is based on *changes* from an initial point (year), and the consumption growth and distribution from this initial point. The question of a 'terminal' year distribution does not arise.

Table 21.1(A) Growth-Inequality-Poverty Connections: Rural India, 1983–99

State	Gini		Change in Gini	Change in Inequality	Growth in Per Capita Cons.	Total Growth	SDE	Change in HCR		HCR	
								Predicted	Actual		
	1983	1999	(1983–99)	(1983–99)	(1983–99)	(1983–99)	1983	(1983–99)	(1983–99)	1983	1999
Andhra Pradesh	29.7	23.8	−22.1	14.6	9.0	23.6	0.80	−19.0	−16.2	27.3	11.0
Assam	20	20.3	1.5	−2.5	1.9	−0.6	1.30	0.9	−3.9	44.3	40.4
Bihar	26.2	20.8	−23.1	7.1	18.6	25.7	0.80	−20.4	−20.9	65.3	44.4
Gujarat	26.6	23.8	−11.1	4.3	17.8	22.1	0.85	−18.9	−16.9	29.3	12.5
Haryana	28.4	24.9	−13.2	7.3	17.5	24.8	0.83	−20.5	−14.0	21.5	7.4
Himachal Pradesh	27.2	24.5	−10.5	10.0	12.1	22.1	0.67	−14.9	−10.3	18.4	8.0
Karnataka	30.9	24.4	−23.6	16.7	13.2	29.9	0.79	−23.7	−19.1	36.3	17.2
Kerala	31.9	28.9	−9.9	7.6	37.0	44.6	0.88	−39.3	−30.7	40.1	9.4
Madhya Pradesh	29.7	25.4	−15.6	10.1	6.9	17.0	0.85	−14.4	−12.8	50.3	37.4
Maharashtra	29.1	26.2	−10.5	5.6	22.1	27.7	0.87	−24.0	−22.9	46.3	23.4
Orissa	27.1	24.7	−9.3	3.2	22.8	26.0	0.82	−21.2	−20.0	68.5	48.4
Punjab	28.8	25.3	−13.0	13.7	6.7	20.4	0.48	−9.8	−7.9	14.1	6.2
Rajasthan	34.6	21.3	−48.5	31.8	1.6	33.4	0.74	−24.7	−20.9	34.3	13.4
Tamil Nadu	36.6	28.4	−25.4	15.4	30.1	45.5	0.79	−35.9	−34.1	54.4	20.4
Uttar Pradesh	29.1	24.9	−15.6	8.1	11.9	20.0	0.85	−17.1	−16.0	47.4	31.4
West Bengal	29.9	22.6	−28.0	14.3	26.2	40.5	0.78	−31.6	−32.8	64.3	31.5
India	30.4	26.3	−14.5	7.8	18.5	26.3	0.92	−24.2	−20.9	48.2	27.3

Notes: 1. SDE is the 'shape of distribution elasticity' defined as the expected change in poverty for each 1 per cent growth assuming the distribution of consumption stayed constant.

2. Inequality change is the (log) change in the consumption share of the poor. This change is computed as the change in share of the bottom 20 per cent, if the HCR for the base year 1983, was below 20 per cent, or of the bottom 40 per cent if the HCR in 1983 was between 25 and 45 per cent, etc.

3. Total growth in incomes is the sum of (log) growth in per capita consumption and log change in inequality.

4. Predicted change in the HCR is given by the product of total growth and SDE.

Source: Unit record NSS data for 1983 and 1999.

Table 21.1(B) Growth-Inequality-Poverty Connections: Urban India, 1983–99

State	Gini		Change in Gini	Change in Inequality	Growth in Per Capita Cons.	Total Growth	SDE	Change in HCR		HCR	HCR
								Predicted	Actual		
	1983	1999	(1983–99)	(1983–99)	(1983–99)	(1983–99)	1983	(1983–99)	(1983–99)	1983	1999
Andhra Pradesh	33.1	31.5	−5.0	1.6	28.8	30.4	0.73	−22.1	−23.7	51.2	27.4
Assam	26.1	32.5	21.9	−13.3	28.9	15.6	0.88	−13.7	−8.6	16.4	7.7
Bihar	30.4	32.3	6.1	−2.9	10.1	7.2	0.76	−5.4	−3.8	38.0	34.2
Gujarat	28.7	29.1	1.4	−2.2	31.6	29.4	1.08	−31.8	−22.3	37.3	15.0
Haryana	38.7	29.1	−28.5		15.6	15.6	0.92		−17.3	27.4	10.1
Himachal Pradesh	44.7	30.7	−37.6	30.0	35.4	65.4	0.42	−27.2	−19.1	22.2	3.1
Karnataka	34.2	32.8	−4.2	4.3	26.4	30.7	0.71	−21.7	−19.1	44.2	25.1
Kerala	40.5	32.6	−21.7	13.4	24.2	37.6	0.64	−24.2	−22.4	42.4	20.0
Madhya Pradesh	30	31.9	6.1	−4.3	21.2	16.9	0.81	−13.7	−15.8	54.3	38.5
Maharashtra	34.6	35.4	2.3	−0.1	−1.6	−1.7	0.60	1.0	0.9	26.3	27.1
Orissa	29.1	29.6	1.7	−0.7	−3.1	−3.8	0.91	3.4	2.3	41.2	43.5
Punjab	35.6	29.4	−19.1	22.6	25.4	48.0	0.56	−26.8	−19.0	24.4	5.4
Rajasthan	33.8	28.5	−17.1	12.6	15.2	27.8	0.78	−21.6	−17.7	37.2	19.5
Tamil Nadu	35.2	38.8	9.7	−5.5	41.2	35.7	0.73	−26.1	−25.7	48.5	22.8
Uttar Pradesh	31.8	33.2	4.3	−3.1	22.6	19.5	0.82	−15.9	−14.2	45.3	31.1
West Bengal	33.5	34.6	3.2	1.8	11.9	13.7	0.75	−10.3	−6.2	21.3	15.0
Delhi	36	36.2	0.6	−2.2	36.9	34.7	0.67	−23.3	−17.8	27.0	9.2
India	33.9	34.7	2.3	−1.8	31.5	29.7	0.76	−22.6	−21.7	45.1	23.4

Table 21.1(C) Growth-Inequality-Poverty Connections: All-India, 1983–99

State	Gini 1983	Gini 1999	Change in Gini (1983–99)	Change in Inequality (1983–99)	Growth in Per Capita Cons. (1983–99)	Total Growth (1983–99)	SDE 1983	Change in HCR Predicted (1983–99)	Change in HCR Actual (1983–99)	HCR 1983	HCR 1999
Andhra Pradesh	31.3	29.8	-4.9	5.8	14.7	20.5	0.80	-16.5	-15.1	35.3	20.2
Assam	21.2	24.5	14.5	-7.1	7.3	0.2	1.17	-0.3	-4.9	41.3	36.5
Bihar	27.8	24.1	-14.3	7.6	18.0	25.6	0.79	-20.3	-17.9	62.1	44.3
Gujarat	28.4	28.6	0.7	-0.9	23.3	22.4	0.87	-19.5	-16.2	33.3	17.1
Haryana	30.6	26.9	-12.9	6.2	17.9	24.1	0.76	-18.3	-14.7	23.5	8.8
Himachal Pradesh	29	27.1	-6.8	8.3	20.1	28.4	0.80	-22.7	-15.0	23.1	8.1
Karnataka	33.2	31.3	-5.9	7.7	18.4	26.1	0.68	-17.7	-15.8	41.1	25.3
Kerala	33.6	30.4	-10.0	6.9	34.0	40.9	0.85	-34.8	-28.1	40.4	12.3
Madhya Pradesh	30.7	29.3	-4.7	3.5	11.3	14.8	0.94	-13.9	-10.2	51.5	41.3
Maharashtra	34.1	35.3	3.5	-2.1	14.4	12.3	0.69	-8.5	-9.0	41.1	32.1
Orissa	28.4	27.8	-2.1	0.7	20.3	21.0	0.85	-17.8	-15.1	65.4	50.3
Punjab	30.3	27.1	-11.2	14.9	12.7	27.6	0.43	-12.0	-11.1	17.2	6.1
Rajasthan	35	24.6	-35.3	27.0	5.2	32.2	0.66	-21.3	-19.7	36.1	16.3
Tamil Nadu	37.1	36.6	-1.4	1.7	36.0	37.7	0.81	-30.6	-26.2	52.4	26.2
Uttar Pradesh	30.2	28.2	-6.9	4.4	14.9	19.3	0.84	-16.3	-15.1	47.4	32.3
West Bengal	32.8	29.8	-9.6	8.1	23.5	31.6	0.78	-24.8	-25.0	54.3	29.3
Delhi	36.2	41.1	12.7	4.7	15.9	20.6	0.65	-18.4	-5.5	11.5	5.9
India	32.5	32	-1.6	1.6	23.6	25.2	0.80	-20.1	-18.9	48.2	29.4

argued by Ravallion (2000a), World Bank (2000), etc. There is no theoretical reason for initial inequality to affect poverty reduction since the inequality that matters is that observed *at or near* the poverty line. And given a fixed poverty line, such inequality is constantly in flux when there is economic growth.

2. There have been large changes towards equality observed in most parts of rural India (15 out of 16 states) and to a lesser degree in urban India (8 out of 17 states). On an all-India basis, the share of the poor (defined according to the HCR in 1983) in the overall consumption distribution *increased in 14 out of the 17 states.* This overwhelming evidence suggests that the claim that inequality has worsened in India over the last two decades is somewhat erroneous.

The impact that a variation in the magnitude of SDE has on poverty reduction is underlined by the results in Table 21.1. For rural Assam, the SDE is a high 1.3 in 1983; for urban Maharashtra, it is a low 0.6 in the same year. Thus, the theoretical, empirical, and policy-related consequences of deriving the headcount elasticity *without* accounting for the variation and/or magnitude in the SDE are enormous. By example, Ravallion and Datt contend that the growth-poverty elasticity for Bihar is low, and that for Kerala is high, noting that 'for the headcount index, the elasticities vary from a low of 0.25 in Bihar to a high of 1.23 in both Kerala and West Bengal' (p. 15). They then proceed to calculate different growth-poverty scenarios based on these estimated elasticities.

However, these elasticities are faulty. The SDE for India has stayed close to 0.8 for the last 20 years; for Kerala, it was 0.70 in 1983, and today, it is 0.57. This means that Kerala today would need about a 20 per cent higher growth to achieve the *same* amount of poverty reduction as in the early 80s. By contrast, Bihar had an SDE of 0.9 in 1983 and 1.16 in 1999. Accordingly, a 20 per cent *lower* rate growth would be sufficient for Bihar to achieve the same amount of poverty reduction as previously. These predictions are diametrically opposite to the assertion of Ravallion and Datt.

Indeed, it is generally the case that if the impact of growth is assessed via the 'mediation' of SDE, then the correct growth-poverty elasticity is often 50 to 100 per cent larger than one which has been conventionally estimated.[11] For instance, in the case of Indian states, this elasticity is estimated to be −3.0, rather than −2.4. On an average basis, the 'improvement' from 2.4 to 3 reflects the fact that adjusted by an SDE of approximately 0.8, the 'net' impact of growth on poverty reduction is 3*.8 = 2.4.

However, as shown above, SDEs can and do vary enormously, so an estimate of the correct elasticity is critical. For example, in the next few years it might be the case that the SDE declines from 0.8 to 0.6. A 10 per cent rate of growth would accordingly lead to a 6-percentage point decline in the HCR (10 per cent multiplied by 0.6), rather than an 8-percentage point decline, as would have been the case previously. If one does not take into account SDE, one would, therefore, be led to conclude erroneously that the importance of growth in decreasing poverty has severely diminished in India. And some might even attribute this purely statistical decline to economic reforms!

Besides adjustment for SDE, a *second* serious conceptual error besets traditional estimates of the growth poverty relationship. It has been variously termed the 'Peter-Paul' problem by Bhalla (2000b, 2002d), and the 'Indian-Chinese' problem by Deaton (2001a). The error is one of using changes in real per capita consumption based on *national accounts* as an estimate of *survey*-based consumption growth, and using survey-based consumption growth for deriving the poverty estimates.

What is happening is the following: most journalists compare the per capita GDP growth from the national accounts with the change in the HCR, as revealed by household surveys. Only if consumption

---

[11] See Bhalla (2002d), for details of estimates for different countries and time periods.

growth from national accounts is approximately equal to consumption growth from household surveys would there be no error in this attribution. Between 1960 and 1983, per capita consumption growth according to surveys was 431 per cent; according to national accounts, 461 percent.[12] Over the last 20 years this previously close correspondence has attenuated. Corresponding to the period 1983–1999, survey consumption grew at 373 per cent, which was considerably lower than the 533 per cent consumption growth reflected in the national accounts.

What happened? Nothing, except that in the 1960s, surveys were capturing upwards of 90 per cent of national accounts; in 1983, the surveys captured approximately 70 to 75 per cent, and in 1999 the surveys captured only 56 per cent. In other, but equivalent, national account terms, average consumption would have to increase by approximately 30 per cent between 1983 and 1999 for one to conclude that there had been absolutely *no* change in the level of average consumption, and therefore no change in the level of Indian poverty! This is an untenable assumption, which yields an untenable conclusion. Therefore, while there is no reason for journalists to change their headline practice of citing NA income growth and survey based change in poverty, there is considerable reason for economists to not commit the same Peter-Paul mistake, i.e. attributing Peter's income to Paul's poverty.

As noted earlier, there is one further problem plaguing the estimation of Indian poverty, pertaining specifically to 1999 – the use of both 7-day and 30-day reference periods in the NSS CES for that year. For the 1999/2000 surveys, the enumerators asked the same household to recall their consumption for each food item according to a 7-day reference period, as well as a 30-day reference period. The corresponding mean food group estimate for the 7-day period was Rs 343 per capita per month. For the 30-day recall period, the corresponding estimate was Rs 323, i.e. 6 per cent lower. If the 30-day period recall is taken as the 'true' estimate, this would imply that surveyed consumption of all items is only 12.4 per cent higher in real terms in 1999/2000, than it was six years earlier, in 1993/94. Note that this figure corresponds to the mean estimate of total consumption. However, the national accounts estimate of growth in mean consumption over the same period is 30 per cent, i.e. two-and-a-half times the equivalent survey estimate. In reality therefore, the food estimate for 1999 is likely to be higher than Rs 323 and some distance towards the 7-day estimate of Rs 343. If the movement is in the other direction, then the survey estimate will be approaching a 0 growth estimate in average consumption, and doing so during a time period when all other estimates suggest a rapid growth in mean consumption and income. Accordingly, it is reasonable to argue that the error in the 30-day recall period is unlikely to be more than a few percentage points, and considerably smaller than the 18-percentage point gap between the survey and national accounts estimate. If this is indeed the case, then the best assessment of poverty levels in India in 1999/2000 can be provided by an assessment of the trends in the survey/national accounts ratio (S/NAS). This is a subject towards which we now turn.

ACCURACY OF SURVEY AND NATIONAL ACCOUNT MEANS

The present method of measuring poverty in India entails an assumption that the survey data is approximately correct both with regard to the mean and distribution of consumption. The number of people whose expenditure is registered below a pre-defined poverty line is then counted. This pre-defined line is fixed at Rs 49.60, and Rs 56.80 for rural and urban areas respectively in 1973/74 prices.

[12] As discussed later, there is more than one estimate of nominal consumption growth in India! The estimate referred to here pertains to the national accounts base (1960/61, 1970/71, 1980/81, or 1993/94) in use at the time of the household survey.

Individual consumer price deflators, for rural and urban areas, respectively, are then used to update the poverty line over time.

There are two sources for the estimate of the mean of the distribution – one available from the surveys, and the other provided by the system of national accounts (NAS). However, the two means are not expected to be exactly equal, because their coverage (by definition) is not identical. For example, NAS means include the consumption of institutional populations, be they prison inmates or non-government organisations (NGOs). The *growth* rates of consumption yielded by the two methods, however, should be broadly similar, since it is not expected that the share of the institutional population *and* their mean consumption would increase significantly on a structural basis.

The law of large numbers suggests that the survey mean of per capita expenditures would be approximately equal to the unknown 'true' number, X. An *alternative* estimate of X is provided by the national accounts data, which, unlike surveys, provides mean estimates for every year, and every quarter. The NAS uses several pieces of data (including NSS when available), to obtain annual estimates of total private consumption expenditure. It is worth noting that the law of large numbers applies with much greater force to the national accounts data. Furthermore, accounting checks and balances used in the NAS should smooth out unwarranted spikes and fluctuations in average consumption.

So, how do we evaluate the data reliability and attributes of the national accounts and NSS estimates? There were several articles in the 1960s on this topic, and a special volume on poverty, edited by Bardhan and Srinivasan (1974) contains some of the major contributions. At that time, the general conclusion was that the survey and national accounts were moving in parallel, and that the survey capture ratio was close to 95 per cent. Thus, it was not surprising that the accepted practice of the Government of India was to use the distribution in per capita expenditure from NSS surveys, and equate the survey mean to the national accounts estimate. Thus, a consistency was achieved, in that the mean survey estimate of per capita expenditure was set equal to the mean national accounts estimate. Accordingly, all poverty or HCR were derived from this *mean-adjusted* NSS survey data.

However, in 1989, the Government of India appointed an Expert Group (EGGOI) to examine the entire set of issues relating to the estimation of poverty in India. This group recommended in its report (GOI, 1993), which was accepted by the Planning Commission in 1996, that henceforth the practice of equating the means of the survey and national accounts should be discontinued, and that estimates of poverty should be exclusively based on the NSS survey estimates.

EGGOI did not empirically *substantiate* the conclusion that poverty calculations should henceforth not adjust the survey data with reference to the NAS, a point noted by both Bhalla (2000a) and Deaton (2001a). They did note conceptual problems with a uniform multiplier, and that there were problems with the accuracy of the national accounts data. However, the choice between NSS and NAS cannot be settled by noting that NAS contains errors. A useful point of departure in making that choice would have been to note also errors in the NSS survey data. Only if there were considerably *less* errors in NSS would one prefer not to use the information contained in national accounts. The Expert Group also did not discuss the possibility that NSS data might not be capturing the entire picture. Notably, this was at a time when the survey and national accounts data were beginning to diverge, with the NA yielding a level of consumption at least 25 per cent higher than the survey estimate. In other words, just when a reconciliation attempt was needed, the EGGOI decided to altogether ignore the question of the reliability of NSS data.

Given that the NA estimates of per capita consumption are considerably higher than the survey estimates, it is a trivial calculation to show that the old Planning Commission method would yield a considerably lower estimate of the HCR than the new EGGOI method. In Bhalla (2000a), several methods are used to test the EGGOI hypothesis of inaccuracy of the NAS data. The conclusion is that the underlying unknown 'true' per capita consumption was likely to be closer to the NAS-based estimate than to the NSS survey estimates. Analysis of NSS wage data in the last section of this chapter (Poverty in India, 1999/2000), also suggests this conclusion.

A 'reliable' estimate of survey consumption mean is provided by an adjusted NA consumption mean (see Bhalla, 2002d). The NA means need to be adjusted downward to reflect two considerations: first, that surveys are likely to miss more of the rich than of the poor; and second, that the degree of under-estimation by the surveyed rich is likely to be higher than the degree of underestimation of the surveyed poor. The total adjustment that is needed is approximately 15 per cent, i.e. the NA means need to be reduced by 15 per cent (10 per cent for the consumption of non-surveyed rich households and 5 per cent for the 'fact' that the rich understate by a larger degree) to arrive at a reasonable approximation for the survey mean (see next section).

However, Ravallion (2000), closely followed by Sundaram and Tendulkar (2001), have questioned the use of even *adjusted* national accounts means. Ravallion argues that since national accounts data on consumption includes that of NGOs, political parties, etc., 'replacing the NSS mean with consumption per capita from the NAS when measuring poverty would imply that campaign spending by politicians trying to get elected would automatically reduce measured poverty even if none of the money goes to the poor'.

Sundaram and Tendulkar (2001) also recommend in their conclusion against adjustment of NSS data. In contrast to Ravallion, they present some empirical evidence for their conclusion, noting that 'our analysis at a disaggregated level across broad items of expenditure and across fractile groups shows that a uniform scalar correction would result in a significant overstatement of the consumer expenditure of the bottom fractile groups'.[13]

Both Ravallion and Sundaram and Tendulkar raise relevant questions, as does the World Bank's *World Development Report 2001: Attacking Poverty*. The central concern of these critics is that the modified adjustment method will contain large errors and wrongly underestimate poverty. Their strong *assumption* is that most of the missing income accrues to the non-poor, and most likely to the rich. So while survey estimates are underestimating average consumption, most of the difference, believe the critics, is *not* accounted for by the bottom half of the population.

The issue of underestimation, and the question of whose consumption is being underestimated, are empirical matters, and can therefore not be addressed merely by assertion. To this end, it should be noted that even in the US, there has been an increase in underestimation. Triplett (1997) notes that national accounts estimates of per capita expenditures in the US have grown at about 1 per cent per year faster than survey estimates. Triplett also finds that the underestimation of food was about the same as that of durable goods – both at about 0.7 per cent per year. The largest amount of underestimation –1.7 per cent per year – affects the item 'durables less motor vehicles'.

The US data provides a perspective on India's underestimation problems. However, the magnitudes involved are radically different – rather than a 1 per cent difference per year in the US, the NSS and NAS data in India have diverged by an average of 1.6 per cent per year, since the early 1980s. Accordingly, NSS has recorded annualised growth of 1.4 per cent per annum versus an annualised NAS consumption growth of 3 per cent per annum. In this context, it is worth noting Lal, Mohan and Natarajan (2001), who use detailed data on expenditure on durables, as well as other items, to show that durable expenditure

[13] That the Sundaram and Tendulkar conclusion does not follow from their own logic, and data analysis, is documented.

is massively underestimated by the NSS, and that this underestimation of durables involves the poor as well.

Trends in the Survey Capture Ratio, S/NAS

These findings open the question of how accurate the survey estimates of mean consumption expenditure are. Since changes in mean expenditure have a very large impact on one's assessment of changes in consumption, and therefore poverty, it is important first of all to set out the correct methodology for assessing the level of, and changes in, this expenditure. Of course, distributional changes also affect poverty, but such changes have been observed to be minimal in India and to move in a direction favouring the poor. Mean changes, meanwhile, are based on differences in *levels*, and *levels* may not be subject to the same systematic proportionate bias over time. In any case, the emphasis of this paper is on accuracy within a rough order of magnitude. Thus, if appropriate NAS-based adjustments only result in minor changes, then the NSS data on expenditures, adjusted by NAS, can be taken to be roughly accurate.

The degree of survey capture, defined as the ratio of survey means to national accounts means, affects the level of consumption and poverty at any point in time. Thus, if there are no trends evident in the survey capture (denoted by S/NA), then surveys can reliably be used to infer trends in the calculation of poverty. But calculations of survey capture assume that the national accounts estimate of current expenditure are known and reliable. This is not evident in India. Twice over the last 15 years, in the 'conversion' years of 1980/81 and 1993/94, the *nominal* expenditures have increased by high percentages. Though estimates of *real* expenditures are known to change because of changes in base year prices, India's case is unusual because of the frequency and magnitude of these changes.

The problem of calculating the appropriate S/NA ratio is complicated by these adjustments of nominal consumption. The 1970/71 and 1980/81 base-year estimates of consumption for 1970/71 are about 9 per cent apart, with the 1980/81 estimate being the higher of the two. For 1993/94, the 1980/81 base and 1993/94 base estimates are about 15 per cent apart, with the latter base year estimate being higher. There are plausible explanations for this. It is likely, for instance, that with development and growth new products arrive on the market, new tastes are created, and statistical systems improve. Any of these factors might cause the latter base year estimate to reveal a different composition of consumption, e.g. with some products showing less consumption than thought before, whereas other products show more. Theoretically, the mean according to both an old and new base should be unaffected. However, the reality is that the *mean* is severely affected, and in the 1970s the impact of upward revisions was a 24 per cent higher consumption, i.e. consumption in the late 1970s was considered to be 24 per cent higher in 1997 than was thought to be the case in 1983.

There are several ways in which this 24 per cent increase can be allocated across the different years. One method would entail making no adjustments to data for the 1960s, and then a gradual adjustment upwards from the 1970s. However, no set of assumptions, or calculations, would support such a large upward adjustment for the 1970s as was performed by the Central Statistical Organisation (CSO) of the Indian national accounts authority.

Table 21.2 reports *four* national accounts estimates for per capita expenditure in current rupees, covering several selected national sample survey years since the mid-fifties. The four different NAS estimates are as follows:

(i) The NAS estimates prevailing at the time of the survey and designated as 'original'. By example, the 1983 estimate is the estimate based on the 1970/71 series of national accounts and the

Table 21.2 Table on S/NAS Adjusted

Year	Population	Consumption Expenditure per Capita per Month (Nominal)				NSS
		National Account				
		Original	RBI	WB	Smoothed	
1954	392.1	17.4				
1957	414.6	20.9			17.4	17.3
1960/61	434.8	29.7	31.0	26.9	20.9	19.8
1967/68	522.8	50.2	54.4	49.2	29.7	23.5
1972/73	586.2	61.1	79.7	69.1	51.4	43.4
1973/74	599.6	72.4	94.4	78.6	64.4	48.3
1977/78	642.1	82.0	108.0	93.8	76.8	56.7
1983	734.1	166.8	198.0	177.1	89.0	73.4
1987/88	798.7	233.8	271.5	251.2	174.8	124.8
1993/94	898.2	463.0	533.3	547.3	254.4	181.1
1998	979.7	970.7	970.7	1,002.7	533.0	327.9
1999/2000	997.5	1,057.2	1,057.2	1,062.7	970.7	462.7
					1,057.2	589.9

Year	Ratio			S/NA (%)			
	RBI/ Original	WB/ Original	Smoothed/ Original	Original	RBI	WB	Smoothed
1954			100.0	99.4			
1957			99.8	94.9			99.4
1960/61	104.5	90.8	100.0	79.2	75.8	87.2	95.0
1967/68	108.3	98.0	102.4	86.4	79.9	88.2	79.2
1972/73	130.5	113.1	105.4	79.1	60.6	69.9	84.4
1973/74	130.4	108.6	106.0	78.3	60.0	72.1	75.0
1977/78	131.7	114.4	108.5	89.5	68.0	78.2	73.9
1983	118.7	106.1	104.8	74.8	63.0	70.5	82.5
1987/88	116.1	107.4	108.8	77.5	66.7	72.1	71.4
1993/94	115.2	118.2	115.1	70.8	61.5	59.9	71.2
1998	100.0	103.3	100.0	47.7	47.7	46.1	61.5
1999/2000	100.0	100.5	100.0	55.8	55.8	55.5	47.7
							55.8

Notes: For all years, the NAS estimates are for the fiscal years. The NSS estimate is the survey based mean estimate for the corresponding year, i.e. for 1983 it is the survey year January–December, for 1999/ 2000 it is the survey year, July 1999/June 2000.

Sources: 1. RBI – From Handbook of Statistics.
2. CSO – National Accounts data for 1993/94 base.
3. WB – From World Development Indicators (WDI).
4. Smoothed – is CSO series 'smoothed' for base adjustments; see text.

1993/94 estimate is the one based on the 1980/81 series. Each new national account base series was developed in the latter half of the decade, e.g. the 1980/81 base series was not published until the late 1980s.

(ii) The 1993/94 base CSO estimates reported in RBI, *Handbook of Statistics in the Indian Economy,* 2001, and designated as RBI.

(iii) The 1993/94 NAS statistics as reported by the World Bank in *World Development Indicators,* 2002, and referred to as WB.

(iv) A 'smoothed' NAS series for the 1993/94 base, with the method of smoothing outlined below.

The table also contains a *fifth* estimate of nominal expenditure (NSS), namely that yielded by the national sample survey for the selected years.

The 'smoothed' estimate is based on the 'Occams razor' principle of straightforward, and logical, assumptions. The key assumptions are that some new information about new expenditure or new products comes to light, and, further, that these new expenditure are not at the expense of existing expenditure, but actually compose part of increased new income. The question then is, how should the *past* estimates of consumption be adjusted?

One method of deriving estimates of new means is to assume a time period for which the adjustment needs to be made, and then derive the 'final' estimates of consumption. Using this method, assume a 15-year adjustment period. A 9 per cent upwards adjustment for the 1980 base is then applied in a compounded manner from 1963 to 1978, and a 15 per cent upward adjustment is applied, again in a compounded manner, for the 15 years, 1979 to 1993.

The second part of the table contains the ratio of the new and original estimates of current per capita expenditure, as well as the (log) percentage difference between the old and new series for the 1970s (1970 to 1980) and the 1980s (1981 to 1993). This table reveals the NAS series as published by the World Bank to be a lot smoother than that published by the CSO. For both time periods, the World Bank series is upgraded by about 10 per cent, specifically 11.8 per cent, in the 1970s and 8.9 per cent in the 1990s. The CSO series, however, shows a 27 per cent increase in the first period and a mean increase of 16 per cent in the second period. The official (CSO) estimates of the ratio seem to be particularly off-base in the 1970s, when nominal expenditure has been upgraded to show a 31.7 per cent increase for 1977/78, as compared to only an 18.7 per cent increase for 1983. In comparison, the World Bank series seems to be considerably better behaved for all the years, and does not show any 'spikes'.

The survey capture ratio yielded by these different methods can now be assessed (Table 21.3). The 'smoothed' NAS series yields one indicator of the trend in the S/NA ratio. Also shown in bold are the relevant ratios for the different years and the different 'base prices'. By example, the relevant S/NAS ratio for the 1960s is the 1970 base, for the 1980s it is the 1980 base, and so forth.

The estimate based on 'original' NAS data shows a consistent trend downwards, and a loss of about 10 percentage points in each decade. In the 1960s this ratio was in the nineties, and accordingly NSS and NAS estimates were virtually identical.[14] In the 1970s, the ratio fell into the eighties, and today,1999/2000, the ratio is only 55 per cent. All other S/NAS estimates show a similar downward trend, i.e. regardless of which series is chosen as being the relevant one, the table evinces a strong trend downward since the 1960s, and a particularly sharp break in the 1990s, equivalent to 55.8 per cent. In light of this, it is somewhat difficult to concur with Sen's conclusion that 'the striking result is that *there is no*

---

[14] The importance of the S/NA ratio is highlighted by the fact that in the 1960s, there was a debate raging over inaccuracies of survey estimates because they diverged by a *few* percentage points from the national accounts estimate. Today, survey estimates are *half* the NAS estimates and scholars like Sundaram and Tendulkar (2001), and Ravallion (2001) maintain that there are no problems with surveys.

Table 21.3 S/NAS Ratio: A Deceptively Large Fall in the 1990s

	1973	1977	1983	1987	1993	1999
Mean consumption – rural (Rs)	53.0	68.9	112.5	158.1	281.4	486.2
Mean consumption – urban (Rs)	70.8	96.2	164.0	250.6	458.0	855.0
Urbanisation ratio (%)	20.7	22.0	23.8	24.8	26.3	28.1
Mean consumption, survey (Rs)	56.7	74.9	124.8	181.0	327.8	589.8
Mean consumption, NA '93 base (Rs)	79.7	108.0	198.0	271.5	533.3	1057.2
Mean consumption, NA '81 base (Rs)	66.3	89.8	166.8	233.8	411.2	
Mean consumption, NA '70 base (Rs)	61.1	82.0	153.9			
Mean consumption, smoothed	76.8	89.0	174.8	254.4	533.0	1057.2
S/NAS ratio, '93 base	71.1	69.4	63.0	66.7	**61.5**	**55.8**
S/NAS ratio, '81 base	85.5	83.4	**74.8**	**77.4**	79.7	
S/NAS ratio, '70 base	**92.8**	**91.4**	81.1			
S/NAS ratio, smoothed	**73.8**	**84.2**	**71.4**	**71.2**	**61.5**	**55.8**

evidence of any large widening of the gap between the NAS and NSS estimates of nominal consumption during the 1990s' (Sen, 2001; p. 19; emphasis in original).

That the estimate of S/NAS has a direct bearing on the estimate of poverty in 1999, and any other year, is discussed in detail in the next section. For the moment, it is important to emphasise that the likely decline in S/NAS between 1983 and 1999 is of the order of around 25 (log) per cent. This corresponds to a decline in the S/NAS from about 72 per cent in 1983 to about 56 per cent today. In turn, this implies that for the NSS survey estimate to show no decline in the HCR, the consumption of the poor would have to have rise by 25 per cent between 1983 and 1999. Equivalently, if the poor increased their consumption by (log) 25 per cent, the NSS would in 1999 actually show that the poor did not reap any increase in their real expenditure! To further highlight the abnormality of this situation, it can be noted that log 15 per cent over 16 years corresponds approximately to an increase of 1.6 per cent a year – an increase recorded by very few countries over such an extended length of time.

SURVEY AND NATIONAL ACCOUNT MEANS – HOW TO ADJUST FOR S/NAS

Based on the previous discussion, there seems to be little doubt that the survey methods are not counting the entirety of household consumption. Furthermore, it seems that the degree of underestimation has perhaps reached alarming proportions.

The *distribution* of the underestimation, however, remains intractable. Sundaram and Tendulkar present per capita estimates of consumption of different items according to the bottom three deciles, and the top decile. However, aggregation by such broad groups is inadequate for assessing the magnitude of underestimation for each item, and its variation across the different deciles or percentiles. Instead, a method which obtains a multiplier for each household and each item can be used to assess the degree of underestimation, and its location. This method is a logical extension of the Sundaram and Tendulkar exercise; the only difference is that it does for each percentile what Sundaram and Tendulkar do for broad groups.

This methodology suggests that the different underestimation levels can be identified to some degree of accuracy, in the following manner: first, the national accounts expenditure is tabulated for each *individual* item – for example cereals, pulses, vegetable, fruits, dry fruits, consumer durables, education, etc. A similar exercise is carried out for the survey data. Thus, two means for each item are obtained – a survey mean and a NA mean. If it is now assumed that the NA means are correct on an item-by-item basis, then the degree of under or over estimation for each household can easily be derived. For each individual, an average multiplier can be obtained, which is the ratio of the adjusted sum of individual and item-specific expenditure, to the sum of expenditure in the survey data.[15]

Table 21.4 documents the different estimates obtained via NSS and national accounts for each item in the 1993/94 fiscal year. Underestimation ranges from a low of 11 per cent for cereals, to a high of 150 per cent for clothing and footwear. These items have multipliers of 1.11 and 1.50 respectively. This means that the NAS estimate for consumption of cereals in 1993/94 was Rs 79.30, compared to a NAS estimate of Rs 87.80.[16] If the latter figure is correct, then each individual's consumption of cereals is

Table 21.4 Item-wise Estimates of Consumption – Survey and National Accounts, 1993/94

Grp. No.	Sl. No.	Item	Per Capita per Month		Multiplier
			NSS	NAS	NAS/NSS
I	A	Cereals + gram + cereal substitute + pulses	79.3	87.8	1.11
	B	Edible oils	14.4		
	C	Sugar + beverages	26.3		
	D	Salt + spices	7.9		
II	E	Edible oils + sugar and beverages + salt and spices	48.6	63.8	1.31
	F	Milk + milk products	31.8		
	G	Meat, egg and fish	10.8		
	H	Fruit and vegetables	24.8		
III	I	Milk and milk products + meat, egg and fish + fruit and vegetables	68.5	129.9	1.90
IV	J	Food (I + II + III)	196.4	281.6	1.43
	K	Paan + tobacco + intoxicants	9.4	10.8	1.16
	L	Clothing	16.8		
	M	Footwear	3.0		
V	N	Clothing + footwear	19.7	49.3	2.50
VI	O	Fuel + light	23.2	20.0	0.86
VII	P	Durable	9.5	15.8	1.67
VIII	Q	Miscellaneous goods + services	62.3	109.3	1.75
IX	R	Non-food (V + VI + VII + VIII)	114.7	194.4	1.70
X	S	Total	311.0	476.0	1.53

Source: Unit record data NSS 1993/94 Consumer Expenditure Survey and National Accounts Statistics (1999).

[15] Since the survey does not contain estimates of imputed rent, house rent is ignored. Further, as documented by Sundaram and Tendulkar, there seems to be a genuine problem with the NAS estimate for clothing. In the 1998 NAS estimate for 1993, clothing expenditure is reported to be Rs 48,350 crore. In the 1999 NAS revised estimates, this expenditure is reduced to only Rs 21,403 crore. Which figure is correct? The first estimate of clothing is taken as the 'correct' figure and the difference between the two figures Rs 48,350 and Rs 21,403 crore, or Rs 26,947 crore, is subtracted from the figure of Rs 1,43,787 crore for miscellaneous goods and services.

[16] All figures are per capita per month and the national population in 1993/94 is taken to be 891 million.

underestimated by the NSS, to the tune of 11 per cent. For milk products, vegetables, etc., the underestimation is a very sizeable 90 per cent, and larger than that for durables, which is 67 per cent.

Given these item-wise ratios, it is now a simple calculation to adjust each individual's consumption to national accounts. Note that the resulting multiplier is *different* for each individual and a function of their consumption pattern. Table 21.5 aggregates individuals according to their per capita expenditure, and reports the resulting average multiplier for each decile of households, arranged according to per capita expenditure. The results are striking – even for the poorest decile, the underestimation is of the order of 30 per cent. The multiplier rises progressively with the wealth of the households, but the variation for the first eight deciles is in the narrow range of 30 to 46 per cent. The border decile for the poor is the 40th percentile. The multiplier for this decile, 1.37, is close to the national average multiplier of 1.41.

Two major results emerge. First, that it is *not* the case that the multiplier is the same across all deciles, though a uniform multiplier holds, within a small margin of error, for the first eight deciles. Second, even for the poorest decile, the adjustment multiplier is large, approximately 25 to 35 per cent. In other words, the adjusted consumption of the poor is some 30 per cent higher than that reported by the NSS. Third, for calculations of HCR, the assumption of a constant multiplier across all households – as suggested in Bhalla (2002a) and questioned by various authors – is surprisingly quite accurate.

But are these multiplier results plausible? Is it reasonable to expect that most of the missing consumption is accounted for by the rich. Indeed it is! The adjustments preserve the original distribution for each *item*. Since the top 20 per cent of the population commands about 45 per cent of expenditure, it can also claim 45 per cent of the missing expenditure. Further, the large underestimation of food items should be noted, which is about 42 per cent, compared to 68 per cent for non-food items. Food items have a low income elasticity – and there is a physical limit to how much extra food the rich can consume. So the 'benefits' of underestimation of food items accrue 'disproportionately' to the poor, as do benefits of underestimation of non-food items accrue 'disproportionately' to the rich. Further to this point, it is

Table 21.5 Decile Consumption and Adjustment Multipliers

Decile	Per Capita Expenditures		Multiplier
	NSS	NSS Adjusted to NA	
1	121	158	1.30
2	163	217	1.33
3	191	258	1.35
4	217	298	1.37
5	245	341	1.39
6	277	391	1.41
7	317	455	1.43
8	375	548	1.46
9	476	707	1.49
10	1,006	1,537	1.53
Average	339	491	1.41

Notes: 1. The NSS adjusted figures for each decile are obtained by matching the total expenditures for each item by the multiplier shown in Table 21.1.
2. The 'multiplier' for each decile is the ratio of the NAS-adjusted survey figure (Column 3), to the NSS estimate (Column 2).
Source: Unit record data NSS 1993/94 Consumer Expenditure Survey and National Accounts Statistics (1999).

worth noting that Item III – milk and milk products and meat, etc., plus fruits and vegetables – is estimated by the survey to be just more than half the national accounts estimate. But the rich cannot possibly be drinking all this milk and eating all the missing food. Accordingly, it must be that the non-rich have also underestimated their food consumption by large proportions. Generally, the large error for the food group suggests that whatever adjustments are done to the Indian survey data on the basis of national accounts data, they will yield the result of a reasonably constant multiplier.

POVERTY IN INDIA, 1999/2000

A non-controversial statement is that there are general problems with both NSS and NAS data, in addition to specific problems with the survey data for 1999, owing to the use of simultaneous 7-day and 30-day recall periods for food consumption. The following section attempts to circumvent these problems by deriving a lower bound estimate of consumption in 1999, and thus consumption growth and poverty trends across the 1990s, using data on growth in wages between 1983 and 1999 drawn from the 'uncontaminated' NSS E&U Survey of the same year. An assessment of poverty trends in the 1990s is important insofar as it is necessary to establish whether economic reforms initiated in that period were anti-poor in their impact. The anti-poor hypothesis can be tested by establishing what happened to both consumption inequality and the incomes of the poor.

Consumption Inequality

As hypothesised by Kuznets (1955 and 1963), it is 'natural' to expect the distribution of income or consumption to first worsen in the context of economic reforms, before peaking and becoming better, yielding an inverted U-curve hypothesis. This has also been verified empirically for several countries (see Bhalla, 2002d). A contrary position is taken by a recent study (Banerjee and Picketty, 2001) that suggests income distribution in India has worsened with rapid growth. However, this study is based on tax-records, and makes several assumptions, the most important of which is the assumption that tax compliance levels have stayed the same for each income group. This position has however been shown to be false (Bhalla, 2002b).

The NSS data is a comprehensive source for trends in consumption inequality, and Table 21.6 documents the evidence that it presents. If there is any trend, it is towards greater equality. Between 1983 and 1999, the Gini has improved sharply in the rural areas, falling from 30.4 to 26.30, and worsened marginally for the urban areas, rising from 33.9 to 34.7. For the entire country, the Gini shows a mild improvement, falling from 32.5 to 32. The first poorest quintile shows the sharpest improvement, equivalent to a 6 per cent increase in its share, from 8.42 to 8.93 per cent.

The conclusion that equality improved in India between 1983 and 1999 is reasonably firm, at least according to the NSS expenditure surveys. Further, there are no signs of a rise in inequality during the so-called 'reform' period, 1993–99. The trend of a small increase in equality continues during this period. Furthermore, as discussed in detail in Bhalla (2002d), the question of whether growth has been pro-poor or not is *identical* to the question of whether there has been an improvement in inequality. No additional assumptions, computations or regressions are required to establish this.

This small improvement in inequality during 1983–1999 suggests that even if there was 0 growth in consumption, poverty in India in 1999 should be approximately a few percentage points lower than the 44.5 per cent poverty level in 1983. This suggests that the 'contaminated' 1999/2000 survey is not

Table 21.6 Trend in Consumption Inequality in India

	1983	1987/88	1993/94	1999/2000
Consumption distribution, NSS				
Rural				
Share of quintile 1	8.9	9.3	9.6	10.1
Quintile 2	13.1	13.2	13.5	14.0
Quintile 3	16.7	16.5	16.9	17.3
Quintile 4	21.7	21.4	21.6	21.9
Quintile 5	39.6	39.6	38.5	36.7
Gini	30.4	29.9	28.6	26.3
Urban				
Share of quintile 1	8.1	8.0	8.0	7.9
Quintile 2	12.1	11.7	11.9	11.7
Quintile 3	15.8	15.5	15.7	15.7
Quintile 4	21.5	21.4	21.6	21.7
Quintile 5	42.6	43.4	42.8	43.0
Gini	33.9	35.0	34.4	34.7
National				
Share of quintile 1	8.4	8.6	8.7	8.9
Quintile 2	12.5	12.4	12.4	12.6
Quintile 3	16.2	15.8	15.9	16.0
Quintile 4	21.4	21.1	21.1	21.1
Quintile 5	41.4	42.1	41.8	41.4
Gini	32.5	32.9	32.5	32.0

Source: Unit record data, National Sample Surveys for the select years.

needed in order to derive a worst-case estimate of poverty. If the worst possible 1983-based distribution is assumed for 1999/2000, then an estimate of growth in mean expenditures between 1983 and 1999, can provide us with a worst-case estimate of poverty in 1999/2000. In Bhalla (2000a), a method was offered to estimate mean consumption growth between 1983 and 1999 using national accounts estimates of change in the availability of major items of consumption like cereals, sugar, and edible oils. However, this method can be criticised for its assumptions, particularly in its part reliance on non-survey data, and with regard to the assumptions about stability of the Engel curve, as well as the assumptions/calculations pertaining to the income and price elasticities.

Estimating Consumption in 1999 from Wage Growth 1983–99

To circumvent such concerns, it is worth exploring an alternative, *exclusively survey*-based method of deriving a *lower-bound* estimate of consumption growth in India between 1983–99. It is based on estimating the growth in wages of the lowest paid workers in India, namely the unskilled labourers in the rural areas and more specifically, the ploughman. Since the absolute poor can be assumed to have zero savings, changes in wage income are expected to translate into changes in mean consumption.

The large scale E&U surveys of the NSS contain estimates of *wages* for all members in the household. This is not a comprehensive income survey, since only limited data is available for households engaged in business or self-employment. But the estimates of wages of casual workers in agriculture, who occupy the least-skilled jobs, should be reasonably accurate. Table 21.7 reports on both the nominal and real wages for the different states between the survey years 1983 and 1999. The latter are deflated by the consumer price index for agricultural labourers. The changes in both the mean and the median wage are then reported, although there is reason to believe that that the estimate for the mean wage is not very reliable, especially for 1983, and that the median wage will be less contaminated by outliers. Rather than attempt to clean the data by 'censoring' such observations, the more defendable method of choosing the median has been adopted.

Table 21.7 also contains wage data from another alternative source, namely, the *Agricultural Situation in India (ASI)*. Since this source contains surveys of labour markets, its data are a useful cross-check on the mean growth observed by asking labourers about the hours they worked, the wages they received, etc. Table 21.7 documents the concomitant increase in consumption and income, and Table 21.8 reports the increase in prices in India for the period 1983–99, according to various indices.

The two sources on nominal wages (NSS and ASI) match to a large degree. The estimated rate of increase based on ASI data is 11.5 per cent per annum, which corresponds closely to the NSS figure for males of 11 per cent and females of 10.8 per cent per annum. The NSS wage data also sheds some light on the inaccuracy of the CSO adjustments to nominal expenditures noted earlier. This annual increase in nominal wages is higher than the annual increase in nominal GDP according to CSO of 10.4 per cent per annum, but lower than the growth recorded by the World Bank of 11.1 per cent per annum, and our 'adjusted' CSO growth of 11.3 per cent per annum (Table 21.8A). Notably, the NSS expenditure survey shows an increase in per capita consumption of only 9.4 per cent per annum, considerably below the

Table 21.7 Wages and Wage Growth in India, 1983/99

	1983	1999	Growth Annualised
Wages			
Avg. daily wages for males, field labour and ploughman (The data reported are for years 1981/82 and 1996/97)			
Current prices	7.7	43.0	11.5
Real	21.4	33.5	3.0
Wages, from NSS data			
Median wage, rural male casual labour (excluding public works)			
Current prices	184.7	1064.8	11.0
Real	418.4	666.8	2.9
Median wage, rural female casual labour (excluding public works)			
Current prices	116.0	651.4	10.8
Real	260.4	405.6	2.8
Median wage, all workers male			
Current prices	309.0	2105.0	12.0
Real	313.5	541.0	3.4
Median wage, all workers female			
Current prices	161.5	1105.0	12.0
Real	169.8	300.0	3.6

Source: Agricultural situation in India and NSS rounds 1983, 1999/2000.

Table 21.8(A) Consumption, Income and Inflation in India, 1983/99

	1983	1999	Growth Annualised
Consumption and GDP per capita, national accounts			
Consumption, current prices			
Expenditure per capita per month			
National accounts, CSO	201.0	1053.4	10.4
National accounts, World Bank	179.8	1058.9	11.1
National accounts, CSO, adjusted	174.8	1057.2	11.3
NSS	124.8	588.9	9.7
Consumption, constant prices			
Expenditure per capita per month			
National accounts, CSO	454.8	660.8	2.3
National accounts, World Bank	423.0	639.9	2.6
Income, current prices			
GDP per capita per month			
National accounts, CSO	253.0	1629.0	11.6
National accounts, World Bank	253.2	1606.4	11.6
Income, constant prices			
GDP per capita per month			
National accounts, CSO	597.6	1054.5	3.6
National accounts, World Bank	599.3	1053.6	3.5

increase of 11 (or 11.5) per cent per annum recorded for unskilled rural wages. This is another indication that the survey-capture ratio in India has declined sharply during the last two decades.

The increase in real wages and, therefore consumption, is a function of the price deflator that is used. Several indices of inflation are reported in Table 21.8B. Deaton and Tarozzi (1999) and Deaton (2001b) report somewhat lower deflators for rural India, deriving these from NSS unit record data, i.e. annual inflation of 7.6 per cent in the rural areas and 8.2 per cent in urban areas.[17] The official price indices used by the Planning Commission show a growth rate of 7.9 per cent rural and 8.3 per cent urban. Thus, a reasonable upper-bound estimate of inflation in rural India is 8.1 per cent per annum between 1983 and 1999. This implies that a reasonable estimate of *real* wage growth in rural India is 2.9 per cent per annum (11 per cent nominal and 8.1 per cent inflation) or 61 per cent for the 16-and-a-half-year period (January/December 1983 to July 1999/June 2000).

This estimate of real wage growth allows us to derive an estimate of real income growth and, therefore, real consumption growth for the period 1983–1999. Given that these are extremely poor people, the easy assumption is one of 0 permanent savings. So by knowing the mean consumption level in 1983, one easily obtains the mean consumption level in 1999 which, as shown above, is 61 per cent higher. As discussed earlier, the worst-case assumption is one of no deterioration in the consumption distribution. So the 1983 consumption distribution can be assumed to apply in 1999 as well.

The implicit assumption is that the per capita consumption of the poor (and non-poor) increases by only the amount of the real wage increase of the *casual worker* in agriculture. It is likely of course that this is a severe *underestimation* of the increase in incomes of the poor and non-poor. The casual worker

[17] Deaton does not report price indices for 1983; for our purpose, the same growth for 1983/87 are assumed as are reflected in the official data; this estimate is then grafted onto the Deaton price indices for 1987, 1993, and 1999.

Table 21.8(B) Inflation in India, Different Measures, 1983–99

	1983	1999	Growth Annualised
Prices			
WPI	112.8	360.9	7.3
Consumption deflator			
CSO	44.2	159.4	8.0
World Bank	42.5	165.5	8.5
GDP deflator			
CSO	42.3	154.4	8.1
World Bank	42.2	152.5	8.0
CPI			
Industrial workers	108.0	428.0	8.6
Agricultural labour	88.3	309.0	7.8
World Bank	35.5	138.4	8.5
Poverty line, Planning Commission			
Rural	89.5	327.6	7.9
Urban	115.6	454.1	8.3
All-India	95.7	363.1	8.1
Deaton price index [1987 = 100]			
(Index for 1983 has been calculated from 1987			
by applying CPI growth)			
Rural	88.9	309.2	7.6
Urban	91.1	352.4	8.2

Sources: 1. RBI Handbook of Statistics, 2002.
2. World Bank: World Development Indicators, 2002.
3. CPI: RBI Handbook of Statistics, 2002.
4. Poverty Line: Planning Commission.
5. Deaton Price Index: see Deaton and Tarozzi (1999) and Deaton (2001c).

is the least skilled worker, and there is considerable evidence to suggest that possession of skills yields a larger return. Nevertheless, since our primary concern is to obtain an upper bound estimate of the evolution of poverty, a lower bound estimate of wage growth will suffice.

The 1983 distribution can be 'shocked' with various estimates of increases in real wages and, therefore, real consumption. Table 21.9 reports these estimates of the growth in consumption, and the corresponding decline in the HCR, and the estimated HCR in 1999 (the HCR for 1983 minus the predicted decline).

As noted earlier, the consumption distribution reported in this table, i.e. for 1983, is a worst-case consumption distribution for 1999. A lower bound survey based estimate of expenditure growth until 1999 is given by the growth in real wages of the worst off and poorest workers in the economy – casual workers in agriculture. Combined, the two worst case assumptions yield an upper-bound estimate of poverty in India for 1999/2000. Crucially, this estimate suggests that poverty in India in 1999/2000 was no more than *15 per cent* – an estimate strikingly lower than the official estimate of 26.1 per cent, and very close to the Engel curve based estimate of poverty of 13 per cent (Bhalla, 2000a). That this estimate is very plausible is also implied by Deaton (2001) who suggests that on the basis of internal NSS survey price-deflators, and proper adjustment for rural-urban price differences, and nominal expenditures as reported in the NSS surveys, poverty in India in 1999/2000 was only 18 per cent.

Table 21.9 Growth in Consumption 1983/99, and Poverty in 1999: Different Estimates

	(log) Growth (in Per cent)	*Predicted Decline in Poverty (in Percentage Points)*	*Predicted HCR in 1999/2000 (in Per cent)*
Avg. per capita consumption (NSS data)	23.2	18.6	26.4
NA private consumption expenditure	34.1	27.3	17.7
Wage growth of casual workers @ 3%	49.5	39.6	5.4
Wage growth of casual workers @ 2.8%	46.2	37.0	8.0
Wage growth of casual workers @ 2.5%	41.3	33.0	12.0
Wage growth of casual workers @ 2.0%	33.0	26.4	6.6

Note: Distribution assumed to be that of 1983 NSS consumer expenditure; uniform real consumption increases assumed as documented in Column 1.

Thus, no matter what the method, the incontrovertible conclusion based on survey data alone, is that poverty in India in 1999/2000 was considerably less than that evidenced by official documents, and considerably less than that suggested by other authors in this volume. While there can be some question about the accuracy of the NAS estimate, there can be little question that the *survey*-based estimate of poverty is in the low teens. What is also important to note is that the method of calculating poverty based on adjusted NAS expenditures reveals an estimate a lot closer to the 'truth' than that estimate dictated by exclusive reliance on the expenditure surveys conducted by the NSS. The fact that the NSS surveys on employment and unemployment and wages also contain estimates at wide variance with NSS consumption, arguably supports this point.

So, how do we conclude and summarise our discussion about growth, inequality, and poverty in India, from 1983 to 1999? Based on a fixed poverty line, and NSS data, the Government of India states that poverty in India has declined from 45 per cent in 1983 to a 26 per cent level in 1999/2000 – a decline of 19 percentage points. The question is whether this result is credible. What happened to inequality? NSS data for the two survey years indicates no increase in inequality. Indeed, the Gini declined over this time period, and the share in consumption of the poor increased. An estimate of per capita consumption growth, therefore, can provide an upper-bound estimate of poverty in India in 1999/2000. This estimate is provided by growth in real wages of the poorest of the poor – unskilled workers in rural agriculture. And a very lower bound conservative estimate of their wage growth (supplied by NSS data) suggests that poverty in India in 1999 was less than 12 per cent. This is in sharp contrast to the official estimate of poverty of 26 per cent for the same year.

ACKNOWLEDGEMENT

This chapter was financed in part by the Planning Commission research project 'Poverty in India: Myth & Reality', and is a complete version of a draft power-point presentation, 'Recounting the Poor,' offered on 11 January 2002 at the World Bank Poverty Monitoring Workshop, New Delhi. I would like to thank Nabhojit Basu for excellent research assistance.

Reprinted from *Economic and Political Weekly*, Vol. 37, 25–31 January 2003.

REFERENCES

Ahluwalia, Montek S. (1977), 'Rural Poverty and Agricultural Performance in India', *Journal of Development Studies*, 22, pp. 298–323.

Ahluwalia, Montek S., Nicholas G. Carter and Holis B. Chenery (1979), 'Growth and Poverty in Developing Countries', World Bank Staff Working Paper No 309, Washington, DC: World Bank.

Asian Development Bank (2002), *The End of Asian Poverty?*, Report prepared for research project RETA-5917 by a team led by Surjit S. Bhalla, Asian Development Bank, Manila, Photocopy, July.

Banerjee, Abhijit and Thomas Piketty (2001), Top Indian Incomes, 1956–98, mimeo, December.

Bardhan, Pranab K. and T.N. Srinivasan (eds) (1974), *Poverty and Income Distribution in India*, Statistical Publishing Society.

Bhalla, Surjit S. (2002e), Report on research project entitled 'The Myth and Reality of Poverty in India', Planning Commission, Government of India, forthcoming.

———— (2002d), *Imagine There's No Country: Poverty, Inequality and Growth in the Era of Globalisation*, Institute of International Economics, September, first draft, 2001.

———— (2002c), Unintended Consequences of Monopoly Funding of Research, Photocopy, May.

———— (2002b), 'Tax Compliance in India', paper prepared as background material for Ministry of Finance, Government of India, February.

———— (2002a), 'Recounting the Poor', Paper presented at a World Bank workshop on Poverty Monitoring and Evaluation, New Delhi, 11 January.

———— (2001c), Poverty and Inequality in a Globalising World: Case Study for India. Paper prepared for the Indian Council for Research on International Economic Relations, New Delhi, 24 December.

———— (2001b) Imagine there is no country: Globalisation and its Consequences for Poverty, Inequality and Growth, mimeo, Presented at Rajiv Gandhi Foundation, New Delhi, January.

———— (2001a), How to Over-Estimate Poverty: Detailed Examination of the NSS 1993 Data, Paper presented for the 50th Anniversary of the National Sample Survey, New Delhi, 8 May.

———— (2000b), Trends in World Poverty: Research and Ideology, Paper presented at the International Monetary Fund, Washington, 28 June.

———— (2000a), Growth and Poverty in India – Myth and Reality, in Govinda Rao (ed.), *Development, Poverty and Fiscal Policy: Decentralisation of Institutions,* Oxford: Oxford University Press, October.

Bhalla, Surjit S. and P. Vashishtha (1988), Income Redistribution in India: A Re-Examination, in *Rural Poverty in South Asia*, T.N. Srinivasan and P. Bardhan (eds), New York: Columbia University Press.

Collier, Paul and David Dollar (2000), 'Can the World Cut Poverty in Half? How Policy Reform and Effective Aid can Meet the International Development Goals', mimeo, Development Research Group, World Bank, July.

Deaton Angus (2001c), 'Computing Prices and Poverty Rates in India, 1999/2000', Research Program in Development Studies, mimeo, Princeton University, December.

———— (2003), 'Adjusted Indian Poverty Estimates for 1999/2000', *EPW*, 25–31 January, (Chapter 12 of this book).

———— (2001a), Counting the World's Poor: Problems and Possible Solutions, Princeton University, Princeton, N.J., Photocopy, August.

Deaton Angus and A. Tarozzi (2000), Prices and Poverty in India, Princeton Research Program on Development Studies, Processed, (Chapter 10 of this book).

Dubuy, A and S. Gangopadhyay (1998), Counting the Poor: Where are the Poor in India? Sarvekshana Analytical Report 1, Department of Statistics, Government of India, New Delhi.

Government of India (1993), Report of The Expert Group on Estimation of Proportion and Number of Poor, Planning Division, Planning Commission, New Delhi.

Kakwani, Nanak (1997), 'On Measuring Growth and Inequality Components of Changes in Poverty with Application to Thailand', forthcoming, *Journal of Quantitative Economics.*

——— (1980), *Income Inequality and Poverty: Methods of Estimation and Policy Applications.* Oxford: Oxford University Press.

Kakwani, Nanak and Ernesto M. Pernia (2000), What Is Pro-poor Growth? *Asian Development Review,* 18, No. 1, pp. 1–16.

Kuznets, Simon (1963), Quantitative Aspects of the Economic Growth of Nations: VIII, Distribution of Income by Size, *Economic Development and Cultural Change*, Part 2, Vol. 11, No. 2, Part II, January, pp. 1–80.

——— (1955), Economic Growth and Income Inequality, *American Economic Review,* Vol. 45, No. 1, March, pp. 1–28.

Lal, Deepak, R. Mohan and I. Natarajan (2001), 'Economic Reforms and Poverty Alleviation: A Tale of Two Surveys', *Economic and Political Weekly*, pp. 1017–28, 25 March.

Quibria M.G. (2002), Growth and Poverty: Lessons from the East Asian Miracle Revisited, ADB Institute Research, Paper 33, Manila: Asian Development Bank.

Ravallion, Martin, (2000b), 'Should Poverty Measures be Anchored to the National Accounts?', *Economic and Political Weekly*, 26 August–2 September, pp. 3245–52.

——— (2000a), 'What is needed for a More Pro-Poor Growth process ', *Economic and Political Weekly*, 25 March, pp. 1089–93.

——— (2001b), 'Inequality Convergence', mimeo, World Bank, 17 July.

Ravallion, Martin and Gaurav Datt (1999), When Is Growth Pro-Poor? Evidence from the Diverse Experiences of India's States, Policy Research Working Paper WPS 2263, World Bank.

Ravallion, Martin and Gaurav Datt (1996), How Important to India's Poor Is the Sectoral Composition of Economic Growth? *World Bank Economic Review,* Vol. 10, No. 1, 1–25 January.

Srinivasan, T.N. and Pranab K. Bardhan (eds) (1988), *Rural Poverty in South Asia,* Oxford: Oxford University Press.

Sundaram, K. (2001), 'Employment and Poverty in India in the Nineteen Nineties: Further Results from NSS 55th Round Employment-Unemployment Survey, 1999/2000', Delhi School of Economics, University of Delhi, May.

Sundaram, K. and Suresh Tendulkar (2001), 'NAS-NSS Estimates of Private Consumption for Poverty Estimation: A Disaggregated Comparison for 1993/94', *Economic and Political Weekly,* 13 January.

Triplett, Jack E. (1997), Measuring Consumption: The Post-1973 Slowdown and the Research Issues, *Federal Bank Review* (Federal Reserve Bank of Saint Louis), May/June, pp. 9–42.

World Bank (2000), *World Development Report: Attacking Poverty*, Oxford University Press, Washington D.C.

——— (1991), Growth, Poverty Alleviation and Improved Income Distribution in Malaysia: Changing Focus of Government Policy Intervention, Report 8667-MA, Washington: World Bank.

——— (1997a), *India: Achievements and Challenges in Reducing Poverty.* World Bank Country Study, Washington: World Bank.

——— (1990), *World Development Report: Poverty and Development*, Oxford University Press, Washington DC.

——— (1991), *World Development Report, The Challenge of Development,* Oxford University Press, Washington DC.

22

Are the Rich Growing Richer?
Evidence from Indian Tax Data

Abhijit Banerjee and Thomas Piketty

INTRODUCTION

It is not often that the methodology of measurement becomes something of a political cause celebre. Yet, over the last few years, newspaper readers in India have been routinely exposed to spirited discussions of the arcana of how to measure poverty. At the heart of this debate, is the question of what happened to poverty in India in this last decade of globalisation and liberalisation. Did the poor get to share the munificence that the rich are so visibly enjoying?

The debate got started with the publication of the results from the 51st, 52nd, 53rd and 54th Rounds of the National Sample Survey (NSS), which, taken together, suggested that, poverty had risen slightly since the 50th Round and was more or less where it had been in the mid- to late-1980s. Since these were the first estimates of what liberalisation had done for the poor, it was read, not unfairly, by the critics of the liberalisation, as direct evidence that liberalisation had failed the poor (Sainath, 2001 and Mehta, 2001), and by more uncommitted observers as a cause for concern (Datt, 1999). The defenders of liberalisation responded by arguing that the data had to be wrong. First, the 51st through 54th Rounds of the NSS were all 'thin' rounds and are, therefore, of dubious reliability. Second these rounds involved various experiments with survey methodology. Neither of these arguments is terribly compelling: as Deaton and Dreze (2002) point out, even the thin rounds are large enough to give fairly tight bounds for nationwide poverty estimates, and the upward trend in poverty between the 52nd and 54th Rounds remain, if we focus on the data generated using a single consistent methodology.

The most compelling argument against these NSS numbers is that they show absolutely no evidence of growth in per capita expenditure, at a time when per capita consumption expenditure according to the National Accounts (NAS) was growing at a real rate of over 3 per cent per annum. Based on this apparent contradiction, dubbed the Indian growth paradox of the 1990s, Bhalla (2000), among others, has argued that the NSS methodology must be missing an increasing fraction of consumption growth and was therefore not fit to be used for poverty measurement.[1] He, therefore, generates alternative

---

[1] As emphasised by Sen (2000), the divergence between the NAS and NSS consumption numbers goes back into the 1970s.

poverty estimates based on the assumption that the distribution of consumption did not change at all in the post-liberalisation period (which allows him to apply the average growth rate of per capita consumption expenditure from the NAS to the poor). Not surprisingly, given that per capita consumption expenditure grew rapidly in this period according to the NAS, he finds evidence of huge declines in poverty (Bhalla, 2002).

The dust settled somewhat after the 55th (1999/2000) Round of the NSS came out. This was a large round and while the methodology was not quite consistent with that in the previous (1993/94) large round, Deaton (2003a) came up with an ingenious method for adjusting the data to make it more or less consistent with the 1993/94 numbers.[2] Based on these adjustments, as well as his recalculations of the price indices (Deaton, 2003b), Deaton (2003a) concludes that poverty did go down substantially between 1993/94 and 1999/2000, though less than it would have had he not made the corrections described above and much less than what Bhalla claims.

Moreover average per capita expenditure did grow over this period even according to the NSS, at 2 per cent per annum. However there is still a substantial amount of *missing growth*: the growth rate for average per capita expenditure that we would get from the NAS is 3.5 per cent. This has meant that those, like Bhalla, who believe the NAS numbers, remain skeptical about the NSS-based poverty estimates (Bhalla, 2002).

One way to reconcile the NSS poverty numbers with the NAS average consumption growth numbers is to assume that the rich are under-represented in the NSS and that average consumption is growing because the consumption of the rich is growing faster than that of everybody else. In the extreme if all the growth is with the rich and the rich are excluded from the survey, average consumption could grow very fast according to the NAS and not at all according to the NSS. Yet the NSS numbers would still be the right ones to use to measure poverty.

While there is no hard evidence that the rich are indeed being undercounted in India[3] (the Indian consumer expenditure surveys do not, for example, report refusal rates by potential income category), there are plausible *a priori* reasons to suppose that this may be the case.[4] NSS surveys are long and relatively intrusive (they ask, for example, about alcohol consumption, a taboo subject for many). The rich may be less intimidated by the fact that the surveyors claim to come from a government organisation, in part because they know their rights better. They may also value their leisure more, or at least have firmer belief in their own right to be left alone to enjoy their leisure. And, of course, the rich often live in buildings where there are doormen, and doormen may be explicitly instructed not to let in surveyors.

However, even if it is true that the rich are being undercounted by the NSS, it would not matter unless it is also true that the rich were getting richer much faster than everyone else in the 1990s. The goal of this note is to present some evidence, based on tax data and culled from our previous paper (Banerjee and Piketty, 2003) on what was happening to the rich in the 1990s.

---

[2] Sundaram and Tendulkar (2001) propose another clever way to adjust the data, which also gives results similar to those obtained by Deaton.

[3] There is one important piece of indirect evidence: Sundaram and Tendulkar (2001) find that the NSS-NAS gap is particularly important for commodities that are more heavily consumed by higher income groups, thereby providing indirect evidence for the explanation based on rising inequality.

[4] See, e.g. Szekely and Hilgert (1999), who look at a large number of Latin American household surveys and find that the 10 largest incomes reported in surveys are often not very much larger than the salary of an average manager in the given country at the time of survey. For a systematic comparison of survey and national accounts aggregates in developing countries, see Ravallion (2001).

The basic pattern that emerges from our data is that in the 1990s, the rich were indeed getting richer much faster than anyone else, but this was entirely driven by what was happening to the very rich, i.e. those who were in the top 0.1 per cent of the population of tax units. Because the extraordinary growth was confined to this one group, the fact that the rich were getting richer cannot by itself explain all of the missing growth in the NSS data. We estimate that its potential contribution may be in the range of 20 per cent of the missing growth over the 1987/88 to 1999/2000 period.

The rest of this chapter is organised as follows. The next section briefly outlines our data and methodology. The section on Dynamics of top Income Shares briefly reports our results on the evolution of the share of the rich in total income. The subsequent section discusses potential problems with this evidence. The last section uses this evidence to shed some light on the Indian growth paradox of the 1990s, and concludes.

DATA AND METHODOLOGY

The tabulations of tax returns published each year by the Indian tax administration in the 'All-India Income-Tax Statistics' (AIITS) series constitute the primary data source used in this paper. The first year for which we have income data is 1956/57 while the last is 1999/2000.[5]

Due to the relatively high exemption levels, the number of taxpayers in India has always been rather small: It was between 0.5 per cent–1 per cent of the population of tax units, till the 1980s but rose sharply during the 1990s to about 3.5 per cent–4 per cent at the end of the decade.[6] To get comparable numbers over a longer period we focus on the top 1 per cent.

The tabulations published in AIITS report the number of taxpayers and the total income reported by these taxpayers for a large number of income brackets. By using standard Pareto extrapolation techniques we computed for each year the average incomes of the top percentile (P99-100), the top 0.5 per cent (P99.5-100), the top 0.1 per cent (P99.9-100), and the top 0.01 per cent (P99.99-100) of the tax unit distribution of total income, as well as the income thresholds P99, P99.5; P99.9; and P99.99 and the average incomes of the intermediate fractiles P99-99.5; P99.5-99.9; and P99.9-99.99.[7]

[5] Financial years run from 1 April to 31 March in India (1956/57 refers to the period running from 1 April 1956 to 31 March 1957, etc., and 1999/2000 to the period running from 1 April 1999 to 31 March 2000). Note also that AIITS publications always refer to assessment years (AY), i.e. years during which incomes are assessed, while we always refer to income years (IY) (IY = AY – 1). For instance, AIITS 1957/58 contains the data on IY 1956/57, etc., and AIITS 1999/2000 contains the data on IY 1998/99. AIITS 2000/01 (IY 1999/2000) was not yet available when we revised this paper, and our IY 1999/2000 figures for top incomes were obtained by inflating the 1998/99 figures by the nominal 1999/2000/1998/99 per tax unit national income growth rate. This approximation probably leads us to underestimate top income growth. We did this because there was no large NSS round for 1998/99 so it was easier to make comparison with 1999/2000 as the end point.

[6] Throughout the paper, 'tax units' should be thought of as individuals (all of our estimates have been obtained by summing up tax returns filed by individuals and those filed by 'Hindu Undivided Families' (HUF), but the latter generally make less than 5 per cent of the total). The total, theoretical number of tax units was set to be equal to 40 per cent of the total population of India throughout the period. This represents a rough estimate of the potential 'positive-income population' of India: this is lower than India's adult population (the 15-year-and-over population makes about 60–65 per cent of total population since the 1950s), but is very close to India's labour force (the labour force consists of about 40–45 per cent of total population since the 1950s).

[7] For a recent use of Pareto extrapolation techniques with similar tax return data, see Piketty (2001) and Piketty and Saez (2001); see also Atkinson (2001).

One thing that immediately emerges from this exercise that is worth emphasising, is that the rich in India, even now, are quite poor by global standards. In 1999/2000, there were 396.4 million tax units in India. Based on the national accounts statistics, the average income of those almost 400 million tax units was around Rs 25,000 per year [$3,000 in Purchasing Power Parity (PPP) terms].[8] To belong to the top percentile (P99), which includes about 4 million tax units, one needed to make more than Rs 88,000 (around $10,000 at PPP). The average income of the bottom half of the top percentile (fractile P99-99.5, about 2 million tax units) was about Rs 99,000 (less than $12,000 at PPP). To belong to the top 0.01 per cent (about 40,000 tax units), one needs to make more than Rs 14 lakh ($160,000 at PPP), and the average income above that threshold was more than Rs 40 lakh ($470,000 at PPP).

As in other countries, the top of India's income distribution appears to be very precisely approximated by the Pareto structural form.[9] The estimates are subject to sampling error: the AIITS tabulations seem to be based upon uniform samples of all tax returns, rather than on the entire population (as in most OECD countries), or stratified sample. However the sampling rate is sufficiently large to guarantee that the estimated trends for top income shares are statistically significant.[10]

AIITS publications also includes tabulations reporting the amounts of the various income categories (wages, business income, dividends, interest, etc.) for each income bracket. In particular, AIITS offers separate tables for wage earners who are by far the largest subgroup. This allowed us to separate estimates for top wage fractiles, which we can compare to our top fractiles estimates for total income.[11]

THE DYNAMICS OF TOP INCOME SHARES

Figure 22.1 illustrates the basic finding from our previous paper:[12] income inequality (as measured by the share of top incomes) has followed a U-shaped pattern over the 1922–2000 period. The top 0.01 per

[8] Our average income series (table A0, Col. 7) was set to be equal to 70 per cent of national income per tax unit (the 30 per cent deduction is assumed to represent the fraction of national income that goes to undistributed profits, non-taxable income, etc.). The national income series was taken from Sivasubramonian (2000), to whom we also owe our population series.

[9] In the same way as for other countries (see above for references), we checked that our extrapolation results are virtually unaffected by the choice of extrapolation thresholds. Pareto coefficients are locally very stable in India, just like in other countries.

[10] According to the *tax administration statistics division*, the sampling rate is about 1 per cent and approximately uniform (no precise information about sampling design and rate is included in AIITS publications). Given India's large population, this implies that our estimate for the top 1 per cent income share (8.95 per cent of total income in 1999/2000, see Bannerjee and Pickety, 2003) has a standard error of about 0.04 per cent, and that our estimate for the top 0.01 per cent income share (1.57 per cent of total income in 1999/2000, see Table A3 of the same paper) has a standard error of about 0.08 per cent. There is some evidence however that the sampling design is changing and that published tabulations are becoming more volatile by the end of the period. In particular, the tabulations for IY 1997/98 (AIITS 1998/99) contain far too many individual taxpayers above Rs 10 lakh, thereby suggesting that something went wrong in the sampling design during that year. The 1997/98 estimates were corrected downwards on the basis of 1996/97 and 1998/99 tabulations.

[11] Published wage tabulations for IY 1996/97 and 1997/98 appear to suffer from sampling design failures (top wages are clearly truncated in 1996/97, and they are too numerous in 1997/98), and our estimates for those two years were corrected on the basis of 1995/96 and 1998/99 data.

[12] Banerjee and Piketty (2003) has a more detailed discussion of the trends, reports the underlying raw data in much greater detail, and provides a comparison between top income shares in India and top income shares in France and the United States.

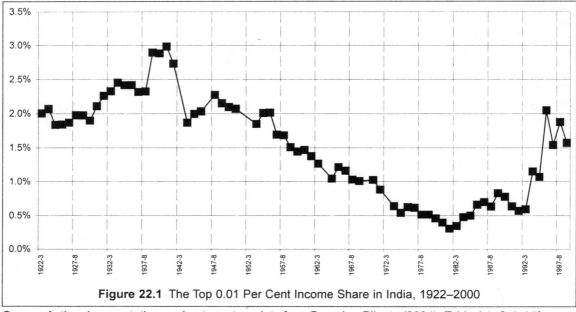

Figure 22.1 The Top 0.01 Per Cent Income Share in India, 1922–2000

Source: Authors' computations using tax return data [see Banerjee-Piketty (2004), Table A4, Col. (4)].

cent income share gradually fell from about 1.5–2 per cent of total income in the 1950s to less than 0.5 per cent in the early 1980s, and then rose during the 1980–1990s, back to 1.5–2 per cent during the late 1990s. What this means is that the average top 0.01 per cent income was about 150–200 times larger than the average income of the entire population during the 1950s. It went down to being less than 50 times as large in the early 1980s, but went back to being 150–200 times larger during the late 1990s.

One also observes a similar (though less pronounced) U-shaped pattern for the top 1 per cent income share, which went from about 12-13 per cent during the 1950s to 4-5 per cent in the early 1980s to 9-10 per cent in the late 1990s (see Figure 22.2). As with the top 0.01 per cent, the turning point seems to be around 1980/81, and over the 1980s, the share of the top 1 per cent also doubles. Then, as with the share of the top 0.01 per cent, there is a period of retrenchment which lasts till 1991/92, followed by a renewed upward movement. However these incomes grow much slower than the very top incomes over the 1990s.

The comparison of these Figures 22.1 and 22.2 reveals another intriguing fact: While in the 1980s the share of the top 1 per cent increases almost as quickly as the share of the top 0.01 per cent, in the 1990s there is a clear divergence between what is happening to the top 0.01 per cent and the rest of the top percentile. To confirm that this is the case, we break up the top percentile into four groups: those between the 99th percentile and the 99.5th percentile, those between the 99.5th percentile and the 99.9th percentile, those between the 99.9th percentile and the 99.99th percentile, and those in the top 0.01 percentile. Table 22.1 below reports what happened to each of these groups in the 1987–2000 period. We see that only those in the top 0.1 per cent enjoyed income growth rates faster than the growth rate of GDP per capita. This contrasts with what we see when we look at the period that includes the 1980s (see Table 22.2): for this period we see evidence of above average growth for the entire top percentile.

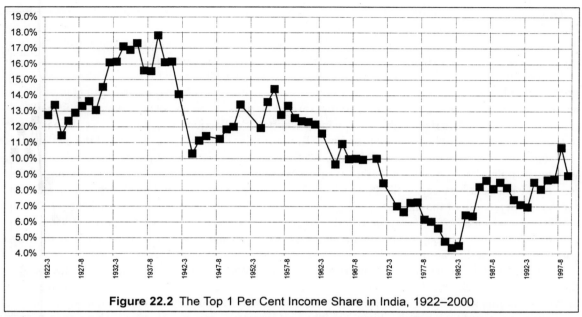

Figure 22.2 The Top 1 Per Cent Income Share in India, 1922–2000

Source: Authors' computations using tax return data [see Banerjee-Piketty (2004), Table A4, Col. (1)].

MEASUREMENT ISSUES

Our presumption so far has been that what we have measured is the actual income share of the rich. There are a number of reasons why this may not be true. First, despite our best efforts, we were unable to discover the actual procedure for generating the sample that is then used to create the tax tables. Our sense, from informal conversations with Indian tax officials, is that, at least in recent years, the procedure is more an informal attempt to sample randomly than a precise random sample. To the extent that this increases the risk of the data being clustered, the implication is that the within sample variance might overstate the precision of our data. While this remains a possibility, we take some consolation from the fact that the trends, for the most part, seem quite stable. While our results for single years or sets of years may reflect sampling variation, the fact that in every year between 1973/74 and 1992/93, the share of the top 0.01 per cent was less than 0.85 per cent (and in every year but two it was less than 0.7 per cent) and that in every year including and after 1995/96 it was greater than 1.5 per cent, seems much more robust. Moreover the intervening two years, 1993/94 and 1994/95 do show, as we might have hoped for, shares for the top 0.01 per cent that were between 0.7 per cent and 1.5 per cent.

A more serious problem is that the surge in top incomes may reflect improvements in the income tax department's ability to measure (and hence tax) the incomes of the wealthy. One reason for this may be that tax cuts in the early 1990s simply reduced the incentives for evading taxes among the wealthy. Note, however, that the overall decline in the top marginal rate, though non-monotonic, was quite moderate: the top marginal tax rate dropped from 50 per cent in 1987/88 to 40 per cent in 1999/2000. By comparison, the change in the share of the top 0.01 per cent was enormous: it went up from 0.7 per cent in 1987/88 to over 1.5 per cent in 1999/2000. If this entire change is to be explained by a shift in tax rates, the implied elasticity would have to be enormous.

Of course, the effect of these tax changes could have been reinforced by a spectacular improvement in the collection technology. There were, after all, a number of innovations in tax collection in the 1990s, such as the introduction of the 'one in six rule' (in 1998) that required everyone who satisfied at least one out of six criteria (owning a car, travel abroad, etc.) to file a tax return.

To see if this is the whole story, we redid the exercise above exclusively for wages. Wages are clearly much less subject to tax evasion than non-wage incomes, since taxes are typically deducted at source and the employer has a strong incentive to report what he pays, since he gets to deduct the wages from his own taxes. Therefore if all that was happening was better collection, we would expect wage incomes to grow much more slowly than other incomes. To see if this is the case, we compared the evolution of top wages with the evolution of top incomes. We find that top wages have increased essentially in step with top incomes during the 1990s. In fact, wage growth among the top percentile of the wage distribution rose by 81 per cent between 1987/88 and 1999/2000, while the corresponding figure was 71 per cent for the top percentile of the income distribution. This is consistent with the fact that the share of wages within the total income of the top percentile has increased somewhat during this period (from 28 per cent to 31 per cent). Although very top incomes are still mostly made up of non-wage income, the wage part has increased during the 1990s.[13]

A final source of concern is that the evolution of the economy might have increased the share of those industries, such as software, which are easier to tax. However much of the increase in the share of the rich seems to be by 1995/96, at which point the software industry was still relatively small and hardly in a position to have such a huge distributional impact.

APPLICATION TO THE GROWTH PARADOX OF THE 1990s

Let us now turn to the growth paradox of the 1980–1990s and how much can be explained by top income growth. Table 22.1 compares the growth performance over the 1987–2000 period of average consumption reported in the NSS, average income and consumption measured by the national accounts (NAS), and top incomes reported in tax returns. The reason for comparing 1987/88 and 1999/2000 is that large NSS surveys were conducted during those two years, so that estimates of the NSS-NAS gap are more precise if one uses those years.[14] To eliminate the effect of using different deflators, we first compare nominal growth performance, and we then compute real growth performance by using the same deflator for all series [namely, the Common Price Index (CPI)].

According to the NSS, real growth was fairly limited in India during the 1990s: per capita consumption increased by only 19 per cent in real terms between 1987/88 and 1999/2000. According to national accounts (NAS), however, the real growth was more than twice as large: both per capita GDP and national income increased by more than 50 per cent in real terms, and per capita household consumption (as measured by national accounts) increased by 40 per cent. This is the NSS-NAS gap that has received so much attention in the recent past.

Table 22.1 shows that the very large growth of top incomes during the 1990s can be a part of the explanation of this puzzle. The average income growth among the top percentile of the tax units was 71 per cent in real terms between 1987/88 and 1999/2000, which is substantially more than average growth

---

[13] The wage results are reported in greater detail in Banerjee and Piketty (2003).

[14] Note that for the NSS 1999/2000 per capita consumption estimates we use the ones reported by Deaton and Dreze (2002), who apply the procedure developed by Deaton (mentioned above), to correct for changes in survey methodology.

Table 22.1 Top Income Growth during the 1990s: 1999/2000 *vs* 1987/88

	1999/2000 vs 1987/88 (Nominal Growth)	1999/2000 vs 1987/88 (Real Growth)
Household consumption/capita (NSS)	+242%	+19%
GDP/capita (NAS)	+337%	+52%
Household consumption/capita (NAS)	+304%	+40%
National income/tax unit (NAS)	+346%	+55%
Top income fractile P99-100 (tax returns)	+392%	+71%
Top income fractile P99.5-100 (tax returns)	+412%	+78%
Top income fractile P99.9-100 (tax returns)	+548%	+125%
Top income fractile P99.99-100 (tax returns)	+1009%	+285%
Top income fractile P99-99.5 (tax returns)	+331%	+50%
Top income fractile P99.5-99.9 (tax returns)	+317%	+45%
Top income fractile P99.9-99.99 (tax returns)	+393%	+71%
Top income fractile P99.99-100 (tax returns)	+1009%	+285%
Consumer price index	+188%	
Share of growth gap accounted for by P99-100		20.1%
Share of growth gap accounted for by P99.5-100		17.2%
Share of growth gap accounted for by P99.9-100		12.7%
Share of growth gap accounted for by P99.99-100		8.0%

Source: Authors' computations using tax return, NAS and NSS data [see Banerjee-Piketty (2004), Table A1, Table A2 and Table A3, row 1999/2000–1987/88)].

according to the national accounts. Moreover, the higher one goes within the top percentile, the higher the growth (up to +285 per cent for the top 0.01 per cent income fractile).

What fraction of the NSS-NAS gap can be explained by the huge growth performance of very top incomes? Let's assume that the NSS is unable to record any of the extra growth enjoyed by the top percentile (say the people in the top percentile do not report their extra growth to the NSS, or do not report anything at all). According to our calculations, the top percentile share in total consumption was around 8 per cent in 1987/88.[15] Since the average income of the top percentile increased by 71 per cent in real terms between 1987/88 and 1999/2000 according to the tax returns (as opposed to +19 per cent for average NSS consumption), this implies that NSS growth was 3.55 per cent less than what would have been without the misreporting.[16] This implies that the growing incomes among the top percentile can explain at most 20.1 per cent of the total NSS-NAS gap (see the bottom panel in Table 22.1).[17] This is significant, but clearly there is a large piece that remains unexplained. The problem lies in the fact that almost all the extraordinary growth was among the top 0.1 per cent and the weight of this group is simply not large enough to have an impact on aggregate statistics of the necessary magnitude. For the rise of inequality to explain fully the NSS-NAS gap, there would have to have been very high income growth at the bottom of the top percentile, and not simply among those in the top 0.1 per cent.

[15] According to our estimates (computed with 70 per cent of national income as the income denominator), the top percentile income share was 8.12 per cent in 1987/88 (see Bannerjee and Pickety, 2003).

[16] $0.0812 \times (1.71/1.19 - 1) = 3.55$.

[17] $3.55/(1.40/1.19 - 1) = 20.1$.

Table 22.2: Top Income Growth during the 1980–1990s: 1999/2000 vs 1981/82

	1999/2000 vs 1981/82 (Nominal Growth)	1999/2000 vs 1981/82 (Real Growth)
Household consumption/capita (NSS)	+487%	+25%
GDP/capita (NAS)	+700%	+70%
Household consumption/capita (NAS)	+599%	+49%
National income/tax unit (NAS)	+688%	+68%
Top income fractile P99-100 (tax returns)	+1508%	+242%
Top income fractile P99.5-100 (tax returns)	+1747%	+293%
Top income fractile P99.9-100 (tax returns)	+2270%	+404%
Top income fractile P99.99-100 (tax returns)	+3980%	+767%
Top income fractile P99-99,5 (tax returns)	+992%	+132%
Top income fractile P99.5-99.9 (tax returns)	+1392%	+217%
Top income fractile P99.9-99.99 (tax returns)	+1698%	+282%
Top income fractile P99.99-100 (tax returns)	+3980%	+767%
Consumer price index	+370%	
Share of growth gap accounted for by P99-100		39.7%
Share of growth gap accounted for by P99.5-100		33.5%
Share of growth gap accounted for by P99.9-100		19.1%
Share of growth gap accounted for by P99.99-100		9.3%

Source: Banerjee and Piketty (2003, Table A0, Table A1, and Table A2, row 1999/2000 vs 1981/82).

Top income growth can explain a larger proportion of the NSS-NAS gap if we start in the 1980s. For instance, under the same assumptions, the top percentile can explain almost 40 per cent of the cumulative NSS-NAS gap over the 1981–2000 periods (see Table 22.2). This is because the bottom of the top percentile enjoyed rapid income growth in the 1980s (see Table 22.2). The more long-term divergence between the NSS and the NAS emphasised, for example, by Sen (2000), is more easily explained by the fact that the rich are getting richer.

The puzzle of the missing growth therefore remains. But our exercise makes it clear why it would be rash to use this as a reason to abandon the use of survey data for poverty measurement, as suggested by Bhalla (2002) and Sala-i-Martin (2002).[18] To be able to say anything useful about changes in poverty levels based on National Accounts data, we need a strong presumption that the income distribution has remained more or less stable. Our evidence, as well as the related work of Piketty and Saez (2001) on the United States, makes it clear that this would be foolhardy.[19] Indeed, one result of what happened in the 1990s is that the weight of the very rich in the income distribution went up very substantially, with the consequence that if the same pattern of divergence between the rich and the rest that we saw over the past decade is repeated over the next decade, the income distribution consequences will be much more drastic than what we have so far seen.

[18] For a detailed critique of the national accounts based approach see Deaton (2003c).
[19] Piketty and Saez show that the share of the top 0.01 per cent in the US went up from 0.6 per cent to over 2.5 per cent between 1980/81 and 1999/2000.

REFERENCES

Atkinson, Anthony B. (2001), 'Top Incomes in the United Kingdom over the Twentieth Century', mimeo, Nuffield College, Oxford.

Banerjee, Abhijit and Thomas Piketty (2003), 'Top Indian Incomes, 1956–2000', mimeo, MIT and Paris-Jourdan.

Bhalla, Surjit S. (2000), 'Growth and Poverty in India: Myth and Reality', mimeo, Oxus Research and Investments, New Delhi.

—— (2002), *Imagine there is no Country: Poverty, Inequality and Growth in an Era of Globalisation*, Washington, DC, Institute for International Economics.

Datt, Gaurav (1999), 'Has Poverty Declined since Economic Reforms', *Economic and Political Weekly*, 11–17 December.

—— (1997), 'Poverty in India 1951–94: Trends and Decompositions', mimeo, The World Bank.

Deaton, Angus (2003c), 'How to Measure Poverty for the Millennium Development Goals', mimeo, Princeton University.

—— (2003b), 'Prices and Poverty in India, 1987–2000', *Economic Political Weekly*, 25 January.

—— (2003a), 'Adjusted Indian Poverty Estimates for 1999/2000', *Economic and Political Weekly*, 25 January.

Deaton, Angus and Jean Dreze (2002), 'Poverty and Inequality in India – A Re-Examination', *Economic and Political Weekly*, 7 September.

Mehta, Jaya (2001), 'Give Poverty a Face, Please', *Alternative Economic Survey 2000/01,* New Delhi: Rainbow Publishers.

Piketty, Thomas (2001), 'Income Inequality in France, 1901–1998', CEPR Discussion Paper, No. 2876 and in *Journal of Political Economy*, 2003.

Piketty, Thomas and Emmanuel Saez (2001), 'Income Inequality in the US, 1913–1998', NBER Working Paper, No. 8467 and in *Quarterly Journal of Economics*, 2003.

Ravallion, Martin (2001), 'Measuring Aggregate Welfare in Developing Countries: How Well do National Accounts and Surveys Agree?', mimeo, The World Bank.

—— (2000), 'Should Poverty Measures Be Anchored to the National Accounts?', *Economic and Political Weekly*, 26 August–2 September.

Sainath, P. (2001), 'Will the Real National Calamity Please Stand Up', *The Hindu*, 25 February.

Sala-i-Martin, Xavier (2002), 'The Disturbing "Rise" of Global Income Inequality', NBER working paper, 8904.

Sen, Abhijit (2000), 'Estimates of Consumer Expenditure and its Distribution', *Economic and Political Weekly,* 16 December.

Sivasubramonian, S. (2000), *The National Income of India in the Twentieth Century*, New Delhi: Oxford University Press.

Szekely, Miguel and Marianne Hilgert (1999), 'What's Behind the Inequality We Measure: An Investigation Using Latin American Data', mimeo, Inter-American Development Bank.

Sundaram K. and Suresh D. Tendulkar (2001), 'NAS-NSS Estimates of Private Consumption for Poverty Estimation', *Economic and Political Weekly,* 13–20 January.

World Bank (2000), 'India – Policies to Reduce Poverty and Accelerate Sustainable Development', Report No. 19471-IN.

Part III

Broader Perspectives on Poverty

23

A Profile and Diagnostic of Poverty in Uttar Pradesh

Valerie Kozel and Barbara Parker

INTRODUCTION

Home to more than 175 million[1] people spread across 112,000 villages and towns, Uttar Pradesh (UP) is the most populous state in India. It also one of the poorest, despite having once seemed a pacesetter for the country's economic and social development, reflecting a rich potential in terms of both human and natural assets. Most of the state's farm land is in the well-watered and naturally fertile Indo-Gangetic Plain, and the western region's tradition of raising wheat and sugarcane made it a strong platform for the Green Revolution in the 1960s and 1970s, which helped UP depart from previously low levels of agricultural growth. In the next decade, the eastern and central regions registered strong advances, spurred by purposeful investments in research, extension, irrigation, and marketing infrastructure. Accordingly, in the 1970s, economic growth in most sectors in Uttar Pradesh was higher than that in the rest of India. Since then however, growth has lagged that of the country as whole. UP has been slow to seize the opportunities created by the liberalisation of the Indian economy that began in 1991.

Reversing this loss of dynamism, and the impact of that loss on the state's 60 million inhabitants who live in poverty, is UP's most important challenge. Because of UP's size and level of poverty, meeting this challenge is of significance not only for UP but also for India, and indeed the world. An estimated 8 per cent of the world's poor live in UP alone.[2]

Against this backdrop, the paper reviews the nature and evolution of poverty in UP. It draws on a range of information, including household surveys, qualitative field studies, and conversations with poor men and women. The aim is to assemble a story about poor people in UP and the constraints – as well as opportunities – which they encounter in their efforts to negotiate and escape deprivation. The narrative that emerges is complex and nuanced; it suggests that while the experience of the nineties provides indications of real progress, it also points at important causes for concern.

---

[1] The discussion in this chapter refers to Uttar Pradesh before the separation of Uttaranchal.
[2] Based on an international poverty line of $1.08/person/day, in 1993 PPP adjusted prices.

Table 23.1 Growth Trends in Uttar Pradesh (Per Cent)

	1971–80	1981–85	1986–90	1991–93	1993–98
Gross Domestic Product					
Uttar Pradesh	3.0	4.0	6.0	1.9	4.0
All-India	3.1	5.0	6.3	4.1	6.7
Agriculture and Allied Services					
Uttar Pradesh	1.9	2.1	3.7	1.7	1.8
All-India	1.5	3.1	3.9	2.4	3.4
Industry					
Uttar Pradesh	5.4	7.4	8.6	1.4	4.8
All-India	4.0	6.4	8.2	3.0	6.6
Manufacturing					
Uttar Pradesh	5.0	9.8	9.2	1.6	3.4
All-India	4.0	7.0	8.2	2.9	7.5
Services, etc.					
Uttar Pradesh	3.6	5.1	7.4	2.5	5.5
All-India	4.3	6.1	7.0	6.0	8.7

Notes: 1980 indicates 1980/81, etc. Since Gross State Domestic Product (GSDP) data are not available prior to 1980, we have used Net State Domestic Product (NSDP) as a proxy for the period 1960–80.

Source: Central Statistical Organisation (CSO).

MEASURING POVERTY: LEVELS, TRENDS, VULNERABILITY, AND VOICE

Measuring poverty, commonly defined as *an unacceptable deprivation in well-being,* is a challenging and complicated task. This is because well-being itself encompasses a multitude of both economic and non-economic dimensions and is therefore difficult to define and quantify. Conventional income or consumption-based measures, while essential to poverty monitoring, may fail to capture many of its critical dimensions. For example, two households with identical income levels cannot be said to be equally impoverished if one has access to free government services, while the other relies on expensive private schools and hospitals. Households may also face different economic prospects if their respective members do not have access to the same work opportunities, due, for example, to ethnic or social discrimination in local labour markets.

In addition to low incomes and inadequate consumption, poverty encompasses low human capabilities, including inadequate skills, lack of education, poor health, and malnutrition. In any country, a variety of economic and non-economic factors must be taken into consideration to obtain an accurate and comprehensive picture of poverty. India, with its rich mosaic of cultural practices and wide variety of social settings and natural environments, presents a special challenge to those wishing to measure and monitor poverty. Poverty is also associated with forms of deprivation situated in specific, local contexts, such as insecurity and violence, vulnerability, social and political exclusion, as well as a lack of dignity and basic rights.

Voices of the Poor

Among the best ways of identifying many dimensions of deprivation is to solicit the perspectives of those who experience it. For this reason, the poverty profile and diagnostic work presented in this paper

---

Box 23.1 People's Perceptions of Rural Poverty

In the context of the UP/Bihar Integrated Poverty Study, discussions were held with local rural inhabitants, both poor and non-poor, about their perceptions of poverty and the factors that influence their upward or downward mobility. Frequently cited factors included the following:

- Landlessness, or possession of only poor-quality, non-irrigated lands.
- Reliance on intermittent, casual wage employment – especially in the agricultural sector, and on foraging or begging.
- Lack of basic literacy, job skills.
- Limited access to social networks, particularly networks that extend outside the village and help residents find better jobs, especially jobs in the non-farm sector.
- Chronic indebtedness.
- Desertion by male spouse, being widowed, or being a woman living alone without an adult male.
- A high dependency ratio, many daughters, and a lack of sons.
- Ill health or disability, particularly of the primary breadwinner.
- Poor quality mud and thatch housing, insecurity of housing tenure.
- Social or caste identity: in several villages, low-caste informants assumed all high-caste households to be rich, while they carefully ranked lower caste households by various economic criteria. Among the higher castes, low-caste status was assumed to be a strong indicator of poverty.

Less tangible factors such as dignity and autonomy were mentioned in numerous cases. One group of harijan (low-caste) informants reported that they had moved from the central village, where they had lived on lands belonging to wealthy traditional patrons, to marginal and non-productive lands on the village periphery. Although they had gained nothing economically by this move and may even have lost an informal safety net, they felt they were better off by virtue of having escaped a demeaning, demoralising, and potentially threatening relationship of dependency.

Source: Field notes, UP/Bihar Poverty Study, 1998/99.

---

draws not only on conventional quantitative data, but also on a range of consultations carried out in poor communities through discussions and open-ended interviews (see Appendix for a description of three

---

Box 23.2 Voices of the Urban Poor

While urban poverty shares some factors with rural poverty, it has a distinctly different face. This is evident from consultations carried out with individuals living in illegal/irregular urban settlements. Many of the urban poor included in the consultations were first generation migrants, and the majority felt that migration had improved their economic position. In urban areas, unlike rural villages, employment opportunities – if only scavenging, petty hawking, and begging – are available year round, typically at higher wages than those paid in rural areas. Furthermore, many of the urban poor said they preferred working in urban areas not only because they earned higher and more regular wages but also because they were 'freer' with respect to the pressure exerted by a powerful patron employer. However, many also complained about their lack of job security and most aspired to more permanent, salaried jobs.

Additional factors linked to urban poverty include the following:

- Very poor housing, lack of secure tenure (extremely important in the eyes of the urban poor), polluted and inadequate water and sanitation services.
- Lack of appropriate job skills and connections – surprisingly, few of the poor in illegal settlements cited formal education as an important factor in determining access to employment, although virtually all respondents felt that basic literacy was important, also for girls.
- The household's asset base at the time of migration was frequently mentioned; households that brought start-up money or had job connections were typically better off than households that came to the city with nothing.
- More than in rural areas, behavioural factors were frequently cited as critical for upward mobility. The poor were considered 'less industrious', less hard working, more prone to alcohol or drug abuse.
- High dependency ratios, particularly in the case of those having young children, and widows without sons or with young children.
- Serious illnesses (TB, cancer, mental illness), and disability of working-age adults.

Source: Field notes, Urban Consultations with the Poor, 2000.

field studies carried out in support of this work – the 1998 UP/Bihar Poverty Study, 1999 Consultations on Poverty Monitoring, and the 2000 Urban Poverty Study). This allows the poor in UP to give voice and context to the story that emerges from the statistical analysis. In so doing, they highlight concerns about lack of land, insecurity of tenure, lack of skills and good education, lack of social networks and lack of access to stable employment. In addition, they speak of poverty in terms of risks, particularly those linked to sudden bouts of poor health, debt, and desertion. The importance of social identity is also sharply highlighted; in rural areas, low caste status was cited as one of the strongest indicators of poverty.

In contrast, the urban poor saw upward mobility as more closed linked to behaviour (e.g. hard work, good business sense) than caste standing.

Poverty as Material Deprivation

In India, and indeed throughout the world, we conventionally equate poverty with material deprivation and define the poor as those individuals whose level of per-capita consumption or income falls below the chosen cut-off point, or poverty line.[3] There is no doubt that material deprivation is a key factor that underlies many other dimensions of poverty. And to be materially poor in India is to be poor indeed. India's official poverty lines represent living standards well below the World Bank international comparator line of $1.08 per person per day, in 1993 PPP-adjusted prices.[4]

But it is misleading to think of poverty as primarily a statistical construct. What does it in fact mean to be poor in India? On the basis of data from the 1993/94 NSS (National Sample Survey), a person living at India's official poverty line[5] would have spent Rs 6.80 per day, equivalent to about 22 cents. And what would this buy? While relative prices have changed since 1994, the change is likely to be marginal. Accordingly, we assume the 1993/94 food basket is still relevant for the poor today. On a typical day therefore, a poor person would consume:

Three scant plates of cooked rice, or 8–10 chapattis
A half cup of cooked pulses
A spoon of edible oil
A spoon of dried chili
One medium-sized potato, or onion
One cup of tea
A handful of brinjal
One half cup of milk
One banana three times each month
An egg every five days

After buying food, two additional rupees each day, equivalent to about 6 cents, would be left over for

[3] India's poverty lines are set by the Planning Commission and use the Expert's Group methodology (GOI, 1997). These poverty lines are based on nutritional norms, and defined in terms of the level of per capita consumer expenditure needed to provide an average daily intake of 2,400 calories per person in rural areas and 2,100 calories in urban areas, plus a minimal allocation for non-food items.

[4] The headcount rate in 1997 in India using the international $1 per day line is 44 per cent, (World Development Report 2000/01) which is considerably higher than the All-India 1993/94 Planning Commission estimate of 37 per cent.

[5] Using the all-India average rural food consumption from the NSS 50th Round, 30–40 per cent fractile.

items like medicines, school books, fuel for cooking, clothing, soap, durable goods, etc. Notably, *one-third of India's rural population cannot even afford this frugal bundle* (World Bank, 1997).

In recent debates, questions have been raised about the methods used to estimate India's official poverty lines (Dubey and Gangopadhyay, 1998; Deaton, 2001 and Deaton and Dreze, 2002) and about the reliability and comparability of the consumption estimates upon which recent poverty estimates are based. However, given their broad acceptability within India, this paper uses India's official poverty lines.

Poverty Trends: Progress and Recent Puzzles

UP has high levels of poverty in comparison to other Indian states. Progress in combating poverty has been uneven over the past two decades, and UP still lags behind many other states in this respect. In the late 1970s, poverty in UP was lower than in Andhra Pradesh and Kerala, as well as the rural and urban all-India average. By 1993/94, however, the latter states had attained lower levels of poverty, while the corresponding level in UP had by then risen above the all-India average. There was, however, evidence of some progress in the 1980s and early 1990s: official estimates for the state suggest a decline in poverty between 1983 and 1987/88, with progress diminishing through 1993/94 (Table 23.2). Moreover, inequality fell substantially between 1983 and 1993/94, and the depth and severity of poverty in both urban and rural areas reduced significantly. However, despite this progress, an estimated 41 per cent of UP's population still lived below the official poverty line in 1993/94, and poverty levels in rural areas, which in 1993/94 accounted for 83 per cent of the state's poor, had fallen very little. This trend compares notably to a steady reduction of urban poverty in UP during the same period.

What happened to poverty in the latter half of the 1990s? Official estimates released by the Planning Commission on the basis of the NSS 55th Round suggest rapid reductions in poverty in UP. The headcount index is estimated to have fallen from 41 per cent of the population (62 million persons) in 1993/94 to 31 per cent (53 million persons) in 1999/2000, a net reduction of 9.1 million persons over six years. Indeed, UP is one of the strongest performing states according to official 55th Round estimates, accounting for 15 per cent of the aggregate drop in poverty in India in the latter half of the 1990s. But it is not clear if the dramatic progress suggested by 55th Round estimates is credible. The interpretation of the most recent official data on welfare and poverty is controversial and subject to intense debate. Changes in survey design for the 55th Round, particularly changes in the reference periods for measuring consumption, rendered 55th Round poverty estimates not comparable to those from earlier rounds of the NSS.

Table 23.2 Trends in Poverty: Uttar Pradesh

Year	NSS Round	Headcount Ratio (Per Cent Poor)		
		Urban	Rural	Overall
1983	38th	51.0	47.4	48.1
1987/88	43rd	45.0	42.3	42.8
1993/94	50th	35.4	42.3	41.0
1999/2000				
– official	55th	30.9	31.2	31.1
– corrected	55th	30.4	33.7	32.9

Source: NSS Consumer Expenditure Surveys, official poverty lines. Corrected estimates from Deaton, 2001.

A number of researchers have offered adjusted figures aimed at restoring comparability between the 55th and earlier Rounds (see papers in this volume). These adjustments suggest that progress has indeed been substantial, if may be less impressive than official statistics indicate. This is particularly the case for rural areas, where new estimates (Table 23.2) suggest that poverty fell by 8.6 percentage points rather than the 11.1 percentage point 'official' reduction in poverty (Deaton, 2001). And even this improvement must be interpreted with care: mean per-capita consumption levels in UP grew at only 1.4 per cent per annum between 1993/94 and 1999/2000. The sharp reduction in the headcount ratio is in part explained by the fact that many households are clustered around the poverty line and the slope of the Lorenz curve is steep in that region. A little growth thus can result in a substantial reduction in the number of people living below the poverty line. However, many of the erstwhile poor still have low consumption levels and remain vulnerable to income and other shocks that can push them back into poverty.

While the debate is not fully resolved, regardless of the method used, there are indications that UP has made significant progress in reducing poverty in the latter half of the 1990s. Further work remains to be done to establish what have been the predominant sources of progress, and more importantly, how these can be further leveraged in order to accelerate the rate of poverty reduction in the future.

Regional Dimensions of Poverty

Not surprisingly, aggregate poverty data for UP conceal considerable regional differences. Home to 175 million people, UP is larger than most countries in the world, and there are longstanding, historic differences across its regions. Levels of poverty vary accordingly, rising from west to east. They are lowest in the western and erstwhile Himalayan Regions – now Uttaranchal state – and rise sharply in the central and eastern regions, peaking in the southern region (Figure 23.1). So stark are the regional contrasts that in 1993/94 southern UP was home to four times as many poor people as is the Himalayan region, even though the two have roughly equal populations. However, with the exception of the southern region, which has been lagging behind the rest of the state, progress in reducing poverty over time has been fairly evenly distributed across regions.

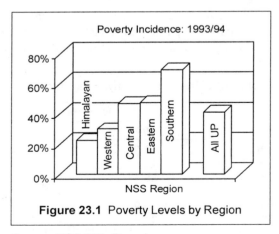

Figure 23.1 Poverty Levels by Region

Source: NSS 50th Round.

Unfortunately, the aforementioned comparability problems associated with the 55th Round make it difficult to assess whether there have been changes in regional patterns of growth and poverty reduction. Instead of analysing these changes using poverty lines, we have looked at the regional composition of the bottom quartile of the population. Figure 23.2 shows the distribution of the poorest quartile of the rural population, defined at the all-UP level, residing in each region.[6] The same figure shows the regional distribution of the total rural population. These data suggest some shifts in the regional distribution of the poor population. In 1999/2000, the central and eastern regions still house a disproportionate share of UP's bottom quartile. However, relative to their population shares, there has been a decrease in the percentage of 'poor' individuals living in the Eastern and Southern regions – historically backward areas accounting for a substantial number of UP's poor and socially marginalised – and a concomitant increase in the percentage of poor living in the Western and central regions. This shift in regional patterns of poverty is consistent with regional trends in agriculture wages (World Bank, 2001 and Deaton and Dreze, 2002). However, further work is needed in order to confirm and better understand these early results.

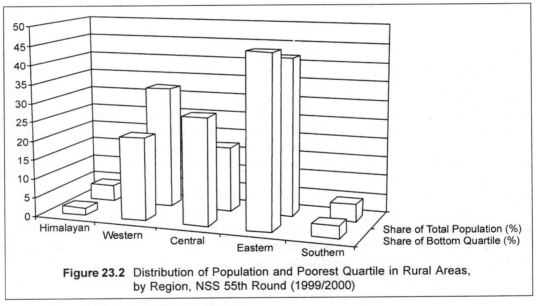

Figure 23.2 Distribution of Population and Poorest Quartile in Rural Areas, by Region, NSS 55th Round (1999/2000)

Source: NSS 55th Round, UP State Sample.

Poverty as Human Deprivation

Deprivation of human resources is another critical dimension of poverty; it is encouraging that despite UP's uncertain success in reducing material deprivation during the 1990s, it enjoyed greater progress in human development. Indicators of human development capture important dimensions of well-being and

[6] This method should not be affected by changes in survey methodology between the 50th and 55th Rounds, since it entails only the assumption that the relative ranking of households will not be affected by the changes in survey methodology described above.

Table 23.3 Highest Educational Attainment of the Population

Educational Attainment	1986/87 (NSS 42nd Round)			1995/96 (NSS 52nd Round)		
	Urban	Rural	Overall	Urban	Rural	Overall
Men (15 years and older)						
Not literate	27	53	48	14	35	30
Less than Primary	8	9	8	8	11	10
Completed Primary	14	12	12	15	17	17
Completed Middle	16	13	14	22	19	20
Completed Secondary	11	6	7	18	10	12
Completed Higher	25	7	10	24	7	11
Overall	*100*	*100*	*100*	*100*	*100*	*100*
Women (15 years and older)						
Not literate	55	85	80	33	67	59
Less than Primary	6	3	3	8	7	7
Completed Primary	9	5	6	14	11	12
Completed Middle	8	3	4	17	9	11
Completed Secondary	7	1	2	13	4	6
Completed Higher	15	3	5	15	2	5
Overall	*100*	*100*	*100*	*100*	*100*	*100*

Source: NSS 42nd and 52nd Rounds.

reflect not just the rate of growth in the economy but also levels and quality of public spending. They also broaden the picture of poverty and provide a wider arena for the fight against it. Effective public spending on basic services, e.g. education, health, water, and sanitation, can compensate for the limited ability of the poor to acquire these services through the market. However, because the impact of spending on public goods and services is not reflected in conventional measures of income poverty, progress in this arena is better reflected in outcome measures, as detailed below.

Education is a key indicator of human development. Many desirable social and economic outcomes are linked to rising levels of education, particularly among women and socially vulnerable groups. Literacy has improved steadily over time in UP, though as of the mid-1990s, two-thirds of rural women were still not able to read or write, and only 15 per cent had more than five years of schooling. Rural men fare better; by the mid-1990s, two-thirds of them were literate, and 36 per cent had completed schooling beyond the primary level. Literacy in urban areas is much higher, although one-third of urban women were still illiterate in the mid-1990s.

Recent results from the 2001 Population Census confirm that UP has made significant progress in boosting literacy levels over the past decade; literacy increased by nearly 17 percentage points between 1991 and 2001. However, the state still compares poorly to many other Indian states – almost 70 million people in UP still cannot read or write.

What of the future? Encouragingly, *enrolment rates* are rising throughout UP, adding to the stock of human capital and boosting prospects for UP's future. UP made better progress in improving enrolments of girls and socially marginalised groups between the mid-1980s and mid-1990s, than did states such as Andhra Pradesh and Karnataka (Table 23.4). However, our understanding of such trends is blurred; there are serious discrepancies among enrolment estimates derived from household surveys such as the NSS, and estimates from administrative sources. Recent information does suggest substantial improvements in school enrolments during the latter half of the 1990s, particularly for girls, and children

Table 23.4 Net School Enrollment Rates in Uttar Pradesh, By Caste and Gender

School Enrolments	1986/87 (NSS 42nd Round)			1995/96 (NSS 52nd Round)		
	Girls	SC/ST Girls	Boys	Girls	SC/ST Girls	Boys
Urban (7 to 12 year olds)						
Uttar Pradesh	60	41	68	75	72	81
All-India	**75**	**63**	**81**	**85**	**80**	**89**
Bihar	52	49	66	76	72	80
Rajasthan	65	40	77	81	62	88
Andhra Pradesh	76	82	78	85	78	89
Karnataka	76	63	78	88	63	89
Kerala	98	97	98	98	97	97
Rural (7 to 12 year olds)						
Uttar Pradesh	29	20	62	52	45	75
All-India	**43**	**31**	**65**	**62**	**53**	**76**
Bihar	27	11	46	41	27	60
Rajasthan	25	14	65	42	41	76
Andhra Pradesh	39	37	66	62	50	71
Karnataka	50	33	69	61	45	79
Kerala	95	94	95	98	98	98

Source: NSS 42nd and 52nd Rounds.

from scheduled caste and tribal families. For instance, recent estimates based on the second round of the National Family Health Survey (NFHS-2, 1998/99) point to sharp increases in aggregate school attendance. EMIS (Education Management Information System) data from the Directorate of Basic Education in UP, suggest that in the districts where the District Primary Education Project (DPEP) was active, enrolments may have doubled since 1993. And early analysis of schooling data from the NSS 55th Round shows significant increases in enrolment rates of rural girls, so much so that it has nearly closed the gap in enrolment rates for boys and girls. Enrolments of rural SC/ST (Scheduled Caste/Scheduled Tribe) girls are estimated to have risen from 45 per cent in 1995/96 to 60 per cent in 1999/2000, and in urban areas from 72 per cent to 76 per cent over the same time period. What is worrisome, however, is an early indication that increases in boys' enrolments may have slowed in the latter half of the 1990s, and there are still very low enrolments among the urban poor – even lower than among the rural poor.

Health status is another key indicator of human development. The people of UP suffer a high burden of health problems and illnesses, particularly compared to the rest of India. Based on estimates from the Office of the Registrar General (ORG, 1999), life expectancy at birth in UP is 61 years for both males and females – well below the national average of 62.4 years for males, and 63.4 years for females. Moreover, the total fertility rate was estimated at 4.8 births in 1997, considerably higher than the national average of 3.5. Similarly, the UP maternal mortality rate was estimated at 707 deaths per 100,000 live births in 1997, compared to 408 in India as a whole. However, recent trends in demographic and health indicators for women are encouraging. According to results of the National Family Health Survey (NHHS-2) of 1998/99, fertility rates have been declining and contraceptive prevalence is slowly on the rise. However, sterilisation, which is not useful for birth spacing, still accounts for three-quarters of contraceptive use (IIPS, 2000).

The health status of children in UP is of particular concern. The Office of the Registrar General (ORG) estimates that infant mortality in the state was 85 deaths per 1,000 births in 1997, compared to a national average of 71 per 1,000 live births. Estimates from NFHS-2 are similar. However, as shown in Figure 23.3, they do suggest slow but steady progress over cohort groups (IIPS, 2000). Also, the percentage of children without any immunisations dropped from 43 per cent (1992/93) to 30 per cent (1998/99), although there was very little improvement in the percentage of children who were fully vaccinated, which is recorded as 20 per cent in NFHS-1, and 21 per cent in NFHS-2. Lastly, stunting[7] (low height-for-age) was prevalent; in 1998/99, 55.5 per cent of children were stunted in UP as compared to 45.5 per cent nationwide, with only modest improvements over the decade.

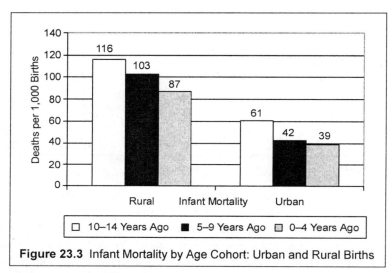

Figure 23.3 Infant Mortality by Age Cohort: Urban and Rural Births

Note: NFHS 1998/99 Base for Age Cohorts.
Source: IIPS, 2000.

Vulnerability, Powerlessness, Exclusion, Social Identity

Just as the reality of poverty goes beyond material deprivation, it also encompasses more than shortcomings in human development. The poor, in Uttar Pradesh as elsewhere, are highly vulnerable. Voiceless and powerless, they also lack access to and influence over the institutions of the state and the resources and services it can provide. Exclusion and social marginalisation is often at the root of this problem. For many poor people, low-caste status and gender operate as social barriers that exclude them from many realms of social and economic opportunity. To describe these barriers, the paper draws on a substantial body of work based on Indian village studies, as reviewed by Jayaram and Lanjouw (1999), Srivastava (1996), and Lieten (2000) as well as on studies of urban and rural poverty in UP. Key findings from the urban study are summarised in Box 23.3.

Vulnerability

Vulnerability to adverse shocks is a fact of life for poor men and women. They are distressed not only

[7] Percentage below 2 standard deviations (-2 SD) from the International Reference Population median.

Box 23.3 Vulnerability to Shocks

In the recent qualitative study of urban poverty in UP, the poorest urbanites were found very often to dwell on the banks of rivers or drainage canals that are prone to flooding during the monsoon season. During this time, entire communities may find their homes under water. In one area of Lucknow, informal settlements were found on the banks of canals (*nallas*) that drain waste water, including sewage, from the city. These also serve as toilets for the settlements. These *nallas* normally flood their banks once a year, leaving homes knee-deep in untreated sewage. Having nowhere else to go, many residents attempt to remain in their huts even under flooded conditions. Accordingly, not only are their homesteads and possessions damaged or lost to the rising waters, but their health is often severely affected. When disease outbreaks such as cholera epidemics follow , illness, which is normally an idiosyncratic shock, becomes covariant throughout the community. The most vulnerable in these communities become destitute as a result of the cost of curative care for those who fall ill and from the necessity of replacing housing or other essential assets. In many cases, these shocks are regular seasonal events in the lives of the poor. In these cases, recurrent shocks prevent them from escaping the precarious shantytown environment, and may force them to resort to begging or other coping strategies associated with the truly destitute.

Source: Field visits, Urban Poverty Study in Uttar Pradesh, 2000.

---

by current low levels of resources and incomes, but also by the possibility of falling into deeper poverty and destitution. Once destitute, it can be difficult to recover. Poverty, as seen by the poor, is a precarious condition; it can easily become worse and only by struggle, hard work, and good fortune does it become better. The poor are at risk because they lack the income, the assets, and the social ties that protect the better-off from the impact of unexpected setbacks. Idiosyncratic shocks are common, such as an illness that requires expensive treatment, the temporary or permanent disability of a breadwinner, and a natural disaster (such as the recent drought affecting a number of states) can obliterate a poor household's small savings. In both urban and rural field studies, death, disability, and disease were cited frequently as factors linked to vulnerability. Widowhood, or more frequently, desertion by a spouse, often led to destitution in poor and low-caste women (see Unni, 1998 and Dreze, 1990). Economy-wide or systemic shocks also are common. Crops may fail due to poor weather conditions, agricultural wages move with the vagaries of the local economy, and land may become eroded or salinised due to flooding or inadequate supplies of ground water. If shocks are severe, repeated, or long-lasting, a household may be forced to sell or pawn its few productive assets and, in the worst cases, may fall into chronic life-long debt.

Perceptions of risk and concomitant fears of destitution strongly influences the economic behaviour of both the poor and the near-poor. It is a truism that the threat of a potential loss is most keenly felt by a household with little saved to cushion against it. Examples of extreme deprivation, hunger, and hopelessness are evident throughout society; the risks are real, not imagined. Even when potential returns are significant, the poor may therefore shun certain ventures if failure would exhaust their limited reserves, or draw them into debt. Relevant undertakings may include leasing cultivable land, purchasing a dairy cow, diversifying crops, or abandoning a subsistence-level livelihood in order to seek better employment. The end result is that many of the poor limit themselves to static, unproductive, and low-paying economic activities, to preserve security of livelihood, even at the cost of potential improvements in economic status, perpetuating the vicious cycle of poverty.

Voice and Power

Poor individuals and communities are generally deprived of political influence, and therefore also lack the leverage to ensure that state institutions serve them fairly. Accordingly, they often lack access to public facilities, or have access only to goods or facilities of inferior quality. Poor public sector governance impinges disproportionally on them. While Indian citizens of all castes and income levels frequently have

---

Box 23.4 Political Organisation and the Urban Poor:
Many Voices are Better than One

Raidas Vihar, in Jajmau, Kanpur, is an informal settlement of low-caste Hindus and Muslims which is not formally recognised by government even though it has been in existence for about 20 years. Its founding family, whose head was employed in an adjacent tannery, discovered that the land around the tannery was unoccupied and set up the first of many shanties on the site. Since then, the smell and stigma of the tannery has discouraged any but unskilled tannery workers from attempting to utilise the site. The city government allotted the land to a private owner, but he never appeared to claim it. The settlement continued undisturbed until 1992, when the Kanpur Development Authority (KDA) sent a contingent of bulldozers to obliterate it. For three days, the bulldozers destroyed homes, shops and infrastructure, including a water point installed by an international NGO. During this time, the community quickly organised a political action group which they called the 'Raidas Vihar Dalit and Minority Committee'. The Committee appealed to local politicians for assistance, and they received it from a former Member of Parliament from the Communist Party. With his help, they were able to get a 'stay' order from the courts. Although the local association has not been successful in gaining formal recognition for their community, they have at least been able to prevent its eradication.

Source: Field visits, Urban Poverty Study in Uttar Pradesh, 2000.

---

to deal with an unresponsive public bureaucracy, the burden of non-responsiveness falls particularly upon poor men and women. For instance, studies by India's Public Affairs Center (Sekhar and Balakrishnan, 1999) indicate that the wealthy and middle classes are more likely to be able to resolve their complaints and at lower cost. In Delhi, an average 27 per cent of ordinary households who complained about a particular government service won redress, through an average number of four required visits to the relevant agency. In contrast, only 6 per cent of slum dwellers were able to get their problems solved, and an average slum dweller had to make six visits in order to do so. Corruption also impacts the poor disproportionally. Since bribes require them to part with a larger share of their income than do better-off groups, this phenomenon often operates as a highly regressive tax on the poorest. At times, they may have to pay more even in absolute terms. In the above example, the average bribe paid by ordinary households was Rs 254, compared to Rs 337 for slum dwellers.

Although poor households are at a disadvantage when they confront public bureaucracies, collective action can improve their bargaining power. For instance, urban slum dwellers interviewed in the course of the urban poverty study, reported some degree of success when community members organised to resist slum clearance efforts by city officials.

Stories such as the above suggest that even though the means of the poor are limited, they have a better chance of being heard if they work together, e.g. by forming community organisations for political action. Notwithstanding, it is questionable whether significant political power can be won through collective action by slum residents. In urban consultations carried out for this study, the political successes enjoyed by these communities were achieved primarily in the defence of certain *status quo* objectives, such as preventing the city from destroying the settlement. However, the study found very few cases in which political activity had won legal recognition or improved services for the slum. What is more, there is little evidence that UP's rural poor have developed comparable political awareness or strategies.

Social Identity

Social identity, in particular, caste status and gender, is linked to poverty in UP in a number of ways. Deep and continuing social inequities mark many facets of society. Individuals with low-caste status are far more likely to be employed as low-paid, low-status agriculture labourers, are often illiterate, and live in poorly constructed houses with limited access to water and sanitation. They are also more likely to suffer job discrimination, with research suggesting (World Bank, 2002) that they earn less than other groups with equal levels of education. Social identity erects particular barriers to economic and social mobility, barriers that must be recognised in designing effective policy and programme interventions. Women also suffer various forms of social and economic discrimination. These and other issues of exclusion and social identity are addressed later in the chapter.

Destitution

A small but important subset of the poor are truly destitute, and the fear of joining their ranks, from which there is often no escape, is widely prevalent, and colours the thinking and behaviour of the poor and non-poor alike. This is despite India's extensive array of anti-poverty programmes, which were generally found to operate poorly in the most backward regions of the state. Consultations with poor households in Eastern and Southern UP frequently identified the poorest of the poor as those who had suffered idiosyncratic shocks such as long-term and costly illnesses; loss of a breadwinner through death, desertion, alcohol or substance abuse; or a loss of assets through fire, theft, death of livestock, or other personal tragedies that had permanently undermined their physical or human resource base (Kozel and Parker, 1999). The destitute poor usually have no other sources of income but low-wage, intermittently available casual labour or, in the worst case, foraging and begging. With rare exceptions, destitute households have very weak ties of mutual assistance and support, particularly compared to their wealthier counterparts. They receive less support from family and form fewer relationships based on mutual assistance, in large part because their needs far outweigh their ability to reciprocate. This lack of formal and informal safety nets likely contributed to their becoming destitute; and once they are destitute, the remaining support systems crumble around them.

Poor women, particularly those with low-caste status, face particularly high risks of becoming destitute. Women in rural UP often marry older men and consequently face a high probability of early widowhood. In some cases they are forced to become the sole income earner in a household with young children. In other cases, women become household heads when they are deserted or when their husbands are disabled. They then face a particularly high risk of destitution because they often do not possess the training and skills required to compete for stable, salaried employment. (Unni, 1998; Dreze, 1990 and Dreze and Srinivasan, 1995). Instead, many are reduced to foraging or begging as their primary means of livelihood.

PROFILE OF THE POOR: POVERTY OF RESOURCES, ACCESS, AND RELATIONSHIPS

Conceptually, poverty is a result of low levels of assets, coupled with low returns on these assets. Almost by definition, the poor have very few assets to draw on beyond their own labour. In addition to being deprived of critical material assets such as land, they also lack education, skills and good health. In this sense they can be said to suffer from *poverty of private resources*. In addition, the poor have limited access to such public assets such as community infrastructure, basic services, and government programmes. In this sense they suffer from *poverty of access to public goods and services*. Finally, they are often deprived of informal systems of support and social and political capital – a *poverty of social relationships*. Policy makers must take all these deprivations into account in order to combat poverty in the state.

Private, Public, and Social Assets: Private Resources

Labour is the most important and abundant asset of the poor. However, it provides the overwhelming majority of those living below the poverty line in UP with only tedious, back-breaking, low-paid jobs with no permanent tenure. In consultations with the poor, better jobs – especially jobs outside the agriculture sector and with security of tenure – were cited repeatedly as the most important priority for urban and rural poor households alike. However, the reality is that agricultural employment in UP, which has been rising in recent years, occupies three-quarters of the labour force, and that a high proportion of the rural poor work as casual labourers – the lowest paid and lowest status occupation in the state.

As in many other parts of India, casualisation of the workforce is on the rise in UP (Leiten and Srivastava, 1999). In 1993/94, nearly two-thirds of rural households who were dependent on earnings from casual labour in the agriculture sector were below the poverty line, as were over half of the households dependent on casual labour earnings outside the agriculture sector (Table 23.5). For these

Table 23.5 Uttar Pradesh: Poverty Incidence by Occupation of Household Head*

Rural Areas Main Occupation	Poverty Incidence	Percentage of Population	Poor	Urban Areas Main Occupation	Poverty Incidence	Percentage of Population	Poor
1983							
S.E. non-agriculture	52.3	13	14	Self-employed	51.6	52	60
Agriculture labour	66.3	16	22				
Other labour	48.2	4	4				
S.E. Agriculture	43.3	61	55				
Other	30.4	7	4	Other	37.1	48	40
Overall	*47.4*	*100*	*100*	Overall	*44.7*	*100*	*100*
1993/94							
S.E. non-agriculture	44.3	13	14	Self-employed	39.9	53	61
Agriculture labour	63.5	18	26	Reg. wage/salary	17.4	31	16
Other labour	52.3	5	6	Casual labour	66.7	11	20
S.E. Agriculture	36.4	58	50				
Other	25.9	6	4	Other	25.8	5	3
Overall	*42.3*	*100*	*100*	Overall	*35.0*	*100*	*100*
1999/2000							
S.E. non-agriculture	28.3	9	7	Self-employed	31.4	44	43
Agriculture labour	50.6	26	40	Reg. wage/salary	18.8	30	17
Other labour	43.9	5	6	Casual labour	62.5	16	31
S.E. Agriculture	27.1	54	44				
Other	14.9	6	3	Other	28.8	10	9
Overall	*33.2*	*100*	*100*	Overall	*32.4*	*100*	*100*

Notes: S.E. = Self-employed.

* Profile tables presented here use official poverty lines and data from the 38th, 43rd, 50th and 55th Rounds of the NSS. All tabulations are based on the NSS central sample. As discussed earlier, changes in survey design may impact on the comparability of 55th Round estimates, in relation to those from earlier rounds of the NSS. Thus, comparisons between the 55th and earlier rounds should be made with care.

Source: 1983, 1993/94, and 1999/2000 NSS.

households, poverty levels remained virtually unchanged from the mid-eighties to the mid-nineties (1983/84 to 1993/94), a period when, in contrast, poverty fell sharply for farm households, self-employed households in the rural non-farm sector and for households with salaried employment. These trends continued through the latter part of the 1990s; rural poverty is increasingly associated with casual labour in agriculture as well as in the rural non-farm sector.

The urban poor are more likely to be involved in casual wage labour, or work in the informal sector, both associated with high levels of poverty. In 1993/94, 11 per cent of urban households were primarily dependent on casual work, and two-thirds of these households lived below the poverty line. By 1999/2000, 16 per cent of the population were dependent on casual work and two-thirds of them still lived below the poverty line. In contrast, the self-employed are evidencing significant gains in terms of rising incomes and falling poverty.

After labour, *land* is the most crucial asset for the rural poor; poverty falls as land ownership rises. However, many of the poorest households own little or no land, and land holdings in UP have become more fragmented over time, with implications for the structure of rural poverty (Table 23.6). In 1983, 27 per cent of the population, corresponding to 30 per cent of the rural poor, owned less than a half

Table 23.6 Uttar Pradesh: Rural Poverty Incidence by Land Ownership

Amt. of land owned	Poverty Incidence	Percentage of	
		Population	Poor
1983/84			
No land owned	37.6	3	2
0–0.4 hectares	57.4	24	28
0.4–1 hectares	58.5	13	15
1-2 hectares	51.7	18	20
2–4 hectares	45.6	20	19
4+ hectares	30.7	23	15
Overall	47.5	100	100
1993/94			
No land owned	51.5	6	8
0–0.4 hectares	52.7	37	46
0.4–1 hectares	41.5	25	24
1-2 hectares	34.6	17	14
2–4 hectares	24.8	10	6
4+ hectares	19.8	5	2
Overall	42.4	100	100
1999/2000			
No land owned	40.6	4	5
0–0.4 hectares	40.7	47	57
0.4–1 hectares	31.3	24	22
1-2 hectares	22.4	15	10
2–4 hectares	17.7	7	4
4+ hectares	10.4	3	1
Overall	33.2	100	100

Source: 1983, 1993/94, and 1999/2000 NSS.

hectare of land. By 1993/94, the number of households owning less than a half hectare had risen to 43 per cent and accounted for 54 per cent of the rural poor. By 1999/2000 nearly two-thirds of the rural population, or 62 per cent of the poor, owned less than a half hectare of land – far less than what is needed to provide for a family's subsistence needs. The trend toward rising poverty among landless and near-landless households suggests that either the rural non-farm sector has failed to provide employment, or that the poor lack the education or skills to take advantage of the opportunities available. Both hypotheses are probably true.

Because rural power is traditionally associated with land ownership, land is more than a material asset in UP; it is also a political arbitrator. Rural landlords control the livelihoods of those working on their land and have historically used these relationships of dependency to maintain economic, social, and political dominance. And while land ownership is becoming less closely linked to power, rural elites continue to have influence in many spheres of rural life and politics.

Human capital is also an important asset for the poor. While land is difficult to redistribute, *education* is provided by the public sector and should be universally available in the state. Indeed, 'Education for All' is an important national as well as state-level objective. Schooling can play a potentially powerful role in promoting economic mobility and reducing poverty, and the poor are not likely to benefit from reform-led growth unless they have the skills and education to take advantage of the opportunities it offers. Concomitantly, in many regions of UP, lack of educational opportunity deepens a vicious cycle of poverty and illiteracy.

Poverty is strongly associated with levels of formal education. This is most strikingly the case in urban areas, but the relationship holds in rural areas as well. In 1993/94, 59 per cent of urban households headed by illiterates were poor, in contrast to only 7 per cent of households whose heads had completed tertiary education (Table 23.7). The link between poverty outcomes and education was marginally

Table 23.7 Uttar Pradesh: Poverty Incidence by Education of the Household Head

Highest Educational Attainment of Head	Incidence of Poverty			Percentage of	
	Urban	Rural	Overall	Population	Poor
1993/94					
Not literate	58.6	50.6	51.6	53	66
Less than primary	43.1	36.7	37.9	11	11
Completed primary	46.3	33.5	35.9	10	9
Completed middle	26.5	32.3	31.0	10	7
Completed secondary	18.9	25.6	23.3	6	4
Completed higher level	6.8	19.6	13.4	10	3
Overall	*35.0*	*42.4*	*40.9*	*100*	*100*
1999/2000					
Not literate	40.4	51.7	41.8	48	61
Less than primary	34.2	41.9	35.6	11	12
Completed primary	32.6	42.2	34.2	9	9
Completed middle	23.9	29.4	24.8	11	8
Completed secondary	20.7	23.2	21.3	9	6
Completed higher level	14.0	8.6	11.8	12	4
Overall	*33.2*	*32.5*	*33.1*	*100*	*100*

Note: Less than primary includes those who are literate, but have no formal schooling.
Source: 1993/94, 1999/2000 NSS.

weaker in rural areas, where 51 per cent of 'illiterate' households and 20 per cent of households whose head had a tertiary education were poor. However, by 1999/2000, the link between poverty and education had become stronger in rural areas: 52 per cent of illiterates were poor, as compared to only 9 per cent of households whose head had a tertiary education. More research remains to be done on this topic. However, these results suggest that even a little education does help to open economic opportunities in rural areas. Because of a threshold effect in UP's urban areas, much higher levels of education may be necessary to open up employment opportunities there.

The Urban Poverty Study, which was carried out in poor, unrecognised settlements and included focus groups with urban youths, helps to explain these findings. While many young people are literate, surprisingly few aspire to more education, and many do not see how having more education would help them get better jobs. Rather, respondents stressed the importance of work skills, informal training, and personal contacts. It was not that education did not matter, but rather that the kinds of jobs open to young people living in very poor and marginalised urban settings do not require or reward higher levels of education. Poor parents in some of the rural field studies voiced similar views.

As noted in earlier in the chapter, average enrolments have been rising in the state. Comparisons between the NSS 42nd Round (1986/87) and 52nd Round (1995/96) indicate that rural primary school enrolment rates for 7–12-year-old girls from the poorest 40 per cent of households almost doubled over 10 years – from around 20 per cent of the relevant age group to an estimated 40 per cent (Deaton, 2000). More recent estimates from the NSS 55th Round state sample show continuing improvements, particularly in education levels of girls and SC/STs (Table 23.8) in the relevant age group. By the end of the 1990s the gap between boys' and girls' enrolments had virtually closed in urban areas and narrowed considerably in the countryside. Despite this, still less than 60 per cent of children from the poorest 20 per cent of the population were enrolled in school, and school enrollments for poorest quintile living in urban areas were even lower than rural enrolments.

Good health is another productive asset that can be hard for the poor to attain or maintain. Often linked to inadequate calorie intakes and malnutrition, poverty increases the risk of getting sick and exacerbating illnesses. Lower-income settlements in urban areas are often clustered in waterlogged, malarial zones, or in areas where poor sanitation makes exposure to waste water and raw sewage all but inevitable. A recent study in a very poor area of southern UP (Parker, 1998) found that low-income informants know little of disease etiology and prevention, even by developing-country standards. The higher risks associated with poverty are reflected in the gap between health status indicators for the rich

Table 23.8 Average School Enrolment Rates,Children Aged 7–12 Years, 1999/2000 (Per cent)

	Rural Areas			Urban Areas		
	Boys	Girls	Total	Boys	Girls	Total
Poorest 20%	68	51	61	55	51	53
2nd Quintile	74	63	69	71	66	69
3rd Quintile	77	68	74	79	78	78
4th Quintile	78	72	76	81	87	83
Wealthiest 20%	85	79	82	92	90	91
Total State	74	63	69	77	77	77

Source: NSS 55th Round, UP State Sample, survey tabulations.

and poor in India as a whole. Survey data from the first National Family Health Survey (NFHS-1) in 1992/93 indicates that infant and child mortality rates among the poorest 20 per cent of the national population are two-and-a-half times higher than among the wealthiest 20 per cent. Since the cost of treating major health problems is one of the shocks that plunges many of its citizens into destitution, it is imperative that India's health system be better prepared to address the special vulnerability of the poor to infectious diseases and malnutrition.

Based on the National Family Health Survey (NFHS-1, 1992/93), children's health in UP is noticeably affected by poverty (Table 23.9), to the point that stunting is widespread.[8] In addition, unlike all-India estimates, children from all economic strata are likely to be stunted, a reflection of a poor general environment, e.g. one lacking clean air and water and sanitation, as well as the inadequacy of health services for rich and poor alike. Also, children from the poorest households are particularly likely to be un-immunised or only partially immunised. In UP, an estimated 60 per cent of children from the poorest 40 per cent of the population had never been immunised, compared to 45 per cent at the all-India level. Unfortunately, while NFHS-2 results have recently been released for UP, wealth-based tabulations are not yet available.

Table 23.9 Comparison of Health Status of Children in Uttar Pradesh, by Quintile

	Poorest 20%	Quintile 2	Quintile 3	Quintile 4	Wealthiest 20%	Total
Stunting						
UP	61.5	65.0	58.7	61.6	59.3	61.7
All India	*55.6*	*54.0*	*48.6*	*43.4*	*30.9*	*47.1*
No Immunisations						
UP	56.9	60.3	44.3	47.4	33.4	48.5
All India	*48.4*	*40.8*	*27.5*	*18.0*	*7.9*	*30.0*
All Immunisations						
UP	9.8	10.8	17.5	17.3	27.9	16.6
All India	*17.1*	*21.7*	*34.7*	*48.2*	*65.0*	*35.4*

Source: NFHS-1, 1992/93, World Bank Tabulations.

Access to Public Goods and Services

As highlighted by the above discussion on health outcomes, government policy operates to reduce poverty both indirectly by enhancing growth, and directly through the delivery of basic services, particularly in health and education, and effective safety-net and anti-poverty programmes. Spending on roads, agriculture research, and education have been shown to make particularly strong impacts on rural productivity and poverty reduction in India. Power and irrigation are likewise important for enhancing rural productivity, while health and rural development projects implemented primarily as anti-poverty programmes, are designed to address poverty directly (Fan, Hazell, and Thorat, 2000). There is indeed widespread evidence that local public goods – for example roads, communication systems, irrigation, schools and health facilities – exert a strong influence on returns to private capital (for agriculture, see Schiff and Montenegro, 1997; Dev and Ranade, 1998; for health outcomes, see Hughes and Dunleavy, 2000; and Jalan and Ravallion, 2000). However, while agriculture terms-of-trade have improved in the 1990s, they have not resulted in improvements in productivity or levels of output, nor in lower rates of

---

[8] Stunting is often considered an indicator of longer term poor nutrition status.

poverty. Non-price incentives, such as under-investment in infrastructure and problems linked to the business environment, are in large part responsible for this lagging response by the agricultural sector.

Compared to better performing states, levels of infrastructure development are low in Uttar Pradesh. For example, per capita consumption of electricity was only 194 kWh in UP but 332 kWh per capita in Andhra Pradesh and 338 kWh in Karnataka. As of March 1999, UP had 1.21 telecom connections per 100 inhabitants, whereas Andhra Pradesh had 2.36 and Karnataka, 3.25 per 100 inhabitants (Kurian, 2000). Inadequate infrastructure and, in particular, the decreasing availability and reliability of power supply and water for irrigation, have lowered productivity in both agriculture and industry. This has contributed to lower rates of poverty reduction. In addition, government spending on infrastructure, social sectors, and rural development has been sluggish in recent years, and O&M significantly underfunded. Not only are spending levels low: weak institutions reduce the efficiency of spending, and produce outputs – as measured in delivery of services – that are themselves poor. Higher spending does not necessarily mean better services.

Whether underfunded or underserved, the regions of UP with high concentrations of poor people tend to have lower endowments of infrastructure and other basic services. The UP/Bihar Poverty Study assessed the status of community infrastructure as well as geographic access to such basic facilities and services as electricity, drinking water, public schools, public and private health care providers, the Anganwadi Centre (Integrated Child Development Services), and the PDS fair-price shop. Even within a village, poor and socially disadvantaged households tend to live further from basic services such as hand pumps and public wells, sanitation systems, public health facilities and schools, the PDS ration shop, and public transportation facilities. Few have piped water or other sources of drinking water on their premises, and, although the majority of villages in India are electrified, few poor and socially disadvantaged households are connected to the electricity grid (Box 23.5).

Early tabulations from the NSS 55th Round highlight continuing inequities across UP between the access enjoyed by the poorest and wealthiest households[9] to basic community services and housing amenities. In rural areas, the poorest households are far more likely to live in housing made of temporary materials, and most lack access to electricity, water, and sanitation. Disparities also are evident in UP's cities and towns. Many of the poor still live in temporary housing and over 40 per cent do not have access to electricity, even for basic lighting. Generally, many of the poorest urban households live in 'unrecognised' settlements, without access to public services or facilities of any kind.

Box 23.5 Access to Facilities in Rural Uttar Pradesh

A study of poverty in four districts in Eastern and Southern UP highlights the gap in access between better-off and less well-off households:

Services Available in the Dwelling Unit	Poorest 20%	Wealthiest 20%
Electricity	4%	28%
Drinking water	25%	66%
Services Available in the Hamlet		
(only if available in revenue village)	Poorest 20%	Wealthiest 20%
Primary school	59%	61%
Middle school	6%	83%
Anganwadi centre	38%	60%
PDS fair-price shop	43%	57%

Source: UP/Bihar Poverty Study, survey tabulations.

---

[9] Ranked by per capita expenditure levels.

Box 23.6 Signs of Transition

Location matters a great deal within a rural village, as does security of tenure. Take the example of a group of Kols (Scheduled castes) living in a village in Banda District. In the pre-Independence era, the Kols lived in the main village, on land owned by wealthy high-caste families, mostly from the Thakur caste. During that time, the Kols were deeply impoverished and most were in debt bondage to their Thakur landlords and suffered daily insults and humiliations when necessity forced them to fetch water from Thakur wells or to defecate in fields owned by Thakurs. After liberation, debt bondage was eliminated and the Kols were freed. The Thakurs, however, refused to allow the Kols to use wells or build houses unless they agreed to serve Thakur families under a system similar to the old one. The older Kols were ready to agree, but the younger generation threatened to rebel. Faced with the possibility of social unrest, the Pradhan agreed to grant public lands to the Kols for the creation of their own *tola* (settlements or small communities). These lands were waterlogged and largely unproductive, but they provided homestead plots which allowed most of the Kol families to move out of the control of their former Thakur landlords. Now, the Kol families rely in part on the collection and sale of forest products, and supplement this by undertaking 'work for any caste who calls them' at the prevailing wage rate. In addition, they now have their own well and are no longer harassed and humiliated when collecting water. Several Kol families remained behind in the Thakur *tola*, but other Kols feel they are poorer than those who have moved. Thakurs interviewed in the same village indicated that in cases of illness or disaster, they provide interest-free loans for Kol families whom they know and trust. These families, however, are only those who work for them on a continuing basis. Thus, by leaving the Thakurs behind, the Kol households who relocated have lost a source of interest-free help in time of trouble. Nevertheless, most of them find that their gains – in dignity and economic independence – have more than compensated for this loss.

Source: Field visits, UP/Bihar Poverty Study, 1998.

Notably, according to our evidence, even when a facility such as a public tap or well was physically available, many of the poor, especially those from lower castes, were either discouraged or actively prevented from using it. Indeed, as illustrated by Box 23.6, social access is as important in many parts of rural UP, as is physical access.

The urban poor, many of whom live in unrecognised settlements lacking services of any kind, face similar problems (Box 23.7). In many communities, the biggest drawback is lack of access to clean, potable water and sanitary facilities such as public toilets. Many respondents were aware of the role of poor sanitation and contaminated water in causing illness, but few thought they had any control over the situation. Women often complained of having to walk long distances to fetch water from public taps.

Box 23.7 Unrecognised Settlements: The Urban Underclass

Although poverty is the norm in UP's urban slums and informal settlements, conditions that most impinge on economic opportunity are found in its 'unrecognised' settlements. Most poor urban neighbourhoods, or 'notified slums,' are recognised by local governments and receive basic city services including water, sewage processing, garbage removal and, in most cases, electrical connections. The most precarious of the informal settlements, however, are located on land that is either owned by government or by a private individual or organisation that has no interest in using or developing the site. The residents of these neighbourhoods, or bustees, have no legal right to their home sites, though they have often paid a significant fee to a neighbourhood leader for squatting privileges. The urban poverty study team visited an unrecognised settlement in Lucknow that has been in existence for nearly 25 years, though the city authorities still record the site as unoccupied land. Located on the banks of a *nalla*, or drainage ditch, it had no source of clean drinkable water until residents were able to gather the money to tap (illegally) into a city water main and establish a public tap. Now, about 95 families use this one water source, and most of the friction in the community is said to arise over the water queues. There are no latrines; all residents use the canal banks for defecation. There is also no public school in or near the *bustee*, but a NGO has hired a teacher to instruct 20-30 of the children for a few hours a week. In many unrecognised bustees, however, none of the children are in school. Their parents recognise that without basic literacy, these children will not be able to break out of deep poverty. However, no public schooling is provided for unrecognised settlements and bustee residents cannot afford private school fees.

Source: Field visits, Urban Poverty Study in Uttar Pradesh, 2000.

Social Capital

In our discussion of assets that are in short supply among the poor, we turn finally to *social capital* – the stock of relationships, networks, and institutions that an individual or household invests in and can call on for assistance and support when needed. Social capital can be utilised in different ways. It can serve a 'protective' function – for example, rural consultations identified cases in which associations were formed amongst groups of scheduled castes for purposes of mutual protection, such as when SC women travel together when they go to the forest to collect firewood. Social ties also can be used for 'productive' purpose and economic advancement. An example of this is caste associations which help members obtain labour contracts or jobs.

The poor in UP were found to have less social capital, and in particular fewer horizontal social ties, and to more frequently utilise protective rather than productive forms of social capital. Most networks are open only to those who have something to contribute, which means that the poor are generally excluded. Occasionally, however, poor individuals have banded together and built their own networks and organisations, often with the help of a local NGO. One example of this is the recent upsurge in savings groups set up for poor women, which are being organised through the facilitation of government programmes as well as non-government organisations. Women in the group contribute a very small sum of money on a regular basis; the aggregate savings are eventually deposited in an account in a local bank, which helps to establish a link with formal financial institutions. Women in the group can then borrow from the aggregate savings in times of need, and some groups have even used the accumulated savings to set up a joint business.

But the general picture remains bleak. Drawing on qualitative field studies buttressed by analysis of household surveys, we find that poor households rarely enjoy any advantageous ties or contacts outside their own poor neighbourhoods. Their social capital is primarily restricted to patron-client relationships with landowners/employers and occasional exchanges with equally poor households in times of need, and is therefore rarely of the type that will lift them out of poverty. However, even potentially exploitative linkages are worth maintaining as possible sources of limited assistance in a short-term crisis. Such

---

Box 23.8 Why Invest in Social Relations?

B** is a large village comprising some 700 households and constitutes a panchayat on its own. Politically and economically the village is dominated by Patidars (approximately 35 per cent), who are known as a progressive farming caste [now classified as Other Backward Caste (OBC)]. The rest of the population forms a mixture of other OBCs, various SCs as well as a small population of STs. The Sarpanch is a woman from the Patidar caste. Her husband and his relatives however, largely carry out her work. In comparison with other Gram Panchayats people in B** are not too dissatisfied with the community works implemented by the Panchayat. Gutters, roads, and tube-well have been built in various parts of the village during the last five years. However, there is a commonly held perception that individual benefits can only be accessed by people who have a relationship with the Sarpanch's family. Such relationships are formed on the basis of frequent labour work for the Sarpanch and her kin, purchasing goods from shops owned by them, and voting in their favour. Many of these people are dependent on the Patidars for their livelihoods. Some of them also fall into the more vulnerable sections of the village and most of them are SCs and STs. The people who feel that they are excluded from the individual benefits of the Panchayat emphasise that they lack the awareness of what to do to change the situation and they do not know whom to turn to outside the Panchayat. One Wardpanch said that he has no powers, but that he and other Wardpanches have to go along with whatever the Patidars decide in the Panchayat as many of them are also dependent on the Patidars for labour. A few villagers spoken to stressed that it is not in their hands to improve the Panchayat and that turning to higher officers will not help as they will say that it is not their business and direct them back to the Gram Panchayat.

Source: Consultations on Poverty Monitoring, 1999.

assistance may include a sack of grain in times of scarcity or a short-term loan to purchase food. Moreover, the poor generally have limited influence in the political sphere. In contrast, the better-off tend to possess a strong network of high-value ties and contacts that help not only to mitigate risk and improve overall welfare levels but often also to enable the better-off to capture more than their fair share of public resources. In the aforementioned studies, higher caste and well-off households, unlike poor and SC/ST households, were found to have useful contacts outside the village. Links with political party officials, for example, helped wealthy households to secure recognition of questionable land rights and to ensure that community infrastructure improvements would be located in the affluent neighbourhoods. Close relations between richer households and both political and administrative arms of government are often used to undermine democratic processes.

SOCIAL IDENTITY AND ECONOMIC EXCLUSION

Economic growth is a powerful force for poverty reduction, but few, if any, modern societies deliver equal opportunities to benefit from such growth to all their citizens. Evidence from around the world suggests that the rising tide of economic growth does not lift all boats equally, and there are forces at work that limit opportunities for some individuals and groups. To varying degrees, countless groups ranging from indigenous populations in Bolivia and Guatemala to ethnic minorities in Sri Lanka and Vietnam, as well as groups and communities in such countries as Australia, Russia, and the United States, experience some form of social discrimination that impacts on economic well-being and limits the returns on the material, human and social assets which they possess. Throughout the world – again to varying degrees – women also experience these disadvantages. In Uttar Pradesh, exclusion based on gender and social identity is not only deeply ingrained, it is also a powerful contributing factor to the persistence of poverty. In light of this, this section looks at the role played by gender and caste in limiting or barring opportunities to escape poverty.

Links between Caste and Poverty

Consultations in rural villages for the 1998 UP/Bihar Poverty Study and the 1999 Consultations on Poverty Monitoring paint a vivid picture of the many links that exist between social identity and poverty in UP. The vast majority of respondents, rich and poor alike, identified a poor household as one at the low end of the caste hierarchy – most often a member of the scheduled castes or scheduled tribes. Indeed, social identity is a strong predictor of who is and is not poor, who is illiterate, who is employed in low-paid, low status agricultural labour, and who lives in poorly constructed housing with limited access to basic services. Despite decades of effort on the part of successive governments, SC/STs are twice as likely to suffer poverty as material deprivation, as are 'majority' individuals, i.e. the aggregate of all non-SC/STs. Accordingly, while SC/STs accounted for only 23 per cent of the UP population in 1993/94, they comprised one-third of the total poor in the state. Worryingly, recent estimates for 1999/2000 suggest at best limited progress in remedying this imbalance[10] (Table 23.10).

A number of factors explain the gap in living standards between SC/ST and majority households. First, SC/STs tend to possess fewer private assets, in particular, less and poorer quality land, as well as lower levels of human capital. The latter trend is particularly disadvantageous: in light of difficulties in

---

[10] 1999/2000 headcount estimates are not strictly comparable to estimates based on earlier rounds of the NSS.

Table 23.10 Poverty Incidence by Caste, 1987/88, 1993/94, and 1999/2000

Year	Caste Group	Incidence of Poverty			Percentage of	
		Urban	Rural	Overall	Population	Poor
1987/88	SC / ST	48.3	56.2	55.3	24	32
	Other	35.7	37.5	37.2	76	68
	Overall	*37.4*	*42.3*	*41.5*	*100*	*100*
1993/94	SC / ST	57.5	58.6	58.4	23	33
	Other	31.3	37.0	35.7	77	67
	Overall	*35.0*	*42.4*	*40.9*	*100*	*100*
1999/2000	SC/ST	44.1	44.0	44.0	26	35
	Other	30.3	29.4	29.6	74	65
	Overall	*32.5*	*33.2*	*33.1*	*100*	*100*

Source: NSS 1987/88, 1993/94, 1999/2000. ·

redistributing land, and the importance of opportunities in the non-farm sector, education could play an important role in improving welfare for poor and socially-marginalised households. Recent evidence suggests that children from (rural) SC/ST households are less likely to be enrolled in school than children from majority households, although the gap has been closing. In 1995/96 (NSS 52nd Round), 41 per cent of SC/ST girls 6–14 years of age were enrolled in school in rural areas, as compared to 50 per cent of girls from majority households. The gap in boys' school enrolments was smaller – 78 per cent of SC/ST boys were enrolled in comparison to 83 per cent of boys from other households. Enrolment gaps were particularly notable for SC/STs from the poorest households. By 1999/2000 (NSS 55th Round), enrolments for rural SC/ST girls had risen to 55 per cent as compared to 61 per cent enrolments for girls from majority households. Interestingly however, there is a wider gap in enrolments between SC/STs and girls from majority households in urban areas – 67 per cent of SC/ST girls in urban areas are enrolled in school, as compared to 75 per cent for girls from majority households.

Why are children from lower-caste households less likely to attend school? One reason has to do with expected returns. In discussions with lower-caste households, education was only rarely described as a means to facilitate economic mobility. One notable symptom of this was that despite significant progress in boosting girl's enrolment rates over the past 10 years, not a single SC/ST girl was attending school in several of the villages visited during the qualitative phase of the work. Heirs to a social identity that places them at a disadvantage in interactions with higher castes, the SC/STs see the stigma they carry as life long, a burden to be inherited in turn by their own children. In many cases, this stigma may cancel the advantage conferred by secondary or higher education in the competition for high-paying jobs (see Table 23.11). On the other hand, few SC/ST informants saw opportunities for advancement in the traditional village economy. With prospects at home being limited, most looked elsewhere for opportunities for social and economic advancement – to the rural non-farm sector or to jobs in the city. Encouragingly, research in urban areas suggests that barriers linked to social identity begin to break down as poor households move out of the traditional economy (Parker, Kukreja and Kozel, 2001). If this trend continues, the motivation of SC/ST's to invest in the higher education of children may grow, particularly in urban areas.

Returns to Assets

Findings from a recent study (Lanjouw and Zaidi, 2001) suggest that low-caste households are not only

Table 23.11 Differential Returns to Assets: Scheduled Caste/Tribe and Other Castes (Per Cent)

Dependent Variable: Log Per Capita Consumption	All-India		Uttar Pradesh	
	Majority	Scheduled Caste	Majority	Scheduled Caste
Rural areas				
Household size	−0.026	−0.035	−0.014	−0.029
Per capita land owned	0.069	0.067	0.186	0.164
Proportion of adults with:				
Education below primary level	0.162	0.117	0.215	0.073
Primary education	0.255	0.199	0.230	0.215
Middle school education	0.353	0.268	0.298	0.284
Matriculation	0.561	0.501	0.430	0.413
Higher secondary or more	0.819	0.781	0.626	0.478
Urban areas				
Household size	−0.074	−0.069	−0.056	−0.048
Proportion of adults with:				
Primary education or below	0.177	0.151	0.226	0.125
Middle school or matriculation	0.420	0.327	0.403	0.417
Higher secondary or more	0.864	0.697	0.804	0.595

Source: From Lanjouw and Zaidi (2001) based on the 1993/94 NSS Consumer Expenditure Survey.

worse-off in terms of levels of assets, but also experience lower economic returns to the minimal stock they do possess, including their human capital. According to NSS data from the mid-1990s, per capita consumption of SC/ST households in Uttar Pradesh is about 30 per cent lower on average than in other (majority) households. To some extent, this gap is due to the fact that the lower caste households own less land as well as other assets, in particular human capital. For instance, at 0.26 acres per person, per capita landholdings of scheduled caste households in UP are a little more than a third those of majority households, at 0.70 acres per person. Similarly, the survey data show that about 80 per cent of adults in rural scheduled caste households in UP had received no education, as compared to 58 per cent in majority households. Similar disadvantages exist in urban areas. 57 per cent of adults in urban scheduled caste households had received no education, in comparison to only 34 per cent in majority households.

But differences in welfare levels are not just explained by differences in stocks of assets. A regression model employing data from the 1993/94 NSSO survey was used to estimate determinants of per capita consumption separately for SC/ST households and majority households for Uttar Pradesh, as well as the all-India population. These results indicate that while about half the difference in welfare between the two groups could be attributed to differences in asset holdings, a roughly equal share was due to differences in returns to asset stocks. Although the results for Uttar Pradesh did not differ significantly in this respect from those for India as a whole, this finding nonetheless raises some troubling questions about possible causes of these differences.

Further analysis yielded a number of interesting findings. Not surprisingly, increases in household size for both SC/ST and majority households were associated with lower per capita consumption. Similarly, returns to land were found to be positive and significant for both groups of households, as were returns to education in both the majority and SC/ST group. However, closer examination of the results reveals some significant differences between the parameter estimates for the two groups (Table 23.10). Specifically, as noted above, not only did SC/ST households own less land, they also experienced lower returns to the land they did own. In education, SC/STs with low levels of education (primary or less) experienced lower returns than did majority households. Notably, the gap is larger in UP than in the all-India findings. Returns to higher education also appear low in rural UP relative to the rest of rural India – a finding that probably reflects the relative scarcity of good opportunities for people with high education levels, as well as restricted access to employment opportunities for SC/ST job seekers. Returns to higher education in urban UP are similar to all-India urban returns, although returns for SC/ST workers are clearly lower than those for well-educated workers from majority households, at the all-India level, and particularly for urban UP.

Further work is needed in order to understand the factors behind these results, particularly in light of India's wide range of 'affirmative action' programmes and policies. One important message does emerge from the current exercise, namely that while policies to raise the human capital of SC/ST households and strengthen their other productive assets holdings must remain a priority, these alone will not be sufficient to close the gap between the two groups.

Location and Land Ownership

Location and Land Ownership distinguish many low-caste households. SC and ST families often live in separate hamlets at the edge of the village, although a few may occupy a homestead plot in the village, belonging to an upper-caste employer. In surveys, lack of a homestead plot was seen as a particularly grave form of landlessness, leaving homeless households at the mercy of wealthy landlords. Hamlets occupied by SC/ST households also tend to be located at some distance from public facilities such as clean wells and paved roads, as well as schools, public health centres, including even Integrated Child Development Services (ICDS) and the PDS fair-price shops that are specifically intended to serve the poor.

In addition, landlessness, entailing a lack of access to fertile, well-watered agricultural land, was mentioned as a cause and characteristic of poverty in every village covered in the UP/Bihar Poverty Study. SCs and STs rarely own land, and when they do, it is of such marginal quality that few households can support themselves by tilling only these plots. Most, accordingly, depend on earnings from casual labour. Some low-caste workers, however, become attached labourers, typically receiving from an upper-caste patron a small plot of land, either a homestead and/or an agricultural plot, as well as other benefits, such as access to credit and food during lean periods. Some become deeply indebted to their supposed patron. Such labourers must work on the agricultural fields of the patron whenever called upon to do so, usually at a wage that is no more than half the rate for unattached casual labour. It is not rare for a whole family to become attached in this way, to the point that even children are apportioned labour or service obligations.

Employment

Employment is another arena in which social identity is linked to poverty. Individuals from low-caste households work disproportionately in low-paid, low-status jobs as agricultural labourers or low-skill labourers in the non-agriculture sector. Indeed, along with female workers, they form the mainstay of the agricultural labour force. And poor women from low-caste households are invariably trapped in the lowest paid and least desirable kinds of work. Although the traditional occupations associated with India's various castes and sub-castes generally do not determine the livelihood of individuals in today's labour market, members of low-caste groups are nevertheless still clustered in less desirable and lower paid activities (Box 23.9). Except in the case of agricultural labour, where all workers earn equally low

---

Box 23.9 Patterns of Employment in Rural UP – Poverty and Caste

Unlike the NSS, the survey undertaken for the UP/Bihar Poverty Study provides detailed information on time spent by various household members in income earning activities. Based on this information, the poorest households were found to depend heavily on earnings from casual labour in both the farm and non-farm sectors. Few have salaried employment. Time spent on own-farm activities increases steadily with income levels, and the best-off among rural households combine earnings from salaried employment with farming.

Distribution of Employment Days	Per capita consumption quintile					
	1st	2nd	3rd	4th	5th	Overall
Self-employed farming	14.6	27.8	30.5	37.4	49.9	33.4
Self-employed non-farm	21.5	19.3	22.1	19.6	14.4	19.1
Agriculture labourer	23.7	11.9	15.1	9.1	6.0	12.5
Non-farm labourer	25.9	25.0	18.9	19.3	5.0	18.0
Salaried employment	8.8	13.1	9.5	12.2	22.8	13.8

Very low-caste households (viz., SC/STs) also were heavily represented in the agriculture sector, particularly as casual labours. And those who did not work as casual labourers in agriculture were likely to be working as casual labourers in non-farm activities. Few members of the low-caste households had permanent or secure jobs.

Distribution of Employment Days	Upper	Other Backward	SC/ST
Self-employed farming	39.1	42.2	20.5
Self-employed non-farm	14.8	19.9	11.8
Agriculture labourer	1.5	7.6	29.4
Non-farm labourer	11.0	17.5	23.6
Salaried employment	31.6	11.2	12.0

Source: UP/Bihar Poverty Study, survey tabulations.

---

wages, SC/STs earn less on average than do individuals from upper castes in all other occupations in rural areas. Notably, other Backward Castes (OBCs) and Muslims face similar, if not as extreme earnings differentials (Srivastava, 2000).

Links between Gender and Poverty

As noted in the introduction to this paper, gender also is linked in many ways to poverty. A disproportionate number of the very poor and destitute live in female-headed households. Many of these women are destitute because their gender forecloses many occupations and other opportunities to participate equally with men in political and economic life. In addition, the returns to their most basic asset – labour – are lower than those obtained by men. When a village woman becomes her family's chief breadwinner, she may find work in agriculture, but she is commonly paid only a half to two-thirds of the wage a man receives for performing the same work. Particularly if her parents were poor, she is unlikely to be literate or to have any qualifications for non-agricultural employment. Some women are even reluctant to enrol any of their daughters in school, since married daughters take their educational benefits, if any, to their husbands' families. These barriers enhance the likelihood that the women will fall into destitution in case of a shock such as desertion, disability, or death of a spouse. Clear evidence of the disadvantage imposed on women in Uttar Pradesh is provided by demographic data from the 1998/99 National Family

Health Survey (NFHS-2, IIPS, 2000), which found only 927 females for every 1,000 males in the general population. This is lower than the all-India average (NFHS-2, IIPS, 2000) of 949 females for every 1,000 males and is strikingly different than sex ratios in many other countries. Usually, the biological advantage of females leads to higher survival rates and sex ratios.

Economic Contributions of Women

One of the many complex issues on which this study touches is the interplay between the valuation of women on the basis of their perceived and actual economic contribution. In the supporting qualitative research, women in many parts of the state and particularly in rural areas, were perceived as having little or no potential for adding to the economic standing of the household. Moreover, cultural ideals in UP society dictate that respectable women should remain in the home and not engage in work for pay. Poor families are rarely able to conform to this ideal, yet even they undervalue women's economic contribution. Indeed, women were often regarded as a burden because they often possess fewer skills and earn lower pay, and because female offsprings usually require dowry for marriage. However, some respondents also recognised that some low-caste households improve their economic situation when their women supplement family income through employment in the fields or homes of others. This awareness may indicate a trend that could, in the longer term, result in full acceptance of women operating economically outside the household. If so, women's autonomy may ultimately increase. On the negative side, until women are more fully empowered, it is likely that the pattern of the 'triple' economic, social, and reproductive burden of women will continue.

Employment Patterns of UP Women

Women are under-represented in the labour force in UP, even more so than in most other states. Comparable estimates show that the workforce participation rates of women are lower than the national level, and significantly lower than in the southern states. According to recent estimates (NSS 55th Round), 16.4 per cent of rural females aged 5 years and older were working[12] in UP, as compared to 25.3 per cent at the all-India level.[13] Female employment is also lower in the cities. In UP, 8.4 per cent of urban females were employed outside the household, as compared to 12.8 per cent for the country as a whole. (NSSO, 2000) Unfortunately, analysis of NSS as well as employment rates from the Population Census (Dreze and Gazdar, 1997) suggest that there has been little change in either the level or structure of women's employment over the past few decades. This is a concern, given current patterns of female employment; women who do work are typically engaged in the lowest-paid activities, including day labour in the fields, foraging for firewood and dung, piecework, or unskilled construction work.

Indeed, a high proportion of female workers is concentrated in low-paid casual work, primarily in the agriculture sector (Table 23.11). While participation in non-farm employment has increased for both men and women, the rate of increase for females has been relatively slow. In 1993/94, only 10 per cent of rural female workers were engaged in non-agricultural activities. In consequence, there has been a feminisation of the agricultural workforce, as the relative proportion of both female cultivators and female agricultural labourers has grown. One possible cause of this shift is male migration in search of

---

[12] Work participation is defined as the average number of persons employed in a week, based on reported current weekly employment status. See the recent NSS report on employment and unemployment for the 55th Round for a more detailed discussion (NSSO, 2000).

[13] Average employment rates mask considerable variation in women's employment patterns over the calendar year, because during peak planting and harvest seasons a high percentage of rural women are pulled into the workforce.

Table 23.12 Distribution of Employment by Gender

Distribution of Employment Days	Male	Female	Total
Self emp.: farming	29.7	47.5	33.4
Self-emp.: non-farm	20.3	14.4	19.1
Agriculture labourer	8.7	27.3	12.5
Non-farm labourer	21.6	4.1	18.0
Salaried employment	16.6	2.8	13.8
Total	100.0	100.0	100.0

Source: UP/Bihar Poverty Study, 1998.

better-paid off-farm employment. As men move away to seek higher wages, many of the women left behind take up casual employment in the agriculture sector – low-paid, low-status, dead-end work. Cultural factors constrain women's ability to move freely in order to seek economic opportunity.

HETEROGENEITY OF THE POOR: THE IMPORTANCE FOR POLICY AND PROGRAMME DESIGN

The term 'poverty' may in itself be misleading if it suggests that all low-income households share a common set of characteristics. In fact, the poor are a heterogeneous group. As discussed above, deprivation has many dimensions; and not all poor households are deprived in the same ways. Poor households differ with respect to the depth of poverty they experience, the material, human and social resources they can marshal, the opportunities offered by their surroundings, and the strategies they employ in their struggles against deprivation. As a result of their differing constraints and endowments, the potential of individuals and households for escaping poverty, either independently or with outside assistance, also varies considerably.

Dimensions of Heterogeneity

Throughout the history of poverty research, the heterogeneity of the poor has been acknowledged insofar as chronic poverty has been distinguished from transitory poverty, and the poorest of the poor, or destitute, have been recognised as constituting a group apart from the less poor. These distinctions do capture some basic differences between poor households, but the factors that underlie and perpetuate these differences have received less attention. In addition, it is only recently that the research community has begun to examine the differing forces that may limit economic opportunities among various types of poor households – and the implications of these limitations for the household's future economic prospects.

By example, the qualitative component of the UP/Bihar Poverty Study revealed that at least three syndromes or patterns of poverty can be found in rural communities. The poorest of the poor were usually described as those who possess no source of income other than intermittently available casual labour, or in the worst cases, begging and foraging. Few of these households maintain significant kinship or social ties beyond the nuclear family, and little informal assistance is available to help them meet emergency or long-term needs. Thereby they are deprived of most of the informal safety nets that cushion other households in times of shortage or emergency need. Since they lack material, human and social assets, the research team characterised these households as *the destitute poor*. Fear of descending to this level of destitution is a large component of the vulnerability experienced by other poor households.

In most cases, informants attributed the destitution of these households to the fact that they had experienced a catastrophic shock or series of serious shocks. A large proportion of these destitute households may thus be described as downwardly mobile, in that their economic well-being has deteriorated from previous levels as a result of misfortune or poor management. Their poverty is unlikely to be transitory, however, because the 'traps' of destitution, such as the sale of assets and chronic indebtedness, prevent them from taking advantage of future opportunities. Self-support is thus no more than a distant dream for the majority of such households.

Other very poor households were found to have maintained a basic equilibrium over long periods, perhaps even over generations. Most of these households rely for their incomes on casual agricultural labour, and very few own any significant assets beyond the household plot, if that. Their literacy levels and school enrolment rates are low, and they tend to occupy temporary shacks (*kacha* housing) with little access to clean water or sanitary facilities. Social identity is a strong predictor of who will be in this group. As discussed above, the disadvantages encountered by the lower castes are multiple and mutually reinforcing, and so many SC and ST households remain caught in a perpetual web of poverty. The poor who are characterised by a stigmatised social identity may be described, for lack of a better term, as *the stigmatised poor*. They are vulnerable to downward mobility, for which reason a member of a stigmatised social or ethnic group may also be destitute. With few prospects for advancement, the best hope for most is to maintain a steady state in which they do not descend into destitution, but retain the basic requirements of survival, self-support, and human decency.

Not all poor households face such low expectations, however. A few of the households encountered were described by informants as upwardly mobile, although they were also low-income and living in conditions characterised by poor housing and sanitation. These households are free of long-term debt and may possess a small stock of potentially productive assets, such as dairy cattle, other livestock or a small amount of arable land. In UP, many of them were members of middle-to-lower caste groups classified as Other Backward Castes (OBCs), but a few were members of higher castes, or of SC/STs. Their relative advantage over other families in the same caste and income group was often said to be due to the fact that they had more than one member earning an income, and had relatively few dependents. These households, who may be termed *the mobile poor*, demonstrate the potential for accumulating surplus resources, investing in productive enterprises, and, in the absence of unexpected shocks, eventually climbing out of poverty.

To some extent, these categories are overlapping. Specific households may partake of the characteristics of more than one type. This should not obscure the fact that various types of poor households – the poorest, the poor and the less poor – face differing sets of circumstances in terms of the barriers and possibilities they encounter and that some households are doubly disadvantaged by social and structural constraints. Household economic strategies will vary accordingly. Some households are able to strive for continuous, if gradual, economic improvement, while others are preoccupied with fending off the threat of further impoverishment and destitution. Still others who are already destitute, are too busy securing the day's basic consumption requirements to imagine long-term strategies for economic betterment.

Why does Heterogeneity Matter?

As the above discussion suggests, it is important for several reasons to take into account the heterogeneity of the poor. First, it is clear that within any society, some types of poor households are in a better position to benefit from economic growth than are others. Expansion of job opportunities in the high-tech sector, for example, will be of little benefit to households unable to afford investments in education; and reforms in the agricultural sector will most favour those who own or possess agricultural land. Those without human or material assets are likely to be left behind by new growth opportunities. Therefore, an effective approach to poverty alleviation will not be uniform across all types of poverty. Separate tools and tactics will be required if the specific needs of all poor households are to be met. For planners and research analysts, recognition of this heterogeneity may offer an opportunity to better identify and build on factors leading to success. In the parlance of health and nutrition specialists, poor but upwardly mobile households could serve as 'models of positive deviance', in that their successful tactics and strategies could be replicated across other poor households with similar characteristics.

The Challenges

In their attempts to reduce poverty, state authorities, NGOs and other local stakeholders in Uttar Pradesh face three kinds of challenges. First, there is the challenge of developing a wider array of economic opportunities that will assist the poor in their struggle to escape poverty and deprivation. A primary means to this end is to recover the dynamism and growth momentum demonstrated in the 1960s and 1970s, which can furnish an environment conducive to the creation of jobs in many sectors and at all levels. As noted earlier, UP's poverty levels have fallen during periods of rapid growth, and stagnated during times of slow growth. Recovering the growth momentum demonstrated in the 1960s and 1970s therefore is a critical concern if UP is to see significant progress in reducing poverty.

However, many of the poor are ill-equipped to take advantage of new employment opportunities; they may lack education and job skills; be ill, disabled or elderly; live in isolated regions cut-off from opportunities and markets; or lack access to basic infrastructure and economic services. Providing the enabling factors – such as high-quality education and health care – that will permit a broader spectrum of the potential work force to participate in the fruits of accelerated growth is the second challenge faced by policy and decision-makers in UP.

Even if these challenges are met, however, there will always be a subset of the poor who are either temporarily or permanently unable to achieve full economic participation. These individuals might include the permanently disabled, single mothers of small children, the mentally ill, or simply those who have suffered a series of shocks and setbacks that may have overwhelmed their coping capacity. The third and final challenge for UP, therefore, is to provide a more effective set of public safety nets that can protect the most vulnerable from the impact of shocks and misfortunes.

ACKNOWLEDGEMENT

This article draws on work done in preparation for *Poverty in India: The Challenge of Uttar Pradesh*, World Bank Report No. 22323-IN, 8 May 2002. The authors would like to acknowledge the contributions of the report team, as well as helpful comments from Michael Walton, Angus Deaton, Ravi Srivastava, Martin Ravallion, Lionel Demery, and Madhavi Kuckreja. These are the views of the authors and should not be attributed to the World Bank or any affiliated organisation.

An earlier version of this paper was published in *Economic and Political Weekly*, Vol. 37, 25–31 January, 2003.

REFERENCES

Bhatty, K. (1998), India's Educational Deprivation: Survey of Field Investigations, Mimeo, New Delhi: Indian Social Institute, *Economic and Political Weekly*.

Datt, G. and M. Ravallion (1998), Why Have Some States Done Better than Others at Reducing Poverty, *Economica*, 65, pp. 17–38.

Datt, G., V. Kozel and M. Ravallion (2001), A Model-based Assessment of India's Progress in Reducing Poverty in the 1990s, World Bank, Washington DC.

Deaton, A. (2001), Adjusted Indian Poverty Estimates for 1999/2000 (forthcoming in EPW), November.

———— (2001), Preliminary Notes on Reporting Periods in the Indian NSS 52nd–54th Rounds, processed, Research Programme in Development Studies, Princeton University.

———— (2000), Enrollment of Children in School in the 42nd (1986/87) and 52nd (1995/96) Rounds of the NSS, Department of Economics, Princeton University, (processed) New Jersey.

———— and Jean Dreze (2002), Poverty and Inequality in India: A Re-examination, *Economic and Political Weekly*, September 7.

Deaton, A. and A. Tarozzi (1999), Prices and Poverty in India, processed, Research Program in Development Studies, Princeton University.

Dev, M. and Ranade (1998), Food Prices and the Poor, *Economic and Political Weekly,* September 26.

Dreze, J. (1990), *Widows in Rural India,* STICERD DEP No. 26, London School of Economics, London.

Dreze, J. and P.V. Srinivasan (1995), Widowhood and Poverty in Rural India: Some Inferences from Household Survey Data, IGIRD, Discussion Paper No. 25.

Dreze, J. and H. Gazdar (1997), 'Uttar Pradesh: The Burden of Inertia' in Jean Dreze and Amartya Sen (eds) op. cit.

Dubey, A. and S. Gangopadhyay (1998), *Counting the Poor,* Sarvekshana Analytical Report No. 1, Department of Statistics, GOI.

Fan, S., P. Hazell and S.K. Thorat (2000), Impact of Public Expenditure on Poverty in Rural India, *Economic and Political Weekly*, September, pp. 35–40.

Government of India (1997), 'Report of the Task Force on Projections of Minimum Needs and Effective Consumption', Planning Commission, New Delhi.

Government of India (2000b), *Household Consumer Expenditure in India: 1999/2000: Key Results*, NSS 55th Round (July 1999–June 2000), Ministry of Statistics and Programme Implementation, National Sample Survey Organisation, New Delhi, December.

———— (2000a), *Choice of Reference Period for Consumption Data,* National Sample Survey Organisation, March.

———— (1999), *Economic Survey 1998/99*, Ministry of Finance.

———— (1998), Attending an Educational Institution in India: Its Level, Nature, and Cost, based on tabulations from the NSS 52nd Round, 1995/96, Ministry of Statistics and Programme Implementation, National Sample Survey Organisation, New Delhi.

Hughes, G., K. Lvovsky and M. Dunleavy. (2001), Environmental Health in India: Priorities in Andhra Pradesh, Environment and Social Development Unit, South Asia Region, World Bank, July.

International Institute for Population Studies, IIPS (2000), National Family Health Survey (NFHS-2): 1998/99, Maryland: ORC Macro, October.

Jalan, J. and M. Ravallion (2000), Does Piped Water Improve Child Health for Poor Families in Rural India?, World Bank, Processed.

Jayaram, R. and P. Lanjouw (1999), The Evolution of Poverty and Inequality in Indian Villages, Policy Research Working Paper 1870, World Bank, Washington DC.

Kozel, V. and B. Parker (1999), Poverty in Rural India: The Contribution of Qualitative Research in Poverty Analysis, Poverty Reduction and Economic Management, South Asia Region, World Bank, Washington, DC.

Kriesal, S. (1999), Child Labour in Rural Uttar Pradesh: The Burden of Caste and Poor Education, Poverty Reduction and Economic Management, South Asia Region, World Bank, Washington DC, Processed.

Kurian, N.J. (2000), Widening Regional Disparities in India: Some Indicators, *Economic and Political Weekly*, 12 February.

Lanjouw, Jene and P. Lanjouw (2001), How to Compare Apples and Oranges: Poverty Measurement Based on Different Definitions of Consumption, *Review of Income and Wealth*, 47(1), pp. 25–42.

Lanjouw, P. and S. Zaidi (2001), Determinates of Household Welfare in India: The Differential Returns of Scheduled Castes, World Bank Poverty Policy Note, Washington DC, processed.

Lieten, G.K. (2000), Children, Work and Education – Fieldwork in two UP villages, *Economic and Political Weekly*, 17 June.

Lieten, G.K. and R. Srivastava (1999), *Power Relations, Devolution, and Development in Uttar Pradesh*, Indo-Dutch Studies on Development Alternatives no. 23, Sage Publication.

Ministry of Health and Family Welfare (2000), Bulletin of Rural Health Statistics in India, Directorate General of Health Statistics, New Delhi, June.

Office of the Registrar General, ORG (1999).

Parker, B. (1998), A Study of Health Conditions in Chitrakoot District, background study for World Bank.

Parker, B., M. Kukreja and V. Kozel (2001), In Search of a Chance: A Qualitative Study of Urban Poverty in Uttar Pradesh, World Bank Poverty Policy Note, Washington DC, processed.

Planning Commission, Press Release, 22 February 2001.

Ravallion, M. and G. Datt (2001), When is Growth Pro-Poor? The Diverse Experience of India's States, Policy Research Working Paper 2263, World Bank, Washington DC, February.

Sekhar, S. and S. Balakrishnan (1999), *Voices from the Capital: A Report Card on Public Service in Delhi*, Public Affairs Center, Bangalore, June.

Sen, Abhijit (2001), Estimates of Consumer Expenditure and its Distribution: Statistical Priorities After the NSS 55th Round, *Economic and Political Weekly*.

Srivastava, R. (1996), *Agricultural Reforms and the Rural Poor in Eastern Uttar Pradesh*, Draft Report prepared for World Bank, 27 March.

——— (2000), A Descriptive Note on the Pattern of Non-farm Employment in Uttar Pradesh, based on the UP/Bihar Living Standards Survey, processed.

Unni, J. (1998), *Gender Dimensions of Poverty*, Informal Sector Unit, Self-employed Women's Association (SEWA) and Gujarat Institute of Development Research, processed.

Visaria, Pravin (1999), Poverty in India During 1994–98: Alternative Estimates, processed, Institute of Economic Growth, Delhi.

——— (2000), *Attacking Poverty, World Development Report 2000/1*, World Bank, Washington DC.

World Bank (1997), *India: Achievements and Challenges in Reducing Poverty*, A World Bank Country Study, Washington, DC.

World Bank (2002), Monitoring Poverty in Uttar Pradesh: Developing Baseline of Poverty and Social Impact Indicators', SASPR Poverty Policy Note, Poverty and Economic Management, South Asia Region.

Appendix

DATA SOURCES AND DATA CONCERNS

The paper makes use of a wide range of information, including data from household surveys, administrative records, and participatory studies and consultations. However, the survey data present a number of challenges; in particular, the interpretation of the most recent official data on welfare and poverty is controversial and intensely debated, and while more generally accepted data are available, they are often out-of-date and of dubious current relevance. Many of GOI's (Government of India) less controversial official surveys date from the early-to-mid 1990s and may no longer represent the realities of living conditions in the state. In addition, statistics derived from various data sources are often inconsistent. We raise these issues at various points in the paper. *One of the key findings to emerge from this work is the urgent need to improve the quality and timeliness of statistics on poverty and living conditions, not only for UP but for India more widely.*

Overview of Data Sources

The primary sources of information on poverty and living conditions in India are the National Sample Surveys (NSS), which are conducted on an annual basis by the National Sample Survey Organisation (NSSO), in GOI's Department of Statistics. Every five years, NSSO conducts an extensive consumer expenditure survey (with a 'thick' sample of approximately 150,000 households) that is used by the Planning Commission to develop 'official' poverty estimates at the state and national level. In intervening years, surveys are conducted on special topics, e.g. health and education, small-scale enterprises, etc. As part of these surveys, data is collected on consumer expenditures from a smaller sample of households than in the quinquennial surveys; these 'thin' rounds are not fully comparable with the 'thick' rounds, not only because they have a smaller sample size, but also because their different purposes mandate a different sample design. In consequence, the GOI's official poverty statistics make no use of those rounds, though many outside researchers have done so (Visaria, 2000; Sen, 2001; Datt and Ravallion, 1998; Ravallion and Datt, 2001). In the 1980s and 1990s, thick sample consumption surveys were conducted in 1983 (NSS 38th Round), 1987/88 (NSS 43rd Round), 1993/94 (NSS 50th Round) and 1999/2000 (NSS 55th Round). Extensive surveys of heath and education services were conducted in 1986/87 (NSS 42nd Round) and 1995/96 (NSS 52nd Round). This paper uses data from the official series of consumption surveys (with a caveat on the 55th round, discussed shortly) as well as the health and education surveys.

Several other government agencies and research organisations undertake household surveys – a large national survey of rural households was carried out by the National Centre for Applied Economic Research (NCAER) in 1993/94, and two rounds of the National Family Health Surveys (NFHS-1, NFHS-2), were carried out under the overall supervision of the International Institute for Population Studies (IIPS) in 1992/93 with a follow on survey in 1998/99. Initial results of the follow-on survey are just becoming available to researchers and policy-makers in India. Statistics from these surveys are also used in the paper.

There are problems of consistency between data sources, and in particular between statistics based on administrative records (e.g. on school enrolment and drop-outs) and statistics derived from household surveys. The paper cites diverse sources and notes inconsistencies where they exist – as they do all too frequently. These inconsistencies are particularly severe in the case of education and assessing impacts of anti-poverty programmes.

The Poverty Debate and the NSS 55th Round

The NSS 55th Round, conducted between July 1999 and June 2000, has been the subject of intense debate in India. It is GOI's most recent quinquennial survey of consumer expenditures, designed to draw a sufficiently large sample of households to derive official estimates of poverty at the state as well as national level. The 55th Round was eagerly awaited by policy-makers and researchers throughout India, with the aim of establishing what has been the impact on poverty of recent economic reforms and India's high levels of economic growth through the latter part of the 1990s.

Unfortunately changes in survey methodology have rendered the 55th Round results incompatible, not only with the earlier 'thick' rounds, such as the 50th and 43rd Rounds, but also with the 'thin' rounds from the 51st to 54th inclusive. As a result, estimates of poverty based on the NSS 55th Round are not comparable with those from earlier rounds of the National Sample Survey, based on either the official estimates (for example from the 50th Round) or unofficial estimates made within the Bank or by other commentators.

Since India's NSS began in the 1950s, it has used a 30-day recall for consumption. In the thin samples of the 51st, 52nd, 53rd, and 54th Rounds, households were randomly divided and some given an experimental questionnaire with a 7-day recall period for some items (including foods) and either 30-day or 365-day recall for others, while others were given the traditional 30-day questionnaire for all items. The results from those rounds showed that the experimental questionnaire, and particularly the 7-day recall period for food, yielded higher reported rates of monthly purchases and, in consequence, much lower rates of poverty than the traditional questionnaires. Although further work remains to be done to fully understand why the different recall periods produce such different results, the *ratios* of average reported expenditures from one questionnaire to another (7-day as compared to 30-day recall) are remarkably constant across these experimental thin rounds.

In the 55th Round, *all* households were given *both* questionnaires, a procedure which invited them (or possibly the enumerators) to reconcile the rates of consumption over the two reporting periods. As a result, although expenditures reported from the experimental questionnaire are still higher than those from the traditional questionnaire, the ratio of one to the other is much closer to one than was the case in the 51st through 54th Rounds. Hence, although the procedure in the 55th Round may have yielded good consumption estimates in itself, they are not comparable with earlier results. More particularly, consumption estimates from the traditional 30-day questionnaire are higher than would have been the case had households been given only the traditional questionnaire, while consumption estimates from the experimental questionnaire are lower than would have been the case had households only been given the experimental questionnaires. The official poverty counts from the 55th Round 30-day questionnaire may therefore be good poverty counts on their own terms, but they are artificially low compared with the counts in the 43rd and 50th Rounds. The 10-percentage point fall in the national poverty rate between 1993/94 and 1999/2000 (using 30-day recall) is therefore certainly too high, though we have no way of knowing by how much. Nor can we use the 55th Round to compare with the thin rounds from the 51st to the 54th Rounds, which themselves showed little or no decline in poverty rates. If we did so, there would be an artificially inflated *increase* in poverty, because the experimental consumption estimates are lowered in the 55th Round by the presence of the traditional questions (see for example,

Sen, 2001). It is no more valid to use this purported increase in poverty to criticize the reforms as it is to use the purported decrease to support them.

Again, the 55th Round consumption estimates are useful in themselves, and can reasonably be used to compare poverty and living standards across regions or states within the Round. They might even be superior to earlier rounds, yielding more accurate measures of poverty. But the poverty estimates cannot be compared with those from earlier rounds, because there is no basis for estimating from the 55th Round what the poverty counts would have been had any earlier survey methodology been followed. In order to get some idea of time trends in poverty, it is necessary to use other methods. One that we shall use below is based on linking earlier poverty trends to plausible determining factors, and using information on those factors to calculate what we might expect poverty to be. Such calculations suggest that there has indeed been a fall in national and state poverty rates over recent years though less than would be suggested by comparing the (incomparable) 30-day recall results from the 50th and 55th Rounds.

While India's poverty monitoring system has been seriously compromised by the way in which the 55th Round was conducted, this should not detract attention from a number of other longstanding problems with the Indian poverty statistics. One of the most serious is on the use of price indexes. Although the price indexes used to update the lines over time appear to be quite accurate, the same cannot be said of the price differentials between states and between the urban and rural sectors that are implicit in the official poverty lines. The introduction of the new methodology following the recommendations of the Expert Group in 1993 resulted in a subsequent serious overestimation of urban relative to rural poverty in a number of the large Indian states (see Dubey and Gangopadhyay, 1998; Deaton and Tarozzi, 1999).

The Poverty Module: UP's State Sample, NSS 55th Round

Despite the limitations of the NSS 55th Round for measuring poverty trends, the UP state-sample[13] for the 55th Round includes some important innovations designed to provide more information about the relative living conditions of the poor within the state. These innovations are a part of the UP Poverty and Social Monitoring System (UP PSMS) that the Government of UP began to implement in mid-1999. In the context of ongoing institutional reforms, the UP PSMS seeks to monitor the evolution of a range of poverty and social outcome indicators. While the system cannot attribute causality between the changes observed and specific reforms, it nonetheless provides important information on how living standards respond to overall economic conditions in the state. It also provides information to assess how well the public sector is performing in delivering services to the poor.

In designing the system, GoUP identified a set of monitoring indicators and baseline information on these indicators was collected in conjunction with the state sample of the 55th Round. The indicators include for example measures of: (i) private consumption; (ii) poverty statistics (headcount index, poverty gap, severity of poverty), (iii) employment and wage rates, (iv) health outcomes (immunisation, infant mortality rates), (v) education outcomes (literacy, enrolments, drop-outs), (vi) housing and infrastructure (access to clean water, sanitation, electricity), (vii) use of special anti-poverty schemes and welfare programmes, (viii) awareness of social rights, and (ix) measures of satisfaction and quality of services.

[13] NSSO collects information at the all-India level using a sample frame that ensures that survey statistics are representative at the state level. In addition, state-level Directorates of Economics and Statistics (DES) collect a 'matching sample' of households and communities, drawn at random from population. The matching samples are the same size as the NSS samples (approximately 15,000 households) and were designed to provide a cross-check on national survey statistics.

Attached to the state sample, a special Poverty Module (Schedule 99) was administered at the same time and for the same households as the conventional NSS 55th Round schedules (Schedules 1.0 and 10.0). The new module includes information on many of the monitoring performance indicators, for example, access to education and health services, basic infrastructure (water, sanitation), and coverage and use of specific Anti-Poverty Programmes (APPs). It also includes questions on awareness and satisfaction with key government programmes. This paper includes some of the very early findings from these new data. The process of preparing a comprehensive report, based on the 55th Round Poverty Module to establish a statistical baseline for its Poverty and Social Monitoring System, is now underway. This paper presents some initial findings from early analysis of the 55th Round poverty module, with the aim of highlighting concerns and issues to be addressed in the joint baseline report.

Additional Field Studies

The paper also builds on three World Bank-sponsored studies of poverty initiated in the late 1990s and carried out in close collaboration with local researchers and NGOs in the state. The findings of these studies are used throughout the paper; they help to enrich the analysis and extend the work to better address social issues and the perspectives of the poor themselves.

The studies were launched prior to the NSS 55th Round, with the aim of filling in gaps in the existing survey data in some of the poorest regions, and adding a stronger qualitative dimension, missing from much of the previous research on poverty in the state. For example, prior to the Poverty Module in the UP 55th Round, there was little up-to-date information available on the impact of GOI's anti-poverty programs on the poor, and limited information on access and use of basic services. Nor had much research been done to look at poverty from the perspective of the poor themselves, using methods developed from Participatory Rural Appraisal (PRA) work. These include qualitative research methods such as focus group discussions, semi-structured interviews, and a series of sorting, ranking and mapping exercises that are aimed at eliciting community-level perceptions and priorities.

The three studies are described below.

UP/Bihar Poverty Study

In 1997/98, a study of poverty in eastern and southern UP and central Bihar was carried out in collaboration with Indian academics and NGO and community workers. Fieldwork took place over a period of 9 months, from June 1997 through February 1998. The study used a mix of qualitative research techniques and more conventional survey-based methods. It began with a qualitative examination of perceptions of poverty in 30 rural villages. This component of the study utilised PRA methods. These included social mapping, which provides a visual display of community members' perceptions of their village and its resources in social as well as economic terms; wealth ranking exercises, which examine local perceptions of the characteristics and concomitants of wealth and poverty; as well as case history interviews, and assessments of the role of services and programmes, social capital and gender in determining who is and who remains poor.

In addition to providing important insights in their own right, the PRA findings were used to enrich and sharpen the design of the study's household and community questionnaires, which were designed as integrated living standards surveys. The field survey was carried out between November 1997 through February 1998, in 120 villages (including the 30 covered in the qualitative component) with an overall sample size of 2,250 households. Approximately half the households were drawn at random from three districts in Southern and Eastern UP – Banda, Allahabad, and Gorakhpur. In addition to self-standing analysis, the findings of the qualitative portion of the study are being used to inform, validate, and add explanatory material to the survey-based analyses. Joint use of the two methods yields a rich picture of the situation of the poor in rural UP and the broad factors that determine their well-being. The qualitative component allowed the researchers to better comprehend the significance to rural Indians of the economic and social patterns identified and documented by the survey results. Since the two methods produce different but complementary types of information, the combined methodology yielded a more comprehensive view of the multiple dimensions of poverty than could be obtained through either approach alone.

Findings of this initial study led to the implementation of two follow-on studies aimed at elucidating and clarifying points that had emerged as ambiguous during the data analysis. Since poor health was found to be an unexpectedly common cause of impoverishment, a district health assessment was implemented in one of the study areas to assess the strengths and weaknesses of the primary health care available to the poor. The on-the-ground functioning of the Targeted Public Distribution System (TPDS), a government food subsidisation programme that was praised by many informants, was the subject of the second mini-study. Its goal was to examine whether improvements in this much-criticised programme were real or illusory, and to document the amount of leakage that occurs.

Consultations on Poverty Monitoring

Consultations with villagers and other important stakeholders were held in four districts (one each in the Hill, West, Central, and Eastern regions of UP) during November-December 1999. The goal of the consultations was to guide the Government of Uttar Pradesh in the selection of better and more widely-shared indicators, meaningful for the poor and population at large, for tracking progress at reducing poverty. The government had developed a set of indicators reflecting their objectives and linked to the state's strategy for poverty reduction – for example, the proportion of people below the poverty line, wage rates for agriculture labour, primary school enrolments for children from poor and socially marginalised families. Further consultations were carried out under this study to determine how the poor themselves measure and judge progress at reducing poverty and improving living conditions. The fieldwork and reporting were carried out by a local NGO – Sahbhagi Shikshan Kendra (SSK). The team discussed key aspects of poverty with a variety of stakeholders in order to draw community-level viewpoints and understandings into the development of a set of indicators to measure changes in the social components of poverty. Findings were discussed with government, and will influence future efforts to develop a qualitative component for the UP PSMS.

Urban Poverty in Uttar Pradesh

During February and March 2000, a field study examining the condition of the urban poor was carried out in UP by Vanangana, an NGO located in UP. The study built on the 1997 UP/Bihar Poverty Study and, to facilitate a comparison of rural and urban patterns of response, it employed an adapted version of qualitative research instruments initially developed for the rural study. Survey teams visited low-income urban communities in two large cities (Lucknow and Kanpur), two medium-sized cities, and five smaller towns. The goal was to explore the forces and factors supporting the persistence of poverty in the urban setting and to identify the coping strategies of the urban poor; particularly in terms of the economic and social strategies they pursue, the opportunities they recognise and exploit, and the barriers to success that they encounter.

24

Calorie Deprivation in Rural India Between 1983 and 1999/2000
Evidence from Unit Record Data

J.V. Meenakshi and Brinda Viswanathan

There is a consensus now that the post-reforms period appears to have witnessed a decline in income poverty; a continuation of the trend since the 1980s, at least according to the quinquennial consumer expenditure surveys conducted by the National Sample Survey Organisation (NSSO). Indeed, the debate has had much more to do with the impact of methodological changes (in survey design, for example) or of different price deflators on the magnitude of the decline; the fact of the decline is not much disputed.

There has been much less focus on trends in *calorie* deprivation in the country. It is now well established that there has been a secular decline in calorie intakes in rural areas – to the extent of approximately 70 calories per capita over the period 1983 to 1999/2000. This decrease can be discerned in virtually all states, and has translated into a corresponding *increase* in the headcount ratios of calorie deprivation. Thus while the magnitude of income poverty has declined, that of calorie deprivation has increased.

This chapter, therefore, focuses on calorie deprivation, its magnitude, depth and distribution. It highlights the centrality of the norm used to calculate headcount ratios of calorie deprivation and demonstrates that the choice of a particular norm significantly influences not just the magnitude of deprivation, but also the direction of change. Furthermore, the direction of change is also sensitive to the choice of poverty measure. The chapter argues that there is need for a fresh debate on the determination of the norm, and more generally on defining the poverty line.

More specifically, it seeks to:

- Document the extent of calorie deprivation, and examine the sensitivity of these measures to the choice of a calorie norm. We propose an alternative, household-specific calorie norm, one which is attentive to the household's demographic composition.
- Estimate, using alternative norms, three of the popular Foster-Greer-Thorbecke measures, assessing respectively, the magnitude, depth and severity of deprivation.

- Document changes in nutrient-intake distributions.
- Examine the extent of overlap between income poverty and calorie deprivation.

The study focuses on rural areas of sixteen states, and on the changes that have occurred during the period between 1983 and 1999/2000. The analysis is based on household-level (unit record) data on consumer expenditure surveys of the National Sample Survey Organisation for the years 1983 (38th Round) and 1999/2000 (55th Round). The rural sample consists of nearly 80,000 households in 1983 and 70,000 households in 1999/2000.

Calorie intakes are calculated by applying conversion factors to the quantities (of an exhaustive list) of commodities reported as being consumed by the household during the previous 30 days.[1] To the extent that there may be inadequate coverage of certain food items, and that methods of cooking and preparation influence nutrient content that the conversion factors may not capture entirely, these intakes are not free from measurement error. However, meaningful comparisons over time may still be made, since the magnitudes of these errors are unlikely to have changed over time.

We compute three measures of deprivation, using the well-known Foster-Greer-Thorbecke (FGT) class of indices (1984):

$$\text{FGT}(\alpha) = \frac{1}{H} \sum_{k=1}^{q} \left(\frac{g^h}{z} \right)^{\alpha}$$

where $g^h = z - m^h$, if $z > m^h$ and is the gap between the calorie norm (z) and the hth individual's calorie intake (m^h); $g^h = 0$, if $z \leq m^h$; H is the total population and q is the number of calorie-deprived persons.

When $\alpha = 0$, the index collapses to the familiar headcount ratio (henceforth HCR) of those with insufficient calories. When $\alpha = 1$, the index measures the average deficit of calories with respect to the norm, weighted by the proportion of those who are thus deprived; we term this the *calorie-gap ratio*. When $\alpha = 2$, the index measures the severity of deprivation, as it gives a higher weight to those who are the most deprived (whose intakes are far below the norm).

We also compute and compare the cumulative distribution functions of calorie intakes in 1983 and 1999/2000. If the cumulative distribution function for one of the years lies everywhere to the right side of the other, then it is said to exhibit first-order stochastic dominance over the other, and is associated with higher welfare. These comparisons have the added advantage of not being referenced with any particular norm. The cumulative distributions are estimated by fitting non-parametric kernel densities, using Gausian weights (see Deaton, 1997 and Engel and Kneip, 1994).[2]

ON THE CHOICE OF ALTERNATIVE NORMS

Before turning to the evidence, a few words on the calorie norm should be discussed. First, pegging the level of the norm has long been open to question, so that there is, in fact, more than one norm. For example, the average calorie norm prescribed by the FAO is far lower at 2,110 calories per capita per day for South Asia (FAO, 1996) than the 2,400 calories that is conventionally adopted in India for rural areas. The FAO also uses another cut-off of 1,810 calories for India (FAO, 2000), which represents the lower end of the range of food requirements. In principle, the figure 2,400 represents an 'average' and

---

[1] The methodological changes in the 55th Round (and in particular the use of two different recall periods) do not require substantial adjustments or corrections to the cereal-dominated calorie intake figures, and hence are not attempted here.

[2] Each of the observations is weighted by the product of the NSS combined multiplier and household size.

includes a margin of 'safety' while the figure 1,810 represents a 'minimum' amount necessary for good health.

Furthermore, the FAO norm would appear to have decreased over time, presumably to account for the fact that lifestyles have become more sedentary, and that improved hygiene and sanitation have meant fewer calories need to be budgeted for fighting water-borne diseases.

There have been debates over the use of a norm at all. For example, P.V. Sukhatme (1993) has suggested that the body's adaptation mechanisms enable those with lower body weights to metabolise a lower amount of calories more efficiently, thus invalidating the use of a biologically derived nutrient norm.

Although the problem of the 'troublesome norm' is certainly not a new one, the debate has by and large been inconclusive. For this reason, this paper simply uses three alternative norms – one set at 1,800 calories, the second at 2,400 calories, and the third at an arbitrarily defined 2,200 calories for rural areas – and examines the sensitivity of the results to the choice of a norm.

It is, perhaps, also useful to reiterate what may seem obvious: that nutritional requirements vary not only by climate, but also by gender, age and activity status. In fact, the figure of 2,400 calories corresponds to the National Institute of Nutrition's Recommended Daily Allowance (RDA) for an adult male weighing 60 kg and engaged in sedentary work. The RDA for an adult woman (in sedentary activity) is 1,875 calories per day. The corresponding recommendations for moderate work are 2,875 and 2,225 calories respectively, while those for children below 18 are much lower (Gopalan et al., 2000). The use of the single norm – whatever may be the level at which it is pegged – cannot capture these differential 'requirements'. At best, it provides an estimate of the aggregate nutritional deficit.

One method of incorporating these differing needs is to define the norm in terms of consumer units. An adult male is taken as the reference individual (unity), and age and gender-specific conversion factors (less than unity) are then applied to other members of the household to obtain the total number of consumer units per household. The corresponding norm has been determined as 2,700 calories per consumer unit per day. This paper also presents evidence on the percentage of persons whose per consumer unit intakes are less than 2,700 calories.

This paper tries to capture the different calorie requirements of individual members by exploiting information on the age and sex composition of household members, and individual-specific norms prescribed by the Indian Council of Medical Research and reported in Gopalan et al. (2000), to derive a *household-specific norm*. Thus instead of using a single norm for all households, the norm varies according to the demographic characteristics of the household. A household is then categorised as having a calorie deficit if the household's calorie intake is below the household's calorie requirements. This is one way of assessing whether demographic changes explain the observed trends in calorie deprivation.

The age- and gender-norms used in this computation are taken from Gopalan et al. and are as follows:

$$z^h = \text{n1*713 + n2*1240 + n3*1690 + n4*1950 + b1*2190 + b2*2450 + b3*2640 + g1*1970 + g2*2060 + g3*2060 + am*2875 + af*2225}$$

Where the variables represent the number of household members in different gender and age groups:

n1 = children below 1 year,
n2 = children between 1 and 3 years,
n3 = children between 4 and 6 years,

n4 = children between 7 and 9 years,
b1(g1) = boys (girls) between 10 and 12 years,
b2(g2) = boys (girls) between 13 and 15 years,
b3(g3) = boys (girls) between 16 and 18 years, and
am (af) = men (women) above 18 years.

In this case, the superscript h in the FGT measures given above indexes households. By appropriately modifying the sampling weights, we compute the percentage of *persons* living in households with insufficient intakes, thus enabling a direct comparison of the two HCRs. This modification, necessitated by the absence of data on consumption by individuals within the households, represents an attempt to capture the impact of demographic composition, and changes in this structure, on the prevalence of undernutrition.

A different approach to the estimation of norms is adopted by Minhas (1991) who suggests that these can be derived behaviourally. He evaluates intake levels at which households cease being net recipients of meals, and may, therefore, be deemed to be calorie-sufficient. These calculated levels vary substantially by geographic region: with Punjab, for example, recording higher cut-offs than Gujarat. Thus, people of Punjab appear to need a far greater number of calories than do people of Gujarat, who tend to be more parsimonious in their calorie intakes.

As an approximation – albeit a crude one – to this behaviourally derived norm, we use the *median* calorie intake in the rural areas of each state as yet another cut-off in computing indices of deprivation.[3] The median has the merit that it takes into account differences in climatic conditions and in consumption patterns across states, although it also allows the cut-off to vary over time. It is a measure of *relative* deprivation, and is thus similar to the use of the two-thirds or half-median income cut-off in the income poverty literature.

CHANGES IN CALORIE DEPRIVATION, 1983 TO 1999/2000

Table 24.1 sets out some summary statistics relating to average calorie intake, calorie deprivation, and income poverty. In 1983, average intakes were below 2,400 calories in all but six states; and were above this per capita norm only in the Northern region. By 1999/2000 intakes declined in all states except Kerala, Orissa and West Bengal. Median intakes in both years were lower than average intakes, and these, too, witnessed a decline between 1983 and 1999/2000.

These declining intake levels have translated, as expected, into increased headcount ratios of calorie deprivation. As indicated in columns 5 to 8 of Table 24.1, while income poverty has declined, calorie poverty appears to have increased.

Even in absolute terms, headcount ratios of calorie deprivation are far higher than those based on income poverty. For example, in 1999/2000, the HCR of calorie deprivation in rural Andhra Pradesh was 81 per cent, although the income headcount ratio was only 11 per cent.

In principle, the determination of the poverty line is anchored in the cost of a food basket that would yield the requisite calories. Therefore, one would expect both classes of measures to yield similar results, at least qualitatively. Clearly, this is not the case. It is this discordance (also corroborated by Palmer Jones and Sen, 2001) that further underscores the need to examine nutrient deprivation separately.

[3] Except, of course, the HCR, for it would by definition be 50 per cent.

Table 24.1 Some Summary Statistics on Calorie Intake and Poverty

	Average Calorie Intake Per Capita per Day (Kcal)		Median Calorie Intake Per Capita per Day (Kcal)		Headcount Ratios (% Consuming below 2,400 Calories per Day)		Headcount Ratios of Poverty (% with below OPL Incomes)		Required Calories per Day (Demographically Adjusted) Kcal per Capita	
	1983	1999/2000	1983	1999/2000	1983	1999/2000	1983	1999/2000	1983	1999/2000
	(1)	(2)	(3)	(4)	(5)	(6)	(7)	(8)	(9)	(10)
Andhra Pradesh	2,204	2,021	1,988	1,955	68.5	80.7	35.8	11.1	1,932	2,041
Bihar	2,189	2,121	2,081	2,034	67.6	74.9	60.5	44.0	1,920	2,000
Gujarat	2,113	1,986	1,988	1,904	72.6	80.5	39.0	13.2	1,959	2,036
Haryana	2,554	2,455	2,325	2,313	54.1	55.1	27.5	8.3	1,926	2,032
Himachal Pradesh	2,636	2,454	2,499	2,307	44.5	56.5	23.9	8.0	1,933	2,040
Jammu & Kashmir	2,569	2,631	2,480	2,577	44.5	39.7	31.6	4.0	1,952	2,055
Karnataka	2,260	2,028	2,097	1,905	64.0	78.9	40.0	17.4	1,933	2,042
Kerala	1,884	1,982	1,749	1,904	81.5	81.2	48.5	9.4	1,931	2,057
Madhya Pradesh	2,323	2,062	2,175	1,932	62.5	78.4	53.7	37.1	1,925	2,011
Maharashtra	2,144	2,012	2,021	1,926	73.1	83.3	54.6	23.7	1,938	2,035
Orissa	2,103	2,119	1,995	2,051	70.9	74.6	66.2	48.0	1,935	2,034
Punjab	2,677	2,381	2,479	2,221	46.2	62.8	18.5	6.4	1,954	2,046
Rajasthan	2,433	2,425	2,324	2,292	54.2	56.7	46.7	13.7	1,933	1,996
Tamil Nadu	1,861	1,826	1,720	1,727	80.6	86.5	59.1	20.6	1,945	2,059
Uttar Pradesh	2,399	2,327	2,252	2,176	58.4	64.5	50.8	31.2	1,935	1,991
West Bengal	2,027	2,095	1,902	2,009	76.0	75.6	66.7	31.9	1,947	2,036

Note: OPL – Official Poverty Line.

Extent of Deprivation: Headcount Ratios

The use of a different calorie norm significantly influences the magnitude of headcount ratios, as indicated in Table 24.2, which presents calorie HCRs using alternative norms. These HCRs based on a 2,200 cut-off are lower than the HCRs computed using 2,400 calories (Table 24.1) by a full 10 percentage points. Thus an approximately 10 per cent decrease in the norm results in a more than proportionate 15 per cent decrease in headcount ratios in many states. In some states, the decrease is as much as 30 per cent. The same pattern is obtained with the use of an 1800 norm – headcount ratios here are less than half those using the 2,400 norm. This implies that a high proportion of people have calorie intakes that are close to the norm.

More significantly, the use of a different norm alters conclusions about whether or not the magnitude of calorie deprivation has increased between 1983 and 1999/2000. Thus while the 2,400 norm indicates rising deprivation in fifteen of sixteen states, the 2,200 norm suggests that calorie deprivation *decreased* slightly in four states (Jammu & Kashmir, Kerala, Rajasthan and West Bengal) and increased in the remaining twelve states. Similarly, using an 1,800 norm suggests that HCRs of calorie deprivation declined in eight states.[4]

[4] Note however that the use of a different norm does not appreciably change the ranking of states by HCRs – the Spearman rank correlations are high and not significantly different from unity.

Table 24.2 Headcount Ratios of Calorie Deprivation, Alternative Norms

	2,200 Norm		1,800 Norm		2,700 (per Consumer Unit Norm)		Demographically Adjusted Norm	
	1983	1999/2000	1983	1999/2000	1983	1999/2000	1983	1999/2000
Andhra Pradesh	56.9	69.7	30.0	36.9	53.8	68.1	40.1	57.8
Bihar	56.9	62.4	32.4	32.5	53.3	60.3	39.7	48.9
Gujarat	63.8	70.4	36.6	41.0	62.0	68.4	48.2	58.8
Haryana	42.8	43.5	19.3	18.4	40.1	44.5	30.7	33.4
Himachal Pradesh	33.8	42.7	14.8	12.1	30.3	40.7	21.9	27.5
Jammu & Kashmir	31.9	28.9	13.0	7.3	30.4	27.6	22.4	20.8
Karnataka	55.2	69.9	35.7	41.8	53.2	68.6	42.1	60.0
Kerala	74.0	70.3	53.2	42.8	72.3	67.2	60.9	61.4
Madhya Pradesh	51.6	68.0	24.9	38.5	47.9	66.7	32.5	54.4
Maharashtra	61.6	70.5	34.2	39.2	58.8	69.2	46.0	59.1
Orissa	60.6	61.7	35.1	29.1	58.7	60.4	44.9	49.3
Punjab	36.8	48.1	19.8	20.6	35.6	46.0	26.0	35.4
Rajasthan	43.4	43.0	22.7	15.5	40.2	40.1	29.8	26.0
Tamil Nadu	74.6	78.7	54.4	55.4	72.7	77.7	62.8	72.8
Uttar Pradesh	47.1	52.0	24.0	23.0	43.3	48.7	32.0	36.0
West Bengal	67.3	63.3	43.8	34.1	67.0	64.2	53.2	52.4

Once family composition is taken into account, HCRs of calorie deprivation – based on per consumer intakes lower than 2,700 calories – are much lower than those based on the per capita 2,400 calorie norm in both the years. In fact, the figures are similar – both in magnitude and in trend – to those based on the lower 2,200 per capita norm.

Before comparing the household's caloric intake with a *household-specific* norm, it is useful to examine how these new norms themselves vary across states and over time, for these reflect how demographic composition influences the norm. While state-level differences are to be expected, what is interesting is that over time, the norm itself has increased, largely due to the fewer number of children per household. This is clearly demonstrated in last two columns of Table 24.1, which presents data normalised to per capita terms for ease of interpretation. Indeed, in several states, actual intakes are, on average, *higher* than these new norms (in 1983), unlike the case with the use of the 2,400 norm.

One impact of the use of this norm is that headcount ratios of calorie deprivation fall sharply (Table 24.2), certainly as compared to the HCR corresponding to 2,400 calories per capita per day. In fact, these headcount ratios are now closer, in absolute terms, to the income poverty rates. However, what is unaffected is the increase in HCRs of calorie deprivation over time in all states except Rajasthan and West Bengal. Thus, even after accounting for demographic changes, intakes have declined over time in most states.

Depth of Deprivation: Calorie Gap Ratio

Despite an increase in the extent of calorie deprivation, its depth seems to have declined in many states. For example, with the 2,400 calorie cut-off, this decrease occurred in eight states (Table 24.3). The

Table 24.3 Calorie Gap Ratios FGT(1), Alternative Norms

	2,400 Norm		2,200 Norm		1,800 Norm		Median		Demographically Adjusted	
	1983	1999/2000	1983	1999/2000	1983	1999/2000	1983	1999/2000	1983	1999/2000
Andhra Pradesh	17.1	20.1	12.9	15.0	6.0	6.4	8.9	8.1	7.5	10.7
Bihar	17.5	17.5	13.4	12.8	6.4	5.0	11.1	9.3	7.9	8.1
Gujarat	19.5	20.8	15.1	15.9	7.2	6.8	10.6	8.9	8.9	11.3
Haryana	12.4	11.3	9.1	7.8	4.4	2.5	11.1	9.7	4.9	4.8
Himachal Pradesh	10.0	9.5	7.4	5.8	3.6	1.2	11.5	7.7	4.5	3.0
Jammu & Kashmir	9.0	6.3	6.3	3.8	2.8	0.8	10.2	9.0	3.6	2.2
Karnataka	18.5	21.7	14.7	16.9	7.9	8.1	12.9	10.2	9.5	12.7
Kerala	27.2	22.7	22.6	16.8	13.4	7.9	12.2	10.0	15.5	13.1
Madhya Pradesh	14.8	20.0	10.9	15.2	4.9	6.5	10.5	9.1	6.1	10.2
Maharashtra	18.1	20.4	13.6	15.3	5.9	6.5	9.8	9.0	7.5	10.8
Orissa	19.5	16.6	15.3	11.9	7.8	4.4	11.2	8.7	9.8	7.1
Punjab	11.5	12.5	8.8	8.5	4.5	2.7	12.7	8.9	5.4	5.3
Rajasthan	16.1	10.5	13.1	6.8	8.7	2.0	14.9	8.4	9.1	3.4
Tamil Nadu	30.2	27.0	25.9	21.9	17.1	11.6	15.5	9.9	19.6	17.6
Uttar Pradesh	13.6	13.6	10.1	9.6	4.5	3.5	11.0	9.2	5.6	5.4
West Bengal	23.7	17.9	19.4	13.2	11.2	5.2	13.1	9.0	13.5	8.9

number of states which witnessed an improvement in the calorie deficit increases to eleven when a norm of 2,200 calories per day is used instead; and to twelve, when an 1800 norm is used. Interestingly, the state of Andhra Pradesh with a well-functioning public distribution system does *not* figure in the list of states where the calorie gap ratio has decreased. However, when median calorie intakes are used as the cut-off, the depth of deprivation would appear to have declined unambiguously in all sixteen states.

When a household-specific norm is applied, the resulting calorie gap ratios are lower than the case with the 2,400 norm, but show an increase over time in nearly half the states considered here.

Further, in 1999/2000 the magnitudes of the calorie gap ratio were much higher than the corresponding poverty gap ratio based on the official poverty line (results are available with the authors). Thus the calorie deficit is higher than the income deficit, a result driven in large measure by the high magnitudes of headcount ratios of calorie deprivation.[5]

Severity of Deprivation: The FGT(2)

The trends in the severity of calorie deprivation are qualitatively different (Table 24.4). The use of the 2,400 norm suggests that the severity of calorie inadequacy increased only in four states, and declined in the remaining twelve states. Twelve states exhibited a lower FGT(2) in 1999/2000 when the 2,200 norm is used; in all sixteen states if either the 1,800 norm or the median intake is used to compute the index; and in five states if the household-specific norm is used. Thus in contrast to trends in income poverty, where the direction of change appears largely invariant to the choice of FGT measure, trends

[5] No ranking between calorie and income gap ratios can be established if the 1,800 norm is used instead; similarly, the pattern for 1983 was also more mixed.

Table 24.4 Severity of Calorie Deprivation FGT(2), Alternative Norms

	2,400 Norm		2,200 Norm		1,800 Norm		Median		Demographically Adjusted	
	1983	1999/ 2000	1983	1999/ 2000	1983	1999/ 2000	1983	1999/ 2000	1983	1999/ 2000
Andhra Pradesh	6.1	6.8	4.5	4.8	2.1	1.9	3.0	2.3	2.5	3.1
Bihar	6.3	5.6	4.6	3.8	2.0	1.3	3.7	2.5	2.5	2.1
Gujarat	7.3	7.1	5.4	4.9	2.5	1.8	3.7	2.4	2.8	3.1
Haryana	4.7	3.2	3.6	2.0	2.1	0.6	4.3	2.7	2.2	1.1
Himachal Pradesh	4.0	2.3	3.1	1.2	2.0	0.2	4.5	1.7	2.3	0.6
Jammu & Kashmir	3.2	1.5	2.3	0.8	1.3	0.1	3.6	2.3	1.5	0.4
Karnataka	7.4	7.9	5.6	5.7	2.8	2.4	4.8	3.1	3.4	4.0
Kerala	11.8	7.7	9.3	5.6	4.9	2.2	4.5	2.9	5.8	4.0
Madhya Pradesh	5.2	6.8	3.8	4.8	1.8	1.8	3.6	2.6	2.2	2.9
Maharashtra	6.2	6.8	4.3	4.7	1.7	1.7	3.0	2.5	2.1	3.0
Orissa	7.5	5.1	5.6	3.3	2.7	1.1	4.0	2.3	3.4	1.7
Punjab	4.7	3.5	3.6	2.2	2.2	0.6	5.1	2.3	2.5	1.3
Rajasthan	9.1	2.8	8.0	1.7	6.6	0.4	8.6	2.1	6.4	0.8
Tamil Nadu	15.6	10.6	13.2	8.0	9.1	3.6	8.4	2.9	10.1	5.9
Uttar Pradesh	4.7	4.1	3.4	2.7	1.5	0.9	3.7	2.6	1.8	1.4
West Bengal	10.3	5.7	8.1	3.9	4.6	1.3	5.4	2.4	5.6	2.4

in calorie deprivation are sensitive to this choice. Also note that unlike the case with the calorie gap ratio above, the income FGT(2) is higher than the calorie FGT(2).

Changes in Calorie Distributions – First-order Stochastic Dominance

To understand more completely the nature of changes in nutrient deprivation, we compute the cumulative distribution function (henceforth CDF) of calorie intakes using non-parametric kernel density estimates for each of the sixteen states. Our earlier work, comparing the rural 1983 calorie density with that in 1993/94, had indicated that this decade was characterised by an inward shift in the densities at both the left and right tails, with a far greater percentage of people consuming near-average calories (Viswanathan and Meenakshi, 2001). Thus inequality in intakes declined in most states, even as average intakes also decreased. In particular, the shifting-in of the left tail of the calorie probability density implies that the proportion of people consuming extremely low quantities of calories (for example, those consuming less than 60 per cent of the norm) declined over this period.

This characterisation would appear to hold true broadly for the comparison between 1983 and 1999/ 2000. The CDFs for each state are presented in Figure 24.1. It is apparent that in no state can one discern first-order stochastic dominance between the two years, thus implying that an unambiguous welfare ranking cannot be assigned. In each state, the CDFs intersect; the CDF for 1983 is higher than that for 1999/2000 at lower calorie-intake levels, but the ranking soon reverses.

The calorie level at which the two CDFs intersect – the intake below which there was a clear-cut decline in headcount ratios of calorie deprivation – varies from state to state (Table 24.5). For example, there has been a decline in percentage of people consuming less than 1,300 calories per day in Andhra

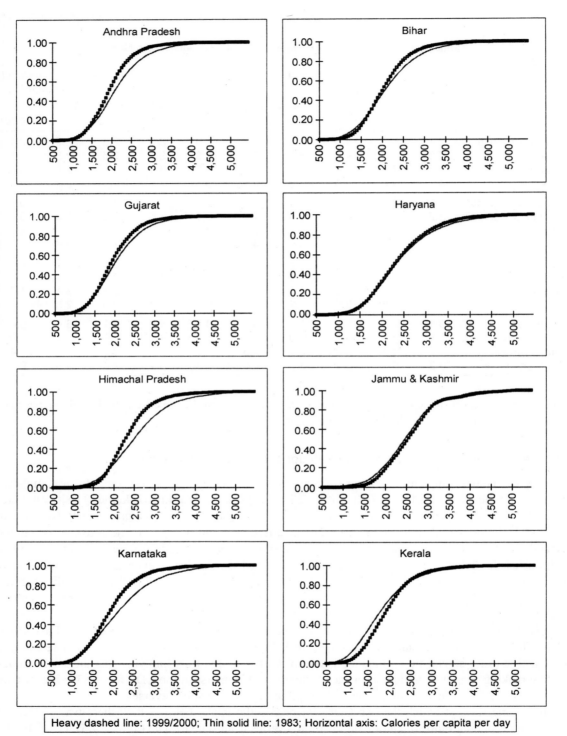

Heavy dashed line: 1999/2000; Thin solid line: 1983; Horizontal axis: Calories per capita per day

Figure 24.1 Cumulative Distribution Functions for Calorie Intakes, 1983 and 1999/2000

(Contd...)

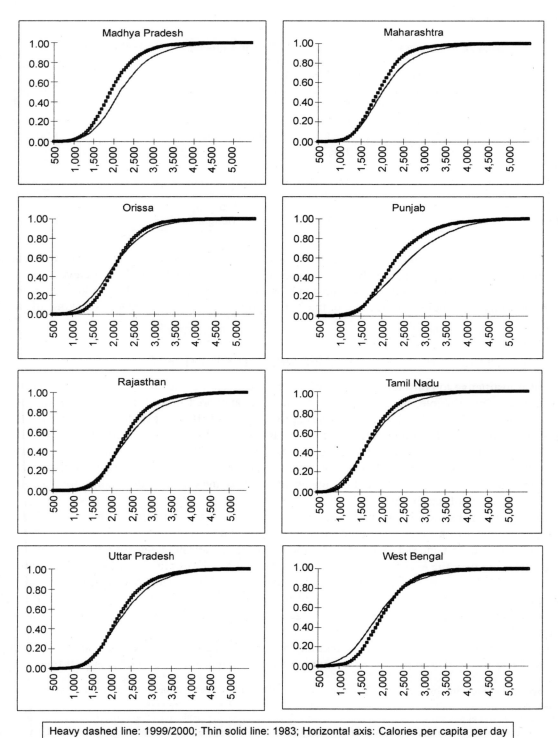

Heavy dashed line: 1999/2000; Thin solid line: 1983; Horizontal axis: Calories per capita per day

Figure 24.1 Cumulative Distribution Functions for Calorie Intakes, 1983 and 1999/2000

Table 24.5 Caloric Intake Levels at which Calorie Cumulative Distribution Functions for 1983 and 1999/2000 Intersect and Cross-over
(*Calories per Capita per Day*)

State	Intersection Level	State	Intersection Level
Andhra Pradesh	1,300	Madhya Pradesh	1,000
Bihar	1,700	Maharashtra	1,200
Gujarat	1,350	Orissa	2,100
Haryana	1,700	Punjab	1,650
Himachal Pradesh	1,850	Rajasthan	1,950
Jammu & Kashmir	3,050	Tamil Nadu	1,550
Karnataka	1,200	Uttar Pradesh	1,850
Kerala	2,450	West Bengal	2,400

Pradesh; a similar decline in Orissa can be observed at a level of 2,100 calories. For Jammu & Kashmir, the intersection occurs at a relatively high calorie intake level of 3,050 calories. In eleven states, the cross-over point exceeds 1,440 calories; thus in most states there has been a decline in the percentage of people consuming below 60 per cent of the 2,400 norm, a continuation, broadly speaking, of earlier trends.

THE RELATIONSHIP BETWEEN INCOMES AND CALORIE INTAKES

It is also instructive to consider the extent of overlap between income and calorie deprivation, for as noted earlier, in principle, the income poverty line was anchored in a norm for calorie intakes. As indicated in Table 24.6, while HCRs of calorie deprivation are 98–100 per cent for the poorest quintile as expected, nutrient HCRs among the rich are substantial as well. In fact, HCRs among the richest 20 per cent exceed 40 per cent in several states, and are between 10 and 20 per cent only in the northern states. Thus while low incomes are clearly associated with low calorie intakes, high incomes by themselves do not imply sufficient calories. In fact, these high magnitudes of the calorie deprivation among the richest quintiles are not really credible.

To examine the relationship between income poverty and calorie deprivation further, Table 24.6 also presents estimates of average calorie intake by quintile expenditure group.[6] To highlight contrasts, the focus is on the poorest and richest quintiles. Average calorie intake among the poorest quintile increased in all states but two: the exceptions being Maharashtra and Madhya Pradesh. In fact, the magnitude of increase in intake among the poor was much greater in the poorer states of Bihar, Orissa and West Bengal than that in states with an established record of rural prosperity such as Andhra Pradesh, Haryana, and Punjab. These numbers are larger than what would be expected from a 'low base' phenomenon.

By the same token, average calorie intake among the richest 20 per cent declined substantially in all states. There would thus appear to be a tendency for convergence in calorie intakes over time.

[6] See related literature by Mehta and Venkataraman (2000) who observe that due to the decrease in average calorie intakes the expenditure required to maintain a calorie intake level of 2,400 kcal per capita per day would be much higher than the (updated) official poverty line. Palmer-Jones and Sen (2001) compare the headcount ratio using the calorie norm as well as the official poverty lines and find that over the years the divergence between the two ratios has increased. They mainly attribute this to the methodological issues related to the recording of consumption information by the NSS.

Table 24.6 Average Caloric Intake by Quintile Expenditure Group

States	Calorie Headcount Ratios 1999/2000 among		Poorest Quintile		Richest Quintile	
	Poorest Quintile	Richest Quintile	1983	1999/2000	1983	1999/2000
	(Per cent)		(Calories/Cap/Day)		(Calories/Cap/Day)	
Andhra Pradesh	98.9	44.4	1,513	1,522	2,822	2,592
Bihar	98.1	31.7	1,426	1,601	3,072	2,797
Gujarat	98.3	43.8	1,459	1,534	2,865	2,558
Haryana	98.1	16.5	1,671	1,713	3,654	3,156
Himachal Pradesh	94.1	16.2	1,757	1,981	3,384	3,116
Jammu & Kashmir	83.6	11.1	1,838	2,228	3,295	3,266
Karnataka	98.6	44.8	1,362	1,464	3,076	2,676
Kerala	100.0	43.9	1,054	1,398	2,409	2,627
Madhya Pradesh	99.0	39.9	1,592	1,528	3,243	2,703
Maharashtra	98.3	56.6	1,593	1,546	2,751	2,479
Orissa	99.8	33.9	1,300	1,578	2,910	2,684
Punjab	98.0	12.0	1,644	1,733	3,790	3,277
Rajasthan	95.5	15.9	1,233	1,836	3,622	3,182
Tamil Nadu	99.7	58.4	847	1,294	2,763	2,427
Uttar Pradesh	96.4	22.8	1,646	1,758	3,352	3,091
West Bengal	97.7	37.5	1,148	1,550	2,994	2,712

The observed shifts in the pattern of calorie intakes must be interpreted in the light of changes in the commodity composition of calories. Our earlier work (Viswanathan and Meenakshi, 2004) suggests that the contribution of cereals to total calories has declined both in absolute and relative terms for all but the lowest income groups in most states. Instead, the contribution of milk, edible oils and processed foods to total calories has increased. Although the poor have also seen changes in their diets towards greater diversification, an increase in cereal consumption can nevertheless be discerned in many states among this group; this explains the increased calorie intakes among the first quintile.

Finally, despite the apparent divergence between calorie- and income-poverty trends, income continues to be a powerful determinant of calorie intakes. Our earlier paper (2001), based on a comparison of 1983 and 1993/94 intakes, indicated that calorie elasticities with respect to income were in the range of 0.5 to 0.7 for the poorest quintile in 1983, and were higher a decade later. A similar exercise, conducted in 1999/2000 reinforces this conclusion: calorie elasticities for the poor are reasonably high (results available with the authors on request).

CALORIE DEPRIVATION IN URBAN AREAS

Nutrient deprivation patterns in urban areas are quite distinct and merit separate study. Unlike the rural areas, average and median urban intakes increased in most states between 1983 and 1999/2000. Thus, headcount ratios of calorie deprivation witnessed a *decline* in 13 of 16 states.[7] Also, the magnitude, depth and severity of nutrient deprivation are all much lower in urban than rural areas, when evaluated at the 2,100 and 2,400 calorie norms, respectively or the demographically adjusted norms.

[7] The urban results are discussed in Viswanathan and Meenakshi (2004).

However, like rural areas, these magnitudes do depend on the choice of a particular norm and are higher than the income poverty rates. Further, there is no unambiguous first-order stochastic dominance between 1983 and 1999/2000, so that clear welfare rankings cannot be assigned in urban areas either.

CONCLUSION

Between 1983 and 1999/2000, the incidence of calorie deprivation in rural India would appear to have increased in most states. At first glance, this may be viewed as an indictment of the reforms process; but this would only be a superficial assessment.

First, the increase is highly sensitive to the choice of a particular norm; the direction of change alters substantially with changed levels of the norm. Also, the trend is scarcely consistent with other evidence on nutrient intakes which points to a less cereal-dependent, more diversified diet, typically associated with higher, and not lower welfare.

This paper also proposes an alternative norm: one that takes into account the demographic composition of a household, and the gender- and age-specificities to calorie requirements. The use of this norm results in far lower estimates of calorie deprivation, with numbers that are closer to the income poverty figures. However, it does not influence conclusions about the relative rankings of states by calorie deprivation, or about changes over time.

In addition, the depth and severity of calorie deprivation has declined in many states when a 2,200 calorie or lower norm is used, and in all states if the median is used. Finally, the incidence of abject deprivation has declined, as is evident from a comparison of the cumulative distribution functions of calorie intake in 1983 and 1999/2000.

This study also highlights the relationship between income and calorie deprivation. Calorie deprivation can be discerned among all income quintiles, although the poorest 20 per cent of the population has the largest percentage of people below the norm and this decreases as one moves up the income quintiles. Yet, calorie deprivation among the highest income groups is of a large order of magnitude.

Most people familiar with poverty statistics would not be surprised by the apparent divergence between the calorie-based measures and income-based measures. A part of the problem lies in the fact that the income-poverty line was established nearly 30 years ago, by inverting an Engel function to yield the minimum level of income that would enable the purchase of a 2,400 calorie food basket. Tastes have changed significantly since then (see, Radhakrishna and Ravi, 1992; Meenakshi, 1996; Meenakshi and Ray, 1999) so that food baskets are far more diversified today than they were then; the commodity weights clearly do not capture this entirely.

There is a renewed need to reconsider the level of nutritional norm whether they be the 'low' norms set out by the FAO or the 'high' ones recommended by the National Institute of Nutrition. There is an informal understanding, albeit unwritten, that the 2,400 norm is 'too high.' Yet, there are no alternatives. This is especially important given that the policy focus is shifting increasingly to ensuring 'nutrition security' rather than 'food security' alone.

Furthermore, the normative basis of the official (income) poverty line also needs to be re-examined. Notions of minimum standards of living have changed substantially since the first attempts to define such a poverty line were made several decades ago. The focus on an adequate food basket needs to give way to a more comprehensive view – one that includes access to adequate shelter, a safe living environment, and good health.

ACKNOWLEDGEMENT

We are grateful to Priya Bhalla for research assistance, and to Mr Sanjeev Sharma for help with the data. An earlier version of this paper appeared in the *Economic and Political Weekly,* 25–31 January 2003.

REFERENCES

Deaton, Angus (1997), *The Analysis of Household Surveys: A Microeconometric Approach to Development Policy,* The John Hopkins University Press, Maryland.

Engel, J. and Alois Kneip (1994), 'Recent Approaches to Estimating Income Distributions, Engel Curves and Related Functions', Discussion Paper No. A-442, Sonderforschungsbereich 303, Rheinische Friedrich Wilhelms Universitat, Bonn.

Food and Agricultural Organisation (1996), *The Sixth World Food Survey*, Rome.

——— (2000), 'Food Insecurity: When People Live with Hunger and Fear Starvation', *The State of Food Insecurity in the World 2000*, Rome.

Foster, J, J. Greer and E. Thorbecke (1984), 'A Class of Decomposable Poverty Measures', *Econometrica*, Vol. 52, pp. 761–65.

Gopalan, C., B.V. Ramasastri and S.C. Balasubramanian (2000), *Nutritive Value of Indian Foods,* revised and updated by B.S. Narasinga Rao, Y.G. Deosthale and K.C. Pant, National Institute of Nutrition, Hyderabad.

Meenakshi, J.V. (1996), 'How Important are Changes in Taste? A State-Level Analysis of Food Demand', *Economic and Political Weekly*, 14 December 1996.

Meenakshi, J.V. and Ranjan Ray (1999), 'Regional Differences in India's Food Expenditure Pattern: A Complete Demand Systems Approach', *Journal of International Development*, Vol. 11.

Mehta, J. and S. Venkataraman, (2000), 'Poverty Statistics: Bermicide's Feast', *Economic and Political Weekly,* Vol. 35, July, pp. 2377–82.

Minhas, B.S. (1991), 'On Estimating the Inadequacy of Energy Intakes: Revealed Food Consumption Behaviour Versus Nutritional Norms (Nutritional Status of the Indian People in 1983)', *Journal of Development Studies* Vol. 28, No. 1.

National Sample Survey Organisation (2001), *Nutritional Intake in India 1999/2000*, (Report No. 471).

——— (1996), *Nutritional Intake in India,* Fifth Ouinquenial Survey on Consumer Expenditure 1993/94 (Report No. 405).

Palmer-Jones, Richard and Kunal Sen (2001), 'On India's Poverty Puzzles and Statistics of Poverty', *Economic and Political Weekly*, Vol. XXXVI, No. 3.

Radhakrishna, R. and R. Ravi (1992), Effects of Growth, Relative Prices and Preferences on Food and Nutrition, *Indian Economic Review*, Special Number 1992, pp. 303–23.

Sukhatme, P.V. (1993), Note in *Report of the Expert Group on Estimation of Proportion and Number of Poor*, Perspective Planning Division, Planning Commission, Government of India.

Suryanarayana, M.H. (1996), 'Food Security and Calorie Adequacy Across States: Implications for Reforms', *Journal of Indian School of Political Economy*, Vol. VIII, No. 2.

Viswanathan, Brinda and J.V. Meenakshi (2001), 'Developing Country Nutrition does Improve with Income: A Look at Calorie and Protein Intakes, 1983 to 1993/94', *Sarvekshana,* Vol. XXIV, No. 2 and 3, 85th issue, October 2000–March 2001, pp. 9–47.

——— (2004), 'Changing Pattern of Undernutrition in India: A Comparative Analysis Across Regions', Mimeograph, Madras School of Economics, Chennai.

25

Measuring Poverty in Karnataka
The Regional Dimension

Rinku Murgai, M.H. Suryanarayana and Salman Zaidi

INTRODUCTION

Poverty in India has received considerable attention in policy formulation and discussion. Official poverty estimates at the national and state level are periodically prepared by the Government of India's Planning Commission using detailed household consumption and expenditure data from the National Sample Survey Organisation's (NSSO) quinquennial consumer expenditure surveys. While there is considerable evidence available of regional (i.e. sub-state) variation in poverty, typically the Planning Commission does not compute poverty estimates below the state level because of limitations of survey sample sizes. Many state government's Departments of Economics and Statistics (DES) conduct households surveys on a matching basis with NSSO, but few if any pool data from these surveys with the central (i.e. NSSO) sample to derive regionally disaggregated estimates, both on account of delays in processing the state sample and because often they lack the requisite in-house capacity to conduct this analysis.

In this context, a noteworthy initiative was undertaken by the Government of Karnataka to estimate poverty incidence at the district level from pooled 1993/94 NSS 50th Round data for the Karnataka Human Development Report (Government of Karnataka, 1999). This chapter updates these estimates to 1999/2000 by combining the central and state samples for Karnataka from the 55th Round to examine regional variation in poverty across the state. The section on Regional Poverty Indices presents poverty estimates for different levels of regional disaggregation for Karnataka based on pooled central and state sample data, along with a brief description of the methodology followed to derive them. A subsequent section on Sensitivity Analysis presents the main findings of sensitivity analysis undertaken to explore the robustness of the conclusions emerging from this regional analysis. Finally, the chapter concludes by summarising the main findings of the paper, as well discusses some policy applications where the results derived may prove useful.

REGIONAL POVERTY INDICES: METHODOLOGY AND RESULTS

The methods we use in this paper to estimate the poverty indices are the same as those followed by the

Planning Commission. Poverty incidence – the headcount ratio (P0) – is defined as the proportion of the population below the official Government of India urban and rural poverty lines for Karnataka. In addition to the headcount, poverty gap (P1) estimates are also derived from the data, as the two measures in conjunction are potentially more informative about the extent and depth of poverty levels rather than the headcount alone (Foster et al., 1984). Monthly per capita expenditure (MPCE) aggregates from the 55th Round Consumer Expenditure Survey are used as an indicator of welfare, and compared to the urban and rural poverty lines for Karnataka to classify the population as either poor or non-poor. An important caveat to bear in mind is the recent debate on the non-comparability of 55th Round data with earlier NSS surveys, given the changes in design of the questionnaire (see e.g. Deaton, 2001; Sundaram, 2001 and Datt and Ravallion, 2002).[1] While the poverty estimates derived from these data may therefore not be directly comparable to those based on earlier rounds (e.g. those in the 1999 Karnataka HDR), since the revised questionnaire was presumably administered uniformly across regions, the unadjusted consumption aggregates can still be used to study regional variation in poverty incidence.

As noted above, difficulties in estimating poverty rates below the state level using the central sample alone arise because of inadequate sample size. While small sample size does not *per se* generate bias in the poverty estimates, it can result in quite high variances in the derived estimates (Deaton and Dreze, 2002). We attempt to ameliorate this problem by combining the central and state samples for Karnataka state, which then provides a greater number of observations per district or region. The central and state samples of the NSS 55th Round for Karnataka include 5,233 and 5,244 households, respectively, leading to a combined sample of over 10,000 households. Pooling the two samples is straightforward, provided appropriate sampling weights are calculated to derive representative estimates from the pooled samples. In calculating the sampling weights, we follow the same basic methodology as recommended by Minhas and Sardana (1990), but adapt it to take into account changes in the sample design strategy introduced in the 55th Round.

Table 25.1 reports the headcount and poverty gap measures derived from the pooled sample. These estimates are fairly close to the official central sample-based Planning Commission poverty estimates for the state (16.8 rural and 24.6 urban). Compared to the all-India poverty level, rural poverty in Karnataka is nearly 7 percentage points lower, and the poverty gap is also considerably lower. By contrast, urban poverty in Karnataka – both headcount rate and poverty gap – is about the same as the

Table 25.1 Official Headcount and Poverty Gap Estimates, by Sector

Sector	Headcount Rate (P0)		Poverty Gap (P1)	
	Karnataka	*All-India*	*Karnataka*	*All-India*
Rural	18.2	26.8	3.0	5.2
Urban	24.5	24.1	5.1	5.2
Overall	20.1		3.6	

Note: Estimates are based on the pooled Karnataka sample, using the official poverty lines.

[1] The source of the problem lies in the recall periods used for food, paan, tobacco, and intoxicants. In the 55th Round, the 30-day and 7-day recall periods were simultaneously canvassed (in adjacent columns in the questionnaire) for the same households, while earlier NSS quinquennial rounds employed only the 30-day recall period. The new questionnaire design is expected to have led to reconciliation of expenditures between the 7-day and 30-day reports, which would have raised the expenditures based on the 30-day recall. As a result, headcount ratios in the 55th Round are likely to be biased down compared to what would have been obtained on the basis of the traditional questionnaire.

all-India level. Table 25.1 also shows that urban poverty in Karnataka is much higher than rural poverty, a somewhat anomalous finding given differentials across urban and rural areas in other living standards indicators. We shall return to this apparent puzzle in the next section.

Further disaggregating poverty estimates for Karnataka by agro-climactic regions shows that state-wide and sectoral poverty measures conceal considerable variation within the state. Table 25.2, which reports poverty by NSS agro-climactic regions,[2] reveals that the extent and depth of poverty in Karnataka are greatest in the inland northern region, in both rural and urban areas. In sharp contrast, the rural coastal and ghat region, and the inland eastern region have very low levels of rural poverty.

Table 25.2 Official Headcount and Poverty Gap Estimates, by NSS Region

Karnataka	Rural Areas		Urban Areas	
NSS Region	Headcount	Poverty Gap	Headcount	Poverty Gap
Coastal and Ghat	3.4	0.7	18.5	4.3
Inland Eastern	4.5	0.6	20.6	3.3
Inland Southern	18.8	3.6	15.2	2.6
Inland Northern	23.7	3.6	39.9	9.1

Note: Estimates are based on the pooled Karnataka sample, using the official poverty lines.

We also compute poverty estimates disaggregated to the district-level (Table 25.3), although the estimates are not separated by rural and urban sectors on account of smaller sample sizes.[3] These estimates confirm that the northern districts of Karnataka tend to be poorer than the rest of the state.[4] There is also evidence of considerable variation within divisions. For example, Kolar district in Bangalore (rural) division is among the poorest in the state, even though poverty incidence in other districts of this division is not nearly as high. The general patterns for the poverty gap index are similar to those indicated by the headcount rates. Indeed, the poverty-gap series is highly correlated with the corresponding HCR series, with a correlation coefficient of 0.98 or a Spearman's rank correlation coefficient of 0.97.

Combining the poverty incidence rates with the distribution of the population across districts shows that in absolute numbers as well, the poor are concentrated in the northern districts (Table 25.4). While Gulbarga and Belgaum divisions account for about 40 per cent of the state's population, nearly 60 per cent of the poor reside in these areas. By contrast, Mysore division accounts for 26 per cent of the state's population, but only 14 per cent of its poor.

SENSITIVITY ANALYSIS

Are these sectoral and regional poverty estimates presented in the paper reasonable measures of living standards differences within the state? Or are they simply an artefact of data or methodological quirks?

[2] NSS region classification is as follows: Inland Northern consists of Gulbarga, Bidar, Raichur, Bellary, Belgaum, Dharwad, Chitradurga, and part of Bijapur. Inland Eastern consists of Kodagu, Chickmagalur, Shimoga, part of Bijapur, and part of Hassan. Inland Southern is Mandya, Mysore, Kolar, Tumkur, Bangalore Rural, and Bangalore Urban. Coastal and Ghat region is Dakshina Kannada and Uttara Kannada.

[3] To conserve sample size, the current 27 districts have been classified into the 20 districts that existed prior to the recent re-organisation.

[4] Although district-level poverty estimates have not been available, the fact that regional disparities persist in Karnataka has been widely noted for a number of decades (e.g. Nanjappa, 1968; Iyengar et al., 1981; Iyengar and Sudarshan, 1983; Vyasulu and Vani, 1997).

Table 25.3 Official Headcount and Poverty Gap Estimates, by District

District	Headcount Rate	Poverty Gap
Gulbarga Division		
Bellary	33.1	6.0
Bidar	30.4	5.2
Gulbarga	26.8	4.9
Raichur	45.6	6.3
Belgaum Division		
Belgaum	17.9	3.2
Bijapur	32.1	6.8
Dharwad	21.4	4.2
Mysore Division (I)		
Chickmagalur	2.3	0.4
Hassan	11.5	1.5
Kodagu	4.9	0.6
Mandya	16.6	2.8
Mysore	15.5	2.0
Mysore Division (II)		
Dakshina Kannada	7.4	1.7
Uttara Kannada	6.7	1.4
Bangalore Division (R)		
Bangalore Rural	5.2	0.7
Chitradurga	16.3	2.8
Kolar	41.9	10.3
Shimoga	8.1	1.4
Tumkur	18.5	2.7
Bangalore Division (U)		
Bangalore Urban	9.9	1.5

Note: Estimates are based on the pooled Karnataka sample, using the official poverty lines.

In order to explore this further, we carried out a range of sensitivity analyses to assess the extent to which the findings presented were good indicators of variation in living standards across regions. However, we first explore the degree of similarity between the state and central samples to ascertain the extent to which pooling the two together appears to be driving the poverty estimates.

Figure 25.1 compares the cumulative distribution functions (CDFs) and Lorenz curves of MPCE separately for the rural and urban sectors, in the two samples.[5] It is readily apparent that the central and state samples have nearly identical MPCE distributions in both sectors, suggesting that rural or urban estimates of poverty from the pooled sample are unlikely to be very different from what would have been obtained with the central sample alone. Similarly, the extremely close correspondence between the two sets of Lorenz curves implies that inequality estimates using either sample are also likely to be very similar: for instance, the gini coefficients are 0.25 and 0.24 for the rural state and central samples, and 0.31 and 0.33 for the urban state and central samples, respectively. On the whole, it is safe to conclude

[5] CDFs plot the cumulative fraction of population that has per capita expenditure below different per capita expenditure levels. Lorenz curves plot the cumulative fraction of population, starting from the poorest, on the x-axis against the cumulative fraction of resources on the y-axis.

Table 25.4 Distribution of the Poor in Karnataka, by District

District	Share of Total State Population of Poor	Share of Total State Population
Gulbarga Division	*33.7*	*20.0*
Bellary	7.1	4.3
Bidar	4.0	2.6
Gulbarga	10.0	7.5
Raichur	12.6	5.5
Belgaum Division	*24.9*	*21.2*
Belgaum	6.4	7.2
Bijapur	10.7	6.7
Dharwad	7.8	7.4
Mysore Division (I)	*11.0*	*17.2*
Chickmagalur	0.2	2.0
Hassan	1.8	3.1
Kodagu	0.3	1.1
Mandya	3.2	3.8
Mysore	5.6	7.2
Mysore Division (II)	*3.0*	*9.3*
Dakshina Kannada	2.0	5.5
Uttara Kannada	0.9	2.6
Bangalore Division (R)	*21.9*	*22.0*
Bangalore Rural	1.0	3.8
Chitradurga	3.7	4.6
Kolar	11.9	5.7
Shimoga	1.6	3.9
Tumkur	3.7	4.1
Bangalore Division (U)	*5.7*	*11.5*
Bangalore Urban	5.7	11.5

Note: Estimates are based on the pooled Karnataka sample, using the official poverty lines.

that poverty indices estimated from the combined sample are not unduly driven by peculiarities in either the central or the state sample.

Turning to whether the poverty estimates are indeed measuring differences in welfare across regions, we consider related evidence on living standards from three additional sources – agricultural wages, district domestic products, and employment shares in agricultural labour, and non-farm activities. There is a considerable evidence that the rural poor in India are highly represented amongst agricultural labourers (see e.g. Singh, 1990), suggesting therefore that the share of the population employed as agricultural labourers and agricultural wages are likely to be good correlates of poverty (see also Datt and Ravallion, 1998; Sundaram, 2001). Figure 25.2, which plots district specific daily agricultural wages for males against district poverty rates, provides some tentative indication of the plausibility of the disaggregated poverty estimates.[6] District poverty rates are found to be highly (and negatively) correlated with agricultural

[6] Wage data are from the Department of Economics and Statistics, Government of Karnataka, which collects monthly district-level data on agricultural wages separately for different categories of land, and further disaggregated by gender and by skilled and unskilled labour. The district agricultural wage used in Figure 25.2 is an average monthly wage for male agricultural labour across the different land types and skill levels. While the usual caveats regarding limitations of such

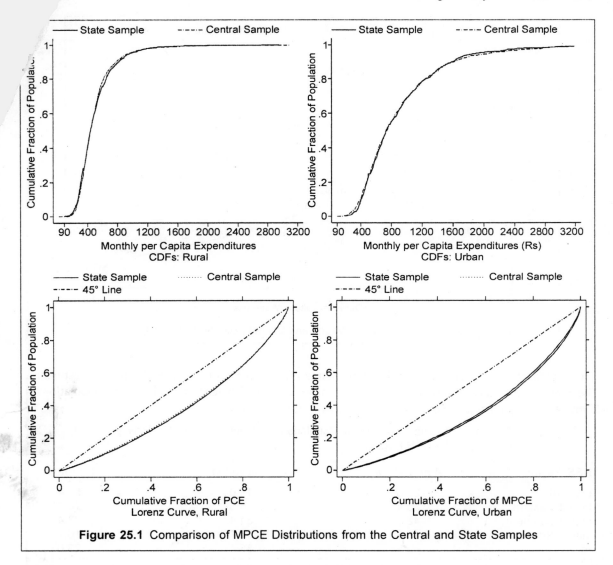

Figure 25.1 Comparison of MPCE Distributions from the Central and State Samples

wages, with a correlation coefficient of –0.63. Similarly, if poverty rates at the NSS region level are compared with agricultural wages derived from the NSS survey itself, workers in the coastal and ghat region are found to command over twice the wage earned by those in the inland northern regions that have higher levels of poverty.[7]

---

averages apply (issues of comparability, etc.), these measures are nonetheless a reasonably good indication of wage labourers' expected income earning potential in different parts of the state.

[7] While a day's work in the coastal region purchased about 5 kg of rice in 1999/2000, in the inland northern region a day's work purchased around 2 kg. We are grateful to Yoko Kijima and Peter Lanjouw for providing the NSS region-wise estimates of agricultural daily wages and employment shares.

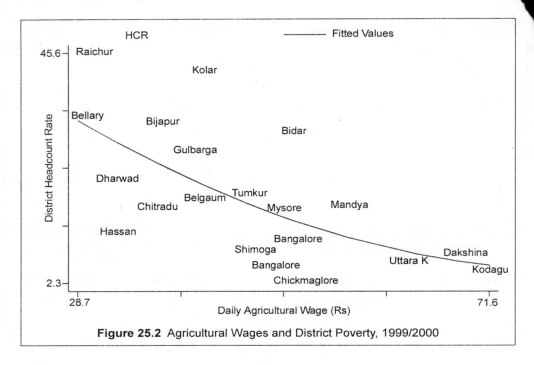

Figure 25.2 Agricultural Wages and District Poverty, 1999/2000

Complementary evidence on employment shares (Table 25.5) corroborates the poverty estimates. The employment share in agricultural labour (as a percentage of the economically active population) is higher in the poorer inland southern and northern districts.

Table 25.5 Distribution of Rural Population by Principal Economic Activity, by NSS Region

NSS Region	Agri. Labour	Cultivation	Non-farm
Coastal	27.6	15.0	57.4
Inland Eastern	35.4	38.5	26.1
Inland Southern	42.3	34.4	23.4
Inland Northern	45.5	37.7	16.7
All	42.0	35.1	23.0

Note: Estimates are based on the 55th Round NSS Employment-Unemployment Survey (Schedule 10) for Karnataka.

Further note that the pattern of district poverty rates is also reasonably consistent with independent estimates of per capita net district domestic product (see Figure 25.3).[8] The correlation between the two series is –0.60, increasing to –0.68 if the three outlier districts – Bangalore Urban, Dakshina Kannada, and Kodagu – are excluded.

---

[8] We should note that there may be a significant margin of error in district domestic product estimates, given the difficulties inherent in attributing state domestic product to different districts. These estimates are at best an indicative measure of the level of economic activity in the region.

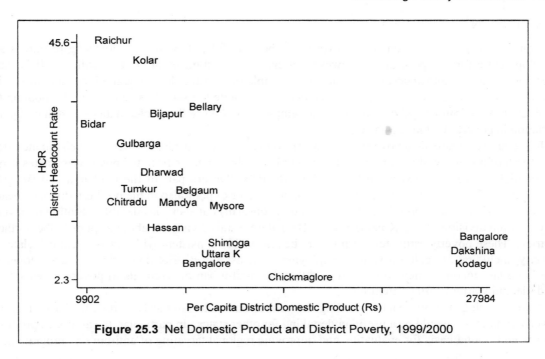

Figure 25.3 Net Domestic Product and District Poverty, 1999/2000

Finally, while poverty estimates disaggregated by district and NSS region are largely consistent with other measures of living standards, the rural-urban poverty gap indicated by the estimates reported in Table 25.1 is hard to believe.[9] The finding that urban poverty is 6 percentage points higher than rural poverty is difficult to reconcile with other evidence such as superior educational attainments, access to services, etc., in urban areas. Higher urban poverty rates come from the fact that the urban poverty line, at Rs 511.44 is around 65 per cent higher than the rural poverty line of Rs 309.59. The large gap between the Planning Commission's urban and rural poverty lines for Karnataka stems from the choice of price indices used for adjusting the poverty lines over time (Deaton, 2001).[10] Using Deaton's proposed poverty lines that explicitly account for urban-rural price differentials within the state in updating the poverty lines over time, the estimated headcount rate in urban Karnataka declines sharply, to 6.6 per cent. In tentative support of the poverty line adjustments, the correlation coefficient between poverty levels and district domestic products improves significantly, from –0.59 to –0.68. Revising the official poverty lines so as to more accurately measure the extent of poverty in the state and identify regions where the concentration of poverty is high will be a valuable exercise.

[9] This peculiarity has been noted by Deaton and Dreze (2002) who report rural and urban poverty estimates for Karnataka based on the central sample. They also note concerns about the urban-rural price differential implicit in official state-level poverty lines for a number of other states (e.g. Andhra Pradesh) as well.

[10] Following the recommendations of the Expert Group in 1993, the original rural and urban all-India poverty lines were adjusted for state-wise differences in price levels, separately for the urban and rural sectors. The adjustment procedure, however, did not explicitly consider the urban to rural differentials within states when setting the poverty lines, and after the adjustment, the all-India urban to rural differential implicit in the official lines increased from 15 per cent prior to the adoption of the Expert Group recommendations to nearly 40 per cent in 1999/2000. In some cases, as in Karnataka, the urban to rural differential implicit in the official poverty lines became unbelievably large.

CONCLUSION

Evidence on regional differences in poverty can be a useful policy tool for focusing resources and development efforts in poor areas. However, disaggregated estimates of poverty within India's states are typically not computed because of inadequate sample sizes available for geographic or administrative units below the state level. This paper attempts to ameliorate the sample-size problem by pooling the 1999/2000 NSS 55th Round central and state sample data. We use the pooled data to examine regional variation in poverty within Karnataka.

Regionally disaggregated poverty estimates show that there is considerable heterogeneity in the extent and depth of poverty within the state. The broad picture that emerges from the poverty estimates is one of: (i) higher levels of poverty in the northern districts, that are part of the Gulbarga and Belgaum divisions; (ii) highest concentration of the absolute number of poor also in the northern districts: nearly 60 per cent of the state's poor live in these two divisions; (iii) but also considerable variation in poverty levels within divisions – e.g. Kolar district in Bangalore (rural) division is about as poor as the northern districts. These poverty estimates are found to be reasonably consistent with independent correlates of poverty, including agricultural wages, employment shares, and district domestic products. However, one important inconsistency worth noting is that the rural-urban differentials in poverty rates are not credible and warrant further attention.

Analysis using this approach – pooling the central and state sample NSS data to derive regional poverty estimates – would be a useful undertaking for other states. In particular, the approach promises to provide a sound basis for evaluating and improving regional targeting of anti-poverty programmes.

ACKNOWLEDGEMENT

An earlier version of this paper was published in *Economic and Political Weekly*, Vol. 37, 25–31 January, 2003.

REFERENCES

Datt, G. and M. Ravallion (2002), 'Is India's Economic Growth Leaving the Poor Behind?', mimeo, World Bank, Washington DC.

———— (1998), 'Farm Productivity and Rural Poverty in India', *Journal of Development Studies,* Vol. 34, pp. 62–85.

Deaton, A. (2001), 'Adjusted Indian Poverty Estimates for 1999/2000', Research Programme in Development Studies, Princeton University, Processed.

Deaton, A. and J. Dreze (2002), 'Poverty and Inequality in India: A Re-examination', Princeton University and Delhi School of Economics, Processed.

Foster, J., J. Greer and E. Thorbecke (1984), 'A Class of Decomposable Poverty Measures', *Econometrica,* 52, pp. 761–65.

Government of Karnataka (1999), *Human Development in Karnataka 1999*, Planning Department, Government of Karnataka, Bangalore.

Iyengar, N.S. and P. Sudarshan (1983), 'On a Method of Classifying Regions from Multivariate Data', in Tate Planning Commission (ed.), *Regional Dimensions of India's Economic Development,* Planning Department, Government of Uttar Pradesh, Lucknow, pp. 732–45.

Iyengar, N.S., M.B. Nanjappa and P. Sudarshan (1981), 'A Note on Inter-District Differentials in Karnataka's Development', *Journal of Income and Wealth,* Vol. 5(1), pp. 79–83.

Minhas, B.S. and M.G. Sardana (1990), 'A Note on Pooling of Central and State Samples Data of national Sample Survey', *Sarvekshana*, Vol. XIV, No. 1, Issue No. 44, pp. 1–4.

Nanjappa, M.B. (1968), 'Backward Areas in Mysore State: A Study in Regional Development', *Southern Economist.*

Singh, I. (1990), *The Great Ascent: The Rural Poor in South Asia,* Baltimore Johns Hopkins University Press.

Sundaram, K. (2001), 'Employment and Poverty in 1990s: Further Results from NSS 55th Round Employment-Unemployment Survey', 1999/2000, *Economic and Political Weekly*, 11 August.

Vyasulu, V. and B.P. Vani (1997), 'Development and Deprivation in Karnataka: A District-Level Study', *Economic and Political Weekly,* Vol. XXXII, No. 46, pp. 2970–75.

Index